AUSTRALIAN INTELLECTUAL PROPERTY LAW

Fourth edition

The fourth edition of *Australian Intellectual Property Law* provides a detailed and comprehensive, yet concise and accessible, discussion of intellectual property law in Australia. It has been thoroughly revised to cover the most recent developments in intellectual property law, including significant case law and the proposed and enacted amendments to the *Copyright Act 1968* (Cth), the *Patents Act 1990* (Cth) and the *Plant Breeder's Rights Act 1994* (Cth) made in response to the recommendations of the 2016 Productivity Commission inquiry report *Intellectual Property Arrangements*.

The new edition provides a comprehensive discussion of the black-letter aspects of the law with its primary emphasis on legal principles and complexities. The content has been restructured for clarity and accessibility: the book now commences with copyright and related regimes such as protection for performers' rights and circuit layouts, followed by design law, confidential information, patents, plant breeder's rights, and finally trademarks and passing off. The final chapter covers general aspects of enforcement of legal rights and civil remedies that are particularly pertinent to intellectual property.

Written by highly respected intellectual property law researchers, *Australian Intellectual Property Law* is an invaluable resource for both undergraduate and postgraduate students, academics and other professionals working with intellectual property.

Mark J. Davison is Professor in the Centre for Commercial Law and Regulatory Studies in the Faculty of Law at Monash University, Special Counsel with

Knightsbridge Lawyers and a member of the Intellectual Property Committee of the Law Council of Australia.

Ann L. Monotti is Professor in the Centre for Commercial Law and Regulatory Studies in the Faculty of Law at Monash University and the Centre's former inaugural Director. She is a member of the Intellectual Property Committee of the Law Council of Australia.

Leanne Wiseman is Professor in the Law School at Griffith University and Associate Director of the Australian Centre for Intellectual Property in Agriculture (ACIPA). She is also a member of the Intellectual Property Committee of the Law Council of Australia.

AUSTRALIAN INTELLECTUAL PROPERTY LAW

FOURTH EDITION

Mark J. Davison, Ann L. Monotti
and Leanne Wiseman

CAMBRIDGE
UNIVERSITY PRESS

University Printing House, Cambridge CB2 8BS, United Kingdom

One Liberty Plaza, 20th Floor, New York, NY 10006, USA

477 Williamstown Road, Port Melbourne, VIC 3207, Australia

314–321, 3rd Floor, Plot 3, Splendor Forum, Jasola District Centre, New Delhi – 110025, India

79 Anson Road, #06–04/06, Singapore 079906

Cambridge University Press is part of the University of Cambridge.

It furthers the University's mission by disseminating knowledge in the pursuit of education, learning and research at the highest international levels of excellence.

www.cambridge.org
Information on this title: www.cambridge.org/9781108746953

© Mark J. Davison, Ann L. Monotti & Leanne Wiseman 2008, 2012, 2016, 2020

This publication is copyright. Subject to statutory exception
and to the provisions of relevant collective licensing agreements,
no reproduction of any part may take place without the written
permission of Cambridge University Press.

First published 2008
Second edition 2012
Third edition 2016
Fourth edition 2020

Cover designed by Cate Furey
Typeset by SPi Global
Printed in China by C & C Offset Printing Co. Ltd, March 2020

A catalogue record for this publication is available from the British Library

A catalogue record for this book is available from the National Library of Australia

ISBN 978-1-108-74695-3 Paperback

Reproduction and communication for educational purposes
The Australian *Copyright Act 1968* (the Act) allows a maximum of one chapter or 10% of the pages of this work, whichever is the greater, to be reproduced and/or communicated by any educational institution for its educational purposes provided that the educational institution (or the body that administers it) has given a remuneration notice to Copyright Agency Limited (CAL) under the Act.

For details of the CAL licence for educational institutions contact:

Copyright Agency Limited
Level 12, 66 Goulburn Street
Sydney NSW 2000
Telephone: (02) 9394 7600
Facsimile: (02) 9394 7601
E-mail: memberservices@copyright.com.au

Cambridge University Press has no responsibility for the persistence or accuracy of URLs for external or third-party internet websites referred to in this publication and does not guarantee that any content on such websites is, or will remain, accurate or appropriate.

For Rachel, Sara, Lyllie, Leif and Oliver
For Alan, Louise, Tim, Henry, Mia and Greta
For Lucy

CONTENTS

Preface	page xxix
Acknowledgements	xxxi
Table of cases	xxxiii
Table of statutes	lxvi
Table of statutory instruments	lxxxviii

PART I INTRODUCTION   1

1 Introduction   3

- **1.1** The nature of intellectual property — 4
- **1.2** Theories of intellectual property — 4
  - 1.2.1 The 'property' in intellectual property — 5
  - 1.2.2 Natural or personality rights — 5
  - 1.2.3 Incentive to create and disseminate — 6
  - 1.2.4 Protection for investment — 7
  - 1.2.5 Rent seeking — 7
  - 1.2.6 A combination of all the above — 8
- **1.3** The intellectual property regimes — 8
  - 1.3.1 Copyright and related rights — 9
  - 1.3.2 Designs — 10
  - 1.3.3 Confidential information — 10
  - 1.3.4 Patents — 11
  - 1.3.5 Plant breeder's rights — 11
  - 1.3.6 Passing off — 12
  - 1.3.7 Registered trade marks — 12
- **1.4** Impact of new technology — 13
- **1.5** Internationalisation of intellectual property — 15
  - 1.5.1 World Intellectual Property Organization — 16
  - 1.5.2 *TRIPS* — 16
  - 1.5.3 Plurilateral and bilateral agreements — 17
  - 1.5.4 Investor–state dispute settlement — 18
  - 1.5.5 Harmonisation of intellectual property procedures — 18

1.6	Intellectual property in Australia	19
	1.6.1 History of Australian intellectual property law	19
	1.6.2 Constitutional law issues	20
1.7	Scheme of the book	21

PART II COPYRIGHT, DESIGNS AND RELATED RIGHTS — 23

2 Copyright: introduction — 25

2.1	Introduction	26
2.2	Justifications	27
	2.2.1 Utilitarian arguments	28
	2.2.2 Natural rights arguments	29
2.3	History	30
	2.3.1 The British legacy	31
	2.3.2 *The Copyright Act 1968* and its reforms	32
	2.3.2.1 Reprographic reproduction	33
	2.3.2.2 CLRC and other reviews	34
	2.3.2.3 Digital agenda reforms	34
	2.3.2.4 *AUSFTA* and WIPO commitments	35
	2.3.2.5 Film directors' rights	36
	2.3.2.6 Technological protection measures	36
	2.3.2.7 Resale royalty rights	37
	2.3.2.8 Digital economy and online piracy	38
	2.3.2.9 Productivity Commission review	39
	2.3.2.10 Disability access	40
	2.3.2.11 Copyright modernisation	40
	2.3.2.12 Administration of copyright licences	41
2.4	International influences	41
	2.4.1 *Berne Convention*	41
	2.4.2 *Universal Copyright Convention*	42
	2.4.3 *Rome Convention*	42
	2.4.4 *TRIPS*	42
	2.4.5 WIPO internet treaties	43
	2.4.6 *AUSFTA*	43
	2.4.7 *Marrakesh Treaty*	44
	2.4.8 *Beijing Treaty*	44
	2.4.9 *Anti-Counterfeiting Trade Agreement*	45
	2.4.10 Future reforms	46

3 Copyright: subsistence — 48

3.1	Introduction	49
3.2	Subject matter	49
	3.2.1 Works (Part III)	50

		3.2.1.1	Literary works	50
		3.2.1.2	Dramatic works	55
		3.2.1.3	Musical works	57
		3.2.1.4	Artistic works	57
	3.2.2	Subject matter other than works (Part IV)		62
		3.2.2.1	Films	62
		3.2.2.2	Sound recordings	62
		3.2.2.3	Broadcasts	63
		3.2.2.4	Published editions	64

3.3 Recorded in material form — 64
3.4 Connected to Australia — 65
3.5 'Originality' — 67
  3.5.1 Original literary, dramatic, musical and artistic works — 67
  3.5.2 Subject matter other than works — 74

4 Copyright: authorship, first ownership, and nature and duration of rights — 75

4.1 Introduction — 76
4.2 'Authorship' and first ownership — 76
  4.2.1 Who is the author? — 77
    4.2.1.1 Literary, dramatic, musical and artistic works — 77
    4.2.1.2 Cinematograph films — 77
    4.2.1.3 Sound recordings — 77
    4.2.1.4 Broadcasts — 78
    4.2.1.5 Published editions — 78
  4.2.2 Joint authorship — 78
  4.2.3 Orphan works — 79
4.3 Exceptions to first ownership — 80
  4.3.1 Works created by employees — 81
    4.3.1.1 Who is an employee? — 81
    4.3.1.2 Was the work created 'in pursuance of the terms of employment'? — 82
  4.3.2 Works created by journalists — 82
  4.3.3 Commissioned works — 83
  4.3.4 Crown copyright — 84
4.4 Nature of the rights — 85
  4.4.1 The right of reproduction — 86
  4.4.2 The right to publish the work — 88
  4.4.3 The right to perform the work in public — 88
  4.4.4 The right to communicate the work to the public — 89
  4.4.5 The right to make an adaptation of the work — 91
  4.4.6 The right of commercial rental — 92

	4.5	Technological protection measures	92
		4.5.1 Anti-circumvention	94
		4.5.1.1 Circumventing an access control TPM	94
		4.5.1.2 Aiding and abetting in the circumvention of a TPM	96
		4.5.1.3 Providing a circumvention service	97
		4.5.1.4 Criminal actions	98
		4.5.1.5 Defences to liability for criminal actions	99
		4.5.2 Rights management information	99
		4.5.3 Unauthorised access to encoded broadcasts	100
	4.6	Duration	101
5	**Copyright: exploitation, infringement and defences**		**103**
	5.1	Introduction	104
	5.2	Exploitation	104
		5.2.1 Assignment	104
		5.2.2 Licences	105
		5.2.2.1 Express licences	105
		5.2.2.2 Implied licences	106
		5.2.2.3 Compulsory and statutory licences	106
		5.2.3 Collective administration	110
		5.2.3.1 Collecting societies	110
		5.2.3.2 The Copyright Tribunal of Australia	111
	5.3	Infringement	112
		5.3.1 Direct infringement	113
		5.3.1.1 Activities within copyright owner's exclusive control	113
		5.3.1.2 Alleged infringing work derived from copyright work	114
		5.3.1.3 Unauthorised act done on whole or substantial part of copyright work	116
		5.3.1.4 Authorisation	120
		5.3.2 Indirect infringement	131
		5.3.2.1 Parallel importation	131
		5.3.2.2 Books	132
		5.3.2.3 Sound recordings	134
		5.3.2.4 Books, periodicals and printed music in electronic format, and computer programs	135
		5.3.2.5 Non-infringing accessories to the article	136
	5.4	Relief for copyright infringement	137
		5.4.1 Injunctions	137
		5.4.2 Damages	138
		5.4.2.1 Additional damages	138
		5.4.3 Innocent infringement	139
		5.4.4 Conversion or detention	139

		5.4.5	Groundless threats to sue	140
		5.4.6	Criminal offences	141
	5.5	Defences and limitations		142
		5.5.1	Fair dealing	143
			5.5.1.1 Permitted purposes	144
			5.5.1.2 The dealing must be 'fair'	151
		5.5.2	Time shifting	154
		5.5.3	Format shifting	155
		5.5.4	Exceptions for archives, libraries and key cultural institutions	157
		5.5.5	Educational uses	159
		5.5.6	Organisations assisting persons with a disability	160
		5.5.7	Artistic works	160
		5.5.8	Computer programs	161
		5.5.9	Temporary and incidental reproductions	162
		5.5.10	Legal materials	163
		5.5.11	Government uses	163
		5.5.12	Reading or recitation in public	164
		5.5.13	Sound recordings	164
		5.5.14	Films	164
		5.5.15	Public interest	165
		5.5.16	Contracting out of the defences	165
		5.5.17	Future reforms	167
6	**Areas related to copyright: moral rights, performers' rights, artist's resale rights, and other rights**			**168**
	6.1	Introduction		169
	6.2	Moral rights		169
		6.2.1	The right of attribution	171
		6.2.2	The right of integrity	172
		6.2.3	The right to object to false attribution	175
		6.2.4	Limits on moral rights	176
			6.2.4.1 'Reasonable in all the circumstances'	176
			6.2.4.2 Consent	178
		6.2.5	Remedies for infringement of moral rights	179
		6.2.6	Indigenous communal moral rights?	180
	6.3	Performers' rights		181
		6.3.1	Performers' moral rights	183
	6.4	Artist's resale rights		185
	6.5	Circuit layouts		188
		6.5.1	Nature and scope of circuit layouts	189
		6.5.2	Subsistence	190
		6.5.3	Exclusive rights	190

		6.5.4	Ownership	191
		6.5.5	Exploitation	191
		6.5.6	Duration	191
		6.5.7	Infringement	191
		6.5.8	Exceptions and defences	192
			6.5.8.1 Innocent commercial exploitation	192
		6.5.9	Remedies	193
		6.5.10	Overlap with copyright and design protection?	194
	6.6	Public and educational lending rights		194
7	**Designs**			**196**
	7.1	Introduction		197
	7.2	History		197
	7.3	The registration process		199
		7.3.1	Who can apply?	200
		7.3.2	Requirements of the application	201
		7.3.3	Request for registration or publication	201
		7.3.4	Publication	202
		7.3.5	Registration	202
		7.3.6	Priority date	202
		7.3.7	Duration	203
		7.3.8	Post-registration examination	203
	7.4	Criteria for protection		203
		7.4.1	Meaning of 'design'	203
			7.4.1.1 Visual features	204
			7.4.1.2 Product	205
		7.4.2	New and distinctive	206
	7.5	Ownership		209
	7.6	Rights		209
	7.7	Infringement		209
		7.7.1	Primary infringement	209
		7.7.2	Secondary infringement	211
	7.8	Defences		211
		7.8.1	The right of repair for spare parts defence	212
			7.8.1.1 'Repair'	213
			7.8.1.2 'Overall appearance of a product'	213
			7.8.1.3 Onus of proof	214
		7.8.2	Consent and parallel importation	214
		7.8.3	Crown use and supply	214
	7.9	Remedies		215
		7.9.1	Unjustified threats	215

7.10	Copyright–design overlap		216
	7.10.1 Registration of a corresponding design		216
	7.10.2 Industrial application of a corresponding design		217
7.11	Future reforms		218

PART III CONFIDENTIAL INFORMATION, PATENTS AND PLANT BREEDER'S RIGHTS 219

8 Equitable doctrine of breach of confidence 221

8.1	Introduction		222
	8.1.1 Overview		222
	8.1.2 Subsistence of equitable obligations of confidence alongside comparable contractual obligations		223
8.2	Origins of the equitable doctrine of breach of confidence		224
8.3	Elements of the action		226
	8.3.1 Must be able to identify the information with specificity		228
	8.3.2 Information must have the necessary quality of confidence		229
		8.3.2.1 Ideas	230
		8.3.2.2 Concept of relative secrecy and the public domain	231
		8.3.2.3 Information based on public knowledge and ideas	234
		8.3.2.4 Guidelines for necessary quality of confidence for business or trade secrets	234
	8.3.3 Information given or received to import an obligation of confidence		235
		8.3.3.1 Receipt of information in circumstances that import an obligation of confidence	235
		8.3.3.2 Encrypted information	236
		8.3.3.3 Verbal confidences: inadvertent eavesdropping	237
		8.3.3.4 Verbal confidences: eavesdropping and telephone tapping	237
		8.3.3.5 Inadvertent acquisition of written confidences	238
		8.3.3.6 Surreptitious acquisition through theft or use of telephoto lens	239
	8.3.4 Unauthorised use or disclosure of the information		239
	8.3.5 The scope of the obligation		241
	8.3.6 The need to show detriment		242
	8.3.7 Reasonableness of obtaining a remedy		243
8.4	How long does the obligation last?		244
	8.4.1 Express contractual obligations		244
	8.4.2 Equitable obligations		244
	8.4.3 Disclosure by the confider		244
	8.4.4 Disclosure by the confidant		245
	8.4.5 Disclosure by third party after confidence is imposed		245

8.5	Entitlement		246
8.6	Special circumstances: during employment		248
8.7	Special circumstances: after employment		249
	8.7.1 Contract		250
		8.7.1.1 Express terms	250
		8.7.1.2 Implied duty of good faith	251
	8.7.2 Equitable principles of confidence		252
8.8	Defences: public interest in disclosure		254
	8.8.1 Background		254
	8.8.2 Nature of a justification for disclosure in the public interest in Australia		256
8.9	Remedies		258
	8.9.1 General		258
	8.9.2 The springboard principle		259
	8.9.3 Damages		260
8.10	Relationship between confidential information and patents		261
8.11	Relationship between confidential information and copyright		262
8.12	International dimensions		262

9 Patents for inventions: introduction — **264**

9.1	What is a patent for invention?		265
9.2	Origins of patent protection		266
9.3	Development of patent law in Australia		268
9.4	Rationales of patent protection		269
9.5	Types of patent		270
	9.5.1 Standard and innovation patents		270
	9.5.2 Selection patents		271
	9.5.3 Combination patents		271
9.6	Types of application		271
	9.6.1 Convention applications		271
	9.6.2 *PCT* applications		272
	9.6.3 Divisional applications		273
	9.6.4 Patents of addition		273
9.7	Procedure for obtaining a standard patent		274
	9.7.1 The application		274
	9.7.2 Pre-examination		275
	9.7.3 Examination		275
	9.7.4 Acceptance and publication		276
	9.7.5 Opposition		277
	9.7.6 Re-examination		278
	9.7.7 Grant		278

9.8	Processing an application for an innovation patent		278
9.9	Patent term		279
9.10	Extension of term of standard patents for pharmaceutical substances		280
	9.10.1	The application	280
	9.10.2	Calculation of the term of extension	282
9.11	Requirement of claims to have a priority date		282
	9.11.1	Complete applications	283
	9.11.2	Convention applications	283
	9.11.3	*PCT* applications	283
	9.11.4	Required disclosure in a priority document	283
9.12	The role of priority dates		285
9.13	Withdrawal and lapsing of applications and ceasing of patents		286
	9.13.1	Withdrawal of patents	286
	9.13.2	Lapsing of patents	286
	9.13.3	Ceasing of patents	286
9.14	International aspects		286
	9.14.1	*Paris Convention*	287
	9.14.2	*TRIPS*	287
	9.14.3	*Budapest Treaty*	288
	9.14.4	*European Patent Convention*	289
	9.14.5	*Patent Law Treaty* and proposed Substantive Patent Law Treaty	290

10 Patents for inventions: validity — 291

10.1	Statutory requirements		292
10.2	A two-tier system		292
10.3	The concept of invention		294
10.4	Manner of manufacture		295
	10.4.1	Time at which manner of manufacture is raised	295
	10.4.2	Background to the meaning of 'manner of manufacture'	295
	10.4.3	*NRDC v Commissioner of Patents*: meaning of 'manner of manufacture'	297
		10.4.3.1 The judgment	297
		10.4.3.2 *NRDC* guiding factors	299
	10.4.4	Application of *NRDC* principles to expand scope and remove classes of unpatentable inventions	300
	10.4.5	Computer programs and computer-implemented methods	302
		10.4.5.1 Computer programs	302
		10.4.5.2 Computer-implemented methods	303
	10.4.6	Genes and biological materials	307
	10.4.7	Methods of medical treatment for humans	313

	10.4.8	Discoveries, ideas, intellectual information and other unpatentable subject matter	318
	10.4.9	Reform proposals	320
10.5	Generally inconvenient	320
10.6	Novelty	323
	10.6.1	Introduction	323
	10.6.2	Time at which novelty is raised	323
	10.6.3	Statutory requirements: overview	324
	10.6.4	Time at which to construe and read documentary disclosures	326
	10.6.5	Prior art base	327
		10.6.5.1 Historical provisions	327
		10.6.5.2 Current prior art base	327
	10.6.6	Person skilled in the relevant art: the skilled addressee	328
	10.6.7	The meaning of 'prior information made publicly available'	329
	10.6.8	Test for 'anticipation'	330
		10.6.8.1 General principles	330
		10.6.8.2 Anticipation through prior use	334
		10.6.8.3 Implicit disclosure and inevitable outcome	335
	10.6.9	Prohibition on 'mosaics'	337
	10.6.10	Making information available in certain circumstances: disclosure with consent	338
		10.6.10.1 Showing, use and publication at recognised exhibition	339
		10.6.10.2 Publication before learned society	340
		10.6.10.3 Working the invention in public for purposes of reasonable trial	341
		10.6.10.4 General grace period	343
	10.6.11	Making information available in certain circumstances: non-consensual disclosure	344
	10.6.12	Novelty by way of selection	345
	10.6.13	Relationship with inventive step and innovative step	346
10.7	Inventive and innovative step: principles	347
	10.7.1	Introduction	347
	10.7.2	Time at which inventive or innovative step is raised	348
	10.7.3	Statutory requirements: overview	348
	10.7.4	Inventive step: prior art base and relevant information for purposes of comparison	350
		10.7.4.1 *Patents Act 1952*	350
		10.7.4.2 *Patents Act 1990*: 30 April 1991 to 31 March 2002	350
		10.7.4.3 *Patents Act 1990*: 1 April 2002 to 14 April 2013	351
		10.7.4.4 From 15 April 2013 to present	352

	10.7.5	Innovative step: prior art base and relevant information for purposes of comparison	353
	10.7.6	Innovative step: level of advance and assessment	354
	10.7.7	Summary of differences	355
10.8	Inventive step: elements in the assessment		356
	10.8.1	Obvious: very plain	356
	10.8.2	Person skilled in the relevant art	357
	10.8.3	Common general knowledge	358
	10.8.4	Information a skilled person could be reasonably expected to ascertain, understand and regard as relevant	360
	10.8.5	Standard required: scintilla of inventiveness	361
	10.8.6	Expert evidence 'tainted by hindsight'	361
	10.8.7	Secondary factors to assist assessment of obviousness	361
		10.8.7.1 Long-felt want and its successful solution	362
		10.8.7.2 Commercial success	363
		10.8.7.3 Expectation of success	363
		10.8.7.4 Problem and solution	365
	10.8.8	Objection to reliance on hindsight	366
10.9	Threshold quality of 'inventiveness'		366
	10.9.1	The issue	366
	10.9.2	Assessment of the threshold quality of 'inventiveness'	368
	10.9.3	Innovation patents and the threshold issue	370
10.10	Utility		370
	10.10.1	General	370
	10.10.2	Meaning of 'useful'	370
10.11	Secret use		372
	10.11.1	General	372
	10.11.2	Rationale	373
	10.11.3	The relationship with novelty	373
	10.11.4	The meaning of 'secret'	374
	10.11.5	The meaning of 'use'	374
	10.11.6	Use for reasonable trial or experiment only	376
	10.11.7	Use occurring solely in a confidential disclosure	377
	10.11.8	Patentee use for any purpose other than trade or commerce	378
	10.11.9	Use on behalf of the government	378
	10.11.10	Onus of proof	378
	10.11.11	Grace period	379
10.12	Express exclusions from patentability		379
	10.12.1	Human beings and biological processes for their generation	379
	10.12.2	Plants and animals	380
	10.12.3	Contrary to law	381

		10.12.4	Mere mixtures	382
		10.12.5	International obligations	382
	10.13	Internal requirements for patent specifications: s 40		383
		10.13.1	Evolution of the specification and function of claims	383
		10.13.2	Statutory provisions for internal requirements for patent specifications	384
		10.13.3	Construction of specification for s 40 purposes	386
		10.13.4	Stages for consideration of s 40 requirements	387
		10.13.5	The relationship between s 40 and other grounds of invalidity	387
		10.13.6	Requirements relating to provisional specifications: s 40(1)	387
		10.13.7	Requirements relating to complete specifications: s 40(2)(a), (aa)	388
			10.13.7.1 Requirement to describe the invention fully	389
			10.13.7.2 Best method	391
			10.13.7.3 Time for meeting the requirements to describe the invention fully	393
		10.13.8	End with claims defining the invention: s 40(2)(b), (c)	394
		10.13.9	Claims must be clear and succinct: s 40(3)	394
		10.13.10	Claims must be supported by the matter disclosed in the specification: s 40(3)	395
		10.13.11	Consistory clause and fair basing	397
		10.13.12	Comparison with fair basis assessment: priority dates	398
		10.13.13	Claims must relate to one invention only: s 40(4)	399
11	**Patents for inventions: allocation of rights and ownership, the Register and dealings**			**400**
	11.1	Entitlement to grant		401
		11.1.1	Criteria for inventorship	403
			11.1.1.1 The invention, conception of the invention or inventive concept	404
			11.1.1.2 The nature of the contribution	404
			11.1.1.3 Joint inventorship	406
		11.1.2	Entitled to have patent assigned to person: s 15(1)(b)	407
		11.1.3	Derives title to invention from inventor: s 15(1)(c)	407
	11.2	Ownership and co-ownership		408
		11.2.1	The notion of co-ownership	408
		11.2.2	Rights of co-owners	409
		11.2.3	Directions to co-owners	409
		11.2.4	Grant of patent	410
		11.2.5	Proprietary rights in the patent	410

11.3	Employee inventions		411
	11.3.1 Express provisions in the employment contract		412
	11.3.2 Implied duty to assign inventions: the duty of good faith		413
	11.3.3 Fiduciary duties		416
11.4	Crown use of patents for inventions		417
	11.4.1 Introduction		417
	11.4.2 Exploitation of inventions by the Crown		418
	11.4.3 Scope of the exploitation right		419
	11.4.4 'For the services of the Commonwealth or a State'		419
	11.4.5 Obligations of the Crown		420
	11.4.6 Procedures available to a patentee		420
	11.4.7 Remuneration and terms for exploitation		420
	11.4.8 Exploitation of invention to cease under court order		421
	11.4.9 Supply of products by Commonwealth to foreign countries		421
	11.4.10 Acquisition of inventions or patents by the Commonwealth		421
	11.4.11 Assignments of inventions to the Commonwealth		422
	11.4.12 Review of Crown use		422
11.5	Dealings with inventions		422
	11.5.1 General principles		422
	11.5.2 Assignments		423
	11.5.3 Exclusive licences		424
	11.5.4 Non-exclusive and sole licences		425
11.6	Compulsory licences		425
	11.6.1 Application		425
		11.6.1.1 Court is satisfied that certain conditions exist	426
		11.6.1.2 Court is satisfied that there is anti-competitive behaviour	427
	11.6.2 Effect of compulsory licence on other patents		428
	11.6.3 Operation of the order		429
	11.6.4 Remuneration payable		429
	11.6.5 Revocation		429
	11.6.6 Other circumstances for compulsory licence		429
	11.6.7 International requirements		430
	11.6.8 Patented pharmaceutical inventions		431
11.7	Contracts		431
	11.7.1 Void conditions		431
	11.7.2 Conditions that are not void		433
	11.7.3 Defence to infringement proceedings		433
	11.7.4 Termination of contract after patent ceases to be in force		434
11.8	The Register and official documents		436
	11.8.1 Contents of the Register		436
	11.8.2 Inspection and access to the Register		437
	11.8.3 False entries		437

		11.8.4	Evidence	438
		11.8.5	Power of patentee to deal with patent	438

12 Patents for inventions: exploitation, infringement and revocation — 440

12.1	The role of the patent specification		441
12.2	General principles for construction of patent specification		441
12.3	Claim construction		444
	12.3.1	Introduction	444
	12.3.2	'Pith and marrow'	445
	12.3.3	Purposive construction	446
12.4	Exclusive rights of the patentee		449
	12.4.1	Nature of exclusive rights	449
	12.4.2	Concept of an implied licence on sale	450
	12.4.3	No grant of positive rights	451
12.5	Direct infringement		452
	12.5.1	Exclusive right to make a patented product	453
	12.5.2	Exclusive right to use	455
	12.5.3	Exclusive right to keep	456
	12.5.4	Exclusive right to import the invention	458
	12.5.5	Concept of parallel importation	459
	12.5.6	Authorisation	460
	12.5.7	Liability as a joint tortfeasor through 'common design' or 'procurement'	462
12.6	Contributory infringement		464
	12.6.1	Introduction	464
	12.6.2	'Supply' of a 'product': s 117(1)	465
	12.6.3	Infringing uses: s 117(2)	468
		12.6.3.1 Section 117(2)(a)	468
		12.6.3.2 Section 117(2)(b)	469
		12.6.3.3 Section 117(2)(c)	472
	12.6.4	Infringement of a product patent by supply of component parts	473
12.7	Misleading and deceptive conduct		474
12.8	Defences to infringement		474
	12.8.1	Use in or on foreign vessels, aircraft or vehicles	475
	12.8.2	Prior use of an invention: s 119	475
		12.8.2.1 Overview	475
		12.8.2.2 Current provision	477
	12.8.3	Acts for obtaining regulatory approval of pharmaceuticals and non-pharmaceuticals	479
	12.8.4	Private acts	479
	12.8.5	Experimental and research use	480

12.9	Infringement proceedings		483
12.10	Relief for infringement		484
12.11	Non-infringement declarations		485
12.12	Unjustified threats of infringement proceedings		485
12.13	Revocation of patents		487
	12.13.1	Statutory provisions	487
	12.13.2	Lack of entitlement	488
	12.13.3	Fraud and false suggestion or misrepresentation	489
	12.13.4	Litigation: parties to proceedings	492

13 Plant breeder's rights — 493

13.1	Introduction		494
13.2	Plant breeding: technical background		494
13.3	Subject matter of PBR		496
13.4	Registrability and grant of PBR		496
	13.4.1	The variety has a breeder	496
		13.4.1.1 Meaning of 'discovery'	497
		13.4.1.2 Meaning of selective propagation	497
	13.4.2	The variety is distinct	498
		13.4.2.1 Common knowledge	498
	13.4.3	The variety is uniform	499
	13.4.4	The variety is stable	499
	13.4.5	The variety has not been exploited or has only recently been exploited	499
	13.4.6	Time at which the variety must meet the DUS criteria	501
13.5	PBR applications		501
	13.5.1	Right to apply for PBR	502
	13.5.2	Form of application for PBR	503
	13.5.3	Priority dates	503
	13.5.4	Acceptance and rejection	504
	13.5.5	Variation of the application after acceptance	504
	13.5.6	Application after acceptance: substantive examination and test growing requirements	504
	13.5.7	Objections	505
	13.5.8	Access to the application and any objection	505
	13.5.9	Status of accepted applications	505
	13.5.10	Deposit of propagating material	505
13.6	Grant of PBR		506
	13.6.1	Requirements	506
	13.6.2	Entry of details in the Register	506
	13.6.3	Effect of grant of PBR	507
	13.6.4	Term of protection	507

13.7	Rights in PBR		507
	13.7.1	General nature of PBR in propagating material	507
	13.7.2	Extension beyond propagating material: essentially derived varieties	508
	13.7.3	Extension beyond propagating material: certain dependent plant varieties	510
	13.7.4	Extension beyond propagating material: harvested material	511
	13.7.5	Extension beyond propagating material: products obtained from harvested material	512
	13.7.6	Concept of exhaustion of rights	512
13.8	Limitations on PBR		513
	13.8.1	Private, experimental or breeding purposes	513
	13.8.2	Farmer's rights	514
	13.8.3	Breeder's rights in harvested material and products from crops grown with farm-saved seed	516
	13.8.4	Other restrictions on rights	516
	13.8.5	Reasonable public access	517
13.9	Ownership and co-ownership		517
13.10	Exploiting PBR: licensing and other forms		518
	13.10.1	Assignment of PBR	518
	13.10.2	Licences	518
13.11	Revocation of PBR		519
13.12	Surrender of PBR		519
13.13	Infringement of rights		520
	13.13.1	What amounts to infringement?	520
	13.13.2	Exemptions from infringement	520
	13.13.3	Prior user rights	521
13.14	Enforcement of rights		521
	13.14.1	Actions for infringement	521
	13.14.2	Non-infringement declarations	521
	13.14.3	Unjustified threats of infringement proceedings	522
	13.14.4	Jurisdiction	522
	13.14.5	Offences and conduct by directors, servants and agents	523
13.15	The Register		523
13.16	Remedies		523
13.17	Relationships between PBR and other intellectual property regimes		524
	13.17.1	PBR and patents	524
	13.17.2	PBR and trade marks	525
13.18	Other international conventions		525

PART IV TRADE MARKS — 527

14 Passing off — 529

- **14.1** History of passing off — 530
  - 14.1.1 Common law and passing off — 530
  - 14.1.2 Equity and passing off — 530
- **14.2** Elements of passing off — 531
- **14.3** The reputation of the plaintiff — 532
  - 14.3.1 Location of reputation — 534
  - 14.3.2 Ownership of reputation — 536
  - 14.3.3 Joint ownership of reputation — 536
  - 14.3.4 Dual ownership: honest concurrent user and use of own name — 537
  - 14.3.5 Reputation in descriptive words and insignia: secondary meanings — 539
  - 14.3.6 Reputation in packaging and appearance — 540
  - 14.3.7 Reputation of marketing image — 542
  - 14.3.8 Reputation in personality — 542
  - 14.3.9 Abandonment of reputation — 543
- **14.4** The misrepresentation — 544
  - 14.4.1 Misrepresentation, confusion and deception — 544
  - 14.4.2 The target of the representation — 546
  - 14.4.3 Misrepresentations of the trade origin of goods — 546
  - 14.4.4 Different quality of goods — 547
  - 14.4.5 Character merchandising — 547
- **14.5** Passing off and the internet — 550
  - 14.5.1 Domain names — 551
  - 14.5.2 Australian passing off cases and the internet — 552
  - 14.5.3 Uniform dispute resolution policy — 554
  - 14.5.4 Australian uniform dispute resolution policy — 556
  - 14.5.5 Meta-tags — 556
  - 14.5.6 Keyword advertising — 557
- **14.6** Effect of disclaimers — 558
- **14.7** A holistic perspective — 560
- **14.8** Damage — 561
- **14.9** Statutory causes of action — 562
  - 14.9.1 Application of the legislation — 562
  - 14.9.2 'In trade or commerce' — 563
  - 14.9.3 'Engage in conduct' — 563
  - 14.9.4 'Misleading or deceptive' — 563
- **14.10** Comparison with passing off — 565

	14.10.1	Sections 29, 33 and 34 of sch 2	566
	14.10.2	Comparison with trade mark infringement	566
14.11	Remedies		566

15 Registered trade marks — 569

15.1	History of registered trade marks		570
15.2	Drawbacks of passing off		571
15.3	Functions of trade marks		572
	15.3.1	Reducing search costs	572
	15.3.2	Managing property interests	573
	15.3.3	Promoting the product	573
15.4	Overview of the registration process		574
15.5	Definition of a trade mark		575
15.6	Definition of a sign		575
	15.6.1	Aspect of packaging, shape	576
	15.6.2	Colour	578
	15.6.3	Sounds	578
	15.6.4	Scents	579
15.7	'Used or intended to be used'		579
	15.7.1	Unconditional intention	579
	15.7.2	Objective test of intention	580
	15.7.3	Use by others	580
15.8	Distinguishing goods or services		581
	15.8.1	'Dealt with or provided'	581
	15.8.2	'In the course of trade'	582
	15.8.3	'By a person'	583
15.9	Ownership		583
	15.9.1	First use in Australia	584
	15.9.2	Distributorship arrangements	585
	15.9.3	Creation or adoption of an overseas trade mark	586
	15.9.4	Persons who can own a trade mark	587
15.10	Certification trade marks		587
	15.10.1	Requirements for registration	588
	15.10.2	Certification by other means	590
15.11	Collective trade marks		590
15.12	Defensive trade marks		590
15.13	Overview of requirements at examination of standard trade mark applications		592
15.14	National signs not to be used as trade marks		593
15.15	Signs prescribed under s 39(2)		593

15.16	Trade mark cannot be represented graphically: s 40	594
15.17	Trade mark not distinguishing goods or services: s 41	594
	15.17.1 Inherent distinctiveness	595
	15.17.2 Partial inherent distinctiveness: use and intended use	599
	15.17.3 Distinctiveness through use	599
	15.17.4 Functional shapes	600
	15.17.5 Colour trade marks	603
15.18	Scandalous trade marks: s 42	604
15.19	Use contrary to law: s 42	605
15.20	Deceptive or confusing trade marks: s 43	605
15.21	Trade marks identical or similar to existing trade marks: s 44	607
	15.21.1 Substantially identical with	607
	15.21.2 Or deceptively similar to	608
	15.21.3 The context of the comparison	610
	15.21.4 Similar goods	611
	15.21.5 Similar services	612
	15.21.6 Closely related goods and services	613
	15.21.7 A global assessment	613
15.22	Honest concurrent user	614
15.23	Prior continuous user	616
15.24	Other legislation	617
	15.24.1 Protection of sporting events	617
	15.24.2 Business names	617
	15.24.3 *Wine Australia Act 2013*	618
	15.24.4 Protection for particular industries	619
15.25	Overview of grounds of opposition	619
15.26	Another trade mark's prior reputation: s 60	620
	15.26.1 Relationship with honest concurrent user and prior continuous user provisions	622
15.27	Geographical indications: s 61	623
	15.27.1 Definition of a geographical indication	623
	15.27.2 Interpretation	624
	15.27.3 Exceptions	625
15.28	Application made in bad faith	625
15.29	Overview of rectification of the Register	627
15.30	Amendment or cancellation by the Registrar	627
15.31	Overview of rectification by the court	629
	15.31.1 Aggrieved person	629
15.32	Errors and omissions: s 85	630

15.33	Contravention of conditions or limits: s 86		630
15.34	Effect of ss 24 and 25 on s 87		631
15.35	Cancellation, removal or amendment: s 88(2)		633
15.36	Transitional provisions and presumptive validity		633
	15.36.1	Fraud	634
	15.36.2	Contrary to s 28 of the repealed legislation	634
	15.36.3	Not distinctive when proceedings commence	634
15.37	General discretion not to rectify		635
15.38	Grounds for opposition		635
15.39	Fraud, false suggestion or misrepresentation		636
15.40	Use likely to deceive or cause confusion		637
15.41	Rectification not granted if registered owner not at fault		637
15.42	Removal for non-use		640
	15.42.1	General discretion	642
	15.42.2	Changes to non-use under the *Trade Marks Amendment Act 2006*	642

16 Exploitation of registered trade marks — 643

16.1	Overview of infringement of trade marks		644
	16.1.1	Use as a trade mark	644
	16.1.2	Use as descriptive term rather than as trade mark	645
	16.1.3	Sign used to distinguish goods and services from others	646
	16.1.4	Substantially identical with or deceptively similar to	647
	16.1.5	Relevance of the defendant's conduct	649
	16.1.6	Relevance of the plaintiff's trade mark's reputation	650
16.2	Section 120(1)		652
	16.2.1	The goods or services for which the trade mark is registered	653
16.3	Section 120(2)		653
16.4	Section 120(3)		654
	16.4.1	Anti-dilution	655
	16.4.2	Well known	656
	16.4.3	Used in relation to unrelated goods or services	657
	16.4.4	Indicating a connection with the owner	658
	16.4.5	Owner's interests adversely affected	660
	16.4.6	Anti-dilution or passing off?	660
	16.4.7	Comparison with passing off	661
16.5	Oral use of a trade mark		662
16.6	Two-dimensional device infringed by three-dimensional shape		662

16.7	Parallel importing	662
	16.7.1 Parallel importing and exclusive licensees	666
	16.7.2 Section 122A	666
	16.7.3 Parallel importing and passing off	667
16.8	Second-hand goods	668
16.9	Trade mark infringement and the internet	669
16.10	Breach of certain restrictions: s 121	671
16.11	Groundless threats of legal proceedings	672
16.12	Acts not constituting infringement	673
	16.12.1 In good faith	674
	16.12.2 Good faith use of a name: s 122(1)(a)	675
	16.12.3 Good faith use of a sign: s 122(1)(b)	675
	16.12.4 Good faith used to indicate purpose: s 122(1)(c)	676
	16.12.5 Use of trade mark for comparative advertising: s 122(1)(d)	676
	16.12.6 Exercising right to use trade mark: s 122(1)(e)	677
	16.12.7 Defendant may obtain registration of similar trade mark: s 122(1)(f)	677
	16.12.8 Non-infringement due to condition or limitation: s 122(1)(g)	678
	16.12.9 Disclaimers: s 122(1)(h)	678
16.13	Trade mark applied by or with consent of registered owner	679
16.14	Prior continuous use defence: s 124	679
16.15	No damages for infringement during non-use period: s 127	680
16.16	Remedies	680
16.17	Assignment of trade marks	681
	16.17.1 Process of assignment	681
	16.17.2 Assignment of certification trade marks	683
	16.17.3 Assignment of collective trade marks	683
	16.17.4 Assignment of defensive trade marks	683
16.18	Licensing of trade marks	683
	16.18.1 Quality control	684
	16.18.2 Financial control	685
	16.18.3 Other forms of control	686
	16.18.4 Franchising	686
	16.18.5 Assignment of licences	687
16.19	Voluntary recording of interests and claims	687
16.20	International treaty obligations	688

PART V ENFORCEMENT OF RIGHTS 691

17 Remedies and miscellaneous issues 693

17.1 Introduction 694
17.2 Pre-trial remedies 694
    17.2.1 Anton Piller orders 694
    17.2.2 Representative orders 696
    17.2.3 Interlocutory injunctions 697
17.3 Permanent injunctions 698
17.4 Groundless threats 699
17.5 Damages 700
17.6 Account of profits 700
17.7 Criminal liability 702
17.8 Customs seizure 702
17.9 Jurisdiction 703
17.10 Intellectual property and freedom of competition 704
    17.10.1 *Per se* prohibitions 704
    17.10.2 Rule of reason prohibitions 705
    17.10.3 Abolition of exemptions under s 51(3) 706

Index *707*

PREFACE

As with the previous three editions of this book, this edition attempts to provide a detailed and scholarly insight into Australian intellectual property law. Its primary emphasis is on the principles of and complexities in that law. The authors have made a deliberate decision to focus on these issues to the exclusion of the wider policy issues surrounding intellectual property law. They have done so for a number of reasons. The first of these is that space constraints make it impractical to adequately deal with those policy considerations in a meaningful way. Consequently, they are flagged throughout the book and detailed references are made to the many excellent works that already discuss those matters and to the numerous reviews of intellectual property that have been undertaken. The second and related reason is that an adequate investigation into and analytic examination of the legal principles and complexities of Australian intellectual property law require the sort of detailed treatment that has been undertaken and, again, space constraints demanded a choice about which issues to focus on. The intention is, therefore, to provide an in-depth and scholarly analysis of intellectual property law. By so doing, we aim to increase the stock of knowledge in this important area of the law.

It is no surprise that in the time that has elapsed since the third edition, the law has continued to expand and develop in ways both expected and unexpected. Key developments include a number of complex cases and the proposed and enacted amendments to the *Copyright Act 1968* (Cth), the *Patents Act 1990* (Cth) and the *Plant Breeder's Rights Act 1994* (Cth) made in response to recommendations of the 2016 Productivity Commission inquiry report *Intellectual Property Arrangements*. The consequence is the need for a new edition that takes account of that expansion and development. In addition, there have been a number of important cases on a wide range of issues, including the inevitable question of what constitutes a manner of manufacture for patenting purposes in the context of increasingly sophisticated advances in digital technology and the life sciences. In the areas of copyright and designs, some of the recent case law developments on copyright in photographs, moral rights and designs infringement are discussed, as are the Australian Law Reform Commission's report on copyright in the digital economy and the Advisory Council on Intellectual Property's review of the designs legislation.

In trade mark law, there have been significant case law developments in relation to licensing of trade marks and what constitutes necessary control together with both case law and statutory developments in parallel importing. In addition to these major developments, myriad smaller but still significant developments have occurred in relation to issues such as the concept of substantial identity. The law as covered by the fourth edition is current to 24 March 2019.

The authors have been responsible for authoring the following chapters:

Mark Davison
Chapters 1 and 14–17
Ann Monotti
Chapters 8–13
Leanne Wiseman
Chapters 2–7

ACKNOWLEDGEMENTS

For the first edition, Mark Davison records his thanks to Sarah Wilkins for her research assistance.

Ann Monotti records her thanks to the partners of Davies Collison Cave, Melbourne, and in particular Mr Raymond Hind, for providing her with a quiet haven in which to write sections of this book during a period of sabbatical leave. She also thanks the following people for their help with a variety of secretarial and other tasks: Maryanne Cassar, Erica Contini, Garmia Dewa and Sarah Weinberg.

Leanne Wiseman would like to thank her colleagues at the Australian Centre for Intellectual Property in Agriculture and Jodi Gardner for her research efforts.

We would like to acknowledge the insightful comments of the anonymous referees and the assistance of the production team at Cambridge University Press, including Zoe Hamilton, Kate Indigo and Greg Alford, and the initial involvement of Jill Henry as Commissioning Editor.

For the second edition, we would like to acknowledge the assistance of the production team at Cambridge University Press, including Kim Armitage (Publishing Manager), Bridget Ell (Commissioning Editor), Jodie Howell (Managing Editor) and Angela Damis (copy editor).

For the third edition we would like to acknowledge the assistance of the production team at Cambridge University Press, including Lucy Russell (Senior Commissioning Editor), Jodie Fitzsimmons (Managing Editor) and Angela Damis (copy editor).

For the fourth edition, we would like to acknowledge the assistance of the production team at Cambridge University Press, including Lucy Russell (Senior Commissioning Editor), Rose Albiston (Academic Development Editor) and Lilla Wendoloski (copy editor). Ann Monotti would like to thank Jordan Finch and Joseph Okraglik for their research assistance and for checking references. Leanne Wiseman would like to thank Prof Jay Sanderson for his collegial support and Anna Stirling and Courtney Thorne for their research assistance.

***

We are grateful to the following individuals and organisations for permission to use their material in *Australian Intellectual Property Law*.

Extracts from Federal Court Reports; Commonwealth Law Reports: Reproduced with permission of Thomson Reuters (Professional) Australia Limited, legal.thomsonreuters.com.au.

Extract from Final Report on the Review of the Designs System by The Advisory Council on Intellectual Property (ACIP): © Advisory Council on Intellectual Property 2014, reproduced under a Creative Commons Attribution 3.0 Australia licence.

Extract from TRIPS Agreement: Reproduced with the permission of the World Trade Organization.

Extract from *General Tire & Rubber Co v Firestone Tyre & Rubber Co Ltd* [1972] RPC 457: Reproduced by permission of Oxford University Press.

Extracts from Explanatory Memorandum, Intellectual Property Laws Amendment (Raising the Bar) Bill 2011 (Cth); *Circuits Layouts Act 1989*; *Competition and Consumer Act 2010*; *Copyright Act 1968*; *Copyright Amendment Act 2006*; *Designs Act 1906*; *Designs Act 2003*; *Intellectual Property Laws Amendment Act 2006*; *Intellectual Property Laws Amendment (Raising the Bar) Act 2012*; *Patents Act 1952*; *Patents Act 1990*; *Patents Regulations 1991*; *Plant Breeder's Rights Act 1994*; *Resale Royalty Right for Visual Artists Act 2009*; *Trade Marks Act 1955*; *Trade Marks Act 1995*; *US Free Trade Agreement Implementation Act 2004*: Sourced from the Federal Register of Legislation. Reproduced under Creative Commons Attribution 4.0 International (CC BY 4.0). For the latest information on Australian Government law please go to www.legislation.gov.au.

Extracts from Intellectual Property Reports and Australian Law Reports originally published by LexisNexis.

Every effort has been made to trace and acknowledge copyright. The publisher apologises for any accidental infringement and welcomes information that would rectify the situation

TABLE OF CASES

A v Hayden (No 2) (1984) 156 CLR 532, **254, 256**
A & M Records Inc v Napster Inc (2000) 50 IPR 232, **120**
A Schroeder Music Publishing Co Ltd v Macauley [1974] 3 All ER 616, **105, 248**
AA Levey v Henderson-Kenton (Holdings) Ltd [1974] RPC 617, **544**
Abbott Laboratories v Corbridge Group Pty Ltd (2002) 57 IPR 432, **372**
Abernethy v Hutchinson (1825) 47 ER 1313, **225**
Abrahams v Biggs [2011] FCA 1475, **231, 235**
Abundant Earth Pty Ltd v R & C Products Pty Ltd (1985) 7 FCR 233, **559**
Accor Australia & New Zealand Hospitality Pty Ltd v Liv Pty Ltd [2017] FCAFC 56, **608, 648**
ACI Australia Ltd v Glamour Glaze Pty Ltd (1988) 11 IPR 269, **544**
Acme Bedstead Co Ltd v Newlands Brothers Ltd (1937) 58 CLR 689, **330–1, 334, 337**
Acohs Pty Ltd v Ucorp Pty Ltd (2010) 86 IPR 492, **72**
Acorn Computer Ltd v MCS Microcomputer Systems Pty Ltd (1984) 6 FCR 277, **682**
Actavis Pty Ltd v Orion Corp [2016] FCAFC 121, **397**
Actavis UK Ltd v Janssen Pharmaceutica NV [2008] FSR 35, **332**
Actavis UK Ltd v Merck & Co Inc [2009] 1 WLR 1186, **449**
Ad Lib Club Ltd v Granville [1972] RPC 673, **543**
Adair v Young (1879) LR 12 Ch D 13, **457**
Adams v Quasar Management Service Pty Ltd (2002) 56 IPR 385, **175**
Adamson v Kenworthy (1932) 49 RPC 57, **413–14**
Adamson v New South Wales Rugby League Ltd (1991) 31 FCR 242, **412**
Adelaide City Corporation v Australasian Performing Right Association Ltd (1928) 40 CLR 481, **462**
Adhesives Pty Ltd v Aktieselskabet Dansk Gaerings-Industri (1935) 55 CLR 523, **489**
Adidas AG v Pacific Brands Footwear Pty Ltd (No 3) (2013) 308 ALR 74, **646, 650, 652**
Advanced Building Systems Pty Ltd v Ramset Fasteners (Australia) Pty Ltd (1995) AIPC 91-129, **461, 474**
Advanced Building Systems Pty Ltd v Ramset Fasteners (Australia) Pty Ltd (1998) 194 CLR 171, **297, 367–8, 371**
Advantage-Rent-A-Car v Advantage Car Rental Pty Ltd (2001) 52 IPR 24, **605**
Aerial Taxi Cabs Co-operative Society Ltd v Lee (2000) 102 FCR 125, **412**
Aerotel Ltd v Telco Holdings Ltd; Macrossan's Application [2007] 1 All ER 225, **306**
AG Australia Holdings Ltd v Burton (2002) 58 NSWLR 464, **222, 238, 256–7**
AG Spalding & Brothers v AW Gamage Ltd (1915) 32 RPC 273, **12, 532, 547, 561, 680**
AGL Sydney Ltd v Shortland County Council (1989) 17 IPR 99, **149**
Ahiida Pty Ltd v JB Trading Group Pty Ltd [2016] FCCA 3146, **215**
Aircraft Pty Ltd v Dickson [2014] SASC 108, **261**

Ajinomoto Co Inc v NutraSweet Australia Pty Ltd (2008) 166 FCR 530, **351**
Aktiebolaget Hassle v Alphapharm Pty Ltd (1999) 44 IPR 593, **359**
Aktiebolaget Hassle v Alphapharm Pty Ltd (2000) 51 IPR 375, **325, 347, 359, 443**
Aktiebolaget Hassle v Alphapharm Pty Ltd (2002) 212 CLR 411, **347, 350, 356–7, 361, 363, 366, 405**
Aktiebolaget Manus v RJ Fullwood & Bland Ltd (1949) 66 RPC 71, **641**
Alain Bernadin & Cie v Pavilion Properties Ltd [1967] RPC 581, **535**
Albany Molecular Research Inc v Alphapharm Pty Ltd (2011) 90 IPR 457, **490–1**
Albert & Sons Pty Ltd v Fletcher Construction Ltd [1974] 2 NZLR 107, **104**
Aldi Foods Pty Ltd v Moroccanoil Israel Ltd [2018] FCAFC 93, **598**
Aldi Stores Ltd Partnership v Frito-Lay Trading Co GmbH (2001) 54 IPR 344, **677–8**
Alexander v Henry (1895) 12 RPC 360, **680**
Alexander v Tait-Jamison (1993) 28 IPR 103, **584**
Alexander Pirie & Sons Ltd's Application [1933] All ER 956, **614**
Alfa Laval Cheese Systems Ltd v Wincanton Engineering Ltd [1990] FSR 583, **233**
Allaway v Lancome Investments Ltd (2002) 58 IPR 346, **407**
Allen Hardware Products v Tclip [2008] ADO 8, **200**
Allen Manufacturing Co Pty Ltd v McCallum & Co Pty Ltd (2001) 53 IPR 400, **463**
Allied Mills Industries Pty Ltd v Trade Practices Commission (1981) 34 ALR 105, **257–8**
Alphapharm Pty Ltd v H Lundbeck A/S (2008) 76 IPR 618, **282, 459, 479**
Alphapharm Pty Ltd v Merck & Co Inc [2006] FCA 1227, **370**
Amalgamated Television Services Pty Ltd v Clissold (2000) 52 IPR 207, **533**
American Cynamid Co v Ethicon Ltd [1975] AC 396, **697**
American Geophysical Union v Texaco Inc (2006) 60 F 3d 913, **145**
AMI Australia Holdings Pty Ltd v Fairfax Media Publications Pty Ltd [2010] NSWSC 1395, **257**
Amoco Australia Pty Ltd v Rocca Bros Motor Engineering Co Pty Ltd (1973) 133 CLR 288, **412–13**
AMP Inc v Commissioner of Patents (1974) 48 ALJR 278, **397**
AMP Inc v Utilux Pty Ltd (1971) 45 ALJR 123, **204, 294, 386, 389**
Amrad Operations Pty Ltd v Genelabs Technologies Inc (1999) 45 IPR 447, **426**
Amway Corp v Eurway International Ltd [1973] FSR 213, **228**
Anaesthetic Supplies Pty Ltd v Rescare Ltd (1994) 50 FCR 1, **284, 299, 301, 313–14, 321, 387, 399, 466, 468, 473**
Ancher, Mortlock, Murray & Woolley Pty Ltd v Hooker Homes Pty Ltd [1971] 2 NSWLR 278, **60**
Anchorage Capital Partners Pty Ltd v ACPA Pty Ltd [2018] FCAFC 6, **620, 635, 648**
Andrew Shelton & Co Pty Ltd v Alpha Healthcare Ltd (2002) 5 VR 577, **231**
Aneeta Window Systems (Vic) Pty Ltd v K Shugg Industries Pty Ltd (1996) 34 IPR 95, **414, 416**
Angoves Pty Ltd v Johnson (1982) 66 FLR 216, **608, 675**
Anheuser-Busch Inc v Budejovicky Budvar (1984) 4 IPR 260, **535**
Anheuser-Busch Inc v Budejovicky Budvar (2002) 56 IPR 182, **674**
Ansell Rubber Co Pty Ltd v Allied Rubber Industries Pty Ltd [1967] VR 37, **226, 230, 234, 236, 253–4**
Anton Piller KG v Manufacturing Processes Ltd (1976) Ch 55, **694**
Apand Pty Ltd v Kettle Chip Co Pty Ltd (1994) 52 FCR 474, **540, 567, 646**
Apand Pty Ltd v Kettle Chip Co Pty Ltd (1999) 88 FCR 568, **701–2**
Apotex Inc v Wellcome Foundation Ltd [2002] 4 SCR 153, **403**

Apotex Pty Ltd v AstraZeneca AB (No 4) (2013) 100 IPR 285, **343, 471**
Apotex Pty Ltd v Les Laboratories Servier [2013] FCA 1426, **392, 489–90**
Apotex Pty Ltd v Les Laboratories Servier (No 2) (2012) 293 ALR 272, **461**
Apotex Pty Ltd v Les Laboratories Servier (No 4) (2010) 89 IPR 274, **461–2**
Apotex Pty Ltd v Sanofi-Aventis (2009) 82 IPR 416, **334, 338, 346, 369**
Apotex Pty Ltd v Sanofi-Aventis Australia Pty Ltd (2013) 253 CLR 284, **270, 299–301, 313, 315–18, 322, 449, 468, 471–2**
Apotex Pty Ltd v Sanofi-Aventis Australia Pty Ltd (No 2) (2012) 204 FCR 494, **332**
Apotex Pty Ltd v Warner-Lambert Co LLC (No 2) (2016) 122 IPR 17, **491**
Apotex Pty Ltd (formerly GenRx Pty Ltd) v Sanofi-Aventis (2008) 78 IPR 485, **334, 338, 369, 370**
Apple Computer Inc v Computer Edge Pty Ltd (1983) 50 ALR 581, **52**
Apple Computer Inc v Computer Edge Pty Ltd (1984) 53 ALR 225, **53**
Apple Inc [2017] ADO 6, **204–5**
Apple Inc v Registrar of Trade Marks [2014] FCA 1304, **600**
Aquaculture Corp v New Zealand Green Mussel Co Ltd [1990] 3 NZLR 299, **261**
Aquaculture Corp v New Zealand Green Mussel Co Ltd (No 2) (1986) 10 IPR 319, **630**
Architects (Australia) Pty Ltd v Witty Consultants Pty Ltd [2002] QSC 139, **552, 555**
Argyll v Argyll [1967] 1 Ch 302, **222, 230**
Aristocrat Leisure Industries Pty Ltd v Pacific Gaming Pty Ltd (2000) 105 FCR 153, **55**
Aristocrat Technologies Australia Pty Ltd [2016] APO 49, **306**
Arrow Pharmaceuticals Ltd v Merck & Co Inc (2004) 63 IPR 85, **329, 369, 448**
Arsenal Football Club plc v Reed (No 2) [2003] 3 All ER 865, **549–50, 645**
Artcraft Urban Group Pty Ltd v Streetworx Pty Ltd (2016) 245 FCR 485, **371**
Ashdown v Telegraph Group Ltd [2002] Ch 149, **143, 145**
Asia Television Ltd v Yau's Entertainment Pty Ltd (2000) 49 IPR 264, **582**
Aspirating IP Ltd v Vision Systems Ltd (2010) 88 IPR 52, **338**
Association for Molecular Pathology v Myriad Genetics Inc (2013) 569 US 576, **308–9**
Aston v Harlee Manufacturing Co (1960) 103 CLR 391, **587**
AstraZeneca AB v Apotex Pty Ltd (2014) 226 FCR 324, **325, 330, 332–8, 349, 351–2, 359–60, 365–6, 368–9, 402–3, 466, 468–70, 472, 488**
AstraZeneca AB v Apotex Pty Ltd (2015) 257 CLR 356, **349, 352, 357–8, 360, 362**
AT Poeton (Gloucester Plating) Ltd v Horton [2000] EWCA Civ 180, **254**
AT&T Corp's Application [2001] ATMO 96, **592, 658**
Atlantis Corp Pty Ltd v Schindler (1997) 39 IPR 29, **398, 490**
Attorney-General (Cth) v Adelaide Steamship Co Ltd [1913] AC 781, **266, 480**
Attorney-General (NSW) v Brewery Employees Union of New South Wales (1908) 6 CLR 469, **20**
Attorney-General (NSW) ex rel Elisha v Holy Apostolic and Catholic Church of the East (Assyrian) Australia New South Wales Parish Association (1989) 14 IPR 609, **563**
Attorney-General (UK) v Guardian Newspapers Ltd (No 2) [1988] 3 All ER 545, **224, 230, 232, 236, 238, 243–5**
Attorney-General (UK) v Heinemann Publishers Australia Pty Ltd (1987) 10 NSWLR 86, **230, 257**
Attorney-General (UK) v Heinemann Publishers Australia Pty Ltd (1987) 8 NSWLR 341, **258**
Attorney-General (UK) v Heinemann Publishers Australia Pty Ltd (No 2) (1988) 165 CLR 30, **230**
Attorney-General (UK) v Jonathan Cape Ltd [1976] QB 752, **230, 243**
Ausdoc Office Pty Ltd v Complete Office Supplies Pty Ltd (1996) 136 ALR 659, **538**

Austal Ships Pty Ltd v Stena Rederi AB (2005) 66 IPR 420, **448**
Austereo Pty Ltd v DMG Radio (Australia) Pty Ltd (2004) 209 ALR 93, **595–6**
Austoft Industries Ltd v Cameco Industries Inc (1995) 33 IPR 251, **342**
Australasian Performing Right Association Ltd v Ceridale Pty Ltd (1990) 19 IPR 1, **706**
Australasian Performing Right Association Ltd v Metro on George Pty Ltd (2004) 61 IPR 575, **462**
Australasian Performing Right Association Ltd v Telstra Corp (1993) 46 FCR 131, **88**
Australian Broadcasting Corporation v Lenah Game Meats Pty Ltd (2001) 208 CLR 199, **4**, **227**, **232**, **236**, **239**
Australian Broadcasting Corporation v O'Neill (2006) 227 CLR 57, **697**
Australian Capital Territory v Munday (2000) 99 FCR 72, **412**
Australian Competition and Consumer Commission v Chen (2003) 132 FCR 309, **699**
Australian Football League v The Age Co Ltd (2006) 15 VR 419, **233**, **256–7**
Australian Marketing Development Pty Ltd v Australian Interstate Marketing Pty Ltd [1972] VR 219, **618**
Australian Meat Group Pty Ltd v JBS Australia Pty Ltd [2018] FCAFC 207, **611**, **652**
Australian Medic-Care Co Ltd v Hamilton Pharmaceutical Pty Ltd (2009) 261 ALR 501, **223–4**, **227**, **233**, **243**
Australian Mud Company Pty Ltd v Coretell Pty Ltd (2010) 88 IPR 270, **447**
Australian Postal Corporation v Digital Post Australia (2013) 308 ALR 1, **675**
Australian Tape Manufacturers Association Ltd v Commonwealth (1993) 176 CLR 480, **21**, **62**, **154**, **462**
Australian Video Retailers Association Ltd v Warner Home Video Pty Ltd (2001) 53 IPR 242, **54**, **87**, **92**
Austshade Pty Ltd v Boss Shade Pty Ltd (2016) 118 IPR 93, **451**
Autocaps (Australia) Pty Ltd v Pro-Kit Pty Ltd (1999) 46 IPR 339, **52**
Autodesk Australia Pty Ltd v Cheung (1990) 94 ALR 472, **138**
Autodesk Inc v Dyason (No 1) (1992) 173 CLR 330, **53**, **117**, **119**
Autodesk Inc v Dyason (No 2) (1993) 176 CLR 300, **54**, **119–20**
Autodesk Inc v Yee (1996) 68 FCR 391, **140**
Avel Pty Ltd v Multicoin Amusements Pty Ltd (1990) 18 IPR 443, **88**
Avel Pty Ltd v Wells (1992) 23 IPR 353, **190**, **193–4**
Azuko Pty Ltd v Old Digger Pty Ltd (2000) 51 IPR 43, **377**
Azuko Pty Ltd v Old Digger Pty Ltd (2001) 52 IPR 75, **330**, **373–7**, **456**

Bacich v Australian Broadcasting Corporation (1992) 29 NSWLR 1, **257**
Badische Anilin & Soda Fabrik v Henry Johnson & Co (1897) 14 RPC 919, **457**
Bailey v Namol Pty Ltd (1994) 53 FCR 102, **139**
Balston Ltd v Headline Filters Ltd [1990] FSR 385, **249–50**
Bank of New South Wales v Commonwealth (1948) 76 CLR 1, **378**
Banks v Transport Regulation Board (Vic) (1968) 119 CLR 222, **424**
Banner Universal Motion Pictures Ltd v Endemol Shine Group Ltd [2017] EWHC 2600, **56**
Barnet Instruments Ltd v Overton (1949) 66 RPC 315, **414**
Baume & Co Ltd v AH Moore Ltd [1958] Ch 907, **674**
Bavaria NV v Bayerischer Brauerbund eV (2009) 177 FCR 300, **623–4**
Bayer Pharma Pty Ltd v Farbenfabriken Bayer AG (1965) 120 CLR 285, **581**
Bayer Pharma Pty Ltd v Henry York & Co Pty Ltd [1964] FSR 143, **544**
Baygol Pty Ltd v Foamex Polystyrene Pty Ltd (2005) 66 IPR 1, **446**, **448**

Bayley & Associates Pty Ltd v DBR Australia Pty Ltd [2013] FCA 1341, **416**
Bedford Industries Rehabilitation Association Inc v Pinefair Pty Ltd (1998) 40 IPR 438, **452–3, 456, 480**
Bedford Industries Rehabilitation Association Inc v Pinefair Pty Ltd (1998) 87 FCR 458, **480**
Beecham Group Ltd v Bristol Laboratories International SA [1978] RPC 521, **345**
Beecham Group Ltd v Bristol Laboratories Ltd (No 1) [1978] RPC 153, **453, 459**
Beecham Group Ltd v Bristol Laboratories Pty Ltd (1968) 118 CLR 618, **697**
Belegging-en-Exploitatiemaatschappij Lavender BV v Witten Industrial Diamonds Ltd [1979] FSR 59, **464**
Beloff v Pressdram Ltd [1973] RPC 765, **148, 153, 165, 255**
Bennetts v Board of Fire Commissioners of New South Wales (1967) 87 WN (Pt 1) (NSW) 307, **232**
Berkeley Hotel Co Ltd v Berkeley International (Mayfair) Ltd [1972] RPC 237, **544**
Berlei Hestia Industries v Bali Co Inc (1973) 129 CLR 353, **598, 610**
BEST Australia Ltd v Aquagas Marketing Pty Ltd (1988) 83 ALR 217, **462, 464**
Betts v Neilson (1868) LR 3 Ch App 429, **457**
Betts v Willmott (1871) LR 6 Ch App 239, **451, 460**
Bihari v Gross (2000) 119 F Supp 2d 309, **557**
Billhöfer Maschinenfabrik GmbH v TH Dixon & Co Ltd [1990] FSR 105, **116**
Bilski v Kappos (2010) 561 US 593, **303**
Biogen Idec MA Inc [2014] APO 25, **328, 338, 344**
Biogen Inc v Medeva plc [1997] RPC 1, **308, 396**
Bismag v Amblins [1940] Ch 667, **677**
Bitech Engineering v Garth Living (2010) 86 IPR 468, **444**
Blackie & Sons Ltd v Lothian Book Publishing Co Pty Ltd (1921) 29 CLR 397, **91**
BLH Engineering & Construction Pty Ltd v Pro 3 Products Pty Ltd (2015) 114 IPR 105, **486**
Bloomsbury Publishing Group Ltd v News Group Newspapers Ltd [2003] FSR 45, **239**
Blount Inc v Registrar of Trade Marks (1998) 83 FCR 50, **599**
Blue Gentian LLC v Product Management Group Pty Ltd (2014) 110 IPR 453, **425, 473**
Blueport Nominees Pty Ltd v Sewerage Management Services Pty Ltd (2015) 251 FCR 127, **462**
BlueScope Steel Ltd v Gram Engineering Pty Ltd [2014] FCAFC 107, **211**
BM Auto Sales Pty Ltd v Budget Rent A Car System Pty Ltd (1976) 12 ALR 363, **535**
Boehringer Ingelheim International GmbH v Commissioner of Patents (No 2) (2001) 112 FCR 595, **281**
Bohemia Crystal Pty Ltd v Host Corp Pty Ltd [2018] FCA 235, **598**
Bollinger v Costa Brava Wine Co Ltd [1960] Ch 262, **531, 536, 546, 561**
Bombala Council v Peter Wilkshire [2009] ATMO 33, **626**
Booth v Federal Commissioner of Taxation (1987) 164 CLR 159, **410**
Bosch's Application (1909) 26 RPC 710, **345**
Bostitch Trade Mark [1963] RPC 183, **684**
Bowden Wire Ltd v Bowden Brake Co Ltd (1914) 31 RPC 385, **683**
Boyce v Morris Motors Ltd (1927) 44 RPC 105, **334**
BP Refinery (Westernport) Pty Ltd v Shire of Hastings (1977) 180 CLR 266, **252**
Brabazon v Western Mail Ltd (1985) 58 ALR 712, **568**
Breen v Williams (1996) 186 CLR 71, **4, 226, 245–6, 410**
Brent v Federal Commissioner of Taxation (1971) 125 CLR 418, **225**
Bresagen Ltd v Austin Research Institute (2004) 60 IPR 174, **308**
Breville Pty Ltd v Warehouse Group (Australia) Pty Ltd (2005) 67 IPR 576, **448**

Bridge v Deacons [1984] AC 705, **413**
Bridge Stockbrokers Ltd v Bridges (1984) 4 FCR 460, **559, 564**
Bristol-Myers Co v Beecham Group Ltd [1974] AC 646, **330, 334, 373–4, 376**
Bristol-Myers Squibb Co v Apotex Pty Ltd (No 5) (2013) 104 IPR 23, **424–5, 450, 461**
Bristol-Myers Squibb Co v Baker Norton Pharmaceuticals Inc [1999] RPC 253, **449**
Bristol-Myers Squibb Co v FH Faulding & Co Ltd (1998) 41 IPR 467, **301, 314, 321, 461, 464, 466, 473**
Bristol-Myers Squibb Co v FH Faulding & Co Ltd (2000) 97 FCR 524, **301, 313, 315, 321, 332–3, 337, 359, 367–9, 461, 464, 466, 472**
Britax Childcare Pty Ltd v Infa-Secure Pty Ltd (2012) 290 ALR 47, **273**
Britax Childcare Pty Ltd v Infa-Secure Pty Ltd (No 3) [2012] FCA 1019, **279, 449, 484**
British American Tobacco Exports v Trojan Trading Co Pty Ltd (2010) 90 IPR 392, **702**
British American Tobacco (Investments) Ltd v Philip Morris Ltd (1999) 47 IPR 351, **330**
British Dynamite Co v Krebs (1896) 13 RPC 190, **389**
British Franco Electric Pty Ltd v Dowling Plastics Pty Ltd [1981] 1 NSWLR 448, **259–60**
British Leyland Motor Corp Ltd v Armstrong Patents Co [1986] AC 577, **59**
British Motor Syndicate Ltd v Taylor & Son [1901] 1 Ch 122, **458**
British Nylon Spinners Ltd v Imperial Chemical Industries Ltd [1952] 2 All ER 780, **437**
British Ore Concentration Syndicate Ltd v Minerals Separation Ltd (1909) 26 RPC 124, **337**
British Reinforced Concrete Engineering Co v Lind (1917) 34 RPC 101, **414**
British Steel Corporation v Granada Television Ltd [1981] AC 1096, **165**
British Syphon Co Ltd v Homewood [1956] 1 WLR 1190, **413**
British Telecommunications v One-in-a-Million [1998] NLJR 1179, **551**
British Thomson-Houston Co Ltd v Corona Lamp Works Ltd (1922) 39 RPC 49, **390**
British Thomson-Houston Co Ltd v Metropolitan-Vickers Electrical Co Ltd (1928) 45 RPC 1, **326**
British United Shoe Machinery Co Ltd v A Fussell & Sons Ltd (1908) 25 RPC 631, **383–4, 388, 441**
British United Shoe Machinery Ltd v Simon Collier Ltd [1910] 27 RPC 567, **455, 457**
Brodel v Telstra Corp [2004] FCA 505, **51**
Broderbund Software Inc v Computermate Products (Australia) Pty Ltd (1991) 22 IPR 215, **705**
Brook v Canon Kabushiki Kaisha (1994) 30 IPR 525, **615**
Brookfield Communications Inc v West Coast Entertainment Corp (1999) 174 F 3d 1036, **556**
Brother Industries Ltd v Dynamic Supplies Pty Ltd (2007) 163 FCR 530, **665**
Buchanan v Alba Diagnostics Ltd [2004] RPC 34, **424**
Buchanan Turf Supplies Pty Ltd v Premier Turf Supplies Pty Ltd [2003] FCA 230, **520**
Budget Eyewear Australia Pty Ltd v Specsavers Pty Ltd (2010) 86 IPR 479, **51, 73**
Buffet v Fersing [1962] D Jur 570, **174**
Buildcorp Contracting NSW Pty Ltd v Build Corp Construction Pty Ltd [2019] FCA 90, **699**
Bulun Bulun v R & T Textiles Pty Ltd (1998) 41 IPR 513, **32, 79**
Burge v Swarbrick (2005) 149 FCR 193, **60, 62**
Burge v Swarbrick (2007) 232 CLR 336, **60**
Burger King Corp v Registrar of Trade Marks (1973) 128 CLR 417, **595, 598**
Burke & Margot Burke Ltd v Spicers Dress Designs [1936] Ch 400, **115**
Burroughs Wellcome Co v Barr Laboratories Inc (1994) 40 F 3d 1223, **403**
Burrows v Smith [2010] EWHC 22 (Ch), **231**
Butler v Board of Trade [1971] Ch 680, **236**
Byrne v Australian Airlines Ltd (1995) 185 CLR 410, **252**

C Van der Lely NV v Bamfords Ltd [1963] RPC 61, **323, 333, 336, 357, 445, 447**
C Van der Lely NV v Ruston's Engineering Co Ltd [1993] RPC 45, **391**
CA Henschke & Co v Rosemount Estates Pty Ltd (2000) 52 IPR 42, **545, 611, 642, 651, 686**
Cadbury Schweppes Pty Ltd v Darrell Lea Chocolate Shops Pty Ltd (No 4) (2006) 229 ALR 136, **533, 541**
Cadbury Schweppes Pty Ltd v Pub Squash Co Pty Ltd [1980] 2 NSWLR 851, **531, 533, 542, 545**
Caesarstone Ltd v Ceramiche Caesar SpA (No 2) [2018] FCA 1096, **616**
Calidad Pty Ltd v Seiko Epson Corp (2019) 142 IPR 381, **451, 454, 458**
Calvin Klein Inc v International Apparel Syndicate [1995] FSR 515, **534**
Camilleri v Steel Foundations Ltd (2003) AIPC 91-837, **407–8, 410**
Campbell v MGN Ltd [2004] 2 AC 457, **239**
Campomar SL v Nike International Ltd (2000) 202 CLR 45, **563, 566, 629, 634, 637, 656**
Canadian Shredded Wheat Co Ltd v Kellogg Co of Canada Ltd [1938] 1 All ER 618, **533**
Cancer Voices Australia v Myriad Genetics Inc (2013) 99 IPR 567, **308**
Canon Kabushiki Kaisha v Brook (1996) 69 FCR 401, **615**
Cantarella Brothers Pty Ltd v Kona Coffee Roastery & Equipment Supplies Pty Ltd (1993) 28 IPR 176, **625**
Cantarella Brothers Pty Ltd v Modena Trading Pty Ltd (2014) 315 ALR 4, **581, 596, 598**
Cantor Fitzgerald International v Tradition (UK) Ltd [2000] RPC 95, **119**
Career Step LLC v TalentMed Pty Ltd (No 2) [2018] FCA 132, **78**
Carindale Country Club Estate Pty Ltd v Astill (1993) 42 FCR 307, **228**
Carlton United Breweries v Royal Crown Co Inc (2001) 53 IPR 599, **606**
Castrol Australia Pty Ltd v EmTech Associates Pty Ltd (1980) 33 ALR 31, **230, 241, 255–7**
Caterpillar Inc v Amco (Vic) Pty Ltd (2000) 49 IPR 407, **613**
Caterpillar Inc v John Deere Ltd (1999) 48 IPR 1, **461–2**
Caterpillar Inc v Kozo Miyake [2000] APO 3, **341**
Caterpillar Loader Hire (Holdings) Pty Ltd v Caterpillar Tractor Co (1983) 77 FLR 139, **618**
Catnic Components Ltd v Hill & Smith Ltd [1982] RPC 183, **357, 444, 446–8**
Cave-Brown-Cave's Application for a Patent [1958] RPC 429, **342**
CBS Records Australia v Telmak Teleproducts (Australia) Pty Ltd (1987) 9 IPR 440, **62**
CBS Songs Ltd v Amstrad Consumer Electronics plc [1988] AC 1013, **122, 462**
CCH Canadian Ltd v Law Society of Upper Canada [2004] 1 SCR 339, **144**
CCOM Pty Ltd v Jiejing Pty Ltd (1993) 27 IPR 577, **463–4, 477**
CCOM Pty Ltd v Jiejing Pty Ltd (1994) 51 FCR 260, **284, 299, 301–3, 320, 396–8**
Centronics Systems Pty Ltd v Nintendo Co Ltd (1992) 39 FCR 147, **189**
Challender v Royle (1887) 36 Ch D 425, **673**
Challenge Engineering Ltd v Fitzroy Milk Tanks Pty Ltd (1997) 40 IPR 647, **586**
Chan v Zacharia (1984) 154 CLR 178, **416**
Chatterton v Cave (1878) 3 App Cas 483, **146**
Children's Television Workshop Inc v Woolworths Ltd (1981) 1 NSWLR 273, **543**
Chiron Corp v Murex Diagnostics Ltd [1996] RPC 535, **271**
Chiropedic Bedding Pty Ltd v Radburg Pty Ltd (2008) 170 FCR 560, **207**
Chiropedic Bedding Pty Ltd v Radburg Pty Ltd (2009) 181 FCR 446, **210**
Chocolaterie Guylian NV v Registrar of Trade Marks (2009) 180 FCR 60, **594**
Cincinnati Grinders (Inc) v BSA Tools Ltd (1931) 48 RPC 33, **371**
Clark v Adie (1875) 10 Ch App 667, **445**

Clark v Associated Newspapers Ltd (1998) 40 IPR 262, **175**
Clark Equipment Co v Registrar of Trade Marks (1964) 111 CLR 511, **595**
Clifford Davis Management Ltd v WEA Records Ltd [1975] 1 All ER 237, **105**
Clipsal Australia Pty Ltd v Clipso Electrical Pty Ltd (No 3) [2017] FCA 60, **545–6, 627, 677**
Clissold v Amalgamated Television Services Pty Ltd (2000) 52 IPR 207, **606**
Clorox Australia Pty Ltd v International Consolidated Business Pty Ltd (2005) 66 IPR 506, **437**
Clorox Australia Pty Ltd v International Consolidated Business Pty Ltd (2006) 68 IPR 254, **444, 448**
CLS Bank International v Alice Corp Pty Ltd (2013) 717 F 3d 1269, **303**
Clyde Nail Co Ltd v Russell (1916) 33 RPC 291, **345**
CMI-Centers for Medical Innovation GmbH v Phytopharm plc [1999] FSR 235, **228**
Coca-Cola Co v All-Fect Distributors Ltd (1998) 43 IPR 47, **657, 659**
Coca-Cola Co v All-Fect Distributors Ltd (1999) 96 FCR 107, **576, 581, 610, 646, 648, 651, 657–9, 661**
Coca-Cola Co v PepsiCo Inc (No 2) (2014) 109 IPR 429, **541, 560, 647, 649**
Coca-Cola Trade Marks [1986] FSR 472, **576**
Coco v AN Clark (Engineers) Ltd [1969] RPC 41, **224, 226–7, 230–1, 233–5, 237–8, 241–2, 245, 249, 260, 262**
Colbeam Palmer Ltd v Stock Affiliates Pty Ltd (1968) 122 CLR 25, **4, 680, 700–1**
Coles Supermarkets Australia Pty Ltd v FKP Ltd [2008] FCA 1915, **224**
Colgate Palmolive v Markwell Finance Ltd [1989] RPC 497, **664, 667**
Collier Constructions v Foskett (1990) 19 IPR 44, **165**
Collins v Northern Territory (2007) 161 FCR 549, **464–6, 469–71**
Collymore v Courier Pete Pty Ltd (2008) 79 IPR 608, **200**
Colorado Group Ltd v Strandbags Group Pty Ltd (2007) 164 FCR 506, **585, 611, 653**
Columbia Pictures Industries Inc v Luckins (1996) 34 IPR 504, **139**
Comite Interprofessionnel des Vins des Cotes de Provence v Bryce (1996) 69 FCR 450, **619**
Commercial Plastics Ltd v Vincent [1964] 3 WLR 820, **250**
Commissioner of Patents v AbbVie Biotechnology Ltd (2017) 253 FCR 436, **280–1, 449**
Commissioner of Patents v Emperor Sports Pty Ltd (2006) 149 FCR 386, **352, 360–1**
Commissioner of Patents v Microcell Ltd (1959) 102 CLR 232, **296, 367, 382**
Commissioner of Patents v RPL Central Pty Ltd (2015) 238 FCR 27, **302–7, 312**
Committee of Direction of Fruit Marketing v Australian Postal Commission (1980) 144 CLR 577, **419**
Commonwealth v John Fairfax & Sons Ltd (1980) 147 CLR 39, **148, 165, 226–7, 230, 235–6, 239, 243**
Commonwealth Industrial Gases Ltd v MWA Holdings Pty Ltd (1970) 180 CLR 160, **366, 449**
Companhia Souza Cruz Industria & Comercio v Rothmans of Pall Mall (Australia) Ltd (1998) 41 IPR 497, **598**
Computer Edge Pty Ltd v Apple Computer Inc (1986) 161 CLR 171, **50, 52**
ConAgra Inc v McCain Foods (Australia) Pty Ltd (1992) 33 FCR 302, **531–2, 536**
Concrete Constructions (NSW) Pty Ltd v Nelson (1990) 169 CLR 594, **378, 563**
Concrete Pty Ltd v Parramatta Design & Developments Pty Ltd [2004] FCA 1312, **140**
Concut Pty Ltd v Worrell (2000) 176 ALR 693, **224**
Conor Medsystems Inc v Angiotech Pharmaceutical Inc [2008] UKHL 49, **365**
Conor Medsystems Inc v University of British Columbia (2005) 223 ALR 74, **361–3**
Conor Medsystems Inc v University of British Columbia (No 2) (2006) 68 IPR 217, **489–90**
Coogi Australia Pty Ltd v Hysport International (1998) 41 IPR 593, **61**

Cooper v Universal Music Australia Pty Ltd (2006) 156 FCR 380, **113, 125**
Cooper Engineering Co Pty Ltd v Sigmund Pumps Ltd (1952) 86 CLR 536, **609**
Coopers Animal Health Australia Ltd v Western Stock Distributors Pty Ltd (1986) 6 IPR 545, **371**
Coopers Animal Health Australia Ltd v Western Stock Distributors Pty Ltd (1987) 15 FCR 382, **388**
Copyright Agency Ltd v Department of Education of New South Wales (1985) 59 ALR 172, **110**
Copyright Agency Ltd v Haines [1982] 1 NSWLR 182, **142**
Copyright Agency Ltd v Victoria University of Technology (1994) 53 FCR 56, **159**
Corby v Allen & Unwin Pty Ltd (2013) 101 IPR 181, **138**
Corby v Allen & Unwin Pty Ltd (2013) 297 ALR 761, **139, 171**
Coretell Pty Ltd v Australian Mud Company Pty Ltd (2017) 250 FCR 155, **273, 279, 284, 373, 376, 379, 399, 452, 484–5**
Corrs Pavey Whiting & Byrne v Collector of Customs (Vic) (1987) 14 FCR 434, **222, 227–9, 239, 243, 254–7**
Cortis Exhaust Systems Pty Ltd v Kitten Software Pty Ltd (2001) ATPR 41-837, **50, 64, 71**
Cosmetic, Toiletry and Fragrance Association Foundation v Fanni Barns Pty Ltd (2003) 57 IPR 594, **604**
Costa v GR & IE Daking Pty Ltd (1994) 29 IPR 241, **330, 334, 342, 405**
Coulthard v South Australia (1995) 63 SASR 531, **238, 243**
County Laboratories Ltd v J Mindel Ltd [1957] 1 Ch 295, **672**
Cowell v British American Tobacco Australia Services Ltd [2007] VSCA 301, **257**
Crane v Price (1842) 1 WPC 393, 4 M & G 580, 134 ER 239, **295**
Cranleigh Precision Engineering Ltd v Bryant [1964] 3 All ER 289, **241, 244, 246**
Cray Valley Ltd v Deltech Europe Ltd [2003] EWHC 728, **260**
Creation Records Ltd v News Group Newspapers Ltd (1997) 39 IPR 1, **232, 236, 239**
Crowley v Murphy (1981) 52 FLR 123, **222**
CSR Building Products Ltd v Abnoos (2009) 81 IPR 641, **403**
CSR Ltd v Resource Capital Australia Pty Ltd (2003) 128 FCR 408, **553, 669**
Cuisenaire v Reed [1963] VR 719, **60, 114**
Cullen v Welsbach Light Co of Australasia Ltd (1907) 4 CLR 990, **331**
Cultivaust Pty Ltd v Grain Pool Pty Ltd (2004) 62 IPR 11, **511–13, 515–16, 519**
Cultivaust Pty Ltd v Grain Pool Pty Ltd (2005) 147 FCR 265, **508, 511–13, 516**
Cummins v Bond [1927] 1 Ch 167, **68, 77**
Cummins v Vella [2002] FCAFC 218, **114**

D Sebel & Co Ltd v National Art Metal Co Pty Ltd (1965) 10 FLR 224, **204**
Daiquiri Rum Trade Mark [1969] RPC 600, **611, 653**
Dallas Buyers Club LLC v iiNet Ltd [2015] FCA 317, **130**
Damorgold Pty Ltd v Blindware (2017) 130 IPR 1, **486**
Damorgold Pty Ltd v JAI Products Pty Ltd (2014) 105 IPR 60, **461–4**
Damorgold Pty Ltd v JAI Products Pty Ltd (2015) 229 FCR 68, **332**
Darcy v Allin (1602) 77 ER 1260, **266**
D'Arcy v Myriad Genetics Inc (2014) 224 FCR 479, **298–9, 301, 308–10**
D'Arcy v Myriad Genetics Inc (2015) 258 CLR 334, **14, 294, 297, 299–300, 302, 305, 308, 310, 312–13, 315, 319, 321–2, 368, 444**
D'Arcy v Myriad Genetics Inc [2015] HCA Trans 12, **310**
Dart Industries Inc v David Bryar & Associates Pty Ltd (1997) 38 IPR 389, **240, 259**
Dart Industries Inc v Décor Corp Pty Ltd (1989) 15 IPR 403, **208, 210**

Dart Industries Inc v Décor Corp Pty Ltd [1994] FSR 567, **701**
Darvall McCutcheon (a firm) v HK Frost Holdings Pty Ltd (in liq) (2002) 4 VR 570, **231**, **260–1**
Darwin Fibreglass Pty Ltd v Kruhse Enterprises Pty Ltd (1998) 41 IPR 649, **60**
Data Access Corp v Powerflex Services Pty Ltd (1999) 202 CLR 1, **50**, **53–4**, **117**, **119**, **302**
Datadot Technology Ltd v Alpha Microtech Pty Ltd (2003) 59 IPR 402, **468**, **472**
David McNicol v Australian Capital Territory Health Authority [1988] ACTSC 55, **341**
David Syme & Co Ltd v GMH Ltd [1984] 2 NSWLR 294, **256–7**
Davis v Commonwealth (1988) 166 CLR 79, **20**
DB Breweries v Domain Name Co Ltd (2001) 52 IPR 280, **671**
DC Payments Pty Ltd v Next Payments Pty Ltd [2016] VSC 315, **228**
De Garis v Neville Jeffress Pidler Pty Ltd (1990) 37 FCR 99, **144–9**, **153**
De Maudsley v Palumbo [1996] FSR 447, **230–1**
Deckers Outdoor Corp Inc v Farley (No 2) (2009) 176 FCR 33, **636**
Deckers Outdoor Corp Inc v Farley (No 5) (2009) 83 IPR 245, **59**
Decor Corp Pty Ltd v Dart Industries Inc (1988) 13 IPR 385, **371**, **441–4**
Del Casale v Artedomus (Australia) Pty Ltd (2007) 73 IPR 326, **223–4**, **230**, **234**, **249**, **251–4**
Delphic Wholesalers v Elco Food Co (1987) 8 IPR 545, **666**
Demon Ale Trade Mark [2000] RPC 345, **625**
Dempsey Group Pty Ltd v Spotlight Pty Ltd [2018] FCA 2016, **118**
Dennison Manufacturing Co v Monarch Marking Systems Inc (1983) 1 IPR 431, **329**
Dent v Turpin (1861) 2J & H 139, 70 ER 1003, **537**
Desktop Marketing Systems Pty Ltd v Telstra Corp Ltd (2002) 119 FCR 491, **4**, **19**, **52**, **71–2**
Deta Nominees Pty Ltd v Viscount Plastic Products Pty Ltd [1979] VR 167, **223–4**, **239**
Diamond v Chakrabarty (1980) 447 US 303, **307**, **309**
Diamond v Diehr (1991) 450 US 175, **302**
Dias Aluminium Products Pty Ltd v Ullrich Aluminium Pty Ltd (2006) 66 IPR 561, **205**
Digga Australia Pty Ltd v Norm Engineering Pty Ltd (2008) 166 FCR 268, **217**
Docker v Somes (1834) 39 ER 1095, **702**
Dominion Rent A Car Ltd v Budget Rent A Car Systems (1970) Ltd [1987] 2 NZLR 395, **538**
Donaldson v Beckett (1774) 4 Burr 2408, 98 ER 257, **31–2**
Donoghue v Allied Newspapers Ltd [1938] Ch 106, **77–8**
Dormeuil Freres SA v Feraglow [1990] RPC 449, **680**
Douglas v Hello! Ltd (No 3) [2006] QB 125, **230**, **232**, **235**, **239**
Dow Chemical AG v Spence Bryson & Co Ltd [1982] FSR 397, **463**
Dowson & Mason Ltd v Potter [1986] 1 WLR 1419, **260**
DP World Sydney Ltd v Guy [2016] NSWSC 1072, **251**, **258**
Dr Reddy's Laboratories (UK) Ltd v Eli Lilly & Co Ltd [2010] RPC 9, **334**, **345**
DSI Australia (Holdings) Pty Ltd v Garford Pty Ltd (2013) 100 IPR 19, **342**, **373**, **376**, **446**
Dunford & Elliott Ltd v Johnson & Firth Brown Ltd [1978] FSR 143, **227**, **243**
Dunlop Aircraft Tyres Ltd v The Goodyear Tire & Rubber Co [2018] FCA 1014, **627**, **641**
Dunlop Pneumatic Tyre Co Ltd v British & Colonial Motor Car Co (1901) 18 RPC 313, **453**, **457**
Dunlop Pneumatic Tyre Co Ltd v David Moseley & Sons Ltd [1904] 1 Ch 612, **464**
Dura-Post (Australia) Pty Ltd v Delnorth Pty Ltd (2009) 81 IPR 480, **349**, **354**, **370**
Durkan v Twentieth Century Fox Film Corp (2000) 47 IPR 651, **606–7**
Dynamic Supplies Pty Ltd v Tonnex International Pty Ltd (No 3) (2014) 312 ALR 705, **138–9**
Dynamite Games Pty Ltd v Aruze Gaming Australia Pty Ltd (2013) 103 IPR 373, **365**
Dyno Nobel Asia Pacific Ltd v Orica Australia Pty Ltd (1999) 99 FCR 151, **330**, **478**

E & J Gallo Winery v Lion Nathan Australia Pty Ltd (2008) 77 IPR 69, **654**
E & J Gallo Winery v Lion Nathan Australia Pty Ltd (2009) 175 FCR 386, **612, 654**
E & J Gallo Winery v Lion Nathan Australia Pty Ltd (2010) 241 CLR 144, **572, 584, 586**
E Worsley & Co Ltd v Cooper [1939] 1 All ER 290, **252**
Eagle Rock Entertainment Ltd v Caisley (2005) 66 IPR 554, **139**
Earl v Nationwide News Pty Ltd [2013] NSWSC 839, **227**
Earthquake Commission v Krieger [2014] 2 NZLR 547, **239**
Eastland Technology Australia Ltd v Ritract Ltd [2005] WASC 125, **424**
eBay v MercExchange (2006) 126 S Ct 1837, **699**
EdSonic v Cassidy (2010) 189 FCR 271, **82**
Edwards Hot Water Systems v SW Hart Pty Ltd (1985) 9 FCR 537, **58, 205**
EI Du Pont de Nemours & Co v ICI Chemicals & Polymers Ltd (2005) 66 IPR 462, **328, 361**
EI Du Pont de Nemours & Co v Imperial Chemical Industries plc (2002) 54 IPR 304, **357**
EI Du Pont de Nemours (Witsiepe's) Application [1982] FSR 303, **346**
Elconnex Pty Ltd v Gerard Industries Pty Ltd (1991) 32 FCR 491, **357, 395, 443, 449**
Elconnex Pty Ltd v Gerard Industries Pty Ltd (1992) 25 IPR 173, **357, 362–3**
Elecon Australia Pty Ltd v PIV Drives GmbH (2010) 93 IPR 174, **247**
Electric & Musical Industries Ltd v Lissen Ltd [1938] 4 All ER 221, **394, 441–4**
Electrolux Ltd v Electrix Ltd (No 2) (1954) 71 RPC 23, **678**
Electrolux Ltd v Hudson [1977] FSR 312, **248, 412–13**
Eli Lilly Canada Inc v Apotex Inc (2008) 75 IPR 625, **449**
Eli Lilly & Co v Pfizer Overseas Pharmaceuticals (2005) 64 IPR 506, **389, 391, 393–4**
Eli Lilly & Co Ltd v Apotex Pty Ltd (2013) 100 IPR 451, **345–6**
Elliott v Ivey [1998] NSWSC 116, **241**
Elmslie v Boursier (1869–70) LR 9 Eq 217, **458–9**
Elwood Clothing Pty Ltd v Cotton On Clothing Pty Ltd (2008) 76 IPR 83, **51**
Elwood Clothing Pty Ltd v Cotton On Clothing Pty Ltd (2008) 172 FCR 580, **59, 115**
EMI Songs Australia Pty Ltd v Larrikin Music Publishing Pty Ltd (2011) 191 FCR 444, **116–18**
Emory University v Biochem Pharma Inc (1998) 86 FCR 1, **492**
Encompass Corp Pty Ltd v InfoTrack Pty Ltd [2018] FCA 421, **306**
Encompass Corp Pty Ltd v InfoTrack Pty Ltd [2019] FCAFC 161, **304, 306**
English & American Insurance Co Ltd v Herbert Smith [1988] FSR 232, **228, 238**
Eos (Australia) Pty Ltd v Expo Tomei Pty Ltd (1998) 42 IPR 277, **635**
EPI Environmental Technologies Inc v Symphony Plastic Technologies plc [2005] 1 WLR 3456, **241, 260**
EPP (Australia) Pty Ltd v Levy [2001] NSWSC 482, **232**
Erickson's Patent (1923) 40 RPC 477, **443**
Erven Warnink BV v J Townend & Sons (Hull) Ltd [1979] AC 731, **531, 537, 561**
ESCO Corp v Ronneby Road Pty Ltd (2018) 131 IPR 1, **371–2, 442**
Esso Australia Resources Ltd v Plowman (1995) 183 CLR 10, **222, 256**
Esso Petroleum Co Ltd v Harper's Garage (Stourport) Ltd [1968] AC 269, **413**
Esteban Zone Industrielle v Digital Crown Holdings (2004) 64 IPR 122, **624**
Estex Clothing Manufacturers Pty Ltd v Ellis & Goldstein Ltd (1967) 116 CLR 254, **582**
European Communities v United States WT/DS160, **158**
European Ltd v Economist Newspaper Ltd [1996] FSR 431, **540**
European Ltd v Economist Newspaper Ltd [1998] FSR 283, **540**
EV Hawtin Ltd v John F Hawtin & Co Ltd [1960] RPC 95, **538**
Expo-Net Danmark A/S v Buono-Net Australia Pty Ltd (No 2) [2011] FCA 710, **392**

Express Newspapers plc v Liverpool Daily Post & Echo plc [1985] 3 All ER 680, **73**
Exxon Corp v Exxon Insurance Consultants International Ltd [1982] RPC 69, **50–1**
EZYDVD Pty Ltd v Lahrs Investments Qld Pty Ltd [2010] 2 Qd R 517, **251**

F Hoffmann-La Roche AG v Chiron Corp (2000) 47 IPR 516, **362**
F Hoffmann-La Roche & Co AG v Harris Pharmaceuticals Ltd [1977] FSR 200, **457**, **481**
Faccenda Chicken Ltd v Fowler [1985] FSR 105, **246**, **251–2**
Faccenda Chicken Ltd v Fowler [1987] Ch 117, **223**, **246**, **248–53**
Facton Ltd v Toast Sales Group Pty Ltd (2012) 205 FCR 378, **666**
Facton Ltd v Xu (2015) 111 IPR 103, **59**
FAI Insurance v Advance Bank of Australia (1986) 7 IPR 217, **59**
Fairfax Media Publications Pty Ltd v Reed International Books Australia Pty Ltd (2010) 189 FCR 109, **51**, **70**, **72**, **117**, **149**
Falcon v Famous Players Film Co [1926] 2 KB 474, **122**
Fanfold Ltd's Application (1928) 45 RPC 325, **597**
Farah Constructions Pty Ltd v Say-Dee Pty Ltd (2007) 230 CLR 89, **225–6**, **246–7**
'Farah' Trade Mark [1978] FSR 234, **598**
Fastening Supplies Pty Ltd v Olin Mathieson Chemical Corp (1969) 119 CLR 572, **426**
Fawcett v Homan (1896) 13 RPC 398, **371**
Federal Commissioner of Taxation v United Aircraft Corp (1943) 68 CLR 525, **4**, **225**, **247**
Fei Yu (t/as Jewels 4 Pools) v Beadcrete Pty Ltd (2014) 107 IPR 516, **443**, **468**, **472–3**
Feist Publications v Rural Telephone Service Co Inc (1991) 499 US 340, **72**
Fellows v Thomas William Lench Ltd (1917) 34 RPC 45, **384**
Fermiscan Pty Ltd v James [2009] NSWCA 355, **424**
Ferodo Ltd's Application [1945] Ch 334, **591**
Festo Corp v Shoketsu Kinzoku Kogyo Kabushiki Co (2000) 234 F 3d 538, **7**
Festo Corp v Shoketsu Kinzoku Kogyo Kabushiki Co (2002) 535 US 722, **7**
FH Faulding & Co Ltd v Imperial Chemical Industries of Australia & New Zealand Ltd (1964) 112 CLR 537, **631**, **650**
Figgins Holdings Pty Ltd v Registrar of Trade Marks (1995) 59 FCR 147, **630**
Fine Industrial Commodities Ltd v Powling (1954) 71 RPC 253, **412**
Firebelt Pty Ltd v Brambles Australia Ltd (2000) 51 IPR 531, **391**
Firebelt Pty Ltd v Brambles Australia Ltd (2002) 188 ALR 280, **349**, **352**, **354**, **360–2**
Firth Industries Ltd v Polyglas Engineering Pty Ltd (1975) 132 CLR 489, **464**
Flamingo Park Pty Ltd v Dolly Dolly Creations Pty Ltd (1986) 6 IPR 431, **567–8**
Fletcher Challenge Ltd v Fletcher Challenge Pty Ltd [1981] 1 NSWLR 196, **535**
Flexible Steel Lacing Co v Beltreco Ltd (2000) 49 IPR 331, **395**, **441–4**
Flocast Australia Pty Ltd v Purcell (No 3) (2000) 52 IPR 147, **696**
FNH Investments Pty Ltd v Sullivan (2003) 59 IPR 121, **139**
Fomento Industrial SA & Biro Swan Ltd v Mentmore Manufacturing Co Ltd [1956] RPC 87, **329–30**
Food Channel Network Pty Ltd v Television Food Network GP (2010) 185 FCR 9, **579**
Football League Ltd v Littlewoods Pools Ltd [1959] Ch 637, **52**
Fortuity Pty Ltd v Barcza (1995) 32 IPR 517, **139**
Foster v Mountford & Rigby Ltd (1976) 14 ALR 71, **222**, **247**
Foster's Australia Ltd v Cash's (Australia) Pty Ltd (2013) 219 FCR 529, **407**
Foxtel Management Pty Ltd v TPG Internet Pty Ltd [2018] FCA 933, **138**
Franchi v Franchi [1967] RPC 149, **231–2**, **244**, **261**

Francis Day & Hunter v Bron [1963] Ch 587, **115**
Francis Day & Hunter v Bron [1964] 1 WLR 273, **87**
Francis Day & Hunter Ltd v Twentieth Century Fox Corp Ltd [1940] AC 112, **51**
Francome v Mirror Group Newspapers Ltd [1984] 2 All ER 408, **237–8**
Franconi Holdings Ltd v Gunning (1982) 1 SR (WA) 341, **618**
Frank M Winstone (Merchants) Ltd v Plix Products Ltd (1985) 5 IPR 156, **115**
Franklin v Giddins [1978] Qd R 72, **222, 227, 235, 237, 239**
Fraser v Evans [1969] 1 QB 349, **165, 239, 246, 255**
Fraser v Thames Television Ltd [1984] QB 44, **226, 230–1**
Frearson v Loe (1878) 9 Ch D 48, **481**
French v Mason [1999] FSR 597, **413**
Fresenius Medical Care Australia Pty Ltd v Gambro Pty Ltd (2005) 67 IPR 230, **442, 444–6**
Frisby v British Broadcasting Corporation [1967] Ch 932, **105**
Frito-Lay Trading Co GmbH v Aldi Stores Ltd Partnership (2001) 52 IPR 410, **678**
Fry Consulting Pty Ltd v Sports Warehouse Inc (No 2) (2012) 201 FCR 565, **626**
FSS Travel & Leisure Systems Ltd v Johnson [1999] FSR 505, **250**
Funk Brothers Seed Co v Kalo Inoculant Co (1948) 333 US 127, **319**

G v Day [1982] 1 NSWLR 24, **240**
GA Cramp & Sons Ltd v Frank Smythson Ltd [1944] AC 239, **73**
Galaxy Electronics Pty Ltd & Gottlieb Enterprises Pty Ltd v Sega Enterprises Ltd (1997) 75 FCR 8, **54, 193**
Gambro Pty Ltd v Fresenius Medical Care South East Asia Pty Ltd (2000) 49 IPR 321, **280**
Gambro Pty Ltd v Fresenius Medical Care South East Asia Pty Ltd (2004) 61 IPR 442, **358, 362, 366**
Garden City Planters Pty Ltd v Vivre Veritas Pty Ltd (2012) 99 IPR 403, **430**
Garford Pty Ltd v DYWIDAG-Systems International Pty Ltd (2015) 110 IPR 30, **342, 356, 362, 365, 376**
Gartside v Outram (1857) 26 LJ Ch 113, **255–6**
Gates v City Life Mutual Assurance Society Ltd (1986) 160 CLR 1, **568**
Gazal Apparel Pty Ltd v Fine Lines Extraordinary Apparel Pty Ltd (2000) AIPC 91-543, **599**
GE Trade Mark [1973] RPC 297, **538**
Genentech Inc v Wellcome Foundation Ltd [1989] RPC 147, **357**
General Electric Co v General Electric Co Ltd [1969] RPC 418, **684**
General Nutrition Investment Co v Little Vienna Pty Ltd [2009] ATMO 44, **612**
General Steel Industries Inc v Commissioner for Railways (NSW) (1964) 112 CLR 125, **418–20**
General Tire & Rubber Co v Firestone Tyre & Rubber Co Ltd [1972] RPC 457, **326, 330, 332, 357**
Generic Health Pty Ltd v Bayer Pharma AG (2014) 222 FCR 336, **364–5, 395**
Generic Health Pty Ltd v Bayer Pharma AG (2018) 137 IPR 1, **484**
Generic Health Pty Ltd v Otsuka Pharmaceutical Co Ltd (2013) 296 ALR 50, **465, 468, 470–1**
George C Warner Laboratories Pty Ltd v Chemspray Pty Ltd (1967) 41 ALJR 75, **488–9**
George Hensher v Restawhile Upholstery [1976] AC 64, **60–1**
George Weston Foods Ltd v Peerless Holding Pty Ltd (1999) 48 IPR 145, **612**
Giller v Procopets (2008) 79 IPR 489, **261**
Gillette Australia Pty Ltd v Energizer Australia Pty Ltd (2002) 193 ALR 629, **677**
Gillette Co v Pharma-Goods Australia Pty Ltd (1997) 38 IPR 509, **676–7**
Glaverbel SA v British Coal Corporation [1994] RPC 443, **394**

GlaxoSmithKline Australia Pty Ltd v Reckitt Benckiser Healthcare (UK) Ltd (2013) 305 ALR 363, **444, 446**
GlaxoSmithKline Australia Pty Ltd v Reckitt Benckiser Healthcare (UK) Ltd (2016) 120 IPR 406, **449**
GlaxoSmithKline Australia Pty Ltd v Ritchie (2008) 77 IPR 306, **234, 254**
GlaxoSmithKline Consumer Healthcare Investments (Ireland) (No 2) Ltd v Generic Partners Pty Ltd (2018) 131 IPR 384, **390–3, 397**
Global Brand Marketing Inc v YD Pty Ltd (2008) 76 IPR 161, **577**
GM Global Technology Operations LLC v SSS Auto Parts Pty Ltd [2019] FCA 97, **212–14**
GM Holden Ltd v Paine (2011) 281 ALR 406, **567**
Goddard v Nationwide Building Society [1987] QB 670, **238**
Gold Peg International Pty Ltd v Kovan Engineering (Australia) Pty Ltd (2005) 67 IPR 497, **105, 216–18**
Google Inc v Australian Competition and Consumer Commission (2013) 249 CLR 435, **557–8**
Google LLC v Weeks [2018] FCCA 3150, **657**
Gorne v Scales [2006] EWCA Civ 311, **260**
Grain Pool of Western Australia v Commonwealth (2000) 202 CLR 479, **20, 428, 479, 494, 496, 508–9**
Grant v Australian Temporary Fencing Pty Ltd [2003] QSC 194, **425**
Grant v Commissioner of Patents (2005) 67 IPR 1, **266, 298, 301, 480**
Grant v Commissioner of Patents (2006) 154 FCR 62, **298, 300–1, 303–4, 306, 311, 319–20, 322, 370–1**
Graver Tank & Manufacturing Co Inc v Linde Air Products Co (1950) 339 US 605, **445**
Great Western Corp Pty Ltd v Grove Hill Pty Ltd [2001] FCA 423, **330, 464, 473**
Greater Dandenong City Council v Australian Municipal, Administrative, Clerical and Services Union (2001) 112 FCR 232, **84**
Greater Glasgow Health Board's Application [1996] RPC 207, **412, 414**
Green v Broadcasting Corporation of New Zealand [1989] 3 NZLR 18, **55, 71**
Green v Broadcasting Corporation of New Zealand [1989] RPC 469, **56**
Greenfield Products Pty Ltd v Rover-Scott Bonnar Ltd (1990) 17 IPR 417, **59**
Griffin v Isaacs (1938) 1B IPR 619, **329–30**
Grimme Landmaschinenfabrik GmbH & Co KG v Scott [2010] EWCA Civ 1110, **466, 474**
Gromax Plasticulture Ltd v Don & Low Nonwovens Ltd [1999] RPC 367, **625**
Grove Hill Pty Ltd v Great Western Corp Pty Ltd (2002) 55 IPR 257, **336, 342, 373–4, 376, 379, 388, 397, 448, 464, 473**
GS Technology Pty Ltd v Elster Metering Pty Ltd (2008) 167 FCR 444, **402**
Guinness Peat Properties Ltd v Fitzroy Robinson Partnership [1987] 1 WLR 1027, **238**
Gum v Stevens (1923) 33 CLR 267, **323**

H Lundbeck A/S v Alphapharm Pty Ltd (2009) 177 FCR 151, **325–6, 328, 333–5, 337, 357, 371, 442, 452**
H Lundbeck A/S v Sandoz Pty Ltd (2018) 137 IPR 408, **485**
Habib Bank Ltd v Habib Bank AG Zurich [1982] 99 RPC 1, **538**
Haines v Copyright Agency Ltd (1982) 64 FLR 184, **110**
Half Court Tennis Pty Ltd v Seymour (1980) 53 FLR 240, **59**
Hallen Co v Brabantia (UK) Ltd [1991] RPC 195, **271, 346**
Hansen v Magnavox Electronics Co Ltd [1977] RPC 301, **434, 436**
Hard Coffee Pty Ltd v Hard Coffee Main Beach Pty Ltd [2009] ATMO 26, **626**

Harkness v Commonwealth Bank of Australia Ltd (1993) 32 NSWLR 543, **232**
Harpur v Lambourne (1999) 45 IPR 213, **52**
Harris v CSIRO (1993) 26 IPR 469, **405–6**
Harris' Patent [1985] RPC 19, **413–14**
Harrison v Project & Design Co (Redcar) Ltd (No 1) [1978] FSR 81, **376, 378**
Hawkes & Son (London) Ltd v Paramount Film Service Ltd [1934] Ch 593, **117–18**
Health World Ltd v Shin-Sun Australia Pty Ltd (2008) 75 IPR 478, **637, 685**
Health World Ltd v Shin-Sun Australia Pty Ltd (2010) 240 CLR 590, **629**
Heavener v Loomes (1924) 34 CLR 306, **258**
Heller Financial Services Ltd v Brice (1987) 9 IPR 469, **544**
Hellewell v Chief Constable of Derbyshire [1995] 1 WLR 804, **232, 235**
Helmet Integrated Systems Ltd v Tunnard [2007] FSR 16, **249**
Henderson v Radio Corp Pty Ltd (1960) 60 SR (NSW) 576, **543, 548, 567**
Henley Arch Pty Ltd v Lucky Homes Pty Ltd (2016) 120 IPR 317, **139**
Henrick v Granite Works Pty Ltd (2008) 79 IPR 361, **405–6**
Henry Brothers (Magherafelt) Ltd v Ministry of Defence and Northern Ireland Office [1999] RPC 442, **409**
Hepples v Federal Commissioner of Taxation (1990) 22 FCR 1, **410**
Herbert Morris Ltd v Saxelby [1915] 2 Ch 57, **253**
Herbert Morris Ltd v Saxelby [1916] 1 AC 688, **250, 253, 412**
Hexagon Pty Ltd v Australian Broadcasting Commission (1975) 7 ALR 233, **536, 543**
Hickton's Patent Syndicate v Patents & Machine Improvements Co Ltd (1909) 26 RPC 339, **318, 366**
Hill v Evans (1862) 4 De GF & J 288, **331–5**
Hivac Ltd v Park Royal Scientific Instruments Ltd [1946] Ch 169, **248–9, 413, 416**
HK Frost Holdings Pty Ltd (in liq) v Darvall McCutcheon (a firm) [1999] FCA 570, **230–1**
Hodgkinson & Corby Ltd v Wards Mobility Services Ltd [1995] FSR 169, **546, 564**
Hoechst Celanese International Corp v BP Chemicals Ltd [1999] RPC 203, **701**
Hoechst UK Ltd v Chemiculture Ltd [1993] FSR 270, **222**
Hogan v Koala Dundee Pty Ltd (1988) 20 FCR 314, **531, 549, 567**
Hogg v Scott (1874) LR 18 Eq 444, **29**
Hollinrake v Truswell [1894] 3 Ch 420, **50**
Home Box Office Inc v Florenca (2010) 90 IPR 164, **625**
Honey v Australian Airlines Ltd (1990) 18 IPR 185, **543, 550**
Honiball v Bloomer (1854) 10 Exch 538, **342**
Hornsby Building Information Centre Pty Ltd v Sydney Building Information Centre Ltd (1978) 140 CLR 216, **564**
Hosokawa Micron International Inc v Fortune (1990) 26 FCR 393, **205**
Hospital Products Ltd v United States Surgical Corp (1984) 156 CLR 41, **249, 416**
Hotel Cipriani Srl v Cipriani (Grosvenor Street) Ltd [2010] EWCA Civ 110, **534, 539**
Howard v Reid (1993) 31 NSWLR 298, **696**
Howard Auto-Cultivators Ltd v Webb Industries Pty Ltd (1946) 72 CLR 175, **597**
HRC Project Design Pty Ltd v Orford Pty Ltd (1997) 38 IPR 121, **430**
HRH Prince of Wales v Associated Newspapers Ltd [2006] EWHC 522, **232, 234**
Hubbard v Vosper [1972] 2 QB 84, **148, 151, 153**
Hughes Aircraft Systems International v Airservices Australia (1997) 76 FCR 151, **222**
Hugo Boss Trade Mark Management GmbH & Co Kg v Sasalili Oxford Fia (2014) 110 IPR 74, **680**

Humpherson v Syer (1887) 4 RPC 407, **329, 374**
Hunter Pacific International Pty Ltd v Martec Pty Ltd [2016] FCA 796, **207–8**
HVE Electric Ltd v Cufflin Holdings Ltd [1964] RPC 149, **486**
Hy-Line Chicks Pty Ltd v Swifte (1966) 115 CLR 159, **616, 675**
Hyperion Records Ltd v Sawkins [2005] EWCA Civ 565, **57**

Ibcos Computers v Barclays Mercantile Highland Finance Ltd [1994] FSR 275, **115**
IceTV Pty Ltd v Nine Network Australia Pty Ltd (2009) 239 CLR 458, **4, 19, 28, 52, 67–9, 71–2, 116–18**
ICI Chemicals & Polymers Ltd v Lubrizol Corp Inc (1999) 45 IPR 577, **325, 443**
ICI Chemicals & Polymers Ltd v Lubrizol Corp Inc (2000) 106 FCR 214, **280, 325–6, 347, 357, 359–60, 443, 491–2**
Idenix Pharmaceuticals LLC v Gilead Sciences Pty Ltd (2017) 134 IPR 1, **284, 359, 389, 391, 398**
IG Farbenindustrie AG's Patents (1930) 47 RPC 289, **345–6**
Illinois Tool Works Inc v Autobars Co (Services) Ltd [1972] FSR 67, **399**
Imperial Chemicals Industries Pty Ltd v Commissioner of Patents (2004) 213 ALR 399, **345**
Imperial Group Ltd v Philip Morris & Co Ltd [1982] FSR 72, **580, 640**
Improver Corp v Remington Consumer Products Ltd [1990] FSR 181, **441**
Independent Management Resources Pty Ltd v Brown [1987] VR 605, **228, 413**
Industrial Rollformers Pty Ltd v Ingersoll-Rand (Australia) Ltd [2001] NSWCA 111, **244**
Infabrics Ltd v Jaytex Shirt Co Ltd [1981] 1 All ER 1057, **88**
Infopaq International A/S v Danske Dagblades Forening (Case C-5/08) [2009] ECDR 16, **68**
Inform Design & Construction Pty Ltd v Boutique Homes Melbourne Pty Ltd (2008) 77 IPR 523, **114**
Initial Services Ltd v Putterill [1968] 1 QB 396, **255, 258**
Inland Revenue Commissioners v Muller & Co's Margarine Ltd [1901] AC 217, **534**
Innes v Short & Beal (1898) 15 RPC 449, **464**
Innovative Agricultural Products Pty Ltd & Jacek v Cranshaw (1996) 35 IPR 643, **330, 395**
Insight SRC IP Holdings Pty Ltd v Australian Council for Educational Research Ltd (2012) 211 FCR 563, **81**
Insta Image Pty Ltd v KD Kanopy Australasia Pty Ltd (2008) 78 IPR 20, **329–31, 349**
Integrated Medical Technology Pty Ltd v Gilbert [2014] QSC 227, **223**
Interfirm Comparison (Australia) Pty Ltd v Law Society of New South Wales [1975] 2 NSWLR 104, **243, 254, 260, 700**
Interlego AG v Toltoys Pty Ltd (1973) 130 CLR 461, **395, 444**
International Business Machines Corp v Commissioner of Patents (1991) 33 FCR 218, **14, 296, 302, 306**
International Hair Cosmetics Group Pty Ltd v International Hair Cosmetics Ltd [2011] FCA 339, **583–4**
International News Service v Associated Press (1918) 248 US 215, **7, 29**
Interstate Parcel Express Co Pty Ltd v Time-Life International (Nederlands) BV (1977) 138 CLR 534, **460**
Inverness Medical Switzerland GmbH v MDS Diagnostics Pty Ltd (2010) 85 IPR 525, **371, 461, 463**
Isaac v Dargan Financial Pty Ltd [2018] NSWCA 163, **244, 258**
ISTIL Group Inc v Zahoor [2003] 2 All ER 252, **238, 254**

J Bernstein Ltd v Sydney Murray Ltd [1981] RPC 303, **59**
Jafferjee v Scarlett (1937) 57 CLR 115, **609**
James Minifie & Co v Edwin Davey & Sons (1933) 49 CLR 349, **582**
James North Australia Pty Ltd v Blundstone Pty Ltd (1978) 18 IPR 596, **586**
Jardin v Metcash Ltd (2011) 285 ALR 677, **251, 258**
Jelinnek's Application (1946) 63 RPC 59, **611–12**
Jennings v Stephens [1936] 1 All ER 409, **89**
Jerry's Famous Deli Inc v Papanicolaou (2004) 383 F 3d 998, **533**
JH Coles Pty Ltd v Need (1933) 49 CLR 499, **618**
Jian Tools for Sales Inc v Roderick Manhattan Group Ltd [1995] FSR 924, **534**
JMVB Enterprises Pty Ltd v Camoflag Pty Ltd (2005) 67 IPR 68, **326, 332, 361, 374, 401, 405–6, 410, 488–90**
JMVB Enterprises Pty Ltd v Camoflag Pty Ltd (2006) 154 FCR 348, **360, 403, 407**
John Fairfax & Sons Pty Ltd v Australian Consolidated Press Ltd [1960] SR (NSW) 413, **52**
John Fitton & Co Ltd's Application (1949) 66 RPC 110, **616**
Johns v Australian Securities Commission (1993) 178 CLR 408, **226–7, 236, 239, 244, 258**
Johns-Manville Corp's Patent [1967] FSR 327, **358, 365**
Johnson v Mortgage Processing Centre [2003] FMCA 483, **698**
Johnson & Johnson v Unilever Australia Ltd [1994] AIPC 91-038, **580**
Johnson & Johnson (Australia) Pty Ltd v Sterling Pharmaceuticals Pty Ltd (1991) 30 FCR 326, **645, 675**
Jonathan Cape Ltd v Consolidated Press Ltd [1954] 1 WLR 1313, **105**
Joos v Commissioner of Patents (1972) 126 CLR 611, **313**
JR Consulting & Drafting Pty Ltd v Cummings [2014] NSWSC 1252, **55**
JR Consulting & Drafting Pty Ltd v Cummings (2016) 329 ALR 625, **246**
JT International SA v Commonwealth (2012) 250 CLR 1, **21, 644**
Julia Fiona Roberts v Russell Boyd D2000–0210 (WIPO, 29 May 2000), **555**
Jupiters Ltd v Neurizon Pty Ltd (2005) 65 IPR 86, **331, 334, 442–4, 448, 490**
Just Group Ltd v Peck [2016] VSCA 334, **251**

Kabushiki Kaisha Sony Computer Entertainment v Stevens (2003) 132 FCR 31, **54, 87**
Kabushiki Kaisha Sony Computer Entertainment v Stevens (2005) 224 CLR 193, **87**
Kafataris v Davis (2016) 120 IPR 206, **388, 403, 406**
Kalamazoo (Australia) Pty Ltd v Compact Business Systems Pty Ltd (1985) 5 IPR 213, **52, 72, 139**
Kalman v Packaging (UK) Ltd [1982] FSR 406, **463**
KCI Licensing Inc v Smith & Nephew plc [2010] EWCA Civ 1260, **466, 474**
Keech v Sandford (1726) 22ER 629, **413**
Keith Henry & Co Pty Ltd v Stuart Walker & Co Pty Ltd (1958) 100 CLR 342, **413**
Keller v LED Technologies Pty Ltd (2010) 185 FCR 449, **201, 207–8, 210, 463**
Kellogg Co v National Biscuit Co (1938) 305 US 111, **533**
Kenman Kandy Australia Pty Ltd v Registrar of Trade Marks (2002) 122 FCR 494, **577, 595–6, 598, 600–2**
Kenrick & Co v Lawrence & Co (1890) 25 QBD 99, **58, 78**
Kestos Ltd v Kempat Ltd & Kemp (1935) 53 RPC 139, **204**
Kettle Chip Co Pty Ltd v Pepsico Australia Pty Ltd (1995) 132 ALR 286, **674–5**
Kimberly-Clark Australia Pty Ltd v Arico Trading International Pty Ltd (1998) 42 IPR 111, **462**
Kimberly-Clark Australia Pty Ltd v Arico Trading International Pty Ltd (2001) 207 CLR 1, **294, 328, 386, 389, 391, 393–5, 397, 404, 443–4, 450**

Kinabalu Investments Pty Ltd v Barron & Rawson Pty Ltd [2008] FCAFC 178, **441–2**
King v Milpurrurru (1996) 66 FCR 474, **462**
King Features Syndicate Inc v O & M Kleeman Ltd [1941] AC 417, **114**
Kirin-Amgen Inc v Board of Regents of University of Washington (1995) 33 IPR 557, **301, 319**
Kirin-Amgen Inc v Hoechst Marion Roussel Ltd [2005] RPC 169, **390, 442, 444–6, 448**
Kitchen & Sons Pty Ltd v Inman (1939) AOJP 1383, **605**
Klissers Bakeries v Harvest Bakeries Ltd (1986) 5 IPR 399, **117**
Knead (Holding) SAL v Fiordelli [2018] FCCA 1472, **59**
Knott Investments Pty Ltd v Winnebago Industries Inc (2013) 211 FCR 449, **536, 560, 610, 635, 639, 650**
Kockums AB v Commonwealth [2001] FCA 398, **242**
Koninklijke Philips Electronics NV v Remington Products Australia Pty Ltd (2000) 100 FCR 90, **210, 542, 571, 577, 600–1, 645, 650, 662**
Kromschroder AG's Patent [1960] RPC 75, **490**
Krueger Transport Equipment Pty Ltd v Glen Cameron Storage & Distribution Pty Ltd (2008) 78 IPR 262, **234**
KSR International Co v Teleflex Inc (2007) 550 US 398, **365**
Kwan v Queensland Corrective Services Commission (1994) 31 IPR 25, **407, 412**
Kyowa's Application (No 1) [1968] RPC 101, **385**

LAC Minerals v International Corona Resources (1989) 69 OR (2d) 287, **258**
Ladbroke (Football) Ltd v William Hill (Football) Ltd [1964] 1 WLR 273, **51, 77, 86, 119**
Lamb v Evans [1893] 1 Ch 218, **51, 252**
Lancashire Fires Ltd v SA Lyons & Co Ltd [1996] FSR 629, **249, 413**
Lane Fox v Kensington & Knightsbridge Electric Lighting Co (1892) 9 RPC 413, **318**
Lansing Linde Ltd v Kerr [1991] 1 WLR 251, **251**
Larrikin Music Publishing Pty Ltd v EMI Songs Australia Pty Ltd (2010) 263 ALR 155, **118**
Law v Razer Industries Pty Ltd (2010) 190 FCR 166, **430**
Leather Cloth Co v Lorsont (1869) LR 9 Eq 345, **412**
LED Technologies Pty Ltd v Elecspess Pty Ltd (2008) 80 IPR 85, **200, 209**
Lego Australia Pty Ltd v Paul's (Merchants) Pty Ltd (1982) 42 ALR 344, **565**
Lego System A/S v Lego M Lemelstrich Ltd [1983] FSR 155, **545, 548, 567**
Leica Geosystems Pty Ltd v Koudstaal (No 3) (2014) 109 IPR 1, **222**
Lend Lease Homes Pty Ltd v Warrigal Homes Pty Ltd [1970] 3 NSWLR 265, **60**
Leonardis v Sartas No 1 Pty Ltd (1996) 67 FCR 126, **284, 357, 359, 397, 443–4**
Leonardis v Theta Developments Pty Ltd (2000) 78 SASR 376, **466**
Leroy SA v Regal Grange Pty Ltd (2001) 51 IPR 199, **607**
Les Laboratoires Servier v Apotex Pty Ltd (2016) 247 FCR 61, **388, 391–2**
Lewis v Hall (2005) 68 IPR 89, **449**
Liberty Financial Pty Ltd v Scott [2002] FCA 345, **695**
Lido Manufacturing Co Pty Ltd v Meyers & Leslie Pty Ltd [1964] 5 FLR 443, **486**
Life Savers (Australasia) Ltd's Application (1952) 22 AOJP 3106, **576**
Lifeplan Australia Friendly Society Ltd v Woff [2016] FCA 248, **562**
Lift Shop Pty Ltd v Easy Living Home Elevators Pty Ltd [2013] FCA 900, **558**
Lift Shop Pty Ltd v Easy Living Home Elevators Pty Ltd (2014) 311 ALR 207, **670**
Lincoln Industries Ltd v Wham-O Manufacturing Co (1984) 3 IPR 115, **58–9, 630**
Lindner v Murdock's Garage (1950) 83 CLR 628, **250, 413**

Link 2 Pty Ltd v Ezystay Systems Pty Ltd [2016] NSWCA 317, **234**
Linter Group (in liq) v Price Waterhouse [2000] VSC 90, **84**
Liquideng Farm Supplies Pty Ltd v Liquid Engineering 2003 Pty Ltd (2009) 175 FCR 26, **702**
Littlewoods Organisation Ltd v Harris [1977] 1 WLR 1472, **251**
LJ Fisher & Co Ltd v Fabtile Industries Pty Ltd (1979) 49 AOJP 3611, **204**
Lockwood Security Products Pty Ltd v Doric Products Pty Ltd (2004) 217 CLR 274, **284, 346, 384, 386–7, 389–90, 395–8**
Lockwood Security Products Pty Ltd v Doric Products Pty Ltd (No 2) (2007) 235 CLR 173, **318, 348–9, 351, 356–62, 365, 367–8, 405**
Lockwood Security Products Pty Ltd v Doric Products Pty Ltd (No 3) (2005) 226 ALR 70, **294, 388, 452**
Lodestar Anstalt v Campari America LLC [2016] FCAFC 92, **640, 685**
London Printing & Publishing Alliance Ltd v Cox [1891] 3 Ch 291, **105**
London Regional Transport v Mayor of London [2001] EWCA Civ 1491, **239**
Lone Star Steakhouse & Saloon Inc v Zurcas (2000) 48 IPR 325, **618, 651**
Longworth v Emerton (1951) 83 CLR 539, **341–2**
Lord Ashburton v Pape [1913] 2 Ch 469, **235, 237–8**
Lott v JBW & Friends Pty Ltd [2000] SASC 3, **51**
Louis Vuitton Malletier v Sonya Valentine Pty Ltd (2013) 106 IPR 203, **652**
Lucasfilm Ltd v Ainsworth (2008) 78 IPR 145, **58**
Lux Traffic Controls Ltd v Pike Signals Ltd [1993] RPC 107, **334**

Mack Innovations (Australia) Pty Ltd v Rotorco Pty Ltd [2011] 2 Qd R 217, **339**
MacKay v McKay (2004) 63 IPR 441, **414**
Macmillan & Co Ltd v Cooper (1923) 93 LJPC 113, **29, 91**
Macmillan & Co Ltd v Cooper (1924) 40 TLR 186, **72**
Macquarie Bank Ltd v Seagle (2005) 146 FCR 400, **553**
Maeder v Busb (1938) 59 CLR 684, **313**
Maggbury Pty Ltd v Hafele Australia Pty Ltd (2001) 210 CLR 181, **223, 230, 244–5, 250, 412**
Majestic Selections Pty Ltd v Bushland Flora [2016] APBRO 1, **498, 519, 521**
Major Brothers v Franklin & Son (1908) 25 RPC 406, **582**
Malleys Ltd v JW Tomlin Pty Ltd (1961) 180 CLR 120, **204**
Malone v Metropolitan Police Commissioner (No 2) [1979] 2 All ER 620, **165, 236–8**
Mander v O'Brien [1934] SASR 87, **52**
Manderson M & F Consulting (a firm) v Incitec Pivot Ltd [2011] VSCA 444, **228**
Mantra Group Pty Ltd v Tailly Pty Ltd (No 2) (2010) 183 FCR 450, **557, 669, 674, 676**
Marconi v British Radio Telegraph & Telephone Co Ltd (1911) 28 RPC 181, **445**
Mark Foy's Ltd v Davies Co-op & Co Ltd (1956) 95 CLR 190, **597**
Mark Foys Pty Ltd v TVSN (Pacific) Ltd (2000) 104 FCR 61, **544**
Mars Australia Pty Ltd v Sweet Rewards Pty Ltd (2009) 81 IPR 354, **651**
Mars UK Ltd v Teknowledge Ltd [2000] FSR 138, **233, 236, 259**
Martin v Scribal Pty Ltd (1954) 92 CLR 17, **394–5, 441–4, 490**
Martin Engineering Co v Nicaro Holdings Pty Ltd (1991) 20 IPR 241, **463**
Martin Engineering Co v Trison Holdings Pty Ltd (1989) 14 IPR 330, **371**
Master Plumbers & Mechanical Services Association (Australia) v Master Plumbers & Mechanical Contractors Association (NSW) (2003) 60 IPR 156, **599**
Matthews v Clifton (2014) 99 ACSR 265, **229**

Mayne Industries Pty Ltd v Advanced Engineering Group Pty Ltd (2008) 166 FCR 312, **632**
Mayne Nickless Ltd v Multigroup Distribution Services Pty Ltd (2001) 114 FCR 108, **568**
McCain International Ltd v Country Fair Foods Ltd [1981] RPC 69, **539**
McCormick & Co Inc [2017] APO 62, **307**
McCormick & Co Inc v McCormick (1998) 42 IPR 515, **622**
McCormick & Co Inc v McCormick (2001) 51 IPR 102R 515, **622**
McCulloch v Lewis A May (Produce Distributors) Ltd [1947] 2 All ER 845, **547**
McDonald v Graham [1994] RPC 407, **457**
McDonald's Corp v McDonald's Corp Ltd [1997] FSR 200, **534**
McGill University v Bionomics Ltd (2007) 72 IPR 149, **406**
McWilliam's Wines Pty Ltd v LS Booth Wine Transport (1992) 25 NSWLR 723, **538**
McWilliam's Wines Pty Ltd v McDonald's System of Australia Pty Ltd (1980) 33 ALR 394, **545, 564**
Meat & Livestock Australia Ltd v Cargill Inc (2018) 129 IPR 278, **312**
Mediaquest Communications LLC v Registrar of Trade Marks (2012) 205 FCR 205, **682**
Melbourne v Terry Fluid Controls Pty Ltd (1993) 26 IPR 292, **330, 374, 376–7**
Mellor v William Beardmore & Co Ltd (1927) 44 RPC 175, **412**
Memcor Australia Pty Ltd v GE Betzdearborn Canada Co (2009) 81 IPR 315, **449**
Mense & Ampere Electrical Manufacturing Co Pty Ltd v Milenkovic [1973] VR 784, **253**
Mentmore Manufacturing Co Ltd v National Merchandising Manufacturing Co Inc (1978) 89 DLR (3d) 195, **463**
Merchandising Corp of America Inc v Harpbond [1983] FSR 32, **58**
Merck & Co Inc v Arrow Pharmaceuticals Ltd (2003) 59 IPR 226, **281**
Merck & Co Inc v Arrow Pharmaceuticals Ltd (2006) 154 FCR 31, **313, 329, 333, 338, 367–70, 403**
Merial New Zealand Ltd v Jurox Pty Ltd [2016] APO 63, **338**
Merrell Dow Pharmaceuticals Inc v HN Norton & Co Ltd (1995) 33 IPR 1, **334**
Meskenas v ACP Publishing Pty Ltd (2006) 70 IPR 172, **175–6**
Meters Ltd v Metropolitan Gas Meters Ltd (1911) 29 RPC 157, **680**
Metix (UK) v GH Maughan Plastics Ltd [1997] FSR 718, **58**
Meyers Taylor Pty Ltd v Vicarr Industries Ltd (1977) 137 CLR 228, **332, 361, 366**
MG Distribution Pty Ltd v Luthra [2004] FMCA 1027, **698**
Microsoft Corp v ATIFO Pty Ltd (1997) 38 IPR 643, **138**
Microsoft Corp v Auschina Polaris Pty Ltd (1996) 71 FCR 231, **463**
Microsoft Corp v Blanch (2002) AIPC 91-813, **87**
Microsoft Corp v CX Computer Pty Ltd (2002) AIPC 91-780, **696**
Microsoft Corp v Ezy Loans Pty Ltd (2004) 63 IPR 54, **138**
Microsoft Corp v Goodview Electronics Pty Ltd (1999) FCA 754, **695**
MID Sydney Pty Ltd v Australian Tourism Co Ltd (1998) 90 FCR 236, **612**
Miles v Genesys Wealth Advisers Ltd (2009) 201 IR 1, **223, 228, 251**
Millar v Taylor (1769) 4 Burr 2303, 98 ER 201, **29–30**
Milpurrurru v Indofurn Pty Ltd (1994) 54 FCR 240, **131, 138–9**
Milwell Pty Ltd v Olympic Amusements Pty Ltd (1999) 85 FCR 436, **52, 78, 139**
Minerals Separation North America Corp v Noranda Mines Ltd (1952) 69 RPC 81, **444**
Minister for Immigration and Citizenship v Kumar (2009) 238 CLR 448, **256**
Minnesota Mining & Manufacturing Co v Beiersdorf (Australia) Ltd (1980) 144 CLR 253, **271, 297, 332, 337, 350, 356, 358, 363, 395, 442–3**
Minnesota Mining & Manufacturing Co v Tyco Electronics Pty Ltd (2001) 53 IPR 32, **452**
Minnesota Mining & Manufacturing Co v Tyco Electronics Pty Ltd (2002) 56 IPR 248, **357, 361**

Minter v Williams (1835) 31 ER 781, **480**
Mirage Studios v Thompson (1994) 28 IPR 517, **585**
Mirror Newspapers Ltd v Queensland Newspapers Pty Ltd (1982) 59 FLR 71, **52**
MK Hutchence v South Sea Bubble Co Pty Ltd (1986) 64 ALR 330, **543, 549**
Molins & Molins Machine Co Ltd v Industrial Machine Co Ltd (1936) 54 RPC 94, **481**
Molnlycke AB v Procter & Gamble Ltd (No 4) [1992] 1 WLR 1112, **462**
Monaco v TGSG Group Pty Ltd (2001) 51 IPR 191, **599**
Monsanto Co v Kamp (1967) 154 USPQ 259, **406**
Monsanto Co v Stauffer Chemical Co (NZ) Ltd [1984] FSR 559, **480**
Monsanto Co v Syngenta Participations AG (2005) AIPC 92-128, **361**
Mont Adventure Equipment Pty Ltd v Phoenix Leisure Group Pty Ltd (2009) 175 FCR 575, **343**
Montana Wines Ltd v Villa Maria Wines Ltd [1985] FSR 400, **677**
Montgomery v Thompson [1891] AC 217, **558**
Moorgate Tobacco Co Ltd v Philip Morris Ltd (No 2) (1984) 156 CLR 414, **7, 224–6, 229–30, 236, 242, 245, 531, 584, 587**
Morellini v Mizzi Family Holdings Pty Ltd (2016) 116 IPR 411, **491**
Morgan v Seaward (1837) 150 ER 874, **373, 490**
Morison v Moat (1851) 9 Hare 241, 68 ER 492, **225**
Morris Communications Corp v PGA Tour Inc (2004) 364 F 3d 1288, **7**
Morrison Leahy Music Ltd v Lightbond Ltd [1993] EMLR 144, **173**
Morton-Norwich Products Inc v Intercen Ltd [1978] RPC 501, **462**
MPEG LA LLC v Regency Media Pty Ltd (2014) 105 IPR 202, **432, 434–6**
Mueller Brass Co v Reading Industries Inc (1972) 352 F Supp 1357, **405**
Mullard Radio Valve Co Ltd v Philco Radio & Television Corp of Great Britain Ltd (1936) 53 RPC 323, **396**
Multigate Medical Devices Pty Ltd v B Braun Melsungen AG (2016) 117 IPR 1, **284, 397, 399**
Multisteps Pty Ltd v Source & Sell Pty Ltd (2013) 214 FCR 323, **201, 205, 208, 211, 354**
Multisteps Pty Ltd v Speciality Packaging Aust Pty Ltd (2018) 132 IPR 399, **330–1, 461**
Muntz v Foster (1844) 2 WPC 93, **481**
Murex Diagnostics Australia Pty Ltd v Chiron Corp (1995) 55 FCR 194, **462, 705**
Musca v Astle Corp Pty Ltd (1988) 80 ALR 251, **568**
My Kinda Town Ltd v Soll [1982] FSR 147, **702**
Mylan Health Pty Ltd (formerly BGP Products Pty Ltd) v Sun Pharma ANZ Pty Ltd (formerly Ranbaxy Australia Pty Ltd) (2019) 138 IPR 402, **459, 472**

National Basketball Association v Motorola Inc (1997) 105 F 3d 841, **7**
National Phonograph Co of Australia Ltd v Menck (1911) 12 CLR 15, **451, 458–9, 479**
National Research Development Corporation v Commissioner of Patents (1959) 102 CLR 252, **266, 292, 294, 297, 299, 301, 303, 309, 313, 318–19, 367**
National Roads and Motorists' Association v Geeson (2001) 40 ACSR 1, **232, 241, 254**
National Surgical Pty Ltd v McPhee (2010) 87 IPR 602, **227, 259**
Nationwide News Pty Ltd v Copyright Agency Ltd (1996) 65 FCR 399, **64, 119**
Neobev Pty Ltd v Bacchus Distillery Pty Ltd (admin apptd) (No 3) (2014) 104 IPR 249, **247–8, 405–6, 436**
Nesbit Evans Group Australia Pty Ltd v Impro Ltd (1997) 39 IPR 56, **371–2, 442, 448, 489**
Network Ten Pty Ltd v TCN Channel Nine Pty Ltd (2004) 218 CLR 273, **7, 63–4, 147**
Neumann v Sons of the Desert SL [2008] FCA 1183, **605**
Neurizon Pty Ltd v Jupiters Pty Ltd (2004) 62 IPR 569, **448**

New South Wales Dairy Corporation v Murray Goulburn Co-operative Co Ltd (1989) 14 IPR 75, **630**
New South Wales Dairy Corporation v Murray Goulburn Co-operative Co Ltd (1990) 171 CLR 363, **634, 638–9**
Newspaper Licensing Agency Ltd v Marks & Spencer plc [2000] 4 All ER 239, **143, 145**
Newspaper Licensing Agency Ltd v Meltwater Holdings BV [2010] EWHC 3099, **51**
Nexus Adhesives Pty Ltd v RLA Polymers Pty Ltd (2012) 97 IPR 160, **259**
Nicaro Holdings Pty Ltd v Martin Engineering Co (1990) 16 IPR 545, **333, 335, 337, 476**
Nichia Corp v Argos [2007] FSR 38 Ltd, **365**
Nichia Corp v Arrow Electronics Australia Pty Ltd [2019] FCAFC 2, **365**
Nine Films & Television Pty Ltd v Ninox Television Ltd (2005) 67 IPR 46, **56, 140**
Nine Network Australia Pty Ltd v Australian Broadcasting Corporation (1999) 48 IPR 333, **55**
Nine Network Australia Pty Ltd v IceTV Pty Ltd (2007) 73 IPR 99, **67**
Nintendo Co Ltd v CARE (2000) 52 IPR 34, **657**
Nintendo Co Ltd v Centronics Systems Pty Ltd (1994) 181 CLR 134, **20–1, 192–3**
Nobel's Explosives Co Ltd v Jones, Scott & Co (1881) 17 Ch D 721, **457**
No-Fume Ltd v Frank Pitchford & Co Ltd (1935) 52 RPC 231, **389, 391, 394**
Norbrook Laboratories Ltd v Bomac Laboratories Ltd [2006] UKPC 25, **240**
Nordenfelt v Maxim Nordenfelt Guns & Ammunition Co [1894] AC 535, **248**
Norman v Federal Commissioner of Taxation (1963) 109 CLR 9, **410**
Norowzian v Arks Ltd (No 2) [2000] FSR 363, **55**
Northern Territory v Collins (2008) 235 CLR 619, **465–9, 473**
NorthWest Bay Ships Pty Ltd v Austal Ships Pty Ltd (2010) 87 IPR 214, **361**
Norwich Pharmacal Co v Customs and Excise Commissioners [1974] AC 133, **230**
Notaras v Barcelona Pty Ltd [2019] FCA 4, **621**
Novartis Vaccines & Diagnostics Srl [2015] APO 2, **280**
Novozymes A/S v Danisco A/S (2013) 99 IPR 417, **326, 328, 330, 333, 335, 369, 395, 442**
Novozymes North America, Inc v DSM IP Assets BV [2018] APO 37, **338**
NP Generations Pty Ltd v Feneley (2001) 80 SASR 151, **227**
NSI Dental Pty Ltd v University of Melbourne (2006) 69 IPR 542, **339, 344, 360**
NT Power Generation Pty Ltd v Power and Water Authority (2004) 219 CLR 90, **427**
NutraSweet Australia Pty Ltd v Ajinomoto Co Inc (2005) 224 ALR 200, **357–8, 360**
NV Philips Gloeilampenfabrieken v Mirabella International Pty Ltd (1993) 44 FCR 239, **389, 391**
NV Philips Gloeilampenfabrieken v Mirabella International Pty Ltd (1995) 183 CLR 655, **292, 296, 366–9**

Oakley Inc v Franchise China Pty Ltd (2003) 58 IPR 452, **582**
O'Brien v Komesaroff (1982) 150 CLR 310, **227–8, 232**
Occupational & Medical Innovations Ltd v Retractable Technologies Inc (2007) 73 IPR 312, **486**
Occupational & Medical Innovations Ltd v Retractable Technologies Inc (2008) 77 IPR 570, **485**
Ocean Spray Cranberries Inc v Registrar of Trade Marks (2000) 47 IPR 579, **596, 599**
Ofrex Ltd v Rapesco Ltd [1963] RPC 169, **653**
Old Digger Pty Ltd v Azuko Pty Ltd (2000) 51 IPR 43, **327–8, 330**
Olin Corp v Super Cartridge Co Pty Ltd (1977) 180 CLR 236, **284, 331, 396–7, 446, 452**
Olin Mathieson Chemical Corp v Biorex Laboratories Ltd [1970] RPC 157, **363**
Olympic Amusements Pty Ltd v Milwell Pty Ltd (1998) 40 IPR 180, **73**
O'Mustad & Son v S Alcock & Dosen Co Ltd [1963] 3 All ER 416, **230–1, 244, 247, 261**
Optical 88 Ltd v Optical 88 Pty Ltd (No 2) (2010) 275 ALR 526, **622, 674–5, 679**

Optus Networks Pty Ltd v Telstra Corp Ltd (2010) 265 ALR 281, **224, 227, 244, 258**
Orica Australia Pty Ltd v Dyno Nobel Inc (2003) 57 IPR 545, **394**
Orion Corp v Actavis Pty Ltd (No 3) (2015) 116 IPR 102, **424–5**
Ormonoid Roofing & Asphalts Ltd v Bitumenoids Ltd (1930) 31 SR(NSW) 347, **249**
O'Sullivan v Management Agency & Music Ltd [1985] QB 428, **105**
Otsuka Pharmaceutical Co Ltd v Generic Health Pty Ltd (No 4) (2015) 113 IPR 191, **449, 459, 468, 470**

Pacific Brands Sport & Leisure Pty Ltd v Underworks Pty Ltd (2006) 149 FCR 395, **423, 687**
Pacific Dunlop Ltd v Hogan (1989) 23 FCR 553, **536, 549**
Pacific Publications Pty Ltd v IPC Media Pty Ltd (2003) 57 IPR 28, **540**
Painaway Australia Pty Ltd v JAKL Group Pty Ltd (2011) 249 FLR 1, **247–8**
Paragon Shoes Pty Ltd v Paragini Distributors (NSW) Pty Ltd (1988) 13 IPR 323, **641**
Paramount Design v Awaba Group (2003) AIPC 91-331, **698**
Parkdale Custom Built Furniture Pty Ltd v Puxu Pty Ltd (1982) 149 CLR 191, **60, 559, 563, 565**
Parker-Knoll Ltd v Knoll International Britain (Furniture & Textiles) Ltd [1961] RPC 346, **674**
Parker-Knoll Ltd v Knoll International Ltd [1962] RPC 265, **538–9**
Parramatta Design & Developments Pty Ltd v Concrete Pty Ltd (2005) 144 FCR 264, **106**
Patent Gesellschaft AG v Saudi Livestock Transport & Trading Co (1996) 33 IPR 426, **371**
Paul's Retail Pty Ltd v Lonsdale Australia Ltd (2012) 294 ALR 72, **663–4, 666**
PB Foods Ltd v Malanda Dairy Foods Ltd (1999) 47 IPR 47, **614–15**
Penn v Bibby (1866) LR 2 Ch 127, **384**
Pepsico Australia Pty Ltd v Kettle Chip Co Pty Ltd (1996) 135 ALR 192, **540, 542, 646**
Perard Engineering Ltd (Hubbard's) Application [1976] 14 RPC 363, **342**
Perez v Fernandez (2012) 260 FLR 1, **173**
Performing Right Society Ltd v Ciryl Theatrical Syndicate Ltd [1924] 1 KB 1, **463**
Pessers and Moody v Haydon & Co (1909) 26 RPC 58, **382**
Peter Isaacson Publications v Nationwide News Pty Ltd (1984) 6 FCR 289, **538, 565**
Peter Pan Manufacturing Corp v Corsets Silhouette Ltd [1964] 1 WLR 96, **223, 240–1**
Peters (WA) Ltd v Petersville Ltd (2001) 205 CLR 126, **250, 412**
Petrofina (Great Britain) Ltd v Martin [1966] Ch 146, **413**
Pfizer Corp v Commissioner of Patents (No 2) (2006) 69 IPR 525, **281**
Pfizer Corp v Ministry of Health [1965] AC 512, **420, 453, 455, 457–8, 480**
Pfizer Inc v Commissioner of Patents (2005) 141 FCR 413, **345**
Pfizer Overseas Pharmaceuticals v Eli Lilly & Co (2005) 68 IPR 1, **357, 360, 387, 389, 391, 393, 489–90**
Pham Global Pty Ltd v Insight Clinical Imaging Pty Ltd [2017] FCAFC 83, **608, 648, 674–5**
Pharmacia Italia SPA v Interpharma Pty Ltd (2005) 67 IPR 397, **424–5**
Pharmacia Italia SPA v Mayne Pharma Pty Ltd (2005) 66 IPR 84, **394, 444, 448–9**
Pharmacia Italia SPA v Mayne Pharma Pty Ltd (2006) 69 IPR 1, **281**
Philip Morris Products SA (Switzerland) v Uruguay, ICSID Case No ARB/10/7 Award (8 July 2016), **18**
Philmac Pty Ltd v Registrar of Trade Marks (2002) 126 FCR 525, **599, 603–4**
Phoenix Eagle Co Pty Ltd v Tom McArthur Pty Ltd [2017] WASC 130, **256**
Phonographic Performance Ltd v Pontin's Ltd [1968] Ch 290, **164**
PhotoCure ASA v Queen's University at Kingston (2002) 56 IPR 86, **222**
PhotoCure ASA v Queen's University at Kingston (2005) 64 IPR 314, **325, 359, 395, 441, 443–4, 448**

Pierre Fabre SA v Marion Laboratories Inc (1986) 7 IPR 387, **641**
Pinefair Pty Ltd v Bedford Industries Rehabilitation Association Inc (1998) 87 FCR 458, **375, 453, 456**
Pioneer Concrete Services Ltd v Galli [1985] 675, **251**
Pioneer Electronic Corp v Registrar of Trade Marks (1977) 137 CLR 670, **683–5**
Pitman Training Ltd v Nominet UK (1997) 38 IPR 341, **552**
Playboy Enterprises v Welles (2002) 279 F 3d 796, **557**
PLG Research Ltd v Ardon International Ltd (No 2) [1993] FSR 197, **334**
Pollock v JC Williamson Ltd [1923] VLR 225, **91**
Polo/Lauren Co LP v Ziliani Holdings Pty Ltd (2008) 173 FCR 266, **217**
Polo Textile Industries v Domestic Textile Corp Pty Ltd (1993) 42 FCR 227, **685**
Polwood Pty Ltd v Foxworth Pty Ltd (2008) 165 FCR 527, **258, 260, 403–6, 409–10**
Polygram Pty Ltd v Golden Editions Pty Ltd (1994) 30 IPR 183, **139**
Polygram Records Inc v Raben Footwear Pty Ltd (1996) 35 IPR 426, **62, 139–40**
Polysius Corp v Fuller Co (1989) 709 F Supp 560, **469**
Populin v HB Nominees Pty Ltd (1982) 41 ALR 471, **441, 445–6**
Powerflex Services Pty Ltd v Data Access Corp (No 2) (1997) 37 IPR 436, **54**
Pracdes Pty Ltd v Stanilite Electronics Pty Ltd (1995) 35 IPR 259, **371**
Prejay Holdings Ltd v Commissioner of Patents [2002] FCA 881, **466, 473**
Prejay Holdings Ltd v Commissioner of Patents (2003) 57 IPR 424, **281**
Prestige Group (Australia) Pty Ltd v Dart Industries Inc (1990) 26 FCR 197, **489–91, 636**
Preston Erection Pty Ltd v Speedy Gantry Hire Pty Ltd (1998) 43 IPR 74, **407–8**
Primary Health Care Ltd v Commissioner of Taxation (2010) 186 FCR 301, **70, 74, 118**
Primary Health Care Ltd v Commonwealth [2017] FCAFC 174, **598, 605–6**
Prince Albert v Strange (1849) 47 ER 1302, **225, 230, 243**
Prince Jefri Bolkiah v KPMG [1999] 2 AC 222, **222**
Prince Manufacturing Inc v ABAC Corp Australia Pty Ltd (1984) 4 FCR 288, **568**
Prince plc v Prince Sports Group Inc [1998] FSR 21, **552, 672**
Printers & Finishers Ltd v Holloway [1965] RPC 239, **234, 246, 250–2, 254**
Prior v Lansdowne Press Pty Ltd [1977] VR 65, **138**
Pro Sieben Media AG v Carlton UK Television Ltd [1999] FSR 610, **143, 145**
Proctor v Bayley & Son (1888) 6 RPC 106, **481**
Product Management Group Pty Ltd v Blue Gentian LLC (2015) 240 FCR 85, **354, 442**
Pugh v Riley Cycle Co Ltd [1912] 1 Ch 613, **204**
Pussy Galore Trade Mark [1967] RPC 265, **580**

Quadramain Pty Ltd v Sevastapol Investments Pty Ltd (1976) 133 CLR 390, **413**
Quantel Ltd v Spaceward Microsystems Ltd [1990] RPC 83, **334**

R v Commissioner of Patents; Ex parte Martin (1953) 89 CLR 381, **490–1**
R v Department of Health; Ex parte Source Informatics Ltd [2001] QB 424, **239**
R v Patents Appeal Tribunal; Ex parte Swift & Co [1962] 1 All ER 610, **330**
R v Wheeler (1819) ER 392, **318**
R & A Bailey & Co Ltd v Boccaccio Pty Ltd [1986] 4 NSWLR 701, **137**
Raben Footwear Pty Ltd v Polygram Records Inc (1997) 75 FCR 88, **131, 138**
Radio Corp Pty Ltd v Disney (1937) 57 CLR 448, **620**
Raleigh Cycle Co Ltd v H Miller & Co Ltd (1948) 65 RPC 141, **449**
Ralph M Parsons Co (Beavon's) Application [1978] FSR 226, **340, 344**

Ramsay v Nicol [1939] VLR 330, **544**

Ramset Fasteners (Australia) Pty Ltd v Advanced Building Systems Pty Ltd (1996) 66 FCR 151, **326, 369**

Ramset Fasteners (Australia) Pty Ltd v Advanced Building Systems Pty Ltd (1999) 44 IPR 481, **323, 332, 336, 463, 465**

Ranbaxy Australia Pty Ltd v Warner-Lambert Co LLC (2008) 77 IPR 449, **345–6, 490–1**

Ranbaxy Australia Pty Ltd v Warner-Lambert Co LLC (No 2) (2006) 71 IPR 46, **370**

Rank Film Distributors Ltd v Video Information Centre [1982] AC 380, **696**

Rapid Metal Developments (Australia) Pty Ltd v Anderson Formrite Pty Ltd [2005] WASC 255, **228, 241, 243, 258**

Ravenscroft v Herbert & New English Library Ltd [1980] RPC 193, **138**

Rawhide Trade Mark [1962] RPC 133, **579**

RD Werner & Co Inc v Bailey Aluminium Products Pty Ltd (1989) 25 FCR 565, **323, 346**

Re Alsop's Patent (1907) 24 RPC 733, **490–1**

Re Application by Bovingdon (1946) 64 RPC 20, **296**

Re Application by CSIRO and Gilbert (1995) 31 IPR 67, **408**

Re Application by Hamish Robertson & Co Ltd (1998) 13 IPR 69, **576**

Re Application by Notetry Ltd (1999) 45 IPR 547, **600**

Re Application by SPHC(IP) Pty Ltd (2001) 49 IPR 655, **599**

Re Application by Veuve Clicquot Ponsardin, Maison Fondee En 1772 (1999) 45 IPR 525, **599**

Re Application for Type Font in the Name of Microsoft (2007) 71 IPR 664, **204**

Re Application of Eli Lilly & Co [1982] 1 NSWLR 526, **459**

Re Applications by Comshare Inc (1991) 23 IPR 145, **205**

Re Applications of Tashounidis (1995) 35 IPR 305, **682**

Re C & W's Application for a Patent (1914) 31 RPC 235, **313**

Re Cementation Co Ltd, Abram Ruper Neelands & Peckersgill's Patents (1945) 62 RPC 151, **296**

Re Charles Selz Ltd's Application (1954) 71 RPC 158, **414**

Re Colgate-Palmolive Co Inc (2010) 88 IPR 434, **205**

Re Ducker's Trade Mark (1928) 45 RPC 397, **579**

Re Eli Lilly & Co's Application [1975] RPC 438, **313**

Re Elton & Leda Chemicals Ltd's Application [1957] RPC 267, **296**

Re Estee Lauder Cosmetics Ltd (2000) 50 IPR 131, **599**

Re GEC's Application (1942) 60 RPC 1, **295**

Re Hatschek's Patents; Ex parte Zerenner [1909] 2 Ch 68, **426**

Re Hwang (2004) AIPC 92–031, **380**

Re Imperial Chemical Industries Ltd; Ex parte British Nylon Spinners Ltd (1963) 109 CLR 336, **424**

Re Institut Francais du Petrole des Carburants et Lubricants' Application [1972] FSR 147, **345**

Re International Stem Cell Corp (2016) 123 IPR 142, **380**

Re Lawson [2001] AIPC 91-693, **628**

Re Lenard's Application (1954) 71 RPC 190, **298**

Re Luminis Pty Ltd and Fertilitescentrum AB (2004) 62 IPR 420, **380**

Re Multix Pty Ltd (1999) 47 IPR 153, **600, 604**

Re Newall and Elliot (1858) 140 ER 1087, **342**

Re Parry-Husband's Application [1965] RPC 382, **490**

Re Pfizer Inc (2004) 62 IPR 627, **280**

Re Pfizer Products Inc (2004) 61 IPR 165, **592, 657, 660**

Re Rantzen's Application for a Patent (1946) 64 RPC 63, **296**

Re Rau Gesellschaft's Application (1935) 52 RPC 362, **296**
Re Sakata Rice Snacks (Australia) Pty Ltd (1998) 43 IPR 378, **599**
Re Sanyo Electric Co Ltd and Commissioner of Patents (1997) 36 IPR 470, **430**
Re Smithkline Beecham plc (2000) 50 IPR 169, **278**
Re Standard Oil Development Co's Application (1951) 68 RPC 114, **296**
Re Trade Mark 'Orlwoola' (1909) 26 RPC 850, **605**
Re Vono's Application (1949) 66 RPC 305, **591**
Re Wheatley's Patent Application (1984) 2 IPR 450, **330, 374–5, 377**
Re Wolanski's Registered Design (1953) 88 CLR 278, **204**
Re Yanx Registered Trade Mark; Ex parte Amalgamated Tobacco Corp Ltd (1951) 82 CLR 199, **584**
Reckitt & Colman Products Ltd v Borden Inc [1990] 1 All ER 873, **532, 541, 546**
Reddaway v Banham [1896] AC 199, **539**
Redrock Holdings Pty Ltd v Hinkley (2001) 50 IPR 565, **81**
Redwood Music Ltd v B Feldman & Co Ltd [1979] RPC 1, **79**
Reed Business Information Pty Ltd v Seymour [2010] NSWSC 790, **230**
Reed Executive plc v Reed Business Information Ltd [2003] Info TLR 660, **680**
Refaat v Barry [2015] VSCA 218, **234**
Registrar of Trade Marks v Woolworths Ltd (1999) 45 IPR 411, **13, 614, 621, 651, 658**
Rehm Pty Ltd v Websters Security Systems (International) Pty Ltd (1988) 11 IPR 289, **284, 371, 397–8, 443, 446**
Reiss Engineering Co Ltd v Harris [1985] 14 IRLR 232, **412**
Rescare Ltd v Anaesthetic Supplies Pty Ltd (1992) 25 IPR 119, **314–15, 370–2, 391, 466**
Research Affiliates LLC v Commissioner of Patents (2014) 227 FCR 378, **299–300, 302, 304, 306–7**
Retractable Technologies v Occupational & Medical Innovations Ltd (2007) 72 IPR 58, **228, 236**
Review 2 Pty Ltd v Redberry Enterprise Pty Ltd (2008) 173 FCR 450, **207–8, 210**
Review Australia Pty Ltd v Innovative Lifestyle Investments Pty Ltd (2008) 166 FCR 358, **215**
Review Australia Pty Ltd v New Cover Group Pty Ltd (2008) 79 IPR 236, **208**
Revlon Inc v Cripps & Lee Ltd [1980] FSR 85, **685**
RGC Mineral Sands Pty Ltd v Wimmera Industrial Minerals Pty Ltd (1998) 89 FCR 458, **280**
Richards v Kadian (2005) 64 NSWLR 204, **254**
Richwood Creek Pty Ltd v Williams (2009) 82 IPR 385, **403**
Richwood Creek Pty Ltd v Williams (2010) 85 IPR 378, **407**
Ritz Hotel Ltd v Charles of the Ritz Ltd (1988) 15 NSWLR 158, **630, 685**
Riv-Oland Marble Co (Vic) Pty Ltd v Settef SpA (1988) 19 FCR 569, **586**
RLA Polymers Pty Ltd v Nexus Adhesives Pty Ltd (2011) 280 ALR 125, **233, 245, 260**
Roadshow Films Pty Ltd v iiNet Ltd (2011) 194 FCR 285, **90, 123–4, 126–9, 462**
Roadshow Films Pty Ltd v iiNet Ltd (No 3) (2010) 83 IPR 430, **90**
Roadshow Films Pty Ltd v Telstra Corp Ltd (2016) 248 FCR 178, **138**
Roadshow Films Pty Ltd v Telstra Corp Ltd (2018) 132 IPR 1, **138**
Robb v Green [1895] 2 QB 315, **224, 249, 251, 413**
Robin Jig & Tool Co Ltd v Taylor [1979] FSR 130, **105**
Rodi & Wienenberger AG v Henry Showell Ltd [1969] RPC 367, **441, 446**
Roger Bullivant Ltd v Ellis [1987] 13 FSR 172, **250**
Rokt Pte Ltd v Commissioner of Patents [2018] FCA 1988, **306**
Rolls-Royce Ltd's Application [1963] RPC 251, **296**
Root Quality Pty Ltd v Root Control Technologies Pty Ltd (2000) 49 IPR 225, **357, 385, 441, 443, 448, 462–3**

Rose Holdings Pty Ltd v Carlton Shuttlecocks Ltd (1957) 98 CLR 444, **396**
Rosedale Associated Manufacturers Ltd v Airfix Products Ltd [1956] RPC 360, **140, 215, 486**
Rothmans Ltd v WD & HO Wills (Australia) Ltd (1955) 92 CLR 131, **584**
Rotocrop International Ltd v Genbourne Ltd [1982] FSR 241, **462–4, 473**
Roussel-Uclaf SA v Hockley International Ltd [1996] RPC 441, **451**
Row Weeder Pty Ltd v Nielsen (1997) 39 IPR 400, **405–6, 408**
Royal Children's Hospital v Alexander [2011] APO 94, **414**
Royal Typewriter Co v Remington Rand Inc (1948) 168 F 2d 691, **445**
Rozenblit v VR TEK Pty Ltd (2013) 104 IPR 153, **403**
RPL Central Pty Ltd v Commissioner of Patents [2013] FCA 871, **14**
RS Components Ltd v Holophane Corp (1999) 46 IPR 451, **606**
Rutter v Brookland Valley Estate (2009) 81 IPR 549, **179**
Ryan v Lum (1989) 16 NSWLR 518, **462, 464, 488–9**

Sabaf SpA v MFI Furniture Centres Pty Ltd [2005] RPC 10, **369**
Saccharin Corp Ltd v Anglo-Continental Chemical Works Ltd (1900) 17 RPC 307, **453, 459**
Sachtler GmbH & Co KG v RE Miller Pty Ltd (2005) 65 IPR 605, **441, 445, 448**
Safe Sport Australia Pty Ltd v Puma Australia Pty Ltd (1985) 4 IPR 120, **218**
SAI Global Property Division Pty Ltd v Johnstone (2016) 122 IPR 210, **223, 248**
Saltman Engineering Co Ltd v Campbell Engineering Co Ltd (1948) 65 RPC 203, **224–6, 229–31, 233, 235, 240–1, 245**
Sami S Svendsen Inc v Independent Products Canada Ltd (1968) 119 CLR 156, **397**
Samsung Electronics Co Ltd v Apple Inc (2011) 286 ALR 257, **484**
Samuel Smith & Son Pty Ltd v Pernod Ricard Winemakers Pty Ltd [2016] FCA 1515, **676**
San Remo Macaroni Co Pty Ltd v San Remo Gourmet Coffee Pty Ltd (2000) 50 IPR 321, **657**
Sands & McDougall Pty Ltd v Robinson (1917) 23 CLR 49, **58, 71, 77**
Sandvik Intellectual Property AB v Quarry Mining & Construction Equipment Pty Ltd (2017) 126 IPR 427, **358, 391–3, 442**
Sanofi-Synthelabo Canada Inc v Apotex Inc [2008] 3 SCR 265, **365**
SAP Australia Pty Ltd v Sapient Australia Pty Ltd (1999) 48 IPR 593, **608, 611**
Sartas No 1 Pty Ltd v Koukourou & Partners Pty Ltd (1994) 30 IPR 479, **278, 363, 388, 464, 466**
Scandinavian Tobacco Group Eersel BV v Trojan Trading Co Pty Ltd [2016] FCAFC 91, **666**
Schering Chemicals Ltd v Falkman [1981] 2 WLR 848, **232, 241**
Schott Musik International GmbH & Co v Colossal Records of Australia Pty Ltd (1997) 75 FCR 321, **173**
Schütz (UK) Ltd v Werit UK Ltd [2013] UKSC 16, **454**
'Sea Island Cotton' Certification Trade Marks [1989] RPC 87, **589**
Seafolly Pty Ltd v Fewstone Pty Ltd (2014) 313 ALR 41, **115, 118, 217**
Seager v Copydex Ltd [1967] 2 All ER 415, **224, 240–1, 260**
Seager v Copydex Ltd (No 2) [1969] 2 All ER 718, **260, 700–1**
Sebel Furniture Ltd v Acoustic & Felts Pty Ltd (2009) 80 IPR 244, **601**
Sega Enterprises Ltd v Galaxy Electronics Pty Ltd (1998) 39 IPR 577, **106**
Sega Enterprises Ltd & Avel Pty Ltd v Galaxy Electronics Pty Ltd (1996) 69 FCR 268, **62, 194**
Seiko Epson Corp v Calidad Pty Ltd (2017) 133 IPR 1, **452, 455, 460**
Sent v John Fairfax Publication Pty Ltd [2002] VSC 429, **228**
Settef SpA v Riv-Oland Marble Co (Vic) Pty Ltd (1987) 10 IPR 402, **582**
Seven Network Ltd v Commissioner of Taxation (2014) 109 IPR 520, **62**
Seven-Up Co v Bubble Up Co Inc (1987) 9 IPR 259, **605**

SGS Australia Pty Ltd v Australian Laboratory Services Pty Ltd [2012] FCA 711, **239**
Sharp & Dohme Inc v Boots Pure Drug Co Ltd (1927) 44 RPC 367, **337**
Shave v HV McKay Massey Harris Pty Ltd (1935) 52 CLR 701, **390, 397**
Sheldon & Hammond Pty Ltd v Metrokane Inc (2004) 135 FCR 34, **62**
Shell Co of Australia Ltd v Esso Standard Oil (Australia) Ltd (1963) 109 CLR 409, **608, 644**
Shelley Films Ltd v Rex Features Ltd [1994] EMLR 134, **232, 236**
Sheraton Corp of America v Sheraton Motels [1964] RPC 202, **534**
Sigma Pharmaceuticals (Australia) Pty Ltd v Wyeth (2009) 81 IPR 339, **369**
Sigma Pharmaceuticals (Australia) Pty Ltd v Wyeth (2011) 119 IPR 194, **402, 407, 410, 491–2**
Sillitoe v McGraw Hill Book Co (UK) Ltd [1983] FSR 545, **147–8**
Skids Programme Management Ltd v McNeill (2012) 98 IPR 324, **261**
Smith Bartlet & Co v British Pure Oil Grease & Carbide Co Ltd (1934) 51 RPC 157, **616**
Smith Kline & French Laboratories (Australia) Ltd v Registrar of Trade Marks (1967) 116 CLR 628, **576, 579**
Smith Kline & French Laboratories (Australia) Ltd v Secretary, Department of Community Services and Health (1990) 22 FCR 73, **4, 225–6, 235, 241–3, 256–7**
Smith Kline & French Laboratories (Australia) Ltd v Secretary, Department of Community Services and Health (1991) 28 FCR 291, **226, 242**
Smith Kline & French Laboratories Ltd v Attorney-General (NZ) (1991) 22 IPR 143, **480**
Smith Kline & French Laboratories Ltd v RD Harbottle (Mercantile) Ltd [1980] RPC 363, **457**
Smith Kline v Registrar of Trade Marks [1976] RPC 511, **576**
Smith & Nephew Pty Ltd v Wake Forest University Health Sciences (2009) 82 IPR 467, **271, 297**
SNF (Australia) Pty Ltd v Ciba Specialty Chemicals Water Treatments Ltd (2011) 92 IPR 46, **461, 486**
Snow v Eaton Shopping Centre (1982) 70 CPR (2d) 105, **173**
Société Anonyme des Manufactures de Glaces v Tilghman's Patent Sand Blast Co Ltd [1884] LR 25 Ch D 1, **460**
Société Technique de Pulverisation Step v Emson Europe Ltd [1993] RPC 513, **446**
Societe des Usines Chimiques Rhone-Poulenc v Commission of Patents (1958) 100 CLR 5, **284, 397**
Solar Thomson Engineering Co Ltd v Barton [1977] RPC 537, **454**
Sony Music Australia Ltd v Tansing (1993) 27 IPR 649, **560**
Southcorp Wines Pty Ltd v Coy [2001] AIPC 91-715, **607**
Southern Cross Refrigerating Co v Toowoomba Foundry Pty Ltd (1954) 91 CLR 592, **612, 621–2**
Southorn v Reynolds (1865) 12 LT 75, **537**
Spedley Securities Ltd (in liq) v Bond Brewing Investment Pty Ltd (1991) 9 ACLC 522, **696**
Speed Seal Products Ltd v Paddington [1986] 1 All ER 91, **244–5**
Speedy Gantry Hire Pty Ltd v Preston Erection Pty Ltd (1998) 40 IPR 543, **407, 489, 491**
Spencer Industries Pty Ltd v Collins (2003) 58 IPR 425, **407, 412, 414**
SPI Spirits (Cyprus) Ltd v Diageo Australia Ltd (No 6) (2008) 77 IPR 62, **630, 682**
Spiral Foods Ltd v Valio Ltd (2000) 50 IPR 473, **607**
Spirit Pharmaceuticals Pty Ltd v Mundipharma Pty Ltd (2013) 102 IPR 55, **281**
Sporte Leisure Pty Ltd v Paul's International Pty Ltd (No 3) (2010) 275 ALR 258, **666**
Sports Data Pty Ltd v Prozone Sports Australia Pty Ltd (2014) 107 IPR 1, **52, 229**
Sports Warehouse Inc v Fry Consulting Pty Ltd (2010) 186 FCR 519, **594**
Spring Form Inc v Toy Brokers Ltd [2002] FSR 17, **484**
Stack v Brisbane City Council (1995) 59 FCR 71, **84, 378, 417–20**
Stack v Brisbane City Council (1999) 47 IPR 525, **361, 487–9**

Stack v Brisbane City Council (No 2) (1996) 67 FCR 510, **424, 436**
Stack v Davies Shephard Pty Ltd (2001) 108 FCR 422, **401–2, 405–7, 410, 488–9**
Standard Cameras Ltd's Application (1952) 69 RPC 125, **597**
Stanway Oyster Cylinders Pty Ltd v Marks (1996) 66 FCR 577, **329–32, 374, 395**
Star Industrial Co Ltd v Yap Kwee Kor [1976] FSR 256, **544**
Star Micronics Pty Ltd v Five Star Computers Pty Ltd (1991) 22 IPR 473, **667**
Star Micronics Pty Ltd v General Synthetics Pty Ltd (Unreported, No V G390 of 1991 Fed No 868), **695**
State Street Bank & Trust Co v Signature Financial Group (1998) 149 F 3d 1368, **303**
Statuscard Australia Pty Ltd v Rotondo [2009] 1 Qd R 559, **64**
Steers v Rogers [1893] AC 232, **479**
Stena Rederi AB v Irish Ferries Ltd [2003] EWCA Civ 66, **475**
Stephens v Avery [1988] Ch 449, **226, 245**
Stephenson Jordan & Harrison Ltd v MacDonald & Evans (1952) 69 RPC 10, **81, 236**
Sterling Engineering Co Ltd v Patchett [1955] AC 534, **407, 414**
Stevens v Brodribb Sawmilling Co Pty Ltd (1986) 160 CLR 16, **81**
Stevens v Kabushiki Kaisha Sony Computer Entertainment (2005) 224 CLR 193, **96**
Stoke-on-Trent City Council v W & J Wass Ltd [1988] 1 WLR 1406, **680**
Stone & Wood Group Pty Ltd v Intellectual Property Development Corp Pty Ltd [2018] FCAFC 29, **530, 540, 673**
Streetscape Projects (Australia) Pty Ltd v City of Sydney (2013) 85 NSWLR 196, **224, 236**
Streetworx Pty Ltd v Artcraft Urban Group Pty Ltd (2014) 110 IPR 82, **354, 461–2**
Streetworx Pty Ltd v Artcraft Urban Group Pty Ltd (2015) 110 IPR 544, **484**
Sullivan v FNH Investments Pty Ltd (2003) 57 IPR 63, **139**
Sullivan v Sclanders & Goldwell International Pty Ltd (2000) 77 SASR 419, **227, 235, 239, 254, 257**
Sumitomo Electric Industries Ltd v Metal Manufacturers Ltd (1993) AIPC 91-000, **345**
Sun World International Inc v Registrar, Plant Breeder's Rights (1998) 87 FCR 405, **432, 508**
Sunbeam Corp v Morphy-Richards (Australia) Pty Ltd (1961) 180 CLR 98, **329, 346**
Sunrider Corp v Vitasoy International Holdings Ltd [2009] ATMO 42, **612**
Surface Technology plc v Young [2002] FSR 25, **238**
Sutherland Publishing Co Ltd v Caxton Publishing Co Ltd [1936] Ch 323, **138**
Sydney Markets Ltd v Sydney Flower Market Pty Ltd (2002) ATPR 46-216, **553, 558**
Synthetic Turf Development Pty Ltd v Sports Technology International Pty Ltd [2004] FCA 1179, **491**

Taco Co (Australia) Inc v Taco Bell Pty Ltd (1982) 42 ALR 177, **535, 564**
Talbot v General Television Corp Pty Ltd [1980] VR 224, **227, 230–1, 234, 236, 240, 260**
Talk of the Town v Hagstrom (1990) 19 IPR 649, **59**
Talmex Pty Ltd v Telstra Corp Ltd [1997] 2 Qd R 444, **543, 550**
Tate v Haskins (1935) 53 CLR 594, **284, 384**
Tavener v Sheridan [2000] FCA 219, **413**
TCN Channel Nine Pty Ltd v Network Ten Pty Ltd (2001) 108 FCR 235, **63, 147, 151, 153**
TCN Channel Nine Pty Ltd v Network Ten Pty Ltd (2002) 118 FCR 417, **62–3, 119, 146–8, 151**
Telefon A/B LM Ericsson's Application [1975] FSR 49, **296**
Television Broadcasts Ltd v Telstra Corp Ltd [2018] FCA 1434, **138**
Telstra Corp Ltd v Australasian Performing Right Association Ltd (1997) 191 CLR 140, **89**
Telstra Corp Ltd v First Netcom Pty Ltd (1997) 78 FCR 132, **235**

Telstra Corp Ltd v Nuclear Marshmallows D2000–0003 (WIPO, 18 February 2000), **555**
Telstra Corp Ltd v Phone Directories Co Pty Ltd (2010) 194 FCR 142, **52, 69–74**
Telstra Corp Ltd v Royal & Sun Alliance Insurance Australia Ltd (2003) 57 IPR 453, **55**
10th Cantanae Pty Ltd v Shoshana Pty Ltd (1987) 79 ALR 299, **543, 550**
Terrapin Ltd v Builders Supply Co (Hayes) Ltd [1967] RPC 375, **227, 233, 241, 259–60**
TF Industrial Pty Ltd v Career Tech Pty Ltd [2011] NSWSC 1303, **229**
TGI Friday's Minnesota Inc v TGI Friday's Australia Pty Ltd (1999) 48 IPR 65, **686**
The Gadget Shop Ltd v The Bug.Com Ltd [2001] FSR 26, **228**
Thermawear Ltd v Vedonis Ltd [1982] RPC 44, **544**
Theta Developments Pty Ltd v Leonardis (2002) 59 IPR 368, **469**
Thomas Hunter Ltd's Patent [1965] RPC 416, **432**
Thomas Marshall (Exports) Ltd v Guinle [1979] Ch 227, **251, 253–4**
Thompson v Eagle Boys Dial-A-Pizza Australia Pty Ltd [2001] FCA 741, **161**
Thomson v B Seppelt & Sons Ltd (1925) 37 CLR 305, **581**
Thorsten Nordenfelt v Maxim Nordenfelt Guns & Ammunition Co [1894] AC 535, **412**
Thunderbird Products Corp v Thunderbird Marine Products Pty Ltd (1974) 131 CLR 592, **584**
TICA Default Tenancy Control Pty Ltd v Datakatch Pty Ltd (2016) 120 IPR 98, **227**
Tidy v Trustees of the Natural History Museum (1995) 39 IPR 501, **173**
Tidy Tea Ltd v Unilever Australia Ltd (1995) 32 IPR 405, **352**
Titan Group Pty Ltd v Steriline Manufacturing Pty Ltd (1990) 19 IPR 353, **224**
Tivo Inc v Vivo International Corp Pty Ltd [2012] FCA 252, **614, 635**
Toddler Kindy Gymbaroo Pty Ltd v Gymboree Pty Ltd (2000) 100 FCR 166, **634–5**
Tony Blain Pty Ltd v Jamieson (1993) AIPC 90-990, **697**
Tool Metal Manufacturing Co Ltd v Tungsten Electric Co Ltd [1955] 1 WLR 761, **432**
Torrington Manufacturing Co v Smith & Sons (England) Ltd [1966] RPC 285, **241**
Totally and Permanently Disabled Soldiers' Association v Australian Federation of Totally and Permanently Incapacitated Ex-Service Men & Women Ltd (2001) 52 IPR 626, **615**
Townsend v Haworth (1875) 12 Ch D 831, **464**
Townsend v Haworth (1879) 48 LJ Ch 770, **464**
Toys 'R' Us Inc v Akkaoui (1996) 40 USPQ 2d 1836, **656**
Tramanco Pty Ltd v BPW Transpec Pty Ltd (2014) 105 IPR 18, **389–90, 442**
Transfield Pty Ltd v Arlo International Ltd (1980) 144 CLR 83, **432, 706**
Transport Tyre Sales Pty Ltd v Montana Tyres Rims & Tubes Pty Ltd (1999) 93 FCR 421, **582, 636, 663–4, 673, 679**
Trevorrow v South Australia (No 4) (2006) 94 SASR 64, **238, 260**
Triplex Safety Glass Co Ltd v Scorah [1938] Ch 211, **223, 412–14, 416–17**
TS & B Retail Systems Pty Ltd v 3fold Resources Pty Ltd (2003) 57 IPR 530, **247**
Turner v General Motors (Australia) Pty Ltd (1929) 42 CLR 352, **535**
TVBO Production Ltd v Australia Sky Net Pty Ltd (2009) 82 IPR 502, **90**
Twentieth Century Fox Film Corp v Die Hard (2001) 52 IPR 455, **621**
Twentieth Century Fox Film Corp v South Australian Brewing Co Ltd (1996) 66 FCR 451, **543, 545, 559, 561, 567**
Ty Inc v Perryman (2002) 306 F 3d 509, **7**
Tye-Sil Corp Ltd v Diversified Products Corp (1991) 20 IPR 574, **395**

U & I Global Trading (Australia) Pty Ltd v Tasman-Warajay Pty Ltd (1995) 60 FCR 26, **486, 672**

Unilever Australia Ltd v PB Foods Ltd (1999) 47 IPR 358, **678**
Unilever plc v Gillette (UK) Ltd [1989] RPC 583, **462**
Uniline Australia Ltd v S Briggs Pty Ltd (2009) 81 IPR 42, **486**
Union Nationale Inter-Syndicate des Marques Collectives Application (1922) 39 RPC 346, **589**
United Indigo Chemical Co Ltd v Robinson (1939) 49 RPC 178, **252–3**
United States Surgical Corp v Hospital Products International Pty Ltd [1983] 2 NSWLR 175, **260**
United Telephone Co v Sharples (1885) 2 RPC 12, **481**
United Wire Ltd v Screen Repair Services (Scotland) Ltd [2000] 4 All ER 353, **454, 460**
Universal Music Australia Pty Ltd v Australian Competition and Consumer Commission (2003) 131 FCR 529, **705**
Universal Music Australia Pty Ltd v Cooper (2005) 150 FCR 1, **90, 113, 125, 131**
Universal Music Australia Pty Ltd v Sharman License Holdings Ltd (2005) 222 FCR 465, **90, 120, 124, 695**
Universal Music Australia Pty Ltd v TPG Internet Pty Ltd (2017) 348 ALR 493, **138**
University of British Columbia v Conor Medsystems Inc (2006) 155 FCR 391, **402, 407–8, 411, 437, 488**
University of Georgia Research Foundation Inc v Biochem Pharma Inc (2000) 51 IPR 222, **346**
University of London Press Ltd v University Tutorial Press Ltd [1916] 2 Ch 601, **7, 50, 71**
University of New South Wales v Moorhouse (1975) 133 CLR 1, **107, 110, 121–2, 461**
University of Nottingham v Fishel [2000] ICR 1462, **249, 416**
University of Western Australia v Gray (2009) 179 FCR 346, **82, 224, 248, 403–4, 414–15**
University of Western Australia v Gray (No 20) (2008) 246 ALR 603, **411, 415**
Uprising Dragon Ltd v Benedict Trading & Shipping Pty Ltd (1987) 16 FCR 93, **424**

Vac-U-Flex Trade Mark [1965] FSR 176, **653**
Valensi v British Radio Corp Ltd (No 1) [1972] FSR 273, **389, 490**
Vasco Investment Managers Ltd v Morgan Stanley Australia Ltd (2014) 108 IPR 52, **230–1, 234, 241, 260**
Vehicle Monitoring Systems Pty Ltd v SARB Management Group Pty Ltd (No 2) (2013) 101 IPR 496, **354, 479**
Vertical Leisure Ltd v Skyrunner Pty Ltd [2014] FCCA 2033, **138**
Veuve Clicquot Ponsardin, Maison Fondee en 1772 [1999] ATMO 29, **604**
Victoria v Pacific Technologies (Australia) Pty Ltd (No 2) (2009) 177 FCR 61, **51**
Victoria Park Racing and Recreation Grounds Co Ltd v Taylor (1937) 58 CLR 479, **7, 27**
Victoria University of Technology v Wilson (2004) 60 IPR 392, **82, 407, 412, 414, 416–17**
Vidal Dyes Syndicate Ltd v Levenstein Ltd & Read Holliday & Sons Ltd [1912] 29 RPC 245, **391**
Vine Products Ltd v McKenzie & Co Ltd (No 3) [1969] RPC 1, **537**
Virgin Enterprises Ltd v Klapsas (2002) AIPC 91-670, **657**
Vitamins Australia Ltd v Beta-Carotene Industries Pty Ltd (1987) 9 IPR 41, **424, 437**
Vivo International Corp Pty Ltd v Tivo Inc [2012] FCAFC 159, **614, 635**
Vokes Ltd v Heather (1945) 62 RPC 135, **223, 249, 414**
Von Heyden v Neustadt (1880) 14 Ch D 230, **458–9**

Wagdy Hanna & Associates Pty Ltd v National Library of Australia [2014] ACTCA 32, **239**
Wake Forest University Health Sciences v Smith & Nephew Pty Ltd (No 2) (2011) 92 IPR 496, **461**
Walker v Alemite Corp (1933) 49 CLR 643, **384, 441, 453, 462–4**
Wallis Nominees (Computing) Pty Ltd v Pickett (2013) 45 VR 657, **244, 251**
Wal-Mart Stores Inc v Samara Brothers Inc (2000) 529 US 205, **541**

Walt Disney Productions v H John Edwards Publishing Co Pty Ltd (1954) 71 WN (NSW) 150, **114**
Walter v Lane [1900] AC 539, **29, 71, 77**
Wanem Pty Ltd v Tekiela (1990) 19 IPR 435, **140, 216, 486**
Ward Group Pty Ltd v Brodie & Stone plc (2003) 132 FCR 309, **553, 562**
Ward Group Pty Ltd v Brodie & Stone plc (2005) 143 FCR 479, **583–4, 670, 679**
Warner-Lambert Co LLC v Apotex Pty Ltd (2014) 311 ALR 632, **468, 470**
Warner-Lambert Co LLC v Apotex Pty Ltd (2017) 249 FCR 17, **450**
Warner-Lambert Co LLC v Apotex Pty Ltd (No 2) (2018) 129 IPR 205, **389, 391, 459**
Washex Machinery Corp v Roy Burton & Co Pty Ltd (1974) 49 ALJR 12, **371**
WD & HO Wills (Australia) Ltd v Rothmans Ltd (1956) 94 CLR 182, **583–4**
Webster v James Chapman & Co [1989] 3 All ER 939, **238**
Welch Perrin & Co Pty Ltd v Worrel (1961) 106 CLR 588, **297, 369, 371, 386, 395, 397, 441–4**
Welcome Real-Time SA v Catuity Inc (2001) 113 FCR 110, **14, 301, 303, 322, 371, 477–8**
Welcome Real-Time SA v Catuity Inc (No 2) (2001) AIPC 91-736, **473**
Wellcome Foundation Ltd v Commissioner of Patents [1979] 2 NZLR 591, **315**
Wellcome Foundation Ltd v VR Laboratories (Australia) Pty Ltd (1981) 148 CLR 262, **350, 357, 361–3, 366, 403**
Weller Hotels & Taverns Pty Ltd v TGI Friday's Inc (1994) 30 IPR 631, **613**
Wells Fargo v WhenU.com (2003) 293 F Supp 2d 734, **558**
Wessex Dairies Ltd v Smith [1935] 2 KB 80, **223, 251, 413**
West Australian Newspapers Ltd v Bond [2009] 40 WAR 164, **256**
Western Australia's Application (1934) AOJP 557, **615**
Westpac Banking Corp v John Fairfax Group Pty Ltd (1991) 19 IPR 513, **227**
Wheatley v Bell [1982] 2 NSWLR 544, **227, 236**
Whirlpool Trade Mark [1997] FSR 905, **534**
Wilderman v FW Berk & Co Ltd [1925] Ch 116, **459**
William Edge & Sons Ltd v William Niccolls & Sons Ltd [1911] AC 693, **541, 602**
Wilson v Ferguson [2015] WASC 15, **261**
Wilson Parking Australia 1992 Pty Ltd v Rush [2008] FCA 1601, **259**
Windsurfing International Inc v Petit [1984] 2 NSWLR 196, **462, 464, 473**
Wingate Marketing Pty Ltd v Levi Strauss & Co (1994) 49 FCR 89, **547, 609, 650, 668**
Winnebago Industries Inc v Knott Investments Pty Ltd (No 4) [2015] FCA 1327, **561, 567**
Wissen Pty Ltd v Lown (1987) 9 IPR 124, **426**
WM Wrigley Jr Co v Cadbury Schweppes Pty Ltd (2005) 66 IPR 298, **297, 369, 382, 491**
WMC Ltd v Westgold Resources NL (1997) 39 IPR 319, **544**
Woodtree Pty Ltd v Zheng (2007) 211 FLR 18, **59**
Woodward v Hutchins [1977] 2 All ER 751, **255**
Woolly Bull Enterprises Pty Ltd v Reynolds (2001) 107 FCR 166, **641**
Woolworths Ltd v BP plc (No 2) (2006) 154 FCR 97, **575, 604**
Woolworths Ltd v Olson [2004] NSWCA 372, **251**
Woolworths Ltd v Olson (2004) 184 FLR 121, **89, 416**
Woolworths Ltd v Registrar of Trade Marks (1998) 45 IPR 445, **606–7, 609–10, 613, 652**
Woolworths Ltd v Registrar of Trade Marks (1999) 45 IPR 411, **606–7, 609–10, 613, 652**
World of Technologies (Australia) Pty Ltd v Tempo (Australia) Pty Ltd (2007) 71 IPR 307, **206**
Worldgroup (Australia) Pty Ltd v Shimmersea (Australia) Pty Ltd (1998) 43 IPR 641, **613**
WR Grace & Co v Asahi Kasei Kogyo Kabushiki Kaisha (1993) 25 IPR 481, **358**

Wright v Gasweld Pty Ltd (1991) 22 NSWLR 317, **223, 230, 244, 246, 250–4**
Wright v Hitchcock (1870) LR 5 Exch 37, **459**

X v Twitter Inc (2017) 95 NSWLR 301, **234, 236, 249**

Yarra Valley Dairy Pty Ltd v Lemnos Foods Pty Ltd (2010) 191 FCR 297, **635**
Yorke v Ross Lucas Pty Ltd (1982) 45 ALR 299, **568**
Young v Wilson (1955) 72 RPC 351, **409**
Young v Wyllie [2010] FCA 283, **90**

TABLE OF STATUTES

Commonwealth
Acts Interpretation Act 1901
  s 2B, **324, 351**
  s 23, **409**
Archives Act 1983, **199**
Australian Bicentennial Authority Act 1980, **20**
Australian Consumer Law, **130**
Australian Grape and Wine Authority Act 2013, **625**
Australian Securities and Investments Commission Act 2001
  s 12CB, **130**
Australian Wine and Brandy Corporation Amendment Act 1993, **618**
Australian Wine and Brandy Corporation Regulations 2010
  sch 1, **618**
Banking Act 1959
  s 66, **619**
Broadcasting Services Act 1992, **63, 66, 78**
Business Names Registration Act 2011, **617**
  s 17, **617**
  s 18, **617**
Circuit Layouts Act 1989, **10, 57, 189, 194**
  div 3, **192**
  s 5, **189–91**
  s 8, **190**
  s 8(2), **190**
  s 9, **190**
  s 10, **190**
  s 10(b), **190**
  s 11, **190**
  s 13, **191**
  s 14, **190**
  s 15, **190–1**
  s 16(1), **191**
  s 16(2), **191**
  s 16(3), **191**
  s 17, **190**

  s 18, **191**
  s 19, **191**
  s 19(3), **192**
  s 20, **192**
  s 20(1), **192**
  s 20(2), **193**
  s 20(3), **193**
  s 21, **192**
  s 22, **192**
  s 23, **192**
  s 24(1), **190, 193**
  s 24(2), **193**
  s 27, **192, 700**
  s 27(2), **699**
  s 27(2)–(4), **193**
  s 27(4), **193**
  s 42, **190**
  s 44, **191**
  s 45(1), **191**
  s 45(2), **191**
  s 45(3), **191**
  s 45(4), **191**
  s 46, **672**
  s 48, **190**
Competition and Consumer Act 2010, **686, 699, 703**
  pt IV, **257, 423, 426–7, 589, 694, 704–6**
  s 24(1), **631**
  s 45AD, **704**
  s 46, **704, 706**
  s 48, **704**
  s 51(3), **423, 704, 706**
  s 150A, **426–7**
  sch 2, **566**
  sch 2 pt 2-2, **589**
  sch 2 pt 3-1, **589**
  sch 2 pt 5-2, **568**
  sch 2 s 2(2)(a), **563**
  sch 2 s 2(2)(b), **563**

sch 2 s 2(2)(c), 563
sch 2 s 18, 12, 60, 166, 378, 474, 520, 532, 538, 553, 562–3, 565–6, 568, 630, 653–4, 662, 667, 677, 703
sch 2 s 29(c), 566
sch 2 s 29(d), 566
sch 2 s 30(c), 566
sch 2 s 30(d), 566
sch 2 s 34, 566
sch 2 s 236, 565, 568

Constitution
   s 51(i), 21
   s 51(xviii), 20–1, 32, 268
   s 51(xxix), 21
   s 51(xxxi), 21
   s 55, 21, 154

Copyright Act 1905, 32
Copyright Act 1912, 19, 32
Copyright Act 1968, 32, 35–6, 38–9, 49, 106, 111, 141, 190, 192, 194, 198
   pt III, 9, 26, 49, 85, 118
   pt III div 5A, 107, 121
   pt IV, 9, 26, 49–50, 55, 62, 64, 74, 76, 85, 118, 194
   pt IV div 3, 111
   pt IVA, 40
   pt IVA div 4, 109
   pt IVA div 5, 109
   pt V div 2A, 93
   pt V div 5 sub-div E, 98
   pt V div 7, 702
   pt V sub-div A, 94, 97
   pt VA, 40, 105, 108, 112
   pt VAA, 100
   pt VB, 40, 105, 108, 112, 142, 159
   pt VC, 105, 107
   pt VII div 1, 84
   pt VII div 2, 84, 107
   pt IX, 9, 76, 183
   pt XIA, 49, 181
   s 6, 160
   s 10, 40, 50, 52–3, 58, 64, 66, 72, 141, 144, 147, 156, 160, 163, 194
   s 10(1), 50, 54–5, 57, 59–60, 62–4, 77–8, 87–9, 91, 94, 96–9, 105, 139, 155, 193
   s 10(1)(a), 91, 137
   s 10(1)(a)–(e), 137
   s 10(1)(b), 91, 137
   s 10(1)(ba), 91
   s 10(1)(c), 91, 137
   s 10(1)(d), 91, 137
   s 10(1)(f), 137
   s 10(1)(g), 137
   s 10(2), 157
   s 10A, 158
   s 10AA, 134
   s 10AA(2)(c), 134
   s 10AA(3), 134
   s 14, 116
   s 21, 114
   s 21(1), 87
   s 21(1A), 87, 114
   s 21(3), 91, 216
   s 21(3)(a), 115
   s 21(3)(b), 115
   s 21(5), 87, 115
   s 22(1), 49, 64
   s 22(2), 49
   s 22(3), 77
   s 22(3)(a), 74
   s 22(3A), 78, 183
   s 22(3B), 81, 183
   s 22(3C), 81
   s 22(4), 77
   s 22(5), 78
   s 22(6), 89
   s 22(6A), 90
   s 23, 62
   s 24, 62
   s 27(1)(a), 88
   s 27(1)(b), 88
   s 27(2), 88
   s 27(3), 88
   s 27(4), 88
   s 28, 89, 159
   s 28(3), 89
   s 28(4), 89
   s 29(1)(a), 65, 88
   s 29(1)(b), 65
   s 29(1)(c), 65
   s 29(3), 88
   s 29(4), 65
   s 29A, 65, 80
   s 31, 4, 106
   s 31(1), 112
   s 31(1)(a), 86
   s 31(1)(a)(iii), 88
   s 31(1)(a)(vi), 91

s 31(1)(a)(vii), 91
s 31(1)(b), 86
s 31(1)(c), 86, 92
s 31(1)(d), 86, 92
s 31(6), 86, 92
s 32, 4, 49, 64, 67
s 32(1), 49, 66
s 32(2), 66
s 32(2)(c), 70
s 32(3)(a), 66
s 32(4), 66, 76
s 33, 80
s 33(2), 76, 101
s 35, 64, 80
s 35(2), 76
s 35(3), 80
s 35(4), 82
s 35(5), 83
s 35(5)(a), 83
s 35(6), 81–2
s 35(7), 83
s 36(1), 113, 120
s 36(1A), 122–3
s 37, 112, 131, 134
s 37(2), 131
s 38, 113, 131, 134
s 39, 113, 122, 131
s 39(2), 131
s 39(3), 131
s 39A, 123
s 39B, 122
s 40, 142, 144, 151–2
s 40(1), 146
s 40(1A), 146
s 40(2), 152–3
s 40(3), 144, 152–3
s 40(3)–(5), 152–3
s 40(4), 144, 152–3
s 40(5), 153–4
s 40(6), 152
ss 40–43, 143
s 41, 144, 146
s 41A, 144, 149
s 42, 144, 148
s 42(1)(a), 148
s 42(1)(b), 148
s 42(2), 148
s 43(1), 149, 163
s 43(2), 144, 149

s 43A, 162
s 43B, 87, 162
s 43C, 155
s 44A, 132
s 44E, 136
s 44F, 136
s 45, 164
s 47(3), 105, 107
s 47A, 107
s 47B, 166
s 47B(1), 161
s 47B(3), 162
s 47C(1)(c)(i), 161
s 47C(1)(c)(ii), 161
s 47C(2), 161
s 47D, 120, 162
s 47E, 161
s 47E(d), 161
s 47F, 162
s 47H, 162
s 47J, 156, 160
s 48A, 158
s 49, 121–2, 157
s 49(9), 157
s 50, 157–8
s 50(10), 157
s 51, 158
s 51A, 158
s 51AA, 158
s 52, 158
s 53, 157
s 53B, 142
ss 54–64, 105, 107
s 55, 173
s 65, 160
ss 67–68, 160
s 68, 160
s 70, 160
s 70(3), 105, 107
s 72, 161
s 73, 161
s 74, 216
s 74(1), 217
s 74(2), 217
ss 74–77, 160, 216
ss 74–77A, 10
s 75, 216–18
s 76, 217
s 77, 217

s 77(1)(a), 60, 218
s 77(1)(d), 218
s 77(1A), 218
s 77(5), 218
s 77A, 217–18
s 78, 78
s 79, 66
s 84, 66
s 85, 88
s 85(1), 86
s 85(1)(a), 88
s 85(2), 86
s 86, 86, 88
s 86(a), 88
s 87(a), 63, 88
s 87(b), 88
s 88, 86, 88
s 89, 74
s 89(1)–(3), 66
s 90, 74
s 90(1), 66
s 90(3), 66
s 91, 74
s 91(a)–(b), 66
s 92, 74
s 92(1), 66
s 93, 164
s 95(2), 74
s 97, 76
s 97(1), 77
s 97(2), 77
s 98, 76
s 98(1), 77
s 98(2), 77
s 99, 76, 78
s 100, 76, 78
s 100A, 146
s 100AF, 78
s 101, 461
s 101(1), 113, 120, 126
s 101(1A), 122, 127
s 101(1A)(a), 127
s 101(1A)(b), 127
s 101(1A)(c), 127
s 102, 113, 131, 134
s 103, 113, 131, 134
s 103A, 144, 146
s 103AA, 149–50
s 103B, 144, 148

s 103B(1), 148
s 103C, 144
s 103C(2), 153
s 104(a), 163
s 104(b), 149
s 104(c), 149
s 104B, 123
s 106(1)(a), 164
s 106(1)(b), 164
s 107(3), 105, 107
s 108, 107
ss 108–109, 105
s 109, 107
s 109A, 156
s 109A(1)(c), 156
s 110(1), 164
s 110(2), 165
s 110(3), 164
s 110A, 158
s 110AA, 156
s 110B, 158
s 111, 155
s 111(1), 155
s 111(3), 155
s 111(4), 155
s 111A, 162
s 111B(1), 162
s 111B(2), 162
s 112A, 132
s 112AA, 158
s 112B, 122
s 112DA, 136
s 112E, 123, 125–6
s 113E, 93, 144, 153
s 113E(1), 151
s 113E(2), 153
s 113F, 93, 160
s 113F(b), 160
s 113G, 157
s 113L, 157
s 113N, 109
s 113P, 40, 93, 109
s 113P(1)(d), 109
s 113Q, 109
s 113R, 109
s 113S, 109
s 115, 700
s 115(2), 137, 699–700
s 115(3), 139

s 115(4), 138–9
s 115A, 39, 138
s 115A(2), 39, 138
s 116, 139, 699
s 116(1B), 140
s 116(1C), 140
s 116(2), 140
s 116(2)(c), 139
s 116A, 94, 97, 124
s 116AAA, 78
s 116ABA, 40
ss 116AC–116AF, 124
ss 116AD–116AE, 124
s 116AE, 124
s 116AF, 124
s 116AG, 123
s 116AH, 124
ss 116AK–116D, 93
s 116AN, 94, 96, 98
s 116AN(1), 94
s 116AN(2), 95
s 116AN(2)–(9), 94
s 116AN(3), 95
s 116AN(4), 95
s 116AN(5), 95
s 116AN(6), 95
s 116AN(7), 96
s 116AN(8), 95, 99
s 116AN(9), 96
s 116AN(9)(c), 93
s 116AN(10), 95
s 116AO, 94, 96, 98
s 116AO(1), 96
s 116AO(2), 97
s 116AO(2)–(6), 97
s 116AO(3), 97
s 116AO(4), 97
s 116AO(5), 97
s 116AO(6), 97
s 116AO(7), 97
s 116AP, 94, 97–8
s 116AP(1), 97
s 116AP(2), 98
s 116AP(2)–(6), 98
s 116AP(3), 98
s 116AP(4), 98
s 116AP(5), 98
s 116AP(7), 98
s 116AQ(2), 96

s 116B(1)(a), 99
s 116B(1)(b), 99
ss 117–125, 106
ss 126–129, 113
s 126A, 113
s 126B, 113
s 129A, 113
s 130A, 113, 134
s 130AAA, 113
s 130B, 113, 136
s 130C, 136
s 132(5C), 100
s 132(5EA), 100
s 132(6A), 100
s 132A, 113
s 132AD(5), 141
s 132AE(5), 141
s 132AF(7), 141
s 132AG(7), 141
s 132AG(8), 142
s 132AH(5), 142
s 132AI, 141–2
s 132AI(7), 142
s 132AJ(5), 142
s 132AL, 141
s 132AL(8), 142
s 132AM, 113
s 132AN, 141
s 132AO, 141
s 132AO(5), 142
s 132APC, 98
s 132APC(2)–(8), 99
s 132APD, 98
s 132APD(2)–(7), 99
s 132APE, 98
s 132APE(2)–(7), 99
s 132AT(1)–(2), 141
s 132B, 113
s 132C, 113
s 133B, 142
s 134, 137
s 135AL, 100
ss 135AL–135ANA, 100
s 135AN(4), 100
s 135AN(6), 100
s 135ANA(6), 100
s 135AOB, 101
s 135ASI, 101
s 135ASJ, 101

s 135C, 108
ss 135ZH–135ZM, 108
s 135ZV(2), 112
s 135ZX(2A), 108
s 138, 111
s 153F, 163
s 157AB, 112
ss 176–179, 84
s 176(1), 84
s 178(1), 84
s 182A, 163
s 182A(3), 163
ss 182B–182E, 84
ss 182B–183E, 105, 107
s 183, 84, 163
s 183(1), 84
s 183(3), 84–5
s 183(4), 84–5, 163
s 183A, 85
ss 183A–183D, 85
s 183C, 85
s 189, 171, 184
ss 189–195AZG, 9, 76
s 190, 171, 175
s 191, 171
s 193, 171
s 194(1), 171
s 194(2), 171
s 195, 171
s 195AA, 171
s 195AB, 171
s 195ABA, 184
s 195ABA(1), 184
s 195ABA(2), 184
s 195ABB(1), 184
s 195ABB(2), 184
s 195ABC(3), 184
s 195ABD, 184
s 195AC(1), 175
s 195AD(a), 175
s 195AD(b)–(c), 175
s 195AD(d), 175
s 195AE(a), 175–6
s 195AE(b)–(d), 175
s 195AF(1), 175
s 195AF(2), 175
s 195AG, 175
s 195AHA, 184
s 195AHB(1)–(7), 184

s 195AHC, 185
s 195AHC(2)(a), 185
s 195AHC(2)(b), 185
s 195AI(1), 172
s 195AI(1)–(2), 172
s 195AI(2), 172
s 195AJ(a), 172
s 195AJ(b), 172
s 195AK, 173
s 195AL(a), 172
s 195AL(b), 172
s 195ALA, 184–5
s 195ALB, 185
s 195AM(1), 170–1
s 195AN(1), 170
s 195AN(2), 170
s 195AN(3), 170
s 195AO, 171
s 195AQ(3), 172
s 195AQ(4), 172
s 195AQ(5), 172
s 195AR, 172, 176
s 195AR(1), 176
s 195AR(2), 176
s 195AR(2)(a), 176
s 195AR(2)(b), 177
s 195AR(2)(c), 177
s 195AR(2)(d), 177
s 195AR(2)(e), 177
s 195AR(2)(h)(i), 177
s 195AS, 176
s 195AS(1), 176
s 195AS(2), 176
s 195AS(2)(a), 174
s 195AS(2)(b), 177
s 195AS(2)(c), 177
s 195AS(2)(d), 177
s 195AS(2)(e), 177
s 195AS(2)(g)(i), 177
s 195AT, 174
s 195AT(1), 174
s 195AT(2), 174
s 195AT(2A)–(4A), 174
s 195AT(5), 174
s 195AVA, 172
s 195AW, 172
ss 195AW–195AWA, 170
s 195AWA, 172, 178
s 195AWA(3), 178

s 195AWA(4), 178
s 195AWB, 178–9
s 195AXA, 184
s 195AXC, 185
s 195AXJ, 185
s 195AXJ(1), 185
s 195AXK, 185
s 195AZA, 179
s 195AZA(1), 179
s 195AZA(2), 179
s 195AZA(3), 180
s 195AZB(1), 179
s 195AZM(2), 171
s 195AZN(1), 175
s 195AZQ(2), 184
s 196(2)(a), 104
s 196(2)(a)–(c), 104
s 196(2)(b), 104
s 196(2)(c), 104
s 196(3), 105
s 196(4), 105
s 197(1), 105
s 199(2), 164
s 200, 158–9
s 200(1)(b), 159
s 200(2), 159
s 200(2A), 159
s 200AAA, 87, 90
s 200AAA(1)(a)–(d), 87
s 200AB, 149, 158, 160
s 200AB(1)(a), 158
s 200AB(1)(c), 158
s 200AB(1)(d), 158
s 200AB(2)(b), 158
s 200AB(2)(c), 158
s 200AB(3), 93
s 200AB(4), 144, 151
s 200AB(6), 158
s 200AB(7), 158
s 202, 140, 672
s 202(2), 140
s 202(3), 140
s 202A, 140
ss 203A–203H, 140
s 213(2), 83
s 248(1), 183
s 248A, 181
s 248A(1), 181–2
s 248A(2), 181

s 248A(3), 183
s 248CA(1), 182
s 248CA(3), 182
s 248G, 182–3
s 248G(1)(b), 182
s 248G(2), 182
s 248J, 183
s 249, 96
Copyright (Parallel Importation) Act 2003, 136
Copyright (World Trade Organization Amendments) Act 1994, 86
Copyright Amendment Act 1980
  s 7, 152
  s 14, 121
Copyright Amendment Act 1984, 50, 53
  ss 47AB–47AH, 53
Copyright Amendment Act 1989, 108
Copyright Amendment Act 1998
  pt VB, 108
  sch 3, 139
  sch 4, 163
Copyright Amendment Act 2006, 37, 90, 94, 100, 108, 112–13, 140–1, 143, 153, 157, 183
  schs 1–5, 37
  sch 2, 113
  sch 6, 152
  sch 6 pt 1, 155
  sch 6 pt 2, 155
  sch 6 pt 4 item 11, 98
  schs 6–8, 37, 143
  sch 9, 37, 100
  sch 10 items 4–33, 112
  sch 10 pt 1, 112
  sch 10 pt 3, 111
  schs 10–11, 37
  sch 11, 112
  sch 12, 37, 92
  sch 12 item 9, 94, 97
Copyright Amendment (Computer Programs) Act 1999, 53
  s 47B, 192
Copyright Amendment (Digital Agenda) Act 2000, 35, 43, 53, 92, 99–100, 108, 121–2, 139, 161
Copyright Amendment (Disability Access and Other Measures) Act 2017, 40, 44, 65, 80, 101, 109, 143–4, 151, 160, 164

s 113E, **40**
s 113F, **40**
Copyright Amendment (Film Directors' Rights) Act 2005, **36**
Copyright Amendment (Moral Rights) Act 2000, **9**, **175**
Copyright Amendment (Online Infringement) Act 2015, **39**, **138**
Copyright Amendment (Online Infringement) Act 2018, **39**, **130**
Copyright Amendment (Service Providers) Act 2018, **40**
Copyright Amendment Regulations (No 1) 2004
   sch 10 pts 1–6, **124**
Copyright Legislation Amendment Act 2004, **181**
Copyright Legislation Amendment (Technological Protection Measures) Regulations 2017, **93**
Copyright Regulations 1969, **93**, **218**
   pt 6A, **142**
   reg 17, **218**
   reg 25, **163**
Copyright Regulations 2017, **93**
   reg 40, **93**
Copyright Tribunal (Procedure) Regulations 1969, **93**
Corporations Act 2001, **667**
   s 183(1), **222**, **249–50**
Crimes Act 1914
   s 4AA, **99–101**, **141**
Designs Act 1906, **197–200**, **203–4**, **206**, **210**, **216**
   s 4, **204–5**, **218**
   s 4(1), **203–4**
   s 15(2), **206**
   s 17, **206**
   s 17(1), **206**
   s 30, **198**
   s 47, **207**
Designs Act 2003, **194**, **197–200**, **203**, **206**, **216**
   s 4(1), **194**
   s 5, **10**, **201**, **212**
   s 6, **204**, **218**
   s 6(1), **205**
   s 6(2), **205**, **212**
   s 6(3), **206**
   s 6(4), **205**
   s 7(1), **205**
   s 7(2), **205**
   s 7(3), **205**
   s 10, **209**
   s 10(1), **209**
   s 10(2), **209**
   s 11, **209**
   s 11(1)–(3), **209**
   s 13(1), **200**
   s 13(1)(a), **200**
   s 13(1)(b), **200**
   s 13(2), **200**
   s 13(3), **200**
   s 15, **206**
   s 15(2), **206**
   s 16, **210**
   s 16(1), **207**
   s 16(2), **207**
   s 16(3), **207**
   s 17, **207**
   s 19, **201**, **207**
   s 19(1), **207**, **209–11**
   s 19(2), **208**, **210**
   s 19(2)(a), **208**, **210**
   s 19(2)(b), **201**, **208**, **210**
   s 19(2)(c), **208**, **210**
   s 19(2)(d), **210**
   s 19(3), **208**, **211**
   s 19(4), **208**, **211**
   s 21, **200**
   s 21(2), **200–1**
   s 21(3), **200**
   s 22, **201**
   s 27(1), **202**, **207**
   s 27(2), **207**
   s 27A, **203**
   s 28(3), **202**
   s 29, **201**
   s 33(1)(a), **202**
   s 35, **201**
   s 36(1), **202**
   ss 39–40, **202**
   s 41, **202**
   s 43(1), **202**
   s 43(1)(c)(i), **194**
   s 45, **202**
   s 46, **203**
   s 46(1), **10**

s 47, **203**
s 51, **201**
s 52, **201**
s 63(1), **200, 203**
s 65, **203**
s 66(3), **203**
s 67, **203**
s 68, **203**
s 68(6), **203**
s 69, **201**
s 71(1)(a), **209, 211**
s 71(1)(a)–(e), **210**
s 71(1)(b)–(e), **211**
s 71(2), **211, 214**
s 71(3), **209, 211**
s 72, **211, 213**
s 72(1), **212**
s 72(2), **214**
s 72(3)(a), **213**
s 72(4), **213**
s 72(5), **212–13**
s 73, **200**
s 73(3), **203, 209**
s 75(1), **215**
s 75(2), **209**
s 75(2)(a)(i)–(ii), **211, 215**
s 75(2)(b), **211**
s 75(3), **215, 700**
s 75(4), **215**
s 75(5), **209**
s 77, **699**
s 77(1), **215**
s 77(2), **215**
s 77(3), **215**
s 79, **216**
s 80, **215**
s 84, **703**
s 93, **209**
ss 95–105, **211, 214**
s 150, **197**
ss 151–161, **198**
s 152, **198**
s 156, **198**
Designs (Consequential Amendments) Act 2003, **198, 216**
   sch 1 item 1, **60**
Designs Regulations 2004
   reg 2.01, **207**
   reg 3.01, **200–1**

reg 3.06, **202**
reg 4.04(f), **201**
reg 11.01, **201**
sch 4, **201, 203**
Federal Court of Australia Act 1976
   s 23, **484**
Gaming Machine Control (Amendment) Act 1993, **619**
Intellectual Property Laws Amendment Act 2006, **479, 628**
   sch 2 item 1, **479**
   sch 6, **476**
   sch 6 item 1, **476, 478**
   sch 7, **475**
   sch 7 item 4, **475**
Intellectual Property Laws Amendment Act 2015, **199, 269, 422**
   sch 1, **431**
   sch 2, **431**
Intellectual Property Laws Amendment (Productivity Commission Response Part 1 and Other Measures) Act 2018, **402, 494**
   sch 1 item 7, **399**
   sch 1 pt 2, **509**
   sch 2 pt 7 item 182, **395**
   sch 2 pt 8 item 200, **486**
   sch 2 pt 8 item 202, **522**
   sch 2 pt 8 item 209(4), **522**
   sch 2 pt 9 item 212, **502**
   sch 2 pt 9 item 217, **523**
   sch 2 pt 11 items 221–3, **524**
   sch 3 pt 8, **522**
Intellectual Property Laws Amendment (Raising the Bar) Act 2012, **268, 324, 441, 449, 484, 680**
   s 18(2), **379–80**
   s 18(3), **380**
   s 18(4), **381**
   s 24, **328**
   s 50(1)(a), **381**
   sch 1 item 3, **352**
   sch 1 item 4, **354**
   sch 1 item 6, **372**
   sch 1 item 7, **385**
   sch 1 item 8, **385**
   sch 1 item 9, **385, 396**
   sch 1 item 12, **370**

sch 1 item 13, 348
sch 1 item 17, 348, 370, 387
sch 1 item 20, 348, 370
sch 1 item 21, 279
sch 1 item 29, 393
sch 1 item 55, 385
sch 1 item 55(1), 352, 354
sch 2 pt 2, 482
sch 6 item 17, 295
sch 6 item 23, 295
sch 6 item 28, 379
sch 6 item 29, 379
sch 6 item 31, 488
sch 6 item 33, 344
sch 6 item 43, 395
sch 6 item 54, 277
sch 6 item 101, 328
sch 6 item 102, 328
sch 6 item 133(7), 395
Intellectual Property Legislation Amendment (Raising the Bar) Regulation 2013 (No 1)
sch 6 item 7, 339
Olympic Insignia Protection Act 1987, 202, 617
Patents Act 1903, 268, 323
s 32(3), 401
s 62, 452
s 124, 341
Patents Act 1952, 268, 289, 292, 300, 323, 326, 328–9, 341, 347, 350, 373, 386, 419, 424, 456, 458–9, 480
s 34(1), 401, 407
s 34(1)(a), 407
s 40(1), 386
s 40(1)(a), 289
s 40(1A)(b), 293
s 40(3)–(7), 289
s 48(3), 327
s 48(3)(b), 323
s 48(3)(d), 323
s 48(3)(d)–(e), 327
s 48(3)(e), 323
s 49A(11)(c)–(e), 327
s 59(1)(c)–(d), 327
s 59(1)(c)–(e), 323
s 59(1)(d)–(e), 327
s 59(1)(g), 323
s 59(1)(h), 323, 327

s 64, 407
s 69, 452
s 100(1), 490
s 100(1)(e), 330, 350, 358
s 100(1)(e)–(g), 323
s 100(1)(f), 327
s 100(1)(g), 327
s 100(1)(k), 373
s 100(1)(l), 476
s 100(3)(a), 341
Patents Act 1977, 401
s 40(2)(b), 394
s 40(2)(c), 394
s 40(3), 394–9
s 40(3A), 395
s 40(4), 399
s 45(1)(a), 399
s 102, 393, 395
s 102(1), 393
sch 1, 393
Patents Act 1990, 200, 268, 270, 273, 287, 293–4, 297, 300–1, 308, 314–15, 317, 321, 323, 326, 328–9, 334, 347, 459, 481
ch 6 pt 3, 274
ch 6A, 273
ch 7, 274
ch 9A pt 2, 279
ch 9A pt 3, 279
ch 11 pt 2, 424
ch 12, 426, 431, 433
ch 12 pt 3, 431
ch 14, 423, 431
ch 17, 378, 417, 420
ch 19, 438
s 3, 401
s 3(1), 343
s 5, 274
s 6, 300
s 7, 324, 352
s 7(1), 324–6, 335, 337, 354, 373, 476
s 7(1)(a)–(c), 325
s 7(1)(b), 337–8
s 7(2), 285, 348–53, 356, 360, 365, 369
s 7(2)–(5), 347
s 7(3), 285, 348–53, 356, 359–60, 365, 369
s 7(4), 285, 348–9, 353, 355, 359
s 7(5), 285, 348–9, 353, 355, 359
s 7A, 372
s 9, 373, 375–7, 379, 455, 476

Table of statutes lxxv

s 9(a), 342, 376
s 9(b), 374, 377
s 9(c), 378
s 9(e), 261, 379
s 13, 410, 438
s 13(1), 408–9, 423, 425, 431, 449–50, 452, 460–1, 464, 466
s 13(2), 408, 410, 422, 450
s 13(3), 450
s 14, 424
s 15, 274–5, 401–2, 407, 411, 488–9
s 15(1), 401, 407, 437, 488
s 15(1)(a), 403
s 15(1)(b), 407, 411
s 15(1)(b)–(d), 488
s 15(1)(c), 407–8, 410–11
s 16, 406, 410
s 16(1)(a), 409
s 16(1)(b), 409
s 16(1)(c), 409
s 16(2), 409
s 16(3), 409
s 17, 410
s 18, 265, 292, 314, 324, 348, 366, 369, 379, 387, 403–4, 428, 441, 450, 476, 487
s 18(1), 4, 292, 294, 296, 307, 325, 348, 366–70, 372, 382
s 18(1)(a), 276, 295, 297, 301, 315, 366–8
s 18(1)(b), 276, 285, 366–7
s 18(1)(b)(i), 323–4, 373
s 18(1)(b)(ii), 262, 307, 323, 348, 369
s 18(1)(c), 276, 370
s 18(1)(d), 261, 277, 285, 373, 476
s 18(1A), 292, 294, 296, 307, 325, 370, 372, 487
s 18(1A)(a), 297, 301
s 18(1A)(b), 285
s 18(1A)(b)(i), 323–4, 373
s 18(1A)(b)(ii), 262, 323, 348, 353
s 18(1A)(d), 285, 373
s 18(2), 276, 300
s 18(3), 293
s 20(1), 265, 276
s 22A, 403, 488
s 23, 274, 324
s 23(a), 285
s 23(b), 285
s 24, 379, 475
s 24(1), 338–9, 343

s 24(1)(a), 339, 478
s 24(1)(b), 344
s 24(2), 344
s 24(2)(a), 344
s 24(2)(b), 344
s 27(1), 276, 278
s 29, 274, 401
s 29(1), 274–5
s 29(2)–(4), 274
s 29(4), 283
s 29A, 283
s 29A(1), 272
s 29B(1), 272
s 29B(2), 272
s 29B(3), 272
s 29B(4), 272
s 29C, 273
s 30, 272, 274, 282
s 31, 274, 401
s 32, 402–3
s 33, 402, 408
ss 33–35, 403
ss 33–36, 285
s 34, 402, 408
s 35, 408
s 36, 402, 411
s 37, 274
s 38, 274, 283, 286
s 38(1), 283, 340–1, 343–4
s 38(1A), 272
s 40, 274, 294, 370, 387, 441, 450, 490
s 40(1), 282, 385–8, 398–9
s 40(2), 282, 325, 348, 385–7, 487
s 40(2)–(4), 275, 387
s 40(2)(a), 6, 11, 289, 385–94, 398–9, 404
s 40(2)(aa), 385, 388–94
s 40(2)(b), 293, 348
s 40(2)(b)–(c), 325
s 40(2)(c), 293, 348
s 40(3), 284, 385–6, 441, 449, 487
s 40(3A), 385
s 40(4), 385–6, 404
s 41, 274, 289, 300, 385
s 41(1), 386, 389
s 41(1A), 386, 388
s 41(2), 386
s 41(3), 289, 386
s 41(6), 386
s 42, 289, 300, 386

s 43, 274, 324, 348, 401
s 43(1), 282
s 43(2), 282, 325, 348
s 43(2)(b), 284
s 43(2A), 282, 387
s 43(2A)(b), 283–4
s 43(3), 325
s 43(4), 282
s 43A, 275
s 43AA, 283
s 44, 275
s 44(1), 275
s 44(2), 275
s 44(3), 275
s 45(1)–(2), 275
s 45(1)(a), 387
s 45(1)(b), 285, 295, 323, 348, 370, 476
s 45(1A), 324, 348
s 48(1A), 324, 348
s 49(1), 276
s 49(2), 276
s 49(5), 277
s 49(6), 277
s 49(7), 276
s 49A, 276
s 50, 276, 300
s 50(1)(a), 276, 320, 382
s 50(1)(b), 276, 382
s 50(2), 277
s 50A, 277
s 51, 276
s 52, 295, 381
s 52(1), 279
s 52(2), 279
s 53, 275
s 53(2), 273
s 54(3), 285
s 54(3)(b), 328
ss 54–5, 275
s 55, 483, 485
s 56A, 273
s 57, 273, 275, 279, 411, 483–4
s 57(3), 483
s 59, 277, 286, 373, 381, 402, 408, 476, 486
s 59(b), 277, 295, 323, 348, 370, 373, 381, 476
s 59(c), 387
s 60(3A), 277
s 60(3B), 277

s 60(4), 277
s 61, 348, 410–11, 438
s 61(1), 278, 323, 438
s 62, 295, 348, 381
s 63, 410
s 64, 278
s 64(2), 285
s 65, 274, 280, 450
s 67, 11, 265, 279, 293, 411, 450
s 68, 265, 280, 293, 450
s 68A, 293
s 70, 11, 280, 282, 316
s 70(2), 280
s 70(2)(a), 280–1
s 70(2)(b), 280–1
s 70(3), 280
s 70(3)(a), 281
s 70(3)(b), 281
s 70(4), 280–1
s 70(5), 281
s 70(5A), 282
s 70(6), 281
s 71(2), 282
s 71(5A), 281
s 77(2), 282
s 79B, 273, 280
s 79C, 273, 280
s 83, 274, 280
s 83(1), 280
s 83(3), 274
s 83(4), 274
s 85, 487
s 97, 277
s 97(2), 278
s 97(3), 278
s 97(4), 278
s 98, 278, 348, 370
s 98(2), 324, 348
s 98(b), 285, 295, 323, 348
s 100A, 278
s 101, 278
s 101A, 279
s 101B, 295, 348, 370
s 101B(1), 382
s 101B(2), 285
s 101B(2)(b), 295, 324, 348
s 101B(2)(d), 382
s 101B(2)(e), 382
s 101B(2)(f), 382

s 101B(2)(h), 285
s 101B(3), 324, 348
s 101E, 483
s 101E(1)(a), 279
s 101E(1)(b), 279
s 101E(2), 279
s 101F, 382
s 101G, 295
s 101G(1A)(3)(b), 295
s 101G(3), 285
s 101G(3)(b), 324, 348
s 101J, 279
s 101M, 295, 402
s 101M(c), 295
s 102(1), 387
s 104, 276
s 107, 276, 286
s 112, 432
s 113, 408, 411
s 114(1), 282
s 117, 461–2, 464–6, 470, 472–4
s 117(1), 465–8, 472–3
s 117(2), 465, 468, 474
s 117(2)(a), 468, 470
s 117(2)(b), 467, 469–72
s 117(2)(c), 471–3
s 118, 474–5
s 118(a), 475
s 118(b), 475
s 119, 261, 285, 316, 474–9
s 119(1), 478–9
s 119(2), 478
s 119(3), 477
s 119(4), 478–9
s 119A, 317, 475, 479
s 119B, 474, 479
s 119C, 474, 482, 525
s 119C(1), 482
s 119C(2), 482
s 120, 409, 424–5, 483
s 120(1), 483
s 120(1A), 279, 483
s 120(2), 424, 484
s 120(3), 484
s 120(4), 484
s 121, 484, 487
s 121A, 484
s 121A(3), 484
s 122(1), 484, 699

s 122(1A), 484, 700
s 122(2), 485
s 123(2), 485
s 123(3), 485
s 125(2), 485
s 125(3), 485
ss 125–127, 485
s 126(1)(a), 485
s 126(1)(b), 485
s 127, 485
s 128, 486
s 128(1), 486
s 128(A), 486
ss 128–132, 672
s 129A, 486
s 129A(1), 486
s 129A(3), 486
s 130(1), 486
s 130(2), 486
s 131, 486
s 132, 486
s 133, 431
s 133(1), 426
s 133(1A), 426
s 133(2)(a)(i), 426
s 133(2)(a)(ii), 426
s 133(2)(a)(iii), 426
s 133(2)(b), 426–7, 431
s 133(3), 427
s 133(3)(a), 427
s 133(3)(b), 427
s 133(3B), 428
s 133(3B)(c), 428
s 133(4), 429
s 133(5), 429
s 133(6), 429
s 134, 431, 487
s 134(1), 429
s 135, 427
s 135(1), 427
s 135(2), 427
s 136, 429
s 137, 487
s 138, 324, 348, 381
s 138(1A), 487
s 138(3), 265, 487
s 138(3)(a), 401–2, 487–9
s 138(3)(b), 295, 324, 348, 370, 373, 381, 476, 487

s 138(3)(c), **487**
s 138(3)(d), **381, 487, 489–90**
s 138(3)(e), **487, 489–90**
s 138(3)(f), **387, 487**
s 138(4), **403, 488–9**
s 139(1), **492**
s 141(1), **286**
s 141(1)(b), **286**
s 142(1), **274, 286**
s 142(2), **275, 286**
s 142(2)(e), **276**
s 143, **286**
s 143A, **279, 286**
s 143B, **286**
s 144, **432–3**
s 144(1)(a), **432**
s 144(1)(b), **432–3**
s 144(1A), **433**
s 144(2), **433**
s 144(2)(a), **434**
s 144(3), **434**
s 144(4), **433**
s 144(5), **434**
s 145, **435–6**
s 145(1), **432, 434**
s 145(2), **434**
s 146, **433**
s 146(a), **433**
s 152, **421**
s 155, **703**
s 155(1), **421**
s 162, **378, 418**
s 163, **418, 421**
s 163(1), **419–21**
s 163(2), **419**
s 163(3), **421**
s 164, **420**
s 165(2), **420**
s 165(3), **420**
s 165(4), **421**
s 165A(1), **421**
s 165A(2), **421**
s 166, **419**
s 167(1), **419**
s 167(2), **419**
s 168, **418**
s 168(a), **421**
s 168(b), **421**
s 168(c), **421**

s 169(1), **420**
s 169(2)(a), **420**
s 169(2)(b), **420**
s 169(3), **420**
s 169(4), **420**
s 171, **418**
s 171(1), **421**
s 171(2), **421**
s 171(3)(b), **421**
s 171(4), **422**
s 172, **418**
s 172(1), **422**
s 172(2), **422**
s 173, **421**
s 186, **436**
s 187, **436**
s 188, **436**
s 189(1), **423, 436, 438**
s 189(2), **438**
s 189(2A), **437–8**
s 189(3), **424, 439**
s 189(4), **439**
s 190, **437**
s 191, **437**
s 192, **437**
s 193, **437**
s 194, **437**
s 195, **438**
s 195(1), **438**
s 196(1)(a), **438**
s 196(1)(b)(i), **438**
s 196(1)(b)(ii), **424, 438**
s 197, **438**
s 199, **373**
s 223, **429**
s 223(9), **430**
s 223(10), **430**
s 230, **268**
sch 1, **11, 278, 280, 292, 323–5, 327–8, 343, 348, 350, 353, 367, 378, 409, 420–1, 424, 432, 450, 452, 458, 460–1, 466, 476–7**
Patents (World Trade Organization Amendments) Act 1994, **92, 287, 430**
    s 4, **279**
Patents Amendment Act 1984, **289, 386**
Patents Amendment Act 2001, **327, 351**
    sch 1 pt 1 item 1, **326**

sch 1 pt 1 item 3, **351**
sch 1 pt 1 item 4, **351**
Patents Amendment (Innovation Patents) Act 2000, **293**, **327**, **347**, **353**
   sch 2 pt 1, **280**
Patents Regulations 1991, **268**
   ch 3, **274**
   ch 3 pt 1 div 2, **325**, **387**
   reg 2.2, **339**, **475**
   reg 2.2(1A), **339**, **343**
   reg 2.2(2)(a), **339**
   reg 2.2(2)(b), **339**
   reg 2.2(2)(c), **340**
   reg 2.2(2)(d), **342**, **344**
   reg 2.2(3), **340**
   reg 2.2(d), **478**
   reg 2.2A, **340**
   reg 2.2A(2), **340**
   reg 2.2A(3), **341**
   reg 2.2A–2.2D, **475**
   reg 2.2B, **341–2**, **478**
   reg 2.2B(3), **343**
   reg 2.2C, **343**
   reg 2.2D, **344**
   reg 2.3, **343**, **475**
   reg 2.3(1)(a), **340**
   reg 2.3(1)(b), **341**
   reg 2.3(1)(c), **343**
   reg 2.3(1A), **343**
   reg 2.3(2), **344**
   reg 2.5, **276**
   reg 3.1(2)(a), **402**
   reg 3.2B, **279**
   reg 3.5, **274**, **282**
   reg 3.5AA, **272**, **274**
   reg 3.5AG, **272**
   reg 3.9, **274**
   reg 3.10, **274**, **283**, **286**, **340–1**, **343–4**
   reg 3.12, **348**
   reg 3.12(1)(b), **284**
   reg 3.12(1)(c), **399**
   regs 3.12–3.14, **282**
   reg 3.13, **348**
   reg 3.13A, **283**
   reg 3.13B, **283**
   reg 3.13C, **283**
   reg 3.14, **282**, **348**
   reg 3.14A, **275**
   reg 3.14B, **275**
   reg 3.15(1), **275**
   reg 3.15(2), **402**
   reg 3.16, **275**
   reg 3.17, **275**
   reg 3.18(2), **276**
   reg 4.1, **275**
   reg 4.2(3), **285**, **328**
   regs 4.2–4.3, **275**
   reg 4.4, **273**
   reg 5.4, **277**
   reg 6.3, **450**
   reg 6.3(7), **280**
   reg 6.3(8), **280**
   reg 9.1, **277**
   reg 9.2, **278**
   reg 9A.1, **279**
   reg 12.1(1), **426**
   reg 12.2(1), **429**
   reg 13.1A, **286**
   reg 13.1B, **286**
   reg 13.1C, **286**
   reg 13.6, **286**
   reg 22.11, **430**
   reg 22.21, **430**
Patents Regulations (Amendment) 1987, **289**, **386**
Personal Property Securities Act 2009, **437–8**, **687–8**
   ch 2 pt 2.5, **439**
   ch 2 pt 2.6, **439**
   ch 4, **439**
   s 10, **438**
   s 12(1), **438**
   s 12(5), **438**
Personal Property Securities (Consequential Amendment) Act 2009, **438**
   sch 2 item 9, **438**
Plant Breeder's Rights Act 1994, **20**, **494**
   pt 3, **501**
   s 3, **502**, **506**, **512**
   s 3(1), **495–6**, **500**, **502–3**, **505**, **508**, **511**, **518**
   s 4, **509**
   s 5, **497**
   s 5(1), **497**
   s 5(2), **502**
   s 6, **495**
   s 11, **496**, **508–9**, **511–13**, **515–16**, **518**, **520–1**
   ss 11–15, **513**
   s 12, **496**, **507**, **509**, **514**
   ss 12–15, **508**, **513**

s 13, 496, 510, 514, 521
s 13(a), 510
s 13(b), 510
s 14, 496, 511–13, 515–16
s 14(1), 511–12, 516
s 14(1)(b), 511
s 14(2), 516
s 15, 496, 512–13, 515–16
s 16, 11, 508, 511–13, 515, 520
ss 16–18, 513
s 16(a), 515
s 17, 511–12, 515–17, 519–20
s 17(1), 513, 516
s 17(1)(a), 515
s 17(1)(a)–(c), 515
s 17(1)(c), 515
s 17(1)(d), 515
s 17(1)(e), 515
s 18, 512, 515–16, 520
s 18(2), 517
s 19, 505, 512, 517, 520
s 19(1), 517
s 19(2), 517
s 19(3), 517
s 19(4), 517
s 19(11), 517
s 20(1), 518
s 20(2), 518
s 20(3), 518
s 21, 523
s 22, 11
s 22(1), 507
s 22(2), 507
s 22(4), 507
s 22(5), 507
s 23, 512, 520
s 23(3), 517
s 24(1), 501–2
s 24(2), 502
s 24(3), 502, 517
s 24(4), 502
s 25, 401
s 25(1), 502
s 25(2), 502
s 26, 503–4
s 26(2)(e), 501, 503
s 26(2)(ga), 505
s 26(2)(i), 504
s 27, 496, 503

s 27(1), 503
s 27(2)(a), 503
s 27(2)(b), 503
s 27(3), 503
s 27(4), 503
s 27(5), 503
s 27(5)(e), 525
s 27(6), 503
s 28(1), 503
s 28(3), 502
s 29, 503
s 30(2), 498, 504
s 30(3), 504
s 30(4), 504
s 30(5), 504
s 31(1), 502, 504
s 31(5), 504
s 31(6), 504
s 32, 504
s 33(l), 501
s 34, 503
s 34(1), 499, 504
s 34(4), 503–4
s 34(4)(b), 499
s 34(6), 501, 504
s 35, 505
s 36, 505
s 36(3), 505
s 37, 499, 504
s 38, 499, 504
s 39, 505
s 39(1), 521
s 39(6), 521
s 40, 496, 507, 509–10
s 40(1C), 510
s 40(2), 510
s 40(6), 510
s 41, 496, 499, 504, 507, 510
s 41A, 510
s 41A(2), 510
s 41A(8), 510
ss 41A–41F, 507, 510
s 41E, 499, 504
s 41G, 510
s 43, 11, 496, 498, 500–1, 503
s 43(2), 498
s 43(3), 499
s 43(4), 499
s 43(5), 499

s 43(6), 499–500
s 43(7), 500
s 43(7A), 500
s 43(7B), 501
s 43(7C), 501
s 43(8), 498
s 43(9), 498
s 43(10), 499
s 44, 505
s 44(1)(b), 506
s 44(1)(b)(vii), 505
s 44(1)(b)(viii), 506
s 44(2), 506
s 44(4), 506
s 44(5), 506
s 44(7), 505
s 44(8), 505
s 44(9), 505
s 44(11), 502, 506, 517
s 45(1), 502, 521
s 45(2), 518
s 46, 506, 523
s 48, 502
s 48(1)(a), 507
s 48(1)(b), 507
s 48(2), 507
s 48(2)(c), 507
s 48(3), 518
s 49, 506, 518
s 49(2), 522
s 50, 523
s 50(1), 498, 519
s 50(1)(a), 519
s 50(1)(b), 519
s 50(2), 519
s 50(8), 519
s 50(10), 519
s 51(1)(a), 523
s 51(1)(b), 523
s 51(2), 519
s 51(3), 523
s 52, 519, 523
s 53, 518, 521
s 53(1)(a), 520
s 53(1)(b), 520
s 53(1)(c), 520
s 53(1A), 520
s 53(2), 520
s 53(3), 520

s 53(4), 520
s 54, 510, 521, 523, 703
s 54(1), 518, 521
s 54(2), 521
s 54(3), 521
s 54A, 521
s 54A(1)(a), 519
s 54A(1)(b), 519
s 55, 522
s 55(1), 521
s 55(2), 522
s 55(3), 522
s 55(5), 522
s 55(6), 522
s 55(7), 522
s 55(8), 522
s 56(1), 522
s 56(2), 522
s 56(3), 524, 699–700
s 56(3A), 524
s 56A(1), 522
s 56A(2), 522
s 56A(3A), 524
s 57(1), 524
s 57(2), 524
s 57A, 522
s 57A(2), 522–3
s 57B, 522
s 57C, 522
s 57D, 522
s 57E, 522
s 58, 523
s 60(1), 502
s 61, 523
s 62, 523
s 62A, 523
s 70(2), 505
s 71, 505–6
s 74, 523
s 74(1), 521
s 75, 523
s 76, 523
s 77, 517, 519, 522
Plant Variety Rights Act 1987, 20, 494, 496
  s 14, 500
Probibition of Human Cloning for
  Reproduction Act 2002, 382
Public Interest Disclosure Act 2013,
  222

Public Lending Right Act 1985, 194
  s 5(4)(a), 195
  s 5(4)(c), 195
  s 6, 195
  s 8(1), 195
  s 10(1), 195
  s 10(2), 195
  s 30, 195
Resale Royalty Right for Visual Artists Act 2009, 37, 186
  s 6(2), 187
  s 6(3), 187
  s 7(2), 187
  s 9, 187
  s 10(1)(a), 187
  s 11, 187
  s 12, 186
  s 14, 186
  s 18, 187
  s 21(1)–(3), 187
  s 22, 187
  ss 22–31, 187
  s 33, 186
  s 34, 186
  s 53, 186
Sydney 2000 Games (Indicia and Images) Protection Act 1996, 617
Tax Laws Amendment (Resale Royalty for Visual Artists) Act 2009, 37, 186
Therapeutic Goods Act 1989, 281, 471, 479
  ch 9, 281
  s 23(2)(ba), 471
Tobacco Plain Packaging Act 2011
  s 3(2)(a), 574
Trade Marks Act 1905, 570
Trade Marks Act 1955, 570, 582, 644–5, 662, 675
  s 6, 572
  s 28, 633–4, 638–9, 656
  s 28(a), 634, 637–9
  s 28(d), 638
  s 56, 631
  s 61(1), 633
  s 64, 645
  s 74(2), 684
  s 74(3), 683
  s 82(1), 681
  s 82(2), 681
  s 82(2)(b), 681

s 123, 663, 665–7
s 123(1), 664
Trade Marks Act 1994, 570–1
  s 39, 600
  s 121(4), 671
  s 134, 669
  s 134(2), 668
Trade Marks Act 1995, 618
  pt 4 div 2, 593
  pt 4 div 3, 574
  pt 5 div 2, 619, 635
  pt 8, 627
  pt 8 div 1, 627
  pt 8 div 2, 629
  pt 9, 640
  pt 11, 682, 687
  pt 13, 702
  s 6, 575, 590, 647, 681
  s 6(1), 597–8
  s 7(2), 662
  s 7(4), 669
  s 8, 640
  s 8(1), 684
  s 8(3), 684, 686
  s 8(3)–(5), 684
  s 8(4), 685–6
  s 8(5), 686
  s 10, 608
  s 14, 12
  s 14(1), 611
  s 14(2), 612
  s 17, 575, 594, 601
  s 20, 677
  s 20(1), 644
  s 20(2), 644
  s 21, 13, 571
  s 21(1), 573
  s 22, 682, 688
  s 22(2A), 688
  s 24, 629, 631–3
  s 24(1), 631
  s 24(2), 632
  s 24(3), 632
  s 24(4), 632
  s 25, 629, 631–3
  s 27(1), 580, 583
  s 27(1)(b)(ii), 580
  s 27(1)(b)(iii), 580
  s 27(2A), 587, 590

s 33, 593–4, 616, 657
s 39(1), 593
s 39(2), 593
s 40, 593–4
s 41, 573, 593–4, 606, 624, 635
s 41(2), 594
s 41(3), 571, 577, 594, 599, 601–2, 604, 622, 634
s 41(4), 594, 599, 622
s 41(5), 676
s 41(6), 602–4, 676, 678
s 42, 593, 604–5, 636
s 43, 573, 605–7, 634
s 44, 574, 593, 606–7, 610, 615, 620–2, 635
s 44(1), 614, 616, 651
s 44(2), 614, 616, 651
s 44(3), 593, 614–15, 674, 678
s 44(3)–(4), 573
s 44(4), 593, 614, 616, 619, 679
s 55, 616
s 57, 619
s 58, 616, 619
s 58A, 616, 620
s 59, 620
s 60, 591, 606, 616, 619–23, 634–6, 639, 678
s 61, 620, 623–5
s 61(1), 624
s 61(2), 624
s 61(2)(b), 625
s 61(2)(c), 618, 625
s 61A, 620
s 62, 620
s 62A, 625
s 72, 574
s 81, 627
s 82, 627
s 83(1)(a), 627
s 83(1)(b), 627
s 83(1)(c), 627
s 83(2), 629
s 83A, 627
s 84, 628
s 84A, 628
s 84B, 628
s 85, 629–30
s 86, 629–30
s 87, 629, 631–3, 637
s 87(1), 632
s 88, 629, 640

s 88(2), 629, 633, 635, 640
s 88(2)(a), 635, 639
s 88(2)(c), 589, 636–7, 685
s 88(2)(e), 636
s 89, 634–5, 637–40
s 92(4)(a), 640
s 94, 641
s 97, 641
s 100, 642
s 100(2), 641
s 100(3), 641
s 100(3)(c), 641
s 101, 642
s 101(4), 642
s 102, 642
s 106, 682
s 106(1), 681–2
s 106(2), 681
s 106(3), 572, 681
s 107, 682
s 111, 688
s 113(1), 687
s 116, 687
s 120, 607
s 120(1), 12, 591, 650–2, 657, 659
s 120(1)–(3), 644
s 120(1)(e), 661
s 120(2), 12, 591, 630, 651–4, 657–9, 661
s 120(3), 13, 573, 591–2, 630, 651–2, 654–62, 668
s 120(4), 13, 656–7
s 121, 671–2
s 121(2), 671
s 121(3), 671
s 121(4)(b), 671
s 122, 673–4
s 122(1)(a), 675, 678
s 122(1)(b), 675–6
s 122(1)(c), 676
s 122(1)(d), 676
s 122(1)(e), 677
s 122(1)(f), 677–8
s 122(1)(fa), 678
s 122(1)(g), 678
s 122(1)(h), 678
s 122(2), 678
s 122A, 662, 666–9
s 122A(2), 667
s 122A(c), 667

s 123, 662, 671, 679
s 123(1)(b), 667
s 123(1)(c), 667
s 124, 679
s 126, 680, 699
s 126(2), 680, 700
s 127, 680
s 129, 672–3, 699
s 129(1), 673
s 129(5), 673
s 162, 590
s 166, 683
s 169, 587
s 170, 588
s 171, 588
s 172, 588
s 173, 588–9
s 175, 589
s 177, 588
s 177(1), 588
s 180, 683
s 180(3), 683
s 180A, 683
s 181, 629
s 185, 657, 659
s 185(1), 590–1, 659
s 185(2), 590
s 186, 590
s 189, 683
s 195, 703
s 230(2), 567
s 234, 633–4
s 234(2), 633
Trade Marks Amendment Act 2006, 622, 624, 642, 682
Trade Marks Regulations 1995, 597
  pt 17A, 574
  reg 4.14, 593
  reg 8.1, 640
  reg 10.4, 682, 688
  reg 16.6, 589
  sch 2, 593
Trade Practices Act 1974
  pt IV, 257, 589
  pt IVA, 589
  pt V, 257, 589
  s 52, 12, 56, 166, 378, 474, 520, 646, 669
  s 53(d), 56

Treasury Laws Amendment (2018 Measures No 5) Act 2019, 706
  sch 4 item 1, 423
US Free Trade Agreement Implementation Act 2004, 9, 35–6, 44, 65, 99–101, 181–3
  sch 8 item 1, 370, 373
  sch 8 item 5, 487
  sch 9 pt 2, 36
  sch 9 pt 2 items 16–58, 181, 183
  sch 9 item 2, 81
  sch 9 item 131, 101
  sch 9 item 136, 100
  sch 9 item 137, 100
  sch 9 item 139, 100
  sch 9 item 141, 100
  sch 9 item 141(25), 100
  sch 9 item 142, 100
  sch 9 item 188, 162
  sch 9 item 189, 162
Wine Australia Act 2013, 619, 623, 625

AUSTRALIAN CAPITAL TERRITORY
Business Names Act 1963, 617
Public Interest Disclosure Act 2012, 222

NEW SOUTH WALES
Business Names Act 2002, 617
Public Interest Disclosures Act 1994, 222
Restraints of Trade Act 1976, 413

NORTHERN TERRITORY
Business Names Act 1963, 617
Public Interest Disclosure Act 2008, 222

QUEENSLAND
Business Names Act 1962, 617
City of Brisbane Act 1924
  s 6, 418
Public Interest Disclosure Act 2010, 222

SOUTH AUSTRALIA
Aboriginal Heritage Act 1988
  s 35, 222
Business Names Act 1996, 617
Public Sector Act 2009, 222
Whistleblowers Protection Act 1993, 222

TASMANIA
Business Names Act 1962, **617**
Public Interest Disclosures Act 2002, **222**

VICTORIA
Business Names Act 1962, **617**
Commonwealth Games Arrangements Act 2001, **617**
Protected Disclosure Act 2012, **222**

WESTERN AUSTRALIA
Business Names Act 1962, **617**
Public Interest Disclosure Act 2003, **222**

Canada
Copyright Act (RSC, c C-30)
   s 29, **144**
   s 29(1), **144**
   s 29(2), **144**

New Zealand
Copyright Act 1994
   s 42, **144**
   s 43, **144**

United Kingdom
An Act for Amending the Law for Granting Patents for Inventions 1852
   s VI, **384**
   s IX, **384**
Australian Courts Act 1828, **31**
Calico Printers Act 1787, **197**
Calico Printers Act 1794, **197**
Colonial Laws Validity Act 1865, **31**
Copyright Act 1911, **19**, **32**
Copyright Act 1956, **33**
Copyright, Designs and Patents Act 1988, **57**
   s 3(1), **57**
   s 21(3), **59**
   s 29(1), **144**
   s 30(1), **144**
Fine Art Copyright Act 1862, **31**
Literary Property Act of 1842, **106**
Patents Act 1883, **384**
Patents Act 1949, **268**, **480**
   s 51(3), **341**
Patents Act 1977, **268**, **317**, **480**
   s 2, **325–6**

   s 14(3), **388**
   ss 39–42, **411**
   s 60(1), **452**
   s 60(2), **474**
   s 60(3), **469**
   s 60(5)(d), **475**
Patents and Designs Act 1907, **432**
Patents, Designs and Trade Marks Act 1883, **268**
Semiconductor (Protection of Topography) Regulations 1987, **188**
Statute of Anne (1709), **31**, **50**
Statute of Monopolies 1623, **267**, **366–7**
   s 6, **266**, **276**, **292**, **295**, **297–9**, **314**, **320**, **323**, **381**, **432**, **480**
Trade Marks Act 1938
   s 4(1)(b), **677**
Trade Marks Registration Act 1875, **570**

United States
15 USC
   s 1125 (1946), **573**, **603**, **655**
35 USC
   s 101, **309**
   s 271, **452**
   s 271(c), **469**
   s 287(c), **318**
Copyright Act 1976
   s 107, **143**, **153**
   s 110(5), **158**
Federal Trademark Dilution Act of 1995, **655**
Lanham (Trademark) Act 1946, **655**
   s 2(e)(5), **603**
   s 125, **573**
Semiconductor Chip Protection Act 1984, **188–9**

European Union
Council Directive 87/54/EEC of 16 December 1986 on the Legal Protection of Semiconductor Products, **188**
Council Directive 89/104/EEC of 21 December 1988 to Approximate the Laws of the Member States Relating to Trademarks
   art 5(1), **645**

Directive 96/9/EC of the European Parliament and of the Council of 11 March 1996 on the Legal Protection of Databases, **10**
Directive 98/44/EC of the European Parliament and of the Council of 6 July 1998 on the Legal Protection of Biotechnological Inventions, **308**
Directive (EU) 2015/2436 of the European Parliament and of the Council of 16 December 2015 to Approximate the Laws of the Member States Relating to Trade Marks
art 4(1)(e), **603**
art 10(2)(c), **573**, **655**
Regulation (EU) No 1257/2012 of the European Parliament and of the Council of 17 December 2012 Implementing Enhanced Cooperation in the Area of the Creation of Unitary Patent Protection, **290**

TABLE OF STATUTORY INSTRUMENTS

Agreement on Trade-Related Aspects of
    Intellectual Property, 16–17, 42, 134,
    136–7, 189, 269, 287–8, 318, 431, 570,
    688
  art 4, 17, 288
  art 13, 158
  art 16(2), 654
  art 16(3), 654
  art 25, 197
  art 26, 197
  art 27(1), 288
  art 27(2), 288, 309, 320, 322, 383
  art 27(3), 288, 383
  art 27(3)(a), 314, 317
  art 27(3)(b), 524
  art 28, 288
  art 28(2), 408
  art 29, 288
  art 30, 288, 418, 474
  art 31, 288, 418, 430
  art 33, 288
  art 34, 288
  art 35, 189
  arts 36–38, 189
  art 39, 262
  art 39(1), 262
  art 39(2), 263
  art 39(3), 263
Anti-Counterfeiting Trade Agreement, 45–6
Australia–United States Free Trade
    Agreement, 9, 19, 35–6, 43, 92, 101,
    123, 169, 181–3, 372
  art 3, 383
  art 17.4.7, 96
  art 17.4.7(a)(i), 98
  art 17.4.7(e), 95
  art 17.9, 381, 383
  art 17.9.3, 418
  art 17.9.7, 418, 430

art 17.9.7(a), 430
art 17.9.7(b), 430
Beijing Treaty on Audiovisual Performances,
    44–5
Berne Convention for the Protection of
    Literary and Artistic Works, 15–16,
    41–3, 65, 134, 136–7, 159
  art 6*bis*, 169
  art 9(2), 159
  art 14*ter*, 186
Brussels Act of the Berne Convention for the
    Protection of Literary and Artistic
    Works, 33
Budapest Treaty on the International
    Recognition of the Deposit of
    Microorganisms for the Purposes of
    Patent Procedure, 288, 300
Canada – Patent Protection of
    Pharmaceutical Products,
    16–17
Competition Principles Agreement, 418
Comprehensive and Progressive Agreement
    for Trans-Pacific Partnership, 17
Convention on Biological Diversity, 525
Convention Establishing the World
    Intellectual Property Organization
  art 2(viii), 4
Convention on the Grant of European
    Patents, 268, 289–90, 317
  pt II, 289
  pt V, 289
  pt VI, 289
  art 2, 289
  art 14, 290
  art 52(4), 314
  art 64, 289
  art 65, 290
  art 83, 388
  art 84, 396

Convention Relating to International
    Exhibitions
  art 1, 339
Geneva Act of the Hague Agreement
    Concerning the International
    Registration of Industrial Designs, 10
Hague Agreement Concerning the
    International Registration of
    Industrial Designs, 199
India – Patent Protection for Pharmaceutical
    and Agricultural Chemical Products,
    16
International Code of Nomenclature for
    Cultivated Plants 1995
  s 27(6), 503
International Convention for the Protection
    of New Varieties of Plants, 288, 494,
    513, 524
  art 14(5)(a)(i), 514
  art 14(5)(a)(ii), 514
  art 15(1), 513–15
  art 15(2), 514
International Convention for the Protection
    of Performers, Producers of
    Phonograms and Broadcasting
    Organisations, 42–3, 47, 181
International Treaty on Plant Genetic
    Resources for Food and Agriculture
    2001, 525
Joint Recommendation Concerning
    Provisions on the Protection of Well-
    Known Marks
  art 2(1)(b), 657
  art 2(2), 656
  art 2(3), 656
Locarno Agreement Establishing an
    International Classification for
    Industrial Designs, 201
Marrakesh Agreement Establishing the World
    Trade Organization, 15, 17, 40
  annex 1C, 16, 42, 134, 189, 197, 287, 408,
    524, 570, 654
Marrakesh Treaty to Facilitate Access to
    Published Works for Persons Who Are
    Blind, Visually Impaired or Otherwise
    Print Disabled, 44
Nice Agreement Concerning the
    International Classification of Goods
    and Services for the Purposes of the
    Registration of Marks, 689
Paris Convention for the Protection of
    Industrial Property, 15–16, 271–2, 287,
    688
  art 4, 274
  art 4(B), 476
  art 4*bis*, 287
  art 4*quater*, 287
  art 5, 287
  art 5A, 430
  art 5*ter*, 475
  art 10, 262
  art 10*bis*, 262
  art 11, 339
  art 15(5), 275
Patent Cooperation Treaty, 272
  ch I, 272
  ch II, 273
  art 1, 272
  art 2(xi), 272
  art 3, 272
  art 6, 396
  art 8, 272
  art 9, 272
  art 10, 272
  art 11(3), 272
  art 11(4), 272
  art 15, 272
  art 16, 272
  art 20, 272
  art 21, 273
  art 29, 273
  art 30, 273
  art 30(2)(a)(i), 273
  art 33, 273
Patent Law Treaty, 290
Protocol Relating to the Madrid Agreement
    Concerning the International
    Registration of Marks, 18, 574, 689
Trademark Law Treaty, 689
Treaty on Intellectual Property in Respect of
    Integrated Circuits, 189
Uniform Domain Name Dispute Resolution
    Policy, 20, 554–6
Universal Copyright Convention, 42
Universal Declaration of Human Rights
  art 27(2), 29

World Intellectual Property Organization Copyright Treaty, **43**, **47**, **92**, **181**
World Intellectual Property Organization Performances and Phonograms Treaty, **35**, **43**, **47**, **50**, **181**, **183**

art 5, **181**
art 6, **181**
arts 7–10, **181**

PART I

INTRODUCTION

1

INTRODUCTION

1.1 The nature of intellectual property

Intellectual property is now a term that is widely used within the legal profession and society at large. Despite this extensive use, a comprehensive definition of the term remains elusive, especially as some forms of 'intellectual property', such as 'sweat of the brow' copyright,[1] are not intellectual and others, such as confidential information, are very arguably not property.[2] On the other hand, most forms of intellectual property are clearly regarded as just that – forms of property that are recognised as flowing from the exercise of intellectual activity. For example, copyright, designs, patents, plant breeder's rights, and registered trade marks are expressly stated by legislation to be property. In addition, various statutory requirements evidence the need for the exercise of intellectual activity to obtain that property status. For example, patent applications must demonstrate an inventive step before they acquire registration[3] and literary, dramatic, musical and artistic works must be original in order to qualify for copyright protection.[4]

In the absence of a satisfactory exhaustive definition of intellectual property, probably the best that can be done is to rely on an inclusive list of categories of legal rights that are generally recognised as constituting intellectual property. Article 2(viii) of the *Convention Establishing the World Intellectual Property Organization* states:

'intellectual property' shall include the rights relating to:

- literary, artistic and scientific works,
- performances of performing artists, phonograms, and broadcasts,
- inventions in all fields of human endeavor,
- scientific discoveries,
- industrial designs,
- trade marks, service marks, and commercial names and designations,
- protection against unfair competition, and all other rights resulting from intellectual activity in the industrial, scientific, literary or artistic fields.[5]

1.2 Theories of intellectual property

Even more elusive than a simple and satisfactory definition of intellectual property is a consensus about the underlying rationale or rationales for intellectual property. This book

---

1. *Desktop Marketing Systems Pty Ltd v Telstra Corp Ltd* (2002) 119 FCR 491. Sweat of the brow is no longer protected by copyright in Australia: see *IceTV Pty Ltd v Nine Network Australia Pty Ltd* (2009) 239 CLR 458.
2. See *Federal Commissioner of Taxation v United Aircraft Corp* (1943) 68 CLR 525, 534; *Breen v Williams* (1996) 186 CLR 71, 81, 90, 111, 128; *Australian Broadcasting Corporation v Lenah Game Meats Pty Ltd* (2001) 208 CLR 199, 271. See also *Smith Kline & French Laboratories (Australia) Ltd v Secretary, Department of Community Services and Health* (1990) 22 FCR 73, 592–4. Compare *Colbeam Palmer Ltd v Stock Affiliates Pty Ltd* (1968) 122 CLR 25, 34.
3. *Patents Act 1990* (Cth) s 18(1).
4. *Copyright Act 1968* (Cth) ss 31, 32.
5. Opened for signature 28 September 1979, WIPO Lex No TRT/CONVENTION/001 (entered into force 1 June 1984).

does not attempt to resolve these issues[6] but it is important to have some idea of the various justifications put forward for intellectual property. These will be discussed briefly below.

1.2.1 The 'property' in intellectual property

In order to understand any of those rationales it is first important to understand the unique nature of the 'property' aspect of intellectual property. Most property rights, such as those in chattels or real estate, are relatively easily justified in a capitalist society by the potential consequences of what is known as 'the tragedy of the commons'.[7] For example, if a piece of land is owned by no-one but available for use by everyone, the likely consequence will be that the land will be overused and deteriorate in value because the cost of using it is nil and there is no incentive for anyone to maintain or improve the land because they will not derive the benefit of their investment. Exclusive rights over the land solve this problem by conferring exclusive rights of enjoyment of the land on one party who then has the incentive to maintain and improve it in return for that exclusive enjoyment.[8] The net result is that the land is maintained and improved with consequent benefits to everybody.

Intellectual property is different. It does not deteriorate through use; that is, IP rights are non-rivalrous and non-excludable. For example, if an intellectual property owner gives you the right to copy their book or make their invention, their freedom to copy their book or make their invention is still intact and they may continue to do so, unimpeded by the fact that you now also have that right. The position remains the same even if the right is given to another hundred, thousand or even a million people.

On the other hand, while intellectual property is different from other forms of property in this important sense, there remains the need to ensure that there is an incentive to create that property in the first place and then to distribute that property. It is argued that exclusive property rights are needed to provide the incentive to create expressive works and inventions and to invest in the development of the reputations associated with trade marks. The critical decisions for both legislators and courts relate to how they achieve a balance between the need for an incentive for investment in the creation and distribution of intellectual property and the need to ensure that the products of that investment are not locked up by individuals indefinitely. Consequently, there are considerable debates about issues such as the appropriate period of protection for patents and copyright and the appropriate exceptions to the rights of owners.

1.2.2 Natural or personality rights

In addition to the incentive argument, there is no doubt that the concept of natural rights has influenced the development of some aspects of intellectual property law. Hence, it is often

---

[6] For further reference, see B. Sherman and L. Bently, *The Making of Modern Intellectual Property Law* (Cambridge: Cambridge University Press, 1999); P. Drahos, *A Philosophy of Intellectual Property* (Aldershot: Dartmouth Publishing, 1996).

[7] A term popularised by economist William Forster Lloyd in relation to overgrazing on common land: W. F. Lloyd, *Two Lectures on the Checks to Population* (1833).

[8] See R. A. Posner, *Economic Analysis of Law* (6th edn, New York: Aspen Publishers, c. 2003); R. Cooter and T. Ulen, *Law and Economics* (4th edn, Boston: Pearson Addison Wesley, c. 2004).

argued that copyright material such as literary and artistic works is the extension of the creator's personality and, as such, should be respected and protected. This argument clearly influences copyright in Continental Europe. It is a basis for moral rights, such as the right of an author to be attributed as such and the right of integrity, that is the right to prevent alterations to an author's work that would adversely affect their honour or reputation. These rights have been recognised for many years in Europe but have only recently been recognised in common law countries that usually adopt an approach to copyright that is driven by economic considerations.[9]

1.2.3 Incentive to create and disseminate

Another frequently made argument is that intellectual property laws are necessary to encourage both the creativity involved in producing the subject matter of intellectual property and the dissemination of that subject matter. Hence, it is argued that there is no incentive to write a novel, produce an artistic work or make a film if it can be copied by anyone who chooses to do so. Similarly, even if the work may be created without the incentive of intellectual property rights, there is little incentive for a creator to undertake the further and possibly even more difficult task of disseminating the subject matter to the public at large. For example, where is the incentive to widely advertise a new invention and establish an expensive marketing regime for it if others can freely copy the invention and take a free ride on the marketing efforts of the original inventor?

A particular manifestation of the dissemination argument is that the process of registering patents requires the patent holder to reveal the best known method for the working of their invention.[10] This dissemination of information to the public via the patents register is the public benefit gained from providing exclusive rights to the owner of the invention for a limited period of time. In the absence of such rights, there would be no incentive to make the information publicly available. Similarly, with copyright, the copyright owner gains little, if any, benefit from their copyright unless they disseminate their material to the public, and so they have an incentive to make it available to people who are willing and able to pay for the material.[11]

It is also important to recognise that the 'return' for a person who innovates or creates can be, and usually is, more than the economic return to them and, similarly, that the need and desire of users to access and utilise innovative or creative material is more than a simple economic imperative. Hence, the legal acknowledgment of the issues of personality referred to above[12] can be an important driver of innovation and creativity while simultaneously crafting a legal system that ensures that maximum access to innovation and creativity by users is also important.

---

[9] E. Adeney, *The Moral Rights of Authors and Performers: An International and Comparative Analysis* (2nd edn, Oxford: Oxford University Press, 2006).
[10] *Patents Act 1990* (Cth) s 40(2)(a).
[11] M. Richardson, J. Gans, F. Hanks and P. Williams, *The Benefits and Costs of Copyright: An Economic Perspective* (Discussion Paper prepared by the Centre for Copyright Studies, 2000); The Allen Consulting Group, *Economic Perspectives on Copyright Law* (Sydney: Centre for Copyright Studies, 2003).
[12] At 1.2.2.

1.2.4 Protection for investment

The argument that legal protection is needed to encourage the creation and dissemination of information is often transformed into an argument that any commercial investment should be protected. For example, the digital information revolution led to a significant increase in the number of databases of value, and these did not acquire copyright protection because they did not meet the originality requirements of many copyright regimes. In response, the European Union created a new sui generis database protection right. That new right is acquired simply by proving that a substantial investment has been made in obtaining, verifying or presenting data.[13]

This general approach has led to calls to implement a general principle of protecting investment from unfair competition and claims that 'what is worth taking is worth protecting'.[14] To date, these calls have largely been resisted, especially in Australia, where the High Court has explicitly rejected this proposition as a test for copyright infringement and rejected the notion of a general tort of unfair competition.[15] On the other hand, many European countries have such a civil action[16] and the majority of American states have a common law tort of misappropriation that does not require proof of deception but is aimed at preventing commercial free riding on the efforts of others in certain defined and quite limited circumstances.[17]

There are some obvious difficulties with the idea of protecting investment per se. Apart from the uncertainty of determining that investment should be protected, there is no immediately obvious justification for determining that all investment is necessarily worthy of protection, either from a natural rights perspective or from an economic perspective. There may even be the possibility of encouraging too much investment by providing too much protection.[18]

1.2.5 Rent seeking

Related to the discussion above are attempts to moderate 'rent seeking' behaviour. In this context, 'rent seeking' refers to the tendency of interest groups to devote considerable resources to obtaining benefits from the introduction or expansion of legal rights for members

---

13   *Directive 96/9/EC of the European Parliament and of the Council of 11 March 1996 on the Legal Protection of Databases*, OJ L 77/20.
14   *University of London Press Ltd v University Tutorial Press Ltd* [1916] 2 Ch 601.
15   *Victoria Park Racing & Recreation Grounds Co Ltd v Taylor* (1937) 58 CLR 479; *Moorgate Tobacco Co Ltd v Philip Morris Ltd (No 2)* (1984) 156 CLR 414. See *Network Ten Pty Ltd v TCN Channel Nine Pty Ltd* (2004) 218 CLR 273.
16   A. Kamperman Sanders, *Unfair Competition Law: The Protection of Intellectual and Industrial Creativity* (New York: Oxford University Press, 1997).
17   *International News Service v Associated Press*, 248 US 215 (1918). See also *National Basketball Association v Motorola Inc*, 105 F 3d 841 (2nd Cir, 1997); *Festo Corp v Shoketsu Kinzoku Kogyo Kabushiki Co*, 234 F 3d 538, 627 (Fed Cir, 2000) (en banc) (Linn J, dissenting), reversed 535 US 722 (2002) (where the court debated the proper role of patent law's doctrine of equivalents in terms of whether it permits free riding); *Morris Communications Corp v PGA Tour Inc*, 364 F 3d 1288 (11th Cir, 2004) (where the court permitted the imposition of a private intellectual property–like restriction that would otherwise violate the antitrust laws on the grounds that the restriction is necessary to prevent free riding on data created by the restrictor). See further *Ty Inc v Perryman*, 306 F 3d 509, 512 (7th Cir, 2002) (where the court rejected intellectual property claims because it could not find evidence of free riding).
18   Prices Surveillance Authority, *Inquiry into Book Prices and Parallel Imports* (Report No 61, April 1995).

of those interest groups.[19] For example, patent holders may seek to increase their 'rents' or wealth by lobbying the government to lengthen the term of their monopoly rights. Rent seeking is not a justification for intellectual property rights but a partial explanation of some aspects of intellectual property law. That is, one possible explanation for why some groups have successfully lobbied for the expansion of intellectual property rights is that it has been in their interests to do so. Related to this point is the frequent lack of organisation of, and therefore lack of opposition from, groups that would benefit from a reduction in intellectual property rights or the containment of them. For example, the many millions in developing countries suffering from AIDS might have had a particular interest in the minimisation of intellectual property rights in relation to pharmaceutical drugs but it was difficult for their combined voices to be effectively heard in the international trade negotiations that resulted in a global expansion of such rights. In contrast, pharmaceutical companies in the United States had one full-time lobbyist for every two members of the United States Congress in 2000, and 2.3 lobbyists for every member of Congress in 2009.[20] Some aspects of intellectual property law might be a product of the disproportionate investment in securing legal protection.

1.2.6 A combination of all the above

The likely reality is that our present intellectual property laws are a combination of these and many other factors whose respective influences wax and wane over time. Hence, as Sherman and Bently have stated:

> [I]n spite of what many present-day commentators would have us believe, the emergence of modern intellectual property law was neither natural nor inevitable, nor was it an example of the law coming to occupy its proper philosophical position.[21]

The diversity and complexity of today's intellectual property laws reflect the various principles and forces that have influenced their development, and so no easy explanation for the existence of any particular law is readily forthcoming.

1.3 The intellectual property regimes

With the inclusive description of the categories of intellectual property and the possible rationales for legal protection of those categories of rights in mind, we can turn to a consideration of the individual intellectual property regimes. Below is a very brief summary of the major intellectual property regimes, together with some comments on the various rationales for those regimes.

---

19   W. M. Landes and R. A. Posner, *The Economic Structure of Intellectual Property Law* (Cambridge, MA: Harvard University Press, 2003).
20   P. Drahos, *Information Feudalism: Who Owns the Knowledge Economy?* (London: Earthscan, 2002) 160–1; K. Tumulty and M. Scherer, 'How drug-industry lobbyists won on health-care', Time.com (22 October 2009).
21   Sherman and Bently, *The Making of Modern Intellectual Property Law*, above n 6, 141.

1.3.1 Copyright and related rights

Copyright confers rights in relation to the reproduction and dissemination of material that expresses ideas or information. The *Copyright Act 1968* (Cth) defines the categories of material that receive copyright protection as literary, artistic, dramatic and musical works,[22] and subject matter other than works that are sound recordings, cinematograph films, broadcasts and published editions of works.[23] Copyright does not prevent alternative or independently created expressions of the same ideas or information and in this regard the scope of a copyright owner's rights are more limited than those of other intellectual property owners, such as patentees and owners of trade marks.

Moreover, unlike trade marks, designs, patents and plant breeder's rights, copyright is not registered and is generated automatically when the copyright material is reduced to a material form. The main justification given for copyright protection in common law jurisdictions is that it provides an incentive for the creation and subsequent distribution of the material in question.

In addition to this economic justification for copyright and the consequent conferral of economic rights on copyright owners, copyright legislation confers moral rights on authors. Moral rights permit authors to insist that others give them proper attribution of their authorship and to restrain others from interfering with the integrity of their works. Moral rights are the consequence of the view that some copyright works are an expression of an author's personality and, as such, the author has a personal interest in the attribution of their work and in ensuring that it is not altered in a manner that would be disparaging of the author. For this reason, moral rights differ from the economic rights of authors in a number of critical respects. For example, moral rights cannot be transferred to another person.

Both economic and moral rights last, as a general rule, for the life of the author plus seventy years. This period of protection was introduced as a consequence of the *Australia–United States Free Trade Agreement*[24] (*AUSFTA*). The duration of protection for copyright is and has been a controversial issue. If copyright is based on natural rights arguments, protection should probably be perpetual. On the other hand, if the purpose of copyright is to provide an incentive to create and disseminate copyright material, the duration of copyright need only be sufficiently long to provide the necessary incentive and no longer.

Part IX of the *Copyright Act 1968* (Cth) also confers rights on performers in certain circumstances.[25] These rights presently differ from and are less than those of a copyright owner although those rights were extended in 2005 as a consequence of the *AUSFTA*.[26] The justification for performers' rights is that those who perform and thus interpret copyright material such as musical works contribute a significant amount of creativity to the process of disseminating and exploiting that underlying material.

Similarly, a resale royalty right for some visual artists came into effect in 2010 via the *Resale Royalty Right for Visual Artists Act 2009* (Cth). The right is held by an artist or their successor in title and is payable in respect of the resale of the original artistic work in question.

---

22   *Copyright Act 1968* (Cth) pt III.
23   *Copyright Act 1968* (Cth) pt IV.
24   Signed 18 May 2004, [2005] ATS 1 (entered into force 1 April 2005).
25   *Copyright Act 1968* (Cth) ss 189–195AZG came into operation on 21 December 2000 as a result of the *Copyright Amendment (Moral Rights) Act 2000* (Cth).
26   *US Free Trade Agreement Implementation Act 2004* (Cth).

There are other forms of statutory protection that are similar to copyright. For example, the *Circuit Layouts Act 1989* (Cth) provides separate protection for a circuit layout, defined in s 5 as the 'representation . . . of the three-dimensional location of the active and passive elements and interconnections making up an integrated circuit'. In the European Union, databases receive protection that is over and above the protection provided by copyright under the copyright provisions that apply there.[27] These pieces of legislation deal with specific issues that relate to perceived gaps in the copyright regime.

1.3.2 Designs

A design in relation to a product is 'the overall appearance of the product resulting from one or more visual features of the product'.[28] The design of a product is often critical to its commercial success. In addition, designs have industrial and commercial application that results in them often having a functional aspect as well as an aesthetic aspect. Partly for that reason, it is important to restrict the extent of protection conferred on them. The period of protection for designs is a maximum of ten years.[29]

This limited period of protection contrasts with the lengthy period of protection for copyright; and as designs usually also constitute artistic works, there are important issues about the overlap between copyright and designs. In Australia, these overlap issues are dealt with by denying copyright protection to some designs once they have been industrially applied.[30] In addition, designs law differs markedly from copyright in that design protection, like patent and trade mark protection, is subject to a system of registration.

In addition, unlike copyright, independent creation of the same or a substantially similar design is not permitted. Partly for that reason, there needs to be a balance between creating an incentive to produce new designs while preventing indefinite monopolisation of functional designs.

1.3.3 Confidential information

In Australia, common law and equitable principles combine to protect confidential information with commercial or other value from being acquired, disclosed or used by others in circumstances where an obligation of confidentiality arises. The obligation may arise from any one or a combination of sources, such as contract or the fact that the circumstances in which a person acquired the confidential information are such that the courts consider that those circumstances impose an obligation of confidentiality.

---

27 See *Directive 96/9/EC of the European Parliament and of the Council of 11 March 1996 on the Legal Protection of Databases*, OJ L 77/20. See also M. Davison, *The Legal Protection of Databases* (Cambridge: Cambridge University Press, 2003).
28 *Designs Act 2003* (Cth) s 5 (definition of 'design').
29 *Designs Act 2003* (Cth) s 46(1). The period is fifteen years under the *Geneva Act of the Hague Agreement Concerning the International Registration of Industrial Designs*, opened for signature 2 July 1999, 2279 UNTS 156 (entered into force 23 December 2003). Consideration is being given to Australia becoming a party to that treaty: see ch 7 at 7.2.
30 *Copyright Act 1968* (Cth) ss 74–77A.

There are a number of possible benefits flowing from the laws imposing such obligations. For example, they encourage people to innovate and discover valuable information, they make it possible for people to share that information with potential business partners and thus increase its value without running the risk of losing control of it, and they reduce the extent to which others will devote resources to 'stealing' information rather than acquiring their own information via their own intellectual efforts. They also allow the information to stay protected indefinitely so that as long as the information is not publicly disclosed it is not subject to a term limit.

1.3.4 Patents

Patents confer an exclusive right to exploit an invented product or process.[31] A patent owner must demonstrate the following: their invention is useful in the sense that it achieves the outcomes claimed by the inventor; the patent is inventive in the sense that it is not an obvious addition to pre-existing knowledge or inventions;[32] and the invention is novel in the sense that it has not been previously made publicly available via publication or use by either the patent owner or another person. Unlike copyright, independent 'creation' or invention does not justify infringement of the exclusive rights of the original inventor.

While the threshold for obtaining protection is quite high and certainly much higher than for copyright, the rights obtained are also much stronger and, partly for this reason, the period of protection is restricted to twenty years,[33] although there is provision for extending that period of protection for pharmaceuticals to twenty-five years.[34]

The registration process is meant to produce a social contract between the patentee and society by ensuring the full disclosure of the invention[35] in return for which the patentee receives exclusive property rights in respect of their patent for a limited period of time. On the expiry of the patent, the invention becomes available for all to use and exploit for free.

1.3.5 Plant breeder's rights

Plant breeder's rights confer exclusive rights on those who develop new plant varieties that are stable, uniform and distinct, and prevent others from propagating or commercially dealing with those varieties of plant.[36] Some exemptions apply to farmers who may use seeds obtained from their crops for their own private purposes.[37] The rights last for twenty-five years for trees and vines and twenty years for other plants.[38]

---

31 The word 'exploit' is defined in the Dictionary of sch 1 of the *Patents Act 1990* (Cth) as: '(a) where the invention is a product – make, hire, sell or otherwise dispose of the product, offer to make, sell, hire or otherwise dispose of it, use or import it, or keep it for the purpose of doing any of those things; or (b) ... use [a] method or process or do any act mentioned in paragraph (a) in respect of a product resulting from such use.'
32 An innovation patent has an even lower requirement of inventiveness or innovation.
33 *Patents Act 1990* (Cth) s 67.
34 Ibid s 70 (discussed in ch 9 at 9.10).
35 Ibid s 40(2)(a).
36 *Plant Breeder's Rights Act 1994* (Cth) s 43.
37 Ibid s 16.
38 Ibid s 22.

The purpose of the rights is to encourage constant investment in the development of new plant varieties. New varieties are required that in turn respond to problems such as the adaptation of insects and diseases to previously developed plant varieties.

1.3.6 Passing off

The tort of passing off protects a trader from reputational harm that flows from misrepresentations by another trader (the defendant) to prospective customers of the defendant or those who may ultimately acquire the defendant's goods or services. The classic form of passing off is for the defendant to represent that its goods are those of the plaintiff, but the cause of action has been expanded to almost any misrepresentation that wrongly suggests an association between the defendant's product and the plaintiff. It has also been extended to more general misrepresentations where the defendant has not suggested any association between its goods and the plaintiff but the defendant has nevertheless misappropriated the plaintiff's reputation in a misleading manner.[39] Consequently, the plaintiffs may be other traders who compete directly with the defendant or they may be well-known celebrities, such as sporting heroes or famous actors, objecting to the misuse of their celebrity status to promote the defendant's products by the suggestion of an association between those products and the celebrity.

The tort has a twofold justification. From the plaintiff's perspective, the benefit of the tort is to prevent the misappropriation of its commercial image or goodwill by another. In this sense, it protects business investment by providing a vehicle through which the owners of a commercial image or reputation may protect it. However, in doing so, the tort also protects consumers from deceptive conduct and misinformation concerning the products that they may choose to buy. This protection performs an important economic function. In order for a market economy to work efficiently, buyers and sellers need reliable and accurate information concerning the products they are buying and selling. By giving a cause of action to those with a valuable reputation to protect, the tort provides an incentive to the owners of that reputation to promote the public benefit of preventing the deception of consumers.

A number of statutory consumer protection provisions, such as s 18 of sch 2 of the *Competition and Consumer Act 2010* (Cth),[40] have a similar effect to passing off, although their focus is on consumer protection and the protection of reputations is a side effect of that focus. For that reason, there are some differences between these consumer protection provisions and passing off that need to be considered.

1.3.7 Registered trade marks

Trade marks are signs used to distinguish one person's products, be they goods or services, from another person's products. A registered trade mark owner can proceed to use their trade mark in respect of their products with confidence that others may not use it or a deceptively similar trade mark in respect of similar goods or services or closely related goods or services.[41]

---

39 *AG Spalding & Brothers v AW Gamage Ltd* (1915) 32 RPC 273.
40 Formerly *Trade Practices Act 1974* (Cth) s 52.
41 *Trade Marks Act 1995* (Cth) s 120(1), (2). Section 14 of the Act defines goods and services as being 'similar goods' and 'similar services' if they are: (a) the same as the other goods/services; or (b) of the

Well-known trade marks also get additional protection under the current legislation.[42] Registration therefore provides some guaranteed national protection for investing in the development of goodwill; by contrast, the tort of passing off only applies after the investment has been made and only in the location where the reputation has actually been developed. The registration system therefore provides not only protection for investment but an incentive for traders to differentiate their products from the products of others. Again, consumers gain a benefit from this differentiation as it indicates the various characteristics of the products. As long as the trade mark continues to perform its role of distinguishing the owner's products from other products, the trade mark protection may be continued indefinitely by paying the relevant registration fees.

Once registered, trade marks constitute personal property in their own right,[43] but if they are used extensively they may also signify in shorthand form the reputation of a trader and as such may have significant additional commercial value. Consequently, there is some overlap between protection for registered trade marks and passing off, with the latter the common law precursor to the former.

1.4 Impact of new technology

Intellectual property law is inherently influenced by technological change and is intended to also drive that technological change by providing the incentive for investment in technological development. One of the great challenges for intellectual property law is and always has been to cope with and respond to massive technological developments that fundamentally affect industries or create new industries.

For example, copyright itself only became relevant as a consequence of the invention of the printing press, because prior to that invention the time and cost involved in copying was so great that the lack of the technological capability to copy obviated the need for legal protection against copying. After the printing press, new technology eventually emerged, including photography, film, sound recording, and radio and television broadcasting. Each new development presented new challenges for intellectual property law.

In more recent times, intellectual property law has had to respond to the implications of the digital revolution. The mass adoption of digital devices, such as personal computers and mobile phones, together with the pervasive influence of the internet has fundamentally altered the manner in which business is done and personal relationships are conducted. In the copyright arena alone, some of the legal issues arising from this have included determining the best means of protecting computer software, and the appropriate response to the creation and distribution of software and systems that readily facilitate both legal and illegal copying of sound recordings and films on a massive scale.[44] Also under discussion has been the extent to

---

        same description as that of the other goods/services. 'Closely related' goods and services may be defined by the function of the service with respect to the good, for example, televisions and television repair services: *Registrar of Trade Marks v Woolworths Ltd* (1999) 45 IPR 411.
42   *Trade Marks Act 1995* (Cth) s 120(3), (4).
43   Ibid s 21.
44   See, for example, R. Giblin, 'Evaluating graduated response' (2014) 37 *Columbia Journal of Law and the Arts* 147 on the possible effects of denying internet connection to serial infringers.

which copyright owners can and should be permitted to circumvent copyright exceptions by combining contractual provisions with digital processes for denying access to copyright material to those who do not comply with those contractual provisions.

In the patent area, the use of computers and the increasing use of the internet for transacting business have led to attempts to patent business systems, such as the electronic systems by which transactions are both made and recorded, and the patenting of software itself has been a contentious issue.[45] The patent area has also been affected by the use of genetic information to create transgenic life forms. Both technical and moral issues arise concerning the patentability of these new life forms and the nature and extent of legal protection, if any, which should be accorded to genetic information.[46]

Perhaps less obvious but no less important are the implications for trade mark law of new global systems of marketing. One well-documented issue that has led to enormous litigation and/or arbitration proceedings is the rules relating to obtaining and maintaining registration of domain names, vital means by which businesses advertise and promote their products over the internet. Globalisation of commercial activity and the consequent rise in global marketing of megabrands facilitated by the ease of modern communication and liberalisation of trade has led to an increasing emphasis and push for protection of famous trade marks.

Finally, some technological changes have demonstrated the gaps in intellectual property law and they have resulted in differing regulatory responses, including the development of new sui generis legislation to address specific issues. Circuit layout legislation and European database protection laws, mentioned above,[47] are examples of this approach of using sui generis legislation to address perceived gaps in protection. One of the difficulties for law reform is with playing technological catch-up, and specific solutions to specific problems are often soon outdated. For example, the legislation protecting circuit layouts has had very little practical application in recent years.

Consequently, one possible response is to stipulate that law operates by reference to general standards and principles applied in a specific context by courts rather than clearly defined rules applying only to very particular circumstances that may cease to be relevant. An example of this approach is the American doctrine of fair use in copyright – this outlines principles by which possible case-by-case exceptions to copyright are considered and contrasts sharply with the current Australian copyright law approach of having a relatively long list of very specific exceptions.[48]

---

45   A proposed European Union Directive on the patenting of computer software was voted for by the European Parliament on 23 September 2003 but rejected by the European Council on 17 March 2004. See *Welcome Real-Time SA v Catuity Inc* (2001) 113 FCR 110, *International Business Machines Corp v Commissioner of Patents* (1991) 33 FCR 218 and *RPL Central Pty Ltd v Commissioner of Patents* [2013] FCA 871 for analyses of Australian cases on patenting of computer programs and business systems.

46   Australian Law Reform Commission (ALRC), *Protection of Human Genetic Information* (Discussion Paper No 66, 2002). See also *D'Arcy v Myriad Genetics Inc* (2015) 258 CLR 334.

47   At 1.3.1.

48   See ALRC, *Copyright and the Digital Economy* (Report No 122, November 2013). See also G. W. Austin, '"This is a complex issue": A few more questions about fair use' (2018) 28(3) *Australian Intellectual Property Journal* 97.

1.5 Internationalisation of intellectual property

No introduction to Australian intellectual property law would be complete without some explanation of the increasingly important international and global aspects of intellectual property law that directly affect Australian domestic law. Some very important international treaties concerning intellectual property have been in place for many decades and have had the effect of producing some degree of consistency in relation to general standards of intellectual property protection. The *Berne Convention for the Protection of Literary and Artistic Works*[49] (*Berne Convention*) and the *Paris Convention for the Protection of Industrial Property*[50] (*Paris Convention*) are important examples of the influence of international treaties.

Yet despite the undoubted influence of these treaties over a long period of time, many nations either did not join the treaties or did not fully meet their obligations under those treaties. For example, the United States did not join the *Berne Convention* until 1989 and many developing nations did not regard it as in their national interest to join the *Berne Convention* either. In addition, common law nations did not strictly comply with the obligation to protect the moral rights of attribution and integrity until many years after they joined the *Berne Convention*, and some common law countries are arguably still in breach of that obligation.

Differences in approach from country to country are attributable to various factors. In particular, different rationales for intellectual property protection prevailed in different countries. For example, the influence of economic perspectives of the role of copyright in common law countries in contrast to the natural rights arguments in some civil law countries may well explain the difference in approaches to the protection of moral rights. The nature and degree of protection afforded by any nation has also varied according to its perception of its national interest in doing so. Consequently, developing countries have tended not to provide high levels of protection while developed countries have provided higher protection. Some countries, such as Japan and the United States, significantly increased their protection of intellectual property as their economies developed and it became increasingly in their economic interest to provide that greater degree of protection. Many European nations did not provide patent protection for drugs until the 1980s and many developing nations provided little or no protection until they were obliged to in order to meet their obligations under the *World Trade Organization Agreement*.[51]

These differences in approach reveal important but conflicting aspects of intellectual property law. One of these is the territorial aspect of intellectual property. As a creature of the statutes or case law of individual nations, intellectual property is territorial in nature. On the other hand, there are also numerous and increasing pressures to harmonise intellectual property protection across international borders. There are obvious advantages to intellectual property owners that flow from consistency in rights across international borders if those rights are sufficiently

---

[49] Opened for signature 9 September 1886, WIPO Lex No TRT/BERNE/001 (as amended 28 September 1979, entered into force 19 November 1984).

[50] Opened for signature 14 July 1967, WIPO Lex No TRT/PARIS/001 (as amended 28 September 1979, entered into force 3 June 1984).

[51] *Marrakesh Agreement Establishing the World Trade Organization*, opened for signature 15 April 1994, 1867 UNTS 3 (entered into force 1 January 1995) (*World Trade Organization Agreement*).

powerful. As intellectual property has been seen by major economic powers as constituting a major comparative economic advantage, there has been a major push for international agreements on greater protection for intellectual property. Key institutions and aspects of the current international intellectual property environment that assist in achieving the standardisation of and increase in intellectual property protection standards are discussed below.

1.5.1 World Intellectual Property Organization

The largest international organisation dealing primarily with intellectual property matters is the World Intellectual Property Organization (WIPO). WIPO has been a specialised agency of the United Nations since 1974 with a mandate to administer intellectual property matters.[52] It administers some twenty-two intellectual property treaties and has 180 member states. As a vehicle for the creation of international treaties, dissemination of information concerning intellectual property and a forum for discussion of intellectual property generally, it has a significant influence on the development and shape of intellectual property regimes throughout the world.

1.5.2 *TRIPS*

While WIPO has a significant role in shaping international norms concerning the protection of intellectual property, it has few, if any, teeth in ensuring compliance with the treaties that it administers. The only means of enforcing the WIPO treaties directly is by referring a matter to the International Court of Justice. No country has ever done so.

The teeth needed to enforce international intellectual property agreements have been supplied by the *World Trade Organization Agreement* and that part of the agreement dealing with intellectual property known as the *Agreement on Trade-Related Aspects of Intellectual Property*[53] (*TRIPS*). *TRIPS* specifies minimum intellectual property standards that each member of the World Trade Organization (WTO) must abide by and it also requires member states to take enforcement measures that give effect to those standards. More importantly, failure to create and enforce the minimum standards leaves each member state vulnerable to the dispute resolution processes of the WTO that provide that member states defaulting on their obligations under the WTO may be subjected to retaliatory trade sanctions. These processes provide an effective means of ensuring that member states honour their obligations under *TRIPS*.[54]

There is also a close connection between several of the most important treaties administered by WIPO and the minimum intellectual property standards imposed by *TRIPS*. As the WTO is a trade organisation rather than an organisation predominantly concerned with intellectual property, it adopted most of its intellectual property standards from two WIPO-administered treaties rather than attempting to 'reinvent the wheel'. Consequently, *TRIPS* requires member states to implement key provisions of the major WIPO treaties such as the *Berne Convention* and *Paris Convention*, although it also adds some other requirements, such

---

52 See World Intellectual Property Organization (WIPO), www.wipo.int.
53 *World Trade Organization Agreement*, above n 51, annex 1C (*Agreement on Trade-Related Aspects of Intellectual Property*) (*TRIPS*).
54 See *Canada – Patent Protection of Pharmaceutical Products*, WTO Doc WT/DS114/R (adopted 7 April 2000); *India – Patent Protection for Pharmaceutical and Agricultural Chemical Products*, WTO Doc WT/DS 79/R (adopted 24 August 1998).

as those relating to the protection of geographical indications. In this way, *TRIPS* enforces the major provisions of the relevant WIPO treaties.

In addition, by specifically referring to those treaties and their provisions, it imports into the interpretation of *TRIPS* all those matters relevant to the interpretation of those WIPO treaties, such as the negotiating history of the treaties.[55]

TRIPS also imposes two other important requirements. One derives from the pre-existing intellectual property treaties and the other is a cornerstone of the *World Trade Organization Agreement*. The principle of national treatment derives from the major pre-existing treaties. It requires member states to confer on foreign nationals the same or better protection than it provides for its own nationals. For example, Australia must confer the same or better copyright protection on a book written by a French author as it does on books written by Australian authors. This requirement has obvious implications for consistency and transparency.

The second and related requirement of *TRIPS* is that of most favoured nation status. This requires member states to ensure that 'any advantage, favour, privilege or immunity granted by a Member to the nationals of any other country shall be accorded immediately and unconditionally to the nationals of all other Members'.[56] This requirement ensures that any protection conferred on one nation will lead to the same protection being conferred on others.

1.5.3 Plurilateral and bilateral agreements

One consequence of the need for national treatment and compliance with most favoured nation status is that, since the signing of *TRIPS* and even before its implementation, intellectual property standards have been ratcheted up via the use of plurilateral and bilateral agreements. The United States and the European Union have done this by requiring agreement to '*TRIPS* plus' intellectual property standards in trade agreements.[57] The effect of this approach is to increase intellectual property standards generally. Hence, most changes to intellectual property as a consequence of plurilateral or bilateral agreements have multilateral as well as plurilateral and bilateral effects. One example of a recent plurilateral agreement, albeit without either the United States or the European Union, is the *Comprehensive and Progressive Agreement for Trans-Pacific Partnership* which came into effect in Australia on 30 December 2018.[58]

One exception to most favoured nation and national treatment requirements relates to sui generis legislation that is regarded as falling outside the ambit of intellectual property as it is understood for the purposes of *TRIPS*. For example, the European Union's protection for database owners is only extended to those with the necessary connection with the European Union or the citizens of other countries that have reciprocal arrangements with the European Union concerning the protection of databases. This approach is justified on the basis that the European Union's database laws constitute a sui generis form of protection that is not the subject of *TRIPS* and therefore not subject to its requirements of national treatment and the accordance of most favoured nation status.

---

55 See *Canada – Patent Protection of Pharmaceutical Products*, above n 54.
56 *TRIPS* art 4.
57 See the list of bilateral agreements in Drahos, *Information Feudalism*, above n 20, xi–xv.
58 Signed 8 March 2018 [2018] ATS 23 (entered into force 30 December 2018).

1.5.4 Investor–state dispute settlement

One of the most controversial issues in recent times is the use of investor–state dispute settlement clauses in plurilateral and bilateral trade and investment treaties. Most treaties, such as *TRIPS*, can be enforced exclusively by member states that are signatories to those treaties. However, under international agreements that have investor–state dispute settlement clauses, individual investors who claim that their interests have been adversely affected by a breach of the agreement may be able to institute arbitration proceedings directly against the nation that is allegedly in breach of the agreement. The purpose of the clauses is to give security to investors that they will be able to seek redress in the event of their overseas investments receiving treatment in a manner inconsistent with international obligations. One of the many criticisms of such clauses is that the cost of such disputes can be very significant, with some multinational companies expending enormous amounts of money on resolving them, leading to a possible chilling effect over regulatory responses. An example of such a dispute involving intellectual property was the dispute between Philip Morris Products SA (Switzerland) and Uruguay in relation to Uruguayan tobacco packaging regulations.[59] The dispute was based on alleged breaches of a bilateral agreement between Switzerland and Uruguay. While Uruguay was ultimately successful, there was a prospect of it paying both legal costs and damages if it had lost. Much of its legal costs was met by the philanthropist Michael Bloomberg and it is unclear whether Uruguay would have been able to effectively resist the claim without that support.

1.5.5 Harmonisation of intellectual property procedures

While many multilateral agreements (such as *TRIPS*) and other agreements deal with substantive aspects of intellectual property protection, there are also a number of international agreements governing key aspects of procedural matters that are relevant to the registration of intellectual property rights, such as patents and trade marks. For example, an agreement regulates the classes of goods and services for registered trade marks. In addition, the *Madrid Protocol*,[60] to which Australia is a party, permits the one trade mark application to be made for registration in a number of different countries.

In the patent area, there are agreements regulating the deposit of patented organisms[61] and agreements concerning the classification of patents and the process of assessing them for novelty.[62]

---

[59] See, for example, *Philip Morris Products SA (Switzerland) v Uruguay*, ICSID Case No ARB/10/7 Award (8 July 2016).

[60] *Protocol Relating to the Madrid Agreement concerning the International Registration of Marks*, opened for signature 27 June 1989, WIPO Lex No TRT/MADRIDP-GP/001 (entered into force 1 December 1995, as amended 12 November 2007).

[61] *Budapest Treaty on the International Recognition of the Deposit of Microorganisms for the Purposes of Patent Procedure*, opened for signature 28 April 1977, WIPO Lex No TRT/BUDAPEST/001 (entered into force 19 August 1980, as amended 26 September 1980).

[62] *Patent Cooperation Treaty*, opened for signature 19 June 1970, WIPO Lex No TRT/PCT/001 (entered into force 24 January 1978, as modified 3 October 2001).

1.6 Intellectual property in Australia

The foregoing discussion of the nature of intellectual property, the rationales for its protection, and the technological and international pressures that help to shape its domestic form need to be borne in mind when considering and explaining specific aspects of Australian intellectual property law. Apart from these general considerations, which affect the formation of the intellectual property laws of all nations, there are some specific issues directly relevant to Australia that determine our intellectual property laws. Some of these issues are discussed below.

1.6.1 History of Australian intellectual property law

As with many aspects of Australian law, the vast majority of Australian intellectual property law was originally inherited from the United Kingdom and there was little, if any, divergence from the legislative and common law leads provided from there. For example, Australia's *Copyright Act 1912* (Cth) simply adopted the *Copyright Act 1911* (UK).

Case law also tended to follow United Kingdom case law precedent. For example, until recently, the Australian judicial tests for originality of literary works followed older English case law despite the fact that the United Kingdom had changed its legislation on the point in response to a European Union Directive requiring the change. Hence, in at least this one respect, Australian law remained tied to a bygone era of English law.[63] As United Kingdom law continues to be significantly affected by European Union Directives on all aspects of intellectual property law, which are a reflection of the European Union's desire to harmonise its laws, even more differences are emerging between United Kingdom and Australian law. It appears that European influence on the intellectual property law of the United Kingdom will remain in place, despite the impending withdrawal of the United Kingdom from the European Union.

In addition, American law is having an increasing influence as Australian courts take a more eclectic view of the precedents that they will consider, both indirectly as a consequence of the United States continuing to be a large player in the world economy, and more directly as a consequence of the *AUSFTA*. For example, there has been considerable discussion about adopting the American copyright defence of fair use and referencing American case law if such an approach were adopted by the legislature.[64]

In other respects, Australian law and regulatory regimes have gone their own way. For example, both the European Union and the United States have express statutory limitations on the registration of functional shapes as trade marks because of the potential anti-competitive effects of giving monopoly rights over such shapes. The Australian legislation has no such express provision and the issue is dealt with very differently by the Australian courts via the concept of distinctiveness. In addition, the policies concerning the allocation of '.au' domain names and the resolution of disputes concerning ongoing registration of those domain names

---

63   *Desktop Marketing Systems Pty Ltd v Telstra Corp Ltd* (2002) 119 FCR 491. But that authority itself has been since overturned, in *IceTV Pty Ltd v Nine Network Australia Pty Ltd* (2009) 239 CLR 458.
64   ALRC, *Copyright and the Digital Economy*, above n 48.

are specifically adapted to some Australian requirements and in the light of international experience of difficulties with the *Uniform Domain Name Dispute Resolution Policy*.[65] Consequently, those policies differ from the policies in respect of generic top-level domain names.

1.6.2 Constitutional law issues

The constitutional power to legislate in relation to intellectual property matters lies with the Commonwealth government via s 51(xviii) of the *Constitution*, which confers exclusive power on the Commonwealth to make laws with respect to 'copyrights, patents of inventions and designs and trade marks'. The section has only twice been an impediment to legislation and more recent statements by the High Court have adopted an expansive interpretation. In *Attorney-General (NSW) v Brewery Employees Union of New South Wales*,[66] the High Court struck down legislation conferring trade mark registration on signs used by a trade union to indicate that goods marked with the sign were produced by members of a particular trade union, thus excluding the possibility that they were produced with non-union labour. The majority held that the trade union signs were not trade marks because a trade mark is 'a visible symbol of a particular kind of incorporeal or industrial property consisting in the right of a person engaged in trade to distinguish by a special mark goods in which he deals, or with which he has dealt, from the goods of other persons'. The other case where s 51(xviii) was held not to support aspects of the legislation in question is *Davis v Commonwealth*,[67] where the power in respect of trade marks was not considered sufficient to justify provisions of the *Australian Bicentennial Authority Act 1980* (Cth), which conferred exclusive rights on the Bicentennial Authority to use certain descriptive expressions, such as '200 years'.

A restrictive interpretation of the wording of s 51(xviii) seems to have been rejected in later cases where the High Court has adopted a more dynamic view of the particular categories of intellectual property and focused on the essential characteristics of the categories rather than the particular definitions in place at the time the Constitution came into effect. Hence, in *Nintendo Co Ltd v Centronics Systems Pty Ltd*,[68] the High Court had no difficulty in treating circuit layout rights as falling within the provision even though such rights are conferred by sui generis legislation. Similarly, in *Grain Pool of Western Australia v Commonwealth*,[69] the High Court had no objection to the *Plant Variety Rights Act 1987* (Cth) and the *Plant Breeder's Rights Act 1994* (Cth), on the basis that even in 1900 intellectual property regimes were in a state of flux, and dynamic interpretations of the words used in the relevant section should be adopted in the context of legal regimes that are constantly changing, partly as a response to technological developments. Consequently, plant variety rights were accepted because they could be considered a type of invention.

---

65 Opened for signature on 26 August 1999 (entered into force on 24 October 1999). See ch 14 at 14.5.3.
66 (1908) 6 CLR 469.
67 (1988) 166 CLR 79.
68 (1994) 181 CLR 134.
69 (2000) 202 CLR 479.

The result of these decisions is that while the specific reference to categories of intellectual property is probably undesirable,[70] and generates some uncertainty, it is unlikely that it will frequently generate an obstacle to legislation in the area. In any event, the increasing influence of multilateral, plurilateral and bilateral agreements concerning intellectual property means that any difficulties posed by the interpretation of s 51(xviii) can usually be overcome by reliance on other powers. In particular, additional power to legislate in respect of intellectual property flows from the external affairs power in s 51(xxix) of the *Constitution* and the trade and commerce power in s 51(i). Both these sources of power are particularly useful in the light of the many trade agreements, such as *TRIPS* and the *AUSFTA*, that contain provisions relating to intellectual property.

Other aspects of the *Constitution* may have an indirect effect on intellectual property legislation. For instance, in *Australian Tape Manufacturers Association Ltd v Commonwealth*,[71] the High Court struck down legislation providing for the imposition of a levy on blank cassette tapes. The levy was intended to compensate copyright owners for copying of their works onto blank tapes and was described as a royalty to be paid to copyright collecting agencies that would then distribute the royalty to copyright owners. The levy was found to be unconstitutional because it was a tax rather than a royalty and, as such, did not comply with s 55 of the *Constitution*.

Another constitutional issue raised from time to time in the context of intellectual property is the requirement that if the Commonwealth acquires property it must do so on just terms (s 51(xxxi)). In *Nintendo Co Ltd v Centronics Systems Pty Ltd*,[72] the High Court held that rights granted under s 51(xviii) did not constitute an acquisition of property but rather 'the adjustment of the competing rights, claims or obligations of persons in a particular relationship or area of activity' and that s 51(xviii) of the *Constitution* was not subject to s 51(xxxi), as legislation in the area would necessarily impact on existing property rights.[73] The issue was also addressed more recently in the High Court decision relating to the plain packaging of tobacco products. The plain packaging legislation prevents the use of certain trade marks at a retail level on tobacco products. By a six to one majority, the High Court rejected the challenge on the basis that while the legislation limits the use of trade marks by their owners, it does not provide for their acquisition by the government or any third party.[74]

1.7 Scheme of the book

This book is divided into parts dedicated to the individual intellectual property regimes or a regime and its closely related regimes. Each part is intended to be self-contained so that those with a particular interest in a particular regime may read it without reference to other parts of the book, except perhaps this introduction and the last chapter of the book concerning

---

70   A more expansive version of the section was recommended by Constitutional Commission, *Final Report* (1988) vol 1 [10.140]–[10.153].
71   (1993) 176 CLR 480.
72   (1994) 181 CLR 134.
73   However, see *Australian Tape Manufacturers Association Ltd v Commonwealth* (1993) 176 CLR 480 (where the court held that a levy imposed on sales of blank tapes affected property rights in the tapes).
74   *JT International SA v Commonwealth* (2012) 250 CLR 1.

remedies and miscellaneous matters. Consequently, each individual part deals with the history of the particular regime, Australian law on the topic and, to some extent, the international aspects of the topic as they impact on Australian law and practice.

In Part II we start with copyright and related regimes, such as protection for performers' rights and circuit layouts, and then address design law. This is followed in Part III with a discussion of confidential information, patents and plant breeder's rights. In Part IV, the final discussion of intellectual property categories relates to trade marks and commences with passing off, the common law precursor of the registered trade mark system. The last chapter of the book (Part V) deals with some general aspects of the means of enforcing legal rights and civil remedies that are particularly pertinent to intellectual property. It also deals with some miscellaneous matters such as the relationship between intellectual property and Part IV of the *Competition and Consumer Act 2010* (Cth).

PART II

COPYRIGHT, DESIGNS AND RELATED RIGHTS

2

COPYRIGHT: INTRODUCTION

2.1 Introduction

Copyright law regulates the creation, dissemination and use of a range of different types of 'works'[1] ranging from books, plays, musical works, computer programs and films through to sound recordings and television broadcasts. In developing the legal framework to regulate copyright, the law has attempted to balance the interests and concerns of copyright owners with those of authors, users and the public more generally. For example, in setting the duration of copyright protection, the law has balanced the interests of copyright owners, who have always argued for longer protection, with those of the public more generally, who have an interest in the duration of protection being more limited.

Unlike the case with other intellectual property rights, such as patents, trade marks and designs, copyright protection arises automatically on the creation of the copyright work. In order to qualify for protection, a work needs to fall within one of the categories of subject matter that are recognised under the *Copyright Act 1968* (Cth). One of the features of Australian copyright law is that a general distinction is drawn between Part III authorial works (literary, dramatic, artistic and musical works) and Part IV entrepreneurial works or, as the *Copyright Act* prefers, 'subject matter other than works' (films, sound recordings, television and sound broadcasts, and published editions). This distinction is important because it influences the criteria that need to be satisfied for a creation to qualify for protection, the nature and duration of the rights that are granted, and the defences that are available.

To be protected by copyright, a work must be original, recorded in material form and connected to Australia. Copyright initially vests in the author of the work ('author' is the term used to refer to the creator, whether of books, computer programs or paintings). There are certain situations, however, where copyright will vest in someone other than the creator, such as an employer or a person who commissions the creation of a work. Copyright gives the author (or owner) the right to exploit their works in a range of different circumstances. These include the ability to copy (or reproduce) the work, to publish the work, to perform the work in public, to communicate the work to the public, to make an adaptation of the work and to authorise someone else to carry out any of these activities. Copyright as an economic right is, like other forms of intellectual property, able to be sold outright, licensed, used as security or gifted. Copyright provides the owner with the right to prevent copying of their works. In essence, if there is no copying, there is no infringement. In this sense, copyright is different to the rights granted under patent, trade mark and design law, which give the holder of the intellectual property right the ability to sue for infringement even if the infringing creation was independently developed without reference to the protected invention, mark or design.

A key concept in copyright law, related to the nature and scope of the copyright work, is the so-called idea–expression dichotomy. In effect, this provides that copyright protection does not apply to the underlying idea or information but only to the expression of the idea. The rationale usually given for the idea–expression dichotomy is that if a person were given protection over ideas or information, this would stifle subsequent creations. As in many cases

---

[1] Work is the term that is used to describe subject matter protected under pt III of the *Copyright Act 1968* (Cth) – namely, literary, dramatic, artistic and musical works. See B. Sherman, 'What is a copyright work?' (2011) 12 *Theoretical Inquiries in Law* 99.

with copyright, the key question here turns on where and how the line between expression and idea is to be drawn.

It is important to note that the copyright in a work is distinct from the physical object in which the work exists. For example, copyright in an artistic image, such as a painting, is separate from the physical painting. This means that if you buy a painting you can choose where you hang it. As you own the painting as an object, you can also sell the painting if you no longer like looking at it. You do not, however, own the image represented in the painting. This remains with the artist (unless the copyright has been transferred to a third party).[2] The owner of the copyright in the image, in this case the artist, can prevent you from copying the image. If the artist decides to reproduce that image on tea towels, coffee cups or T-shirts, there is nothing you can do to prevent this. The separate existence of the intangible property from the physical object is a fundamental principle of copyright and of intellectual property more generally.[3]

2.2 Justifications

One of the greatest successes that copyright owners achieved in the literary property debates of the eighteenth century, when British publishers unsuccessfully argued that copyright protection was perpetual, was the widespread acceptance of the idea that copyright was a public good that was a necessary part of cultural policy-making.[4] While there have been occasional exceptions, for the most part it has been generally assumed that copyright protection is a good thing that should be supported. The history of copyright in Australia has followed a similar pattern.[5]

Over time, a number of different arguments have been given to justify the existence of copyright. These arguments are typically raised in situations where pressure groups are lobbying for changes to the law (often for the law to accommodate new types of subject matter or new ways of creating or consuming artistic and cultural creations). While discussions of copyright usually focus on whether or not copyright should be recognised at all, in practice most policy discussions tend to focus on specific issues, typically in response to the advent of a new technology or to changes in the way that cultural objects are created and consumed.

While the arguments used to justify and support copyright protection have taken many different forms, they can be broken down into two general types of arguments. The first, which is by far the most commonly used in Australia, falls under the general label of utilitarian-based arguments, which focus on ways of encouraging or promoting the creation and dissemination of new cultural and artistic objects. The second set of arguments, which are often lumped together as natural rights arguments, are less concerned with regulatory techniques to

---

2   See ch 5 at 5.2.1 on assignment. The artist, however, would have moral rights in the work: see ch 6 at 6.2 on moral rights.
3   See, for example, the distinction drawn by Dixon J in *Victoria Park Racing and Recreation Grounds Co Ltd v Taylor* (1937) 58 CLR 479, 498, 509 where he pointed out that the law does not necessarily protect any form of effort, enterprise, organisation or labour that may result in something of value for which others are prepared to pay.
4   B. Sherman and L. Bently, *The Making of Modern Intellectual Property Law* (Cambridge: Cambridge University Press, 1999) 40–2.
5   See P. Drahos, *A Philosophy of Intellectual Property* (Aldershot: Dartmouth, 1996) ch 9.

promote social, cultural and economic goals than with a belief that copyright ought to exist because it is proper and correct for it to do so. The differences between these two approaches were summed up in this comment:

> [T]he Australian tradition in intellectual property law is more explicitly utilitarian: in the sense of seeking to maximise social welfare, rather than focusing on [intellectual property] as having intrinsic value and hence merit. In this context, maximising social welfare involves maximising the difference between the social value of [intellectual property] created and used, and the social cost of its creation, including the cost of administering the system of intellectual property rights itself.[6]

2.2.1 Utilitarian arguments

The first general set of arguments that are used to justify the existence of copyright can be conveniently labelled as utilitarian in nature, meaning that they focus on the broader policy implications of copyright law. One of the most common utilitarian justifications of copyright is usually referred to as the 'incentive theory'. Given that the copyright initially vested in an author can be assigned to a third party, copyright is said to provide an incentive for third parties to invest in the creation, production and dissemination of copyright works that benefit society. The High Court expressed its support for the incentive theory in *Ice TV v Nine Network Australia*[7] when it said that copyright operated on the basis 'that an author could obtain a monopoly, limited in time, in return for making a work available to the reading public'.[8]

Underlying the incentive-based argument is the fact that copyright works, such as books, software, DVDs, CDs and films, are often very costly to produce. For a party to invest in the creation of new cultural and artistic objects, they usually need a guaranteed way of obtaining a return on their initial investment. One way of attempting to recoup the initial investment is to charge very high prices for the initial sale of a limited number of copies of a particular work. While this approach may be used in some limited circumstances, such as the sale of limited editions of artistic works, for the most part a different business model has been used – that of widespread distribution of the work, with a percentage of the sale price being returned to the owner. The problem with this model is that once objects such as books, DVDs, CDs and films are placed on the market, they can easily be copied. If these works were not copyright protected, competitors and consumers could simply wait until a new product was placed on the market at which time they would reproduce the work without having to contribute to the costs of production.

According to the incentive argument, if cultural and artistic objects were not given legal protection, people would not invest in their creation, production and dissemination. While some cultural and artistic objects would continue to be created, overall there would be a decline in the quality and quantity of works that were produced and consumed. Insofar as

---

6   Intellectual Property and Competition Review Committee, *Review of Intellectual Property Legislation under the Competition Principles Agreement* (Final Report, 2000) 32.
7   (2009) 239 CLR 458.
8   Ibid 471 (French CJ, Crennan and Kiefel JJ).

copyright protects against the unauthorised copying of protected works, it ensures that the mass-production business model is able to function. From this perspective, copyright provides a 'legal means by which those who invest time and labour in producing cultural and informational goods can be confident that they will not only be able to recoup that investment, but also to reap a profit proportional to the popularity of their work'.[9] The legal protection given by copyright rectifies the 'market failure' and as a result provides an incentive for parties to invest in the production and dissemination of works.[10]

2.2.2 Natural rights arguments

According to natural rights arguments, copyright protection is not granted for the greater public good, but because it is right and proper that it be granted. More specifically, it is 'right' to recognise a property right in intellectual productions *because* such productions emanate from the mind of an individual author. The natural rights theory is often described by reference to the landmark decision of *Millar v Taylor*,[11] where it was said that 'it is not agreeable to natural justice that a stranger should reap the pecuniary produce of another's work'.[12] Natural rights arguments require that the resulting creation is recognised as the exclusive property of its creator. The corollary of this is that the copying of another person's work is a usurpation of their property, which is equivalent to theft. It is also an imposition on the creator's personality. Copyright 'is the positive law's realisation of this self-evident, ethical precept'.[13] It has been suggested that the natural law approach

> sees the foundation of the rights of an author in the very nature of things. Laws have no other purpose but to recognise the existence of the author's rights, and to give them a more precise formulation. These rights are not created by the laws because they have always existed in the legal conscience of man. Copyright is thus a natural right growing out of natural law. The rights of an author in his intellectual product are equated with the property of incorporeal things.[14]

---

9   L. Bently, B. Sherman, D. Gangee and P. Johnson, *Intellectual Property Law* (5th edn, Oxford: Oxford University Press, 2018) 42; *Millar v Taylor* (1769) 4 Burr 2303, 98 ER 201. See also *Walter v Lane* [1900] AC 539 (Lord Halsbury); *Hogg v Scott* (1874) LR 18 Eq 444, 458; *Macmillan & Co Ltd v Cooper* (1923) 93 LJPC 113, 119; *International News Service v Associated Press*, 248 US 215, 239–41 (1918).
10 C. Arup, 'Innovation, policy strategies and law' (1990) 12 *Law and Policy* 247, 248–9. See also C. Arup, *Innovation, Policy and Law* (New York: Cambridge University Press, 1993); W. van Caenegem, *Intellectual Property Law and Innovation* (Melbourne: Cambridge University Press, 2007).
11 (1769) 4 Burr 2303, 98 ER 201.
12 Ibid 218 (Wiles J). It could be argued that the natural rights theory is embodied at an international level in art 27(2) of the *Universal Declaration of Human Rights*, which states, 'Everyone has the right to protection of the moral and material interests resulting from scientific, literary or artistic production of which [she or] he is the author': GA Res 217A (III), UN GAOR, UN Doc A/810 (10 December 1948).
13 Bently et al, *Intellectual Property Law*, above n 9, 40.
14 F. Kase, *Copyright Thought in Continental Europe: Its Development, Legal Theories and Philosophy* (South Hackensack: FB Rothman & Co, 1971) 8; H. Spector, 'An outline of a theory justifying intellectual property and intellectual property rights' (1989) 8 *European Intellectual Property Review* 270. See also J. Hughes, 'The philosophy of intellectual property' (1988) 77 *Georgetown Law Journal* 287, which draws on the philosophical approaches of John Locke and Georg Hegel to justify intellectual property rights.

At its most extreme, a natural rights conception of copyright leads to longer and stronger protection for authors (and copyright owners) than an incentive-based (utilitarian) conception. This is because a natural rights argument for copyright is assumed to result in a form of property that is perpetual and unqualified.[15]

For the most part, natural law notions (which are generally seen as a foreign, civil law concept) have had little place in the self-styled hard-nosed commercial world of Australian copyright law. As Machlup and Penrose wrote: 'Natural rights theories ... have never been particularly fashionable in common law jurisdictions' where copyright is usually 'viewed in more instrumentalist terms, as an institution given the sanction of positive rule for a social purpose.'[16] Having said that, natural law ideals do underpin some of the arguments about copyright law in Australia. One area where this can be seen is in the so-called reward arguments, which hold that copyright protection is granted because it is fair to reward an author for the effort they have expended in creating a work and giving it to the public. Under this approach, copyright is seen as the 'legal expression of gratitude to an author for doing more than society expects or feels that they are obliged to do. In a sense, the grant of copyright is similar to the repayment of a debt'.[17] Another area in which the natural law theories can be seen to operate is in relation to the idea that it is unfair (and therefore wrong) for a defendant to 'reap where they haven't sown'. This metaphor, which is often used by courts in copyright infringement actions, is used to argue that where a plaintiff has gone to the effort of creating a new cultural or artistic object, it is unfair for a defendant to copy that work.[18]

2.3 History

With a few notable exceptions, the history of copyright law in Australia is a subject that is yet to be written.[19] To date, most accounts have focused on the impact of British law and international treaties on the development of Australian copyright law. While these are important issues, there are many other areas that could be addressed, including the role that Australian law played in influencing other copyright regimes (particularly British and Imperial copyright), and the history of the interrelationship between copyright protection and Indigenous art and culture. While Australian copyright law is a rich and complex subject, this chapter will be limited to a chronology that highlights key moments in the development of the law.

---

15   See *Millar v Taylor* (1769) 4 Burr 2303, 98 ER 201, 218–22 (Aston J), 252 (Mansfield CJ).
16   F. Machlup and E. Penrose, 'The patent controversy in the nineteenth century' (1950) 10 *Journal of Economic History* 11.
17   'An exclusive privilege is of all rewards the best proportioned, the most natural, and the least bothersome': J. Bentham, 'Manual of political economy' in J. Bowring (ed), *The Works of Jeremy Bentham*, iii (1843) 31, 71.
18   See generally Bently et al, *Intellectual Property Law*, above n 9.
19   Some of the exceptions are B. Atkinson, *The True History of Copyright: The Australian Experience 1905–2005* (Sydney: Sydney University Press, 2007); L. Bently, 'Copyright and the Victorian internet: Telegraphic property laws in colonial Australia' (2004) 38 *Loyola of Los Angeles Law Review* 71; R. Burrell, 'Copyright reform in the early twentieth century: A view from Australia' (2006) 27 *Journal of Legal History* 239; S. Ricketson and C. Creswell, *The Law of Intellectual Property* (2nd edn, Sydney: LBC Information Services, 1999).

2.3.1 The British legacy

Like many areas of Australian law, copyright law in Australia owes much of its legacy to British law, which was first received into Australia by virtue of the *Australian Courts Act 1828* (UK) (9 Geo IV c 83). British copyright law is typically traced back to events in the late seventeenth century when the Stationers' Company (a London-based guild of printers, binders and booksellers) lost the statutory monopoly it had previously exercised over the printing of books in England. To overcome this loss, the Stationers' Company successfully lobbied the British parliament for the introduction of the first copyright statute, the 1709 *Statute of Anne* (8 Anne c 19). This provided fourteen or, in some cases, twenty-eight years of protection to authors of literary works. Importantly, authors were able to assign (or transfer) their rights to third parties. Allowing publishers to justify copyright, or as it was then called 'literary property', on the basis that it protected the specific interests of authors, while at the same time reaping the financial benefits of the copyright that authors had transferred to them, established a pattern that continues today.

While the publishers achieved a victory of sorts with the introduction of a property right in literary works, the fact that protection was limited to fourteen or twenty-eight years meant that, by the 1730s, copyright over valuable books had begun to lapse. As the rights that the publishers had obtained (via authors) under the *Statute of Anne* began to come to an end, the Stationers' Company adopted a number of other techniques to continue to exercise the control that it had previously exercised over the book trade. One strategy was to argue that in addition to the limited protection available under the *Statute of Anne*, authors also had a perpetual common law copyright. In 1774, the British House of Lords dismissed the Stationers' claim when it held that copyright was limited to the provisions recognised by the *Statute of Anne*.[20] In so doing, the House of Lords reinforced the statutory nature of copyright law – an issue that has had important ramifications in Australia for Aboriginal and Torres Strait Islander creators.

One of the notable characteristics of copyright law from the later part of the eighteenth century through to the nineteenth century was that the *Statute of Anne* acted as a legislative blueprint for the extension of copyright to new types of subject matter. When British copyright law was received in Australia in 1828, it had been extended beyond literary property to include engravings and sculptures. It was further extended over the course of the nineteenth century to include other forms of subject matter, including paintings, drawings and photographs.[21]

By the time of Australia's Federation in 1901, a number of Australian colonies (later states) had enacted copyright laws.[22] In part, these were prompted by the inadequacy of the protection afforded to Australian authors by the British legislation at the time. These laws remained in place after the federal Commonwealth was established in 1901 and operated concurrently with the British copyright law that had been received into the colony. When the Constitution was being drafted, it was decided that copyright legislation (and intellectual property more generally) should be a matter for Commonwealth rather than state governments. To this end,

---

20   *Donaldson v Beckett* (1774) 4 Burr 2408, 98 ER 257.
21   *Fine Art Copyright Act 1862* (25 & 26 Vict c 68).
22   Victoria in 1869, South Australia in 1878, New South Wales in 1879 and Western Australia in 1895. See the *Colonial Laws Validity Act 1865* (28 & 29 Vict c 63).

s 51(xviii) of the Commonwealth Constitution provides that 'the Parliament shall, subject to this Constitution, have power to make laws for the peace, order, and good government of the Commonwealth with respect to, inter alia, copyrights, patents of inventions and designs, and trade marks'.[23] One of the immediate consequences of this was that copyright lawmaking shifted from the colonial, now state, legislatures to the federal parliament.

In 1905, the Commonwealth passed the *Copyright Act 1905* (Cth).[24] As well as marking Australia's first national copyright statute, the 1905 *Copyright Act* was 'a succinct and elegant codification of copyright law that was markedly superior to the inconsistent and complex body of copyright acts then in force in the UK'.[25] While the 1905 Act overrode the state Copyright Acts, existing rights under state Acts were preserved. The 1905 Act stipulated that before a plaintiff could bring an infringement action, they had to register their copyright and/or performing rights at the Commonwealth Copyright Office. After this relatively brief attempt to develop an Australian copyright law, the Commonwealth reverted to the nineteenth-century sycophantic practice of mimicking the law of Britain when in 1912 it replaced the 1905 Act with the British *Copyright Act 1911*. This occurred with the passage of the *Copyright Act 1912* (Cth), which declared that the British *Copyright Act 1911* was in force in Australia from 1 July 1912. This was subject to any modifications that Australia made to the Australian Act itself.[26]

While the adoption of British Imperial copyright law in Australia may have delayed the development of local laws, the British *Copyright Act 1911* marked an important development in copyright law and practice. In particular it marked a shift from the previous situation where 'copyright' consisted of a series of piecemeal and subject-specific laws to a more general and forward-looking codified law. By abolishing the common law right in unpublished works, the 1911 Act also completed the process that had begun with the 1774 House of Lords decision in *Donaldson v Beckett*[27] of ensuring that copyright is primarily a creature of statute.[28]

2.3.2 The Copyright Act 1968 and its reforms

The *Copyright Act 1912* (Cth) laid the foundation for Australian copyright law for the first half of the twentieth century. During this time, the subject matter that was protected was expanded to include types of works (whether published or not) that had not been included before, such as architecture, sound recordings and films. The 1912 Act remained in force until it was repealed and replaced by the *Copyright Act 1968* (Cth) which came into operation on 1 May 1969 and which remains in force today. It was enacted partly in response to the

---

23 *Commonwealth of Australia Constitution Act 1900*, s 51(xviii).
24 This Act came into operation on 1 January 1907 and provided the first uniform copyright law for Australia. The Act was based on the nineteenth-century British legislation.
25 S. Ricketson, 'Intellectual property administration and policy in Australia: An examination of the Australian situation, past and present, and recommendations for future change' (Paper presented at the National Innovation Summit, Melbourne, 9–11 February 2000).
26 Pursuant to s 8 of the *Copyright Act 1912* (Cth). The limited differences between Australian and United Kingdom law arose because of Australia's obligations under the *Berne Convention for the Protection of Literary and Artistic Works*.
27 (1774) 1 ER 837.
28 This has raised difficulties in recognising legal concepts drawn from Indigenous customs, such as communal ownership, that are not recognised by statute. See *Bulun Bulun v R & T Textiles Pty Ltd* (1998) 41 IPR 513, 525.

recommendations of the Spicer Committee, which had been appointed by the Australian Attorney-General in 1958 to review the *Copyright Act 1912* (Cth) and determine what changes were necessary[29] for Australia to ratify the *Brussels Act 1948* of the *Berne Convention for the Protection of Literary and Artistic Works*. It was also prompted by the collapse of the Imperial system that occurred with the passage of a new British *Copyright Act* in 1956. The 1968 Act has been modified on several occasions.

2.3.2.1 Reprographic reproduction

The first major review of the *Copyright Act 1968* occurred in 1974 when the Whitlam government appointed the Copyright Law Committee, chaired by Justice Franki, to examine the impact of reprographic reproduction on copyright law in Australia.[30] Specifically, the Committee was asked to examine the impact of photocopying of works and 'to recommend any alterations to the Australian copyright law to effect a proper balance of interest between owners of copyright and the users of copyright material in respect of reprographic reproduction'.[31]

In commencing the review, the Franki Committee reminded itself of what it saw as the primary purpose of copyright law – namely

> to give to the author of a creative work his just reward for the benefit he has bestowed on the community and also to encourage the making of further creative works. On the other hand, as copyright is in the nature of a monopoly, the law should ensure, as far as possible, that the rights conferred are not abused and that study, research and education are not unduly hampered.[32]

In its deliberations, the Franki Committee observed that Australia should be careful that it did not adopt too radical a solution given that it was a net importer of copyright material.[33]

---

29 *Report of the Committee Appointed by the Attorney-General of the Commonwealth to Consider what Alternatives are Desirable in the Copyright Law of the Commonwealth* (Canberra: AGPS, 1965) (*Spicer Committee Report*).

30 Copyright Law Committee, *Report on Reprographic Reproduction* (Canberra: AGPS, 1976) (*Franki Committee Report*). The Franki Committee had the benefit of studying a number of earlier reports on copyright. These included *Report of the Copyright Committee, 1951, of the United Kingdom* (CMD 8662) (Gregory Committee) (which recommended most of the provisions now contained in the *Copyright Act 1956* (UK)); *Report on Copyright of the Canadian Royal Commission on Patents, Copyright, Trade Marks and Industrial Designs* dated 1 Aug 1957; *Report of the Copyright Committee* (1959) of New Zealand; *Report of the Australian Copyright Law Review Committee* (1959); and *Report on Intellectual and Industrial Property of the Economic Council of Canada* (1971).

31 *Franki Committee Report*, above n 30, 10 [1.09]–[1.11]. The main issue before the Franki Committee was whether reprographic reproduction of a copyright work should be excluded from the rights that a copyright owner enjoys in respect of the reproduction of their work in a material form only where greater public interest clearly requires such an exclusion, or whether the proper balance of interest between owners of copyright and users of copyright material in respect of reprographic reproduction should be achieved on a broader basis.

32 Ibid 9 [1.05]. 'Stress has been laid by a number of witnesses before the Committee on the importance of the free flow of information for education and for scientific, technical and social development in Australia': 16 [1.40].

33 Ibid 15 [1.35]–[1.56].

Ultimately, the Franki Committee recommended, inter alia, the adoption of a statutory licensing scheme.[34]

2.3.2.2 CLRC and other reviews

This was followed in the 1980s and 1990s by a range of inquiries into many aspects of copyright law. One of the key drivers of these reviews was the establishment in 1983 of the Copyright Law Review Committee (CLRC) as an advisory body concerned with copyright reform. The CLRC was disbanded in 2005 by the federal government. In this period, the CLRC produced a number of reports on a range of issues. During the 1980s these included *The Meaning of Publication in the Copyright Act* (1984), *Use of Copyright Materials by Churches* (1985), *Performers' Protection* (1987), *Moral Rights* (1988) and *Importation Provisions* (1988). Reports produced during the 1990s included *Conversion Damages* (1990), *Report of Journalists' Copyright* (1994), *Computer Software Protection* (1994), *Simplification of the Copyright Act: Part 1* (1998) and *Part 2* (1999). Reports produced in the early 2000s included *Jurisdiction and Procedures of the Copyright Tribunal* (2002), *Copyright and Contract* (2002) and *Crown Copyright* (2005).

In addition to the various reports of the CLRC, a number of other reports reviewed specific areas of copyright. These included *Highways to Change* (1994),[35] *Stopping the Rip-Offs* (1994),[36] the *Simpson Report* (1995),[37] the *Bently and Sherman Report* (1995),[38] the *Janke Report* (1998)[39] and the *Ergas Committee Report* (2000).[40]

The proliferation of reports over the last twenty or so years has been accompanied by a number of legislative reforms. These have included the introduction of moral rights, changes to the rules for parallel importation and the introduction of new rights for performers. These reforms will be looked at in detail below and in chapters 3–7.

2.3.2.3 Digital agenda reforms

Copyright reform in the 1990s and 2000s was dominated by the so-called digital agenda reforms. While copyright law in Australia has been dealing with computer technologies since

---

[34] Ibid 49 [6.39]. No recommendation of the Franki Committee was the subject of more discussion and counter-proposal than the recommendation to provide a statutory licence scheme to operate in non-profit educational institutions. See L. Farrell, 'Copyright Amendment Act 1980: Photocopying in educational institutions' (1980) *Australian Current Law Digest* 53, 54. The recommendation that 'provision be made for multiple copying when carried out in non-profit educational establishments' was described as 'possibly the most significant advanced by the [Franki] Committee': Commonwealth, *Parliamentary Debates*, House of Representatives, 9–11 September 1980, 1012 (Ian Viner).

[35] Copyright Convergence Group, *Highways to Change: Copyright in the New Communications Environment* (1994).

[36] Attorney-General's Department, *Stopping the Rip-Offs: Intellectual Property Protection for Aboriginal and Torres Strait Islander Peoples* (1994).

[37] S. Simpson, *Review of Australian Copyright Collecting Societies* (Report to the Minister for Communications and the Arts and the Minister for Justice, 1995).

[38] B. Sherman and L. Bently, *Performers' Rights: Options for Reform* (Report to the Interdepartmental Committee, 1995).

[39] T. Janke, *Our Culture, Our Future: Report on Australian Indigenous Cultural and Intellectual Property Rights* (Report prepared for Australian Institute of Aboriginal and Torres Strait Islander Studies and the Aboriginal and Torres Strait Islander Commission, 1998).

[40] Intellectual Property and Competition Review Committee (Chair, Henry Ergas), *Review of Intellectual Property Legislation under the Competition Principles Agreement* (Final Report, 2000).

the 1960s, the question of the scope of digital copyright began to be considered in earnest in the mid 1990s, when the federal government's digital agenda reforms to the *Copyright Act 1968* got under way. This set in place several years of heated, often vitriolic, debate about the shape that copyright law should take in the digital environment which reached a conclusion, of sorts, when the *Copyright Amendment (Digital Agenda) Act 2000* (Cth) (*Digital Agenda Act*) came into operation in March 2001.

The *Digital Agenda Act* introduced a number of important changes that will be dealt with in following chapters. The most important included the introduction of the right to communicate works to the public, which is a technology-neutral right that applies to all subject matter except published editions. The new right was given to copyright owners so that they could control the use that was made of their works online – for example, the digitising and uploading of material onto an internet server. To balance this new right, the *Digital Agenda Act* also introduced a number of exceptions. In addition, it introduced:

- a statutory licence scheme for the payment of equitable remuneration for works contained in retransmitted, free-to-air broadcasts;
- new remedies for the circumvention of technical protection measures, including the removal or alteration of rights management information; and
- provisions dealing with the liability of internet providers.

2.3.2.4 *AUSFTA* and WIPO commitments

While many of the recent changes to Australian copyright law have been prompted by a combination of international treaties and domestic concerns, the reform process took a different turn when Australia entered into a bilateral trade agreement with the United States in 2004. The *Australia–United States Free Trade Agreement* (*AUSFTA*) was implemented in Australia by the *US Free Trade Agreement Implementation Act 2004* (Cth) and came into effect on 1 January 2005. The *AUSFTA* included a number of specific provisions in relation to copyright.[41] In particular, it required that a number of key changes be made to Australian copyright law, notably in relation to duration of protection, the definitions of 'reproduction in material form' and 'copy', electronic rights management, broadcast decoding devices and the liability of internet service providers. Changes were also required to be made in relation to performers. These changes will be discussed in the following chapters where relevant.

As well as ensuring that Australian law complied with some of the requirements of the *AUSFTA*, the 2004 Act made changes to ensure that the law complies with the *WIPO Performances and Phonograms Treaty*. The key changes were:

- a longer term of protection for most copyright subject matters;
- a change to the term of protection for photographs, so that it is now the same as for other artistic works – namely, the life of the author plus seventy years;

---

41 See generally C. Arup, 'The *United States–Australia Free Trade Agreement*: The intellectual property chapter' (2004) 15 *Australian Intellectual Property Journal* 204.

- changes to the definitions of 'reproduction in material form' and 'copy' to ensure that storage of a work or other subject matter will infringe even if the stored material is unable to be reproduced;
- granting of copyright in sound recordings to performers, jointly with the owner of the material in which the performance was recorded (as well as moral rights[42]);
- changes to the scope of protection for performers' rights;
- changes to the law in relation to electronic rights management and broadcast decoding devices; and
- the introduction of a safe harbour scheme for online and internet service providers, which provides immunity from financial remedies for infringement if providers comply with certain conditions.

2.3.2.5 Film directors' rights

The next change to Australian copyright law took place when the *Copyright Amendment (Film Directors' Rights) Act* (Cth) was assented to on 8 November 2005. The Act, which came into force on 8 May 2006, amended the *Copyright Act 1968* (Cth) to provide film directors with copyright in the films they create. Importantly, these rights are limited to a right to share as copyright owners in the remuneration for the retransmission of films included in free-to-air broadcasts.

2.3.2.6 Technological protection measures

While the *US Free Trade Agreement Implementation Act 2004* (Cth) ensured that Australia complied with many of its copyright-related obligations under the *AUSFTA*, a number of areas still required reform.[43] In light of this, the federal government released an exposure draft of the Copyright Amendment (Technological Protection Measures) Bill 2006 in September 2006. As part of the reform process, the government established the House of Representatives Legal and Constitutional Affairs Committee Inquiry into Technological Protection Measures to consider what additional possible exceptions should be introduced into Australian copyright law.[44] After a very quick review, the government broadened the scope of the reforms. To this end, the Copyright Amendment (Technological Protection Measures) Bill 2006 was amended and incorporated into the Copyright Amendment Bill 2006. As well as implementing some of the recommendations of the reviews conducted by the federal government into aspects of copyright law, the Bill aimed to give effect to Australia's remaining copyright obligations under the *AUSFTA*. In particular, it proposed to introduce a liability scheme for the circumvention of technological protection measures (TPMS).[45] On 19 October 2006, the Senate referred the provisions of the Copyright Amendment Bill 2006 to the Standing Committee on Legal and

---

42 *US Free Trade Implementation Act 2004* (Cth) sch 9 pt 2. These new rights came into force when the *WIPO Performances and Phonograms Treaty* came into force on 26 July 2007.
43 Under the *AUSFTA*, the federal government was obliged to implement a new liability regime for circumventing technological protection measures by 1 January 2007.
44 This served as an administrative review for the purpose of this last category of allowable exceptions under the *AUSFTA*. For further information see ch 4 at 4.5.
45 As explained by the Explanatory Memorandum to the Copyright Amendment Bill 2006 (Cth).

Constitutional Affairs.[46] After submissions had been received from numerous stakeholders, a series of amendments were made to the Copyright Amendment Bill 2006.[47] After a relatively brief debate,[48] the Copyright Amendment Bill received Royal Assent on 11 December 2006.[49] The *Copyright Amendment Act 2006* (Cth) made a number of important changes to Australian copyright law that will be discussed in the following chapters.[50] The main changes were the introduction of new fair dealing defences for the purpose of parody and satire, as well as new defences for time shifting and format shifting. The Act also introduced a defence that allows libraries, archives, educational institutions and people with a disability to use copyright material in 'special cases'. As well as altering the criminal penalties, the 2006 Act made changes in relation to TPMs, the Copyright Tribunal and the unauthorised reception of encoded broadcasts.

The 2006 scheme came into effect on 1 January 2007. The operation of the TPM provisions was reviewed by the Attorney-General's Department in its 2012 *Review of Technological Protection Measure Exceptions made under the Copyright Act 1968*. The main aim of this review was to consider the appropriateness of the TPM exceptions and whether new additional exceptions should be added. This issue was also considered by the Australian Law Reform Commission (ALRC) in its 2013 review, and noted in its *Copyright and the Digital Economy* discussion paper. As a result of these reviews, amendments were introduced in 2017 which expanded the operation of the TPM provisions and updated some exceptions for circumvention of TPMs. The revised TPM scheme is discussed in detail in chapter 4 at 4.5.

2.3.2.7 Resale royalty rights

After many years of lobbying by non-salaried artists who argued that there was often very little, if any, capacity for them to recoup money from the reproductions of their original creations, the federal government passed the *Resale Royalty Right for Visual Artists Act* in 2009. The resale royalty scheme, which came into effect from 9 June 2010,[51] grants artists a royalty on the

---

46 See Senate Standing Committee on Legal and Constitutional Affairs, *Report on the Copyright Amendment Bill 2006* (2006).
47 See Amendments to the Copyright Amendment Bill 2006 (29 November) Supplementary Explanatory Memorandum, Copyright Amendment Bill 2006 (Cth) (amendments to be moved on behalf of the government) 11. See the discussion in Commonwealth, *Parliamentary Debates*, Senate, 30 November 2006, 3133–84.
48 Commonwealth, *Parliamentary Debates*, House of Representatives, 19 October 2006, 2 (Philip Ruddock).
49 Not all of the provisions came into force on that day. Some came into force immediately on 11 December 2006: schs 6–8 (on private copying, the new 'special case' exception, other exceptions for libraries and educational institutions, parody and satire) and schs 10 and 11 (on the Copyright Tribunal). Other came into force at later dates, including schs 1–5 (new criminal provisions and enforcement measures), sch 12 (technological protection measures) on 1 January 2007, and sch 9 (encoded broadcasts) on 8 January 2007.
50 In December 2006, the *Final Report of the Gowers Review of Intellectual Property* was released in the United Kingdom. Some key recommendations related to enforcement (such as stronger penalties for online infringement); introduction of a private copying exception to enable consumers to 'format shift' in certain circumstances; amendments to the exceptions for education establishments and libraries, so that they apply in the digital environment; and that the term of protection for sound recordings not be extended. Many of these recommendations mirrored the approach taken by the Australian government in the 2006 reforms of the *Copyright Act 1968*.
51 The *Resale Royalty Right for Visual Artists Act 2009* (Cth) was complemented by the *Tax Laws Amendment (Resale Royalty for Visual Artists) Act 2009* (Cth).

resale of original artworks. A resale royalty right entitles the artist to a percentage payment when a work of art that they have created is resold (typically in a commercial gallery).[52] One of the motivations for the introduction of the resale royalty scheme was to provide better protection for Aboriginal and Torres Strait Islander artists.

Another change that was proposed to protect Indigenous artists was the possible introduction of Indigenous communal moral rights. These rights would recognise communal moral rights based on an agreement between the artist and their community. To date, no federal government has committed to introducing this proposed scheme.[53]

2.3.2.8 Digital economy and online piracy

In June 2012, the ALRC was asked to consider whether the exceptions and statutory licences in the *Copyright Act 1968* (Cth) were adequate and appropriate in the digital environment, and whether further exceptions should be recommended. Among other things, the ALRC was to consider whether further exceptions should be provided to 'facilitate legitimate use of copyright works to create and deliver new products and services of public benefit; and allow legitimate non-commercial use of copyright works for uses on the internet such as social networking'.[54]

A discussion paper was released in June 2013, and the ALRC's final report, *Copyright and the Digital Economy*, was released in November 2013 and tabled in parliament on 13 February 2014.[55] The final report made a number of recommendations: one was that the federal government recognise 'fair use' of copyright materials to create and deliver new products and services of public benefit; another was that changes be made to allow appropriate access to, use of, interaction with and production of copyright materials online for social, private or domestic purposes. In its response, the government disregarded the ALRC's recommendations; it focused instead on the issue of online piracy, primarily because this was seen to be more important to copyright owners. To this end, it released the *Online Copyright Infringement Discussion Paper* in July 2014. The discussion paper outlined three proposals to address online piracy: extending authorisation liability for copyright infringement, facilitating the blocking of infringing overseas websites by internet service providers, and expanding the operation of the current 'safe harbour' scheme.

In December 2014, the Attorney-General and the Communications Minister wrote to industry leaders, asking them to develop an industry anti-piracy code. In February 2015, a draft industry code of practice was released for public comment by the Communications Alliance.[56] The final version was submitted for approval by the Australian Communications and Media

---

52   In August 2004, a discussion paper was released that was designed to stimulate debate about whether it would be desirable to introduce a resale royalty arrangement in Australia: Australian Government, Department of Communications, Information Technology and the Arts, *Report of the Contemporary Visual Arts and Craft Enquiry* (Canberra: 2002) (*Myer Report*) rec 4, 13.
53   For further discussion of Indigenous communal moral rights, see ch 6 at 6.2.6.
54   ALRC, 'Terms of Reference: Copyright and the Digital Economy', www.alrc.gov.au.
55   ALRC, *Copyright and the Digital Economy: Final Report* (ALRC Report No 122, February 2014).
56   Communications Alliance Ltd, *Industry Code C653:2015 Copyright Notice Scheme* (Public Comment Version 20/2/2015). The following rights holders were involved in the development of the industry code: APRA, AMCOS, ARIA, Australian Screen Association, Copyright Agency, Foxtel, Free TV Australia, Music Rights Australia, News Corp Australia, Village Roadshow Ltd and World Media.

Authority (ACMA) in April 2015. It provided that the majority of Australian internet service providers must send notices to alleged copyright infringers at the request of a copyright owner. If a user received three notices in a twelve-month period, the internet service provider would then be required to assist the copyright owner if it applied to the court for preliminary discovery to identify the alleged infringers.[57] This became known as the 'three-strikes piracy code'. There were a number of unresolved issues with the code, such as concerns over privacy and the significant costs to be incurred in its implementation, which meant the code was never registered by the ACMA. Later that year, the focus of the federal government changed to website blocking so the code appears to have gone into abeyance.

In 2015 the *Copyright Amendment (Online Infringement) Act 2015* (Cth) came into operation. This amended the *Copyright Act 1968* (Cth) to extend the operation of the safe harbour scheme to a broader range of service providers, including educational institutions, libraries, archives, key cultural institutions and organisations assisting persons with a disability. Section 115A was inserted to enable copyright owners to apply to the Federal Court for injunctions against carriage service providers to prevent access to online locations outside Australia that have infringement as their primary purpose. The injunctions require the carriage service provider to take reasonable steps to disable access to the online location.[58]

2.3.2.9 Productivity Commission review

In 2015 the Australian Government asked the Productivity Commission to undertake a twelve-month public inquiry into Australia's intellectual property system. An issues paper was released in October 2015,[59] and the final report, *Intellectual Property Arrangements*, was publicly released on 20 December 2016.[60] This was a major and detailed review of all of Australia's intellectual property arrangements. The Commission made a number of recommendations to improve the system's operation.

Put simply, the Commission found that copyright protection in Australia suffers from a number of shortcomings. It observed that 'copyright is overly broad, to the detriment of intermediate users and consumers' and that rights have expanded over time, despite little evidence of benefits, meaning 'innovative firms, universities and schools, and consumers bear the costs'.[61] It also found that the term of protection is overly long, reducing access to valuable works and that the protection lasts far longer than is needed.[62] The Commission also recognised that a fairer system of user rights was needed, as 'Australia's fair dealing exceptions are too narrow and prescriptive, do not reflect the way people consume and use content in today's digital age, and do not readily accommodate new legitimate uses of copyright material'.[63] Several issues that affect the use and licensing of copyright material, including geoblocking and

---

57   Communications Alliance Ltd, *Industry Code*, above n 56, [3.12.8].
58   *Copyright Act 1968* (Cth) 115A(2) as later amended by the *Copyright Amendment (Online Infringement) Act 2018* (Cth).
59   Productivity Commission, *Intellectual Property Arrangements* (Issues Paper, October 2015).
60   Productivity Commission, *Intellectual Property Arrangements* (Inquiry Report No 78, September 2016).
61   Productivity Commission, 'Reforming Australia's intellectual property arrangements' (PC News, August 2017).
62   Ibid.
63   Ibid.

restrictions on the parallel importation of books, were also examined. The Commission found that 'the use of geoblocking technology is widely imposed on Australian consumers who are frequently offered a lower level of digital service (such as a more limited music or TV streaming catalogue) at a higher price than in overseas markets and that policy reform was needed around parallel importation'.[64]

The government signalled in August 2017 that it would consult on options for copyright reforms arising from the government's response to the Productivity Commission's report.[65]

2.3.2.10 Disability access

Further copyright reform took place in 2017 and 2018. In December 2017, the *Copyright Amendment (Disability Access and Other Measures) Act 2017* (Cth) became law. This Act introduced a raft of measures to assist those copyright users with disabilities. This fulfils Australia's commitments as a signatory to the *Marrakesh Treaty* (discussed below)[66] which aims to facilitate the import and export of accessible copies of published works. The 2017 Act introduced a fair dealing exception for access to copyright material by a person with a disability.[67] It also introduced a new definition of 'person with a disability' to account for a wider range of disabilities and learning difficulties.[68] The new definition covers all persons with a disability that causes difficulty in reading, viewing, hearing or comprehending copyright material. The defence extends to people who act on behalf on a person with a disability. Educational institutions and not-for-profit organisations with a principal function of providing assistance to persons with a disability are also covered by this defence.[69] This means that teachers and educational institutions can make format-appropriate versions of educational materials for students with disabilities. A new streamlined educational statutory licence is provided for in s 113P of the *Copyright Act 1968*, replacing the former Parts VA and VB.

The *Copyright Amendment (Service Providers) Act 2018* (Cth) commenced on 29 December 2018. The most substantial change resulting from this Act is the introduction of s 116ABA into the *Copyright Act 1968*. The new section redefines the term 'service provider' to include educational institutions, libraries, archives, key cultural institutions and organisations assisting persons with disabilities, thus extending the operation of the safe harbour scheme to a broader range of service providers.

2.3.2.11 Copyright modernisation

Marking 50 years since the enactment of the *Copyright Act 1968*, in March 2018 the federal government began a review into copyright modernisation.[70] This review implemented a

---

64   Ibid.
65   Department of Industry, Innovation and Science, *Australian Government Response to the Productivity Commission Inquiry into Intellectual Property Arrangements* (August 2017).
66   At 2.4.7.
67   *Copyright Amendment (Disability Access and Other Measures) Act 2017* (Cth) s 113E.
68   *Copyright Act 1968* (Cth) s 10. The definition appears in a new pt IVA ('Uses that do not infringe copyright').
69   *Copyright Amendment (Disability Access and Other Measures) Act 2017* (Cth) s 113F.
70   Department of Communication and the Arts, 'Copyright Modernisation consultation', www.communications.gov.au.

suggestion made by the Productivity Commission in its 2016 report.[71] The focus of the review is to consider whether modernisation of the Act is required, particularly given the impact of the digital world when creating, accessing and distributing copyright material. The consultation paper released in March 2018 by the Department of Communications and the Arts sought views on three areas: flexible exceptions, contracting out of copyright exceptions and access to orphan works.[72]

A series of roundtables was held in late April and early May 2018 on a range of issues including quotation and educational uses, orphan works, contracting out and government uses. A wide range of submissions were made by stakeholders as part of the consultation process. At August 2019, there has been no further progress on the review.

2.3.2.12 Administration of copyright licences

As part of its response to the Productivity Commission's review of intellectual property arrangements in Australia (specifically recommendation 5.4),[73] the government also committed to review the Code of Conduct of Collecting Societies, in an effort to strengthen governance and increase transparency.[74] In April 2019, the government's Bureau of Communications and Arts Research released the final report of the review of the code.[75] The review examined the extent to which the code remains the best mechanism to promote efficient, effective and transparent administration of copyright licences, and supports overall confidence in Australia's collective copyright management system. The recommendations outlined in the report seek to increase clarity around the role of the code, improve the transparency of collecting societies' operations and strengthen governance arrangements for collecting societies and the code.

2.4 International influences

Australia is a party to a number of international treaties and agreements that impact on and shape domestic copyright law. These treaties and agreements set out the minimum standards of protection required by their member states.

2.4.1 *Berne Convention*

One of the concerns of legislators in the nineteenth century was how copyright was to be protected in foreign countries. While bilateral treaties provided some assistance, they became increasingly complicated. In part, this prompted the establishment in 1886 of a specific multilateral treaty dealing with copyright, the *Berne Convention for the Protection of Literary and Artistic Works*[76] (*Berne Convention*). The *Berne Convention* lays down minimum

---

71 Productivity Commission, *Intellectual Property Arrangements*, above n 60.
72 Department of Communication and the Arts, *Copyright Modernisation* (Consultation Paper, March 2018).
73 Productivity Commission, *Intellectual Property Arrangements*, above n 60.
74 Department of Industry, Innovation and Science, *Australian Government Response*, above n 65.
75 Bureau of Communications and Arts Research, *Review of Code of Conduct for Australian Copyright Collecting Societies* (Final Report, April 2019).
76 Opened for signature 9 September 1886, WIPO Lex No TRT/BERNE/001 (as amended 28 September 1979, entered into force 19 November 1984) (*Berne Convention*).

standards of protection for literary and artistic works, and films. It also introduced the important concept of national treatment or reciprocity, which provides that a copyright owner in one member country ought to be entitled to equal treatment in other member states. When combined with art 5(2), which provides that copyright protection arises automatically without formalities, reciprocity ensures that once a work is created it is immediately protected in all member states.

The *Berne Convention* has been modified on a number of occasions and is supplemented by two 1996 WIPO treaties (discussed below).[77] The *Berne Convention* is administered by the World Intellectual Property Organization (WIPO), a specialised agency of the United Nations, and has a membership of 177 countries.[78] The United Kingdom became a member in 1887; Australia, then a dependent territory of the United Kingdom, became a member at the same time. In 1928 Australia became a party to the *Berne Convention* and its revisions in its own right.

2.4.2 Universal Copyright Convention

The *Universal Copyright Convention* (*UCC*) was concluded in 1952, with membership comprising many *Berne Convention* member states and the United States, which was not then a member of *Berne*. Australia ratified the *UCC* in 1969.[79] The *UCC* applied to the same range of works as were protected by *Berne*, but the standards of protection were lower and more general. Since the United States joined the *Berne Convention* in 1989, the international importance of the *UCC* has diminished.

2.4.3 Rome Convention

The *International Convention for the Protection of Performers, Producers of Phonograms and Broadcasting Organisations*[80] (*Rome Convention*) sets out protection for sound recordings, broadcasts and performances. The Convention is administered by WIPO. Until the introduction of *TRIPS*, it was the only international instrument protecting performers' and broadcasters' rights. Australia became a signatory to the *Rome Convention* in 1992.

2.4.4 TRIPS

The *Agreement on Trade-Related Aspects of Intellectual Property* (*TRIPS*) commences with a statement of the desires of the members:

> To reduce distortions and impediments to international trade, and taking into account the need to promote effective and adequate protection of intellectual property rights, and to ensure that measures and procedures to enforce intellectual property rights do not themselves become barriers to legitimate trade.[81]

---

77 At 2.4.5.
78 As at March 2019: WIPO, 'Contracting parties: Berne Convention', www.wipo.int.
79 The *Second Protocol of the UCC* (the Paris Text) was ratified in 1978.
80 Opened for signature 26 October 1961, WIPO Lex No TRT/ROME/001 (entered into force 18 May 1964).
81 *Marrakesh Agreement Establishing the World Trade Organization*, opened for signature 20 December 1996 (entered into force 6 March 2002) annex 1C (*Agreement on Trade-Related Aspects of Intellectual Property*) (*TRIPS*).

TRIPS requires member states to implement the protection prescribed by the *Berne Convention*, except for the moral rights provisions. *TRIPS* represents a change in the intellectual property–specific conventions insofar as it contains extensive provisions for the enforcement of intellectual property rights. Australia became a party to *TRIPS* on 1 January 1995 when the agreement first came into force.[82] *TRIPS* was negotiated following the Uruguay Round of the General Agreement on Tariffs and Trade. Today it is administered by the World Trade Organization.

2.4.5 WIPO internet treaties

In recognition of the fact that the latest substantial revision of the *Berne Convention* was in 1971, WIPO convened a committee of experts in 1991 to consider the possible development of a protocol to the *Berne Convention*. A second committee of experts was formed, in effect, to update the *Rome Convention*. This eventually led to the establishment of two new treaties which were passed at the WIPO Diplomatic Conference held in Geneva in December 1996. They are often referred to as the 'internet treaties'.

- The *WIPO Copyright Treaty*[83] is a protocol between members of the *Berne Convention*, but uses the *TRIPS* device so that non-*Berne* members can join, provided they implement all the obligations of the *Berne Convention*.
- The *WIPO Performances and Phonograms Treaty*[84] deals with the intellectual property rights of performers and producers of phonograms.

The main obligations under these treaties were implemented in Australian law through the *Copyright Amendment (Digital Agenda) Act 2000* (Cth). That Act included measures providing for a new online right of communication to the public for rights holders, and sanctions for the circumvention of technological protection of copyright materials. Accession to the two WIPO treaties is part of Australia's copyright obligations under the *AUSFTA*.[85]

2.4.6 *AUSFTA*

In addition to the multilateral treaties discussed above, Australia has entered a number of bilateral trade agreements that impact on copyright law in this country. One of the most important of these is the *Australia–US Free Trade Agreement*[86] (*AUSFTA*) which was concluded in May 2004.[87] The *AUSFTA* was implemented by the *US Free Trade Agreement Implementation Act*

---

82   C. Arup, '*TRIPS*: Across the global field of intellectual property' (2004) 26 *European Intellectual Property Review* 7; P. Mavroidis, *The General Agreement on Tariffs and Trade: A Commentary* (Oxford: Oxford University Press, 2005).
83   Opened for signature 20 December 1996, WIPO Lex No TRT/WCT/001 (entered into force 6 March 2002).
84   Opened for signature 20 December 1996 (entered into force 20 May 2002).
85   A third WIPO treaty concerning protection for non-original databases was also proposed at the WIPO Diplomatic Conference. The introduction of this treaty has, however, been deferred for the present. For a useful commentary on database protection, see M. Davison, *The Legal Protection of Databases* (Cambridge: Cambridge University Press, 2003).
86   Signed 18 May 2004, [2005] ATS 1 (entered into force 1 April 2005).
87   Chapter 17 of the *AUSFTA* specifically deals with intellectual property rights.

2004 (Cth), which came into effect on 1 January 2005.[88] As noted above,[89] the key changes to Australian copyright law brought about by the *AUSFTA* were in relation to duration of protection, the definitions of 'reproduction in material form' and 'copy', electronic rights management, broadcast decoding devices, and the liability of internet service providers. Changes were also made in relation to performers. These will be discussed where relevant in the following chapters.

2.4.7 Marrakesh Treaty

In June 2013, after four years of intense negotiations between publishers, copyright owners and the visually impaired and blind communities, the *Marrakesh Treaty to Facilitate Access to Published Works for Persons Who Are Blind, Visually Impaired or Otherwise Print Disabled*[90] (*Marrakesh Treaty*) was adopted in Marrakesh, Morocco. The treaty improves access to copyright works for people who are blind, visually impaired or otherwise print-disabled. It does this by promoting the making and distribution of copies of books and other published materials in formats accessible to people with print disabilities. The treaty obligates signatory countries to adopt exceptions in their copyright laws that permit the making of copies in accessible formats as well as the distribution of those copies both domestically and internationally.

The *Marrakesh Treaty* came into force on 20 September 2016. The *Copyright Amendment (Disability Access and Other Measures) Act 2017* (Cth) implements this treaty into Australian copyright law.

2.4.8 Beijing Treaty

The *Beijing Treaty on Audiovisual Performances*[91] (*Beijing Treaty*) was adopted in Beijing on 24 June 2012. The treaty deals with the intellectual property rights of performers in audiovisual performances. It grants performers four kinds of economic rights for their performances fixed in audiovisual fixations (such as motion pictures):

- the right of reproduction;
- the right of distribution;
- the right of rental; and
- the right of making available.[92]

The treaty also grants a number of rights in relation to (live) performances that are not fixed, including:

- the right of broadcasting (except in the case of rebroadcasting);
- the right of communication to the public (except where the performance is a broadcast performance); and
- the right of fixation.

---

88 See generally C. Arup, 'The *United States–Australia Free Trade Agreement*', above n 41, 204.
89 At 2.3.2.4.
90 Opened for signature 27 June 2013, WIPO Lex No TRT/MARRAKESH/001 (entered into force 20 September 2016).
91 Opened for signature 24 June 2012, WIPO Lex No TRT/BEIJING/001 (not yet in force).
92 WIPO, 'Summary of the *Beijing Treaty on AudioVisual Performances* (2012)' www.wipo.int.

The *Beijing Treaty* grants performers the moral right to be identified as the performer and, taking into account the nature of the audiovisual fixations, the right to object to any distortion, mutilation or other modification that would be prejudicial to their reputation.

While the provisions may not necessarily provide performers in Australia with an increased revenue stream, they would improve performers' ability to control how their audiovisual performances are used. The *Beijing Treaty* will only enter into force three months after thirty eligible parties have deposited their instruments of ratification or accession. While a number of countries have signed the treaty, the number has not yet reached thirty, so the treaty has not yet come into force.[93]

2.4.9 Anti-Counterfeiting Trade Agreement

The *Anti-Counterfeiting Trade Agreement*[94] (*ACTA*) is a controversial proposed multinational treaty that aims to establish stronger international standards for intellectual property rights enforcement, particularly in relation to counterfeit goods, generic medicines and online copyright infringement.[95] The agreement was signed in October 2011 by Australia, Canada, Japan, Morocco, New Zealand, Singapore, South Korea and the United States. It will come into force if it is ratified in the parliaments of six of the signatories. Japan is the only country so far to ratify the agreement.[96]

The aim of *ACTA* is to 'establish international standards for enforcing intellectual property rights in order to fight more efficiently the growing problem of [trade mark] counterfeiting and [copyright] piracy'.[97] A new international body would be established to oversee *ACTA*, which countries would be able to join on a voluntary basis. The proposed agreement, which has been widely criticised for the fact that it was negotiated in private and because of the potential impact it would have on consumers,[98] reflects a new direction in international intellectual property law.

It does not seem that the proposed agreement will have much of a direct impact on Australian copyright law,[99] although Australia's signing is indicative of the copyright-related priorities of the Australian government.[100] The government has said that *ACTA* would 'create a more secure trading environment for Australia's knowledge economy by strengthening the

---

93 As of March 2019, twenty-six countries had acceded to or ratified the *Beijing Treaty*.
94 Opened for signature 1 October 2011 (not yet in force).
95 Negotiations for *ACTA* began in 2006 by the United States, the European Community, Japan and Switzerland. Subsequently, Australia, Canada, Jordan, Mexico, Morocco, New Zealand, Singapore, South Korea and the United Arab Emirates joined the negotiations.
96 As at March 2019.
97 Office of the United States Trade Representative, '*ACTA*: Summary of key elements under discussion' (November 2009) www.ustr.gov.
98 See M. Geist, 'The trouble with the *Anti-Counterfeiting Trade Agreement (ACTA)*' (2010) 30 *School of Advanced International Studies Review* 137; P. Sugden, 'The *Anti-Counterfeiting Trade Agreement (ACTA): Why?*' (2010) 28 *Copyright Reporter* 137.
99 C. Emerson, Minister for Trade, 'Anti-counterfeiting agreement to benefit creative industries' (Media Release, 16 November 2010).
100 See L. Wiseman, 'Copyright and the creative arts: Emerging Issues' in K. Bowrey, M. Handler and D. Nicol (eds), *Emerging Challenges in Intellectual Property* (Melbourne: Oxford University Press, 2011).

enforcement of intellectual property rights in foreign markets'.[101] Given the widespread hostility to *ACTA*, it is highly unlikely that it will be adopted, at least in the near future.

2.4.10 Future reforms

A number of changes currently underway at the international level may impact on Australian copyright law in the future.

The first area of reform underway at WIPO relates to the intellectual property aspects of traditional knowledge. The Intergovernmental Committee on Intellectual Property, Genetic Resources, Traditional Knowledge and Folklore was formed by WIPO to consider and advise on appropriate actions concerning:

- the economic and cultural significance of tradition-based creations;
- the issues of conservation, management, sustainable use and sharing of benefits from the use of genetic resources and traditional knowledge; and
- the enforcement of rights to traditional knowledge and folklore.[102]

After some delays, a 'negotiating document' for a Protection of Traditional Cultural Expressions treaty was formulated in February 2011.[103] This was used in March 2011 to form the basis of a draft text on objectives and principles that is intended to lay the foundation for the new agreement. In July 2014, draft articles on traditional knowledge and traditional cultural expressions were forwarded to the WIPO General Assembly. These drafts, along with a draft on intellectual property and genetic resources, could form the basis of one or more international legal instruments. It is difficult to assess the impact that this 'treaty', if passed, would have on copyright law in Australia. At this stage, however, it seems that it will have little real impact, considering that the protection given to traditional cultural expression is either meant to complement intellectual property laws or to be subservient to those laws.[104] There continues to be work on the protection of traditional knowledge and traditional cultural expressions. For example, in 2017 the WIPO General Assembly requested the Secretariat to 'update the 2008 gap analyses on the existing protection regimes related to [traditional knowledge] and [traditional cultural expressions]. They were published and distributed as two working documents: *The Protection of Traditional Cultural Expressions*[105] and *The Protection of Traditional Knowledge*.[106]

The second area of reform that WIPO is involved with relates to broadcast copyright, specifically attempts to formulate a new treaty to deal with the reported increase in piracy suffered by broadcasters, cablecasters and webcasters. To prevent such piracy, the proposed

---

101 Emerson, above n 99.
102 The Intergovernmental Committee was established in the Twenty-Sixth Session (Twelfth Extraordinary Session) of the WIPO General Assembly, held in Geneva from 25 September to 3 October 2000.
103 WIPO Secretariat, *The Protection of Traditional Cultural Expressions: Draft Articles*, WIPO/GRTKF/ IC/18/4 (18 February 2011).
104 Ibid, art 10 options 1 and 2.
105 *The Protection of Traditional Cultural Expressions: Updated Draft Gap Analysis*, WIPO/GRTKF/IC/37/7 (6 July 2018).
106 *The Protection of Traditional Knowledge: Updated Draft Gap Analysis*, WIPO/GRTKF/IC/37/6 (20 July 2018).

treaty, the Draft Basic Proposal for the WIPO Treaty on the Protection of Broadcasting Organizations,[107] aims to provide new rights to broadcasters, cablecasters and webcasters. It would also extend the scope and duration of the rights presently given to broadcasting organisations under the *Rome Convention*, the *WIPO Performances and Phonograms Treaty*, the *WIPO Copyright Treaty* and *TRIPS*. Following reconfirmation in November 2010 by WIPO's Standing Committee on Copyright and Related Rights of its ongoing commitment to an international treaty to protect broadcasters,[108] in 2011 WIPO agreed on a work plan and undertook informal consultations on the protection of broadcasting organisations.[109] In March 2014, the Standing Committee produced a working document for a treaty protecting broadcasting organisations.[110]

---

107   Revised Draft Basic Proposal for the WIPO *Treaty on the Protection of Broadcasting Organizations*, last revised in September 2006.
108   WIPO, Standing Committee on Copyright and Related Rights, Twenty-First Session, 8–12 November 2010.
109   WIPO, *Informal Consultation Meeting on the Protection of Broadcasting Organizations*, WIPO/CR/Consult/GE/11/2/1 (2 February 2011). See also WIPO, 'Protection of broadcasting organizations' (Background Briefs) www.wipo.int.
110   WIPO, Standing Committee on Copyright and Related Rights, *Working Document for a Treaty on the Protection of Broadcasting Organizations*, Twenty-Seventh Session (28 April–2 May 2014) www.wipo.int.

3
COPYRIGHT: SUBSISTENCE

3.1 Introduction

There are a number of different criteria that a creation must meet in order for it to be protected by copyright law. These are the requirements of subject matter, material form, connection to Australia, and originality. While copyright arises automatically on creation, a work will only be protected if it satisfies these different criteria (or at least those criteria that apply). The first threshold that must be met is that the creation must fall within one of the categories of subject matter recognised under the *Copyright Act 1968* (Cth). Copyright law divides subject matter into two general categories: 'works'[1] (literary, dramatic, musical and artistic works) and 'subject matter other than works' (sound recordings, cinematograph films, sound and television broadcasts, and published editions of works).

Once it has been established that a creation falls within one of the categories of subject matter, it is then necessary to show that it meets the requisite criteria for protection. The particular criteria that need to be met differ depending on the type of subject matter in question.[2] The first of these is that for a work to qualify for protection, it must be recorded in material form. This requirement only applies to literary, dramatic, musical and artistic works. The next requirement that must be satisfied, which applies to all categories of subject matter, is that the creation must be sufficiently connected to Australia to qualify for protection under Australian law. The final requirement, and the requirement that often requires closest examination, is that the work must be original.[3] This requirement only applies to literary, dramatic, musical and artistic works. Part IV works (that is, subject matter other than works) only need to satisfy the lower threshold that the subject matter has not been copied. Each of these criteria will be examined in turn.

3.2 Subject matter

One of the very first questions to be decided when determining whether a creation is protected by copyright law is whether it falls within one of the categories of subject matter recognised under the *Copyright Act 1968* (Cth). As was discussed in chapter 2, books, pamphlets and other literary works were the first type of subject matter protected by copyright. Over time, the categories of subject matter have expanded to include a range of new types of creative and artistic output, the latest instance being computer programs in the 1980s. While patent law subject matter is based on a relatively open-ended definition of invention,[4] copyright law provides an exhaustive list of the types of subject matter that are protected. If a creation does not fall within the scope of one of these categories, it will not be protected by copyright.

As noted above, the *Copyright Act 1968* (Cth) distinguishes between two categories of subject matter.[5] The first, which is found in Part III of the *Copyright Act*, covers literary,

---

1 See B. Sherman, 'What is a copyright work?' (2011) 12 *Theoretical Inquiries in Law* 99.
2 In the case of works and subject matter other than works it is also necessary to distinguish between those that are 'published' and those that are 'unpublished'. This is largely because the place of first publication becomes significant in determining subsistence of copyright: *Copyright Act 1968* (Cth) ss 32, 22(1), (2).
3 *Copyright Act 1968* (Cth) s 32(1).
4 See ch 10 at 10.3.
5 See 3.1. *Copyright Act 1968* (Cth) pt XIA provides separately for rights against specified unauthorised uses of performances. These rights are more commonly referred to as performers' rights. Performers

dramatic, musical and artistic works. These forms of subject matter, which are united by the fact that they usually have an identifiable author, are commonly referred to as 'works'. The second category of subject matter, which is found in Part IV of the *Copyright Act*, covers sound recordings, cinematograph films, sound and television broadcasts, and published editions of works. These are usually called 'subject matter other than works', entrepreneurial rights or neighbouring rights. The categorisation of subject matter is important because the criteria for protection, as well as the length and scope of protection, differ depending on the type of subject matter in question.[6]

3.2.1 Works (Part III)

There are four types of work recognised in Part III of the *Copyright Act 1968* (Cth). These are literary works, dramatic works, musical works and artistic works.

3.2.1.1 Literary works

Literary works, which were first protected under the 1709 *Statute of Anne*, are the oldest form of subject matter recognised by copyright law. Literary works have been defined as creations that are 'intended to afford either information or instruction, or pleasure, in the form of literary enjoyment'.[7] It has also been said that a literary work supplies information capable of conveying an intelligible meaning.[8] There is no requirement that a literary work must have literary merit or that it is of a particular quality.[9] As such, it covers a wide range of creations, ranging from novels, articles, poems, short stories and song lyrics through to instructions, catalogues and databases as well as more mundane creations, such as railway timetables and university exam papers. Literary work is defined in s 10(1) of the *Copyright Act 1968* (Cth) to include tables or compilations expressed in words, figures or symbols. As a result of changes introduced in 1984, it also expressly covers computer programs and compilations of computer programs.[10] Most literary works (with the obvious exception of computer programs) are recorded in writing.[11]

The question of whether something qualifies as a literary work is, for the most part, relatively straightforward. There are, however, a number of areas that warrant separate attention. These are names, titles and trade marks; tables and compilations; and computer programs.

---

now have moral rights in their performances since the *WIPO Performances and Phonograms Treaty* (WPPT) became law in Australia on 26 July 2007: see ch 2 at 2.4.5. Moral rights of creators are contained in pt IX of the Act and are discussed in more detail, along with performers' rights, in ch 6.

6   A further distinction is made between published and unpublished creations, whether they are works or subject matter other than works.
7   *Hollinrake v Truswell* [1894] 3 Ch 420, 428, approved in *Exxon Corp v Exxon Insurance Consultants International Ltd* [1982] RPC 69.
8   See, for example, *Computer Edge Pty Ltd v Apple Computer Inc* (1986) 161 CLR 171. But compare *Data Access Corp v Powerflex Services Pty Ltd* (1999) 202 CLR 1; *Cortis Exhaust Systems Pty Ltd v Kitten Software Pty Ltd* (2001) ATPR 41-837, [31]–[33].
9   *University of London Press Ltd v University Tutorial Press Ltd* [1916] 2 Ch 601, 608–10.
10 By the *Copyright Amendment Act 1984* (Cth).
11 'Writing' is defined in *Copyright Act 1968* (Cth) s 10 to mean a mode of representing or reproducing words, figures or symbols in a visible form, and 'written' has a corresponding meaning.

3.2.1.1.1 NAMES, TITLES AND TRADE MARKS

Single words, names and titles are generally not protected by copyright.[12] There are many examples of titles and single words that have been held to fall outside the scope of copyright protection, including 'The Man Who Broke the Bank at Monte Carlo',[13] 'Opera in the Outback',[14] 'Exxon',[15] and a phrase used by taxi drivers in distress: 'Help-Help-Driver-In-Danger-Call-Police-Ph-000'.[16] In some situations, however, copyright may subsist in a title; whether it does is a question of fact in each case depending on the originality and nature of the title.[17] While the majority of headlines are short, factual statements of the subject of an article, this, as Bennett J said in *Fairfax Media Publications Pty Ltd v Reed International Books Australia Pty Ltd*, 'does not exclude the possibility of establishing a basis for copyright protection of an individual headline'.[18] A similar view was expressed in *Budget Eyewear Australia Pty Ltd v Specsavers Pty Ltd*,[19] which held that it was arguable that the way a concept was expressed in an advertisement may be original. One explanation of why names and titles do not qualify for protection (which overlaps with the originality requirement) is that they are not substantial enough to attract copyright protection. As Bennett J explained in *Fairfax*:

> Headlines generally are, like titles, simply too insubstantial and too short to qualify for copyright protection as literary works. The function of the headlines is as a title to an article as well as a brief statement of its subject, in a compressed form comparable in length to a book title or the like. It is, generally, too trivial to be a literary work, much as a logo was held to be too trivial to be an artistic work ... even if skill and labour has been expended on creation.[20]

It has also been suggested that there is no need for copyright protection to be given to single words as they are adequately protected by trade mark law, passing off and artistic copyright.[21]

---

12 See *Francis Day & Hunter Ltd v Twentieth Century Fox Corp Ltd* [1940] AC 112, 123 (Lord Wright). Compare *Lamb v Evans* [1893] 1 Ch 218; *Exxon Corp v Exxon Insurance Consultants International Ltd* [1982] RPC 69. See also *Brodel v Telstra Corp* [2004] FCA 505.
13 *Francis Day & Hunter Ltd v Twentieth Century Fox Corp Ltd* [1940] AC 112, 123 (Lord Wright).
14 See *Lott v JBW & Friends Pty Ltd* [2000] SASC 3 (title of the brochure 'Opera in the Outback' was not a literary work).
15 *Exxon Corp v Exxon Insurance Consultants International Ltd* [1982] RPC 69.
16 *Victoria v Pacific Technologies (Australia) Pty Ltd (No 2)* (2009) 177 FCR 61. The phrase was too 'trivial, ordinary, insubstantial and commonplace' to constitute an original literary work. The help words did no more than express an 'idea'. There were also public policy issues, as no-one should be able to own help words: 'It would be inappropriate for the Help Words not to be available for use by anybody without consent of *Pacific Technologies*' (at [24]). In *Elwood Clothing Pty Ltd v Cotton On Clothing Pty Ltd* (2008) 76 IPR 83, the Full Federal Court held that T-shirt designs that contained words and numbers were too insubstantial and vague to represent a literary work.
17 *Lamb v Evans* [1893] 1 Ch 218, 227; *Ladbroke (Football) Ltd v William Hill (Football) Ltd* [1964] 1 WLR 273, 286.
18 (2010) 189 FCR 109, [50]. Compare *Newspaper Licensing Agency Ltd v Meltwater Holdings BV* [2010] EWHC 3099 (Ch) where it was held that 'headlines are capable of being literary works, whether independently or as part of the articles to which they relate': at [77].
19 (2010) 86 IPR 479, [17].
20 *Fairfax Media Publications Pty Ltd v Reed International Books Australia Pty Ltd* (2010) 189 FCR 109, 122.
21 J. Lahore, *Copyright and Designs*, looseleaf service (Sydney: LexisNexis Butterworths) [6020]. See also L. Bently, B. Sherman, D. Gangee and P. Johnson, *Intellectual Property Law* (5th edn, Oxford: Oxford University Press, 2018) 64.

3.2.1.1.2 TABLES AND COMPILATIONS

It is clear from s 10 of the *Copyright Act 1968* (Cth) that tables and compilations expressed in words, figures or symbols – as well as compilations of computer programs – are literary works. There are many examples of compilations that have been recognised as literary works. For example, in *Kalamazoo (Australia) Pty Ltd v Compact Business Systems Pty Ltd*,[22] a system of blank accounting forms for use in a mechanical device known as a peg board was held to be a compilation that fell within the definition of literary works. Other examples are telephone directories,[23] race programs,[24] a list of numbers for a game of Bingo[25] betting information for football match figures,[26] columns of birth and death announcements in a newspaper,[27] a list of the different prizes to be used in video gaming machines,[28] a list of radiator caps and fuel tank caps,[29] and tables of data and statistics relating to sporting events.[30] Given that tables and compilations usually consist of the collection and arrangement of pre-existing materials, protection usually turns on whether the work is original (discussed below),[31] rather than on whether it is a literary work.

3.2.1.1.3 COMPUTER PROGRAMS

In the 1970s and 1980s, there was widespread debate in many countries as to whether computer programs should be protected by copyright, patents or sui generis legislation. In Australia, as elsewhere, there was confusion and uncertainty about whether computers could and should be protected by copyright law. These problems were highlighted in the 1983 decision of *Apple Computer Inc v Computer Edge Pty Ltd*,[32] the first Australian case to consider whether computer programs could be protected by copyright law. While the threshold to convey 'intelligible meaning' is fairly low, Beaumont J nonetheless held that a computer program in object code was not a literary work. This was because the object code was not intelligible to humans, largely because the series of electrical impulses was not visible.[33]

---

22 (1985) 5 IPR 213.
23 *Telstra Corp Ltd v Phone Directories Co Pty Ltd* (2010) 194 FCR 142; *Desktop Marketing Systems Pty Ltd v Telstra Corp Ltd* (2002) 119 FCR 491 (overturned in relation to originality by *IceTV Pty Ltd v Nine Network Australia Pty Ltd* (2009) 239 CLR 458 and *Telstra* in 2010); *Harpur v Lambourne* (1999) 45 IPR 213 (where a directory of businesses in the boating industry that was arranged in a manner similar to a yellow pages telephone listing was held to be a literary work).
24 *Mander v O'Brien* [1934] SASR 87.
25 *Mirror Newspapers Ltd v Queensland Newspapers Pty Ltd* (1982) 59 FLR 71.
26 *Football League Ltd v Littlewoods Pools Ltd* [1959] Ch 637.
27 *John Fairfax & Sons Pty Ltd v Australian Consolidated Press Ltd* [1960] SR (NSW) 413.
28 In *Milwell Pty Ltd v Olympic Amusements Pty Ltd* (1999) 85 FCR 436, the Full Federal Court held that prize scales developed for draw poker video gaming machines were protected by copyright as a table or compilation as they were plainly intended to convey information and instructions regarding the prizes available.
29 *Autocaps (Australia) Pty Ltd v Pro-Kit Pty Ltd* (1999) 46 IPR 339.
30 *Sports Data Pty Ltd v Prozone Sports Australia Pty Ltd* (2014) 107 IPR 1, [75]–[77].
31 At 3.5.
32 (1983) 50 ALR 581. It is important to note that the decision is based on the law as it stood before the *Copyright Amendment Act 1984* (Cth) took effect on 15 June 1984.
33 See, for example, *Computer Edge Pty Ltd v Apple Computer Inc* (1986) 161 CLR 171 (noting that a literary work may be a mere collection of letters, numerals or symbols that are in themselves meaningless, but made up in merely mechanical ways, such as codes, ciphers, mathematical tables, and systems of shorthand).

On appeal, the Full Federal Court held that there was copyright in the computer program as the source code was a literary work and the object code was an adaptation of the literary work (on the basis of it being a translation).[34]

This decision was reaffirmed on appeal by the High Court which held that while the computer program in source code was a literary work, the object code did *not* constitute a literary work.[35] This was largely because although the object code was 'original', it was not 'visible or otherwise perceptible and thus was not intended to be capable by [itself] of conveying a meaning which could be understood by human beings'.[36]

Despite (or more probably because of) this decision, Australia followed the lead of many other countries and decided to protect computer programs as literary works (although patent protection is now commonly used to protect computer programs). To this end, the *Copyright Act 1968* (Cth) was amended in 1984 to include computer programs within the definition of 'literary works'.[37] This definition, which came into effect in 1984, was later replaced by the *Copyright Amendment (Digital Agenda) Act 2000*.[38] Under current law, a computer program is defined as 'a set of statements or instructions to be used directly or indirectly in a computer to bring about a certain result'.[39] As a result, it was made clear that computer programs are protected as literary works, whether expressed in source code or object code, and whether stored electronically or not.[40]

Something that the 1984 and 2000 definitions have in common is that they define a computer program as a set of statements or instructions. One question that has arisen in this context, which relates to the scope of the work, is whether there are some minimum criteria

---

34   *Apple Computer Inc v Computer Edge Pty Ltd* (1984) 53 ALR 225. The court drew a distinction between the functioning of the machine (due to the electrical impulses) and the computer program itself, which could be understood by suitably trained people and which contained the instructions for the storage and reproduction of the information.

35   *Computer Edge Pty Ltd v Apple Computer Inc* (1986) 161 CLR 171. Gibbs CJ, Mason, Wilson and Brennan JJ held that the Apple source codes were literary works. Mason and Wilson JJ (at 194) held that a computer program in object code was a literary work, and Gibbs CJ and Brennan J (at 184) held that it could not be a literary work. See also *Autodesk Inc v Dyason (No 1)* (1992) 173 CLR 330.

36   Note *Copyright Act 1968* (Cth) ss 47AB–47AH, which allow decompilation of computer programs for interoperability, introduced by the Digital Agenda amendments.

37   By virtue of the *Copyright Amendment Act 1984* (Cth), which came about after industry concerns about the lack of protection for computer programs were expressed at the National Symposium on Legal Protection of Computer Software in March 1984. The 1984 provision, which has now been replaced, defined computer program as 'an expression, in any language, code or notation, of a set of instructions (whether with or without related information) intended, either directly or after either or both of the following: (a) conversion to another language, code, or notation; (b) reproduction in different material form; to cause a device having digital information facilities to perform a particular function'.

38   In 1988, the Copyright Law Review Committee (CLRC) was given the task of examining the adequacy of copyright protection for computer programs. Its report was released in 1995. While the key CLRC recommendations were enacted in the *Copyright Amendment (Computer Programs) Act 1999* (Cth), the changes to the definition of computer program were not adopted until 2000.

39   *Copyright Act 1968* (Cth) s 10 (definition of 'computer program'). Prior to the *Copyright Amendment (Digital Agenda) Act 2000* (Cth), it was defined in s 10 as 'an expression, in any language code or notation, of a set of instructions (whether with or without related information) intended, either directly or after either or both of the following; (a) conversion to another language, code or notation; (b) reproduction in a different material form; to cause a device having digital information processing capabilities to perform a particular function'.

40   *Data Access Corp v Powerflex Services Pty Ltd* (1999) 202 CLR 1.

that must be met before something qualifies as a computer program in copyright law. This issue was considered in the 1999 decision of *Data Access Corp v Powerflex Services Pty Ltd*,[41] where the High Court was asked whether an individual word in a computer language (Huffman compression table), although representing a computer program, was a literary work.[42] The High Court defined a computer program in a negative way:

> Something is not a 'computer program' within the meaning of the definition in s 10(1) unless it is intended to express, either directly or indirectly, an algorithmic or logical relationship between the function desired to be performed and the physical capabilities of the 'device' having digital processing capabilities. Thus, in the sense employed by the definition, a program in object code causes a device to perform a particular function 'directly' when executed. A program in source code does so 'after … conversion to another language, code or notation'.[43]

On the basis that the reserved words (in the Huffman compression table) expressed neither an algorithmic nor a logical relationship intended to cause a computer to function, the High Court concluded that the compression table was not a computer program and thus not a literary work for purposes of the *Copyright Act 1968* (Cth).[44] While the High Court's decision is based on the 1984 definition of computer program, nonetheless the comments on the way that the 'set of instructions' is to be construed are still relevant today.

When thinking about copyright protection for computer programs, it is important to note that computer programs consist (at least potentially) of both functional and non-functional components. That is, a computer program may consist of instructions (code) that serve a specific purpose (such as word processing), as well as non-functional material (for example, the data).[45] The copyright protection of a computer program is not intended to extend to the content of the computer programs (for example, the audiovisual and caption content of DVDs are not program instructions and thus not part of a computer program).[46] However, in *Kabushiki Kaisha Sony Computer Entertainment v Stevens*,[47] a computer game was held to be both a literary work and a cinematograph film.[48] Updates of computer software programs

---

41 Ibid.
42 At first instance, Jenkinson J held that each of the reserved words was a computer program within the 1984 definition, as they were translations of the set of instructions in source code and object code that were intended to cause the computer to function: *Data Access Corp v Powerflex Services Pty Ltd* (1999) 202 CLR 1, 197–8. This decision was overturned on appeal to the Full Federal Court, when the court held that the words were mere 'triggers' that activated the underlying set of instructions and not themselves an expression of the set of instructions by which the computer was caused to function: *Powerflex Services Pty Ltd v Data Access Corp (No 2)* (1997) 37 IPR 436, 451.
43 *Data Access Corp v Powerflex Services Pty Ltd* (1999) 202 CLR 1, 248.
44 Ibid 251.
45 The data is not incidental, as 'in many cases it will be necessary for instructions to be accompanied by related information if those devices are to perform quite ordinary computer functions': Gaudron J in *Autodesk Inc v Dyason (No 2)* (1993) 176 CLR 300, 329.
46 *Australian Video Retailers Association Ltd v Warner Home Video Pty Ltd* (2001) 53 IPR 242, 258.
47 (2003) 132 FCR 31, [62].
48 Following *Galaxy Electronics Pty Ltd & Gottlieb Enterprises Pty Ltd v Sega Enterprises Ltd* (1997) 75 FCR 8.

have also been held to be copyright works as long as the programmer expended some independent intellectual effort.[49]

3.2.1.2 Dramatic works

The second category of works that are recognised under the *Copyright Act 1968* (Cth) is dramatic works. The *Copyright Act* defines a dramatic work to include a choreographic show or other dumb show (pantomime).[50] Plays, screenplays, scripts and possibly firework displays[51] fall within the category of dramatic works. While a script for a film is included in the definition of a dramatic work, the film itself is not a dramatic work. Instead, the film is a separate type of subject matter that is recognised in Part IV of the *Copyright Act*.[52]

A dramatic work must be 'capable of being performed'.[53] In *Aristocrat Leisure Industries Pty Ltd v Pacific Gaming Pty Ltd*, it was held that a video game was not a dramatic work on the basis that there was no apparent plot, choreography, script, characterisation or interaction between characters and there was a strong element of unpredictability and randomness.[54] While there is no copyright protection of the plots or themes of dramatic works, it is still possible to infringe copyright in a dramatic work if the plot or theme is reproduced and it constitutes a substantial part of the original dramatic work.[55] Interestingly, in the United Kingdom decision of *Norowzian v Arks Ltd (No 2)*,[56] the court gave a generous interpretation of what could be protected as a dramatic work. In this case, copyright protection was given for a particular form of film editing (jump-cutting) used in the film *Joy* and copied in the Guinness stout commercial on which the advertisement was based. While the copied dance could not be performed, as the film was a result of the editing process, it was held that as the film could be played, the film itself was 'capable of being performed'. Some doubt has been cast on the *Norowzian* decision in Australia by *Telstra Corp Ltd v Royal & Sun Alliance Insurance Australia Ltd*.[57] In this case, Telstra claimed infringement of its 'Goggomobil' advertisement by the defendant insurance company. Telstra claimed that its advertisement was a dramatic work (a series of dramatic events making up a short story) even though there was no written script of the work and hence no reduction into material form. Telstra failed in its claim for copyright infringement as, even though the defendant's ad campaign had featured similar

---

49   *JR Consulting & Drafting v Cummings* [2014] NSWSC 1252.
50   *Copyright Act 1968* (Cth) s 10(1).
51   In *Nine Network Australia Pty Ltd v Australian Broadcasting Corporation* (1999) 48 IPR 333, Channel Nine applied for an injunction to restrain the Australian Broadcasting Corporation from broadcasting the 2000 Millennium Fireworks spectacular at the Sydney Harbour Bridge. In exchange for a financial contribution to the staging of the event, the Sydney City Council had granted Channel Nine the status of official broadcaster and the exclusive right to record and televise the 'fireworks spectacular and associated events'. It was not clear whether the grant of the exclusive rights had a firm legal basis on which others could be excluded from broadcasting the same event; one of the issues was whether an outdoor fireworks spectacular was able to be protected by copyright.
52   See the discussion of films as subject matter below at 3.2.2.1. On the question of the relationship between a dramatic work and a film, see *Norowzian v Arks Ltd (No 2)* [2000] FSR 363.
53   *Green v Broadcasting Corporation of New Zealand* [1989] 3 NZLR 18.
54   (2000) 105 FCR 153. See also *Nine Network Australia Pty Ltd v Australian Broadcasting Corporation* (1999) 48 IPR 333 (FC) (doubting whether a fireworks display was a dramatic work).
55   See Lahore, *Copyright and Designs*, above n 21, 34, 300–20.
56   [2000] FSR 363.
57   (2003) 57 IPR 453.

concepts (that is, a memorable character and unusual car), there was only the taking of the idea rather than the expression of the idea.[58]

The requirement that a dramatic work must be capable of being performed has had important ramifications for the protection given to game shows and franchised television programs such as *Big Brother*, *The Block*, *Survivor* and *The Biggest Loser*. While aspects of these programs (such as the theme tune and logo) may be protected by copyright and trade marks, a problem facing the creators of these programs is that the courts have, with one or two exceptions, refused to accept that the formats of television programs are a form of dramatic work able to be protected by copyright. For example, in *Green v Broadcasting Corporation of New Zealand*,[59] the owner of the popular British game show *Opportunity Knocks* brought an infringement action against a rival program screened in New Zealand that adopted many of the features of the British program. As part of the action, the Privy Council was called on to decide whether *Opportunity Knocks* was protected as a dramatic work. The Privy Council held that although the program followed a specific format, used particular catchphrases, and adopted a special technical device called a 'clapometer' to measure audience response, nonetheless, when looked at as a whole it was not protected by copyright.[60] This was because the program lacked the specificity or detail that enabled it to be performed – an element that was required for it to qualify as a dramatic work. The Privy Council held that the rival program had only copied the idea or concept, which was not able to be protected under copyright law.[61] This decision, which has been followed in a number of cases, led some academics to lobby for legislative change to provide specific protection for television format rights.[62] To date, the legislators in Australia have resisted the temptation to extend the reach of copyright protection to format rights. However, it is interesting to note that in *Banner Universal Motion Pictures Ltd v Endemol Shine Group Ltd*,[63] even though the claim of copyright infringement failed, the English High Court confirmed that television formats are arguably capable of being protected as dramatic works. This is provided that the format contained, as a minimum, a sufficient number of distinguishing features presented in a coherent framework that can be repeatedly applied so as to enable the television show to be reproduced in recognisable form.[64]

---

58 Telstra was, however, successful in a claim for passing off under *Trade Practices Act 1974* (Cth) ss 52, 53(d). Even though the ideas had been expressed differently (the defendant thereby avoiding copyright infringement), the court found that as the defendant had used similar concepts in its advertising campaign, the defendant had falsely represented an affiliation with Telstra.

59 [1989] RPC 469 (PC) (on appeal from the New Zealand Court of Appeal). This case is further discussed below at n 162.

60 Ibid 1058 (Lord Bridge).

61 Ibid.

62 Initially in the United Kingdom: see Anon, 'Programme formats: A further consultative document' (1996) *Entertainment Law Review* 216; R. Bridge and S. Lane, 'Programme formats: The write-in vote' (1996) *Entertainment Law Review* 212. This position was followed in Australia: see J. Malbon, 'All the eggs in one basket: The new TV formats global business strategy' in M. Keane, A. Moran and M. Ryan (eds), *Audiovisual Works, TV Formats and Multiple Markets*, Australian UNESCO Orbicom Working Papers in Communications No 1 (Brisbane: Griffith University, 2003); A. Moran (with J. Malbon), *Understanding the Global TV Format* (Bristol: Intellect Books, 2006). See also *Nine Films & Television Pty Ltd v Ninox Television Ltd* (2005) 67 IPR 46.

63 [2017] EWHC 2600.

64 Ibid [44].

3.2.1.3 Musical works

The next category of works that are recognised in the *Copyright Act 1968* (Cth) is that of 'musical works'. While there is no definition of musical work in the *Copyright Act*, it is taken to refer to the non-literary aspects of a song[65] – that is, to the sound, melody, harmony and rhythm. A compact disc may contain a number of different types of copyright, including copyright in the lyrics (as a literary work), in the musical score (as a musical work), and in the recording of the song (as a sound recording). There may also be copyright in the artwork on the cover.[66] There is no need for a musical work to possess any creative or artistic merit for it to attract copyright protection. An interesting example of the types of musical creation that constitute a copyright work was given by the 2005 English Court of Appeal decision *Hyperion Records Ltd v Sawkins*.[67] In this decision, musicologist Lionel Sawkins claimed that he owned copyright in the performing edition of French Baroque composer Michel-Richard de Lalande's (out-of-copyright) music. This was on the basis that the intense research involved in creating the edition entitled him to the same rights as the author of a work. In response, refusing to pay royalties for use of the performing edition, Hyperion Records argued that an edition of an existing musical work that was a faithful reproduction of Lalande's music could not itself be an original music work. The Court of Appeal held that while the work of Sawkins did not involve a re-composition of Lalande's music, nonetheless the production of the performing editions required sufficient effort, skill and time on the part of Sawkins for the work to attract copyright protection under the *Copyright, Designs and Patents Act 1988* (UK).

3.2.1.4 Artistic works

The fourth and final category of works listed in the *Copyright Act 1968* (Cth) is 'artistic works'. Artistic work is exhaustively defined in s 10(1) of the *Copyright Act* to mean paintings, sculptures, drawings, engravings, photographs, buildings or models of buildings, and works of artistic craftsmanship.[68] Following the approach that is adopted with other copyright works, there is no requirement that paintings, sculptures, drawings, engravings, photographs, buildings or models of buildings have artistic merit or quality. The one exception to this general rule is in relation to works of artistic craftsmanship – these need to exhibit some artistic quality in order for them to qualify for protection.

---

[65] In the United Kingdom, a musical work is defined in *Copyright, Designs and Patents Act 1988* (UK) s 3(1) to mean 'a work consisting of music exclusive of any words or action intended to be sung, spoken or performed with the music'.

[66] A strange example of an avant-garde musical work was given in a copyright dispute in the United Kingdom in 2002. John Cage's song, which was called '4 minutes 33 seconds' (it consisted of four minutes thirty-three seconds of silence), was allegedly copied by The Planets when the group reproduced sixty seconds of silence on its recording. The case was settled, with Cage being paid a relatively large five-figure sum. See Bently et al, *Intellectual Property Law*, above n 21, 71–2, referring to a report in *The Independent*, 22 June 2002.

[67] [2005] EWCA Civ 565.

[68] The definition expressly excludes circuit layouts within the meaning of the *Circuit Layouts Act 1989* (Cth).

3.2.1.4.1 PAINTINGS

Generally, there is little trouble in determining whether something is a painting. Thus, paintings will include framed objects hung in art galleries or on lounge room walls. Occasionally, however, questions arise as to where the limits of the category lie. In *Merchandising Corp of America Inc v Harpbond*,[69] 1970s pop star Adam Ant found that his image had been reproduced without permission on a series of posters. In the absence of a right of personality or some equivalent means of protection, it was argued that Adam Ant's distinctive make-up (which consisted of two horizontal stripes across his cheeks) was a painting that was protected by copyright as an artistic work. The English Court of Appeal rejected this argument on the basis that it was ridiculous to suggest that the make-up on a person's face could be a painting. More specifically, the court held that a painting required a surface and that Adam Ant's face was not a surface: '[A] painting is not an idea: it is an object; and paint without a surface is not a painting.'[70]

3.2.1.4.2 SCULPTURES

The next type of artistic work recognised under the *Copyright Act 1968* (Cth) is sculptures. As well as objects commonly recognised as sculptures, such as Henry Moore's works, 'sculpture' is defined to include a 'cast or model made for purposes of sculpture'.[71] In a decision that highlights some of the problems with an overly literal interpretation of statutory language, the New Zealand Court of Appeal held in *Lincoln Industries Ltd v Wham-O Manufacturing Co*[72] that the wooden model used as a mould to make frisbees was a sculpture. Somewhat bizarrely, the court held that the frisbee itself was not a sculpture since it was created by injecting plastic into a mould and was thus not the expression of a sculptor's ideas.[73] In a preferable approach, English courts have construed sculpture in a less legalistic manner to suggest that a sculpture is a three-dimensional work made by an artist's hand.[74] While this issue has not been addressed in Australia, it seems that the current approach is more in tune with that of the United Kingdom than that of New Zealand.

3.2.1.4.3 DRAWINGS

A 'drawing' includes a diagram, map,[75] chart or plan.[76] While the term 'drawing' conjures up thoughts of sketches of landscapes or people, it includes more functional and simple items, such as architects' plans, the sketch of a hand holding a pencil,[77] designs for exhaust

---

69 [1983] FSR 32.
70 Ibid 46.
71 *Copyright Act 1968* (Cth) s 10.
72 (1984) 3 IPR 115.
73 Ibid 131.
74 *Metix (UK) v GH Maughan Plastics Ltd* [1997] FSR 718, 722 (holding that functional cartridges in a double-barrel shape were not sculptures). In the United Kingdom case *Lucasfilm Ltd v Ainsworth* (2008) 78 IPR 145, the trial Judge, Mann J, suggested that a sculpture should have an 'instrinsic quality of being intended to be enjoyed as a visual thing', and this view was ultimately upheld in the Court of Appeal decision *Lucasfilm Ltd v Ainsworth* [2009] EWCA Civ 1328, [75].
75 *Sands & McDougall Pty Ltd v Robinson* (1917) 23 CLR 49.
76 *Edwards Hot Water Systems v SW Hart Pty Ltd* (1985) 9 FCR 537.
77 *Kenrick & Co v Lawrence & Co* (1890) 25 QBD 99, holding that the sketch of a hand holding a pencil in the act of drawing a cross within a square (a how-to-vote card that helped illiterate voters) was merely

pipes,[78] dresses[79] and logos.[80] It seems, however, that it will need to exhibit some type of visual rather than, for example, merely 'semiotic' function.[81] Protection for the two-dimensional drawings of an object also provides protection for the three-dimensional product and thus prevents the reproduction of the drawing into the three-dimensional form.[82]

3.2.1.4.4 ENGRAVINGS

An 'engraving' includes an etching, lithograph, product of photogravure, woodcut, print or similar work, but not a photograph.[83] The term 'engraving' refers to the process of cutting, marking or otherwise working the surface of an object, as well as the product resulting from the process. In *Lincoln Industries Ltd v Wham-O Manufacturing Co*,[84] it was held that both the mould from which a frisbee was pressed and the frisbee itself were protected as engravings. Following the approach that has been adopted in the United Kingdom in relation to sculptures (rejecting the *Wham-O* decision), this legalistic approach was rejected in Australia in *Greenfield Products Pty Ltd v Rover-Scott Bonnar Ltd* where it was held that the drive mechanism of a lawnmower was not an engraving.[85]

3.2.1.4.5 PHOTOGRAPHS

A 'photograph' means a product of photography, xerography or a process similar to photography.[86] The definition excludes cinematograph films but is broad enough to include digital photographs where there is no film.

3.2.1.4.6 BUILDINGS OR MODELS OF A BUILDING

A 'building' includes a structure of any kind.[87] A half-court tennis court (made of concrete with steel posts) has been held to be a building,[88] as has a plug and mould used for

---

the representation of an idea, not the expression. A square can only be drawn as a square and a cross can only be drawn as a cross. There were very few ways to draw the hand or the pencil that is held in the hand. See also *FAI Insurance v Advance Bank of Australia* (1986) 7 IPR 217 (no copyright in a how-to-vote and proxy form because it would mean an overlap of idea and expression).

78 *British Leyland Motor Corp Ltd v Armstrong Patents Co* [1986] AC 577.
79 *J Bernstein Ltd v Sydney Murray Ltd* [1981] RPC 303.
80 *Deckers Outdoor Corp Inc v Farley (No 5)* (2009) 83 IPR 245; *Facton Ltd v Xu* (2015) 111 IPR 103, [26]–[31]; *Knead (Holding) SAL v Fiordelli* [2018] FCCA 1472.
81 *Elwood Clothing Pty Ltd v Cotton On Clothing Pty Ltd* (2008) 172 FCR 580, [154], [50]: 'whether a work is a "drawing" depends on whether it has a visual rather than a "semiotic" function.' As the Full Federal Court stated, 'the work on the New Deal T-shirt, front and back, is an artistic work. The artistic quality of the work consists of the layout, balancing, form, font, positioning, shaping and interrelationship of the various elements. Any meaning conveyed by the numerals and text is so obscure, subjective to the reader and subservient to the artistic aspect that the numerals and text do not amount to a literary work': at [62]. See also *Woodtree Pty Ltd v Zheng* (2007) 211 FLR 18, where a work made up of words and photographs was held not to be a drawing.
82 *Copyright Act 1968* (Cth) s 21(3).
83 Ibid s 10(1) (definition of 'engraving').
84 (1984) 3 IPR 115, 128.
85 (1990) 17 IPR 417; *Talk of the Town v Hagstrom* (1990) 19 IPR 649.
86 *Copyright Act 1968* (Cth) s 10(1) (definition of 'photograph').
87 Ibid s 10(1) (definition of 'building').
88 *Half Court Tennis Pty Ltd v Seymour* (1980) 53 FLR 240.

manufacturing pre-cast fibreglass swimming pools.[89] Copyright will also subsist in plans for buildings.[90]

3.2.1.4.7 ARTISTIC CRAFTSMANSHIP

Works of artistic craftsmanship are the final category of artistic work recognised under the *Copyright Act 1968* (Cth). This category is referred to within the definition of 'artistic work' in s 10(1) of the Act. Creations such as quality furniture, jewellery, crafts, pots, quilts and glassware would be classified as works of artistic craftsmanship.[91] As a result of amendments made to the Act in 2003, sculptures and other artistic works qualify both as artistic works and as works of artistic craftsmanship.[92] Section 18 of sch 2 of the *Competition and Consumer Act 2010* (Cth) also provides some protection from misleading and deceptive conduct in relation to the appearance of articles.[93]

Works of artistic craftsmanship differ from the other categories of works recognised under the *Copyright Act* in that to qualify for protection they must exhibit some degree of artistic quality. For many years the leading authority on the scope of artistic craftsmanship in Australian law was *George Hensher v Restawhile Upholstery*.[94] In this case, the House of Lords held that a 'cheap' and 'flashy' lounge suite fell outside the realm of artistic craftsmanship. While the mass-produced chair was held to be distinctive, it was not 'artistic'. Lord Reid said that objects could be said to be artistic if a person gets 'pleasure or satisfaction ... from contemplating it'.[95] As many commentators have noted, the House of Lords decision, which is wideranging and often contradictory, provides little real assistance in determining the meaning of artistic craftsmanship.

Many of the uncertainties as to the meaning of artistic craftsmanship under Australian law have now been clarified as a result of the High Court decision of *Burge v Swarbrick*.[96] In the case, the High Court was called on to decide whether a mould for the hull and deck fittings of a 30-foot yacht (which was known as the 'Plug') was a work of artistic craftsmanship. In holding

---

89   *Darwin Fibreglass Pty Ltd v Kruhse Enterprises Pty Ltd* (1998) 41 IPR 649. For the purposes of the copyright–design overlap provisions, in particular s 77 of the *Copyright Act 1968* (Cth), a building or model of a building does *not* include a portable building such as a shed, pre-constructed swimming pool, demountable building or similar portable building. The copyright–design overlap is discussed in ch 7 at 7.10.

90   See *Lend Lease Homes Pty Ltd v Warrigal Homes Pty Ltd* [1970] 3 NSWLR 265; *Ancher, Mortlock, Murray & Woolley Pty Ltd v Hooker Homes Pty Ltd* [1971] 2 NSWLR 278.

91   In *Cuisenaire v Reed* [1963] VR 719, wooden coloured rods used to teach children addition and subtraction were not works of artistic craftsmanship.

92   The definition of 'artistic work' in *Copyright Act 1968* (Cth) s 10(1) was amended by *Designs (Consequential Amendments) Act 2003* (Cth) sch 1 item 1. The Full Federal Court in *Burge v Swarbrick* (2005) 149 FCR 193 clarified that something (in this case a plug for a yacht) could be a work of artistic craftsmanship for the purpose of *Copyright Act 1968* (Cth) s 77(1)(a) even if it could also qualify as a sculpture. Between the hearing of first instance and the appeal, the definition of artistic work in s 10 was amended to make this clear.

93   See *Parkdale Custom Built Furniture Pty Ltd v Puxu Pty Ltd* (1982) 149 CLR 191, which was decided under *Trade Practices Act 1974* (Cth) ss 52 and 53 (now *Competition and Consumer Act 2010* (Cth) sch 2 s 18).

94   [1976] AC 64.

95   Ibid 78.

96   (2007) 232 CLR 336.

that the yacht was not a work of 'artistic craftsmanship', the High Court provided some useful guidance as to the meaning of that term.

The High Court began by noting that the question of whether something was a 'work of artistic craftsmanship' was not to be decided by the intentions of the creator of the work. Instead, the question, 'like many other issues calling for care and discrimination, is one for objective determination by the court, assisted by admissible evidence and not unduly weighed down by the supposed terrors for judicial assessment of matters involving aesthetics'.[97]

The High Court also noted that the question of whether something was a work of artistic craftsmanship was particularly difficult in relation to functional works – that is, where the shape of an object was dictated, or partially dictated, by the task that it had to perform. In deciding how a functional object was to be dealt with, the High Court said:

> [D]etermining whether a work is 'a work of artistic craftsmanship' does not turn on assessing the beauty or aesthetic appeal of a work or on assessing any harmony between its visual appeal and its utility. The determination turns on assessing the extent to which the particular work's artistic expression, in its form, is unconstrained by functional considerations.[98]

In essence, the High Court said that the key consideration in deciding whether a functional object was a work of artistic craftsmanship was whether the person who created the work was able to shape or mould the resulting object. As the court said, with 'wallpaper, a tapestry, stained glass window, piece of jewellery or Tiffany artefact, there is considerable freedom of design choice relatively unconstrained by the function or utility of the article so produced'.[99] In these cases, the High Court said, there was little doubt that these objects were works of artistic craftsmanship. At the other extreme, following Lord Simon in *Hensher*, the High Court also said that objects such as the works of a cobbler or dental mechanic, and a wheelwright, where there was little design choice, were not works of artistic craftsmanship. Applying this logic to the facts of the case, the High Court said that as the design brief for the new yacht 'focused on utilitarian considerations,' there was little scope for the encouragement of real or substantial artistic effort. On this basis, the court said that the mould for the yacht hull and deck fittings were not works of artistic craftsmanship.

As well as helping to clarify the status of functional objects as works of artistic craftsmanship, the High Court clarified that, contrary to the view that craftsmanship requires that the work be 'hand made', it is possible for a mass-produced item to be a work of artistic craftsmanship. In this sense, the court reiterated the finding in *Coogi Australia Pty Ltd v Hysport International*[100] that the uniquely coloured and knitted fabrics that were made into

---

97   Ibid [63]. Compare Lord Kilbrandon in *George Hensher v Restawhile Upholstery* [1976] AC 64, who said that the artistic quality question was to be determined by whether the author had the 'desire to produce a thing of beauty which would have an artistic justification for its own existence': at 98. Lord Simon disagreed and suggested that it was the intention of the creator and their result that was the crucial question: at 92.
98   (2007) 232 CLR 336, [83].
99   Ibid [73].
100 (1998) 41 IPR 593.

jumpers were works of artistic craftsmanship. This was despite the fact the fabric was made using a computer-controlled knitting machine.[101]

3.2.2 Subject matter other than works (Part IV)

This section examines the second category of subject matter recognised in the *Copyright Act 1968* (Cth), which is commonly referred to, rather unhelpfully, as 'subject matter other than works'. Four different types of subject matter are recognised in Part IV of the *Copyright Act*: sound recordings, cinematograph films, sound and television broadcasts, and published editions of works.

3.2.2.1 Films

A 'cinematograph film' is defined as the aggregate of the visual images embodied in an article or thing and capable of being shown as a moving picture.[102] The definition of cinematograph film is a broad one, as illustrated by *Sega Enterprises Ltd & Avel Pty Ltd v Galaxy Electronics Pty Ltd*[103] where it was held that a computer game represented a 'cinematograph film'. Films attract separate copyright protection from copyright in the underlying dramatic work. The underlying scenario or script for a film is a dramatic work.[104] The soundtrack of a film is considered to be part of the film (not part of a sound recording).[105] 'Sound-track' is also defined to include a record (disc, tape, paper or other device) made available by the film maker for use in conjunction with the film.[106]

3.2.2.2 Sound recordings

The next type of subject matter recognised in Part IV is sound recordings.[107] Section 10 defines 'sound recording' to mean the aggregate of the sounds embodied in a record. The word 'record' is used in a special sense to mean a disc, tape, paper or other device in which sounds are embodied. Sounds are considered to have been embodied in a record if the sounds are capable of being reproduced from it.[108] As such, it would cover MP3 audio and the now older

---

101 A similar approach was taken by the Full Federal Court (at least on this issue) in *Burge v Swarbrick*, when it noted that 'craftsmanship should not be limited to handicraft: the word "artistic" is not incompatible with machine production': (2005) 149 FCR 193, [55]. See also *Sheldon & Hammond Pty Ltd v Metrokane Inc* (2004) 135 FCR 34.
102 Ibid [52]. *Copyright Act 1968* (Cth) s 24. On the scope of the provision see *TCN Channel Nine Pty Ltd v Network Ten Pty Ltd* (2002) 118 FCR 417, 444–5. See also the discussion of the meaning of 'embodied' in *Seven Network Ltd v Commissioner of Taxation* (2014) 109 IPR 520, where it was held that there was no embodiment of an aggregate of visual images in the data signal since no visual image or sounds were capable of being reproduced from it.
103 (1996) 69 FCR 268.
104 For the relationship between copyright in pt III works incorporated into films and copyright in the films themselves, see above at 3.2.1.2.
105 *Copyright Act 1968* (Cth) s 23.
106 Ibid s 10(1) (definition of 'sound-track').
107 See *CBS Records Australia v Telmak Teleproducts (Australia) Pty Ltd* (1987) 9 IPR 440; *Australian Tape Manufacturers Association Ltd v Commonwealth* (1993) 176 CLR 480.
108 *Copyright Act 1968* (Cth) s 24. A compact disc is a 'record' for the purposes of the Act, and the original multi-track or 'grand master' recording is a 'record' in which sounds are embodied, whether digitally recorded or not: *Polygram Records Inc v Raben Footwear Pty Ltd* (1996) 35 IPR 426.

technologies of CDs, records, tapes and so on. The protection of copyright in a sound recording is a recognition of the skill needed to capture musical works (or sounds) in a more permanent format.

3.2.2.3 Broadcasts

A 'broadcast' is defined as a communication to the public[109] delivered by a broadcasting service within the meaning of the *Broadcasting Services Act 1992* (Cth).[110] A broadcast includes either a television or radio broadcast. Unlike all other subject matter in copyright, there is no requirement that a broadcast be in a material form for it to qualify for protection. As with the other types of subject matter recognised in Part IV, broadcast copyright is recognition of the (often) considerable investment needed to make television and radio broadcasts. Here, the focus of the law is less on the creation of the copyright material and more on the development of ways to encourage its dissemination.

The meaning and scope of a broadcast was examined in detail in *TCN Channel Nine v Network Ten* (the *Panel* decision).[111] The facts of this case were as follows. Channel Nine alleged that Channel Ten had infringed its copyright in a television broadcast by replaying extracts (ranging from eight to forty-two seconds) from a number of Channel Nine programs on the Channel Ten show *The Panel*. The show involved a number of personalities discussing and critiquing current events, including clips from other television programs. At trial, a single judge of the Federal Court, Conti J, found in favour of Channel Ten.[112] The Full Federal Court upheld the appeal by Channel Nine and found, interestingly, that copyright would be infringed whenever any single image contained within a television broadcast was reproduced, regardless of whether that image was a substantial part of the broadcast.[113] This decision was in contrast to the level of protection that is given to all other types of subject matter, where, for an infringement to take place, the whole or a substantial part of a work needs to be taken. On appeal, the High Court rejected the Full Federal Court's approach, holding that separate copyright did not subsist in each of the visual signals transmitted by a television broadcast.[114] The Full Court's approach would have given broadcasters a 'privileged position' compared to other copyright owners.[115] The High Court held that while 'there can be no absolute precision as to what if any of an infinite possibility of circumstances will constitute a television

---

109 The general public or part of the public: *Copyright Act 1968* (Cth) s 10(1) (definition of 'sound-track').
110 *Copyright Act 1968* (Cth) s 10(1) (definition of 'broadcast'). A broadcasting service does not include a service (for example, a tele-text service) that provides only data or only text, with or without associated images, or a service that makes programs available on demand on a point-to-point basis (for example, transmissions intended for a particular recipient).
111 See *Network Ten Pty Ltd v TCN Channel Nine Pty Ltd* (2004) 218 CLR 273, overturning the Full Federal Court decision in *TCN Channel Nine Pty Ltd v Network Ten Pty Ltd* (2002) 118 FCR 417 that had held that copyright in a television broadcast relates to each and every single visual image as a discrete subject matter. See M. de Zwart, 'The *Panel* case' in A. Kenyon, M. Richardson and S. Ricketson (eds), *Landmarks in Australian Intellectual Property Law* (Melbourne: Cambridge University Press, 2009) ch 15.
112 *TCN Channel Nine Pty Ltd v Network Ten Pty Ltd* (2001) 108 FCR 235, which dealt with the issue of infringement of individual images comprising the excerpts from the various Channel Nine broadcasts (*Copyright Act 1968* (Cth) s 87(a)).
113 *TCN Channel Nine Pty Ltd v Network Ten Pty Ltd* (2002) 118 FCR 417.
114 *Network Ten Pty Ltd v TCN Channel Nine Pty Ltd* (2004) 218 CLR 273.
115 Ibid 278.

broadcast', the television programs (such as *Today Show* and *Nightline*) would attract separate broadcast copyright. This was because they were put out to the public and were discrete periods of broadcasting. The court also noted that while a prime-time news television broadcast may consist of a number of stories, items or segments, this does not necessarily mean that each of these constitutes a television broadcast.[116] As Channel Ten raised a defence of fair dealing in relation to use of the extracted program, the *Panel* decision also provided a useful examination of the defence of fair dealing (discussed in chapter 5).[117]

3.2.2.4 Published editions

The final category of subject matter recognised in Part IV of the *Copyright Act 1968* (Cth) is 'published editions'.[118] A published edition of a literary, dramatic, musical or artistic work refers to the typographical arrangement – that is, the layout and formatting of the printed pages as published. Published edition copyright recognises the labour, skill and effort that are invested in the layout of published works.[119] Published edition copyright is distinct from copyright in the material that is being typeset. This means, for example, that a newspaper article may consist of both copyright in the literary work and published edition copyright in the way that the article is set out and organised.

3.3 Recorded in material form

The next requirement that must be satisfied for a work to qualify for copyright protection is that the work must be recorded in material form. It is important to note that this requirement only applies to literary, dramatic, musical and artistic works. For copyright to subsist in literary, dramatic, musical and artistic works, there must be some physical embodiment of the creation. As the *Copyright Act 1968* (Cth) provides, a 'work' must exist in a material form before copyright can subsist in it.[120] Section 22(1) of the Act provides that a literary, dramatic, musical or artistic work is made when it is first reduced 'to writing or some other material form'.[121] In this context, writing means a 'mode of reproducing or representing words, figures or symbols in a visible form'.[122] In turn, 'material form' is defined in s 10 of the Act to include

---

116 Ibid.
117 See M. Handler and D. Rolph, '"A real pea-souper": The *Panel* case and the development of the fair dealing defences to copyright infringement in Australia' (2003) 27 *Melbourne University Law Review* 381, 395; de Zwart, 'The *Panel* case', above n 111, 233.
118 See J. Bannister, 'Published edition copyright: A "rather curious copyright" in an age of electronic publishing' (1997) 15 *Copyright Reporter* 22.
119 Accounting software that was not produced by a 'photographic process' was held not to be a published edition: *Cortis Exhaust Systems Pty Ltd v Kitten Software Pty Ltd* (2001) ATPR 41-837. On the scope of published edition copyright, see *Nationwide News Pty Ltd v Copyright Agency Ltd* (1996) 65 FCR 399.
120 *Copyright Act 1968* (Cth) ss 32, 35.
121 In *Statuscard Australia Pty Ltd v Rotondo* [2009] 1 Qd R 559, [89] it was noted: '[T]here is, I think, a real question whether something as evanescent as a computer screen display can be a work for the purposes of the [Copyright] Act.'
122 *Copyright Act 1968* (Cth) s 10(1) (definition of 'writing').

in relation to a work or an adaptation of a work ... any form (whether visible or not) of storage of the work or adaptation, or a substantial part of the work or adaptation (whether or not the work or adaptation, or a substantial part of the work or adaptation, can be reproduced).[123]

The requirement that literary, dramatic, musical and artistic works need to be reduced to material form often poses particular problems for Aboriginal and Torres Strait Islander cultures to the extent that creations such as stories and songs remain in an oral form. Hence, no copyright protection is afforded unless the knowledge is recorded into some material form.

3.4 Connected to Australia

In order for copyright protection to subsist in a work, or in subject matter other than a work, the work or subject matter must be sufficiently connected to Australia. This requirement, which is often known as the requirement of qualification, applies to all types of subject matter recognised under the *Copyright Act 1968* (Cth). It is important to note that the principle of reciprocity, which was mentioned in chapter 2, means that Australian copyright law treats foreign works as it does Australian works.[124] In these cases, the fact that a work is protected in a foreign *Berne Convention*[125] country means that it will qualify for protection in Australia. The upshot of this is that the requirement of connection to Australia only applies to works that are first protected in Australia, which will then, via the principle of reciprocity, be automatically protected in other *Berne Convention* countries.

In practice, there are a number of different ways in which a work or subject matter other than a work can qualify for protection in Australia. These vary depending on the type of subject matter in question. They also differ depending on whether the work is published or unpublished.

The criteria that need to be satisfied for *literary, dramatic, musical* and *artistic* works differ depending on whether the works have been published. In this context, a work is published if 'reproduction of the work or edition has been supplied or otherwise to the public'.[126] After the commencement of the *Copyright Amendment (Disability Access and Other Measures) Act 2017* (Cth) on 1 January 2019, a new s 29A definition of 'made public' was inserted into the *Copyright Act 1968* (Cth). This ensures that a broader range of public uses will be included under publication and this then applies to the period of duration of copyright. Publications that are 'not intended to satisfy the reasonable requirements of the public' are not considered to be publications.[127] Copyright will subsist in an unpublished literary, dramatic, musical or artistic work if the author of the work (a) was a qualified person at the time when the work was made,

---

123 The definition was amended as a result of the *US Free Trade Agreement Implementation Act 2004* (Cth).
124 Otherwise known as the principle of national treatment. See ch 2 at 2.4.1.
125 *Berne Convention for the Protection of Literary and Artistic Works*, opened for signature 9 September 1886, WIPO Lex No TRT/BERNE/001 (as amended 28 September 1979, entered into force 19 November 1984).
126 *Copyright Act 1968* (Cth) s 29(1)(a). This is the case with sound recordings as well: at s 29(1)(c). For what constitutes publication of films, see s 29(1)(b).
127 *Copyright Act 1968* (Cth) s 29(4).

or (b) where the making of the work extended over a period of time – was a qualified person for a substantial part of that period.[128] In order for copyright to subsist in a literary, dramatic, musical or artistic work that has been published[129] (publication is given the same meaning as above), it is necessary to be able to show that (a) first publication of the work took place in Australia, (b) the author of the work was a qualified person at the time when the work was first published, or (c) the author died before that time, but was a qualified person immediately before their death.[130] In the case of a work of joint authorship, it is enough if one or more of the authors of the work was a qualified person at the relevant time.[131] A 'qualified person' is defined as an Australian citizen, an Australian protected person or a person resident in Australia.[132]

Copyright is available in a *sound recording* if (a) the maker was a qualified person when the recording was made, (b) the recording was made in Australia, or (c) first publication of the recording took place in Australia.[133] A 'qualified person' for the purpose of determining subsistence of copyright in sound recordings is the maker who is an Australian citizen, an Australian protected person, a person resident in Australia other than a body corporate, or a body corporate incorporated under the law of the Commonwealth or of a state.[134]

Copyright is available in a *cinematograph film* if (a) the maker of the film was a qualified person for at least a substantial part of the period during which the film was made, (b) the film was made in Australia, or (c) first publication of the film took place in Australia.[135] 'Qualified person' is the same as for sound recordings.

Copyright is available in a *television and sound broadcast* made from a place in Australia if it is made by the Australian Broadcasting Corporation or the Special Broadcasting Service, or by the holder of a licence for a television or radio station under the *Broadcasting Services Act 1992* (Cth).[136]

Copyright is available in a *published edition* of a literary, dramatic, musical or artistic work or of two or more literary, dramatic, musical or artistic works if (a) first publication of the edition took place in Australia, or (b) the publisher of the edition was a qualified person at the date of the first publication of the edition.[137] In this context, a 'qualified person' is the publisher of a published edition who is (1) an Australian citizen, (2) a person resident in Australia other than a body corporate, or (3) a body corporate incorporated under the law of the Commonwealth or of a state.[138]

---

128   Ibid s 32(1).
129   Copyright is available in a building as an artistic work if it is situated in Australia or in a country to which the Act applies: *Copyright Act 1968* (Cth) s 32(3)(a).
130   Ibid s 32(2).
131   Ibid s 79.
132   Ibid ss 32(4), 10.
133   Ibid s 89(1)–(3).
134   Ibid s 84.
135   Ibid s 90(1), (3).
136   Ibid s 91(a)–(b).
137   Ibid s 92(1).
138   Ibid s 84.

3.5 'Originality'

The final requirement that a work must satisfy in order to qualify for copyright protection is that it must be 'original'. It is important to note that the originality requirement only applies to literary, dramatic, musical and artistic works.[139] A lower standard – namely, that the work has not been copied – is applied to subject matter other than works (that is, to sound recordings, cinematograph films, sound and television broadcasts, and published editions of works). Each of these requirements will be examined separately.

3.5.1 Original literary, dramatic, musical and artistic works

The requirement that literary, dramatic, musical and artistic works need to be 'original' has attracted a lot of attention in recent years. After some uncertainty, the law in this area has been modified and clarified as a result of the 2009 High Court decision of *IceTV Pty Ltd v Nine Network Australia Pty Ltd*.[140] This was an infringement action brought by the Nine Network against IceTV in relation to television program guides produced by Nine. Nine Network put together a 'Weekly Schedule' of the television programs to be broadcast, which included information about the day, time and title of the programs. Nine provided the Weekly Schedule to specialist organisations (known as 'aggregators') that used the information from Nine, along with information from other television stations, to produce aggregated television guides, which were then published in places such as newspapers and magazines. IceTV produced a subscription-based electronic television program guide, called the 'IceGuide', which included details of the television programs to be broadcast on the Nine Network. The IceGuide was produced in a number of stages. Initially, IceTV employees watched television for three weeks in August 2004 and noted the day, time and title of the programs that had been screened. This information was used to develop a weekly template for the different television stations. Importantly, on legal advice the template was created independently of the aggregated guides to avoid infringement. To ensure that variations in programs were accurate and up to date, and that unexpected changes to the program schedule were included, IceTV compared the data in its template with the information published in the aggregated guides. As a result, the time and title information in the IceGuide was virtually identical to the information in the aggregated television guides.

Nine Network argued that, in producing its guide, IceTV had infringed copyright in Nine's weekly television guides. More specifically, Nine argued that insofar as IceTV reproduced the time and title information included in Nine's Weekly Schedules, IceTV had reproduced a substantial part of the Weekly Schedules and had thus infringed Nine's copyright. At first instance, Bennett J held that as IceTV had not reproduced a substantial part of the Weekly Schedules it had not infringed Nine's copyright.[141] After the Full Federal Court overturned this decision, IceTV appealed to the High Court, which, in two joint judgments,[142] unanimously

---

139   Ibid s 32.
140   (2009) 239 CLR 458.
141   *Nine Network Australia Pty Ltd v IceTV Pty Ltd* (2007) 73 IPR 99.
142   One given by French CJ, Crennan and Kiefel JJ, and the other by Gummow, Hayne and Heydon JJ.

upheld the appeal and held that the IceGuide did not infringe the copyright in Nine's Weekly Schedules. The *IceTV* decision – which is one of the few occasions where the High Court has considered the originality requirement in any detail – is a very important case. The decision is somewhat complicated, however, by the fact that IceTV conceded that copyright subsisted in the Weekly Schedules, and argued instead that it had not copied a substantial part of the Weekly Schedules.[143]

In rejecting Nine Network's claim, the High Court made a number of comments pertaining to originality. While the High Court's discussion of originality was primarily in relation to infringement, nonetheless these remarks are also relevant in the context of subsistence of copyright. The first, which builds on the idea that 'authorship' and 'original work' are correlatives,[144] is that originality requires that the work should have *originated* with the author and that it was not merely copied from another work'.[145] This meant that for a work to be original, it was necessary to show that an author had exercised some control over the resulting work.[146] The High Court stressed that while the creation of the work requires some independent intellectual effort, it does not require literary merit, novelty or inventiveness (as in patent law).[147] On the facts before them, the High Court judges said that as the time and title information were limited forms of expression, which could only be expressed in a small number of ways, they lacked the requisite originality for it to constitute a substantial part of the Weekly Schedule: 'The authors of the Weekly Schedule had little if any choice in the particular form adopted, as the expression was essentially dictated by the nature of the information. That expression lacks the requisite originality.'[148]

The High Court also stressed that the focus of an originality inquiry should be on the form or expression that the work takes, rather than on the activities that precede the expression. The skill and labour of Nine's employees was not 'directed to the originality of the particular form of expression of the time and title information. The level of skill and labour required to express the time and title information was minimal'.[149] Although IceTV had appropriated the skill and labour that Nine Network had invested in compiling the Weekly Schedules, as Gummow, Hayne and Heydon JJ stressed, this did not mean that IceTV had infringed Nine's copyright.

While the High Court was limited in the extent to which it could discuss originality as a requirement for substantiality, nonetheless the ramifications of the High Court decision in *IceTV* for the originality inquiry have become much clearer as a result of the Full Federal Court

---

143 The discussion of originality is made all the more problematic because it is largely discussed through the lens of the 'author' and the concept of 'authorship,' which, as French CJ, Crennan and Kiefel JJ said, were central to copyright: Ice TV v Nine Network Australia (2009) 239 CLR 458, [22]. Like the 2009 *Infopaq* decision in the European Court of Justice, the High Court decision marks a return to the author and all that is beneficial and problematic about this concept. See *Infopaq International A/S v Danske Dagblades Forening* (Case C-5/08) [2009] ECDR 16.
144 *IceTV v Nine Network Australia* (2009) 239 CLR 458, 474 [34] (French CJ, Crennan and Kiefel JJ).
145 Ibid 474 [33] (French CJ, Crennan and Kiefel JJ) (emphasis in original).
146 See also *Cummins v Bond* [1927] 1 Ch 167, where the court held that the plaintiff was the author of the chronicle as she was more than a conduit and she had exercised skill in reproducing the communications.
147 *IceTV v Nine Network Australia* (2009) 239 CLR 458, 474 [33] (French CJ, Crennan and Kiefel JJ).
148 Ibid 477 [42] (French CJ, Crennan and Kiefel JJ). The form of the expression 'was essentially dictated by the nature of that information': 481 [54] (French CJ, Crennan and Kiefel JJ).
149 Ibid 481 [54] (French CJ, Crennan and Kiefel JJ).

decision in *Telstra Corp Ltd v Phone Directories Co Pty Ltd*.[150] This was an infringement action brought by Telstra against the Phone Directories Company in relation to the white pages and yellow pages telephone directories produced by Telstra. The directories listed the names, addresses, telephone numbers and other information for residential and business customers in specific geographic locations in Australia. The key issue in the appeal was whether Telstra's directories were original and protected by copyright.

As Perram J in the Full Court said, the production of the telephone directories occurred in three phases. The first, so-called, collection phase involved the maintenance, updating and editing of a database containing relevant information about customers. In the second 'extraction phase', information was extracted from the database and automatically placed in the relevant directory. The third 'production phase' involved the typesetting of the form of the directories and the physical production of the directories. Telstra argued that its employees had applied independent intellectual effort at 'every stage of the process of compilation', including the process of gathering and organising the collection of material ('the collection phase'), and in ordering and arranging the fixation or settlement of the directories in a material form ('the extraction phase'). The Full Federal Court rejected Telstra's claim and held that the telephone directories were not original and thus not protected by copyright.

While the court agreed with Telstra that there was intellectual effort in the collection phase, it did not accept that it was the right type of effort. As Perram J said: 'Whatever else might be said of the kinds of efforts required of an author, they must be efforts which result in the material form of the work ... [T]his is because what is protected by the copyright monopoly is the form of a work and not the ideas which presage or prefigure it.'[151] While there may have been a lot of skill and hard work (or sweat of the brow) involved in the steps 'preparatory to the making of the material form of a work', unfortunately that type of labour was 'not what is protected by copyright and [is] relevant only to show that the work is not copied'.[152] As Perram J said:

> Once one accepts [following *IceTV*] that the focus of the copyright is on the creation of the material form by an author it is analytically difficult to identify any role for labour or skill in the collection of material beyond the question posed by the statute, namely, whether the work is 'original' in the sense of not being copied from anywhere else.[153]

Keane CJ summed up the approach of the Full Court in respect to the labour exercised at the collection phase when he said:

> [The] dicta in *IceTV* shift the focus of inquiry away from a concern with the protection of the interests of a party who has contributed labour and expense to the production of a work, to the 'particular form of expression' which is said to constitute an original literary work, and to the requirements of the Act 'that the work originates with an author or joint authors from some independent intellectual effort'.[154]

---

150 (2010) 194 FCR 142.
151 Ibid 754 [104].
152 Ibid. 'It seems unlikely, given the context, that [Gummow, Hayne and Heydon JJ] intended that gathering and organizing the collection of material was, by itself, an authorial activity': at 756 [109] (Perram J).
153 Ibid 757 [112] (Perram J).
154 Ibid [82] (Keane J). 'The reasons of the High Court in *IceTV* authoritatively establish that the focus of attention in relation to subsistence of copyright is not upon a general concern to prevent

The court held that the only type of labour that is relevant when considering whether a work is original is labour that contributes to the material form (expression) of the work in question. While there might be some situations where independent intellectual effort that is directed at some anterior pre-expression activity might be relevant, in this case the court held that the effort involved in collecting information could not confer originality on the directories in question. The intellectual effort exerted in the collection phase was not directed to the creation of the material form of the directories and was therefore irrelevant for the purposes of establishing originality.[155]

In relation to the extraction phase, the court found that as this was the stage where the work was given its form, this was where the originality potentially may have arisen. Unfortunately for Telstra, however, the court held that as the form of the work originated from an automated computerised process, rather than from an individual or group of individuals, the directories were not original.[156] The court found that the directories were not original because they were 'compiled not by individuals engaged to facilitate the process, but by a computerized process of storing, selecting, ordering and arranging the data to produce the directories in the form in which they were produced'.[157] While the issue was not discussed, it seems that the telling factor here was that none of the purported authors of the works in question actually shaped or controlled the form that the works took.[158] As Perram J said:

> Whilst humans were ultimately in control of the software which did reduce the information to a material form, their control was over a process of automation and they did not shape or direct the material form themselves (that process being performed by the software). The directories did not therefore, have an author and copyright cannot subsist in them.[159]

This is reinforced by Perram J's earlier remark that 'had the tasks been attended to manually an original work would have ensued'.[160]

---

misappropriation of skill and labour but upon the protection of copyright in literary works which originate from individuals': ibid 752 [96] (Keane CJ).
155   Ibid 753 [101] ff (Perram J).
156   Ibid 751 [90] (Keane J), 769 [169] (Yates J).
157   Ibid 727 [7] (Keane J). The human input involved in the directories' creation was found to be of a relatively trivial nature and ancillary to the actual creation of the directories.
158   Where a work has been generated by a large number of authors, 'identification by name of each and every author is not necessary in order to make out a claim that copyright subsists under s 32(2)(c): what is necessary, however, is that it be shown that the work in question originates from an individual author or authors': at 743 [57] (Keane CJ), see also Yates J at 761–2 [127]. Compare *Fairfax Media Publications Pty Ltd v Reed International Books Australia Pty Ltd* (2010) 189 FCR 109; *Primary Health Care Ltd v Commissioner of Taxation* (2010) 186 FCR 301, [125] (where Stone J noted that it is 'necessary for the author of each work to be identified').
159   *Telstra Corp Ltd v Phone Directories Co* (2010) 273 ALR 725, 759–60 [119].
160   Ibid 757 [113] (Perram J): 'I have no doubt if the galley file (or some physical analogue of it) had been generated by humans this would have meant that the directories were original works. Since the Act stipulates that compilations are literary works it follows generally that those who reduce a compilation to material form are likely to be its authors provided there is sufficient intellectual or literary effort involved in the process of reduction'.

Similar reasoning was adopted in relation to the production phase of the directories. In particular, as the process of organising the layout of the directories was dictated by the nature of the work in question, the court held that the effort involved in the production phase was not sufficient for the work to be original. A key factor here was that the independent human intellectual effort of a literary nature was missing.

There are a number of observations that can be made about *IceTV* and *Telstra* and the impact that they have had on originality in Australian copyright law. The first is that, when considering whether a work is original, the only intellectual effort that is relevant is the effort that contributes to the material form of the work.[161] No matter how much effort, skill or expense goes into preliminary steps, this effort cannot confer originality on a work. In many ways this simply reaffirms a key principle of copyright law – namely, that protection is granted for the expression of ideas and not for the ideas themselves, or for the effort that goes into formulating those ideas.[162] This was reflected in the judgment of Peterson J in *University of London Press Ltd v University Tutorial Press Ltd*[163] where the English court held that mathematics examination papers were original even though they were made up of information that was 'stock of knowledge' common to people in the field. As Peterson J said, copyright law 'does not require that the expression must be in a creative or novel form, but that the work must not be copied from another work – that it should originate from the author'.[164] The upshot of this is that if it can be shown that a work originates from an author in the sense that it is the result of their skill and labour and is not copied from another, then the resulting work will be original for purposes of copyright law.[165] The application of this general idea can be seen in the 1917 Australian High Court decision of *Sands & McDougall Pty Ltd v Robinson*,[166] where the plaintiffs alleged infringement of copyright in a map of Europe they had produced. The High Court held that there was nothing novel about the drawing of a map of Europe: the outline sizes were part of the common stock of information in Australia. Nevertheless, the High Court said that the plaintiffs had applied sufficient skill, labour and judgment to produce a map that presented as a whole and in specific parts distinct differences from other existing maps. As such it was an 'original work' within the meaning of the *Copyright Act 1968* (Cth).[167]

---

161 One of the consequences of this is that the 2010 Full Federal Court decision in *Telstra Corp Ltd v Phone Directories Co Pty Ltd* (2010) 194 FCR 142 effectively overruled *Desktop Marketing Systems Pty Ltd v Telstra Corp Ltd* (2002) 119 FCR 491 (at least on this point).

162 This is a version of the so-called idea–expression dichotomy, which provides that mere ideas are not protected by copyright. See *Green v Broadcasting Corporation of New Zealand* [1989] 3 NZLR 18 (PC), a case discussed above at 3.2.1.2. Hughie Green was a longstanding host of the British talent quest television show *Opportunity Knocks*. The salient features of the show were the use of a 'clapometer' to capture audience claps, and catchphrases to address the audience and competitors. The show was replicated in New Zealand with a different host. Green claimed copyright in the title and format of the show and the catchphrases. The Privy Council held that the phrases were hackneyed expressions and that the ideas of the program were not protected by copyright.

163 [1916] 2 Ch 601, 608–10.

164 Ibid.

165 See *Sands & McDougall Pty Ltd v Robinson* (1917) 23 CLR 49. Compare *Cortis Exhaust Systems Pty Ltd v Kitten Software Pty Ltd* (2001) ATPR 41-837 [31]–[33] (holding that a simple logo, SIM, 'written in a digital style', was trivial and non-original and therefore did not attract copyright).

166 (1917) 23 CLR 49.

167 In *Walter v Lane* [1900] AC 539, the House of Lords held that journalists who took down speeches in shorthand and then transcribed them were not mere scribes, but had exercised enough effort to qualify as the authors of the copyright works.

The decisions in *IceTV* and *Telstra* that the only intellectual effort that can confer originality on a work is effort that contributes to the material form of the work, has important ramifications for businesses that specialise in information storage and retrieval.[168] Historically, one area where special problems have arisen is in relation to tables and compilations.[169] Section 10 of the *Copyright Act 1968* (Cth) makes it clear that tables and compilations expressed in words, figures or symbols as well as compilations of computer programs are literary works. Here, the main question is whether the skill, labour and effort involved in the creation of a table or compilation are sufficient to give rise to an *original* literary work. It is important to note that the requisite skill, labour and effort potentially arise in both the way that the material is collected and the way the resulting information is organised. Following the decisions in *IceTV* and *Telstra*, and contrary to the 2002 Federal Court decision in *Desktop Marketing Systems v Telstra*,[170] the exercise of skill, labour and effort in the preparation of tables and compilations will not be sufficient to give rise to an original work.[171]

The second point to draw from *IceTV* and *Telstra* is that for a person to confer originality on a work, it is necessary for them to have some control or input over the form of the resulting work. That is, there must be some contribution by way of skill, labour and effort from the author that is sufficient to warrant copyright protection.[172] Thus, where a telephone directory or a source code was automatically generated by computer program,[173] or a newspaper headline merely repeated a phrase from the body of the text,[174] the work in question was held to be non-original. One of the notable things about most of the post-*IceTV* decisions is that they have dealt with the straightforward situation where the would-be author has not exercised any real control or influence over the form (or expression) of the work. What they share in common is the fact that the form of the work has been shaped by some 'external' factors. In these situations, it is clear that the would-be 'author' has not exercised any influence over the work in question.

---

167 In *Walter v Lane* [1900] AC 539, the House of Lords held that journalists who took down speeches in shorthand and then transcribed them were not mere scribes, but had exercised enough effort to qualify as the authors of the copyright works.
168 See also, in the United States, *Feist Publications v Rural Telephone Service Co Inc*, 499 US 340 (1991) (white pages telephone directory was denied copyright protection because it was not original).
169 *Kalamazoo (Australia) Pty Ltd v Compact Business Systems Pty Ltd* (1985) 5 IPR 213.
170 (2002) 119 FCR 491 (Telstra's telephone directories, both the white and yellow pages, were original works protected by copyright). Distinguished and partly overturned in *IceTV Pty Ltd v Nine Network Australia Pty Ltd* (2009) 239 CLR 458; *Telstra Corp Ltd v Phone Directories Co Pty Ltd* (2010) 194 FCR 142.
171 The United States Supreme Court decision that held there was insufficient originality in telephone directories: *Feist Publications v Rural Telephone Service Co Inc*, 499 US 340 (1991).
172 It 'is necessary that labour, skill and capital should be expended sufficiently to impart to the product some quality or character which the raw material did not possess, and which differentiates the product from the raw materials': *Macmillan & Co Ltd v Cooper* (1924) 40 TLR 186, 188, 190 (Lord Atkinson).
173 *Acohs Pty Ltd v Ucorp Pty Ltd* (2010) 86 IPR 492, [50]: 'The problem is ... that the source code as a work – ie, as a complete entity – was not written by any single human author. It was generated by a computer program.'
174 'A headline that does no more than repeat a phrase from the article is not an original literary work': *Fairfax Media Publications Pty Ltd v Reed International Books Australia Pty Ltd* (2010) 189 FCR 109, 131.

While this much is clear, what is less clear is whether there are any limits on the type or level of effort that needs to be exerted on the material form of the work in question for that work to be original. It is unclear, for example, whether there is a *de minimus* level of creativity needed to establish originality. There is no guidance as to exactly how much skill, labour or effort is required for a creation to be considered an original work.[175] Given that authorship is synonymous with originality, and that the focal point of subsistence and infringement actions is the copyright work, it is not much assistance to use the 'author' as a touchstone for originality. One possible answer to this question is that there is no real threshold: any type of 'intellectual effort' will suffice. This is what Keane CJ alluded to in *Telstra* when he said: '[It] may also be accepted that the level of intellectual effort necessary to produce an original literary work is not required to rise to the level of "creativity" or "inventiveness". In determining whether a literary work is original, the focus of consideration is not upon creativity or novelty, but upon the origin of the work in some intellectual effort of the author.'[176] Perram J also seemed to suggest something similar when, in explaining the situations in which a work produced through a computer might be original, he said:

> [A] computer program is a tool and it is natural to think that the author of a work generated by a computer program will ordinarily be the person in control of that program. However care must be taken to ensure that the efforts of that person can be seen as being directed to the reduction of a work into a material form. Software comes in a variety of forms and the tasks performed by it range from the trivial to the substantial. So long as the person controlling the program can be seen as directing or fashioning the material form of the work there is no particular danger in viewing that person as the work's author.[177]

Where some skill is exercised in the reduction of the work into writing, or in the creation of the dramatic, musical or artistic work, it is likely the resulting work will attract copyright protection.[178] A pre-*IceTV* situation where minimal skill and labour gave rise to copyright protection was the decision of *Express Newspapers plc v Liverpool Daily Post & Echo plc*.[179] In this case, a rival newspaper published the plaintiff newspaper's list of winning letters (in a scratch-it game) and it was claimed that the rival's list infringed the plaintiff's copyright. It was held that there was copyright in the list of letters (as the sequence offered some information and instruction to the readers) that had been infringed by the unauthorised reproduction by the rival newspaper.[180] More recently (and adopting *IceTV*) it was held in *Budget Eyewear Australia Pty Ltd v Specsavers Pty Ltd* that while the way a concept was expressed in an advertisement may be

---

175 In *Olympic Amusements Pty Ltd v Milwell Pty Ltd* (1998) 40 IPR 180, 'the boundar[ies] of copyright protection were examined. At what level of meagreness does it become impossible to describe an original composition as a "literary work" within the meaning of the *Copyright Act 1968*?': at 181 (Wilcox J).
176 *Telstra Corp Ltd v Phone Directories Co Pty Ltd* (2010) 194 FCR 142, [58].
177 Ibid [118].
178 Exceptions include a pocket diary, where the selection and arrangement was held to be commonplace and obvious and the degree of skill and judgment involved in the selection was negligible, thus not worthy of copyright protection: *GA Cramp & Sons Ltd v Frank Smythson Ltd* [1944] AC 239.
179 [1985] 3 All ER 680.
180 Ibid 685 (Whitford J).

original, this was not the case with the legal terms and conditions that appeared in the advertisements.[181]

At this stage, it is difficult to predict whether in light of *IceTV* and *Telstra* the courts will impose limits on the type or level of effort that needs to be exerted on the material form of the work in question for that work to be original. If they do impose some type of qualitative limitation on the type of labour that can be used to confer form on a work, it will serve to limit, even further, the types of works that can be protected by copyright. Even if this does not occur, it seems clear that the decision to exclude effort that is not addressed to the form of the work (such as the collection of data) has important ramifications for many information-based industries. Given the current approach of the courts on this matter, it seems that the only possible remedy to this situation is legislative reform.[182]

3.5.2 Subject matter other than works

As explained above,[183] it is not necessary to show that Part IV subject matter is original. Instead, all that needs to be established is that the film,[184] sound recording,[185] broadcast[186] or published edition[187] is not copied from another film, sound recording, broadcast or published edition. In part, the lower threshold can be explained by the fact that the scope of protection for Part IV subject matter is much more restricted in nature than the protection available to literary, dramatic, artistic and musical works.

---

181   (2010) 86 IPR 479, [17]–[18]. The courts may now be more inclined to afford copyright protection to advertising copy to recognise that such material may require creative activity of a higher order. See also *Primary Health Care Ltd v Commissioner of Taxation* (2010) 186 FCR 301, where medical expertise used in writing notes on patients was held to lie 'behind the formulation of the idea; it is not, however, directed to the expression of the idea': at [38]. On this basis it was held that prescription and health summaries were not original (at [135]), while letters that referred patients to specialists were: at [136].
182   *Telstra Corp Ltd v Phone Directories Co Pty Ltd* (2010) 194 FCR 142, [97].
183   At 3.5.1.
184   *Copyright Act 1968* (Cth) s 90. The making of a cinematograph film means the doing of the things necessary for the production of the *first* copy of the 'film'.
185   *Copyright Act 1968* (Cth) s 89 provides that copyright subsists in a sound recording of which the maker was a qualified person at the time when the recording was made or if the sound recording was made in Australia. A sound recording, for example, is deemed to be made at the time when the *first* record embodying the recording is produced: at s 22(3)(a).
186   *Copyright Act 1968* (Cth) s 91. If a television or radio broadcast is recorded and a further broadcast is made from that recording, no additional copyright protection is conferred on the broadcaster. Copyright will subsist in a completely new broadcast whether or not the material broadcast is the same as that contained in the previous broadcast: s 95(2).
187   Copyright only subsists in a published edition of a work if the edition does not reproduce a previous edition of that work: *Copyright Act 1968* (Cth) s 92.

4

COPYRIGHT: AUTHORSHIP, FIRST OWNERSHIP, AND NATURE AND DURATION OF RIGHTS

4.1 Introduction

This chapter looks at one of the key notions within copyright law – namely, the idea of the 'author'. As we will see, while authorship carries with it certain consequences, including the right to first ownership of copyright, there are a number of exceptions to this general rule. This chapter also looks at the nature and duration of the rights that are given to the copyright owner.

4.2 'Authorship' and first ownership

One of the notable differences between common law copyright systems (such as those in Australia, New Zealand, the United Kingdom and Canada) and the *droit d'auteur* systems of many European countries, concerns the prominence which the latter systems give to the 'author' as creator of copyright works. Despite this, the author has long played a pivotal role in common law copyright systems. It has also been suggested that the modern idea of the author was effectively invented by British publishing houses in the eighteenth century in their attempt to have the courts recognise perpetual copyright protection.[1] The key role given to the author in Australian copyright law is reflected in the fact that copyright law uses the author as the focus or fulcrum point for many rules. For example, the period of protection given to a copyright work is based on the life of the author.[2] In turn, the fact that an author is connected to Australia helps determine whether the copyright work qualifies for protection,[3] and the moral rights associated with a copyright work attach to the author.[4] Perhaps most importantly, the author is treated as the first owner of copyright in a work.[5]

While the author plays a central role in relation to literary, dramatic, musical and artistic works, this is not the case with films, sound recordings, broadcasts and published editions ('Part IV subject matter'), where the law is more concerned with ensuring that a work is distributed to the public, than with the creation of the work in the first place. In the case of Part IV works, the law is more concerned with the person who made the creation of the work possible in the first place (often through some financial arrangement) than with the person who actually created the work. This is reflected in the fact that with films, sound recordings and broadcasts, initial ownership of the copyright is given to the *maker* rather than the creator of the relevant Part IV work. It is also reflected in the fact that with published editions the initial owner of any copyright is the *publisher* of the edition. The copyright in Part IV works is separate from, and additional to, any copyright subsisting in the underlying Part III copyright work that is recorded, filmed or broadcast, or published in the form of an edition.[6]

---

1 M. Rose, *Authors and Owners: The Invention of Copyright* (Cambridge, MA: Harvard University Press, 1993).
2 *Copyright Act 1968* (Cth) s 33(2).
3 Ibid s 32(4).
4 Ibid pt IX (ss 189–195AZG).
5 Ibid s 35(2).
6 See ibid s 98 in relation to the first owner of a film, s 97 in relation to sound recordings and s 99 in relation to broadcasts. The publisher is the first owner of a published edition: at s 100.

4.2.1 Who is the author?

4.2.1.1 Literary, dramatic, musical and artistic works

Despite the central role that authorship plays in copyright law, the *Copyright Act 1968* (Cth) does not define who is an author.[7] In most cases, it is relatively easy to determine who is the author of a literary, dramatic, musical or artistic work. It has been suggested that an author is the person who originates the particular form of literary, dramatic, musical or artistic expression.[8] Usually the author will have to show that they expended skill, labour and effort in creating the work in its material form.[9] A mere scribe, amanuensis, copier or transcriber of a work will not be treated as an author.[10] This is because there is insufficient skill, labour or effort that has resulted in the change in the original work.[11] Merely contributing ideas in the process of creating a work will not entitle a person to be treated as an author.[12]

4.2.1.2 Cinematograph films

The 'maker' of a film is the person (including a corporation) who undertakes the arrangements for the production of the film.[13] The maker is usually the investor who makes the creation of the film, broadcast or published edition possible; that is, the producer and not the director will be initial owner of copyright in the film.[14] The directors, actors and others involved in the making of the film have no copyright interests in the film unless they are a 'maker' of the film.

4.2.1.3 Sound recordings

The initial owner of any copyright in a sound recording (other than a sound recording of a live performance) is the maker of the sound recording.[15] The maker of a sound recording (other than a sound recording of a live performance) is the person who owned the first record of the sound recording.[16] A 'record' is defined as the disc, tape, paper or other device in which the sounds are embodied, and the 'sound recording' is defined as the aggregate of the sounds embodied in a 'record'.[17] The maker and therefore the initial owner is the person who owns the master tape at the time the recording is made. The maker of sound recordings of a *live*

---

[7] With the exception of photographs, where the author is defined as the person who took the photograph: *Copyright Act 1968* (Cth) s 10(1) (definition of 'author').
[8] Isaacs J in *Sands & McDougall Pty Ltd v Robinson* (1917) 23 CLR 49, 55, stated: '[I]n copyright law the two expressions "author" and "original work" have always been correlative; the one connotes the other, and there is no indication in the Act that the Legislature intended to depart from the accepted signification of the words as applied to the subject matter.'
[9] *Ladbroke (Football) Ltd v William Hill (Football) Ltd* [1964] 1 WLR 273, 277–8 (Lord Reid).
[10] See W. van Caenegem, *Intellectual Property* (2nd edn, Sydney: LexisNexis Butterworths, 2006) 45. Compare *Walter v Lane* [1901870] AC 539.
[11] This can be contrasted with the decision of *Cummins v Bond* [1927] 1 Ch 167, where the spiritualist and medium who reduced spirits and communications in an unknown tongue into archaic English language was held to be an author as she was more than a mere conduit and because she had exercised some skill in reproducing the communications.
[12] *Donoghue v Allied Newspapers Ltd* [1938] Ch 106.
[13] *Copyright Act 1968* (Cth) s 98(1), (2) (subject to any assignment or Crown copyright).
[14] Ibid s 22(4).
[15] Ibid s 97(1), (2) (subject to any assignment or Crown copyright).
[16] Ibid s 22(3).
[17] Ibid s 10(1) (definitions of 'record' and 'sound recording').

performance is the person who owns the record on which the first recording was made and the performer(s) who performed the performance unless that is also the person who owns the first recording.[18]

4.2.1.4 Broadcasts

The initial owner of any copyright in a radio or television broadcast[19] is the maker of the broadcast – namely the Australian Broadcasting Corporation, the Special Broadcasting Service or a person who has a television or radio licence or a radio-communications licence.[20] The maker of a broadcast is the person who provided the broadcasting service.[21]

4.2.1.5 Published editions

The initial owner of any copyright in an edition of a work is the publisher of the edition.[22]

4.2.2 Joint authorship

In recognition of the fact that many works are created through a collaborative process involving two or more authors, the *Copyright Act 1968* (Cth) provides for 'joint authorship'.[23] A 'work of joint authorship' is defined in s 10(1) as a work that has been produced by the collaboration of two or more authors and in which the contribution of each author is not separate from the contribution of the other author(s).[24]

Each party must contribute to the joint work as an 'author'. Thus, a person who merely supplies ideas or facts to another person who is creating the work is not a joint author.[25] Similarly, a person who supplies an artistic idea to an artist who then creates a work is not, on that ground alone, a joint author with the artist.[26] The contribution of each author must not be distinct or separable from that of the others.[27] If one author's contribution can be separately identified, the work will be treated as separately authored works rather than as a co-authored

---

18 Ibid s 22(3A). Special provisions ensure that parties who owned copyright in sound recordings prior to 1 January 2005 either are able to continue to exercise their rights as they had done previously (s 100AF) or will receive appropriate compensation for their losses: at s 116AAA.
19 A 'broadcast' is defined as a communication to the public delivered by a broadcasting service within the meaning of the *Broadcasting Services Act 1992* (Cth): *Copyright Act 1968* (Cth) s 10(1) (definition of 'broadcast').
20 *Copyright Act 1968* (Cth) s 99 (subject to any assignment or Crown copyright).
21 Ibid s 22(5).
22 Ibid s 100 (subject to any assignment or Crown copyright).
23 T. Lauterbach, 'Joint authorship in a copyright work revisited' (2005) 3 *European Intellectual Property Review* 119–21; L. Longding, 'Collaborative authorship of distance learning materials: Cross-border copyright and moral rights problems' (2005) *European Intellectual Property Review* 1.
24 For a general discussion of joint authorship, see *Milwell Pty Ltd v Olympic Amusements Pty Ltd* (1999) 85 FCR 436, [32]–[33]. A reference to the 'author' of a work in the *Copyright Act* is to be read as a reference to all the authors of a joint work: *Copyright Act 1968* (Cth) s 78.
25 See *Donoghue v Allied Newspapers Ltd* [1938] Ch 106; *Kenrick & Co v Lawrence & Co* (1890) 25 QBD 99.
26 *Kenrick & Co v Lawrence & Co* (1890) 25 QBD 99.
27 See *Career Step LLC v TalentMed Pty Ltd (No 2)* [2018] FCA 132, where the Federal Court highlighted a number of important questions to be considered when making an assessment as to whether a copyright work is the product of joint authorship. It focused on the definition of the copyright work in question (which is directly relevant to identifying the author of the work) and the possibility of identifying separate contributions of different authors.

work. For example, if in a co-authored book of twelve chapters each author contributes six chapters, the contribution is separable and distinguishable; this is not the case if the authors write all the chapters jointly and correct and edit them.[28]

There was an attempt to expand the notion of joint ownership in the decision of *Bulun Bulun v R & T Textiles Pty Ltd*.[29] In that case, the issue arose as to whether the courts should recognise communal ownership of copyright in Aboriginal traditional ritual knowledge and, in particular, Aboriginal artwork. Von Doussa J held that while the *Copyright Act 1968* (Cth) recognised joint authorship, it provided no grounds for recognising communal ownership as was being suggested in this case. It was held that the artist, Johnny Bulun Bulun, owed a fiduciary obligation to his communal group, the Ganalbingu people, meaning that if he failed to bring a copyright infringement action (which he had) the elders of his community, as beneficiaries, would have been able to bring an action in their own name against the infringer. As Bulun Bulun had fulfilled his obligation and brought an action, there was no basis for finding that the Ganalbingu people had an equitable interest in the work.[30]

4.2.3 Orphan works

In some situations, it is not possible to determine who the author of a work is. This may be because there is no attribution of the author on the work or the work was published anonymously or under a false name or a pseudonym. In the United States and now Australia, the term 'orphan works' is used to describe works where the owner is unknown or untraceable.[31] Orphan works raise a number of difficult issues for copyright users. This is largely because, with no known author, the period of protection is difficult to ascertain. Orphan works also create problems where a person wants to use a copyright work and is willing to pay a licence fee, but is unable to determine from whom they should seek the relevant permissions. The difficulties encountered when using orphan works have been well documented in a number of copyright reform reviews.[32] Given the amount of time and money that is spent, particularly by institutional users such as libraries and educational institutions, in trying to obtain permission to use orphan works, in February 2006 the Attorney-General's Department

---

28 *Redwood Music Ltd v B Feldman & Co Ltd* [1979] RPC 1, 385.
29 (1998) 41 IPR 513.
30 Ibid 531.
31 In January 2006, the United States Copyright Office released a report on orphan works. The report was submitted to the Senate Judiciary Committee on 31 January 2007. In April 2008, the United States Congress considered two Bills: the Orphan Works Act of 2008 (Bill No HR 5889) and the Shawn Bentley Orphan Works Act of 2008 (Bill No S 2913). These were intended to limit the consequences of using orphan works without permission. Neither Bill passed both the Senate or House of Representatives to become law. See Australian Copyright Council, 'Orphan Works: Proposed Changes in the US and Issues for Australia' (Information Sheet G 101 v 03, December 2008). See also D. Kravets, '"Orphan works" copyright law dies quiet death', *Wired* (30 September 2008) www.wired.com.
32 See, for example, the issues that were raised in relation to orphan works in the Attorney-General's review of fair use and also the *Australia–US Free Trade Agreement 2004* (*AUSFTA*) discussions, particularly by institutional users such as libraries and universities. See Australian Vice-Chancellors' Committee, Submission to Attorney-General, *Fair Use and Other Copyright Exceptions* (Issues Paper, May 2005); Australian Digital Alliance, Submission to Attorney-General, *Fair Use and Other Copyright Exceptions* (Issues Paper, May 2005); Department of Communications and the Arts, 'Roundtable on Orphan Works' (May 2018).

announced that it would conduct a review into this issue.[33] The Productivity Commission's final report into Australia's intellectual property system, released publicly in December 2016, provided additional support for reform around orphan works.[34]

The *Copyright Amendment (Disability Access and Other Measures) Act 2017* (Cth) made a number of changes to duration of copyright generally, but of particular relevance here is the amendment made to s 33 of the *Copyright Act 1968* (Cth) on duration where the creator of the copyright material cannot be identified.

Put simply, in relation to unpublished works, copyright in works not made public[35] before 1 January 2019 will expire 70 years after the death of the creator, regardless of the date of first publication. Prior to the 2017 amendments, unpublished materials could potentially remain in copyright indefinitely. However, amendments that came into effect in 2019 provide that where the creator of the copyright material cannot be identified, the standard term of protection will be the *date made* plus 70 years. However, if the material is made public within 50 years of its making, copyright will last from the date the material was *first made public* plus 70 years. The Australian Copyright Council has provided some useful examples to illustrate the operation of the amendments:

- if the author cannot be identified, but the work is dated 1980, then copyright will last for 70 years from that date (ie., until 2050); however
- if the author cannot be identified, the work is dated 1980, *but the work is first made public in 2020*, then copyright will last 70 years from the date of being made public (ie., until 2090).[36]

In 2017, the government committed to public consultation on orphan works in the first half of 2018. On 11 May 2018, the Department of Communications and the Arts held a roundtable on orphan works as part of the copyright modernisation review.[37]

4.3 Exceptions to first ownership

As a general rule, the author, maker or publisher is treated as the first owner of the copyright in the resulting creation. This is, however, subject to a number of important exceptions. These relate to works created in the course of employment (in particular, special rules apply to journalists); certain commissioned artistic works; and works created under the direction and control of the Crown.[38] Each exception will be dealt with in turn. It is important to note that these exceptions can be modified or excluded by agreement.[39]

---

33 H. Daniels, presentation to ACIPA Copyright Conference, Brisbane, 17 February 2006.
34 Productivity Commission, *Intellectual Property Arrangements* (Productivity Commission Inquiry Report No 78, September 2016). See ch 2 at 2.3.2.9.
35 For the definition of 'made public', see *Copyright Act 1968* (Cth) s 29A, inserted by the *Copyright Amendment (Disability and Other Measures) Act 2017* (Cth).
36 Australian Copyright Council, 'Duration of Copyright' (Information Sheet G 023 v 19, January 2019) 5 (emphasis in original).
37 Department of Communications and the Arts, 'Roundtable on Orphan Works', above n 32).
38 Arguably, future assignment of copyright (discussed in ch 5) could be seen as another exception.
39 Section 35(3) provides that any of the general rules of ownership set out in s 35 of the *Copyright Act 1968* (Cth) can be excluded or modified by agreement. An assignment of copyright must be in writing to be effective. Assignment is discussed in ch 5.

4.3.1 Works created by employees

Section 35(6) of the *Copyright Act 1968* (Cth) provides that where a literary, dramatic, musical or artistic work is made by 'the author in pursuance of the terms of his or her employment', the employer is owner of the copyright.[40] It is important to note that this provision may be modified by agreement.[41] To determine whether s 35(6) applies, it is necessary to ask two related questions: (1) Is the creator of the work an employee? and (2) Was the work in question created in pursuance of the terms of employment?

4.3.1.1 Who is an employee?

The first question that should be asked when determining whether a work is caught by s 35(6) is whether the creator is an employee. General principles of employment law apply to this question and a number of factors are taken into account to determine the employment status or otherwise of a creator. These include the nature and scope of the creator's duties;[42] how and when the creator is being paid (is tax being deducted from their pay?); the hours of work; and whether there is a provision for holidays.[43] In *Stephenson Jordan & Harrison Ltd v MacDonald & Evans*, Denning LJ considered that a key factor when deciding whether a person is an employee is whether they are an integral part of a business or only an accessory to it.[44] The fact that a creator is being paid for their work does not necessarily mean that they will be treated as an employee for the purposes of s 35(6). In some situations, if a business exercises direction and control as to the manner in which a person carries out their work, it is more likely that they will be treated as an employee (working under a contract *of* service), rather than an independent contractor or consultant (working under a contract *for* service).

However, for employees who exercise a greater amount of skill, the control test becomes less significant. This is because the employer will not always be able to control the manner in which their tasks are performed. This was the case in *Redrock Holdings Pty Ltd v Hinkley*.[45] The defendant, Mr Hinkley, argued that, as he was not an employee of Redrock, he retained copyright in software programs that he had developed. The main reason for this was that he was not subject to Redrock's control and direction. It was held that legal authority to control is no longer the sole determining factor when determining whether a person is an employee, particularly where a person exercises a high degree of professional skill and expertise in the

---

[40] A performance by an employee is taken to have been made by the employer unless modified or excluded by agreement: *Copyright Act 1968* (Cth) s 22(3B), (3C), introduced by *US Free Trade Agreement Implementation Act 2004* (Cth) sch 9 item 2.
[41] *Copyright Act 1968* (Cth) s 35(3).
[42] *Insight SRC IP Holdings Pty Ltd v Australian Council for Educational Research Ltd* (2012) 211 FCR 563.
[43] *Stevens v Brodribb Sawmilling Co Pty Ltd* (1986) 160 CLR 16, 27 (Mason J).
[44] (1952) 69 RPC 10.
[45] (2001) 50 IPR 565. Denning LJ's test in *Redrock Holdings* was referred to in *Stephenson Jordan & Harrison Ltd v MacDonald & Evans* (1952) 69 RPC 10 by Harper J who considered that the defendant had been an integral part of the business. The court in *Redrock Holdings* also held that the following were relevant considerations when determining whether there was an employment relationship: evidence of fixed salary; the deduction of group tax; the completion of an ATO employees declaration form; annual, sick and long service leave entitlements; superannuation contributions; and the provision of tools and equipment. All these pointed towards a contract of service. While Mr Hinkley was held to be the owner of the 'Hotline' computer program, an associated program was held to be owned by his employer.

performance of their duties. In situations such as this, the key question will be whether the creator is being paid to perform specified services rather than being in a position of being able to be asked to perform any number of duties as an employee may be.[46]

4.3.1.2 Was the work created 'in pursuance of the terms of employment'?

Once it has been determined that the work in question has been made by an employee, it is then necessary to ask whether the work was 'made by the author in pursuance of the terms of his or her employment'. As Nettle J said in *Victoria University of Technology v Wilson*, a decision concerned with ownership of patents but which arguably also applies to copyright:

> [T]he mere existence of the employer/employee relationship will not give the employer ownership of inventions made by the employee during the term of the relationship. And that is so even if the invention is germane to and useful for the employer's business. This is also the case even though the employee may have made use of the employer's time and resources in bringing the invention to completion.[47]

Instead, ownership of copyright under s 35(6) turns on whether the work was made in the normal course of employment.

The test for determining whether a work is made in pursuance of the terms of employment is whether the making of the work falls within the types of activity that an employer could reasonably expect from an employee. In other words, was the work one that the employee could have been directed to create? The scope of the expression 'is made by the author in pursuance of the terms of his or her employment' was explored for the first time in *EdSonic v Cassidy* where Moore J noted:

> What the expression raises for consideration ... is not the bare question of whether the author is employed under a contract of service at the time a work is made but whether the relevant work is made in furtherance of the contract of employment with the employer. That is, did the employee make the work because the contract of employment expressly, or impliedly, required or at least authorised the work to be made?[48]

4.3.2 Works created by journalists

The second exception to the general rule that the author is the first owner of the work relates to journalists. Journalists are placed in a special position that can be contrasted with the position of all other employees. Section 35(4) lays down special rules for literary, dramatic or artistic

---

46 See *Noah v Shuba* [1991] FSR 14, 25–7.
47 (2004) 60 IPR 392, 422. For a general discussion of ownership within universities, see A. Monotti (with S. Ricketson), *Universities and Intellectual Property: Ownership and Exploitation* (Oxford, New York: Oxford University Press, 2003); A. Monotti, 'Who owns my research and teaching materials – my university or me?' (1997) 19 *Sydney Law Review* 425.
48 *EdSonic Pty Ltd v Cassidy* (2010) 189 FCR 271, [41]. While this was partially based on the patent decision of *University of Western Australia v Gray* (2009) 179 FCR 346, Moore J stressed that it was more important to give effect to the words of the *Copyright Act*.

(but not musical) works created for the purpose of being published in a newspaper, magazine or similar periodical under a contract of service or apprenticeship. Copyright in these works is divided between the employed journalist and the owner of the newspaper, magazine or periodical.[49] An employed journalist is the owner of the copyright for the reproduction of the work for the purpose of inclusion in a book *and* the reproduction of the work in the form of a hard copy facsimile.[50] In all other cases, the proprietor of the employing newspaper, magazine or similar periodical is the owner of the copyright.[51] The division drawn between electronic and analogue versions of the work enables journalists to pursue commercial opportunities in relation to their writings (the traditional formats for their works being books and articles), without impacting on the ability of newspaper proprietors to exploit the electronic version of their works in online newspapers.

4.3.3 Commissioned works

Another exception to the general rule that the author is the first owner of copyright is in relation to commissioned works. Prior to 1998, the general rule was that even though a literary, dramatic, musical or artistic work had been commissioned by another person, the author was the initial owner of the copyright. The commissioner only gained ownership of the copyright in the commissioned work if the copyright in the work was assigned to them by way of contract. While the general rule still operates, rules were introduced in 1998 relating to commissioned photographs, portraits and engravings.[52] In part, these were prompted by photographers selling personal photographs, such as wedding photographs, to newspapers. In this situation, the commissioners were powerless to prevent photographers from selling and newspapers from publishing their private photographs. To prevent this from happening, the *Copyright Act 1968* (Cth) was amended to provide that the owner of copyright in a portrait, engraving or photograph taken 'for a private and domestic purpose'[53] will be the commissioner (as opposed to the author). A private or domestic purpose includes a portrait of family members, of a wedding party, or of children.[54] Thus, with the exception of photographs taken for private and domestic purposes and subject to agreements to the contrary, the photographer will be the copyright owner.[55]

---

49   Copyright is shared between the author and the owner of the relevant media if the work was created on or after 30 July 1998.
50   Defined in *Copyright Act 1968* (Cth) s 35(7) (definition of 'hard copy facsimile').
51   This is in relation to works created after 30 July 1998. In relation to works created prior to 30 July 1998, the media proprietor owns the copyright in relation to the publication of the work in the newspaper, magazine or similar periodical; the broadcasting of the work; or the reproduction of the work for such publication or broadcasting. In all other cases, the employee is the owner of copyright.
52   *Copyright Act 1968* (Cth) s 35(5). This section does not apply to a work made at any time in pursuance of an agreement made before 1 May 1969: at s 213(2).
53   *Copyright Act 1968* (Cth) s 35(5)(a), in relation to works made after 30 July 1998.
54   As defined in *Copyright Act 1968* (Cth) s 35(7) (definition of 'private or domestic purpose').
55   In relation to works made prior to 30 July 1998, the copyright in a commissioned photograph, portrait or engraving is owned by the photographer.

4.3.4 Crown copyright

Part VII div 1 of the *Copyright Act 1968* (Cth) (ss 176–9) gives the Commonwealth, states and territories ownership of copyright in literary, dramatic, musical and artistic works, sound recordings and films made or first published by them or under their 'direction or control',[56] unless a contrary written agreement applies.[57] Section 183(1) provides that where the use of copyright material is 'for the services of the Crown it will not infringe copyright in that material'. Importantly, Crown copyright covers the activities of both public servants and government agencies, as well as parties authorised by the government to do something for the services of the Crown.[58] Part VII div 2 provides for Crown use of copyright materials, allowing a form of statutory licence for government use of works and other subject matter in circumstances which would otherwise constitute infringement.[59]

A wide range of activities are covered by the phrase 'for the services of the Crown'. Copyright works may be copied for training purposes for display on government websites, for inclusion in reports produced by government departments or their employees, or any activities engaged in by government employees in the course of their duties. Section 183(4) provides that as soon as possible after the doing of any act under the s 183 licence, the Commonwealth or state shall give the copyright owner such information as the owner 'from time to time reasonably requires' (unless doing so would be contrary to the public interest).

The Crown copyright provisions have been criticised on a number of occasions primarily because they place the government in what is seen as an unfair and privileged position.[60] In December 2003, the Copyright Law Review Committee (CLRC) was asked to examine the law relating to government ownership of copyright material. The CLRC's report, *Crown Copyright*, was released in April 2005.[61] Two important themes formed the basis for the CLRC's recommendations. These were, first, that the government should as far as possible be placed on the same footing as other parties and, second, that the provisions should aim to promote the widest possible access to government-owned materials.[62] The CLRC recommended that the special Crown subsistence and ownership provisions should be repealed.[63]

---

56 See *Linter Group (in liq) v Price Waterhouse* [2000] VSC 90, [6], [7].
57 *Copyright Act 1968* (Cth) ss 176(1), 178(1) also provide that where copyright would not otherwise subsist in works, sound recordings and films, copyright subsists by virtue of the sections.
58 The authority can be given before or after the doing of the relevant act: *Copyright Act 1968* (Cth) s 183(3). The Crown copyright provisions also apply to local councils: see *Greater Dandenong City Council v Australian Municipal, Administrative, Clerical and Services Union* (2001) 112 FCR 232; *Stack v Brisbane City Council* (1995) 59 FCR 71.
59 *Copyright Act 1968* (Cth) ss 182B–182E.
60 See, for example, Intellectual Property and Competition Review Committee, *Review of Intellectual Property Legislation under the Competition Principles Agreement* (Final Report, September 2000).
61 This report was the final report of the CLRC before it was disbanded by the Commonwealth government.
62 CLRC, *Crown Copyright Report* (Canberra: AGPS, 2005), 11. See also C. Bond, 'Reconciling Crown copyright and reuse of government information: An analysis of the CLRC Crown Copyright Review' (2007) 12 *Media and Arts Law Review* 343.
63 First, the subsistence provisions are not clearly drafted and it is difficult to envisage situations where they would be relied on. Second, the ambit of the ownership provisions was uncertain and there was no justification for government to have a privileged position compared with other copyright owners. In particular, the CLRC considered that the term 'direction or control' was potentially too broad. Ownership of copyright in works commissioned by government from independent parties should not be determined by default provisions that alter the usual copyright ownership rules. Not only do these

In March 2018, as part of the copyright modernisation review,[64] the government held a roundtable on government uses. The roundtable discussed a number of related, potential changes:

- extending the declared society provisions in relation to the government statutory licence (ss 183A–183D) to include communication and performance (not just copying);
- extending the government statutory licence (s 183A) to allow communication (not just copying);
- making notifications of government uses to copyright owners simpler and easier (by amending s 183(4));
- enabling parties to agree to estimate a fair price for government uses without a survey or other kind of sampling (by amending ss 183(3) and 183C); and
- providing more clarity on equitable remuneration.[65]

While the roundtable discussed whether there would be benefit to having greater alignment between agreements for the Commonwealth and each state and territory government, it did not reach agreement on the best option for dealing with the Crown copyright issues that had been identified.

4.4 Nature of the rights

The *Copyright Act 1968* (Cth) gives the copyright owner the right to control the protected subject matter in a number of different ways.[66] While copyright allows the owner to control the use that can be made of a work (Part III), or subject matter other than a work (Part IV), in various ways, the rights are not absolute. Unless a defendant's activity falls within one of the activities that are given to the copyright owner, the activity will be non-infringing. This means, for example, that while a person may infringe copyright when they photocopy a book, they will not infringe when they read the book.

It is important to note that the particular activities that fall within the owner's control vary depending on the type of work protected. Given this, the various activities that attach to different types of subject matter will be examined first. Then the scope of some of these rights will be examined in more detail.

The owner of the copyright in a *literary, dramatic* or *musical work* has the exclusive right to:

- reproduce the work in a material form;
- publish the work;

---

provisions give government a negotiating advantage, but the CLRC also heard evidence that many creators have been unaware that in the absence of a written contractual provision with government, they have lost copyright in their creations: CLRC, *Crown Copyright Report*, above n 62, 11.

64   See ch 2 at 2.3.2.11.
65   Department of Communications and the Arts, 'Copyright modernisation consultation' www.communications.gov.au/have-your-say.
66   While the *Copyright Act* presents the rights in a positive sense, many commentators like to speak of copyright as a negative right, in that it allows the owner to prevent third parties from doing something.

- perform the work in public;
- communicate the work to the public;
- make an adaptation of the work; and
- do any of the first four acts in relation to an adaptation of the work.[67]

An exclusive right of commercial rental is provided in computer programs and works embodied in sound recordings.[68]

The owner of copyright in an *artistic work* is given the exclusive right to:

- reproduce the work in material form;
- publish the work; and
- communicate the work to the public.[69]

In relation to *sound recordings*[70] and *films*,[71] the owner is given the exclusive right to:

- make a copy of the recording;
- cause the recording to be heard and seen in public; and
- communicate the recording or film to the public.

The owner of copyright in a sound recording (but not a film) is also given the right to enter into a commercial rental arrangement in respect of the sound recording.[72] The owners of copyright in television and sound broadcasts are given the exclusive right to rebroadcast it or to communicate the broadcast to the public. In the case of television broadcasts insofar as they consist of visual images, the owner also has the right to make a film of the broadcast or a copy of such a film. In the case of sound recordings or a television broadcast insofar as it consists of sounds, the owner has the right to make a sound recording of the broadcast or a copy of such a recording.

The owner of copyright in *published editions* of works is given the exclusive right to make a facsimile copy of the edition.[73]

4.4.1 The right of reproduction

One of the broadest and most commonly exercised rights in relation to Part III works is the right of reproduction. In *Ladbroke (Football) Ltd v William Hill (Football) Ltd*, Lord Reid observed that 'reproduction means copying, and does not include cases where an author or compiler produces a substantially similar result by independent work without copying'.[74]

---

[67] *Copyright Act 1968* (Cth) s 31(1)(a).
[68] Ibid s 31(1)(c), (d), introduced by the *Copyright (World Trade Organization Amendments) Act 1994* (Cth). Generally, the right will not apply to commercial dealings in sound recordings and computer programs purchased before 1 January 1996 if the purchase was made in the course of an established commercial rental business: *Copyright Act 1968* (Cth) s 31(6).
[69] *Copyright Act 1968* (Cth) s 31(1)(b).
[70] Ibid s 85(1).
[71] Ibid s 86.
[72] Ibid s 85(2) sets out a number of exceptions to the rental rights.
[73] Ibid s 88.
[74] [1964] 1 WLR 273, 277.

Wilmer LJ in *Francis Day & Hunter v Bron* said that to show reproduction it was necessary to establish that there was 'a sufficient degree of objective similarity between the two works' and 'some causal connection between the plaintiff's and the defendant's works'.[75]

The reproduction right is exercised when a literary, dramatic or musical work is copied in any material form.[76] 'Material form' includes any visible or non-visible form of storage, irrespective of whether the work or an adaptation can be reproduced.[77] A reproduction of a work will have taken place where that work is converted from a hard copy or analogue form into a digital form.[78] Where the work is a computer program, a reproduction will take place if an object code is derived from its source code, and vice versa.[79] Thus, the temporary or incidental storage of a computer program (or a substantial part thereof) in the RAM of a computer is an infringement of copyright.[80]

One question that caused some concern for copyright owners as their works were increasingly being accessed online was whether the right of reproduction covers the practice of 'caching' (that is, where frequently accessed material is temporarily copied onto a local computer system in order to facilitate faster and more cost-effective access). Section 200AAA of the *Copyright Act 1968* (Cth), which was introduced in 2006, clarified that proxy caching does not infringe copyright and as such is not a remunerable activity. More specifically, s 200AAA provides that copyright is not infringed where a computer system automatically makes a temporary electronic reproduction or copy of works or other subject matter available online. It also provides that the later communication of the work or other subject matter to a user of the system is also non-infringing. These provisions are subject to provisos: that the computer system is operated by or on behalf of a body administering an educational institution; that the system is operated primarily to enable staff and students of the institution to use the system to gain online access for educational purposes to works and other subject matter (whether they are made available online using the internet or merely the system); and that the reproductions and copies are made by the computer system merely to facilitate efficient later access to the works and other subject matter by users of the system.[81]

---

75 [1963] Ch 587, 614.
76 *Copyright Act 1968* (Cth) s 21(1).
77 Ibid s 10(1) (definition of 'material form'). For acts carried out prior to 1 January 2005, it is necessary to show that the work can be reproduced from its stored form. See *Kabushiki Kaisha Sony Computer Entertainment v Stevens* (2002) 200 ALR 55, [137] (Federal Court), reversed (2003) 132 FCR 31 (Full Federal Court), reversed (2005) 224 CLR 193 (High Court).
78 *Copyright Act 1968* (Cth) s 21(1A) provides that a work is taken to have been reproduced if it is converted into or from a digital or other electronic machine-readable form, and any article embodying the work in such a form is taken to be a reproduction of the work. The section further provides that the reference to the conversion of a work into a digital or other electronic machine-readable form includes the first digitisation of the work.
79 *Copyright Act 1968* (Cth) s 21(5).
80 For acts carried out on or after 1 January 2005, copyright protection extends to include non-reproducible forms of storage. This overturned *Kabushiki Kaisha Sony Computer Entertainment v Stevens* (2003) 132 FCR 31; *Microsoft Corp v Blanch* (2002) AIPC 91-813; *Australian Video Retailers Association Ltd v Warner Home Video Pty Ltd* (2001) 53 IPR 242. In January 2005, a related defence was provided where a reproduction is made as part of a technical process by virtue of *Copyright Act 1968* (Cth) s 43B.
81 *Copyright Act 1968* (Cth) s 200AAA(1)(a)–(d).

The copyright owners of sound recordings, films, and television and sound broadcasts are given the right to make copies of their works.[82] In turn, the copyright owner of a published edition is given a narrow right to make a facsimile copy of the work.[83]

4.4.2 The right to publish the work

The *Copyright Act 1968* (Cth) provides the owner of copyright in a literary, dramatic, musical or artistic work with the right to publish the work. A work is published if reproductions of the work have been supplied to the public by sale or otherwise.[84] Publication requires that the public is able to read or visually perceive the work on the copies supplied to it; it is therefore not a publication of a work to supply records of it to the public.[85] The publication right only allows control of the first publication of the work in the relevant territory.[86] There are caveats to this in relation to rental rights, public lending and imports. Section 29(3) provides that certain acts do not constitute publication.

4.4.3 The right to perform the work in public

The right of the copyright owner to perform the work in public[87] includes both live performance and any visual or aural presentation of the work (such as presentations on television, radio, film or other form of reception equipment).[88] The operation of 'reception equipment' (which is defined as equipment, such as a television, that enables people to see or hear a work) constitutes a performance by the display or emission of the images or sounds received by that equipment.[89] A performance also includes the delivery of a work by way of a lecture, address, speech or sermon.[90] The copyright owner of a film or sound recording has the exclusive right to cause it to be seen or heard in public.[91]

A key feature of the right is that the performance is 'in public'. While there is some uncertainty about what is meant by the 'public' (other than that 'it is often defined broadly so as to favour the copyright owners'),[92] in *Australasian Performing Right Association Ltd v Telstra Corp*,[93] the High Court provided some guidance by noting that 'in public' was probably broader than 'to the public', which was the subject of discussion before the High Court.

---

82   Ibid ss 85(a), 86(a), 87(a), (b).
83   Ibid s 88.
84   Ibid s 29(1)(a).
85   Ibid s 29(3).
86   *Avel Pty Ltd v Multicoin Amusements Pty Ltd* (1990) 18 IPR 443, following *Infabrics Ltd v Jaytex Shirt Co Ltd* [1981] 1 All ER 1057.
87   *Copyright Act 1968* (Cth) s 31(1)(a)(iii).
88   Ibid s 27(1)(a). For definitions of 'reception equipment', 'wireless telegraphy apparatus', 'cinematograph film' and 'record' see s 10(1).
89   Ibid s 27(2), (3). The occupier of the premises where the apparatus is situated is considered to be the person giving the performance if the apparatus was provided by or with their consent: at s 27(4).
90   Ibid s 27(1)(b). Section 29(3) provides that the performance of a literary, dramatic or musical work is not a publication of it.
91   Ibid ss 85, 86.
92   L. Bently, B. Sherman, D. Gangee and P. Johnson, *Intellectual Property Law* (5th edn, Oxford: Oxford University Press, 2018) 150.
93   (1993) 46 FCR 131.

The court held that playing music on hold to people in their homes was a broadcast 'to the public'. The High Court tended to prefer the test of whether the performance impacted on the copyright owner's relationship with their audience – that is, whether it was to the copyright owner's public.[94]

Further guidance as to when a work is performed in public is provided by s 28. This states that where a literary, dramatic or musical work is performed by a teacher or student in class or otherwise in the presence of an audience for the purpose of non-profit educational instruction, that performance is deemed *not* to be a performance in public. This is subject to the proviso that the audience is limited to persons who are taking part in the instruction or are otherwise directly[95] connected with the place where the instruction is given. Similar provisions apply in relation to film and sound recordings.[96]

4.4.4 The right to communicate the work to the public

As part of the digital agenda reforms of 2000,[97] copyright owners were given a general right of communication of the work to the public.[98] 'Communicate' is defined to mean 'to make available online or electronically transmit (whether over a path, or combination of paths, provided by a material substance or otherwise) a work or subject-matter'.[99] In turn, 'to the public' is defined to include the public within or outside Australia.[100] This means that material directed to overseas audiences would fall within this right. The scope of the right does not extend, however, to communications that occur within non-profit educational institutions in certain specified circumstances which are deemed *not* to be communications to the public.[101]

Section 22(6) of the *Copyright Act 1968* (Cth) provides that a communication (other than a broadcast) is taken to have been made by the person responsible for determining the content

---

94   Rather than whether the performance was a domestic as opposed to a public one. Wright MR and Romer LJ discussed this in *Jennings v Stephens* [1936] 1 All ER 409, 418 where, by way of contrast, Greene LJ (at 420) looked closely at the relationship between the audience and the copyright owner.
95   *Copyright Act 1968* (Cth) s 28(3): 'For the purposes of this section, a person shall not be taken to be directly connected with a place where instruction is given by reason only that he or she is a parent or guardian of a student who receives instruction at that place.'
96   *Copyright Act 1968* (Cth) s 28(4).
97   See ch 2 at 2.3.2.3.
98   This right applies in cases of literary, musical, artistic and dramatic works, and sound recordings, films and broadcasts. The right does not apply, however, to published editions.
99   *Copyright Act 1968* (Cth) s 10(1). See *Woolworths Ltd v Olson* (2004) 184 FLR 121 [332] (the sending of two emails containing copyright materials by a husband to his wife did not breach the copyright owner's right of communication to the public; the downloading of the emails did, however, breach the copyright owner's right of reproduction).
100 *Copyright Act 1968* (Cth) s 10(1). This right enables the control of acts previously subject to distinct rights of broadcast and of diffusion, notably via wire, whether the members of the public are in one place or scattered in separate places. See *Telstra Corp Ltd v Australasian Performing Right Association Ltd* (1997) 191 CLR 140, where it was held that transmitting recorded on-hold music over an only partially wired network to users of mobile telephones was in part broadcast and in part diffusion – now, effectively, communication – 'to the public'.
101 *Copyright Act 1968* (Cth) s 28. This applies to literary, dramatic and musical works; film and sound recordings; television and radio broadcasts (including works embodied in those broadcasts); and artistic works.

of the communication.[102] The scope of this provision was clarified in 2006[103] by the insertion of a new s 22(6A) which makes it clear that a person who merely accesses or browses material online is not responsible for determining the content of the communication.[104] This means that a person who merely clicks on a hyperlink to gain access to a web page is not exercising the right of communication and thus not infringing.[105] The new provision also confirms that a person who clicks on a link to gain access to a page will not be responsible for determining the content of a communication for the purposes of the communication right.[106] As discussed above, it is also now clear that the communication of a work or other subject matter which has been automatically reproduced (or cached) by a computer system operated by an educational institution is non-infringing.[107]

One of the questions that arose in *Roadshow Films Pty Ltd v iiNet Ltd*[108] was whether one-on-one (or peer-to-peer) communication of a single film on the internet (using BitTorrent) was a communication to the public.[109] At first instance,[110] Cowdroy J rejected the arguments of the film companies that iiNet committed a new act of infringement each and every time a computer containing an infringing film was connected to the internet and the film. This was on the basis that the electronic communication occurred between internet users and the community of peer-to-peer users as a whole (the 'swarm') and not between individuals *per se*.[111] This argument was rejected by the Full Federal Court which found that iiNet users were repeat infringers insofar as they repeatedly made works available online.[112] As the Full Court said:

---

102 See *TVBO Production Ltd v Australia Sky Net Pty Ltd* (2009) 82 IPR 502 where it was held that a party who retransmitted a television program from its base station in Taiwan to subscribers in Australia without approval of the copyright owner 'determined the content of the communication' and thus infringed.
103 By the *Copyright Amendment Act 2006* (Cth).
104 This issue was raised as part of the government's Digital Agenda Review. See *Digital Agenda Review – Government Responses to Phillips Fox Recommendations and Related Matters* (2006) 13 ('Additional matters considered as part of the Digital Agenda Review'). The Explanatory Memorandum to the Copyright Amendment Bill 2006 (Cth) stated: 'Although it was never intended that a person doing no more than merely accessing copyright material online could be considered to be exercising the communication right in relation to what was accessed, some have argued that this interpretation is possible': at 130, as cited in M. Neilsen and R. Bell, *Copyright Amendment Bill 2006*, Parliament of Australia, Department of Parliamentary Service (22 November 2006, Bill Digest 51) 18.
105 *Universal Music Australia Pty Ltd v Cooper* (2005) 150 FCR 1. See also *Universal Music Australia Pty Ltd v Sharman License Holdings Ltd* (2005) 222 FCR 465; *Young v Wyllie* [2010] FCA 283, [69] (films that had been reproduced on DVDs had not been electronically transmitted).
106 In part this was in response to Copyright Agency Limited's argument in the Copyright Tribunal in 2005 that 'telling students to view' a website should be a remunerable act. See Copyright Agency Ltd, 'Umpire to set value of schools digital copying' (Press Release, 17 August 2005). See *Copyright Agency Ltd v Queensland Department of Education* [2006] ACopyT 1.
107 *Copyright Act 1968* (Cth) s 200AAA.
108 (2011) 194 FCR 285.
109 In response to iiNet's argument that a one-on-one (or peer-to-peer) communication was not a communication to the public, the Full Federal Court said it was 'very difficult to reach a conclusion on the question of whether iiNet users have electronically transmitted a substantial part of any of the films to the public': ibid [170], [352] point 2.
110 *Roadshow Films Pty Ltd v iiNet Ltd (No 3)* (2010) 83 IPR 430 (overturned on appeal).
111 Ibid 431.
112 *Roadshow Films Pty Ltd v iiNet Ltd* (2011) 194 FCR 285, [158] ff, [322]–[346], [699].

Connection to the internet is an essential element in making available online, in that communication cannot occur if there is no connection to the internet. Where a particular modem is not connected to the internet, that modem could not be making a film available online. Every time that a modem is connected to the internet and makes a film available, there is a new making of the film available online, a separate act is engaged in each time a modem is connected to the internet and goes online.[113]

It seems that the difference between the decisions turned on how the peer-to-peer (BitTorrent) system was characterised. While Cowdroy J saw peer-to-peer as a series of single acts, the Full Federal Court said that 'BitTorrent use is an ongoing process of communication for as long as one wishes to participate. Therefore, the term "electronically transmit" cannot sensibly be seen ... as anything other than a single ongoing process, even if the iiNet user transmits more than 100% of the film back to the swarm'.[114]

4.4.5 The right to make an adaptation of the work

A copyright owner of a literary, dramatic or musical work has the exclusive right to make an adaptation of the work.[115] An adaptation of a literary work is defined to mean a version of a dramatic literary work in a non-dramatic form, or vice versa; a translation of a literary work; and a version of a literary work in which a story or action is conveyed solely or principally by means of pictures.[116] An adaptation of a computer program means a version of the work, whether or not in the language, code or notation in which the work was originally expressed, not being a reproduction of the work.[117] In relation to a musical work, an adaptation of a musical work means an arrangement or transcription of a musical work.[118]

The adaptation right gives the copyright owner protection beyond the mere expression of the ideas. A common example of the adaptation right is the right of an author of a novel to make a movie from the book – in other words, a pictorial version of the literary work. The adapted work may attract copyright protection in its own right. Copyright has been held to subsist in a translation,[119] an annotated edition of a work,[120] and an anthology of songs and lyrics.[121] Copyright owners have the same rights in relation to the adaptation as they have in relation to the work that was adapted.[122]

The copyright owner of an artistic work has similar adaptation rights; for example, an artist has the exclusive right to make a two-dimensional version of a work in a three-dimensional form, and a three-dimensional work in a two-dimensional form.[123]

---

113 Ibid [152], [664]–[673].
114 Ibid [601].
115 *Copyright Act 1968* (Cth) s 31(1)(a)(vi).
116 Ibid s 10(1) (definition of 'adaptation' (a), (b), (c)).
117 Ibid s 10(1) (definition of 'adaptation' (ba)).
118 Ibid s 10(1) (definition of 'adaptation' (d)).
119 *Pollock v JC Williamson Ltd* [1923] VLR 225.
120 *Blackie & Sons Ltd v Lothian Book Publishing Co Pty Ltd* (1921) 29 CLR 397.
121 *Macmillan & Co Ltd v Cooper* (1923) 93 LJPC 113.
122 *Copyright Act 1968* (Cth) s 31(1)(a)(vii).
123 Ibid s 21(3).

4.4.6 The right of commercial rental

An exclusive right of commercial rental is provided in computer programs and literary, musical and dramatic works embodied in sound recordings.[124] The right only applies where the essential object of the rental is the program itself. Thus, the rental of a DVD that embodied a computer program was *not* a rental of the computer program, because the essential object of the rental was to gain access to the video and audio content and not the computer program.[125]

4.5 Technological protection measures

With the increase in the number of digital works that were made available on the internet in the 1990s, copyright owners began to use technological measures to lock up their copyright works to prevent them being transferred, copied and printed. While the technological locks or technological protection measures (TPMs) relied on by copyright owners provided some relief from online piracy, they were not infallible because users were able to circumvent the locks and decrypt the encoded works.

Seeking to strengthen the TPMs, copyright owners lobbied the federal government for the legal means to reinforce the existing technological protection systems. In particular, they wanted the measures that they had adopted to be legitimised through statutory sanctions that would prohibit users from circumventing the locks.

The government accepted the copyright owners' arguments and in the 2000 digital agenda reforms introduced a raft of enforcement provisions to enable copyright owners to enforce their rights in the digital environment.[126] Two key technological protection measures were introduced in the *Copyright Amendment (Digital Agenda) Act 2000* (Cth): (1) provisions dealing with circumvention devices and services, and (2) provisions in relation to rights management information.

The TPM scheme established by the *Digital Agenda Act* was subsequently modified as a result of Australia's entry into the *Australia–US Free Trade Agreement*[127] (*AUSFTA*) which required Australia to introduce a stronger TPM scheme.[128] To implement these requirements, the Attorney-General released an Exposure Draft of the Copyright Amendment (Technological Protection Measures) Bill in September 2006.[129] After public consultation, the Bill was incorporated into the *Copyright Amendment Act 2006* (Cth) (as sch 12). The *Copyright Amendment Act 2006* (Cth) repealed the existing TPM scheme and introduced an expanded regime which

---

124 Ibid s 31(1)(c), (d), introduced by the *Copyright (World Trade Organization Amendments) Act 1994* (Cth), effective 1 January 1996. Generally, the right will not apply to commercial dealings in sound recordings and computer programs purchased before 1 January 1996, if the purchase was made in the course of an established commercial rental business: *Copyright Act 1968* (Cth) s 31(6).
125 *Australian Video Retailers Association Ltd v Warner Home Video Pty Ltd* (2001) 53 IPR 242.
126 In part, the *Copyright Amendment (Digital Agenda) Act 2000* (Cth) was enacted in response to the *World Intellectual Property Organization Copyright Treaty 1996.*
127 Signed 18 May 2004, [2005] ATS 1 (entered into force 1 April 2005).
128 When announcing the new Bill, the Attorney-General claimed that the 'new laws aimed at preventing unauthorised access to material protected by copyright should increase the availability of music, film and games in digital form': P. Ruddock, Attorney-General, 'DVDs, CDs and computer games: Good news for consumers, bad news for pirates' (Media Release, 4 September 2006).
129 *Copyright Amendment (Technological Protection Measures) Bill 2006.*

complies with Australia's obligations under the *AUSFTA*. This TPM scheme came into effect on 1 January 2007.

In 2012, the Attorney-General's Department undertook a review of the operation of the TPM scheme.[130] The aim of the review was to consider whether the exceptions for TPMs were appropriate and whether new additional exceptions should be added relating to bypassing, disabling or otherwise circumventing access controls on certain technologies.

The Australian Law Reform Commission, in its 2013 review,[131] also considered the operation of the TPM scheme in relation to the 'contracting out' of copyright defences. Much of the concern over the operation of the TPM regimes was highlighted by libraries and cultural institutions as 'the increasing tendency of digital content licences to contract libraries out of existing copyright exceptions, and ways in which TPMs impede preservation and long term access to copyright works in the public interest'.[132]

The Department of Communication and the Arts, in September to October 2017, consulted on the draft *Copyright Regulations 2017* (Cth) and *Copyright Legislation Amendment (Technological Protection Measures) Regulations 2017* (Cth) (*TPM Regulations*). The latter was developed 'to update the exceptions in the current regulations that allow consumers to bypass a [TPM]. Examples include a password or software that controls access to copyright content.'[133]

As part of the copyright amendments that took effect in 2017, a new div 2A was introduced into Part V of the *Copyright Act 1968* (Cth) to expand the operation of the TPM regime.[134] In particular, new s 116AN(9)(c) provides that a person may circumvent an access control TPM to enable the person to do an act if 'the doing of the act by the person is prescribed by the regulations'. In 2017 the *TPM Regulations* revoked the 1969 Regulations[135] and updated some of the exceptions in the Copyright Regulations for the circumvention of TPM in certain circumstances (known as 'TPM exceptions').[136] The TPM exceptions commenced on 1 April 2018.

From 22 December 2017, educational and cultural institutions are permitted to circumvent a TPM for any of the following purposes: relying on the streamlined statutory licence in s 113P; relying on either of the two new disability copying exceptions in ss 113E and 113F; and/or relying on s 200AB(3) (the flexible dealing exception which allows education institutions to copy material for educational instruction in limited circumstances).[137] This reform enables education and disability organisations to rely upon the TPM exceptions to provide disabled students with copyright content in accessible formats.

---

130   Australian Government, Attorney-General's Department, *Review of Technological Protection Measure Exceptions made under the Copyright Act 1968* (2012).
131   Australian Law Reform Commission (ALRC), *Copyright and the Digital Economy* (Discussion Paper No 79, June 2013) [11.127]–[11.130].
132   Australian Digital Alliance and Australian Libraries Copyright Committee, Submission No 213 to ALRC, *Copyright and the Digital Economy* (Issues Paper No 42, August 2012) 39.
133   Department of Communications and the Arts, 'Review of Copyright Regulations 1969 and the Copyright Tribunal (Procedure) Regulations 1969' www.communications.gov.au/have-your-say.
134   *Copyright Act 1968* (Cth) pt V div 2A (ss 116AK–116D).
135   *Copyright Regulations 1969* (Cth) and *Copyright Tribunal (Procedure) Regulations 1969* (Cth), remade as the *Copyright Regulations 2017* (Cth): see Explanatory Statement, Copyright Regulations 2017 (Cth).
136   Department of Communications and the Arts, 'Review of Copyright Regulations 1969 and the Copyright Tribunal (Procedure) Regulations 1969', above n 133.
137   *Copyright Regulations 2017* (Cth) reg 40.

4.5.1 Anti-circumvention

The technological protection measures scheme essentially prohibits three activities:

- circumventing an access control TPM (s 116AN);
- manufacturing a circumvention device for a TPM (s 116AO); and
- providing a circumvention service for a TPM (s 116AP).[138]

To limit the scope of the prohibitions, a number of exceptions were also introduced.[139] The Senate recommended that a prohibition on contracting out of the defences to the anti-circumvention provisions should be introduced into the *Copyright Amendment Act 2006* (Cth) to protect consumers from 'contracting away' their rights. However, the government did not accept this recommendation[140] and this very issue of contracting out is still the subject of consideration by the government.[141]

A key feature of the TPM scheme is that it provides for both civil and criminal sanctions.

4.5.1.1 Circumventing an access control TPM

One of the most important features of the TPM scheme was the introduction of provisions dealing with 'access control technological protection measures'. While the old scheme protected devices that restricted the infringement of copyright,[142] the current scheme protects devices that control access to the work or other subject matter. The ability to control access to copyright material (rather than merely to prevent copyright infringement) marks an important extension of the copyright owner's rights.

Section 116AN(1) of the *Copyright Act 1968* (Cth) provides that an owner or exclusive licensee of copyright in a work or other subject matter that is protected by an access control TPM is able to bring an action against a person who does an act that results in the circumvention of the measure. To be liable, a person must have known, or ought reasonably to have known, that the act in question would lead to the circumvention of the access control TPM.

An 'access control technological protection measure' is defined as:

- a device, product, technology or component (including a computer program) that is used in Australia or a qualifying country;
- by, with the permission of, or on behalf of, the owner or the exclusive licensee of the copyright in a work or other subject matter, and in connection with the exercise of the copyright; and
- that controls access to the work or other subject matter.[143]

---

138   *Copyright Amendment Act 2006* (Cth) sch 12 item 9 repealed *Copyright Act 1968* (Cth) s 116A (the provision that formerly regulated the use of TPM circumvention devices) and substituted a new sub-div A into pt V.
139   *Copyright Act 1968* (Cth) s 116AN(2)–(9).
140   Senate Standing Committee on Legal and Constitutional Affairs, *Copyright Amendment Bill 2006 [Provisions]* (Report, November 2006) rec 14.
141   See ch 5 at 5.5.16.
142   *Copyright Act 1968* (Cth) s 116A (replaced by a new section in 2006).
143   Ibid s 10(1).

While this definition excludes geographic market segmentation technologies (e.g., region coding and computer technologies) that are aimed at preventing competition in non-copyright goods,[144] it is still very broad. It would include, for example, most of the access control systems currently in use, such as Apple's digital rights management system used with the iPhone and iPod, which 'envelopes each song purchased from the iTunes store in special and secret software so that it cannot be played on unauthorised devices'.[145]

4.5.1.1.1 EXCEPTIONS

To some extent, the potential of the access control TPMs to lock up digital works is alleviated by the fact that there are situations where copyright users are able to circumvent a copyright owner's TPMs. There are a number of exceptions to liability for circumventing access control TPMs; in all cases, the defendant bears the burden of proof for these exceptions.[146]

Section 116AN(2) of the *Copyright Act 1968* (Cth) provides that a person will not be liable where they have the permission (either express or implied) of the copyright owner or exclusive licensee to circumvent the access control TPM.[147] A number of other exceptions are made to protect specific activities. For example, the Act provides that a person will not be liable where the circumvention is for the sole purpose of:

- achieving interoperability of an independently created computer program with the original program;[148]
- identifying and analysing flaws and vulnerabilities of encryption technology;[149]
- testing, investigating or correcting the security of a computer, computer system or computer network;[150]
- providing online privacy;[151] or
- allowing libraries, archives and educational institutions to make a decision as to whether they want to buy the copyright material.[152]

These exceptions are subject to the proviso that the act in question will not infringe the copyright in the work or other subject matter.

An additional exception provides that a person who circumvents an access control TPM will not be liable if their conduct is for the purpose of law enforcement, national security, or

---

144 Ibid.
145 S. Jobs, 'Thoughts on music' (6 February 2007).
146 *Copyright Act 1968* (Cth) s 116AN(10). These exceptions correspond to the exceptions allowed in *AUSFTA* art 17.4.7(e).
147 *Copyright Act 1968* (Cth) s 116AN(2).
148 Ibid s 116AN(3).
149 Ibid s 116AN(4).
150 Ibid s 116AN(5).
151 Ibid s 116AN(6). This would permit circumvention in order to identify and disable an undisclosed capability to collect or disseminate personally identifying information about a person's online activities: see Supplementary Explanatory Memorandum, Copyright Amendment Bill 2006 (Cth) (amendments to be moved on behalf of the government).
152 *Copyright Act 1968* (Cth) s 116AN(8).

performing a statutory function, power or duty of Commonwealth, state or territory governments and agencies.[153] The scheme also allows for additional exceptions to be prescribed in the regulations.[154]

The civil remedies that are available for breach of s 116AN include an injunction, damages or an account of profits, or (where relevant) an order that the circumvention device be destroyed or otherwise dealt with. In assessing remedies, the courts may take account of any relevant matters including those listed in s 116AQ(2).

4.5.1.2 Aiding and abetting in the circumvention of a TPM

The second prohibited activity is concerned with people who assist or otherwise facilitate third parties to circumvent TPMs. Section 116AO of the *Copyright Act 1968* (Cth) provides that an owner or exclusive licensee of copyright in a work or other subject matter that is protected by a TPM is able to bring an action against a person who manufactures, imports, distributes, offers to the public or otherwise provides to another person a device that enables the user to circumvent a TPM.[155] This is subject to the proviso that the person knew, or ought reasonably to have known, that the device is a circumvention device for a TPM, and that the work or other subject matter in question is protected by the TPM. The civil remedies for breach of s 116AO are the same as for breach of s 116AN, discussed above.[156]

There are two key components of the provision: 'technological protection measure' and 'circumvention devices'. A 'technological protection measure' includes an access control TPM (defined above).[157] It also includes a device, product, technology or component (including a computer program) that in the normal course of its operation prevents, inhibits or restricts the doing of an act that would infringe copyright.[158] The device must be used in Australia or a qualifying country with the permission of, or on behalf of, the owner or the exclusive licensee of the copyright in a work or other subject matter.[159] In relation to films and computer programs (including computer games), the definition of a 'technological protection measure' does not extend to regional coding devices. To encourage the provision of spare parts, the scope of the provision is also limited by the fact that in relation to computer programs, the definition does not include devices to the extent that they restrict the use of goods (other than the work) or services in relation to the machine or device. This ensures that the TPM scheme cannot be used to restrict competitors from developing devices (such as remote controls) that embody an encrypted computer program.

---

153   Ibid s 116AN(7).
154   Ibid s 116AN(9). The process for making regulations is contained in s 249.
155   Ibid s 116AO(1).
156   At 4.5.1.1.1.
157   At 4.5.1.1. The meaning of a 'technological protection measure' under the pre-2006 scheme was discussed by the High Court in *Stevens v Kabushiki Kaisha Sony Computer Entertainment* (2005) 224 CLR 193; see, in particular, Kirby J at [224].
158   Under the *AUSFTA*, a TPM is 'any technology, device or component that, in the normal course of its operation, controls access to a protected work, performance, phonogram, or other subject matter': at art 17.4.7.
159   *Copyright Act 1968* (Cth) s 10(1).

In turn, a 'circumvention device' is either:

- a device promoted, advertised or marketed as having the purpose or use of circumventing a TPM (that is, it does not require the device to have an actual circumvention purpose or use);
- a device with only a limited commercially significant purpose or use, or no such purpose or use, other than the circumvention of a TPM; or
- a device which is primarily or solely designed or produced to enable or facilitate the circumvention of a TPM.[160]

4.5.1.2.1 EXCEPTIONS

There are a number of exceptions that a person who aids or abets in the circumvention of TPM may be able to rely on.[161] In all cases, the defendant bears the burden of proving the exception to the usual civil standard.[162] In addition to excluding activities carried out for law enforcement, national security, performing a statutory function and so on,[163] exceptions are made: for activities that promote interoperability,[164] for activities that are part of research that aims to identify and analyse flaws and vulnerabilities in encryption technology;[165] and where the circumvention is undertaken to test, investigate or correct the security of a computer, computer system or computer network[166] (similar to those mentioned above). An exception is also made where the promotion, advertising or marketing of the device is carried out without the defendant's authority or approval and where the particular device does not actually have the capacity to be used as a circumvention device.[167]

4.5.1.3 Providing a circumvention service

The third activity prescribed in the TPM scheme[168] relates to the provision of a service that circumvents a TPM. Section 116AP of the *Copyright Act 1968* (Cth) provides that an owner or exclusive licensee of copyright in a work or other subject matter that is protected by a TPM may bring an action against a person who provides a TPM circumvention service to another person or who offers such a service to the public.[169] To be liable, the person must have known, or ought reasonably to have known, that the service is a 'circumvention service' for a TPM. A 'circumvention service' for a TPM is defined as a service that:

- is promoted, advertised or marketed as having the purpose or use of circumventing a TPM;

---

160 Ibid s 10(1) (definition of 'circumvention device').
161 Ibid s 116AO(2)–(6).
162 Ibid s 116AO(7).
163 Ibid s 116AO(6).
164 Ibid s 116AO(3).
165 Ibid s 116AO(4).
166 Ibid s 116AO(5).
167 Ibid s 116AO(2).
168 *Copyright Amendment Act 2006* (Cth) sch 12 item 9 repealed *Copyright Act 1968* (Cth) s 116A (the provision that previously regulated the use of TPM circumvention devices) and substituted a new sub-div A into pt V.
169 *Copyright Act 1968* (Cth) s 116AP(1).

- only has a limited commercially significant purpose or use, or no such purpose or use, other than to circumvent a TPM; or
- is primarily or solely designed or produced to enable or facilitate the circumvention of a TPM.[170]

The civil remedies available for breach of s 116AP are the same as for breach of ss 116AN, discussed above.[171]

4.5.1.3.1 EXCEPTIONS

There are a number of exceptions to civil liability under s 116AP.[172] For example, a person is not liable where a service is promoted as a circumvention service without their authority and where the service is not actually able to be used to circumvent a TPM.[173] Exceptions are also made where the activity is for the sole purpose of promoting interoperability,[174] for encryption-related research,[175] or for testing, investigating or correcting the security of a computer, computer system or computer network.[176] Activities that are carried out for law enforcement, national security or performing a statutory function, power or duty of Commonwealth, state or territory governments and their agencies are also exempt.[177] In all cases, the defendant bears the burden of proof.[178]

4.5.1.4 Criminal actions

As mentioned above,[179] a key component of the TPM scheme is that it provides for both civil and criminal sanctions. The criminal actions regarding TPMs are similar to the civil actions in that they target three activities:[180] circumventing an access control TPM,[181] dealing with a circumvention device for a TPM,[182] and providing a circumvention service for a TPM.[183] A criminal action is only available where the circumvention is carried out for the purpose of commercial advantage or profit.[184] Actions are also subject to the evidential and procedural standards used in criminal law. The scale of the penalties for breach varies depending on the activity in question. While the penalty for circumventing an access control TPM is 60 penalty

---

170 Ibid s 10(1) (definition of 'circumvention service').
171 At 4.5.1.1.1.
172 *Copyright Act 1968* (Cth) s 116AP(2)–(6).
173 Ibid s 116AP(2).
174 Ibid s 116AP(3).
175 Ibid s 116AP(4).
176 Ibid s 116AP(5).
177 Ibid s 116AP(7).
178 Ibid s 116AP(7).
179 At 4.5.1.
180 *Copyright Amendment Act 2006* (Cth) sch 6 pt 4 item 11 inserted new sub-div E into *Copyright Act 1968* (Cth) pt V div 5.
181 *Copyright Act 1968* (Cth) s 132APC.
182 Ibid s 132APD. The section applies where a person manufactures, imports, distributes, offers to the public, provides to another person or communicates a circumvention device.
183 Ibid s 132APE.
184 These provisions implement *AUSFTA* art 17.4.7(a)(i).

units,[185] in contrast the penalty for manufacturing a TPM circumvention device or providing a TPM circumvention service is 550 penalty units and/or five years' imprisonment.

4.5.1.5 Defences to liability for criminal actions

The defences that are available to a criminal action for breach of the TPMs are, with two exceptions, the same as those that are available for the corresponding civil provision (discussed above).[186] The first difference is that the standard and burden of proof is that which is ordinarily applied in a criminal action. The second difference is that non-profit libraries, archives, educational institutions and public non-commercial broadcasters are exempt from criminal liability in respect of anything lawfully done by them in performing their functions. This defence, which has no real civil law equivalent,[187] applies to all three forms of criminal liability.

4.5.2 Rights management information

The second TPM introduced in the *Copyright Amendment (Digital Agenda) Act 2000* (Cth), which was extended and strengthened by the *US Free Trade Agreement Implementation Act 2004* (Cth), makes it an offence for someone to intentionally remove or alter 'electronic rights management information'.[188] Electronic rights management information is electronic information, such as a digital watermark that is attached to or embodied in a copy of a work.[189] It also includes numbers or codes which represent such information in an electronic format.

Rights management information typically includes details about the copyright owner and the way the copyright material may be used.[190] One of the main advantages of rights management information is that it acts as a footprint that helps copyright owners to track the uses of their works online. This information effectively acts as a moral right of attribution, not for the author, but for the work itself. The practical effect of the protection of rights management information is that copyright owners are better able to police the use that is made of their works online. As such, rather than the internet being an unregulated domain where

---

185   See *Crimes Act 1914* (Cth) s 4AA for the definition of a 'penalty unit'.
186   See *Copyright Act 1968* (Cth) ss 132APC(2)–(8), 132APD(2)–(7), 132APE(2)–(7).
187   With the exception of the defence that allows libraries, archives and educational institutions to circumvent TPMs when deciding whether to purchase copyright materials, there is no equivalent exemption from civil liability: *Copyright Act 1968* (Cth) s 116AN(8).
188   *Copyright Act 1968* (Cth) s 116B(1)(a), (b) provides that copyright is infringed by the removal or alteration of any electronic rights management information attached to a copy of a copyright work or other subject matter without the permission of the copyright owner or exclusive licensee.
189   A new definition of rights management information was introduced as a result of the *US Free Trade Agreement Implementation Act 2004* (Cth). It explicitly requires electronic rights management information to be 'electronic' and extends the coverage of electronic rights management information protection to information that 'appears or appeared in connection with a communication, or making available, of the work'.
190   *Copyright Act 1968* (Cth) s 10(1) defines 'electronic rights management information' as electronic information that identifies the work or subject matter that is attached to, or embodied in, a copy of a work or other subject matter, or 'appears or appeared in connection with a communication, or the making available of the work or other subject-matter', or any numbers or codes that represent such information in electronic form (eg, digital watermarks) and terms and conditions of use.

'information is free', digital technologies enable copyright owners to more readily track use than they have been able to do with other technologies, such as the photocopier.

There are civil remedies and criminal sanctions for the intentional removal and alteration of electronic rights management information. To be criminally liable, a person must know, or be reckless as to whether, the information in question is protected.[191] The criminal offence requires an element of commercial or profit-making motivation.[192] In the civil action, knowledge can be implied if the person ought reasonably to have known that they would induce, enable, facilitate or conceal infringement of copyright.[193] A special defence ensures that not-for-profit libraries, archives, educational institutions and public non-commercial broadcasters who are 'performing their functions' are able to alter and remove electronic rights management information without falling foul of these sanctions.[194]

4.5.3 Unauthorised access to encoded broadcasts

On 8 January 2007, a scheme providing for unauthorised access to encoded broadcasts came into operation.[195] This scheme replaced the earlier scheme that dealt with the unauthorised manufacture, advertising, sale, marketing, use or supply of devices intended to decode cable and satellite television transmissions.[196] The 2007 scheme introduced by the *Copyright Amendment Act 2006* (Cth) implemented the recommendations of the government's digital agenda review.[197]

---

191 *Copyright Act 1968* (Cth) s 132(5C), amended by *US Free Trade Agreement Implementation Act 2004* (Cth) sch 9 item 141. Where a person is criminally liable, the maximum fine payable is 550 penalty units and/or imprisonment for not more than five years: *Copyright Act 1968* (Cth) s 132(6A), introduced by the *Copyright Amendment (Digital Agenda) Act 2000* (Cth). See *Crimes Act 1914* (Cth) s 4AA for the definition of a 'penalty unit'.
192 As a result of amendments introduced by the *US Free Trade Agreement Implementation Act 2004* (Cth) sch 9 items 139, 141(25).
193 The criminal offence would require an element of commercial or profit-making motivation (inserted by the *US Free Trade Agreement Implementation Act 2004* (Cth) sch 9 items 136, 137).
194 *Copyright Act 1968* (Cth) s 132(5EA), inserted by *US Free Trade Agreement Implementation Act 2004* (Cth) sch 9 item 142.
195 This was the Broadcast Decoding Devices Scheme, introduced in 2001 by the *Copyright Amendment (Digital Agenda) Act 2000* (Cth) and strengthened by the *US Free Trade Agreement Implementation Act 2004* (Cth). It was repealed by *Copyright Amendment Act 2006* (Cth) sch 9.
196 *Copyright Act 1968* (Cth) pt VAA (former ss 135AL–135ANA). The offence related to the commercial dealing with a broadcast decoding device (defined in s 135AL to mean a device, including a computer program, that is designed or adapted to enable a person to gain access to an encoded broadcast without the authorisation of the broadcaster by circumventing, or facilitating the circumvention of, the technical means or arrangements that protect access in an intelligible form to the broadcast) rather than the actual use of the device itself. A court was able to grant an injunction and order either damages or an account of profits: *Copyright Act 1968* (Cth) s 135AN(4). The court was also, having regard to all relevant matters, able to direct that the relevant broadcast decoding device be destroyed: *Copyright Act 1968* (Cth) ss 135AN(6), 135ANA(6).
197 See Attorney-General's Department, *Protecting Subscription Broadcasts: Policy Review Concerning Unauthorised Access to and Use of Subscription Broadcasts* (Discussion Paper, 2005), where the government decided that it should be a criminal offence to dishonestly access a subscription broadcast without authorisation and payment of the subscription fee and that it should be an offence for pay television subscribers to distribute a subscription broadcast to others or use it for commercial purposes without the broadcaster's authorisation. See Hon P. Ruddock, MP, Attorney-General, 'Pay TV signal theft to be criminal offence' (Media Release, 30 June 2005).

In addition to simplifying the existing civil and criminal provisions, the 2007 scheme also introduced new civil actions and offences. A new civil cause of action is provided where a decoding device is made available online.[198] The new scheme also established an indictable offence for a person gaining unauthorised access to a subscription broadcast.[199] Where unauthorised access is gained to a decrypted encoded broadcast, three separate indictable offences are created.[200] They correspond to the civil actions in ss 135AOD and 135AOC.[201]

4.6 Duration

The question of the appropriate period of protection that ought to be given to copyright works has attracted a lot of attention in copyright law. The duration of copyright protection used to depend on the category of copyright work in question; however, since 1 January 2019, this is no longer the case. New standard terms of copyright protection for original published and unpublished materials apply from 1 January 2019.

Prior to 2005, the period of protection for literary, dramatic, musical and artistic works was the life of the author plus fifty years. The period of protection was extended as a result of the *US Free Trade Agreement Implementation Act 2004* (Cth), which required that Australia extend protection to bring it into line with the United States provision on duration, which is the life of the author plus seventy years.[202] The *AUSFTA* also changed the period of protection for photographs from fifty years to the life of the author plus seventy years (bringing photographs into line with other artistic works).[203] These changes, which applied retrospectively,[204] took place with little if any discussion in Australia of the pros and cons of the extension of term. Australia's protection for literary, dramatic, musical and artistic works, which is now the life of the author plus seventy years, is in line with Europe and the United States.

Substantial changes to the duration of copyright were introduced on 1 January 2019 by the *Copyright Amendment (Disability Access and Other Measures) Act 2017* (Cth).[205] From 1 January 2019, there is a new way of calculating the term of copyright.

The changes simplify and harmonise the copyright terms of unpublished and published materials by introducing standard terms:

- For works (including literary, dramatic, musical and artistic works), the standard term is 70 years after the death of the author of the work.

---

198 *Copyright Act 1968* (Cth) s 135AOB.
199 Ibid s 135ASI, which carries a penalty of 60 penalty units. See *Crimes Act 1914* (Cth) s 4AA for the definition of a 'penalty unit'.
200 *Copyright Act 1968* (Cth) s 135ASJ.
201 The maximum penalty is a fine of 550 penalty units and/or five years' imprisonment. See *Crimes Act 1914* (Cth) s 4AA for the definition of a 'penalty unit'.
202 *Copyright Act 1968* (Cth) s 33(2).
203 The period of copyright protection for photographs is now the same as other artistic works – that is, the life of the author plus seventy years. These *US Free Trade Agreement Implementation Act 2004* (Cth) amendments apply to all photographs protected by copyright as of 1 January 2005. Special provisions ensure that parties who, prior to 16 August 2004, entered into agreements to exploit photographs on the assumption that they would be in the public domain, are not adversely affected by these changes.
204 *US Free Trade Agreement Implementation Act 2004* (Cth) sch 9 item 131.
205 For useful tables of periods of duration, see Australian Copyright Council, 'Duration of Copyright', above n 36.

- For works where the author in unknown, the standard term is 70 years after the making of the work or 70 years after the work has first been made public (provided it is within 50 years of its making).
- For sound recordings and films, the standard terms is 70 years after the making of the sound recording or film, or 70 years after the material has first been made public (provided it is within 50 years of its making).
- For Crown copyright material (where the Commonwealth or a state or territory is the copyright owner), the standard terms will be 50 years after the making of the material.[206]

---

206 Department of Communications and the Arts, 'Fact sheet: Upcoming changes to copyright duration' (December 2017) www.communications.gov.au/documents.

5

COPYRIGHT: EXPLOITATION, INFRINGEMENT AND DEFENCES

5.1 Introduction

This chapter examines the ways in which a copyright work can be exploited. It also examines the different ways in which copyright can be infringed and the defences that a party may rely on to escape liability for an act that would otherwise be infringing.

5.2 Exploitation

When exploiting a copyright work, the owner has a number of different options. One possibility is that the owner exploits the work themself. Another option is for the owner to sell (or assign) copyright to a third party. In this situation, ownership of the copyright work passes to the third party; the initial owner no longer has any legal interest in the copyright work. Another option is for the copyright owner to retain ownership of the work, but to allow (or license) third parties to exploit the work for them. Copyright is divisible as to the exclusive rights comprising copyright, the time of exploitation and the place of exploitation.[1] An assignment or licence of copyright may be limited to apply to one or more of the acts that the copyright owner has the exclusive right to do: for example, it may apply to broadcasting rights, film rights or paperback reprint rights.[2] An assignment or licence may be also limited to apply to a place in or part of Australia or other countries.[3] Finally, an assignment or licence may be limited to apply to part of the copyright term.[4] Thus, a licence in a work may be granted for the broadcast rights for one year in Australia only.

In many situations, the decision as to the mode of exploitation is determined by the copyright owner. While they will need to comply with relevant rules and procedures (notably Australian consumer law), the owner is largely free to do as they wish with the copyright. In some situations, however, the owner is given virtually no say in how the work is exploited. This is the case where a statutory licensing scheme is established that dictates when a work is able to be used and the remuneration that the owner should receive in return.

5.2.1 Assignment

An assignment of copyright is the transfer of the ownership of copyright. Once an assignment of copyright is given, the author no longer retains any economic rights in the work (they will, however, retain their moral rights: see chapter 6). The rights of the copyright owner are divisible; for example, copyright may be assigned in part or as a whole. If copyright is assigned and limits are placed on the time, place or duration of the assignment, this is known as a partial assignment.[5] Thus it is possible for a number of persons to hold different rights (for different acts, for different times, in different places) in the same copyright work.[6]

---

1 *Copyright Act 1968* (Cth) s 196(2)(a)–(c).
2 Ibid s 196(2)(a).
3 Ibid s 196(2)(b).
4 Ibid s 196(2)(c).
5 Ibid s 16.
6 Ibid s 30 provides that should any action need to be brought in relation to the work, the person who is entitled to the particular limited rights at issue will be entitled to sue. See *Albert & Sons Pty Ltd v Fletcher Construction Ltd* [1974] 2 NZLR 107.

To be enforceable, an assignment of copyright must be in writing and signed by or on behalf of the assignor.[7] There is no particular form of writing that is required;[8] however, the terms of the agreement should make it clear that the owner intends to grant an assignment (or a licence).[9]

Future copyright[10] may be assigned.[11] This commonly occurs in employment contracts to clarify an employee's position in relation to ownership of their copyright works. It also occurs in particular industries, such as the music industry where music contracts often contain assignment of future as well as existing copyright. This is done to ensure that all works created by up-and-coming musicians are owned. This type of arrangement came under scrutiny in the courts in the mid 1970s when young or inexperienced musicians entered into contracts that assigned existing and future copyright to their recording companies, who in return gave no undertaking to exploit the copyright assigned to them. These cases highlighted the inequality of bargaining relationships between the relevant parties and accepted that, in certain circumstances, undue influence could be brought over the weaker party, resulting in what some would see as unconscionable contracts that were able to be rescinded.[12]

5.2.2 Licences

Copyright owners commonly use licences as a means to exploit their works; it is one of the best ways for copyright owners to do so. By licensing use of their works, copyright owners can place conditions on that use. This enables copyright owners to retain ownership and control over the work while allowing others to use the work. Copyright owners may grant either an express licence (an exclusive or non-exclusive licence) or an implied licence to utilise the work in certain circumstances.[13] Within the *Copyright Act 1968* (Cth) there is provision for statutory and compulsory licences.[14]

5.2.2.1 Express licences

When thinking about licensing the use of a copyright work, a copyright owner has the choice of granting either an exclusive licence or a non-exclusive licence over their copyright work. An exclusive licence gives the licensee the sole right to use of the copyright work.[15] An exclusive

---

7   *Copyright Act 1968* (Cth) s 196(3). See *Robin Jig & Tool Co Ltd v Taylor* [1979] FSR 130.
8   A letter has been held to be sufficient: *London Printing & Publishing Alliance Ltd v Cox* [1891] 3 Ch 291.
9   See *Jonathan Cape Ltd v Consolidated Press Ltd* [1954] 1 WLR 1313; *Frisby v British Broadcasting Corporation* [1967] Ch 932; *Gold Peg International Pty Ltd v Kovan Engineering (Australia) Pty Ltd* (2005) 67 IPR 497, [71]–[113].
10 'Future copyright' is defined as copyright that is to come into existence at a future time or upon the happening of a future event: *Copyright Act 1968* (Cth) s 10(1).
11 *Copyright Act 1968* (Cth) s 197(1).
12 See *A Schroeder Music Publishing Co Ltd v Macauley* [1974] 3 All ER 616; *Clifford Davis Management Ltd v WEA Records Ltd* [1975] 1 All ER 237; *O'Sullivan v Management Agency & Music Ltd* [1985] QB 428 (each case holding that the contracts containing the assignments were unenforceable, each on different grounds of restraint of trade, unconscionable contracts and undue influence).
13 A licence granted by a copyright owner binds every successor in title of the licensor to the same extent as the licensor: *Copyright Act 1968* (Cth) s 196(4).
14 See *Copyright Act 1968* (Cth) ss 47(3), 54–64, 70(3), 107(3), 108–9, pts VA, VB, VC, ss 182B–183E.
15 An exclusive licence allows 'the licensee, to the exclusion of all other persons, to do an act that by virtue of the *Copyright Act*, the owner of copyright would but for the licence, have the exclusive right to do': *Copyright Act 1968* (Cth) s 10(1) (definition of 'exclusive licence').

licence must be in writing and signed by the licensor.[16] An exclusive licensee is given the same rights of action in relation to the licensed work as if they were the copyright owner.[17] Where an exclusive licence is sought, the copyright owner should consider a premium for that exclusivity as no-one else can make use of the copyright work.[18] A non-exclusive licence can be granted by the copyright owner to a licensee, enabling them to exercise any or all of the exclusive rights of the copyright owner (as set out in s 31 of the *Copyright Act 1968* (Cth)). A non-exclusive licence does not prevent the copyright owner from entering into other licences in relation to other uses of the work. Non-exclusive licences do not need to be in writing.

5.2.2.2 Implied licences

In certain situations, a copyright licence may be impliedly granted over works. This may occur, for example, where plans for buildings are commissioned. In this case, the commissioner is usually granted an implied licence to use the architectural drawings for the purpose for which they were prepared – for example, the construction of the building. An implied licence will also be granted by the architect to subsequent owners of the land.[19] There are many other situations where implied licences to use work are given. For example, where a person writes a letter to an editor of a newspaper, in the absence of an express permission to publish the letter, it is clear that the person will have impliedly given a licence allowing publication.

5.2.2.3 Compulsory and statutory licences

As copyright owners may use their control over copyright works to create a monopoly over their works, the legislature has recognised the need to grant a compulsory or statutory licence to ensure the public interest is served. Since the grant of the first compulsory licence in the *Literary Property Act of 1842* (5 & 6 Vict c 45), the grant and operation of compulsory or statutory licences has been a controversial area of debate within copyright law.

The *Copyright Act 1968* (Cth) provides for a number of statutory or compulsory licences. A main feature of the statutory licence is that while the copyright owner may not withhold permission to use their copyright works, they are entitled to be paid reasonable compensation for the use of their works. For parties that enjoy the benefit of a statutory licence, they are relieved of the obligation to seek permission from numerous copyright owners for the use of copyright works.[20]

The largest statutory licence schemes operating in Australia that generate significant income for the relevant collecting societies are the educational copying licences. There are, however, a number of specific statutory licences that will be discussed briefly first. Of these,

---

16   *Copyright Act 1968* (Cth) s 10(1) (definition of 'exclusive licensee').
17   Ibid ss 117–25.
18   For a definition of 'exclusive licence', see *Sega Enterprises Ltd v Galaxy Electronics Pty Ltd* (1998) 39 IPR 577.
19   Compare *Parramatta Design & Developments Pty Ltd v Concrete Pty Ltd* (2005) 144 FCR 264.
20   In Copyright Law Review Committee (CLRC), *Copyright and Contract* (Report, 2002), it was noted that '[t]he statutory licences are an efficient means of overcoming market failure … On the one hand, the copyright owners' power to withhold a licence is taken away to save users from having to seek them out to obtain a licence. On the other hand the users are made liable to pay for the use in a way that ensures remuneration to the copyright owners without the latter having to seek out the users to obtain payment': at [7.32], [7.33].

there are two broad categories: statutory licences in relation to musical works and sound recordings, and a statutory licence scheme that operates for Crown copyright material.

5.2.2.3.1 MUSICAL WORKS, SOUND RECORDINGS, BROADCASTS AND CROWN COPYRIGHT

There are a number of specific provisions that allow the playing and replaying of sound recordings. For example, ss 108 and 109 allow sound recordings to be played (or broadcast) in public, or broadcast, if the person who plays or broadcasts the sound recording pays, or agrees to pay, equitable remuneration to the copyright owner. A statutory licence is also granted for the making of records of musical works that have been previously recorded.[21] In addition, a statutory licence is granted for the use of sound recordings, or film of a work or sound recording, for the purposes of making a broadcast where the maker of the broadcast and the maker of the recording are different.[22] Special schemes also regulate the making of a sound broadcast of a literary or dramatic work, or its adaptation, by the holder of a print disability radio licence.[23] Statutory licence schemes also exist for the payment of equitable remuneration for works contained in retransmitted, free-to-air broadcasts[24] and for the use of Crown copyright material.[25]

5.2.2.3.2 EDUCATIONAL STATUTORY LICENCES

One of the most important ways in which the copying of copyright works is regulated in educational institutions is via statutory licence. The first statutory licence for educational copying in Australian universities was introduced in 1980.[26] The main catalyst for its introduction was the increasing reliance on the photocopier in the provision of educational materials in Australian universities. Other contributing factors were the time and money spent in seeking copyright owners' permissions for the enormous number of works used in universities, and the 1975 High Court decision of *University of New South Wales v Moorhouse*,[27] which held that universities were liable for authorising copyright infringements that occurred on photocopiers placed in university libraries. The aim of the educational statutory licence was 'to strike a balance between the public interest in the provision of multiple copies of works for use in educational institutions and the public interest in the provision of reasonable and practical opportunities for recompense by copyright owners for use of their work'.[28]

Under the 1980 statutory licence, record keeping was required; the copies made by educational institutions were tracked for the purpose of reimbursing the copyright owners. This was an onerous, time-consuming and expensive exercise for all parties. In 1987, educational institutions and the statutorily appointed collecting society, Copyright Agency Limited,[29] began entering into voluntary licences that largely adapted the statutory licence provisions, to

---

21   *Copyright Act 1968* (Cth) ss 54–64.
22   Ibid ss 47(3), 70(3), 107(3).
23   Ibid s 47A.
24   Ibid pt VC.
25   Ibid pt VII div 2 (ss 182B–183E).
26   *Copyright Amendment Act 1980* (Cth) s 14 inserted div 5A of pt III of the *Copyright Act 1968* (Cth).
27   (1975) 133 CLR 1.
28   CLRC, *Educational Institutions and Copying under the Copyright Act 1968* (Issues Paper, 1997) 1.
29   Now referred to as 'Copyright Agency'.

avoid the detailed record-keeping requirements. Under the new, voluntary licences, the parties agreed to forgo detailed record keeping in favour of a sampling system that distributed to copyright owners royalty payments that were calculated as an amount to be paid for each enrolled student.

In 1989, the 1980 statutory licence was repealed and replaced by a new statutory licence under Part VB ('Copying of works etc. by educational and other institutions') of the *Copyright Act 1968* (Cth).[30] In essence, Part VB provided that in return for payment of equitable remuneration, multiple copies of literary works could be made within educational institutions for educational purposes. This meant that in carrying out their teaching functions, academics were able to make multiple copies of works without fear of infringement. This has allowed universities to make copies of works, to provide course-packs (or anthologies) to students, and to place copies of works on limited access reserves in university libraries. The statutory licence was extended in 2001 to allow academics to digitise literary works and to make digital works available to students in an electronic format.[31]

A compulsory licensing scheme that enabled educational institutions to copy broadcasts, sound recordings or films included in the broadcast was provided for in Part VA of the *Copyright Act 1968* (Cth). The regime only related to copies made for educational purposes or for the purpose of assisting intellectually disabled persons. Part VA specified that payment must be made to a collecting society (the Audio-Visual Copyright Society, now known as Screenrights) and the amount was calculated on the basis of either the number of copies made (records system) or the number of students in the institution (sampling system).[32] In December 2006, the Part VA statutory licence used by educational institutions to copy broadcast material was extended to include copying of material from online sources, such as free-to-air podcasts and webcasts.[33] These could be copied for educational use as long as they were originally 'born' as free broadcasts.[34]

Since the introduction of the educational copying licences, there has been a long, and sometimes difficult, history of voluntary licensing arrangements between educational institutions and the Copyright Agency and Screenrights.[35] The rates payable per enrolled student have always been contentious and thus difficult to negotiate. Similarly, the complexity and unsuitability for the digital age of the educational copying provisions also added tension to the

---

[30] By the *Copyright Amendment Act 1989* (Cth) inserting ss 135ZH–135ZM into the *Copyright Act 1968* (Cth).

[31] There have been relatively few major amendments of the 1989 statutory scheme since its introduction. A number of streamlining improvements were made to the educational copying scheme under *Copyright Amendment Act 1998* (Cth) pt VB. However, a number of substantial amendments were made in 2001 when the pt VB licence was amended to cover digital copying: *Copyright Amendment (Digital Agenda) Act 2000* (Cth).

[32] *Copyright Act 1968* (Cth) s 135ZX(2A), which was introduced in 2006, allows educational institutions and collecting societies to agree on aspects of the records notice scheme under the pt VA licences. If the parties cannot agree, the Copyright Tribunal may make a determination about these additional issues.

[33] As a result of the *Copyright Amendment Act 2006* (Cth).

[34] *Copyright Act 1968* (Cth) s 135C. This implements ALRC, *Copyright and the Digital Economy* (Report No 122, November 2013) rec 9-1. See Explanatory Memorandum, Copyright Amendment Bill 2006 (Cth) 132; D. Browne, *A Summary of the Copyright Act 2006*, National Copyright Unit, Schools Resourcing Taskforce (2007).

[35] L. Wiseman, *Copyright in Universities* (Canberra: Department of Education, Training and Youth Affairs, 1999).

relationship between the collecting societies and educational institutions. These were just some of the matters raised in many submissions made on the educational copying provisions to the Australian Law Reform Commission (ALRC) review of copyright and the digital economy in 2013.[36] In response, the ALRC proposed the repeal of the statutory licences for government, educational institutions, and institutions assisting persons with a print disability.[37]

In December 2017, the educational copying provisions were significantly simplified and updated by the passage of the *Copyright Amendment (Disability Access and Other Measures) Act 2017* (Cth). The new div 4 ('Educational institutions – statutory licence') and div 5 ('Collecting societies') in Part IVA of the *Copyright Act 1968* (Cth) remove the record-keeping requirements of the old educational copying provisions and facilitate the negotiation of rates of equitable remuneration between collecting societies and educational institutions. The new provisions apply to both copying and communication of works and broadcasts.[38] Section 113N provides that an educational institution may copy or communicate certain copyright material for educational purposes if the body administering the educational institution agrees to pay equitable remuneration to a collecting society. So long as a remuneration notice[39] is in force, an educational institution will not infringe copyright if the copying or communicating is done for educational purposes. There is no longer any limit on the amount of a work that can be copied or communicated; the only limitation is that the amount copied or communicated 'does not unreasonably prejudice the legitimate interest of the copyright owner'.[40] Where a remuneration notice is in force, the educational institution must assist the collecting society with collection and distribution of the money.[41] The removal of the prescriptive rule of the previous statutory licences gives educational institutions and collecting societies flexibility in the administrative arrangements that will apply. The amount of equitable remuneration is either agreed between the educational institution and the collecting society or determined by the Copyright Tribunal.[42]

Despite the simplification of the educational copying provisions, it appears that the value and worth of educational copying is still contentious. In November 2018, the Copyright Agency commenced proceedings in the Copyright Tribunal to determine the value of the copyright licence, claiming that the 'annual cost of the university licence is currently $32.5 million, or 9 cents per student per day. The fee has been decreasing in real terms, given inflation, the rapid growth in student numbers and the fact there has been a huge increase in the digital platforms available for copying and sharing material.'[43] Universities Australia responded by saying, 'Universities pay hundreds of millions of dollars directly each year to publishers and copyright owners and that amount continues to grow', and stating that this is a 'fair price' for content.[44] Given the previous tensions between educational institutions and collecting societies over

---

36 See ALRC, *Copyright and the Digital Economy* (Discussion Paper No 79, May 2013) [6.38]–[6.96].
37 Ibid [6.38].
38 *Copyright Act 1968* (Cth) s 113P.
39 Ibid s 113Q.
40 Ibid s 113P(1)(d).
41 Ibid s 113S.
42 Ibid s 113R.
43 Copyright Agency, 'Action launched in Copyright Tribunal' (Media Release, 12 November 2018).
44 M. Johnston, 'Digital copyright costs lands Universities Australia before tribunal' (itnews, 13 November 2018) www.itnews.com.au.

educational copying, it is likely that recourse to the Copyright Tribunal will continue when parties are determining the value and cost of educational copying.

5.2.3 Collective administration

One of the problems that arise in relation to the exploitation of copyright works relates to the difficulties that copyright owners experience when attempting to collect payment for the use of their works. One of the techniques that copyright owners have adopted to remedy this problem is to group together into collecting societies to regulate the way that their members' copyright works are used. Copyright owners rely on collecting societies to collect licence fees for copies of the works that are made; the fees are collected and returned to the creator, less an administrative charge.

5.2.3.1 Collecting societies

Copyright collecting societies are non-profit organisations that license certain uses of copyright material on behalf of their members, and distribute the fees collected to their members.[45] Since 1 January 2002, the collecting societies have been governed by a voluntary code of conduct designed to strengthen accountability and transparency. All the major collecting societies are signatories to the Code of Conduct for Copyright Collecting Societies. The principal societies that operate in Australia are Copyright Agency, Screenrights, APRA AMCOS and Phonographic Performance Company of Australia (PPCA). Compliance by participating collecting societies with the Code's standards of conduct is the subject of an independent annual review. In August 2017, the government announced that a review would be undertaken of the extent to which the Code promotes fair and efficient outcomes for both members and licensees of copyright collecting societies in Australia.[46] On 14 February 2018, the Bureau of Communications and Arts Research released its draft report of the review.[47] It made three broad sets of recommendations aimed at increasing clarity around the Code's role and objectives,[48] encouraging greater transparency,[49] and strengthening governance arrangements.[50]

It is useful to briefly outline the interests of each of the copyright collecting societies.

5.2.3.1.1 COPYRIGHT AGENCY

Copyright Agency was set up in 1974 by authors and publishers principally to deal with the changing economics of the publishing market resulting from the impact of the photocopier. Although the organisation was formed in 1974, it did not commence operations until 1986 when the universities started paying for educational copying.[51] Copyright Agency acts

---

[45] For the practices of collecting societies, see S. Simpson, *Review of Australian Copyright Collecting Societies* (1995).
[46] Department of Communication and the Arts, 'Review of Code of Conduct for Collecting Societies' (2017) www.communications.gov.au. See also discussion in ch 2 at 2.3.2.12.
[47] Ibid.
[48] Bureau of Communications and Arts Research, *Review of Code of Conduct for Australian Copyright Collecting Societies* (Draft Report, February 2018) 4.
[49] Ibid 16–25.
[50] Ibid 27–41.
[51] See *University of New South Wales v Moorhouse* (1975) 133 CLR 1; *Haines v Copyright Agency Ltd* (1982) 64 FLR 184; *Copyright Agency Ltd v Department of Education of New South Wales* (1985) 59 ALR 172. These cases set the rate for equitable remuneration for copying under the statutory licences.

as an agent for its members and affiliated reproduction rights organisations overseas to collectively administer and protect their copyright reproduction rights.

In November 2017, Copyright Agency merged with Viscopy, a body established in October 1995 as the collecting society for the visual arts. Viscopy members became members of Copyright Agency which now also licenses the reproductions of visual or graphic artistic works on behalf of visual artists, including craft workers, photographers, sculptors, multimedia artists and designers.

5.2.3.1.2 SCREENRIGHTS

Originally known as the Audio-Visual Copyright Society, Screenrights is the collecting society for film producers and distributors, scriptwriters and music copyright owners. Established in 1990, it administers the statutory licence that allows educational institutions to copy radio and television broadcasts, and more recently other uses of audiovisual material.

5.2.3.1.3 APRA AMCOS

APRA AMCOS was formed in 1997 from an alliance between the Australasian Performing Right Association (APRA) and the Australasian Mechanical Copyright Owners' Society (AMCOS). The members of the allied organisation are songwriters, composers and music publishers. APRA AMCOS licenses the broadcast, public performance and cable transmission of live and recorded musical works and distributes royalties to members.

5.2.3.1.4 PPCA

PPCA licenses the broadcast and public performance of sound recordings (which are protected separately to any music and lyrics on the recording). The members of PPCA are owners of copyright in sound recordings (principally, record companies).

5.2.3.2 The Copyright Tribunal of Australia

The Copyright Tribunal of Australia (hereinafter 'Copyright Tribunal')[52] is established by the *Copyright Act 1968* (Cth).[53] It has jurisdiction to determine a variety of applications and references for the grant of copyright licences and the determination of royalties and remuneration.[54] One of the reasons for the establishment of the tribunal was the concern that collecting societies would not only be able to charge high royalty rates but also grant and withhold licences at their whim.[55]

In 2000, the Copyright Law Review Committee (CLRC) conducted a review of the jurisdiction and procedures of the Copyright Tribunal.[56] One of the recommendations made by the CLRC was that the jurisdiction of the tribunal should be extended to apply to collectively

---

[52] The tribunal's former official name was 'Copyright Tribunal'. The name was amended by *Copyright Amendment Act 2006* (Cth) sch 10 pt 3.
[53] *Copyright Act 1968* (Cth) s 138.
[54] See *Copyright Act 1968* (Cth) pt IV div 3.
[55] The 'legislative purpose of the Copyright Tribunal in Australia is to act as a curb on potential abuse of the monopoly power or near monopoly power gained by a voluntary collecting society by aggregating the right of individual copyright owners': *Re Applications by Australasian Performing Right Association* (1999) 45 IPR 53, 73.
[56] CLRC, *Jurisdiction and Procedures of the Copyright Tribunal* (Final Report, April 2000).

administered licences covering all types of copyright material and copyright users.[57] This recommendation (and others) was brought into effect in December 2006 by the *Copyright Amendment Act 2006* (Cth).

One of the changes made by the 2006 Act was in respect of the provisions dealing with the remuneration paid under the statutory licences in Parts VA and VB of the *Copyright Act 1968* (Cth).[58] As a result, it is now possible to charge different amounts depending on the class of material that is copied, the nature of the institution and the type of student.[59] Changes were also made to the way that collecting societies are established (the Attorney-General now has power to refer the decision to the Copyright Tribunal),[60] the way in which royalties for the copying of musical works are paid, the record-keeping requirements[61] and in relation to alternative dispute resolution.[62] Of particular importance, the tribunal can, where appropriate, now join the Australian Competition and Consumer Commission (ACCC) as a party to proceedings before the tribunal.[63]

5.3 Infringement

One of the questions that constantly arises in copyright law concerns the scope of the rights that are recognised in artistic and cultural creations and their impact on the users of those creations. While these conflicting interests are mediated and moderated in a number of different ways (such as via the duration of protection), these issues are most visible when considering the situations where copyright is infringed. This is because the question of whether copyright has been infringed depends on the scope and nature of the rights that are given to the copyright owner, as well as the defences that a defendant may rely on to avoid liability.

Copyright can be infringed either directly or indirectly. Direct infringement occurs when a person other than the copyright owner carries out any of the activities that fall within the exclusive rights of the copyright owner without the requisite permission.[64] In turn, a person will indirectly infringe copyright where, without permission, they deal[65] with articles that are themselves infringing articles or, in the case of imported articles, articles that would have been

---

57   Ibid [11.12].
58   *Copyright Amendment Act 2006* (Cth) sch 10 pt 1.
59   *Copyright Act 1968* (Cth) s 135ZV(2).
60   *Copyright Amendment Act 2006* (Cth) sch 10 items 4–33.
61   Ibid sch 11. The changes made to the record-keeping system were opposed by the education sector on the grounds that the changes would impact on the costs for educational institutions.
62   Further implementing some of the recommendations from the CLRC's review, *Jurisdiction and Procedures of the Copyright Tribunal*, above n 56.
63   By virtue of *Copyright Act 1968* (Cth) s 157AB. In April 2019, the Australian Competition and Consumer Commission (ACCC) published *ACCC Guidelines: To assist the Copyright Tribunal in the Determination of Copyright Remuneration*.
64   *Copyright Act 1968* (Cth) s 31(1) sets out the exclusive rights for works; ss 85–88 set out the exclusive rights for subject matter other than works.
65   The unauthorised dealings that constitute an indirect infringement of copyright are sale, hire, offering or exposing for sale or hire, distributing or exhibiting in public for trade purposes, distributing for other purposes prejudicial to the copyright owner, and importation for these purposes: *Copyright Act 1968* (Cth) s 37.

infringing articles if they had been made in Australia by the importer.[66] A person will also indirectly infringe copyright if they permit a place of public entertainment to be used for the public performance of a literary, dramatic or musical work.[67]

As part of the wide-ranging review of copyright that took place in 2006, the federal government made a number of changes, operative from 1 January 2007, to the way that the burden of proof operates in infringement actions.[68] These aim to make it easier for copyright owners to prove subsistence and ownership of copyright. In addition to general presumptions in relation to subsistence and ownership of copyright in civil[69] and criminal cases,[70] the *Copyright Act 1968* (Cth) contains specific presumptions relating to computer programs,[71] sound recordings[72] and films.[73]

5.3.1 Direct infringement

When considering whether there has been a direct infringement of copyright,[74] it is necessary to ask three subsidiary questions.[75] These are:

1. Has the defendant carried out one of the activities that falls within the copyright owner's exclusive control?
2. Was the alleged infringing work derived from the plaintiff's copyright work?
3. Was the unauthorised act done in relation to either the whole or a substantial part of the work?

We will look at each of these in turn.

5.3.1.1 Activities within copyright owner's exclusive control

As explained in chapter 4, copyright owners are not given absolute control over all uses of the copyright work. Instead, they are only given the exclusive right to prohibit others from dealing with the protected work in a limited number of ways. More specifically, the copyright owner is given the exclusive right to carry out certain types of activities in relation to the protected work. While the particular activities that fall within the copyright owner's control vary from work to work, they might include, for example, the exclusive right to reproduce the work or the right to communicate the work to the public. When thinking about whether a person has infringed copyright in a work, the first question to be asked is whether the defendant has exercised any

---

66   *Copyright Act 1968* (Cth) ss 37, 38, 102, 103. On the application of s 103, see *Universal Music Australia Pty Ltd v Cooper* (2005) 150 FCR 1; and on appeal to the Full Federal Court: *Cooper v Universal Music Australia Pty Ltd* (2006) 156 FCR 380.
67   *Copyright Act 1968* (Cth) s 39.
68   Introduced by *Copyright Amendment Act 2006* (Cth) sch 2.
69   *Copyright Act 1968* (Cth) ss 126–9, 126A, 126B (amended by *Copyright Amendment Act 2006* (Cth)).
70   *Copyright Act 1968* (Cth) s 132A (which applies to all offences in div 5 except s 132AM).
71   *Copyright Act 1968* (Cth) ss 129A, 130B, 132AAA (amended by the *Copyright Amendment Act 2006* (Cth)).
72   *Copyright Act 1968* (Cth) ss 130, 130A, 132B (amended by the *Copyright Amendment Act 2006* (Cth)).
73   *Copyright Act 1968* (Cth) s 132C (amended by the *Copyright Amendment Act 2006* (Cth)).
74   *Copyright Act 1968* (Cth) ss 36(1), 101(1).
75   See L. Bently, B. Sherman, D. Gangee and P. Johnson, *Intellectual Property Law* (5th edn, Oxford: Oxford University Press, 2018) 194.

of the copyright owner's exclusive rights without the requisite permission. As the scope and nature of these activities were discussed in detail in chapter 4, it is not necessary to repeat them here.[76]

5.3.1.2 Alleged infringing work derived from copyright work

Once it has been established that the defendant has carried out one of the activities that falls within the copyright owner's control, the next issue that needs to be established is that the alleged infringing work has been derived from the plaintiff's copyright work. That is, it needs to be shown that there is a causal connection between the two works.

The need to show derivation or copying is a key feature of copyright protection which distinguishes it from other areas of intellectual property law, such as patents, which can be infringed independently. In contrast, in copyright an independently created work does not infringe. Where two identical works may be created and there is no evidence of copying, both works will attract copyright protection.

When proving derivation, it is necessary to show that there is a degree of similarity between the copyright work and the alleged infringing work. It is not sufficient that there is similarity in the underlying idea; instead, the similarity must be in the way the idea is expressed – that is, in the material form of the work. This means that copyright will not be infringed if the idea behind a work, as distinct from the expression of the idea, is taken.[77] This also means that a person will not infringe if they merely draw inspiration from a copyright work.[78]

While it is usual for us to talk of the infringement of physical objects, such as books, CDs and so on, these objects may consist of more than one form of copyright. It is important to note that the type of subject matter in question will dictate that aspect of the tangible object that must be copied for the work to be infringed. This will mean, for example, that artistic works will be judged according to visual criteria[79] and musical works judged aurally.

As explained in chapter 2[80] one of the key features of copyright protection is that it is intangible. One of the consequences of this is that it is not necessary to show that the allegedly infringing copy has been derived from the *original* work; an infringing copy can be made from

---

[76] The most common type of direct infringement occurs when a work is copied (or reproduced) in a material form (discussed in ch 4 at 4.4.1). While the term 'reproduction' is not defined in the *Copyright Act 1968* (Cth), s 21 has a number of deeming provisions where works will be deemed to have been reproduced in a material form. Section 21 provides that a reproduction of a literary, musical or artistic work includes the recording of a film of the work and that an artistic work can be reproduced in another dimension. Note also s 21(1A) which clarifies that the conversion of a work from analogue to digital (including the first digitisation) and vice versa is a reproduction.

[77] See *Cuisenaire v Reed* [1963] VR 719, where the idea of coloured rods could not be protected. See also *Inform Design & Construction Pty Ltd v Boutique Homes Melbourne Pty Ltd* (2008) 77 IPR 523 (copyright law does not protect philosophy or design principles employed in planning project homes: 'these are mere ideas').

[78] *Cummins v Vella* [2002] FCAFC 218, [36].

[79] *Walt Disney Productions v H John Edwards Publishing Co Pty Ltd* (1954) 71 WN (NSW) 150, where the court referred to the test in *King Features Syndicate Inc v O & M Kleeman Ltd* [1941] AC 417, 426 by Lord Wright: the 'test to be applied in deciding an artistic work is purely visual, the work and the alleged infringement being compared *occulis subject a fidelibus*'. In this case, it was held that the idea of Donald Duck and his three nephew ducklings involved in adventures with a dog (Goofy) and a donkey (Basil) were not infringed unless the drawings were actually copied.

[80] See, for example, ch 2 at 2.1.

a copy of an original work. For example, an image that is copied from a drawing of a painting will still infringe the artistic copyright in the painting if there is sufficient similarity between the two works.[81] Similarly, the *Copyright Act 1968* (Cth) provides that a two-dimensional artistic work (such as a plan) can be reproduced in three-dimensional form (such as a building).[82] Similar provisions apply for the transformation of a three-dimensional work into a two-dimensional form.[83] In *Frank M Winstone (Merchants) Ltd v Plix Products Ltd*,[84] a tray for holding kiwi fruit made by the appellants was held to have infringed copyright in the respondent's drawings of the trays. This was the case even though the trays were made from written and oral instructions given by the appellant, rather than the drawings themselves. The *Copyright Act* also makes it clear that copyright in a computer program will be held to have been reproduced where an object code version of the program is derived from the source code. Similar provisions apply where a source code version of a program is reproduced from object code.[85]

It does not matter that the defendant was unaware that the work was protected by copyright. In this sense there is strict liability in that, if there is a causal link between the works, the defendant will be liable for infringement even though they might have been unaware that they were infringing. Obviously, the question of whether or not the defendant had access to the plaintiff's work is a relevant factor in determining a causal connection. Where the plaintiff is unable to show that the defendant had access to their work, an action for infringement is likely to fail, even though the works are similar.[86] In some cases, copyright may be infringed innocently or subconsciously.[87] In other words, liability is strict for direct infringement unless some defence or exception applies.

Copying can be proved in a number of ways. One common way of establishing copying is for the copyright owner to include deliberate mistakes in a work. This might consist of false names and addresses being placed in a telephone directory. If a plaintiff can show that a defendant's work includes the false names, the defendant will be unable to claim that they independently created the work; this is sometimes argued where informational works, such as tables, compilations, databases and computer programs, have been copied. An example of a situation where copying of this nature was held to have taken place was the decision of *Ibcos Computers v Barclays Mercantile Highland Finance Ltd*.[88] In this case, involving an allegation of copying of computer programs, the fact that the defendant had included spelling errors and

---

81 See *King Features Syndicate Inc v O & M Kleeman Ltd* [1941] AC 417; *Burke & Margot Burke Ltd v Spicers Dress Designs* [1936] Ch 400; *Elwood Clothing Pty Ltd v Cotton On Clothing Pty Ltd* (2008) 76 IPR 83 (finding no infringement where the pattern of arranging pictures and text on a T-shirt design was taken, but no actual pictures or text were taken), reversed (2008) 172 FCR 580 (allowing infringement in the taking of an artistic layout found to give rise to a specific look and feel). See also *Seafolly Pty Ltd v Fewstone Pty Ltd* (2014) 313 ALR 41, where it was held that design elements of artworks on flag fabrics were taken (in particular, the selection, layout, style and arrangement) even though there were many differences between the visual elements in each of the competing designs.
82 *Copyright Act 1968* (Cth) s 21(3)(a).
83 Ibid s 21(3)(b).
84 (1985) 5 IPR 156.
85 *Copyright Act 1968* (Cth) s 21(5).
86 *Francis Day & Hunter v Bron* [1963] Ch 587.
87 Ibid where the court accepted that as a matter of law unconscious copying was possible.
88 [1994] FSR 275, 298.

redundant code from the plaintiff's computer program in their own program was sufficient evidence for the court to conclude that copying had occurred. In other situations, evidence of copying may be gathered from someone close to the copying (for example, an ex-employee of a company that has allegedly infringed). In other cases, the courts may need to view the works side by side to reach a decision about whether there has been copying. In these instances, the courts rely on the similarities between the work and the copy to decide infringement.[89]

Once a causal connection between the alleged infringing work and the copyright work has been shown, the onus shifts to the defendant to prove that the work was created independently. One way in which this may be achieved is if the defendant is able to show a record of the process by which the alleged infringing work was created.[90]

5.3.1.3 Unauthorised act done on whole or substantial part of copyright work

The third point that needs to be established in an infringement action is that the defendant's unauthorised activities were carried out in relation to the copyright work or a substantial part thereof. In many situations, this will be a straightforward issue. This will be the case, for example, where a defendant reproduces all of a CD or photocopies all of a book. In these circumstances the unauthorised activity clearly occurs in relation to the work as a whole. Problems arise, however, where only part of a work is used. In these circumstances, the *Copyright Act 1968* (Cth) provides that copyright will only be infringed where an act is carried out in relation to a *substantial part* of the work or other subject matter.[91] It follows that it is not an infringement to copy an insubstantial portion of a work or other subject matter. The substantial part test, which allows third parties 'a measure of legitimate appropriation of an original work', is said to achieve an 'appropriate balance between protection of original works and promotion of the public interest in the encouragement of [copyright] works by providing a just reward for the creator, while at the same time maintaining the public interest of ensuring a robust public domain in which further works are produced'.[92]

The Act does not define what is meant by a 'substantial part'. Over time the courts have attempted to develop a number of tests to explain what is meant by a substantial part of a work. While not always helpful, they do provide some guidance as to how this issue is addressed by the courts. One of the factors that the courts will look at when deciding whether a defendant has taken a substantial part is the *quantity* of the work that is taken. Clearly, the more that it is taken or used by a defendant, the more likely it is that that they will infringe. In some situations it is possible to take a small portion of work and still infringe.

---

89   For a discussion of infringement of literary and dramatic plots, see S. Rebikoff, 'Restructuring the test for copyright infringement in relation to literary and dramatic plots' (2001) 25 *Melbourne University Law Review* 340.

90   See *Billhöfer Maschinenfabrik GmbH v TH Dixon & Co Ltd* [1990] FSR 105, 123, where Hoffman J stated: 'It is the resemblance in inessentials, the small redundant even mistaken elements of the copyright work which carry the greatest weight. This is because they are least likely to have been the result of independent design.'

91   *Copyright Act 1968* (Cth) s 14.

92   *IceTV Pty Ltd v Nine Network Australia Pty Ltd* (2009) 239 CLR 458, [71], [28]. See also *EMI Songs Australia Pty Ltd v Larrikin Music Publishing Pty Ltd* (2011) 191 FCR 444, [56].

While the amount of the work that has been taken is important, the courts also place a lot of emphasis on the *quality* of the part that is reproduced. In *IceTV* the High Court stressed that when determining whether a part that has been copied is substantial, the 'quality of what is copied is critical'.[93] This may mean, for example, that a person will infringe where they reproduce a small part of a work, such as the core of a poem, the chorus of a song, or the results of a lengthy experiment. This may not necessarily mean that the taking of a small part will infringe. In contrast, it may mean that there will be no infringement even if a large portion of a work is copied where the portion copied is not original (e.g., where the defendant only takes facts or data). The decision to focus on the quality of the part taken gives rise to the question: what criteria are used to judge quality?

In many cases, the courts have focused on the characteristics of the part that has been reproduced. If the part taken represents the application of a high degree of skill and labour on the part of the author, it may be regarded as a substantial part, even though it is comparatively small in quantitative terms. Following from this, the courts have suggested that substantiality should be determined by 'considering the originality of the part allegedly taken'.[94] This was reiterated in the *IceTV* decision where the High Court was called on to consider whether the reproduction of time and title information from Nine's Weekly Schedule – that is, the time at which programs were to be broadcast on the Nine Network and the title of those programs – was a substantial reproduction of the copyright in those schedules. In considering this question, the court stressed that when determining whether a substantial part had been reproduced, it was necessary to focus on the nature of the skill and labour, and, in particular, to ask whether it is directed to the originality of the particular form of expression.[95] More specifically, the High Court said that when determining whether the part taken is substantial, a 'critical question is the degree of originality of the particular form of expression of the part'.[96] On the basis that the time and title information was not original, required neither particular mental effort nor exertion and was essentially dictated by function,[97] the High Court held that IceTV had not reproduced a substantial part of the Weekly Schedules and, as such, had not infringed Nine's copyright.

A similar approach was adopted in *Fairfax Media Publications Pty Ltd v Reed International Books Australia*[98] where the question for consideration was whether, in reproducing headlines and by-lines from articles in the *Australian Financial Review*, Reed had reproduced

---

[93] *IceTV Pty Ltd v Nine Network Australia Pty Ltd* (2009) 239 CLR 458, [30], [155], [170]. See also *Hawkes & Son (London) Ltd v Paramount Film Service Ltd* [1934] Ch 593.

[94] *Data Access Corp v Powerflex Services Pty Ltd* (1999) 202 CLR 1, quoting Mason CJ in *Autodesk Inc v Dyason (No 1)* (1992) 173 CLR 330, 305. See *Klissers Bakeries v Harvest Bakeries Ltd* (1986) 5 IPR 399 (a substantial reproduction is not necessarily reproduction of a 'substantial part' where that part has no originality).

[95] *IceTV Pty Ltd v Nine Network Australia Pty Ltd* (2009) 239 CLR 458 [30], [49]. The 'more simple or lacking in substantial originality the copyright work, the greater the degree of taking will be needed before the substantial part test is satisfied': at [40]. See also *EMI Songs Australia Pty Ltd v Larrikin Music Publishing Pty Ltd* (2011) 191 FCR 444, [55].

[96] *IceTV Pty Ltd v Nine Network Australia Pty Ltd* (2009) 239 CLR 458, [52].

[97] As the authors of the Weekly Schedule had little if any choice in the expression adopted, as that expression was essentially dictated by function, it lacked the requisite originality: ibid [41]–[42], [532]–[554].

[98] (2010) 189 FCR 109.

a substantial part of the articles in question. Following *IceTV*, it was held that the 'reproduction of a part which by itself has no originality will not normally be a substantial part of the copyright work and therefore not protected ... If the author would not have copyright in the part standing alone, the part reproduced will not be a substantial part'.[99] Specifically, the plaintiff would 'not succeed in claiming infringement by taking the headline because the headline has not been shown to be an original, and therefore, substantial part of the work'.[100]

While the originality of the part taken may be particularly relevant where what has been copied is no more than a 'sliver of information' (as in *IceTV*),[101] in other cases the decision to use originality as a test for substantiality may open up as many problems as it solves. Given this, it is not surprising that in some cases the courts have relied on external criteria, such as the fact that the part taken is easily recognisable by the public, as virtual proof that the part taken was substantial. Thus in *Hawkes & Son (London) v Paramount Film Service*,[102] a key factor in Lord Hanworth's decision that the copying of twenty seconds of a four-minute musical work was an infringement was the fact that 'it would be recognised by any person'.[103] So too, a key factor in the decision in *Larrikin Music* that the reproduction of two bars from 'Kookaburra Sits in the Old Gum Tree' as the flute riff in the Men at Work song 'Down Under', was a substantial reproduction (and thus infringing) was the fact that the lead singer, Colin Hay, had occasionally sung the words of 'Kookaburra' when performing 'Down Under' in concert.[104]

The decision of *Dempsey Group Pty Ltd v Spotlight Pty Ltd*,[105] provides further guidance on what constitutes reproduction of a substantial part of a copyright work. This case involved an allegation of copyright infringement of bed linen fabric design (an artistic work). Davies J observed:[106]

> [I]t is unnecessary that the two works bear an overall resemblance to each other[;] nor is it appropriate to dissect the copyright work piecemeal and focus on the differences. If similarities are identified, the question is the qualitative significance of such similarities. Reproduction does not strictly require a complete and accurate correspondence to a 'substantial part' of the work.[107]

As explained in chapter 3, one of the ways in which Part IV subject matter ('subject matter other than works') differs from Part III works is that subsistence of copyright does not depend on the need to show originality. Instead, all that needs to be shown is that the work has not been copied. One of the consequences of this is that the courts tend to look more to the quantity

---

99 Ibid [116].
100 Ibid [117].
101 See *Primary Health Care Ltd v Commissioner of Taxation* (2010) 186 FCR 301, [832].
102 [1934] Ch 593, 604.
103 Ibid. Slessor LJ held that it was a substantial part 'looked at from any point of view, whether it be quantity, quality or occasion': at 604.
104 *EMI Songs Australia Pty Ltd v Larrikin Music Publishing Pty Ltd* (2011) 191 FCR 444, [57], citing the trial judge in *Larrikin Music Publishing Pty Ltd v EMI Songs Australia Pty Ltd* (2010) 263 ALR 155, [227] (Colin Hay's 'performance of the words of Kookaburra to the tune of the flute riff in Down Under' was 'sufficient illustration that the qualitative test is met'). Strictly speaking this seems to go more to objective similarity than to the question of whether a substantial part had been reproduced.
105 [2018] FCA 2016.
106 Relying on Dodds-Streeton J's observation in *Seafolly Pty Ltd v Fewstone Pty Ltd* (2014) 313 ALR 41, [345].
107 [2018] FCA 2016, [117].

rather than the quality of the part taken when determining whether there has been an infringement of subject matter other than works.[108]

One issue that has arisen in recent years relates to the question of what it means to reproduce a substantial part of a computer program. One of the first occasions where this arose was in *Autodesk v Dyason (No 1)*,[109] where a majority of the High Court[110] suggested that to infringe, a person needed to reproduce the functional features of a program. As Dawson J said:

> Whilst the 127-bit look-up table does not of itself constitute a computer program within the meaning of the definition – it does not by itself amount to a set of instructions – it is a substantial part of Widget C and its reproduction in the Auto Key lock is a reproduction of a substantial part of that program.[111]

The minority said that the question of whether a substantial part had been reproduced should be determined by reference to the originality of the part in question.[112] Mason CJ, in dissent, quoted Lord Pearce's statement in *Ladbroke (Football) Ltd v William Hill (Football) Ltd*[113] and commented that 'in the context of copyright law, where emphasis is to be placed upon the "originality" of the work's expression, the essential or material features of a work should be ascertained by considering the originality of the part allegedly taken'.[114]

The next occasion where the High Court considered the question of what it means to reproduce a substantial part of a computer program was in the 1999 decision of *Data Access Corp v Powerflex Pty Ltd*.[115] In *Data Access*, a majority of the High Court recognised that the reasoning in *Autodesk* was problematic:

> There is great force in the criticism that the 'but for' essentiality test which is effectively invoked by the majority in *Autodesk No 2* is not practicable as a test for determining whether something which appears in a computer program is a substantial part.[116]

The majority then indicated that it preferred Mason CJ's view in *Autodesk* (quoted above).[117] In light of this, the majority in *Data Access* held that the question of whether a substantial part of a

---

108   *Nationwide News Pty Ltd v Copyright Agency Ltd* (1996) 65 FCR 399. The Full Federal Court in *TCN Channel Nine Pty Ltd v Network Ten Pty Ltd* (2002) 118 FCR 417 (at first instance (2001) 108 FCR 235) provided an interesting discussion of what constituted a substantial taking in relation to a television broadcast. See also M. Handler, 'The *Panel* case and television broadcast copyright' (2003) 25 *Sydney Law Review* 391.
109   *Autodesk Inc v Dyason (No 1)* (1992) 173 CLR 330. In *Autodesk Inc v Dyason (No 2)* (1993) 176 CLR 300, the High Court refused to reopen its judgment in *Autodesk Inc v Dyason (No 1)*.
110   Dawson, Brennan and Gaudron JJ (majority).
111   *Autodesk Inc v Dyason (No 1)* (1992) 173 CLR 330, 346. All members of the court agreed with this conclusion.
112   Mason CJ and Deane J (minority).
113   [1964] 1 WLR 273.
114   *Autodesk Inc v Dyason (No 1)* (1992) 173 CLR 330, 305.
115   (1999) 202 CLR 1.
116   Ibid 248 (Gleeson CJ, McHugh, Gummow and Hayne JJ).
117   Ibid. In *Cantor Fitzgerald International v Tradition (UK) Ltd* [2000] RPC 95, Pumfrey J criticised the approach of the majority in *Autodesk* stating that its approach was too simplistic as 'the reasoning would result in any part of any computer program being substantial since without any part the program would not work': at 130.

computer program had been taken was to be decided by reference to the originality of the part taken and not its functionality.[118] Some of the confusion in this area has been clarified by the introduction of s 47D of the *Copyright Act 1968* (Cth), which details a number of situations where copyright in a computer program will not be infringed.[119]

5.3.1.4 Authorisation

One of the notable characteristics of many types of copyright works is that they are able to be consumed and used by a vast number of people at once. This provides owners with the opportunity to recoup money from a large number of people (although there are often problems and costs associated with the collection of small sums of money from a large number of users). At the same time, the fact that copyright works may be simultaneously used by a number of different people also presents owners with the problem that their copyright may be infringed by a number of different people. These problems were exacerbated by technological changes such as the introduction of the photocopier, the tape player and digital technologies. New modes of distributing copyright works, particularly those based on peer-to-peer technology, have further aggravated these problems.

To remedy problems of this nature, copyright owners have been given the capacity to bring an action against a person who authorises an infringing activity.[120] This operates alongside the owner's right to bring an action against a person who directly infringes copyright (for example, against a person who manually operates a photocopy machine or downloads an infringing copy of a song). The ability to sue parties who authorise infringement means that copyright owners are able to concentrate their efforts on a smaller number of more visible and financially stable parties who, ideally, will then take on the role of policing copyright on behalf of the copyright owner. This technique has been used by copyright owners to sue large institutional users, such as libraries and universities. More recently, copyright owners have also relied on the fact that a party will infringe where they authorise infringement in their attempt to regulate and control copying and downloading on the internet. While copyright owners have brought a limited number of high-profile cases against individual users, it is clear that it is not practical to litigate against everyone who, for example, downloads pirated music. Instead, copyright owners have targeted third parties who have facilitated and fostered digital copyright infringement. Instead of suing each of the millions of individuals who used peer-to peer technology to download songs, copyright owners decided to sue the companies (for example, in cases such as *Napster*[121] and *Sharman*[122]) that provided the technical means that supported the peer-to-peer technology used by individual users.

---

118 The High Court (other than Gaudron J) said that it would have decided *Autodesk (No 2)* differently, stating: '[T]hat being so, a person who does no more than reproduce those parts of a program which are "data" or "related information" and which are irrelevant to its structure, choice of commands and combination and sequencing of commands will be unlikely to have reproduced a substantial part of the computer program. We say "unlikely" and not "impossible" because it is conceivable that the data considered alone could be sufficiently original to be a substantial part of the computer program': *Data Access Corp v Powerflex Services Pty Ltd* (1999) 202 CLR 1, 249.
119 This largely covers situations where reproductions are made for the purposes of making interoperable products.
120 See *Copyright Act 1968* (Cth) ss 36(1), 101(1).
121 *A & M Records Inc v Napster Inc* (2000) 50 IPR 232.
122 *Universal Music Australia Pty Ltd v Sharman License Holdings Ltd* (2005) 222 FCR 465.

5.3.1.4.1 THE MEANING OF 'AUTHORISATION'

The leading case on the meaning of authorisation in Australia is the 1975 High Court decision of *University of New South Wales v Moorhouse*.[123] The case was brought to test the system of unsupervised coin-operated photocopying machines in university libraries. While the subject matter in hand was of little importance, leave was nonetheless granted for the matter to be heard by the High Court because of the public interest issues involved.[124]

This decision arose when the novelist Frank Moorhouse sued the University of New South Wales for infringement of the copyright in his collection of short stories called *The Americans, Baby*. As was common at the time, the university supplied a number of coin-operated photocopier machines for use by its staff and students. The university adopted a number of measures to prevent the photocopying machines being used to commit copyright infringements. Notices were displayed on the machines in accordance with s 49 of the *Copyright Act 1968* (Cth), which provided that copyright is not infringed by the making of a copy by or on behalf of a librarian on the conditions set out in s 49.[125] This section provided a defence to copying done by a librarian, but not by others. The university also issued a library guide each year advising students, inter alia, of their rights to make a copy of a work for research or private study. However, it did not set out the permissible limits or details of what constituted a fair dealing of a work.[126] Beyond this, the use of the photocopiers in the library was largely unsupervised.

Paul Brennan, who was a graduate of the University of New South Wales, used one of the coin-operated self-service photocopying machines in the university library to make two photocopies of a story from *The Americans, Baby*. Moorhouse and his publisher, Angus & Robertson, sued the university, alleging that it had infringed copyright in the book by reproducing or authorising the reproduction of part of the book. Moorhouse alleged that the university had effectively authorised the infringement because it had placed photocopying machines in its libraries, but had failed to supervise or control what was being copied. It was also argued that the university was indifferent to whether persons using the machines infringed copyright. In essence, the question before the High Court was whether the University of New South Wales had authorised the copyright infringement that had taken place on the

---

123 (1975) 133 CLR 1. The case also added weight to the review by the Franki Committee of copying within universities, which was largely responsible for introduction of the first statutory licence in 1980. *Copyright Amendment Act 1980* (Cth) s 14 inserted new div 5A of pt III of the *Copyright Act 1968* (Cth). See S. Ricketson and D. Catterns, 'Of vice-chancellors and authors: *UNSW v Moorhouse*' in A. Kenyon, M. Richardson and S. Ricketson (eds), *Landmarks in Australian Intellectual Property Law* (Melbourne: Cambridge University Press, 2009) ch 6.
124 *University of New South Wales v Moorhouse* (1975) 133 CLR 1, 3.
125 At the time, *Copyright Act 1968* (Cth) s 49 permitted librarians to copy reasonable portions and periodical articles for a user if requests were made and certain conditions met. The section is similar today; however, amendments were made by the *Copyright Amendment (Digital Agenda) Act 2000* (Cth) to take into account electronic copies of works.
126 The trial judge went so far as to say that much photocopying was taking place in the university that was not fair dealing, and this was evidenced by the fact that the university had failed to attach to the machines a notice in the form prepared by the Australian Vice-Chancellor's Committee and sent to the university in October 1969. This was rejected by the High Court as an unsupportable conclusion: *University of New South Wales v Moorhouse* (1975) 133 CLR 1, 14 (Gibbs J).

photocopying machines in the university library because it exercised control or supervision over the machines.

The High Court began by noting that the university had reasonable grounds to suspect that some infringements would occur if adequate precautions were not taken.[127] It then went on to hold that the measures taken by the university, such as the section 49 notice (which protected librarians from infringement) and the library guides, did not amount to reasonable or effective precautions against infringement of copyright by the use of the photocopying machines.[128] As such, the High Court held that the university had authorised the infringement.[129] As Gibbs J said:

> The University had the power to control both the use of the books and the use of the machines. In the circumstances, if a person who was allowed to use the library made a copy of a substantial part of a book taken from the open shelves of the library, and did so otherwise than by way of fair dealing for the purpose of research or private study, it can be inferred that the University authorized him to do so, unless the University had taken reasonable steps to prevent an infringing copying of that kind from being made.[130]

The next important occasion where the meaning of authorisation was considered was the British House of Lords decision of *CBS Songs Ltd v Amstrad Consumer Electronics plc*.[131] The question before the House of Lords in this case was whether in selling a high-speed twin-tape recorder, Amstrad had authorised the infringements that were inevitably going to be made on the tape recorder. The Lords held that the sale of the tape player did not amount to an authorisation. The key reason for this was that advertisements for the tape recorder specifically warned users that the recording of some material was only possible with permission of the copyright owner. While the tape players provided the means to infringe, the Lords were persuaded that Amstrad had not granted or purported to grant the right to do the act complained of. In so doing, the Lords defined 'authorisation' very restrictively.[132]

In 2001, a number of changes were made to the *Copyright Act 1968* (Cth) to clarify what was meant by 'authorisation'.[133] These apply both to infringement of works[134] and to subject matter other than works.[135] Under these provisions, the following factors are to be taken into consideration when deciding whether a person has illicitly authorised the doing of an act:

---

127 *University of New South Wales v Moorhouse* (1975) 133 CLR 1, 7 (McTiernan ACJ), 14 (Gibbs J), 23 (Jacobs J).
128 Ibid 17 (Gibbs J).
129 Ibid.
130 Ibid 14 (Gibbs J). As a result of this decision, s 39 of the *Copyright Act 1968* (Cth) was inserted. It provided that, if a notice was displayed at a photocopying machine that advised people of their obligations under the *Copyright Act 1968* (Cth), then there could be no responsibility sheeted home to an institution for authorising infringements that may have taken place on that machine. In effect the High Court followed earlier decisions that had held that authorise means to sanction, countenance or approve. See *Falcon v Famous Players Film Co* [1926] 2 KB 474, 491.
131 [1988] AC 1013.
132 Ibid 493–4.
133 As a result of the *Copyright Amendment (Digital Agenda) Act 2000* (Cth) amendments. See *Copyright Act 1968* (Cth) s 39B for works and s 112B for subject matter other than works.
134 *Copyright Act 1968* (Cth) s 36(1A).
135 *Copyright Act 1968* (Cth) s 101(1A).

- the extent of the person's power to prevent the doing of the act concerned;
- the nature of any relationship existing between the person and the person who did the act concerned; and
- whether the person took any reasonable steps to prevent or avoid the doing of the act, including whether the person complied with any relevant industry codes of practice.

Special provisions protect libraries and archives from liability for authorising infringement of a copyright work on copiers and computers, so long as an appropriate sign is placed near the machine in question.[136] The *Copyright Act 1968* also provides that if a person makes an infringing copy of a published edition of a work or audiovisual item on a machine, including a computer, in a library or archive, the library or archive will not be taken to have authorised the infringement if a prescribed notice is given on or near the machine.[137]

5.3.1.4.2 LIABILITY OF INTERNET SERVICE PROVIDERS

As mentioned above,[138] the fact that parties who authorise other parties to infringe copyright are themselves potentially liable for infringement has been used by copyright owners in an attempt to control online uses of copyright works.

The same principles apply to authorisation of online infringements as apply in other contexts. This means that a person will only be directly liable for copyright infringement where they have determined the content of that communication. In light of concerns raised by internet service providers (ISPs) about their liability for infringements by users of their services,[139] the *Copyright Act 1968* (Cth) was amended in 2001 to make it clear that ISPs and telecommunications carriers will not be liable 'merely because another person uses the facilities to do something'.[140] The scope of s 112E was considered by the Full Federal Court in *Roadshow Films Pty Ltd v iiNet Ltd*.[141] The court held that where an ISP authorised an infringement, it would never merely be 'providing facilities' and as a result would not be protected by s 112E.[142] As the Full Federal Court noted, given that a person who merely 'uses facilities to do something' would never be found liable for authorisation in the first place, it seems that s 112E is redundant.

The legal standing of ISPs and telecommunication carriers was clarified by changes made to the *Copyright Act 1968* (Cth) in 2004 to bring copyright law into line with the *Australia–US Free Trade Agreement 2004*. Under these amendments, ISPs and telecommunication carriers (referred to in the Act as 'carriage providers') are deemed to be immune from monetary remedies for copyright infringement in the course of carrying out certain 'relevant activities'.[143] For a carriage provider to rely on these so-called safe harbour provisions, they must comply with certain 'relevant conditions'.

---

136   *Copyright Act 1968* (Cth) s 39A.
137   *Copyright Act 1968* (Cth) s 104B.
138   At 5.3.1.4.1.
139   *Copyright Act 1968* (Cth) s 36(1A).
140   *Copyright Act 1968* (Cth) s 112E.
141   (2011) 194 FCR 285.
142   Ibid [212]–[228], [452]–[470], [784]–[797].
143   *Copyright Act 1968* (Cth) s 116AG.

The relevant conditions that carriage providers must comply with to avoid liability change depending on the way that the carriage provider interacts with the copyright material.[144] The only requirements that apply in all situations is that the carriage provider must adopt and apply a policy that provides for the termination of the accounts of repeat infringers, as well as comply with any relevant industry code in force. The scope of these conditions was explored, in passing, in the 2011 Full Federal Court decision of *Roadshow Films Pty Ltd v iiNet Ltd*.[145] While the trial judge had found that the ISP (iiNet) had, and had reasonably implemented, a policy that would have entitled it to the protection offered by the safe harbour provisions, the Full Federal Court rejected the claims, arguing that iiNet had neither adopted nor reasonably implemented a policy that provided for termination in appropriate circumstances of the accounts of repeat infringers. While there is little clear guidance as to what an appropriate policy might look like, it seems that it must be in writing and clearly deal with repeat infringers.

Beyond this, the requirements that a carriage provider must comply with to rely on the safe harbour provisions vary depending on how they interact with the copyright material. In this sense, the *Copyright Act 1968* (Cth) distinguishes between three different situations. The first is where a carriage service provider provides facilities or services for transmitting or routing of copyright materials or for the storage of such material while in transmission. In this case, to avoid financial liability for infringement the carriage service provider must not initiate or direct a third party to undertake the transmissions. The Act also states that they must not make substantive modifications to the copyright material that is being transmitted.[146]

The second situation is where a carriage service provider automatically caches copyright material. Here, to avoid financial liability for infringement the provider must ensure that all parties who have access to the cached material comply with any obligations that are imposed on users at the site where the materials originated. The carriage service provider must also comply with any industry codes of conduct in force, as well as remove or disable access to cached material upon notification in the 'prescribed form'[147] that the material has been removed from the originating site. To benefit from the safe harbour provisions, the carriage provider must not make any substantive modifications to the cached material when it is transmitted to users (other than that which occurs as part of a technical process).[148]

The third scenario is where a carriage service provider stores copyright material at the discretion of a user[149] or refers or links users to an online location.[150] In this situation, to escape financial liability for infringement, the provider must not receive any financial benefits as a result of the infringing activity. They must also remove or disable access to the copyright material if they become aware that the copyright material is, or is likely to be, infringing.[151]

The meaning of authorisation for online uses of infringing works was further clarified in three recent decisions. The first of these was *Universal Music Australia Pty Ltd v Sharman*

---

144   Ibid ss 116AC–116AF (defining 'relevant activities'), 116AH (defining the 'relevant conditions').
145   (2011) 194 FCR 285.
146   *Copyright Act 1968* (Cth) s 116AH condition 2.
147   The form of the take-down notices is set out in *Copyright Amendment Regulations (No 1) 2004* (Cth) sch 10 pts 1–6.
148   *Copyright Act 1968* (Cth) ss 116AC, 116AH condition 3.
149   Ibid s 116AE.
150   Ibid s 116AF.
151   Ibid ss 116AD–AE, 116AH conditions 3–4.

License Holdings Ltd.[152] In this case, an infringement action was brought against Sharman License Holdings, a company that provided the software and website that underpinned a peer-to-peer network that was widely used for the exchange of pirated music. While the *Copyright Act 1968* (Cth) provides that the mere provision of facilities such as a peer-to peer sharing network does not of itself constitute an authorisation,[153] nonetheless Sharman was held to have infringed copyright insofar as it authorised users of the system to make copies of pirated sound recordings. An important consideration in the court's deliberations was the fact that Sharman had encouraged users to share music files and had used advertising that 'conveyed the idea that it was "cool" to defy the record companies and their stuffy reliance on their copyrights'.[154]

The second decision where the nature of online authorisation was considered was *Universal Music Australia Pty Ltd v Cooper*.[155] While the defendant (Cooper) was not directly involved in any infringing activities, he hosted a website that provided hyperlinks to remote websites that contained pirated sound recordings that could be downloaded by users. Cooper was held to have authorised the infringement of copyright by internet users who downloaded music from the remote websites. He was also held to have authorised the infringement of copyright by the operators of the remote websites. In the Federal Court, Tamberlin J said that although Cooper was aware that at least some of the music on the internet was pirated, he had not even attempted to ascertain whether the sites that he was directing users to contained recordings that were made in breach of copyright.[156] On appeal, the Full Federal Court affirmed the reasoning of Tamberlin J, holding that Cooper (the website designer) and E-talk (the hosting ISP) were both liable for having authorised infringement of copyright insofar as they provided links to infringing music.[157] In so doing, the Full Federal Court provided an expansive reading of the meaning of authorisation. This was exemplified by Branson J when she said:

> [A] person's power to prevent the doing of an act comprised in a copyright includes the person's power not to facilitate the doing of that act by, for example, making available to the public a technical capacity calculated to lead to the doing of that act. The evidence leads to the inexorable inference that it was the deliberate choice of Mr Cooper to establish and maintain his website in a form which did not give him the power immediately to prevent, or immediately to restrict, internet users from using links on his website to access remote websites for the purpose of copying sound recordings in which copyright subsisted.[158]

While Kenny J provided a more conventional approach to the question of whether a person has authorised an infringement – focusing on a combination of factors including knowledge,

---

152 (2005) 222 FCR 465.
153 *Copyright Act 1968* (Cth) s 112E.
154 *Universal Music Australia Pty Ltd v Sharman License Holdings Ltd* (2005) 222 FCR 465.
155 (2005) 150 FCR 1.
156 Ibid. See J. Ginsburg and S. Ricketson, 'Inducers and authorisers: A comparison of the US Supreme Court's *Grokster* decision and the Australian Federal Court's *KaZaa* ruling' (2006) 11 *Media and Arts Law Review* 1; G. Austin, '*Kazaa* and *Grokster* across borders' (2006) 11 *Media and Arts Law Review* 355.
157 *Cooper v Universal Music Australia Pty Ltd* (2006) 156 FCR 380.
158 Ibid [41].

inactivity and control – nonetheless she also emphasised the fact that Cooper could have prevented the infringing acts

> either by not establishing the link in the first place or, subsequently, by disabling or removing the link. The fact that internet users could make other online copies of the sound recordings by other means does not detract from the fact that there were infringements as a consequence of effective activations of the links on the website operated by Mr Cooper.[159]

The third and most recent decision to explore what it means to authorise an infringement online was the 2011 Full Federal Court decision of *Roadshow Films Pty Ltd v iiNet Ltd*.[160] This was an infringement action brought by thirty-four Hollywood film companies against iiNet, the third largest ISP in Australia. The film companies argued that iiNet users had infringed copyright of Hollywood films by engaging in peer-to-peer file sharing using the BitTorrent peer-to-peer network. Like many other authorisation decisions, the iiNet litigation was part of a wider campaign on behalf of copyright owners to prevent infringement. As occurred with the photocopier, the tape-to-tape player and the video recorder, copyright owners were frustrated with their inability to prevent end-users from infringing copyright. As often happens, the copyright owners turned to focus on the parties who acted as intermediaries – here the ISPs – who were a steadier and more fixed target.

Between July 2008 and March 2009, the Australian Federation Against Copyright Theft (AFACT), who acted on behalf of the film companies, sent weekly notices to iiNet that detailed the alleged infringements that had taken place. The infringement notices also demanded that iiNet suspend or terminate the internet services of the (alleged) infringers. iiNet did not dispute the fact that many of its customers infringed copyright. iiNet also agreed that it could identify the customers on whose accounts the alleged infringements occurred, and that it had both a contractual right and the technical capacity to terminate the accounts of customers. iiNet did not believe, however, that it had responsibility to regulate the copyright activities of their users. Instead, iiNet simply forwarded the information that AFACT had sent it on to the police.

Frustrated with iiNet's response, the film companies brought an action in the Federal Court in November 2008 arguing that iiNet had authorised the copyright infringement of its customers. iiNet denied that it had authorised infringement.[161] At first instance, Cowdroy J found in favour of iiNet, arguing that iiNet had not authorised the copyright infringement of its users. In particular, Cowdroy J held that although iiNet had provided the necessary preconditions for infringement (namely, access to the internet), it had not provided the necessary 'means' of infringement, which was the *use* of BitTorrent in a 'deliberate or calculated manner to infringe copyright'.[162]

The film companies appealed Cowdroy J's decision to the Full Federal Court, where the key question was whether iiNet had authorised the copyright infringement by its customers under s 101(1) of the *Copyright Act 1968* (Cth). The majority of the Full Federal Court (Emmett and Nicholas JJ) rejected the appeal (with Jagot J dissenting) and held that iiNet had *not* authorised

---

159 Ibid [148], [149].
160 (2011) 194 FCR 285.
161 iiNet also argued that it was protected by s 112E and by the safe harbour provisions.
162 *Roadshow Films Pty Ltd v iiNet Ltd (No 3)* (2010) 83 IPR 430.

the infringements by its customers. While the Full Court upheld Cowdroy J's decision, it disagreed with his reasoning. In particular, the court rejected the distinction that Cowdroy J had drawn between a 'precondition' and a 'means' of infringement. Instead, the court unanimously agreed that when determining whether a person had authorised an infringement, it was necessary to take account of the three factors set out in s 101(1A). These were:

- the extent (if any) of iiNet's power to prevent the infringing act;
- the nature of the relationship between the iiNet and the primary infringers; and
- whether iiNet took any other reasonable steps to prevent or avoid infringing act.

While the Full Federal Court stressed that these factors were non-exhaustive and that it was necessary to take account of other relevant factors, such as those outlined in *University of New South Wales v Moorhouse*,[163] the court concentrated on the factors set out in s 101(1A) in deciding whether iiNet had authorised the copyright infringement of its customers.

In relation to the first factor, all three judges of the Full Court found (contrary to the trial judge) that iiNet had both the technical capacity[164] and the contractual right to adopt and implement a scheme of warnings and suspension or termination of customer accounts.[165] Moreover, 'it had other technical capacities available to it which it routinely used in other circumstances, particularly shaping (slowing the speed at which downloading can occur)'.[166] On this basis, all three of the judges held that iiNet had 'the capacity to control the use of its services by its customers and to take steps to prevent acts of infringement' and that the 'presence of such provisions amounted to a degree of power to prevent further acts of infringement'.[167]

The second factor set out in s 101(1A)(b), which requires the court to take account of the nature of the relationship between iiNet and its customers, was effectively subsumed within the inquiry under s 101(1A)(a) and, as such, was not considered in any real detail.[168]

While the three judges agreed that iiNet had the power to prevent the infringing act, they were divided in relation to the third factor set out in s 101(1A)(c): namely, whether iiNet's failure to suspend or terminate the internet services of the alleged infringers was 'reasonable' in the circumstances and, as such, whether iiNet had authorised the primary infringements. While the majority (Emmett and Nicholas JJ) held that iiNet had not acted unreasonably in the circumstances and as such had not authorised the primary infringements, Jagot J dissented and held that it would have been reasonable for iiNet to have terminated or suspended the accounts of infringers. Given that iiNet had not done so, Jagot J held that iiNet had authorised the primary infringements.

---

163 Discussed above at 5.3.1.4.1.
164 The majority found that iiNet had the technical power to prevent copyright infringement, including warning customers, blocking websites, and suspending and terminating accounts: *Roadshow Films Pty Ltd v iiNet Ltd* (2011) 194 FCR 285, [182], [399]–[427], [719]–[725].
165 iiNet also had contractual power, under its customer relationship agreement, to cancel, suspend or restrict the internet service without liability for the subscriber's breach of the agreement, including the use of the service to infringe another person's rights: *Roadshow Films Pty Ltd v iiNet Ltd* (2011) 194 FCR 285 [181].
166 *Roadshow Films Pty Ltd v iiNet Ltd* (2011) 194 FCR 285, [426].
167 Ibid [193].
168 Ibid [428]–[430].

In reaching its decision, the majority highlighted the fact that iiNet received more than 5000 allegations of infringement a week, many of which were automatically generated. While iiNet accepted that it had general knowledge about the alleged infringements, it argued that it did not have sufficiently specific information to act on.[169] The majority accepted iiNet's argument, holding that 'it was not reasonable to require iiNet to undertake the immense amount of work, cost and effort to set out, review and analyse the allegations in the information provided with the Infringement notices'.[170] As Nicholas J said, the infringement notices issued by AFACT did not contain any information as to how the information was gathered, or any statement verifying the accuracy of the data or the reliability of the methods used to collect it. Given this, Nicholas J held that the 'AFACT notices were not sufficient to provide the respondent with knowledge that its network was being utilized by users of particular accounts to infringe appellant's copyright'.[171] Given that iiNet had hundreds of thousands of customers and that it received hundreds of infringement notices each day, Nicholas J said, 'I do not think the respondent could reasonably be expected to issue warnings, or to terminate or suspend particular accounts, in reliance upon any such notice in circumstances where it has been told nothing at all about the methods used to obtain the information which lead to the issue of the notice'.[172]

Emmett J provided a checklist of the things that would have to have occurred for him to conclude that it was reasonable for iiNet to have suspended or terminated customers' accounts. These were:

1. iiNet has been informed in writing of particular specific primary acts of copyright infringement by use of particular internet protocol (IP) addresses of iiNet customers.
2. iiNet has been requested in writing to take specific steps, such as:
    (a) inform its customers about the allegations;
    (b) invite customers to respond;
    (c) warn customers either to refute the allegations or give assurances that there will be no more infringements;
    (d) warn customers that if no satisfactory response is received within a reasonable time, say, seven days, the iiNet service will be suspended;
    (e) warn customers that their service will be terminated if there are any more infringements;
    (f) terminate the accounts in the event of further infringements.
3. iiNet has been provided with 'unequivocal and cogent evidence' of the alleged infringements: mere assertions would not suffice. This would include information as to the way that material supporting the allegations was derived, so that iiNet could verify the allegations.
4. Copyright owners have undertaken to reimburse iiNet for reasonable costs of verifying the particulars of the primary acts of infringement and to indemnify iiNet in respect of

---

169 Ibid [204], [207].
170 Ibid [205].
171 Ibid [762]–[763].
172 Ibid [764].

any liability incurred as a result of them mistakenly suspending or terminating a service based on allegations made by the copyright owner.[173]

While Emmett J felt that the first two requirements had been met by the infringement notices issued by AFACT, he agreed with Nicholas J that the third factor had not. Interestingly, and unlike Nicholas J, Emmett J also stressed that it would only have been reasonable for iiNet to have acted upon infringement notices if the film companies had promised to reimburse iiNet for the reasonable costs of implementing a system to verify the allegations and monitor its service, and also to indemnify iiNet in respect of any liability it might incur as a consequence of mistaken suspensions or terminations.

While Jagot J agreed with the majority that iiNet had the power to prevent further acts of infringement, he differed from the majority in finding that there were a series of reasonable steps that iiNet could have, but did not, take including adopting and implementing a policy to deal with AFACT notices leading to shaping, suspension or termination of alleged infringers.[174] The key difference between Jagot J and the majority turned on how the respective judges viewed AFACT's infringement notices. While the majority felt that AFACT had not provided iiNet with sufficient information, Jagot J felt that the infringement notices did not make bare allegations of copyright infringement. Instead, Jagot J felt that they 'provided substantial supporting information which, on its face, indicated that considerable time, effort and money had been expended to provide iiNet with credible evidence of substantial and repeated copyright infringement by persons using the service provided by iiNet'.[175] They also enabled iiNet to identify customers (via their IP addresses).[176] Drawing on the view that to authorise meant to 'sanction, approve, countenance', Jagot J also said that iiNet had not only 'countenanced the primary infringements', but had also 'moved beyond mere indifference to at least tacit approval of those primary infringements'.[177]

While the primary judge's reason seemed to 'imply that an ISP which provides internet connectivity will never be liable for its subscribers' acts of copyright infringement because it could never be said that the ISP had supplied the means of infringement',[178] the Full Federal Court decision opened the way to greater ISP liability. It may also lend more impetus to the development of industry guidelines. While the upshot of the Full Federal Court decision is that copyright owners are now in a better position to pressure ISPs to act, in effect, as their agents in the policing of copyright infringement, one factor that needs to borne in mind is Nicholas J's remark that '[u]nintended consequences may follow if adverse inferences are too readily drawn against ISPs who refuse, in good faith, to act on infringement notices received from copyright owners ... ISPs might be driven to act on infringement notices out of a desire to avoid involvement in potentially expensive and uncertain copyright litigation rather that any well founded acceptance of the substance of a copyright owner's complaints'.[179]

173 Ibid [210].
174 Ibid [431].
175 Ibid [402].
176 Ibid [476].
177 Ibid [477].
178 Ibid [694].
179 Ibid [782].

An interesting development in relation to ISP liability occurred in the Federal Court decision of *Dallas Buyers Club LLC v iiNet Ltd*, which was handed down on 7 April 2015.[180] This was a preliminary discovery application by Dallas Buyers Club LLC requesting several ISPs (including iiNet, Internode, Amnet Broadband, DoDo Services, Adam Internet and Wideband Networks) to disclose the identities of subscribers who had shared the movie *Dallas Buyers Club* online. The applicants claimed that there were 4726 unique IP addresses from which *Dallas Buyers Club* was shared, with the ISP subscribers using BitTorrent, a peer-to-peer file sharing technology, without authorisation. The ISP respondents raised a number of arguments in defence, including the privacy of information about their account holders; the trivial nature of the infringement (each copy of the film was worth less than $10); and their concern that the applicants would engage in 'speculative invoicing' – the practice whereby copyright owners 'write to account holders demanding a large sum of money and offering to settle for a smaller sum which was still very much in excess of what might actually be recovered in any actual suit',[181] which could amount to sharp practice in Australia. Perram J did not accept any of these arguments and ruled in favour of Dallas Buyers Club's application, on the basis that a case could be made against some of the ISP subscribers, and that the copyright owners could not readily identify who these people were but the ISPs could. Perram J ordered that 'the ISPs divulge the names and physical addresses of the customers associated in their records with each of the 4726 IP addresses'.[182]

To address some of the privacy concerns raised by the ISPs, Perram J imposed a condition on the applicants that 'this information only be used for the purposes of recovering compensation for the infringement and is not otherwise to be disclosed without the leave of the [Federal] Court'.[183] To address the ISPs' concern that the practice of 'speculative invoicing' would be engaged in by the applicants should they be successful, Perram J also imposed a condition that they submit a draft of any letter that they propose to send to account holders associated with the IP addresses that were identified[184] to ensure they did not trangress Australian law, such as the misleading and deceptive conduct and unconscionability provisions of the *Australian Consumer Law* or s 12CB of the *Australian Securities and Investments Commission Act 2001* (Cth).[185]

It would seem that this decision not only sends a strong signal to those who have been taking advantage of BitTorrent peer-to-peer file sharing technology, it also sends a message to other copyright holders to pursue the account information of ISPs' subscribers who engage in online infringement. As was discussed earlier,[186] the *Copyright Amendment (Online Infringement) Act 2018* (Cth) gives copyright owners the ability to go to a Federal Court judge to seek the blocking of overseas websites or 'online locations' that have the 'primary purpose' of facilitating copyright infringement.

---

180   [2015] FCA 317.
181   Ibid [73]. Perram J accepted that the applicant had previously engaged in this practice in similar litigation in the United States: at [81].
182   [2015] FCA 317, [5].
183   Ibid.
184   Ibid.
185   (2015) 112 IPR 1, [82].
186   See ch 2 at 2.3.2.8.

5.3.2 Indirect infringement

Copyright law has long recognised that to protect the investment that copyright owners make in the creation and distribution of artistic and cultural objects, it is not enough merely to provide recourse against parties who directly infringe their copyright. As such, the law also provides copyright owners with the capacity to control parties who assist in the process of infringement. This is known as indirect infringement.

The *Copyright Act 1968* (Cth) recognises two types of indirect infringement. The first is where a person permits a place of public entertainment to be used for the public performance of a literary, dramatic or musical work.[187] The second form of indirect infringement is where a person without permission 'deals' with articles that are themselves infringing articles or, in the case of imported articles, articles that would have been infringing articles if they had been made in Australia by the importer.[188] Dealing is defined broadly to include the sale, hire, offering or exposing for sale or hire, distributing or exhibiting in public for trade purposes, or distributing for other purposes prejudicial to the copyright owner.[189]

In order to bring an action for indirect infringement of copyright, it is necessary to show that the defendant had either actual or constructive knowledge that they were infringing copyright. This general rule applies to all forms of indirect infringement (except a number of special cases in relation to the importation of copyright works, discussed below). To show that a defendant has constructive knowledge, it is necessary to show that they 'ought reasonably to have known' having regard to their 'knowledge, capacity and circumstances' that they were infringing copyright.[190] The chief exception to this general rule arises where the action is brought against a person who imports non-infringing copies into Australia. In a number of specific instances (listed below), copyright owners no longer have to prove that the importer knew or ought reasonably to have known that the making of the imported accessory to an article would have infringed copyright if it had been made in Australia by the importer.[191] Instead, the onus of proof falls on the defendant to show that the items in question are non-infringing.[192]

5.3.2.1 Parallel importation

One of the rights that are given to copyright owners is the right to prevent the importation of protected works into Australia. Importantly, the right to control the importation of copyright works, which is commonly referred to as the right to control the parallel importation of works, applies to both pirated and non-pirated works. The ability to prevent pirated works from being

---

187   *Copyright Act 1968* (Cth) s 39. See the defence in s 39(2) and the definition of 'place of public entertainment' in s 39(3).
188   *Copyright Act 1968* (Cth) ss 37, 38, 102, 103. On the application of s 103, see *Universal Music Australia Pty Ltd v Cooper* (2005) 150 FCR 1.
189   *Copyright Act 1968* (Cth) s 37.
190   *Raben Footwear Pty Ltd v Polygram Records Inc* (1997) 75 FCR 88, 91. See also *Milpurrurru v Indofurn Pty Ltd* (1994) 54 FCR 240.
191   *Copyright Act 1968* (Cth) s 37(2).
192   These changes only apply in relation to the importers and not to the distributors of unauthorised articles. As such, where an action is brought against a distributor under *Copyright Act 1968* (Cth) s 38 or s 103, it is still necessary for the copyright owner to prove, in relation to imported articles, that the distributors knew or ought reasonably to have known that if the article had been made in Australia by the importer, it would have constituted an infringement.

introduced into Australia has not proved to be controversial. However, this is not the case with the ability of copyright owners to prevent copyright works that are legitimately purchased overseas from being imported into Australia. The ability to prevent parallel importations has enabled copyright owners to divide the world into separate markets. More specifically, it has enabled them to charge higher prices for the same product in different markets, safe in the knowledge that competitors will not be able to import the cheaper products from overseas to keep local costs down. The power to prevent the parallel importation of non-infringing copies of works confers a 'significant advantage on copyright owners and can be seen as a corresponding serious disadvantage to consumers and users of copyright material'.[193] Given this, it is not surprising that the federal government has limited the copyright owner's right to control importation into Australia in a number of different areas.

5.3.2.2 Books

Publishers have long used their rights to control importation in an anticompetitive manner to divide the world into discrete markets. In Australia, this led to the undesirable position where consumers were forced to pay higher prices for books than consumers in other countries were being charged. Consumers were also faced with the problem, at least in relation to certain types of books, that the books were not available in Australia or at best there was a long delay before they were made available. To remedy some of the problems that had arisen as a result of the way copyright owners controlled the importation of books into Australia, the government amended the *Copyright Act 1968* (Cth) in 1991. These amendments changed the law to allow the free importation of non-infringing copies of books from abroad where there was a failure to supply the Australian market.[194] Under the scheme, the copyright owner's ability to control the importation of works into Australia is restricted in two situations. First, the importation provisions do not apply to books that are published overseas but have never been released in Australia, and to books not published in Australia within thirty days of being published overseas. In these circumstances, non-pirated copies may be imported from overseas without the approval of the copyright owner. Second, in relation to books first published in Australia (whatever the date) and books first published overseas but subsequently published in Australia within thirty days, these books can only be imported where it is necessary to 'satisfy local orders which have remained unfulfilled for at least 90 days'.[195]

As will be seen below, while there have been attempts to broaden these provisions, the provisions have remained in place; the only changes that have been made are in relation to the importation of books, periodicals and printed music that are in an *electronic* format.

On 7 November 2008, the federal government asked the Productivity Commission to examine the parallel importation provisions of the *Copyright Act 1968* (Cth). In particular, the commission was asked 'to examine whether the restrictions further the objectives of the *Copyright Act* and whether they provide a net benefit to Australians'.[196] The commission

---

193   S. Ricketson and C. Creswell, *The Law of Intellectual Property* (2nd edn, Sydney: LBC Information Services, 1999) [9.615].
194   Ibid.
195   *Copyright Act 1968* (Cth) ss 44A, 112A.
196   C. Bowen, Assistant Treasurer and Minister for Competition Policy and Consumer Affairs, 'Parallel import restrictions on books to be reviewed' (Media Release, 7 November 2008).

released its report, *Copyright Restrictions on the Parallel Importation of Books*, on 14 July 2009. The commission concluded that the parallel importation restrictions placed 'upward pressure on book prices and that, at times, the price effect is likely to be substantial'.[197] It recommended that the government repeal Australia's parallel import restrictions for books and that the repeal should take effect three years after the date that it is announced. It also recommended that the government 'review the current subsidies aimed at encouraging Australian writing and publishing, with a view to better targeting of cultural externalities' and that the outcomes should be monitored and assessed five years after implementation.[198]

The Australian Society of Authors (ASA) publicly rejected the findings of the Productivity Commission, stating: 'Removing the territorial copyright of books will simply destroy our hard-won literary culture. There will be no benefit to anyone – authors, booksellers, publishers, printers and readers will all suffer.'[199] The Australian Publishers Association also strongly opposed the findings and to bolster its cause, commissioned its own report, which contested the economic analysis used in the Productivity Commission's report.[200] In May 2009 a lobby group, the Coalition for Cheaper Books, was formed to campaign for the removal of parallel importation restrictions on books in Australia.[201]

The parallel importation debate was brought to a close in November 2009, when the government announced that it would not repeal the parallel importation restrictions, thus rejecting the recommendations of the Productivity Commission.[202] The government considered compromise proposals, involving reductions in the length of the thirty-day publication rule and the ninety-day resupply rule. However, 'in the circumstances of intense competition from online books and e-books, the government judged that changing the regulations governing book imports was unlikely to have any material effect on the availability of books in Australia'.[203] Two recent reports, the Harper Competition Policy Review[204] and the Productivity Commission's Review,[205] have again supported the repeal of the remaining parallel importation provisions that relate to books. It is likely that the existence of the parallel importation restrictions will once again become the subject of intense public debate in the future.

---

197   Productivity Commission, *Restrictions on the Parallel Importation of Books* (Research Report, Canberra: 2009) xiv 'Key points'.
198   Ibid xxv recs 1–3.
199   Australian Society of Authors, 'ASA rejects findings of Productivity Commission' (Press Release, 2009).
200   See O. Maurer and M. Walzl, *A Review of 'Restrictions on the Parallel Importation of Books' Research Report by the Productivity Commission June 2009* (Australian Publishers Association, 2009).
201   The coalition described itself on its (now defunct) website as 'a group of booksellers made up of the major book store chain Dymocks as well as the Discount Stores of Woolworths, Kmart, Coles and Big W. Together we sell 40% of books in Australia. We formed the Coalition because we believe our customers want cheaper book prices.'
202   C. Emerson, Minister for Competition Policy and Consumer Affairs, 'Regulatory regime for books to remain unchanged' (Media Release, 11 November 2009).
203   Ibid.
204   I. Harper, P. Anderson, S. McClusky and M. O'Bryan, *Competition Policy Review* (Final Report, 2015) rec 13.
205   Productivity Commission, *Intellectual Property Arrangements* (Inquiry Report No 78, 2016) rec 5.3.

5.3.2.3 Sound recordings

Given the relative success that consumer groups had in limiting the copyright owner's ability to control the importation of books into Australia, it is not surprising that they also targeted other types of copyright works, notably copyright in sound recordings. In many ways, the debates in relation to the importation of sound recordings were similar to those in relation to books. As with books, a key driving force behind this push for reform was the belief that Australian consumers were paying higher prices for records, tapes and CDs than consumers were being charged for the same products overseas. While in other cases the market might have corrected this discrepancy, this was restricted by the copyright owner's ability to control parallel importation. Faced with this problem, in 1991 the Prices Surveillance Authority recommended that changes be made to the copyright owner's ability to control the importation of sound recordings.

After the initial Bill lapsed,[206] amendments were made to the *Copyright Act 1968* (Cth) in 1998 that made it easier to import non-infringing sound recordings into Australia. The explicit aim of this change was to provide lower prices for CDs in Australia. The amended law allowed for the unauthorised importation of a non-infringing copy of a sound recording into Australia.[207] An imported sound recording is a 'non-infringing copy' if it can be shown that the copy was made: without infringement in the country of manufacture, and there is no copyright protection in that country; or with the consent of the copyright owner in the country of first recording.[208]

Where the sound recording is subject to copyright in Australia, it must also be shown that:

- copyright subsists in the work under the law of the 'copy country';
- the making of the copy does not infringe the copyright in the work under the law of the 'copy country'; and
- the 'copy country' is a party to the *Berne Convention for the Protection of Literary and Artistic Works*[209] (*Berne Convention*) and is compliant with the *Agreement on Trade-Related Aspects of Intellectual Property*[210] (*TRIPS*).[211]

To appease industry fears that these changes to allow for the parallel importation of non-infringing copies would increase the risk of the importation of pirated copies, the government made a number of additional changes. As well as increasing and simplifying penalties for copyright piracy offences generally, changes were also made in relation to the onus of proof. Once a plaintiff has established the necessary elements to sue for infringement of copyright,[212] the onus of proof then shifts to the defendant to establish that the imported copies are 'non-infringing copies'.[213]

---

206 Copyright Amendment Bill 1992 (Cth) (lapsed).
207 A non-infringing copy is defined in s 10AA of the *Copyright Act 1968* (Cth).
208 *Copyright Act 1968* (Cth) s 10AA.
209 Opened for signature 9 September 1886, WIPO Lex No TRT/BERNE/001 (as amended 28 September 1979, entered into force 19 November 1984) (*Berne Convention*).
210 *Marrakesh Agreement Establishing the World Trade Organization*, opened for signature 15 April 1994, 1867 UNTS 3 (entered into force 1 January 1995) annex 1C (*Agreement on Trade-Related Aspects of Intellectual Property*) (*TRIPS*).
211 *Copyright Act 1968* (Cth) s 10AA(2)(c), (3).
212 Ibid ss 37, 102 (importation) or ss 38, 103 (distribution).
213 Ibid s 130A.

5.3.2.4 Books, periodicals and printed music in electronic format, and computer programs

The next area where the copyright owner's ability to control importation has been limited is in relation to books, periodical publications and printed music in an electronic format, as well as articles that embody a computer program. These reforms grew out of plans that began in 2000 to abolish all of the remaining limitations on parallel importation.[214] While anecdotal evidence suggested that the changes made in 1991 provided some benefits to consumers, there were still a number of problems. One of the concerns was that there was still a significant difference in the price charged for books sold in Australia and overseas, particularly for bestseller titles in paperback form, denying consumers reduced prices and improved product range. The Minister for Communications, Information Technology and the Arts and the Attorney-General said in a joint statement in 2002, 'the current outdated copyright law creates a lucrative distribution monopoly for foreign multinationals and prevents local retailers from sourcing cheaper copyrighted materials from overseas, even though individuals can make purchases directly over the Internet'.[215] These concerns were reinforced by research that found that the 1991 amendments had not improved competition.[216] Studies done at the time showed that the price of books in Australia was still significantly higher than overseas. For example, from July 1988 to December 2000, Australians paid around forty-four per cent more for fiction paperbacks than United States readers and around nine per cent more than United Kingdom readers for best-selling paperback fiction.[217] A survey carried out by the ACCC in 2002 found that a selection of technical and professional books was around twenty-three per cent more expensive in Australia than in the United States, and eighteen per cent more expensive than in the United Kingdom.[218]

To remedy problems of this nature, the government introduced the Parallel Importation Bill (Cth) into parliament in 2001. The Bill aimed to improve access on a fair, competitive basis to a wide range of products, including books, periodical publications and printed music. It also aimed 'to prevent international price discrimination that exists under present arrangements to the detriment of Australian consumers and facilitate efficiency in the Australian book publishing industry, while protecting copyright'.[219] To do this the Bill proposed to allow the commercial importation of non-pirated electronic books and printed books without the permission of the Australian rights holder. It was argued that the removal of the parallel importation restrictions would reduce prices, improve product range for consumers, and provide an 'impetus for local suppliers to seek greater operational efficiencies, with consequent flow-on effects in terms of reduced costs and prices and improved service levels'.[220]

Unsurprisingly, publishers and (certain) author groups were opposed to the removal of the parallel importation scheme. Their major concern was that if copyright owners were unable to

---

214 Reflecting the ongoing importance of the film industry, the one proposed exception to this was in relation to films.
215 R. Alston, Minister for Communications, Information Technology and the Arts, and D. Williams, Attorney-General, 'Cheaper books and software' (Media Release, 13 March 2002).
216 Prices Surveillance Authority, *Book Prices and Parallel Imports* (Report No 61, April 1995).
217 Alston and Williams, above n 215.
218 Ibid.
219 Explanatory Memorandum, Copyright Amendment (Parallel Importation) Bill 2001 (Cth).
220 Ibid.

prevent the parallel importation of books this would displace the sales of books by Australian authors and books generated by Australian publishers. As the ASA said:

> [A]ny move that weakens the positions of copyright owners now will be seen as incredibly short sighted in a few years time. At a time when Australia is being criticised for being out of step with the burgeoning knowledge-based economies of the world, it will be seen as remarkable that we should even contemplate undermining our home grown copyright creating industries.[221]

After considerable debate, the *Copyright (Parallel Importation) Act 2003* (Cth) was passed by parliament. This Act repealed the 1991 provisions on the parallel importation of books, periodical publications and printed music in an electronic format.[222] As a result, it provides consumers with improved access to digital copyright works. However, earlier proposals to allow the parallel importation of books, periodical publications, and printed music that would have provided the Australian reading public with cheaper copyright works did not appear in the final Act. Thus, while the final amendments improved the position of readers (at least in relation to literary works in an electronic format), the position in relation to books and publications in a hard-copy form, which still constitute the bulk of the income for publishers, did not change.[223]

The *Copyright (Parallel Importation) Act 2003* (Cth) also made changes in relation to the importation of non-infringing copies of computer programs. More specifically, s 44E of the *Copyright Act 1968* (Cth) provides that the literary copyright in a computer program will not be infringed where a person imports an article that has embodied within it a non-infringing copy of a computer program previously published in Australia or in a *Berne Convention* or *TRIPS* country.

As was the case when changes were made in relation to the importation of sound recordings, to appease copyright owners the federal government changed the burden of proof so that defendants have the obligation of proving that the work in question was non-infringing. The change in onus of proof applies to books, periodical publications and printed music in an electronic format, as well as to articles that embody a computer program.[224]

5.3.2.5 Non-infringing accessories to the article

The final area where the rights of the copyright owner to control importation have been curtailed is in relation to what are called 'non-infringing accessories'. Initially this provision arose when copyright owners realised that while the changes made in 1998 meant that they could no longer use copyright in sound recordings to prevent the importation of CDs into Australia, nonetheless they could still rely on other forms of copyright in CDs (such as copyright in the artwork) to prevent CDs from being imported into Australia. The use of these 'incidental' forms of copyright clearly had the potential to undermine the reforms made to allow for the parallel importation of non-infringing sound recordings. To prevent this, further

---

221 Commonwealth, *Parliamentary Debates*, Senate, 23 May 2001, 27,066 (Robert McMullan).
222 *Copyright Act 1968* (Cth) ss 44F (works), 112DA (published editions).
223 The total sales of books in Australia in 2002–03 amounted to $814.5 million; of this, sales of electronic books amounted to only $7.1 million: Australian Government, Bureau of Statistics, 2004.
224 *Copyright Act 1968* (Cth) ss 130B, 130C.

changes were made to the *Copyright Act 1968* (Cth) that allowed for the importation of a non-infringing accessory to a non-infringing copy of a sound recording. Faced with similar problems in other areas,[225] from January 2000 these provisions were extended beyond sound recordings to apply to 'articles' more generally.

The law now provides that it will not be an infringement of copyright in a work to import an article for commercial purposes where the work is on, or embodied in, a non-infringing accessory to the article.[226] An 'accessory' is defined broadly and includes labels, packaging, written instructions and other information provided with the article, and records embodying an instructional sound recording or a copy of an instructional film provided with the article.[227] An accessory is 'non-infringing' if it was made in a country that was a party to the *Berne Convention* and complies with *TRIPS* in relation to copyright,[228] and the owner of the copyright in that country authorised the making of any copy of the work that is on or embodied in the accessory.[229]

5.4 Relief for copyright infringement

An action for infringement of copyright may be brought by the owner of a copyright or an exclusive licensee.[230] The action for infringement must be brought within six years of the time of the infringement or of the making of the copy.[231] Remedies include injunctions, damages or conversion awards, additional damages, accounts of profits, and delivery-up of infringing copies or devices (as well as costs).[232] While the remedies for infringement of copyright are similar to the remedies that are available for the infringement of other forms of intellectual property (which are discussed separately),[233] there are a number of important differences in relation to damages that warrant separate attention. In a limited number of situations, criminal sanctions may also be available where a person infringes copyright.

5.4.1 Injunctions

Courts may grant injunctions where there has been unauthorised use or threatened use of copyright material.[234] Injunctions are one of the most common remedies sought when there has been an unauthorised use of copyright material. Injunctions at an interlocutory stage are often granted to prevent the offending conduct continuing before trial. Anton Pillar order may

---

225 *R & A Bailey & Co Ltd v Boccaccio Pty Ltd* [1986] 4 NSWLR 701 (use of artistic copyright in a label to prevent the importation of Bailey's Irish Cream Liqueur into Australia).
226 *Copyright Act 1968* (Cth) s 44C.
227 Ibid s 10(1)(a)–(e). It is also provided that any label, packaging or container on which the Olympic signal is reproduced and a manual sold with computer software for use in connection with that software are not 'accessories': at s 10(1)(f), (g).
228 *Copyright Act 1968* (Cth) s 10(1)(a), (b).
229 Ibid s 10(1)(c), (d).
230 A licensee may not sue the owner of the copyright.
231 *Copyright Act 1968* (Cth) s 134.
232 Ibid s 115(2).
233 See ch 17 on remedies.
234 *Copyright Act 1968* (Cth) s 115(2).

also be sought with an injunction to allow a copyright owner to enter into premises and seize the material that is the subject of the unauthorised conduct.

Copyright owners were given additional rights to apply for injunctions against carriage service providers to prevent access to online locations outside Australia that have infringement as their primary purpose by the addition of s 115A of the *Copyright Act 1968* (Cth) in 2015.[235] Section 115A(2) provides that the carriage service providers must take reasonable steps to disable access to the online location.

5.4.2 Damages

Alongside the injunction, damages is the most common remedy for the infringement of copyright.[236] The purpose of damages is to 'compensate the defendant for the loss suffered as a result of the defendant's breach'.[237] The courts use a number of different tests to determine the amount of damages that needs to be paid including lost profits, a notional royalty rate or, if it exists, the going royalty rate.[238] Where the infringement has the potential to expose the copyright owner to embarrassment and contempt, the assessment of damages may also include compensation for personal suffering, humiliation and personal distress.[239]

5.4.2.1 Additional damages

In exceptional cases, the court will award additional damages for infringement of copyright.[240] Additional damages, which are also known as exemplary or punitive damages, will be awarded where the infringement is clearly deliberate or the conduct of the defendant is otherwise objectionable. In deciding whether to grant additional damages, the court will take account of a range of factors including the flagrancy of the infringement;[241] the need to deter similar infringements;[242] the defendant's conduct after the infringing act or, if relevant, after being informed that they had allegedly infringed the plaintiff's copyright; whether the

---

235 *Copyright Amendment (Online Infringement) Act 2015* (Cth). See *Roadshow Films Pty Ltd v Telstra Corp Ltd* (2016) 248 FCR 178; *Universal Music Australia Pty Ltd v TPG Internet Pty Ltd* (2017) 348 ALR 493; *Roadshow Films Pty Ltd v Telstra Corp Ltd* (2018) 132 IPR 1; *Foxtel Management Pty Ltd v TPG Internet Pty Ltd* [2018] FCA 933; *Television Broadcasts Ltd v Telstra Corp Ltd* [2018] FCA 1434.
236 'Damages are an incorporeal right which are measured by the depreciation caused by the infringement to the value of the copyright, as a chose in action': *Sutherland Publishing Co Ltd v Caxton Publishing Co Ltd* [1936] Ch 323, 336 (Lord Wright MR).
237 *Autodesk Australia Pty Ltd v Cheung* (1990) 94 ALR 472, 475.
238 *Microsoft Corp v Ezy Loans Pty Ltd* (with Corrigendum dated 4 February 2005) (2004) 63 IPR 54, [88].
239 See *Milpurrurru v Indofurn Pty Ltd* (1994) 54 FCR 240.
240 *Copyright Act 1968* (Cth) s 115(4).
241 The term 'flagrancy' has been interpreted a number of ways: see *Prior v Lansdowne Press Pty Ltd* [1977] VR 65, 70 ('calculated disregard of the plaintiff's rights, or cynical pursuit of benefit'); *Raben Footwear Pty Ltd v Polygram Records Inc* (1997) 75 FCR 88, 103 (Tamberlin J) ('glaring, notorious, scandalous or blatant conduct'); *Ravenscroft v Herbert & New English Library Ltd* [1980] RPC 193 ('scandalous conduct, deceit and such like [including] deliberate and calculated copyright infringement'); *Microsoft Corp v ATIFO Pty Ltd* (1997) 38 IPR 643, 648 ('deliberate, deceitful and serious' conduct); *Corby v Allen & Unwin Pty Ltd* (2013) 101 IPR 181, 200–1 ('flagrant disregard' of the copyright owner's rights suggested a need to 'deter the respondent and others from conduct of a similar kind'); *Vertical Leisure Ltd v Skyrunner Pty Ltd* [2014] FCCA 2033 ('deliberate and calculated disregard').
242 *Dynamic Supplies Pty Ltd v Tonnex International Pty Ltd (No 3)* (2014) 312 ALR 705; *Vertical Leisure Ltd v Skyrunner Pty Ltd* [2014] FCCA 2033.

infringement involved the conversion of copyright material from hard copy or analog form into digital or other machine-readable form; any benefits that accrued to the infringer; and all other relevant matters.[243] Additional damages have been awarded to Indigenous plaintiffs whose artworks were reproduced on carpets because of the cultural harm that the infringement created for the plaintiff and his community.[244] Additional damages have also been awarded for the repeated importation of infringing copies, as well as the 'aggressive and flagrant infringement' of the plaintiff's copyright works.[245]

5.4.3 Innocent infringement

Under s 115(3) of the *Copyright Act 1968* (Cth) the court will not award damages if at the time of the infringement the defendant was not aware or had no reasonable grounds for suspecting that they were infringing copyright. The owner is still entitled, however, to an account of profits. A defendant will not be able to maintain innocence where they were put on notice that they are infringing, but failed to make any positive inquiries.[246] For the 'defence' to operate, the defendant must establish 'an active, subjective, lack of awareness that the act constituting the infringement was an infringement of the copyright', and that 'objectively considered [the defendant] had no reasonable grounds for suspecting that the act constituted an infringement'.[247] A defendant who was mistaken about the scope of copyright law will not be able to avoid damages.[248] If the defendant makes an error when trying to identify the copyright owner, but has otherwise acted reasonably, they may still be able to rely on s 115(3).[249]

5.4.4 Conversion or detention

Section 116 of the *Copyright Act 1968* (Cth) also provides that the copyright owner can bring an action for conversion or detention in relation to infringing copies or devices that are used to make infringing copies.[250] An 'infringing copy' is defined as a reproduction or copy the making of which constituted an infringement of copyright or, in the case of an imported article, would have been an infringement if it had been made in Australia by the importer.[251] In effect,

---

243 *Copyright Act 1968* (Cth) s 115(4).
244 *Milpurrurru v Indofurn Pty Ltd* (1994) 54 FCR 240. See *Bailey v Namol Pty Ltd* (1994) 53 FCR 102; *Fortuity Pty Ltd v Barcza* (1995) 32 IPR 517.
245 *Sullivan v FNH Investments Pty Ltd* (2003) 57 IPR 63 ($15 000 additional damages awarded for flagrant breach), affirmed *FNH Investments Pty Ltd v Sullivan* (2003) 59 IPR 121 (Full Federal Court); *Eagle Rock Entertainment Ltd v Caisley* (2005) 66 IPR 554 ($90 000 additional damages awarded for the deliberate and deceitful pirating of DVDs). See also *Polygram Records Inc v Raben Footwear Pty Ltd* (1996) 35 IPR 426; *Columbia Pictures Industries Inc v Luckins* (1996) 34 IPR 504; *Corby v Allen & Unwin Pty Ltd* (2013) 297 ALR 761; *Dynamic Supplies Pty Ltd v Tonnex International Pty Ltd (No 3)* (2014) 312 ALR 705; *Henley Arch Pty Ltd v Lucky Homes Pty Ltd* (2016) 120 IPR 317.
246 See *Polygram Pty Ltd v Golden Editions Pty Ltd* (1994) 30 IPR 183.
247 *Milwell Pty Ltd v Olympic Amusements Pty Ltd* (1999) 85 FCR 436.
248 See ibid.
249 See *Kalamazoo (Australia) Pty Ltd v Compact Business Systems Pty Ltd* (1985) 5 IPR 213; *Polygram Pty Ltd v Golden Editions Pty Ltd* (1994) 30 IPR 183, 193–4.
250 *Copyright Act 1968* (Cth) s 116, amended by the *Copyright Amendment (Digital Agenda) Act 2000* (Cth). *Copyright Amendment Act 1998* (Cth) sch 3 substituted 'device' for 'plate' in *Copyright Act 1968* (Cth) s 116(2)(c).
251 *Copyright Act 1968* (Cth) s 10(1) (definition of 'infringing copy').

conversion damages compensate the copyright owner for acts that are inconsistent with their right to possess infringing copies and devices. This might occur, for example, where a defendant is ordered to 'deliver up' infringing copies but has already sold them. Any relief granted under this section is in addition to the owner's right to bring an action for damages or account of profits.[252] Despite this, conversion or detention damages will not be available where the court believes that damages or account of profits provides 'a sufficient remedy'.[253] The measure of conversion damages is the value of the copies and devices at the date of the conversion, not the depreciation caused by any infringement to the value of the copyright.[254] Defendants have a defence to any claim for conversion or detention if they can prove either that they were not aware, or that they did not have reasonable grounds for suspecting, that the materials to which the action relates were protected by copyright, or that the copies they made or dealt in were infringing.[255]

5.4.5 Groundless threats to sue

Section 202 of the *Copyright Act 1968* (Cth) permits a person who is subject to a groundless threat of an action for infringement of copyright to bring proceedings against the person making the threat. Section 202A also provides for relief against groundless threats for legal proceedings in relation to technological protection measures.[256] The remedies available against a person making a groundless threat include a declaration, an injunction and damages. Similar provisions exist in the other intellectual property regimes.

The mere notification of the existence of copyright does not constitute a threat of an action or proceedings.[257] However, the courts are quick to infer a threat if a person's conduct goes beyond notifying another party that a work is protected by copyright.[258] Legal representatives are not liable for threats that they make on their clients' behalf but the clients will be liable for such threats.[259]

Numerous cases have been brought pursuant to this section by parties seeking to resolve their legal position prior to proceeding to exploit copyright material. Examples include proceedings by Channel Nine seeking a declaration that its television program *The Block* did not infringe any copyright in a similar reality television program produced in New Zealand. By initiating proceedings, it forced the other party into instituting a counterclaim for infringement and it then sought security for its costs as the other party had no assets in Australia.[260]

---

252 Ibid s 116(1B).
253 Ibid s 116(1C).
254 See *Polygram Records Inc v Raben Footwear Pty Ltd* (1996) 35 IPR 426; *Autodesk Inc v Yee* (1996) 68 FCR 391.
255 *Copyright Act 1968* (Cth) s 116(2). There are a number of offences in relation to making, retaining and inspecting records of copying under the various provisions of the Act dealing with reprographic reproduction: at ss 203A–203H.
256 This was added by the *Copyright Amendment Act 2006* (Cth).
257 *Copyright Act 1968* (Cth) s 202(2).
258 *Rosedale Associated Manufacturers Ltd v Airfix Products Ltd* [1956] RPC 360, 363.
259 *Copyright Act 1968* (Cth) s 202(3). See *Wanem Pty Ltd v Tekiela* (1990) 19 IPR 435, 444.
260 *Nine Films & Television Pty Ltd v Ninox Television Ltd* (2005) 67 IPR 46. See also *Concrete Pty Ltd v Parramatta Design & Developments Pty Ltd* [2004] FCA 1312.

5.4.6 Criminal offences

The *Copyright Act 1968* (Cth) provides for offences and penalties for specified dealings in infringing copies and devices. There is no limitation on the time within which criminal proceedings may be brought. The criminal remedies under the *Copyright Act 1968* were substantially modified by the *Copyright Amendment Act 2006* (Cth).

From 1 January 2007 the criminal offences in the *Copyright Act 1968* (Cth) are divided into indictable, summary and strict liability offences. The main difference between these tiered offences is in relation to the level of fault that must be satisfied and the penalties that apply.

To establish an *indictable offence*, it is necessary to show that the infringement was either intentional or reckless. Indictable offences have maximum penalties of five years' imprisonment and/or between 550 and 850 penalty units for natural persons.[261] For corporations, the fine can be up to five times the maximum fine of a natural person.

Most *summary offences* require intention (by default) and/or negligence, and have maximum penalties of two years' imprisonment and/or 120 penalty units.

The *strict liability offences*, which do not contain a fault requirement, were introduced by the *Copyright Amendment Act 2006* (Cth) to target lower levels of commercial piracy, such as the sale of pirated works at street markets. This means that a person will be liable for infringement irrespective of intention, negligence or fault. The government's rationale for introducing strict liability offences was that 'it would give police and prosecutors a wider range of enforcement options depending on the seriousness of the relevant conduct'.[262]

One of the fears that were raised about the strict liability offences was that they had the potential to criminalise activities that were considered to be a legitimate part of commercial life. To ensure that this did not occur, the strict liability offences only apply in a limited number of cases.[263] There are also a number of defences to the strict liability offences.[264] The strict liability offences arise where a person:

- makes an infringing copy[265] in preparation for, or in the course of, selling it, letting it for hire, or obtaining a commercial advantage or profit;[266]
- sells or lets for hire an infringing copy;[267]
- exposes or offers for sale or hire an infringing copy by way of trade;[268]
- exhibits an infringing copy in public, by way of trade;[269]

---

261 See *Crimes Act 1914* (Cth) s 4AA for the definition of a 'penalty unit'.
262 Explanatory Memorandum, Copyright Amendment Bill 2006 (Cth) 2.
263 The offences that do not have strict liability include *Copyright Act 1968* (Cth) ss 132AI, 132AL, 132AN, 132AO (introduced by the *Copyright Amendment Act 2006* (Cth)).
264 For example, see *Copyright Act 1968* (Cth) s 132AT(1)–(2) (introduced by the *Copyright Amendment Act 2006* (Cth)).
265 *Copyright Act 1968* (Cth) s 10 defines an 'infringing copy' as 'an article that infringes copyright in a work or other subject matter where copyright subsists in the work or other subject matters at the time when the article is made'.
266 *Copyright Act 1968* (Cth) s 132AD(5).
267 Ibid s 132AE(5).
268 Ibid s 132AF(7).
269 Ibid s 132AG(7).

- exhibits an infringing copy in public in preparation for, or in the course of, obtaining a commercial advantage or profit;[270]
- imports an infringing copy to be used for a commercial purpose;[271]
- distributes an infringing copy in preparation for, or in the course of, trading or obtaining a commercial advantage or profit;[272]
- possesses an infringing copy in preparation for, or in the course of, doing any of the above acts (selling, letting for hire, exhibiting, distributing, etc);[273]
- makes a device for the purpose of making an infringing copy;[274]
- causes images or sound from a cinematographic film to be seen or heard in public at a place of public entertainment, where causing the hearing or seeing infringes copyright in the recording or film.[275]

The maximum penalty for a strict liability offence is 60 penalty units for a natural person.[276] It is also possible for an alleged offender to be issued with an infringement notice in lieu of prosecution, which gives them the option of paying one-fifth of the maximum fine and to forfeit the alleged infringing article or device.[277] The possibility of issuing what is effectively an on-the-spot fine may provide copyright owners with a useful strategy against small-scale pirates.

5.5 Defences and limitations

While the rights conferred on copyright owners have expanded greatly over the last century or so, they are not absolute. As with all forms of intellectual property, the rights granted to owners are subject to a number of limitations. In addition to the compulsory licence schemes that are discussed above,[278] copyright law recognises a series of defences or exceptions to copyright infringement.[279]

The limits placed on the copyright owner's rights serve to balance the rights of copyright owners with the rights of the public to use copyright works.[280] The *Copyright Act 1968* (Cth) includes different types of defence. Some, such as the fair dealing defences, are general in

---

270   Ibid s 132AG(8).
271   Ibid s 132AH(5).
272   Ibid s 132AJ(5).
273   Ibid s 132AI(7).
274   Ibid s 132AL(8).
275   Ibid s 132AO(5).
276   See *Crimes Act 1914* (Cth) s 4AA for the definition of a 'penalty unit'.
277   *Copyright Act 1968* (Cth) s 133B; *Copyright Regulations 1969* (Cth) pt 6A.
278   At 5.2.2.3.
279   The relationship between the fair dealing defence and the educational statutory licences was considered in *Copyright Agency Ltd v Haines* [1982] 1 NSWLR 182. The issue in dispute was whether persons who have the benefit of a statutory licence are nevertheless entitled to rely on the fair dealing provisions. This case did not rule out reliance by teachers and schools on s 40 fair dealing for copying within the educational context. McLelland J granted relief to restrain the threatened authorisation of infringement. This was based on the fact that a memorandum had stated that virtually the same copying as could be done under s 53B (later replaced by the pt VB statutory licence provisions) could also be done under s 40, without the need for the payment of equitable remuneration to copyright owners.
280   CLRC, *Copyright and Contract*, above n 20, [2.01].

nature, whereas others, such as special provisions to deal with computer programs, were designed to deal with specific issues.

In May 2005, the Attorney-General's Department published an issues paper (*Fair Use and Other Copyright Exceptions*) to encourage public consultation on a number of issues relating, inter alia, to fair dealing. One of the questions that was raised was whether Australia should adopt a United States–style open-ended fair use defence (instead of the specific purpose-driven fair dealing exception). Following the public consultation process in May 2006, the Attorney-General announced that the government intended to reform the law of fair dealing in Australia.[281] However, the government decided not to adopt a United States–style open-ended fair use exception. Instead, the *Copyright Amendment Act 2006* (Cth) introduced a number of new exceptions to infringement including copying for the purpose of parody and satire, time shifting or format shifting, as well as a number of specific exceptions for libraries, archives and educational institutions.[282] In 2013, the ALRC recommended the introduction of a defence of fair use[283] and this was supported in 2016 by the Productivity Commission's review of intellectual property arrangements.[284] As part of its copyright modernisation review in 2018, the government has consulted on the possible introduction of more flexibility into the copyright defences, including re-examining fair use for an Australian context.[285] However, the current fair dealing provisions remain, allowing a 'fair dealing' with copyright material only for the specified purposes set out in the *Copyright Act 1968* (Cth).

5.5.1 Fair dealing

The main fair dealing provisions that operate in Australia are found in ss 40–43 of the *Copyright Act* (Cth). Unlike the open-ended fair use regime that operates in the United States,[286] the defence of fair dealing, for what would otherwise be an infringing act, is permitted in six[287] specific circumstances (which are listed below). Once it has been established that a particular dealing falls within the scope of one of the specified purposes, it is then necessary to show that the dealing was 'fair'. All that is meant by 'dealing' in this context is that the copyright work has been used in some way or another.[288]

In December 2006, a number of important amendments were made to the fair dealing provisions in the *Copyright Act 1968* (Cth). In addition to adding a fifth permitted purpose (of

---

281   Hon P. Ruddock, Attorney-General, 'Major copyright reforms strike balance' (Media Release, 14 May 2006).
282   See *Copyright Amendment Act 2006* (Cth) schs 6–8.
283   ALRC, *Copyright and the Digital Economy* (Report No 122, November 2013) rec 4.1.
284   Productivity Commission, *Intellectual Property Arrangements* (Inquiry Report No 78, September 2016) rec 6.1.
285   Department of Communication and the Arts, 'Copyright modernisation consultation' www.communications.gov.au.
286   *Copyright Act*, 17 USC § 107 (1976).
287   Prior to the passage of the *Copyright Amendment Act 2006* (Cth), there were only four permitted purposes. The fifth purpose of 'parody or satire' was added in 2006, the sixth of access by persons with a disability was added in 2017 as part of the *Copyright Amendment (Disability Access and Other Measures) Act 2017* (Cth).
288   Bently et al, *Intellectual Property Law*, above n 75, 229. See *Newspaper Licensing Agency Ltd v Marks & Spencer plc* [2000] 4 All ER 239, 257 (Chadwick LJ); *Pro Sieben Media AG v Carlton UK Television Ltd* [1999] FSR 610, 620; *Ashdown v Telegraph Group Ltd* [2002] Ch 149, 172 [64].

parody or satire), the *Copyright Amendment Act 2006* (Cth) made changes to the research and study defence by repealing s 40(3) and (4) and substituting new provisions to clarify the meaning of 'reasonable portion' for the purposes of s 40, and to align the definition with that used elsewhere in the Act.[289]

5.5.1.1 Permitted purposes

In order for a defendant to rely on the fair dealing defence, they need to be able to show that the dealing in question was carried out for one of the six specific purposes listed in the Act. In this respect the situation is similar to the United Kingdom, Canadian and New Zealand fair dealing provisions.[290] Under current law, the defence of fair dealing, for what would otherwise be an infringing act, is permitted for the purpose of:

- research or study;[291]
- criticism or review;[292]
- reporting news;[293]
- professional advice given by a legal practitioner or patent attorney;[294]
- parody or satire;[295] or
- access by persons with a disability.[296]

The purpose of the copying is determined by an objective test (whether a reasonable person would have understood that copying was being done for one of the specified purposes), rather than by the subjective intention of the person doing the copying (whether the copier intends to use the copies for one of the specified purposes).[297]

5.5.1.1.1 RESEARCH OR STUDY

The first type of dealing recognised under the *Copyright Act 1968* (Cth) relates to those activities that are carried out for the purpose of 'research' and 'study'. Under s 40, fair dealing for the purpose of research or study is not an infringement of copyright.[298] This exception to infringement applies to literary, dramatic, musical and artistic works, adaptations of such

---

289 *Copyright Act 1968* (Cth) s 10.
290 *Copyright, Designs and Patents Act 1988* (UK) ss 29(1), 30(1); (RSC, c C-30) (Can) ss 29, 29(1), 29(2) (see also *CCH Canadian Ltd v Law Society of Upper Canada* [2004] 1 SCR 339); *Copyright Act 1994* (NZ) ss 42, 43.
291 *Copyright Act 1968* (Cth) ss 40, 103C. In 1976, the Franki Committee recommended substantial changes to the fair dealing provisions. One of the significant changes was the removal of the requirement that a fair dealing for the purposes of study had to be for 'private' study, which enabled the reliance on the fair dealing provisions for what has been referred to as 'commercial' research. See *Report of the Copyright Law Committee on Reprographic Reproduction* (1976).
292 *Copyright Act 1968* (Cth) ss 41, 103A.
293 Ibid ss 42, 103B.
294 Ibid s 43(2).
295 Ibid s 41A.
296 Ibid s 113E, introduced by *Copyright Amendment (Disability Access and Other Measures) Act 2017* (Cth). Section 113E replaced the former exception in s 200AB(4).
297 Bently et al, *Intellectual Property Law*, above n 75, 229.
298 *Copyright Act 1968* (Cth) s 40. As to the meaning of 'research' and 'study' see *De Garis v Neville Jeffress Pidler Pty Ltd* (1990) 37 FCR 99.

works, sound recordings, films, broadcasts and published editions of works. The terms 'research' and 'study' are not defined in the *Copyright Act 1968*. One of the leading cases on the meaning of these terms is the decision of *De Garis v Neville Jeffress Pidler Pty Ltd*.[299] In this case the defendant's press clipping service located and scanned newspaper articles at the request of subscribers. The defendant provided no commentary or additional input, leading Beaumont J to conclude that the defendant had not dealt with the plaintiff's copyright works for the purposes of criticism or review within the meaning of the Act. Beaumont J did not need to define the terms 'criticism' and 'review' to come to this conclusion: under any interpretation of these terms, the defendant's activities were clearly not for the prescribed statutory purpose. Beaumont J said that the terms 'research' and 'study' should be given their ordinary dictionary meaning. In so doing, he relied on the *Macquarie Dictionary* definition of research as the 'diligent and systematic enquiry or investigation into a subject in order to discover facts or principles'. In turn, Beaumont J defined study as '(1) the application of the mind to the acquisition of knowledge, as by reading, investigation or reflection; (2) the cultivation of a particular branch of learning, science or art; (3) a particular course of effort to acquire knowledge ... (5) a thorough examination and analysis of a particular subject'.[300] It was also said that as the media-monitoring agency was merely involved in the collection of data, rather than the *evaluation* and *analysis* of that data, the copying fell outside the research or study defence.[301] In so doing, the court emphasised that for the defence to apply, a person needs to engage with the material that has been copied. The court also held that it was the purpose of the copier and not the purpose of the ultimate user of the copies that was important.[302]

While it has been suggested that the specified purposes have been construed narrowly in Australia,[303] it seems that the definition of research or study as set out in *De Garis* (and other decisions) would cover many of the activities that would ordinarily be expected to qualify as research and study. It would seem, for example, that it would cover much of the copying undertaken by staff and students in Australian universities (at least copying for academic reasons), as well as the situation where academics, researchers and writers copy parts of books or articles for use in the preparation of the writing of new articles and books.[304] It would

---

299 (1990) 37 FCR 99.
300 Ibid.
301 Ibid.
302 Ibid.
303 K. Weatherall and E. Hudson, *Response to the Issues Paper: Fair Use and Other Copyright Exceptions*, Intellectual Property Research Institute of Australia and Centre for Media and Communications Law (Melbourne: University of Melbourne, 2005) 11. In contrast, the specified purposes have been construed liberally in the United Kingdom: see Bently et al, *Intellectual Property Law*, above n 75, 242–4. See *Newspaper Licensing Agency Ltd v Marks & Spencer plc* [2000] 4 All ER 239, 257 (Chadwick LJ); *Pro Sieben Media AG v Carlton UK Television Ltd* [1999] FSR 610, 620; *Ashdown v Telegraph Group Ltd* [2002] Ch 149, 172.
304 This is supported by reasoning that was put forward by the United States Court of Appeals for the Second Circuit in *Texaco* when it distinguished the systematic copying being done by Texaco Inc from a situation where 'a professor or independent scientist [is] engaged in copying and creating files for independent research': *American Geophysical Union v Texaco Inc*, 60 F 3d 913, 916 (2006), as cited in M. Ryan, 'Fair use and academic expression: rhetoric, reality, and restriction on academic freedom' (1999) 8 *Cornell Journal of Law and Public Policy* 541, 550. 'The court's decision in *Texaco* may serve a useful purpose in shaking academia from its complacency. Unless a critical distinction can be made regarding academic use of academic scholarship and research in the university setting, we must prepare

also cover the copying of works by students studying for exams or writing assignments.[305] It is also clear that the defence applies where the copying is carried out for the purpose of, or associated with, an approved course of study or research by an enrolled external student of an educational institution.[306]

5.5.1.1.2 CRITICISM OR REVIEW

Section 41 of the *Copyright Act 1968* (Cth) provides that a fair dealing with a literary, dramatic, musical or artistic work, or with an adaptation of a work, is not an infringement of copyright in the work if the fair dealing is for the purpose of criticism or review.[307] A similar exception exists for sound recordings, cinematograph films, television and radio broadcasts.[308] Insofar as the exception prevents the copyright owner from controlling the work, and thus controlling reviews of the work, it recognises the importance of criticism or review for public debate.[309] In an odd version of evolutionary jurisprudence, the defence is often justified on the basis that it allows creators to build on and thus progress existing cultural and artistic works.[310] The exception, which allows for what Americans like to call transformative use, is 'based on the policy that all copyright subject matter is published with an expectation of critical review, and as such, it is reasonable to freely take portions from the original in order to illustrate the review'.[311]

For the defence to apply, a defendant must 'sufficiently acknowledge' the work. That is, they must identify the name or title of the work that is being criticised or reviewed, as well as

---

ourselves for the possibility that copyright restrictions on such academic expression may invade academia': at 551.

[305] '[D]uring the early stages of writing an article, conference paper, essay or thesis any copying that is done usually consists of obtaining extracts of earlier published and unpublished works. Such copies are made for a variety of reasons – to allow reading to be done at the researcher's convenience, because material is held in a distant library or archive to which the researcher has to travel and does not have time to read all potentially relevant material on site, and sometimes because the researcher has not finally decided what questions she is asking and thus may need to review the material several times. A second type of copying occurs when the researcher's results are presented, for example, in an essay, thesis, published paper or book and the researcher wishes to make reference to source material': R. Burrell and A. Coleman, *Copyright Exceptions: The Digital Impact* (Cambridge: Cambridge University Press, 2005) 116.

[306] *Copyright Act 1968* (Cth) s 40(1A). Ricketson and Creswell, *The Law of Intellectual Property*, above n 193, [11.32] states: 'A fair dealing with a literary work (other than lecture notes) does not constitute an infringement of the copyright in the work if it is for the purpose of, or associated with, an approved course of study or research by an enrolled external student of an educational institution.' As the authors suggest, 'It is unclear what section 40(1A) adds to what is already allowed under s 40(1), in the absence of any deeming effect. It is noteworthy that the provision was added as result of non-governmental amendment and that the government of the day regarded the amendment as unnecessary'. Ricketson and Creswell were referring to CLRC, *Simplification Report – Part 1: Exceptions to the Exclusive Rights of Copyright Owners* (1998) 81 and the fact that the CLRC itself recommended the repeal of s 40(1).

[307] *Copyright Act 1968* (Cth) s 41. See, for example, *De Garis v Neville Jeffress Pidler Pty Ltd* (1990) 37 FCR 99; *TCN Channel Nine Pty Ltd v Network Ten Pty Ltd* (2002) 118 FCR 417 (on the meaning of 'criticism' and 'review'), overturned on other grounds (2004) 218 CLR 273.

[308] *Copyright Act 1968* (Cth) ss 103A, 100A.

[309] Bently et al, *Intellectual Property Law*, above n 75, 234.

[310] Weatherall and Hudson, *Response to the Issues Paper*, above n 303, 11–12.

[311] D. Brennan, 'Copyright and parody in Australia: Some thoughts on *Suntrust Bank v Houghton Mifflin Company*' (2002) 13 *Australian Intellectual Property Journal* 161, 163, citing *Chatterton v Cave* (1878) 3 App Cas 483, 492.

the name of the author.[312] It is not necessary to identify the author if the work is anonymous or pseudonymous or the author has previously agreed or directed that an acknowledgement of his or her name is not to be made. It has been held in this context that the fact that the 'Channel Nine' logo appeared on the bottom of a television image shown on Channel Ten was 'sufficient acknowledgement' of the television station that originally broadcast the work.[313]

The main issue relates to whether a particular activity falls within the meaning of 'criticism' and 'review'. The scope and meaning of these terms was considered in the *Panel* decision (*TCN Channel Nine v Network Ten*).[314] The *Panel* decision concerned the claim by Channel Nine that by showing extracts from twenty of its broadcast programs as part of commentary on *The Panel* program, Channel Ten had infringed Nine's copyright in those programs. The extracts were of various lengths, ranging from eight seconds to forty-two seconds in duration, and were taken from a variety of news, sport and entertainment programs. *The Panel*, broadcast weekly on Wednesday evenings, was a sixty-minute television program on which a panel of regulars and guests discussed the events of the preceding week including news, current affairs, entertainment and sport. Channel Ten responded that by screening extracts from various programs discussed by the panellists, it had not taken a substantial part of the programs sufficient to constitute infringement and, even if it had, that use could be excused on the grounds that such uses were fair dealing, either for the purpose of criticism or review, or in the alternative for the purpose of reporting the news.[315] Given that the courts were called on to consider the status of a large number of different extracts, the decision provides useful guidance as to how these factual issues are addressed.[316] While this decision had the potential to provide some important guidance as to what is meant by criticism and review, at best it provides indirect guidance. At worst, it only confuses things further.[317]

It has been suggested that 'criticism' means 'the act or art of analysing and judging the quality of a literary or artistic work'.[318] It is 'the act of passing judgement as to the merits of something ... A critical comment, article or essay; a critique'.[319] In turn 'review' has been

---

312   *Copyright Act 1968* (Cth) s 10. See *Sillitoe v McGraw Hill Book Co (UK) Ltd* [1983] FSR 545.
313   *TCN Channel Nine Pty Ltd v Network Ten Pty Ltd* (2001) 108 FCR 235, 236, upheld, issue not discussed on appeal (2002) 118 FCR 417; *Network Ten Pty Ltd v TCN Channel Nine Pty Ltd* (2004) 218 CLR 273.
314   *TCN Channel Nine Pty Ltd v Network Ten Ltd* (2002) 118 FCR 417 (later in the High Court).
315   M. de Zwart, 'Seriously entertaining: *The Panel* and the future of fair dealing' (2003) 8 *Media and Arts Law Review* 1, 8.
316   At first instance, Conti J concluded that Channel Nine had not succeeded in showing that a substantial part of the subject matter of each of the program segments originally broadcast on Channel Nine had then been shown on *The Panel*. Therefore, there was no infringement and it was not necessary to consider if use of the excerpts was justified on the basis of fair dealing. Nevertheless, Conti J went on to consider whether the uses would have been justified on the basis of fair dealing. The decision was appealed and the Full Court disagreed with Conti J at first instance. See also M. Handler and D. Rolph, '"A real pea-souper": The *Panel* case and the development of the fair dealing defences to copyright infringement in Australia' (2003) 27 *Melbourne University Law Review* 381; Brennan, 'Copyright and parody in Australia', above n 311, 161, 163.
317   Handler and Rolph, 'A real pea-souper', above n 316, 381, 390.
318   In *De Garis v Neville Jeffress Pidler Pty Ltd* (1990) 37 FCR 99, 299 (Beaumont J relied on the *Macquarie Dictionary*).
319   Ibid. Despite referring to the need to interpret criticism and review broadly, the court in the *Panel* case still applied narrow, dictionary-based definitions of 'criticism' and 'review'. These definitions require that the use involve the 'passing of judgement': *TCN Channel Nine Pty Ltd v Network Ten Pty Ltd* (2001) 108 FCR 235, 285, as cited in Weatherall and Hudson, *Response to the Issues Paper*, above n 303, 11.

described as a 'critical article or report, as in a periodical, on some literary work, commonly some work of recent appearance; a critique'.[320] In the *Panel* decision, Conti J said that criticism and review are words of wide and infinite scope that should be interpreted liberally; nevertheless criticism and review involve the passing of judgement; criticism and review may be strongly expressed.[321]

The copying may be for the purpose of criticising or reviewing either the work itself, or another work. The criticism or review can be aimed at the work, or the underlying ideas that are used in the work.[322] Criticism and review must be genuine and not a pretence for some other purpose. If criticism is genuine, there is no need for it to be balanced.[323] Given that the *Copyright Act 1968* (Cth) does not specifically link the criticism or review to the work itself, it may be possible for the provision to be used as a basis to criticise the author and their motives. It is not necessary that the defendant be able to show that criticism or review was the sole reason for the copying in question. Instead, it is only necessary that the copying was 'substantially' for the purpose of criticism or review. This allows the use to be made for both criticism and another related purpose, such as education.[324] However, it seems that the defence will not apply where a person has an 'oblique or hidden motive ... particularly where the infringer is a trade rival who uses the copyright subject matter for its own benefit, particularly in a dissembling way'.[325]

5.5.1.1.3 REPORTING NEWS

The third type of dealing protected by the fair dealing defences are those dealings that are carried out for the purpose of 'reporting news'. The defence applies both to literary, dramatic, musical and artistic works,[326] and to sound recordings, cinematograph films, and television and radio broadcasts.[327] The reporting of news must take place in a newspaper, magazine or similar periodical[328] (in which case the original work must be sufficiently acknowledged). Alternatively, the dealing must take place for the purpose of reporting the news by means of a communication or in a cinematograph film.[329] Given that it is increasingly difficult to

---

[320] *De Garis v Neville Jeffress Pidler Pty Ltd* (1990) 37 FCR 99, [41]. This approach has been criticised on the basis that only certain *Macquarie Dictionary* definitions were adopted by Beaumont J, and others, such as 'censure' and 'fault-finding' for 'criticism' or a 'general survey of something' for 'review', were not considered. It has also been suggested that Beaumont J failed to consider whether there were more expansive definitions available in other dictionaries: Handler and Rolph, 'A real pea-souper', above n 316, 381, 399, citing A. Delbridge et al (eds), *The Macquarie Dictionary* (1981).
[321] *TCN Channel Nine Pty Ltd v Network Ten Pty Ltd* (2002) 118 FCR 417 (later in the High Court).
[322] Ibid. (Criticism and review extends to thought underlying the expression of the copyright works or subject matter.) See *Hubbard v Vosper* [1972] 2 QB 84, 94–5, 98.
[323] *TCN Channel Nine Pty Ltd v Network Ten Ltd* (2002) 118 FCR 417 (later in the High Court).
[324] *Sillitoe v McGraw Hill Book Co (UK) Ltd* [1983] FSR 545. It is not a fair dealing of a work for the purpose of criticism or review to publish the work knowing that it has been improperly obtained, although the work is published for the purpose of criticism and comment. See *Beloff v Pressdram Ltd* [1973] RPC 765; *Commonwealth v John Fairfax & Sons Ltd* (1980) 147 CLR 39.
[325] *TCN Channel Nine Pty Ltd v Network Ten Ltd* (2002) 118 FCR 417 (later in the High Court).
[326] *Copyright Act 1968* (Cth) s 42.
[327] Ibid s 103B.
[328] *De Garis v Neville Jeffress Pidler Pty Ltd* (1990) 37 FCR 99 (a media-monitoring service was not 'a newspaper, magazine or similar periodical').
[329] *Copyright Act 1968* (Cth) ss 42(1)(a), (b), 103B(1). Section 42(2) provides that, in the case of a musical work, the playing of the work forms part of the news being reported.

distinguish between news and entertainment, particularly in light of the growth of 'infotainment' programs, it has been held that 'news' may involve the use of humour.[330] It has also been said that the fact that a party is motivated by commercial considerations does not preclude a finding that its use is a fair dealing.[331] While 'reporting news' usually refers to providing information about current events, it may also extend to the provision of historical material. The fact that subscribers had access to a database of abstracts – 'an entire history of material' – did not alter the nature, effect and content of the abstracts.[332]

It seems that the reporting of news requires at least some type of input on behalf of the reporter. Thus, while the provision of newspaper articles as part of a media-monitoring service was held not to fall within the scope of the defence,[333] the provision of abstracts (or summaries) of newspaper articles was held to be a reporting of the news. The key difference was that in the latter case the 'preparation of the Abstracts involve[d] significantly more than the mere copying of headlines from news publications. The contribution of the abstracted article [made] the use of the headline a "transformative use" by "adding something new, with a further purpose or character"'.[327]

5.5.1.1.4 PROFESSIONAL ADVICE AND LEGAL PROCEEDINGS

A fair dealing may also be made of a literary, dramatic, musical or artistic work for the purpose of giving advice, if that advice is given by a legal practitioner, a patent attorney or a trade mark attorney.[334] Similarly, copyright will not be infringed by anything done for the purposes of a judicial proceeding or of a report of a judicial proceeding.[335] Section 104 provides a similar defence in relation to Part IV works; however, this section is worded more broadly in that it covers *'anything done'* for the purpose of giving *or seeking* such advice.[336]

5.5.1.1.5 PARODY OR SATIRE

In 2006,[337] the government introduced a new s 41A (and the corresponding s 103AA for audiovisual works) to allow for fair dealing for the purpose of parody or satire.[338] The

---

330 *TCN Channel Nine Pty Ltd v Network Ten Pty Ltd* (2002) 118 FCR 417, decision overturned on other grounds on appeal to the High Court (2004) 218 CLR 273). See also de Zwart, 'Seriously entertaining', above n 315, 1, 8.
331 *Fairfax Media Publications Pty Ltd v Reed International Books Australia Pty Ltd* (2010) 189 FCR 109, 143.
332 Ibid [136].
333 *De Garis v Neville Jeffress Pidler Pty Ltd* (1990) 37 FCR 99.
334 *Copyright Act 1968* (Cth) s 43(2).
335 Ibid s 43(1).
336 Ibid s 104(b), (c).
337 From 11 December 2006. The pre-2006 position of parody and satire in Australian law is unclear. See *AGL Sydney Ltd v Shortland County Council* (1989) 17 IPR 99, 105 (the *Copyright Act 1968* (Cth) 'grants no exemption, in terms, in the case of works of parody or burlesque').
338 In the Copyright Amendment Bill 2006 (Cth) the government originally proposed to amend s 200AB of the *Copyright Act 1968* (Cth) to provide for parody and satire. However, after numerous submissions pointing out the limits of placing the parody and satire defence within this section, the government in its response to the Senate inquiry indicated that it would insert a new provision in the fair dealing section of the Act to provide for parody and satire. See Senate Standing Committee on Legal and Constitutional Affairs, *Copyright Amendment Bill 2006 [Provisions]* (Report, 2006) [3.72]. See also Supplementary Explanatory Memorandum, Copyright Amendment Bill 2006 (Cth) (amendments to be moved on behalf of the government) 11.

government felt that it was 'appropriate to require that a use for the purpose of parody and satire should be "fair"'.[339] Section 41A provides that a fair dealing with a literary, dramatic, musical or artistic work, or with an adaptation of a literary, dramatic or musical work, does not constitute an infringement of the copyright in the work if it is for the purpose of parody or satire.[340]

A range of justifications have been given to support parody and satire including their importance to free speech, criticism and public debate and because they aim to provide humour in an effective and creative way.[341] As there is no definition of parody or satire in the Act, the courts will probably rely on standard techniques (such as the use of dictionaries) to define the limits of these activities. While there is no clear consensus, parody and satire tend to employ irony, sarcasm and ridicule in a humorous manner. Where they differ is in the focus of their attention. The term 'parody' is associated more with ridicule and is generally directed at criticism of a work.[342] On the other hand, the purpose of satire is to draw attention to characteristics or actions that are external to an author's work. Despite the fact that a parody 'may appear to treat its target in a manner similar to satire in making it the object of laughter, one major factor which distinguishes parody from satire is ... the parody's use of the performed material of its "target" as a constituent part of its own structure'. In contrast, satire uses the target material to make fun of something external to the target.[343] Parody, by its nature, is likely to involve holding a creator or performer up to scorn or ridicule. Satire does not involve such direct comment on the original material but, in using material for a general point, should also not be unfair in its effect for the copyright owner.[344]

Given that an aim of parody and satire is to usurp or undermine the way that an author intends their work to be viewed, it is not surprising that questions have arisen about the relationship of a defence that protects parody and satire with the author's moral right of integrity (which aims to protect the work from certain abuses). For example, in discussions about moral rights in 1997 it was said that 'the introduction of moral rights, in particular the right of integrity, is not intended to impede or adversely affect the time-honoured practices of parody and burlesque. The moral right of integrity is not intended to stifle satire, spoof or lampoon any more than does the existing law of defamation'.[345] While the government was keen to stress that the parody or satire fair dealing defence was not intended to detract from the

---

[339] Many countries have a special exception for parody (but none appear to have a special exception for satire). See Australian Copyright Council, *Copyright Amendment Act 2006* (Information Sheet G 096) 5.

[340] *Copyright Act 1968* (Cth) s 103AA is a mirror provision that relates to fair dealing for parody and satire of audiovisual items: a fair dealing with an audiovisual item does not constitute an infringement of the copyright in the item or in any work or other audiovisual item included in the item if it is for the purpose of parody or satire.

[341] Attorney-General and Department of Communications and the Arts, *Proposed Moral Rights Legislation for Copyright Creators* (Discussion Paper, 1994) [3.66].

[342] Ibid.

[343] M. Rose, *Parody: Ancient, Modern, Post-Modern* (Cambridge: Cambridge University Press, 1993) 81–2.

[344] Supplementary Explanatory Memorandum, Copyright Amendment Bill 2006 (Cth) (amendments to be moved on behalf of the government) 11.

[345] The government was careful to make this observation in its introduction of the first Moral Rights Bill in 1997: Commonwealth, *Parliamentary Debates*, House of Representatives, 18 June 1997, 5548 (Daryl Williams).

creator's moral rights in their works, it will be interesting to see how the courts manage the obvious and clear conflicts that exist between these two provisions.[346]

5.5.1.1.6 ACCESS BY PERSONS WITH A DISABILITY

As part of the 2017 amendments of the *Copyright Act 1968* (Cth),[347] a new defence was introduced for fair dealing with copyright materials for the purposes of access by one or more persons with a disability.[348] This fair dealing exception will permit enlarging text and graphics and making changes to the format to assist persons with a disability. This defence can be relied upon by the person with the disability or by other people on their behalf.

5.5.1.2 The dealing must be 'fair'

Once it has been shown that dealing was carried out for one of the specified purposes recognised in the Act, for the defence to apply it is then necessary to show that the dealing was 'fair'. It has long been recognised that it is very difficult to determine how 'fair' is to be judged in this context. In part this is because it is a question of fact that will depend on the circumstances of the case. As Lord Denning said:

> [It is] impossible to define what is 'fair dealing'. It must be a question of degree. You must first consider the number and the extent of the quotations and the extracts. Are they altogether too many and too long to be fair? Then you must consider the use made of them. If they are used as a basis for comment, criticism and review, that may be a fair dealing. If they are used to convey the same information as the author, for a rival purpose, that may be unfair. Next you must consider the proportions. ... But after all is said and done, it must be a matter of impression.[349]

Conti J adopted a similar approach in the *Panel* decision when he said that 'fair dealing involves questions of degree and impression: it is to be judged by the criterion of a fair-minded and honest person, and is an abstract concept'.[350]

Fairness is judged objectively in relation to the relevant purpose; that is to say, 'the purpose of criticism or review or the purpose of reporting news; in short, it must be fair and genuine for the relevant purpose'.[351] Of the six different permitted purposes recognised in the Act, the question of what is meant by a *fair* dealing is easiest to answer in relation to dealings that are undertaken for the purpose of criticism and review under s 40. Prior to 1980, the question of whether a dealing was 'fair' under s 40 was open-ended. This created problems for librarians and universities who in their daily dealings with copyright works had to determine when a

---

346   Australian Copyright Council, *Copyright Amendment Act 2006*, above n 339, 5. See also P. Loughlan, 'Parody, copyright and the new four-step test' (2006) 67 *Intellectual Property Forum* 46.
347   *Copyright Amendment (Disability Access and Other Measures) Act 2017* (Cth).
348   *Copyright Act 1968* (Cth) s 113E(1). This replaces the s 200AB(4) flexible dealing exception for people with disability.
349   *Hubbard v Vosper* [1972] 2 QB 84, 94. 'The notion of fairness is not personal or idiosyncratic, but rather is to be assessed objectively, with sound reasons for judgment given in support': Handler and Rolph, 'A real pea-souper', above n 316, 381.
350   *TCN Channel Nine Pty Ltd v Network Ten Pty Ltd* (2001) 108 FCR 235, 285.
351   Ibid 381, approved on appeal by the Full Court (2002) 118 FCR 417.

dealing was fair and thus non-remunerable,[352] a problem that became particularly acute after the decision of *University of New South Wales v Moorhouse*.[353]

In part, concerns of this nature led the federal government in 1974 to establish the Copyright Law Committee (the Franki Committee) to examine the impact of reprographic reproduction on copyright law in Australia. One of the issues considered by the committee was the scope and operation of the fair dealing defences, particularly in relation to reprographic copying.

Many institutional copyright users, such as educational institutions and libraries, made it clear in their submissions that they were not only concerned generally about the future of the fair dealing provisions but more specifically about what would amount to a 'fair' dealing. In other words, their concern was about the practical question of *how much* could be copied.[354]

In an effort to alleviate some of the uncertainty associated with fair dealing, the Franki Committee suggested in its 1976 report that the *Copyright Act 1968* (Cth) should be amended to provide guidelines as to when a dealing is 'fair'.[355] Following these recommendations, the government introduced qualitative (s 40(2)) and quantitative guidelines (s 40(3), (4))[356] that help determine whether a particular dealing for the purpose of research or study is fair.[357] As is shown below, the s 40(3) and (4) quantitative guidelines introduced in 1980 were repealed and replaced by the new guidelines (now found in s 40(3)–(5)).[358]

Section 40(2) provides a list of qualitative factors that are taken into account when considering whether a dealing for the purpose of research or study is fair. These are:

(a) the purpose and character of the dealing;[359]
(b) the nature of the work or adaptation;

---

352   Ricketson and Creswell, *The Law of Intellectual Property*, above n 193, [11.35].
353   (1975) 133 CLR 1.
354   This concern was articulated by the State Library of Tasmania. 'The area of the *Copyright Act* which causes us particular concern in the State Library is section 40 where closer thought needs to be given to stating the amount that is permissible to copy. There also seems little point in requiring that copies should be for research or private study because of the difficulty of proving that copies are not used for this and the inability of the librarian to control this if they were': Submission to Copyright Law Committee on Reprographic Reproduction by the State Library of Tasmania, 14 October 1974.
355   *Report of the Copyright Law Committee on Reprographic Reproduction*, above n 291, 29 [2.60]. See also *Copyright Amendment Act 1980* (Cth) s 7. Interestingly, the Franki Committee went on to state that 'a person coming within the general provisions of section 40 may be entitled to make more than one copy of a substantial part of a work for research or study if, for example, he is engaged on a research project which requires him to assemble for his own use part of a work under different headings or, for example, where he wished to make certain references on one copy and certain comment or criticism on another': at 30 [2.61].
356   Also added in 1980. See Ricketson and Creswell, *The Law of Intellectual Property*, above n 193, [11.35]. Subsections (3) and (4) of s 40 were amended in 2006.
357   In an attempt to provide further guidance as to what constitutes a fair dealing, the Franki Committee recommended the introduction of a quantitative test that is now laid down in *Copyright Act* 1968 (Cth) s 40(3) (replaced in 2006): *Report of the Copyright Law Committee on Reprographic Reproduction*, above n 291, 29 [2.60].
358   *Copyright Amendment Act 2006* (Cth) sch 6 repealed the quantitative test in s 40(5) and (6) and inserted new quantitative limits.
359   Including anything which has a commercial flavour to it: Ricketson and Creswell, *The Law of Intellectual Property*, above n 193, [11.35].

(c) the possibility of obtaining the work or adaptation within a reasonable time at an ordinary commercial price;[360]
(d) the effect of the dealing on the potential market for, or value of, the work or adaptation;
(e) where only part of the work is reproduced, the amount of the part copied in relation to the whole work or adaptation.[361]

As the Franki Committee acknowledged[362] the guidelines in s 40(2) still leave considerable room for judicial interpretation.[363]

For the new defence of copyright for persons with a disability that was added as part of the 2017 amendments, the matters to which regard must be had, in determining whether the dealing is a fair dealing for the purposes of s 113E, include:

(a) the purpose and character of the dealing;
(b) the nature of the copyright material;
(c) the effect of the dealing upon the potential market for, or value of, the material;
(d) if only part of the material is dealt with – the amount and substantiality of the part dealt with, taken in relation to the whole material.[364]

The second change to fair dealing initiated by the Franki Committee was the introduction of the s 40(3) quantitative guidelines. These provisions were replaced[365] by new quantitative guidelines in s 40(3)–(5). These sections provide specific guidance as to when certain types of copying will be fair. The quantitative guidelines introduced in 2006 provide that it is a fair dealing for the purpose of research or study to reproduce one article from a periodical publication,[366] or more than one article from the same periodical publication only when those articles are required for the same research or the same course of study.[367]

In relation to a *published literary, dramatic* or *musical work* (or of an adaptation thereof), s 40(5) provides that a person will not infringe where they reproduce a 'reasonable portion' of a work for the purpose of research or study. In this context, a 'reasonable portion' is defined as

---

360   This suggests that the defence should not be used as a matter of convenience. If the work can be purchased at a reasonable price then the court would consider that the defendant should have licensed the work rather than copying it.
361   The factors in *Copyright Act 1968* (Cth) s 40(2) represent the sort of factors that the courts took into account when deciding cases such as *Beloff v Pressdram Ltd* (1973) 1 All ER 241 and *Hubbard v Vosper* [1972] 2 QB 84. See Ricketson and Creswell, *The Law of Intellectual Property*, above n 193, [11.35]. These factors are similar to those in s 107 of the United States *Copyright Act 1976*. For fair dealings with respect to audiovisual works see s 103C(2) of the *Copyright Act 1968* (Cth).
362   The Franki Committee admitted that given the section was 'mainly directed to the acts of an individual, there are so many factors which may have to be considered in deciding whether a particular instance of copying is "fair dealing" we think it is quite impracticable to attempt to remove entirely from the Court the duty of deciding the question whether or not a particular instance constitutes "fair dealing"': *Report of the Copyright Law Committee on Reprographic Reproduction*, above n 291, 29.
363   Ricketson and Creswell, *The Law of Intellectual Property*, above n 193, [11.35]. The operation and scope of the defence has rarely been tested in Australian courts. See *De Garis v Neville Jeffress Pidler Pty Ltd* (1990) 37 FCR 99; *TCN Channel Nine Pty Ltd v Network Ten Pty Ltd* (2001) 108 FCR 235, approved on appeal by the Full Court (2002) 118 FCR 417.
364   *Copyright Act 1968* (Cth) s 113E(2).
365   By the *Copyright Amendment Act 2006* (Cth).
366   *Copyright Act 1968* (Cth) s 40(3).
367   Ibid s 40(4).

ten per cent of the number of pages in the edition; or if the work or adaptation is divided into chapters, a single chapter.

Section 40(5) also provides that in relation to a *published literary work in electronic form* (except a computer program or an electronic compilation, such as a database), a published dramatic work in electronic form, or an adaptation published in electronic form of such a literary or dramatic work, a person will not infringe where they reproduce a 'reasonable portion' of a work for the purpose of research or study. In this context, a 'reasonable portion' is defined as ten per cent of the number of words in the work or adaptation; or if the work or adaptation is divided into chapters, a single chapter.

The statutory guidance as to when a dealing will be fair only applies where the dealing is for the purpose of research or study. In all other cases – that is, in relation to dealings for the purpose of criticism or review, reporting of news, the provision of professional advice and legal proceedings, parody or satire, and disability access – fairness is assessed by the court according to the general guidelines discussed above. While it is not possible to provide precise details as to when a dealing will be fair, it is possible to identify a number of factors that may influence the way this question is answered. Following suggestions made about equivalent provisions in the United Kingdom, some of the factors that are likely to be important when deciding whether a dealing is fair include whether the work is unpublished; how the work was obtained; the amount taken; the use made of the work; the motives for, and consequences of, the dealing; and whether or not the purpose could be achieved by different means.[368]

5.5.2 Time shifting

The question of private copying has been an issue in Australian law since the advent of the video recorder and the tape-to-tape player. Both of these technologies, which allow individuals to copy in the privacy of their homes, were seen as a threat to the interests of copyright owners. Faced with the realisation that it was very difficult, if not impossible, to regulate such copying, copyright owners turned their attention to the parties who facilitated the copying – namely, the companies that sold video and tape players, as well those companies that sold blank tapes and videos. In light of decisions that suggested that the sale of tape-to-tape players did not amount to an authorisation of infringement, copyright owners argued that a levy should be imposed on the sale of blank tapes to offset the private copying. When challenged, however, the scheme was overturned by the High Court on the basis that the levy was a tax that should have been dealt with in separate legislation.[369] Since downloading music onto computers, iPods and iPhones became popular, private copying has again received a lot of attention. Faced with concerns that copyright could hinder the uptake and use of new technologies, in 2006 the government introduced two new exceptions for private copying.

One of the exceptions introduced as part of the federal government's review of copyright in 2006 was a defence of 'time shifting'. In essence, this allows people to record broadcasts for

---

368   Bently et al, *Intellectual Property Law*, above n 75, 229–32.
369   *Australian Tape Manufacturers Association Ltd v Commonwealth* (1993) 176 CLR 480. Section 55 of the *Constitution* provides: 'Laws imposing taxation shall deal only with the imposition of taxation, and any provision therein dealing with any other matter shall be of no effect.'

replaying at a more convenient time without infringing copyright.[370] Section 111(1) of the *Copyright Act 1968* (Cth) provides a defence to copyright infringement where a person records a cinematograph film or sound recording of a broadcast to watch or listen to at a more convenient time. The defence applies to 'private and domestic uses', which is defined to mean 'private and domestic use on or off domestic premises'.[371] The fact that the new definition of 'private and domestic use' makes it clear that the new exception applies to the use of time-shifted material 'on or off domestic premises' means that the recording can be played on a portable device (such as a DVD or an MP3 player). It also means that the time-shifted recording need not be made 'in domestic premises'. The person making the recording is able to lend the recording to a member of their family or household so long as it is used for that person's private and domestic use.[372] If a copy is sold, let for hire, offered for sale or hire, or distributed for trade or other purposes, then the recording becomes an infringing copy, in respect of both its making and subsequent dealing.[373]

The upshot of the 2006 changes is that it is possible to tape a broadcast of a radio or television program to watch or listen to for private and domestic use at a more convenient time.[374] The exception allows a person to record a television program that is shown while they are at work to be watched at a later time.

5.5.3 Format shifting

As well as providing individuals with the ability to make recordings for the purpose of time shifting, in 2006 a 'format shifting' defence was introduced.[375] In essence, this allows a person to reproduce copyright material in a different format for private use without infringing copyright. The government gave two reasons why an individual might want to copy material into a different format. One is to have a private copy to carry around – for example, music on an iPod instead of the original CD form. The second reason for format shifting is because one format has become obsolete, and an individual wants to move their collection of music into a new format (for example, from vinyl records to CDs).

The format-shifting defence, which applies to four categories of copyright material, provides that it is permissible to copy, without infringing copyright:

- the content of a book, newspaper or periodical into another format (for example, making a digital copy of the work by scanning it or uploading onto the internet);[376]

---

370   *Copyright Amendment Act 2006* (Cth) sch 6 pt 1.
371   *Copyright Act 1968* (Cth) s 10(1). The definition of 'private and domestic use' was inserted after the Senate Committee highlighted the limitations of the previous requirement that the recording needed to be made in domestic premises. Senate Standing Committee on Legal and Constitutional Affairs, *Copyright Amendment Bill 2006 [Provisions]*, above n 338, recs 4 and 5. The insertion of the definition of private and domestic use to mean use *on or off premises* overcame the previous physical limitation and legitimised the use of MP3 players, iPods and iPhones.
372   *Copyright Act 1968* (Cth) s 111(4).
373   Ibid s 111(3).
374   Ibid s 111.
375   *Copyright Amendment Act 2006* (Cth) sch 6 pt 2.
376   *Copyright Act 1968* (Cth) s 43C.

- a photograph from hard copy into electronic format, or from electronic format into hard-copy form;[377]
- a sound recording from CD, tape, record, or digital download to any other format[378] (except podcasts[379]);
- a film from video to electronic format.[380]

There are a number of conditions that must be satisfied before the defence can operate:

- An individual is only able to copy for their own 'private and domestic use'. This is defined in s 10 to mean private or domestic use inside or outside premises. This enables a person, for example, to copy a CD onto their iPod or iPhone to listen to on their way to work.
- An individual can only copy from a legitimately purchased or owned original. This means that it is not permissible to copy from a borrowed or pirated copy. The owner is not required to store the original, and may choose to read, view or listen to the original or the main copy.[381] However, the main copy must be in a different format to the original.
- The exception will not apply if the main copy is sold, hired, traded or distributed. The main copy becomes an infringing copy if the owner disposes of the original to another person. This is said to avoid the situation where a person acquires an article, makes a free copy of it for ongoing use and then disposes of the original to another person who might repeat the process. However, loaning the copy to a member of the lender's family or household for the member's private use is allowed.
- An individual is only able to make one (direct) copy in any given format.[382] With the exception of sound recordings, all incidental copies made as a consequence of the format shifting must be 'destroyed at the first practicable time'. As a result of changes made in the Senate, there is no longer a requirement to destroy any 'temporary copy' made in the course of shifting music to another format.[383] This means that a person is able to copy music from a CD onto their computer as a part of the process of shifting the CD format to an MP3 format.

---

377   Ibid s 47J.
378   Ibid s 109A.
379   Ibid s 109A(1)(c).
380   Ibid s 110AA.
381   The copy that is made through the process of 'format shifting' – that is, the digital version of a CD – is referred to as the 'main copy'.
382   While the format-shifting defence requires a person making a copy to destroy any incidental copies as soon as practicable, this does not apply in the case of sound recordings.
383   The Senate Committee said that to allow legitimate use of digital music players there should not be a requirement that 'temporary copies' made in the course of shifting music to another format be destroyed: Senate Standing Committee on Legal and Constitutional Affairs, *Copyright Amendment Bill 2006 [Provisions]*, above n 338, rec 5.

5.5.4 Exceptions for archives, libraries and key cultural institutions

Libraries, archives[384] and key cultural institutions[385] play an important role in collecting and maintaining information, in providing access to information, and in disseminating that information to the wider community. To ensure that copyright law does not hamper these institutions in their efforts to collect, preserve and disseminate information, the *Copyright Act 1968* (Cth) provides them with a number of special exceptions to infringement. Traditionally copyright owners did not seem to be overly concerned about the exceptions for libraries, archives and key cultural institutions. Over the last decade, however, owners have become more wary of these exceptions. One reason for this is that certain libraries have become more concerned with commercial considerations – a factor that makes it more difficult for them to argue that they operate in the public good (and thus should be exempt from liability). This has been compounded by the argument that as more and more information has become available digitally, libraries have changed from information holders to publishers of sorts. The changing status of at least some libraries has been used to argue against these exceptions, primarily on the basis that they threaten the markets that copyright owners have in electronic works. Despite pleas of this nature, the *Copyright Act 1968* still contains a number of important exceptions to copyright infringement specifically targeted at libraries, archives and key cultural institutions.

Sections 49 and 50 form the basis of the library and archives copying provisions. Section 49 provides that non-profit-making libraries or archives may make copies of published literary, dramatic, musical and artistic works for the purpose of research or study of users of the library or archives without payment to the copyright owner on certain conditions.[386] The definition of a library was revised in 2006 so that it now means a library 'all or part of whose collection is accessible to members of the public directly or through interlibrary loans'.[387] This means that a library of a commercial company, such as a law firm or an engineering firm, now can rely on the library copying provisions. A librarian or archivist has the right to reproduce the whole of a work or more than a reasonable portion of a work[388] where a new copy of the work cannot be obtained within a reasonable time and at a reasonable price.[389] A librarian of a non-profit library may reproduce and supply one article in a periodical journal, part of one article, two or more articles on the same subject matter in a periodical journal or a reasonable portion of a published work for a person who has requested a copy for their research or study and has made a declaration to that effect. 'Supply' includes making the article available to a person online or electronically transmitting it to them. This is subject to the proviso that where a work is communicated in this way, the library or archive must destroy any reproduction made for the

---

384 Defined in *Copyright Act 1968* (Cth) ss 49(9), 50(10), 113G.
385 Defined in *Copyright Act 1968* (Cth) s 113L.
386 Also for artistic works that are accompanying illustrations: see s 53 of the *Copyright Act 1968* (Cth). See also J. Lahore, *Copyright and Designs*, looseleaf service (Sydney: LexisNexis Butterworths) [44,025].
387 *Copyright Act 1968* (Cth) s 49(9), as amended by the *Copyright Amendment Act 2006*.
388 A 'reasonable portion' is defined as not more than ten per cent of the number of pages of a published edition of the work of not less than ten pages, or the whole or part of a single chapter of the work, where the work is divided into chapters: *Copyright Act 1968* (Cth) s 10(2).
389 *Copyright Act 1968* (Cth) s 49.

purpose of the communication as soon as is possible. A library cannot digitise a hard-copy work under this section. Section 50 allows libraries and archives to reproduce and communicate works for the purpose of supplying the works to other libraries and archives. Sections 49 and 50 do not apply if the library or archive imposes a charge that is more than the cost of reproducing and supplying the reproduction. Other exceptions allow libraries and archives to reproduce and communicate published and unpublished works for libraries and archives.[390] As a result of changes in 2006, libraries and archives are able to make preservation non-infringing copies of significant published editions in key cultural institutions' collections.[391]

From December 2006 libraries and archives are also able to rely on a 'special case exemption' to copyright infringement (s 200AB). While the special case exemption began as an attempt to provide copyright users with a flexible and open-ended exception (similar to the United States' fair use model),[392] there is so much uncertainty about the provision in its final form that it is unlikely to be of much use to libraries or archives.[393] For the exemption to operate it must be shown that:

- the material was used for the purpose of maintaining or operating a library or archive;[394]
- the material was not used partly for the purpose of obtaining a commercial advantage or profit;[395]
- the circumstances of the use amount to a 'special case';[396]
- the use does not conflict with the normal exploitation of the work;[397] and
- the use does not 'unreasonably prejudice the legitimate interests of the owner of the copyright or a person licensed by the owner of the copyright'.[398]

One of the key limitations of the defence is that it only operates in 'special cases', which is given the same meaning as in art 13 of *TRIPS*.[399] The fact that the defence only operates in 'special cases', which ultimately need to be decided by Australian courts on the basis of World Trade Organization jurisprudence, means that the scope of the defence is, and is likely to

---

390 Ibid s 51. Additional exceptions can be found in ss 10A, 48A, 49, 50, 51, 110A, 51AA, 51A, 52, 110B.
391 Ibid s 112AA.
392 Explanatory Memorandum, Copyright Amendment Bill 2006 (Cth) 109 [6.53].
393 The exception will not apply if (a) the use is not an infringement of copyright, or (b) the use would not be an infringement of copyright assuming the conditions or requirements of that other provision were met: *Copyright Act 1968* (Cth) s 200AB(6).
394 *Copyright Act 1968* (Cth) s 200AB(2)(b).
395 Ibid s 200AB(2)(c). Section 200 provides that the use does not fail to meet the condition in para (2)(c) merely because of the charging of a fee that (a) is connected with the use, and (b) does not exceed the costs of the use to the charger of the fee.
396 *Copyright Act 1968* (Cth) s 200AB(1)(a). Section 200AB(7) gives 'special case' the same meaning as in *TRIPS* art 13.
397 *Copyright Act 1968* (Cth) s 200AB(1)(c). Section 200AB(7) gives 'conflict with normal exploitation' the same meaning as in *TRIPS* art 13.
398 *Copyright Act 1968* (Cth) s 200AB(1)(d). Section 200AB(7) gives 'unreasonably prejudice the legitimate interests' the same meaning as in *TRIPS* art 13.
399 TRIPS art 13 provides: 'Members shall confine limitations or exceptions to exclusive rights to certain special cases which do not conflict with a normal exploitation of the work and do not unreasonably prejudice the legitimate interests of the right holder.' The meaning of art 13 was discussed in *European Communities v United States* WT/DS160, in relation to s 110(5) of the United States' *Copyright Act* (home-style exemption).

remain, uncertain. This is compounded by the fact that, in many cases, it will be unclear whether a use conflicts with the normal exploitation of the work, and unreasonably prejudices the legitimate interests of the owner. While these three requirements (which make up the 'three-step test')[400] may be of use in deciding whether the legalisation of a particular country complies with *TRIPS* or the *Berne Convention*, they only hinder the operation of the defence. Given that one of the key complaints by libraries, archives and educational institutions about copyright law is its uncertainty, it is highly unlikely that this exception will provide much assistance to copyright users in their day-to-day work.

5.5.5 Educational uses

Educational institutions have always had special privileges or exceptions from infringement. This is largely because of the important public roles that schools and universities serve in the community. For universities, schools and other educational institutions to fulfil their educative roles, they need to be able to access and use copyright works. To facilitate the delivery of research, education and training, the *Copyright Act 1968* (Cth) allows certain uses of copyright works to be made without the acts constituting an infringement of copyright. In addition to the compulsory licence schemes that are discussed above,[401] there are a range of exceptions in the Act that apply to educational uses of copyright works. Section 200 allows copyright works, or adaptations of a work, to be used as part of an exam question or in answer to an exam question. It also provides that such material can be displayed on a screen, an overhead, or a part of a PowerPoint presentation (this does not extend to multiple copying, such as photocopying or digital copying).[402]

Where sound broadcasts are used for educational instruction, there is no infringement of either the copyright in the broadcast or the underlying works if a copy is made by an educational institution for educational instruction at that institution or at another institution.[403] A teacher or student may perform a work, show a film or play a sound recording without infringing the relevant performance in public rights so long as the act is done in the course of an educational instruction (that is, to the students in the course rather than a performance to the 'public' or parents).[404]

Short extracts of works are able to be included in a collection of readings, films or sound recordings produced by educational institutions so long as the collection consists principally of *non-copyright works*. It is the fact that the collection must contain non-copyright works that means institutions rarely rely on this as a defence and instead rely on the Part VB statutory licence to produce course-packs of copyright works for students, which has been (and will continue to be) a point of controversy with copyright owners.[405]

---

400 *Berne Convention* art 9(2) provides that members shall confine limitations or exceptions to exclusive rights to *certain special cases* that do not conflict with a *normal exploitation* of the work and do *not unreasonably prejudice* the legitimate interests of rights holders.
401 At 5.2.2.3.
402 *Copyright Act 1968* (Cth) s 200(1)(b).
403 Ibid ss 200(2), (2A).
404 Ibid s 28.
405 See *Copyright Agency Ltd v Victoria University of Technology* (1994) 53 FCR 56.

Educational institutions are also able to rely on the 'special case exemption' contained in s 200AB (which was discussed above).[406] The defence covers non-commercial uses. This is subject to the proviso that the use is a 'special case', does not conflict with the 'normal exploitation' of the work, and does not 'unreasonably prejudice' the interests of the copyright owner. As mentioned above, the scope of this provision is unclear.

5.5.6 Organisations assisting persons with a disability

The *Copyright Amendment (Disability Access and Other Measures) Act 2017* (Cth) inserted a new exception for an 'organisation assisting persons with a disability' into s 113F of the *Copyright Act 1968* (Cth). For the exception to apply, the organisation must first be satisfied that the material cannot be obtained in the appropriate format within a reasonable time at an ordinary commercial price.[407] Educational institutions and not-for-profit organisations with a principal function of providing assistance to persons with a disability will be deemed to be 'organisations assisting persons with a disability'.[408] This new exception replaces the print disability statutory licence in Part VB of the Act. This means that organisations no longer need to be declared as an organisation assisting persons with a disability.

5.5.7 Artistic works

Artistic works, particularly architectural and visual artistic works, figure prominently in our urban landscape. The fact that many of these artistic works are protected by copyright has the potential to restrict the way that we operate in public spaces. It has the potential, for example, to restrict landscape artists, photographers and film makers.[409] To minimise the negative impact of copyright in these situations, the *Copyright Act 1968* (Cth) allows buildings, sculptures, and works of artistic craftsmanship that are on permanent display in a public place or on premises open to the public[410] to be reproduced in a two-dimensional form (that is, in photographs, paintings or drawings).[411] As discussed above,[412] from 2006 the format-shifting defence allows the owner of a photograph to reproduce the photograph in a different format for private use. This allows a person to translate a photograph from hard copy into electronic format, or from electronic format into hard-copy form without infringing copyright in the photograph.[413]

The Act also provides that copyright in an artistic work is not infringed when it is reproduced in a film or television broadcast where its inclusion is incidental to the principal matters represented.[414] This would mean, for example, that a person could make a film of a car chase in a city without first having to obtain permission to use the artistic works (such as

---

406 At 5.5.4.
407 *Copyright Act 1968* (Cth) s 113F(b).
408 Ibid s 10.
409 As discussed in ch 7 at 7.10, *Copyright Act 1968* (Cth) ss 74–77 set a series of special rules in relation to the reproduction of artistic works as designs.
410 *Copyright Act 1968* (Cth) ss 65, 68.
411 Ibid ss 65, 66.
412 At 5.5.3.
413 *Copyright Act 1968* (Cth) s 47J.
414 Ibid ss 67–68, 70.

buildings or sculptures) that might be included in the background. Clearly, the key issue here is determining when an image is 'incidental' to a film or broadcast. This question was considered in *Thompson v Eagle Boys Dial-A-Pizza Australia Pty Ltd*,[415] an infringement action brought by the American-owned Pizza Hut in relation to a television advertisement made by the Australian-owned Eagle Boys Pizza. In the advertisement in question, the presenter placed a pizza box used by Pizza Hut on an airport trolley and wheeled it to a United Airlines airplane waiting on the tarmac. On the basis that the Pizza Hut packaging was protected as an artistic work, Pizza Hut argued that its inclusion in the advertisement was a breach of artistic copyright. While the issue was not finalised, Wilcox J said that although the Pizza Hut packaging was deliberately used in the advertisement, nonetheless its inclusion was incidental to the primary purpose of the advertisement – namely, communicating the importance of buying products from Australian, rather than foreign-owned, companies.[416]

One of the problems that potentially confront an artist who relinquishes copyright in a particular artistic work is that the new copyright owner may be able to prohibit the artist from reusing or developing the ideas or themes in subsequent works. Problems may also arise if they wish to reuse moulds, casts, sketches, plans or models that formed the basis of an earlier work. To prevent these problems from arising, s 72 allows artists to reproduce part of one of their earlier works in a later work. This is subject to the proviso that the artist does not repeat or initiate the main design of the earlier work.[417] Equivalent provisions also provide that copyright in a building, and in any drawing or plan of the building, are not infringed by the reconstruction of that building.[418]

5.5.8 Computer programs

One of the key features of the package of reforms introduced by the federal government to adapt copyright law to digital technologies was the introduction of a number of specific defences in relation to the use and operation of computer programs. Copyright in a computer program is not infringed by a reproduction that is 'incidentally and automatically made as part of the technical process of running a copy of the program for the purposes for which the program was designed'.[419] A person will not infringe copyright if they make, store or use a back-up copy of a computer program in case the original is lost, destroyed or rendered unusable.[420] Similar provisions allow a person to make a back-up copy for security purposes.[421] Special rules also provide that a reproduction of a computer program is non-infringing where it is made for the purpose of:

- correcting an error in the original program that prevents it from operating;[422]

---

415   [2001] FCA 741.
416   Ibid [19].
417   *Copyright Act 1968* (Cth) s 72.
418   Ibid s 73.
419   Ibid s 47B(1).
420   Ibid s 47C(1)(c)(i), (ii).
421   Ibid s 47C(2) (as amended by the *Copyright Amendment (Digital Agenda) Act 2000* (Cth)).
422   This exemption is subject to the condition that an error-free copy must not be available within a reasonable time at an ordinary commercial price. The exception will not apply where the reproduction is made from an infringing copy of the computer program: *Copyright Act 1968* (Cth) ss 47E, 47E(d).

- testing, in good faith, the security of the original program, a computer system, or the network of which the program is a part;[423]
- studying the ideas behind the program and the way in which it functions;[424] or
- obtaining information necessary to enable the owner, a person acting on behalf of the owner, or a licensee to make a new program or article that is interoperable with the original program.[425]

In order to ensure that these exceptions are not undermined, the Act specifically provides that a party cannot contract out of these exceptions.[426]

5.5.9 Temporary and incidental reproductions

A number of provisions ensure that the copying that occurs as an incidental part of a technical process will not constitute an infringement. For example, ss 43A and 111A of the *Copyright Act 1968* (Cth) provide that copyright in works and audiovisual items will not be infringed when they are temporarily reproduced as part of the technical process of making or receiving a communication.[427] This exception, which includes temporary reproductions made when caching, browsing or viewing copyright material online, is intended to ensure that copyright owners are not able to interfere unduly with internet and like technologies. Users are also exempt from infringement where the incidental reproductions are made as part of a technical process of using a copy of the work.[428] Similar exceptions apply to incidental reproductions of sound recordings, cinematograph films, television and sound broadcasts, and published editions.[429]

One of the questions that arose in the discussions that preceded the introduction of the format-shifting defence in 2006 was the status of incidental copies made in the course of translating a work from one format to another. In relation to books, newspapers and periodicals, photographs and films, the Act places an obligation on the person making the copy to destroy any temporary reproductions that may arise 'at the first practicable time during or after the making of the copy'. This obligation does not apply, however, in relation to sound

---

423 *Copyright Act 1968* (Cth) s 47F. This exemption does not apply where the reproduction is made from an infringing copy of the computer program.
424 Ibid s 47B(3). This decompilation exemption will not apply to the making of a reproduction from an infringing copy of the computer program.
425 Ibid s 47D. This is subject to the requirement that the 'necessary information' must not be readily available to the owner or licensee from another source. Nor does the exception apply where the reproduction is made from an infringing copy.
426 *Copyright Act 1968* (Cth) s 47H.
427 Ibid s 43A.
428 Ibid s 43B (introduced by *US Free Trade Agreement Implementation Act 2004* (Cth) sch 9 item 188).
429 Ibid s 111B(1) (introduced by *US Free Trade Agreement Implementation Act 2004* (Cth) sch 9 item 189). In both cases, the defence only applies to acts carried out on or after 1 January 2005. This exception does not apply if the reproduction of the subject matter is made from an infringing copy of the subject matter: at s 111B(2) (introduced by *US Free Trade Agreement Implementation Act 2004* (Cth) sch 9 item 189). This difference suggests that the defence may not apply for the private non-commercial playing of pirated CDs or DVDs. Such playing could render the user liable for infringement under the new definition of 'copy' that means that mere storage will infringe, even if it is not in a form that can be reproduced.

recordings. The upshot of this is that a person copying a CD onto their computer as a part of the process of transferring the music onto their iPhone is not under an obligation to remove the music that was incidentally copied onto their computer.

5.5.10 Legal materials

Access to legal information, particularly to legislation and judgments, is a central tenet of our legal and political system. Given this, it is not surprising that the *Copyright Act 1968* (Cth) provides that a person will not infringe copyright or any prerogative right or privilege of the Crown where they make a single reprographic copy of Commonwealth or state legislation, statutory instruments, or of judgments, orders and awards of courts and tribunals whether they be Commonwealth, state or territory.[430] The exception does not apply to works that are based on legal materials (such as headnotes and summaries of facts).[431] While it is possible for a person to charge a fee for the making and supplying of a copy (which is allowed under the provision), the fee must not exceed the cost of making and supplying the copy. Similar provisions also apply to copying undertaken for judicial proceedings. Specifically, s 43(1) provides that copyright in a literary, dramatic, musical or artistic work will not be infringed by anything done for the purposes of a judicial proceeding or of a report of a judicial proceeding.[432] A judicial proceeding is defined as a proceeding before a court, tribunal, or person having power by law to hear, receive and examine evidence on oath.[433]

5.5.11 Government uses

There is an exemption from infringement where copyright material is used for the services of the Crown.[434] In particular, s 183 provides that copyright is not infringed if the Commonwealth or a state, or a person authorised in writing by the Commonwealth or a state, does an act that would otherwise be an infringement for the services of the Commonwealth or a state. Until 1998,[435] the Commonwealth and state governments were obliged to enter into an agreement with the copyright owner about the terms on which the copyright material was to be used.[436] This scheme was changed in 1998 when a scheme for government copying similar to that in place between educational institutions and collecting societies was established. Under the scheme, which is administered by the Copyright Agency,[437] the government pays equitable remuneration for any copies made.

---

430 *Copyright Act 1968* (Cth) s 182A.
431 Ibid s 182A(3).
432 Ibid ss 43(1), 104(a).
433 Ibid s 10.
434 Ibid s 183.
435 *Copyright Amendment Act 1998* (Cth) sch 4.
436 *Copyright Act 1968* (Cth) s 183(4); *Copyright Regulations 1969* (Cth) reg 25.
437 *Copyright Act 1968* (Cth) s 153F.

5.5.12 Reading or recitation in public

It is not an infringement to read or recite in public, or to include in a sound or television broadcast of a reading or recitation, a reasonable length extract from a published literary or dramatic work or an adaptation of such a work.[438]

5.5.13 Sound recordings

A number of exceptions to infringement apply in relation to sound recordings. In addition to the format-shifting defence discussed above,[439] a person who plays a sound recording in public at premises where persons reside or sleep will not be liable for infringement of copyright in the sound recording. This is on the condition that no charge is made to listen to the music[440] and that the music is exclusively for residents of the premises and their guests.[441] Non-profit clubs and societies (who pursue charitable ends or the advancement of religion, education or social welfare) are also exempt from infringement where they play a sound recording in public.[442] The defence does not apply if a charge is made for admission to the place where the recording is to be heard. Section 199(2) also provides that copyright in a sound recording is not infringed where as a result of playing a television or sound broadcast in public, the sound recording is heard in public.[443]

5.5.14 Films

In addition to the time-shifting and format-shifting defences discussed above,[444] the *Copyright Act 1968* (Cth) provides a number of defences to an action for infringement of copyright in films. These ensure, for example, that a film that primarily consists of old news images can be shown in public without infringing copyright;[445] and that copyright in a film is not infringed by any use of a record that embodies a film soundtrack.[446] Prior to 2019, the duration of unpublished film copyright[447] (fifty years) was often less than copyright in literary, dramatic, musical and artistic works (life of the author plus seventy years). Given this, where a literary, dramatic, musical or artistic work is included in a film, it has the potential to extend the time period in which the showing and use of a film is controlled by copyright. To avoid this, the *Copyright Act 1968* (Cth) provides that the public exhibition of a cinematograph film after

---

[438] Ibid s 45.
[439] At 5.5.3.
[440] This is the case even if the charge is only partly related to the sound recording and is partly for other purposes.
[441] *Copyright Act 1968* (Cth) s 106(1)(a). See *Phonographic Performance Ltd v Pontin's Ltd* [1968] Ch 290.
[442] *Copyright Act 1968* (Cth) s 106(1)(b).
[443] Ibid s 199(2). Note there is no diffusion right in sound recordings.
[444] At 5.5.2 and 5.5.3, respectively.
[445] *Copyright Act 1968* (Cth) s 110(1).
[446] Ibid s 110(3).
[447] *Copyright Amendment (Disability Access and Other Measures) Act* 2017 introduced new terms of duration for films: seventy years after the making of the film or seventy years after the work has been made public (provided it is within fifty years of its making): *Copyright Act 1968* (Cth) s 93.

copyright has expired in the film does not infringe copyright in any literary, dramatic, musical or artistic work that is included in the film.[448]

5.5.15 Public interest

The final exception to copyright infringement that is examined is the non-statutory public interest defence. Unlike the position in the United Kingdom, where the public interest defence has been accepted by the courts, its status in Australia is unclear. To the extent that the defence operates in Australia, it is usually taken into account when the court is deciding whether or not to grant injunctive relief.[449] To date, the defence has only been applied to prevent copyright from being used to suppress publication of information that has the potential to cause destruction, damage or harm, as well as the disclosure of information that involves danger to the public.[450] In other cases, the defence has been used to deal with fraud and breach of national security.[451]

5.5.16 Contracting out of the defences

While the provisions in the *Copyright Amendment (Digital Agenda) Act 2000* (Cth) were designed to balance the interests of copyright users and owners, the particular terms of online contracts depend on the negotiating power of the parties involved. This is because in drawing on the basic principles of freedom of contract, copyright law allows the parties relatively free rein to decide the terms on which an information service may be offered. In practice, the inequality of bargaining power that exists between providers and users of information means that users are often confronted with a 'take it or leave it' situation. With online contracts, copyright users are led through a series of online screens that require them to click 'yes' to proceed. In clicking 'yes', the user might agree to terms of access to a work that would be unacceptable in an analog world.

Online contracts are often drafted in favour of copyright owners, allowing very few, if any, of the normal uses that are allowed under copyright law. For example, before readers are able to access the Adobe Glassbook e-book version of Lewis Carroll's classic *Alice in Wonderland*, they must agree not to copy, print, loan or give the book to someone else, nor to read the book aloud. One of the consequences of copyright owners being able to determine the terms on which a work can be used is that online contracts can be overly restrictive of the public's right to access and use copyright works. For example, a copyright owner is able to use a contract to restrict access to a work beyond the term of copyright protection. Online contracts can also take away a user's right to access or browse works. The Attorney-General admitted as much

---

448   *Copyright Act 1968* (Cth) s 110(2).
449   *Fraser v Evans* [1969] 1 QB 349; *Beloff v Pressdram Ltd* [1973] RPC 765; *Commonwealth v John Fairfax & Sons Ltd* (1980) 147 CLR 39; *British Steel Corporation v Granada Television Ltd* [1981] AC 1096; *Collier Constructions v Foskett* (1990) 19 IPR 44. In the latter case Gummow J said that the defence did not exist, focusing instead on the equitable principle that a court has the capacity not to grant injunctive relief when a party has 'unclean hands'.
450   Compare *Commonwealth v John Fairfax & Sons Ltd* (1980) 147 CLR 39 with *Malone v Metropolitan Police Commissioner (No 2)* [1979] 2 All ER 620.
451   *Commonwealth v John Fairfax & Sons Ltd* (1980) 147 CLR 39.

when he said that while the *Digital Agenda Act* allows 'free browsing ... this is not to say that copyright owners may not charge for the browsing of their copyright material made available online under specific licensing arrangements'.[452]

An important issue that arises in this context is whether contracts entered into between owners and users can override the operation of copyright defences. If this is the case, it will further shift the balance away from users and authors of copyright and towards owners and publishers. Copyright law gives the parties free rein when deciding the terms of a contract. It is becoming increasingly common for online contracts to include terms that stipulate that the user will not exercise rights such as fair dealing. (This is referred to as 'contracting out' of copyright defences.) If this were allowed, the policy objectives of the copyright defences, such as ensuring that the public is able to freely access and use copyright works for certain purposes, would not be achieved.[453] To ensure that individuals are unable to use their bargaining position, in 2002 the CLRC recommended that parliament should legislate to ensure that the parties cannot contract out of the defences set out in the *Copyright Act 1968* (Cth).[454] There is precedent for this in the *Copyright Act 1968* that overturns any attempt to contract out of the provisions that allow parties to make a back-up copy of a computer program.[455]

The ALRC in its 2013 review was supportive of making contractual terms unenforceable if they restricted libraries and archives from relying upon actions that were permitted under the Copyright Act.[456] The Productivity Commission was also supportive of a restriction on the ability to contract out of copyright defences more generally.[457] Both of these recommendations were supported in principle by the government and the vexed issue of 'contracting out' of copyright defences was the subject of a roundtable as part of the government's copyright modernisation consultation in 2018.[458] While no consensus was reached as to the reforms needed in this area, there was agreement that contracting out is a problem of the fair dealing exception, and that the government needed to look more closely at developments in other jurisdictions before proceeding with reform in this area.

Until changes of this nature are made, the only legal relief available to copyright users is provided by the so-called vitiating factors of contract law, such as the equitable ground of unconscionability.[459]

---

[452] D. Williams, 'Government progress on copyright issues' (1999) 12 *Australian Intellectual Property Law Bulletin* 62.
[453] P. B. Hugenholtz, 'Copyright, contract and technology: What will remain of the public domain? Is copyright a right to control access to works?' (2000) 18 *Cahiers Du Centre de Recherches Informatique et Droit* 77.
[454] CLRC, *Copyright and Contract*, above n 20, rec 7.49.
[455] *Copyright Act 1968* (Cth) s 47B.
[456] ALRC, *Copyright and the Digital Economy* (Discussion Paper No 79, May 2013).
[457] Productivity Commission, *Intellectual Property Arrangements*, above n 205, rec 5.1.
[458] Department of Communication and the Arts, 'Copyright modernisation consultation', above n 285.
[459] It is also possible that overly restrictive contractual terms, like those in the Adobe e-book version of *Alice in Wonderland*, contravene consumer protection legislation, such as *Competition and Consumer Act 2010* (Cth) sch 2 s 18 (formerly *Trade Practices Act 1974* (Cth) s 52). While contract law's vitiating factors and the safeguards of the consumer protection legislation may provide copyright users with some relief, nonetheless the obligation falls on the user to initiate legal actions to seek relief, which may be an expensive and time-consuming process.

5.5.17 Future reforms

One issue that has troubled researchers in the past is whether research undertaken for commercial purposes could be regarded as fair dealing for the purpose of research or study. Unfortunately this issue was not clarified in the 2006 or the 2017 reforms. The ALRC recommended that the *Copyright Act 1968* (Cth) be amended to provide that commercial research is 'research' for the purposes of the fair dealing exceptions.[460] To date, there has been no clear response by the federal government to this proposal.

---

460   ALRC, *Genes and Ingenuity: Gene Patenting and Human Health* (Report No 99, 2004) [28.56]–[28.60].

6

AREAS RELATED TO COPYRIGHT: MORAL RIGHTS, PERFORMERS' RIGHTS, ARTIST'S RESALE RIGHTS, AND OTHER RIGHTS

6.1 Introduction

This chapter examines some of the rights that are closely associated with but not usually seen as part of copyright law. The first section examines the moral rights that are given to creators upon creation of a copyright work. Moral rights are independent of copyright but arise where copyright subsists in a work, and continue to exist even though the creator may have sold (assigned) their copyright in the work. This is followed by an examination of the protection given to performers under the *Copyright Act 1968* (Cth). The law in this area has undergone a number of recent changes, principally as a result of the *Australia–US Free Trade Agreement 2004* (*AUSFTA*), which extended the protection to include control over authorised sound recordings of performances,[1] as well as providing moral rights for certain types of performances. Later sections of this chapter consider resale royalty rights, circuit layout rights, and the public and educational lending rights schemes.

6.2 Moral rights

One of the recurring themes of twentieth-century Australian copyright law was the question of whether Australia complied with its requirements under the *Berne Convention for the Protection of Literary and Artistic Works*[2] (*Berne Convention*) to protect the moral rights of authors. In particular, art 6*bis* of the *Berne Convention* requires member states to provide authors with the right to claim authorship of the work and to object to any distortion, mutilation or other modification of the work that would be prejudicial to the author's honour or reputation. While the Commonwealth government and many others argued that the existing laws of defamation and passing off provided adequate protection, creators and commentators continually expressed their dissatisfaction with the level of protection afforded by Australian law.[3] After nearly seventy years of debate,[4] the government capitulated in 2000 and admitted that the existing laws were 'fragmentary and incomplete'.[5] To remedy this deficiency, in December 2000 the government introduced a moral rights legislative scheme into Australian copyright

---

1   These new rights took effect from 1 January 2005.
2   Opened for signature 9 September 1886, WIPO Lex No TRT/BERNE/001 (as amended 28 September 1979, entered into force 19 November 1984) (*Berne Convention*).
3   See S. Ricketson, *The Berne Convention for the Protection of Literary and Artistic Works: 1886–1986* (London: Kluwer, 1987); J. Crawford, 'Opinion of Australia's obligation under the *Berne Convention* to introduce moral rights' (1989) 7 *Copyright Reporter* 8; S. Ricketson, 'Is Australia in breach of its international obligations with respect to the protection of moral rights?' (1990) 17 *Melbourne University Law Review* 462; P. Anderson and D. Saunders (eds), *Moral Rights Protection in a Copyright System* (Brisbane: Griffith University, 1992).
4   Copyright Law Review Committee (CLRC), *The Importation of Provisions of the Copyright Act 1968* (Canberra: AGPS, 1988); CLRC, *Report on Moral Rights* (Canberra: AGPS, 1988); Attorney-General and Department of Communications and the Arts, *Proposed Moral Rights Legislation for Copyright Creators* (Discussion Paper, 1994).
5   Commonwealth, *Parliamentary Debates*, House of Representatives, 8 December 1999 (Daryl Williams). Prior attempts to introduce such rights had failed. See Joint Statement of the Minister for the Arts and the Minister for Justice of 26 August 1993 in Attorney-General and Department of Communications and the Arts, *Proposed Moral Rights Legislation for Copyright Creators*, above n 4.

law.[6] A limited regime of moral rights for performers, which is discussed below,[7] was also introduced in 2007.

Typically, moral rights are defined in relation to copyright. Copyright provides an alienable economic right to control certain uses (notably reproduction) of protected works. In contrast, moral rights are personal rights that provide specific protection for authors, their reputation and, in some cases, the work itself.[8] Moral rights are personal to the creator. They are non-economic rights that are distinct from copyright and are often justified on similar non-economic grounds.[9]

As with many legal regimes, moral rights perform, or at least are said to perform, a number of different roles. At the most general level, they provide a limited form of protection for authors and their works. This is particularly important where creators no longer own copyright in their works, or where they 'no longer own the physical items in which their copyright is embodied, and ... therefore do not have an opportunity to contract with users for the protection of those rights'.[10] Moral rights, unlike copyright, cannot be assigned; however, authors may 'consent' in writing to infringements of their moral rights.[11] Moral rights are also meant to ensure that people who make use of artistic and cultural creations do so in a manner that is respectful to the interests of the creator. Moral rights also play a role in protecting and promoting the author's or creator's reputation.

Australian law recognises three moral rights: the right of attribution of authorship, the right of integrity of authorship and the right to prevent false attribution.[12] Except in the case of the makers of cinematograph films and sounds recordings, all moral rights continue in force until copyright ceases to exist in the work.[13] When the author of a work dies, the author's moral rights may be exercised and enforced by the author's legal personal representative.[14] In relation to cinematograph films, the moral rights are held by the director, producer and

---

[6] For more detailed discussion of moral rights, see E. Adeney, 'The moral rights of integrity: The past and future of "honour"' (2005) 2 *Intellectual Property Quarterly* 111–35; E. K. Giles, 'Mind the gap: Parody and moral rights' (2005) 18 *Australian Intellectual Property Law Bulletin* 69; E. Adeney, *The Moral Rights of Authors and Performers: An International and Comparative Analysis* (Oxford: Oxford University Press, 2006); K. Garnett and G. Davies, *Moral Rights* (London: Sweet & Maxwell, 2010).

[7] At 6.3.1.

[8] See generally J. Ginsburg, 'Moral rights in a common law system' (1990) 14 *Entertainment Law Review* 121.

[9] Moral rights are often said to derive from romantic notions of authorship, including ideas from natural law that liken the author's creation of a work to the creation of a child. The 'good manners' argument also stems from these ideas: S. Ricketson and C. Creswell, *The Law of Intellectual Property: Copyright, Designs and Confidential Information* (2nd edn, Sydney: LBC Information Services, 1999) [10.15]. See generally M. Sainsbury, *Moral Rights and Their Application in Australia* (Sydney: Federation Press, 2003).

[10] V. Morrison, 'The new moral rights legislation' (2000) 18 *Copyright Reporter* 170, 178.

[11] *Copyright Act 1968* (Cth) ss 195AW–195AWA. See discussion below at 6.2.5.

[12] The moral rights recognised under the *Copyright Act 1968* (Cth) are not transmissible by assignment, by will or by devolution by operation of law: at s 195AN(3). However, if the author of a work dies, the author's moral rights (other than the right of integrity of authorship in respect of a cinematograph film) may be exercised and enforced by the author's legal personal representative: at s 195AN(1).

[13] *Copyright Act 1968* (Cth) s 195AM(1).

[14] Ibid s 195AN(1). See also s 195AN(2) (where the affairs of an author are lawfully administered by another person, other than by way of bankruptcy or insolvency).

screenwriter[15] (as long as they are individuals and not corporations)[16] and the right of integrity lapses when the last of these creators dies.[17]

The potential impact of moral rights was weakened by the fact that when the government introduced the new rights in 2000, it imposed two limitations on the operation of these rights. These are the defence of reasonableness and the ability of authors to consent to their moral rights being infringed. The scope of these limitations will be examined after each of the individual rights are looked at in turn.

6.2.1 The right of attribution

The right of attribution provides authors with the right to be identified as author of the works they have created.[18] For literary works, the right of attribution applies where the work is reproduced, published, performed, communicated to the public or adapted.[19] The author of an artistic work has the right to be identified as author where the work is reproduced, published, exhibited publicly or communicated to the public.[20] The director, producer[21] and screenwriter of a film[22] have the right to be named as such where the film is copied, exhibited publicly or communicated to the public.[23] In all these situations (which are called 'attributable acts'), the author has the right to be identified as author of the work in question. The right of attribution will be infringed where a person performs an 'attributable act' but fails to identify the author in an appropriate manner.[24] A party will also infringe where they authorise someone else to act in a manner such that they infringe the author's right of attribution.[25]

The author of a work may be identified by any reasonable form of identification:[26] the main requirement is that the identification is clear and reasonably prominent.[27] The identification of an author will be reasonably prominent if it is included on each reproduction, adaptation or copy in such a way that a person acquiring the item would have notice of the author's identity.[28] It has been suggested that a reasonably distinct identification of the author at the

---

15 Ibid s 191.
16 Ibid s 190.
17 Ibid s 195AM(1).
18 Ibid s 193. In relation to literary works, the right of attribution applies to works that were made before the commencement of the moral rights regime (21 December 2000). However, the right only applies to acts carried out after 21 December 2000: at s 195AZM(2).
19 *Copyright Act 1968* (Cth) s 194(1).
20 Ibid s 194(2).
21 Ibid s 189.
22 Ibid.
23 Ibid s 195.
24 See *Corby v Allen & Unwin Pty Ltd* (2013) 297 ALR 761. Although a breach of the right of attribution was found in relation to the publication by Allen & Unwin of Corby family photographs in the book, *Sins of the Father*, without the Corby family's permission, it was held that no loss was suffered, as the Corbys would not have wished their names to be published in connection with the photos. Their distress and outrage arose as 'family members, not as authors of the photographs': at [135]. The infringement was held to be one of 'form rather than substance': at [136].
25 *Copyright Act 1968* (Cth) s 195AO.
26 Ibid s 194(1).
27 Ibid s 195AA.
28 Ibid s 195AB. A person infringes an author's right of attribution if the person deals with the work, or authorises another to deal with the work, without identifying the author: s 195AO. The factors to be

beginning or end of the work would satisfy this requirement.[29] Industry practice may also have an impact on what is considered to be a reasonable attribution.[30] Attribution is not required where it was 'reasonable in all the circumstances not to identify the author' or where the author has consented in writing to not being identified.[31]

The matters to be taken into account in determining whether an infringement has been authorised are the extent (if any) of the person's power to prevent the doing of the act concerned; the nature of any relationship existing between the person and the person who did the act concerned; and whether the person took any reasonable steps to prevent or avoid the doing of the act, including whether the person complied with any relevant industry codes of practice.[32] Attribution is still required under the educational statutory licences and the fair dealing provisions.

6.2.2 The right of integrity

The second moral right granted to authors is the right of integrity of authorship.[33] In essence, the right of integrity provides that authors have the right not to have their work subject to derogatory treatment in relation to certain specified uses of the work.[34]

In relation to literary, dramatic and musical works, the right of integrity applies where the work is reproduced, published, performed, communicated to the public or adapted.[35] In relation to artistic works, the right applies where the work is reproduced, published, or communicated to the public.[36] With cinematograph films, the right of integrity applies where the film is copied, exhibited or communicated to the public.[37]

In relation to *literary, dramatic and musical works and films*, derogatory treatment means:

- the doing of anything that results in the material distortion of, the mutilation of, or a material alteration to the work that is prejudicial to the author's honour or reputation;[38] or
- the doing of anything in relation to the work that is prejudicial to the author's honour or reputation.[39]

---

taken into account when determining whether there has been an 'authorisation' are outlined in s 195AVA.

29 Ricketson and Creswell, *The Law of Intellectual Property*, above n 9, [10.70].
30 V. Morrison, *Moral Rights: A Practical Guide* (Sydney: Australian Copyright Council, 2000) 11.
31 *Copyright Act 1968* (Cth) ss 195AR, 195AW, 195AWA.
32 Ibid s 195AVA.
33 Ibid s 195AI(1), (2). See B. Ong, 'Why moral rights matter: Recognising the intrinsic value of integrity rights' (2002) 26 *Columbia Journal of Law and the Arts* 297.
34 In relation to literary, dramatic, musical and artistic works, other than those included in films, the right of integrity subsists with respect to works made before or after 21 December 2000. In relation to films and to literary, dramatic, musical and artistic works included in films, the right of integrity subsists only in films made *after* 21 December 2000: *Copyright Act 1968* (Cth) s 195AI(1)–(2).
35 *Copyright Act 1968* (Cth) s 195AQ(3).
36 Ibid s 195AQ(4).
37 Ibid s 195AQ(5).
38 Ibid ss 195AJ(a), 195AL(a).
39 Ibid ss 195AJ(b), 195AL(b). See also ss 195AJ(a), 195AL(a).

In relation to *artistic works*, derogatory treatment means:

- the doing of anything that results in the material distortion of, the destruction or mutilation of or a material alteration to the work that is prejudicial to the author's honour or reputation;
- an exhibition in public that is prejudicial to the author's honour or reputation because of the manner in which the exhibition occurs; or
- the doing of anything in relation to the work that is prejudicial to the author's honour or reputation.[40]

When determining whether an author's moral right of integrity has been infringed the key issue is whether or not the treatment in question was 'derogatory'. Under the *Copyright Act 1968* (Cth), to be derogatory the treatment must be prejudicial to the author's honour or reputation. This might occur, for example, where part of a work is taken out of context in such a way that it changes its meaning,[41] or where a work is inappropriately placed alongside another work in a manner that is deemed to be derogatory: for example, where an article written by a Jewish author is placed in a collection of neo-Nazi writings or a painting by an artist who is inspired by Christian ideals is placed in a gallery of pornographic 'art'. The task of determining whether an author's honour and reputation has been harmed is often very difficult.[42] One of the problems that potentially arises here is that a particular artist may be hypersensitive or overly controlling in relation to the way that their works are used. If the courts were to allow the subjective judgement of the author to determine whether a work had been used in a derogatory manner, it could have far-reaching consequences. This question was addressed in the Canadian decision of *Snow v Eaton Shopping Centre*,[43] where O'Brien J said that 'the words "prejudicial to his honour or reputation" involve a certain subjective element or judgement on the part of the author so long as it is reasonably arrived at'.[44] It would seem that this approach is the most sensible way of determining whether a particular treatment was derogatory.

The decision in *Perez v Fernandez*[45] is Australia's first decision on the moral right of integrity. This case involved infringement of both copyright in the musical work and the moral right of integrity by Fernandez's modification of Perez's song 'Bon Bon'. Mr Perez was better

---

40	Ibid s 195AK. In *Tidy v Trustees of the Natural History Museum* (1995) 39 IPR 501, 504, Ratee J referred to the test used in *Snow v Eaton Shopping Centre* (1982) 70 CPR (2d) 105, stating: 'Even if I accept that statement of principle, the fact remains that before accepting the plaintiff's view that the reproduction in the book complained of is prejudicial to his honour or reputation, I have to be satisfied that that view is one which is reasonably held, which inevitably involves the application of an objective test of reasonableness.'
41	In *Morrison Leahy Music Ltd v Lightbond Ltd* [1993] EMLR 144, the singer George Michael, via his first record company, claimed a violation of his right of integrity after the release of a recording of a 'megamix' containing altered portions of his work. The moral right issue was not clearly dealt with by the judges because a copyright violation had been established.
42	On the problems that arise when the courts are asked to assess the artistic merits of a work to determine whether a work has been 'debased' under *Copyright Act 1968* (Cth) s 55, see *Schott Musik International GmbH & Co v Colossal Records of Australia Pty Ltd* (1997) 75 FCR 321, where a 'techno' dance remix of the 'O Fortuna' chorus from the work *Carmina Burana* 'debased' the original work. The appeal was dismissed.
43	(1982) 70 CPR (2d) 105.
44	Ibid 106.
45	(2012) 260 FLR 1.

known in the music industry as the performing artist 'Pitbull'. Mr Fernandez was a Perth DJ and promoter who ran the Suave website. Fernandez replaced ten words from Perez's song with an audio drop Fernandez had created to promote Perez's tour to Australia and streamed the song from his website. The focus in this case was the harm to Perez's reputation caused by the audio drop's false association with Fernandez. The Federal Court, in awarding $10 000 for infringement of Perez's moral right of integrity, took into account the distortion of Perez's song and held that the false association created by it injured his reputation as an artist.[46] In addition, the court took into account the fact that Perez's original recording of his song 'Bon Bon' had not yet been released in Australia at the time and listeners of the remixed song would have incorrectly thought that Perez had authored the remixed song.[47]

One factor that may influence the decision as to whether a treatment was derogatory was the motive of the infringer, particularly where they were motivated by malice. The nature or type of work may also be relevant when determining whether a treatment of a work is derogatory.[48] The courts may adopt a different attitude to works that have been created as a result of intellectual creativity as opposed to works that are more utilitarian in nature.[49] In the latter case, it would be more likely to expect that the work (such as the shape of a petrol bowser) would be modified and changed compared to a work (such as a painting) that was perceived to be more 'artistic or cultural' in nature.[50]

Special rules apply to movable artistic works and buildings.[51] The destruction of a movable artistic work is not an infringement of the author's right of integrity if the person who destroyed the work gave the author or their representative a reasonable opportunity to remove the work from the place where it was situated.[52] Similarly, the rights of integrity in a building will not be infringed where the building is relocated, demolished or destroyed on the condition that either the 'author' or their representative cannot be located after reasonable inquiries, or the author was given reasonable opportunity to remove the work.[53] The *Copyright Act 1968* (Cth) also provides that the right of integrity in an artistic work will not be infringed where a person sets out to restore or preserve that work.[54]

---

46 Ibid [103].
47 Ibid [86].
48 *Copyright Act 1968* (Cth) s 195AS(2)(a).
49 See generally I. Eagles and L. Longdin, 'Technological creativity and moral rights: A comparative perspective (2004) 12 *International Journal of Law and Information Technology* 209.
50 In *Buffet v Fersing* [1962] D Jur 570 (Cour d'appel, Paris) the dismantling of an artistically painted refrigerator into six parts for sale as separate artworks was held to be an infringement of the artist's right of integrity under French law. For discussion, see J. H. Merryman, 'The refrigerator of Bernard Buffet' (1976) 27 *Hastings Law Journal* 1023.
51 *Copyright Act 1968* (Cth) s 195AT. There have been a number of disputes in Australia involving architects and their moral rights (e.g., the National Gallery of Australia, the National Museum of Australia, New Parliament House, the Queensland Performing Arts Complex and Brisbane's Riverside Centre). Most of these have been resolved without litigation. See M. Rimmer, 'Crystal palaces: Copyright law and public architecture' (2002) 14 *Bond Law Review* 320. See also K. Stammer and H. Macpherson, 'Moral rights in the Australian building industry: What's been happening' (2006) 18 *Australian Intellectual Property Law Bulletin* 137.
52 *Copyright Act 1968* (Cth) s 195AT(1).
53 Ibid s 195AT(1), (2). The procedures that must be followed in these circumstances are set out in s 195AT(2A)–(4A).
54 Ibid s 195AT(5).

It is interesting to note that there is a potential for conflict between the exercise of the moral right of integrity and the defence of fair dealing for the purposes of parody or satire. While the right of integrity gives the author the right to object to derogatory treatment of their work, the defence of parody or satire allows users to use those same works to parody or make satirical acts or observations about the work or the author. Thus, while Sainsbury observes, 'the use of the author's own work to attack or criticise the author or his or her work may be argued to be a use which is prejudicial to that author's honour or reputation',[55] she concludes that while these issues may arise from the same factual situation, the defence of fair dealing should be argued and considered separately from the consideration of the moral rights of the author.[56]

6.2.3 The right to object to false attribution

The third moral right recognised in Australian copyright law, and the oldest of the three moral rights, is the right of authors not to have authorship of their work falsely attributed.[57] The right to object to false attribution, which existed in Australian copyright law prior to 2000, was reinforced and extended by the *Copyright Amendment (Moral Rights) Act 2000* (Cth).[58] This right allows authors to prevent someone else affixing or inserting a person's name to a work (or a reproduction of a work) in a way that falsely implies that that person is the author of the work.[59] It also prevents commercial dealings with the work carrying a false attribution.[60]

The right applies where someone inserts or affixes another person's name in or on the work or film, or in or on a reproduction of the work or film, in such a way as to imply falsely that the other person is its author.[61] In all cases, the right applies where the wrongly attributed work is published, sold, let for hire, offered or exposed for sale or hire, or exhibited or communicated to the public.[62] False attribution can be shown even where there is no intention to falsely attribute, as 'falsely' bears the meaning of 'objectively incorrect'.[63] In the case of literary, dramatic or musical works, and films, the right also applies where a named work is performed in public under someone else's name.[64] In relation to artistic works, the right also applies where a party authorises the use of a person's name in connection with the work or

---

55 M. Sainsbury, 'Parody, satire, honour and reputation: The interplay between economic and moral rights' (2007) 18 *Australian Intellectual Property Journal* 149.
56 Ibid 150.
57 *Copyright Act 1968* (Cth) s 195AC(1). This right subsists in works made before or after 21 December 2000. However, the right only applies in relation to acts of false attribution done after that date: at s 195AZN(1). For a discussion of the now repealed s 190 see *Adams v Quasar Management Service Pty Ltd* (2002) 56 IPR 385.
58 *Copyright Act 1968* (Cth) s 195AC(1). This expanded right subsists in works or films made before or after 21 December 2000, but only applies in relation to acts of false attribution done after that date. The prior right against false attribution of authorship, somewhat more restricted in scope, applies to acts before that date: at s 195AZN(1).
59 *Copyright Act 1968* (Cth) ss 195AD(a), 195AE(a).
60 Ibid s 195AG. This is subject to the requirement that the offender knows that the work has been altered.
61 Ibid ss 195AD(a), 195AE(a), 195AF(1), (2): Directors, producers and screenwriters have the right not to have authorship of their work falsely attributed where the work is a cinematograph film.
62 Ibid ss 195AD(b)–(c), 195AE(b)–(d). For a discussion of United Kingdom provisions, see *Clark v Associated Newspapers Ltd* (1998) 40 IPR 262.
63 *Meskenas v ACP Publishing Pty Ltd* (2006) 70 IPR 172, [31].
64 *Copyright Act 1968* (Cth) s 195AD(d).

with a reproduction of the work, in such a way as to imply falsely that the other person is the author of the work.[65] This might occur, for example, where a sign is placed beside a painting that falsely suggests that the work was created by someone other than the actual artist. In what is thought to be the first reported decision on moral rights in Australia, *Meskenas v ACP Publishing Pty Ltd*, the court suggested that the fact that the artist had a well-established reputation would mean that the false attribution would have had less of an impact on their reputation.[66] In other words, a well-established artist would have to prove significant damage to reputation from a lack of attribution to succeed in a substantial award of damages.

6.2.4 Limits on moral rights

While moral rights have the potential to protect the interests that authors have in their creations, even when they may have assigned away their copyright, the impact that moral rights have on the way works are used ultimately depends on a number of factors.[67] This is because, in response to fears[68] that moral rights would have imposed unreasonable burdens on industry, the Commonwealth government imposed two limitations on the operation of an author's moral rights. The first is the so-called reasonableness defence, which provides that if a person performs an attributable act or subjects a work to a derogatory treatment, there will be no infringement if the act or treatment of the work was 'reasonable in all the circumstances'.[69] The second limit is that authors are able to consent to acts that may otherwise infringe their moral rights. Given that the reasonableness defence and the ability of authors to consent to moral rights infringements have the potential to erode the impact that moral rights have in regulating the way in which works are used, it may be helpful to look at each in turn.

6.2.4.1 'Reasonable in all the circumstances'

One of the most important limitations on the moral rights regime is that the right of attribution and the right of integrity will not be infringed where the treatment in question was 'reasonable in all the circumstances'.[70] The question of whether the conduct of a party is reasonable will vary depending on the circumstances of the case.

The *Copyright Act 1968* (Cth) outlines some of the matters to be taken into account when determining whether a treatment of a work was 'reasonable in all the circumstances'.[71] The nature or type of work will be relevant.[72] In particular, works of 'high art' will be treated

---

65 Ibid s 195AE(a).
66 (2006) 70 IPR 172, [40].
67 As more and more works are made available online, authors also find it close to impossible to enforce their moral rights when infringement occurs on the internet. See F. Cantatore and J. Johnston, 'Moral rights: Exploring the myths, meanings and misunderstandings in Australian copyright law' (2016) 21(1) *Deakin Law Review* 71
68 Particularly from the film and advertising industries.
69 *Copyright Act 1968* (Cth) ss 195AR(1), 195AS(1).
70 Ibid ss 195AR, 195AS.
71 Ibid ss 195AR(2), 195AS(2). The Act provides no guidance as to how the reasonableness factors are to be balanced against each other. In the absence of such guidance, it can be assumed that each factor weighs equally with the others.
72 *Copyright Act 1968* (Cth) s 195AR(2)(a).

differently from more mundane or 'lowbrow' works.[73] Another factor to be taken into account when deciding whether an act or treatment of a work was reasonable is the purpose,[74] manner[75] and context[76] in which the work is used. In relation to the purpose of the use, a relevant consideration is whether the work was used for a private or public purpose and whether the purpose of the intended use was commercial or non-commercial.[77] Where the use was for the greater public good, the conduct in question may be considered to be reasonable in the circumstances. In contrast, where the use is private and likely to result in commercial gain for the user, the use may not be considered to be reasonable. This may also refer to the permanency of the use of the work – that is, whether the work is used, for example, in a permanent publication or a transitory handout. Where a work is used for private, non-commercial ends (for example, where it is disseminated as part of a public seminar series) there may be circumstances in which a failure to attribute authorship or to deal with the work in an otherwise derogatory way would be reasonable. This may especially be the case where the work is circulated on a one-off basis and the recipients were not expected to retain the publication. However, where a work is used for a commercial purpose, for example, as part of a full-fee seminar that is continuously on offer, it would be reasonable to expect proper attribution and treatment of the work that does not prejudice the author's honour or reputation.

The manner in which a work is used is also relevant when deciding whether an act or treatment was reasonable.[78] In relation to attribution, a failure to attribute authorship may occur for a number of reasons. For example, only a small portion of a work may have been used, or a work may have a very large number of authors, or there may be limits on the amount of space or time.[79] In these situations, it may be reasonable not to attribute authorship.

The context in which the work is used is also relevant when deciding whether an act or treatment was reasonable.[80] For example if an artist's painting is displayed as part of an exhibition titled *Ten Worst Paintings of the Twentieth Century*, then this would clearly prejudice the artist's honour or reputation. Another factor that may be relevant when deciding whether an act or treatment was reasonable is whether there is any practice in the industry in which the work is used that is relevant to the work or the use of the work.[81] This was introduced in recognition of the fact that certain industries already had in place practices that regulated how creators and their works should be treated. It was also designed to encourage other industries to adopt similar best practice models.[82]

Another factor that may influence the decision as to whether the way that a work was used was reasonable is the fact that the work was made in the course of the author's employment.[83]

---

73 Morrison, *Moral Rights*, above n 30, 13.
74 *Copyright Act 1968* (Cth) ss 195AR(2)(b), 195AS(2)(b).
75 Ibid ss 195AR(2)(c), 195AS(2)(c).
76 Ibid ss 195AR(2)(d), 195AS(2)(d).
77 Ricketson and Creswell, *The Law of Intellectual Property*, above n 9, [10.175].
78 *Copyright Act 1968* (Cth) ss 195AR(2)(c), 195AS(2)(c).
79 Ricketson and Creswell, *The Law of Intellectual Property*, above n 9, [10.175].
80 *Copyright Act 1968* (Cth) ss 195AR(2)(d), 195AS(2)(d).
81 Ibid ss 195AR(2)(e), 195AS(2)(e).
82 Some peak industry bodies have developed industry codes of conduct. For example, the Australian Publishing Association in conjunction with the Australian Society of Authors has implemented a code.
83 *Copyright Act 1968* (Cth) ss 195AR(2)(h)(i), 195AS(2)(g)(i). Together with the issue of consent (formerly the waiver provision) this was one of the more controversial aspects of the moral rights legislation. This

While this does not mean that an employed author has no moral rights, it does suggest that it may be more reasonable for employers to breach the moral rights of their employees than is the case with non-employed authors. Some employers of large organisations would argue that it would be impractical and inconvenient for them to consult with their employed authors constantly in relation to normal uses of the work, such as editing, particularly where the employer already owns the copyright in the work.[84]

6.2.4.2 Consent

One of the defining characteristics of moral rights in many regimes (particularly those based on European models) is that moral rights are inalienable. That is, while an author may be able to assign their copyright in a work to a third party, they are unable to transfer their moral rights to anyone else. In the same way in which many human rights cannot be overruled by contract or other legal instruments, moral rights, at least in some jurisdictions, always remain with the author. In drafting the moral rights regime, the government decided that this approach should not be adopted in Australia. Instead, the government decided that authors should be able to consent (in writing) to acts that would otherwise infringe their moral rights.[85]

Reflecting the impact that the film industry had on the moral rights regime, the consent provisions differ between films (including literary, dramatic, musical and artistic works that are included in a film) on the one hand, and literary, dramatic, musical and artistic works (other than those included in a film) on the other.[86]

In relation to films (including literary, dramatic, musical and artistic works that are included in a film), the *Copyright Act 1968* (Cth) provides that it is not an infringement of moral rights to do, or omit to do, something if the act or omission is within the written consent given by the author or by a person representing the author.[87] Consent can be granted in relation to specified existing works when the consent is given, or to works of a particular description that do not yet exist.[88] Generally, the consent must be in relation to specified acts or omissions, or classes or types of acts or omissions.[89] A distinction is made where the author is an employee, insofar as an employee can grant consent in relation to all works made in the course of employment.[90]

---

is largely because of the concern that employed authors are in a much less favourable position than other authors. That is, because of the nature of the employment relationship, it may be considered 'reasonable in the circumstances' for employers to breach their employees' moral rights.

84 Ricketson and Creswell, *The Law of Intellectual Property*, above n 9, [10.175].
85 See generally W. Rothnie, 'Moral rights: Consents and waivers' (2002) 20 *Copyright Reporter* 145.
86 *Copyright Act 1968* (Cth) ss 195AWA, 195AWB.
87 See Commonwealth, *Parliamentary Debates*, House of Representatives, 8 December 1999 (Daryl Williams): 'As recognised by the Government when withdrawing the original legislation, the most controversial and divisive issue was whether it should be possible for authors, artists and film-makers to waive their moral rights. Understandably, creators saw the provision for waiver in the original legislation as a means by which economically powerful users of their copyright works could force them to agree to give up these new rights completely. In response to these concerns the concept of waiver has been dropped from this Bill.'
88 *Copyright Act 1968* (Cth) s 195AWA(3).
89 For works that are not films.
90 See *Copyright Act 1968* (Cth) s 195AWA(4), which provides that consent may be given by an employee for the benefit of their employer in relation to all or any acts or omissions (whether occurring before or after the consent is given) and in relation to all works made or to be made by the employee in the course of their employment.

Where such a broad consent is given, a waiver of moral right is effectively granted. Consents must be granted by the author, who may or may not be the copyright owner. Where consent is obtained as a result of duress or false or misleading statements, the consent will be invalid.[91]

While the provisions in relation to literary, dramatic, musical and artistic works (other than those included in a film) are similar to those dealing with films, there are a number of subtle differences. The first is that the written consent has to be 'genuinely given by the author'. Another difference is that no mention is made of the possibility of consents applying retrospectively. Beyond this, the provisions are much the same as for films.

6.2.5 Remedies for infringement of moral rights

Authors are able to bring an action for infringement of their moral rights by virtue of s 195AZA of the *Copyright Act 1968* (Cth).[92] The existence of moral rights does not preclude the possibility of authors protecting their honour and reputation under different causes of action, such as defamation or passing off.[93]

The courts have the power to award an injunction and/or damages, or to declare that the defendant make a public apology. To prevent 'double counting' when calculating quantum for breach of moral rights, the courts are required to take account of any related copyright damages.[94] The court can also order that any false attribution of authorship or derogatory treatment must be removed or reversed.[95] In exercising its discretion as to which relief to grant, the court may take into account:[96]

(a) whether the defendant was aware, or ought reasonably to have been aware, of the author's moral rights;
(b) the effect on the author's honour or reputation resulting from any damage to the work;
(c) the number, and categories, of people who have seen or heard the work;
(d) anything done by the defendant to mitigate the effects of the infringement;
(e) if the moral right that was infringed was a right of attribution of authorship – any cost or difficulty that would have been associated with identifying the author;
(f) any cost or difficulty in removing or reversing any false attribution of authorship, or derogatory treatment, of the work.

---

91 See *Copyright Act 1968* (Cth) s 195AWB. This section was introduced in the Senate: see Commonwealth, *Parliamentary Debates*, Senate, 7 December 2000 (Daryl Williams). It was welcomed by many. Film critic Julie Rigg stated, '[T]he legislation was further strengthened by opposition amendments in the Senate, invalidating "consent" obtained under duress. What this exactly means no one knows. One view of film and television industry negotiations is that contract negotiations all involve duress: as in "sign this or you don't eat". It is a field rife with lawyers ... A test case on this might be very interesting': ABC Radio National, 'Moral rights legislation Q&A' (Arts Today, 12 December 2000) 2.
92 *Copyright Act 1968* (Cth) s 195AZA(1) provides that the court may award an injunction and/or damages, make a declaration that a moral right of an author has been infringed, make an order that the defendant make a public apology or that any false attribution of authorship or derogatory treatment be removed or reversed, or any combination of these remedies. See also s 195AZA(2).
93 *Copyright Act 1968* (Cth) s 195AZB(1).
94 *Rutter v Brookland Valley Estate* (2009) 81 IPR 549, [114].
95 *Copyright Act 1968* (Cth) s 195AZA.
96 Ibid s 195AZA(2).

Where the court is considering whether to grant an injunction, it must consider whether the parties have made any attempt to negotiate a settlement, through mediation or otherwise.[97]

6.2.6 Indigenous communal moral rights?

When the new moral rights legislation was being debated in parliament at the end of 1999, Senator Aden Ridgeway argued that the law should recognise Indigenous communal moral rights.[98] While the proposal was not accepted by the Senate, nonetheless the government gave an assurance that 'serious consideration' would be given to the principles underlying Senator Ridgeway's proposal.[99] After pledges were made by all political parties, copies of the draft Copyright Amendment (Indigenous Communal Moral Rights) Bill 2003 were distributed to a limited group of stakeholders in mid-2003.[100] The Bill recognised '[I]ndigenous communal moral rights in relation to a work or film based on an agreement between the author/artist and the [I]ndigenous community'. It proposed that communities (and not merely individual artists) be allowed to 'take legal action to protect against inappropriate, derogatory or culturally insensitive use of such material'. In order for a community to claim Indigenous communal moral rights, the draft Bill proposed that five formal requirements would need to be met:[101]

- There must be copyright subject matter.
- The work must draw on the particular body of traditional observances, customs or beliefs held in common by the Indigenous community.
- There must be a voluntary agreement (which could be oral) between the Indigenous community and the creator of the work (the copyright holder).
- There must be an acknowledgement of the Indigenous community's involvement with the work.
- Interested parties in the work need to have consented to the rights arising, and this consent must be provided through written notice.[102]

Submissions were made to the government by the limited group of stakeholders and in March 2006, the federal Attorney-General at the time, Philip Ruddock, confirmed the government's commitment to introduce a new version of the Copyright Amendment (Indigenous Communal Moral Rights) Bill into parliament. However, as at August 2019, there has been no further support from the federal government for the introduction of communal moral rights.[103]

---

97   Ibid s 195AZA(3).
98   Commonwealth, *Parliamentary Debates*, Senate, 7 December 2000 (Aden Ridgeway) 21062–4.
99   I. MacDonald, 'Indigenous communal moral rights back on the agenda' (2003) 16 *Australian Intellectual Property Law Bulletin* 47.
100 For critical comments, see J. Anderson, 'Indigenous Communal Moral Rights Bill: A failure of language and imagination' (2004) 17 *Australian Intellectual Property Law Bulletin* 26.
101 J. Anderson, 'The politics of Indigenous knowledge' (2004) 27 *University of New South Wales Law Journal* 585, 597.
102 Ibid.
103 See T. Janke et al, 'Legal protection of Indigenous knowledge in Australia' (Supplementary Paper No 1, IP Australia and Department of Industry, Innovation, and Science, August 2017) 9–10.

6.3 Performers' rights

Until 1989, performers had no specific protection for their live performances under Australian law.[104] There was nothing that a performer could do to prevent others from recording and using their performances where they had not already been fixed in a material form. The situation changed in 1989 when the government amended the *Copyright Act 1968* (Cth) to provide specific protection for performers.[105] Essentially, the new rights meant that performers could prevent 'unauthorised uses' of their live performances in Australia. Performers' rights were strengthened as a result of Australia's accession to two treaties of the World Intellectual Property Organization (WIPO) – the *WIPO Copyright Treaty*[106] and the *WIPO Performances and Phonograms Treaty*[107] – which occurred on 26 July 2007.[108] The *AUSFTA* also required Australian law to be changed to grant moral rights to performers in relation to live performances and to performances recorded in sound recordings.[109] A 'performance' is defined to mean a live performance of a dramatic work (including a puppet show); a musical work; a reading, recitation or delivery of a literary work; a dance performance; a circus act or variety act; or an expression of folklore.[110] A performance includes the improvisation of a literary, dramatic or musical work. It is not necessary that the performance be in the presence of an audience.[111] A performance does not include a reading, recital or delivery of any item of news and information; performance of a sporting activity; participation in a performance as a member of the audience; or certain performances by teachers and students in the course of educational instruction.[112]

Performers' rights are separate from and additional to copyright in the material that is performed and to the creator's or author's moral rights. Performers have the right to control their performances in two situations. First, performers have the right to control the recording and communication of their performances. An unauthorised use of a performance is an unauthorised recording of a live performance directly or indirectly off-air (that is, a bootleg

---

104 Performers' rights were recognised in the *Rome Convention* as a right given to performers to prevent unauthorised dealing with sound recordings of musical performances: *International Convention for the Protection of Performers, Producers of Phonograms and Broadcasting Organizations*, opened for signature 26 October 1961, WIPO Lex No TRT/ROME/001 (entered into force 18 May 1964).
105 With effect from October 1989, the *Copyright Act 1968* (Cth) was amended by the insertion of a new pt XIA that introduced a system of protection for performers. This followed the recommendations of the CLRC in its 1987 report *Performers' Protection* and involved the minimum legislation necessary to enable Australia to join the *Rome Convention* (which it subsequently did, in 1992).
106 Opened for signature 20 December 1996, WIPO Lex No TRT/WCT/001 (entered into force 6 March 2002).
107 Opened for signature 20 December 1996 (entered into force 20 May 2002).
108 *WIPO Performances and Phonograms Treaty* arts 7–10 require contracting parties to provide performers with economic rights in their performances embodied in sound recordings. Article 6 requires parties to grant performers the exclusive right of authorising the broadcasting and communication to the public of their unfixed performances, and art 5 concerns moral rights for performers. See the *US Free Trade Agreement Implementation Act 2004* (Cth) and the *Copyright Legislation Amendment Act 2004* (Cth).
109 The *Copyright Act 1968* (Cth) was amended by *US Free Trade Agreement Implementation Act 2004* (Cth) sch 9 pt 2 (items 16–58).
110 *Copyright Act 1968* (Cth) s 248A.
111 The performance is protected if it is a live performance given in Australia or given by an Australian qualified person: *Copyright Act 1968* (Cth) s 248A(1) (definition of 'performance').
112 *Copyright Act 1968* (Cth) s 248A(1), (2).

version), or an unauthorised broadcast or transmission of a live performance. Second, as a result of the *AUSFTA*, performers also now have rights over authorised sound recordings of their performances. In particular, performers are the owners of the copyright in sound recordings of their performances along with the owner of the master recording (which is usually the record company). This ownership is shared equally between the owner of the record and the performers. This enables performers to exercise some control over sound recordings in which their performances are recorded. As a result of the *US Free Trade Agreement Implementation Act 2004* (Cth), performers also have the exclusive right to authorise the communication of their unrecorded performances to the public, either directly from the performance or indirectly from an unauthorised recording of it.[113] These rights came into effect from 1 January 2005.

Performers' rights to authorise the making of a sound recording last for fifty years from the year in which the performance was made.[114] In contrast, a performer's right to control the communication of their performance to the public or its inclusion in a soundtrack only lasts for twenty years.

The rights given to performers will be infringed where there has been an 'unauthorised use'. The requisite consent can be written or oral. The *Copyright Act 1968* (Cth) distinguishes between primary unauthorised uses (which do not require any knowledge on the part of the unauthorised user) and secondary unauthorised uses.[115] A primary unauthorised use occurs if a person makes a direct or indirect recording of the performance;[116] or broadcasts or rebroadcasts the performance, either directly from the live performance or from an unauthorised recording of it.[117] A number of secondary types of unauthorised uses are also provided for in the *Copyright Act*.[118] These include the making of and dealing in copies of recordings of performances. For liability to be established, it must be shown that there is actual or constructive knowledge on the part of the defendant.

Certain types of indirect recordings are exempt from the performers' rights scheme.[119] These include private uses, uses solely for teaching or scientific research, and uses that fall under any of the permitted fair dealing purposes (notably use for the purpose of research or study, criticism or review, or reporting of the news).[120] In 2006, the definition of 'exempt recording' was amended to include an indirect film or sound recording made in domestic premises from a broadcast for private and domestic use by watching or listening to the

---

113 Ibid s 248G(1)(b). This right took effect on 1 January 2005, replacing a prior right relating to broadcasting.
114 Ibid s 248CA(1), (3) in relation to sound recordings.
115 Ibid s 248G.
116 A 'direct' recording is defined as a sound recording or film made directly from a live performance. An 'indirect' recording is defined as a sound recording or film made from a broadcast of a live performance: *Copyright Act 1968* (Cth) s 248 A(1).
117 *Copyright Act 1968* (Cth) s 248G(1)(b).
118 *Copyright Act 1968* (Cth) s 248G(2) sets out the circumstances where a person will have made an unauthorised use that falls into the second category.
119 *Copyright Act 1968* (Cth) s 248A(1).
120 The fair dealing provisions provide that a sound recording, or a copy of a sound recording that is an exempt recording, ceases to be an exempt recording if it is used for any other purpose without the authority of the performer.

performance at a more convenient time.[121] This ensures that the time-shifting defence operates effectively.[122] The blanket exemption that was previously granted to educational institutions assisting people with disabilities for the indirect sound recordings of performances has been repealed.[123]

As discussed above, performers are now recognised as co-owners, with the maker, of copyright in their sound recordings.[124] There are a number of limits on the performers' right in sound recordings. These are similar to the rules of ownership of copyright works insofar as they provide that the performer will not be first owner where a sound recording is commissioned or produced in the course of employment. The *Copyright Act 1968* (Cth) provides that the permission of a performer to use their performance captured in a sound recording is deemed to have been given if the performance was recorded for a particular purpose and the recording is used in accordance with the performer's original consent. Performers' copyright in sound recordings lasts for the same period as copyright in the sounds recording (that is, seventy years). In certain cases, performers' rights cease to expire when a performer authorises certain uses of fixations of their sound recordings and films of their performances.

Performers are only given certain rights to prevent or claim damages for 'unauthorised uses' of their performances in Australia.[125] Where there has been an 'unauthorised use'[126] of their performance, a performer may bring an action seeking an injunction and/or damages, including exemplary damages.[127]

6.3.1 Performers' moral rights

In order to comply with the *AUSFTA*, Part IX of the *Copyright Act 1968* (Cth) was amended to include moral rights for performers. These provisions came into effect on 26 July 2007.[128] The moral rights granted to performers only apply in relation to live performances and to performances recorded in sound recordings, and do not extend to audiovisual performers.[129] The lack of moral rights protection for audiovisual performers is one of the issues that WIPO is attempting to rectify in the proposed Audiovisual Performance Treaty.[130] Although the

---

121 *Copyright Amendment Act 2006* (Cth). Without this amendment, a performer might have been able to bring an action for an unauthorised use of a performance against a person who records a broadcast of a performance under the 'time-shifting provision'.
122 See ch 5 at 5.5.2.
123 As a result of changes to 'exempt recording' in *Copyright Act 1968* (Cth) s 248(1) introduced by the *US Free Trade Agreement Implementation Act 2004* (Cth).
124 As a result of changes introduced to *Copyright Act 1968* (Cth) s 22(3A), (3B) by the *US Free Trade Agreement Implementation Act 2004* (Cth).
125 *Copyright Act 1968* (Cth) s 248G.
126 The unauthorised use may relate to either the whole performance or a substantial part of the performance: *Copyright Act 1968* (Cth) s 248A(3).
127 *Copyright Act 1968* (Cth) s 248J.
128 The *Copyright Act 1968* (Cth) was amended by the *US Free Trade Agreement Implementation Act 2004* (Cth) sch 9 pt 2 (items 16–58).
129 *WIPO Performances and Phonograms Treaty*.
130 See WIPO, *Informal Consultation Meeting on the Protection of Broadcasting Organizations*, WIPO/CR/Consult/GE/11/2/1 (2 February 2011) 3; WIPO, Standing Committee on Copyright and Related Rights, *Background Document on the Main Questions and Positions Concerning the International Protection of Audiovisual Performances*, SCCR/19/9 (30 November 2009).

proposal, adopted on 24 June 2012, will provide audiovisual performers with the moral right to be identified as author of their performance and also the ability to object to distortion, mutilations or other modifications of their performances, it is not yet in force.[131] At present, however, moral rights protection is only granted for live performances and for performances recorded in sound recordings.

There are three moral rights given to performers: the right of attribution of performership,[132] a right not to have performership falsely attributed[133] and a right of integrity of performership.[134] 'Performership' is the rather unattractive name given to a person who undertakes a performance.[135]

The right of attribution is the right to be identified as a performer in a live performance, whenever the performance is staged or communicated to the public.[136] In relation to a performance recorded on a sound recording, the right of attribution arises whenever that recording is copied or communicated to the public.[137] Where there are a number of performers, each of the performers has the right to be known as author of the performance.[138] A performer's moral right of attribution will be infringed where an 'attributable act' is carried out in relation to the performance without properly attributing the performer.[139] In relation to a live performance, the attributable acts are communicating or staging the live performance in public. The attributable acts for a recorded performance are the making of a copy of the recorded performance or communicating the recorded performance to the public.[140] Any 'reasonable' form of identification that is 'clear' and 'reasonably prominent' or audible may be used.[141] If a performance is presented by performers who use a group name, identification using the group name is sufficient.[142]

Performers also have the right not to have performances falsely attributed to them.[143] In the case of a live performance, a person staging a performance will infringe the right not to have performership falsely attributed where they state or imply falsely that a person is, was, or will be a performer in the performance; or the performance is being, was, or will be presented by a particular group of performers.[144] In the case of a recorded performance, false attribution involves implying falsely that a person (or group) is a performer in the recording when in fact they are not. The act of false attribution will usually occur where a person affixes or inserts a name to, or on, a recording. A person will also infringe the right where they deal with a recording or communicate a sound recording to the public knowing that a person (or group)

---

131   WIPO, 'Summary of the Beijing Treaty on Audiovisual Performances' (2012) www.wipo.int.
132   *Copyright Act 1968* (Cth) s 195ABA.
133   Ibid s 195AHA.
134   Ibid s 195ALA.
135   'Performership' is defined to mean participation in a performance, as the performer or one of the performers: *Copyright Act 1968* (Cth) s 189 (definition of 'performership'). 'Performance' is defined above in the text accompanying n 110.
136   *Copyright Act 1968* (Cth) ss 195ABB(1), 195ABA.
137   Ibid s 195ABB(2).
138   Ibid s 195AZQ(2).
139   Ibid s 195AXA.
140   Ibid s 195ABA(1), (2).
141   Ibid s 195ABD.
142   Ibid s 195ABC(3).
143   Ibid s 195AHA.
144   Ibid s 195AHB(1)–(7).

named in, or on, the sound recording is not a performer. The right will also be infringed where they deal with a recorded performance that has been altered by someone other than the performer as an unaltered performance knowing that it is not[145] (except if the effect of the alteration was insubstantial or required by law).[146]

The right of integrity of performership is the right not to have a live or recorded performance subject to derogatory treatment.[147] Derogatory treatment is the doing of anything that results in a material distortion or mutilation of the performance, or a material alteration to the performance, that is prejudicial to the performer's reputation.[148] The question of whether a treatment is derogatory will be decided in a similar manner to the way this question is decided in relation to an author's right of integrity (discussed above).[149]

There are two key defences to infringement of performers' moral rights. These are where the performer has consented to the infringing act and where the infringement was reasonable in the circumstances. The consent provisions for performers are similar to those that relate to the moral rights for authors.[150] A failure to attribute a performance, false attribution of a performer, or a derogatory treatment of a performance does not infringe the performer's moral rights if the performer consented to the action or omission.[151] The consent has no effect if it was given under duress or because of a false misrepresentation.[152] Consent can be given for all or any acts or omissions occurring before or after the consent is given; or in relation to specific performances or to particular performances or for performances where the performer is an employee.[153]

The reasonableness defence is only available in relation to the right of attribution of performership and the right of integrity of performership. There are a number of factors that the court can take into account when determining whether a failure to attribute a performer or derogatory treatment of a performance was reasonable. These include the nature of the performance; the purpose, manner and context in which the performance is being used; and any relevant industry practices.[154]

6.4 Artist's resale rights

While authors are able to recoup royalties when their works are reproduced – their royalties increase with the number of copies sold – artists tend to rely on the first sale of their works for the bulk of their income. One of the problems that many artists face is that the initial sale of their artwork may be at a very low price, particularly compared to the price the work subsequently sells at. To remedy this problem, many countries have introduced *droit de suite* schemes that entitle artists to a percentage payment when a work of art that they have created

---

145   Ibid s 195AHC.
146   Ibid s 195AHC(2)(a), (b).
147   Ibid ss 195ALA, 195AXC.
148   Ibid s 195ALB.
149   At 6.2.2.
150   *Copyright Act 1968* (Cth) s 195AXJ.
151   Ibid s 195AXJ(1).
152   Ibid s 195AXK.
153   Ibid s 195AXJ.
154   Ibid s 195AXJ.

is resold (typically in a commercial gallery).[155] Although it has been suggested that the *droit de suite* scheme is not really a form of copyright,[156] it is recognised in art 14*ter* of the *Berne Convention*.

The optional *droit de suite* scheme set out in art 14*ter* has been adopted in more than thirty jurisdictions.[157] For many years, artists have lobbied for the introduction of a similar scheme in Australia. In particular, non-salaried artists have argued that there has often been very little, if any, capacity for them to recoup money from the reproductions of their original creations; the main source of income arises from the initial sale of their artworks. The 2002 *Report of the Contemporary Visual Arts and Crafts Inquiry*, which resulted from a wide-ranging review by Rupert Myer into the contemporary visual arts and craft sector, accepted this argument and suggested that an artist's resale royalty scheme be introduced in Australia. This was followed in 2004 by a discussion paper that explored the relative advantages and disadvantages of introducing a resale right in Australia.[158] The impetus for a new scheme continued in 2006 when the Artist's Resale Rights Bill was introduced into federal parliament as a Private Member's Bill. The government of the time did not support the introduction of the resale royalty right on the basis that it would 'not provide a meaningful source of income for the majority of Australian artists'.[159] Despite this setback, the resale scheme remained on the agenda and after successful lobbying by arts organisations and artists, the *Resale Royalty Right for Visual Artists Act 2009* (Cth) came into effect from 9 June 2010.[160]

The resale royalty right, which subsists for seventy years after the death of the artist, is inalienable[161] and unable to be waived;[162] it is, however, able to be transferred upon the death of the artist to a successor in title.[163] The resale royalty right only applies where the holder of the right (either the artist or their successor) is an Australian citizen, a permanent resident of Australia, or a national or citizen of a prescribed reciprocating country.[164] The scheme grants

---

155   Department of Communications, Information Technology and the Arts, *Report of the Contemporary Visual Arts and Craft Enquiry* (2002) (*Myer Report*).
156   It has been said that while the resale royalty 'right is closely associated with copyright, it is not a copyright right as it arises from the physical object (i.e., the painting) rather than the reproduction of the image in the painting: A. Stewart, P. Griffith and J. Bannister, *Intellectual Property in Australia* (4th edn, Sydney: Lexis Nexis, 2010) 291.
157   *Myer Report*, above n 155, 94.
158   Minister for the Arts and Sport, *Proposed Resale Royalty Arrangement* (Discussion Paper, 2004); P. Ruddock, Attorney-General, 'DVDs, CDs and computer games: Good news for consumers, bad news for pirates' (Media Release, 4 September 2006).
159   See P. Ruddock, Attorney-General, and R. Kemp, Minister for Arts and Sports, 'New support for Australia's visual artists' (Media Release, 9 May 2006). In 2008 the federal Minister for the Arts announced that Australia would establish a national *droit de suite* scheme, commenting: 'By enshrining in law the right of artists and their heirs to receive a benefit from the secondary sale of their work, we are building an environment where the talent and creativity of visual artists receives greater reward.' See P. Garrett, Minister for the Environment, Heritage and the Arts, 'Artists to benefit from resale royalty right' (Media Release, 3 October 2008).
160   The Act is complemented by the *Tax Laws Amendment (Resale Royalty for Visual Artists) Act 2009* (Cth). For a general discussion see Stewart, Griffith and Bannister, *Intellectual Property in Australia*, above n 156, 291 n 146, 291 ff.
161   *Resale Royalty Right for Visual Artists Act 2009* (Cth) s 33.
162   Ibid s 34.
163   Ibid s 12.
164   Ibid s 14. Section 53 provides for the making of regulations prescribing matters for the purposes of the Act.

artists a royalty on the resale of original artworks. More specifically, royalties are received from 'resales of original works of visual art sold through the secondary art market where the seller has acquired the work after the legislation takes effect' and the work is resold for a minimum of $1000.[165] The fact that the scheme only applies to resales 'through the secondary art market' (that is, by an art market professional) is one of the major limitations of the scheme.[166] This means that resales that take place between private individuals are excluded from the operation of scheme. The resale royalty scheme applies to original works of visual art, which are defined in the Act to include traditional fine arts, such as paintings, sculptures, drawings and engravings, along with applied or decorative arts, such as jewellery, glassware, ceramics and tapestries, installations, digital video and multimedia artworks.[167] The new scheme only applies to works created, or acquired by the seller, on or after the date of commencement of the Act when they are later resold through the secondary commercial art market.[168] This protects the owners of existing artworks who bought them before the scheme was introduced. The royalty is calculated on the sale price when an artwork is resold, after the first transfer of ownership in the commercial market. The royalty rate payable is five per cent of the sale price of the commercial resale of the artwork.[169]

To ensure that the resale royalty scheme operates effectively, it was decided that a collecting society should be established to collect resale royalties and enforce resale royalty rights on behalf of the holder of the resale royalty right.[170] Copyright Agency Limited (now called Copyright Agency) is the collecting society established to deal with the reproduction of literary works and currently administers the resale royalty scheme. In administering the scheme, Copyright Agency is required to publish information about commercial resales that it is aware of on its website 'as soon as it is reasonably practicable'.[171] If the holder of a resale royalty right does not notify Copyright Agency within twenty-one days post-publication that it does not want the collecting society to collect royalties or enforce relevant rights,[172] the agency is obliged to collect and distribute royalties and to enforce rights. In addition, vendors – directly or through their agents – must provide Copyright Agency with sufficient information about all commercial resales for the agency to ensure, together with the buyer and seller, that royalties are paid to it for payment to artists and their beneficiaries. This information can be provided to Copyright Agency by galleries, auction houses or dealers.[173]

As is often the case with the imposition of a new tax, the resale scheme has proved to be controversial, particularly among commercial gallery owners. In this sense, the experience in Australia is not dissimilar to the reactions that the *droit de suite* scheme provoked in the United Kingdom. While there was concern about the relative costs and benefits of the resale scheme, it is interesting to note that as of June 2018, the scheme has generated over $6.3 million in

---

165 Ibid s 10(1)(a).
166 Ibid s 6(2), (3).
167 Ibid s 7(2). Buildings, plans or models for buildings, circuit layouts and manuscripts are expressly excluded from the definition: at s 9.
168 Ibid s 11.
169 Ibid s 18.
170 Ibid ss 22–31 are the relevant provisions.
171 Ibid s 22.
172 Ibid s 21(1)–(3).
173 See further Copyright Agency, 'Sellers and resale royalties' (14 April 2011) www.resaleroyalty.org.au.

royalties for more than 1,600 artists from more than 17,000 resales.[174] Importantly, 63% of paid artists were Aboriginal or Torres Strait Islander artists and they have received 38% of the total royalties.[175] This is despite some critics suggesting that the scheme was destined to fail because it did not take account of the particular place that Indigenous art and artists occupy within Indigenous communities.[176]

6.5 Circuit layouts

Intellectual property law has been grappling with the various changes introduced by the growth in computers and information technologies since the 1970s. During this time, the law has granted protection to computer programs, and has been modified to deal with new methods of creation, distribution and use. One area that attracted special attention in the 1980s was the protection available to 'computer chips' (also known as circuit layouts, semiconductor chips, integrated circuits and silicon chips). A computer chip is a very small electronic device that allows data to be stored, arranged and accessed. As such, it is a key component in many computer-based systems. The specific form that a chip takes will vary depending on a range of factors, including the program that it operates with and what it is to be used for. The layout of the circuitry on the chips (which often look like topographic maps) gives them a distinctive appearance.

In the early 1980s, it was estimated that United States industry was losing millions of dollars as a result of unauthorised copying of semiconductor chips.[177] One of the problems facing the computer industry was that as the designs of the chips were largely dictated by function, it was unlikely that the physical layout of computer chips would have been protected by copyright. To overcome this problem, the computer industry argued that specific sui generis legal protection for the layout of computer chips should be introduced. In 1984, the United States passed the *Semiconductor Chip Protection Act* for the protection of circuit layouts. In order to ensure that American interests were protected in other jurisdictions, the United States was only prepared to recognise the rights of foreign-owned semiconductor chips where their country of origin recognised the rights of United States semiconductor chip designers. This approach saw the European Commission introduce an equivalent system in 1986.[178] The European Directive required all Member States to introduce protection for semiconductor chips. In the United Kingdom, the *Semiconductor (Protection of Topography) Regulations* were passed in 1987. These were later repealed and replaced by the *Design Right (Semiconductor Topographies) Regulations 1989* (UK). In the United Kingdom, semiconductor topographies are now protected as unregistered designs with a number of modifications.

---

174 Copyright Agency, 'Resale royalty' www.resaleroyalty.org.au. See also Janke et al, 'Legal protection of Indigenous knowledge in Australia', above n 103.
175 Janke et al, 'Legal protection of Indigenous knowledge in Australia', above n 103.
176 R. Quiggin, 'The resale royalty and Indigenous art: An opportunity for the recognition of economic and cultural rights' in F. Macmillan and K. Bowrey (eds), *New Directions in Copyright Law, Volume 3* (Cheltenham: Edward Elgar Publishing, 2006).
177 See House Report on the *Semiconductor Chip Protection Act 1984*, HR Rep 781, 98th Cong, 2d, Sess (1984).
178 *Council Directive 87/54/EEC of 16 December 1986 on the Legal Protection of Semiconductor Products* [1986] OJ L 24/36.

The United States *Semiconductor Chip Protection Act of 1984* also prompted WIPO to develop the *Treaty on Intellectual Property in Respect of Integrated Circuits*[179] (*Washington Treaty*). While the treaty prompted a number of countries to adopt their own national sui generis schemes for semiconductor chip protection (including Australia), few countries became formal signatories to it. The later *Agreement on Trade-Related Aspects of Intellectual Property*[180] (*TRIPS*) requires member states to provide protection for circuit layouts in accordance with the *Washington Treaty*.[181] In this section, the sui generis legal regime introduced into Australian law in 1989[182] to protect circuit layouts will be discussed.[183]

6.5.1 Nature and scope of circuit layouts

Circuit layouts and semiconductor chips are protected in Australia under the *Circuit Layouts Act 1989* (Cth). This legislation was introduced in anticipation of the 1989 *Washington Treaty*. The Act protects 'plans which show the three-dimensional location of the electronic components of an integrated circuit and gives the owner of the plans certain rights, including the right to make an integrated circuit from the plans'.[184]

A *circuit layout* is defined as a representation, fixed in any material form, of the three-dimensional location of the active and passive elements and interconnections making up an integrated circuit.[185] An *integrated circuit* means a circuit, whether in a final form or an intermediate form, the purpose, or one of the purposes, of which is to perform an electronic function, being a circuit in which the active and passive elements, and any of the interconnections, are integrally formed in or on a piece of material.[186] Both the originals of circuit layouts and copies of circuit layouts and integrated circuits are protected.[187]

The *Circuit Layouts Act 1989* (Cth) protects what are called 'eligible layouts'. An 'eligible layout' is defined to mean an original circuit layout (a) the maker of which was, at the time the layout was made, an eligible person; or (b) that was first commercially exploited in Australia or in an eligible foreign country.[188]

---

179 WIPO Lex No TRT/WASHINGTON/001 (opened for signature 26 May 1989).
180 *Marrakesh Agreement Establishing the World Trade Organization*, opened for signature 15 April 1994, 1867 UNTS 3 (entered into force 1 January 1995) annex 1C (*Agreement on Trade-Related Aspects of Intellectual Property*) (*TRIPS*).
181 TRIPS art 35. Articles 36–38 set out the minimum requirements for the scope of protection of circuit layouts, as well as exceptions and duration.
182 *Circuit Layouts Act 1989* (Cth).
183 When the Intellectual Property and Competition Review Committee was reviewing the intellectual property laws to assess the effect of competition, it received no submissions on circuit layout legislation. Therefore, it was held that the legislation has no adverse effects. However, the committee did question 'the value of, and the need for, sui generis laws such as the *Circuit Layouts Act*. By their nature such laws are highly specialised, technology-specific and narrowly defined. Their ability to keep pace with technological changes is limited': Intellectual Property and Competition Review Committee, *Review of Intellectual Property Legislation under the Competition Principles Agreement* (Final Report, 2000).
184 Department of Communication and the Arts, *Short Guide to Copyright* (November 2016). Northrop J outlined the characteristics of the statutory scheme in *Centronics Systems Pty Ltd v Nintendo Co Ltd* (1992) 39 FCR 147, 148–9.
185 *Circuit Layouts Act 1989* (Cth) s 5.
186 Ibid.
187 Ibid.
188 Ibid.

6.5.2 Subsistence

For a circuit layout to be eligible for protection, it needs to be original, in a 'material form', and connected to Australia. The Act defines originality in a negative sense: a circuit layout shall be taken not to be original if its making involved no creative contribution by the maker; if it was commonplace at the time it was made; or its features are dictated solely by function.[189] It has been suggested that the threshold of originality that a circuit layout must meet to qualify for protection requires more intellectual input than is required under the *Copyright Act 1968* (Cth).[190]

An eligible layout is deemed to have been made when it was first fixed in material form.[191] Material form includes any form of storage (whether visible or not) from which the layout, or a substantial part of it, can be reproduced.[192] There must be a necessary connection with Australia. The maker[193] of the circuit layout must be an Australian citizen, resident or incorporated company. Alternatively, the place of the first commercial exploitation of the layout must be in Australia.[194] Reciprocal rights are given to citizens, residents or incorporated companies of designated countries.[195]

6.5.3 Exclusive rights

The exclusive rights of the maker of an eligible layout or integrated circuit are referred to as eligible layout rights.[196] The owner of the rights in an eligible layout has the exclusive right to copy the layout, directly or indirectly, in material form; to make an integrated circuit in accordance with the layout or a copy of the layout; and to exploit the layout commercially in Australia.[197] A circuit layout is taken to have been *commercially exploited* if the layout or a copy of the layout is sold, let for hire or otherwise distributed by way of trade; offered or exposed for sale or hire, or other distribution by way of trade; or imported for the purpose of sale, letting for hire, or other distribution by way of trade.[198] The exclusive right to exploit the layout commercially in Australia extends to parallel importation. However, it should be noted that where an authorised computer chip is first put on the market by the owner of the eligible layout rights, the circuit layout or integrated circuit may be freely imported into Australia.[199] Thus, parallel importation is permitted in these circumstances. The owner also has the right to authorise another person to exercise any of these rights.[200]

---

189   Ibid s 11.
190   J. Lahore, *Copyright and Designs* (Sydney: LexisNexis Butterworths) [52,040].
191   *Circuit Layouts Act 1989* (Cth) s 10(b).
192   Ibid s 5.
193   See definitions in *Circuit Layouts Act 1989* (Cth) ss 10, 14, 15.
194   *Circuit Layouts Act 1989* (Cth) s 5.
195   Ibid ss 5, 42, 48.
196   *Avel Pty Ltd v Wells* (1992) 23 IPR 353, 360–2.
197   *Circuit Layouts Act 1989* (Cth) s 17.
198   Ibid s 8. Section 8(2) contains a similar provision relating to the sale, hire or distribution by way of trade of a copy of a circuit layout or an integrated circuit made in accordance with a circuit layout.
199   *Circuit Layouts Act 1989* (Cth) s 24(1).
200   Ibid s 9.

6.5.4 Ownership

The person who makes an eligible layout is the first owner of any eligible layout rights.[201] Where an eligible layout is made in the course of employment, the employer will be the first owner of the eligible layout.[202] The parties may agree to exclude or modify the employment provisions of the Act.[203] The Act recognises that circuit layouts are often made by more than one person and hence joint makers are recognised unless there is a contrary intention.[204]

6.5.5 Exploitation

Eligible layout rights are the personal property of the holder, transmissible by assignment, will, devolution or by operation of law.[205] Eligible layout rights may be assigned or licensed. Eligible layout rights may be wholly or partially assigned to another party.[206] Limits can be placed on what rights are assigned as well as the area and the duration. An assignment of eligible layout rights does not have effect unless it is in writing signed by or on behalf of the assignor.[207] Future eligible layout rights may be also assigned or licensed.[208] The grant of a licence over eligible layout rights will bind the grantor's successors.[209]

6.5.6 Duration

The period of protection for an eligible layout is ten years after the calendar year in which the layout was made.[210] Where a circuit layout has been commercially exploited within the first ten years of its creation, it will be protected for a further ten years calculable from the end of the year in which the first commercial exploitation took place.[211]

6.5.7 Infringement

A person commits a primary infringement of a layout right where they exercise one of the exclusive rights of the eligible layout rights holder without permission.[212] To infringe, the unauthorised act must be carried out in relation to the protected layout or a *substantial part* thereof.[213] To infringe, the infringer must know or ought reasonably to have known that they

---

201 Ibid s 16(1).
202 Ibid s 16(2).
203 Ibid s 16(3).
204 A reference to joint makers refers to all the makers of the layout, unless the contrary intention appears: *Circuit Layouts Act 1989* (Cth) s 15. Where only some of the makers are eligible persons under the Act, eligible layout rights will subsist in the layout but will only vest in those who are eligible persons: at s 18.
205 *Circuit Layouts Act 1989* (Cth) s 45(1).
206 Ibid s 45(2).
207 Ibid s 45(3).
208 Ibid s 44.
209 Ibid s 45(4).
210 Ibid s 5.
211 See ibid for the definition of 'protected period'.
212 Ibid s 19.
213 Ibid s 13.

were not licensed by the owner of that right to do the acts that they are doing.[214] Hence a person who innocently exploits an eligible layout will not infringe.[215] Damages will not be available in certain cases of innocent infringement.[216] In *Nintendo v Centronics Systems*,[217] it was held that it is not enough for the defendant to be aware that the plaintiff has not provided authorisation for use of their layout. To establish infringement the defendant must have known (or had reason to know) that the plaintiff is the owner of the layout rights. However, in the same case, the High Court also held that a person would be infringing if they had that knowledge even if they were not aware that their particular use would amount to a commercial exploitation.[218]

6.5.8 Exceptions and defences

The defences to an infringement of eligible layout rights[219] are similar to the copyright defences in that they allow use of an eligible layout for research or teaching purposes,[220] for private use[221] and for evaluation or analysis.[222] The evaluation or analysis defence has been likened to the reverse engineering provisions of the *Copyright Act 1968* (Cth).[223] There is also a defence where there has been innocent commercial exploitation of the eligible layout, discussed in more detail below.[224]

6.5.8.1 Innocent commercial exploitation

For this defence to operate, the infringer needs to be able to show that at the time the eligible layout was acquired they did not know and could not reasonably have been expected to have known that eligible layout rights subsisted in the layout. The infringer also needs to pay equitable remuneration to the owner or exclusive licensee of the rights from the time of awareness.[225] The policy underlying this defence has been described as being

> to make special provision for circumstances in which it would be unjust to impose liability for infringement on a person who innocently acquires and subsequently deals with an unauthorised integrated circuit. One can readily envisage circumstances in which an ordinary person who innocently acquires, and subsequently commercially deals with,

---

214 Ibid s 19(3). See also *Nintendo Co Ltd v Centronics Systems Pty Ltd* (1994) 181 CLR 134; A. Christie, *Integrated Circuits and their Contents: International Protection* (Sydney: LBC Information Services, 1995) 120.
215 *Circuit Layouts Act 1989* (Cth) s 20.
216 Ibid s 27.
217 (1994) 181 CLR 134.
218 This concept is summed up by Stewart, Griffith and Bannister, who say that 'ignorance of the existence of layout rights or the identity of their owner may constitute a defence; but ignorance as to the extent of those rights may not': *Intellectual Property in Australia*, above n 156, 270.
219 *Circuit Layouts Act 1989* (Cth) div 3.
220 Ibid s 22.
221 Ibid s 21.
222 Ibid s 23.
223 Van Caenegem states that an interesting parallel can be drawn between s 23 and the provisions introduced by the *Copyright Amendment (Computer Programs) Act 1999* (Cth) s 47B ff: W. van Caenegem, *Intellectual Property* (2nd edn, Sydney: LexisNexis Butterworths, 2006) 327.
224 *Circuit Layouts Act 1989* (Cth) s 20(1).
225 Ibid s 20(1).

an item of electronic equipment would have no means of knowing or ascertaining that some concealed integrated circuit in the article was an unauthorised copy of an eligible circuit layout in which [eligible layout] rights subsist.[226]

Following *Nintendo Co Ltd v Centronics Systems Pty Ltd*,[227] a defendant will only be liable if they knew or ought reasonably to have known the identity of the owner of the eligible layout rights *and* that the owner had not licensed the defendant to exploit the layout.[228] Once a person becomes aware, or could reasonably be expected to have become aware, that their use of the integrated circuit was unauthorised, a compulsory or statutory licence comes into operation. The defence ceases to apply to any subsequent commercial exploitation of the circuit unless the person pays equitable remuneration to the owner or exclusive licensee of the eligible layout rights in the layout.[229] An integrated circuit is unauthorised if it is made without the licence of the owners of the eligible layout rights in the layout.[230]

Where a circuit or a copy of a circuit has been acquired as a result of an authorised commercial exploitation either in Australia or overseas, then the commercial exploitation of that circuit is excused by virtue of s 24(1). In this situation, the owner of the eligible layout cannot prevent parallel importation of an integrated circuit obtained overseas from being imported into Australia. Given that integrated circuits often contain a computer program (which will be protected as a literary work), there is the possibility that the owner of the copyright may be able to prevent the importation of the integrated circuit into Australia.[231] To prevent this from happening, s 24(2) provides that copyright in a work embedded in a computer chip cannot be relied on to prohibit the importation of that integrated circuit into Australia.

6.5.9 Remedies

Where an infringement action is successfully brought, the owner or exclusive licensee of an eligible layout may be awarded an injunction and either damages or an account of profits.[232] Damages will not be awarded against a person who neither knew nor reasonably should have known that they were committing an infringement.[233] Courts have the power to award punitive damages where the infringement is flagrant. In deciding whether to grant punitive damages, the court will look at a range of factors, including the benefit derived by the defendant.[234]

---

226 *Nintendo Co Ltd v Centronics Systems Pty Ltd* (1994) 181 CLR 134, 154.
227 (1994) 181 CLR 134.
228 Van Caenegem, *Intellectual Property*, above n 223, 327.
229 *Circuit Layouts Act 1989* (Cth) s 20(2).
230 Ibid s 20(3).
231 *Avel Pty Ltd v Wells* (1992) 23 IPR 353 (s 24(2) applied both to works embodied in a circuit at the time it was manufactured and to works subsequently stored there by someone other than the maker of the chip); *Galaxy Electronics Pty Ltd & Gottlieb Enterprises Pty Ltd v Sega Enterprises Ltd* (1997) 75 FCR 8 (a video game with computer-generated images was held to be a 'cinematograph film' under *Copyright Act 1968* (Cth) s 10(1). This resulted in it being protected against parallel importation).
232 *Circuit Layouts Act 1989* (Cth) s 27(2)–(4).
233 Ibid.
234 Ibid s 27(4).

6.5.10 Overlap with copyright and design protection?

One of the questions that often arise when sui generis legislation is introduced is how the tailor-made law relates to more general forms of intellectual property protection. The specific protection given to semiconductor chips is no exception to this problem, particularly in relation to the way it overlaps with copyright and design protection. Given that the protection afforded by the *Circuit Layouts Act 1989* (Cth) is for the physical aspects of the design of the integrated circuit on the computer chips, it is unlikely that these features would also fall within the subject matter of copyright. However, to ensure that there is no overlap, amendments were made to the definition of relevant categories of subject matter under the *Copyright Act 1968* (Cth) and the *Designs Act 2003* (Cth).[235] As computer chips store large amounts of information (as 'embodiments' or 'aggregates' of information), it is possible that some of the information stored on the computer chip, as distinct from the chip itself, will be protected by copyright.[236]

6.6 Public and educational lending rights

The public lending right (PLR)[237] and educational lending right (ELR)[238] schemes are regimes designed to compensate Australian authors and publishers for income that is 'lost' when their books are made available in public lending libraries and educational libraries (in schools, TAFEs and universities). In contrast with the rights conferred on authors by the *Copyright Act 1968* (Cth), the schemes do not create a 'right' in authors to demand payment for the lending of their works. Instead, the two schemes provide payments to authors and publishers on the basis

---

235 The definition of artistic work in *Copyright Act 1968* (Cth) s 10 excludes 'a circuit layout within the meaning of the *Circuit Layouts Act 1989*'. The definition of 'article' in *Designs Act 1906* (Cth) s 4(1) excluded an 'integrated circuit, or part of an integrated circuit within the meaning of the *Circuit Layouts Act 1989*', or a mask used to make such a circuit. Designs of integrated circuits are expressly excluded from registration under *Designs Act 2003* (Cth) s 43(1)(c)(i).

236 The question of dual protection has been considered by the Australian courts in *Avel Pty Ltd v Wells* (1992) 23 IPR 353 and *Sega Enterprises Ltd & Avel Pty Ltd v Galaxy Electronics Pty Ltd* (1996) 69 FCR 268. In *Sega Enterprises* Burchett J held that certain computer games that were stored in integrated circuits imported in Australia were 'cinematograph films' as recognised under *Copyright Act 1968* (Cth) pt IV. Burchett J rejected the idea that the computer games (being stored on a computer) should only find protection (if at all) under the *Circuit Layouts Act 1989* (Cth). He said at 168: 'The fact that there are here integrated circuits and that these give rise to the application of particular statutory provisions, does not subtract from the further and relevant fact that the use of the integrated circuits is capable of bringing to the screen, so as to be shown as a moving picture, the aggregate of visual images making up [the computer program]. That attracts the operation of the *Copyright Act* in respect of cinematograph films.'

237 From the mid 1960s, the Australian Society of Authors lobbied successive Commonwealth governments for a PLR scheme. Since 1974, this scheme has compensated Australian authors, compilers, translators, editors, illustrators and publishers for royalties lost in sales to the public because their books are freely available in public libraries. See A. Jordens, 'Assisting Australian authors: Recording the history of the public lending right and educational lending right schemes' (2005) 2 *History Australia* [47.1]–[47.5]. The PLR regime was established by the *Public Lending Right Act 1985* (Cth).

238 In the 1990s the Australian Society of Authors campaigned for an ELR scheme to compensate for books held in the libraries of educational institutions. Such a scheme was agreed to by the Keating Labor government in 1994, abandoned by the Howard government in 1996, and finally funded for four years in 2000 as part of a compensation package to the book industry for the imposition of the GST on books. Funding was renewed in 2005 for a further four years. Authors eligible for royalties whose books are used in school, university and other tertiary educational libraries, benefit from this scheme. See Jordens, 'Assisting Australian authors', above n 237.

of the number of copies of their books that are held in relevant libraries. The schemes are open to creators (authors, editors, illustrators, translators and compilers)[239] and publishers[240] who have been involved in the development of a book with an International Standard Book Number (ISBN) that has been offered for sale and has no more than five creators.[241] The amount distributed is based on a sample survey of the number of books that are held in relevant libraries.[242]

---

[239] Publishers are eligible for PLR payments where their businesses consist wholly or substantially of the publication of books and they regularly publish (at least once in the preceding two years in Australia). Self-publishing authors may also be eligible: *Public Lending Right Act 1985* (Cth) s 6.

[240] *Public Lending Right Act 1985* (Cth) s 5(4)(a), (c).

[241] Ibid s 10(1), (2) and, more generally, s 30. The PLR scheme is administered by the Public Lending Right Committee, which distributes funds set aside by the federal government. The committee's functions are outlined at s 8(1).

[242] For more information, see Department of Communications and the Arts, 'Australian Lending Right Schemes (ELR/PLR)' www.arts.gov.au/funding-and-support/lending-rights.

7 DESIGNS

7.1 Introduction

From the chairs that we sit on, to the pens that we write with and the clothes that we wear, design plays an important role in many aspects of our lives. Design impacts on objects in a range of ways, from the way that objects look through to the way that they function. Given this, it is not surprising that design is pivotal to the commercialisation and marketing of many different products.[1] In this chapter, we look at the law that encourages and protects the skill, labour and effort that goes into the creation of new designs.[2] Intellectual property protection for designs focuses on the visual appearance of commercial or industrial articles, rather than their function or the means of producing them. In Australia, the law in this area is set out in the *Designs Act 2003* (Cth).[3] This Act repealed the *Designs Act 1906* (Cth), which had governed Australian designs law for most of the twentieth century.

7.2 History

Design law occupies an awkward position in contemporary intellectual property law, where it is often regarded as the stepchild of patents and copyright. In part, this has been reinforced by the fact that unlike these other categories of intellectual property law, there has never been a specific international treaty that deals with design protection.[4] Despite this, design law is one of the oldest forms of intellectual property.[5] Designs for certain textiles, such as linens, cottons, calicoes and muslins, were first protected in the United Kingdom by the 1787 and 1794 *Calico Printers Acts*.[6] This was followed in 1839 and then in 1842 and 1843 by design legislation that not only laid the groundwork for modern design law but also for modern intellectual property law more generally.[7]

Design law in Australia was first introduced by the *Designs Act 1906* (Cth). This provided the framework for the protection of registered designs for nearly a century. In light of growing criticism of the 1906 Act, in 1992 the Australian Law Reform Commission (ALRC) was commissioned to produce a report on the system as it then was.[8] After a wide-ranging review, the

---

1   Australian Law Reform Commission (ALRC), *Designs* (Report No 74, 1995) 31.
2   Compare the work of the Bureau of Industry Economics, which noted that although it has been economically demonstrated that intellectual property rights such as patents are vital to innovation and growth, there is no empirical evidence to support such a claim with respect to any form of design right: Bureau of Industry Economics, *The Economic Rights of Intellectual Property Rights for Design* (Occasional Paper, 27 May 1995) 3.
3   *Designs Act 2003* (Cth) s 150 (superseding the *Designs Act 1906* (Cth), effective 17 June 2004). See J. Cooke and K. O'Connell, 'Rags to riches? Changes in Australian and European design laws' (2003) 14 *Australian Intellectual Property Journal* 65.
4   Except for *Agreement on Trade-Related Aspects of Intellectual Property* (TRIPS) arts 25 and 26 (setting out the requirements and scope of protection) in *Marrakesh Agreement Establishing the World Trade Organization*, opened for signature 15 April 1994, 1867 UNTS 3 (entered into force 1 January 1995) annex 1C.
5   See B. Sherman and L. Bently, *The Making of Modern Intellectual Property Law* (Cambridge: Cambridge University Press, 1999) chs 3, 4.
6   27 Geo c 23 and 34 Geo c 23, respectively.
7   2 Vict c 17. See Sherman and Bently, *The Making of Modern Intellectual Property Law*, above n 5, 61–76.
8   ALRC, *Designs*, above n 1. The ALRC recommended the enactment of a new Act to replace the *Designs Act 1906*, based on six key principles: (1) definition of a design – define it by one or more visual features

ALRC suggested that the law needed to be modernised and simplified. In explaining why designs had been underutilised for so long, the ALRC highlighted the mismatch between modern design requirements (such as technological and interactive designs) and legislative protection.[9]

After a period of deliberation, the federal government repealed and replaced the 1906 *Designs Act* when it passed the *Designs Act 2003* (Cth) and the *Designs (Consequential Amendments) Act 2003* (Cth). These Acts, which came into operation in June 2004, aimed to clarify a number of issues, including the overlap between copyright and design protection. Although the period of protection was reduced from sixteen to ten years and, in some respects, the criteria for protection are now more arduous, it was thought that the new system would be more cost-effective and straightforward and thus more attractive to designers. To overcome problems that had developed under the old law, the 2003 Act also added a 'right to repair' defence against infringement.

Given that the term of maximum protection under the 1906 *Designs Act* was sixteen years, a large number of designs registered under the 1906 Act were still protected when the 2003 *Designs Act* came into force. To deal with these registered designs, ss 151–161 of the 2003 *Designs Act* provides that the 1906 Act will still operate in limited circumstances. The main areas affected by these transitional provisions are duration of protection,[10] rectification of the design register and conduct of infringement proceedings.[11] In some cases, decisions under the 1906 Act will also continue to be relevant in interpreting the new provisions under the 2003 Act.

In May 2012, the Parliamentary Secretary for Industry and Innovation, Mark Dreyfus, directed the Advisory Council on Intellectual Property (ACIP) to 'investigate the effectiveness of the design system in stimulating innovation by Australian users and the impact the designs system has on economic growth'.[12] The following terms of reference were endorsed:

> Inquire, report and make recommendation to the Australian Government on the operation and effectiveness of the *Designs Act 2003* in supporting innovation, having regard to any new opportunities for enhancing the Act's effectiveness and efficiency; and any deficiencies and unintended consequences arising from the Act's implementation.

In December 2014, ACIP released an options paper that outlined three possible ways of responding to these problems:[13] (1) fix the details in the 2003 Act,[14] (2) fix the 2003 Act and

---

of a product; (2) new threshold test for protection – adopt a test ensuring the design is new *and* distinctive; (3) new test for infringement – determine whether there is infringement by an 'informed user' of the product (the court should also give more weight to the similarities between competing designs than the differences); (4) duration of product – set the maximum term at fifteen years with renewal at five years; (5) spare parts protection – continue protection for spare parts subject to procedure for referring anti-competitive actions to the Australian Competition and Consumer Commission; (6) copyright–designs overlap – repeal the provisions in the *Copyright Act 1968* (Cth) dealing with the overlap and introduce a new adaptation right for artistic works.

9   ALRC, *Designs*, above n 1, [2.1].
10 For example, all 1906 registrations will have a maximum period of protection of sixteen years: *Designs Act 2003* (Cth) s 152.
11 An action for infringement of a design registered under the 1906 Act will be determined under the 1906 infringement provisions (s 30): *Designs Act 2003* (Cth) s 156.
12 Advisory Council on Intellectual Property (ACIP), *Review of the Designs System* (Issues Paper, September 2013) 6.
13 ACIP, *Review of the Designs System* (Options Paper, December 2014) 59.
14 Ibid.

adopt some changes designed to improve the system and bring Australian design law into line with international standards[15] or (3) undertake a wholesale reconsideration and revision of the role of the designs system.[16] In the course of its review, ACIP found that a number of improvements could be made to the designs system and that evidence of the effectiveness of the 2003 Act was mixed. ACIP also found that technological trends warranted more reconsideration of the role of design protection, particularly given the increasing use of 'virtual design'.[17]

In March 2015, ACIP released its final report.[18] The report made twenty-three recommendations focused on improving the effectiveness and efficiency of the designs system. The recommendations aimed to improve design protection, clarify designs law for owners and third parties, streamline the processing of design applications, and improve harmonisation with international practices.

On 6 May 2016, the government responded[19] to ACIP's report, agreeing to the majority of ACIP's recommendations.[20] However, the issue of whether or not Australia should join the Hague Agreement (1925) for designs, which allows designers to file into seventy territories through a single application, was given to IP Australia to investigate. In 2016, the Productivity Commission recommended that Australia delay joining the Hague Agreement.[21] In 2018, IP Australia published an economic analysis which explored the costs and benefits of Australia joining the Hague Agreement.[22] It concluded that the costs of acceding to the Hague Agreement outweighed the benefits, but that, in the future, as more countries accede to the Agreement, it may become desirable for Australia to do so.

7.3 The registration process

As with patents and trade marks, a design will only be protected if it has been duly registered. The process of design registration is administered by the Designs Office in IP Australia, headed by the Registrar for Designs. The *Designs Act 2003* (Cth) provides a more streamlined registration system for the protection of designs than was afforded under the 1906 Act.

---

15 Ibid 60.
16 Ibid 61.
17 I. Hargraves, *Digital Opportunity: A Review of Intellectual Property and Growth* (Independent Report, 2011) [7.10]. See also M. Hall, '3D printing – some of the IP challenges' (2013) 23 *Australian Intellectual Property Law Bulletin* 213; L. Miller, 'Protecting designs in the age of 3D printing' (2014) 27 *Australian Intellectual Property Law Bulletin* 118; D. Mendis, M. Lemley and M. Rimmer (eds.), *3D Printing and Beyond: Intellectual Property and Regulation* (Cheltenham: Edward Elgar, 2019).
18 ACIP, *Review of the Designs System* (Final Report, March 2015).
19 See IP Australia, 'Government response – ACIP Review of the Designs System', www.ipaustralia.gov.au.
20 The *Intellectual Property Laws Amendment Act 2015* (Cth) received royal assent on 25 February 2015. Although some changes under the Act came into force on 26 February 2015 (and with retrospective effect), the main changes came into effect on 25 August 2015. These changes repealed various document retention provisions in the *Designs Acts* which were already provided for under the *Archives Act 1983* (Cth).
21 Productivity Commission, *Intellectual Property Arrangements* (Inquiry Report No 78, September 2016) 351.
22 IP Australia, *The Hague Agreement Concerning the International Registration of Industrial Designs: A Cost-Benefit Analysis for Australia* (March 2018).

There are two notable features of the design registration process. The first is that, unlike the case with patents and trade marks, there is no substantive examination of the design application during the registration process. Instead, the application is only checked to see that it contains certain information, such as the name and contact details of the applicant and the prescribed number of representations of the design.[23] This makes the registration process similar to that of the innovation patent. The absence of substantive examination means that the registration process is simpler, faster and less expensive than was previously the case under the 1906 *Designs Act*. While examination may not occur as a matter of course during the registration process, a registered design may be examined after grant if this is requested. The request for examination can be made by anyone, including the applicant, the Registrar or a court.[24] One of the main reasons for examination is that an infringement action can only be brought once a design has been examined.[25] The second notable feature of the 2003 *Designs Act* is that the applicant is given the option to publish, as opposed to register, the design. While publication of the design does not give the applicant any rights in the design, publication places the design in the 'prior art base' (discussed below).[26] As this destroys the novelty of the design, it prevents others from registering similar designs. As this option is not often used, the government has indicated that it has accepted ACIP's recommendation[27] to remove this option of publication; however, public consultations will be conducted in 2019 before any amendments are made.[28]

7.3.1 Who can apply?

While there are no restrictions on who can apply to have a design registered,[29] only certain people are able to be registered as the owner of a design.[30] These are the author of the design (that is, the 'designer');[31] the employer of the author, if the author made the design in the course of their employment;[32] the person who contracted the author to make the design;[33] and the person to whom the author has assigned the design (the assignment must be in writing).[34] A design can be owned by more than one person.[35] Where there is a dispute between

---

23   *Designs Act 2003* (Cth) s 21(2); *Designs Regulations 2004* (Cth) reg 3.01.
24   *Designs Act 2003* (Cth) s 63(1).
25   Ibid s 73.
26   At 7.4.2.
27   ACIP, Final Report, above n 18, rec 5.
28   IP Australia, 'Government response', above n 19, 2.
29   *Designs Act 2003* (Cth) s 21.
30   Ibid s 13(1).
31   Ibid s 13(1)(a). The *Designs Act* does not define what is meant by a 'designer' beyond describing them as 'the person who created the design'. Reflecting the ambivalent status of design law within intellectual property law, the 'designer' is said to draw both from the notion of 'author' in copyright law (see *LED Technologies Pty Ltd v Elecspess Pty Ltd* (2008) 80 IPR 85, 96) and from patent law (*Allen Hardware Products v Tclip* [2008] ADO 8, [19]: '[T]he principles relating to inventorship under the *Patents Act 1990* apply generally to designership under the *Designs Act 2003*').
32   *Designs Act 2003* (Cth) s 13(1)(b). See *Collymore v Courier Pete Pty Ltd* (2008) 79 IPR 608, 611; *Allen Hardware Products v Tclip* [2008] ADO 8, [19].
33   *Designs Act 2003* (Cth) s 13(1)(b).
34   Ibid s 13(2).
35   Ibid ss 13(3), 21(3).

parties as to joint ownership, the Registrar may make a determination as to how the application is to proceed.[36]

7.3.2 Requirements of the application

A design application must comply with the 'minimum filing requirements' set out in s 21(2) of the *Designs Act 2003* (Cth). These are that the application include a completed application form, at least one representation of the design[37] and the application fee.[38] A representation is a drawing, photograph or specimen of the design.[39] Photographs of the article are also acceptable. The representations should show the article as the eye would see it. Traditional views from the front, side and top are preferred to perspective or isometric views.[40] The inclusion of a representation in the design application allows the public to determine the details of the design and the scope of the protection. Registered designs must be reasonably clear and succinct. This means that the design must 'appear with reasonable clarity, and without necessity for unreasonably prolonged or complicated series of deductions from the registered representation'.[41]

While an application can be filed in respect of one design applied to a product, s 22 allows for a single application to cover a 'common design' that applies to more than one product or multiple designs that apply to a particular product. Where an application relates to several designs for several products, the products must all fall within the same class of products as set out in the *Locarno Agreement Establishing an International Classification for Industrial Designs*.[42]

A 'statement of newness and distinctiveness' may also be included in the application form.[43] This sets out any visual feature(s) of the design that the applicant believes are novel and distinctive. It is not compulsory to include a statement of newness and distinctiveness, but it may assist in the determination of whether the design is new and distinctive when compared to prior art of disclosed designs.[44]

7.3.3 Request for registration or publication

One of the notable features of the design system is that applicants have the option of having their design registered or published.[45] Whereas registration of the design gives the applicant

---

36 Ibid s 29. The Registrar may also consider an application to revoke the design on the basis that one of the owners was not an entitled person: at ss 51, 52.
37 *Designs Regulations 2004* (Cth) reg 4.04(f).
38 See ibid reg 3.01. A fee must be paid for each design in the design application: see reg 11.01, sch 4.
39 *Designs Act 2003* (Cth) s 5.
40 IP Australia, 'Prepare drawings' in 'Designs' www.ipaustralia.gov.au.
41 *Keller v LED Technologies Pty Ltd* (2010) 185 FCR 449, 491–2 where it was accepted that a person would not only have access to the representations of the design on the IP Australia website, but also that they would magnify the image to improve clarity.
42 Opened for signature 28 September 1979, WIPO Lex No TRT/LOCARNO/001 (entered into force 23 November 1981).
43 *Designs Act 2003* (Cth) s 69.
44 Ibid s 19 provides a list of factors to be taken into account when determining infringement. Section 19(2)(b) of the 2003 Act expressly states how statement of newness and distinctiveness may be used. On this see *Keller v LED Technologies Pty Ltd* (2010) 185 FCR 449, 503–4; *Multisteps Pty Ltd v Source & Sell Pty Ltd* (2013) 214 FCR 323, [56], [111], [198]–[210].
45 *Designs Act 2003* (Cth) s 35.

rights in the design, publication merely serves to ensure that the design is part of the prior art. As publication destroys the novelty and distinctiveness of the design, it prevents other parties from registering similar designs. Applicants must decide whether they want to publish or register their design either at the time the application is lodged or within six months of the priority date of the application, or the application will lapse.[46]

7.3.4 Publication

If an applicant decides that they want their application to be published (rather than registered), the application will be checked to see that it satisfies the minimum filing requirements.[47] Where an application complies with the necessary requirements, it will be published in the *Australian Official Journal of Designs* and in the Australian Designs Data Searching system. While no rights arise from the publication of a design, it may be useful in that it prevents others from registering the design. It is important to note that a person who wishes to ensure that similar designs are not registered does not need to go to the trouble and expense of using the design system to destroy the novelty of the design. This is because a design will become part of the public domain and thus not be able to be protected if it is made available to the public (by any means) before the priority date of the application.

7.3.5 Registration

Registration of the application will occur after an initial formalities check.[48] If the application complies with the requisite requirements, and the registration is not prohibited by s 43(1) of the *Designs Act 2003* (Cth),[49] the design will be registered. Where this occurs, details including the representation of the design will be published in the *Australian Official Journal of Designs* and in the Australian Designs Data Searching system. The Registrar will issue a certificate of registration and the successful design will be recorded in the Register of Designs.[50] If the Registrar is not satisfied with the application, the applicant will be given an opportunity to amend the application.[51]

7.3.6 Priority date

The priority date of the application is the date when the application was filed, unless there is a claim to an earlier priority date from an overseas design application, or from a design excluded from an earlier Australian design application.[52]

---

46   Ibid s 33(1)(a). An applicant can choose publication for some designs in the application and registration for others: at s 36(1).
47   Ibid ss 39–40.
48   Ibid.
49   *Designs Act 2003* (Cth) s 43(1) declares that certain designs must be refused, such as integrated circuits and those protected by the *Olympic Insignia Protection Act 1987* (Cth).
50   *Designs Act 2003* (Cth) s 45.
51   Ibid s 41, so long as it is not amended as to matters of substance: at s 28(3).
52   *Designs Act 2003* (Cth) s 27(1); *Designs Regulations 2004* (Cth) reg 3.06.

7.3.7 Duration

The term of protection for a registered design is five years from the filing date of the design application, and is renewable for up to a total of ten years.[53] Under the 1906 *Designs Act*, the maximum period of protection was sixteen years.[54]

7.3.8 Post-registration examination

The *Designs Act 2003* (Cth) has a formal, post-registration examination system. Any person or relevant court may request that a design be examined.[55] As discussed above, a registered design must be examined and a certificate of examination issued before proceedings for infringement can be brought.[56] When examining the design, the Registrar must determine whether the design should be revoked.[57] The main grounds for revocation are that there is no 'design', or that the design is not 'novel and distinctive' as compared with the prior art base[58] (both requirements are discussed below).[59] If the Registrar decides that there is no ground for revocation, a certification of examination will be issued.[60] If the Registrar decides, however, that there is a ground of revocation, the applicant will be given an opportunity to amend their application.[61] If the amendment does not rectify the problem(s), the parties are given a further hearing, after which, if the Registrar is still not satisfied, the registration will be revoked and the register amended.[62]

7.4 Criteria for protection

A number of factors must be satisfied for a design to be registered. The two key criteria are that there is a 'design' that is 'new and distinctive'.

7.4.1 Meaning of 'design'

While designs are always closely connected to the object in which they are embodied, it has long been recognised that a design must be something that is separate and distinct from the article or product to which it is applied.[63] This is reflected in the fact that a 'design' is defined in the 2003 Act to mean 'the overall appearance of the product resulting from one or more visual

---

53 *Designs Act 2003* (Cth) ss 46 and 47. The fee for renewal of registration is set out in sch 4 of the *Designs Regulations 2004* (Cth).
54 Ibid s 27A. The sixteen-year period was made up of a twelve-month period from the date of registration: an extension for six years from the priority date (which included the initial twelve-month period) and two additional five-year extensions.
55 *Designs Act 2003* (Cth) s 63(1).
56 Ibid s 73(3).
57 Ibid s 65.
58 Ibid s 15.
59 At 7.4.
60 *Designs Act 2003* (Cth) s 67.
61 Ibid s 66(3).
62 Ibid s 68. The unsuccessful registrant may appeal to the Federal Court: at s 68(6).
63 This was the case under *Designs Act 1906* (Cth) s 4(1), which referred to 'features ... applicable to an article'.

features of the product'.[64] The requirement that the design be separate to the article itself was raised in *Re Wolanski's Registered Design*,[65] a case decided under the 1906 Act that is still relevant today. When discussing the design of a 'neck-tie support' Kitto J observed that a design is 'a conception or suggestion as to shape, configuration, pattern or ornament ... and accordingly what the proprietor of a design gets by its registration is a monopoly for one thing only, and that is "one particular individual and specific appearance"'.[66] The need for a design to be applied to an article was also a telling factor in the decision to reject Microsoft's application for design registration for a type font. This was on the basis that the 'type font is not built into, or to be applied to, anything at all. What Microsoft seeks to register is nothing other than the characteristics of the type font itself ... The design does not specify a tangible thing'.[67] It is worth noting that the Registrar will not register designs for graphical user interfaces.[68]

There are two features of the 2003 definition of design that need further attention. These are, first, the requirement that the design's appearance results from one or more visual features, and second, the requirement that a design must be embodied in a 'product'. We will look at each in turn.

7.4.1.1 Visual features

The first requirement is that the design's appearance results from one or more visual features. Unlike the position under the 1906 *Designs Act*, there is no longer a requirement that a design consists of features 'that, in the finished article, can be judged by the eye'.[69] The requirement that there be eye appeal (under the 1906 Act) was interpreted to mean that the design must have sufficient individuality of appearance to distinguish it from the fundamental form.[70] This proved to be a difficult requirement to satisfy. The problems that arose when attempting to establish eye appeal were illustrated by *D Sebel & Co Ltd v National Art Metal Co Pty Ltd*,[71] a decision that concerned a design applied to the fundamental form of a chair (that is, the back, legs and seat). The problem of showing eye appeal in this context was highlighted by Jacobs J's comment that in relation to a chair, startling novelty or originality should not be expected,

---

64   *Designs Act 2003* (Cth) s 6. A design was defined in s 4 of the *Designs Act 1906* (Cth) to mean 'features of shape, configuration, pattern or ornamentation applicable to an article, being features that, in the finished article, can be judged by the eye, but does not include a method or principle of construction'.
65   (1953) 88 CLR 278.
66   Ibid 79–280 (Kitto J), citing *Pugh v Riley Cycle Co Ltd* [1912] 1 Ch 613, 619 and A. D. Russell-Clarke, *Copyright in Industrial Designs* (1930) 17; *Kestos Ltd v Kempat Ltd & Kemp* (1935) 53 RPC 139, 151. See also *Malleys Ltd v JW Tomlin Pty Ltd* (1961) 180 CLR 120.
67   *Re Application for Type Font in the Name of Microsoft* (2007) 71 IPR 664, [33].
68   *Apple Inc* [2017] ADO 6.
69   *Designs Act 1906* (Cth) s 4(1). This did not necessarily mean that there had to be some aesthetic features or that the design was appealing to the eye. The question was often raised 'whose' eye? It was held that it was to be the eye of the court, which must assess novelty or originality, and that expert evidence enabled the court's eye to be an 'instructed eye': *LJ Fisher & Co Ltd v Fabtile Industries Pty Ltd* (1979) 49 AOJP 3611, 572. In the United Kingdom it was to be determined by the eye of the customer: *AMP Inc v Utilux Pty Ltd* (1971) 45 ALJR 123. The removal of the requirement of eye appeal followed the recommendation of the ALRC in its report *Designs*, above n 1.
70   *Malleys Ltd v JW Tomlin Pty Ltd* (1961) 180 CLR 120.
71   (1965) 10 FLR 224.

as 'the element of novelty or originality will of necessity be likely to be within a small compass'.[72]

The fact that the 2003 definition of 'design' no longer contains a requirement of eye appeal means that the law is more straightforward and thus clearer. Although eye appeal is no longer a requirement for protection, the 2003 Act specifically includes the visual features of a product in the definition of design. 'Visual feature' is defined to mean including the 'shape, configuration, pattern or ornamentation' of the product.[73] This definition covers both three-dimensional articles (such as the shape of a tea cup and saucer) and two-dimensional patterns on products (such as the floral pattern applied to the tea cup and saucer).[74] The feel of a product and the materials used in the creation of a product are excluded from the definition of a visual feature.[75] This is because these features do not contribute to the overall visual appearance of the product.

A visual feature may, but need not, serve a functional purpose. Under Australian law, a functional design may be validly registered even if it consists of, or includes, features of shape or configuration that serve a functional purpose.[76] In *Multisteps Pty Ltd v Source & Sell Pty Ltd*,[77] the court took into account the fact that the functional aspects of the plastic punnet containers intended for small tomatoes and strawberries 'limited the freedom of the designer to innovate'. While the registered designs themselves were valid, the individual features were held not to 'signify aspects of design innovation'.[78]

7.4.1.2 Product

The second notable aspect of the way that a design is defined is that it applies to a 'product'. A product is defined as something 'that is manufactured or handmade'.[79] A product includes the component parts of a complex product if it is made separately,[80] and a kit when it is assembled.[81] While we usually think of a product as a single isolated object with fixed dimensions, in certain circumstances something may still qualify as a product even where it is of an indeterminate length. This might include, for example, plastic pipes, corrugated iron, or roof guttering, all of which are manufactured in continuous lengths. A computer screen has been held not to be registerable as a design on the basis that the physical screen or monitor is the 'product', and that the appearance of the screen was ephemeral.[82] It was also confirmed

---

72   Ibid 226. Similarly, in *Dias Aluminium Products Pty Ltd v Ullrich Aluminium Pty Ltd* (2006) 66 IPR 561, it was observed that startling novelty or originality cannot be expected with a sliding wardrobe door design.
73   *Designs Act 2003* (Cth) s 7(1). The expression 'features of shape, configuration, pattern or ornamentation' was also used in *Designs Act 1906* (Cth) s 4.
74   *Designs Act 2003* (Cth) s 7(2).
75   Ibid s 7(3). If the surface or the feel of a product constitutes visual features of the product, it may be able to be registered.
76   Ibid s 7(2). Compare *Edwards Hot Water Systems v SW Hart Pty Ltd* (1985) 9 FCR 537; *Hosokawa Micron International Inc v Fortune* (1990) 26 FCR 393 (discussing a similar provision under the *Designs Act 1906* (Cth)).
77   (2013) 214 FCR 323 [85].
78   Ibid [154]–[156].
79   *Designs Act 2003* (Cth) s 6(1).
80   Ibid s 6(2). See *Re Colgate-Palmolive Co Inc* (2010) 88 IPR 434, [15]–[20].
81   *Designs Act 2003* (Cth) s 6(4).
82   *Apple Inc* [2017] ADO 6, following the approach of *Re Applications by Comshare Inc* (1991) 23 IPR 145.

that a screen display was not a 'product' as the pattern or ornamentation that was displayed on the screen was a result of the use of software that was separate from the computer screen.[83] In order for something that has one or more indefinite dimensions to qualify as a product, it is necessary to show that: (a) a cross-section taken across any indefinite dimension is fixed or varies according to a regular pattern; (b) all the dimensions remain in proportion; (c) the cross-sectional shape remains the same throughout, whether or not the dimensions of that shape vary according to a ratio or series of ratios; or (d) it has a pattern or ornamentation that repeats itself.[84]

7.4.1.2.1 SPARE PARTS

Design protection is available under both the 1906 and 2003 *Designs Acts* for new or original designs for spare parts. As part of its review of designs, the ALRC received a number of submissions asking for the protection of these designs to be maintained, arguing that protection for spare parts designs is necessary as an incentive for manufacturers to invest in design.[85] However, a number of submissions called for the protection of designs for spare parts to be excluded or limited. These views were based on the fact that design protection reduces competition in the supply of repair and replacement parts, which adversely affects consumers and excludes potential competitors.[86] In response to concerns of this nature, the 'right of repair for spare parts' defence, discussed below,[87] was introduced into Australian law in 2003.

7.4.2 New and distinctive

The second condition that must be satisfied for a design to be protected is that the design is new *and* distinctive.[88] This is a more difficult threshold to satisfy than that under the 1906 *Designs Act* where it was only necessary to show that the design was new *or* original.[89] When determining whether a design is new and distinctive, it is necessary to compare the design as set out in the application with similar designs that fall within the 'prior art base'.[90] The prior art base includes designs that have been used in Australia, published in a document in Australia or overseas,[91] or disclosed in a published design application.[92] This expands the breadth of the

---

83 *Apple Inc* [2017] ADO 6, [4.32].
84 *Designs Act 2003* (Cth) s 6(3).
85 ALRC, *Designs*, above n 1, [16.18] referring to submissions by Ford and Holden Australia.
86 Ibid [16.1].
87 At 7.8.1.
88 *Designs Act 2003* (Cth) s 15. The ALRC found this test to be too lenient: ALRC, *Designs*, above n 1, rec 32. The problem was that as long as the Registrar had regard to the differences between the two designs (as required by *Designs Act 1906* (Cth) s 17) and found that the design differed in at least one aspect from a design already registered, published or used in Australia, then it would be accepted for registration.
89 *Designs Act 1906* (Cth) s 17(1).
90 *Designs Act 2003* (Cth) s 15.
91 Ibid s 15(2). This means that the prior art base outside Australia must be considered (which is a change to the law of invalidity as it stood under the 1906 *Designs Act*). Regarding the delivery of a sample vacuum cleaner to a potential retailer (Godfreys), or to a state government department to obtain a certificate of approval to sell an electrical product, neither delivery was a public use within the context of s 15(2) of the *Designs Act 2003* (Cth). See *World of Technologies (Australia) Pty Ltd v Tempo (Australia) Pty Ltd* (2007) 71 IPR 307, [67]–[68].
92 *Designs Act 1906* (Cth) s 15(2). *Icon Plastics Pty Ltd* [2007] ADO 2, [10] (expressly recognising that the prior art base includes earlier registered designs).

prior art base beyond Australia.[93] Importantly, the prior art base only includes designs that were made available before the design's priority date.[94] Section 17 of the *Designs Act 2003* (Cth) provides that certain things (such as publication with the consent of the owner in prescribed circumstances)[95] are to be disregarded in deciding whether a design is new and distinctive. Newness and distinctiveness are two separate requirements.

A design is *new* unless it is identical to a design that forms part of the prior art base for the design.[96] A design is *distinctive* if it is not substantially similar in overall impression to a design that already exists.[97] In determining whether two designs are substantially similar in overall impression, more weight is to be given to the similarities between the designs than to the differences.[98] However, as Kenny J observed,[99] the inquiry under the Designs Act is more complex and sophisticated than that, particularly where the design field is crowded and due consideration must be given to the state of the development of the prior art.

In *Hunter Pacific International Pty Ltd v Martec Pty Ltd*,[100] Nicholas J provided a useful analysis of s 19 of the *Designs Act 2003* (Cth). This decision concerned an alleged infringement of the applicant's registered design for a ceiling fan hub (the Registered Design) by the respondent's Martec Razor (the Razor). Nicholas J observed:

> Section 19 of the Act contemplates that the Court will have regard to all the similarities and the differences between the visual features of the two designs in coming to its ultimate conclusion. Hence the relevant comparison cannot be based upon a fleeting or casual inspection of the drawings or object in question or some 'imperfect recollection' of either of them. That is not to deny that the comparison to be undertaken is essentially impression based.[101]

Nicholas J followed the reasoning of Yates J in *Multisteps Pty Ltd v Source & Sell Pty Ltd*,[102] who held that the 'notion of "imperfect recollection" familiar in trade mark law – has no application when determining design similarity'.[103]

---

93 *World of Technologies (Australia) Pty Ltd v Tempo (Australia) Pty Ltd* (2007) 71 IPR 307, [61] (the design for which the applicant secured registration was substantially similar in overall impression to that which appeared on the printed brochure for the MC-801 vacuum cleaner distributed at the Canton Fair in April 2005; the latter was a design published in a document outside Australia and, accordingly, part of the prior art base for the purposes of registrability).
94 *Designs Act 2003* (Cth) ss 15, 27(1), 27(2). Section 16(3) provides that the newness or distinctiveness of a design is not affected by the mere publication or public use of the design in Australia on or after the priority date of the design, or by the registration of another design with the same or a later priority date.
95 *Designs Regulations 2004* (Cth) reg 2.01 sets out the prescribed circumstances and deals with uses and publications of designs that may occur at an official or officially recognised international exhibition. For a discussion of the meaning of the equivalent provision under the 1906 Act (s 47) see *Chiropedic Bedding Pty Ltd v Radburg Pty Ltd* (2008) 170 FCR 560.
96 *Designs Act 2003* (Cth) s 16(1).
97 *Designs Act 1906* (Cth) s 16(2). See at s 19 for factors to be used in assessing substantial similarity in overall impression. For discussion, see *Keller v LED Technologies Pty Ltd* (2010) 185 FCR 449, [44] ff.
98 *Designs Act 2003* (Cth) s 19(1).
99 *Review 2 Pty Ltd v Redberry Enterprise Pty Ltd* (2008) 173 FCR 450, [37]–[38].
100 [2016] FCA 796.
101 Ibid [39].
102 (2013) 214 FCR 323.
103 Ibid [55].

Nicholas J held that the Razor did infringe the applicant's Registered Design as the obvious differences in the shape and configuration of the ceiling fan hub were unable to overcome the 'significant and eye-catching similarities'.

The prior art was examined in comparison to both the Registered Design and the Razor and guidance was gleaned from Lockhart J in *Dart Industries Inc v Décor Corp Pty Ltd* who observed:

> Small differences between the registered design and the prior art will generally lead to a finding of no infringement if there are equally small differences between the registered design and the alleged infringing article. On the other hand, the greater the advance in the registered design over the prior art, generally the more likely that a court will find common features between the design and the alleged infringing article to support a finding of infringement.[104]

As the expert witnesses in *Hunter Pacific* agreed that there was freedom to innovate in the field, and the applicant's Registered Design was considered to be significantly different to the prior art, Nicholas J held that he must give more weight to the similarities of the designs than to the differences between them.[105]

Distinctiveness is assessed by 'the standard of the informed user'.[106] The concept of an informed user is 'flexible enough to incorporate where relevant the views of consumers, experts, specialists and skilled tradespersons. At the same time it does not, and should not, require that the expert or consumer be the test in all cases'.[107] The informed user need not have used the product but must be 'familiar with the product to which the design relates'.[108] The examination focuses on whether there is any substantial similarity in the overall impression to any of the prior art, taking into account any statement of newness and distinctiveness as well as the other factors set out in s 19(2) of the *Designs Act 2003* (Cth), such as the freedom of the designer to innovate as well as the amount, quality and importance of the part of the design that may be substantially similar.[109] This is the same test that is used to determine whether infringement has taken place. Interestingly, Nicholas J in *Hunter Pacific*[110] observed that the product should be viewed by the informed user in its intended installed position. In that case, the overall visual appearance was evaluated assuming the ceiling fan was fully installed and thus the design was seen by looking up at the hub embodying the Registered Design as

---

104   (1989) 15 IPR 403, 409.
105   [2016] FCA 796, [65]. 'Precise mathematical comparisons or analyses of measurements or ratios have no role to play in determining whether or not the two designs create an overall impression that is substantially similar ... The overall impression created by a design arises from looking at a registered design or a product made to a particular design rather than measuring it': at [64] (Nicholas J).
106   *Designs Act 1906* (Cth) s 19(4).
107   ALRC, *Designs*, above n 1, [5.17]. The decision of *Review 2 Pty Ltd v Redberry Enterprise Pty Ltd* (2008) 173 FCR 450 provides a good example of how the courts decide similarity under ss 19(2)(a), (b) and 19(3): see [19]–[26]. See also *Keller v LED Technologies Pty Ltd* (2010) 185 FCR 449; *Review Australia Pty Ltd v New Cover Group Pty Ltd* (2008) 79 IPR 236 [22]–[30]; *Multisteps Pty Ltd v Source & Sell Pty Ltd* (2013) 214 FCR 323, [50]–[56].
108   *Designs Act 2003* (Cth) s 19(4). See also Yates J in *Multisteps Pty Ltd v Source & Sell Pty Ltd* (2013) 214 FCR 323, [57]–[68] (highlighting differences between the United Kingdom and Australian statues in relation to 'informed user').
109   *Designs Act 2003* (Cth) ss 16–17.
110   [2016] FCA 796.

compared to the hub of the Razor. This attaches particular importance to those features likely to draw the attention of the eye in that position.

7.5 Ownership

The owner may assign all or part of their interest in the registered design. To be valid, the assignment must be in writing and signed by or on behalf of the assignor and assignee.[111] A registered design can also be transferred or devolved by will or through the operation of law.[112]

7.6 Rights

The owner of a registered design has the exclusive right to control the way in which products that embody a design are used in certain circumstances.[113] Under the Act, the registered owner has the exclusive right to: make a product that embodies the design; import the product for sale; sell, hire or otherwise dispose of the product; use a product; and authorise another person to do any of the foregoing.[114]

7.7 Infringement

A registered design must be examined and a certificate of examination issued before proceedings for infringement can be initiated under the *Designs Act 2003* (Cth).[115] Once a design has been examined, the owner of a registered design is able to bring an action for either primary or secondary infringement.[116] In both cases, the onus is on the registered owner of the design to show infringement.[117] In infringement proceedings, a defendant may counterclaim for rectification of the Register by virtue of s 74.[118]

7.7.1 Primary infringement

Primary infringement occurs when a person, without the licence or authority of the registered owner of the design, does one of a range of activities in relation to a product that embodies a design that is *identical or substantially similar* in overall impression to the registered design.[119] 'Infringement is determined by comparing the allegedly infringing product against the registered design, not by comparing a product embodying the registered design against the infringing product'.[120] The activities that fall with the owner's control are the rights to: 'make or

---

111 *Designs Act 2003* (Cth) s 11.
112 Ibid ss 10(2), 11(1)–(3).
113 Ibid s 10.
114 *Designs Act 1906* (Cth) s 10(1).
115 *Designs Act 2003* (Cth) s 73(3).
116 Ibid s 75(5).
117 Ibid s 72(2).
118 Under ibid s 93.
119 Ibid ss 71(1)(a), 71(3), 19(1).
120 *LED Technologies Pty Ltd v Elecspess Pty Ltd* (2008) 80 IPR 85, [77].

offer to make; import for sale or use in trade or business; sell, hire or otherwise dispose of (or offer to do any of those things); use in any way for a trade or business or keep the product that embodies the design for any of those purposes'.[121]

For infringement to have occurred, the defendant must have undertaken one of the activities that fall within the owner's exclusive control *and* this activity must have been carried out in relation to a product that embodies a design that is *identical or substantially similar* in overall impression to the registered design. When determining whether a product is *identical or substantially similar* in overall impression to the registered design, the court takes into account the range of factors that are set out in s 19(2) of the *Designs Act 2003* (Cth) and that are relevant to a determination of whether the design is 'distinctive' (under s 16).[122] Section 19(1) requires the court to give more weight to the similarities between the competing designs than the differences.[123] As a result, small differences between an allegedly infringing design and a registered design will be insufficient to avoid a finding of infringement, if the overall impression of the infringing design remains the same.[124] This means that

> [s]mall differences between the registered design and the prior art will generally lead to a finding of no infringement, if there are equally small differences between the registered design and the alleged infringing article. On the other hand, the greater the advance in the registered design over the prior art, the more likely that the court will find common features between the design and the alleged infringing article to support a finding of infringement.[125]

When assessing substantial similarity in overall impression, the courts should have particular regard to the features identified in the statement of newness and distinctiveness that the applicant has the option to file.[126] Other factors to be taken into account are the state of development of the prior art[127] and the freedom of the designer to innovate.[128] In situations where only part of the design is substantially similar to another design, the court will take account of the amount, quality and importance of that part in the context of the design as a whole.[129] Where the application did not include a statement of newness and distinctiveness,

---

121 *Designs Act 2003* (Cth) s 71(1)(a)–(e).
122 Ibid s 71(3).
123 Ibid s 19(1). If a design is registered for a particular colour, the design may be limited to that colour (as distinct from a design that was registered for black and white): *Review 2 Pty Ltd v Redberry Enterprise Pty Ltd* (2008) 173 FCR 450.
124 Contrast *Koninklijke Philips Electronics NV v Remington Products Australia Pty Ltd* (2000) 100 FCR 90, where no infringement was found due to differences in the dimensions of the two razors but it was clear that there was, in effect, copying of the product.
125 *Keller v LED Technologies Pty Ltd* (2010) 185 FCR 449, 462. See also *Dart Industries Inc v Décor Corp Pty Ltd* (1989) 15 IPR 403, 409.
126 *Designs Act 2003* (Cth) s 19(2)(b). 'Section 19 does not simply refer to the prior art base, but to the *state of development* of the prior art base': *Keller v LED Technologies Pty Ltd* (2010) 185 FCR 449, 464. Under the 1906 *Designs Act*, the weight to be placed on a statement of novelty was largely left to the courts (for discussion see *Chiropedic Bedding Pty Ltd v Radburg Pty Ltd* (2009) 181 FCR 446). Section 19(2)(b) of the 2003 Act, however, expressly states how a statement of newness and distinctiveness may be used (see *Keller v LED Technologies* at 503–4).
127 *Designs Act 2003* (Cth) s 19(2)(a).
128 Ibid s 19(2)(d).
129 Ibid s 19(2)(c).

the court must have regard to the appearance of the design as a whole.[130] The assessment must be made through the eyes of an informed user – in other words, a person familiar with the product to which the design relates.[131] Although '[b]reaking down the Design and the prior art into its constituent elements may be helpful in the comparison', the courts have stressed that 'it must not be allowed to obscure the general appearance of the Design and prior art'.[132] It is the overall impression conveyed of the design that will make the design distinctive over the prior art.[133]

Where an action is brought for primary infringement of a registered design, the court may refuse to award damages, reduce the damages that would otherwise be awarded, or refuse to make an account of profits if the defendant can show that they were not aware that the design was registered and that, before that time, the defendant had taken all reasonable steps to ascertain whether the design was registered.[134]

7.7.2 Secondary infringement

A person will be liable for secondary infringement where they import, sell, hire or otherwise dispose of a product that embodies a design that is identical or substantially similar in overall impression to the registered design.[135] Secondary infringement will also occur where a person uses such a product for the purposes of trade or business; or where they keep such a product for the purposes of sale, hire, disposal or any trade or business.[136] If a defendant can satisfy the court that at the time of the infringement they were not aware, and could not reasonably have been expected to have been aware, that the design was registered, then the court may refuse to award damages, reduce the damages that would otherwise be awarded, or refuse to make an order for an account of profits.[137] This makes the test for secondary infringement more lenient than that for primary infringement.

7.8 Defences

There are two defences to infringement under the *Designs Act 2003* (Cth): the right of repair for spare parts defence[138] and the defence of consent.[139] The Crown is also given special rights in relation to the use and supply of design via compulsory licence provisions.[140]

---

130   Ibid s 19(3).
131   Ibid s 19(4).
132   *BlueScope Steel Ltd v Gram Engineering Pty Ltd* [2014] FCAFC 107, [72].
133   *Multisteps Pty Ltd v Source & Sell Pty Ltd* (2013) 214 FCR 323.
134   *Designs Act 2003* (Cth) s 75(2)(a)(i)–(ii).
135   Ibid ss 71(1)(a), 71(3), 19(1).
136   Ibid s 71(1)(b)–(e).
137   Ibid s 75(2)(b).
138   Ibid s 72.
139   Ibid s 71(2).
140   Ibid ss 95–105.

7.8.1 The right of repair for spare parts defence

This defence was introduced into the *Designs Act 2003* (Cth) in response to the longstanding difficulties design law has had in relation to complex objects, such as motor vehicles and machinery, which are made up of a number of separate and distinct but necessarily interrelated parts.[141] The problem here is that as spare parts must fit or match existing equipment for them to function, the owner of the design of the spare part is given a monopoly not only over the manufacture of the part, but also over replacement parts. The fear is the design monopoly may restrict competition for the repair and servicing of the original equipment and enable the design owner to charge consumers higher prices for parts.[142]

To remedy some of these problems, the *Designs Act 2003* (Cth) allows complex products and their component parts to be registered,[143] subject to a right of repair defence. Specifically, s 72(1) provides that a design is not infringed where:

- a person uses,[144] or authorises another to use, a product in relation to which the design is registered;
- the product embodies a design that is identical or substantially similar to the registered design;
- that product is a component of a complex product;[145] or
- the purpose of the use or authorisation is the repair of the complex product so as to restore its overall appearance in whole or in part.[146]

It is useful to examine the concepts of 'repair' and 'overall appearance of a product' in more detail.

---

141 Spare parts have been examined by the Industry Commission, the Bureau of Industry Economics, the ALRC and the Intellectual Property Competition Committee. The federal government undertook at the time of the introduction of this defence to review its operation in 2005: see Commonwealth, *Parliamentary Debates*, Senate, 2 December 2003 (Nick Minchin). IP Australia conducted the review in 2005. The final report (which recommended that no changes be made) is entitled *Review of the 'Spare Parts' Provision in the Designs Act 2003* (2005).

142 Intellectual Property Competition Committee, *Review of Intellectual Property Legislation under the Competition Principles Agreement* (Final Report, 2000), 183. Interestingly, in 2019, the government signalled its intention to consider the design of a mandatory scheme for access to motor vehicle service and repair information. Between February and March 2019, Treasury undertook consultation to gauge the suitability of possible elements of a mandatory scheme for the sharing of motor vehicle service and repair information and the establishment of a Service and Repair Information Sharing Advisory Committee. Subject to the outcome of consultation on these elements, the government intends to implement a scheme in 2019: see Treasury, *Mandatory Scheme for the Sharing of Motor Vehicle Service and Repair Information* (Consultation Paper, February 2019).

143 *Designs Act 2003* (Cth) s 6(2).

144 The definition of 'use' in *Designs Act 2003* (Cth) s 72(5) extends the defence not only to consumers but also to spare parts manufacturers, dealers and importers by virtue of the reference to 'make', 'import' and 'sell' the product.

145 A 'complex product' means a product comprising at least two replaceable component parts permitting disassembly and reassembly of the product: *Designs Act 2003* (Cth) s 5.

146 See *GM Global Technology Operations LLC v SSS Auto Parts Pty Ltd* [2019] FCA 97, where it was held the onus rests on the design owner to show that the alleged infringer knew that the purpose of its sale of the part was not repair. If the alleged infringer is supplying the parts to third parties, the relevant purpose that is relevant to the defence is still that of the supplier.

7.8.1.1 'Repair'

In order for the right of repair for spare parts defence to operate, the part that needs to be repaired must be damaged or decayed. This is reflected in the definition of 'repair' in the *Designs Act 2003* (Cth). In relation to a complex product, repair includes:

(a) restoring a decayed or damaged component part of the complex product to a good or sound condition;
(b) replacing a decayed or damaged component part of the complex product with a component part in good or sound condition;
(c) necessarily replacing incidental items when restoring or replacing a decayed or damaged component part of the complex product;
(d) carrying out maintenance on the complex product.[147]

The scope of the defence was considered in *GM Global Technology Operations LLC v SSS Auto Parts Pty Ltd*.[148] Holden brought design infringement proceedings against the defendant, SSS Auto Parts (SSS), alleging that it was importing, offering for sale, keeping for sale and selling motor vehicle parts which infringed Holden's registered designs. Holden held numerous designs registered under the Designs Act covering vehicle parts such as bonnets, radiator grilles, lamps and fascias. It became aware that SSS was importing non-genuine parts designed for use on Holden Special Vehicles and certain sports models of the VE Commodore. While SSS accepted that the parts were infringing, it argued that it had a defence under s 72 of the *Designs Act 2003* because the parts were to be used for the purposes of repair.

The issues in dispute in this case were relatively confined. Holden and SSS agreed that the SSS parts were identical, or substantially similar in overall impression, to Holden's registered designs, and that the SSS parts were 'component parts' of a 'complex product', being a motor vehicle. Where the parties differed concerned whether the SSS parts were to be used for the purpose of repair of the complex product (the motor vehicle) so as to restore its overall appearance in whole or part. Burley J held at [25] that in only a small number of instances was Holden able to discharge the onus of proving that the registered spare parts were being used for non-repair purposes.

7.8.1.2 'Overall appearance of a product'

The right of repair for spare parts defence only covers repairs that restore the overall appearance of a product. Thus, if a design of a front bumper of a car is used to repair the car's appearance, then the repairer may be able to rely on the repair defence. The overall appearance is restored if, to a person familiar with the complex product (otherwise known as an 'informed user'),[149] there is no material difference in the appearance of the product before and after the use of the component part.[150]

---

147 *Designs Act 2003* (Cth) s 72(5) (definition of 'repair').
148 [2019] FCA 97.
149 An 'informed user', in relation to the overall appearance of a complex product, means a person who is familiar with the complex product, or with products similar to it: *Designs Act 2003* (Cth) s 72(4).
150 Ibid s 72(3)(a).

7.8.1.3 Onus of proof

While the right of repair provides a defence against infringement, the use of a part that is protected by a registered design for purposes other than repair will still infringe. Where a defendant raises 'the spare parts defence' in design infringement proceedings, the registered owner of the design bears the onus of proving that the registered spare parts were being used for non-repair purposes.[151] This places the registered design owner in a difficult position as the alleged infringer's purpose is best known to the alleged infringer.[152]

In the *GM Global Technology Operations* decision,[153] various factors were put forward by Holden in support of its argument that SSS ought reasonably to have known that the parts were not to be used for the purpose of repair. These included:

- there was consumer demand for the parts to be used for the purpose of 'customisation and enhancement' of Holden vehicles;
- there was limited demand for the parts to be used for the purpose of repairing the vehicles to which the parts were originally fitted; and
- the nature and name of the businesses to which SSS supplied the parts indicated that the parts would be not be used for a repair purpose.

In response, SSS argued that it had a number of 'repair only' policies and used stickers on parts stating 'authorized for use only in repairs' which proved an intention that the parts be used for repair only.

While there were over 1300 alleged infringements in this case, Burley J held that Holden only discharged the onus of proving there was not a repair purpose in a small number of instances. Burley J held at [82] that the repair defence required Holden to establish that SSS knew or ought reasonably to have known that the parts were not intended to be used for repair; it was insufficient that SSS knew that they might not be used for that purpose.

7.8.2 Consent and parallel importation

A defence to infringement is provided by s 71(2) of the *Designs Act 2003* (Cth) where a person imports a product with an infringing design if a licence or authority is given by the registered owner of the design. The 2003 Act does not make it clear who is the 'registered owner' (that is, whether the design needs to be registered in Australia or an overseas jurisdiction), so it is not clear whether parallel importation is allowed.[154]

7.8.3 Crown use and supply

The Crown is granted a compulsory licence by virtue of ss 95–105 of the 2003 *Designs Act*. This is consistent with the ability of the Crown to use other forms of intellectual property, such as patents and copyright material.

---

151   Ibid s 72(2).
152   *GM Global Technology Operations LLC v SSS Auto Parts Pty Ltd* [2019] FCA 97.
153   Ibid.
154   See R. Reynolds, N. Stoinanoff and A. Roy, *Intellectual Property: Text and Essential Cases* (5th edn, Sydney: Federation Press, 2015) 578.

7.9 Remedies

The relief awarded where a registered design has been infringed includes an injunction and either damages or an account of profits.[155] Additional damages may also be awarded in certain circumstances.[156] In situations where there has been an unjustified threat of infringement proceedings, there is provision for declarations, injunctions and damages.

As was discussed in relation to the actions for infringement above,[157] the court may refuse to award damages or an account of profits, or reduce the amount of damages awarded if the defendant satisfies the court:

- for *direct infringement* – that the defendant was not aware that the design was registered and that the defendant had taken all reasonable steps to ascertain whether the design was registered;[158] or
- for *secondary infringement* – that at the time of the infringement, the defendant was not aware, and could not reasonably have been expected to be aware, that the design was registered.[159]

The defendant will be taken to have been aware that the design was registered if the product or its packaging is marked so as to indicate registration of the design.[160]

7.9.1 Unjustified threats

A person threatened by another person with infringement proceedings in respect of a design may seek: a declaration that the threat is unjustified, an injunction preventing the continuation of the threat, and damages.[161] A threat made before a certificate of examination has been issued in respect of a design is an unjustified threat.[162] The threat may be made by means of circulars, advertisements or otherwise.[163]

The mere notification of the existence of a registered design does not constitute an unjustified threat.[164] However, the courts will be quick to infer a threat if a person goes beyond this and says something like 'our clients are prepared to protect their interests with the utmost vigour'.[165] Legal representatives, patent attorneys and trade mark attorneys will not be liable

---

155 *Designs Act 2003* (Cth) s 75(1).
156 Ibid s 75(3). For flagrant infringement, see *Review Australia Pty Ltd v Innovative Lifestyle Investments Pty Ltd* (2008) 166 FCR 358 where $10 000 damages were awarded as additional damages. See also *Ahiida Pty Ltd v JB Trading Group Pty Ltd* [2016] FCCA 3146, where $20 000 was awarded as additional damages, not for flagrancy but for 'other relevant matters': see at [85], [88].
157 At 7.7.
158 *Designs Act 2003* (Cth) s 75(2)(a)(i)–(ii).
159 Ibid s 75(4).
160 Ibid s 75(2)(a)(i)–(ii).
161 Ibid s 77(1).
162 Ibid s 77(3).
163 Ibid s 77(2).
164 Ibid s 80.
165 *Rosedale Associated Manufacturers Ltd v Airfix Products Ltd* [1956] RPC 360, 363.

for threats made on behalf of their clients.[166] However, a client cannot escape liability by saying 'My lawyer did that; not me'.[167]

7.10 Copyright–design overlap

The protection offered by the registered design system has the potential to overlap with copyright protection[168] because the owner of copyright in a two-dimensional artistic work has the right to reproduce the work in a three-dimensional format.[169] For example, a chair protected as a registered design could also potentially be protected as an artistic work (on the basis of copyright in the drawing of the chair). As the two-dimensional drawing is also able to be protected when the chair is reproduced in three dimensions, this means that the design of the chair would be, potentially, protected by both design and copyright law. There is also the possibility that the chair may be protected as a sculpture. Dual protection enables owners to manipulate the protection they receive in a way that undermines the policy goals of intellectual property law. The main concern is that while design law is limited to ten-year protection and is only available for designs that are new and distinctive, copyright protection is not only available for much longer (the life of the author plus seventy years), but is also easier to acquire.

While there are a number of exceptions, Australian law largely rejects cumulative protection of a design by both copyright and design laws. The law in this area is governed by ss 74–77 of the *Copyright Act 1968* (Cth).[170] The broad policy approach that underpins these provisions is that artistic works that are commercially exploited 'as three-dimensional designs should generally be denied copyright protection and be protected, if at all, under the designs legislation'.[171] A submission to ACIP's 2014 review of the designs system noted that the level of confusion in relation to the copyright–design overlap compels reform.[172]

As the law stands, there are two situations where copyright protection will no longer be available to protect an artistic work. These are: (1) where a corresponding design has been registered, and (2) where a corresponding design has been industrially manufactured.

7.10.1 Registration of a corresponding design

Section 75 of the *Copyright Act 1968* (Cth) provides that where copyright subsists in an artistic work and a 'corresponding design' is or has been registered under the *Designs Act 1906* (Cth) or the *Designs Act 2003* (Cth), it is not an infringement of that copyright to reproduce the work by embodying the corresponding design in a product. A 'corresponding design' is defined in s 74 of the *Copyright Act 1968* as the visual features of shape or configuration that, when

---

166   *Designs Act 2003* (Cth) s 79.
167   *Wanem Pty Ltd v Tekiela* (1990) 19 IPR 435, 444.
168   See C. Golvan, 'The copyright/design overlap: An appropriate balance under the new design legislation?' (2004) 59 *Intellectual Property Forum* 36.
169   *Copyright Act 1968* (Cth) s 21(3).
170   Amended by the *Designs (Consequential Amendments) Act 2003* (Cth), effective from 17 June 2004.
171   *Gold Peg International Pty Ltd v Kovan Engineering (Australia) Pty Ltd* (2005) 67 IPR 497, [201].
172   Submission by Law Council Australia to ACIP, 'Options Paper', above n 13.

embodied in a product, result in a reproduction of that work.[173] This definition was intended to reflect the policy that the restrictions on dual protection should only arise in relation to three-dimensional designs. In line with this, most commentators have suggested that s 75 will not apply where an artistic work (such as a painting) is applied to a flat surface (such as a T-shirt).[174] Accordingly, artistic works exploited in two dimensions as visual features of pattern or ornamentation (but not 'embodied in a product') will retain copyright protection as they will be excluded from the operation of s 75.[175] It would apply, however, to deny copyright protection for an engineering drawing of a chair that was subsequently registered as a three-dimensional design.

Unlike the case where a corresponding design has been applied industrially, s 75 applies where the artistic work is a building, a model of a building or a work of artistic craftsmanship. The upshot of s 75 is that where a registered design is a three-dimensional reproduction of an artistic work, copyright in the artistic work will not be infringed where an object that embodies the artistic work is reproduced. One of the consequences of registration is that the designer is no longer able to rely on copyright to protect the artistic work when it is reproduced in a three-dimensional format.[176]

The scope of the prohibition on dual protection was extended by the 2003 *Designs Act*, which introduced a new defence of s 77A into the *Copyright Act 1968* (Cth).[177] While s 75 primarily deals with the reproduction (or manufacturing) of a product that embodies an artistic work, s 77A extends the defence to include situations where the reproduction occurs in the course of, or is incidental to, the making, selling or letting for hire of the product that embodies the artistic work. That is, the defence now applies to marketing materials such as packaging and advertisements as well as activities that occur during the manufacturing process. This might occur, for example, where a person uses technical drawings or where they make a cast or a mould embodying a corresponding registered design in relation to the artistic work.

7.10.2 Industrial application of a corresponding design

The second limitation on the potential for dual protection arises under s 77 of the *Copyright Act 1968* (Cth). Subject to a limited number of exceptions, this provides a defence to an action for infringement of copyright in an artistic work where a 'corresponding design' has not been registered as a design, but has been 'applied industrially' whether in Australia or overseas.[178] The section also applies where a complete patent specification or a representation of the

---

173   See *Polo/Lauren Co LP v Ziliani Holdings Pty Ltd* (2008) 173 FCR 266, 279–83; *Digga Australia Pty Ltd v Norm Engineering Pty Ltd* (2008) 166 FCR 268, [84].
174   *Copyright Act 1968* (Cth) s 74(1). 'Embodied in a product includes "woven into, impressed on or worked into the product"': at s 74(2). It is unclear whether this would include situations where an image is reproduced on a flat surface, such as wallpaper or a T-shirt (although it is possible that in this context it could be argued that as the polo player device was stitched on that the image has been 'impressed on' the product): see *Polo/Lauren Co LP v Ziliani Holdings Pty Ltd* (2008) 173 FCR 266.
175   In *Seafolly Pty Ltd v Fewstone Pty Ltd* (2014) 313 ALR 41, consistent with the Full Federal Court's reasoning in *Polo/Lauren Co LP v Ziliani Holdings Pty Ltd* (2008) 173 FCR 266, the Senorita diamond pattern embroidery (smocking) design was held not to be 'embodied' in the Senorita garments. Dodds-Streeton J noted at [482] that the smocking had stronger claims to being conceptually indistinguishable from the garment than the logo in *Polo/Lauren*, as it was not able to exist independently.
176   This is subject to the proviso in relation to false registration set out in *Copyright Act 1968* (Cth) s 76.
177   *Digga Australia Pty Ltd v Norm Engineering Pty Ltd* (2008) 166 FCR 268.
178   *Gold Peg International Pty Ltd v Kovan Engineering (Australia) Pty Ltd* (2005) 67 IPR 497, [203].

product is published in Australia.[179] While the meaning of 'corresponding design' in this context is the same as with s 75, the exception does not apply where the artistic work is a building, a model of a building or a work of artistic craftsmanship.[180] The prohibition on dual protection under s 77 was extended in 2003 by the introduction of s 77A. The upshot is that s 77 now operates where the reproduction occurs in the course of, or is incidental to, the making, selling or letting for hire of the product that embodies the artistic work. Section 77(1)(d) provides that for s 77 to operate, the corresponding design must not have been registered or registrable under either the 2003 or 1906 *Designs Act*.

According to the *Copyright Regulations 1969* (Cth), a design is taken to be 'applied industrially' if it is applied to more than fifty articles or to one or more articles (other than handmade articles) manufactured in lengths or pieces. For the purposes of the regulation, a design is taken to be applied to an article if the design is applied to the article by a process (whether a process of printing, embossing or otherwise); or the design is reproduced on or in the article in the course of the production of the article.[181] While reg 17 stipulates that a design is taken to have been applied industrially where it is applied to fifty or more articles, this is not an exhaustive definition.[182]

7.11 Future reforms

In November 2019, IP Australia began a review of the Australian designs system 'to better understand what drives visual design innovation and what changes may be needed to realise greater benefits to the Australian economy'.[183] IP Australia is seeking views on proposed options for improving the design system, to implement accepted recommendations from ACIP's review. Three topics are being examined: the scope of design protection; increased flexibility for designers; and simplifying and clarifying the system.

Perhaps this review is an opportunity for IP Australia to engage with the emerging international Right to Repair movement.[184] The movement, which began as car repair legislation in Massachusetts in 2012 and spread to the European Union in 2018 through amendments to the Ecodesign Directive[185] puts pressure on manufacturers to make their products easier to repair and fix. It empowers consumers with rights to repair their goods, and supports environmental goals by pushing back against growing levels of e-waste and planned obsolescence of goods. Australia's design system would benefit from reflecting on developments in Right to Repair as well as in 3D printing.[186]

---

179   *Copyright Act 1968* (Cth) s 77(1A).
180   Ibid s 77(1)(a). A building or a model of a building does not include a portable building such as a shed: at s 77(5).
181   *Copyright Regulations 1969* (Cth) reg 17.
182   See *Safe Sport Australia Pty Ltd v Puma Australia Pty Ltd* (1985) 4 IPR 120, 126 (King J), cited in *Gold Peg International Pty Ltd v Kovan Engineering (Australia) Pty Ltd* (2005) 67 IPR 497, [210].
183   IP Australia, *Talking Design: Views from Australia's Visual Design Ecosystem* (2019).
184   L. C. Grinvald and O. Tur-Sinai, 'Intellectual property and the right to repair' (2019) 88 *Fordham Law Review* (forthcoming).
185   See European Parliament News, 'Ecodesign directive: From energy efficiency to recycling' (24 May 2018) www.europarl.europa.eu/news/en.
186   D. Mendis, M. Lemley and M. R. Rimmer, *3D Printing and Beyond: Intellectual Property and Regulation* (Cheltenham: Edward Elgar Publishing, 2019).

PART III

CONFIDENTIAL INFORMATION, PATENTS AND PLANT BREEDER'S RIGHTS

8

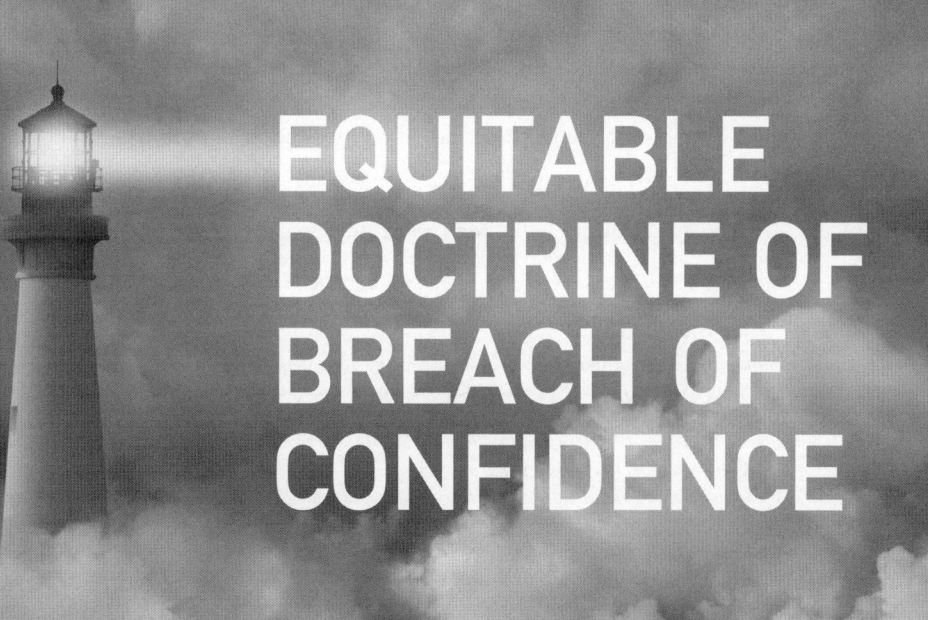

EQUITABLE DOCTRINE OF BREACH OF CONFIDENCE

8.1 Introduction

8.1.1 Overview

The creation and open transmission of ideas and information are important features of a democratic society. However, many occasions arise when a person wants to communicate information to another in confidence on the understanding that there will be no further dissemination or use of the information without consent. This may arise in the context of business, government, personal and other kinds of relationships. The value of information in each type of context will differ. Businesses and corporations are usually concerned to protect information that has commercial value.[1] Governments need to protect their ability to make decisions on sensitive issues. Individuals are concerned about protection of reputation and privacy.[2] In the case of Indigenous groups, their concern may be to protect the secrets of their tribal group.[3] Secrets in business are especially vulnerable to indirect acquisition and industrial espionage using improper and surreptitious means.[4]

No discrete body of law in Australia protects confidential information. Duties of confidence may arise in many different legal contexts, including protection of government secrets, business secrets and personal privacy, and requests for information under the relevant freedom of information legislation.[5] The doctrine of legal professional privilege imposes obligations of confidentiality,[6] but we distinguish these from confidential information that is the source of the plaintiff's rights.[7] People who have statutory powers to obtain information may owe specific duties,[8] and issues of confidentiality can arise in connection with arbitration proceedings.[9] There are also some statutory provisions that impose specific obligations of confidence[10] and others that deal with protecting those who disclose confidential information.[11] In certain types

---

[1] See generally G. A. Hughes (ed), *Dean's Law of Trade Secrets and Privacy* (3rd edn, Sydney: Law Book Company, 2018); J. D. Heydon, M. J. Leeming and P. G. Turner, *Meagher, Gummow and Lehane's Equity: Doctrines and Remedies* (5th edn, Sydney: Butterworths, 2015); J. Glover, *Equity, Restitution and Fraud* (Sydney: LexisNexis Butterworths, 2004) ch 6; F. Gurry, *Breach of Confidence* (Oxford: Clarendon Press, 1984); T. Aplin and F. Gurry, *Gurry on Breach of Confidence: The Protection of Confidential Information* (2nd edn, Oxford: Oxford University Press, 2012).

[2] For example, *Argyll v Argyll* [1967] 1 Ch 302. See also *Dean's Law of Trade Secrets and Privacy*, above n 1, pt 2.

[3] *Foster v Mountford & Rigby Ltd* (1976) 14 ALR 71.

[4] *Franklin v Giddins* [1978] Qd R 72.

[5] M. Paterson, *Freedom of Information and Privacy in Australia: Information Access 2.0* (Chatswood: LexisNexis Butterworths, 2015); Australian Law Reform Commission, *For Your Information: Australian Privacy Law and Practice* (Report No 108, May 2008).

[6] S. B. McNicol, *The Law of Privilege* (Sydney: Law Book Company, 1992); *PhotoCure ASA v Queen's University at Kingston* (2002) 56 IPR 86, 95–9; *Prince Jefri Bolkiah v KPMG* [1999] 2 AC 222; *AG Australia Holdings Ltd v Burton* (2002) 58 NSWLR 464.

[7] *Corrs Pavey Whiting & Byrne v Collector of Customs (Vic)* (1987) 14 FCR 434, 455; *Crowley v Murphy* (1981) 52 FLR 123, 145–6.

[8] See, for example, *Aboriginal Heritage Act 1988* (SA) s 35; *Hughes Aircraft Systems International v Airservices Australia* (1997) 76 FCR 151; *Hoechst UK Ltd v Chemiculture Ltd* [1993] FSR 270.

[9] *Esso Australia Resources Ltd v Plowman* (1995) 183 CLR 10.

[10] *Corporations Act 2001* (Cth) s 183(1). See, for example, *Leica Geosystems Pty Ltd v Koudstaal (No 3)* (2014) 109 IPR 1.

[11] See, for example, *Public Interest Disclosure Act 2013* (Cth); *Public Interest Disclosure Act 2012* (ACT); *Public Interest Disclosures Act 1994* (NSW); *Public Interest Disclosure Act 2008* (NT); *Public Interest Disclosure Act 2010* (Qld); *Public Sector Act 2009* (SA); *Whistleblowers Protection Act 1993* (SA); *Public Interest Disclosures Act 2002* (Tas); *Protected Disclosure Act 2012* (Vic); *Public Interest Disclosure Act 2003* (WA).

of relationships of trust and confidence, such as client and solicitor, patient and doctor, customer and banker, and employee and employer, the law will imply a term to respect confidences into the relationship.[12] An obligation of confidence may also arise in consequence of a court order to disclose confidential information to a restricted range of persons, such as nominated experts and lawyers.[13]

In many instances, the source of the duty of confidence will be contractual.[14] Nevertheless, equitable obligations of confidence may coexist with comparable contractual obligations, thus providing the aggrieved party with access to the equitable remedy of an account of profits.[15] The courts will often imply a contractual term to fill the void if there is no express term, or if the term of the contract is in restraint of trade and unenforceable.[16] Express terms that impose obligations of confidentiality, often in combination with a restrictive covenant, commonly appear in situations where there is an employment contract, a deed of release,[17] business or industry source funding of research within a university, or disclosure of an invention to a potential business partner.[18] Such covenants may involve a direct restraint against the use of confidential information[19] or a restraint on engaging in certain conduct where use could be made of the confidential information to the promisee's detriment.[20]

While recognising the multiple sources for protection of confidences, this chapter is concerned principally with the protection that is available under the equitable action for breach of confidence.

8.1.2 Subsistence of equitable obligations of confidence alongside comparable contractual obligations

When a contract contains express confidentiality obligations, an issue may arise whether the parties have *excluded* equitable obligations of confidence or whether the obligations coexist. Coexistence becomes an issue especially when the injured party seeks an account of profits,[21] a discretionary remedy that is available for a successful equitable claim for breach of confidence.[22] A pecuniary remedy in contract is limited to damages.

---

12   See Glover, *Equity, Restitution and Fraud*, above n 1, chs 2–4.
13   *Integrated Medical Technology Pty Ltd v Gilbert* [2014] QSC 227.
14   *Maggbury Pty Ltd v Hafele Australia Pty Ltd* (2001) 210 CLR 181; *Faccenda Chicken Ltd v Fowler* [1987] Ch 117, 135; *Meagher, Gummow and Lehane's Equity*, above n 1, [42.050].
15   See below at 8.4.1.
16   *Triplex Safety Glass Co Ltd v Scorah* [1938] Ch 211; *Wessex Dairies Pty Ltd v Smith* [1935] 2 KB 80; *Vokes Ltd v Heather* (1945) 62 RPC 135); *Deta Nominees Pty Ltd v Viscount Plastic Products Pty Ltd* [1979] VR 167; *Maggbury Pty Ltd v Hafele Australia Pty Ltd* (2001) 210 CLR 181.
17   *Miles v Genesys Wealth Advisers Ltd* (2009) 201 IR 1.
18   *Maggbury Pty Ltd v Hafele Australia Pty Ltd* (2001) 210 CLR 181.
19   *Wright v Gasweld Pty Ltd* (1991) 22 NSWLR 317; *Del Casale v Artedomus (Australia) Pty Ltd* (2007) 73 IPR 326.
20   *Miles v Genesys Wealth Advisers Ltd* (2009) 201 IR 1.
21   *SAI Global Property Division Pty Ltd v Johnstone* (2016) 122 IPR 210 [42]. It is relevant also in the context of employment. See below at 8.9.1.
22   *Australian Medic-Care Co Ltd v Hamilton Pharmaceutical Pty Ltd* (2009) 261 ALR 501, [674]; *Peter Pan Manufacturing Corp v Corsets Silhouette Ltd* [1964] 1 WLR 96.

In *Optus Networks Pty Ltd v Telstra Corp Ltd*,[23] the Full Federal Court confirmed that the equitable duty of confidence coexists alongside the contractual duty of confidence unless the contract excludes access to equitable principles and rights. The court distinguished the facts from a number of authorities[24] that questioned coexistence of rights of confidentiality and confirmed that '[t]he notion that no equitable duty of confidence arises where there is a comparable contractual duty is opposed to much authority'.[25]

In some cases, the contractual effect of a confidentiality clause may be 'only to the extent that information falling within the three stipulated species [supplier, business of the supplier, products of the supplier] is itself confidential information under the general law'.[26] In such a case, Finn J described the contractual duty as 'parasitic upon the equitable duty of confidence' and found it necessary to refer only to the breach of confidence principles.[27]

It is clear that a contract might exclude the operation of the equitable obligation.[28] In *Gold & Copper Resources Pty Ltd v Newcrest Operations Ltd*, Stevenson J concluded that a statement that the agreement is 'the entire agreement and understanding between the parties on everything connected with the subject matter of this Agreement'[29] is effective to exclude the equitable obligation of confidence.

When the contract includes an *implied* obligation of confidence, a substantial body of authority supports its coexistence with equitable obligations of confidence and courts usually do not differentiate between the two sources for the content of the confidentiality obligations.[30]

8.2 Origins of the equitable doctrine of breach of confidence

In the absence of contract, relief is available on equitable grounds under the breach of confidence action.[31] The apparent origins of this action lie in the practice of equity to protect secrets confided by one party to another in recognised relationships of trust and

---

23 (2010) 265 ALR 281, [29], [34]–[38].
24 *Coles Supermarkets Australia Pty Ltd v FKP Ltd* [2008] FCA 1915, [63]–[64]; *Del Casale v Artedomus (Australia) Pty Ltd* (2007) 73 IPR 326, [118]; *Deta Nominees Pty Ltd v Viscount Plastic Products Pty Ltd* [1979] VR 167, 195. See also *Streetscape Projects (Australia) Pty Ltd v City of Sydney* (2013) 85 NSWLR 196, [149]–[162].
25 *Optus Networks Pty Ltd v Telstra Corp Ltd* (2010) 265 ALR 281, [38]; *Titan Group Pty Ltd v Steriline Manufacturing Pty Ltd* (1990) 19 IPR 353, 388.
26 *Australian Medic-Care Co Ltd v Hamilton Pharmaceutical Pty Ltd* (2009) 261 ALR 501, [659].
27 Ibid [628]–[629].
28 Meagher, Gummow and Lehane's *Equity*, above n 1, [42.050]; *Deta Nominees Pty Ltd v Viscount Plastic Products Pty Ltd* [1979] VR 167, 191; *Del Casale v Artedomus (Australia) Pty Ltd* (2007) 73 IPR 326, [18].
29 [2013] NSWSC 281, [89]–[96].
30 *Concut Pty Ltd v Worrell* (2000) 176 ALR 693, [26]; *University of Western Australia v Gray* (2009) 179 FCR 346, [161]–[162]; *Robb v Green* [1895] 2 QB 315. See generally *Gurry on Breach of Confidence*, above n 1, [4.48]–[4.63].
31 *Moorgate Tobacco Co Ltd v Philip Morris Ltd (No 2)* (1984) 156 CLR 414, 438 (Deane J); *Attorney-General (UK) v Guardian Newspapers Ltd (No 2)* [1988] 3 All ER 545; *Saltman Engineering Co Ltd v Campbell Engineering Co Ltd* (1948) 65 RPC 203; *Seager v Copydex Ltd* [1967] 2 All ER 415; *Coco v AN Clark (Engineers) Ltd* [1969] RPC 41.

confidence.[32] However, the doctrine soon encompassed a wider range of circumstances in which disclosure amounts to a breach of confidence. The wider doctrine originated in two lines of cases in the eighteenth and nineteenth centuries where courts of Chancery intervened to protect confidences outside the usual relationships of trust.[33] One basis seemed to be the common law right of property that was akin to copyright protection. Here, courts of Chancery restrained unauthorised use or publication of unpublished literary or artistic works. An example is that of *Prince Albert v Strange*,[34] where the court restrained publication of any information whatsoever concerning an unpublished catalogue of etchings made by Prince Albert and Queen Victoria for their own private enjoyment. This line of authority required the information to exist in a tangible form. It ceased when copyright protection extended to unpublished works in 1911.

The jurisdictional basis for the second line of cases was unclear, but arose independently of any contractual obligation or common law right of property in an unpublished work. In *Abernethy v Hutchinson*,[35] a remedy was available to prevent an intending publisher from reproducing lectures that Mr Abernethy delivered orally to a limited audience of students. It was not possible to base the action on the common law right of property in unpublished lectures because there were no written lectures. Furthermore, there was no contractual basis for a remedy because there was no contract between the lecturer and the intending publisher. An underlying sense of unconscionability that appears in the judgment may have influenced the decision.

These early cases lay the foundation for the modern action, but there is no clear definition as to the jurisdictional basis for the action. In some cases, property provided the basis;[36] in others it was founded on contract[37] and in yet others on trust and confidence.[38] Although scholars debate the appropriate jurisdictional basis for the protection of confidential information,[39] Australian authorities are clear that property provides no rational basis for the action.[40] Nevertheless, it is clear that 'trade secrets may be transferred, held in trust and charged'[41] and the effect of protection provided under the doctrine of breach of confidence

---

32 L. S. Sealy, 'Fiduciary Relationships' (1962) 20(1) *Cambridge Law Journal* 69; P. D. Finn, *Fiduciary Obligations* (Sydney: Law Book Company, 1977) ch 19.
33 *Abernethy v Hutchinson* (1825) 3 LJOS (Ch) 209, 1 H & Tw 28, 47 ER 1313; *Prince Albert v Strange* (1849) 1 H & Tw 1, 47 ER 1302; *Morison v Moat* (1851) 9 Hare 241, 68 ER 492.
34 (1849) 1 H & Tw 1, 47 ER 1302.
35 (1825) 3 LJOS (Ch) 209, 1 H & Tw 28, 47 ER 1313.
36 *Morison v Moat* (1851) 9 Hare 241, 68 ER 492; *Prince Albert v Strange* (1849) 1 H & Tw 1, 47 ER 1302.
37 *Saltman Engineering Co Ltd v Campbell Engineering Co Ltd* (1948) 65 RPC 203.
38 *Morison v Moat* (1851) 9 Hare 241, 68 ER 492.
39 J. Stuckey, 'The equitable action for breach of confidence: Is information ever property?' (1981) 9 *Sydney Law Review* 402; S. Ricketson, 'Confidential information – a new proprietary interest? Part I' (1977) 11 *Melbourne University Law Review* 223; S. Ricketson, 'Confidential information – a new proprietary interest? Part II' (1978) 11 *Melbourne University Law Review* 289.
40 See, for example, *Moorgate Tobacco Co Ltd v Philip Morris Ltd (No 2)* (1984) 156 CLR 414, 437–8; *Federal Commissioner of Taxation v United Aircraft Corp* (1943) 68 CLR 525, 534; *Brent v Federal Commissioner of Taxation* (1971) 125 CLR 418, 425. Compare *Smith Kline & French Laboratories (Australia) Ltd v Secretary, Department of Community Services and Health* (1990) 22 FCR 73, 121.
41 *Farah Constructions Pty Ltd v Say-Dee Pty Ltd* (2007) 230 CLR 89, [118]. For the meaning of 'trade secret', see below at 8.7.1.

can imbue certain types of confidential information with proprietary characteristics.[42] Rather, the better explanation is in terms of the 'notion of an obligation of conscience arising from the circumstances in or through which the information was communicated or obtained'.[43] This emphasises that a person who receives information in confidence must not take unfair advantage of it; the action requires an unconscientious use of the information.[44]

The existence of the jurisdiction for an equitable action in breach of confidence in Australia is clear.[45] The general thrust of the action is to provide a person who discloses secret ideas and information to another in confidence with rights to restrain the threatened or actual unauthorised use or disclosure. An obligation to protect confidences arises because of the subject matter and circumstances in which the subject matter comes into the hands of the person charged with the breach.[46] There is no requirement for a tangible record of the secrets and remedies apply equally to protect the conveyance of ideas in confidence either orally or in some material form.[47] However, such cases that involve oral disclosure may not proceed far in practice due to problems of proof.

8.3 Elements of the action

The modern doctrine emerged from *Saltman Engineering Co Ltd v Campbell Engineering Co Ltd*.[48] Its significance was that Lord Greene recognised that an action for breach of confidence was possible in the absence of a contract. The elements of the action were later summarised by Megarry J in *Coco v AN Clark (Engineers) Ltd*.[49] That case involved the disclosure of details including the prototype, drawings and other information in pre-contractual negotiations for a joint venture for the production of a motor-assisted cycle ('Coco') that the plaintiff had designed. The negotiations collapsed and the plaintiff claimed unsuccessfully that the defendant had made unauthorised use of information communicated in the course of negotiations. The elements of the action were summarised as follows:

- that the information was of a confidential nature – not in the public domain;
- that the information was communicated in circumstances importing an obligation of confidence;

---

42 *Smith Kline & French Laboratories (Australia) Ltd v Secretary, Department of Community Services and Health* (1990) 22 FCR 73, 121; *Farah Constructions Pty Ltd v Say-Dee Pty Ltd* (2007) 230 CLR 89, [118]. See below at 8.5.
43 *Moorgate Tobacco Co Ltd v Philip Morris Ltd (No 2)* (1984) 156 CLR 414, 438; *Breen v Williams* (1996) 186 CLR 71, [12] (Brennan CJ); *Saltman Engineering Co Ltd v Campbell Engineering Co Ltd* (1948) 65 RPC 203; *Stephens v Avery* [1988] Ch 449, 456.
44 *Smith Kline & French Laboratories (Australia) Ltd v Secretary, Department of Community Services and Health* (1991) 28 FCR 291, 304.
45 See, for example, *Moorgate Tobacco Co Ltd v Philip Morris Ltd (No 2)* (1984) 156 CLR 414; *Commonwealth v John Fairfax & Sons Ltd* (1980) 147 CLR 39; *Johns v Australian Securities Commission* (1993) 178 CLR 408, 427 (Brennan J), 436 (Dawson J), 455 (Toohey J), 474 (McHugh J), 459–60 (Gaudron J).
46 *Ansell Rubber Co Pty Ltd v Allied Rubber Industries Pty Ltd* [1967] VR 37, 40.
47 *Fraser v Thames Television Ltd* [1984] QB 44, 64.
48 (1948) 65 RPC 203.
49 [1969] RPC 41.

- that there has been unauthorised use of the information to the detriment of the person communicating it.

These early principles have been refined to respond to the complex circumstances in which a person might seek to protect confidences.[50] For example, it is clear that:

- no relationship of confidence is required;[51]
- there can be threatened misuse;[52]
- the information must be identified with specificity before there can be a successful action;[53]
- the imposition of the obligation must be reasonable;[54]
- the information was received (as contrasted with communicated) in such circumstances as to import an obligation of confidence;[55] and
- an action can be brought to restrain disclosure by third parties.[56]

A necessary implication is that the information must be traceable to a particular source. It cannot be something 'which has become so completely merged in the mind of the person informed that it is impossible to say from what precise quarter he derived the information which led to the knowledge which he is found to possess'.[57]

While the need for detriment has appeared in the past as an element that normally is required,[58] it may not necessarily be the case or appear when courts list the required elements for the action.[59] The issue of detriment occasionally appears in discussion of the effect of use of the confidential information,[60] but it is more likely to arise in the context of remedies. In *Australian Medic-Care Co Ltd v Hamilton Pharmaceutical Pty Ltd*,[61] Finn J was satisfied that an unauthorised disclosure of a manufacturing method had occurred, but no use was ever made of it. Accordingly, although the duty of confidence was breached, 'no loss (other than nominal damages for breach of contract) was suffered by it, nor was any profit made using it'.[62]

---

50 *Corrs Pavey Whiting & Byrne v Collector of Customs (Vic)* (1987) 14 FCR 434, 443.
51 *Franklin v Giddins* [1978] Qd R 72; *Sullivan v Sclanders & Goldwell International Pty Ltd* (2000) 77 SASR 419; *Australian Broadcasting Corporation v Lenah Game Meats Pty Ltd* (2001) 208 CLR 199.
52 *Commonwealth v John Fairfax & Sons Ltd* (1980) 147 CLR 39, 50–1; *O'Brien v Komesaroff* (1982) 150 CLR 310, 326–8.
53 *O'Brien v Komesaroff* (1982) 150 CLR 310, 326.
54 *Dunford & Elliott Ltd v Johnson & Firth Brown Ltd* [1978] FSR 143, 148.
55 *Corrs Pavey Whiting & Byrne v Collector of Customs (Vic)* (1987) 14 FCR 434, 443; *Franklin v Giddins* [1978] Qd R 72, 80.
56 *Talbot v General Television Corp Pty Ltd* [1980] VR 224; *Wheatley v Bell* [1982] 2 NSWLR 544, 550; *Johns v Australian Securities Commission* (1993) 178 CLR 408, 460, 474; *Earl v Nationwide News Pty Ltd* [2013] NSWSC 839, [17]; *TICA Default Tenancy Control Pty Ltd v Datakatch Pty Ltd* (2016) 120 IPR 98, [146]; J. Stuckey, 'The liability of innocent third parties implicated in another's breach of confidence' (1981) 4 *University of New South Wales Law Journal* 73.
57 *Terrapin Ltd v Builders Supply Co (Hayes) Ltd* [1967] RPC 375, 391.
58 *Coco v AN Clark (Engineers) Ltd* [1969] RPC 41, 48; *Westpac Banking Corp v John Fairfax Group Pty Ltd* (1991) 19 IPR 513, 524; *Commonwealth v John Fairfax & Sons Ltd* (1980) 147 CLR 39, 51–4.
59 *Optus Networks Pty Ltd v Telstra Corp Ltd* (2010) 265 ALR 281, [39]; *Australian Medic-Care Co Ltd v Hamilton Pharmaceutical Pty Ltd* (2009) 261 ALR 501, [632]; *Corrs Pavey Whiting & Byrne v Collector of Customs (Vic)* (1987) 14 FCR 434, 443; *NP Generations Pty Ltd v Feneley* (2001) 80 SASR 151, 157–8.
60 *National Surgical Pty Ltd v McPhee* (2010) 87 IPR 602, [37], [41]–[42].
61 (2009) 261 ALR 501.
62 Ibid [660].

It seems that a person may impose a duty of confidence *after* communication of information as long as the material remains confidential and the confider informs the recipient of the obligation before they read the information.[63]

8.3.1 Must be able to identify the information with specificity

The plaintiff must identify the relevant confidential information with precision in an action for breach of confidence so that identification is possible.[64] However, the degree of particularity will depend on the circumstances of each case.[65] Very precise identification of confidential information will be especially important in cases where the parties are involved in 'closely substitutable fields of common endeavour', such as supply of immediately substitutable retractable syringes.[66] In contrast, an 'overly narrow' approach to the degree of specificity required for a pleading may be inappropriate in an application for summary judgment.[67] Interlocutory proceedings do not justify less precision in the identification of the confidential parts.[68] However, compliance with the standard in an application for an interlocutory injunction may not require the plaintiff to provide the confidential documents as exhibits in evidence in support when the entire contents of those documents are claimed to be confidential and the defendant knew what the listed documents were.[69]

Merely identifying a document or range of documents that contain confidential information, or making claims in general or global terms, is insufficient to found the cause of action. It is necessary to identify the particular contents of the documents for which the confider asserts protection, for two reasons.[70] First, such claims provide insufficient detail to satisfy a court that the 'information so described was imparted or received or retained ... in circumstances which give rise to an obligation of confidence.'[71] Second, the lack of precision makes it impossible for the court to frame a clear injunction in terms that enable people to determine what they can freely use,[72] should relief against misuse of confidential information be granted.[73]

However, not all circumstances require disaggregation of information 'with a view to determining which information is available in the public domain and which is not'.[74]

---

63   *English & American Insurance Co Ltd v Herbert Smith* [1988] FSR 232.
64   *Mancini v Mancini* [1999] NSWSC 800, [7]; *O'Brien v Komesaroff* (1982) 150 CLR 310, 326–7; *The Gadget Shop Ltd v The Bug.Com Ltd* [2001] FSR 26, [65]; *Sent v John Fairfax Publication Pty Ltd* [2002] VSC 429, [65]–[71]; *Carindale Country Club Estate Pty Ltd v Astill* (1993) 42 FCR 307, 314–5.
65   *Sent v John Fairfax Publication Pty Ltd* [2002] VSC 429, [67]–[69]; *Rapid Metal Developments (Australia) Pty Ltd v Anderson Formrite Pty Ltd* [2005] WASC 255.
66   *Retractable Technologies v Occupational & Medical Innovations Ltd* (2007) 72 IPR 58, [104].
67   *Manderson M & F Consulting (a firm) v Incitec Pivot Ltd* [2011] VSCA 444, [13]–[21].
68   *CMI-Centers for Medical Innovation GmbH v Phytopharm plc* [1999] FSR 235, [27].
69   *The Gadget Shop Ltd v The Bug.Com Ltd* [2001] FSR 26, [65].
70   *O'Brien v Komesaroff* (1982) 150 CLR 310, 324–8; *Corrs Pavey Whiting & Byrne v Collector of Customs (Vic)* (1987) 14 FCR 434, 443.
71   *Independent Management Resources Pty Ltd v Brown* [1987] VR 605, 609 [40]; *Carindale Country Club Estate Pty Ltd v Astill* (1993) 42 FCR 307, 314–5.
72   *Miles v Genesys Wealth Advisers Ltd* (2009) 201 IR 1, [23]; *Amway Corp v Eurway International Ltd* [1973] FSR 213, 219; *Corrs Pavey Whiting & Byrne v Collector of Customs (Vic)* (1987) 14 FCR 434, 443.
73   *Carindale Country Club Estate Pty Ltd v Astill* (1993) 42 FCR 307, 314.
74   *DC Payments Pty Ltd v Next Payments Pty Ltd* [2016] VSC 315, [59].

The protection provided by equity recognises that information that is constructed solely from materials in the public domain with 'skill, effort, time and money expended in acquiring, collating and producing the information in a readily workable and useful form' can possess the necessary quality of confidence.[75] Examples are customer lists and compilations of statistics. However, as Wigney J observed in *Sports Data Pty Ltd v Prozone Sports Australia Pty Ltd*, the consequence of specifying confidential information as a compilation or compendium of data may be that 'it is difficult to see how there could be said to be unauthorised use unless the entire compendium, or at least a substantial part of it, is used'.[76]

Practical difficulties with identification of the confidential information can arise also when parties merge their individual databases but fail to keep the data sourced from each database separate and identifiable.[77] They may also arise when the plaintiff no longer has access to the information to be able to identify it with specificity. In *Matthews v Clifton*,[78] the directors of two companies in liquidation and receivership intervened in proceedings taken by the appointed liquidator for an order that the receivers give up possession and control of four company computers. They sought an order for equitable protection of confidential information contained on those computers: information that was unrelated to the company business and that included privileged communications with their solicitor in emails. One of the liquidator's objections was a failure of the directors to detail the confidential information with specificity. The directors identified the confidential content on the computers with reference to categories of documents including emails, taxation returns and financial statements. A number of considerations persuaded White J to accept what would otherwise be a general level of specificity. First, the court could order a regime under which to identify the specific confidential material. Second, the claim identified the categories of documents said to be confidential. Third, his Honour was wary of ignoring claims of professional privilege to some of the correspondence. Finally, it was plausible that the computers would contain information that is unrelated to the business of the two companies.[79]

8.3.2 Information must have the necessary quality of confidence

Information will not be protected unless it has 'the necessary quality of confidence about it, namely, it must not be something which is public property and public knowledge'.[80] This is an elusive concept: Finn wrote in 1977, 'no general definition can be given of confidential information – secrecy in this context is a chameleon'.[81] An exception may be 'information as to crimes, wrongs and misdeeds' that lacks the necessary quality of confidence for a successful action on the basis that there is no confidence in an iniquity.[82] It is also clear that not every item

---

75 Ibid [60]. See below at 8.3.2.3.
76 (2014) 107 IPR 1, [41].
77 *TF Industrial Pty Ltd v Career Tech Pty Ltd* [2011] NSWSC 1303, [109].
78 (2014) 99 ACSR 265.
79 Ibid [43]–[60].
80 *Saltman Engineering Co Ltd v Campbell Engineering Co Ltd* (1948) 65 RPC 203, 215; *Moorgate Tobacco Co Ltd v Philip Morris Ltd (No 2)* (1984) 156 CLR 414, 437.
81 Finn, *Fiduciary Obligations*, above n 32, 148.
82 *Corrs Pavey Whiting & Byrne v Collector of Customs (Vic)* (1987) 14 FCR 434, 456. See below at 8.8.

of confidential information will merit protection by the courts. In *Coco v AN Clark (Engineers) Ltd*, Megarry J thought that equity should not be invoked merely to protect 'trivial tittle tattle', however confidential.[83]

The range of protectable information is extremely wide and extends to personal information,[84] government secrets,[85] business information and trade secrets[86] and a range of other ideas.[87] The action will protect confidential information given by citizens to governments and their departments and agencies,[88] but 'not all information given to a government department, whether voluntarily or under compulsion is of this confidential character'.[89] In addition, the information must be significant in the sense that 'the preservation of its confidentiality or secrecy is of substantial concern to the plaintiff'.[90] This may not necessarily be in a commercial sense.[91]

The requirement that information has the necessary quality of confidence means that a person cannot impose obligations of confidentiality when the information is in the public domain.[92] This differs from a contractual imposition of an obligation of confidence, where the parties can agree to keep information secret even though it may already be in the public domain.[93]

8.3.2.1 Ideas

A preliminary matter concerns the meaning of 'information' and the extent to which a person must develop ideas before they satisfy this criterion. It is clear that the ideas must be 'sufficiently developed'.[94] This issue arises in cases that involve television, theatre and entertainment where there may be no tangible finished product, such as a detailed written script.[95] Protection is available for an idea that is developed to the stage of being a concept that is

---

83 [1969] RPC 41, 48.
84 *Argyll v Argyll* [1967] 1 Ch 302; *Prince Albert v Strange* (1849) 1 H & Tw 1, 47 ER 1302; *Douglas v Hello! Ltd (No 3)* [2006] QB 125.
85 *Commonwealth v John Fairfax & Sons Ltd* (1980) 147 CLR 39; *Attorney-General (UK) v Guardian Newspapers Ltd (No 2)* [1988] 3 All ER 545; *Attorney-General (UK) v Heinemann Publishers Australia Pty Ltd (No 2)* (1988) 165 CLR 30; *Attorney-General (UK) v Jonathan Cape Ltd* [1976] QB 752; *Castrol Australia Pty Ltd v EmTech Associates Pty Ltd* (1980) 33 ALR 31.
86 *Ansell Rubber Co Pty Ltd v Allied Rubber Industries Pty Ltd* [1967] VR 37; *O'Mustad & Son v S Alcock & Dosen Co Ltd* [1963] 3 All ER 416; *Saltman Engineering Co Ltd v Campbell Engineering Co Ltd* (1948) 65 RPC 203; *Coco v AN Clark (Engineers) Ltd* [1969] RPC 41. See below at 8.7.2.
87 *Talbot v General Television Corp Pty Ltd* [1980] VR 224; *De Maudsley v Palumbo* [1996] FSR 447.
88 *Castrol Australia Pty Ltd v EmTech Associates Pty Ltd* (1980) 33 ALR 31; *Attorney-General (UK) v Heinemann Publishers Australia Pty Ltd* (1987) 10 NSWLR 86, 191.
89 *Norwich Pharmacal Co v Customs and Excise Commissioners* [1974] AC 133, 189.
90 *Moorgate Tobacco Co Ltd v Philip Morris Ltd (No 2)* (1984) 156 CLR 414, 436.
91 *Argyll v Argyll* [1967] 1 Ch 302, 329.
92 *Coco v AN Clark (Engineers) Ltd* [1969] RPC 41, 47.
93 *Maggbury Pty Ltd v Hafele Australia Pty Ltd* (2001) 210 CLR 181, [50]; *Wright v Gasweld Pty Ltd* (1991) 22 NSWLR 317, 329, 335, 340–1; *Del Casale v Artedomus (Australia) Pty Ltd* (2007) 73 IPR 326, [51], [77], [92], [134], [140]; *Reed Business Information Pty Ltd v Seymour* [2010] NSWSC 790, [36]. See below at 8.4.
94 *HK Frost Holdings Pty Ltd (in liq) v Darvall McCutcheon (a firm)* [1999] FCA 570, [60]; *Vasco Investment Managers Ltd v Morgan Stanley Australia Ltd* (2014) 108 IPR 52, [274]; *Fraser v Thames Television Ltd* [1984] QB 44, 65–6.
95 *De Maudsley v Palumbo* [1996] FSR 447, 453; *Talbot v General Television Corp Pty Ltd* [1980] VR 224; *Fraser v Thames Television Ltd* [1984] QB 44, 65–6.

attractive as a television program and is capable of being realised as an actuality.[96] However, it is unnecessary to develop fully the literary or dramatic idea in the permanent form of a synopsis or treatment.[97]

Ideas that give rise to commercial transactions may also warrant protection if they are sufficiently developed.[98] The extent to which a person must develop the idea will depend on the circumstances and the context in which they provide the information.[99] Sometimes a short unelaborated statement of an idea will satisfy the requirement; other ideas may be too vague and unable to be realised in actuality without further development, or may be expressions of broad concepts and in global terms. For instance, Jessup J found in *Abrahams v Biggs* that the broad disclosure about the use of Teflon as an effective bed bug barrier on bed legs was no more than an idea and could not give the confider rights that 'encompass every form of bed bug barrier made from Teflon which sits on a bed leg'.[100]

Not only must the idea have a degree of particularity but it must also have 'some significant element of originality not already in the realm of public knowledge'.[101] A unique combination of ideas that results in a strategy, as opposed to an expression at a high level of abstraction, satisfies the requirement.[102] For instance, a commercial plan for recapitalisation of a group of companies was developed sufficiently and capable of protection, even though some aspects of the plan changed or were excluded as it 'moved through negotiation to finality through the various stakeholders'.[103]

8.3.2.2 Concept of relative secrecy and the public domain

The revelation to others of something that is already public property or public knowledge is not a breach of confidence.[104] However, protection for confidential information does not require absolute secrecy in the sense that no members of the public can access the information. Rather, relative secrecy is the standard,[105] although the actual meaning of this will depend on the facts of each case. A number of circumstances in which information enters the public domain provide a guide as to the meaning of the public domain:

- Secret information will enter the public domain in a country when it is published in a patent specification within that country.[106]

---

96   *Talbot v General Television Corp Pty Ltd* [1980] VR 224, 230; *Fraser v Thames Television Ltd* [1984] QB 44, 65–6; *Darvall McCutcheon (a firm) v HK Frost Holdings Pty Ltd (in liq)* (2002) 4 VR 570, [59]–[60]; *Burrows v Smith* [2010] EWHC 22 (Ch), [34].
97   *De Maudsley v Palumbo* [1996] FSR 447, 455–6. See W. Cornish, 'Confidence in ideas' (1990) 1 *Intellectual Property Journal* 3; J. Stuckey-Clarke, 'Remedies for the misappropriation of ideas' [1989] *European Intellectual Property Review* 333.
98   *Vasco Investment Managers Ltd v Morgan Stanley Australia Ltd* (2014) 108 IPR 52, [280]–[281].
99   Ibid [274]; *HK Frost Holdings Pty Ltd (in liq) v Darvall McCutcheon (a firm)* [1999] FCA 570, [60].
100 [2011] FCA 1475, [68].
101 *De Maudsley v Palumbo* [1996] FSR 447, 455; *Fraser v Thames Television Ltd* [1984] QB 44, 65; *Andrew Shelton & Co Pty Ltd v Alpha Healthcare Ltd* (2002) 5 VR 577, [86]–[94].
102 *Vasco Investment Managers Ltd v Morgan Stanley Australia Ltd* (2014) 108 IPR 52, [304]–[311].
103 Ibid [308].
104 *Coco v AN Clark (Engineers) Ltd* [1969] RPC 41, 47; *Saltman Engineering Co Ltd v Campbell Engineering Co Ltd* (1948) 65 RPC 203, 215.
105 *Franchi v Franchi* [1967] RPC 149, 152.
106 *O'Mustad & Son v S Alcock & Dosen Co Ltd* [1963] 3 All ER 416.

- A published patent specification may also be within the public domain of another country if patent attorneys in that country regularly search those foreign specifications.[107]
- Confidential information may enter the public domain when it receives a degree of publicity among those in the relevant community, industry or profession that effectively destroys the utility of maintaining its secrecy.[108]

In contrast, information previously disclosed may not enter the public domain. This may be because the source of the information is the confider who provides it in confidence to the confidant for commercial purposes.[109] It may also be when the disclosure is to a limited public.[110] For example, in *Douglas v Hello! Ltd (No 3)*, the United Kingdom Court of Appeal said:

> Information will be confidential if it is available to one person (or a group of people) and not generally available to others, provided that the person (or group) who possesses the information does not intend that it should become available to others.[111]

Not everything said at a meeting of a company's board of directors is necessarily confidential and an obligation of confidence does not arise in respect of every item discussed.[112] In addition, not everything performed on private property will have the necessary quality of confidence. There is likely to be a difference between activities filmed on private property and the filming of private activities.[113] The concept of private activities imports the notion of confidentiality that is not present merely because the location of the activities is private property. Something further is necessary; there must be evidence that a person took special precautions to avoid unauthorised people seeing or hearing the secret activities.[114] Such precautions might involve the imposition of obligations of confidence on those people before they enter the private property, or the erection of appropriate signage.[115] It is not enough to impose an obligation of confidence that a person obtained the information because of a trespass or other tortious action.[116]

Information that is accessible to the public on the internet will not necessarily result in the information entering the public domain. Although Barrett J in *EPP (Australia) Pty Ltd v Levy* regarded 'everything which is accessible through resort to the internet as being in the public

---

107 *Franchi v Franchi* [1967] RPC 149.
108 Ibid; *O'Brien v Komesaroff* (1982) 150 CLR 310, 326; *Australian Broadcasting Corporation v Lenah Game Meats Pty Ltd* (2001) 208 CLR 199, 235–6.
109 *Schering Chemicals Ltd v Falkman* [1981] 2 WLR 848, 879.
110 *Attorney-General (UK) v Guardian Newspapers Ltd (No 2)* [1988] 3 All ER 545, 595; *HRH Prince of Wales v Associated Newspapers Ltd* [2006] EWHC 522 (Ch); *Franchi v Franchi* [1967] RPC 149, 152–3.
111 [2006] QB 125, 151.
112 *National Roads and Motorists' Association v Geeson* (2001) 40 ACSR 1, [30]; *Bennetts v Board of Fire Commissioners of New South Wales* (1967) 87 WN (Pt 1) (NSW) 307, 310; *Harkness v Commonwealth Bank of Australia Ltd* (1993) 32 NSWLR 543, 552.
113 *Australian Broadcasting Corporation v Lenah Game Meats Pty Ltd* (2001) 208 CLR 199, 224–6; *Douglas v Hello! Ltd (No 3)* [2006] QB 125; *Hellewell v Chief Constable of Derbyshire* [1995] 1 WLR 804, 807G–H.
114 *Australian Broadcasting Corporation v Lenah Game Meats Pty Ltd* (2001) 208 CLR 199, 221.
115 *Shelley Films Ltd v Rex Features Ltd* [1994] EMLR 134; *Creation Records Ltd v News Group Newspapers Ltd* (1997) 39 IPR 1. See R. Arnold, 'Note: Circumstances importing an obligation of confidence' (2003) 119 *Law Quarterly Review* 193.
116 *Australian Broadcasting Corporation v Lenah Game Meats Pty Ltd* (2001) 208 CLR 199, 222.

domain',[117] this may depend on how viewers regard the reliability and authority of the source of that information. For instance, we might expect a newspaper or a television or radio station to have internal and external controls over the accuracy of the information appearing on a website they operate. That information would enter the public domain. In contrast, information that appears in postings on sites that enable 'opinions, gossip, trivia, rumour and speculation to be published as an assertion of fact by anonymous contributors'[118] is unlikely to enter the public domain. The lack of accountability for the credibility of the anonymous publication of information leaves the disclosures in the 'realm of speculation'.[119] Kellam J identified undesirable consequences of allowing such disclosures to enter the public domain in *Australian Football League v The Age*:

> If speculation, gossip or even assertion from an anonymous source, thus being incapable of being verified or in any way held accountable, is to be regarded as the putting of information in the public domain, then the opportunity for the unethical, and the malicious, to breach confidentiality and then claim that there is no confidentiality is unrestrained.[120]

Generally, information will enter the public domain when a product that incorporates that information is freely available for purchase. The release of a product onto the market leaves purchasers free to reverse-engineer the product.[121] This may be true also where the manufacturer encrypts information contained in the product on the basis that people with skills to de-encrypt have access to that information. As Jacob J held in *Mars UK Ltd v Teknowledge Ltd*, a case involving encrypted information, the full right of ownership in a chattel gives an entitlement 'to dismantle the machine to find out how it works and tell anyone he pleases'.[122] However, an evaluation of whether the information is released into the public domain in any given case remains a question of degree. It will depend on the extent of the expenditure of time, effort and money on experimentation that would be required to disclose those secrets through this process.[123] At some point, a court may find that the extent of these activities is of 'such a degree that it cannot be said to be "publicly available" or in the "public domain"'.[124] A person who steals information would be in a different position[125] from the person who legitimately acquires the means to discover the information.

---

117 [2001] NSWSC 482, [20].
118 *Australian Football League v The Age Co Ltd* (2006) 15 VR 419, [55].
119 Ibid [56].
120 Ibid [55].
121 *Saltman Engineering Co Ltd v Campbell Engineering Co Ltd* (1948) 65 RPC 203.
122 [2000] FSR 138, 149 [31]; *Alfa Laval Cheese Systems Ltd v Wincanton Engineering Ltd* [1990] FSR 583. See M. Richardson, 'Of shrink-wraps, "click-wraps" and reverse engineering: Rethinking trade secret protection' (2002) 25 *University of New South Wales Law Journal* 748. See also *Saltman Engineering Co Ltd v Campbell Engineering Co Ltd* (1948) 65 RPC 203, 215 (CA); *Coco v AN Clark (Engineers) Ltd* [1969] RPC 41, 47.
123 *Australian Medic-Care Co Ltd v Hamilton Pharmaceutical Pty Ltd* (2009) 261 ALR 501, [633].
124 *RLA Polymers Pty Ltd v Nexus Adhesives Pty Ltd* (2011) 280 ALR 125, [52].
125 *Terrapin Ltd v Builders Supply Co (Hayes) Ltd* [1967] RPC 375.

8.3.2.3 Information based on public knowledge and ideas

Information may lack the necessary quality of confidence when it is no different from knowledge or ideas that are in the public domain. However, this does not preclude confidentiality subsisting in information that is constructed solely from materials in the public domain. What is required to convert public knowledge into confidential information is the application of intellectual skill and ingenuity to that material that results in something that is new and confidential. This concept of 'newness' must not be confused with terms such as 'novel' that have precise meanings within patent law. As Megarry J said in *Coco v AN Clark (Engineers) Ltd*, 'whether it is described as originality or novelty or ingenuity or otherwise, I think there must be some product of the human brain which suffices to confer a confidential nature upon the information'.[126] This would be a result 'which can only be achieved by somebody who goes through the same process'.[127]

A person may exercise a sufficient degree of skill and ingenuity to compile information into a business manual,[128] write a diary to describe public events[129] or build on freely circulating ideas about television programs to develop something new.[130] What takes the information in the latter example out of the realm of public knowledge may be a particular novel slant on the program – such as a 'commercial twist'. This is clear from the facts of *Talbot v General Television Corp Pty Ltd*.[131] The case involved the plaintiff, an independent filmmaker, who devised a format for a proposed television series entitled *To Make a Million*. He submitted confidentially to the Channel Nine network a fully developed format for the series. Although ideas about programs featuring millionaires were relatively common, the theme for the successful self-made millionaires to give recipes for their success was new.

8.3.2.4 Guidelines for necessary quality of confidence for business or trade secrets

Business or commercial information is often referred to as 'trade secrets' but that terms has no special meaning in Australian law. It usually arises in the context of confidential information that an employee learns during employment, 'the confidentiality of which, as an employee of ordinary honesty and intelligence would acknowledge, must be maintained even after employment has come to an end.'[132] Some authorities suggest that this principle and concept of trade secrets may apply not only in an employment context but also in a partnership context.[133] The guidelines for identifying information as a 'trade secret' are discussed below.[134]

---

126 [1969] RPC 41, 47; *Vasco Investment Managers Ltd v Morgan Stanley Australia Ltd* (2014) 108 IPR 52, [310]; *Krueger Transport Equipment Pty Ltd v Glen Cameron Storage & Distribution Pty Ltd* (2008) 78 IPR 262, [92]; *Del Casale v Artedomus (Australia) Pty Ltd* (2007) 73 IPR 326 [103].
127 *Ansell Rubber Co Pty Ltd v Allied Rubber Industries Pty Ltd* [1967] VR 37, 49.
128 *Link 2 Pty Ltd v Ezystay Systems Pty Ltd* [2016] NSWCA 317, [126]–[127].
129 *HRH Prince of Wales v Associated Newspapers Ltd* [2006] EWHC 522 (Ch).
130 *Talbot v General Television Corp Pty Ltd* [1980] VR 224.
131 [1980] VR 224.
132 *GlaxoSmithKline Australia Pty Ltd v Ritchie* (2008) 77 IPR 306, [50]; *Printers & Finishers Ltd v Holloway (No 2)* [1965] RPC 239, 255.
133 *Refaat v Barry* [2015] VSCA 218, [132]–[135]; *X v Twitter Inc* (2017) 95 NSWLR 301, [5].
134 At 8.7.2.

8.3.3 Information given or received to import an obligation of confidence

The early exposition of this element for a successful action for breach of confidence referred to the *communication* of the information in circumstances importing an obligation of confidence.[135] In *Coco v AN Clark (Engineers) Ltd*, Megarry J proposed a 'reasonable man' test in the following terms:

> It seems to me that if the circumstances are such that any reasonable man standing in the shoes of the recipient of the information would have realised that upon reasonable grounds the information was being given to him in confidence, then this should suffice to impose upon him the equitable obligation of confidence.[136]

The test envisages a direct disclosure of confidential information from one person to another. In such a case, Megarry J felt that the recipient would carry a heavy burden if they were to deny an obligation of confidence.[137] However, the reasonable man test necessarily implies that the disclosure of some information in the course of a confidential discussion may not attract an obligation of confidence. For instance, the casual imparting of an idea 'in the nature of an aside' by one person to another in the course of a confidential discussion about a business venture would not raise an obligation of confidence when the idea is unrelated to that venture.[138]

8.3.3.1 Receipt of information in circumstances that import an obligation of confidence

Imparting information in confidence is one means by which to impose an obligation of confidence. However, protection for confidences is not limited to receipt of information by a direct communication. As Lord Greene stated in *Saltman Engineering*:

> If a defendant is proved to have used confidential information, directly or indirectly obtained from a plaintiff, without the consent, express or implied, of the plaintiff, he will be guilty of an infringement of the plaintiff's rights.[139]

Indirect acquisition of information may arise from the use of improper or surreptitious means. These latter means on the one hand and imparting information in confidence on the other 'are treated as two species of the same genus.'[140] As the emphasis is upon receipt of information, the equitable doctrine of breach of confidence accommodates such cases as surreptitious acquisition or theft,[141] eavesdropping,[142] telephoto lens photography[143] and phone

---

135 *Coco v AN Clark (Engineers) Ltd* [1969] RPC 41.
136 Ibid 48; *Telstra Corp Ltd v First Netcom Pty Ltd* (1997) 78 FCR 132, 138.
137 *Coco v AN Clark (Engineers) Ltd* [1969] RPC 41, 48.
138 *Abrahams v Biggs* [2011] FCA 1475, [71].
139 *Saltman Engineering Co Ltd v Campbell Engineering Co Ltd* (1948) 65 RPC 203, 213.
140 *Smith Kline & French Laboratories (Australia) Ltd v Secretary, Department of Community Services and Health* (1990) 22 FCR 73, 86 [49].
141 *Franklin v Giddins* [1978] Qd R 72; *Sullivan v Sclanders & Goldwell International Pty Ltd* (2000) 77 SASR 419, 424, 429; *Commonwealth v John Fairfax & Sons Ltd* (1980) 147 CLR 39, 50; *Lord Ashburton v Pape* [1913] 2 Ch 469.
142 *Hellewell v Chief Constable of Derbyshire* [1995] 1 WLR 804, 807.
143 *Douglas v Hello! Ltd (No 3)* [2006] QB 125.

tapping.[144] These circumstances all share some form of reprehensible conduct in circumstances where the reasonable person would expect the imposition of an obligation of confidence on the person who acquires the information. Such things as the presence of signs forbidding entry and restriction of access to an otherwise public area can create the circumstances in which an objective assessment of confidentiality is likely.[145]

It is clear also that an obligation of confidence can be imposed where a third party receives information from a person who breaches a duty of confidence to another in respect of that information, knowing that it has been disclosed in breach of that duty.[146] Even when the third party is an innocent recipient of the information, he will be subject to a duty of confidence when he subsequently learns of the confidential quality of that information.[147] This principle is equally applicable to individuals as it is to all types of media, including online social networking platforms such as Twitter.[148] The case of *Stephenson Jordan & Harrison Ltd v MacDonald & Evans*[149] established that a third party could not publish information once they learnt of its confidentiality, despite the fact that its acquisition was innocent. The rationale for imposing this obligation lies in the notion that the 'duty of confidence has devolved' on that innocent third party because of the circumstances in which the information was acquired.[150] Hence, a court will examine those circumstances, beyond merely the fact that the innocent party is now on notice, to determine whether their conscience should be bound.[151]

8.3.3.2 Encrypted information

It seems that the mere encryption of information contained in an article that is purchased in the open market will not impose an obligation of confidentiality on the purchaser.[152] According to Jacob J in *Mars UK Ltd v Teknowledge Ltd*,[153] the express notice to the effect 'confidential – you may not de-encrypt' would make no difference. He continued:

> As pure matter of common sense I cannot see why the mere fact of encryption makes that which is encrypted confidential or why anyone who de-encrypts something in code, should necessarily be taken to be receiving information in confidence. He will appreciate

---

144   *Malone v Metropolitan Police Commissioner (No 2)* [1979] 2 All ER 620.
145   *Shelley Films Ltd v Rex Features Ltd* [1994] EMLR 134; *Creation Records Ltd v News Group Newspapers Ltd* (1997) 39 IPR 1. See Arnold, 'Note: Circumstances importing an obligation', above n 115, 193.
146   *Australian Broadcasting Corporation v Lenah Game Meats Pty Ltd* (2001) 208 CLR 199, 224–5; *Attorney-General (UK) v Guardian Newspapers Ltd (No 2)* [1988] 3 All ER 545, 578–9; *Ansell Rubber Co Pty Ltd v Allied Rubber Industries Pty Ltd* [1967] VR 37; *Commonwealth v John Fairfax & Sons Ltd* (1980) 147 CLR 39. See Stuckey, 'The liability of innocent third parties', above n 56, 73.
147   *Wheatley v Bell* [1982] 2 NSWLR 544, 549–50; *Retractable Technologies v Occupational & Medical Innovations Ltd* (2007) 72 IPR 58, [81]–[87]; *Johns v Australian Securities Commission* (1993) 178 CLR 408, 460, 474; *Butler v Board of Trade* [1971] Ch 680, 690 (Goff J); *Streetscape Projects (Australia) Pty Ltd v City of Sydney* (2013) 85 NSWLR 196, [153]; *Moorgate Tobacco Co Ltd v Philip Morris Ltd (No 2)* (1984) 156 CLR 414, 438.
148   *X v Twitter Inc* (2017) 95 NSWLR 301, [19].
149   (1952) 69 RPC 10; *Talbot v General Television Corp Pty Ltd* [1980] VR 224.
150   *Johns v Australian Securities Commission* (1993) 178 CLR 408, 460.
151   *Retractable Technologies v Occupational & Medical Innovations Ltd* (2007) 72 IPR 58, [86]–[87].
152   *Mars UK Ltd v Teknowledge Ltd* [2000] FSR 138.
153   [2000] FSR 138.

that the source of the information did not want him to have access, but that is all. He has no other relationship with that source.[154]

In the application of the reasonable person test, Jacob J distinguished this type of situation from the case of an actual transfer of information from one person to another. The de-encryption of information contained in a product purchased on the open market was 'just about finding out information from a product on the market. I do not think [de-encrypting] would be regarded as anything other than fair game for competitors'.[155]

8.3.3.3 Verbal confidences: inadvertent eavesdropping

It is clear that no obligation can be imposed if the information is 'blurted out in public'.[156] According to Megarry V-C in *Malone v Metropolitan Police Commissioner (No 2)*, a person who carelessly discusses confidential matters in such places as a bus, over the back fence or in an office must accept the risk that someone nearby might overhear the conversation.[157] In his view, an obligation of confidence cannot be imposed on the accidental eavesdropper. Similarly, a person who speaks on a telephone takes the risks of being overheard that are inherent in the system.[158] Although the confider may impose the obligation on the person to whom they are speaking, this imposition of an obligation would not extend to a person who accidentally overhears the conversation through an imperfection in the system.

This type of inadvertent eavesdropping shares some common features. First, the information is spoken and it is received in an environment that possesses no inherent secrecy and security in itself. This may be the communications systems or public places, such as a bus or a restaurant. A person does not need to be proactive in order to overhear the information. In fact, the recipient has no opportunity to refuse to hear the information. Second, the confidant may be oblivious to the fact that the information has been overheard and by whom. Hence, there may be no opportunity to seek the agreement of the eavesdropper to keep the information confidential. It seems that a person who chooses to communicate confidential information in an environment that is inherently vulnerable to inadvertent overhearing by people conducting their day-to-day lives may impose a moral obligation of secrecy but no more. It is not clear whether a person can impose an obligation of confidence directly on the inadvertent recipient at a later time by asking them to keep the information secret. Perhaps it is more likely that the person is responsible for protecting confidentiality before the obligation can be imposed on others.

8.3.3.4 Verbal confidences: eavesdropping and telephone tapping

The position will be different when there is deliberate illegal eavesdropping[159] or surreptitious acquisition of the information.[160] In the case of a telephone call, it has been held that the lawful interception for the purposes of a police investigation will not impose any obligation on the

---

154 Ibid 150.
155 Ibid.
156 *Coco v AN Clark (Engineers) Ltd* [1969] RPC 41, 48.
157 [1979] 2 All ER 620, 645–6.
158 Ibid 646; *Francome v Mirror Group Newspapers Ltd* [1984] 2 All ER 408, 415.
159 *Francome v Mirror Group Newspapers Ltd* [1984] 2 All ER 408, 415.
160 *Franklin v Giddins* [1978] Qd R 72; *Lord Ashburton v Pape* [1913] 2 Ch 469.

eavesdropper to keep the information confidential.[161] However, in another decision it was held that the obligation of confidence may be imposed on a private person who overhears the conversation using unlawful telephone tapping on the basis that the confidant would not be expected to accept this risk.[162] An alternative explanation for this result may be that the action is only available because the recipient engaged in unlawful conduct.[163]

8.3.3.5 Inadvertent acquisition of written confidences

An obviously confidential document may inadvertently come to the attention of a person in a variety of ways. It may be emailed, posted or faxed in error to the wrong person. In contrast to the inadvertent verbal disclosure of information, a person who comes across an obviously confidential document can choose not to read it. According to Lord Goff in *Attorney-General (UK) v Guardian Newspapers (No 2)*,[164] this type of receipt would impose an obligation of confidence on the recipient. The reason for this was expressed by Debelle J in *Trevorrow v South Australia (No 4)*[165] in the hypothetical context of the person who inadvertently leaves confidential information in a satchel on a bus that another passenger finds. The obligation of confidence would arise from the fact that the finder came into possession of the information in circumstances in which it was not intended that the confidential information could be used by the finder. Expressing this in terms of the reasonable person test in *Coco v AN Clark (Engineers) Ltd*, the finder would understand from the nature of the information and the fact that the bag was obviously left by mistake that the information should be kept in confidence.

All the judges in *Trevorrow* confirmed that the relevant consideration is the circumstance by which the person has acquired possession of the confidential information contained in a document rather than the circumstances in which the information was imparted to the initial recipient. Those circumstances are judged according to their impact on the reasonable person who is the recipient in those circumstances.[166] Such things as the nature of the material, the presence of an express notice of confidentiality and the inadvertent nature of the disclosure or otherwise will be relevant to the imposition of an obligation of confidence.

United Kingdom courts have developed principles to deal with the special case of inadvertent disclosure of secret information that is also protected by legal privilege.[167] However, the approach in Australia favours the application of the traditional principles articulated in *Coco v AN Clark (Engineers) Ltd*.[168] The test has been expressed as would 'a reasonable person

---

161 *Malone v Metropolitan Police Commissioner (No 2)* [1979] 2 All ER 620.
162 *Francome v Mirror Group Newspapers Ltd* [1984] 2 All ER 408, 415. See Richardson, 'Of shrink-wraps, "click-wraps" and reverse engineering', above n 122.
163 See G. Wei, 'Surreptitious takings of confidential information' (1992) 12 *Legal Studies* 302.
164 *Attorney-General (UK) v Guardian Newspapers Ltd (No 2)* [1988] 3 All ER 545, 657–8.
165 (2006) 94 SASR 64, [80]–[81].
166 *Coco v AN Clark (Engineers) Ltd* [1969] RPC 41, 48; *Coulthard v South Australia* (1995) 63 SASR 531, 534–5, 548–9; *Trevorrow v South Australia (No 4)* (2006) 94 SASR 64, [41]; *AG Australia Holdings Ltd v Burton* (2002) 58 NSWLR 464 (privileged documents that accidentally come into the hands of opponent to litigation).
167 *Goddard v Nationwide Building Society* [1987] QB 670; *English & American Insurance Co Ltd v Herbert Smith* [1988] FSR 232; *Guinness Peat Properties Ltd v Fitzroy Robinson Partnership* [1987] 1 WLR 1027; *Surface Technology plc v Young* [2002] FSR 25, [27]; *Webster v James Chapman & Co* [1989] 3 All ER 939; *Lord Ashburton v Pape* [1913] 2 Ch 469; *ISTIL Group Inc v Zahoor* [2003] 2 All ER 252, 269.
168 [1969] RPC 41; *Trevorrow v South Australia (No 4)* (2006) 94 SASR 64, [81]–[83]. Debelle J applied the approach of the United Kingdom courts: see *ISTIL Group Inc v Zahoor* [2003] 2 All ER 252, 269.

standing in [the recipient's] shoes have appreciated that a mistake had been made, and that confidential information was being disclosed unintentionally?'[169] An obligation of confidence would be imposed if an affirmative answer were given.

8.3.3.6 Surreptitious acquisition through theft or use of telephoto lens

Surreptitious acquisition or theft of confidential information can also be restrained under the doctrine of breach of confidence.[170] The circumstances in which this may arise include theft of bud wood from a private orchard,[171] and the taking of photographs of secret and private activities or information.[172] In the United Kingdom, the taking of unauthorised photographs of a private celebrity wedding has been held to impose a duty of confidence on the holders of those photos.[173]

8.3.4 Unauthorised use or disclosure of the information

If the information that possesses the necessary quality of confidence is disclosed or received in circumstances that impose an obligation of confidence, the recipient will breach this obligation when they use or disclose the information or threaten to do so, in ways that were not permitted. This does not require the confidential disclosures to be used in their entirety or in an original form. Use of the principal elements of a confidential plan as the starting point or 'catalyst' for the final plan that is exploited will amount to an unauthorised use when most of those elements remain in that final plan. It may be difficult to establish unauthorised use or disclosure of confidential information in reliance on circumstantial evidence.[174] For instance, although similarities may be present between a confidential tender document and a product developed by the successful tenderer, it will be necessary to show that this product could only have been built with access to the information contained in the other party's tender.[175]

A court will intervene where the circumstances are such that it is unconscionable for a party to use confidential information.[176] The New Zealand High Court expressed the test as 'whether the conscience of the recipient of the confidential information should have been troubled by disclosing the information in question'.[177] There is no requirement for this use or disclosure to

---

169   *Trevorrow v South Australia (No 4)* (2006) 94 SASR 64, [142].
170   *Lord Ashburton v Pape* [1913] 2 Ch 469, 475; *Johns v Australian Securities Commission* (1993) 178 CLR 408, 424, 426–7, 459, 474; *Commonwealth v John Fairfax & Sons Ltd* (1980) 147 CLR 39, 50; *Corrs Pavey Whiting & Byrne v Collector of Customs (Vic)* (1987) 14 FCR 434, 450; *Sullivan v Sclanders & Goldwell International Pty Ltd* (2000) 77 SASR 419; *Bloomsbury Publishing Group Ltd v News Group Newspapers Ltd* [2003] FSR 45; *Creation Records Ltd v News Group Newspapers Ltd* (1997) 39 IPR 1.
171   *Franklin v Giddins* [1978] Qd R 72.
172   *Australian Broadcasting Corporation v Lenah Game Meats Pty Ltd* (2001) 208 CLR 199.
173   *Douglas v Hello! Ltd (No 3)* [2006] QB 125 (CA). See also *Campbell v MGN Ltd* [2004] 2 AC 457. See Richardson, 'Of shrink-wraps, "click-wraps" and reverse engineering', above n 122, 673.
174   *SGS Australia Pty Ltd v Australian Laboratory Services Pty Ltd* [2012] FCA 711, [137].
175   *Wagdy Hanna & Associates Pty Ltd v National Library of Australia* [2014] ACTCA 32, [57].
176   *Fraser v Evans* [1969] 1 QB 349, 361; *Deta Nominees Pty Ltd v Viscount Plastic Products Pty Ltd* [1979] VR 167, 191.
177   *Earthquake Commission v Krieger* [2014] 2 NZLR 547, [56], citing *R v Department of Health; Ex parte Source Informatics Ltd* [2001] QB 424, [14]; *London Regional Transport v Mayor of London* [2001] EWCA Civ 1491, [39].

be deliberate or for there to be 'conscious plagiarism'.[178] However, the person must be aware (or have reason to be aware) at some stage of the confidential character of the information.[179] The Privy Council determined that a remedy was available from a person who disclosed the information after he incorrectly believed that it had entered the public domain.[180] Also, a genuine belief that the person was the originator of the information is irrelevant if it is established that this belief is false, and that the idea had been conveyed but forgotten.[181]

A remedy will be available to restrain the use of information that is in the public domain if this use will result in the unauthorised disclosure of other information that is confidential. In a case involving a proposed broadcast of a report on police informers, the court restrained the use in the broadcast of a publicly available photograph of a police informer who had since been given a new secret identity. It was considered that the combination of the photograph with the report could lead to his identification.[182]

Any unauthorised attempt to use, vary or modify confidential information can be restrained because it allows the party using the confidential information to achieve a particular result without having to go through the expense, time and effort of discovering the information themselves.[183] The use of information as the starting point of a new design gives the person an unfair advantage or 'springboard' into the marketplace:

> In short, if a person wishes to design a product without it being alleged that the person has used confidential information he must proceed through an independent design sequence and not use confidential information as a springboard to jump through that sequence.[184]

The presence of differences in the information confided and anything made using that information is irrelevant.[185]

Compliance with the obligations imposed on confidants can be difficult in some circumstances. First, in *Seager v Copydex*, it was pointed out that a confidant who seeks to use public information that is mixed with the confidential information that was disclosed in circumstances of confidence must 'take special care to use only the material which is in the public domain'.[186] In that case, Lord Denning MR stated that such circumstances may influence the remedy that is appropriate in the circumstances:

> He should go to the public source and get it: or, at any rate, not be in a better position than if he had gone to the public source. He should not get a start over others by using the information which he received in confidence. At any rate, he should not get a start without

---

178 *Seager v Copydex Ltd* [1967] 2 All ER 415, 418.
179 *Talbot v General Television Corp Pty Ltd* [1980] VR 224.
180 *Norbrook Laboratories Ltd v Bomac Laboratories Ltd* [2006] UKPC 25, [29].
181 *Talbot v General Television Corp Pty Ltd* [1980] VR 224.
182 *G v Day* [1982] 1 NSWLR 24.
183 *Dart Industries Inc v David Bryar & Associates Pty Ltd* (1997) 38 IPR 389, 408–9; *Peter Pan Manufacturing Corp v Corsets Silhouette Ltd* [1964] 1 WLR 96.
184 *Dart Industries Inc v David Bryar & Associates Pty Ltd* (1997) 38 IPR 389, 408; *Saltman Engineering Co Ltd v Campbell Engineering Co Ltd* (1948) 65 RPC 203, 215. See below at 8.9.2.
185 *Dart Industries Inc v David Bryar & Associates Pty Ltd* (1997) 38 IPR 389, 409.
186 [1967] 2 All ER 415, 417.

paying for it. It may not be a case for injunction but only for damages, depending on the worth of the confidential information to him in saving him time and trouble.[187]

It may be that this means that the recipient must take care only to use the public information; the private information must be paid for.[188] A second complex situation may arise where parties are engaged in a joint venture of some kind that requires exchange of information concerning the activities of products of the joint venture. There is the risk that both parties can exchange confidential information in such a way that it becomes intermingled. If the relationship unravels, neither the confider nor the confidant can use the other's confidential information as a 'springboard for activities detrimental to the person who made the confidential communication'[189] without permission. Again, courts can address these difficulties through their choice of the appropriate remedy to suit the circumstances.

8.3.5 The scope of the obligation

The equitable duty of confidence requires that 'he who has received information in confidence shall not take unfair advantage of it'.[190] However, the test in *Coco v AN Clark (Engineers) Ltd*[191] does not give guidance as to the scope of the obligation of confidence. As a general principle, a person can limit the scope for which a confidant may use confidential information. In such cases, the duty of confidence crystallises around that limited purpose.[192] When a person claims to have imparted confidential information to another to be used for a limited purpose only, the recipient either must know or ought to have known of that limitation for their conscience to be bound.[193] A person may also disclose information and consent to its use on condition that a reasonable level of remuneration is paid for that use. Use of the information without payment would then amount to unauthorised use.[194]

The extent and limits of the obligation of confidentiality may be expressly stated at the time of the communication of clearly specified information. In other cases, an absolute obligation or one of limited scope may be implied from the circumstances.[195] The scope may differ according to each of the particular pieces of confidential information in the recipient's possession.[196]

---

187 Ibid 417.
188 *EPI Environmental Technologies Inc v Symphony Plastic Technologies plc* [2005] 1 WLR 3456, 3464 [48].
189 *Terrapin Ltd v Builders Supply Co (Hayes) Ltd* [1967] RPC 375, 391; *Cranleigh Precision Engineering Ltd v Bryant* [1964] 3 All ER 289, 301; *Saltman Engineering Co Ltd v Campbell Engineering Co Ltd* (1948) 65 RPC 203, 215; *Seager v Copydex Ltd* [1967] 2 All ER 415, 417; *Peter Pan Manufacturing Corp v Corsets Silhouette Ltd* [1964] 1 WLR 96. See below at 8.9.2.
190 *Seager v Copydex Ltd* [1967] 2 All ER 415, 417.
191 [1969] RPC 41.
192 *Castrol Australia Pty Ltd v Emtech Associates Pty Ltd* (1980) 33 ALR 31, 46; *Elliott v Ivey* [1998] NSWSC 116; *Rapid Metal Developments (Australia) Pty Ltd v Anderson Formrite Pty Ltd* [2005] WASC 255, [60]; *Schering Chemicals Ltd v Falkman* [1981] 2 WLR 848, 879; *Torrington Manufacturing Co v Smith & Sons (England) Ltd* [1966] RPC 285, 301.
193 *Smith Kline & French Laboratories (Australia) Ltd v Secretary, Department of Community Services and Health* (1990) 22 FCR 73, 95.
194 *Vasco Investment Managers Ltd v Morgan Stanley Australia Ltd* (2014) 108 IPR 52, [321]–[324].
195 *Smith Kline & French Laboratories (Australia) Ltd v Secretary, Department of Community Services and Health* (1990) 22 FCR 73.
196 *National Roads and Motorists' Association v Geeson* (2001) 40 ACSR 1, [30].

The scope of a limited purpose may not always be able to be determined by reference only to the confider's purpose. This is particularly the case where each party's interest is quite different. This is more likely to arise where a private person provides confidential information to a government authority or department.[197] In *Smith Kline & French Laboratories (Australia) Ltd v Secretary, Department of Community Services and Health*,[198] the Full Federal Court listed some of the multiple factors that can help a court to determine the existence of confidentiality and its scope in a particular fact situation, namely:

- whether the information is provided gratuitously or for consideration;
- evidence of past practice of such a kind as to give rise to an understanding of confidence;
- sensitivity of the information;
- whether the confider has an interest in the purpose for which information is to be used;
- express warning by the confider to the confidant against a particular disclosure or use;
- existence of restraint of trade provisions in an employment contract; and
- value of the information to the confider.[199]

When information is provided to a government department, for example, a person would ordinarily assume that the government would keep the information for later use – perhaps to justify a decision. Although there is an obligation to avoid taking unfair advantage of the information, this does not mean that a department must use it only for the confider's purpose, when such a restriction could interfere with the vital functions of government. The obligation is to refrain from unconscientious use of the information. Similarly, a prospective employee would not assume that the employer would destroy confidential information in the employee's application file if their application were successful.[200]

8.3.6 The need to show detriment

The question was left open in *Coco v AN Clark (Engineers) Ltd*[201] of whether it is necessary to show detriment to obtain relief for a breach of confidence. Although the summarised elements of the action of breach of confidence require detriment, Megarry J noted that his summary stated the general propositions in their stricter form. He could find no general requirement for detriment among past authorities, some of which made no mention of detriment. As he conceived there may be a need for equity to intervene in the absence of detriment, he left open the possibility for a remedy. in such a case.[202] Although most claimants suffer clear detriment, financial or personal, 'in the sense that the preservation of its confidentiality or secrecy is of substantial concern to the plaintiff',[203] the need for them to do so is still not

---

197   *Smith Kline & French Laboratories (Australia) Ltd v Secretary, Department of Community Services and Health* (1990) 22 FCR 73, affirmed (1991) 28 FCR 291; *Kockums AB v Commonwealth* [2001] FCA 398, [99]–[100].
198   (1991) 28 FCR 291.
199   Ibid 302–3.
200   Ibid 304
201   [1969] RPC 41.
202   Ibid.
203   *Moorgate Tobacco Co Ltd v Philip Morris Ltd (No 2)* (1984) 156 CLR 414, 438.

decided.[204] As Gummow J stated in *Smith Kline & French Laboratories (Australia) Ltd v Secretary, Department of Community Services and Health*:

> The obligation of conscience is to respect the confidence, not merely to refrain from causing detriment to the plaintiff. The plaintiff comes to equity to vindicate his right to observance of the obligation, not necessarily to recover loss or to restrain infliction of apprehended loss.[205]

Even if detriment is required, it may be simple to satisfy. For example, in personal matters, it may be enough that a person will suffer sufficient detriment where disclosure of information relating to their affairs has exposed them to public discussion and criticism.[206] It may also be enough to merely suffer an unwanted disclosure.[207] Another suggestion is that, as equity is concerned to uphold the obligation of confidence, the question of detriment might go only to the discretion to grant the remedy.[208] Courts have awarded nominal damages where no detriment has been proved.

However, it seems clear that the application of the doctrine to protect the secrets of government would require not merely detriment, but a level of detriment that is higher than merely exposing government actions to criticism and review. In *Commonwealth v John Fairfax & Sons Ltd*,[209] Mason J drew a distinction between private actions and actions involving government secrets. He noted that the remedy is fashioned to protect personal, private and proprietary interests of the individual, not to protect the very different interests of the executive government. As governments act in the public interest, disclosure will be restrained if it appears to be 'inimical to the public interest because national security, relations with foreign countries or the ordinary business of government will be prejudiced'.[210]

8.3.7 Reasonableness of obtaining a remedy

A court has discretion as to whether it provides a remedy. One circumstance in which it may deny a remedy is where it is not reasonable to require the maintenance of a confidence, either because the stipulation at the time was unreasonable or because in the course of subsequent happenings, it becomes unreasonable that it should be enforced.[211]

---

204 *Corrs Pavey Whiting & Byrne v Collector of Customs (Vic)* (1987) 14 FCR 434, 443. See above at 8.3; Meagher, Gummow and Lehane's Equity, above n 1, [41.050]–[41.055].
205 (1990) 22 FCR 73, 112.
206 *Commonwealth v John Fairfax & Sons Ltd* (1980) 147 CLR 39; *Prince Albert v Strange* (1849) 1 H & Tw 1, 47 ER 1302.
207 *Rapid Metal Developments (Australia) Pty Ltd v Anderson Formrite Pty Ltd* [2005] WASC 255, [78]; *Attorney-General (UK) v Guardian Newspapers Ltd (No 2)* [1988] 3 All ER 545, 639, 658.
208 *Coulthard v South Australia* (1995) 63 SASR 531, 546; *Interfirm Comparison (Australia) Pty Ltd v Law Society of New South Wales* [1975] 2 NSWLR 104, 120; *Australian Medic-Care Co Ltd v Hamilton Pharmaceutical Pty Ltd* (2009) 261 ALR 501, [660].
209 (1980) 147 CLR 39.
210 Ibid 52; *Attorney-General (UK) v Jonathan Cape Ltd* [1976] QB 752, 770–1.
211 *Dunford & Elliott Ltd v Johnson & Firth Brown Ltd* [1978] FSR 143.

8.4 How long does the obligation last?

8.4.1 Express contractual obligations

Where express contractual terms impose the obligation of confidence, construction of the contract will resolve the matter.[212] Parties to a contract can agree to keep information in confidence, irrespective of whether that information possesses or retains the quality of confidence that is necessary for a breach of confidence action. In the absence of an express contrary intention, ordinarily a court will construe the obligations as limited to subject matter that remains confidential at the time of breach.[213] However, such terms are enforceable only if they survive the application of the restraint of trade doctrine.[214]

8.4.2 Equitable obligations

The position with the doctrine of breach of confidence is different because it only protects information that has the necessary quality of confidence. Hence, protection is not available for information that is in the public domain[215] at the time the obligation is purportedly imposed. However, information that possesses the necessary quality of confidence at that time may subsequently enter the public domain. This may occur through disclosure by the confider, the confidant or a third party. The requirement for information to be confidential means that a court would usually only restrain its use or disclosure if the information retained the quality of confidentiality at the time of breach or threatened breach of those obligations.[216]

8.4.3 Disclosure by the confider

A confider can no longer enforce equitable obligations of confidence once the information is disclosed in public by the confider[217] or as a necessary consequence of their actions in setting that disclosure in train. This may occur with the filing of a patent application that is later published,[218] the tender in open court of information claimed to be confidential without seeking a confidentiality order,[219] or with the release of products into the marketplace that

---

212 *Maggbury Pty Ltd v Hafele Australia Pty Ltd* (2001) 210 CLR 181, [50], [63], [89]; *Isaac v Dargan Financial Pty Ltd* [2018] NSWCA 163; *Optus Networks Pty Ltd v Telstra Corp Ltd* (2010) 265 ALR 281.
213 *Maggbury Pty Ltd v Hafele Australia Pty Ltd* (2001) 210 CLR 181, [45]; *Isaac v Dargan Financial Pty Ltd* [2018] NSWCA 163, [137]–[140].
214 *Maggbury Pty Ltd v Hafele Australia Pty Ltd* (2001) 210 CLR 181, [54]–[59]; *Wallis Nominees (Computing) Pty Ltd v Pickett* (2013) 45 VR 657, [14]; *Wright v Gasweld Pty Ltd* (1991) 22 NSWLR 317; *Industrial Rollformers Pty Ltd v Ingersoll-Rand (Australia) Ltd* [2001] NSWCA 111; *Restraints of Trade Act 1976* (NSW).
215 See above at 8.3.2.2.
216 *Maggbury Pty Ltd v Hafele Australia Pty Ltd* (2001) 210 CLR 181, [45].
217 *Attorney-General (UK) v Guardian Newspapers Ltd (No 2)* [1988] 3 All ER 545, 661; *Maggbury Pty Ltd v Hafele Australia Pty Ltd* (2001) 210 CLR 181, [48]; *Speed Seal Products Ltd v Paddington* [1986] 1 All ER 91, 94 (CA) (Fox LJ); *Cranleigh Precision Engineering Ltd v Bryant* [1964] 3 All ER 289, 300.
218 *O'Mustad & Son v S Alcock & Dosen Co Ltd* [1963] 3 All ER 416; *Franchi v Franchi* [1967] RPC 149.
219 *Isaac v Dargan Financial Pty Ltd* [2018] NSWCA 163, [174]; *Johns v Australian Securities Commission* (1993) 178 CLR 408.

could be pulled apart to discover the secret information.[220] In either case, once the information enters the public domain, the confidant would be released thereafter from the obligation of confidence. However, as the essence of the doctrine is the 'notion of an obligation of conscience arising from the circumstances in or through which the information was communicated or obtained',[221] a remedy may be available when the obligation is breached prior to its release into the public domain and the information is used to gain an unfair advantage in the marketplace.[222]

8.4.4 Disclosure by the confidant

The disclosure by the person who owes the obligation of confidence (the confidant) will be an actionable breach of confidence and will destroy the value of the information for the confider if the information enters the public domain. The principal issue in this case concerns the available remedies. It is clear that the confider would be entitled to damages.[223] Whether this eventuates will depend on the extent of the disclosure and the number of traders seriously competing in the market in which the confider operates. An injunction to restrain further disclosure may still be appropriate relief if it would afford the plaintiff real protection in the particular case.[224] For example, where it is only the parties to the action who are serious competitors in the market, it may be important for the confider to restrain the confidant's continuing use of the information. If the information has become generally known among other traders in the market, an injunction may be less useful.[225]

8.4.5 Disclosure by third party after confidence is imposed

Once information enters the public domain, a confidant is free to have recourse to the public domain for that information. The continuation of the equitable obligation of confidence in these circumstances would seem to depend on whether a confidant would abuse the confidence if released from the duty.[226] There is no general principle that a confidant remains bound by the duty of confidence when a third party releases the information into the public domain.[227] It is different where the imposition of the obligation of confidence is contractual or pursuant to the employment relationship. An express contractual obligation of confidence that does not violate the doctrine of restraint of trade may continue after a third-party disclosure.[228]

---

220 *Coco v AN Clark (Engineers) Ltd* [1969] RPC 41, 51; *RLA Polymers Pty Ltd v Nexus Adhesives Pty Ltd* (2011) 280 ALR 125, [52]. See above at 8.3.2.2.
221 *Moorgate Tobacco Co Ltd v Philip Morris Ltd (No 2)* (1984) 156 CLR 414, 438; *Breen v Williams* (1996) 186 CLR 71, 81; *Saltman Engineering Co Ltd v Campbell Engineering Co Ltd* (1948) 65 RPC 203, 213; *Stephens v Avery* [1988] Ch 449.
222 See below at 8.9.2.
223 *Speed Seal Products Ltd v Paddington* [1986] 1 All ER 91, 95.
224 *Speed Seal Products Ltd v Paddington* [1986] 1 All ER 91.
225 Ibid 95.
226 Ibid.
227 *Maggbury Pty Ltd v Hafele Australia Pty Ltd* (2001) 210 CLR 181, 200–1; *Attorney-General (UK) v Guardian Newspapers Ltd (No 2)* [1988] 3 All ER 545, 661.
228 *Maggbury Pty Ltd v Hafele Australia Pty Ltd* (2001) 210 CLR 181.

Similarly, an employee may be restrained from use or disclosure if the confidant becomes aware of the third-party disclosure by reason of his employment.[229]

8.5 Entitlement

To describe a person as 'owning' information implies a proprietary quality that is unlikely to be appropriate as an explanation of the legal basis upon which protection is available for breaches of confidence.[230] Nevertheless, while the High Court of Australia has confirmed that there is no property in information per se,[231] it has confirmed that trade secrets, at least, are capable of assignment.[232]

Confidential information is therefore in a different category from other forms of intellectual property that are all identified as personal property. In this area, the more helpful approach is to consider which party has the right to restrain unauthorised use or disclosure of the information, rather than to ask who 'owns' it. The person who is entitled to bring an action for breach of confidence is the person who is 'entitled to the confidence and to have it respected. He must be a person to whom the duty of good faith is owed'.[233] In the vast majority of cases, the plaintiff will be the person who communicated the information in confidence to the defendant or to the person from whom the defendant obtained such information. However, when that person is an employee, different and more complicated principles apply to determine who has rights in the information and who can restrain its use.[234]

An action will not lie at the hands of a person merely because they will be affected by the disclosure. In *Fraser v Evans*,[235] a public servant (the plaintiff) prepared a report for the Greek military government on its public relations in Europe. The plaintiff was given no undertaking on behalf of the government to keep this report secret. Some time later, the *Sunday Times* obtained a copy of the report and proposed to publish an article and selected extracts that the plaintiff believed would damage him. His application for an injunction to restrain publication was unsuccessful on the grounds that the newspaper owed no duty to him. Only the Greek government was entitled to the information in the report and could control its communication and publication. It alone had the standing to complain if anyone obtained the information surreptitiously or proposed to publish it,[236] and it made no complaint about the proposed publication.

---

229 Ibid 200, [47]; *Cranleigh Precision Engineering Ltd v Bryant* [1964] 3 All ER 289.
230 See above at 8.2.
231 *Breen v Williams* (1996) 186 CLR 71, 81, 90, 111, 129; *Farah Constructions Pty Ltd v Say-Dee Pty Ltd* (2007) 230 CLR 89, [118].
232 *Farah Constructions Pty Ltd v Say-Dee Pty Ltd* (2007) 230 CLR 89, [118]; *JR Consulting & Drafting Pty Ltd v Cummings* (2016) 329 ALR 625, [387]–[388]. As to 'trade secrets', see below at 8.7.2.
233 *Fraser v Evans* [1969] 1 QB 349, 361.
234 *Faccenda Chicken Ltd v Fowler* [1985] FSR 105, [1987] Ch 117; *Wright v Gasweld Pty Ltd* (1991) 22 NSWLR 317; *Printers & Finishers Ltd v Holloway (No 2)* [1965] RPC 239. As for universities, see A. L. Monotti (with S. Ricketson), *Universities and Intellectual Property: Ownership and Exploitation* (New York: Oxford University Press, 2003) [3.76]–[3.102]; as to rights among 'co-owners', see at [5.172]–[5.182]. See below at 8.6.
235 [1969] 1 QB 349.
236 Ibid 361.

An unusual situation involving entitlement to seek a remedy for breach of confidence arose in the context of tribal secrets in *Foster v Mountford & Rigby Ltd*.[237] Dr Mountford, an anthropologist, was given confidences by elders of a tribe of Aboriginal people. Members of an unincorporated body known as the Pitjantjara Council, but suing on their own behalf, brought an action against Dr Mountford for breach of confidence. The members were concerned that the disclosure of secrets to their women, children and uninitiated men could disrupt their social system. The court held that the individuals had standing to sue as individuals who were threatened with damage from disclosure of the secrets. This decision was likely to have been influenced by the special circumstances that surround tribal secrets.

There is past authority to the effect that confidential information is incapable of assignment because confidential information is not property.[238] However, the High Court recognised that '[c]ertain types of confidential information share characteristics with standard instances of property. Thus trade secrets may be transferred, held in trust and charged'.[239] It is unlikely that the court intended to limit its observations to so-called trade secrets, as equitable remedies provided under the doctrine of breach of confidence in respect of any confidential information can produce these characteristics. It is more likely that this distinction is referable to that class of confidential information that an employee cannot take with them after termination of employment. Commercial sale agreements commonly deal with 'confidential information', 'trade secrets' and 'know-how' as an asset of a business that is sold to a purchaser. In *TS & B Retail Systems Pty Ltd v 3fold Resources Pty Ltd*,[240] Finkelstein J characterised what is assigned as the right to enforce an obligation to keep information confidential rather than the information itself. In consequence, the information is acquired by the purchaser, in the sense of it being imparted,[241] and the purchaser can seek and obtain a remedy from a court of equity to restrain the disclosure or use of that information by a third party.[242]

While the rights of the 'owner' in the information in this sense are assignable, the rights of the user who received the information in confidence cannot be transferred to a third party in the absence of agreement. In *Neobev Pty Ltd v Bacchus Distillery Pty Ltd (admin apptd) (No 3)*,[243] the administrators of Bacchus Distillery sought to sell its business as a going concern. The assets included various patents and the rights granted by Neobev to Bacchus Distillery under a licence agreement to use confidential information contained in various documents relating to recipes, compositions, process instructions, testing specifications and operating and laboratory procedures. This information was received by Bacchus in such circumstances as to import an obligation of confidence. In deciding that the right to use confidential information is unassignable, Besanko J observed:

---

237 (1976) 14 ALR 71.
238 *TS & B Retail Systems Pty Ltd v 3fold Resources Pty Ltd* (2003) 57 IPR 530, 537 [24]; *Federal Commissioner of Taxation v United Aircraft Corp* (1943) 68 CLR 525, 534.
239 *Farah Constructions Pty Ltd v Say-Dee Pty Ltd* (2007) 230 CLR 89, [118].
240 (2003) 57 IPR 530.
241 Ibid [25]; *Elecon Australia Pty Ltd v PIV Drives GmbH* (2010) 93 IPR 174, [35].
242 *Painaway Australia Pty Ltd v JAKL Group Pty Ltd* (2011) 249 FLR 1, [320]–[330]; *TS & B Retail Systems Pty Ltd v 3fold Resources Pty Ltd* (2003) 57 IPR 530, 537 [25]; *O'Mustad & Son v S Alcock & Dosen Co Ltd* [1963] 3 All ER 416.
243 (2014) 104 IPR 249.

It seems fundamentally inconsistent with that feature to allow assignment by the person who owes the obligation of confidence. ... One cannot transfer the right to use without the obligation and the obligation is incapable of assignment.[244]

However, when a licence to use confidential information contains an express provision that allows assignment without the licensor's prior written consent, it may be possible for the licensee to authorise others to similarly make use of that information. This will be a matter of interpretation of the terms of the licence agreement.[245]

8.6 Special circumstances: during employment

Confidentiality in employment requires some qualification of the above principles.[246] This is because the courts recognise

> [t]he prima facie right of any person to use and to exploit for the purpose of earning his living all the skill, experience and knowledge which he has at his disposal, including skill, experience and knowledge which he has acquired in the course of previous periods of employment.[247]

The employer's ability to protect information from unauthorised disclosure or use will depend on the presence of an enforceable express term and whether the use or disclosure is threatened during or after the term of employment.

Unreasonable restrictions on use of the skill, experience or knowledge in subsequent employment may constitute a restraint of trade.[248] Such a restraint may arise when an employer attempts to assert unqualified rights to control and take the benefit of information created or acquired during employment.

In the area of employee obligations of confidence, 'the law is an unhappy mixture of equitable obligation (the duty of confidence and fiduciary obligation) and implied terms (particularly, but not only, the duty of good faith and fidelity)'.[249] Express terms as to confidentiality will be interpreted and applied, unless they are found to impose unreasonable restrictions on use of the skill, experience or knowledge that constitute a restraint of trade in subsequent employment.[250] In the absence of an express term, the implied duty of good faith

---

244   Ibid [141].
245   *Painaway Australia Pty Ltd v JAKL Group Pty Ltd* (2011) 249 FLR 1, [310]–[325]; *Neobev Pty Ltd v Bacchus Distillery Pty Ltd (admin apptd) (No 3)* (2014) 104 IPR 249, [141].
246   *Dean's Law of Trade Secrets and Privacy*, above n 1, [40.1900]–[40.6590]; A. Stewart et al, *Creighton and Stewart's Labour Law* (6th edn, Sydney: Federation Press, 2016) [17.19]–[17.26]; *Hivac Ltd v Park Royal Scientific Instruments Ltd* [1946] Ch 169, 174.
247   *Faccenda Chicken Ltd v Fowler* [1987] Ch 117, 128.
248   The classic formulation of restraint of trade is in *Nordenfelt v Maxim Nordenfelt Guns & Ammunition Co* [1894] AC 535, 565. See also *Electrolux Ltd v Hudson* [1977] FSR 312; *A Schroeder Music Publishing Co Ltd v Macauley* [1974] 3 All ER 616, 623.
249   *University of Western Australia v Gray* (2009) 179 FCR 346, [159].
250   The equitable doctrine may be relevant when the confider seeks an account of profits as the remedy for breach: *SAI Global Property Division Pty Ltd v Johnstone* (2016) 122 IPR 210, [42]. See above at 8.1.2 on coexisting rights.

or fidelity imposes obligations on the employee in respect of the use and disclosure of information.[251] This implied contractual term inevitably overlaps with the equitable duty of confidence.[252]

In addition, an employee may owe fiduciary duties to their employer.[253] Fiduciary obligations may arise in employment from specific contractual obligations and are recognised by equity as additional and more stringent duties than those that exist under the duty of fidelity. However, they are not a necessary incident of employment.[254] When fiduciary obligations exist, they sit alongside any express or implied terms in the employment contract.[255] Any obligation 'must accommodate itself to the terms of the contract so that it is consistent with and conforms to them. The fiduciary relationship cannot be superimposed upon the contract in such a way as to alter the operation which the contract was intended to have according to its true construction'.[256]

Equitable obligations of confidence may arise independently of the contract of employment if they satisfy the requirements for the equitable action of breach of confidence.[257] The dependence on proof that the information possesses the necessary level of confidentiality makes this a less attractive cause of action when an employer can rely on the more expansive duties of fidelity or implied contractual terms of employment.[258] Although the principles discussed above arise in the context of employment law cases, it seems that they apply equally to partnership relationships:

> The contractual obligation, and a correlative equitable obligation, subsist during partnership or employment, and continue after the cessation of partnership or employment.[259]

8.7 Special circumstances: after employment

When employment ends, the employer's ability to restrain use or disclosure of their secrets becomes more limited. In these circumstances, the obligation of an employee to preserve

---

251 *Robb v Green* [1895] 2 QB 315; *Del Casale v Artedomus (Australia) Pty Ltd* (2007) 73 IPR 326; *Faccenda Chicken Ltd v Fowler* [1987] Ch 117, 135.
252 *Lancashire Fires Ltd v SA Lyons & Co Ltd* [1996] FSR 629, 647–8.
253 As to fiduciary relationships, see *Hivac Ltd v Park Royal Scientific Instruments Ltd* [1946] Ch 169; *Hospital Products Ltd v United States Surgical Corp* (1984) 156 CLR 41; *University of Nottingham v Fishel* [2000] ICR 1462; *Balston Ltd v Headline Filters Ltd* [1990] FSR 385. See generally *Dean's Law of Trade Secrets and Privacy*, above n 1, [40.05] ff; Finn, *Fiduciary Obligations*, above n 32; J. Glover, *Commercial Equity: Fiduciary Relationships* (Sydney: Butterworths, 1995).
254 *University of Nottingham v Fishel* [2000] ICR 1462, 1491–2; *Helmet Integrated Systems Ltd v Tunnard* [2007] FSR 16, [36]–[38].
255 *Lancashire Fires Ltd v SA Lyons & Co Ltd* [1996] FSR 629, 648; *Ormonoid Roofing & Asphalts Ltd v Bitumenoids Ltd* (1930) 31 SR(NSW) 347; *Robb v Green* [1895] 2 QB 315; *Vokes Ltd v Heather* (1945) 62 RPC 135, 141–2.
256 *Hospital Products Ltd v United States Surgical Corp* (1984) 156 CLR 41, 97; *University of Nottingham v Fishel* [2000] ICR 1462, 1491–2.
257 *Coco v AN Clark (Engineers) Ltd* [1969] RPC 41.
258 Additional rights are available for corporations under *Corporations Act 2001* (Cth) s 183(1).
259 *X v Twitter Inc* (2017) 95 NSWLR 301, [5].

secrecy of information properly gained in the course of employment will depend on a variety of factors, including the nature of the information,[260] the existence of any express covenants, and the circumstances in which the information is removed by the employee for use.[261] Actions to protect secret information are still framed in contract or under the equitable action for breach of confidence but only under the duty of fidelity in strictly limited circumstances.[262]

8.7.1 Contract

8.7.1.1 Express terms

If the employer wishes to control disclosure of information after employment ceases, it can use an express term in the contract of employment. However, any express terms in a contract are unenforceable if they involve a restraint of trade against the former employee.[263]

In *Herbert Morris Ltd v Saxelby*,[264] a case involving an attempt by an employer to prevent a former employee disclosing and using information gained in the course of his employment, Lord Atkinson considered the extent to which it was permissible to impose a covenant in restraint of trade against a former employee. The classic formula that subsequent courts adopt was stated as follows:

> He [the employer] is undoubtedly entitled to have his interest in his trade secrets protected, such as secret processes of manufacture which may be of vast value. And that protection may be secured by restraining the employee from divulging these secrets or putting them to his own use. He is also entitled not to have his old customers by solicitation or such other means enticed away from him. But freedom from all competition per se apart from both these things, however lucrative it might be to him, he is not entitled to be protected against. He must be prepared to encounter that even at the hands of a former employee.[265]

Thus, for a covenant in restraint of trade to be reasonable, the employer must prove that (a) the covenant protects some legitimate interest of the employer and (b) the covenant extends no further than is strictly necessary to protect the employer's legitimate interest.[266]

In *Herbert Morris v Saxelby*,[267] the court recognised two legitimate interests of an employer as suitable for protection by restrictive covenants, one of which is trade secrets.[268] The

---

260 *Faccenda Chicken Ltd v Fowler* [1987] Ch 117; *Balston Ltd v Headline Filters Ltd* [1990] FSR 385; *Wright v Gasweld Pty Ltd* (1991) 22 NSWLR 317; *Dean's Law of Trade Secrets and Privacy*, above n 1, 186–203; *Creighton and Stewart's Labour Law*, above n 246, [17.27]–[17.41].
261 *Faccenda Chicken Ltd v Fowler* [1987] Ch 117, 137–8; *Printers & Finishers Ltd v Holloway (No 2)* [1965] RPC 239, 255; *Roger Bullivant Ltd v Ellis* [1987] 13 FSR 172.
262 Additional rights are available for corporations under *Corporations Act 2001* (Cth) s 183(1).
263 *Nordenfelt v Maxim Nordenfelt Guns & Ammunition Co* [1894] AC 535; J. D. Heydon, *The Restraint of Trade Doctrine* (4th edn, Sydney: LexisNexis Butterworths, 2018).
264 [1916] 1 AC 688.
265 Ibid 702.
266 *Maggbury Pty Ltd v Hafele Australia Pty Ltd* (2001) 210 CLR 181; *Peters (WA) Ltd v Petersville Ltd* (2001) 205 CLR 126.
267 [1916] 1 AC 688.
268 Ibid 702, 710; *Lindner v Murdock's Garage* (1950) 83 CLR 628, 633–5, 645, 649–50, 653–4; *Printers & Finishers Ltd v Holloway* [1965] RPC 239, 256; *Commercial Plastics Ltd v Vincent* [1964] 3 WLR 820; *FSS Travel & Leisure Systems Ltd v Johnson* [1999] FSR 505. For restrictive covenants in employment, see

meaning of this term is imprecise and a variety of factors assists courts with their decision.[269] The preferable approach in the current context is to equate 'trade secrets' with the 'far end of the spectrum' which has trivial information at one end and 'secrets that attract equitable protection whether or not there is a contractual agreement' at the other.[270] The composite phrase 'confidential information and trade secrets' appears commonly to describe the scope of this legitimate interest along with the employer's customer connections.[271]

Courts will enforce covenants that restrain employment of the former employee by a trade rival where it might be anticipated that the employee's use of the information after termination of the employment might give the employee an advantage in competing with the employer for the period of the restraint.[272] However, as stated above, the restraint must be reasonable[273] and is assessed at the date of the contract.[274] A court will construe the clause to ensure that it does not exceed what is necessary to protect the legitimate interests of the employer.[275]

8.7.1.2 Implied duty of good faith

As mentioned above, the implied duty of good faith or fidelity imposes obligations on the employee in respect of the use and disclosure of information.[276] The general understanding is that the implied duty of an employee to act in good faith towards their employer ceases on termination of the employment contract.[277] Subject to limited exceptions, the duty does not provide the source of rights to restrain post-employment breaches of confidence.[278] An exception is when the employee deliberately acquires or memorises the information during the period of employment. In this case, an employer may have a remedy for breach of contract if the employee seeks to use or disclose that information after he leaves employment.[279]

The rights of an employer to restrain post-employment breaches of confidence imposed by the implied duty of good faith were considered in the *Faccenda Chicken Ltd v Fowler*

Heydon, *The Restraint of Trade Doctrine*, above n 263, chs 4–7; *Creighton and Stewart's Labour Law*, above n 246, [17.34]–[17.41].

269 *Thomas Marshall (Exports) Ltd v Guinle* [1979] Ch 227, 248; *Lansing Linde Ltd v Kerr* [1991] 1 WLR 251, 259; *Del Casale v Artedomus (Australia) Pty Ltd* (2007) 73 IPR 326, [40]–[41], [108]–[138]. See below at 8.7.2.
270 *Wright v Gasweld Pty Ltd* (1991) 22 NSWLR 317, 333–4.
271 *Pioneer Concrete Services Ltd v Galli* [1985] 675, 710–11; *Lindner v Murdock's Garage* (1950) 83 CLR 628, 633–4; *Just Group Ltd v Peck* [2016] VSCA 334, [33]–[34].
272 *Littlewoods Organisation Ltd v Harris* [1977] 1 WLR 1472, 1479, 1485; *Printers & Finishers Ltd v Holloway* [1965] RPC 239; *Jardin v Metcash Ltd* (2011) 285 ALR 677, [98]–[104].
273 *Just Group Ltd v Peck* [2016] VSCA 334, [30]–[37]; *Wallis Nominees (Computing) Pty Ltd v Pickett* (2013) 45 VR 657, [14], [18]; *Miles v Genesys Wealth Advisers Ltd* (2009) 201 IR 1, [63]; *EZYDVD Pty Ltd v Lahrs Investments Qld Pty Ltd* [2010] 2 Qd R 517 (restraint in a franchising agreement found to be unreasonable); Heydon, *The Restraint of Trade Doctrine*, above n 263, ch 7.
274 *Miles v Genesys Wealth Advisers Ltd* (2009) 201 IR 1, [43]; *Woolworths Ltd v Olson* [2004] NSWCA 372, [40]
275 *Just Group Ltd v Peck* [2016] VSCA 334, [38]–[39]. For commencement of a restraint period when the employee is placed on 'gardening leave', see *DP World Sydney Ltd v Guy* [2016] NSWSC 1072.
276 *Robb v Green* [1895] 2 QB 315; *Del Casale v Artedomus (Australia) Pty Ltd* (2007) 73 IPR 326; *Faccenda Chicken Ltd v Fowler* [1987] Ch 117, 135.
277 *Del Casale v Artedomus (Australia) Pty Ltd* (2007) 73 IPR 326. Compare *Faccenda Chicken Ltd v Fowler* [1987] Ch 117, 137.
278 *Robb v Green* [1895] 2 QB 315; *Del Casale v Artedomus (Australia) Pty Ltd* (2007) 73 IPR 326; *Dean's Law of Trade Secrets and Privacy*, above n 1.
279 *Wessex Dairies Ltd v Smith* [1935] 2 KB 80; *Del Casale v Artedomus (Australia) Pty Ltd* (2007) 73 IPR 326, [33]; *Faccenda Chicken Ltd v Fowler* [1987] Ch 117, 136.

litigation.[280] The need to balance the employee's right to continue using their skills and knowledge with the employer's right to maintain confidences[281] led Goulding J to classify knowledge acquired in employment into knowledge that the employee can use freely both in and out of employment and two categories of confidential information.[282] The first class is confidential information that becomes part of the stock of knowledge and skill applied in the course of the employer's business – often referred to as 'know-how'. Courts are reluctant to grant a remedy where the ex-employee is using that information in circumstances that render it artificial to sever the know-how from the confidential information.[283] The only way an employer can protect this class of information is to use a reasonable restrictive covenant that restrains the employee from competing with the employer for a period of time within a particular distance.[284]

The second class of confidential information in Goulding J's taxonomy is 'trade secrets' – information that is 'so confidential that ... [it] cannot lawfully be used for anyone's benefit but the master's.'[285] The Court of Appeal in *Faccenda Chicken Ltd v Fowler* confirmed the principle that only 'trade secrets' can be protected post-employment when no express term exists in the employment contract under an implied term that is more restricted in its scope than the general duty of good faith.[286] In *Del Casale v Artedomus (Australia) Pty Ltd*,[287] the New South Wales Court of Appeal considered the extent to which an implied term in an employment contract imposing a duty of good faith operates after employment to protect confidences. All members of the court doubted the proposition of the English Court of Appeal in *Faccenda Chicken Ltd v Fowler* that an implied duty of good faith continues to operate in post-employment situations to restrain unauthorised use or disclosure of trade secrets.[288] According to Hodgson JA in *Del Casale*, the preferable way in which to deal with these issues is under the equitable action for breach of confidence. An alternative approach discussed in the case is to impose an implied term in law as an incident of the relationship or a matter of business efficacy.[289]

8.7.2 Equitable principles of confidence

An employer may be able to rely on the equitable doctrine of breach of confidence to restrain the unauthorised disclosure of secrets by a former employee, but its operation requires modification to address the special considerations that apply to the acquisition and use of

---

280 [1985] FSR 105, 114–16 (HC); [1987] Ch 117 (CA).
281 *Wessex Dairies Ltd v Smith* [1935] 2 KB 80, 89; *United Indigo Chemical Co Ltd v Robinson* (1939) 49 RPC 178, 187; *E Worsley & Co Ltd v Cooper* [1939] 1 All ER 290, 309.
282 *Faccenda Chicken Ltd v Fowler* [1985] FSR 105, 114–16, accepted on appeal [1987] Ch 117; *Wright v Gasweld Pty Ltd* (1991) 22 NSWLR 317.
283 *Del Casale v Artedomus (Australia) Pty Ltd* (2007) 73 IPR 326, [43]–[47].
284 *Printers & Finishers Ltd v Holloway* [1965] RPC 239, 253; *Wright v Gasweld Pty Ltd* (1991) 22 NSWLR 317; *Faccenda Chicken Ltd v Fowler* [1985] FSR 105, 115. Compare *Faccenda Chicken Ltd v Fowler* [1987] Ch 117, 137.
285 *Faccenda Chicken Ltd v Fowler* [1985] FSR 105, 115.
286 [1987] Ch 117, 136.
287 (2007) 73 IPR 326.
288 Ibid [34], [79]–[91].
289 Ibid [34], [100]; *Lamb v Evans* [1893] 1 Ch 218; *BP Refinery (Westernport) Pty Ltd v Shire of Hastings* (1977) 180 CLR 266, 282–3; *Byrne v Australian Airlines Ltd* (1995) 185 CLR 410, 422.

knowledge by employees.[290] These considerations relate particularly to protecting the rights of an individual to use in subsequent employment all knowledge and skill in the nature of 'know-how' that has been acquired in previous employment.[291] There is obiter to the effect that equitable relief may be granted to prevent disclosure of confidential information to a third party but not to prevent the former employee using the information.[292]

There have been numerous attempts to formulate guidelines to identify business information that would have the necessary quality of confidence to enable an employer to benefit from equitable protection after employment terminates. Guidelines and lists provide 'useful aids to decision-making'[293] and are supplemented as circumstances arise for consideration.[294] In *Ansell Rubber Co Pty Ltd v Allied Rubber Industries Pty Ltd*, the following criteria were adapted from the American Law Institute's *Restatement (First) of Torts*:

> (1) the extent to which the information is known outside of [the owner's] business; (2) the extent to which it is known by employees and others involved in [the] business; (3) the extent of measures taken by [the owner] to guard the secrecy of the information; (4) the value of the information to [the owner] and to [their] competitors; (5) the amount of effort or money expended by [the owner] in developing the information; (6) the ease or difficulty with which the information could be properly acquired or duplicated by others.[295]

Another set of four guidelines appears in the judgment of Megarry V-C in *Thomas Marshall (Exports) Ltd v Guinle*:

> First, ... the information must be information the release of which the owner believes would be injurious to him or of advantage to his rivals or others. Second, ... the owner must believe that the information is confidential or secret, i.e. that it is not already in the public domain ... Third, ... the owner's belief under the two previous heads must be reasonable. Fourth, ... the information must be judged in the light of the usage and practices of the particular industry or trade concerned.[296]

Other factors include:

- that the obligation of confidentiality was impressed upon the employee;[297]
- that information was jealously guarded;[298]

---

290 See above at 8.6 and 8.7.1.2.
291 *Faccenda Chicken Ltd v Fowler* [1987] Ch 117, 136; *Herbert Morris Ltd v Saxelby* [1916] 1 AC 688, 714.
292 *Del Casale v Artedomus (Australia) Pty Ltd* (2007) 73 IPR 326, [47]; *Herbert Morris Ltd v Saxelby* [1916] 1 AC 688, 710; *United Indigo Chemical Co Ltd v Robinson* (1939) 49 RPC 178, 187.
293 *Del Casale v Artedomus (Australia) Pty Ltd* (2007) 73 IPR 326, [138].
294 *Wright v Gasweld Pty Ltd* (1991) 22 NSWLR 317, 334; *Del Casale v Artedomus (Australia) Pty Ltd* (2007) 73 IPR 326, [40]; *Faccenda Chicken Ltd v Fowler* [1987] Ch 117, 137–8.
295 [1967] VR 37, 50 (Gowans J); *Mense & Ampere Electrical Manufacturing Co Pty Ltd v Milenkovic* [1973] VR 784, 795–8.
296 [1979] Ch 227, 248.
297 See, for example, *Lancashire Fires Ltd v SA Lyons & Co Ltd* [1996] FSR 629, 673–4; *Cray Valley Ltd v Deltech Europe Ltd* [2003] EWHC 728 (Ch), [55]–[56]; *Gurry on Breach of Confidence*, above n 1; *Wright v Gasweld Pty Ltd* (1991) 22 NSWLR 317, 334; *Faccenda Chicken Ltd v Fowler* [1987] Ch 117, 138.
298 *Ansell Rubber Co Pty Ltd v Allied Rubber Industries Pty Ltd* [1967] VR 37, 50; *Wright v Gasweld Pty Ltd* (1991) 22 NSWLR 317, 334.

- the nature of the employment and the ease with which the information could be isolated from other information the employee was free to use or disclose;[299]
- the expenditure of skill and effort to acquire the information;[300] and
- industry usages and practices that support the assertion of confidentiality.[301]

Guidelines have an important role, and the classification of the information as a trade secret in any particular case will take account of the strength of these factors.[302] Nevertheless, they 'are not a substitute for the different legal tests by which the existence of those different obligations are decided. Such lists should not distract attention from what is the true object of each of those separate inquiries.'[303] What is that true object? It has been described as that which

> should fairly be regarded as a separate part of the employee's stock of knowledge ... which a man of ordinary intelligence and honesty would regard as the property of the former employer.[304]

8.8 Defences: public interest in disclosure
8.8.1 Background

A person may be restrained from using or disclosing the confidential information of another without the owner's consent, irrespective of how they acquire possession of the information.[305] However, rights to restrain unauthorised use or disclosure are not absolute.[306] Although public policy protects the maintenance of confidences, a variety of grounds exist on which a court might refuse a remedy. Apart from the existence of statutory exemptions from infringement or justifications for disclosure, such as under legal compulsion or to assist with the administration of justice,[307] courts might exercise discretion in equity to deny a remedy on grounds that one or more of the traditional equitable defences, such as unclean hands or illegality, are present.[308]

---

299 *Del Casale v Artedomus (Australia) Pty Ltd* (2007) 73 IPR 326, [41]; *Ansell Rubber Co Pty Ltd v Allied Rubber Industries Pty Ltd* [1967] VR 37, 49; *Faccenda Chicken Ltd v Fowler* [1987] Ch 117, 137–8; *AT Poeton (Gloucester Plating) Ltd v Horton* [2000] EWCA Civ 180; *FSS Travel & Leisure Systems Ltd v Johnson* [1999] FSR 505.
300 *Wright v Gasweld Pty Ltd* (1991) 22 NSWLR 317, 334; *Interfirm Comparison (Australia) Pty Ltd v Law Society of New South Wales* [1975] 2 NSWLR 104, 117.
301 *Thomas Marshall (Exports) Ltd v Guinle* [1979] Ch 227, 248; *Wright v Gasweld Pty Ltd* (1991) 22 NSWLR 317, 334.
302 *Del Casale v Artedomus (Australia) Pty Ltd* (2007) 73 IPR 326, [40]–[41].
303 Ibid [138].
304 *Ansell Rubber Co Pty Ltd v Allied Rubber Industries Pty Ltd* [1967] VR 37, 40; *Printers & Finishers Ltd v Holloway (No 2)* [1965] RPC 239, 255; *GlaxoSmithKline Australia Pty Ltd v Ritchie* (2008) 77 IPR 306, [53].
305 *Sullivan v Sclanders & Goldwell International Pty Ltd* (2000) 77 SASR 419, 424 [31].
306 Defences, see *Meagher, Gummow and Lehane's Equity*, above n 1, [42.160]–[42.175].
307 *National Roads and Motorists' Association v Geeson* (2001) 40 ACSR 1, [54]; *Richards v Kadian* (2005) 64 NSWLR 204, [46]; *A v Hayden (No 2)* (1984) 156 CLR 532; *ISTIL Group Inc v Zahoor* [2003] 2 All ER 252, [112].
308 *Corrs Pavey Whiting & Byrne v Collector of Customs (Vic)* (1987) 14 FCR 434, 456; *Meagher, Gummow and Lehane's Equity*, above n 1.

An alternative justification for disclosure of confidential information arises from the principle in *Gartside v Outram* that no confidence exists in the disclosure of iniquity:

> You cannot make me the confidant of a crime or a fraud, and be entitled to close up my lips upon any secret which you have the audacity to disclose to me relating to any fraudulent intention on your part: such a confidence cannot exist.[309]

In that case, Wood V-C found that an employee was not required to maintain confidential the fraudulent operations of the employer. The rule defines 'iniquity' narrowly so that the preservation of confidences remains paramount.[310] Further developments in the United Kingdom introduced an express requirement that the disclosure is in the 'public interest'.[311] It is undeniable that it is in the public interest to permit disclosure of a crime or fraud in breach of confidence, but it is not clear how far this concept of 'iniquity' can extend to provide a defence for disclosure in the public interest. While the historic principle that 'there is no confidence in the disclosure of iniquity' may be source of a public interest defence, no consistent language appears in decisions to define its scope.[312] In *Fraser v Evans,* Denning LJ equated the word 'iniquity' with an arguably broader concept of 'just cause and excuse':

> I do not look upon the word 'iniquity' as expressing principle. It is merely an instance of *just cause and excuse* for breaking confidence. There are some things that require to be disclosed in the public interest, in which event no confidence can be prayed in aid to keep them secret.[313]

Later in *Beloff v Pressdram Ltd*,[314] Ungoed-Thomas J emphasised the gravity of the conduct that would justify the disclosure without reference to 'iniquity', but using an expanded list of conduct:

> The defence of public interest clearly covers ... disclosure, which as Lord Denning MR emphasized must be disclosure justified in the public interest, of matters carried out or contemplated, in breach of the country's security, or in breach of law, including statutory duty, fraud, or otherwise destructive of the country or its people, including matters medically dangerous to the public; and doubtless other misdeeds of similar gravity ... Such public interest, as now recognized by the law, does not extend beyond misdeeds of a serious nature and importance to the country and thus, in my view, clearly recognizable as such.[315]

A 'high-water mark' of a public interest defence arrived in *Woodward v Hutchins*,[316] with the test expressed as 'a question of balancing the public interest in maintaining the confidence

---

309 *Gartside v Outram* (1857) 26 LJ Ch 113, 114.
310 *Corrs Pavey Whiting & Byrne v Collector of Customs (Vic)* (1987) 14 FCR 434, 456.
311 *Initial Services Ltd v Putterill* [1968] 1 QB 396, 405; *Beloff v Pressdram Ltd* [1973] 1 All ER 241, 260; *Castrol Australia Pty Ltd v EmTech Associates Pty Ltd* (1980) 33 ALR 31, 55.
312 See *Dean's Law of Trade Secrets and Privacy*, above n 1, pt 2; S. Ricketson and C. Creswell, *The Law of Intellectual Property: Copyright, Designs and Confidential Information* (Thomson Legal & Regulatory, 2006) [26.5]; *Gurry on Breach of Confidence*, above n 1.
313 *Fraser v Evans* [1969] 1 QB 349, 362 (emphasis added).
314 [1973] RPC 765.
315 Ibid; [1973] 1 All ER 241, 260.
316 *Woodward v Hutchins* [1977] 2 All ER 751, 754.

against the public interest in knowing the truth.'[317] The concept of an 'iniquity' becomes merely 'public interest' with no further definition.[318] That approach may not require the disclosure of an 'iniquity' – merely a balancing act without preference for maintenance of confidences.[319]

8.8.2 Nature of a justification for disclosure in the public interest in Australia

The developments in the United Kingdom of an iniquity rule and a defence in the public interest to this point influenced Australian courts as they searched for a principled approach to justify disclosure of a confidence in breach of an equitable obligation of confidence. Traditional equitable defences such as unclean hands and illegality continue to justify disclosure of confidences. However, while courts recognise additional circumstances in which to justify disclosure in breach of confidence, the present status and scope of any defence in the public interest remains unclear.[320]

A defence to an action for breach of confidence for disclosure of an iniquity is clearly available, although the limits beyond the commission of crimes and frauds[321] remain undefined. In *Corrs Pavey Whiting & Byrne v Collector of Customs (Vic)*,[322] Gummow J (in the Federal Court) concluded that *Gartside v Outram*[323] concerned equitable relief in aid of contractual rights and provided insufficient basis for a public interest defence 'of the kind that ... has developed in the recent English authorities.'[324] However, it could 'inspire' a narrower principle of general application in equity when there is no reliance on contract:

> [I]nformation will lack the necessary attribute of confidence if the subject matter is the existence or real likelihood of the existence of an iniquity in the sense of a crime, civil wrong or serious misdeed of public importance, and the confidence is relied upon to prevent disclosure to a third party with a real and direct interest in redressing such crime, wrong or misdeed.[325]

This focus upon the confidential status of the information avoids any consideration of the public interest in disclosure. The rule is 'one of the content of any such obligation in its inception'[326] that prevents the duty of confidence arising through the lack of the necessary

---

317 Ibid.
318 *Castrol Australia Pty Ltd v EmTech Associates Pty Ltd* (1980) 33 ALR 31, 55.
319 See *Gurry on Breach of Confidence*, above n 1, [16.58]–[16.129] for the subsequent development in the United Kingdom of defences to misuse of private information.
320 *AG Australia Holdings Ltd v Burton* (2002) 58 NSWLR 464, [177] (Campbell J); *Australian Football League v The Age Co Ltd* (2006) 15 VR 419, [83]; *David Syme & Co Ltd v GMH Ltd* [1984] 2 NSWLR 294, 297 (Street CJ); *Esso Australia Resources Ltd v Plowman* (1995) 183 CLR 10, 402 (Mason CJ).
321 *A v Hayden (No 2)* (1984) 156 CLR 532, 544–7; *Minister for Immigration and Citizenship v Kumar* (2009) 238 CLR 448, [26]; *West Australian Newspapers Ltd v Bond* [2009] 40 WAR 164, [44]; *Phoenix Eagle Co Pty Ltd v Tom McArthur Pty Ltd* [2017] WASC 130, [48].
322 (1987) 14 FCR 434.
323 (1857) 26 LJ Ch 113.
324 *Corrs Pavey Whiting & Byrne v Collector of Customs (Vic)* (1987) 14 FCR 434, 454.
325 (1987) 14 FCR 434, 456.
326 *Smith Kline & French Laboratories (Australia) Ltd v Secretary, Department of Community Services and Health* (1990) 22 FCR 73, 110.

quality of confidence.[327] Hence, it may not be a true defence to an otherwise breach of confidence.[328] A number of judges prefer this statement of an 'iniquity rule' for resolving applications to permit disclosure.[329] Other decisions may expressly require consideration of the public interest, but continue to confine the defence to circumstances in which the information exposes a level of disgraceful content. The precise limits of that content – of 'iniquity' or 'misdeeds' – remain unclear.[330] It is also debatable whether the concept of iniquity extends to the tort of negligence.[331]

Nevertheless, the 'iniquity rule' – or defence in the public interest that is limited to confidences in 'iniquities' – clearly permits disclosure of confidences where it would be unconscionable 'for the applicant to insist upon the maintenance of a confidence which would keep the iniquity secret.'[332] Various decisions support this rationale for the continuing application of the rule and endorse the development of equitable principle by reference to what conscionable behaviour demands of the confidant in the circumstances as opposed to 'balancing those demands with matters of public interest'.[333]

A public interest defence that requires some broad balancing of interests without reference to some concept of disclosure of iniquity contrasts diametrically with the above 'iniquity rule'. It has support in cases that involve disclosure of secret information held by governments[334] where different considerations of public interest apply but otherwise may have limited application in Australia. A number of cases reject an approach to a public interest defence that merely requires that public interest in the publication, or the right of the public to know, outweigh the public interest in confidentiality.[335] Gummow J in the Federal Court described such defences as 'picturesque and somewhat imprecise'[336] and 'an invitation to judicial idiosyncrasy'.[337]

---

327 *Corrs Pavey Whiting & Byrne v Collector of Customs (Vic)* (1987) 14 FCR 434, 456; *AMI Australia Holdings Pty Ltd v Fairfax Media Publications Pty Ltd* [2010] NSWSC 1395, [20].
328 *Australian Football League v The Age Co Ltd* (2006) 15 VR 419, [69].
329 *Sullivan v Sclanders & Goldwell International Pty Ltd* (2000) 77 SASR 419, [2], [45]. See also *Australian Football League v The Age Co Ltd* (2006) 15 VR 419, 440 [83]; *Cowell v British American Tobacco Australia Services Ltd* [2007] VSCA 301, [34].
330 For example, there are differences of opinion as to whether breach of the provisions of pt IV and pt V of the *Trade Practices Act 1974* (Cth) – now pt IV of the *Competition and Consumer Act 2010* (Cth) – is an iniquity for the purposes of this defence: *Allied Mills Industries Pty Ltd v Trade Practices Commission* (1981) 34 ALR 105, 142. Compare *AG Australia Holdings Ltd v Burton* (2002) 58 NSWLR 464, [191].
331 *AG Australia Holdings Ltd v Burton* (2002) 58 NSWLR 464, [191].
332 *Cowell v British American Tobacco Australia Services Ltd* [2007] VSCA 301, [34]; *Corrs Pavey Whiting & Byrne v Collector of Customs (Vic)* (1987) 14 FCR 434, 457.
333 *Sullivan v Sclanders & Goldwell International Pty Ltd* (2000) 77 SASR 419, [45]; *AMI Australia Holdings Pty Ltd v Fairfax Media Publications Pty Ltd* [2010] NSWSC 1395, [20].
334 *Attorney-General (UK) v Heinemann Publishers Australia Pty Ltd* (1987) 10 NSWLR 86, 171 (Kirby P); T. Voon, 'Breach of confidence by government, *Smith Kline* and the *TRIPs Agreement*: Public interest to the rescue' (1998) 9 *Australian Intellectual Property Journal* 6. A detailed analysis of the defence in the public interest appears in *Dean's Law of Trade Secrets and Privacy*, above n 1.
335 *David Syme & Co Ltd v General Motors-Holden's Ltd* [1984] 2 NSWLR 294, 298 (Samuels JA), 305 (Hutley AP); *Castrol Australia Pty Ltd v EmTech Associates Pty Ltd* (1980) 33 ALR 31, 55; *Bacich v Australian Broadcasting Corporation* (1992) 29 NSWLR 1, 16.
336 *Corrs Pavey Whiting & Byrne v Collector of Customs (Vic)* (1987) 14 FCR 434, 451.
337 *Smith Kline & French Laboratories (Australia) Ltd v Secretary, Department of Community Services and Health* (1990) 22 FCR 73, 111.

As a final observation, it is likely that Australian courts would defend the disclosure of an iniquity only if it is to the 'appropriate authority'[338] or to those who have a real and direct interest in addressing the problem.[339] In some cases, this may justify disclosure to the public as a whole.

8.9 Remedies
8.9.1 General

As a general principle, a court should not intervene 'unless it is satisfied that there is no risk of disclosure. The risk must be a real one, and not merely fanciful or theoretical'.[340] When breach of confidence is established, a court has the usual array of remedies available.[341] Monetary remedies are available in the form of damages or an account of profits. Where parties to a contract include express provisions relating to confidential information but do not exclude equitable obligations of confidence, it is possible for the injured party to make a claim in equity and to elect between damages for breach under the contract or an account of profits.[342] It may be that the remedies include the imposition of a constructive trust.[343]

An injunction is the most important remedy for apprehended or continuing breaches of confidence and, like other causes of action that originate in equity, is available without the need to establish that damages are an inadequate remedy.[344] It is therefore important to distinguish between the grant of an injunction in relation to the equitable doctrine of breach of confidence, on the one hand, and that in aid of a legal right arising in contract, on the other.[345] As an injunction should be no wider than is necessary for the protection of the rights, it should identify with some precision the confidential information to which it relates.[346] It may also be limited in time according to the existence of a 'springboard' advantage. When the employer places an employee on 'gardening leave', the period of restraint may commence at that time.[347] Injunctive relief has no utility when the aggrieved party disclosed the confidential information in open court without seeking a confidentiality order.[348]

---

338 *Allied Mills Industries Pty Ltd v Trade Practices Commission* (1981) 34 ALR 105, [105].
339 *Attorney-General (UK) v Heinemann Publishers Australia Pty Ltd* (1987) 8 NSWLR 341, 381; *Initial Services Ltd v Putterill* [1968] 1 QB 396, 405–6.
340 *Rapid Metal Developments (Australia) Pty Ltd v Anderson Formrite Pty Ltd* [2005] WASC 255, [95].
341 See ch 17.
342 *Optus Networks Pty Ltd v Telstra Corp Ltd* (2010) 265 ALR 281, [41].
343 *LAC Minerals v International Corona Resources* (1989) 69 OR (2d) 287; *Polwood Pty Ltd v Foxworth Pty Ltd* (2008) 165 FCR 527, [88].
344 *Heavener v Loomes* (1924) 34 CLR 306, 326; K. Barnett and S. Harder, *Remedies in Australian Private Law* (Melbourne: Cambridge University Press, 2014) 233, 261.
345 *Jardin v Metcash Ltd* (2011) 285 ALR 677, [116]; *Meagher, Gummow and Lehane's Equity*, above n 1, [21.010], [21.015], [21.025], [21.035].
346 See above at 8.3.1.
347 *DP World Sydney Ltd v Guy* [2016] NSWSC 1072.
348 *Isaac v Dargan Financial Pty Ltd* [2018] NSWCA 163, [174]; *Johns v Australian Securities Commission* (1993) 178 CLR 408.

8.9.2 The springboard principle

The expressions 'head start' and 'springboard' are used to describe the advantage gained by persons who have misused confidential information before it enters the public domain. The cases in which this doctrine is applied deal with circumstances where a person has gained an advantage which can be measured by reference to the advantage which has followed the misuse of the information. The first explicit mention of the 'springboard' principle occurs in *Terrapin Ltd v Builders' Supply Co (Hayes) Ltd*, when Roxburgh J stated:

> [T]he essence of this branch of the law ... is that a person who has obtained information in confidence is not allowed to use it as a springboard for activities detrimental to the person who made the confidential communication, and springboard it remains even when all the features have been published or can be ascertained by actual inspection by any member of the public ... It is, in my view, inherent in the principle upon which [*Saltman Engineering Co Ltd v Campbell Engineering Co Ltd* (1948) 65 RPC 203] rests that the possessor of such information must be placed under a special disability in the field of competition in order to ensure that he does not get an unfair start.[349]

It is necessary to exercise caution about applying this passage literally. Commenting on it in *British Franco Electric Pty Ltd v Dowling Plastics Pty Ltd*, Wootten J expressed the view:

> This passage contemplates not that a person who has received information in confidence will be enjoined for ever from using it, notwithstanding that it has become public. It contemplates rather the moulding of remedies to place him under special disability to ensure that he does not get an unfair start, in other words, the imposition of some compensating handicap.[350]

Terrapin was concerned with the confidant who would have the benefit of a head start over others in the market only because there would be some delay involved for others to discover the secret information from what was in the marketplace. It was clear that the secret information was not exposed by the product and other materials put into the marketplace.[351] As the doctrine prevents advantages secured through avoiding 'special labours in respect of the product in order to discover its secret',[352] a handicap is unnecessary when the details are immediately available from the public domain. Any person who wants to avoid an allegation of misuse of confidential information 'must proceed through an independent design sequence and not use confidential information as a springboard to jump through that sequence'.[353] The springboard principle may be relevant also in cases that involve restraining a former employee from performing work for a competitor, although authority on this point is scarce. A court would be wary of making an order to this effect, particularly in the absence of a contractual restraint in the employment contract, as this would be 'tantamount to a restraint of trade'.[354]

---

349 *Terrapin Ltd v Builders Supply Co (Hayes) Ltd* [1967] RPC 375, 391–2.
350 [1981] 1 NSWLR 448, 451.
351 *Terrapin Ltd v Builders Supply Co (Hayes) Ltd* [1967] RPC 375.
352 *Mars UK Ltd v Teknowledge Ltd* [2000] FSR 138, [32]; *Gurry on Breach of Confidence*, above n 1.
353 *Dart Industries Inc v David Bryar & Associates Pty Ltd* (1997) 38 IPR 389, 408–9; *Nexus Adhesives Pty Ltd v RLA Polymers Pty Ltd* (2012) 97 IPR 160, [96].
354 *National Surgical Pty Ltd v McPhee* (2010) 87 IPR 602, [52]–[56]. But see *Wilson Parking Australia 1992 Pty Ltd v Rush* [2008] FCA 1601.

In some cases, an injunction will be the appropriate remedy, the handicap being gauged according to the time that others might be expected to take to reverse-engineer the product or research publicly available information to uncover this secret information. In others, a remedy in damages[355] only or an account of profits[356] may be more appropriate. This might be because the head start gained is minor,[357] because such a remedy adequately compensates for the use of the information, or because it is unreasonable to prohibit use when the confidant has mingled their own confidential information with that of the confider.[358] The essence of the doctrine is to prevent the use of information to gain an unfair advantage in the marketplace.[359]

Equity may exercise its discretion not to grant relief or, in particular, an injunction. Reasons could include laches,[360] acquiescence and 'unclean hands'.

8.9.3 Damages

The main pecuniary remedy for breach of confidence is damages, the other being an account of profits. Damages are available where the breach is one of an express or implied contractual obligation of confidence, either alone or in addition to an injunction. They can also be claimed in tort where the defendant is a third party who has induced the breach of confidence. Where liability arises under the equitable doctrine, damages are also available either alone or in addition to an injunction.[361] The value of the information that a defendant takes or misuses depends on its nature.[362] A variety of means exist for the calculation of damages;[363] this may be by reference to the loss of profits that would have been derived but for the defendant's breach,[364] by reference to the cost of a consultant who could provide the same information,[365] or by reference to any licence fee that would be negotiated in a commercial transaction.[366] As stated by the Victorian Court of Appeal in *Darvall McCutcheon (a firm) v HK Frost Holdings Pty Ltd (in liq)*:

---

[355] For example, *Seager v Copydex Ltd* [1967] 2 All ER 415, 417; *Coco v AN Clark (Engineers) Ltd* [1969] RPC 41; *Cray Valley Ltd v Deltech Europe Ltd* [2003] EWHC 728 (Ch), [47]; *Darvall McCutcheon (a firm) v HK Frost Holdings Pty Ltd (in liq)* (2002) 4 VR 570.

[356] *RLA Polymers Pty Ltd v Nexus Adhesives Pty Ltd* (2011) 280 ALR 125, [165], [174], approved in (2012) 97 IPR 160.

[357] *Cray Valley Ltd v Deltech Europe Ltd* [2003] EWHC 728 (Ch), [47].

[358] *Coco v AN Clark (Engineers) Ltd* [1969] RPC 41, 48–9; *Seager v Copydex Ltd* [1967] 2 All ER 415, 417; *EPI Environmental Technologies Inc v Symphony Plastic Technologies plc* [2005] 1 WLR 3456; *Polwood Pty Ltd v Foxworth Pty Ltd* (2008) 165 FCR 527, [89]–[92].

[359] *Terrapin Ltd v Builders Supply Co (Hayes) Ltd* [1967] RPC 375, 391–2; *British Franco Electric Pty Ltd v Dowling Plastics Pty Ltd* [1981] 1 NSWLR 448, 451; *United States Surgical Corp v Hospital Products International Pty Ltd* [1983] 2 NSWLR 175, 229–33.

[360] *Trevorrow v South Australia (No 4)* (2006) 94 SASR 64, [88].

[361] *Talbot v General Television Corp Pty Ltd* [1980] VR 224, 241. *Supreme Court Act 1986* (Vic) s 38.

[362] *Seager v Copydex Ltd (No 2)* [1969] 2 All ER 718, 719.

[363] *Darvall McCutcheon (a firm) v HK Frost Holdings Pty Ltd (in liq)* (2002) 4 VR 570, [66].

[364] *Dowson & Mason Ltd v Potter* [1986] 1 WLR 1419.

[365] *Seager v Copydex Ltd (No 2)* [1969] 2 All ER 718, 719.

[366] *Interfirm Comparison (Australia) Pty Ltd v Law Society of New South Wales* [1975] 2 NSWLR 104, 124; *Gorne v Scales* [2006] EWCA Civ 311; *Seager v Copydex Ltd (No 2)* [1969] 2 All ER 718, 720–1; *Vasco Investment Managers Ltd v Morgan Stanley Australia Ltd* (2014) 108 IPR 52, [327].

The aim in every case is to put the plaintiff, so far as monetary compensation can do so, in the position it would have been in but for the breach of confidence by the defendant.[367]

In doing this, the court will adopt the most appropriate method of measuring the plaintiff's loss. The fact that it may be difficult to assess damages in any situation does not relieve the court of its obligation to do so.[368] The Victorian Court of Appeal has also recognised that monetary awards damages should be available for breach of confidence occasioning mental distress.[369] Although exemplary damages are available for a breach of confidence in New Zealand,[370] Australian courts have not been influenced to award exemplary or punitive damages for equitable wrongs, such as breach of fiduciary duty or breach of confidence. Despite past vigorous debate, it seems clear that exemplary damages are unavailable in cases involving equitable wrongs.[371]

8.10 Relationship between confidential information and patents

At some point, a patentable invention will have existed as confidential information because absolute novelty is required for its protection under a patent. However, once the specification is made available to the public, the information enters the public domain.[372] Broadly speaking, it is not possible to obtain a patent for an invention that has been secretly used by the inventor.[373] Therefore, a person cannot keep something secret and use it in trade and then apply for a patent. A choice must be made between a patent or reliance on the methods that are available to protect confidential information, including contract, physical barriers and the doctrine for breach of confidence. However, it must be noted that a person who has used an invention in secret may have rights to continue that use despite the later grant of a patent for that invention to another person.[374]

The principal differences between seeking a patent or choosing to rely on the protection that the breach of confidence action offers for secret information relate to the type of information that is protected, the term of protection, and the nature of that protection. First, a patent provides a limited monopoly for twenty years (standard patent) or eight years (innovation patent) and is granted on condition that the invention must be made available to the public. In contrast, an action for breach of confidence is dependent on the maintenance of the secrecy and confidentiality of the information. If the information can be kept secret, there is the possibility of perpetual protection of the information.

---

367 (2002) 4 VR 570, [66].
368 *Darvall McCutcheon (a firm) v HK Frost Holdings Pty Ltd (in liq)* (2002) 4 VR 570, [67].
369 *Giller v Procopets* (2008) 79 IPR 489, 588–9 [431], applied in *Wilson v Ferguson* [2015] WASC 15.
370 *Aquaculture Corp v New Zealand Green Mussel Co Ltd* [1990] 3 NZLR 299, 301–2; *Skids Programme Management Ltd v McNeill* (2012) 98 IPR 324, [123].
371 *Aircraft Pty Ltd v Dickson* [2014] SASC 108, [173].
372 See, for example, *Franchi v Franchi* [1967] RPC 149; *O'Mustad & Son v S Alcock & Dosen Co Ltd* [1963] 3 All ER 416.
373 *Patents Act 1990* (Cth) s 18(1)(d). However, certain uses are not to be taken as a 'secret use': at s 9(e). See ch 10 at 10.11.11 on the grace period.
374 *Patents Act 1990* (Cth) s 119. See ch 12 at 12.8.2 on prior use of an invention.

Second, a patent is available only for inventions that are novel and not obvious. They must involve either an inventive step (standard patents) or an innovative step (innovation patents).[375] Therefore, a lot of secret information may not be suitable for patenting. The existence of the protection for confidential information does not depend on novelty or invention, but on its confidential nature; it must be relatively secret and must be reasonably discrete and ascertainable. A very wide range of material can be protected with no need to meet any technical requirements. There is no requirement for it to be in a material form, so even ideas conveyed orally are capable of protection. Apart from some *de minimis* principle – courts will not protect trivial 'tittle tattle'[376] – the breadth for protection is expansive.

Third, upon grant of the patent, the protection is absolute and not dependent on secrecy. It protects against those who independently discover the invention. In contrast, the equitable action does not protect information unless it has the necessary quality of confidence. Hence, there is always a risk that the monopoly will end when others engage in industrial espionage or discover the secret by independent means. It may also be difficult to maintain secrecy because there is no prohibition on reverse-engineering anything that is available in the marketplace.

8.11 Relationship between confidential information and copyright

When confidential information is expressed in a material form, such as a document, two forms of intellectual property rights are created: rights in copyright in the form in which the information is expressed, and rights to restrain unauthorised disclosure of the information itself in breach of confidence. When an author creates secret information and sets this out in a document or other material form, the author can exercise all the exclusive rights under copyright and can also take action for any unauthorised breach of confidence. These rights are exercised by the employer if the creation of the information and the copyright work is in pursuance of employment duties, and no agreement exists to the contrary.

8.12 International dimensions

The most significant substantive obligations with respect to the protection of confidential information are embodied in art 39 of the *Agreement on Trade-Related Aspects of Intellectual Property* [377] (*TRIPS*) and art 10 of the *Paris Convention for the Protection of Industrial Property*[378] (*Paris Convention*). Article 39(1) of *TRIPS* provides that members must afford certain levels of protection for particular classes of undisclosed information in order to ensure that 'effective protection against unfair competition is provided in Article 10*bis* of the *Paris*

---

375 *Patents Act 1990* (Cth) ss 18(1)(b)(ii), 18(1A)(b)(ii).
376 *Coco v AN Clark (Engineers) Ltd* [1969] RPC 41, 48.
377 *Marrakesh Agreement Establishing the World Trade Organization*, opened for signature 15 April 1994, 1867 UNTS 3 (entered into force 1 January 1995) annex 1C (*Agreement on Trade-Related Aspects of Intellectual Property*) (*TRIPS*).
378 Opened for signature 14 July 1967, WIPO Lex No TRT/PARIS/001 (as amended 28 September 1979, entered into force 3 June 1984).

Convention (1967)'. Article 10*bis* provides that any act of competition contrary to honest practices in industrial or commercial matters constitutes an act of unfair competition.

The first class of undisclosed information (protected under art 39(2) of *TRIPS*) is secret information that has commercial value because it is secret and has been subject to reasonable steps taken by the person lawfully in control to keep it secret. The concept of secrecy is used in the sense that it is not 'generally known among or readily accessible to persons within the circles that normally deal with the kind of information in question'.[379] The second class of information (protected under art 39(3)) involves undisclosed test or other data that is originated with considerable effort and is required to be submitted to government or government agencies as a condition for obtaining approval for the marketing of pharmaceutical or agricultural products that utilise new chemical entities.

---

[379] *TRIPS* art 39(2).

9
PATENTS FOR INVENTIONS: INTRODUCTION

9.1 What is a patent for invention?

A patent is granted by the Crown and confers private property rights in the form of a monopoly for the invention of products, methods and processes in all fields of technology. The invention could relate to all manner of things, including pharmaceutical products and processes, engineering products and processes, medical and therapeutic devices, micro-organisms, computer technologies and nano technologies. These things all have in common some human intervention with nature to bring about some physical change or physically observable effect. A patent grants exclusive rights to the patentee in relation to the invention in return for public disclosure of the invention.

Patents are available currently for two tiers of inventions – standard patents and innovation patents – however, amendments to commence the abolition of the innovation patent were introduced into parliament in July 2019[1] Neither patent will be granted for something that is already known. The invention must be novel, in the sense that its details are not published or made publicly available through use anywhere in the world. The invention must also be useful.[2] Different levels of an advance over what is known apply to standard and innovation patents. The standard patent must not be obvious – it must involve an inventive step – whereas an innovation patent requires a substantial contribution to the working of the invention.

Novelty and inventive or innovative step require a comparison with specified documents and acts throughout the world. This base for comparison is referred to as a 'prior art base'. The monopoly is granted for a restricted period, with the public free to utilise and perform the invention at the end of that period. During the term of the patent,[3] the patentee can exclude others from exercising the rights granted. Those exclusive rights are the same for inventions that possess significant inventive merit, for those that possess only a scintilla of inventiveness and for those that possess an innovative step.

An important feature of the patent system is that the mere fact that a patent application satisfies the Commissioner of Patents and results in a patent grant does not guarantee the validity of the patent.[4] A granted patent can be revoked on a variety of grounds, including obviousness and lack of novelty.[5] The requirements for validity of both standard and innovation patents are discussed in chapter 10. Issues that relate to ownership and exploitation of rights in a patent are discussed in chapter 11, and both what constitutes infringement of a patent and the requirements for revocation of a patent are discussed in chapter 12.

This chapter provides an overview of the nature of patents for inventions, including some brief discussion of their origins and the rationales for their existence. It explains some fundamental concepts on which later chapters expand and outlines the procedures for obtaining the grant of a patent.

---

1   Intellectual Property Laws Amendment (Productivity Commission Response Part 2 and Other Measures) Bill 2019 (Cth) sch 1 pt 2. In September 2019, the Senate Economics Legislation Committee recommended that the Bill be passed: Senate, Economics Legislation Committee, Parliament of Australia, *Intellectual Property Laws Amendment (Productivity Commission Response Part 2 and Other Measures) Bill 2019* (Report, September 2019). See ch 10 at 10.2.
2   *Patents Act 1990* (Cth) s 18.
3   Ibid s 67 (standard patent), s 68 (innovation patent).
4   Ibid s 20(1).
5   Ibid s 138(3).

9.2 Origins of patent protection

The statutory concept of a patentable invention appeared originally in s 6 of the *Statute of Monopolies 1623* (21 Jac 1 c 3):

> Provided also ... that any declaration ... shall not extend to any letters-patent and grants of privilege ... of the sole working or making of any manner of new manufacture ... to the true and first inventor and inventors of such manufactures, which others, at the time of making such letters-patent or grant, shall not use so as also they be not contrary to the law, nor mischievous to the state, by raising prices of commodities at home, or hurt of trade, or generally inconvenient.

The purpose of this section was 'to allow the use of the prerogative to encourage national development in a field that already, in 1623, was seen to be excitingly unpredictable'.[6] The context for limiting monopolies was that of trade, the common law having suspicions of such monopolies.[7] Up until the seventeenth century in England, the Crown granted patents in exercise of its prerogative to grant privileges. This system of monopoly grants was lucrative for the Crown. These privileges were granted in an 'open letter' – letters patent – which came to be known as a patent. The grant of some patents was used without objection as an instrument of industrial or economic policy to encourage invention and investment in invention.[8] In the late sixteenth and early seventeenth centuries, Queen Elizabeth I granted monopoly rights for the purpose of conducting trade in a foreign country or area. For example, she granted patents to merchant venturers such as the East India Company in return for royalty payments.[9]

The Crown also granted privileges indiscriminately by way of general monopolies in various industries. These grants were controversial in that they were used merely as a convenient way to raise revenue, rather than as part of an industrial policy. No element of innovation was required, either in terms of bringing something new into the country or in terms of inventing something new. Wide powers were given to monopolists to enforce their rights.[10] Often monopolies were granted in relation to commodities that were already being used and in the public domain, thereby harming existing trade of such commodities. For example, a grant to X to sell playing cards would be detrimental to Y and Z who were already selling playing cards,[11] not to mention the population who derived considerable pleasure from this pursuit. The common law was hostile to monopolies but had no power over them without Crown approval. Outrage was expressed in 1601 in the Parliamentary Debate on Monopolies (Elizabeth I's last parliament) at the nature of monopolies granted for things such as 'currants, iron,

---

6 *National Research Development Corporation v Commissioner of Patents* (1959) 102 CLR 252, 271. For the history of patents, see H. I. Dutton, *The Patent System and Inventive Activity During the Industrial Revolution, 1750–1852* (Manchester: Manchester University Press, 1984); S. Shulman, *Owning the Future* (Boston: Houghton Mifflin, 1999).
7 *Attorney-General (Cth) v Adelaide Steamship Co Ltd* [1913] AC 781, 793; *Grant v Commissioner of Patents* (2005) 67 IPR 1.
8 K. Boehm with A. Silberston, *The British Patent System 1: Administration* (Cambridge: Cambridge University Press, 1967) 2, 14–15.
9 *Darcy v Allin* (1602) 11 Co Rep 84b, 77 ER 1260.
10 G. R. Elton, *England under the Tudors* (London: Methuen, 1955) 463.
11 *Darcy v Allin* (1602) 11 Co Rep 84b, 77 ER 1260.

powder, cards, ox shin-bones, train oil', where there was no element of innovation. Another grant related to 'all the wild swans betwixt London Bridge and Oxford'.[12] Finally, under pressure in 1601, Elizabeth I issued a proclamation in parliament against the principal monopolies complained of and gave the common law courts the power to determine the validity of those that remained.[13]

In 1602 the case of *Darcy v Allin*[14] was decided. The case, which came to be known as the *Case of Monopolies*, concerned the validity of a patent granting Darcy the sole right to manufacture and import playing cards. It was argued in infringement proceedings against Allin that the Queen had a prerogative in matters of pleasure and recreation and that the grant had been given as a means of controlling the numbers of playing cards in circulation and the time that apprentices and servants spent playing cards. Arguments in support of the monopoly related to the type of merchandise – 'things of vanity' – and 'the occasion of loss of time and the decrease of the substance of many, the loss of the service and work of servants, causes of want, which is the mother of woe and destruction, and therefore it belongs to the Queen'. The court declared the grant invalid, saying that such a grant could deprive people of their livelihood. The Queen was not to suppress the making of cards in England, no more than the making of 'dice, bowls, balls, hawks' hoods, bells, lures, dog-couples'.[15]

In the process of deciding the case, the court stated the common law of monopolies comprehensively, that common law being that monopolies are prohibited other than those for patents for invention. The principal reasons for this prohibition on monopolies were economic – that monopolies raise prices, debase quality, cause unemployment by reducing output and are not for the benefit of the public but the benefit of the patentee.

Despite the comprehensive statement of the common law and the later declaration in James I's *Book of Bounty 1610* of common law hostility to monopolies other than patents for invention, abuse continued and the prerogative courts continued to enforce monopolies granted.[16] Finally, after vigorous anti-monopoly debate, parliament passed the *Statute of Monopolies 1623* (21 Jac 1 c 3) which became the first statutory basis in England for the protection of patents for inventions. It provided for the grant of a patent for a period of fourteen years. In return for the monopoly, the patentee would teach the art to two sets of apprentices.[17] According to Edmund Coke, s 6 was merely declaratory of the law before the enactment of the *Statute of Monopolies*.[18]

The patent system in England continued to develop over the next 200 years or so, undergoing periods of cumbersome administration and expensive procedures.[19] The need for reform became particularly evident in the nineteenth century and led to the enactment of

---

12   Ibid 1262.
13   Boehm, *The British Patent System 1*, above n 8, 15.
14   (1602) 11 Co Rep 84b, 77 ER 1260.
15   Ibid 1264.
16   Boehm, *The British Patent System 1*, above n 8, 15–16.
17   E. Coke, *The Third Part of the Institutes of the Laws of England Concerning High Treason, and Other Pleas of the Crown, and Criminal Causes* (1644) (Imprint: W. Clarke, London, 1809) 184–5; Boehm, *The British Patent System 1*, above n 8, 17.
18   Boehm, *The British Patent System 1*, above n 8, 17–18. Boehm refers to the 'curious confusion' surrounding the year of this statute – whether it is 1623 or 1624. This book uses the common citation of 1623, but Boehm identifies the year as 1624.
19   As to the evolution of the patent specification over this period, see ch 10 at 10.13.1.

the *Patents, Designs and Trade Marks Act 1883* (46 & 47 Vict c 57), which provides the foundations of the modern patent system.[20]

9.3 Development of patent law in Australia

Prior to Federation in 1901, each Australian colony had its own *Patents Act* that was based on the *Patents, Designs and Trade Marks Act 1883* (46 & 47 Vict c 57). These Acts continued in force until the Commonwealth parliament enacted the *Patents Act 1903* (Cth) pursuant to its legislative powers under s 51(xviii) of the *Constitution*. The 1903 Act was repealed by the *Patents Act 1952* (Cth), which was repealed in turn by s 230 of the *Patents Act 1990* (Cth). The *Patents Act 1990* came into operation on 1 May 1991 and the *Patents Regulations 1991* (Cth) commenced at the same time.

Many of the provisions in the *Patents Act 1990* (Cth) are drawn in substance from the *Patents Act 1952* (Cth), which was based on the *Patents Act 1949* (UK).[21] However, the United Kingdom legislation changed considerably in 1977 when the *Patents Act 1977* (UK) was enacted to comply with the 1973 *European Patent Convention*.[22] This need for United Kingdom law to be consistent with the convention and to comply with later Directives of the European Community resulted in considerable differences between the *Patents Act 1990* (Cth) and the *Patents Act 1977* (UK).

The *Patents Act 1990* (Cth) has undergone significant amendment since its enactment, with the result that the laws are now more closely aligned with both EU law and the patent law of Australia's main trading partners. The following explains the principal substantive reforms and reform proposals since 2012:

- The *Intellectual Property Laws Amendment (Raising the Bar) Act 2012* (Cth) (*Raising the Bar Act*)[23] reforms chiefly arose following a series of reviews that IP Australia conducted in 2009 that aimed to raise patentability thresholds to align them more closely with overseas markets, to resolve unnecessary differences among jurisdictions, to provide regulatory use and research exemptions, and to simplify processes.[24] In broad terms, the substantive amendments apply to:
  - complete applications – both standard and innovation – on or after 15 April 2013;
  - standard patent applications before 15 April 2013 with no examination request;
  - innovation patents granted on or after 15 April 2013 that relate to a complete application made before that day; and
  - complete applications for innovation patents that are not granted before 15 April 2013.

---

20 Boehm, *The British Patent System 1*, above n 8, 18–30.
21 For the historical development of patents, see S. Ricketson, *The Law of Intellectual Property* (Sydney: Law Book Company, 1984) ch 46, and the sources cited in that text, including A. A. Gomme, *Patents of Invention: Origin and Growth of the Patent System in Britain* (London: Longmans, Green & Co, 1946) and H. G. Fox, *Monopolies and Patents: A Study of the History and Future of the Patent Monopoly* (Toronto: University of Toronto Press, 1947).
22 L. Bently and B. Sherman, *Intellectual Property Law* (4th edn, Oxford: Oxford University Press, 2014) 381–86. See below at 9.14.4.
23 Assented to on 15 April 2012. Item 87 of sch 6 commenced on 16 April 2012. Most of the Act's provisions commenced on 15 April 2013.
24 IP Australia, 'Intellectual property reform in Australia: A summary of important changes' (July 2013), www.ipaustralia.gov.au.

- The *Intellectual Property Laws Amendment Act 2015* (Cth) implements the Protocol amending the *Agreement on Trade-Related Aspects of Intellectual Property (TRIPS)*.[25] The objective of the Protocol is to provide access for least developed and developing countries to cheaper patented medicines under a form of compulsory licence. The amendments 'allow Australian pharmaceutical manufacturers to supply these countries with the patented medicines they need.'[26]
- The Intellectual Property Laws Amendment (Productivity Commission Response Part 2 and Other Measures) Bill 2019 (Cth) contains a number of other reforms that arise from the Productivity Commission inquiry report *Intellectual Property Arrangements*.[27] The Commission concluded that, notwithstanding the *Raising the Bar* reforms in 2012, Australian patent law remained skewed in favour of rights holders. The key substantive reforms set out in the Bill relate to the introduction of an objects clause, staged abolition of the innovation patent system, Crown use of patents and compulsory licensing of patents.[28]

9.4 Rationales of patent protection

Over the years, scholars have identified a number of rationales for patent protection that are more or less relevant according to the times in which they are contextualised.[29] The natural property rights theory, for example, has little application to the contemporary system. Yet other theories remain relevant to support a contemporary patent system, including rationales that are expressed in terms of preventing 'free riding' on inventions and ideas,[30] or providing a reward for services useful to society, or providing an incentive to disclose secrets, to invent or create and to stimulate innovation[31] by investing in technology.

In his second reading speech accompanying the Patents Bill 1990 (Cth), Simon Crean, then Minister for Science and Technology, explained that the 'essence of the patent system is to encourage entrepreneurs to develop and commercialise new technology'.[32] Since that date, various reports and inquiries have reiterated the links between granted patents of high quality and successful innovation. In 2009, IP Australia noted:

> In recent years there has been a greater awareness and use of patent rights both in Australia and around the world. This has been driven by factors such as a growing

---

25 Geneva, 6 December 2005. See below at 9.14.2.
26 Explanatory Memorandum, Intellectual Property Laws Amendment Bill 2014 (Cth) sch 1 ('TRIPS Protocol interim waiver'), sch 2 ('TRIPS Protocol: later commencing amendments'). The changes commenced on 25 August 2015.
27 Productivity Commission, *Intellectual Property Arrangements* (Inquiry Report No 78, September 2016).
28 The Bill was introduced into parliament in July 2019. In September 2019, the Senate Economics Legislation Committee recommended that the Bill be passed: Senate, above n 1.
29 Some of these are discussed in Ricketson, *The Law of Intellectual Property*, above n 21, 868–71.
30 Intellectual Property and Competition Review Committee, *Review of Intellectual Property Legislation under the Competition Principles Agreement* (Final Report, September 2000) 23.
31 Department of Innovation, Industry, Science and Research, *Powering Ideas: An Innovation Agenda for the 21st Century* (Report, May 2009) 56.
32 Commonwealth, *Parliamentary Debates*, House of Representatives, 10 October 1990, 2565 (Simon Crean).

appreciation of the importance of intellectual property rights in the successful commercialisation of technology, the realisation that successful innovation is a primary driver of economic growth, and pressure on public research organisations to commercialise their research and development.[33]

The link between granting patent monopolies and encouraging investment in research and commercialisation of technology makes it ever more important to balance the competing public and private interests that will often be 'in fierce competition with each other'.[34]

The last decade has seen a number of reviews[35] whose recommendations have resulted in a multitude of new statutory provisions introduced to implement significant and constant policy change. One issue that links directly with the rationales for patent protection concerns the lack of an express statement in the *Patents Act 1990* (Cth) of that Act's objective. Although there is wide consensus regarding the economic rationales for the grant of patent monopolies, the express purpose that should guide decision-makers in the interpretation and practical application of the patent legislation remains unclear and unstated. The government accepted the most recent call[36] for the clear articulation of the objective of patent law in the legislation itself. After wide consultation on the issue, the Intellectual Property Laws Amendment (Productivity Commission Response Part 2 and Other Measures) Bill 2019 (Cth) was drafted to insert a new section that captures the appropriate balance of the various interests:

s 2A Object of this Act:
The object of this Act is to provide a patent system in Australia that promotes economic wellbeing through technological innovation and the transfer and dissemination of technology. In doing so, the patent system balances over time the interests of producers, owners and users of technology and the public.[37]

9.5 Types of patent
9.5.1 Standard and innovation patents

The *Patents Act 1990* (Cth) provides protection for two types of patents for invention: the standard patent and the innovation patent. A number of differences apply to standard and innovation patents, which are discussed in the relevant following chapters. For the purposes of this chapter, the essential difference relates to the absence of any substantive form of

---

33   IP Australia, *Exemptions to Patent Infringement: Toward a Stronger and More Efficient IP Rights System* (2009) 3.
34   *Apotex Pty Ltd v Sanofi-Aventis Australia Pty Ltd* (2013) 253 CLR 284, [45].
35   Advisory Council on Intellectual Property (ACIP), *Patentable Subject Matter* (Final Report, December 2010) rec 1; Productivity Commission, *Intellectual Property Arrangements*, above n 27, rec 7.1.
36   ACIP, *Patentable Subject Matter*, above n 35, rec 1; Productivity Commission, *Intellectual Property Arrangements*, above n 27, rec 7.1.
37   The Bill was introduced into parliament in July 2019. In September 2019, the Senate Economics Legislation Committee recommended that the Bill be passed: Senate, above n 1.

examination prior to grant for an innovation patent. The application procedures for both standard and innovation patents are described below.[38]

9.5.2 Selection patents

An invention that selects a group of members or one member from a previously known class, and finds new uses and qualities previously unknown, is called a 'selection patent'. This is not a statutory class of patents but refers to a particular type of invention that may be the subject of a patent application or grant.[39] A selection patent appears most often in the chemical field but is not restricted in that operation.[40] The selection, or sub-class, is united by a common feature that has beneficial properties that distinguish it from the class from which it was selected. Courts have approved three conditions for a valid selection patent that they have followed on 'countless occasions'.[41]

9.5.3 Combination patents

A 'combination patent' is a patent in which the elements or integers in the claim interact with each other to produce a new result or product that constitutes the invention. All the integers in the combination may be old or some may be new; the essence of the combination patent is the result of the interaction.[42] The term is one that courts have developed to describe a particular type of invention that may be the subject of a patent application or grant.

9.6 Types of application

Apart from national applications for standard and innovation patents, which are explained below, four other types of applications should be mentioned here. They are 'Convention' applications, *PCT* applications, divisional applications and applications for patents of addition.

9.6.1 Convention applications

The *Paris Convention for the Protection of Industrial Property*[43] (*Paris Convention*) applies to industrial property generally, including trade marks and designs as well as patents. Its fundamental principle is that it requires member states to accord national treatment in respect of those forms of intellectual property rights.[44] It provides a means of access into national patent systems for foreign patentees. If the applicant makes the first application for a patent in a

---

38 At 9.7 and 9.8.
39 For special principles that apply to selection patents, see ch 10 at 10.6.12.
40 *Hallen Co v Brabantia (UK) Ltd* [1991] RPC 195.
41 *Chiron Corp v Murex Diagnostics Ltd* [1996] RPC 535.
42 *Minnesota Mining & Manufacturing Co v Beiersdorf (Australia) Ltd* (1980) 144 CLR 253, 266; *Smith & Nephew Pty Ltd v Wake Forest University Health Sciences* (2009) 82 IPR 467, [15]–[44].
43 Opened for signature 14 July 1967, WIPO Lex No TRT/PARIS/001 (as amended 28 September 1979, entered into force 3 June 1984) (*Paris Convention*).
44 *Paris Convention* art 2.

country that is a party to the *Paris Convention* ('the basic application'),[45] the applicant has twelve months from that day in which to make the Convention application ('the priority period').[46] Once a Convention application is lodged within this priority period, it is prosecuted as if it were a national application.[47] The priority period gained under the *Paris Convention* complements the streamlined filing procedures under the *Patent Cooperation Treaty*.

9.6.2 *PCT* applications

The *Patent Cooperation Treaty*[48] (*PCT*) established an International Patent Cooperation Union 'for cooperation in the filing, searching, and examination, of applications for the protection of inventions, and for rendering special technical services'.[49] The granting of the patents remains the responsibility of each national office in the countries in which the patentee seeks protection, and commences when the international application enters its 'national phase'. This national application process is described below[50] in the procedure for obtaining an Australian patent.

There are two chapters in the *PCT* that are particularly relevant to the discussion here. Chapter I provides that any national or resident of a *PCT* contracting state can seek patent protection in any number of selected *PCT* contracting states by filing one international application.[51] The application may be filed in Australia with IP Australia, which will act as the *PCT* 'receiving office'.[52] Provided that the application satisfies the minimum requirements in the *PCT*, this single application acts as a national patent application in each designated state,[53] and is regarded as equivalent to a regular national filing within the meaning of the *Paris Convention*.[54] Its international filing date is considered to be the date of actual filing in each designated state.[55] The international filing date becomes the priority date[56] unless an earlier priority date can be claimed on the basis of a prior patent application – national or *PCT* – for the same invention.[57]

Each international patent application is subject to an 'international search' by an 'international searching authority' to discover relevant prior art.[58] Both the application and the search report are sent to the relevant designated national offices.[59]

45　*Patents Act 1990* (Cth) s 29B(1), (2); *Patents Regulations 1991* (Cth) reg 3.11.
46　*Patents Act 1990* (Cth) s 38(1A); *Patents Regulations 1991* (Cth) reg 3.11; *Paris Convention 1883* art 4.
47　*Patents Act 1990* (Cth) s 29B(3), (4); *Patents Regulations 1991* (Cth) reg 3.5AG.
48　Opened for signature 19 June 1970, WIPO Lex No TRT/PCT/001 (entered into force 24 January 1978 (except ch II: 29 March 1978), as modified 3 October 2001) (*PCT*). The *PCT* entered into force for Australia on 31 March 1980.
49　Ibid art 1(1).
50　At 9.7 and 9.8.
51　*PCT* arts 3, 9.
52　Ibid art 10.
53　Ibid art 11(3); *Patents Act 1990* (Cth) s 29A(1).
54　*PCT* art 11(4).
55　Ibid art 11(3); *Patents Act 1990* (Cth) s 30; *Patents Regulations 1991* (Cth) reg 3.5AA.
56　See below at 9.11 and 9.12 for the significance of priority dates generally.
57　*PCT* arts 2(xi), 8.
58　Ibid arts 15, 16.
59　Ibid art 20.

Unless the applicant requests an earlier publication of the international application, it is promptly published with the international search report after eighteen months from its priority date.[60] This publication occurs before the application enters the national phase in each designated state and therefore before it is examined and accepted. After international publication, any third party can request copies of documents contained in the international file,[61] and thereby have the benefit of this published material to help them formulate their opinion about the patentability of the claimed invention. The application will remain unpublished and inaccessible to third parties if the application is withdrawn before international publication.[62]

The effect of this international publication is the same as the effect of compulsory national publication of unexamined national applications under the national law of each designated state.[63] Under the *Patents Act 1990* (Cth), this gives the applicant the same rights as they would have possessed if the patent had been granted on the day when the specification became open to public inspection.[64]

Chapter II of the *PCT* provides the applicant with the opportunity to delay the entry into the national phase by asking for a preliminary examination on the basis of the international search report. The objective of this examination is to provide a preliminary and non-binding opinion on whether the claimed invention appears to be novel, to involve an inventive step and to be industrially applicable.[65]

9.6.3 Divisional applications

It is possible to make a divisional application[66] with respect to both standard and innovation patents prior to grant,[67] and with respect to innovation patents after grant.[68] The 'parent' application may also be a *PCT* application. The applicant can divide some of the subject matter in the parent application into separate applications while retaining the priority date of the claims from the original application. Such an application[69] may be used where, contrary to s 40(4), more than one invention was contained in the complete application. It may also have a variety of practical uses, such as dividing an innovation patent from a pending standard patent to target infringing activities.[70]

9.6.4 Patents of addition

Patents of addition are available to protect improvements to and modifications of a granted standard patent or one for which an application is made. They enable the assembly of clusters

---

60 Ibid art 21; *Patents Act 1990* (Cth) ss 53(2), 56A; *Patents Regulations 1991* (Cth) reg 4.4.
61 *PCT* art 30(2)(a)(i).
62 Ibid art 30.
63 Ibid art 29.
64 *Patents Act 1990* (Cth) s 57.
65 *PCT* art 33.
66 *Patents Act 1990* (Cth) ch 6A; *Patents Regulations 1991* (Cth) ch 6A.
67 *Patents Act 1990* (Cth) s 79B.
68 Ibid s 79C.
69 The application is made under *Patents Act 1990* (Cth) s 29; *Coretell Pty Ltd v Australian Mud Company Pty Ltd* (2017) 250 FCR 155, [28].
70 *Britax Childcare Pty Ltd v Infa-Secure Pty Ltd* (2012) 290 ALR 47, [27].

of standard patents to provide strong protection for the inventive concept.[71] A patent of addition is dependent on the first patent and generally remains in force only while the first patent is in force.[72] Special provisions apply when the term of either the first patent or a patent of addition is extended under Part 3 of Chapter 6 of the *Patents Act 1990* (Cth) (patents relating to pharmaceutical substances).[73]

9.7 Procedure for obtaining a standard patent

9.7.1 The application

Any person, including a body of persons whether incorporated or not, can apply for a patent.[74] Two or more persons can make a joint application.[75] The application may be provisional or complete.[76] However, after filing a complete application and before it has been accepted or made open to public inspection, the applicant can request the Commissioner to treat it as a provisional application.[77]

The application is taken to be made on its filing date.[78] The date of first filing of the specification establishes the priority date for the claims in that specification.[79] It is common practice to file a provisional application to establish that date. In this event, the applicant has twelve months from the filing date to make one or more complete applications associated with the provisional application.[80] The provisional application will lapse if a complete application is not filed in this period.[81] It is possible to refile the application as a provisional, and thereby accept a later priority date, or abandon it altogether. The priority date is significant for a number of reasons, one of which is that later publication or use of the invention will not invalidate a patent application.[82]

The date of filing the complete specification establishes the date of the patent.[83] It is from this date that the term of the patent runs. In the case of a standard patent, the term is twenty years from the date of the patent,[84] whereas the term for an innovation patent is eight years.[85]

The requirements for the content of both provisional and complete specifications are set out in ss 40 and 41 (micro-organisms) of the *Patents Act 1990* (Cth) and Chapter 3 of the *Patents Regulations 1991* (Cth). These requirements will be discussed in more detail in chapter

---

71 *Patents Act 1990* (Cth) ch 7.
72 Ibid s 83.
73 Ibid s 83(3), (4).
74 Ibid ss 15, 29(1).
75 Ibid s 31.
76 Ibid s 29(2)–(4).
77 Ibid s 37; *Patents Regulations 1991* (Cth) reg 3.9.
78 *Patents Act 1990* (Cth) s 30; *Patents Regulations 1991* (Cth) regs 3.5, 3.5AA.
79 *Patents Act 1990* (Cth) s 43.
80 Ibid ss 5, 29, 38; *Patents Regulations 1991* (Cth) reg 3.10; *Paris Convention* art 4.
81 *Patents Act 1990* (Cth) s 142(1).
82 Ibid s 23. See the discussion of the priority date below at 9.11 and 9.12.
83 *Patents Act 1990* (Cth) s 65.
84 Ibid s 67.
85 Ibid s 68.

10. A grant can be made to 'the nominated person', who must be the inventor or a person who gains rights from the inventor. This could be a person entitled to an assignment or grant of the patent, a person who derives title from the inventor, or the legal representative of the relevant person.[86] Following the application, the prescribed details are published in the *Australian Official Journal of Patents* (*Official Journal*).[87] In the case of a complete application, the subject matter is classified using the International Patent Classification and abstracts are prepared for search material.

9.7.2 Pre-examination

Formal examination of a patent application occurs at the request of the applicant.[88] However, the applicant has two ways in which to obtain valuable advance information about the shortcomings of the application. First, in the case of a provisional application, an applicant can request an international-type search under art 15(5) of the *PCT* within ten months of the filing date.[89] Second, the applicant for a complete application for a standard patent made on or after 15 April 2013 may request the Commissioner to conduct a preliminary search and opinion (PSO) prior to submitting a request for examination.[90] The PSO is published when the application becomes open to inspection.

The examination may proceed in any of three ways: the applicant may seek examination (and must do so within five years from filing the complete application);[91] the Commissioner may direct the applicant to ask for examination within two months;[92] or, after the specification is open to public inspection, any person may require the Commissioner to direct the applicant to ask for examination.[93] The application lapses if there is no examination requested or directed.[94]

The Patent Office publishes all complete specifications for standard patents eighteen months after the priority date. At this stage, the specification becomes open to public inspection (or 'OPI').[95] The significance of this date is that infringement of a standard patent is possible after this date, but no proceedings can be commenced until the patent is granted.[96]

9.7.3 Examination

The examination of a standard patent under the *Patents Act 1990* (Cth) requires the Commissioner to carry out the examination in accordance with the regulations and to report on the following matters:[97]

- whether the content of the specification complies with s 40(2)–(4);

---

86   Ibid ss 15, 29(1). See ch 11.
87   *Patents Act 1990* (Cth) s 53; *Patents Regulations 1991* (Cth) reg 4.1.
88   *Patents Act 1990* (Cth) s 44.
89   *Patents Regulations 1991* (Cth) reg 3.14A.
90   *Patents Act 1990* (Cth) s 43A; *Patents Regulations 1991* (Cth) reg 3.14B.
91   *Patents Act 1990* (Cth) s 44(1); *Patents Regulations 1991* (Cth) reg 3.15(1).
92   *Patents Act 1990* (Cth) s 44(2); *Patents Regulations 1991* (Cth) reg 3.16.
93   *Patents Act 1990* (Cth) s 44(3); *Patents Regulations 1991* (Cth) reg 3.17.
94   *Patents Act 1990* (Cth) s 142(2).
95   Ibid ss 54–5; *Patents Regulations 1991* (Cth) regs 4.2–4.3.
96   *Patents Act 1990* (Cth) s 57.
97   Ibid s 45(1)–(2).

- whether, to the best of the Commissioner's knowledge, the invention so far as claimed:
  - is a 'manner of manufacture within the meaning of section 6 of the *Statute of Monopolies*';[98]
  - is both new and inventive;[99] and
  - is useful;[100]
- whether the invention is a patentable invention under s 18(2);
- whether the invention satisfies such other matters as are prescribed in reg 3.18(2), including matters relating to entitlement to the grant.

The *Patents Act 1990* (Cth) provides a process for amending the patent request and specification in response to objections raised in the course of examination.[101] Success with the examination of a standard patent does not ensure its validity.[102]

9.7.4 Acceptance and publication

From the OPI date to immediately before acceptance, anyone can notify the Commissioner that the invention is not a patentable invention because it is not novel or it lacks an inventive step.[103] The Commissioner must accept the patent request and the specification if they are *satisfied* on the balance of probabilities as to the same matters on which they report at examination.[104] However, the Commissioner has discretion to postpone acceptance on their own initiative or at the written request of the applicant.[105] A refusal to accept the application must be notified to the applicant and published and can be appealed to the Federal Court.[106]

In the absence of an obligation to accept under s 49(1) of the *Patents Act 1990* (Cth), the Commissioner may refuse to accept the application but is not compelled to do so.[107] Furthermore, the Commissioner may refuse to accept the patent request and the specification or grant the patent in the three further circumstances set out in s 50, namely:

- The use of the invention would be contrary to law.[108]
- The claimed invention is a substance that is capable of being used as food or medicine (whether for human beings or animals and whether for internal or external use) and is a mere mixture of known ingredients or a process for producing such a substance by mere admixture.[109] This express provision provides the Commissioner with a way in which to

---

98 Ibid s 18(1)(a).
99 Ibid s 18(1)(b).
100 Ibid s 18(1)(c).
101 Ibid ss 104, 107.
102 Ibid s 20(1).
103 *Patents Act 1990* (Cth) s 27(1); *Patents Regulations 1991* (Cth) reg 2.5.
104 *Patents Act 1990* (Cth) s 49(1).
105 Ibid ss 49A, 142(2)(e).
106 Ibid ss 49(7), 51.
107 Ibid s 49(2).
108 Ibid s 50(1)(a). See ch 10 at 10.12.3.
109 Ibid s 50(1)(b). See ch 10 at 10.12.4.

refuse applications for this subject matter without the need to consider the other criteria for validity.
- A claim in the specification includes the name of a person as the name, or part of the name, of the claimed invention.[110]

Once accepted, the application is advertised in the *Official Journal*[111] and various documents associated with the application become OPI if this has not already occurred.[112] The Commissioner has a power to revoke an acceptance of a standard patent that has not yet been granted if the Commissioner is satisfied on the balance of probabilities that the patent request should not have been accepted and it is reasonable to now revoke it. This power is directed to correcting administrative errors that might occur in the process of accepting a patent application. Examination of the application must continue following revocation of acceptance.[113]

9.7.5 Opposition

The advertisement of acceptance makes the public aware of what has been accepted by the Patent Office. The Minister or any member of the public is entitled within three months of the advertisement to oppose the grant.[114] The grounds for opposition in s 59 of the *Patents Act 1990* (Cth) are:

(a) that the nominated person is either:
 (i) not entitled to a grant of a patent for the invention; or
 (ii) entitled to a grant of a patent for the invention but only in conjunction with some other person;
(b) that the invention is not a patentable invention;
(c) that the specification filed in respect of the complete application does not comply with subsection 40(2) or (3).

The ground in s 59(b) that the invention is not a patentable invention introduces the requirement that the claimed invention was not secretly used in the patent area before the priority date.[115]

The Commissioner decides the case and can take into account any of the above grounds for opposition, irrespective of whether the opponent relies on them. The Commissioner may refuse the application if satisfied on the balance of probabilities that a ground of opposition exists and after giving an applicant a reasonable opportunity to amend the specification.[116] Either party can appeal the decision to the Federal Court.[117] There is the possibility for re-examination if the application is opposed.[118]

---

110 Ibid s 50(2).
111 Ibid s 49(5).
112 Ibid s 49(6).
113 Ibid s 50A; *Intellectual Property Laws Amendment (Raising the Bar) Act 2012* (Cth) sch 6 item 54.
114 *Patents Act 1990* (Cth) s 59; *Patents Regulations 1991* (Cth) reg 5.4.
115 *Patents Act 1990* (Cth) s 18(1)(d).
116 Ibid s 60(3A), (3B).
117 Ibid s 60(4).
118 Ibid s 97; *Patents Regulations 1991* (Cth) reg 9.1.

9.7.6 Re-examination

The *Patents Act 1990* (Cth) contains discretion for the Commissioner to instigate the re-examination of an accepted application and a granted patent.[119] According to IP Australia, the discretion will be exercised only if an adverse re-examination report will issue.[120] This may be because some new prior art is brought to the attention of the Commissioner by a member of the public.[121] Granted patents must be re-examined if the patentee or another person requests the Commissioner to do so,[122] unless proceedings in relation to a patent are pending.[123] When the request asserts invalidity based on lack of novelty, inventive or innovative step, it must identify the documents on which that assertion is based.[124] The Commissioner must re-examine a patent upon the direction of a court.[125]

The matters that the Commissioner must ascertain and report on are listed in s 98:

(a) whether the specification does not comply with subsection 40(2) or (3); and
(b) whether, to the best of his or her knowledge, the invention, so far as claimed, does not satisfy the criteria mentioned in paragraph 18(1)(a), (b) or (c); and
(c) whether the invention is not a patentable invention under subsection 18(2).

An adverse re-examination report may result in a refusal to grant the patent in the case of a patent application or revocation of a granted patent.[126]

9.7.7 Grant

The patent is granted by registering prescribed particulars of the patent in the Register of Patents.[127] It is possible for two or more applications for patents for identical or substantially identical inventions to have the same priority date. In this event, neither application will form part of the prior art base for the other for the purposes of assessment of novelty and inventive step. Nor does the grant of one invalidate the other. Hence, the *Patents Act 1990* (Cth) contemplates the possible grant of two independent patents for the one invention, but only where there are different inventors.[128]

9.8 Processing an application for an innovation patent

Chapter 9A of the *Patents Act 1990* (Cth) sets out the procedures for processing an application for an innovation patent. Briefly, an innovation patent application does not undergo

---

119 *Patents Act 1990* (Cth) s 97.
120 IP Australia, *Australian Patent Office: Manual of Practice and Procedures (APO Manual)* [2.22.1].
121 *Patents Act 1990* (Cth) s 27(1).
122 Ibid s 97(2).
123 Ibid s 97(4).
124 *Patents Regulations 1991* (Cth) reg 9.2.
125 *Patents Act 1990* (Cth) s 97(3).
126 Ibid ss 100A, 101. See *APO Manual*, above n 120, [2.22], Annex A.
127 *Patents Act 1990* (Cth) s 61(1).
128 *Patents Act 1990* (Cth) s 64, sch 1 (definition of 'prior art base'). See also *Re Smithkline Beecham plc* (2000) 50 IPR 169; *Sartas No 1 Pty Ltd v Koukourou & Partners Pty Ltd* (1994) 30 IPR 479.

substantive examination. Instead, after the applicant files the patent request and complete specification, the Commissioner only undertakes a formalities check in respect of the application.[129] If satisfied on the balance of probabilities that the application passes the formalities check, the Commissioner must accept the patent request and complete specification.[130] Following its acceptance, the Commissioner must grant the innovation patent by registering the prescribed particulars of the patent in the Register.

An innovation patent will only be examined after grant either because the Commissioner so decides or because the patentee or some other person asks for examination.[131] A patentee may commence infringement proceedings only when the patent is certified, so this is often the reason for a patentee's request for examination.[132] It is possible to infringe a granted standard patent on and from the day when the specification became OPI.[133] In the case of an innovation patent, the relevant date for determining infringement 'is the date of grant of the patent in suit'.[134]

The Commissioner must certify the patent if two conditions are satisfied. First, the Commissioner must be satisfied on the balance of probabilities as to each of the matters for examination and report that are listed in s 101E(1)(a).[135] Second, the patent must not have ceased for any of the reasons set out in s 143A.[136] After a successful examination, the Commissioner issues a certificate of examination, publishes a notice in the *Official Journal* and registers the issue of that certificate.[137] In the event that the conditions are not satisfied, the Commissioner may revoke the patent.[138] Finally, certified patents may be re-examined under Part 2 of Chapter 9A of the Act or opposed under Part 3 of Chapter 9A.

It is important to note that reforms set out in the Intellectual Property Laws Amendment (Productivity Commission Response Part 2 and Other Measures) Bill 2019 (Cth), if enacted, will commence the abolition of the innovation patent.[139]

9.9 Patent term

The term of a standard patent granted on or after 1 July 1995 is twenty years from the date of the patent.[140] The term of an innovation patent is eight years from the date of the

---

129   *Patents Act 1990* (Cth) s 52(1); *Patents Regulations 1991* (Cth) reg 3.2B.
130   *Patents Act 1990* (Cth) s 52(2).
131   Ibid s 101A; *Patents Regulations 1991* (Cth) reg 9A.1.
132   *Patents Act 1990* (Cth) s 120(1A). See above n 95 and accompanying text.
133   Ibid s 57.
134   *Coretell Pty Ltd v Australian Mud Company Pty Ltd* (2017) 250 FCR 155, [97], disagreeing with an earlier decision in which the relevant date was the date of the patent, *Britax Childcare Pty Ltd v Infa-Secure Pty Ltd (No 3)* [2012] FCA 1019, [27].
135   This standard of proof was raised by *Intellectual Property Laws Amendment (Raising the Bar) Act 2012* (Cth) sch 1 item 21.
136   *Patents Act 1990* (Cth) s 101E(1)(b).
137   Ibid s 101E(2).
138   Ibid s 101J.
139   The Bill was introduced into parliament in July 2019. In September 2019, the Senate Economics Legislation Committee recommended that the Bill be passed: Senate, above n 1.
140   *Patents Act 1990* (Cth) s 67. The term was extended by *Patents (World Trade Organization Amendments) Act 1994* (Cth) s 4.

patent.[141] In both cases, the date of the patent is the date of filing the complete specification.[142] In the case of a divisional patent, the date of the patent is the date of its parent patent.[143] In the case of a patent of addition, it remains in force as long as the patent for the main invention remains in force.[144]

9.10 Extension of term of standard patents for pharmaceutical substances

9.10.1 The application

A patentee can apply for one extension of the term of a standard patent.[145] If a patent of addition has been granted for improvements in or modifications of a patent for the main invention, an application for extension of term may relate to either or both the patent of addition and the patent for the main invention.[146] The extension is available only when the patentee satisfies the requirements in s 70(2), (3) and (4) of the *Patents Act 1990* (Cth). Section 70(2) requires either or both of the following conditions to be satisfied – namely, that the patent claims one or more pharmaceutical substances per se,[147] or claims one or more pharmaceutical substances when produced by a process that involves the use of recombinant DNA technology.[148] These conditions have in common the requirement for the *pharmaceutical substance* to be the subject matter of the claim.[149] In each case, the pharmaceutical substance 'must in substance be disclosed in the complete specification of the patent and in substance fall within the scope of the claim or claims of that specification'. A 'pharmaceutical substance' is defined to mean 'a substance (including a mixture or compound of substances) for therapeutic use' with particular defined applications.[150] It does not include a substance to be used solely for in vitro diagnosis or in vitro testing. The phrase 'in substance disclosed' seems to require merely that the pharmaceutical substance is a specific claimed feature of the invention. This phrase appears in various contexts in the patent system[151] and is viewed by the Federal Court as similar to the 'real and reasonably clear disclosure' test developed for fair basing.[152] The requirement that the 'substance fall within the scope of the claim or claims of that specification'

---

141 *Patents Act 1990* (Cth) s 68. For transitional provisions, see *Patents Amendment (Innovation Patents) Act 2000* (Cth) sch 2 pt 1.
142 *Patents Act 1990* (Cth) s 65.
143 Ibid ss 79B, 79C; *Patents Regulations 1991* (Cth) reg 6.3(7), (8).
144 *Patents Act 1990* (Cth) s 83(1).
145 Ibid s 70. For a discussion, see G. McGowan SC and B. Fitzpatrick, 'Pharmaceutical extension law in the 21st century' (2012) 88 *Intellectual Property Forum* 69.
146 *Patents Act 1990* (Cth) s 83.
147 Ibid s 70(2)(a).
148 Ibid s 70(2)(b). The court in *Novartis Vaccines & Diagnostics Srl* [2015] APO 2, [10] stated that this 'does not require the disclosure of a new recombinant process, nor does it require that a claim is limited entirely to a product produced by recombinant DNA technology'.
149 *Commissioner of Patents v AbbVie Biotechnology Ltd* (2017) 253 FCR 436, [55], [56], [60].
150 *Patents Act 1990* (Cth) sch 1.
151 *Re Pfizer Inc* (2004) 62 IPR 627, 630.
152 *Gambro Pty Ltd v Fresenius Medical Care South East Asia Pty Ltd* (2000) 49 IPR 321; *RGC Mineral Sands Pty Ltd v Wimmera Industrial Minerals Pty Ltd* (1998) 89 FCR 458; *ICI Chemicals & Polymers Ltd v Lubrizol Corp Inc* (2000) 106 FCR 214. See ch 10 at 10.13.10.

is not satisfied merely because a pharmaceutical substance is one essential feature in combination with other integers.[153]

Section 70(2)(a) confines extensions to patents that claim invention of the 'pharmaceutical substance *per se*'. Courts have construed this expression to mean the substance itself that is the subject of a claim and would usually be restricted to new and inventive substances.[154] In each case, this question becomes a matter of correctly characterising the claim as one for a product that does not contain elements of 'process'.[155] It is unnecessary for every component of a claimed compound that is said to be a 'pharmaceutical substance *per se*' to be therapeutically useful, and claims for pharmaceutical formulations that include the active ingredient will satisfy the definition.[156]

The Full Federal Court in *Commissioner of Patents v AbbVie Biotechnology Ltd*[157] considered the application of s 70(2)(b) to method or process claims directed to *the use* of a pharmaceutical substance in the manufacture of a medicament for a specified therapeutic use (Swiss type claims). The court confirmed that, although the pharmaceutical substance may have been produced using recombinant DNA technology, that substance must also 'fall within the scope of the claim or claims' for the claim to satisfy this condition.[158] In other words, the pharmaceutical substance must be the subject matter of the claim. A pharmaceutical substance that merely forms part of a method or process claim, is not entitled to extension rights.[159] The policy for this distinction appears to relate to parliament's desire to encourage research and development in inventive substances and recombinant DNA techniques.[160]

Subject to no previous extension of the patent,[161] the patentee must satisfy two further conditions in relation to at least one of the pharmaceutical substances that satisfies the above requirements. First, goods containing or consisting of the substance must be included in the Australian Register of Therapeutic Goods.[162] Section 70(3)(a) does not stipulate any quantity of the substance to be present in the registered goods. Hence, this provision is satisfied even though the substance may be present in only minute quantities.[163] Second, there must be at least five years between the date of the patent and the first regulatory approval date for the substance.[164]

Section 70(5) defines the first regulatory approval date as either the date of the commencement of the first inclusion in the Australian Register of Therapeutic Goods of goods that contain or consist of the substance,[165] or if pre–*Therapeutic Goods Act 1989* marketing approval has

---

153   *Prejay Holdings Ltd v Commissioner of Patents* (2003) 57 IPR 424, [24].
154   *Boehringer Ingelheim International GmbH v Commissioner of Patents (No 2)* (2001) 112 FCR 595, [39]–[42]; *Prejay Holdings Ltd v Commissioner of Patents* (2003) 57 IPR 424, 429 [24] (Wilcox and Cooper JJ).
155   *Pharmacia Italia SpA v Mayne Pharma Pty Ltd* (2006) 69 IPR 1, [55].
156   Ibid [107]; *Spirit Pharmaceuticals Pty Ltd v Mundipharma Pty Ltd* (2013) 102 IPR 55, 73 [65]–[67].
157   (2017) 253 FCR 436.
158   *Commissioner of Patents v AbbVie Biotechnology Ltd* (2017) 253 FCR 436, [59], [61].
159   Ibid; *Prejay Holdings Ltd v Commissioner of Patents* (2003) 57 IPR 424, 429–30.
160   *Boehringer Ingelheim International GmbH v Commissioner of Patents (No 2)* (2001) 112 FCR 595, 599.
161   *Patents Act 1990* (Cth) s 70(4).
162   Ibid s 70(3)(a). This Register is established under *Therapeutic Goods Act 1989* (Cth) ch 9. For a discussion, see *Pfizer Corp v Commissioner of Patents (No 2)* (2006) 69 IPR 525.
163   *Merck & Co Inc v Arrow Pharmaceuticals Ltd* (2003) 59 IPR 226, 232 [28].
164   *Patents Act 1990* (Cth) s 70(3)(b), (5), (6).
165   Ibid s 71(5A) provides circumstances in which the inclusion in the Register of a pharmaceutical substance for the sole purpose of exporting goods to address a public health problem is to be disregarded.

been given, the date of the first approval in relation to the substance.[166] Section 71(2) of the *Patents Act 1990* (Cth) provides that the application must be made during the term of the patent and within six months after the latest of the following dates:

(a) the date the patent was granted;
(b) the date of commencement of the first inclusion in the Australian Register of Therapeutic Goods of goods that contain or consist of pharmaceutical substances referred to in subsection 70(3)...;
(c) the date of commencement of [s 71(2)].[167]

The High Court in *Alphapharm Pty Ltd v H Lundbeck A/S*[168] construed the phrase 'during the term of the patent and within six months' in s 71(2) as comprising two separate time constraints that must both be observed in order to make an application.

9.10.2 Calculation of the term of extension

The extension of term is the period commencing on the date of the patent and ending on the earliest first regulatory approval date (as defined in s 70 of the *Patents Act 1990* (Cth)) reduced by five years (but not below zero). The maximum extension period is five years.[169]

9.11 Requirement of claims to have a priority date

Both a provisional specification and a complete specification must disclose the invention in a manner that is clear and complete enough for the invention to be performed by a skilled person and end with a claim or claims that define the invention.[170] Each claim is required to have a priority date,[171] to establish a date that is used for a variety of purposes set out in the *Patents Act 1990* (Cth) and regulations. The priority date of a claim is the date of filing the specification in which the invention claimed is first disclosed or such date that is otherwise determined by the *Patents Regulations 1991* (Cth).[172] Claims in the same specification may have different priority dates.[173] For instance, an amendment to a specification may claim new matter.[174] Another instance is where two or more provisional specifications are filed at different times in respect of the same complete application. The *Patents Regulations 1991* (Cth) provide particulars for identifying the priority documents in cases of complete, Convention and *PCT* applications.

---

166 Ibid s 70(5), (5A), (6). As to the first regulatory date, see *Alphapharm Pty Ltd v H Lundbeck A/S* (2008) 76 IPR 618.
167 27 January 1999.
168 (2014) 314 ALR 182.
169 *Patents Act 1990* (Cth) s 77(2).
170 Ibid s 40(1), (2).
171 Ibid s 43(1); *Patents Regulations 1991* (Cth) regs 3.12–3.14.
172 *Patents Act 1990* (Cth) ss 43(2), 43(2A), 30; *Patents Regulations 1991* (Cth) reg 3.5.
173 *Patents Act 1990* (Cth) s 43(4).
174 Ibid s 114(1); *Patents Regulations 1991* (Cth) reg 3.14.

9.11.1 Complete applications

In the case of complete applications for both standard and innovation patents – namely, an application that is accompanied by a complete specification[175] – a provisional application that is associated with the complete application is a priority document.[176] This association requires that the complete application was made within twelve months from the filing date of the provisional application.[177]

9.11.2 Convention applications

In the case of a Convention application,[178] the priority documents for a claim in the Convention application are the documents filed for a related basic application at the time when the application was made.[179]

9.11.3 *PCT* applications

A *PCT* application[180] is treated as a complete application for a standard patent.[181] Under art 8 of the *PCT*, an international application for protection of an invention may claim priority of earlier applications filed in a country that is party to the *Paris Convention*. Hence, an initial filing in a Convention country may be able to claim priority for a subsequent Convention application in Australia or a subsequent international filing under the *PCT*.[182]

9.11.4 Required disclosure in a priority document

The default rule for the priority date of a claim in a specification is the date of filing the specification. However, a claim in a complete specification can take the benefit of the earlier priority date of an associated provisional specification[183] or other priority document such as a Convention application[184] or *PCT* application[185] if that priority document (or documents) discloses 'the invention in the claim in a manner that is clear enough and complete enough for the invention to be performed by a person skilled in the relevant art'.[186]

A different test applies to patents that are governed by the provisions of the *Patents Act 1990* (Cth) and the *Patents Regulations 1991* (Cth) in force before the *Raising the Bar* legislation. The claim in a complete specification can take the benefit of the earlier priority date if the claim 'is fairly based on matter disclosed' in the relevant priority

---

175 *Patents Act 1990* (Cth) s 29(4).
176 Ibid s 38; *Patents Regulations 1991* (Cth) reg 3.13C.
177 *Patents Act 1990* (Cth) s 38(1); *Patents Regulations 1991* (Cth) reg 3.10.
178 See above at 9.6.1.
179 *Patents Act 1990* (Cth) s 43AA; *Patents Regulations 1991* (Cth) reg 3.13B.
180 See above at 9.6.2.
181 *Patents Act 1990* (Cth) s 29A.
182 *Patents Regulations 1991* (Cth) reg 3.13A.
183 Ibid reg 3.13C.
184 Ibid reg 3.13B.
185 Ibid reg 3.13A.
186 *Patents Act 1990* (Cth) s 43(2A)(b). See *Encompass Corp Pty Ltd v InfoTrack Pty Ltd* (2018) 130 IPR 387, [181].

document.[187] As the Full Federal Court in *Leonardis v Sartas No 1 Pty Ltd* confirmed, the priority document must contain a 'real and reasonably clear disclosure' of the invention to provide fair basis for the claim.[188] In other words, the claim does not travel beyond that disclosure.[189] Referred to as 'external fair basis', further decisions of the Full Federal Court, most recently *Idenix Pharmaceuticals LLC v Gilead Sciences Pty Ltd*[190] and *Coretell Pty Ltd v Australian Mud Company Pty Ltd*,[191] have confirmed that this test 'is essentially the same' as the test for 'internal fair basis' under s 40(3). This provision requires the claim or claims in the complete specification to be fairly based on matter described in that specification.[192] Bearing in mind nuanced linguistic differences in the respective statutory provisions that govern 'external' and 'internal' fair basis, the essence of both tests remains that there be a 'real and reasonably clear disclosure' of what is claimed in the relevant document.[193] In making the comparison between the claim and a priority document, it is incorrect to apply an 'over meticulous verbal analysis' or to seek to isolate essential integers in the priority document to see whether they correspond with the claim.[194]

A provisional application may provide the level of disclosure that is required by either fair basis or the modified standard that appears in s 43(2A)(b) of the *Patents Act 1990* (Cth), as the case may be, for several complete applications.[195] Two or more provisional applications 'may be taken together' for this purpose, such as where the second provisional application contains language that links it to the first provisional application.[196] Similarly, one provisional application may provide a priority document for more than one complete specification.[197] A claim may benefit from the earlier priority date of a provisional specification, even though that specification also discloses other inventions.[198]

---

187   *Patents Act 1990* (Cth) s 43(2)(b); *Patents Regulations 1991* (Cth) reg 3.12(1)(b) (in force before 15 April 2013).
188   (1996) 67 FCR 126; *Rehm Pty Ltd v Websters Security Systems (International) Pty Ltd* (1988) 11 IPR 289, 304; *Anaesthetic Supplies Pty Ltd v Rescare Ltd* (1994) 50 FCR 1, 20; *Tate v Haskins* (1935) 53 CLR 594, 606.
189   *Olin Corp v Super Cartridge Co Pty Ltd* (1977) 180 CLR 236, 240 (Barwick CJ); *Leonardis v Sartas No 1 Pty Ltd* (1996) 67 FCR 126, 143.
190   (2017) 134 IPR 1, [263], adopting discussion of the topic in *Multigate Medical Devices Pty Ltd v B Braun Melsungen AG* (2016) 117 IPR 1, [184]–[190].
191   (2017) 250 FCR 155.
192   *Lockwood Security Products Pty Ltd v Doric Products Pty Ltd* (2004) 217 CLR 274, [69].
193   *Coretell Pty Ltd v Australian Mud Company Pty Ltd* (2017) 250 FCR 155, [135], citing *Lockwood Security Products Pty Ltd v Doric Products Pty Ltd* (2004) 217 CLR 274, [69]. The 'internal fair basis' test is discussed in depth in ch 10 at 10.13.10.
194   *CCOM Pty Ltd v Jiejing Pty Ltd* (1994) 51 FCR 260, 281; *Societe des Usines Chimiques Rhone-Poulenc v Commission of Patents* (1958) 100 CLR 5, 11; *Multigate Medical Devices Pty Ltd v B Braun Melsungen AG* (2016) 117 IPR 1, [188].
195   *Leonardis v Sartas No 1 Pty Ltd* (1996) 67 FCR 126, 139.
196   Ibid 138.
197   Ibid 140.
198   Ibid 143–4; *Societe des Usines Chimiques Rhone-Poulenc v Commission of Patents* (1958) 100 CLR 5, 28–9.

9.12 The role of priority dates

The priority date of a claim performs a number of important functions to assist in the assessment of the validity of a patent. The main ones are:

1. It is only information in the prior art base as it existed before the priority date of the claim that can be compared with the claim to assess novelty, inventive or innovative step.[199]
2. Only common general knowledge before the priority date of the claim is relevant for the purposes of assessing inventiveness or in the innovative step inquiry.[200]
3. It is before the priority date of the relevant claim that one considers whether a skilled person could be reasonably expected to have combined information for the purposes of an inquiry into inventive step.[201]
4. It is implied that it is before the priority date of the relevant claim that one considers whether a skilled person would treat two or more related documents or two or more related acts as a single source of information for the purposes of an inquiry into innovative step.[202]
5. It is only secret use of the invention before the priority date of the claim that is relevant to the validity of the patent.[203]
6. The priority date defines the time after which the publication or use of the invention claimed in any claim will no longer invalidate that claim.[204]

Some other uses of the priority date include:

- to clarify that the validity of a granted patent is not affected by the grant of another patent that claims the same invention in a claim of the same or later priority date;[205]
- to prevent the grant of multiple patents for the same invention made by the same inventor where the claims in the specifications have the same priority date;[206]
- where, for a variety of reasons, the *Patents Act 1990* (Cth) provides that a grant of a standard or innovation patent may have the benefit of the priority date of an earlier claim;[207]
- to establish a time by which notice must be published of patent specifications being open to public inspection;[208] and
- to establish infringement exemptions for a prior user of a patented invention.[209]

---

199 *Patents Act 1990* (Cth) ss 18(1)(b), 18(1A)(b), 45(1)(b), 98(b), 101B(2), 101G(3).
200 Ibid s 7(2), (4).
201 Ibid s 7(2), (3).
202 Ibid s 7(4), (5).
203 Ibid s 18(1)(d), (1A)(d).
204 Ibid s 23(a).
205 Ibid s 23(b).
206 Ibid ss 64(2), 101B(2)(h).
207 Ibid ss 33–36.
208 Ibid s 54(3); *Patents Regulations 1991* (Cth) reg 4.2(3).
209 *Patents Act 1990* (Cth) s 119.

9.13 Withdrawal and lapsing of applications and ceasing of patents

9.13.1 Withdrawal of patents

Section 141(1) of the *Patents Act 1990* (Cth) governs the circumstances in which applications for standard and innovation patents can be withdrawn.[210] To overcome a former practice of using withdrawal provisions strategically during contested opposition proceedings under s 59, the Commissioner may refuse an applicant's request for leave to withdraw their opposed patent application.[211] *PCT* applications may be withdrawn or are taken to be withdrawn in the circumstances prescribed by reg 13.1C of the *Patents Regulations 1991* (Cth).

9.13.2 Lapsing of patents

A provisional application lapses at the end of the period of twelve months from the filing date of the provisional application.[212] A number of situations will result in the lapse of a standard patent.[213] These include failure to have the patent examined for a variety of reasons, failure to pay continuation fees, non-compliance with directions of the Commissioner to make amendments to the specification under s 107 of the *Patents Act 1990* (Cth), and non-acceptance of the patent request and specification.

9.13.3 Ceasing of patents

There is also provision for a standard patent to cease if renewal fees are not paid or prescribed documents are not filed within the prescribed period.[214] In the case of an innovation patent, it will cease in any of the circumstances listed in s 143A of the *Patents Act 1990* (Cth). These include failure to pay fees and to comply with directions.

9.14 International aspects

An overview of the specific norms that apply to an application for a patent in more than one country, and in particular the application procedures that apply under the *PCT*, was provided above.[215] Other key features of the principal treaties and conventions are set out in the following discussion of the *Paris Convention*, *TRIPS*, the *Budapest Treaty* and the *European Patent Convention*. Brief mention is made also of the *Patent Law Treaty* and the attempts to harmonise patent law in a Substantive Patent Law Treaty. Numerous free trade agreements include a chapter on intellectual property rights.[216]

---

210 *Patents Regulations 1991* (Cth) regs 13.1A (standard patent) and 13.1B (innovation patent) prescribe the period during which withdrawal cannot occur.
211 *Patents Act 1990* (Cth) s 141(1)(b).
212 Ibid ss 38, 142(1); *Patents Regulations 1991* (Cth) reg 3.10.
213 *Patents Act 1990* (Cth) s 142(2).
214 Ibid ss 143, 143B; *Patents Regulations 1991* (Cth) reg 13.6.
215 At 9.11.2 and 9.11.3.
216 See Department of Foreign Affairs and Trade, 'Free trade agreements', https://dfat.gov.au.

9.14.1 Paris Convention

The *Paris Convention for the Protection of Industrial Property*[217] was the first major international treaty designed to assist people to obtain protection for intellectual property rights in more than one country.[218] It contains three categories of substantive provisions: national treatment, right of priority and some general rules. The principle of national treatment enables nationals in any country of the Union to enjoy in all other Union countries the same protection for their industrial property as those countries grant to their own nationals. The right of priority, in the case of patents,[219] enables a means of access into national patent systems for foreign patentees without loss of the priority date given to their first filing. The application procedure was described briefly above.[220]

The common rules relate to a variety of matters, the more important being the following:

- All patents applied for in the various countries of the Union are independent of each other.[221]
- The inventor has the right to be mentioned as such in the patent.[222]
- The grant of a patent shall not be refused, and a patent shall not be invalidated on the ground that the sale of the patented product or of a product obtained by means of a patented process is subject to restrictions or limitations resulting from the domestic law.[223]
- The Convention provides for members to grant compulsory licences.[224] The *Paris Convention* contains no provisions that prescribe standards for patentability, term of patent or subject matter that may be excluded from patentability. Substantive provisions of this nature, and others, are found in *TRIPS*.

9.14.2 TRIPS

The *Patents (World Trade Organization Amendments) Act 1994* (Cth) enacted amendments to the *Patents Act 1990* (Cth) in order to bring Australian law into line with the standards and principles prescribed for patents in the *Agreement on Trade-Related Aspects of Intellectual Property*[225] (*TRIPS*). In addition to a general obligation to comply with the substantive provisions in the *Paris Convention*, the main features of *TRIPS* relevant to patents are as follows:

---

[217] Opened for signature 14 July 1967, WIPO Lex No TRT/PARIS/001 (as amended 28 September 1979, entered into force 3 June 1984) (*Paris Convention*).
[218] S. Ricketson, *The Paris Convention for the Protection of Industrial Property: A Commentary* (Oxford University Press, 2015).
[219] Also, utility models (where these exist), marks and designs.
[220] At 9.6.1.
[221] *Paris Convention* art 4bis.
[222] Ibid art 4ter.
[223] Ibid art 4quater.
[224] Ibid art 5.
[225] *Marrakesh Agreement Establishing the World Trade Organization*, opened for signature 20 December 1996 (entered into force 6 March 2002) annex 1C (*Agreement on Trade-Related Aspects of Intellectual Property*) (*TRIPS*).

- The most-favoured-nation clause requires that a party who gives any advantage to the nationals of another country must extend it immediately and unconditionally to the nationals of all other parties.[226]
- Patents must be available for products and processes in all fields of technology, provided they are new, involve an inventive step and are capable of industrial application. Patents must be available, and rights enjoyable, without discrimination as to various matters including the field of technology.[227]
- There is limited scope for exclusion of inventions from patentability to prevent their commercial exploitation within the territory where it would have certain specified adverse consequences, such as serious prejudice to the environment.[228]
- Members also have discretion to exclude other inventions from patentability, such as diagnostic, therapeutic and surgical methods for the treatment of humans or animals, and plants and animals other than micro-organisms.[229]
- There is an obligation to protect plant varieties, either by patents or an effective sui generis scheme, such as those provided in the *International Convention for the Protection of New Varieties of Plants*.[230]
- Exclusive rights for the owner are prescribed. In the case of process patents, the rights must extend to the products directly obtained by the process.[231]
- Applicants must sufficiently describe their invention and may be required to include the best method for carrying it out.[232]
- Limited exceptions may be provided to the rights conferred.[233]
- There are limitations on compulsory licensing or governmental use of patents without the authorisation of the patent owner.[234]
- A minimum term of protection of twenty years is calculated from the filing date of the complete application.[235]
- The burden of proof for process patents is imposed on the defendant in an infringement action.[236]

9.14.3 Budapest Treaty

Australia acceded to the *Budapest Treaty on the International Recognition of the Deposit of Microorganisms for the Purposes of Patent Procedure*[237] (*Budapest Treaty*) on 7 July 1987. This

---

226 *TRIPS* art 4.
227 Ibid art 27(1).
228 Ibid art 27(2).
229 Ibid art 27(3).
230 Ibid art 27(3).
231 Ibid art 28.
232 Ibid art 29.
233 Ibid art 30.
234 Ibid art 31.
235 Ibid art 33.
236 Ibid art 34.
237 Opened for signature 28 April 1977, WIPO Lex No TRT/BUDAPEST/001 (entered into force 19 August 1980, as amended 26 September 1980) (*Budapest Treaty*).

was made possible through amendments introduced into the *Patents Act 1952* (Cth) by the *Patents Amendment Act 1984* (Cth) and *Patents Regulations (Amendment) 1987* (Cth). The treaty establishes a system where it is necessary to deposit a sample with a prescribed International Depository Institution of inventions that are micro-organisms that cannot be described adequately in the words of the complete specification.[238] The provisions apply also where an invention involves the use, modification or cultivation of a micro-organism that is not reasonably available to a person skilled in the relevant art.[239] According to the World Intellectual Property Organization (WIPO), 'the whole point of depositing a microorganism for patent purposes is to make it available to entitled parties according to the requirements of patent law'.[240]

9.14.4 European Patent Convention

The *Convention on the Grant of European Patents of 5 October 1973*,[241] known as the *European Patent Convention* or *EPC*, is a multilateral treaty that created the European Patent Organisation, based in Munich. The convention established a system of law for the grant of patents that would be common for all contracting states.[242] Part II of the convention provides the substantive provisions with which contracting states must comply.

The *European Patent Convention* provides a single application procedure. The European Patent Organisation undertakes the complete process of search and examination and grants a European patent to a successful applicant. The convention contains provision for opposition to grant of a patent[243] and appeals against decisions.[244] A European patent is not a single patent, but a bundle of national patents for each of the contracting states designated by the applicant. In each of those designated contracting states, the European patent has the effect of and is subject to the same conditions as a national patent granted by that state.[245] Hence, issues of validity and enforcement are dealt with in the local courts of each respective state.[246] Maintenance of the patent registration is also a matter for the local patent offices.

The single application procedure is an alternative to single filings in each country in which protection is sought. There is a certain amount of risk associated with this process, in that failure to be granted a European patent results in no patent grant in any of the designated contracting states. The official languages of the European Patent Organisation are English,

---

238 *Patents Act 1990* (Cth) ss 40(2)(a), 41, 42; *Patents Act 1952* (Cth) s 40(1)(a), (3)–(7).
239 This does not necessarily require that the micro-organism is reasonably available in the patent area: *Patents Act 1990* (Cth) s 41(3).
240 World Intellectual Property Organization (WIPO), *Guide to the Deposit of Microorganisms under the Budapest Treaty* (2010) pt I [87] www.wipo.int.
241 Opened for signature 5 October 1973, 1065 UNTS 199 (entered into force 7 October 1977) (*European Patent Convention*).
242 There were thirty-eight contracting states as at March 2019: European Patent Office, 'Member states of the European Patent Organisation' www.epo.org. Australia is not a member of the *European Patent Convention*.
243 *European Patent Convention* pt V.
244 Ibid pt VI.
245 Ibid arts 2, 64.
246 Ibid art 64.

French and German. European patent applications must be filed in one of these languages.[247] The multiplicity of languages in contracting states can result in significant translation costs.[248]

An alternative to national patents and European patents will be a unitary patent. This is a European patent to which unitary effect is given after grant, at the patentee's request.[249] The unitary patent is to be implemented by two regulations that came into force on 20 January 2013[250] and an Agreement on a Unified Patent Court that was signed by 25 European Union member states on 19 February 2013. That agreement is yet to enter into force, but commencement of the new system is anticipated in the first half of 2020.[251] The Unified Patent Court will provide exclusive jurisdiction for litigation relating to European patents and European patents with unitary effect. The regulations will only apply from the date of entry into force of the Agreement on a Unified Patent Court.

9.14.5 *Patent Law Treaty* and proposed Substantive Patent Law Treaty

The *Patent Law Treaty*[252] harmonises formal procedures, such as the requirements to obtain a filing date for a patent application, the form and content of a patent application, and representation. The treaty was concluded on 1 June 2000. It came into effect generally on 28 April 2005, and for Australia 16 March 2009.

After the adoption of the *Patent Law Treaty*, WIPO's Standing Committee on the Law of Patents[253] commenced work on the harmonisation of substantive requirements of patent law in a Substantive Patent Law Treaty (SPLT). Since May 2001, several versions of a draft SPLT have been discussed. However, work stalled in 2005 after the eleventh session of the committee failed to reach agreement on a variety of issues. WIPO reinvigorated the establishment of an SPLT by holding an open forum in Geneva in March 2006. Since then, the committee continues to examine a variety of substantive issues that include standards and patents, exclusions from patentable subject matter, exceptions and limitations to the rights, the client–patent adviser privilege, dissemination of patent information, transfer of technology, and opposition systems. Its thirtieth session was held in June 2019.

---

247 Ibid art 14.
248 Ibid arts 14, 65.
249 European Patent Office, 'Unitary Patent', www.epo.org.
250 *Regulation (EU) No 1257/2012 of the European Parliament and of the Council of 17 December 2012 Implementing Enhanced Cooperation in the Area of the Creation of Unitary Patent Protection; Council Regulation (EU) No 1260/2012 of the European Parliament and of the Council of 17 December 2012 Implementing Enhanced Cooperation in the Area of the Creation Of Unitary Patent Protection with Regard to the Applicable Translation Arrangements.*
251 European Patent Office, 'When will the Unitary Patent system start?' www.epo.org.
252 Opened for signature 1 June 2000, WIPO Lex No TRT/PLT/001 (entered into force 28 April 2005). As at 10 October 2018, there are forty contracting parties.
253 See WIPO, 'Standing Committee on the Law of Patents (SCP)', www.wipo.int.

10

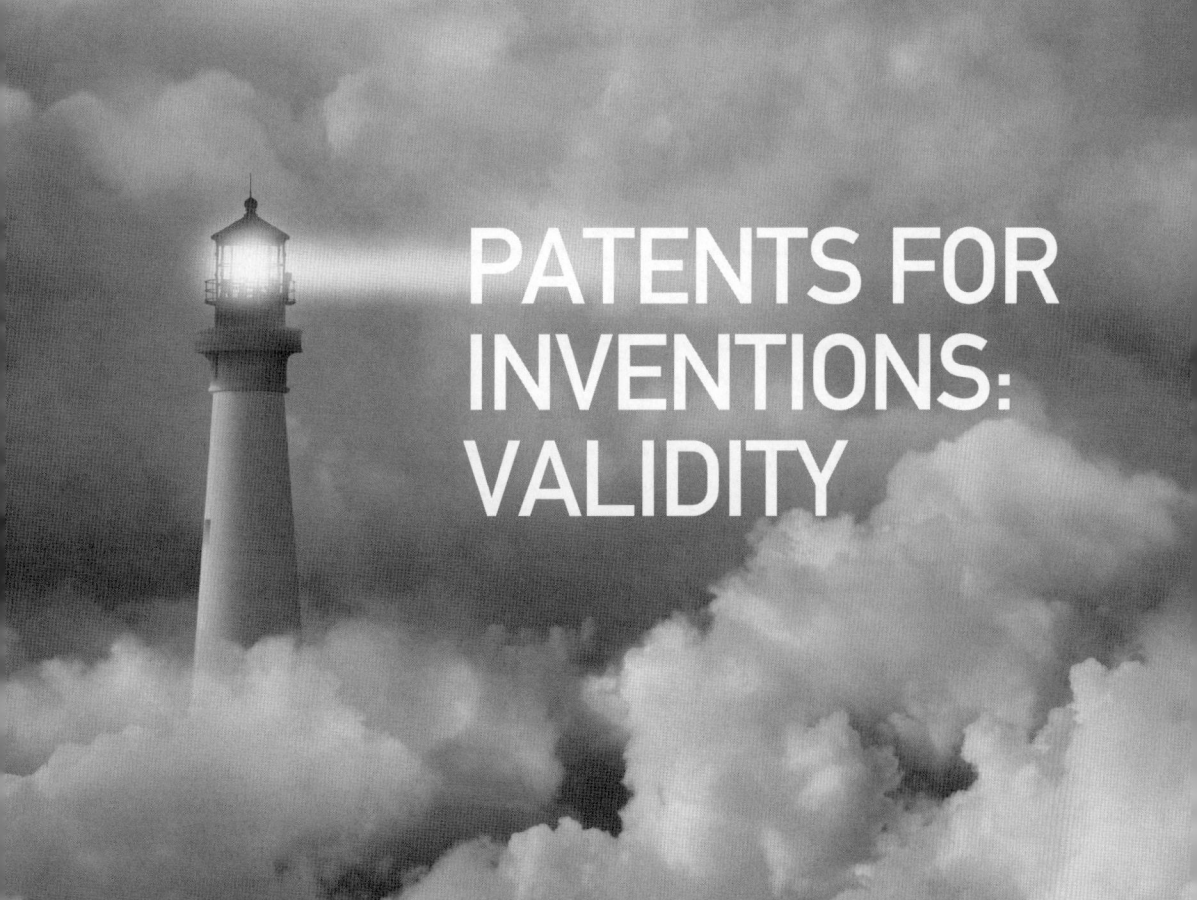

PATENTS FOR INVENTIONS: VALIDITY

10.1 Statutory requirements

The concept of a patentable invention appeared originally in s 6 of the *Statute of Monopolies 1623* (21 Jac 1 c 3)[1] and was expressed in terms of any 'manner of new manufacture'. The purpose of this section was 'to allow the use of the prerogative to encourage national development in a field which already, in 1623, was seen to be excitingly unpredictable'.[2]

There has never been a statutory definition of the phrase 'manner of manufacture'. Over the centuries, judicial interpretation of s 6 gradually fleshed out the requirements of a 'patentable invention', which is now defined in sch 1 of the *Patents Act 1990* (Cth) as meaning 'an invention of the kind mentioned in section 18'. As to the meaning of 'invention', sch 1 provides that the word 'invention' (without any definite or indefinite article before it) means 'any manner of new manufacture the subject of letters patent and grant of privilege within section 6 of the *Statute of Monopolies*, and includes an alleged invention'.[3] The word 'alleged' relates to the word 'new'.[4] The term 'new' in s 6 was a broad and undefined concept that has subsequently been construed by the courts to encompass the separate notions of novelty and inventiveness. Hence, the use of the word 'new' in the context of the phrase 'manner of new manufacture' in the 1990 Act is not to be equated with what we now refer to as 'novelty'.

Patents are available for products and processes. Assuming that there is an 'invention',[5] it is patentable for the purposes of a standard patent if the invention, so far as claimed in any claim, satisfies the remaining requirements set out in s 18(1) of the *Patents Act 1990* (Cth), namely:

(a) is a manner of manufacture within the meaning of section 6 of the *Statute of Monopolies*; and
(b) when compared with the prior art base as it existed before the priority date of that claim:
  (i) is novel; and
  (ii) involves an inventive step; and
(c) is useful; and
(d) was not secretly used in the patent area before the priority date of that claim by, or on behalf of, or with the authority of, the patentee or nominated person or the patentee's or nominated person's predecessor in title to the invention.

The criteria for validity of an innovation patent in s 18(1A) are identical with the exception that it must be shown to involve an innovative step, not an inventive step.

10.2 A two-tier system

Prior to 1979, the *Patents Act 1952* (Cth) provided protection for standard patents only. In 1979, in line with international developments, Australia introduced a second-tier form of patent

---

1. See ch 9 at 9.2 for the text of s 6.
2. *National Research Development Corporation v Commissioner of Patents* (1959) 102 CLR 252, 271 (*NRDC v Commissioner of Patents*).
3. *Patents Act 1990* (Cth) sch 1 (definition of 'invention'). This definition is subject to any contrary intention appearing in the Act.
4. *NV Philips Gloeilampenfabrieken v Mirabella International Pty Ltd* (1995) 183 CLR 655, 663–4.
5. See below at 10.3.

protection known as the petty patent.[6] It was designed to provide protection for small-scale innovations with a short commercial life, such as appliances and accessories. The substantive requirements of patent law were applicable, with both standard and petty patents assessed for novelty and inventive step against the same relevant prior art base. However, there were some important differences in the two regimes. The petty patent specification was limited to a single claim[7] and petty patents were granted a shorter monopoly term to reflect the nature of the inventions for which they would be suitable. The term was limited to a maximum of six years, with an initial period of twelve months and the option for a five-year extension.[8]

The *Patents Act 1990* (Cth) continued to provide a legislative scheme for the protection of standard and petty patents. The differences in the term of protection remained unaltered, at sixteen and six years respectively,[9] but a petty patent was now able to have an independent claim and not more than two dependent claims defining the invention.[10] With the exception of procedural differences, and the expansion of the prior art base against which the novelty of a standard patent was assessed,[11] the essential characteristics of a patentable invention for the purposes of the Act remained identical for both standard and petty patents. Importantly, the invention had to reach the same level of inventiveness and was available for the same forms of subject matter.

On the recommendation of the Advisory Council on Intellectual Property (ACIP) in 1995,[12] the government enacted the *Patents Amendment (Innovation Patents) Act 2000* (Cth) to repeal and replace the petty patent with the innovation patent. The legislative intention was clear that the innovation patent system was to provide a lower level of inventive height for entry: an *innovative* step.[13] It would provide a second tier of protection for inventions that did not meet the criteria for an inventive step. A number of other substantive changes included differentiation in the subject matter for an innovation patent by providing that plants and animals, and the biological processes for the generation of plants and animals, are not patentable inventions.[14] In addition, an innovation patent could now have protection for up to eight years and for up to five independent claims. The principal administrative change was to provide registration of an innovation patent after a formalities check and without substantive examination. Certification of the innovation patent could be sought after grant if, for example, the patentee wished to bring an infringement action. The *Patents Amendment (Innovation Patents) Act 2000* (Cth) brought the prior art base for innovation patents into line with that which applied for standard patents,[15] so that the novelty test was identical, but provided entirely different comparisons for the purposes of testing innovative and inventive step.

6	Advisory Council on Intellectual Property (ACIP), *Review of the Petty Patent System* (Final Report, October 1995).
7	*Patents Act 1952* (Cth) s 40(1A)(b).
8	Ibid s 68 (standard patent sixteen years), s 68A (petty patent six years).
9	*Patents Act 1990* (Cth) ss 67, 68.
10	Ibid s 40(2)(b), (c).
11	See below at 10.6.5.
12	ACIP, *Review of the Petty Patent System*, above n 6.
13	Ibid rec 2; *Introduction of the Innovation Patent: The Government Response to the Recommendations of the ACIP Report* (March 1997); Revised Explanatory Memorandum, Patents Amendment (Innovation Patents) Bill 2000 (Cth). The scheme commenced on 24 May 2001.
14	*Patents Act 1990* (Cth) s 18(3).
15	See below at 10.6.5.1.

The innovation patent system has continued to provoke criticism and concerns regarding its effectiveness and relevance for Australian small and medium-sized enterprises as its intended beneficiaries. In 2014, ACIP published its final report following a review of the innovation patent system. Although doubtful that benefits of innovation patents warranted their retention, ACIP felt constrained by a lack of empirical evidence to make a recommendation to either abolish or retain that system.[16] However, it revised its position in May 2015 and recommended that the government should consider abolition of the system. Also in 2015, the Australian Government requested the Productivity Commission to undertake a wideranging inquiry into Australia's entire intellectual property system. The Commission's 2016 report *Intellectual Property Arrangements* included a recommendation to abolish the innovation patent system: a recommendation that the government subsequently supported.[17] The Intellectual Property Laws Amendment (Productivity Commission Response Part 2 and Other Measures) Bill 2019 (Cth) gives effect to these recommendations and includes amendments to the *Patents Act 1990* (Cth) to commence the abolition process 'by preventing the filing of new applications, subject to certain limited exceptions'.[18] As the draft Bill was yet to be introduced into parliament at the time of writing, a brief reference only appears below where relevant.

10.3 The concept of invention

The term 'invention' appears in various provisions of the *Patents Act 1990* (Cth) but is not used uniformly throughout the Act.[19] For example, it is used in s 18(1) and (1A) to mean the subject matter of the claim. This meaning is not the same as the inventive step taken by the inventor.[20] In contrast, it is used in s 40 to mean 'the embodiment which is described, and around which the claims are drawn'.[21] The essence of invention is that it involves some human intervention. As the plurality in *D'Arcy v Myriad Genetics Inc* stated:

> [A]n invention is something which involves 'making'. It must reside in something. It may be a product. It may be a process. It may be an outcome which can be characterised, in the language of *NRDC*, as an artificially created state of affairs'. Whatever it is, it must be something brought about by human action.[22]

---

16 ACIP, *Review of the Innovation Patent System* (Final Report, June 2014) rec 2.1.
17 Productivity Commission, *Intellectual Property Arrangements* (Inquiry Report No 78, September 2016) rec 8.1; *Australian Government Response to the Productivity Commission Inquiry into Intellectual Property Arrangements* (August 2017) 10, www.industry.gov.au.
18 Explanatory Memorandum, Intellectual Property Laws Amendment (Productivity Commission Response Part 2 and Other Measures) Bill 2019 (Cth) 14. The Bill was introduced into parliament in July 2019. In September 2019, the Senate Economics Legislation Committee recommended that the Bill be passed: Senate, Economics Legislation Committee, Parliament of Australia, *Intellectual Property Laws Amendment (Productivity Commission Response Part 2 and Other Measures) Bill 2019* (Report, September 2019).
19 *Kimberly-Clark Australia Pty Ltd v Arico Trading International Pty Ltd* (2001) 207 CLR 1, 13–14.
20 *Lockwood Security Products Pty Ltd v Doric Products Pty Ltd (No 3)* (2005) 226 ALR 70, [196].
21 *AMP Inc v Utilux Pty Ltd* (1971) 45 ALJR 123, 127 (McTiernan J); *Kimberly-Clark Australia Pty Ltd v Arico Trading International Pty Ltd* (2001) 207 CLR 1, 14–15.
22 (2015) 258 CLR 334, [6] (French CJ, Kiefel, Bell and Keane JJ); *NRDC v Commissioner of Patents* (1959) 102 CLR 252, 276–7.

10.4 Manner of manufacture
10.4.1 Time at which manner of manufacture is raised

The first of the requirements for patentability is that the invention, so far as claimed in any claim, must be a 'manner of manufacture within the meaning of section 6 of the *Statute of Monopolies*'.[23] This requirement is the same for both standard and innovation patents. Compliance with this requirement is considered at both examination[24] and re-examination,[25] and its absence is a ground for opposition[26] and revocation.[27] An innovation patent is granted after a formalities check.[28] Compliance with the requirement that the invention is a manner of manufacture is considered at examination, which occurs after grant,[29] re-examination,[30] opposition[31] and revocation.[32]

10.4.2 Background to the meaning of 'manner of manufacture'

From the time of the *Statute of Monopolies*, the concept of 'manner of manufacture' was always understood to be flexible, although it was not until 1842 that processes were confirmed as patentable subject matter.[33] Although initially thought to apply only to products, it was settled by 1842 that 'manufacture' comprehended both a process and a product.[34] However, the development of patent law over the following decades resulted in a lack of clarity for the patentability of processes. In 1942, Lord Morton proposed guidelines in *Re GEC's Application*[35] for finding a process to be patentable to deal with these concerns. These guidelines required the process to lead to the production, preservation from deterioration, restoration or improvement of some vendible product to which the process is applied. Lord Morton expressly disclaimed any intention that this proposition should become a rule that is applicable in all cases. Despite the disclaimer, subsequent courts tended to apply these guidelines ('Morton's Rules') as a formula or definition that, over time, came to have the potential to limit the scope of patentable subject matter. The 'rules' were applied inconsistently. Some courts required a

---

23 *Patents Act 1990* (Cth) s 18(1)(a).
24 Ibid ss 45(1)(b), 101B(2)(b).
25 Ibid ss 98(b), 101G(1A)(3)(b)
26 Ibid ss 59(b), 101M(c).
27 Ibid s 138(3)(b).
28 Ibid ss 52, 62. Intellectual Property Laws Amendment (Productivity Commission Response Part 2 and Other Measures) Bill 2019 (Cth) sch 1 pt 2 item 4 limits the availability of the formalities check to patents that would (if granted) have a date before the commencement of this subsection.
29 Ibid s 101B.
30 Ibid s 98(b) (standard patents) and s 101G (innovation patents) were amended to include all the substantive grounds considered at examination (in addition to the pre-existing grounds of novelty and inventive step): *Intellectual Property Laws Amendment (Raising the Bar) Act 2012* (Cth) sch 6 items 17, 23. The changes apply to all standard patents and patent applications, regardless of when the applications were made or the patents granted.
31 *Patents Act 1990* (Cth) s 101M.
32 Ibid s 138(3)(b).
33 *Crane v Price* (1842) 1 WPC 393, 4 M & G 580, 134 ER 239, 248, 249.
34 Ibid.
35 (1942) 60 RPC 1.

tangible product to be involved.[36] Others construed the concept of a 'vendible product' more flexibly to deal with advances in science.[37] The limits on patentability were unclear, although it was generally understood that, for instance, a mere abstract idea, intellectual information, natural phenomena, and discoveries had never been patentable. The difficulty was in determining the distinction between these concepts and appropriate patentable subject matter.

This lack of clarity concerning the limits on patentable processes was exacerbated by the lack of any other underlying rationale that could provide a principled justification for defining limits on patentable subject matter in general. Faced with the unpredictability of advances in human ingenuity, courts had been developing progressively a mix of unpatentable classes of inventions that ranged across four broad areas.[38]

The first included intellectual information of all kinds, such as plans, instructions and presentations of information, as well as intellectual conceptions, such as discoveries, mathematical formulae or algorithms, and principles of nature. This type of subject matter was never considered to be patentable, but the reasons were not always clear.

A second group of excluded inventions that fell within a variety of more specific classes of subject matter were also regarded as unpatentable. Methods of medical treatment for humans, horticultural and agricultural methods,[39] computer programs, business methods and living matter were regarded as unpatentable, but there was no principled basis for their exclusion. Methods of medical treatment were rejected on ethical grounds and not because the method disclosed no manner of manufacture. In contrast, computer programs were rejected on the basis of theories that these types of invention were in the realm of the fine arts or merely recited mathematical algorithms.[40] As for business schemes and methods, these were seen also as belonging within the fine arts rather than the useful arts, being intellectual information in the nature of sequences of instructions for solving a problem. In rare cases, the ground of general inconvenience was used to support a decision.[41] Living matter, such as plants, animals and inventions in the area of biotechnology, was also regarded as unpatentable.

The absence of inventiveness best explains the exclusion from patentability of a third class of material referred to as 'the use of a known material in the manufacture of known articles for the purpose of which its known properties make that material suitable'.[42] This subject matter is now excluded from patentability on the basis of the threshold test of inventiveness that appears from the opening words of s 18(1) and (1A) of the *Patents Act 1990* (Cth).[43]

---

36   *Re Standard Oil Development Co's Application* (1951) 68 RPC 114; *Re Application by Bovingdon* (1946) 64 RPC 20.
37   *Re Cementation Co Ltd, Abram Ruper Neelands & Peckersgill's Patents* (1945) 62 RPC 151; *Re Rantzen's Application for a Patent* (1946) 64 RPC 63; *Re Elton & Leda Chemicals Ltd's Application* [1957] RPC 267.
38   See S. Ricketson, *The Law of Intellectual Property* (Sydney: Law Book Company, 1984) [48.27]–[48.54] for discussion of earlier authorities.
39   *Re RauGesellschaft's Application* (1935) 52 RPC 362.
40   An algorithm is a procedure for solving a given type of mathematical problem: *International Business Machines Corp v Commissioner of Patents* (1991) 33 FCR 218, 220.
41   *Rolls-Royce Ltd's Application* [1963] RPC 251 (schemes); *Telefon A/B LM Ericsson's Application* [1975] FSR 49, 56–7 (computer program).
42   *Commissioner of Patents v Microcell Ltd* (1959) 102 CLR 232, 251. See *Patents Act 1990* (Cth) s 18(1); *NV Philips Gloeilampenfabrieken v Mirabella International Pty Ltd* (1995) 183 CLR 655. See below at 10.9.
43   See below at 10.9.

A fourth class is that of 'collocations' or a 'mere collocation of separate parts'. However, the reason for their exclusion is best explained on the basis of lack of inventive step. Something is described as a mere collocation when the combination of its separate parts produces nothing 'new' in that it is obvious.[44] For a combination of separate parts to be patentable, it must be for an invention that involves a combination of a number of separate parts or integers that combine with each other in a way that produces a new result or product that is not obvious.[45] There must be 'a working interrelationship brought about by the collocation of integers claimed'.[46] The discussion of these final two classes of subject matter belongs in the context of s 18(1)(a) and what is known as the threshold concept of newness or inventiveness.

It is important to mention two fundamental principles in assessing whether subject matter claimed satisfies s 18(1)(a) or s 18(1A)(a) of the *Patents Act 1990* (Cth). First, the purpose of s 6 of the *Statute of Monopolies* was to encourage inventions in excitingly unpredictable fields within the useful arts as contrasted with the fine arts. Second, inquiries as to newness are independent issues that are considered only in the assessment of novelty, inventive step or threshold of inventiveness.

The test for patentable subject matter requires consideration of the principles in *NRDC v Commissioner of Patents*.[47] These require the 'terminology of "manner of manufacture" taken from s 6 of the *Statute of Monopolies* ... to be treated as a concept of case-by-case development'.[48] This common law methodology is to be consistent with a 'widening conception of the notion [which] has been a characteristic of the growth of patent law'.[49] Hence, the starting point for the meaning of 'manner of manufacture' is *NRDC v Commissioner of Patents*. Although the government accepted recommendations of two reviews to amend the test for patentable subject matter in the *Patents Act 1990* (Cth), it is unlikely to implement any change.[50]

10.4.3 *NRDC v Commissioner of Patents*: meaning of 'manner of manufacture'

10.4.3.1 The judgment

This combination of judicially created classes of unpatentable subject matter and the use of Morton's Rules to constrain the development of patent law in its application to process and method inventions provides the backdrop for the 1959 landmark decision of the High Court in

---

44 *Advanced Building Systems Pty Ltd v Ramset Fasteners (Australia) Pty Ltd* (1998) 194 CLR 171, 182; *Welch Perrin & Co Pty Ltd v Worrel* (1961) 106 CLR 588; *WM Wrigley Jr Co v Cadbury Schweppes Pty Ltd* (2005) 66 IPR 298, 315, [94] (collocation); *Smith & Nephew Pty Ltd v Wake Forest University Health Sciences* (2009) 82 IPR 467, [15]–[44].
45 *Minnesota Mining & Manufacturing Co v Beiersdorf (Australia) Ltd* (1980) 144 CLR 253, 266; *Advanced Building Systems Pty Ltd v Ramset Fasteners (Australia) Pty Ltd* (1998) 194 CLR 171, 182.
46 *Smith & Nephew Pty Ltd v Wake Forest University Health Sciences* (2009) 82 IPR 467, 474 [43].
47 (1959) 102 CLR 252.
48 *D'Arcy v Myriad Genetics Inc* (2015) 258 CLR 334, [5] (French CJ, Kiefel, Bell and Keane JJ); *NRDC v Commissioner of Patents* (1959) 102 CLR 252, 269.
49 *NRDC v Commissioner of Patents* (1959) 102 CLR 252, 270; *D'Arcy v Myriad Genetics Inc* (2015) 258 CLR 334, [18] (French CJ, Kiefel, Bell and Keane JJ).
50 ACIP, *Patentable Subject Matter* (Final Report, December 2010); ALRC, *Genes and Ingenuity: Gene Patenting and Human Health* (Report No 99, June 2004); *Government Response: Patentable Subject Matter* (2011) (updated April 2016 on www.ipaustralia.gov.au).

National Research Development Corporation v Commissioner of Patents[51] (*NRDC*). The time was ripe for the court to draw together the body of legal precedent into a single, principled approach that would apply to both processes and products.[52]

The invention under consideration was for a process that used a known chemical for a purpose for which it was not known to be useful – namely, eradicating weeds from crop areas so that crops could thrive. The process fell outside a literal interpretation of Morton's Rules as it did not produce, preserve, restore or improve some physical thing. The High Court found the invention to be a manner of manufacture. It stated that any attempt to precisely define 'manufacture' with an exact verbal formula was bound to fail. The court made it clear that the inquiry relates to the 'breadth of the concept which the law has developed by its consideration of the text and purpose of the *Statute of Monopolies*'. Accordingly: 'The right question is: "Is this a proper subject of letters patent according to the principles which have been developed for the application of section 6 of the *Statute of Monopolies?*"'[53]

The court identified the principles that had been developed up to 1959 in broad terms to guide subsequent courts that have the responsibility to continue to develop and mould the notion of what is proper subject matter for a patent. In this context, it approved the use of Morton's Rules as guidelines only as to what is proper subject matter. It effectively abandoned the 'vendible product' analysis by reinterpreting the concept of a 'vendible product' in light of the past development of the law as 'laying proper emphasis upon the trading or industrial character of the processes intended to be comprehended by the Acts – their "industrial or commercial or trading character"'.[54] The court stated:

> The point is that a process, to fall within the limits of patentability which the context of the *Statute of Monopolies* has supplied, must be one that offers some advantage which is material, in the sense that the process belongs to a useful art as distinct from a fine art ... – that its value to the country is in the field of economic endeavour.[55]

The High Court continued to explain that a product, in relation to a process, is 'only something in which the new and useful effect may be observed'; the '"something" need not be a "thing" in the sense of an article; it may be any physical phenomenon in which the effect, be it creation or merely alteration, may be observed'.[56] As for the distinction between fine and useful arts that is expressed in the above passage, this is both difficult and unresolved.[57] The High Court found the agricultural process under consideration to be a manner of manufacture because its effect

> exhibits the two essential qualities upon which 'product' and 'vendible' seem designed to insist. It is a 'product' because it consists in an *artificially created state of affairs*,

---

51 (1959) 102 CLR 252. See S. Hubicki and B. Sherman, 'We have never been modern: The High Court's decision in *National Research Development Corporation v Commissioner of Patents*' in A. T. Kenyon, M. Richardson and S. Ricketson (eds), *Landmarks in Australian Intellectual Property Law* (Melbourne: Cambridge University Press, 2009) ch 5.
52 *D'Arcy v Myriad Genetics Inc* (2014) 224 FCR 479 (FC), [166]; (2015) 258 CLR 334.
53 *NRDC v Commissioner of Patents* (1959) 102 CLR 252, 269.
54 Ibid 275; *Re Lenard's Application* (1954) 71 RPC 190, 192 (Lloyd-Jacob J).
55 *NRDC v Commissioner of Patents* (1959) 102 CLR 252, 275.
56 Ibid 276. See *Grant v Commissioner of Patents* (2006) 154 FCR 62.
57 *Grant v Commissioner of Patents* (2005) 67 IPR 1, 5. For guidance see IP Australia, *Australian Patent Office: Manual of Practice and Procedures* (*APO Manual*) [2.9.2.4].

discernible by observing over a period the growth of weeds and crops respectively on sown land on which the method has been put into practice. And the *significance of the product is economic*; for it provides a remarkable advantage, indeed to the lay mind a sensational advantage ... [The process] achieves a separate result, and the result possesses its own *economic utility*.[58]

10.4.3.2 NRDC guiding factors

Courts have relied upon the above passages from time to time to coin various phrases that capture the essence of the concept of 'manner of manufacture' that previous courts had developed. These include 'a mode or manner of achieving an end result which is an artificially created state of affairs of utility in the field of economic endeavour',[59] an 'artificially created state of affairs of economic significance'[60] and 'an artificially created state of affairs providing economic utility'.[61]

Three points are relevant here. First, despite these and other expressions of the *NRDC* guiding factors, courts are now clear that the terminology used in *NRDC* was not intended to be applied 'as some statutory text',[62] as a definition or rigid formula,[63] or as a 'sufficient or exhaustive statement'[64] of the characterisation of patentable subject matter. The fundamental question remains as the relevant legal principle: 'Is this a proper subject of letters patent according to the principles which have been developed for the application of section 6 of the *Statute of Monopolies?*'[65]

In answering this question, there is consensus that the presence of these guiding factors, however they may be phrased, is 'necessary to the characterisation of an invention claimed as a manner of manufacture' and will 'ordinarily be sufficient'.[66] Importantly, *NRDC* is not to be applied narrowly in answering this question, and questions of novelty and inventive step do not arise.[67]

Second, although courts agree that human action or invention is crucial for an invention to qualify as a manner of manufacture, this element is not explicit in the phrase 'artificially created state of affairs'. In contrast, the plurality in *D'Arcy v Myriad Genetics Inc* addressed the significance of the human factor in its rephrasing of this first factor as '[w]hether the invention as claimed is for a product made, or a process producing an outcome *as a result of human*

---

58   *NRDC v Commissioner of Patents* (1959) 102 CLR 252, 277 (emphasis added).
59   *CCOM Pty Ltd v Jiejing Pty Ltd* (1994) 51 FCR 260, 295.
60   *Research Affiliates LLC v Commissioner of Patents* (2014) 227 FCR 378, [102].
61   *Anaesthetic Supplies Pty Ltd v Rescare Ltd* (1994) 50 FCR 1, 19, endorsed in *Apotex Pty Ltd v Sanofi-Aventis Australia Pty Ltd* (2013) 253 CLR 284, [241] (Crennan and Kiefel JJ).
62   *D'Arcy v Myriad Genetics Inc* (2014) 224 FCR 479 (FC), [113]; (2015) 258 CLR 334, [275] (Gordon J).
63   *D'Arcy v Myriad Genetics Inc* (2015) 258 CLR 334, [21] (French CJ, Kiefel, Bell and Keane JJ), endorsing A. Monotti, 'The scope of "manner of manufacture" under the *Patents Act 1990* (Cth) after *Grant v Commissioner of Patents*' (2006) 34 *Federal Law Review* 461, 465–6.
64   *Research Affiliates LLC v Commissioner of Patents* (2014) 227 FCR 378, [102].
65   *NRDC v Commissioner of Patents* (1959) 102 CLR 252, 269.
66   *D'Arcy v Myriad Genetics Inc* (2015) 258 CLR 334, [20], [28] (French CJ, Kiefel, Bell and Keane JJ).
67   *D'Arcy v Myriad Genetics Inc* (2014) 224 FCR 479 (FC), [185], [206].

action.[68] The implications of the differences in these expressions (if any) await future elucidation. In the meantime, the phrase that continues to appear in judgments remains linked to an artificially created state of affairs.

Third, it is likely that the High Court in *NRDC* was not intending that *significance* of the economic utility of an invention would override a lesser standard of 'economic utility' that also appears in the quoted passage above. It is more likely that the court was merely observing the significance of the invention under consideration as distinct from introducing the requirement of significance in considering the presence of economic utility. The plurality judgment in *D'Arcy v Myriad Genetics* omitted any reference to 'significance' in its phrasing of the second factor as that 'the invention as claimed has economic utility'.[69] A more expansive description of this factor in *Apotex Pty Ltd v Sanofi-Aventis Australia Pty Ltd*, also without reference to significance, is that the subject matter of the patent 'must have some useful application, that is, must be capable of being practically applied in commerce or industry'.[70] As many patented inventions are never exploited commercially, it is unlikely that economic utility is measured with reference to its significance.

10.4.4 Application of *NRDC* principles to expand scope and remove classes of unpatentable inventions

In its 1984 review of the *Patents Act 1952* (Cth),[71] the Industrial Property Advisory Committee (IPAC) concluded that it would be difficult to draft a definition that would adequately reflect the body of law that had progressively fleshed out the concept of a manner of manufacture. The legislature accepted this view and retained the reference to 'manner of manufacture' in the new *Patents Act 1990* (Cth). Both the *Patents Act 1990* (Cth) and the *Budapest Treaty on the International Recognition of the Deposit of Microorganisms for the Purposes of Patent Procedure*[72] (*Budapest Treaty*) made it clear that micro-organisms and processes involving the use of micro-organisms were to be patentable subject matter.[73] With some minor statutory exceptions, such as for human beings and the biological processes for their generation,[74] and despite various reviews of patentable subject matter, the responsibility to define the scope of this concept of manner of manufacture continues to reside with the judiciary.[75]

---

68 *D'Arcy v Myriad Genetics Inc* (2015) 258 CLR 334, [28] (French CJ, Kiefel, Bell and Keane JJ) (emphasis added). The significance of this is explored below at 10.4.6.
69 Ibid [28] (French CJ, Kiefel, Bell and Keane JJ), [125] (Gageler and Nettle JJ); *Grant v Commissioner of Patents* (2006) 154 FCR 62, 72, [42]; *Research Affiliates LLC v Commissioner of Patents* (2014) 227 FCR 378, 32, [115].
70 *Apotex Pty Ltd v Sanofi-Aventis Australia Pty Ltd* (2013) 253 CLR 284, [278] (Crennan and Kiefel JJ).
71 Industrial Property Advisory Committee, *Patents, Innovation and Competition in Australia* (1984).
72 Opened for signature 28 April 1977, WIPO Lex No TRT/BUDAPEST/001 (entered into force 19 August 1980, as amended 26 September 1980).
73 *Patents Act 1990* (Cth) ss 6, 41, 42.
74 Ibid (Cth) ss 18(2), 50.
75 Recommendations for reform await decision and implementation: see ACIP, *Patentable Subject Matter*, above n 50, recommending statutory amendment; ALRC, *Genes and Ingenuity: Gene Patenting and Human Health*, above n 50. For the government response to the recommendations in both reports, see *Government Response: Patentable Subject Matter*, above n 50.

However, with the exception of the plurality decision in *D'Arcy v Myriad Genetics Inc*, judges see themselves as constrained in imposing non-statutory limitations on patentable subject matter, for two historic reasons. The first is the expansive way in which the High Court in *NRDC*[76] defined manner of manufacture. The second is the decision of the legislature in 1990 not to codify, as unpatentable, classes of subject matter that were still thought at the time of the enactment of the *Patents Act 1990* (Cth) to be arguably unpatentable, such as methods of medical treatment and computer programs. Although individual judges have from time to time balanced social costs and benefits[77] or assessed the general inconvenience of an invention[78] to deny an invention the status of a manner of manufacture, this is rare. Most judges are reticent to find that otherwise patentable subject matter is not a manner of manufacture because it raises significant matters of policy and competing interests. They prefer to leave such matters to parliament.[79]

The lack of express statutory exception combined with the breadth of the *NRDC* judgment as construed by successive courts has resulted in a piecemeal erosion of formerly perceived classes of excluded subject matter. The fact that an invention falls within a particular class, such as a method of medical treatment, a computer program or a business method, does not in itself prevent it being properly the subject of letters patent.[80] *NRDC* itself rejected the former exclusion of patents for horticultural and agricultural methods. Since then, courts have applied mechanically the *NRDC* guiding factors of 'artificially created state of affairs' and economic utility to declare claims valid for computer programs,[81] methods of medical treatment for humans,[82] living plants,[83] isolated genetic materials[84] and recombinant DNA techniques.[85] Nevertheless, classes of subject matter remain relevant in identifying what is *not* an 'invention'.[86]

The starting point and principal authority for deciding whether a claimed invention is a manner of manufacture within the meaning of s 18(1)(a) or s 18(1A)(a) continues to be *NRDC*. However, in deciding a case, it is now clear that a court does not start with 'precise guidelines' but must determine whether a 'claimed invention, as a matter of substance not form, is

---

76 *NRDC v Commissioner of Patents* (1959) 102 CLR 252.
77 *Grant v Commissioner of Patents* (2005) 67 IPR 1.
78 *Anaesthetic Supplies Pty Ltd v Rescare Ltd* (1994) 50 FCR 1 (Sheppard J); *Bristol-Myers Squibb Co v FH Faulding & Co Ltd* (1998) 41 IPR 467.
79 *D'Arcy v Myriad Genetics Inc* (2014) 224 FCR 479 (FC), [205]; *Apotex Pty Ltd v Sanofi-Aventis Australia Pty Ltd* (2013) 253 CLR 284, [44] (French CJ); *Anaesthetic Supplies Pty Ltd v Rescare Ltd* (1994) 50 FCR 1; *Bristol-Myers Squibb Co v FH Faulding & Co Ltd* (2000) 97 FCR 524; *Welcome Real-Time SA v Catuity Inc* (2001) 113 FCR 110. See below at 10.5.
80 *Bristol-Myers Squibb Co v FH Faulding & Co Ltd* (2000) 97 FCR 524; *Welcome Real-Time SA v Catuity Inc* (2001) 113 FCR 110, 137; *Grant v Commissioner of Patents* (2006) 154 FCR 62, [26].
81 *CCOM Pty Ltd v Jiejing Pty Ltd* (1994) 51 FCR 260; *Welcome Real-Time SA v Catuity Inc* (2001) 113 FCR 110.
82 *Anaesthetic Supplies Pty Ltd v Rescare Ltd* (1994) 50 FCR 1; *Bristol-Myers Squibb Co v FH Faulding & Co Ltd* (2000) 97 FCR 524.
83 N. Byrne, *Legal Protection of Plants in Australia under Patent and Plant Variety Rights Legislation* (Report to Australian Patent Office and Australian Plant Variety Rights Office, 1990).
84 *D'Arcy v Myriad Genetics Inc* (2014) 224 FCR 479 (FC), reversed on appeal (2015) 258 CLR 334.
85 See, for example, *Kirin-Amgen Inc v Board of Regents of University of Washington* (1995) 33 IPR 557.
86 See below at 10.4.8.

properly the subject of a patent.'[87] This judicial task has spawned various additional *guidance* factors, especially in the area of computer-implemented methods. As with the original *NRDC* factors, it is important that these are not applied as a rigid formula or a sufficient or exhaustive statement of the characterisation of patentable subject matter in that field of technology.

Although claimed inventions are assessed on their merits according to the legal principles arising from *NRDC*, and no longer because they are within an 'excluded' class of otherwise patentable subject matter, the analysis of particular inventions generally proceeds with reference to cases dealing with similar types of subject matter. The categories of subject matter discussed in the following sections are selected because they were once or remain somewhat controversial.

10.4.5 Computer programs and computer-implemented methods

10.4.5.1 Computer programs

A claim that merely recites a mathematical formula, algorithm or scientific principle and seeks patent protection for that formula in the abstract will not be accorded the protection of the patent laws.[88] The former classification of computer programs as a class of unpatentable subject matter could not survive following *NRDC*.[89] It became clear that it is the *application* of the formula to achieve an end or to a method of producing that end that renders it a manner of manufacture. The erosion of the former excluded class commenced with the decision of Burchett J in *International Business Machines Corp v Commissioner of Patents*[90] (*IBM*). His Honour drew upon authorities in the United States and on the broad principles in *NRDC* to conclude that a method of producing and displaying an image of a curve on computer graphics displays was patentable subject matter. He saw no conceptual difference between the use of an algorithm to achieve a particular purpose – namely, the image of the curve – and the use of the compounds in *NRDC*. The application of the mathematics used in *IBM* achieved the improved curve image that was a commercially useful effect in the field of computer graphics.

Three years later, the Full Federal Court in *CCOM Pty Ltd v Jiejing Pty Ltd*[91] confirmed the patentability of computer programs in the context of a method for assembling text on a computer in the Chinese language. The court concluded, with reference to its formulation of the *NRDC* guiding factors, that the storage of data as to Chinese characters and retrieval of graphic representations to enable word processing were a particular mode or manner of achieving an end result that is an artificially created state of affairs.[92] Since then, the High Court has supported the role of patents for computer programs, as when it commented in *Data Access Corp v Powerflex Services Pty Ltd* that 'the definition of a computer program seems to have more in common with the subject matter of a patent than a

---

87 *Commissioner of Patents v RPL Central Pty Ltd* (2015) 238 FCR 27, [97]; *D'Arcy v Myriad Genetics Inc* (2015) 258 CLR 334; *Research Affiliates LLC v Commissioner of Patents* (2014) 227 FCR 378, [107].
88 *International Business Machines Corp v Commissioner of Patents* (1991) 33 FCR 218, 226; *Diamond v Diehr*, 450 US 175 (1981).
89 *NRDC v Commissioner of Patents* (1959) 102 CLR 252.
90 (1991) 33 FCR 218, 224.
91 (1994) 51 FCR 260.
92 Approved in *Research Affiliates LLC v Commissioner of Patents* (2014) 227 FCR 378, [95].

copyright'.[93] The decision in *Welcome Real-Time SA v Catuity Inc*[94] consolidated this line of authority for patentability of computer software in the context of a process for using a smart chip card, the memory space on that card, various computer programs, readers and printers to operate a loyalty scheme for customers.[95] A key feature of these cases is that the claimed inventions do more than recite an abstract idea: they all in substance claim the application of a computer program to achieve a practical result with economic utility. They also involve inventions that produce a physically observable effect, an element of the criteria in *NRDC* that resurfaced in *Grant v Commissioner of Patents*[96] (discussed below) as a requirement for patentability.

10.4.5.2 Computer-implemented methods

The fact that the claimed method may be classified as one used in business or in the financial sector, for instance, does 'prevent it being properly the subject of letters patent':[97] but that is not enough in itself.[98] A claim that recites a mere scheme, plan, directions for performing a mental act or other types of intellectual information does not define an invention. The claimed invention must 'as a matter of substance' satisfy the requirements of a manner of manufacture.[99]

Until the pivotal decision of the Full Federal Court in *Grant v Commissioner of Patents*,[100] courts used the *NRDC* guiding factors alone to answer the broader question of whether the claimed invention was a manner of manufacture.[101] However, while useful, they lacked the subtlety of the entire *NRDC* decision. No reference appeared in reasoning in cases such as *CCOM Pty Ltd v Jiejing Pty Ltd* to the requirement for 'any physical phenomenon in which the effect, be it creation or merely alteration, may be observed'[102] – presumably because a physical effect was apparent in the invention under consideration. Eventually, the mechanical and unqualified application of the *NRDC* guiding factors to assess the patentability of a claimed invention became problematic when there was no physical effect in the invention.

This was the position in *Grant v Commissioner of Patents*.[103] The case involved an alleged invention for structuring a financial transaction designed to protect an individual's assets against the lawful claims of the individual's creditors. It was a scheme that was not limited

---

93	(1999) 202 CLR 1, [20].
94	(2001) 113 FCR 110.
95	Ibid [127].
96	*Grant v Commissioner of Patents* (2006) 154 FCR 62.
97	Ibid [26]; *Welcome Real-Time SA v Catuity Inc* (2001) 113 FCR 110, [125], [126]. As to the position in the United States, see *State Street Bank & Trust Co v Signature Financial Group*, 149 F 3d 1368 (Fed Cir, 1998); *Bilski v Kappos*, 561 US 593 (2010); *CLS Bank International v Alice Corp Pty Ltd*, 717 F 3d 1269 (2013).
98	*Commissioner of Patents v RPL Central Pty Ltd* (2015) 238 FCR 27, [96].
99	See *APO Manual*, above n 57, [2.9.2.7] for its guidelines on this subject matter.
100	(2006) 154 FCR 62. See A. L. Monotti, 'The scope of "manner of manufacture" under the *Patents Act 1990* (Cth) after *Grant v Commissioner of Patents*', above n 63.
101	The issue arose in *Welcome Real-Time SA v Catuity Inc* (2001) 113 FCR 110, [128]. By way of obiter, Heerey J did not accept that a physically observable effect was necessarily required.
102	*NRDC v Commissioner of Patents* (1959) 102 CLR 252, 276. See *Grant v Commissioner of Patents* (2006) 154 FCR 62.
103	(2006) 154 FCR 62. See A. L. Monotti, 'The scope of "manner of manufacture" under the *Patents Act 1990* (Cth) after *Grant v Commissioner of Patents*', above n 63.

by requiring computer implementation: it required no physical component for its operation and produced no physical effect. Furthermore, it took advantage of gaps or loopholes in the laws of Australia, which made it even more controversial. Nevertheless, if the *NRDC* factors were applied rigidly, the claimed invention would result in an artificially created state of affairs in an area of economic utility. It was necessary for decision-makers to define the limits of a manner of manufacture with greater precision in order to justify their eventual decisions to label it as unpatentable subject matter.

The Full Federal Court revisited *NRDC* and clarified that a manner of manufacture within the meaning of s 6 of the *Statute of Monopolies* requires the presence of 'a physical effect in the sense of a concrete effect or phenomenon or manifestation or transformation'.[104] They concluded that the invention failed this test because there was 'no physical consequence at all'. Furthermore, it was 'a mere scheme, an abstract idea, mere intellectual information, which has never been patentable'.[105] The court rejected the basis for the Commissioner's earlier decision to reject the claims, namely, to equate a requirement of an artificially created state of affairs with the application of science and technology.[106] The *Grant v Commissioner of Patents* decision is silent on the extent to which computer implementation of an otherwise unpatentable business scheme would render that subject matter patentable. Hence, the reliance on the need for a physically observable effect 'defers the real battle to another day'.[107]

This question arose for decision by the Full Federal Court in two recent cases before an identical bench:[108] *Research Affiliates LLC v Commissioner of Patents*[109] and *Commissioner of Patents v RPL Central Pty Ltd*.[110] The first case involved a method for generating a securities index for managing a portfolio. The second case concerned a method of gathering evidence to assess an individual's competency or qualification relative to recognised qualification standards. The method involved various steps performed by a standard computer, including using the assessable criteria retrieved via the internet to automatically generate and present questions via the internet to the user's computer. The method could not be carried out without the use of a computer.

In each case, the court concluded that the substance of the respective inventions was nothing more than a mere scheme or business method. Although there may have been a physically observable effect in the sense that a computer performed the method, this aspect of *Grant v Commissioner of Patents* does not feature in either judgment as the reason for finding the claimed inventions to be unpatentable subject matter and therefore outside the scope of a manner of manufacture. Influential factors for the decision in *Research Affiliates v Commissioner of Patents* were the lack of specificity in the specification as to how the computer is utilised, the absence of any indication that it uses or creates any unusual or special technical

---

104   *Grant v Commissioner of Patents* (2006) 154 FCR 62, [32].
105   Ibid.
106   Ibid [38].
107   A. L. Monotti, 'The scope of "manner of manufacture" under the *Patents Act 1990* (Cth) after *Grant v Commissioner of Patents*, above n 63, 478.
108   An enlarged Full Federal Court in *Encompass Corp Pty Ltd v InfoTrack Pty Ltd* [2019] FCAFC 161 did 'not think that the correctness of those decisions [*Research Affiliates* and *RPL Central*] is seriously in doubt': at [77].
109   (2014) 227 FCR 378.
110   (2015) 238 FCR 27.

effect. Ultimately the substance of the invention was implementation of an abstract idea or scheme in a computer without any improvement in technology.[111]

In *Commissioner of Patents v RPL Central*, the court concluded that the computer effectively operated as an intermediary to assist the user to evaluate their competency for a particular course or their ability to obtain a qualification without completing that course. One influential factor for this decision was that the computer was 'not functioning in the nature of an adviser or an artificial intelligence.'[112] There was nothing to show that this was other than the operation of generic software on a generic computer. Even though the court accepted that reframing criteria into questions may be outside the generic use of a computer, 'the idea of presenting questions, by reframing the criteria, is that: an idea. It is not suggested that the implementation of this idea formed part of the invention'.[113] Indeed, no instruction as to the necessary programming appeared in the specification.

The courts developed some guiding principles to assist their decision-making, and these are outlined below. However, it is necessary first to mention the effect of the High Court judgment in *D'Arcy v Myriad Genetics* on computer-implemented inventions, a decision which was delivered in the period between *Research Affiliates* and *RPL Central*. Although the invention in *D'Arcy* related to isolated DNA, the plurality judgment at [28] propounded principles that were not specific to any technology. The judges proposed that the *NRDC* factors will be necessary but insufficient: 'When a new class of claim involves a significant new application or extension of the concept of "manner of manufacture", other factors including factors connected directly or indirectly to the purpose of the Act may assume importance.'[114]

Perhaps unsurprisingly, as there was a history of litigation in relation to computer-implemented inventions, the court in *RPL Central* distinguished the invention under consideration from a new class of claim that would fall within these special circumstances. It approached the issue with reference to *NRDC* factors alone, while recognising them as apposite but 'not conclusive of patentability.'[115] The court concluded:

> This case does not involve a new class of claim involving a significant extension of the concept of manner of manufacture. It is therefore unnecessary to examine any of these wide-ranging considerations. This is fortunate, because the Court does not have the bases for analyses of this kind.[116]

Until a new class of claim arises for decision, these cases clarify that the task for the decision-maker who must assess a computer-implemented invention is to ascertain the substance of the claimed invention:

- Is it a mere idea, scheme, business method or intellectual information (as in *Grant*, *Research Affiliates* and *RPL Central*)? The fact that the claimed method can only be implemented in a computing environment may not alter the fact that the substance of the claimed invention is within one of these classes.

---

111   (2014) 227 FCR 378 [104], [108], [115].
112   *Commissioner of Patents v RPL Central Pty Ltd* (2015) 238 FCR 27, [109].
113   Ibid [110].
114   *D'Arcy v Myriad Genetics Inc* (2015) 258 CLR 334, [28] (French CJ, Kiefel, Bell and Keane JJ).
115   *Commissioner of Patents v RPL Central Pty Ltd* (2015) 238 FCR 27, [117].
116   Ibid [119].

- Alternatively, can it 'broadly be described as an improvement in computer technology'[117] (as in *IBM* and *CCOM v Jiejing*)?

Three principles are clear from these and other decisions. First, there is a distinction between a technological innovation (patentable) and a business innovation (not patentable).[118] Second, a business method is not patentable if it uses well-known and understood functions of a computer.[119] Third, where the claimed invention is a computerised business method, the invention must lie in that computerisation.[120]

Ultimately, it is impossible to clarify for all purposes the nature of a technological innovation or the well-known and understood functions of a computer. Resolution of the above question is likely to lie largely in the realm of the facts of each case. Various sources elaborate a range of useful matters to use for guidance in assessing a claimed invention in this field of technology.[121] Those matters that support its patentability include whether:

- the contribution to the claimed invention is technical in nature;[122]
- the invention solves a technical problem;[123]
- the invention results in an improvement in the functioning of the computer, irrespective of the data being processed;[124]
- the computer is 'integral to the invention';[125] and
- the claimed steps are foreign to the normal use of computers.[126]

Those matters that do not support its patentability include whether:

- the invention requires merely generic computer implementation;[127]
- the computer is merely the intermediary, or a mere tool, configured to carry out the method using program code for performing the method, but adding nothing to the substance of the idea;[128] and

---

117 Ibid [96].
118 Ibid [100]; *Research Affiliates LLC v Commissioner of Patents* (2014) 227 FCR 378, [94].
119 *Commissioner of Patents v RPL Central Pty Ltd* (2015) 238 FCR 27, [96]; *Research Affiliates LLC v Commissioner of Patents* (2014) 227 FCR 378, [105].
120 *Commissioner of Patents v RPL Central Pty Ltd* (2015) 238 FCR 27, [96], [104].
121 APO Manual, above n 57, [2.9.2.7]; *Aristocrat Technologies Australia Pty Ltd* [2016] APO 49, [35]; *Rokt Pte Ltd v Commissioner of Patents* [2018] FCA 1988, [189] (application filed by the Commissioner for leave to appeal 16 January 2019).
122 *Commissioner of Patents v RPL Central Pty Ltd* (2015) 238 FCR 27, [99], citing *Aerotel Ltd v Telco Holdings Ltd; Macrossan's Application* [2007] 1 All ER 225; *Research Affiliates LLC v Commissioner of Patents* (2014) 227 FCR 378, [114]; *Grant v Commissioner of Patents* (2006) 154 FCR 62, [18].
123 *Commissioner of Patents v RPL Central Pty Ltd* (2015) 238 FCR 27, [99]; *Research Affiliates LLC v Commissioner of Patents* (2014) 227 FCR 378, [103].
124 *Commissioner of Patents v RPL Central Pty Ltd* (2015) 238 FCR 27, [99]; *Research Affiliates LLC v Commissioner of Patents* (2014) 227 FCR 378, [101].
125 *Commissioner of Patents v RPL Central Pty Ltd* (2015) 238 FCR 27, [96].
126 *Research Affiliates LLC v Commissioner of Patents* (2014) 227 FCR 378, [94], citing the production of the curved image in *International Business Machines Corp v Commissioner of Patents* (1991) 33 FCR 218.
127 *Commissioner of Patents v RPL Central Pty Ltd* (2015) 238 FCR 27, [99], [102]; *Research Affiliates LLC v Commissioner of Patents* (2014) 227 FCR 378, [94]; *Encompass Corp Pty Ltd v InfoTrack Pty Ltd* [2018] FCA 421, [193], affirmed [2019] FCAFC 161.
128 *Commissioner of Patents v RPL Central Pty Ltd* (2015) 238 FCR 27, [99].

- the significance of the claimed invention 'lies in the content of the data rather than any specific effect generated by the computer'.[129]

It has been observed that consideration of the above factors may introduce prior art into the consideration of manner of manufacture.[130]

A central pillar of s 18(1) and (1A) of the *Patents Act 1990* (Cth) is that each requirement for validity in s 18(1) is separate and distinct. The consideration of manner of manufacture must be without regard to, and is separate and distinct from, inventiveness or 'ingenuity'. A different, and concerning, approach is evident from these cases when the invention is a computer-implemented scheme or idea, if some of the judicial statements are taken literally. In *Research Affiliates*, the court said that '[t]here is no suggestion in the specification or the claims that any part of the inventive step lies in the computer implementation'.[131] And in *RPL Central*:

> A computer-implemented business method can be patentable where the invention lies in the way in which the method is carried out in a computer. This necessitates some ingenuity in the way in which the computer is utilised (*Research Affiliates*).[132]

Theoretically this does not involve an examination of inventive step – that is the province of s 18(1)(b)(ii) – but it does introduce an additional element of ingenuity into any consideration of manner of manufacture when the invention is a computer-implemented method or scheme. Courts appear to determine this with reference to an open-ended list of guiding factors, some of which are set out above. It is not enough for a scheme or method to be ingenious if the manner of its implementation in a computer is a normal use of the computer.

10.4.6 Genes and biological materials

In the rapidly advancing area of biotechnology, the Patent Office and Australian courts have adopted a similar approach to that of the United States Supreme Court in *Diamond v Chakrabarty*.[133] That court cleared the way for future patenting of plants, animals and inventions in the area of biotechnology when it ruled that live human-made genetically engineered bacteria capable of breaking down multiple components of crude oil is patentable subject matter. The bacterium was new and had 'markedly different characteristics from any found in nature'.[134] The majority stated that the 'relevant distinction was not between living and inanimate things, but between products of nature, whether living or not, and human-made inventions'.[135] The court did not limit its decision to genetically engineered living

---

129   Ibid.
130   McCormick & Co Inc [2017] APO 62; M. Summerfield, 'Will an expanded full Bench of the Federal Court bring sense to Australian law on computer-implemented inventions?' *Patentology* (Blog Post, 25 September 2018).
131   *Research Affiliates LLC v Commissioner of Patents* (2014) 227 FCR 378, [119].
132   *Commissioner of Patents v RPL Central Pty Ltd* (2015) 238 FCR 27, [104].
133   447 US 303 (1980).
134   Ibid 310.
135   Ibid 313.

organisms. Although there is continuing debate as to whether some of this subject matter should be patentable, the more usual grounds for attack are those of novelty and inventive step.[136]

Patenting of human genes and genetic material remains controversial, although it is now clear that genetic material in situ is unpatentable subject matter.[137] The controversy continues to affect 'isolated' genetic materials – those that are removed from the environment in which they are found in nature, including synthesised cDNA.[138] In the context of isolated nucleic acid sequences, the term 'isolated' has been explained as follows:

> [T]he naturally occurring nucleic acid found in the cells of the human body, whether it be DNA or RNA, has been removed from the cellular environment in which the material naturally exists and separated from other cellular components also found there.[139]

The principal grounds for objection concern the adverse impacts that patenting of such subject matter has on research on, access to and the cost of, health care. Although there may be chemical, structural and functional differences in the isolated material when it is viewed as a chemical compound, the information it contains remains the same as the genetic material in the body. The issue of whether genetic material and technologies should be excluded from patentability has been reviewed over the past decade by the Australian Law Reform Commission (ALRC) and ACIP,[140] neither of which recommended a specific exclusion. The Senate Community Affairs References Committee also considered these issues within the specific context of a Private Member's Bill – the Patent Amendment (Human Genes and Biological Materials) Bill 2010 (Cth), introduced into the Senate in late 2010.[141] The Bill lapsed after a majority of the Legal and Constitutional Affairs Legislation Committee recommended that the Bill should not be passed. The federal government accepted in principle the recommendation of the ALRC that the *Patents Act 1990* (Cth) should not be amended 'to exclude genetic materials and technologies from patentable subject matter'.[142] The government also accepted ACIP's recommendations for the introduction of a morality exclusion as permitted by art 27(2)

---

136 See, for example, *Biogen Inc v Medeva plc* [1997] RPC 1; *Bresagen Ltd v Austin Research Institute* (2004) 60 IPR 174.
137 *Cancer Voices Australia v Myriad Genetics Inc* (2013) 99 IPR 567, [116]; *D'Arcy v Myriad Genetics Inc* (2014) 224 FCR 479 (FC), [158]; ALRC, *Genes and Ingenuity*, above n 50, [6.53].
138 *D'Arcy v Myriad Genetics Inc* (2014) 224 FCR 479 (FC), [1]; (2015) 258 CLR 334; *Association for Molecular Pathology v Myriad Genetics Inc*, 569 US 576 (2013).
139 *D'Arcy v Myriad Genetics Inc* (2014) 224 FCR 479 (FC), [1].
140 ACIP, *Patentable Subject Matter*, above n 50; ALRC, *Genes and Ingenuity*, above n 50.
141 Senate Community Affairs References Committee, *Gene Patents* (26 November 2010). See further ACIP, *Patentable Subject Matter*, above n 50; ALRC, *Genes and Ingenuity*, above n 50, 114–247; *Government Response: Patentable Subject Matter*, above n 50; Directive 98/44/EC of the European Parliament and of the Council of 6 July 1998 on the Legal Protection of Biotechnological Inventions [1998] OJ L 213/13; D. Nicol, 'On the legality of gene patents' (2005) 29 *Melbourne University Law Review* 809; G. Dutfield, 'Claiming a life: Are organisms inherently unpatentable?' in L. Bently, G. D'Agastino and C. Ng (eds), *The Common Law of Intellectual Property: Essays in Honour of Professor David Vaver* (Oxford: Hart, 2010) ch 8.
142 *Government Response: Patentable Subject Matter*, above n 50; ACIP, *Patentable Subject Matter*, above n 50, rec 7.

of the *Agreement on Trade-Related Aspects of Intellectual Property*[143] (*TRIPS*) that would be technology neutral. IP Australia issued a consultation paper on this matter in 2013,[144] but the way in which to amend the *Patents Act 1990* (Cth) to give effect to the recommendations remains unresolved.

The principal case that guides the law in this area is *D'Arcy v Myriad Genetics Inc*,[145] a case involving a patent concerned with mutations in the BRCA1 gene that are indicative of a predisposition to breast and ovarian cancer. The claimed composition comprised nucleic acid (DNA or RNA molecules) that had been isolated[146] from the cell nucleus. The specific invention related to

> germline (heritable) and somatic (non-heritable) mutations of the BRCA1 gene and their use, including in the screening process, in the diagnosis of a predisposition to breast and ovarian cancer. The invention is also said to relate to somatic mutations in the BRCA1 gene and their use in the diagnosis, prognosis and therapy of human cancers which have a mutation in the BRCA1 gene.[147]

Hence, the examination of a particular sequence of nucleotides may indicate whether a person is susceptible to cancer. Whether there is infringement would not be known until the process of isolation had been carried out. The United States Supreme Court in the corresponding case, *Association for Molecular Pathology v Myriad Genetics Inc*,[148] decided that the similar Myriad patents in the United States that claimed these inventions (but not in identical form) lacked eligible subject matter by reason of the judicially created 'laws of nature' exception in United States patent law.[149] This was possible because the Supreme Court construed the claims as focused on the genetic information in the isolated nucleic acid (which was not altered or created), not on its chemical composition. The crucial similarity with nature was the same sequence of nucleotides. However, the court held that synthesised cDNA was not excluded from patentability under the 'laws of nature' exception.

In contrast, an extended Full Federal Court in *D'Arcy v Myriad Genetics Inc* construed the substance of the claims to isolated nucleic acid as a chemical composition of a particular molecule as distinct from the genetic information that it contained. This meant that the court could reach a different conclusion from the United States Supreme Court when following the reasoning in *NRDC*[150] and *Chakrabarty*.[151] The Full Federal Court concluded that the isolated

---

143 *Marrakesh Agreement Establishing the World Trade Organization*, opened for signature 15 April 1994, 1867 UNTS 3 (entered into force 1 January 1995) annex 1C (*TRIPS*).
144 IP Australia, *Patentable Subject Matter: Consultation on an Objects Clause and an Exclusion from Patentability* (Consultation Paper, July 2013).
145 (2014) 224 FCR 479 (FC); (2015) 258 CLR 334, [18].
146 See above n 139 and accompanying text for an explanation of 'isolated'.
147 *D'Arcy v Myriad Genetics Inc* (2014) 224 FCR 479 (FC), [66].
148 569 US 576 (2013).
149 Ibid. 35 USC §101 provides: 'Whoever invents or discovers any new and useful process, machine, manufacture, or composition of matter, or any new and useful improvement thereof, may obtain a patent therefor, subject to the conditions and requirements of this title'. Courts interpret these categories to exclude laws of nature, natural phenomena and abstract ideas. See United States Patent and Trademark Office, *2014 Interim Guidance on Patent Subject Matter Eligibility*, 37 CFR Part 1 (Docket No PTO-P-2014-0058).
150 *NRDC v Commissioner of Patents* (1959) 102 CLR 252.
151 *Diamond v Chakrabarty*, 447 US 303 (1980).

nucleic acid as a compound is both artificial and structurally and functionally different from nucleic acid as it exists in the body and that it has economic utility. Of critical importance to its decision were the chemical changes in the isolated nucleic acid that resulted from the isolation procedures. The court expressly rejected, with respect, the Supreme Court's consideration of the claims in the United States patent as concerned 'primarily with the information contained in the genetic sequence [rather than] with the specific chemical composition of a particular molecule'.[152] The decision applied to isolated DNA, including cDNA.[153]

An appeal to the High Court was successful.[154] The issue between the parties was ultimately whether the isolated nucleic acid is to be compared with what exists in the body (in which case the focus is on the identical information they both contain) or whether one looks at the isolated nucleic acid itself as a chemical composition and applies the *NRDC* factors to that product to come up with an answer.

All the judges unanimously decided, but with different reasoning, that the disputed claims did not disclose patentable subject matter. Significantly, the court was not concerned with 'gene patenting' generally, but with the substance of the claimed inventions under consideration. All judgments agreed that satisfaction of the *NRDC* factors alone does not mean that the substance of a disputed claim defines a manner of manufacture. However, as discussed above, those factors remain *necessary* for the characterisation of a claimed invention as a manner of manufacture and are likely to suffice 'for a large class of cases in which there are no countervailing considerations'.[155]

The key significant distinction in the reasoning of the plurality judgment of French CJ, Kiefel, Bell and Keane JJ relates to the evaluation of inventions that fall outside the existing scope of manner of manufacture as developed through the courts but nevertheless satisfy the *NRDC* factors. Although *NRDC* did not confine manner of manufacture 'to any verbal formula', it gave no defined pathway for the development of the concept of manufacture 'in its application to unimagined technologies with unimagined characteristics and implications'.[156] In the case of a new class of claim, *NRDC* did not 'preclude consideration of policy factors informed by the purpose of the Act and considerations of coherence in the law in developing the law'.[157]

The judicial methodology for expansion of patentable subject matter is either one of *exclusion* or one of *inclusion*. What is the difference? The earlier approach was one of deciding whether to *exclude* otherwise patentable subject matter because it fell within a recognised *excluded* category of subject matter. This approach risked the elevation of the *NRDC* factors beyond mere guidelines to a rigid formula that, if satisfied, would result in a claimed invention automatically being held to be a manner of manufacture. It was through this process of reasoning that the concept of unpatentable classes of subject matter crumbled when it failed to survive scrutiny. This approach hampered the use of common law methodology to *control* expansion of patentable subject matter into unforeseen areas of technology and left that control to parliament.

---

152 *D'Arcy v Myriad Genetics Inc* (2014) 224 FCR 479 (FC), [216].
153 Ibid [218].
154 *D'Arcy v Myriad Genetics Inc* [2015] HCA Trans 12; *D'Arcy v Myriad Genetics Inc* (2015) 258 CLR 334.
155 *D'Arcy v Myriad Genetics Inc* (2015) 258 CLR 334, [20] (French CJ, Kiefel, Bell and Keane JJ).
156 Ibid [23].
157 Ibid [5].

The plurality in *D'Arcy* turned this approach on its head to embrace an approach of inclusion.[158] The court accepted its authority to develop the concept of manner of manufacture on a case-by-case basis with reference to a number of factors, including a reframed, contemporary expression of the *NRDC* factors:

1. Whether the invention as claimed is for a product made, or a process producing an outcome as a result of human action.
2. Whether the invention as claimed has economic utility.[159]

First, the phrase 'outcome of human action' may be limited in scope by earlier authorities such as *Grant* to 'a physical effect in the sense of a concrete effect or phenomenon or manifestation or transformation',[160] but it is capable of being construed more broadly in later cases. Second, a decision is not constrained by the fact that a claimed invention satisfies the *NRDC* factors. Nevertheless, the plurality declared that in most cases '[w]hen the invention falls within the existing concept of manner of manufacture, as it has been developed through the cases, [the *NRDC* factors] will also ordinarily be sufficient.'[161] They did not engage with the concept of 'artificially created state of affairs', stating that it places patentability in 'too narrow a frame': this invites comparisons with products of nature instead of focusing on whether the claimed invention can be 'made'.[162] That distracts from the central requirement. However, in what will amount to rare instances, the court established a new principle:

> When a new class of claim involves a significant new application or extension of the concept of 'manner of manufacture', other factors including factors connected directly or indirectly to the purposes of the Act may assume importance.[163]

The factors that may then also assume importance are set out at length at [28] of the High Court judgment and include, broadly:

- consistency with the purposes of the Act;
- maintenance of coherence of the law;
- international obligations and laws of other countries; and
- whether according patentability 'would involve law-making of a kind which should be done by the legislature'.

Significantly, it is a matter for judicial decision whether to accord patentability or to leave any expansion of the concept of manner of manufacture to parliament. Neither the judgment of Gageler and Nettle JJ nor that of Gordon J accepted this additional factorial approach.

The plurality in *D'Arcy* provides some guidance on what is a 'new class of claim': it is not within established boundaries; it involves a significant new application or extension of the principles of patentability; it involves far-reaching questions of public policy; and it could affect

---

158 Ibid [37].
159 Ibid [28].
160 *Grant v Commissioner of Patents* (2006) 154 FCR 62, [32].
161 Ibid [28].
162 Ibid [91] (French CJ, Kiefel, Bell and Keane JJ), [222]–[225] (Gordon J).
163 Ibid [28] (French CJ, Kiefel, Bell and Keane JJ).

the balance of important conflicting interests.[164] They concluded that they were dealing with a new class of claim: this was not just information; nor was it just an isolated chemical compound. It was a combination of the two in which the genetic information was an essential integer: 'The product is the medium in which the information resides.'[165] By construing the claims in this way, the plurality concluded that 'the subject matter of the claims lies at the boundaries of the concept of "manner of manufacture".'[166] This essential integer of genetic information took the claims outside that which can be 'made': the existence of the mutations or polymorphisms was a matter of chance.[167] Following consideration of the further additional factors, the plurality concluded that inclusion of this class of claim within the concept of a manner of manufacture was not appropriate for judicial determination.[168] Especially influential were the breadth of the claim and its elusive boundaries, potentially negative effects on innovation, the chilling effect on activities outside the scope of the monopoly, conflicting public and private interests, a failure to contribute to coherence of the law, and no evident support for inclusion from Australia's international obligations and the patent laws of other jurisdictions.[169]

The narrow confines of this approach to new classes of claims limit its impact.[170] The plurality in *D'Arcy* offered a means for future courts to use a more transparent judicial method when deciding whether *to expand* (as distinct from exclude) the concept of manner of new manufacture in cases of highly controversial inventions. However, in *Meat & Livestock Australia Ltd v Cargill Inc*,[171] Beach J was troubled about how to consider these factors. He sought greater clarity of purpose and guidance and asked, among other questions, 'am I obliged to consider each and all of the factors or only some of them?'[172] It is not surprising that judges will be uncomfortable with this approach. However, it is suggested that the High Court in *D'Arcy* was intending to do no more than provide them with a discretion that was previously unavailable to them. That discretion is to refuse an extension of the scope of patentability to a claimed invention in an appropriate case. This is an entirely different exercise from justifying the exclusion of otherwise patentable subject matter in the absence of a statutory exclusion into which the claimed invention would fit.[173] It is suggested with respect that the 'other factors' approach offers no more than a broad discretion, accompanied by some guidelines that may be left deliberately open, to provide an avenue to reject a claimed invention in a rare, and probably extreme case, such as *D'Arcy*: a 'safety net'. It is also suggested with respect that

---

164   Ibid [7], [27], [28] (French CJ, Kiefel, Bell and Keane JJ), [94] (Gageler and Nettle JJ).
165   Ibid [89] (French CJ, Kiefel, Bell and Keane JJ).
166   Ibid [93].
167   Ibid [91].
168   Ibid [94] (French CJ, Kiefel, Bell and Keane JJ), also [284] (Gordon J).
169   Ibid [93]–[94] (French CJ, Kiefel, Bell and Keane JJ). See *Meat & Livestock Australia Ltd v Cargill Inc* (2018) 129 IPR 278, [386]–[500].
170   Distinguished in *Commissioner of Patents v RPL Central Pty Ltd* (2015) 238 FCR 27, [119], applied and distinguished in *Meat & Livestock Australia Ltd v Cargill Inc* (2018) 129 IPR 278, [391], [453].
171   (2018) 129 IPR 278, [391],
172   *Meat & Livestock Australia Ltd v Cargill Inc* (2018) 129 IPR 278, [391]. The case involved method claims for identifying a trait of a bovine subject from a nucleic acid sample of that subject and were thus distinguished at [409] from the product claims in *D'Arcy v Myriad Genetics Inc* (2015) 258 CLR 334.
173   See, for example, the discussion of *Bristol-Myers Squibb Co v FH Faulding & Co Ltd* (2000) 97 FCR 524 below at 10.4.7.

the factors are not intended to be a checklist to be worked through in a specified and methodical manner. As the plurality stated, '[a] number of factors *may* be relevant', and further, 'other factors including factors connected directly or indirectly to the purpose of the Act *may* assume importance.'[174]

10.4.7 Methods of medical treatment for humans

A method of medical treatment for the human body is patentable.[175] Prior to *NRDC*,[176] the traditional view was that methods of surgery and processes for treating the human body were not patentable. The traditional view arose from a couple of early cases. The first, *Re C & W's Application for a Patent*,[177] rejected a process of removing lead from bodies. The second, *Maeder v Busb*,[178] doubted that a method of treating human hair growing on the head could be patentable subject matter, but did not resolve the issue. However, these cases were decided at the time when courts applied Lord Morton's vendible product test, so the lack of a tangible vendible product may have influenced their decisions. The court in *NRDC* seemingly endorsed the exclusion on the basis that such processes are essentially non-economic:

> The exclusion of methods of surgery and other processes for treating the human body may well lie outside the concept of invention because the whole subject is conceived as essentially non-economic.[179]

Subsequent judicial reflections on the exclusion based its existence on 'ethics rather than logic',[180] or on public policy grounds as being 'generally inconvenient'.[181] In *Joos v Commissioner of Patents*,[182] Barwick CJ distinguished between a process for treating the diseases of the body (unpatentable) and a process for improving the cosmetic appearance of the body (patentable). The case-by-case analysis of claimed methods of medical treatment using the broad *NRDC* principles provided no clear development of principle that could support a broad exclusion of the subject matter from patentability.[183] Eventually, two cases came to the Full Court of the Federal Court that exposed the difficulties in maintaining an exclusion without legislative intervention. In both cases, the courts found by way of obiter dicta that the exception did not exist. These decisions applied a broad ratio decidendi from *NRDC* – namely, that if the process results in 'a new and useful effect' so that the new result is

---

174   *D'Arcy v Myriad Genetics Inc* (2015) 258 CLR 334, [28] (French CJ, Kiefel, Bell and Keane JJ) (emphasis added).
175   *Anaesthetic Supplies Pty Ltd v Rescare Ltd* (1994) 50 FCR 1; *Bristol-Myers Squibb Co v FH Faulding & Co Ltd* (2000) 97 FCR 524; *Merck & Co Inc v Arrow Pharmaceuticals Ltd* (2006) 154 FCR 31 (obiter).
176   *NRDC v Commissioner of Patents* (1959) 102 CLR 252.
177   (1914) 31 RPC 235.
178   (1938) 59 CLR 684.
179   *NRDC v Commissioner of Patents* (1959) 102 CLR 252, 275.
180   *Re Eli Lilly & Co's Application* [1975] RPC 438, 445.
181   *Joos v Commissioner of Patents* (1972) 126 CLR 611, 623.
182   (1972) 126 CLR 611.
183   *Apotex Pty Ltd v Sanofi-Aventis Australia Pty Ltd* (2013) 253 CLR 284, [44] (French CJ).

'an artificially created state of affairs' providing economic utility, it may be considered a 'manner of new manufacture' within s 6 of the *Statute of Monopolies*.[184]

The first case, *Anaesthetic Supplies Pty Ltd v Rescare Ltd*,[185] involved a patent for a device and its use in treating sleep apnoea, a syndrome associated with an extreme form of snoring in which the sufferer chokes on their tongue and soft palate repeatedly while asleep. The device comprised a nose mask and tubing, and the treatment comprised continuous positive airways pressure applied via the mask. At first instance, Gummow J[186] concluded that the process claims for methods of human treatment were patentable subject matter. He noted the absence of any express exclusion in s 18 and dismissed arguments that such methods were 'generally inconvenient'. This concept derives from the language of s 6 of the *Statute of Monopolies* that is incorporated by reference in the *Patents Act 1990* (Cth) through the definition of 'invention'.[187] A majority of Lockhart and Wilcox JJ approved Gummow J's decision in the appeal to the Full Federal Court. Lockhart J could see no logic for the past broad exclusion of this class of subject matter, particularly if the object of the patent system were to provide incentives and rewards for research. He could see 'no justification in law or in logic to say that simply because on the one hand substances produce a cosmetic result or a functional result as opposed to a curative result, one is patentable and the other is not'.[188] Both Lockhart and Wilcox JJ were influenced by the absence of any express statutory exclusion of this or any other class of subject matter from the scope of a manner of manufacture. Both rejected the 'generally inconvenient' arguments. Only Sheppard J rejected this subject matter as patentable on the grounds that it would be generally inconvenient. He explicitly invoked ethical considerations and observed that the court should not contemplate giving a monopoly to

> one medical practitioner, or perhaps a group of medical practitioners, a monopoly over, for example, a surgical procedure which might be greatly beneficial to mankind. Its denial might mean the death or unnecessary suffering of countless people.[189]

Sheppard J's decision was influenced also by the body of international thinking which regarded it as undesirable to grant patents for methods of treatment of diseases and other abnormalities in human beings.[190]

The second case, *Bristol-Myers Squibb Co v FH Faulding & Co Ltd*, involved a method of administering a drug used in cancer treatment. At first instance,[191] Heerey J regarded the majority observations in *Anaesthetic Supplies v Rescare* on methods of medical treatment as obiter and proceeded to agree with and adopt the observations of Sheppard J as to general

---

184 For a historical discussion of methods of medical treatment in general see, for example, J. Pila, 'Methods of medical treatment within Australian and United Kingdom patents law' (2001) 24 *University of New South Wales Law Journal* 420.
185 (1994) 50 FCR 1.
186 *Rescare Ltd v Anaesthetic Supplies Pty Ltd* (1992) 25 IPR 119, 151.
187 See above at 10.3.
188 *Anaesthetic Supplies Pty Ltd v Rescare Ltd* (1994) 50 FCR 1, 19.
189 Ibid 41.
190 Ibid 40–1; *TRIPS* art 27(3)(a); *Convention on the Grant of European Patents of 5 October 1973*, opened for signature 5 October 1973, 1065 UNTS 199 (entered into force 7 October 1977) (*European Patent Convention*) art 52(4).
191 *Bristol-Myers Squibb Co v FH Faulding & Co Ltd* (1998) 41 IPR 467.

inconvenience.[192] This decision was overturned by the Full Federal Court,[193] which rejected the proposition that methods of medical treatments of humans, as a class of subject matter, were unpatentable. The Full Federal Court also rejected the application of 'generally inconvenient' on the facts of the case. It is important to note that the court did not reject the possibility of the application of 'generally inconvenient' in the context of methods of medical treatment, but expressed doubt that it could ever be successful. The reasoning of Black CJ and Lehane J relied on two factors. First, their Honours could not rationally explain why a product for treating the human body could be patentable whereas a method of treatment would be denied.[194] This is particularly the case where the claim is for an invention for the administration of the product. Second, Black CJ and Lehane J were strongly influenced by the failure of parliament to exclude methods of medical treatment from patentability when it enacted the *Patents Act 1990* (Cth).[195] The third judge, Finkelstein J, also held that medical treatment and surgical processes are patentable under the legislation. He decided that public policy matters of such complexity must be resolved by parliament. Thus, he refused to exercise any judicial discretion in this area to find a patentable medical treatment process to be 'generally inconvenient'.[196]

The conclusion to be drawn from this authority is that exclusion of a particular invention remains possible only if it fails to satisfy the concept of manner of manufacture within the meaning of *NRDC* or, having satisfied that concept, is found to be generally inconvenient. However, subsequent decisions, as well as the recommendations in the ACIP report *Patentable Subject Matter*, now make it clear that public policy in the form of the generally inconvenient exception is unlikely to be pleaded as the preferable basis, if at all, for excluding methods of medical treatment from patentability.[197]

Almost fifteen years after *Bristol-Myers*, the High Court majority in *Apotex Pty Ltd v Sanofi-Aventis Australia Pty Ltd* confirmed that:

> Assuming that all other requirements for patentability are met, a method (or process) for medical treatment of the human body which is capable of satisfying the *NRDC Case* test, namely that it is a contribution to a useful art having economic utility, can be a manner of manufacture and hence a patentable invention within the meaning of s 18(1)(a) of the 1990 Act.[198]

The relevant patent claimed a method of preventing or treating a skin disorder, namely, psoriasis, in which an effective amount of a pharmaceutical composition containing a compound of nominated formulae (leflunomide) as an active ingredient was administered. Leflunomide, and its use in treating psoriasis, had been the subject matter of an expired patent.

---

192   Ibid 481.
193   *Bristol-Myers Squibb Co v FH Faulding & Co Ltd* (2000) 97 FCR 524.
194   Ibid 530. See also *Wellcome Foundation Ltd v Commissioner of Patents* [1979] 2 NZLR 591, 620 (Davison CJ); *Rescare Ltd v Anaesthetic Supplies Pty Ltd* (1992) 25 IPR 119, 150.
195   French CJ voiced strong objections to invoking legislative inaction as negativing an implied exclusion: *Apotex Pty Ltd v Sanofi-Aventis Australia Pty Ltd* (2013) 253 CLR 284, [49]–[50].
196   *Bristol-Myers Squibb Co v FH Faulding & Co Ltd* (2000) 97 FCR 524, 569.
197   *Apotex Pty Ltd v Sanofi-Aventis Australia Pty Ltd* (2013) 253 CLR 284, [74]–[77] (Hayne J). But see *D'Arcy v Myriad Genetics Inc* (2015) 258 CLR 334, [28], below at 10.5.
198   (2013) 253 CLR 284, [286] (Crennan and Kiefel JJ, Gageler J agreeing).

Apotex had obtained registration of a generic version of leflunomide – apo-leflunomide – to be used in the treatment of different disorders, namely, psoriatic arthritis and rheumatoid arthritis. Sanofi-Aventis brought an action in the Federal Court asserting that the proposed supply would infringe the patent, and the matter came eventually before the High Court.[199] The relevant issue in this context was whether a method of medical treatment, involving the use of a pharmaceutical product, can be the subject of a patent.[200]

Relying on the obiter dicta in *NRDC* quoted earlier in this section, Apotex argued that the subject matter was 'essentially non-economic' and, hence, not patentable subject matter. In the principal judgment, Crennan and Kiefel JJ (with Gageler J agreeing) provided seven reasons for rejecting this submission. These can be summarised as follows:

1. The meaning of 'essentially non-economic' is derived from the requirement of patent law that patentable subject matter must have some useful application – it must be capable of being applied in commerce or industry. It seems that their Honours view 'economic utility' as the opposite of 'non-economic'.

2. There is an absence of any express or implied exception in the legislation. To the contrary, specific provisions in s 70 (extension of term of patents relating to pharmaceutical substances) and s 119A (infringement exemptions for pharmaceutical patents)[201] contemplate the grant of patents that claim a method of medical treatment using or administering a pharmaceutical substance. Moreover, despite numerous amendments of the *Patents Act 1990* (Cth), parliament has chosen not to legislate an express exception.

3. There is no normative distinction between methods of medical treatment that are cosmetic and those that are medical.

4. It is impossible to distinguish on public policy grounds a claim for a new product for therapeutic use, alone or combined with method claims, from the subject matter of a claim for a previously unknown method of treatment using a known product having prior therapeutic uses. Patents should reward both types of research.

5. The claimed invention satisfies the *NRDC* principles: it 'belongs to a useful art, effects an artificially created improvement in something and can have economic utility'.

6. The past practice of the Australian Patent Office is relevant (although not determinative).

7. The obiter dicta in *NRDC* can be distinguished as being referable to *medical treatments*, not to therapeutic uses of pharmaceutical substances as defined in the *Patents Act 1990* (Cth).[202]

These reasons persuaded Gageler J to answer 'yes' to the narrower question – namely, whether the method of medical treatment involving the use of a pharmaceutical product is patentable

---

199 Infringement issues are considered in ch 12 at 12.6.
200 *Apotex Pty Ltd v Sanofi-Aventis Australia Pty Ltd* [2013] HCATrans 123; [2013] HCATrans 124; *Apotex Pty Ltd v Sanofi-Aventis Australia Pty Ltd (No 2)* (2012) 204 FCR 494.
201 See ch 9 at 9.10 and ch 12 at 12.8.3.
202 *Apotex Pty Ltd v Sanofi-Aventis Australia Pty Ltd* (2013) 253 CLR 284, [278]–[285] (Crennan and Kiefel JJ, Gageler J agreeing).

subject matter. He added an eighth reason for coming to this conclusion. He observed that the position reached in *Bristol-Myers* – that a process of using a pharmaceutical product (taxol) to produce a therapeutic result is patentable subject matter – had been regarded subsequently as 'representing orthodoxy in Australian patent law'.[203] It was assumed in framing s 119A that a reversal would 'disappoint commercial expectations legitimately formed and acted upon for at least 13 years'.[204]

Importantly, Crennan and Kiefel JJ acknowledged a distinction between a method of medical treatment that involves a hitherto unknown therapeutic use of a pharmaceutical (having prior therapeutic uses), and other activities or procedures of doctors (and other medical staff) when physically treating patients, such as surgical procedures:

> Although it is unnecessary to decide the point, or to seek to characterise such activities or procedures exhaustively, speaking generally they are, in the language of the *NRDC Case*, 'essentially non-economic' and, in the language of the *EPC* [*European Patent Convention*] and the *Patents Act 1977* (UK), they are not 'susceptible' or 'capable' of industrial application. To the extent that such activities or procedures involve 'a method or a process', they are unlikely to be able to satisfy the *NRDC Case* test for the patentability of processes because they are not capable of being practically applied in commerce or industry, a necessary prerequisite of a 'manner of manufacture'.[205]

Gageler J observed that it was not necessary to determine whether *all* processes for treating the human body ought now to be recognised as patentable subject matter.[206] A strong dissenting judgment of Hayne J concluded that a method of prevention or treatment of human disease is not proper subject matter for the grant of a patent.[207] Only French CJ, in reliance on the lack of any principled development of an exclusion for methods of medical treatment, recognised no exception for methods of medical treatment:

> [T]he exclusion from patentability of methods of medical treatment represents an anomaly for which no clear and consistent foundation has been enunciated. Whatever views may have held in the past, methods of medical treatment, particularly the use of pharmaceutical drugs, cannot today be conceived as 'essentially non-economic'.[208]

If greater certainty is required in this area of inventive activity, it is possible for parliament to introduce an express exclusion into the *Patents Act 1990* (Cth). Article 27(3)(a) of *TRIPS* permits members to exclude 'diagnostic, therapeutic and surgical methods for the treatment of humans or animals' from patentability.

The need for such an express exclusion was considered in 2004 by the ALRC in the context of patents on genetic materials and technologies. In its report *Genes and Ingenuity: Gene Patenting and Human Health*,[209] the ALRC concluded that the introduction of an express

---

203   Ibid [315] (Gageler J), approving the reasoning of Bennett and Yates JJ in *Apotex Pty Ltd v Sanofi-Aventis Australia Pty Ltd (No 2)* (2012) 204 FCR 494, [193].
204   *Apotex Pty Ltd v Sanofi-Aventis Australia Pty Ltd* (2013) 253 CLR 284, [315].
205   Ibid [287] (Crennan and Kiefel JJ), [314] (Gageler J agreeing).
206   Ibid [312].
207   Ibid [165].
208   Ibid [50].
209   ALRC, *Genes and Ingenuity*, above n 50, [7.41].

exclusion for methods of medical treatment of humans in the specific area of genetic materials and technologies would have 'adverse effects on investment in biotechnology, medical research and innovation in healthcare and may not be consistent with Australia's obligations under the *TRIPS Agreement*' that require technological neutrality. The ALRC also rejected an approach that would introduce some form of medical treatment defence of the type introduced into United States patent law in 1996. The effect of this legislation is to provide a defence to an action for infringement against a medical practitioner or against a related health care entity, which includes a hospital with whom the practitioner has an affiliation, with respect to the performance of defined 'medical activities'. In general terms, this means the performance of a medical or surgical procedure on a body.[210]

The reservations expressed in *Apotex v Sanofi-Aventis Australia* by Crennan and Kiefel JJ that this type of subject matter is likely to fall outside the *NRDC* principles, together with the dissenting judgment of Hayne J, may prompt further thought regarding this subject matter. At a minimum, they provide a warning to future courts to be especially vigilant to avoid a mechanical application of *NRDC* principles to this type of subject matter.

10.4.8 Discoveries, ideas, intellectual information and other unpatentable subject matter

A prerequisite for the grant of a patent is that there is an invention. The High Court in *NRDC* distinguished a discovery from an invention 'either because the discovery is of some piece of abstract information without any suggestion of a practical application of it to a useful end, or because its application lies outside the realm of "manufacture"'.[211] However, the difficulty lies in the lack of precision in drawing this distinction: 'The truth is that the distinction between discovery and invention is not precise enough to be other than misleading in this area of discussion.'[212] The difficulty also lies in the open-ended nature of the concept of 'manufacture', which the court said was incapable of definition.[213] The theoretical distinction between a discovery and an invention is that an invention involves some practical application of or mode of carrying into effect the discovery, theory or idea that satisfies the *NRDC* principles.[214] There is a requirement for 'something of a corporeal and substantial nature' when considering the patentability of ideas.[215]

Other intellectual concepts that continue to be regarded as outside the scope of an invention include an abstract idea, mathematical algorithm, formula, calculation, directions for use or some other form of intellectual information, such as scientific principles. In relation to terms such as 'work of nature' and the 'laws of nature' that appear in United States jurisprudence, the High Court observed in *NRDC* that these are 'vague and malleable terms infected with too much ambiguity and equivocation. Everything that happens may be deemed 'the work of

---

210   Ibid [7.42], [21.44]; 35 USC §287(c).
211   *NRDC v Commissioner of Patents* (1959) 102 CLR 252, 264.
212   Ibid.
213   Ibid 269–70.
214   Ibid 263. See also *Lane Fox v Kensington & Knightsbridge Electric Lighting Co* (1892) 9 RPC 413, 416; *Hickton's Patent Syndicate v Patents & Machine Improvements Co Ltd* (1909) 26 RPC 339.
215   *Lockwood Security Products Pty Ltd v Doric Products Pty Ltd (No 2)* (2007) 235 CLR 173, [66], citing *R v Wheeler* (1819) 2 B & Ald 345, 350, 106 ER 392, 395 (Abbott CJ).

nature', and any patentable composite exemplifies in its properties 'the laws of nature'.[216] Despite some discussion of products of nature in *D'Arcy v Myriad Genetics*, there is no express recognition of a 'product of nature', 'work of nature' or 'laws of nature' as a class of unpatentable subject matter. Gordon J rejected the appellant's argument that 'naturally occurring things, or products or phenomena or principles of nature, are excluded as a proper subject matter of a patent'.[217] She approved the above passages from *NRDC*. The plurality in *D'Arcy* refused to engage with the criterion of 'artificially created state of affairs' because it was too narrow and invited distracting debates with the category of 'products of nature'. The central issue according to the plurality is whether an 'essential integer of the claims, the genetic information, takes them outside the category of that which can be "made".'[218] Only the judgment of Gageler and Nettle JJ examined the essence of an invention 'in its artificiality or distance from nature', stating that 'whether a product amounts to an invention depends on the extent to which the product "individualise[s]" nature.'[219]

NRDC drew a distinction between inventions that belong to a useful art (patentable) as distinct from a fine art (not patentable).[220] The distinction is not easy to find, although 'useful art' probably still translates into an area of economic endeavour that is qualified by the requirement that it has an 'industrial, commercial or trading character'.[221] The Full Court in *Grant* considered that the practice of law is outside the concept of a useful art. Although the interpretation and application of law is within an area of economic importance, the court in *Grant* found that this lacks any industrial or commercial or trading character:

> The practice of the law requires, amongst other things, ingenuity and imagination which may produce new kinds of transactions or litigation arguments which could well warrant the description of discoveries. But they are not inventions. Legal advices, schemes, arguments and the like are not a manner of manufacture.[222]

The distinction between an unpatentable discovery and an invention is particularly difficult in the area of biotechnology as evidenced by the *D'Arcy* litigation. One thing is clear: claims to naturally occurring entities are not patentable. In *Kirin-Amgen Inc v Board of Regents of University of Washington*,[223] the distinction was explained in the context of an invention that relied on the discovery of the DNA sequence encoding erythropoietin. The Deputy Commissioner of Patents expressed the distinction as follows:

---

216   *NRDC v Commissioner of Patents* (1959) 102 CLR 252, 264; *Funk Brothers Seed Co v Kalo Inoculant Co*, 333 US 127 (1948); *D'Arcy v Myriad Genetics Inc* (2015) 258 CLR 334, [222]–[225] (Gordon J), cf [126]–[127] (Gageler J).
217   *D'Arcy v Myriad Genetics Inc* (2015) 258 CLR 334, [225].
218   Ibid [91].
219   Ibid [126], adopting the arguments in B. Sherman and L. Bently, *The Making of Modern Intellectual Property Law* 46; B. Sherman, '*D'Arcy v Myriad Genetics Inc*: Patenting Genes in Australia' (2015) 37 *Sydney Law Review* 135, 138–9.
220   *NRDC v Commissioner of Patents* (1959) 102 CLR 252, 275.
221   Ibid; *Grant v Commissioner of Patents* (2006) 154 FCR 62, [34].
222   *Grant v Commissioner of Patents* (2006) 154 FCR 62, [34].
223   (1995) 33 IPR 557.

> In my view, a claim directed to a naturally occurring DNA characterized by specifying the DNA coding for a portion of that molecule would likely be claiming no more than a discovery per se and not be a manner of manufacture.[224]

There is no difficulty in finding a manner of manufacture when the application of a discovery results in some observable effect, such as the weed-free soil in *NRDC* or a new or restored tangible product. However, there is a new dimension to the concept of discovery. The distinction between a discovery and a manner of manufacture is not just the practical application of the discovery to a useful end. It is now evident that the application must produce some physical effect in the sense described in *Grant v Commissioner of Patents* to result in a manner of manufacture. This has been referred to as a 'useful physical result in relation to a material or tangible entity'.[225] For example, the court in *Grant* held that new kinds of legal transactions and other advice, schemes and arguments that are produced in the course of the practice of law may warrant the description of discoveries[226] although they clearly involve some practical application of ideas.

10.4.9 Reform proposals

The controversy that surrounds the patentability of genes and other biological materials, business methods and computer-implemented systems provided a catalyst for the various reviews to determine guidelines for appropriate subject matter for a patent. ACIP released *Patentable Subject Matter* (Final Report) in February 2011 and recommended a number of changes to the legislation. These included introducing a statement of objectives, defining patentable subject matter in clear and contemporary language, and replacing the general inconvenience proviso with a general morality exclusion: one that is permitted by art 27(2) of *TRIPS* and that would preclude the patenting of inventions the commercial exploitation of which would be wholly offensive to the ordinary reasonable and fully informed member of the Australian public.[227] Although the government accepted the recommendations in principle,[228] it is yet to determine the most appropriate way in which to proceed on these complex issues.

10.5 Generally inconvenient

Section 6 of the *Statute of Monopolies* excludes from patentability any inventions that would be contrary to law or mischievous to the state by being generally inconvenient. The 'contrary to law' exclusion is expressly provided in s 50(1)(a) of the *Patents Act 1990* (Cth) and is discussed below. The courts in the United Kingdom and Australia have considered the concept of 'generally inconvenient' rarely and in relation to a narrow range of inventions, including a method of operating an aircraft,[229] but the principal discussion in Australia has arisen in the

---

224 Ibid 569.
225 *CCOM Pty Ltd v Jiejing Pty Ltd* (1994) 51 FCR 260, 291.
226 *Grant v Commissioner of Patents* (2006) 154 FCR 62, [34].
227 ACIP, *Patentable Subject Matter*, above n 50; *Government Response: Patentable Subject Matter*, above n 50.
228 *Government Response: Patentable Subject Matter*, above n 50.
229 *Rolls-Royce Ltd's Application* [1963] RPC 251.

context of methods of medical treatment for humans[230] and more recently in the context of isolated genes.[231] In *Anaesthetic Supplies Pty Ltd v Rescare Ltd*,[232] the majority of the Full Federal Court rejected an argument that an invention for a method of medical treatment that involved the application of continuous airways pressure to the nasal passages using a face mask to treat obstructive sleep apnoea is 'generally inconvenient'. Lockhart J considered that there is no distinction in principle between a product for treating the human body (which is patentable) and a method of treating the human body.[233] However, he did not reject the existence of the exception under the *Patents Act 1990*. Wilcox J appeared to significantly reduce its possible application by stating that the court should not resort to matters of ethics and social policy to 'engraft onto a recently enacted statute an exception that Parliament has chosen not to adopt'.[234] In dissent, Sheppard J considered that the method of treating obstructive sleep apnoea was generally inconvenient. He stated:

> [T]he Court should not contemplate the grant of letters patent which would give to one medical practitioner, or perhaps a group of medical practitioners, a monopoly over, for example, a surgical procedure which might be greatly beneficial to mankind. Its denial might mean the death or unnecessary suffering of countless people. I cannot think that this is really what the medical profession as a whole would seek to achieve. Its whole history is a denial of the proposition.[235]

In *Bristol-Myers Squibb Co v FH Faulding & Co Ltd*, Heerey J followed this approach when he applied the generally inconvenient exception in the context of a method of administering the drug taxol in the treatment of cancer.[236] However, all appeal judges rejected its application. Black CJ and Lehane J followed the majority view in *Rescare* for two reasons. First, they saw it as an insurmountable problem, from a public policy point of view, to draw a logical distinction between allowing patentability of a pharmaceutical product for treating the human body, and denying patentability for a method of treating the human body using a pharmaceutical product. Second, they were influenced by the fact that there was no express exclusion included in the *Patents Act 1990*, even though patents were being granted for methods of medical treatment at the time.[237] While expressing some empathy with the need for a possible special area, such as 'an entirely novel and simple procedure, capable of saving many lives by its application as first aid',[238] the lack of a logical distinction around patenting products to treat medical ailments remained what appeared to be an insurmountable hurdle. Nevertheless, they did not reject the existence of the exception under the Act. Finkelstein J also rejected the application of the 'generally inconvenient' exception to methods of medical treatment, but on the ground that matters of such complex public policy should be resolved by parliament.[239] Arguments based

---

230   See above at 10.4.7.
231   *D'Arcy v Myriad Genetics Inc* (2015) 258 CLR 334, [28] (French CJ, Kiefel, Bell and Keene JJ).
232   (1994) 50 FCR 1.
233   Ibid 18.
234   Ibid 45.
235   Ibid 41.
236   (1998) 41 IPR 467, 479–80.
237   *Bristol-Myers Squibb Co v FH Faulding & Co Ltd* (2000) 97 FCR 524, 528–30 [15]–[16].
238   Ibid 530 [17]
239   Ibid [141]–[142].

on general inconvenience have been similarly unsuccessful in the context of a patent for a process for operating smart cards in connection with traders' loyalty programs.[240]

Following this reluctance of the judiciary to reject the patentability of a variety of inventions on grounds of general inconvenience, the Australian Patent Office Manual instructs its examiners to refrain from taking this objection to a patent application.[241] No-one is clear what 'generally inconvenient' encompasses. Although there is some understanding that it may have ethical or broader public policy functions, the ALRC doubts the ability of the proviso to deal adequately with ethical issues and has recommended its review.[242] ACIP has noted this conclusion and has recommended the removal and replacement of the generally inconvenient proviso with 'a patentability exclusion as permitted by Article 27(2) of the *TRIPS Agreement*'.[243] IP Australia issued a consultation paper in July 2013 on an exclusion clause that would be consistent with art 27(2).[244] This issue remains unresolved.

It seems that the courts recognise that they retain discretion to reject inventions that are generally inconvenient, but are unwilling to exercise that discretion in matters of complex policy if it is possible to reject the inventions on other grounds, such as being a mere scheme or intellectual information.[245] To date, this seems to be a satisfactory means for imposing a threshold on patentable subject matter until there is statutory resolution of this wider issue. As French CJ observed in *Apotex Pty Ltd v Sanofi-Aventis Australia Pty Ltd* in the context of an invention for a method of medical treatment of humans:

> Recognition of the economic dimensions of this question is not inconsistent with the concurrent recognition of the large public policy questions which it raises. They may involve competing philosophies of proprietarianism and instrumentalism and the relative values to be accorded to different public goods: alleged incentives to innovation on the one hand, and the widest possible availability of new methods of medical treatment to relieve suffering on the other. To decide that the concept of 'manner of new manufacture' does not logically exclude methods of medical treatment from patentability does not engage with those large questions, although it may have significant consequences for public policy. This is a case in which such considerations are best left to the legislature. . . . Nor … does 'general inconvenience' (upon which, in any event, Apotex placed no reliance) appear to provide any basis for their exclusion.[246]

While this is likely to remain the approach of the judiciary, the plurality in *D'Arcy v Myriad Genetics* breathed new life into the generally inconvenient proviso with factors that might inform this limitation for those rare situations that require resort to some concept of public policy for their exclusion from patentability.[247] These are the same factors that the plurality regarded as relevant to the judicial development of the concept of manner of manufacture.[248]

---

240 *Welcome Real-Time SA v Catuity Inc* (2001) 113 FCR 110, [132].
241 *APO Manual*, above n 57, [2.9.3.3].
242 ALRC, *Genes and Ingenuity*, above n 50, rec 6-2.
243 ACIP, *Patentable Subject Matter*, above n 50, recs 8, 9.
244 IP Australia, *Patentable Subject Matter*, above n 144.
245 *Grant v Commissioner of Patents* (2006) 154 FCR 62, 72 [40]–[45].
246 (2013) 253 CLR 284, [50].
247 *D'Arcy v Myriad Genetics Inc* (2015) 258 CLR 334, [28]. See A. L. Monotti, 'The scope of "manner of manufacture" under the *Patents Act 1990* (Cth) after *Grant v Commissioner of Patents*', above n 63.
248 See above at 10.4.6.

10.6 Novelty
10.6.1 Introduction

Novelty is a basic requirement of the patent system, because it would be unjust to allow a monopoly over something that is already known and possibly in use. Novelty is a separate inquiry from that which considers whether the invention involves an inventive or innovative step over the relevant prior art.[249]

The crucial question is whether an invention is novel when compared to prior art information made publicly available.[250] Such public disclosure is often referred to as an 'anticipation' of the invention that subsequently becomes the subject of a patent application. Anticipation can occur in a variety of ways. It may be information in a prior publication anywhere in the world, such as a newspaper article, patent specification or advertisement. The publication includes photographs[251] and illustrations. It may be information made publicly available through doing an act anywhere in the world, such as a public demonstration. It makes no difference if there is lack of knowledge of the prior public use or prior public disclosure, or if there is considerable ingenuity in the creation of the invention.

Novelty is derived from the requirements of s 6 of the *Statute of Monopolies* – namely, that the invention be a 'manner of *new* manufacture'. Before separation of the two types of newness that subsequently developed – novelty and inventive step – first in the *Patents Act 1952* (Cth) and then in the *Patents Act 1990* (Cth), the distinction was not clearly drawn. Consequently, early cases decided under the *Patents Act 1903* (Cth) in particular often merged the concepts of novelty (prior disclosure) and inventive step (not obvious).[252] Under the 1952 Act, lack of novelty was a ground for examination, opposition and revocation. Obviousness or lack of invention became a statutory ground for objection in both opposition and revocation proceedings, but this was not available at examination stage.[253] Hence, care is required in reading cases involving the patentability of an invention under the 1952 Act, as they may also merge these concepts.[254] The concepts of novelty and inventive or innovative step are clearly separated for all purposes under the 1990 Act.

10.6.2 Time at which novelty is raised

Under the *Patents Act 1990* (Cth), the issue of novelty can be raised with respect to standard patents[255] at examination stage[256] and in opposition proceedings,[257] and is a ground for

---

249 *Patents Act 1990* (Cth) s 18(1)(b)(ii), (1A)(b)(ii).
250 Ibid s 18(1)(b)(i), (1A)(b)(i).
251 *C Van der Lely NV v Bamfords Ltd* [1963] RPC 61, 71–2; *Ramset Fasteners (Australia) Pty Ltd v Advanced Building Systems Pty Ltd* (1999) 44 IPR 481.
252 *RD Werner & Co Inc v Bailey Aluminium Products Pty Ltd* (1989) 25 FCR 565, 572, 575–6; *Gum v Stevens* (1923) 33 CLR 267 (Isaacs J).
253 *Patents Act 1952* (Cth) s 48(3)(b), (d), (e), s 59(1)(c)–(e), (g), (h), s 100(1)(e)–(g).
254 *RD Werner & Co Inc v Bailey Aluminium Products Pty Ltd* (1989) 25 FCR 565 (Gummow J).
255 *Patents Act 1990* (Cth) s 61, sch 1.
256 Ibid ss 45(1)(b) (examination), 98(b) (re-examination).
257 Ibid s 59(b).

revocation of a patent.[258] In the case of an innovation patent, novelty is a ground for revocation after examination, re-examination[259] or upon an application for revocation under s 138.

The *Intellectual Property Laws Amendment (Raising the Bar) Act 2012* (Cth) (*Raising the Bar Act*) removed the restriction that the Commissioner must not have regard to prior public use at examination, modified examination and re-examination. The rationale for this former limitation[260] was that there is no opportunity for an examiner to obtain information from anyone other than the applicant. The Explanatory Memorandum to the Bill notes:

> [T]he amendments are intended to permit the consideration of prior use information if the examiner is aware of that information in the ordinary course of examination, or where evidence of prior use is provided to the Commissioner under section 27. They are not intended to impose an obligation on the Commissioner to conduct exhaustive searches specifically for prior use.[261]

10.6.3 Statutory requirements: overview

The statutory requirements for novelty are the same for both standard and innovation patents. They are set out in ss 7(1), 18(1)(b)(i) (standard patent), 18(1A)(b)(i) (innovation patent) and sch 1 of the *Patents Act 1990* (Cth). Section 18 provides that the invention, so far as claimed in any claim, must be novel when it is compared with the prior art base as it existed before the priority date of the claim.[262] There is a presumption of novelty unless the invention is not novel in light of specified classes of publicly available information. A person can publish or use the invention after the priority date of the claim without affecting its validity.[263] The current prior art base, defined in sch 1, includes information made publicly available in documents and acts anywhere in the world and certain unpublished Australian complete specifications. This prior art base has expanded over time in response to calls for a stronger patent system.[264]

In all versions of the patent legislation, a 'document' has the meaning given to it in s 2B of the *Acts Interpretation Act 1901* (Cth). It means any record of information and includes

(a) anything on which there is writing; and
(b) anything on which there are marks, figures, symbols or perforations having a meaning for persons qualified to interpret them; and
(c) anything from which sounds, images or writings can be reproduced with or without the aid of anything else; and
(d) a map, plan, drawing or photograph.

---

258 Ibid s 138(3)(b).
259 Ibid s 101B(2)(b) (examination), s 101G(3)(b) (re-examination).
260 Ibid ss 45(1A) and 101B(3) (examination), s 48(1A) (modified examination), ss 98(2) and 101B(3) (re-examination) (pre-*Raising the Bar* versions).
261 Explanatory Memorandum, Intellectual Property Laws Amendment (Raising the Bar) Bill 2011 (Cth).
262 *Patents Act 1990* (Cth) s 43 (priority dates). As to the drafting of s 7 see G. Levy, 'The curious case of the inventive step and innovative step provisions under the Patents Act 1990: A drafting flaw?' (2010) 21 *Australian Intellectual Property Journal* 4.
263 *Patents Act 1990* (Cth) s 23.
264 See below at 10.6.5.

The novelty inquiry relates to each individual claim in the specification,[265] as each claim defines a particular form of the invention for which a patent is sought.[266] Each claim of a specification has a priority date, which is the date of filing the specification[267] or such other date as is determined under the regulations.[268]

The question is whether an invention is novel when compared to prior art information made publicly available before the priority date of the claim. The test is not whether the *invention* itself has been made publicly available.[269] The novelty inquiry is performed by the court through the eyes of the person whom the court identifies as the relevant hypothetical skilled addressee in the relevant art,[270] who construes the specification and prior art in light of the common general knowledge.[271] The notion of common general knowledge is discussed below.[272] Briefly, it refers to information that the skilled person would retain in their mind, and any information they know of and might refer to as a matter of course or habitually consult.[273]

The novelty inquiry proceeds along the following lines:

1. Determine the priority date and the relevant prior art.[274]

2. Interpret claims at their priority date – what are their essential integers? This is a matter of law and for the court to decide. It involves the same method as applies for infringement.

3. Construe the relevant prior art. This is also a matter of law and for the court to decide. It is construed at the priority date of the claim under consideration.

4. Assess lack of novelty at the priority date of the relevant claim.[275] Section 7(1) of the *Patents Act 1990* (Cth) sets the precise boundaries of the information that can be taken into account. It is clear that common general knowledge does not fall within those boundaries and can be used only for the purpose of construing the documents.[276] An invention is taken to be novel when compared with the prior art base unless it is not novel in light of any one of several kinds of publicly available information set out in s 7(1)(a)–(c) (presented below), each of which must be considered separately. Each type of information is described as 'prior art information'. This term is defined in the Dictionary in sch 1 of the Act as information that is part of the prior art base in relation to deciding whether an invention is novel.

---

265 *Patents Act 1990* (Cth) s 18(1), 18(1A) ('so far as claimed in any claim'), s 40(2).
266 Ibid s 40(2)(b)–(c).
267 Ibid s 43(2). A claim may be supported with multiple priority dates when the claim defines more than one form of an invention: at s 43(3). This can result in 'poisonous priority' – where a claim is found to be anticipated by the application from which it claims priority. See M. Caine, 'Poisonous priority arrives in Australia and New Zealand' (Davies Collison Cave, 6 November 2014) https://dcc.com.
268 *Patents Regulations 1991* (Cth) ch 3 pt 1 div 2. See ch 9 at 9.11 and 9.12.
269 H Lundbeck A/S v Alphapharm Pty Ltd (2009) 177 FCR 151, [163] (Bennett J, Middleton J agreeing). Contrast this with *Patents Act 1977* (UK) s 2.
270 See below at 10.6.6.
271 Questions of interpretation and construction are considered in ch 12.
272 At 10.8.3.
273 *ICI Chemicals & Polymers Ltd v Lubrizol Corp Inc* (1999) 45 IPR 577, [112]; *Aktiebolaget Hassle v Alphapharm Pty Ltd* (2000) 51 IPR 375, [73]; *PhotoCure ASA v Queen's University at Kingston* (2005) 64 IPR 314, [31].
274 *AstraZeneca AB v Apotex Pty Ltd* (2014) 226 FCR 324 (FC), [231]–[255].
275 *ICI Chemicals & Polymers Ltd v Lubrizol Corp Inc* (2000) 106 FCR 214.
276 *AstraZeneca AB v Apotex Pty Ltd* (2014) 226 FCR 324 (FC), [311].

The comparison is with information that is disclosed in a single source, within the prior art base, namely

(a) prior art information (other than that mentioned in paragraph (c)) made publicly available in a single document or through doing a single act;

(b) prior art information (other than that mentioned in paragraph (c)) made publicly available in two or more related documents, or through doing two or more related acts, if the relationship between the documents or acts is such that a person skilled in the relevant art[277] would treat them as a single source of that information;

(c) prior art information contained in a single specification of the kind mentioned in subparagraph (b)(ii) of the definition of *prior art base* in Schedule 1.[278]

There is no reference in either the *Patents Act 1952* (Cth) or the *Patents Act 1990* (Cth) to 'disclosure' or 'enablement' of the invention in the context of novelty.[279] The test is not whether the invention has been made publicly available but whether the invention is novel in light of publicly available information. This contrasts with s 2 of the *Patents Act 1977* (UK), which provides two requirements for novelty: that the invention does not form part of the state of the art (disclosure), and that the invention has not been 'made available to the public' (enablement). This latter concept of enablement is similar to the concept of sufficiency under the *Patents Act 1990* (Cth).

The party that alleges lack of novelty bears the onus of proving that the prior art is 'publicly available' before the priority date of the relevant claim.[280] If publication is in issue, it is a question of fact to be decided by reference to the civil standard of proof.[281]

10.6.4 Time at which to construe and read documentary disclosures

A documentary disclosure that forms part of the prior art base is construed by a court through the eyes of the skilled addressee in light of common general knowledge at the priority date of the claim under consideration to assess whether the disclosure amounts to an anticipation of the claimed invention. Practice has resolved[282] the uncertainty identified in *ICI Chemicals & Polymers Ltd v Lubrizol Corp Inc*[283] as to whether the skilled addressee is taken to consider the publication at its date[284] or at the priority date of the claim under consideration.[285]

---

277 *Patents Amendment Act 2001* (Cth) sch 1 pt 1 item 1 removed a limitation to the relevant art 'in the patent area'.
278 *Patents Act 1990* (Cth) s 7(1).
279 *H Lundbeck A/S v Alphapharm Pty Ltd* (2009) 177 FCR 151, [162] (Bennett J, Middleton J agreeing).
280 *JMVB Enterprises Pty Ltd v Camoflag Pty Ltd* (2005) 67 IPR 68, [53].
281 Ibid [56].
282 See, for example, *Novozymes A/S v Danisco A/S* (2013) 99 IPR 417, [101]–[109] (Jessup J, [37] Greenwood J and [238] Yates J agreeing).
283 *ICI Chemicals & Polymers Ltd v Lubrizol Corp Inc* (2000) 106 FCR 214, [41]–[46]. In the face of conflicting judicial statements and assumptions, the Full Court in this case assumed that both the specification and prior art documents are construed at the priority date of the claim under consideration (without finding it necessary to decide the issue).
284 *General Tire & Rubber Co v Firestone Tyre & Rubber Co Ltd* [1972] RPC 457, 479.
285 *Ramset Fasteners (Australia) Pty Ltd v Advanced Building Systems Pty Ltd* (1996) 66 FCR 151, [18]–[19] (priority date assumed, but without deciding the point); *British Thomson-Houston Co Ltd v Metropolitan-Vickers Electrical Co Ltd* (1928) 45 RPC 1, 22 (priority date assumed).

10.6.5 Prior art base
10.6.5.1 Historical provisions
10.6.5.1.1 *PATENTS ACT 1952*
The prior art base for novelty under the *Patents Act 1952* (Cth) was confined to documents and acts that were published in Australia. The same prior art base applied for both standard[286] and petty patents.[287] A concept of 'prior claiming' applied under the *Patents Act 1952* (Cth) – namely, where a comparison was possible with a valid claim of earlier priority date contained in the complete specification of a standard patent or in the petty patent specification of a petty patent.[288] The prior claims had to contain a distinct claim to the subject matter of the later claim. It was not enough to simply disclose the invention.

10.6.5.1.2 *PATENTS ACT 1990*: 30 APRIL 1991 TO 23 MAY 2001
The prior art base for a standard patent comprised information in a document, being a document made publicly available anywhere in the world, and information made publicly available through doing an act anywhere in the patent area. In contrast, the prior art base for a petty patent was limited to a domestic prior art base for both documents and acts.[289] The reference to documents included patent specifications, the information in which was publicly available before the priority date.

Prior unpublished patent specifications provide an additional source of prior art information under the *Patents Act 1990* (Cth) under a 'whole of contents' approach, which is a question of anticipation, rather than the prior claiming.[290] A discussion of the operation of this provision appears below.[291]

10.6.5.1.3 *PATENTS ACT 1990*: 24 MAY 2001 TO 31 MARCH 2002
The *Patents Amendment (Innovation Patents) Act 2000* (Cth) introduced the innovation patent with an identical prior art base to that which was available for assessing the novelty of a standard patent: information in a document that is publicly available anywhere in the world and information made publicly available through doing an act in the patent area.

10.6.5.2 Current prior art base
10.6.5.2.1 DOCUMENTS AND ACTS
The *Patents Amendment Act 2001* (Cth) extended the prior art base from and including 1 April 2002 for both standard and innovation patents to include a worldwide comparison for acts as well as documents.

---

286   *Patents Act 1952* (Cth) ss 48(3)(d)–(e), 59(1)(d)–(e), (h), 100(1)(g).
287   Ibid s 49A(11)(c)–(e).
288   *Patents Act 1952* (Cth) ss 48(3), 59(1)(c)–(d), 100(1)(f).
289   *Patents Act 1990* (Cth) sch 1 (definition of 'prior art base').
290   *Old Digger Pty Ltd v Azuko Pty Ltd* (2000) 51 IPR 43, [83]–[90].
291   At 10.6.5.2.2.

10.6.5.2.2 PRIOR UNPUBLISHED SPECIFICATIONS: 'WHOLE OF CONTENTS'

It is possible that a specification in respect of a complete application may have an earlier filing date but be unpublished at the priority date of the relevant claim. A complete application is not required to become open for public inspection until eighteen months have elapsed from its filing date or the date of making its earliest priority document.[292] Hence, such specifications would not come within the prior art base of publicly available documents at the priority date. However, if that information is ignored, it would be possible for a patent to issue that is not new because it is the same as an invention that was in the pipeline, but unpublished, at its filing date.

The *Patents Act 1952* (Cth) dealt with this issue under the 'prior claiming' concept. In contrast, the *Patents Act 1990* (Cth) includes within the novelty prior art base, information in an unpublished Australian specification whose priority date precedes that of the relevant claim when that information remains in the later published specification.[293] The disclosure need not be within the claims of the filed or published specification,[294] but it would have to be capable of forming the subject of a notional claim.[295] Hence, any information that is introduced after the priority date of the relevant claim would not be within the prior art base against which the comparison is made. It is necessary for the parties to formulate a notional claim that is then used as a point of reference for considering whether the claims in the patent under consideration are novel.[296]

The *Raising the Bar* reforms made two amendments to the definition of prior art base in sch 1. The first clarifies that the specification must be published on or after the priority date of the claim under consideration. The second limits prior art information to that which is contained in the specification on its filing date to reduce complexity and maintain consistency with practice in the United States and Europe.[297]

10.6.6 Person skilled in the relevant art: the skilled addressee

In making a decision on the novelty of an invention as claimed, the court is to place itself 'in the position of some person acquainted with the surrounding circumstances as to the state of [the] art and manufacture' at the priority date of the relevant claim.[298] This is the hypothetical, non-inventive and not particularly imaginative 'skilled addressee', a person 'skilled in the relevant art' who possesses 'ordinary skill',[299] and who works in the art or science connected with the

---

292   *Patents Act 1990* (Cth) s 54(3)(b); *Patents Regulations 1991* (Cth) reg 4.2(3).
293   *Patents Act 1990* (Cth) sch 1 (definition of 'prior art base' (b)(ii)).
294   *Old Digger Pty Ltd v Azuko Pty Ltd* (2000) 51 IPR 43, [85].
295   *EI Du Pont de Nemours & Co v ICI Chemicals & Polymers Ltd* (2005) 66 IPR 462, [80]–[85].
296   *Novozymes A/S v Danisco A/S* (2013) 99 IPR 417, [194]; *EI Du Pont de Nemours & Co v ICI Chemicals & Polymers Ltd* (2005) 66 IPR 462, [80]–[85].
297   *Intellectual Property Laws Amendment (Raising the Bar) Act 2012* (Cth) sch 6 items 101, 102. The grace period in s 24 applies also to a 'whole of contents' objection. See below at 10.6.10. See also *Biogen Idec MA Inc* [2014] APO 25.
298   *Kimberly-Clark Australia Pty Ltd v Arico Trading International Pty Ltd* (2001) 207 CLR 1, [24]. See ch 12 at 12.2.
299   *H Lundbeck A/S v Alphapharm Pty Ltd* (2009) 177 FCR 151, [173] (Bennett J, Middleton J agreeing).

invention. The term does not identify a specific person and may consist of a team of persons with combined skills.[300] This skilled addressee is relevant for a variety of other purposes in patent law.[301]

10.6.7 The meaning of 'prior information made publicly available'

Although novelty was not defined with reference to the phrase 'publicly available' under the *Patents Act 1952* (Cth), the Federal Court applied an established line of authority to the *Patents Act 1990* (Cth) to construe this phrase.[302] This authority established that the requisite degree of publication is met if there is communication to any one member of the public in a manner that left that person free, in law and equity, to make use of that information.[303] Clearly an invention is not publicly available when the disclosure arises in circumstances that impose an obligation of confidence on the recipient of the information.[304] Whether the information disclosed in either a prior publication or use actually anticipates the invention is a separate question.

It is immaterial whether the information becomes known to many or a few people[305] and whether a person availed themselves of access to an invented product.[306] A description in an obscure publication is sufficient and it does not matter if no-one actually reads the information.[307] Members of the public will include persons who purchase subscriptions to magazines, who are on mailing lists, and who buy newspapers over the counter.[308] They will also include persons who are selected by the publisher for commercial reasons, but would exclude the publisher's agent in another country.[309] Information that is made available on a website will be information available to the public,[310] as will information in published patent specifications, irrespective of the language in which they exist.[311]

When disclosure occurs through doing single or related acts, the concept of prior information being made publicly available will require clear evidence that the location of the act or

---

300 *Ranbaxy Australia Pty Ltd v Warner-Lambert Co LLC (No 2)* (2006) 71 IPR 46, [65]–[72].
301 See below at 10.8.2 for a more detailed description of this concept. See also Justice J. Middleton, 'The skilled addressee' (2013) 92 *Intellectual Property Forum* 12.
302 *Merck & Co Inc v Arrow Pharmaceuticals Ltd* (2006) 154 FCR 31, [97]–[103]; *Arrow Pharmaceuticals Ltd v Merck & Co Inc* (2004) 63 IPR 85, [98]–[102]; *Sunbeam Corp v Morphy-Richards (Australia) Pty Ltd* (1961) 180 CLR 98, 111.
303 *Humpherson v Syer* (1887) 4 RPC 407; *Stanway Oyster Cylinders Pty Ltd v Marks* (1996) 66 FCR 577, 581; *Merck & Co Inc v Arrow Pharmaceuticals Ltd* (2006) 154 FCR 31, [98]; *Insta Image Pty Ltd v KD Kanopy Australasia Pty Ltd* (2008) 78 IPR 20 [124].
304 *Griffin v Isaacs* (1938) 1B IPR 619, 621.
305 *Fomento Industrial SA & Biro Swan Ltd v Mentmore Manufacturing Co Ltd* [1956] RPC 87, 99; *Humpherson v Syer* (1887) 4 RPC 407, 413; *Sunbeam Corp v Morphy-Richards (Australia) Pty Ltd* (1961) 180 CLR 98.
306 *Merck & Co Inc v Arrow Pharmaceuticals Ltd* (2006) 154 FCR 31.
307 *Sunbeam Corp v Morphy-Richards (Australia) Pty Ltd* (1961) 180 CLR 98, 111–12 (Windeyer J).
308 *Arrow Pharmaceuticals Ltd v Merck & Co Inc* (2004) 63 IPR 85, [100].
309 Ibid.
310 Ibid [101].
311 *Dennison Manufacturing Co v Monarch Marking Systems Inc* (1983) 1 IPR 431.

use was open to members of the public.[312] This may be on a private property.[313] As to the nature of the acts performed, it seems probable that the word 'act' in s 7 and in the definition of 'prior art base' encompasses the concept of 'prior use' that was relevant in the context of an inquiry as to inventiveness under the *Patents Act 1952* (Cth).[314] Acts will involve the use[315] or demonstration[316] of a device, product or process. Disclosure may occur through distribution of samples,[317] manufacture of devices and products,[318] display of a product at a public event[319] and sales[320] or offers to sell the invention. For instance, the use of a portable collapsible canopy framework at a race meeting, in an area that was open freely to the general public, resulted in the information disclosed by this use becoming publicly available for the purposes of a novelty assessment.[321] The conduct itself must make sufficient disclosure of all the essential integers of the invention. It follows from this discussion that the use of a device that is an embodiment of an earlier patented invention will anticipate the later invention only if the specification itself amounts to anticipation.[322] A disclosure is possible in conversations and a no less stringent test applies to oral disclosures.[323]

10.6.8 Test for 'anticipation'

10.6.8.1 General principles

Novelty is concerned with what the prior art discloses – not with the 'teaching' of a patent.[324] As an enlarged Full Federal Court observed in *AstraZeneca AB v Apotex Pty Ltd*,[325] the 'touchstone' for anticipation of both product and process[326] inventions continues to be the words of the United Kingdom Court of Appeal in *General Tire & Rubber Co v Firestone Tyre & Rubber Co Ltd*:

> When the prior inventor's publication and the patentee's claim have respectively been construed by the Court in the light of all properly admissible evidence ... the question

---

312 *Costa v GR & IE Daking Pty Ltd* (1994) 29 IPR 241, 248; *Insta Image Pty Ltd v KD Kanopy Australasia Pty Ltd* (2008) 78 IPR 20.
313 *Costa v GR & IE Daking Pty Ltd* (1994) 29 IPR 241, 250.
314 *Patents Act 1952* (Cth) s 100(1)(e) (was known or used in Australia). *Dyno Nobel Asia Pacific Ltd v Orica Australia Pty Ltd* (1999) 99 FCR 151, [218].
315 For example, *Stanway Oyster Cylinders Pty Ltd v Marks* (1996) 66 FCR 577; *Azuko Pty Ltd v Old Digger Pty Ltd* (2001) 52 IPR 75; *Great Western Corp Pty Ltd v Grove Hill Pty Ltd* [2001] FCA 423; *Acme Bedstead Co Ltd v Newlands Brothers Ltd* (1937) 58 CLR 689.
316 *Griffin v Isaacs* (1938) 1B IPR 619, 623; *Innovative Agricultural Products Pty Ltd & Jacek v Cranshaw* (1996) 35 IPR 643.
317 *Fomento Industrial SA & Biro Swan Ltd v Mentmore Manufacturing Co Ltd* [1956] RPC 87.
318 *Melbourne v Terry Fluid Controls Pty Ltd* (1993) 26 IPR 292; *R v Patents Appeal Tribunal; Ex parte Swift & Co* [1962] 1 All ER 610; *Bristol-Myers Co v Beecham Group Ltd* [1974] AC 646.
319 *Insta Image Pty Ltd v KD Kanopy Australasia Pty Ltd* (2008) 78 IPR 20.
320 *R v Patents Appeal Tribunal; Ex parte Swift & Co* [1962] 1 All ER 610; *Bristol-Myers Co v Beecham Group Ltd* [1974] AC 646; *Re Wheatley's Patent Application* (1984) 2 IPR 450 (acceptance of an order to purchase).
321 *Insta Image Pty Ltd v KD Kanopy Australasia Pty Ltd* (2008) 78 IPR 20, [143]–[144].
322 *Old Digger Pty Ltd v Azuko Pty Ltd* (2000) 51 IPR 43.
323 *British American Tobacco (Investments) Ltd v Philip Morris Ltd* (1999) 47 IPR 351, [12].
324 *Multisteps Pty Ltd v Speciality Packaging Aust Pty Ltd* (2018) 132 IPR 399, [46].
325 (2014) 226 FCR 324 (FC), [293].
326 *Novozymes A/S v Danisco A/S* (2013) 99 IPR 417, [146] (Jessup J, Greenwood and Yates JJ agreeing).

whether the patentee's claim is new ... falls to be decided as a question of fact. If the prior inventor's publication contains a clear description of, or clear instructions to do or make, something that would infringe the patentee's claim if carried out after the grant of the patentee's patent, the patentee's claim will have been shown to lack the necessary novelty, that is to say, it will have been anticipated. The prior inventor, however, and the patentee may have approached the same device from different starting points and may for this reason, or it may be for other reasons, have so described their devices that it cannot be immediately discerned from a reading of the language which they have respectively used that they have discovered in truth the same device; but if carrying out the directions contained in the prior inventor's publication will inevitably result in something being made or done which, if the patentee's patent were valid, would constitute an infringement of the patentee's claim, this circumstance demonstrates that the patentee's claim has in fact been anticipated.

If, on the other hand, the prior publication contains a direction which is capable of being carried out in a manner which would infringe the patentee's claim, but would be at least as likely to be carried out in a way which would not do so, the patentee's claim will not have been anticipated, although it may fail on the ground of obviousness. To anticipate the patentee's claim the prior publication must contain clear and unmistakable directions to do what the patentee claims to have invented ... A signpost, however clear, upon the road to the patentee's invention will not suffice. The prior inventor must be clearly shown to have planted his flag at the precise destination before the patentee.[327]

Hence, 'whatever is essential to the invention must be read out of the prior publication'.[328] In the case of a claimed product, clear and unmistakable directions to make the product will suffice as long as the claimed product would necessarily result from following those directions.[329]

When the disclosure arises from an act as opposed to a documentary disclosure, the mere public use or circulation of a product that embodies the invention may not necessarily amount to an anticipation. Prior use does not itself invalidate a patent. The act must disclose the essential integers of the invention through provision of the information or because it can be gleaned from inspection of the invention.[330] Courts have inquired as to what information on the nature of the invention was given by the particular act or use. Anticipation occurred in *Insta Image Pty Ltd v KD Kanopy Australasia Pty Ltd*[331] through the use of a portable collapsible canopy framework at race meetings because the evidence established that all essential integers of the invention were disclosed by visual inspection of the product. In contrast, there was no anticipation in *Jupiters Ltd v Neurizon Ltd*,[332] because there was no direct evidence that

---

[327] [1972] RPC 457, 443–4. See also *Hill v Evans* (1862) 4 De GF & J 288, 301; *Multisteps Pty Ltd v Speciality Packaging Aust Pty Ltd* (2018) 132 IPR 399, [46] (no clear directions).
[328] *Hill v Evans* (1862) 4 De GF & J 288, 300; *Acme Bedstead Co Ltd v Newlands Brothers Ltd* (1937) 58 CLR 689, 707.
[329] *Olin Corp v Super Cartridge Co Pty Ltd* (1977) 180 CLR 236, 260–1.
[330] *Stanway Oyster Cylinders Pty Ltd v Marks* (1996) 66 FCR 577, 581; *Jupiters Ltd v Neurizon Pty Ltd* (2005) 65 IPR 86, [144]–[146]; *Cullen v Welsbach Light Co of Australasia Ltd* (1907) 4 CLR 990, 1002–3 (Griffith CJ), 1008 (Barton J).
[331] (2008) 78 IPR 20.
[332] (2005) 65 IPR 86.

observation of the operation of an electronic gaming system in casinos 'would establish that anything of relevance to the patent would be gleaned from mere observation of the system in operation, even by a skilled observer'.[333] Similarly, in *Damorgold Pty Ltd v JAI Products Pty Ltd*[334] mere observation of the operation of roller blinds in a showroom did not communicate all of the essential integers of the invention to customers. Even though the remaining integers were easily accessible from an inspection of the blind after it was disassembled, Bennett J noted the absence of evidence that any customer was interested in the internal componentry, was free to examine the mechanisms or had any opportunity to do so.[335] Even though disassembly and reassembly of the mechanism was a simple matter, the actual conduct did not itself make sufficient disclosure of the invention.[336] The decision may have been different if the blinds had been sold or given to a customer, because the customer would then have the opportunity to examine the product to find its internal workings. However, Yates J stressed that such cases raise different considerations and his decision was not to be taken as dealing with such circumstances.[337]

Cautionary observations were expressed by Bennett and Yates JJ in *Apotex Pty Ltd v Sanofi-Aventis Australia Pty Ltd (No 2)*[338] that the logic of the 'inevitable result' principle expressed above in *General Tire* should not be applied uncritically, particularly where the invention is a new method of medical treatment that involves the use of a known compound for a hitherto unknown and unexpected, but useful, therapeutic use.[339] The enlarged Full Court in *AstraZeneca* noted the importance of these observations and then proceeded to make its own cautionary observations as to the circumstances in which the commonly cited notion of reverse infringement is to be used in assessing anticipatory disclosures. Aickin J articulated the reverse infringement test in *Meyers Taylor Pty Ltd v Vicarr Industries Ltd*:

> The basic test for anticipation or want of novelty is the same as that for infringement and generally one can properly ask oneself whether the alleged anticipation would, if the patent were valid, constitute an infringement.[340]

Infringement occurs when an alleged infringing product or process contains all essential integers of the claimed invention.[341] Hence, the prior art information made publicly available similarly must disclose all those essential features clearly and plainly to the skilled person in the manner expressed in *General Tire*.[342] The words of caution expressed in *AstraZeneca* are that

---

333 Ibid [144].
334 (2015) 229 FCR 68.
335 Ibid [58] (Bennett J).
336 Ibid [54]–[58] (Bennett J), [94] (Yates J).
337 Ibid [98].
338 (2012) 204 FCR 494.
339 Ibid [165] (Bennett and Yates JJ); *AstraZeneca AB v Apotex Pty Ltd* (2014) 226 FCR 324 (FC), [296], referring to this decision and also to *Actavis UK Ltd v Janssen Pharmaceutica NV* [2008] FSR 35, [90] (Floyd J).
340 (1977) 137 CLR 228, 235. See also *General Tire & Rubber Co v Firestone Tyre & Rubber Co Ltd* [1972] RPC 457, 485; *Bristol-Myers Squibb Co v FH Faulding & Co Ltd* (2000) 97 FCR 524, [66].
341 See ch 12 at 12.4 and 12.5.
342 *Minnesota Mining & Manufacturing Co v Beiersdorf (Australia) Ltd* (1980) 144 CLR 253, 298; *Ramset Fasteners (Australia) Pty Ltd v Advanced Building Systems Pty Ltd* (1999) 44 IPR 481; *Hill v Evans* (1862) 4 De GF & J 288, 301; *JMVB Enterprises Pty Ltd v Camoflag Pty Ltd* (2005) 67 IPR 68, [55]; *Stanway Oyster Cylinders Pty Ltd v Marks* (1996) 66 FCR 577, 581.

the reverse infringement test should not be applied 'by simply asking whether something within the prior art document would, if carried out after the grant of the patent, infringe the invention as claimed'. It must be shown that the specification contains 'a clear description of, or clear instructions to do or make, something that would infringe the patentee's claim if carried out after the grant of the patentee's patent'.[343] This may be more difficult to establish when the prior art documents are not patent specifications but ultimately these are questions of fact. Although reports of results of medical research and trials were found not to anticipate the claimed invention in *Bristol-Myers Squibb Co v FH Faulding & Co Ltd*,[344] the Full Federal Court in *Merck & Co Inc v Arrow Pharmaceuticals Ltd* found that details of a 'simple method' – oral administration of a known drug at a specified dosage over a specified period – were conveyed in a news article. Evidence from a medical witness that he would not have followed the suggestion contained in that article for fear of side effects did not mean that the disclosure itself did not anticipate the claimed invention.[345]

An earlier classic novelty principle arises from the following passage in *Hill v Evans*:

> [T]he antecedent statement must be such that a person of ordinary knowledge of the subject would at once perceive, understand, and be able practically to apply the discovery without the necessity of making further experiments and gaining further information before the invention can be made useful ... [T]he information as to the alleged invention given by the prior publication must, for the purposes of practical utility, be equal to that given by the subsequent patent. The invention must be shewn to have been before made known. Whatever, therefore, is essential to the invention must be read out of the prior publication.[346]

The reference to 'experiments'[347] has confused matters somewhat, but it is clearly limited to experiments performed with a view to discovering something not disclosed.[348] It does not include experiments that form part of standard procedure or common general knowledge and ordinary methods of trial and error.[349] A disclosure of all essential elements of the invention may anticipate the invention despite the presence of the words 'needs to be tested' in the prior art document. As the court in *Merck* observed in the case of pharmaceutical patents, 'it is a matter of notoriety that prolonged testing for the purpose of regulatory approval must occur between the stage of patent application and commercial marketing'.[350] The scope of acceptable experimentation is limited by the overall requirement that 'whatever is essential to the

---

343 *AstraZeneca AB v Apotex Pty Ltd* (2014) 226 FCR 324 (FC), [299]–[301], citing and approving *Bristol-Myers Squibb Co v FH Faulding & Co Ltd* (2000) 97 FCR 524, [67].
344 *Novozymes A/S v Danisco A/S* (2013) 99 IPR 417, [107] noting this distinction in respect of *Bristol-Myers Squibb Co v FH Faulding & Co Ltd* (2000) 97 FCR 524, [67].
345 *Merck & Co Inc v Arrow Pharmaceuticals Ltd* (2006) 154 FCR 31, [110]–[112].
346 (1862) 4 De GF & J 288, 301.
347 Ibid 300.
348 *Nicaro Holdings Pty Ltd v Martin Engineering Co* (1990) 16 IPR 545, 549 (Gummow J); *C Van der Lely NV v Bamfords Ltd* [1963] RPC 61, 71–7; *H Lundbeck A/S v Alphapharm Pty Ltd* (2009) 177 FCR 151, [173] (Bennett J, Middleton J agreeing).
349 *H Lundbeck A/S v Alphapharm Pty Ltd* (2009) 177 FCR 151, [173], citing *C Van der Lely NV v Bamfords Ltd* [1963] RPC 61, 71–7.
350 *Merck & Co Inc v Arrow Pharmaceuticals Ltd* (2006) 154 FCR 31, [108].

invention must be read out of the prior publication'.[351] As Giles J remarked in *Apotex v Sanofi-Aventis*, '[a]nticipation is deadly but requires the accuracy of a sniper, not the firing of a 12 gauge shotgun'.[352] In the case of chemical patents, a prior disclosure of a large class of compounds, of which the patented subject matter is but one compound, is not an anticipatory disclosure.[353] This contrasts with the naming of a specific compound in the prior art.[354]

10.6.8.2 Anticipation through prior use

It is not enough to tell a person the 'broad generalities' of the invention if this fails to disclose or make it possible for the person to glean the essential integers.[355] In the case of the composition or internal structure of a product, it may be sufficient disclosure if it is possible for the skilled person to 'discover it and reproduce it without undue burden'.[356] It may be sufficient if the skilled addressee could use available techniques to analyse samples of a product and glean the necessary information,[357] or for a person to have the unrestrained opportunity to reverse-engineer a product to ascertain the information that will render an invention not novel. The demonstration of a video graphics system without supply of the program or oral disclosure of the program would not be sufficient.[358]

On the other hand, it seems there will be no sufficient disclosure if a product is sold in circumstances that render it impossible for any member of the public to ascertain all the essential features of the invention. This could occur when a car is driven on a public road without stopping to allow a member of the public to lift the bonnet and inspect the engine.[359] It could also occur in the kind of circumstances that existed in *Bristol-Myers Co v Beecham Group Ltd*,[360] a case that was concerned with whether the prior use by the patentee was a ground for refusing the patent application. The facts involved the unintentional manufacture of ampicillin trihydrate that was blended with other forms of ampicillin, and the sale of capsules made from the blend. No-one knew that the batch contained the trihydrate form; nor could anyone have extracted it from the batch. A majority in the House of Lords found this to have constituted a prior use of the invention, intention to use being irrelevant. However, this would not amount to anticipation under the *Patents Act 1990* (Cth) because the essential integers of the invention are not made publicly available. No-one is given the relevant information; nor could they glean it from the product that was sold.[361]

---

351 *Hill v Evans* (1862) 4 De GF & J 288, 300; *Acme Bedstead Co Ltd v Newlands Brothers Ltd* (1937) 58 CLR 689, 707.
352 *Apotex Pty Ltd (formerly GenRx Pty Ltd) v Sanofi-Aventis* (2008) 78 IPR 485, 525 [91].
353 *Dr Reddy's Laboratories (UK) Ltd v Eli Lilly & Co Ltd* [2010] RPC 9, [26], [28]; *AstraZeneca AB v Apotex Pty Ltd* (2014) 226 FCR 324 (FC), [285]–[286].
354 *H Lundbeck A/S v Alphapharm Pty Ltd* (2009) 177 FCR 151, [193]–[194]; *Apotex Pty Ltd v Sanofi-Aventis* (2009) 82 IPR 416, [106].
355 *Costa v GR & IE Daking Pty Ltd* (1994) 29 IPR 241, 248.
356 *Jupiters Ltd v Neurizon Pty Ltd* (2005) 65 IPR 86, [142]; *Merrell Dow Pharmaceuticals Inc v HN Norton & Co Ltd* (1995) 33 IPR 1, 11.
357 *PLG Research Ltd v Ardon International Ltd (No 2)* [1993] FSR 197, 226–7; *Jupiters Ltd v Neurizon Pty Ltd* (2005) 65 IPR 86, [141]; *Lux Traffic Controls Ltd v Pike Signals Ltd* [1993] RPC 107.
358 *Quantel Ltd v Spaceward Microsystems Ltd* [1990] RPC 83, 126; *Jupiters Ltd v Neurizon Pty Ltd* (2005) 65 IPR 86, [140].
359 *Boyce v Morris Motors Ltd* (1927) 44 RPC 105, 149.
360 [1974] AC 646.
361 *Merrell Dow Pharmaceuticals Inc v HN Norton & Co Ltd* (1995) 33 IPR 1, 11.

10.6.8.3 Implicit disclosure and inevitable outcome

Clearly there will be anticipation when the relevant prior art information discloses exactly what is claimed.[362] However, as the prior art information is evaluated through the eyes of the skilled addressee, something less than an exact disclosure can also amount to anticipation,[363] provided that all the essential integers can be read out of that prior art information. This might arise through: (a) an implicit disclosure to the skilled addressee from the language as construed; or (b) from following instructions set out in the specification (inevitable disclosure). While an implicit disclosure may amount to anticipation, there are limits on its application, as the passage from *Hill v Evans* above demonstrates: 'the notion of implicit disclosure is confined to what is in fact disclosed by the prior art document'.[364] The issue of claim construction is paramount here – although the skilled addressee construes a specification in light of common general knowledge, this involves a limited use of that knowledge. As the Full Court in *AstraZeneca* emphasised

> s 7(1) does not permit the common general knowledge to be used as a resource that can be deployed complementarily to arrive at a disclosure which the document alone, properly construed, does not make. If it were otherwise, the separate requirement of an inventive step to support a patentable invention ... would be otiose.[365]

The case of *Novozymes A/S v Danisco A/S*[366] demonstrates the distinction between an implicit disclosure of essential integers on the one hand and a disclosure that arises as the inevitable outcome of following instructions on the other. It confirms that anticipation can be established using either approach but not a combination of both. The invention was a process for preparing a food product for consumption, such as bread, that is to contain an emulsifier[367] and a second functional ingredient, such as a preservative. Instead of adding the emulsifier and colouring as ingredients, the patented process generated both the emulsifier and the preservative through the action of an added enzyme. The heat of baking would then denature the enzyme so that it was no longer active and would not need to be declared on the list of the foodstuff ingredients in the loaf of bread.

One item of prior art was an international patent application, published a month before the priority date of the relevant claims (the Novo patent). Novozymes relied on the Novo patent as disclosing the invention in claim 1 to the skilled addressee with reference to her understanding of the prior art, or alternatively on the basis of *General Tire*, as the inevitable outcome of following a method of baking (example 20) contained in the Novo patent.[368] It failed on both counts. First, the Novo patent did not disclose explicitly or implicitly that a second functional ingredient, such as a preservative, was to be generated by the addition of the enzyme in the bread-making process.[369] Second, the *General Tire* approach was of no assistance because

---

362   *H Lundbeck A/S v Alphapharm Pty Ltd* (2009) 177 FCR 151, [180] (Bennett J, Middleton J agreeing).
363   Ibid [180]–[181]; *Nicaro Holdings Pty Ltd v Martin Engineering Co* (1990) 16 IPR 545.
364   *AstraZeneca AB v Apotex Pty Ltd* (2014) 226 FCR 324 (FC), [350].
365   Ibid [352].
366   (2013) 99 IPR 417.
367   An ingredient that is responsible for the softening or anti-staling effect in bread.
368   *Novozymes A/S v Danisco A/S* (2013) 99 IPR 417, [129] (Jessup J, Greenwood and Yates JJ agreeing).
369   Ibid [143].

following the baking method would not inevitably disclose that the enzyme would be denatured in the commercial baking process.

Although the Novo patent did not explicitly disclose the denaturing of the enzyme, the skilled addressee would have had an implicit understanding of this matter from the Novo specification. Therefore, Jessup J asked the question whether a complete case on anticipation can be made by 'reference to express and implicit disclosure for some integers and inevitable outcome for others'.[370] In answering this question as 'no', he concluded that if the *General Tire* approach is taken, it

> may be taken only with respect to the whole of any claim asserted to be anticipated. The 'precise destination' at which the flag must have been planted is one which includes every integer of the claim. The approach cannot, in my view, be taken for some integers only, leaving others to be dealt with by reference to the understanding of the skilled addressee. … It is necessary that they show that, if Example 20 were worked as directed, it would inevitably, as a matter of hard fact, have involved inactivation of the enzyme (to the standard set up under claims 1 and 7 of the patent in suit as identified by the primary Judge) at the baking stage.[371]

The fact that there was no practical ability for a person to carry out those instructions in practice before the priority date, due to the brief period between publication of the Novo patent and the priority date, was not relevant to an evaluation of novelty in s 7(1). The court noted that the *General Tire* test must be 'accommodated to the terms of s 7(1) of the Patents Act, upon which everything depends'.[372] Hence

> the inevitability of outcome to which *General Tire* refers must be such as would arise from recourse to the *information* referred to in the section. … It is not the doing of it, nor even the ability to do it, that amounts to anticipation: it is the content of the information. If the information contains directions which, *if* carried out, *would* constitute an infringement of the patent in suit, the invention under the latter is not novel. … the appellants' *General Tire* case was not compromised by the practical difficulties which would have confronted the skilled addressee putting Example 20 of the Novo patent into effect before the priority date of the patent in suit.[373]

Examples of where anticipation may occur in the apparent absence of all explicit details include these circumstances:

- The claim as properly construed[374] shows the variation to be an inessential integer.[375]
- The skilled addressee would find the information implicit in what is disclosed in the prior art document.[376]

---

370 Ibid [186].
371 Ibid [187].
372 Ibid [177].
373 Ibid [177]–[178].
374 See ch 12 at 12.2.
375 *Ramset Fasteners (Australia) Pty Ltd v Advanced Building Systems Pty Ltd* (1999) 44 IPR 481, [24]; *Grove Hill Pty Ltd v Great Western Corp Pty Ltd* (2002) 55 IPR 257, [253].
376 *C Van der Lely NV v Bamfords Ltd* [1963] RPC 61, 71–7 (Lord Reid); *Ramset Fasteners (Australia) Pty Ltd v Advanced Building Systems Pty Ltd* (1999) 44 IPR 481, [23]; *AstraZeneca AB v Apotex Pty Ltd* (2014) 226 FCR 324 (FC), [350].

- A direction, recommendation or suggestion is implicit in what is described.[377] However, there would be no anticipation if pursuit of those directions requires the exercise of inventive ingenuity or the taking of any inventive step.[378]

10.6.9 Prohibition on 'mosaics'

A prior publication must disclose the whole invention to constitute anticipation. Hence, as a general principle, it is not permissible to make a mosaic for the purposes of a novelty assessment.[379]

The rationale for this prohibition resides in access to a worldwide prior art base that includes all the records of past failure and the ease of finding anything with the benefit of hindsight.[380] The concept of a prohibited mosaic is different from allowing the claim to be read through the eyes of the skilled person, although as the Full Federal Court emphasised in *AstraZeneca*

> s 7(1) does not permit the common general knowledge to be used as a resource that can be deployed complementarily to arrive at a disclosure which the document alone, properly construed, does not make.[381]

However, s 7(1)(b) provides some limited scope for considering the combination of two or more pieces of prior art information as a single source. It permits two or more related documents or two or more related acts to be considered as a single source of information when the relationship between them is such that a person skilled in the relevant art would treat them as a single source of information. It is not possible to combine a document with an act to obtain a single source of information for novelty assessment. As the common law allowed limited situations where two or more documents could be considered as a single source of information for the purposes of a novelty assessment, it offers some guidance as to the meaning of 'related' documents and 'single source' in s 7(1)(b) of the *Patents Act 1990* (Cth). At common law, some connection was necessary between two or more documents, but the degree was a question of fact in each case. The assessment would depend on the nature of the art in which the skilled addressee is to be treated as versed at the priority date.[382] At one end of a continuum the connection will be clear, as when a patentee makes it clear in the specification that they relied on particular named patents.[383] In this case, the documents clearly form one consistent whole. At the other end of the continuum is a description of the

---

377 *Bristol-Myers Squibb Co v FH Faulding & Co Ltd* (2000) 97 FCR 524, [67]; *H Lundbeck A/S v Alphapharm Pty Ltd* (2009) 177 FCR 151, [173].
378 *Nicaro Holdings Pty Ltd v Martin Engineering Co* (1990) 16 IPR 545, 563 (Gummow J).
379 *Minnesota Mining & Manufacturing Co v Beiersdorf (Australia) Ltd* (1980) 144 CLR 253, 292–3; *Nicaro Holdings Pty Ltd v Martin Engineering Co* (1990) 16 IPR 545, 549 (Lockhart J), 558, 565–73 (Gummow J).
380 *British Ore Concentration Syndicate Ltd v Minerals Separation Ltd* (1909) 26 RPC 124, 147 (Fletcher-Moulton LJ); *Acme Bedstead Co Ltd v Newlands Brothers Ltd* (1937) 58 CLR 689, 703–4 (Starke J).
381 *AstraZeneca AB v Apotex Pty Ltd* (2014) 226 FCR 324 (FC), [352].
382 *Nicaro Holdings Pty Ltd v Martin Engineering Co* (1990) 16 IPR 545, 570 (Gummow J); *Sharp & Dohme Inc v Boots Pure Drug Co Ltd* (1927) 44 RPC 367.
383 *Nicaro Holdings Pty Ltd v Martin Engineering Co* (1990) 16 IPR 545, 571 (Gummow J).

prior publication for the purpose of directing or teaching the reader away from it, dismissing it or as disclosing something outmoded or defective.[384] A mere identification of prior art in a schedule of a specification, such as an entry under a heading 'References cited',[385] is probably also insufficient. Something more may be necessary, such as making it clear that the incorporation by reference 'unequivocally and plainly demonstrates that the draftsman has adopted the cross-referencing system solely as a shorthand means of incorporating a writing disclosing the invention'.[386]

Two or more related acts can form a consistent whole for the purposes of s 7(1)(b). For example, in *Aspirating IP Ltd v Vision Systems Ltd*,[387] Dr Cole publicly disclosed the invention during presentations to industry groups and prospective purchasers of the claimed smoke detection system by showing photographs together with an oral explanation of all the essential features of the system.

10.6.10 Making information available in certain circumstances: disclosure with consent

Section 24(1) of the *Patents Act 1990* (Cth) provides that a person making a decision as to novelty or inventive or innovative step must disregard certain types of information made publicly available by or with the consent of the patentee in circumstances prescribed in the regulations. The section is not limited to information that is publicly available before the priority date but can also be relied on to overcome a 'whole of contents' objection to novelty.[388] Until 15 April 2013, s 24(1) provided that the person making the decision must disregard any information made publicly available, *through any publication or use of the invention*. The problem with these italicised words is that they

> could be taken only to apply to information that could deprive an invention of novelty, not to information that could deprive an invention of an inventive or innovative step. For example, the grace period would not apply in a circumstance where the patentee disclosed the work they had done, or a prototype that led directly to their invention.[389]

This problem was addressed under the *Raising the Bar Act* – the words 'through any publication or use of the invention' in s 24(1) were replaced with a reference only to 'information made publicly available'.

Until 15 April 2013, s 24(1) required a person to file a 'patent application' – construed as *either a provisional or complete application* – within the relevant prescribed

---

384   Ibid 571–2.
385   Ibid 572.
386   Ibid 549 (Lockhart J). Examples of this occurring are *Merck & Co Inc v Arrow Pharmaceuticals Ltd* (2006) 154 FCR 31, [34], [39], [62]; *Apotex Pty Ltd v Sanofi-Aventis* (2009) 82 IPR 416, [192]; *Apotex Pty Ltd (formerly GenRx Pty Ltd) v Sanofi-Aventis* (2008) 78 IPR 485, [121]; *AstraZeneca AB v Apotex Pty Ltd* (2014) 226 FCR 324 (FC), [389].
387   (2010) 88 IPR 52, [287]–[288].
388   *Biogen Idec MA Inc* [2014] APO 25.
389   Explanatory Memorandum, Intellectual Property Laws Amendment (Raising the Bar) Bill 2011 (Cth) sch 6 item 32. Two decisions of the Australian Patent Office construed these words widely and not limited to novelty disclosures of the *same* invention: *Merial New Zealand Ltd v Jurox Pty Ltd* [2016] APO 63, [60]–[64]; *Novozymes North America, Inc v DSM IP Assets BV* [2018] APO 37, [62]–[64].

period.[390] This requirement applied to three prescribed circumstances of disclosure set out in reg 2.2: publication or use of the invention at a recognised exhibition, publication before a learned society, and working the invention for the purposes of reasonable trial. In contrast, a *complete application* was required when the prescribed circumstance was the general grace period provided at that time in reg 2.2(1A). An amendment to s 24(1) now provides that the protection from a prior disclosure arising in any of the prescribed circumstances, including the general grace period, is available only if a *complete application* is filed within a prescribed period.[391]

The following sections describe the circumstances prescribed in the *Patents Regulations 1991* (Cth) for the purposes of s 24(1)(a) and their operation both before and from 15 April 2013.[392] While the form of the current regulations differs, the specific treatment of disclosures associated with international exhibitions, learned societies and the public working of the invention remain unchanged. Therefore, the following discussion refers to the current regulations.

10.6.10.1 Showing, use and publication at recognised exhibition

The prescribed circumstance in reg 2.2 is that the information has been made publicly available because the invention was shown or used at a recognised exhibition or published during the exhibition at which the invention was shown or used.[393] A recognised exhibition is an official or officially recognised international exhibition within the meaning of art 11 of the *Paris Convention*[394] or art 1 of the *Convention Relating to International Exhibitions*.[395] It may also be an international exhibition recognised by the Commissioner by a notice published in the *Official Journal* before the beginning of the exhibition.

The prescribed period for filing a complete application on or after 15 April 2013 is twelve months from the day of showing, use or publication. If priority is claimed from a basic application or provisional application that is made within six months of the day of the showing, use or publication, then the complete application must be filed twelve months from the day the basic or provisional application is made. For instance, X shows an invention at an exhibition on 1 July 2014 and files a provisional application on 10 December 2014. X has twelve months from 10 December 2014 in which to file the complete application. In contrast, if no

---

390 *NSI Dental Pty Ltd v University of Melbourne* (2006) 69 IPR 542, [125]; *Mack Innovations (Australia) Pty Ltd v Rotorco Pty Ltd* [2011] 2 Qd R 217, [15] (McMurdo J).
391 The amended s 24(1) and regulations apply to information that is made publicly available on or after 15 April 2013. The former provisions continue to apply to information made publicly available on or before 14 April 2013.
392 *Intellectual Property Legislation Amendment (Raising the Bar) Regulation 2013 (No 1)* (Cth) sch 6 item 7.
393 *Patents Regulations 1991* (Cth) reg 2.2; pre-15 April 2013: reg 2.2(2)(a), (b).
394 *Paris Convention for the Protection of Industrial Property*, opened for signature 14 July 1967, WIPO Lex No TRT/PARIS/001 (as amended 28 September 1979, entered into force 3 June 1984), as in force for Australia on the commencing day of the *Patents Regulations 1991* (Cth).
395 Opened for signature 22 November 1928 (as amended 16 November 1966, entered into force for Australia 6 September 1976), as in force in Australia on the commencing day of the *Patents Regulations 1991* (Cth).

provisional application had been made, the complete application must be filed twelve months from 1 July 2014.[396]

The prescribed period for filing a provisional or complete application before 15 April 2013 was six months after the first showing or use. If priority was claimed from a basic application, then the complete application must be filed twelve months from making the basic application.[397] For instance, X shows an invention at an exhibition on 1 July 2014 and files a basic application on 10 December 2014. X has twelve months from 10 December 2014 in which to file the complete application. In contrast, if no basic application had been made, the complete application must be filed *six* months from 1 July 2014. Before 15 April 2013, because a provisional or complete application was required within the prescribed period, a further twelve-month period would be available if a provisional application associated with the complete application was filed in the prescribed period.[398]

10.6.10.2 Publication before learned society

The prescribed circumstance in reg 2.2A is information made publicly available in a paper read before a learned society or published by or on behalf of a learned society.[399] The requirement for a 'written' paper in the pre-15 April 2013 version of reg 2.2(2)(c) has been removed from the current reg 2.2A. A broad meaning of 'read' is likely so that it would include an oral explanation of the contents of the paper with reference to that paper.[400] An oral disclosure without contemporaneous or subsequent publication of any written paper by or on behalf of the society would not have the benefit of this exemption, although such a disclosure may benefit from the general grace period that is discussed below.

There is no definition of 'learned society', but a decision of the United Kingdom Patent Office (now the United Kingdom Intellectual Property Office) in *Ralph M Parsons Co (Beavon's) Application* provides guidance as to the potential scope of the description 'learned':

> [I]t may follow that the epithet 'learned' is apt to be applied to any properly constituted society made up of persons seeking to promote and organise the study of specific subjects by the provision of a forum for discussion and a means of contact for those of a common interest.[401]

However, failure to publish records of its proceedings was regarded as a contradiction for a learned society. The United Kingdom Patent Office also regarded with suspicion factors such as exclusion of academics from membership and involvement in commercial exploitation.[402] The publication of any such paper must be by, or on behalf of, the learned society. This would not include the situation where journalists obtain a copy of the paper with permission of the inventor and publish the information independently of and without authorisation of the society.[403]

---

396   *Patents Regulations 1991* (Cth) reg 2.2(3).
397   Ibid reg 2.3(1)(a).
398   *Patents Act 1990* (Cth) s 38(1); *Patents Regulations 1991* (Cth) reg 3.10.
399   *Patents Regulations 1991* (Cth) reg 2.2A(2).
400   *Ralph M Parsons Co (Beavon's) Application* [1978] FSR 226.
401   Ibid 231.
402   Ibid 232.
403   Ibid.

The hearing officer in *Caterpillar Inc v Kozo Miyake*[404] found that the Institute of Electrical and Electronics Engineers (IEEE) was a learned society. Assistance might also be drawn from reference to learned societies in cases other than patent cases.[405] For instance, in *David McNicol v Australian Capital Territory Health Authority*, Kelly J listed a number of what he referred to as 'learned societies', including the Royal Australian College of Surgeons and the Australian Orthopaedic Association.[406]

The prescribed period for filing a complete application on or after 15 April 2013 is twelve months from the day of the reading or publication. If priority is claimed from a basic application or provisional application that is made within six months of the day of the reading or publication, then the complete application must be filed twelve months from the day the basic or provisional application is made. For instance, X discloses the invention on 1 July 2014 and files a provisional application on 10 December 2014. X has twelve months from 10 December 2014 in which to file the complete application. In contrast, if no provisional application had been made, the complete application must be filed twelve months from 1 July 2014.[407]

The prescribed period for filing a provisional or complete application before 15 April 2013 was six months after the first reading or publication. If priority was claimed from a basic application made within six months of the date of the first reading or publication, then the complete application must be filed twelve months from making the basic application.[408] For instance, X discloses the invention on 1 July 2014 and files a basic application on 10 December 2014. X has twelve months from 10 December 2014 in which to file the complete application. In contrast, if no basic application had been made, the complete application must be filed *six* months from 1 July 2014. Before 15 April 2013, because a provisional or complete application was required within the prescribed period, a further twelve-month period would be available if a provisional application associated with the complete application was filed in the prescribed period.[409]

10.6.10.3 Working the invention in public for purposes of reasonable trial

The prescribed circumstance in reg 2.2B of the *Patents Regulations 1991* (Cth) is:

> (a) the information has been made publicly available because the invention was worked in public; and
> (b) the working ... was for the purposes of a reasonable trial of the invention; and
> (c) because of the nature of the invention, it was reasonably necessary for the working to be in public.

This provision effectively codifies the common law as it had developed under the *Patents Act 1952* (Cth).[410] The judgment in *Longworth v Emerton*[411] provides some examples of inventions

---

404 [2000] APO 3.
405 *APO Manual*, above n 57, [2.4.4.6.2].
406 [1988] ACTSC 55, [10]–[11].
407 *Patents Regulations 1991* (Cth) reg 2.2A(3).
408 Ibid reg 2.3(1)(b).
409 *Patents Act 1990* (Cth) s 38(1); *Patents Regulations 1991* (Cth) reg 3.10.
410 *Patents Act 1903* (Cth) s 124 (exhibited or tested either publicly or privately: *Longworth v Emerton* (1951) 83 CLR 539); *Patents Act 1952* (Cth) s 100(3)(a) (for the purpose of reasonable trial or experiment only); *Patents Act 1949* (UK) s 51(3) (working was effected for the purpose of reasonable trial only).
411 (1951) 83 CLR 539.

whose nature may require working in public for trial purposes. The first is the invention that must be transported to another location for testing, in the course of which some public exposure is unavoidable. This occurred in *Re Newall and Elliot*.[412] The plaintiff obtained a contract to lay cable in the Black Sea. He had been unable to test his invention for a device for use in laying submarine telegraph cables on land. His decision to test its operation in the Black Sea involved unavoidable disclosure to the public, both in the course of transportation and in operation. The court found this was not a prior public use that would destroy the novelty of the invention.

A second example is the trial of an anchor, a thing not easily made the subject of secret testing.[413] A third example is assorted farm machinery.[414] Not only must the invention be one that necessarily requires public testing, but the working must be for purposes of reasonable trial.[415] One view construes this phrase as requiring a trial that is reasonably necessary to develop a suitable invention for a patent application.[416] This requires some deliberate intention to use the invention with a view to making definite improvements, conducting experiments of a specific character, or developing the actual invention. It is insufficient to have some vague sense of dissatisfaction that the machine's qualities had been fully tested, or uncertainty as to whether some further improvements might increase efficiency. Hence, wide and unguarded use of the invention with no specific purpose for testing or experiment will fail the test.[417] In contrast, working a prototype of a machine that did not function for a period during which numerous changes are made may be a trial or experimental use.[418] The degree of public working that is reasonably necessary will be a question of fact in each case. For example, features of the dimension, strength or rigidity of the components of a gymnastics system to be installed in a school may require a longer period to test than features of assembly and dismantling.[419]

A number of cases have considered whether a prior secret use amounts to a 'reasonable trial and experiment' within s 9(a) of the *Patents Act 1990* (Cth). Some of the observations raised in that context may be useful for purposes of analogy, in view of scant authority on reg 2.2(2)(d) and its recent successor, reg 2.2B.[420]

The prescribed period for filing a complete application on or after 15 April 2013 is from the start of the public working of the invention. If priority is claimed from a basic application or provisional application that is made within twelve months of the start of the public working of

---

412 (1858) 4 CB (NS) 269, 140 ER 1087.
413 *Honiball v Bloomer* (1854) 10 Exch 538.
414 *Longworth v Emerton* (1951) 83 CLR 539.
415 *Austoft Industries Ltd v Cameco Industries Inc* (1995) 33 IPR 251 (no working for reasonable trial); *APO Manual*, above n 57, [2.4.4.6.5].
416 *Longworth v Emerton* (1951) 83 CLR 539, 550–1; *Perard Engineering Ltd (Hubbard's) Application* [1976] 14 RPC 363, 370 (Whitford J).
417 *Longworth v Emerton* (1951) 83 CLR 539, 550; *Cave-Brown-Cave's Application for a Patent* [1958] RPC 429.
418 *Costa v GR & IE Daking Pty Ltd* (1994) 29 IPR 241, 250.
419 *Cave-Brown- Cave's Application for a Patent* [1958] RPC 429; *Perard Engineering Ltd (Hubbard's) Application* [1976] 14 RPC 363, 371 (trial of apparatus in a coal mining operation).
420 For example, *Grove Hill Pty Ltd v Great Western Corp Pty Ltd* (2002) 55 IPR 257, [222]–[233]; *DSI Australia (Holdings) Pty Ltd v Garford Pty Ltd* (2013) 100 IPR 19, [174] (Yates J), affirmed *Garford Pty Ltd v DYWIDAG-Systems International Pty Ltd* (2015) 110 IPR 30.

the invention, then the complete application must be filed twelve months from the day the basic or provisional application is made. For instance, X disclosed the invention on 1 July 2014 and files a provisional application on 30 June 2015. X has twelve months from 30 June 2015 in which to file the complete application. In contrast, if no provisional application had been made, the complete application must be filed twelve months from 1 July 2014.[421]

The prescribed period for filing a provisional or complete application before 15 April 2013 was twelve months from the start of the first public working of the invention.[422] For instance, if X disclosed the invention on 1 July 2014, X must file a complete or provisional application twelve months from the start of the first public working of the invention.[423]

10.6.10.4 General grace period

The prescribed circumstance in reg 2.2C is information made publicly available in circumstances that do not come within the above disclosures associated with international exhibitions, learned societies and the public working of the invention. The period for making a complete application for the invention is twelve months from the day the information was made publicly available.

A twelve-month grace period for patents was introduced as reg 2.2(1A) on 1 April 2002 as a Backing Australia's Ability[424] initiative. The principal reason for its introduction was to provide protection against 'inadvertent disclosures'.[425] It applied to information made publicly available through a publication or use of the invention on or after 1 April 2002,[426] and within twelve months before the filing date of the complete application.[427] Hence, the maximum period after the public disclosure in which to file the complete application is twelve months. In the case of a divisional application, the phrase 'the filing date of the complete application' refers to the parent application and not the divisional application.[428] However, the reference to a 'patent application for the invention' in s 24(1) has been held not to include foreign applications because the 'patent application' is defined in s 3(1) and sch 1 to mean 'an application for a standard patent or innovation patent. In the context of the Act as a whole, these are Australian patents'.[429]

Prior to the *Raising the Bar* reforms, the general grace period overlapped with all the specific activities that are discussed above, but the filing requirements differed because a person could file either a provisional or a complete application in the prescribed period with respect to those activities. For example, if the invention was worked in public for the purposes

---

421 *Patents Regulations 1991* (Cth) reg 2.2B(3).
422 Ibid reg 2.3(1)(c).
423 *Patents Act 1990* (Cth) s 38(1); *Patents Regulations 1991* (Cth) reg 3.10.
424 Department of Industry, Science and Resources, *Backing Australia's Ability: An Innovation Action Plan for the Future* (2001). A review of the general grace period in August 2005 recommended that no changes to the grace period provisions were required at that stage: IP Australia, *Review of the Patent Grace Period* (Report, August 2005). Changes to its operation were introduced in the *Raising the Bar* reforms.
425 A. L. Monotti, 'The impact of the new grace period under Australian patent law on universities' [2002] 24 *European Intellectual Property Review* 475.
426 *Patents Regulations 1991* (Cth) reg 2.2(1A).
427 Ibid reg 2.3(1A).
428 Ibid reg 2.3; *Mont Adventure Equipment Pty Ltd v Phoenix Leisure Group Pty Ltd* (2009) 175 FCR 575.
429 *Apotex Pty Ltd v AstraZeneca AB (No 4)* (2013) 100 IPR 285, [371] (Jagot J).

of reasonable trial,[430] the applicant had twelve months in which to file the provisional specification and another twelve months in which to file the complete application.[431] The general grace period would give only twelve months in which to file the complete application. This inconsistency was removed by an amendment to s 24(1) that specified the filing of a complete patent application.[432]

10.6.11 Making information available in certain circumstances: non-consensual disclosure

The person making the decision on novelty must disregard information made publicly available without the consent of the nominated person or patentee by a person who derived the information from the nominated person or patentee or from a predecessor in title of either.[433] Therefore, if the inventor X tells his friend Y about the invention, Y's public disclosure of the information before the priority date and without X's permission will be disregarded. An assignee of X's rights in the invention also has the benefit of this section. Giving a paper to journalists at a conference will imply consent to publication.[434]

For information that is made publicly available on or after 15 April 2015, the prior publication is disregarded only if a complete patent application is made within twelve months from the day when the information became publicly available.[435] For public disclosures before 15 April 2013, the reference to a patent application for the invention meant that a provisional or complete application could be filed.[436] Therefore, filing the complete application could be delayed for up to two years after the public disclosure.[437]

Other information to be disregarded in deciding whether an invention is novel is that which is given by or with the consent of the patentee, their nominated person, or predecessor in title[438] to:

- the Commonwealth or a state or territory, or an authority of any of these;
- a person authorised by the Commonwealth or a state or territory to investigate the invention.[439] Anything done for the purpose of such an investigation of the invention is also to be disregarded.[440]

The section is not limited to information that is publicly available before the priority date but can also be relied on to overcome a 'whole of contents' objection to novelty.[441]

---

430 *Patents Regulations 1991* (Cth) reg 2.2(2)(d).
431 *Patents Act 1990* (Cth) s 38(1); *Patents Regulations 1991* (Cth) reg 3.10.
432 *Intellectual Property Laws Amendment (Raising the Bar) Act 2012* (Cth) sch 6 item 33.
433 *Patents Act 1990* (Cth) s 24(1)(b).
434 *Ralph M Parsons Co (Beavon's) Application* [1978] FSR 226.
435 *Patents Regulations 1991* (Cth) regs 2.2D, 2.3(2).
436 *NSI Dental Pty Ltd v University of Melbourne* (2006) 69 IPR 542, [125]; *Patents Regulations 1991* (Cth) reg 2.3(2).
437 *Patents Act 1990* (Cth) s 38(1); *Patents Regulations 1991* (Cth) reg 3.10.
438 *Patents Act 1990* (Cth) s 24(2).
439 Ibid s 24(2)(a).
440 Ibid s 24(2)(b).
441 *Biogen Idec MA Inc* [2014] APO 25.

10.6.12 Novelty by way of selection

One form of inventive activity involves trawling through a class of products known to possess certain common features to discover an unpredictable sub-class that is found to possess some special advantage for a particular purpose.[442] It is this discovery, which includes the identification of the characteristics of the sub-class, that amounts to an inventive step.[443] However, there would be little incentive to conduct research of this nature if the prior public disclosure of the sub-class within the wider class could destroy the novelty of any invention. As Crennan J remarked in *Imperial Chemical Industries Pty Ltd v Commissioner of Patents*, the application of the usual novelty principles

> could lead to a finding of a want of novelty based on the disclosure of a whole flag locker without any teaching (ie, disclosure for novelty purposes) of a particular flag. Such an approach in these circumstances might leave little room for patents of addition and selection patents.[444]

A body of law for what are referred to as 'selection patents' developed in the United Kingdom in the context of chemical patents to deal with this issue.[445] Selection patents are not a sui generis category of patents.[446] Although their existence under Australian law has been questioned, the principles have been applied or acknowledged in decisions of both the Australian Patent Office and the Federal Court.[447] As Gyles J remarked in *Apotex Pty Ltd (formerly GenRx Pty Ltd) v Sanofi-Aventis*:

> It seems to me that it is too late in the day to find that the principles explained by Maugham J in *Re IG Farbenindustrie* are not relevant to the question of anticipation under the 1952 Act (and the 1990 Act, for that matter). That is not to recognise a special class of patents – the reference to a selection patent is a convenient shorthand to pick up the relevant principles concerning anticipation.[448]

---

442 *IG Farbenindustrie AG's Patents* (1930) 47 RPC 289, 322–3; *Eli Lilly & Co Ltd v Apotex Pty Ltd* (2013) 100 IPR 451, [375] (Middleton J); *Imperial Chemicals Industries Pty Ltd v Commissioner of Patents* (2004) 213 ALR 399, [66] (Crennan J).
443 *Re Institut Francais du Petrole des Carburants et Lubricants' Application* [1972] FSR 147, 154 (Whitford J). This could not be predicted before the discovery was made: see *IG Farbenindustrie AG's Patents* (1930) 47 RPC 289, 322–3 (Maugham J); *Pfizer Inc v Commissioner of Patents* (2005) 141 FCR 413, [10]–[11]; *Beecham Group Ltd v Bristol Laboratories International SA* [1978] RPC 521, 579.
444 (2004) 213 ALR 399, [66].
445 *IG Farbenindustrie AG's Patents* (1930) 47 RPC 289, 322–3. However, as a member of the European Patent Convention, the Court of Appeal decided to follow decisions of the European Patent Office Boards of Appeal, observing that the 'IG' rules are to be seen as 'part of legal history, not as part of the living law': see *Dr Reddy's Laboratories (UK) Ltd v Eli Lilly & Co Ltd* [2010] RPC 9, [37], [92]–[93].
446 *Eli Lilly & Co Ltd v Apotex Pty Ltd* (2013) 100 IPR 451, [372]; *Dr Reddy's Laboratories (UK) Ltd v Eli Lilly & Co Ltd* [2010] RPC 9, [104].
447 *Eli Lilly & Co Ltd v Apotex Pty Ltd* (2013) 100 IPR 451, [379]–[386]; *Ranbaxy Australia Pty Ltd v Warner-Lambert Co LLC* (2008) 77 IPR 449, [105]; *Imperial Chemicals Industries Pty Ltd v Commissioner of Patents* (2004) 213 ALR 399, [66]. Selection issues could arise also in mechanical and electrical inventions: *Sumitomo Electric Industries Ltd v Metal Manufacturers Ltd* (1993) AIPC 91-000, citing *Clyde Nail Co Ltd v Russell* (1916) 33 RPC 291; *Bosch's Application* (1909) 26 RPC 710.
448 (2008) 78 IPR 485, [79].

These principles of selection[449] – referred to as the 'IG' rules – apply in comparing the claimed invention against prior art information to determine whether the patent involves a selection and whether the sub-class of a prior disclosed class possesses novelty. Novelty is said to reside in the selection because it has particular advantages:

- The selection must be based on some substantial advantage gained or disadvantage avoided.
- All the selected members must possess the advantage in question.
- The selection must be in respect of something peculiar to the selected group.
- The specification must describe that advantage.
- The selection must not be a mere choice of presented alternatives.
- The prior publication of the wider class does not refer to that advantage.[450]

Underlying these principles is the necessity for the prior disclosure (which is usually in an earlier patent specification) to be a disclosure of a class, rather than a disclosure of the individual members of that class as distinct entities.[451] The monopoly is granted to the inventor in return for the public disclosure of the special advantages that the selected members of the class possess.

A selection patent may be valid even if it is later found that there are other members or compounds that also possess the advantage shared by the defined sub-class. This is a question of degree and both the efforts of the patentee to find all the members of the group and the numbers of members that are overlooked in the course of that research are relevant factors.[452] Some selection patents will involve material that is selected from patents that have expired. Other inventions will arise while the earlier patent remains in force. In such a case, a licence will be required if the exercise of the exclusive rights under the selection patent would otherwise infringe the exclusive rights of the earlier patentee.

10.6.13 Relationship with inventive step and innovative step

Novelty and inventive or innovative step are separate and independent requirements for the validity of a patent and must be kept conceptually distinct.[453] Novelty, or newness, is concerned with establishing that no-one has made the invention publicly available anywhere in the world before the priority date of the claim. It is concerned with prior disclosure of the essential integers of the invention. Novelty may be destroyed by a prior publication that is publicly available, regardless of whether that publication became part of the fund of common

---

449   *IG Farbenindustrie AG's Patents* (1930) 47 RPC 289.
450   Ibid; *Ranbaxy Australia Pty Ltd v Warner-Lambert Co LLC* (2008) 77 IPR 449, [105]; *EI Du Pont de Nemours (Witsiepe's) Application* [1982] FSR 303, 310; *Hallen Co v Brabantia (UK) Ltd* [1991] RPC 195, 217.
451   *Apotex Pty Ltd v Sanofi-Aventis* (2009) 82 IPR 416, [117] (Bennett and Middleton JJ); *Eli Lilly & Co Ltd v Apotex Pty Ltd* (2013) 100 IPR 451, [386] (Middleton J).
452   *IG Farbenindustrie AG's Patents* (1930) 47 RPC 289, 323; *University of Georgia Research Foundation Inc v Biochem Pharma Inc* (2000) 51 IPR 222, 242.
453   *Lockwood Security Products Pty Ltd v Doric Products Pty Ltd* (2004) 217 CLR 274, [46]; *RD Werner & Co Inc v Bailey Aluminium Products Pty Ltd* (1989) 25 FCR 565; *Sunbeam Corp v Morphy-Richards (Australia) Pty Ltd* (1961) 180 CLR 98, 111.

general knowledge. In contrast, inventive or innovative step is concerned with establishing an advance on a particular, and more limited, prior art base of knowledge.[454] In many instances, the same prior art will be available for assessment both of novelty and inventive step, but this is not necessarily the case. The general principle is that obviousness is not relevant to a novelty inquiry and vice versa.

10.7 Inventive and innovative step: principles

10.7.1 Introduction

Inventive and innovative step are concerned with finding some advance of an appropriate degree over the relevant prior art information. In the case of a standard patent, an inventive step is required. An innovation patent requires an innovative step. The principal distinction between a standard patent and an innovation patent is the nature of the advance that qualifies the invention as suitable for protection. Whereas the standard patent requires an inventive step, an innovation patent is designed to impose a lesser threshold for patentability – an 'innovative step'. The latter makes no reference to inventiveness or obviousness but instead requires that the variations between the claimed invention and any piece of prior art information make some substantial contribution to the working of the invention. The *Patents Amendment (Innovation Patents) Act 2000* (Cth) brought the provisions on the prior art base for innovation patents into line with those that applied for standard patents, so that the novelty test is identical. The requirement for invention and innovation is a legal one, but the assessment of this requirement involves an objective comparison of the invention claimed as against the existing prior art that comes within the relevant prior art base. The objectivity is provided through the perception of the notional skilled person in the relevant art. The level of the advance that is required is directly related to the breadth of prior art that is available for consideration. The common law provides guidance on the way this is measured.

Patents were available for both standard and petty patents under the *Patents Act 1952* (Cth).[455] Prior to 2001, the *Patents Act 1990* (Cth) also provided protection for both standard and petty patents. Subsequently, the *Patents Amendment (Innovation Patents) Act 2000* (Cth) replaced the petty patent with the innovation patent from 24 May 2001. The intention was to provide a second tier of protection for inventions that did not meet the criteria for an inventive step.[456] The legislative intention was clear that the innovation patent system was to provide a lower level of inventive height for entry.[457] A Bill to commence abolition of the innovation patent was introduced into parliament in July 2019.[458]

---

454 *Patents Act 1990* (Cth) s 7(2)–(5). See below at 10.7.4.
455 Critical cases under the *Patents Act 1952* (Cth) are *Aktiebolaget Hassle v Alphapharm Pty Ltd* (2002) 212 CLR 411, *Aktiebolaget Hassle v Alphapharm Pty Ltd* (2000) 51 IPR 375 and *ICI Chemicals & Polymers Ltd v Lubrizol Corp Inc* (2000) 106 FCR 214.
456 ACIP, *Review of the Petty Patent System*, above n 6.
457 Ibid rec 2; *Introduction of the Innovation Patent: The Government Response*, above n 13; Revised Explanatory Memorandum, Patents Amendment (Innovation Patents) Bill 2000 (Cth).
458 See above at 10.2.

10.7.2 Time at which inventive or innovative step is raised

Under the *Patents Act 1990* (Cth) the issue of inventiveness can be raised with respect to standard patents[459] at the examination stage[460] and in opposition proceedings[461] and is a ground for revocation of a patent.[462] Similarly, in the case of an innovation patent,[463] lack of an innovative step is a ground for revocation after examination[464] or re-examination[465] or upon an application for revocation under s 138. The *Raising the Bar* reforms removed a restriction that the Commissioner must not have regard to prior public use at examination,[466] modified examination[467] and re-examination.[468] The rationale for this former limitation was that there is no opportunity for an examiner to obtain information from anyone other than the applicant.[469] The amendments 'are not intended to impose an obligation on the Commissioner to conduct exhaustive searches specifically for prior use'.[470]

10.7.3 Statutory requirements: overview

The statutory requirements for lack of inventive step for a standard patent are set out in s 18(1)(b)(ii), s 7(2) and (3) and sch 1 of the *Patents Act 1990* (Cth). Lack of innovative step requirements are set out in s 18(1A)(b)(ii), s 7(4) and (5) and sch 1.

Section 18 provides that the invention, so far as claimed in any claim, must involve an inventive or innovative step when it is compared with the prior art base as it existed before the priority date of the claim.[471] This prior art base has expanded over time in response to calls for a stronger patent system.[472] The inquiry relates to each individual claim in the specification,[473] as each claim defines a particular form of the invention for which a patent is sought.[474] Each claim of a specification has a priority date that is the date of filing the specification[475] or such other date as determined under the regulations.[476] The correct approach in assessing obviousness is to identify the inventive concept in the invention as claimed and then to identify the person (or persons) who could be said to be the skilled but non-inventive person in the field

---

459 *Patents Act 1990* (Cth) s 61, sch 1 (definition of 'standard patent').
460 Ibid ss 45(1)(b), 98(b) (re-examination).
461 Ibid s 59(b).
462 Ibid s 138(3)(b).
463 Ibid s 62, sch 1 (definition of 'innovation patent').
464 Ibid s 101B(2)(b).
465 Ibid s 101G(3)(b).
466 Ibid ss 45(1A), 101B(3).
467 Ibid s 48(1A).
468 Ibid ss 98(2), 101B(3).
469 *Intellectual Property Laws Amendment (Raising the Bar) Act 2012* (Cth) sch 1 item 13 (repealing s 45(1A)), items 17, 20 (repealing and substituting ss 98 and 101B, respectively). See above at 10.6.2.
470 Explanatory Memorandum, Intellectual Property Laws Amendment (Raising the Bar) Bill 2011 (Cth) sch 1 item 13.
471 *Patents Act 1990* (Cth) s 43.
472 See below at 10.7.4.
473 *Patents Act 1990* (Cth) s 18(1) ('so far as claimed in any claim'), s 40(2); *Lockwood Security Products Pty Ltd v Doric Products Pty Ltd (No 2)* (2007) 235 CLR 173, 219.
474 *Patents Act 1990* (Cth) s 40(2)(b), (c).
475 Ibid s 43(2).
476 *Patents Regulations 1991* (Cth) regs 3.12, 3.13, 3.14. See ch 9 at 9.11 and 9.12.

who construes the specification and prior art in light of the common general knowledge.[477] The notion of common general knowledge is discussed below.[478] Briefly, it refers to information that the skilled person would retain in their mind, and any information they know of and might refer to as a matter of course or habitually consult.

Section 7(2) is a deeming provision and requires the Commissioner or a court to assume the existence of an inventive step when compared with the prior art base in the absence of evidence that establishes lack of inventive step.[479] The onus for establishing lack of inventive step rests on the party that challenges validity.[480] The method of construing the various iterations of s 7(2) and (3) that are described below[481] may be expressed succinctly as follows:

> Accordingly, whether a claim of a patent is invalid for lack of inventive step is to be determined by comparing the invention, so far as claimed, against the common general knowledge and any s 7(3) information. The question is then whether the invention would have been obvious to the hypothetical person skilled in the art in light of that knowledge considered separately from, or together with, the s 7(3) information.[482]

Anything outside these prescribed limits cannot be considered in the inventive step assessment, even if it appears in the specification.[483]

The Full Federal Court in *AstraZeneca AB v Apotex Pty Ltd*[484] approved a framework for analysis that was laid out in *Insta Image Pty Ltd v KD Kanopy Australasia Pty Ltd*:

> (1) to identify the invention 'so far as claimed in any claim';
> (2) to identify the 'person skilled in the relevant art';
> (3) to identify the common general knowledge as it existed in Australia before the priority date;
> (4) to inquire under s 7(2) whether the invention referred to in (1) above would have been obvious to the person referred to in (2) above in light of the knowledge referred to in (3) above; and
> (5) to inquire whether that invention would have been obvious to that person in the light of that knowledge when that knowledge is considered together with either kind of information mentioned in s 7(3) (additional prior art information).[485]

In the case of an innovation patent, a similar procedure applies but the final test is whether (as a question of fact) the differences between the claimed invention and any item of prior art information amount to a substantial contribution to the working of the invention.[486]

---

477   *Lockwood Security Products Pty Ltd v Doric Products Pty Ltd (No 2)* (2007) 235 CLR 173, 219–21.
478   At 10.8.3.
479   *Patents Act 1990* (Cth) s 7(2) and (3) (inventive step), s 7(4) and (5) (innovative step); *AstraZeneca AB v Apotex Pty Ltd* (2014) 226 FCR 324 (FC), [458], appeal dismissed (2015) 257 CLR 356, [18] (French CJ).
480   *Firebelt Pty Ltd v Brambles Australia Ltd* (2002) 188 ALR 280, [31]; *AstraZeneca AB v Apotex Pty Ltd* (2015) 257 CLR 356, [18] (French CJ).
481   At 10.7.4.
482   *AstraZeneca AB v Apotex Pty Ltd* (2014) 226 FCR 324 (FC), [202], appeal dismissed (2015) 257 CLR 356.
483   Ibid.
484   (2014) 226 FCR 324 (FC), [500].
485   (2008) 78 IPR 20, [80].
486   *Dura-Post (Australia) Pty Ltd v Delnorth Pty Ltd* (2009) 81 IPR 480.

Interpretation and construction of claims and prior art, as well as identification of the skilled addressee, are essential to this process. The principles that apply to construction of claims are considered in chapter 12. The following text looks first at the relevant prior art against which the invention is tested for both a standard and innovation patent. Second, it considers the approaches that courts take to an assessment and the various elements involved in making that assessment.

10.7.4 Inventive step: prior art base and relevant information for purposes of comparison

10.7.4.1 *Patents Act 1952*

The standard of inventiveness was the same for both standard and petty patents under the *Patents Act 1952* (Cth) and was assessed against a prior art base, being 'what was known or used in Australia on or before the priority date of that claim'.[487] The High Court explained this test in terms of

> whether the invention would have been obvious to a non-inventive worker in the field, equipped with the common general knowledge in that particular field as at the priority date, without regard to documents in existence but not part of such common general knowledge.[488]

Therefore, prior publications could not be taken into account if they did not form part of the common general knowledge in Australia. As the High Court noted in *Aktiebolaget Hassle v Alphapharm Pty Ltd*, '[c]ommon knowledge ... is the correlative of subject-matter or inventiveness, and available knowledge the correlative of lack of novelty'.[489]

10.7.4.2 *Patents Act 1990*: 30 April 1991 to 31 March 2002

The *Patents Act 1990* (Cth) raised the threshold of inventiveness by enlarging the prior art base beyond those disclosures proven to be part of the common general knowledge. The prior art base for inventive step of a standard patent under the *Patents Act 1990* was defined as: (1) information in a document that is publicly available anywhere in the world; and (2) information made publicly available through doing an act anywhere in the patent area. A domestic prior art base for both publicly available documents and acts applied for petty patents.[490]

An invention was taken to involve an inventive step when compared to the prior art base unless it was obvious to a person skilled in the relevant art in light of specified items of publicly available information. The comparison is made first with the common general knowledge as it existed in the patent area[491] (Australia) before the priority date of the relevant claim being

---

[487] *Patents Act 1952* (Cth) s 100(1)(e).
[488] *Wellcome Foundation Ltd v VR Laboratories (Australia) Pty Ltd* (1981) 148 CLR 262, 270; *Minnesota Mining & Manufacturing Co v Beiersdorf (Australia) Ltd* (1980) 144 CLR 253, 293–5.
[489] (2002) 212 CLR 411, [43].
[490] *Patents Act 1990* (Cth) s 7(2), (3), sch 1.
[491] Ibid s 7(2) sch 1 (definition of 'patent area'). 'Patent area' is defined as Australia, the Australian continental shelf, the waters above the Australian continental shelf and the airspace above Australia and the Australian continental shelf.

considered. If the invention remains non-obvious after that comparison, it is possible to combine the common general knowledge with either of the following kinds of information:

(a) prior art information made publicly available in a single document or through doing a single act;

(b) prior art information made publicly available in two or more related documents, or through doing two or more related acts, if the relationship between the documents or acts is such that a person skilled in the relevant art in the patent area would treat them as a single source of that information.

Information in these two categories is restricted further to that which the skilled person could, before the priority date of the relevant claim, *be reasonably expected to have ascertained, understood and regarded as relevant to work in the relevant art in the patent area*.[492]

10.7.4.3 *Patents Act 1990*: 1 April 2002 to 14 April 2013

The *Patents Amendment Act 2001* (Cth) repealed and replaced s 7(3) and increased the threshold for an inventive step by expanding the prior art base from which the skilled person might select prior art information for the purposes of comparison with a claimed invention.[493] The prior art base during this period comprises information in a document that is publicly available anywhere in the world and information made publicly available through doing an act anywhere in the world. Any prior art information that s 7(2) and (3) permits the skilled person to combine with common general knowledge must fall within that prior art base. Three features that limited the available prior art information were also removed when the *Patents Amendment Act 2001* (Cth) repealed and replaced s 7(3). The skilled addressee was no longer required to be skilled in the relevant art *in the patent area*; the information was not required to be regarded as relevant *to work in the relevant art in the patent area*; and it would be possible to combine documents and acts into a single source of information.

A summary of the operation of s 7(2) and (3) during this period can be expressed as follows. An invention is taken to involve an inventive step when compared with the prior art base described above unless it is obvious to a person skilled in the relevant art in light of the common general knowledge as it existed in the patent area[494] before the priority date of the claim.[495] That knowledge can be considered separately or together with either of two forms of information.

The first is any single piece of prior art information that a skilled person could before the priority date of the claim be reasonably expected to have ascertained, understood and regarded as relevant. This additional information could be in a document[496] that is publicly available anywhere in the world or that is made publicly available through doing an act anywhere in the world. This would allow the common general knowledge to be combined with any such single document or act.

---

492   See *Ajinomoto Co Inc v NutraSweet Australia Pty Ltd* (2008) 166 FCR 530; *Lockwood Security Products Pty Ltd v Doric Products Pty Ltd (No 2)* (2007) 235 CLR 173.
493   *Patents Amendment Act 2001* (Cth) sch 1 pt 1 items 3, 4.
494   The patent area remained confined to Australia: *Patents Act 1990* (Cth) sch 1 (definition of 'patent area').
495   *AstraZeneca AB v Apotex Pty Ltd* (2014) 226 FCR 324 (FC), [200].
496   *Acts Interpretation Act 1901* (Cth) s 2B (definition of 'document').

The second is a combination of any two or more pieces of prior art information that a skilled person could before the priority date of the claim be reasonably expected to have ascertained, understood and regarded as relevant and combined. This would allow the combination of one or more separate documents with the common general knowledge, one or more separate acts with the common general knowledge, or documents and acts with the common general knowledge. The concept of requiring a 'single source', which applied prior to 1 April 2002 (see above[497]), was replaced with this concept of combination. The change provides a more expansive scope for combining information for the purposes of comparison than applies for both novelty and innovative step.[498]

10.7.4.4 From 15 April 2013 to present

The *Raising the Bar Act* again expanded the prior art base for inventive step to improve the quality of granted patents. It removed the geographical restriction on common general knowledge in s 7(2), and amended s 7(3) to remove the words 'be reasonably expected to have ascertained, understood and regarded as relevant' to address three problems that had been identified as arising from this language.[499] First, relevant information can be excluded because the skilled person will not have ascertained the information.[500] Second, the terms 'understood' and 'regarded as relevant' are implicit in any inventive step test. Third, these restrictions are out of alignment with Australia's major trading partners. As to the intended effect of the amendments, the Explanatory Memorandum notes:

> Importantly, the changes are not intended to substantially change the operation of the existing tests for inventive step as applied to the prior art base or to permit hindsight analysis. While a skilled person is essentially deemed to be aware of and to have carefully read the publically [sic] available information, the inventive step tests are otherwise applied in the context of what the skilled person would have known and done before the priority date of the claims in question. The tests will therefore continue to take account of factors such as whether the skilled person would have understood and appreciated the relevance of the prior art to the problem the invention was seeking to solve and whether it would be considered a worthy starting point for further investigation or development.

The current form of s 7(2) and (3) is:

> (2) For the purposes of this Act, an invention is to be taken to involve an inventive step when compared with the prior art base unless the invention would have been obvious to a person skilled in the relevant art in the light of the common general knowledge as it existed (whether in or out of the patent area) before the priority date of the relevant claim, whether that knowledge is considered separately or together with the information mentioned in subsection (3).

---

497 At 10.7.4.2.
498 For the construction of s 7, see *AstraZeneca AB v Apotex Pty Ltd* (2014) 226 FCR 324 (FC), [192]–[207], appeal dismissed (2015) 257 CLR 356. See also *Tidy Tea Ltd v Unilever Australia Ltd* (1995) 32 IPR 405, 414; *Firebelt Pty Ltd v Brambles Australia Ltd* (2002) 188 ALR 280, [36].
499 *Intellectual Property Laws Amendment (Raising the Bar) Act 2012* (Cth) sch 1 item 3. The amendment applies to applications made on or after 15 April 2013 and to applications made before 15 April 2013 if no prior examination request was made: at sch 1 item 55(1).
500 *Commissioner of Patents v Emperor Sports Pty Ltd* (2006) 149 FCR 386.

(3) The information for the purposes of subsection (2) is:
   (a) any single piece of prior art information; or
   (b) a combination of any 2 or more pieces of prior art information that the skilled person mentioned in subsection (2) could, before the priority date of the relevant claim, be reasonably expected to have combined.

Under this regime, therefore, any publicly available prior art may be added to common general knowledge to assess obviousness. Any prior art could also be combined if the skilled addressee could reasonably be expected to do so, even if it was not common general knowledge.

The Productivity Commission recommended amendments to s 7(2) and (3) of the *Patents Act 1990* (Cth) to raise the threshold for inventive step. It based its recommendation on an assumption that 'Australia still has a lower threshold for inventive step compared to Europe'.[501] Although the government accepted the recommendation in August 2017 that the Australian standard must be equivalent to that of its major trading partners, stakeholders persuaded IP Australia to reconsider the drafting of its proposed changes to the *Patents Act 1990* (Cth).[502]

10.7.5 Innovative step: prior art base and relevant information for purposes of comparison

The *Patents Amendment (Innovation Patents) Act 2000* (Cth) repealed the petty patent and introduced the innovation patent in its place on 24 May 2001. A common prior art base[503] for both standard and innovation patents applied – namely, information in a document that is publicly available anywhere in the world and information made publicly available through doing an act in the patent area.

By virtue of s 18(1A)(b)(ii) of the *Patents Act 1990* (Cth), an invention is a patentable invention 'for the purposes of an innovation patent if the invention, so far as claimed in any claim ... when compared with the prior art base as it existed before the priority date of that claim ... involves an innovative step'. The requirements for an innovative step are provided in s 7(4):

> [A]n invention is to be taken to involve an innovative step when compared with the prior art base unless the invention would, to a person skilled in the relevant art, in the light of the common general knowledge as it existed in the patent area before the priority date of the relevant claim, only vary from the kinds of information set out in subsection (5) *in ways that make no substantial contribution to the working of the invention*.[504]

Subsection (5) refers to information made publicly available in a single document or through doing a single act or in two or more related documents or two or more related acts if the skilled

---

501 Productivity Commission, *Intellectual Property Arrangements* (Inquiry Report No 78, September 2016) 222.
502 IP Australia Response to Public Consultation on Exposure Draft of *Intellectual Property Laws Amendment (Productivity Commission Response Part 2 and Other Matters) Bill 2018* (2019) https://ipaustralia.govcms.gov.au.
503 *Patents Act 1990* (Cth) sch 1 (definition of 'prior art base').
504 Ibid s 7(4) (emphasis added).

person would treat them as a single source of the information. It is likely that the meaning of single source is the same as applies in the context of novelty in s 7(1). The *Raising the Bar Act* removed the geographical restriction on common general knowledge in s 7(4) by substituting the phrase 'in the patent area' with the phrase '(whether in or out of the patent area)'.[505]

By analogy with the position that pertains to inventive step,[506] the onus for establishing lack of innovative step would rest on the party that challenges validity.

10.7.6 Innovative step: level of advance and assessment

An invention – meaning the invention so far as claimed in any claim – will not involve an innovative step when it varies from the information in the prior art base only in ways that make no substantial contribution to the working of that invention as *claimed*.[507] It is not a question of any contribution it might make to the prior art.[508] The meaning of 'substantial contribution' is a contribution that is 'real' or 'of substance'.[509] This substantial contribution must be made to the invention as claimed across the full scope of the claim. This requirement will not be met when the claimed invention includes embodiments that do not include the asserted innovative step.[510] The statutory test does not ask whether the invention works 'in substantially the same way' as a prior disclosure and a finding to that effect does not necessitate a finding of no innovative step.[511] For instance, a substantial contribution to the working of the claimed invention can be satisfied if the invention is adapted to a new purpose, even though it works in substantially the same way as a prior disclosure.[512] In summary, an innovative step represents a lesser threshold for patentability than that of 'inventive step' and is not measured with reference to any 'advance in the art'[513] or advantage.[514]

The test involves a functional and narrow comparison as to the practical working of the invention. This comparison between the claimed invention and each separate and relevant prior disclosure is from the perspective of the skilled addressee who possesses certain background knowledge that is used in identifying and assessing the variations.[515] The test requires the skilled person to identify the differences between the claimed invention and the earlier prior disclosure as a matter of fact and assess whether they make a substantial contribution to the working of the device or process the subject of a claim. The skilled person

---

505 *Intellectual Property Laws Amendment (Raising the Bar) Act 2012* (Cth) sch 1 item 4. The amendment applies to applications made on or after 15 April 2013, and to patents granted on or after 15 April 2013 (application prior to that date) or granted before 15 April 2013 if no decision to examine or request for examination was made before 15 April 2013: at sch 1 item 55(1).
506 *Firebelt Pty Ltd v Brambles Australia Ltd* (2002) 188 ALR 280, [31].
507 *Vehicle Monitoring Systems Pty Ltd v SARB Management Group Pty Ltd (No 2)* (2013) 101 IPR 496, [226]–[227]; *Product Management Group Pty Ltd v Blue Gentian LLC* (2015) 240 FCR 85, [176].
508 *Streetworx Pty Ltd v Artcraft Urban Group Pty Ltd* (2014) 110 IPR 82, [234], [237].
509 *Dura-Post (Australia) Pty Ltd v Delnorth Pty Ltd* (2009) 81 IPR 480, [74]; *Product Management Group Pty Ltd v Blue Gentian LLC* (2015) 240 FCR 85, [175].
510 *Multisteps Pty Ltd v Source & Sell Pty Ltd* (2013) 214 FCR 323, [285].
511 *Product Management Group Pty Ltd v Blue Gentian LLC* (2015) 240 FCR 85, [183].
512 *Vehicle Monitoring Systems Pty Ltd v SARB Management Group Pty Ltd (No 2)* (2013) 101 IPR 496, [235].
513 *Dura-Post (Australia) Pty Ltd v Delnorth Pty Ltd* (2009) 81 IPR 480, [72].
514 *Product Management Group Pty Ltd v Blue Gentian LLC* (2015) 240 FCR 85, [178].
515 *Dura-Post (Australia) Pty Ltd v Delnorth Pty Ltd* (2009) 81 IPR 480, [74], [83].

makes this assessment having regard to the relevant common general knowledge before the priority date.

For example, *Dura-Post (Australia) Pty Ltd v Delnorth Pty Ltd*[516] considered an invention for a 'Roadside Post' – this was a resilient and durable flexible roadside post to support signage or delineate paths, roadways or boundaries. The hypothetical skilled person, who was required to compare the claimed roadside post and an earlier patented flexible roadside post, identified a range of differences that comprised known features, including a barb to anchor the post in the ground, a marker hole to mark the correct depth of the pole in the ground and to aid its extraction, and a tapered end to facilitate it being driven into the ground. The court was satisfied that each of these variations from the prior disclosure made a substantial contribution to the working of the claimed invention. Hence the invention involved an innovative step.

It is important to note that this inquiry has nothing to do with obviousness, does not involve a direct comparison with the common general knowledge as a body of knowledge, and does not involve looking for an 'advance in the art' as identified by reference to common general knowledge. Furthermore, the common general knowledge cannot be combined with a prior disclosure for the purpose of identifying the differences with the claimed invention. This approach contrasts with the assessment of an inventive step, which requires a direct comparison to be made between the invention as claimed and the common general knowledge alone or in combination with prior art information.[517]

The level of the advance was always intended to be lower than that which is required for an inventive step. However, the court's limited construction of s 7(4) and (5) in *Delnorth* provoked consternation over whether that level of advance should be sufficient to entitle a person to a monopoly over the claimed invention. Consequently, the relevance and operation of the innovation patent system was investigated by ACIP in 2014 and the Productivity Commission in 2016.[518] The government subsequently accepted recommendations of both ACIP and the Productivity Commission to abolish the innovation patent, and a Bill to do so was introduced into parliament in July 2019.[519]

10.7.7 Summary of differences

The above discussion identifies a number of differences between the prior art information and how it can be located and combined for the purposes of assessment for inventive and innovative step. These differences, based on the current law, are summarised as follows.

1. Relationship between common general knowledge and other information
   (a) Inventive step: common general knowledge can be considered alone or combined with other information.
   (b) Innovative step: common general knowledge cannot be considered alone and cannot be combined with a prior disclosure. It is relevant as background knowledge that the skilled person uses to identify the variations between the invention

---

516   (2009) 81 IPR 480.
517   Ibid [73].
518   IP Australia, *Review of the Innovation Patent* (Final Report, July 2006); Productivity Commission, *Intellectual Property Arrangements*, above n 501, ch 8.
519   See above at 10.2.

as claimed and a prior disclosure and to assess whether these variations make a substantial contribution to the working of the claimed invention.

2. Combination of documents and acts
   (a) Inventive step: two or more pieces of prior art information, whether documents or acts, can be combined if the skilled person could be reasonably expected to do so. Hence, documents and acts can be combined with each other.
   (b) Innovative step: any related documents and related acts can be combined if the skilled person would view them as a single source. However, no combination of acts and documents is permitted.

10.8 Inventive step: elements in the assessment

An assessment of inventive step is performed in relation to each claim independently of the other claims.[520] In the case of a combination patent, the assessment is of the whole combination of integers and the way they work together, not of each integer in the claim.[521] The test in the current s 7(2) and (3) of the *Patents Act 1990* (Cth) requires that the invention is *obvious* to a *person skilled in the relevant art* in light of the *common general knowledge* as it existed (whether in or out of the patent area) before the priority date of the relevant claim, whether this is considered separately or together with the information mentioned in s 7(3). This assessment of inventive step is a question of fact and of degree.[522] Each of the concepts highlighted above[523] is developed and discussed in the following sections.

10.8.1 Obvious: very plain

The test for inventive step is that the invention itself must not be 'obvious'. This is a question of fact and means 'plain' or 'very plain'.[524] There is no distinction between obviousness and lack of inventive step. In the case of a combination patent, the question is whether the combination of the integers was at the relevant time obvious, not whether each integer regarded in isolation is obvious.[525]

---

520 *Lockwood Security Products Pty Ltd v Doric Products Pty Ltd (No 2)* (2007) 235 CLR 173, [148].
521 *Garford Pty Ltd v DYWIDAG-Systems International Pty Ltd* (2015) 110 IPR 30, [53]–[56], [58]; *Minnesota Mining & Manufacturing Co v Beiersdorf (Australia) Ltd* (1980) 144 CLR 253, [293].
522 *Aktiebolaget Hassle v Alphapharm Pty Ltd* (2002) 212 CLR 411, [79] (Gleeson CJ, Gaudron, Gummow and Hayne JJ).
523 At 10.7.7.
524 Ibid [34] (Gleeson CJ, Gaudron, Gummow and Hayne JJ), [85] (McHugh J), [144] (Kirby J), [190] (Callinan J); *Lockwood Security Products Pty Ltd v Doric Products Pty Ltd (No 2)* (2007) 235 CLR 173, [51].
525 *Lockwood Security Products Pty Ltd v Doric Products Pty Ltd (No 2)* (2007) 235 CLR 173, [69]; *Aktiebolaget Hassle v Alphapharm Pty Ltd* (2002) 212 CLR 411, [6].

10.8.2 Person skilled in the relevant art

As a reference point for the identification of the hypothetical skilled addressee, the court must identify the field of knowledge that is relevant to the claimed invention.[526] Then the court is required to consider what that skilled addressee would have done in hypothetical circumstances.[527] This is the hypothetical, non-inventive and not particularly imaginative 'skilled addressee', a person 'skilled in the relevant art' who possesses 'ordinary skill',[528] who works in the art or science connected with the invention and has a practical interest in the subject matter of the invention.[529] This skilled person is relevant for a variety of other purposes in patent law. It is the person to whom the patent is addressed and who must construe it and the person who will judge whether a patent involves both novelty and an inventive step.[530] This skilled person would be assumed to have whatever language is necessary to read and understand the document[531] and to possess the best available equipment. This may be a single person or a composite being or team, whose combined skills are to be employed where the complexity of the invention demands the skills and information in more than one art.[532] The skilled addressee will be a team where it is normal in the field for a team to work together.[533] The team may be sophisticated and members of the team may possess and apply different skills and knowledge in their approach to the problem in question.[534]

Testing whether there is an inventive step involves considering the obviousness of any particular contribution to the ultimate successful invention by reference individually to the hypothetical members of the team, attributing to each the appropriate skills.[535] This individual or team may be credited with possessing the best available equipment.[536] In the case of research into pharmaceutical products, a PhD qualification would be an entry requirement to be part of the hypothetical team.[537]

The test is applied through the objective standard of the hypothetical skilled person. Therefore, although there may be evidence that an actual person was actually unsuccessful

---

526 *Aktiebolaget Hassle v Alphapharm Pty Ltd* (2002) 212 CLR 411, [152]; *Lockwood Security Products Pty Ltd v Doric Products Pty Ltd (No 2)* (2007) 235 CLR 173, [54]; *AstraZeneca AB v Apotex Pty Ltd* (2015) 257 CLR 356, [9]–[18].
527 *Wellcome Foundation Ltd v VR Laboratories (Australia) Pty Ltd* (1981) 148 CLR 262, 270; *Elconnex Pty Ltd v Gerard Industries Pty Ltd* (1991) 32 FCR 491, 507; *El Du Pont de Nemours & Co v Imperial Chemical Industries plc* (2002) 54 IPR 304, [102].
528 *H Lundbeck A/S v Alphapharm Pty Ltd* (2009) 177 FCR 151, [173].
529 *Catnic Components Ltd v Hill & Smith Ltd* [1982] RPC 183, 242 (Lord Diplock); *NutraSweet Australia Pty Ltd v Ajinomoto Co Inc* (2005) 224 ALR 200, [28]; *Minnesota Mining & Manufacturing Co v Tyco Electronics Pty Ltd* (2002) 56 IPR 248, [39].
530 *Root Quality Pty Ltd v Root Control Technologies Pty Ltd* (2000) 49 IPR 225, [70]. See above at 10.6.6.
531 *C Van der Lely NV v Bamfords Ltd* [1963] RPC 61, 71–2.
532 *Elconnex Pty Ltd v Gerard Industries Pty Ltd* (1992) 25 IPR 173, 178.
533 *General Tire & Rubber Co v Firestone Tyre & Rubber Co Ltd* [1972] RPC 457, 485; *ICI Chemicals & Polymers Ltd v Lubrizol Corp Inc* (2000) 106 FCR 214, [61].
534 *NutraSweet Australia Pty Ltd v Ajinomoto Co Inc* (2005) 224 ALR 200, [28].
535 For example, *General Tire & Rubber Co v Firestone Tyre & Rubber Co Ltd* [1972] RPC 457, 485; *Leonardis v Sartas No 1 Pty Ltd* (1996) 67 FCR 126, 146; *ICI Chemicals & Polymers Ltd v Lubrizol Corp Inc* (2000) 106 FCR 214, [61].
536 *Genentech Inc v Wellcome Foundation Ltd* [1989] RPC 147, 278 (Mustill LJ), 241 (Dillon J).
537 *Pfizer Overseas Pharmaceuticals v Eli Lilly & Co* (2005) 68 IPR 1, [288].

in trying the particular invention, the court may consider this to be atypical of the class.[538] The court must postulate what the 'hypothetical person' would have done in light of common general knowledge, not what an actual person was able to do or not do. The evidence of a particular expert witness does not dictate the answer.[539]

Prior to the enlargement of common general knowledge by the *Raising the Bar Act*, it was clear that a hypothetical skilled person could be attributed with common general knowledge in Australia even if there is no actual skilled person undertaking research in the area of the invention in Australia.[540] According to Finkelstein J in *NutraSweet Australia Pty Ltd v Ajinomoto Co Inc*, the lack of a relevantly skilled person in Australia did not prevent his consideration of what would have been the common general knowledge of the hypothetical skilled addressee. This would include information in widely circulated international textbooks and journals that would ordinarily be referred to by a person interested in the area.[541]

10.8.3 Common general knowledge

The concept of common general knowledge arose from the language in the *Patents Act 1952* (Cth) of 'what was known or used in Australia on or before the priority date of that claim'.[542] The classic formulation of what common general knowledge means is that of Aickin J in *Minnesota Mining & Manufacturing Co v Beiersdorf (Australia) Ltd*:

> The notion of common general knowledge itself involves the use of that which is known or used by those in the relevant trade. It forms the background knowledge and experience which is available to all in the trade in considering the making of new products, or the making of improvements in old, and it must be treated as being used by an individual as a general body of knowledge.[543]

The High Court in *Lockwood Security Products Pty Ltd v Doric Products Pty Ltd (No 2)* emphasised that it is the common general knowledge of the hypothetical non-inventive worker in the particular field of the invention that is relevant.[544] Common general knowledge is distinct from mere public knowledge.[545] It is not to be 'constructed out of a mosaic of prior publications.'[546] When a claimed invention was assessed for inventiveness under the *Patents Act 1952* (Cth), it was necessary to show that each piece of prior art to be considered was part of the common general knowledge. As discussed above,[547] the *Patents Act 1990* (Cth) rejected this narrow approach and permits the common general knowledge to be combined with other

---

538   *Johns-Manville Corp's Patent* [1967] FSR 327, 334.
539   *AstraZeneca AB v Apotex Pty Ltd* (2015) 257 CLR 356, [23]; *Sandvik Intellectual Property AB v Quarry Mining & Construction Equipment Pty Ltd* (2017) 126 IPR 427, [158].
540   *Gambro Pty Ltd v Fresenius Medical Care South East Asia Pty Ltd* (2004) 61 IPR 442; *NutraSweet Australia Pty Ltd v Ajinomoto Co Inc* (2005) 224 ALR 200, [30]–[31].
541   *NutraSweet Australia Pty Ltd v Ajinomoto Co Inc* (2005) 224 ALR 200, [31].
542   *Patents Act 1952* (Cth) s 100(1)(e) (was obvious and did not involve an inventive step having regard to what was known or used in Australia on or before the priority date of that claim).
543   (1980) 144 CLR 253, 292.
544   *Lockwood Security Products Pty Ltd v Doric Products Pty Ltd (No 2)* (2007) 235 CLR 173, [54].
545   *WR Grace & Co v Asahi Kasei Kogyo Kabushiki Kaisha* (1993) 25 IPR 481, 492.
546   *AstraZeneca AB v Apotex Pty Ltd* (2015) 257 CLR 356, [13].
547   At 10.7.4 and 10.7.5.

prior art information within the prior art base that does not form part of the common general knowledge.[548]

The common general knowledge not only includes the information that the skilled person would retain in their mind, but may also include any information they know of and might refer to as a matter of course or habitually consult.[549] This would be subject to the underlying principle that the information 'must be generally accepted and assimilated by persons skilled in the art and known and accepted without question by the bulk of those who are engaged in the particular art'.[550]

It does not include information that the skilled person would find through a routine literature search.[551] The ready access to a publication in a library does not mean that it is part of the common general knowledge.[552] Nor is information common general knowledge merely because it might be found in a journal, even if widely read.[553] Critically, the body of common general knowledge in any case is entirely dependent on the identity and level of skills attributed to the skilled addressee, which in turn flows from identifying the relevant field with which the invention is concerned. The following passage illustrates that comparison of the claimed invention with different bodies of common general knowledge is likely to produce different results in an obviousness assessment of a claimed invention:

> If the field is occupied by practical tradesmen, rather than scientists, claims to an invention should be considered against the background of *that* field, not of some unreal field peopled by a technological elite. What must be taken into account is the common general knowledge and the skill of the relevant calling.[554]

After the decision in *Bristol-Myers Squibb Co v FH Faulding & Co Ltd*,[555] the courts would ordinarily proceed on the basis that the knowledge described in the body of the specification is part of the common general knowledge before the priority date.[556] However, it is clear following the High Court's decision in *Lockwood Security Products Pty Ltd v Doric Products Pty Ltd (No 2)* that admissions in a specification on common general knowledge, while relevant, must be assessed as to their probative force like all other evidence.[557] This might, or might not, lead to a finding that the item of information is common general knowledge or s 7(3) information.[558]

---

548 See *Patents Act 1990* (Cth) s 7(3), (4), (5).
549 *ICI Chemicals & Polymers Ltd v Lubrizol Corp Inc* (2000) 106 FCR 214, [57]; *Aktiebolaget Hassle v Alphapharm Pty Ltd* (2000) 51 IPR 375, [73]; *PhotoCure ASA v Queen's University at Kingston* (2005) 64 IPR 314, [31].
550 *Idenix Pharmaceuticals LLC v Gilead Sciences Pty Ltd* (2017) 134 IPR 1, [192].
551 *Aktiebolaget Hassle v Alphapharm Pty Ltd* (2002) 212 CLR 411, [31], [45], [55].
552 *Aktiebolaget Hassle v Alphapharm Pty Ltd* (1999) 44 IPR 593, [105] (Lehane J); *PhotoCure ASA v Queen's University at Kingston* (2005) 64 IPR 314, [31].
553 *Idenix Pharmaceuticals LLC v Gilead Sciences Pty Ltd* (2017) 134 IPR 1, [192].
554 *Leonardis v Sartas No 1 Pty Ltd* (1996) 67 FCR 126, 146.
555 (2000) 97 FCR 524.
556 Ibid [30]. A specification can include an express statement to exclude this presumption: see, for example, *AstraZeneca AB v Apotex Pty Ltd* (2014) 226 FCR 324 (FC), [33].
557 (2007) 235 CLR 173, [105]–[111].
558 *AstraZeneca AB v Apotex Pty Ltd* (2014) 226 FCR 324 (FC), [204].

It is possible for international experts from outside Australia to give evidence as to the state of the common general knowledge within Australia in cases that fall to be determined on the law in existence before the amendments made to the scope of common general knowledge.[559]

10.8.4 Information a skilled person could be reasonably expected to ascertain, understand and regard as relevant

It is not enough that a piece of prior art information is publicly available at the priority date of the claimed invention. In the period between 1 April 2002 and 14 April 2013, the information in s 7(3) to which a skilled person could refer for the purposes of s 7(2) was qualified by the requirement that the skilled person could, before the priority date of the relevant claim, be reasonably expected to have ascertained, understood and regarded as relevant.[560] The words suggest a person skilled in the relevant art familiar with some, but not necessarily every piece of, publicly available information in the relevant art beyond common general knowledge.[561] To 'ascertain' simply means to discover or find. However, it seems that the skilled person could not be reasonably expected to find a piece of prior art information unless that person 'could reasonably be expected to know where to look'.[562] The test in this version of s 7(3) is not limited to what would be ascertained in the course of a skilled person's ordinary work but applies also where the person is undertaking a particular project.[563]

Having ascertained the relevant information, 'understood' means that the skilled person would have '"comprehended it" or "appreciated its meaning or import"'.[564] The concept of 'relevant to work in the relevant art' that was present in s 7(3) until 1 April 2002 is one that must be restricted to the particular problem or need in respect of which the invention constitutes an advance.[565]

At least in high technology areas, a court will assume, without requiring evidence, that the skilled person is familiar with the major professional or academic journals and would be reasonably expected to consult them.[566] In areas such as pharmaceutical research, they would be expected to carry out literature searches using electronic databases.[567] Published patents will constitute information to be taken into account when it is accepted that a patent literature search would have been routinely undertaken by the hypothetical skilled team in the area.[568] It will not matter that the patent literature is not consulted by all workers in the art. In an area of intense patent activity, it is reasonable to conclude that the skilled person could reasonably be

---

559 *Pfizer Overseas Pharmaceuticals v Eli Lilly & Co* (2005) 68 IPR 1, [292].
560 Legislative history and the construction of s 7(3) are discussed in *Firebelt Pty Ltd v Brambles Australia Ltd* (2002) 188 ALR 280, [31]–[36] and *AstraZeneca AB v Apotex Pty Ltd* (2014) 226 FCR 324 (FC), appeal dismissed (2015) 257 CLR 356.
561 *Lockwood Security Products Pty Ltd v Doric Products Pty Ltd (No 2)* (2007) 235 CLR 173, [149].
562 *Commissioner of Patents v Emperor Sports Pty Ltd* (2006) 149 FCR 386, [30].
563 *NSI Dental Pty Ltd v University of Melbourne* (2006) 69 IPR 542, [198].
564 *Lockwood Security Products Pty Ltd v Doric Products Pty Ltd (No 2)* (2007) 235 CLR 173, [132].
565 Ibid [152]. See above at 10.7.4.2, 10.7.4.3 and 10.7.4.4.
566 *ICI Chemicals & Polymers Ltd v Lubrizol Corp Inc* (2000) 106 FCR 214, [57].
567 *Pfizer Overseas Pharmaceuticals v Eli Lilly & Co* (2005) 68 IPR 1, [280].
568 *NutraSweet Australia Pty Ltd v Ajinomoto Co Inc* (2005) 224 ALR 200, [44]; *JMVB Enterprises Pty Ltd v Camoflag Pty Ltd* (2006) 154 FCR 348, [81].

expected to consult the patent literature.[569] A lower threshold of inventiveness results when information that is relevant and readily understood cannot be considered because the skilled person would not be expected to search for patents.[570]

10.8.5 Standard required: scintilla of inventiveness

Only a small amount of inventiveness needs to be shown. This is usually referred to as a 'scintilla of inventiveness'.[571] It may be something stumbled on by accident.[572] Nevertheless, the standard requires something that is not obvious, in contrast to the test for an innovative step that refers to the contribution that the advance makes to the working of the invention.

10.8.6 Expert evidence 'tainted by hindsight'

Evidence by 'experts' on the question of obviousness is not always likely to be helpful.[573] The court is required to consider what the hypothetical skilled person or research group would have done in hypothetical circumstances.[574] This is an objective test, and the court is to give relatively little weight to evidence from expert witnesses who have been provided with the patent and other prior art documents in advance.[575] In such cases, the evidence is likely to be 'tainted by hindsight': once the solution to a problem is known there is the tendency to think that it was more predictable than it actually was. This is particularly problematic where the conception of the idea involves the use of well-known principles.

10.8.7 Secondary factors to assist assessment of obviousness

A number of factors can contribute to a conclusion that there was an inventive step, but no one factor is decisive alone or together with the others. They are evidentiary only, are admissible and relevant, but are not conclusive. These factors do not replace the statutory test. However, they help courts resist hindsight analysis and help inform a decision in 'a close case when something is required to tip the scales'.[576] An Australian court should be 'slow to ignore secondary evidence or to rely on its own assumed technical expertise to reach conclusions contrary to such evidence'.[577] However, while courts recognise the importance of this evidence, 'its weight will vary from case to case and it will not necessarily be

---

569 *Monsanto Co v Syngenta Participations AG* (2005) AIPC 92-128, 39,426; *Stack v Brisbane City Council* (1999) 47 IPR 525, [178].
570 For example, *Commissioner of Patents v Emperor Sports Pty Ltd* (2006) 149 FCR 386, 393; *North West Bay Ships Pty Ltd v Austal Ships Pty Ltd* (2010) 87 IPR 214, [90].
571 For example, *Meyers Taylor Pty Ltd v Vicarr Industries Ltd* (1977) 137 CLR 228, 249; *Aktiebolaget Hassle v Alphapharm Pty Ltd* (2002) 212 CLR 411, [48].
572 *Wellcome Foundation Ltd v VR Laboratories (Australia) Pty Ltd* (1981) 148 CLR 262, 286.
573 *Firebelt Pty Ltd v Brambles Australia Ltd* (2002) 188 ALR 280, [46].
574 *El Du Pont de Nemours & Co v ICI Chemicals & Polymers Ltd* (2005) 66 IPR 462, [128].
575 *Minnesota Mining & Manufacturing Co v Tyco Electronics Pty Ltd* (2002) 56 IPR 248, [42]. See also *JMVB Enterprises Pty Ltd v Camoflag Pty Ltd* (2005) 67 IPR 68, [100].
576 *Conor Medsystems Inc v University of British Columbia* (2005) 223 ALR 74, [6].
577 *Lockwood Security Products Pty Ltd v Doric Products Pty Ltd (No 2)* (2007) 235 CLR 173, [116]; *Firebelt Pty Ltd v Brambles Australia Ltd* (2002) 188 ALR 280.

determinative.'[578] Any secondary factors must be viewed in a context of the business and the market in which the patentee trades.[579] For example, a competitor who acts in flagrant disregard of a patent is likely to view the patent as invalid. In contrast, a lack of patent challenges or requests for licences indicates that a patent has been evaluated by interested parties and deemed to be valid.[580]

10.8.7.1 Long-felt want and its successful solution

A quick imitation of the product by competitors may reveal an underlying 'long-felt want' for the invention[581] as well as an inference that it is not obvious.[582] On the other hand, imitation may be to match the range of competitive products,[583] or it may suggest that the patent is invalid. Imitation is more likely to have neutral impact,[584] and is thus a weak indicator of non-obviousness if viewed in isolation. However, its weight will depend on the circumstances in which it occurred and other relevant evidence.[585] Particular caution should be exercised when copying occurs in another country.[586]

Evidence of failed attempts to solve a well-known problem or to satisfy a long-felt want may be a powerful indication of inventiveness. The assumption is that problems in the prior art would not persist if the solution were obvious.[587] The evidence required to establish a long-felt want is

>   (a) the existence of the problem and its duration; (b) the nature of the efforts to solve the problem; and (c) the actual successful solution by the patentee.[588]

The mere fact that something has not been previously produced does not mean it involves an inventive step or is non-obvious.[589] There may have been economic, market or other reasons to explain a lack of investment in its development and production. The concept of an unfelt want is said to be 'very closely tied to the commercial success that comes with creating and satisfying the demand for a product the usefulness or desirability of which was not generally appreciated before its conception.'[590]

Not all inventions will reveal a long-felt want, and 'those which reveal an "unfelt want" are as likely, or sometimes more likely, to involve an inventive step'.[591]

---

578 *Lockwood Security Products Pty Ltd v Doric Products Pty Ltd (No 2)* (2007) 235 CLR 173, [116]; *AstraZeneca AB v Apotex Pty Ltd* (2015) 257 CLR 356, [45] (French J).
579 *Gambro Pty Ltd v Fresenius Medical Care South East Asia Pty Ltd* (2004) 61 IPR 442, [428].
580 *Conor Medsystems Inc v University of British Columbia* (2005) 223 ALR 74, [9].
581 *Elconnex Pty Ltd v Gerard Industries Pty Ltd* (1992) 25 IPR 173, 181 (Sheppard and Lockhart JJ); *Firebelt Pty Ltd v Brambles Australia Ltd* (2002) 188 ALR 280, [49].
582 *Conor Medsystems Inc v University of British Columbia* (2005) 223 ALR 74, [10]; *F Hoffmann-La Roche AG v Chiron Corp* (2000) 47 IPR 516; *Wellcome Foundation Ltd v VR Laboratories (Australia) Pty Ltd* (1981) 148 CLR 262, 287.
583 *Elconnex Pty Ltd v Gerard Industries Pty Ltd* (1992) 25 IPR 173, 181 (Lockhart J).
584 Ibid 183 (Lockhart J).
585 *Garford Pty Ltd v DYWIDAG-Systems International Pty Ltd* (2015) 110 IPR 30, [69].
586 *Conor Medsystems Inc v University of British Columbia* (2005) 223 ALR 74, [12].
587 Ibid [7].
588 Ibid.
589 *Elconnex Pty Ltd v Gerard Industries Pty Ltd* (1992) 25 IPR 173, 182–3 (Lockhart J).
590 *Garford Pty Ltd v DYWIDAG-Systems International Pty Ltd* (2015) 110 IPR 30, [92].
591 *Wellcome Foundation Ltd v VR Laboratories (Australia) Pty Ltd* (1981) 148 CLR 262, 287.

10.8.7.2 Commercial success

Commercial success is another factor to take into account. It also is not decisive,[592] principally because it can be explained on grounds other than inventiveness,[593] such as mass advertising.[594]

10.8.7.3 Expectation of success

The main judgment of the High Court in *Aktiebolaget Hassle v Alphapharm Pty Ltd*[595] identified the test for assessing inventive step in the context of a pharmaceutical invention that involved a number of steps in the research process with reference to two authorities. The first was the approach that Aickin J adopted in *Wellcome Foundation Ltd v VR Laboratories (Australia) Pty Ltd*:

> The test is whether the hypothetical addressee faced with the same problem would have taken as a matter of routine whatever steps might have led from the prior art to the invention, whether they be the steps of the inventor or not.[596]

What Aickin J had in mind as 'routine' was then explained in a passage that was paraphrased as follows:

> Were the experiments 'part of' that inventive step claimed in the Patent or were they 'of a routine character' to be tried 'as a matter of course'? If the latter be attributable to the hypothetical addressee of the Patent, such a finding would support a holding of obviousness.[597]

The second authority, which the court said had an 'affinity' with the *Wellcome* test, was *Olin Mathieson Chemical Corp v Biorex Laboratories Ltd*,[598] in which Graham J reformulated what is known as the 'Cripps question':

> *Would* the notional research group at the relevant date, in all the circumstances, which include a knowledge of all the relevant prior art and of the facts ... *directly be led as a matter of course* to try [the solution proposed by the patent application] ... in the expectation that it might well produce a useful [result] ...?[599]

After setting out both approaches, the court in *Alphapharm* concluded, 'That approach should be accepted'[600] but without further specifying the intended approach. Although *Alphapharm* refers both to routine steps to be tried as a matter of course (*Wellcome*) and to the reformulated

---

592   *Minnesota Mining & Manufacturing Co v Beiersdorf (Australia) Ltd* (1980) 144 CLR 253, 298; *Sartas No 1 Pty Ltd v Koukourou & Partners Pty Ltd* (1994) 30 IPR 479, 511.
593   *Elconnex Pty Ltd v Gerard Industries Pty Ltd* (1992) 25 IPR 173, 182–3.
594   *Conor Medsystems Inc v University of British Columbia* (2005) 223 ALR 74, [8]; *Garford Pty Ltd v DYWIDAG-Systems International Pty Ltd* (2015) 110 IPR 30, [87].
595   (2002) 212 CLR 411, [50] (Gleeson CJ, Gaudron, Gummow and Hayne JJ).
596   (1981) 148 CLR 262, 286.
597   *Aktiebolaget Hassle v Alphapharm Pty Ltd* (2002) 212 CLR 411, [52].
598   [1970] RPC 157.
599   *Aktiebolaget Hassle v Alphapharm Pty Ltd* (2002) 212 CLR 411, [53], quoting *Olin Mathieson Chemical Corp v Biorex Laboratories Ltd* [1970] RPC 157, 187–8. The court had been referred to *Olin* in *Wellcome Foundation Ltd v VR Laboratories (Australia) Pty Ltd* (1981) 148 CLR 262, 267.
600   (2002) 212 CLR 411, [53].

Cripps question (*Olin*), subsequent cases have generally accepted the latter as the principle arising from this decision. It is important to note here that neither version of the test is formulated as 'worthwhile to try'.[601]

Two issues of principle that arise from these passages were considered, but not finally resolved, by the Full Federal Court in *Generic Health Pty Ltd v Bayer Pharma AG*,[602] a case involving an invention for an oral contraceptive that included a poorly soluble and acid labile compound, drospirenone (DRSP). The invention lay in creating a rapidly dissolving formulation of DRSP that reduced degradation in the stomach and led to more rapid absorption in the bloodstream. At the priority date, the primary judge found that the obvious solution to this problem of poor solubility and degradation in the stomach would be to coat the formulation with an enteric coating to protect it from stomach acids. Generic Health argued that the appropriate test for obviousness in these circumstances is the *Wellcome* formulation – namely, 'whether the hypothetical addressee, faced with the same problem, would have taken, as a matter of routine, whatever steps might have led from the prior art to the invention'. It argued that the skilled addressee would have carried out some in vivo tests as a matter of routine and thereby be led, as a matter of course, to the invention. The primary judge rejected this argument and concluded that, as the skilled person would already know and expect that DRSP would degrade in the stomach, there would be *no expectation of success* in carrying out the in vivo tests. The obvious course would be to apply an enteric coating. An appeal to the Full Court was unsuccessful and the invention was found not obvious. The High Court refused an application for special leave to appeal.

The first issue of principle considered by the Full Court[603] was whether the reformulated Cripps question, which includes express reference to an expectation of success, was the only applicable test. The court concluded that it was not:

> We do not think that the plurality in *Alphapharm* were saying that the reformulated Cripps question was the test to be applied in every case. Rather, it is a formulation of the test which will be of assistance in cases, particularly those of a similar nature to *Alphapharm*. The plurality did not reject as an alternative expression of the test the question whether experiments were of a routine character to be tried as a matter of course.[604]

It was later observed by Bell J, in the special leave application to the High Court to appeal the decision, that the reformulated Cripps test is 'simply a way of explaining the routine steps in the *Wellcome* test'.[605]

The second related issue of principle considered by the Full Court was whether an expectation of success was a necessary element of the resolution of obviousness, that expectation being that the experiment might well produce the invention or at least something very

---

601   *Generic Health Pty Ltd v Bayer Pharma AG* (2014) 222 FCR 336, [71]; *AstraZeneca AB v Apotex Pty Ltd* (2015) 257 CLR 356, [15].
602   *Generic Health Pty Ltd v Bayer Pharma AG* (2014) 222 FCR 336.
603   The trial judge found it unnecessary to consider the matters of principle due to factual findings.
604   *Generic Health Pty Ltd v Bayer Pharma AG* (2014) 222 FCR 336, [71].
605   *Generic Health Pty Ltd v Bayer Pharma AG* [2014] HCATrans 261 (Bell J). An application for leave to appeal to the High Court on the statutory test of obviousness was refused on the basis that this case was 'an inappropriate vehicle to reconsider settled principles in relation to obviousness'.

like the invention. The court saw no distinction in this regard between the two formulations of the test:

> We do not think there is a divide here in terms of whether an expectation of success is relevant between a test which refers to routine steps to be tried as a matter of course and the reformulated Cripps question. It is difficult to think of a case where an expectation that an experiment might well succeed is not implicit in the characterisation of steps as routine and to be tried as a matter of course.[606]

It is not just the expectation of success that is involved in the reformulated Cripps question, but also the fact that the prior art renders the ultimate invention predictable rather than merely possible or worth trying. As Crennan J observed in the special leave hearing, 'if the prior art renders the ultimate invention unpredictable, you are in non-obviousness territory rather than obvious territory.'[607]

In order to align the High Court test with the approach of the United Kingdom, United States and Canadian courts, the test is best applied only in relation to simple inventions,[608] 'where it is very plain or ... more or less self-evident that what is being tested ought to work',[609] or where there is a fair expectation of success.[610]

10.8.7.4 Problem and solution

Sometimes it may assist to frame the statutory test in the context of the problem that required invention for its resolution and to use the European concept of a 'problem and solution' approach that takes as its starting point the closest prior art.[611] However, as Jacob LJ noted in the United Kingdom Court of Appeal decision in *Nichia Corp v Argos Ltd*, 'attempts to force all questions of obviousness into a 'problem-solution' approach can lead to trouble, though often the test can be a helpful guide'.[612] The enlarged Full Federal Court in *AstraZeneca AB v Apotex Pty Ltd* has made it clear that if a problem is to form the 'starting point' of any inventive step inquiry, it must be within the body of information that s 7(2) and (3) prescribes.

> If the problem addressed by a patent specification is itself common general knowledge, or if knowledge of the problem is s 7(3) information, then such knowledge or information will be attributed to the hypothetical person skilled in the art for the purpose of assessing obviousness. But if the problem cannot be attributed to the hypothetical person skilled in the art in either of these ways, then it is not permissible to attribute a knowledge of the

---

606 *Generic Health Pty Ltd v Bayer Pharma AG* (2014) 222 FCR 336, [71]. See also *Nichia Corp v Arrow Electronics Australia Pty Ltd* [2019] FCAFC 2.
607 *Generic Health Pty Ltd v Bayer Pharma AG* [2014] HCATrans 261.
608 *Johns-Manville Corp's Patent* [1967] FSR 327. An Australian example of its application to a simple invention is *Dynamite Games Pty Ltd v Aruze Gaming Australia Pty Ltd* (2013) 103 IPR 373, [24].
609 *Sanofi-Synthelabo Canada Inc v Apotex Inc* [2008] 3 SCR 265, [65]; *KSR International Co v Teleflex Inc*, 550 US 398 (2007); *Conor Medsystems Inc v Angiotech Pharmaceutical Inc* [2008] UKHL 49, [42].
610 A. L. Monotti, 'Divergent approaches in defining the appropriate level of inventiveness in patent law' in Bently, D'Agastino and Ng (eds), *The Common Law of Intellectual Property*, above n 141, ch 9, 195.
611 *Lockwood Security Products Pty Ltd v Doric Products Pty Ltd (No 2)* (2007) 235 CLR 173, [148]; *AstraZeneca AB v Apotex Pty Ltd* (2014) 226 FCR 324 (FC), [210]; *Garford Pty Ltd v DYWIDAG-Systems International Pty Ltd* (2015) 110 IPR 30, [67].
612 [2007] FSR 38, [22]; *Lockwood Security Products Pty Ltd v Doric Products Pty Ltd (No 2)* (2007) 235 CLR 173, [65].

problem on the basis of the inventor's 'starting point' such as might be gleaned from a reading of the complete specification as a whole.[613]

10.8.8 Objection to reliance on hindsight

To test an invention with the benefit of hindsight involves the consideration of the invention as claimed and then looking back. This presents many dangers to the fair and proper assessment of whether an inventive step was present at the priority date of the relevant claim. Something may appear to be obvious with the solution in hand but non-obvious in its absence. The courts have consistently criticised any approach that allows the benefit of hindsight.[614] The potential for misuse is highlighted when the inventive step is not in the solution of a known problem, but in the conception of the problem itself.[615] Once the problem is perceived, the solution may be found with straightforward experiments.[616] The danger of misusing hindsight is also acute where the invention lies in the combination of known integers.[617] It is not appropriate, with the benefit of hindsight, to merely line up the previously known elements of the claim and assess whether the invention might have been arrived at by taking a series of obvious steps.

10.9 Threshold quality of 'inventiveness'
10.9.1 The issue

The *Statute of Monopolies* protected monopolies for a 'manner of new manufacture', which phrase is synonymous with a patentable invention for the purposes of the *Patents Act 1990* (Cth). We have seen above that s 18 of the Act specifies the various criteria for patentability. Section 18(1)(a) requires that it must be a 'manner of manufacture'. There is no express reference to any requirement for 'newness' in s 18(1)(a). This broad concept of 'newness', which initially encompassed only novelty but expanded to include inventiveness, is set out in s 18(1)(b) as novelty and inventive step.

In *NV Philips Gloeilampenfabrieken v Mirabella International Pty Ltd*,[618] a case involving proceedings for infringement and revocation of a granted standard patent, the High Court considered that the opening words that appeared in s 18(1) at the time – 'a patentable invention is an invention that' – introduce a threshold quality of 'newness' or 'inventiveness' that is to be considered as a separate and additional inquiry to the formal investigation of novelty and inventive step as set out in s 18(1)(b). It does not render those specific requirements otiose, but 'simply means that, if it is apparent on the face of the specification that the

---

613 *AstraZeneca AB v Apotex Pty Ltd* (2014) 226 FCR 324 (FC), [203].
614 *Aktiebolaget Hassle v Alphapharm Pty Ltd* (2002) 212 CLR 411, [21]; *Commonwealth Industrial Gases Ltd v MWA Holdings Pty Ltd* (1970) 180 CLR 160, 163–4; *Meyers Taylor Pty Ltd v Vicarr Industries Ltd* (1977) 137 CLR 228, 242–3.
615 *Hickton's Patent Syndicate v Patents & Machine Improvements Co Ltd* (1909) 26 RPC 339, 347.
616 *Wellcome Foundation Ltd v VR Laboratories (Australia) Pty Ltd* (1981) 148 CLR 262, 280–1; *Meyers Taylor Pty Ltd v Vicarr Industries Ltd* (1977) 137 CLR 228, 241–2 (Aickin J); *Aktiebolaget Hassle v Alphapharm Pty Ltd* (2002) 212 CLR 411, 423–4.
617 *Gambro Pty Ltd v Fresenius Medical Care South East Asia Pty Ltd* (2004) 61 IPR 442, [354].
618 (1995) 183 CLR 655.

quality of inventiveness necessary for there to be a proper subject of letters patent under the *Statute of Monopolies* is absent, one need go no further'.[619]

Relying on the earlier authority of *Commissioner of Patents v Microcell Ltd*,[620] a case involving an application for a patent rather than its revocation, the majority in *NV Philips* reasoned that the words 'a patentable invention is an invention that' introduce this threshold quality of newness or inventiveness into s 18(1). This occurs through the definition of the word 'invention' in sch 1 of the *Patents Act 1990* (Cth) – it includes an 'alleged invention', a phrase that has been interpreted to mean an 'allegedly new invention'. Therefore, the court concluded with reference to traditional patent principle[621] that if a patentable invention must first be an 'invention' as defined in the Dictionary in sch 1 of the *Patents Act 1990*, it must be 'new' or alleged to be 'new'. A mere assertion of newness will not satisfy this threshold requirement if the absence of inventiveness is clearly disclosed on the face of the specification.[622] One circumstance where the threshold will remain unsatisfied is where it is apparent on the face of the specification to the hypothetical skilled person that the claim relates to 'the use of a known material in the manufacture of known articles for the purpose of which its known properties make that material suitable'.[623] In such a case, there is no patentable invention because there is clearly nothing inventive and nothing new.[624]

In contrast, there will be an invention if the new use consists of taking advantage of a previously unknown or unsuspected property of the substance.[625] The High Court did not intend that this threshold requirement would correspond with or 'render otiose' the more specific requirements of novelty and inventive step in s 18(1)(b). It simply means that one need go no further to examine those separate aspects of newness if the invention fails the threshold test.[626]

The High Court majority found it 'strictly speaking' unnecessary to answer the question whether the words in s 18(1)(a) – 'manner of manufacture' – exclude from

---

619	Ibid 664; *Lockwood Security Products Pty Ltd v Doric Products Pty Ltd (No 2)* (2007) 235 CLR 173, [106]: 'The decision in *Microcell* has not always been properly understood; it does not involve a separate ground of invalidity or a discrete "threshold" test.'
620	(1959) 102 CLR 232.
621	*NV Philips Gloeilampenfabrieken v Mirabella International Pty Ltd* (1995) 183 CLR 655, 663–4; *NRDC v Commissioner of Patents* (1959) 102 CLR 252, 262.
622	*NV Philips Gloeilampenfabrieken v Mirabella International Pty Ltd* (1995) 183 CLR 655, 663.
623	This can be shortened to the 'mere new use of a known product': *Commissioner of Patents v Microcell Ltd* (1959) 102 CLR 232, 251 (*Patents Act 1903* (Cth)); *NRDC v Commissioner of Patents* (1959) 102 CLR 252, 262; *NV Philips Gloeilampenfabrieken v Mirabella International Pty Ltd* (1995) 183 CLR 655, 664.
624	*NV Philips Gloeilampenfabrieken v Mirabella International Pty Ltd* (1995) 183 CLR 655, 663–4; *Advanced Building Systems Pty Ltd v Ramset Fasteners (Australia) Pty Ltd* (1998) 194 CLR 171, [38].
625	*NRDC v Commissioner of Patents* (1959) 102 CLR 252, 262; *Merck & Co Inc v Arrow Pharmaceuticals Ltd* (2006) 154 FCR 31, [63].
626	*NV Philips Gloeilampenfabrieken v Mirabella International Pty Ltd* (1995) 183 CLR 655, 663–4; *Advanced Building Systems Pty Ltd v Ramset Fasteners (Australia) Pty Ltd* (1998) 194 CLR 171, [38]. The effect of the decision was to affirm the earlier decision of the Full Court: *NV Philips Gloeilampenfabrieken v Mirabella International Pty Ltd* (1993) 44 FCR 239. See *Bristol-Myers Squibb Co v FH Faulding & Co Ltd* (2000) 97 FCR 524, [20]. A summary of the various propositions that are established in *Microcell*, *NRDC* and *NV Philips* are set out in *Merck & Co Inc v Arrow Pharmaceuticals Ltd* (2006) 68 IPR 511, [63].

their operation a process 'that is merely a new use of a known product'.[627] Nevertheless, they observed that

> the preferable conclusion is that the phrase 'manner of manufacture within the meaning of section 6 of the *Statute of Monopolies*' in s 18(1)(a) should be understood as referring to a process which is a proper subject matter of letters patent according to traditional principle.[628]

The majority concluded by way of obiter dicta that both the trial judge and the majority of the Full Court were correct in holding that the effect of concluding that the relevant process in the case was 'no more than a new use of a particular known product was that it was not a "manner of manufacture" for the purposes of s 18(1)(a)'. An enlarged Full Court in *AstraZeneca AB v Apotex Pty Ltd* commented:

> These observations suggest that s 18(1)(a), considered separately from the threshold requirement, has an operation that would deny patentability to a claimed invention that is in truth nothing more than a 'new use of an old substance' (properly understood) where that fact is not apparent on the face of the specification. However, the majority did not examine that prospect in any more detail.[629]

As these observations were obiter,[630] *NV Philips* is authority only for the majority's construction of the introductory words in s 18(1), which then 'imposes a threshold requirement which must be satisfied before reaching the requirement of s 18(1)(a)'.[631]

10.9.2 Assessment of the threshold quality of 'inventiveness'

The threshold issue is whether an alleged invention appears on the face of the specification.[632] This is not a 'discrete "threshold" test' but a threshold requirement for the invention to be a manner of manufacture.[633] The High Court in *NV Philips* 'does not provide a comprehensive answer to the question: by reference to what body of knowledge is inventiveness (under s 18(1)(a), including the threshold requirement) judged?'[634] Whereas novelty and inventive step

---

627 This was the basis for the majority decision in *NV Philips Gloeilampenfabrieken v Mirabella International Pty Ltd* (1993) 44 FCR 239, 262–3 (Lockhart J, Northrop J concurring).
628 *NV Philips Gloeilampenfabrieken v Mirabella International Pty Ltd* (1995) 183 CLR 655, 667.
629 *AstraZeneca AB v Apotex Pty Ltd* (2014) 226 FCR 324 (FC), [382].
630 Ibid [380]; *Advanced Building Systems Pty Ltd v Ramset Fasteners (Australia) Pty Ltd* (1998) 194 CLR 171, [38]; *Bristol-Myers Squibb Co v FH Faulding & Co Ltd* (2000) 97 FCR 524, [22]. See also M. Padbury, 'Inventiveness apart from novelty and inventive step: The High Court's decisions on manner of manufacture in *Philips* and *Ramset*' (1998) 9 *Australian Intellectual Property Journal* 161; D. Brennan and A. Christie, 'Patent claims for analogous use and the threshold requirement of inventiveness' (1997) *Federal Law Review* 237.
631 *AstraZeneca AB v Apotex Pty Ltd* (2014) 226 FCR 324 (FC), [379].
632 *NV Philips Gloeilampenfabrieken v Mirabella International Pty Ltd* (1995) 183 CLR 655, 664; *Merck & Co Inc v Arrow Pharmaceuticals Ltd* (2006) 154 FCR 31, [22].
633 *Lockwood Security Products Pty Ltd v Doric Products Pty Ltd (No 2)* (2007) 235 CLR 173, [106]; *D'Arcy v Myriad Genetics Inc* (2015) 258 CLR 334, [131] (Gageler and Nettle JJ); *Merck & Co Inc v Arrow Pharmaceuticals Ltd* (2006) 154 FCR 31, [62].
634 *AstraZeneca AB v Apotex Pty Ltd* (2014) 226 FCR 324 (FC), [383].

10 Patents for inventions: validity   369

are determined with reference to a clearly defined body of knowledge that is established with reference to the relevant prior art base, this is not true for this threshold quality of inventiveness in the opening words of s 18(1) of the *Patents Act 1990* (Cth). The majority spoke of 'the specification, when properly construed and understood' by a person skilled in the relevant art.[635] The enlarged Full Court in *AstraZeneca AB v Apotex* clarified, with reference to earlier authority,[636] that the assessment of newness or inventiveness is by reference only to what is disclosed or revealed as known on the face of the specification as properly construed.[637] This could include documents that are incorporated into the specification by reference,[638] but not publications that are referred to merely as a source for statements made in the specification. Otherwise, the specification is to be used as the sole body of information. In contrast with the statutory test for inventive step in s 7(2), the common general knowledge cannot be referred to as a body of knowledge but merely to aid the interpretation of the specification.[639]

The threshold requirement will be satisfied if the body of prior knowledge disclosed by the specification is insufficient to deprive what is claimed of the quality of inventiveness. In such a case, the patentability of the invention proceeds with reference to the subsections in s 18. In the case of lack of inventive step, the assessment is with reference to the body of knowledge described in s 7(2) and (3).[640] This threshold test application must avoid incursion into these specific sections of the *Patents Act 1990* (Cth).[641]

The threshold requirement of inventiveness has practical significance where the lack of inventiveness is so apparent that it is unnecessary to adduce evidence of a prior art base.[642] This may arise where there is a clear collocation of separate parts[643] that, on the face of the specification, provide 'no synergy, or working interrelationship, suggested between the two integers'.[644]

Apart from the above, its application will always overlap with the test for obviousness under s 18(1)(b)(ii), so the principal practical application for the threshold test is likely to be one of expediency to avoid costs and delays associated with proving a lack of inventive step. There is a need to provide an efficient means for the refusal of rubbishy, mischievous and

---

635   *NV Philips Gloeilampenfabrieken v Mirabella International Pty Ltd* (1995) 183 CLR 655, 662. For construction of claims, see ch 12.
636   *Bristol-Myers Squibb Co v FH Faulding & Co Ltd* (2000) 97 FCR 524, [30]; *Merck & Co Inc v Arrow Pharmaceuticals Ltd* (2006) 154 FCR 31, [22], [66], [72]–[75]; *Novozymes A/S v Danisco A/S* (2013) 99 IPR 417, [215], [221].
637   *AstraZeneca AB v Apotex Pty Ltd* (2014) 226 FCR 324 (FC), [391].
638   *Merck & Co Inc v Arrow Pharmaceuticals Ltd* (2006) 154 FCR 31, [34], [39], [62]; *Apotex Pty Ltd v Sanofi-Aventis* (2009) 82 IPR 416, [192]; *Apotex Pty Ltd (formerly GenRx Pty Ltd) v Sanofi-Aventis* (2008) 78 IPR 485, [121]; *Astra-Zeneca AB v Apotex Pty Ltd* (2014) 226 FCR 324 (FC), [389].
639   *AstraZeneca AB v Apotex Pty Ltd* (2014) 226 FCR 324 (FC), [384]–[392].
640   *Bristol-Myers Squibb Co v FH Faulding & Co Ltd* (2000) 97 FCR 524, [30]. The *Patents Amendment Act 2001* (Cth) amended s 7 of the *Patents Act 1990* (Cth).
641   *Merck & Co Inc v Arrow Pharmaceuticals Ltd* (2006) 154 FCR 31, [64]; *Bristol-Myers Squibb Co v FH Faulding & Co Ltd* (2000) 97 FCR 524, [30].
642   *Arrow Pharmaceuticals Ltd v Merck & Co Inc* (2004) 63 IPR 85, [80]; *Sigma Pharmaceuticals (Australia) Pty Ltd v Wyeth* (2009) 81 IPR 339.
643   *Welch Perrin & Co Pty Ltd v Worrel* (1961) 106 CLR 588, 611; *Ramset Fasteners (Australia) Pty Ltd v Advanced Building Systems Pty Ltd* (1996) 66 FCR 151, 168.
644   *WM Wrigley Jr Co v Cadbury Schweppes Pty Ltd* (2005) 66 IPR 298, [94]; *Sabaf SpA v MFI Furniture Centres Pty Ltd* [2005] RPC 10.

manifestly uninventive applications at the earliest possible stage in the patent application process. Although there were early doubts regarding the existence of this test, it is now firmly entrenched as one of the argued grounds of invalidity of a standard patent.[645]

10.9.3 Innovation patents and the threshold issue

Although the opening words of s 18(1) of the *Patents Act 1990* (Cth) are similar to those in s 18(1A), there is no reason to expect that they would be given the same interpretation when the context is that of an innovation patent that requires no inventiveness.[646] Nevertheless, members of the Federal Court in *Dura-Post (Australia) Pty Ltd v Delnorth Pty Ltd*[647] did not question its applicability when Dura-Post argued the point before them.

10.10 Utility

10.10.1 General

Utility is a ground of examination,[648] opposition,[649] re-examination[650] and revocation.[651] Reform proposals implemented by the *Raising the Bar Act* introduced utility as a ground of examination for standard and innovation patents and for re-examination of standard patents. Previously, there was some flexibility for considering utility at examination due to some overlapping between the concepts of utility and that of sufficiency of description of the invention.[652] Therefore, the Commissioner could take utility indirectly into account at examination if the specification did not comply with the requirements of s 40. However, the risk remained that a patent could be accepted and granted for a useless patent in the absence of opposition proceedings. Section 18(1)(c) does not require the invention to remain useful at all times during the life of the patent.[653]

10.10.2 Meaning of 'useful'

An invention, so far as claimed in any claim, must be useful to be patentable.[654] The ground of inutility is not concerned with the question of whether the invention to be used by following

---

645 For example, *Grant v Commissioner of Patents* (2006) 154 FCR 62, [5]; *Merck & Co Inc v Arrow Pharmaceuticals Ltd* (2006) 154 FCR 31, [62]; *Ranbaxy Australia Pty Ltd v Warner-Lambert Co LLC (No 2)* (2006) 71 IPR 46; *Apotex Pty Ltd (formerly GenRx Pty Ltd) v Sanofi-Aventis* (2008) 78 IPR 485.
646 A. L. Monotti, 'Innovation patents: The concept of manner of new manufacture and assessment of innovative step: *Dura-Post (Aust) Pty Ltd v Delnorth Pty Ltd*' (2010) 32 *European Intellectual Property Review* 93.
647 (2009) 81 IPR 480.
648 *Patents Act 1990* (Cth) ss 45(1)(b), 101B, amended by *Intellectual Property Laws Amendment (Raising the Bar) Act 2012* (Cth) sch 1 items 12, 20.
649 *Patents Act 1990* (Cth) s 59(b). The ability to consider utility at opposition was introduced on 16 August 2004 by *US Free Trade Agreement Implementation Act 2004* (Cth) sch 8 item 1.
650 *Patents Act 1990* (Cth) s 98, amended by *Intellectual Property Laws Amendment (Raising the Bar) Act 2012* (Cth) sch 1 item 17.
651 *Patents Act 1990* (Cth) s 138(3)(b).
652 *Rescare Ltd v Anaesthetic Supplies Pty Ltd* (1992) 25 IPR 119, 142.
653 *Alphapharm Pty Ltd v Merck & Co Inc* [2006] FCA 1227, [28], [29].
654 *Patents Act 1990* (Cth) s 18(1)(c).

the directions in the patent would be commercially viable.[655] The basic principle is that the invention is useful if it does what the patentee intended and achieves that promised useful result.[656] This principle can be framed as two questions:

> first, what is the promise of the invention derived from the whole of the specification?; second, by following the teaching of the specification, does the invention, as claimed in the patent, attain the result promised for it by the patentee?[657]

In order to ascertain the intention of the patentee, the whole specification is construed at the priority date.[658] The fact that there may be better ways of performing the invention is irrelevant if the invention is useful for the intended purpose.[659] Hence, identification of the result promised is fundamental in a utility challenge.[660]

The ground of inutility may be established by showing that the invention does not produce any useful result at all.[661] This will arise because the claim omits a necessary feature or features of the invention that cannot be supplied by the skilled addressee.[662] Moreover, a claim is not rendered useful merely because a problem with its utility can be overcome by taking some additional steps.[663] Everything within the claim must be useful.[664] It can also be established by showing that both useful and useless devices and processes fall within the claim and that the language of the claim positively 'points to some useless construction'.[665] The claim cannot be saved by showing that no skilled person would ever try to use that method.[666] However, the court should be reluctant to place a construction on a claim so as to include embodiments that would appear useless to the qualified reader,[667] when they can be construed to give the claim a more limited meaning.[668] It is inappropriate to purposely adopt a form of the invention that would obviously malfunction.[669]

---

[655] *Rescare Ltd v Anaesthetic Supplies Pty Ltd* (1992) 25 IPR 119, 143; *Decor Corp Pty Ltd v Dart Industries Inc* (1988) 13 IPR 385, 394; *Grant v Commissioner of Patents* (2006) 154 FCR 62, [43].
[656] *Fawcett v Homan* (1896) 13 RPC 398, 405 (Lindley LJ); *Rehm Pty Ltd v Websters Security Systems (International) Pty Ltd* (1988) 11 IPR 289, 305; *Advanced Building Systems Pty Ltd v Ramset Fasteners (Aust) Pty Ltd* (1998) 194 CLR 171, [24]; *Welcome Real-Time SA v Catuity Inc* (2001) 113 FCR 110, [160]; *ESCO Corp v Ronneby Road Pty Ltd* (2018) 131 IPR 1, [233].
[657] *Artcraft Urban Group Pty Ltd v Streetworx Pty Ltd* (2016) 245 FCR 485, [121] and cited authorities.
[658] *Rehm Pty Ltd v Websters Security Systems (International) Pty Ltd* (1988) 11 IPR 289, 305.
[659] Ibid 306.
[660] *Artcraft Urban Group Pty Ltd v Streetworx Pty Ltd* (2016) 245 FCR 485, [137].
[661] *Patent Gesellschaft AG v Saudi Livestock Transport & Trading Co* (1996) 33 IPR 426, 458.
[662] *Welch Perrin & Co Pty Ltd v Worrel* (1961) 106 CLR 588, 602; *Washex Machinery Corp v Roy Burton & Co Pty Ltd* (1974) 49 ALJR 12, 18–19; *Rescare Ltd v Anaesthetic Supplies Pty Ltd* (1992) 25 IPR 119, 143.
[663] *Pracdes Pty Ltd v Stanilite Electronics Pty Ltd* (1995) 35 IPR 259, 275.
[664] *H Lundbeck A/S v Alphapharm Pty Ltd* (2009) 177 FCR 151, [217].
[665] *Cincinnati Grinders (Inc) v BSA Tools Ltd* (1931) 48 RPC 33, 73; T. A. Blanco White, *Patents for Inventions and the Protection of Industrial Designs* (4th edn, London: Stevens, 1974) [4-408]; *Rehm Pty Ltd v Websters Security Systems (International) Pty Ltd* (1988) 11 IPR 289, 298.
[666] *Coopers Animal Health Australia Ltd v Western Stock Distributors Pty Ltd* (1986) 6 IPR 545, 572–3 (Wilcox J); *Inverness Medical Switzerland GmbH v MDS Diagnostics Pty Ltd* (2010) 85 IPR 525, [117].
[667] *Rescare Ltd v Anaesthetic Supplies Pty Ltd* (1992) 25 IPR 119, 143.
[668] *Rehm Pty Ltd v Websters Security Systems (International) Pty Ltd* (1988) 11 IPR 289, 307–8, quoting from Blanco White, *Patents for Inventions and the Protection of Industrial Designs*, above n 665, [4-408]; *Welch Perrin & Co Pty Ltd v Worrel* (1961) 106 CLR 588, 601–2; *Nesbit Evans Group Australia Pty Ltd v Impro Ltd* (1997) 39 IPR 56, 96–7.
[669] *Washex Machinery Corp v Roy Burton & Co Pty Ltd* (1974) 49 ALJR 12, 18–20; *Martin Engineering Co v Trison Holdings Pty Ltd* (1989) 14 IPR 330, 338.

It is not necessary that the promise be fulfilled in every instance of its use for utility to be present. Hence, in the case of an invention for a face mask designed to be used in the treatment of sleep apnoea, it was enough for the claimed invention to be of practical utility in the treatment of substantial numbers of persons who are 'patients' within the meaning of the claim.[670] The fact that the mask would not work on some patients did not render the invention useless. There is a distinction here between the embodiment of the invention that works in most instances and an embodiment of an invention that will never work.[671]

The specification might identify an invention that promises multiple enhancements or elements. For instance, an invention for an attachment that reduces the wear occasioned to excavating equipment might offer 'enhanced stability, strength, durability, penetration, safety and ease of replacement'.[672] In *ESCO Corp v Ronneby Road Pty Ltd*,[673] the Full Federal Court construed the specification to identify what the patentee intended to be the promise of the invention. If this is as a composite promise – each claim must fulfil each and every element – a claimed invention will be inutile if it fails to attain all of those elements. In contrast, if it is construed as a disjunctive promise, as was the case in *ESCO*, a claimed invention will be useful as long as it achieves one of those elements.[674]

The *Raising the Bar Act*[675] introduced s 7A to strengthen the concept of utility as recommended in two reviews[676] and in a manner that is consistent with Australia's obligations under the *Australia–US Free Trade Agreement 2004* (*AUSFTA*).[677] The amendment does not displace the existing case law but imposes an additional requirement that 'an invention is taken not to be useful unless a specific, substantial and credible use for the invention (so far as claimed) is disclosed in the complete specification'. This disclosure must enable a person skilled in the relevant art to appreciate the 'specific, substantial and credible use'. The intention expressed in the Explanatory Memorandum is that 'specific, substantial and credible be given the same meaning as is currently given by the US courts and the United States Patent and Trade Mark Office (USPTO)'.[678]

10.11 Secret use
10.11.1 General

A final requirement for patent validity in s 18(1) and (1A) of the *Patents Act 1990* (Cth) is that there has been no secret use of the claimed invention in the patent area before the priority date

---

670 *Rescare Ltd v Anaesthetic Supplies Pty Ltd* (1992) 25 IPR 119, 143; *Nesbit Evans Group Australia Pty Ltd v Impro Ltd* (1997) 39 IPR 56, 96 (Lindgren J).
671 See also *Abbott Laboratories v Corbridge Group Pty Ltd* (2002) 57 IPR 432, [64].
672 *ESCO Corp v Ronneby Road Pty Ltd* (2018) 131 IPR 1.
673 Ibid.
674 Ibid [233].
675 *Intellectual Property Laws Amendment (Raising the Bar) Act 2012* (Cth) sch 1 item 6.
676 Intellectual Property and Competition Review Committee, *Review of Intellectual Property Legislation under the Competition Principles Agreement* (September 2000); ALRC, *Genes and Ingenuity*, above n 50.
677 Signed 18 May 2004, [2005] ATS 1 (entered into force 1 April 2005) art 17.9.13.
678 Explanatory Memorandum, Intellectual Property Laws Amendment (Raising the Bar) Bill 2011 (Cth) sch 1 item 6 summarises the meaning of each of these terms and references under ss 2107–2107.03 of the USPTO's *Manual of Patent Examining Procedure*.

of the claim by, or with the authority of, a patentee or nominated person or their predecessor in title (the patentee).[679] Critically, the specification must be construed before examining whether the use in question falls within the scope of any claim or claims.[680] Secret use by anyone else is irrelevant when considering the patentability of an invention under the *Patents Act 1990*. However, such use may be relevant to establish rights of prior user under s 119. This contrasts with the position under the *Patents Act 1952* (Cth), where secret use of an invention by anyone in Australia before the priority date was a ground for revocation of the patent.[681]

Secret use is a ground of opposition[682] and revocation[683] but not of examination. As with utility, the ability to consider prior secret use at opposition was introduced on 16 August 2004 by the *US Free Trade Agreement Implementation Act 2004* (Cth) sch 8 item 1. The current s 59 of the *Patents Act 1990* (Cth) applies to all applications for a standard patent made after this date and all applications made before this date, but for which a patent has not been granted by 16 August 2004.

10.11.2 Rationale

The rationale underlying the availability of secret use by the patentee as a ground of revocation is to prevent the patentee from gaining a de facto extension of the monopoly period without public disclosure of the invention.[684]

The prohibition on commercial secret use before the priority date is consistent with the interface between patents and protection of trade secrets. The patentee is forced to choose between patent protection and trade secret protection where they exploit the invention commercially. If the patentee chooses to work the invention in secret for purposes of trade or commerce, they cannot subsequently then apply for patent protection to gain a longer monopoly period in which to exploit the invention.

Nevertheless, the *Patents Act 1990* (Cth) recognises certain exceptions to secret use in s 9, and as Burley J concluded in *Coretell Pty Ltd v Australian Mud Company Pty Ltd*, 'use that is a de facto extension of term may be permitted, and not invalidating, if the exceptions apply.'[685]

10.11.3 The relationship with novelty

An invention is no longer novel when it is made publicly available before the priority date.[686] This may arise from a public use of the invention. Secret use is necessarily concerned with disclosures that cannot affect the novelty of the invention because they are secret. It is likely

---

679 *Patents Act 1990* (Cth) s 18(1)(d), (1A)(d).
680 *DSI Australia (Holdings) Pty Ltd v Garford Pty Ltd* (2013) 100 IPR 19, [141]–[176] (example of secret use of a method).
681 *Patents Act 1952* (Cth) s 100(1)(k).
682 *Patents Act 1990* (Cth) s 59(b).
683 Ibid s 138(3)(b).
684 *Grove Hill Pty Ltd v Great Western Corp Pty Ltd* (2002) 55 IPR 257, [212]; *Azuko Pty Ltd v Old Digger Pty Ltd* (2001) 52 IPR 75, [180]–[183]; *Morgan v Seaward* (1837) 2 M & W 544, 559, 150 ER 874, 880 (Parke B); *Bristol-Myers Co v Beecham Group Ltd* [1974] AC 646, 680–1 (Lord Diplock).
685 (2017) 250 FCR 155, [242].
686 *Patents Act 1990* (Cth) ss 7(1), 18(1)(b)(i), 18(1A)(b)(i).

that 'secret use' and 'public use' are mutually exclusive.[687] However, public use does not necessarily amount to a destruction of novelty. For that to occur, the essential integers of the invention must be disclosed to any one member of the public in a manner that leaves that person free, in law and equity, to make use of that information.[688] Mere use of an invention in public may not make the invention publicly available. Therefore, whereas secret use requires 'use' as opposed to disclosure, destruction of novelty through use requires a disclosure that makes publicly available all the essential features of the invention.[689]

10.11.4 The meaning of 'secret'

It seems that there must be deliberate concealment of the use of the invention to satisfy the requirement that the use is 'secret'.[690] The imposition of an obligation of confidence on third parties, either expressly or by implication, is a guide as to whether a use is 'secret'.[691] Employees of the patentee are assumed to be bound by confidence if they are involved in a secret use.[692] An accidental or inadvertent use of the invention in circumstances where the use was not publicly available will not be 'secret' as an intention to conceal is required.[693]

10.11.5 The meaning of 'use'

If no commercial dealing has been finalised prior to the priority date, the disclosure of the invention under circumstances of confidence to employees, or demonstration to a patent attorney or potential purchaser, will not amount to a secret use.[694] The meaning given to 'use' of the invention in this context is not co-extensive with the meaning of to 'exploit' the invention.[695] It is only one aspect of the definition of exploit and therefore has a narrower meaning.[696] At the same time, it is not exclusive of the various aspects of that definition. There may be some overlap among the different types of exploitation, such as where a sale of goods made according to the patent might be seen also as commercial use of the goods. Nevertheless, the distinctions cannot be ignored.[697]

The question came before the Full Federal Court in *Azuko Pty Ltd v Old Digger Pty Ltd* (*Azuko*) whether, before filing a patent application, Old Digger's secret manufacture of fifteen

---

687 *Grove Hill Pty Ltd v Great Western Corp Pty Ltd* (2002) 55 IPR 257, [212].
688 *Humpherson v Syer* (1887) 4 RPC 407; *Stanway Oyster Cylinders Pty Ltd v Marks* (1996) 66 FCR 577, 581; *JMVB Enterprises Pty Ltd v Camoflag Pty Ltd* (2005) 67 IPR 68, 80.
689 *Stanway Oyster Cylinders Pty Ltd v Marks* (1996) 66 FCR 577, 581–2. See above at 10.6.7.
690 *Bristol-Myers Co v Beecham Group Ltd* [1974] AC 646, 702; *Re Wheatley's Patent Application* (1984) 2 IPR 450, 455 (Dillon LJ).
691 *Re Wheatley's Patent Application* (1984) 2 IPR 450; Patents Act 1990 (Cth) s 9(b).
692 *Azuko Pty Ltd v Old Digger Pty Ltd* (2001) 52 IPR 75, [178] (Gyles J); *Melbourne v Terry Fluid Controls Pty Ltd* (1993) 26 IPR 292, 302.
693 *Bristol-Myers Co v Beecham Group Ltd* [1974] AC 646, 702.
694 *Azuko Pty Ltd v Old Digger Pty Ltd* (2001) 52 IPR 75, [149] (Heerey J).
695 Ibid [186]; *Grove Hill Pty Ltd v Great Western Corp Pty Ltd* (2002) 55 IPR 257.
696 *Grove Hill Pty Ltd v Great Western Corp Pty Ltd* (2002) 55 IPR 257, [213]; *Azuko Pty Ltd v Old Digger Pty Ltd* (2001) 52 IPR 75, [186]. For a critique of the latter decision, see A. L. Monotti, 'To make an article for ultimate sale: The secret use provision in the Patents Act 1990 (Cth)' [2005] 27 *European Intellectual Property Review* 446.
697 *Azuko Pty Ltd v Old Digger Pty Ltd* (2001) 52 IPR 75, [186].

to twenty percussive hammers in a condition ready for later commercial sale amounted to a secret use of the claimed invention. A further complication was that Old Digger had received unsolicited orders for five or six hammers from a friend and customer, also before the patent application was filed. The majority expressed the following practical test to determine whether there has been the required type of 'use':

> [H]as what occurred amounted to a de facto extension of the patent term? The answer to this will usually depend upon whether the patentee reaped commercial benefit from what was done before the priority date.[698]

However, the commercial character of an act is not the deciding factor when investigating the existence of secret use, as not all acts that have a commercial aspect necessarily involve a de facto extension of the term.[699] According to the majority, if the invention is a process or method, use of the process to make goods for sale would extend the patent if done before the priority date. However, if the invention is a product, the majority held that manufacture of the product would not involve any de facto extension of the term of a patent claiming the product, even if manufacture was for the purpose of sale.[700] Rather, it would be necessary, in the judges' view, to secretly use the product made according to the patent as part of a manufacturing process to make other goods[701] or to use that product as part of an assembly engaged in a commercial activity.[702] An example of the latter circumstance arose from the facts of *Azuko*. The patent claimed a drill bit, namely, a down-hole reverse-circulation percussive hammer. The use of a hammer made according to the patent as part of a drill rig engaged in commercial drilling in conditions of secrecy before the priority date of the claim would amount to a secret use. Other 'uses' of the tangible products that would satisfy this concept of secret 'use' would include dealing commercially in the products of the invention before the priority date[703] through leasing, sale or agreement for sale.[704] This would include acceptance of an order for the manufacture of the product.[705]

The receipt of an unsolicited order from a person who had been involved in testing a prototype would not amount to secret use as this would not involve the patentee in any activity at all.[706] Other acts that would not constitute a secret use are the manufacture simpliciter with a sale at cost to a person who is intended to, and becomes, the assignee of the patent,[707] and secret use for philanthropy or a hobby.[708]

---

698   Ibid [181].
699   Ibid [183]; *Patents Act 1990* (Cth) s 9.
700   Ibid.
701   An example of how this may arise is in the context of infringement: see *Pinefair Pty Ltd v Bedford Industries Rehabilitation Association Inc* (1998) 87 FCR 458.
702   *Azuko Pty Ltd v Old Digger Pty Ltd* (2001) 52 IPR 75, [183].
703   *Re Wheatley's Patent Application* (1984) 2 IPR 450, 453 (Lawton LJ).
704   *Azuko Pty Ltd v Old Digger Pty Ltd* (2001) 52 IPR 75, 136; *Re Wheatley's Patent Application* (1984) 2 IPR 450, 454 (Oliver LJ), 455 (Dillon LJ).
705   *Re Wheatley's Patent Application* (1984) 2 IPR 450, 452 (Lawton LJ).
706   *Azuko Pty Ltd v Old Digger Pty Ltd* (2001) 52 IPR 75, [177].
707   Ibid [178].
708   Ibid [144].

10.11.6 Use for reasonable trial or experiment only

The *Patents Act 1990* (Cth) does not define secret use. However, the list of acts in s 9 that are taken not to be secret use of the invention provides some guidance.[709] The first is use of the invention by the patentee for the purpose of reasonable trial or experiment only.[710] This exception is essential as virtually all inventions will have been secretly used for experimental or trial purposes.[711] The terms 'reasonable trial or experiment' are not defined but have been held to include trial and evaluation to learn whether a product needs improvement or to learn how it may be improved.[712] They would also include experimental use to refine or prove a concept[713] or use in the course of discovering, perfecting and trying out the invention so as to test its suitability for commercial use.[714] Acts may fall within this exception as long as the 'true purpose' of the use is for trial or experiment and the trial or experiment is reasonable. It does not matter that there is also a collateral commercial advantage to the inventor, such as the production of a commercial crop.[715] Although such a use may provide a de facto extension of term, it is not an invalidating use when the exception applies.[716]

In assessing what is reasonable, it is necessary to take into account the nature of the invention, the tasks for which it is designed and the conditions under which it is to be used. Thus, field trials of an agricultural row cultivator in connection with the cultivation of commercial crops on the patentee's property for a period of just over one year were said to amount to reasonable trial.[717]

In *DSI Australia (Holdings) Pty Ltd v Garford Pty Ltd*, Yates J determined that use of an apparatus before the priority date solely for reasonable trial is not denied that character because material produced in the trial was sold. However, the extent of that commercial dealing may be relevant to whether the trial is 'reasonable'.[718] It is likely that the manufacture of products in a condition ready for commercial sale may not be considered a matter of trial and experiment.[719] It is also likely that the manufacture of products to see if production is commercially viable is not the kind of trial and experiment of which s 9(a) speaks. It will be a matter of fact in each case[720] as to when trial and experiment ceases and commercial production commences, but it seems that the 'commercial quality' of the products and their readiness

---

709   *Patents Act 1990* (Cth) s 9.
710   Ibid s 9(a).
711   *Grove Hill Pty Ltd v Great Western Corp Pty Ltd* (2002) 55 IPR 257, [221]; *Coretell Pty Ltd v Australian Mud Company Pty Ltd* (2017) 250 FCR 155.
712   *Melbourne v Terry Fluid Controls Pty Ltd* (1993) 26 IPR 292, 302.
713   *Grove Hill Pty Ltd v Great Western Corp Pty Ltd* (2002) 55 IPR 257, [226], [231], [233]; *Coretell Pty Ltd v Australian Mud Company Pty Ltd* (2017) 250 FCR 155, [232].
714   *Bristol-Myers Co v Beecham Group Ltd* [1974] AC 646, 680–1 (Lord Diplock).
715   *Grove Hill Pty Ltd v Great Western Corp Pty Ltd* (2002) 55 IPR 257, [229]; *Coretell Pty Ltd v Australian Mud Company Pty Ltd* (2017) 250 FCR 155, [222]–[225], [229], [242].
716   *Coretell Pty Ltd v Australian Mud Company Pty Ltd* (2017) 250 FCR 155, [242].
717   *Grove Hill Pty Ltd v Great Western Corp Pty Ltd* (2002) 55 IPR 257, [232].
718   *DSI Australia (Holdings) Pty Ltd v Garford Pty Ltd* (2013) 100 IPR 19, [174]. The finding of the trial judge that there was no secret use on the facts was reversed on appeal, but this principle was unchallenged: *Garford Pty Ltd v DYWIDAG Systems International Pty Ltd* (2015) 110 IPR 30, [141].
719   *Azuko Pty Ltd v Old Digger Pty Ltd* (2001) 52 IPR 75, [147].
720   See, for example, *Harrison v Project & Design Co (Redcar) Ltd (No 1)* [1978] FSR 81.

'to work' are factors that indicate the experiment has concluded. According to Heerey J in *Azuko*:

> The provision is limited to trial or experiment to see how the product of an invention performs and whether any improvements are needed, as distinct from commercial or marketing assessments.[721]

10.11.7 Use occurring solely in a confidential disclosure

The second act in s 9 that is taken not to be secret use of the invention is use by the patentee occurring *solely* in the course of a confidential disclosure of the invention by the patentee.[722] In the absence of a definition of 'confidential disclosure', this would occur if confidentiality is imposed by contract or satisfies the requirements for the equitable doctrine of breach of confidence.[723] Confidentiality may be implied from the circumstances surrounding the disclosure.[724] The subsection does not exclude from its operation confidential disclosures that are for the purpose of trade or commerce. Hence, the demonstration of a product in confidence before the priority date with the object of bringing about a sale would fall within this exception. Similarly, the demonstration of the invention to a patent attorney or potential purchaser or investor would fall within this exception.[725] It would seem that the subsequent unconditional acceptance of an order to purchase the product would no longer have the benefit of this exemption.[726]

In *Azuko*, von Doussa J exempted the manufacture of drill hammers used in the mining industry from secret use on the basis that this was a confidential use 'which did not involve disclosure of the invention to anyone other than [the] employees' engaged in the manufacture.[727] However, Heerey J in his dissenting opinion on appeal[728] rejected this approach, by way of obiter dicta, for two reasons. First, he considered that the words 'solely in the course of a confidential disclosure' suggested a confidential disclosure of the invention in the course of which the invention was 'used'. He described a use that would satisfy this subsection as a demonstration of the invention to a patent attorney or potential purchaser or investor. In contrast, although the manufacture of the drill hammers for the purposes of sale would have involved a disclosure of the invention in confidence to employees to carry out the manufacture, the disclosure would not have involved the use of the invention. Rather, the disclosure of the information enabled the later 'use' of the invention. Second, and in any event, Heerey J pointed out that such use in manufacture was not *solely* in the course of a confidential disclosure because it was also for the purposes of sale.[729]

---

721   *Azuko Pty Ltd v Old Digger Pty Ltd* (2001) 52 IPR 75, [148].
722   *Patents Act 1990* (Cth) s 9(b).
723   See ch 8.
724   *Melbourne v Terry Fluid Controls Pty Ltd* (1993) 26 IPR 292, 302.
725   *Azuko Pty Ltd v Old Digger Pty Ltd* (2001) 52 IPR 75, [149].
726   *Re Wheatley's Patent Application* (1984) 2 IPR 450.
727   *Azuko Pty Ltd v Old Digger Pty Ltd* (2001) 52 IPR 75, [109] (Heerey J), quoting von Doussa J in *Azuko Pty Ltd v Old Digger Pty Ltd* (2000) 51 IPR 43.
728   *Azuko Pty Ltd v Old Digger Pty Ltd* (2001) 52 IPR 75, [149].
729   Ibid.

10.11.8 Patentee use for any purpose other than trade or commerce

The third act that is taken not to be secret use of the invention is use by the patentee for any purpose other than the purpose of trade or commerce.[730] The terms 'trade or commerce' are not defined in the *Patents Act 1990* (Cth) but would be expected to have their ordinary meaning,[731] qualified by the preceding words 'for any purpose *other than the purpose of* trade or commerce'.[732]

Some assistance in interpreting the phrase 'for any purpose *other than the purpose of* trade or commerce' comes from the following statement of the High Court in *Concrete Constructions (NSW) Pty Ltd v Nelson*,[733] made in the context of the phrase 'in trade or commerce' that appeared in the now repealed s 52 of the *Trade Practices Act 1974* (Cth):

> [T]he words 'in trade or commerce' refer to 'the central conception' of trade or commerce and not to the 'immense field of activities' in which corporations may engage in the course of, or for the purposes of, carrying on some overall trading or commercial business.[734]

The latter comment suggests that the phrase 'for the purpose of trade or commerce' in s 9(c) of the *Patents Act 1990* (Cth) may have a broad scope and encompass an 'immense field of activities'.

10.11.9 Use on behalf of the government

The fourth act that is taken not to be secret use of the invention is use of the invention by or on behalf of the Commonwealth, a State or a Territory where it was disclosed to that person by the patentee. The terms 'Commonwealth' and 'State' are undefined for the purposes of this provision. This contrasts with Chapter 17 of the *Patents Act 1990* (Cth), where a reference to the Commonwealth or a State includes a reference to an authority of the Commonwealth or a State respectively.[735] 'Territory' is defined in sch 1 of the Act to mean 'a Territory in which this Act applies or to which this Act extends'.

10.11.10 Onus of proof

In revocation proceedings, the party who seeks revocation on grounds of secret use by the patentee bears the onus of satisfying the court that there has been a disqualifying secret use,

---

730   *Patents Act 1990* (Cth) s 9(c). This would seem to exclude from secret use the type of circumstances that arose in *Harrison v Project & Design Co (Redcar) Ltd (No 1)* [1978] FSR 81.
731   *Bank of New South Wales v Commonwealth* (1948) 76 CLR 1.
732   Emphasis added.
733   (1990) 169 CLR 594, 602–4.
734   Ibid 603. The equivalent section now appears as s 18 of sch 2 of the *Competition and Consumer Act 2010* (Cth).
735   *Patents Act 1990* (Cth) s 162. For the meaning of 'authority of a State', see *Stack v Brisbane City Council* (1995) 59 FCR 71. Reform of the Crown use of patents contained in Intellectual Property Laws Amendment (Productivity Commission Response Part 2 and Other Measures) Bill 2019 (Cth) sch 2 pt 1 repeals s 162 but inserts a definition of 'relevant authority' in sch 1 of the *Patents Act 1990* (Cth) that has the same effect: at sch 2 pt 1 items 6 and 25, respectively.

having regard to the combined operation of ss 9 and 18 of the *Patents Act 1990* (Cth). Proof of use that may have been for the purpose of trial or experiment only will not discharge the onus. The revoker has the onus of excluding reasonable trial and experiment.[736]

10.11.11 Grace period

A prior *public* disclosure by or on behalf of the patentee that occurs within the twelve months preceding the filing of the complete specification has the benefit of a grace period for the purposes of novelty and inventive step.[737] In the past, there was no similar provision available for a patentee's secret use. A rationale for this distinction is that the public suffers no detriment and the patentee gains no advantage when the information becomes publicly available before the priority date. Secret use for twelve months preceding the filing of the complete application provides a de facto extension of the patent term.

However, the *Raising the Bar* reforms removed this distinction and amended s 9 of the *Patents Act 1990* (Cth) to provide in s 9(e) that any use by or on behalf of the patentee for any purpose within twelve months of making a complete application is not to be taken to be secret use of the invention.[738] The prescribed period of twelve months of filing the complete application corresponds with the existing grace period. Two reasons supported this change. First, it might be difficult in practice to decide whether a particular use will result in information becoming publicly available.[739] The availability of an identical grace period for both secret use and publicly available disclosures avoids this dilemma. Second, as the Explanatory Memorandum points out, the lack of a grace period for prior secret use

> gives rise to an absurd situation in which public use of the invention by a patentee within 12 months of filing a complete application does not impact on patentability of an invention, by virtue of the grace period, but secret use in the same period does.[740]

10.12 Express exclusions from patentability

10.12.1 Human beings and biological processes for their generation

The *Patents Act 1990* (Cth) contains an exclusion from patentability for human beings and the biological processes for their generation, for both standard and innovation patents.[741] The

---

736 *Grove Hill Pty Ltd v Great Western Corp Pty Ltd* (2002) 55 IPR 257, [221] (Dowsett J); *Coretell Pty Ltd v Australian Mud Company Pty Ltd* (2017) 250 FCR 155, [227].
737 *Patents Act 1990* (Cth) s 24. See above at 10.6.10.
738 *Intellectual Property Laws Amendment (Raising the Bar) Act 2012* (Cth) sch 6 items 28, 29.
739 IP Australia, *Review of the Patent Grace Period*, above n 424, 7.
740 Explanatory Memorandum, Intellectual Property Laws Amendment (Raising the Bar) Bill 2011 (Cth) sch 6 items 28, 29,
741 *Patents Act 1990* (Cth) s 18(2). ACIP recommended the retention of these exclusions from patentability in ACIP, *Patentable Subject Matter*, above n 50, rec 6.

Deputy Commissioner of Patents considered the scope of this exclusion in *Re Luminis Pty Ltd and Fertilitescentrum AB*[742] and concluded that:

1. A human being is distinct from a human life form.
2. There is no single point in the reproductive process when a human being comes into existence. Instead, its generation occurs over a substantial period of time.
3. Any entity that might reasonably claim the status of the human being is within the prohibition of 'human beings'. Hence, this would include not only a person that has been born, but also a fertilised ovum and all its subsequent manifestations.
4. The prohibition of 'biological processes' for the generation of human beings covers all biological processes applied from fertilisation to birth, as long as the process is one that directly relates to the generation of human beings. This would include processes of generating the entity that can first claim the status of human being, such as processes of fertilising an ovum, processes for cloning at the four-cell stage by division, and processes for cloning by replacing nuclear DNA.

A number of matters influenced the decision, but particularly the undesirable consequences that would arise if s 18(2) required the identification of a particular stage in the reproductive process when a human being comes into existence. Any decision that specified a particular point would not reflect the diversity of opinion and was therefore better avoided.

The s 18(2) exclusion for a method for generation of a human being has been applied to a method of producing a hybrid embryo created by transferring the nucleus of a human cell into a bovine ovum, and then activating the ovum. The Deputy Commissioner of Patents concluded that the hybrid embryo produced by the claimed method was properly described as human.[743] This exclusion applies also when the claimed method is a biological process for the generation of a human being (within the meaning of this section) but includes further steps that prevent its further development. This might involve its subsequent use for a different purpose or its destruction to allow use of the cells produced.[744] However, a biological process that cannot generate a human being is patentable. In *Re International Stem Cell Corp*, the delegate for the Commissioner of Patents determined that a blastocyst produced by parthenogenesis (without fertilisation by human sperm) has no potential to

> lead to birth so does not lie on the pathway from fertilisation to birth, and thus cannot claim the status of a human being. At each point from oocyte activation to the formation of the blastocyst, as well as developmental stages further down the developmental path, the entity is not a human being.[745]

10.12.2 Plants and animals

In addition to the exclusion for human beings and the biological processes for their generation, s 18(3) of the *Patents Act 1990* (Cth) excludes plants and animals and the biological processes for

---

742 (2004) 62 IPR 420; *Re Hwang* (2004) AIPC 92–031.
743 *Re Hwang* (2004) AIPC 92–031.
744 *Re International Stem Cell Corp* (2016) 123 IPR 142, [22] (APO).
745 Ibid [30].

their generation as subject matter for an innovation patent. This exclusion does not apply if the invention is a microbiological process or a product of such a process.[746] The additional scope of the excluded subject matter arose for political rather than policy reasons.[747] In the light of relatively little public concern expressed over the innovation patent exclusion for animals and processes for their generation, a report of ACIP, *Should Plant and Animal Subject Matter Be Excluded from Protection by the Innovation Patent?*, concluded that there was insufficient reason for change at this stage. This recommendation was accepted by the government. Although the *AUSFTA* does not permit Australia to exclude plants and animals from patentability,[748] it is likely that this applies only in relation to standard patents and that the innovation patent system is not subject to the *AUSFTA*.[749] In *Patentable Subject Matter* (Final Report), ACIP recommended that the specific exclusion in s 18(3) be retained. It argued that the exclusion 'precludes overlap between the innovation patent and plant breeder's rights systems, and should be retained in order to maintain access to plant material for Australian breeders'.[750] ACIP found no persuasive case to remove the exception for animals.[751] This issue will become largely academic if parliament passes the Intellectual Property Laws Amendment (Productivity Commission Response Part 2 and Other Measures) Bill 2019 (Cth) without amendment.[752]

10.12.3 Contrary to law

Section 50(1)(a) of the *Patents Act 1990* (Cth) permits the Commissioner to refuse to accept a patent request and specification relating to a standard patent or to grant a standard patent on the grounds that its use would be contrary to law. This exclusion from patentability derives from s 6 of the *Statute of Monopolies*. The section is rarely invoked.[753] Once a patent application is accepted, there is no express ground for opposition[754] or revocation[755] that the use of the invention would be contrary to law. However, in appropriate cases, it may be possible to revoke the patent on the ground that the patent was obtained by fraud, false suggestion or misrepresentation.[756] An opportunity to oppose or seek revocation of the patent may technically arise on the basis that the invention is 'generally inconvenient', but this is unlikely to succeed.[757] As an innovation patent is granted after a formalities check, an objection on the ground that its use is contrary to law would not be possible prior to grant.[758] However, use

---

746   *Patents Act 1990* (Cth) s 18(4).
747   ACIP, *Should Plant and Animal Subject Matter Be Excluded from Protection by the Innovation Patent?* (2004).
748   *AUSFTA* art 17.9.
749   ACIP, *Review of the Innovation Patent System*, above n 16, [3.2], [8.4].
750   ACIP, *Patentable Subject Matter*, above n 50, [4.1].
751   Ibid rec 6, accepted in *Government Response: Patentable Subject Matter*, above n 50.
752   Intellectual Property Laws Amendment (Productivity Commission Response Part 2 and Other Measures) Bill 2019 (Cth) sch 1 pt 2.
753   ACIP recommended its repeal along with repeal of a corresponding ground for revocation of an innovation patent in s 101B(2): ACIP, *Patentable Subject Matter*, above n 50, rec 7, accepted in *Government Response: Patentable Subject Matter*, above n 50.
754   *Patents Act 1990* (Cth) s 59.
755   Ibid s 138.
756   Ibid s 138(3)(d).
757   Ibid ss 59(b), 138(3)(b). See above at 10.5.
758   Ibid ss 52, 62.

contrary to law is a ground for revocation of the patent following examination.[759] As to the meaning of the phrase 'use of which would be contrary to law', it seems that an invention that can be used for both lawful and unlawful purposes is not necessarily bad.[760] It is likely to be necessary to consider whether the unlawful use is the main purpose of the invention.

Factors to consider in deciding whether use of an invention is contrary to law may be the nature of the legislation that the invention would contravene, whether it is reasonable to expect that what is illegal now will remain illegal throughout the term of the patent, or whether such law would be of an ephemeral nature. For example, the *Prohibition of Human Cloning for Reproduction Act 2002* (Cth) makes it illegal to intentionally create a chimeric embryo. The Deputy Commissioner of Patents considered this legislation was not ephemeral and that a method to create an inter-species hybrid embryo should be refused under s 50(1)(a).[761]

10.12.4 Mere mixtures

Another express ground for refusal to accept a request and specification for a standard patent or to grant a standard patent is set out in s 50(1)(b) of the *Patents Act 1990* (Cth). Discretion for refusal exists where the invention claimed is for a substance that is capable of being used as food or medicine and is a mere mixture of known ingredients, or a process for producing such a substance by mere admixture. These specific products must be more than mere collocations to be patentable: they must have some synergy or working interrelationship that results in something more than what might be expected from a mere mixture.[762] The process of producing the substance by mere admixture is a specific instance of the operation of the concept that 'the use of a known material in the manufacture of known articles for the purpose of which its known properties make that material suitable'.[763] Therefore, the section permits the exclusion from patentability of these kinds of products or processes that demonstrate lack of inventiveness without having to establish lack of inventive step. Its scope is probably limited to simple recipes.[764] A similar provision provides grounds for revocation of an innovation patent.[765] These provisions overlap with the general threshold requirement for inventiveness that the High Court concluded is present in the opening words of s 18(1).[766]

10.12.5 International obligations

Members of *TRIPS* are required to make patents available for any inventions in all fields of technology.[767] However, there are two areas in which they have scope to exclude inventions

---

759   Ibid ss 101B(1), (2)(d), 101F.
760   *Pessers and Moody v Haydon & Co* (1909) 26 RPC 58; *Re Hwang* (2004) AIPC 92-031.
761   *Re Hwang* (2004) AIPC 92-031.
762   For an example of an invention found to be a collocation, see *WM Wrigley Jr Co v Cadbury Schweppes Pty Ltd* (2005) 66 IPR 298, [94]. See also *APO Manual*, above n 57, [2.9.3.2] (food or medicines being mere admixtures).
763   *Commissioner of Patents v Microcell Ltd* (1959) 102 CLR 232, 251.
764   *APO Manual*, above n 57, [2.9.2.16].
765   *Patents Act 1990* (Cth) s 101B(2)(e), (f).
766   See above at 10.9. ACIP recommended its repeal along with the repeal of s 101B(2): ACIP, *Patentable Subject Matter*, above n 50, rec 7, accepted in *Government Response: Patentable Subject Matter*, above n 50.
767   See, for example, *Canada: Patent Protection of Pharmaceutical Products: Complaint by the European Communities and their Member States*, WTO Doc WT/DS114/R (17 March 2000).

from patentability. The first area is defined by the impact of commercial exploitation on the territory. It is not permitted to exclude inventions merely because the exploitation is prohibited by laws of the country. Inventions can be excluded from patentability where it is necessary to prevent the commercial exploitation in order to protect '*ordre public* or morality, including to protect human, animal or plant life or health or to avoid serious prejudice to the environment'.[768] In such cases, legislation that regulates the exploitation would provide insufficient protection.

The second area relates to medical treatments, plants and animals. Article 27(3) of *TRIPS* allows exclusions of inventions for diagnostic, therapeutic and surgical methods for the treatment of humans or animals and plants and animals other than micro-organisms, and essentially biological processes for the production of plants or animals other than non-biological and microbiological processes.

The more limited exclusions in art 17.9 of the *AUSFTA* result in '*TRIPS* plus' restrictions in this field. Australia must give the benefit of these to its nationals and to nationals of all members of *TRIPS*.[769]

10.13 Internal requirements for patent specifications: s 40

10.13.1 Evolution of the specification and function of claims

The modern specification bears little resemblance to its earliest antecedents.[770] Prior to 1852, patents were granted upon a 'title'[771] or meagre 'recital'[772] only of the invention. This was inserted in the patent grant, and apart from any oral instructions given to individuals, it was the only source of information as to the nature of the invention and how it worked.[773]

This was not very satisfactory for either the patentee or the public. Hence, as early as the reign of Queen Anne (1702–14) it became an obligation, within six months of the patent being granted on the title, to describe and ascertain the nature of the invention and the manner of its performance in a written document. If the patentee did not file this 'specification', the patent lapsed at the end of six months. This specification had to be consistent with the title and no wider, but the 'title' or 'recital' contained in the patent grant still formed the basis of the grant.[774]

A change in procedure to improve the information about the invention occurred in consequence of *An Act for Amending the Law for Granting Patents for Inventions 1852* (15 &

---

768 *TRIPS* art 27(2).
769 Ibid art 3.
770 See generally D. J. Brennan, 'The evolution of English patent claims as property definers' [2005] 4 *Intellectual Property Quarterly* 361.
771 S. Thorley, R. Miller, G. Burkill and C. Birss, *Terrell on the Law of Patents* (15th edn, London: Sweet & Maxwell, 2000) [5.01].
772 R. Frost, *Treatise on the Law and Practice Relating to Letters Patent for Inventions* (London: Stevens & Haynes, 1912) vol 1, 170.
773 *British United Shoe Machinery Co Ltd v A Fussell & Sons Ltd* (1908) 25 RPC 631, 650.
774 Ibid.

16 Vict c 83) (Eng). Upon application, applicants were now required to file a statement in writing called a provisional specification, in which they described the nature of the invention.[775] The provisional specification occupied the position of the earlier description in the grant.[776] However, there was no obligation to file a provisional specification independently; the application could be accompanied merely by a complete specification that contained this information. The advantage of filing an initial provisional specification was to give the applicant provisional protection for a six-month period in which to improve the means of carrying out the invention before filing the complete specification[777] 'particularly describing and ascertaining the nature of the said invention, and in what manner the same is to be performed'.[778] The patent was granted after a period of advertisement that allowed for oppositions to grant.

The purpose of the obligation to particularly describe the 'nature of the invention' was to alert the public to the scope of the invention so that people knew what was prohibited during the monopoly period. This obligation equates to the current claims in a complete specification. The description of 'what manner the same shall be performed' translates into the present sufficiency requirements in the modern specification. Members of the public were to know how to perform the invention so that they could enjoy its benefits at the end of the patent term.[779]

Changes in subsequent legislation have refined the procedures. Under the *Patents Act 1883* (46 & 47 Vict c 57) (Eng), both provisional and complete specifications were required to be filed and examined and reported on by officers before grant.[780] Also, applicants were required to insert claims to define the invention for which the monopoly is claimed.[781] This basic structure remains in the present *Patents Act 1990* (Cth). The body of the specification and the claims serve different purposes. The requirements for the body of the specification ensure that the public has the necessary directions to perform the invention after the patent expires. The claims, on the other hand, delineate the monopoly of the invention and are there to warn third parties of what is prohibited conduct during the term of the patent.[782] Anything that is not specifically and definitely claimed is disclaimed.[783]

10.13.2 Statutory provisions for internal requirements for patent specifications

Section 40 of the *Patents Act 1990* (Cth) says nothing about the nature of patentable subject matter but sets out the internal requirements for provisional and complete patent specifications.[784] The *Raising the Bar* reforms made a number of amendments to s 40. Section 40(1)

---

775 *An Act for Amending the Law for Granting Patents for Inventions 1852* (15 & 16 Vict c 83) (Eng) s VI.
776 *Tate v Haskins* (1935) 53 CLR 594, 608.
777 Ibid; *Penn v Bibby* (1866) LR 2 Ch 127, 132.
778 *An Act for Amending the Law for Granting Patents for Inventions 1852* (15 & 16 Vict c 83) (Eng) s IX.
779 Frost, *Treatise on the Law and Practice Relating to Letters Patent for Inventions*, above n 772, vol 1, 193.
780 *Tate v Haskins* (1935) 53 CLR 594, 609.
781 *British United Shoe Machinery Co Ltd v A Fussell & Sons Ltd* (1908) 25 RPC 631, 651.
782 *Lockwood Security Products Pty Ltd v Doric Products Pty Ltd* (2004) 217 CLR 274, [44].
783 *Walker v Alemite Corp* (1933) 49 CLR 643, 656, citing *Fellows v Thomas William Lench Ltd* (1917) 34 RPC 45, 55 (Lord Parker).
784 *Patents Act 1990* (Cth).

provides that a provisional specification must 'disclose the invention in a manner which is clear enough and complete enough for the invention to be performed by a person skilled in the relevant art'.[785] The intention is

> to align the disclosure requirement with that applying in other jurisdictions with the effect that sufficient information must be provided to enable the whole width of the claimed invention to be performed by the skilled person without undue burden, or the need for further invention.[786]

This amended section applies in relation to provisional applications made on or after the day on which sch 1 commenced, namely 15 April 2013.

Amendments made to s 40(2) and (3) apply, inter alia, to patents for which the complete application is made on or after 15 April 2013 or for which no request for examination had been made before this date.[787] Section 40(2) provides that the complete specification must:

(a) disclose the invention in a manner which is clear enough and complete enough for the invention to be performed by a person skilled in the relevant art; and

(aa) disclose the best method known to the applicant of performing the invention;[788] and

(b) where it relates to an application for a standard patent – end with a claim or claims defining the invention; and

(c) where it relates to an application for an innovation patent – end with at least one and no more than 5 claims defining the invention.

An amendment to s 40(3) replaces the 'fair basis' requirement with a 'support' requirement and provides 'that the claim or claims must be clear and succinct and supported by matter disclosed in the specification'.[789] This includes both claims as filed and amended claims.[790] A new s 40(3A) aims to narrow the use of 'omnibus claims' – namely, general claims that define an invention by reference to the whole or part of the specification. Such claims can lack clarity as to the exact scope of the monopoly.[791]

Section 40(4) provides that the claim or claims must relate to one invention only.[792] Special provisions in s 41 apply in relation to compliance with s 40(2)(a) where the invention is a micro-organism.

---

785 *Intellectual Property Laws Amendment (Raising the Bar) Act 2012* (Cth) sch 1 item 7 introduced this language in place of 'describe the invention fully, including the best method known to the applicant of performing the invention'.
786 Explanatory Memorandum, Intellectual Property Laws Amendment (Raising the Bar) Bill 2011 (Cth) sch 1 item 8.
787 *Intellectual Property Laws Amendment (Raising the Bar) Act 2012* (Cth) sch 1 item 55.
788 Ibid sch 1 item 8 repealed the former s 40(2)(a), which provided 'describe the invention fully, including the best method known to the applicant of performing the invention', and substituted s 40(2)(a) and (aa).
789 *Intellectual Property Laws Amendment (Raising the Bar) Act 2012* (Cth) sch 1 item 9 omitted from the former s 40(3) the words 'fairly based on the matter described' and substituted 'supported by matter disclosed'.
790 *Kyowa's Application (No 1)* [1968] RPC 101; *Root Quality Pty Ltd v Root Control Technologies Pty Ltd* (2000) 49 IPR 225, [112].
791 See below at 10.13.9.
792 *Patents Act 1990* (Cth) s 40(4).

In the case of an invention that is a micro-organism, the disclosure of the invention for the purposes of s 40 may be subject to obligations imposed following Australia's accession to the *Budapest Treaty* on 7 July 1987. Accession was made possible through amendments introduced into the *Patents Act 1952* (Cth) by the *Patents Amendment Act 1984* (Cth) and *Patents Regulations (Amendment) 1987* (Cth). The *Budapest Treaty* establishes a system that requires the deposit with a prescribed International Depository Institution (IDI) of a sample of certain inventions that are micro-organisms. The applicant may be required to deposit a sample of the invention when it is impossible to fully describe the invention in words and its preparation from the words is not repeatable.[793] There is no requirement for the deposit to be made in Australia. In fact, although there is an IDI in Australia, most depositories are in other countries. The *Patents Act 1990* (Cth) also makes specific provision for the full description of an invention that involves the use, modification or cultivation of a micro-organism that is not reasonably available to a person skilled in the relevant art.[794] If a person could not be reasonably expected to perform the invention without having a sample, it is necessary to comply with the deposit requirements in relation to this micro-organism.[795] There is also provision for the deposit of the micro-organism if it was reasonably available at the date of filing the complete specification but subsequently ceases to be so available.[796]

10.13.3 Construction of specification for s 40 purposes

A patent specification is a public instrument that describes and defines monopoly rights and is not an instrument that operates *inter partes*.[797] Hence, courts have developed general principles of construction of specifications to take this special nature of a patent into account.[798] These principles apply in relation to each of the distinct grounds in s 40 of the *Patents Act 1990* (Cth).[799] However, some further general principles of construction of s 40 can be identified from the case law. First, the term 'complete specification' in s 40 includes both the claims and the matter that precedes them.[800] Second, the term 'invention' has been construed in the context of s 40(2) to mean 'the embodiment which is described, and around which the claims are drawn'.[801] This term also appears in all other subsections of s 40 except s 40(3). While no case has considered its meaning in either s 40(1)[802] or s 40(4), the context suggests that it should have a common meaning throughout the section.

---

793 Ibid ss 41(1A), (1), 42. See ch 9 at 9.14.3.
794 Ibid s 41(3).
795 Ibid ss 41(2), 6.
796 Ibid s 42.
797 *Kimberly-Clark Australia Pty Ltd v Arico Trading International Pty Ltd* (2001) 207 CLR 1, [34]; *Welch Perrin & Co Pty Ltd v Worrel* (1961) 106 CLR 588, 610.
798 See ch 12 at 12.2.
799 *Lockwood Security Products Pty Ltd v Doric Products Pty Ltd* (2004) 217 CLR 274, [49]; *Welch Perrin & Co Pty Ltd v Worrel* (1961) 106 CLR 588, 610.
800 *Kimberly-Clark Australia Pty Ltd v Arico Trading International Pty Ltd* (2001) 207 CLR 1, [14].
801 Ibid [21]; *Lockwood Security Products Pty Ltd v Doric Products Pty Ltd* (2004) 217 CLR 274, [53].
802 The reference to s 40(1) by the High Court in *Lockwood Security Products Pty Ltd v Doric Products Pty Ltd* (2004) 217 CLR 274, 293–4 [53] is an error, as McTiernan J in *AMP Inc v Utilux Pty Ltd* (1971) 45 ALJR 123 was dealing with s 40(1) of the *Patents Act 1952* (Cth), the counterpart of s 40(2) in *Patents Act 1990* (Cth).

10.13.4 Stages for consideration of s 40 requirements

The Commissioner must report on compliance with s 40(2)–(4) of the *Patents Act 1990* (Cth) in the report on examination of a standard patent.[803] While all these requirements of s 40 are considered at examination, only failure to comply with s 40(2) or (3) are grounds for opposition[804] and for revocation of a patent.[805] Hence, the requirement that the claims relate to one invention only is not considered after examination and acceptance of the request and specification. The *Raising the Bar* reforms introduced failure to comply with s 40(2) or (3) during re-examination of standard and innovation patents.[806] The extent of the disclosure of the invention in the specification is also relevant – for instance, when a complete specification is amended[807] and for purposes of determining its priority date.[808]

10.13.5 The relationship between s 40 and other grounds of invalidity

The High Court in *Lockwood Security Products Pty Ltd v Doric Products Pty Ltd*[809] held as a general principle that it is wrong to employ reasoning relevant to one ground of invalidity in considering another. Certain matters of fact and construction may be relevant to various issues, but all the grounds of invalidity 'are, and must be kept, conceptually distinct'.[810] Hence, s 18 issues, such as inventiveness, have no relevance in construing s 40 grounds of invalidity. This warning is unlikely to apply, however, when the grounds of invalidity being considered are the two aspects of sufficiency of description that are contained in the former s 40(2)(a) of the *Patents Act 1990* (Cth).[811]

10.13.6 Requirements relating to provisional specifications: s 40(1)

The provisional specification enables the applicant to secure an early priority date while they continue to test and improve the invention over the next twelve months before making a decision to file a complete application in Australia or make a 'Convention' or '*PCT*' filing.[812] The *Raising the Bar* amendments provide that the provisional specification 'must disclose the invention in a manner that is clear enough and complete enough for the invention to be

---

803 *Patents Act 1990* (Cth) s 45(1)(a).
804 Ibid s 59(c).
805 Ibid s 138(3)(f).
806 *Intellectual Property Laws Amendment (Raising the Bar) Act 2012* (Cth) sch 1 item 17.
807 *Patents Act 1990* (Cth) s 102(1).
808 Ibid s 43(2A); *Patents Regulations 1991* (Cth) ch 3 pt 1 div 2.
809 (2004) 217 CLR 274.
810 Ibid [46].
811 *Pfizer Overseas Pharmaceuticals v Eli Lilly & Co* (2005) 68 IPR 1, [343].
812 *Anaesthetic Supplies Pty Ltd v Rescare Ltd* (1994) 50 FCR 1, 20 (Lockhart J, Wilcox J agreeing). See ch 9 at 9.6, 9.7, 9.11 and 9.12.

performed by a person skilled in the relevant art'.[813] For instance, 'identification of baccarat as a card game embodiment of the invention' satisfied this requirement.[814]

The section contrasts with the former s 40(1), which merely required the provisional specification to describe generally and fairly the nature of the invention and required no enabling disclosure to teach the public how the invention works. This disclosure requirement contrasted with a more stringent standard in other countries. The amended s 40(1) aligns with the descriptive requirement required for a complete specification in s 40(2)(a) but continues to require no disclosure of the best method of performance. A provisional specification may describe more than one invention[815] whereas the complete specification is for one invention only. There is no requirement for the claims of the patent to appear in the provisional specification.[816]

10.13.7 Requirements relating to complete specifications: s 40(2)(a), (aa)

The grant of a patent represents a bargain whereby the applicant is granted a limited monopoly to exploit the invention in return for making a full public disclosure of the claimed invention. This disclosure must enable a skilled addressee 'to know just what is the claimed invention and how it might be best worked so that they can either seek a licence from the patentee or work outside the area of monopoly or work the invention at the expiry of the patent'.[817] It is not necessary for the specification to identify the inventive step or the advance in the art.[818] In fact, this may be an impossible task.[819]

Prior to the *Raising the Bar* reforms, the complete specification was required to describe the invention fully, including the best method known to the applicant of performing the invention. These are explained as being 'co-ordinate requirements'.[820] The amended s 40(2)(a) of the *Patents Act 1990* (Cth) adopts language that is consistent with the higher standard of disclosure in s 14(3) of the *Patents Act 1977* (UK)[821] and requires the complete specification to disclose the invention in a manner that is clear enough and complete enough for the invention to be performed by a person skilled in the relevant art.[822] The requirement in the pre-amended s 40(2)(a) for the disclosure of the best method of performing the invention remains unchanged in a new s 40(2)(aa). Both best method and the requirement to describe

---

813 For compliance with s 40(1) in the case of inventions that are microorganisms, see *Patents Act 1990* (Cth) s 41(1A).
814 *Kafataris v Davis* (2016) 120 IPR 206, [61].
815 *Coopers Animal Health Australia Ltd v Western Stock Distributors Pty Ltd* (1987) 15 FCR 382, 400 (Beaumont J).
816 *Sartas No 1 Pty Ltd v Koukourou & Partners Pty Ltd* (1994) 30 IPR 479, 496–7 (Gummow J).
817 *Lockwood Security Products Pty Ltd v Doric Products Pty Ltd (No 3)* (2005) 226 ALR 70, [194].
818 Ibid [195]–[197]; *Grove Hill Pty Ltd v Great Western Corp Pty Ltd* (2002) 55 IPR 257, 302 (Dowsett J, French J agreeing).
819 *British United Shoe Machinery Co Ltd v A Fussell & Sons Ltd* (1908) 25 RPC 631, 652.
820 *Les Laboratoires Servier v Apotex Pty Ltd* (2016) 247 FCR 61, [109]–[110].
821 *Patents Act 1977* (UK) s 14(3); *European Patent Convention* art 83.
822 The discussion in *Warner Lambert Co LLC v Apotex Pty Ltd (No 2)* (2018) 129 IPR 205, [99]–[111] may guide the application of the amended s 40(2)(a).

the invention fully under s 40(2)(a) (as it relevantly stood prior to amendment by the *Raising the Bar Act*) are discussed below.[823]

10.13.7.1 Requirement to describe the invention fully

The first element in s 40(2)(a) before its amendment is that the complete specification must describe the invention fully.[824] This limb imports the requirement for sufficiency of description.[825] It involves questions of fact 'to be determined generally by the evidence of addressees of the specification'.[826] When the hypothetical skilled addressee comprises a team, the composition of the members within that team might differ for the purposes of assessing sufficiency of description on the one hand and obviousness on the other.[827] This appears to mean that certain members of the overall hypothetical addressee 'team' may be relevant for different issues. The assessment is made by reference to the terms of the patent as granted,[828] and requires reference to the whole document – namely, the body, any illustrations and the claims of the specification.[829] The specification is construed according to well-settled principles and in light of the common general knowledge and the art before the priority date.[830] The character of the invention will influence the 'nature, scope and extent of the description'.[831] However, as a general principle, it is unnecessary to provide the 'wealth of detail'[832] that may be necessary to instruct a reader who knew nothing of the prior art.[833]

A description will be sufficient even if there are omissions or errors, provided that the skilled person can rectify them without the exercise of any inventive faculty, prolonged research, inquiry or experiment.[834] The common general knowledge attributed to the skilled person becomes critical when the specification contains no express method for producing the claimed invention.[835]

The test for insufficiency was expressed by the High Court in *Kimberly-Clark Australia Pty Ltd v Arico Trading International Pty Ltd* (*Kimberly-Clark*):

---

[823] *Pfizer Overseas Pharmaceuticals v Eli Lilly & Co* (2005) 68 IPR 1, [343]. Similar reasoning may be relevant to both.
[824] For compliance with s 40(2)(a) in the case of inventions that are micro-organisms, see s 41(1).
[825] *Pfizer Overseas Pharmaceuticals v Eli Lilly & Co* (2005) 68 IPR 1, [325] (French, Lindgren JJ).
[826] *NV Philips Gloeilampenfabrieken v Mirabella International Pty Ltd* (1993) 44 FCR 239, 260; *British Dynamite Co v Krebs* (1896) 13 RPC 190, 192.
[827] *Eli Lilly & Co v Pfizer Overseas Pharmaceuticals* (2005) 64 IPR 506, [106], [180].
[828] *Kimberly-Clark Australia Pty Ltd v Arico Trading International Pty Ltd* (2001) 207 CLR 1, [5]; *Pfizer Overseas Pharmaceuticals v Eli Lilly & Co* (2005) 68 IPR 1, 73.
[829] *Kimberly-Clark Australia Pty Ltd v Arico Trading International Pty Ltd* (2001) 207 CLR 1, [14], [16]–[17]; *AMP Inc v Utilux Pty Ltd* (1971) 45 ALJR 123, 127 (McTiernan J); *Lockwood Security Products Pty Ltd v Doric Products Pty Ltd* (2004) 217 CLR 274, [49].
[830] *Kimberly-Clark Australia Pty Ltd v Arico Trading International Pty Ltd* (2001) 207 CLR 1, [24]; *Tramanco Pty Ltd v BPW Transpec Pty Ltd* (2014) 105 IPR 18, [200]. See ch 9 at 9.2.
[831] *Warner Lambert Co LLC v Apotex Pty Ltd (No 2)* (2018) 129 IPR 205, [123].
[832] *No-Fume Ltd v Frank Pitchford & Co Ltd* (1935) 52 RPC 231, 243.
[833] *Kimberly-Clark Australia Pty Ltd v Arico Trading International Pty Ltd* (2001) 207 CLR 1, [25]; *No-Fume Ltd v Frank Pitchford & Co Ltd* (1935) 52 RPC 231, 243.
[834] *No-Fume Ltd v Frank Pitchford & Co Ltd* (1935) 52 RPC 231, 2 43; *Valensi v British Radio Corp Ltd (No 1)* [1972] FSR 273, 309–10.
[835] *Idenix Pharmaceuticals LLC v Gilead Sciences Pty Ltd* (2017) 134 IPR 1, [138], [144], [145].

> The question is, will the disclosure enable the addressee of the specification to produce something within each claim without new inventions or additions or prolonged study of matters presenting initial difficulty?[836]

In relation to the first limb of this test, the full description of one embodiment might be sufficient, subject to it 'enabling' something to be produced within each of the claims contained in the specification. In other cases, the full description of more than one embodiment will be required. In either case, the limited disclosure requirements for satisfying this test permit a claim or claims to cover a wider monopoly than is disclosed to the skilled addressee. The skilled person is taken to be trying to make an invention work. If they realise that one method will work and the other will not, the description in the specification is not insufficient because it is broad enough to encompass both methods.[837] When the invention involves the application of a new principle to achieve a new thing or result, all means by which the thing or result may be achieved can be claimed.[838] However, there is no need to disclose all alternative means for making the invention[839] or to explain why the invention works.[840]

The Full Federal Court in *Tramanco Pty Ltd v BPW Transpec Pty Ltd* observed that some claims might need a slightly different approach from that expressed above in *Kimberly-Clark*, especially 'claims to methods for producing one or more specified results'. The court provided an example of a claim for a method of producing one or more of outcomes A, B or C that might be infringed by using the method to produce outcome A, but not outcome B or C. If the claim is construed to require the use of the method to produce only one of A, B or C, as opposed to A, B and C, the court observed:

> [I]t would seem to me to be wrong in principle to hold that the description of the invention is sufficient if the specification enables the use of the method to achieve outcome A, but not outcomes B or C. It would be inconsistent with the purposes of the Act to confer a monopoly on a patentee for a method of producing any of outcomes A, B or C, if the patentee's disclosure only enabled the use of the method to produce some of those outcomes.[841]

A disclosure will be sufficient when it makes readily apparent to the skilled person the steps that are required to work the invention. Those steps must be standard or routine and within the competence of that skilled person. How is a court to distinguish this type of routine work from that which renders the description insufficient as described in the *Kimberly-Clark* test as being 'without new inventions or additions or prolonged study of matters presenting initial difficulty'?

Once disclosure makes apparent to the skilled person the steps required to work the invention, and it is accepted that those steps are standard or routine and are within their

---

836   *Kimberly-Clark Australia Pty Ltd v Arico Trading International Pty Ltd* (2001) 207 CLR 1, [25]; *Lockwood Security Products Pty Ltd v Doric Products Pty Ltd* (2004) 217 CLR 274, [60].
837   *Kirin-Amgen Inc v Hoechst Marion Roussel Ltd* [2005] RPC 169, 205; *British Thomson-Houston Co Ltd v Corona Lamp Works Ltd* (1922) 39 RPC 49, 89.
838   *Lockwood Security Products Pty Ltd v Doric Products Pty Ltd* (2004) 217 CLR 274, [59]; *Shave v HV McKay Massey Harris Pty Ltd* (1935) 52 CLR 701, 709.
839   *Lockwood Security Products Pty Ltd v Doric Products Pty Ltd* (2004) 217 CLR 274, [60].
840   *GlaxoSmithKline Consumer Healthcare Investments (Ireland) (No 2) Ltd v Generic Partners Pty Ltd* (2018) 131 IPR 384, [170].
841   *Tramanco Pty Ltd v BPW Transpec Pty Ltd* (2014) 105 IPR 18, [207].

competence, 'it is beside the point that ... the person skilled in the art might need to apply considerable skill, effort and resources, or that the work might be complex, time-consuming and expensive'.[842] This latter type of work would not amount to 'prolonged study of matters presenting initial difficulty' as envisaged by the High Court in *Kimberly-Clark*.[843]

10.13.7.2 Best method

The specification must disclose the method known to the applicant of performing the invention and not merely the result to be obtained.[844] The means used to convey the method will differ according to the technology involved but will often involve reference to drawings of specific mechanisms.[845] The obligation under the former s 40(2)(a), now contained in s 40(2)(aa), is to disclose the best method known to the applicant as at the date of filing the complete specification of how to carry out the invention.[846] The obligation is directed to the method of performance of the invention described in the specification – not the invention as claimed.[847] The disclosure itself is usually satisfied through the inclusion in the complete specification of one or more preferred embodiments of the invention.[848] Where more than one method is disclosed, there is no need to identify which method is the best method known to the patentee.[849]

As with the obligation to provide a sufficient description of the invention, the rationale underlying this requirement lies in principles of good faith.[850] The public is to be protected against a patentee gaining the benefit of a monopoly without providing the appropriate consideration through deliberate non-disclosure of something new or unpublished that would give the best results.[851] The Full Federal Court recently said that assessment is done 'in a practical and common sense manner' and with 'regard to the public policy justification that supports the best method requirement'.[852]

---

842 *Warner Lambert Co LLC v Apotex Pty Ltd (No 2)* (2018) 129 IPR 205, [133] (application for special leave to appeal to the High Court dismissed).
843 Ibid [133]; *Idenix Pharmaceuticals LLC v Gilead Sciences Pty Ltd* (2017) 134 IPR 1, [144]–[145] (insufficiency established).
844 *NV Philips Gloeilampenfabrieken v Mirabella International Pty Ltd* (1993) 44 FCR 239, 261; *No-Fume Ltd v Frank Pitchford & Co Ltd* (1935) 52 RPC 231.
845 *Firebelt Pty Ltd v Brambles Australia Ltd* (2000) 51 IPR 531, [53]; *Les Laboratoires Servier v Apotex Pty Ltd* (2016) 247 FCR 61, [108]; *Sandvik Intellectual Property AB v Quarry Mining & Construction Equipment Pty Ltd* (2017) 126 IPR 427, [115].
846 *Pfizer Overseas Pharmaceuticals v Eli Lilly & Co* (2005) 68 IPR 1, [329]; *Rescare Ltd v Anaesthetic Supplies Pty Ltd* (1992) 25 IPR 119, 134–5; *GlaxoSmithKline Consumer Healthcare Investments (Ireland) (No 2) Ltd v Generic Partners Pty Ltd* (2018) 131 IPR 384, [184], [186].
847 *Sandvik Intellectual Property AB v Quarry Mining & Construction Equipment Pty Ltd* (2017) 126 IPR 427, [115]; *Les Laboratoires Servier v Apotex Pty Ltd* (2016) 247 FCR 61, [124].
848 *Firebelt Pty Ltd v Brambles Australia Ltd* (2000) 51 IPR 531, [53]; *Les Laboratoires Servier v Apotex Pty Ltd* (2016) 247 FCR 61, [104]; *Sandvik Intellectual Property AB v Quarry Mining & Construction Equipment Pty Ltd* (2017) 126 IPR 427, [115].
849 *Eli Lilly & Co v Pfizer Overseas Pharmaceuticals* (2005) 64 IPR 506, [205]; *C Van der Lely NV v Ruston's Engineering Co Ltd* [1993] RPC 45, 56.
850 *Firebelt Pty Ltd v Brambles Australia Ltd* (2000) 51 IPR 531, [48]; *Vidal Dyes Syndicate Ltd v Levenstein Ltd & Read Holliday & Sons Ltd* [1912] 29 RPC 245, 269.
851 *Firebelt Pty Ltd v Brambles Australia Ltd* (2000) 51 IPR 531, [48]; *Kimberly-Clark Australia Pty Ltd v Arico Trading International Pty Ltd* (2001) 207 CLR 1, [25].
852 *GlaxoSmithKline Consumer Healthcare Investments (Ireland) (No 2) Ltd v Generic Partners Pty Ltd* (2018) 131 IPR 384, [187].

The best method obligation is necessarily determined subjectively by reference to the knowledge of the applicant. This is a matter of fact and will depend on the circumstances, including the nature of the invention as discerned from the whole of the specification and the attributes of the relevant skilled addressee.[853] A specification may leave the skilled addressee to conduct experimentation that is necessary in order to arrive at the best method known to the applicant, but this is dependent on all the circumstances. As the Full Federal Court explained in *GlaxoSmithKline Consumer Health Investments (Ireland) (No 2) Ltd v Generic Partners Pty Ltd*:

> Whether or not it will be open to the patent applicant to not disclose relevant information on the basis that it is available to the skilled addressee by routine experimentation will depend on the importance of the information in question, the practicality of disclosing it, and the extent of the burden imposed on the skilled addressee who is left to rely upon routine experimentation.[854]

Consequently, in some circumstances, the best method obligation will require the disclosure of further information known to the patentee than will satisfy the separate sufficiency obligation.[855] As the extent of this obligation is dependent on the facts and circumstances pertaining to each particular case, comparisons on factual outcomes in other cases have limited utility.[856]

It is crucial, first, *to identify the invention described in the specification* before proceeding to determine these issues.[857] The description of the best embodiment of that invention may not always comply with the best method obligation.[858] For instance, when a court determined that a critical aspect of the best method of performing an invention for an extension drilling system on a semi-automatic drilling rig was an adequate water seal, the applicant's obligation was to describe the best sealing member known to it, even though the seal was not part of the invention described in the specification.[859]

Additional detail of the method of manufacture of a claimed product invention may be necessary in some cases. In *Les Laboratoires Servier v Apotex Pty Ltd*, the invention of a chemical compound (salt) for use in treatment of arterial hypertension and heart failure possessed advantages of increased stability and storage length over the prior art. A generic methodology in the specification that would present 'blind alleys and pitfalls' was inadequate disclosure of a salt possessing those characteristics in circumstances where the patentee knew a specific method for its production.[860] The court said that a patentee must 'include aspects of

---

853 Ibid [190].
854 Ibid [192].
855 *Les Laboratoires Servier v Apotex Pty Ltd* (2016) 247 FCR 61; *Sandvik Intellectual Property AB v Quarry Mining & Construction Equipment Pty Ltd* (2017) 126 IPR 427.
856 *Sandvik Intellectual Property AB v Quarry Mining & Construction Equipment Pty Ltd* (2017) 126 IPR 427, [126].
857 *Expo-Net Danmark A/S v Buono-Net Australia Pty Ltd (No 2)* [2011] FCA 710, [16]; *Apotex Pty Ltd v Les Laboratories Servier* [2013] FCA 1426, [166]; *Les Laboratoires Servier v Apotex Pty Ltd* (2016) 247 FCR 61; *Sandvik Intellectual Property AB v Quarry Mining & Construction Equipment Pty Ltd* (2017) 126 IPR 427, [117], [125].
858 *Les Laboratoires Servier v Apotex Pty Ltd* (2016) 247 FCR 61, [122], [123], [129].
859 *Sandvik Intellectual Property AB v Quarry Mining & Construction Equipment Pty Ltd* (2017) 126 IPR 427, [125]–[126].
860 *Les Laboratoires Servier v Apotex Pty Ltd* (2016) 247 FCR 61, [134].

the method of manufacture [of a claimed invention] that are material to the advantages it is claimed the invention brings'.[861]

In contrast, a level of generality may suffice when additional details are related to the applicant's own manufacturing methods and are inessential for the purpose of describing the best method known to the applicant of performing the invention. This was the case in *GlaxoSmithKline* where the Full Federal Court found that details in the Marketing Authorisation Application of a specific formulation of an invention for a pharmaceutical composition that the applicant sought to commercialise were applicable only to the commercial embodiment and not the best method of performing the invention.[862]

10.13.7.3 Time for meeting the requirements to describe the invention fully

Although the obligation to describe the invention fully arises on the filing of the specification, sufficiency of that description will not be determined until examination or opposition or in revocation proceedings. Hence, the complete specification that is construed for the purpose of assessment of sufficiency may be in the form in which it was filed, as amended in response to an examiner's report, or as finally granted[863] or, in the case of an innovation patent, as certified.

The same position applies to the disclosure of the best method of performing the invention. Although the best method must be identified at the date of filing, the Federal Court clarified that an invention need only be fully described at the date of the grant of the patent.[864] The regime for amendment of specifications in s 102 of the *Patents Act 1990* (Cth) may allow the best method disclosed at the filing date to be amended subsequently, and it is that amended specification that is construed for its adequacy of description.[865] Therefore, it may be that failure to disclose the best method on filing, or to describe the invention fully, can be remedied by later amendment. Consequently, a patentee may receive protection for an invention that was not fully realised until after they filed the patent application. This contrasted with the patent laws of other countries that required a full description of the invention when the specification was filed and do not allow addition of new material to overcome objections to sufficiency of description.

The *Raising the Bar Act* repealed s 102(1) and substituted a provision that operates consistently with this approach. Section 102(1) now provides that no amendment can claim or disclose matter that is more extensive than the disclosure contained in the complete specification as filed. The applicant would have to either reduce the scope of the claims to accord with the original disclosure or file a later application (with a later priority date) covering the expanded material.[866] Nevertheless, in the event that non-allowable amendments are

---

861 Ibid [135]; *Sandvik Intellectual Property AB v Quarry Mining & Construction Equipment Pty Ltd* (2017) 126 IPR 427, [124], [125].
862 *GlaxoSmithKline Consumer Healthcare Investments (Ireland) (No 2) Ltd v Generic Partners Pty Ltd* (2018) 131 IPR 384, [203].
863 Patents Act 1990 (Cth) s 102, sch 1 (definition of 'complete specification'); *Eli Lilly & Co v Pfizer Overseas Pharmaceuticals* (2005) 64 IPR 506, [182]; *Pfizer Overseas Pharmaceuticals v Eli Lilly & Co* (2005) 68 IPR 1, [337], [347]; *Kimberly-Clark Australia Pty Ltd v Arico Trading International Pty Ltd* (2001) 207 CLR 1.
864 *Pfizer Overseas Pharmaceuticals v Eli Lilly & Co* (2005) 68 IPR 1, [375].
865 Ibid [390], [391].
866 *Intellectual Property Laws Amendment (Raising the Bar) Act 2012* (Cth) sch 1 item 29.

made, the consequence would relate to priority dates of claims rather than invalidity on grounds of lack of sufficiency.

When it comes to construing the specification, there is a difference between the date at which to identify the relevant form of specification that is to be construed for assessment of sufficiency and the date at which that specification is construed.[867] In the case of a granted patent, it seems that the correct approach should be to assess the specification in its form at the date of grant but to construe that specification at its priority date and in the light of the common general knowledge and the art before the priority date.[868] This would mean that the common general knowledge and prior art that the skilled addressee could take into account is that which existed before the priority date.[869] In contrast, the patentee's knowledge of the best method is determined subjectively at the filing date.

10.13.8 End with claims defining the invention: s 40(2)(b), (c)

Where the application relates to a standard patent, s 40(2)(b) of the *Patents Act 1990* (Cth) provides that the complete specification must end with a claim or claims defining the invention. The claims mark out the monopoly and operate 'to disclaim what is not specifically and definitely claimed.'[870] In the case of an innovation patent, s 40(2)(c) requires at least one and no more than five claims that define the invention.[871]

10.13.9 Claims must be clear and succinct: s 40(3)

Section 40(3) of the *Patents Act 1990* (Cth) focuses on the claims in the specification that define the scope of the invention, and requires them to be clear and succinct and 'supported by' (formerly 'fairly based on') the matter described in the specification. Often referred to as the question of ambiguity, the requirement that claims are 'clear and succinct' means that they must 'define clearly and with precision the monopoly claimed, so that others may know the exact boundaries of the area within which they will be trespassers'.[872] The claims will not be clear and succinct if any inherent uncertainty makes it difficult for the skilled addressee to be satisfied that any proposed actions could be performed without infringing the patent.[873] Hence, there will be ambiguity if a person can only determine whether they will infringe the patent by actual experiment with the completed article.[874] On the other hand, this does not mean that the need to experiment to determine the scope of the invention will inevitably

---

867 A. L. Monotti, 'Sufficiency of description: At what time is its adequacy considered?' (2005) 16 *Australian Intellectual Property Journal* 152, 153–7.
868 *Kimberly-Clark Australia Pty Ltd v Arico Trading International Pty Ltd* (2001) 207 CLR 1, [24].
869 Compare *Eli Lilly & Co v Pfizer Overseas Pharmaceuticals* (2005) 64 IPR 506, [183].
870 *Pharmacia Italia SPA v Mayne Pharma Pty Ltd* (2005) 66 IPR 84, [29].
871 *Patents Act 1990* (Cth) s 40(2)(b)–(c). See above at 10.13.2.
872 *Martin v Scribal Pty Ltd* (1954) 92 CLR 17, 102–3 (Taylor J); *Electric & Musical Industries Ltd v Lissen Ltd* [1938] 4 All ER 221, 224; *No-Fume Ltd v Frank Pitchford & Co Ltd* (1935) 52 RPC 231.
873 *Glaverbel SA v British Coal Corporation* [1994] RPC 443, 495; *Orica Australia Pty Ltd v Dyno Nobel Inc* (2003) 57 IPR 545.
874 *No-Fume Ltd v Frank Pitchford & Co Ltd* (1935) 52 RPC 231, 37; *Martin v Scribal Pty Ltd* (1954) 92 CLR 17, 59 (Dixon CJ).

render the claim void for ambiguity. This is a matter of degree.[875] Lack of precise definition is not fatal to the validity of a claim, as long as it provides a workable standard suitable for the intended use.[876]

An assessment of whether claims are clear and succinct is conducted after the claims are construed according to the well-known principles.[877] It is not sufficient to conclude a lack of clarity merely because the parties cannot agree on the construction to be given to them.[878] The court attempts to find a clear meaning that will afford protection for the invention that the patentee has in good faith invented, rather than find the patent void on a technicality.[879] Invalidity will only arise if the claim is 'incapable of resolution by a skilled addressee by the application of common sense and common knowledge'.[880] Any ambiguity can be overcome by amendments, subject to various exceptions listed in s 102 of the *Patents Act 1990* (Cth).

Another cause for lack of clarity as to the precise scope of a claim arises with what is known as an 'omnibus claim'. This defines an invention by reference to the whole or a part of the patent specification, such as the drawings, figures or examples. The *Raising the Bar Act* introduced a new s 40(3A)[881] (amended further in 2019[882]) to enable the exact scope of the monopoly to be ascertained from the claim itself. The current version of the section provides that 'the claim or claims must not rely on references to descriptions, drawings, graphics or photographs unless absolutely necessary to define the invention'. An example might be reference to a specific feature in a figure or drawing when this is the only way of defining a chemical composition or apparatus.

10.13.10 Claims must be supported by the matter disclosed in the specification: s 40(3)

Before its amendment in 2013, s 40(3) of the *Patents Act 1990* (Cth) provided that a claim must be fairly based on matter described in the specification. The High Court clarified the application and operation of the fair basis requirement in *Lockwood Security Products Pty Ltd v Doric Products Pty Ltd*,[883] but noted that recent United Kingdom case law provided no assistance in interpreting the Australian provision.[884]

---

875   *No-Fume Ltd v Frank Pitchford & Co Ltd* (1935) 52 RPC 231.
876   *Minnesota Mining & Manufacturing Co v Beiersdorf (Australia) Ltd* (1980) 144 CLR 253, [81]; *Stanway Oyster Cylinders Pty Ltd v Marks* (1996) 66 FCR 577, 585; *Flexible Steel Lacing Co v Beltreco Ltd* (2000) 49 IPR 331, 349.
877   *Kimberly-Clark Australia Pty Ltd v Arico Trading International Pty Ltd* (2001) 207 CLR 1, [15]; *Welch Perrin & Co Pty Ltd v Worrel* (1961) 106 CLR 588, 610; *Interlego AG v Toltoys Pty Ltd* (1973) 130 CLR 461, 479. See ch 12 at 12.2.
878   *Novozymes A/S v Danisco A/S* (2013) 99 IPR 417, [95].
879   *Elconnex Pty Ltd v Gerard Industries Pty Ltd* (1991) 32 FCR 491, 513–14; *Tye-Sil Corp Ltd v Diversified Products Corp* (1991) 20 IPR 574, 585; *Martin v Scribal Pty Ltd* (1954) 92 CLR 17, 102–3 (Taylor J).
880   *Innovative Agricultural Products Pty Ltd & Jacek v Cranshaw* (1996) 35 IPR 643, 666; *PhotoCure ASA v Queen's University at Kingston* (2005) 64 IPR 314, [117].
881   Intellectual Property Laws Amendment (Raising the Bar) Act 2012 (Cth) sch 6 items 43, 133(7).
882   Intellectual Property Laws Amendment (Productivity Commission Response Part 1 and Other Measures) Act 2018 (Cth) sch 2 pt 7 item 182.
883   *Lockwood Security Products Pty Ltd v Doric Products Pty Ltd* (2004) 217 CLR 274.
884   Ibid [66]. See also *Generic Health Pty Ltd v Bayer Pharma AG* (2014) 222 FCR 336, [108].

Section 40(3) was repealed by the *Raising the Bar Act* to remove the unnecessary complexity and uncertainty for patent applicants arising from differences in terminology in the patent laws of Australia and other countries. An amendment to s 40(3) was intended to align the Australian requirements with those of other countries.[885]

The concept of fair basis was replaced with a requirement that the claims are 'supported by' the matter disclosed in the specification. The Explanatory Memorandum explains that the terms 'support' and 'fully support' pick up two concepts that are similar to 'fair basis':

- There must be a basis in the description for each claim.
- The scope of the claims must not be broader than is justified by the extent of the description, drawings and contribution to the art.

The principles clarified in *Lockwood* remain relevant for those cases that remain subject to the fair basis test. The term 'fairly based' is used in the former s 40(3) to describe the relationship between the claims that define the invention and the matter described in the complete specification.[886] The purpose of this provision is to ensure that the invention claimed in any claim does not 'travel beyond' the description of the invention in the patent specification. The term is not concerned with 'abstract fairness' of the applicant's conduct.[887] If a particular result seems unfair, then it is for the legislature to make changes or for a remedy to be found under other heads of invalidity. Similarly, matters of whether the monopoly claimed would be 'an undue reward for the disclosure',[888] 'inventive step', 'merit'[889] or 'technical contribution to the art'[890] are not relevant considerations.[891] In fact, there is no requirement to state what the inventive step is.[892] Although some pre-statutory decisions appeared to give support for consideration of such concepts, those decisions provide very limited assistance in the interpretation of express statutory provisions and must be treated with caution.[893]

Section 40(3) requires that claims be fairly based on 'matter described in the specification' and, in contrast to the other subsections, contains no express reference to an 'invention'. Nevertheless, the High Court in *Lockwood* considered that the context of s 40 suggests that these words implicitly refer to an 'invention' or an 'alleged invention', which term would bear the same meaning as applies to the other subsections in s 40: 'the embodiment which is described, and around which the claims are drawn'.[894] This is not just the preferred

---

[885] *European Patent Convention* art 84; *Patent Cooperation Treaty* art 6; *Patents Act 1977* (UK) s 14(5)(c); *Intellectual Property Laws Amendment (Raising the Bar) Act 2012* (Cth) sch 1 item 9.
[886] *Lockwood Security Products Pty Ltd v Doric Products Pty Ltd* (2004) 217 CLR 274, 293–4. See A. J. McBratney, 'The problem child in Australian patent law: "Fair" basing' (2001) 12(4) *Australian Intellectual Property Journal* 211.
[887] *Lockwood Security Products Pty Ltd v Doric Products Pty Ltd* (2004) 217 CLR 274, [95]; *CCOM Pty Ltd v Jiejing Pty Ltd* (1994) 51 FCR 260, 281.
[888] *Olin Corp v Super Cartridge Co Pty Ltd* (1977) 180 CLR 236, 240.
[889] Derived from *Mullard Radio Valve Co Ltd v Philco Radio & Television Corp of Great Britain Ltd* (1936) 53 RPC 323, 347.
[890] *Biogen Inc v Medeva plc* [1997] RPC 1.
[891] *Lockwood Security Products Pty Ltd v Doric Products Pty Ltd* (2004) 217 CLR 274, [46], [53], [54].
[892] *Rose Holdings Pty Ltd v Carlton Shuttlecocks Ltd* (1957) 98 CLR 444, 449.
[893] *Lockwood Security Products Pty Ltd v Doric Products Pty Ltd* (2004) 217 CLR 274, [55]–[57]; *Olin Corp v Super Cartridge Co Pty Ltd* (1977) 180 CLR 236, 240.
[894] (2004) 217 CLR 274, [53].

embodiment, but all matter that refers to an invention in the specification.[895] The inquiry is into what the body of the specification read as a whole discloses as the invention.[896] Common general knowledge may be relevant if it casts light on matters of construction, but otherwise only what is said about the invention in the specification itself is relevant for the purposes of this section.[897] It is not merely verbal descriptions that are taken into account for this purpose. A claim may be fairly based on matter contained in drawings that accompany the specification, even though there is no verbal description.[898]

The comparison is then made between the language in the claims and what is described in the specification, to ascertain

> whether there is a real and reasonably clear disclosure in the body of the specification of what is then claimed, so that the alleged invention as claimed is broadly, that is to say in a general sense, described in the body of the specification.[899]

In making the comparison with the claims, the High Court confirmed that it is wrong to adopt an 'over meticulous verbal analysis'.[900] The approach does not require correspondence of essential integers in both the claim and the specification. Rather, a claim is not fairly based if the invention claimed is wider or more extensive than that which is described in the specification.[901] It must not 'travel beyond the matter disclosed in the specification'.[902] The law allows claims to be drafted that are narrower than the subject matter described in the specification.[903]

10.13.11 Consistory clause and fair basing

It is common drafting practice to base the first and broadest claim on what is cast as a 'consistory clause' in the body of the specification.[904] A consistory clause is a 'general description of what the invention is said to consist of'.[905] It is not an essential part of the specification and is not required by the *Patents Act 1990* (Cth). Often there is minimal difference between the wording of the consistory clause and that of the first claim, and it is clear that this

---

895 Ibid [77].
896 Ibid [99]; *Welch Perrin & Co Pty Ltd v Worrel* (1961) 106 CLR 588, 612–13.
897 *Lockwood Security Products Pty Ltd v Doric Products Pty Ltd* (2004) 217 CLR 274, [72]; *GlaxoSmithKline Consumer Healthcare Investments (Ireland) (No 2) Ltd v Generic Partners Pty Ltd* (2018) 131 IPR 384, [161]; *Actavis Pty Ltd v Orion Corp* [2016] FCAFC 121, [139].
898 *Societe des Usines Chimiques Rhone-Poulenc v Commission of Patents* (1958) 100 CLR 5, 11 (Fullagar J); *CCOM Pty Ltd v Jiejing Pty Ltd* (1994) 51 FCR 260, 280; *Leonardis v Sartas No 1 Pty Ltd* (1996) 67 FCR 126; *Multigate Medical Devices Pty Ltd v B Braun Melsungen AG* (2016) 117 IPR 1, [190].
899 *Lockwood Security Products Pty Ltd v Doric Products Pty Ltd* (2004) 217 CLR 274, [69]; *Rehm Pty Ltd v Websters Security Systems (International) Pty Ltd* (1988) 11 IPR 289, 304.
900 *Lockwood Security Products Pty Ltd v Doric Products Pty Ltd* (2004) 217 CLR 274, [68] approving *CCOM Pty Ltd v Jiejing Pty Ltd* (1994) 51 FCR 260, 281.
901 *Olin Corp v Super Cartridge Co Pty Ltd* (1977) 180 CLR 236, 250–1; *Sami S Svendsen Inc v Independent Products Canada Ltd* (1968) 119 CLR 156, 165.
902 *Olin Corp v Super Cartridge Co Pty Ltd* (1977) 180 CLR 236, 240; *Kimberly-Clark Australia Pty Ltd v Arico Trading International Pty Ltd* (2001) 207 CLR 1, [15].
903 *Shave v HV McKay Massey Harris Pty Ltd* (1935) 52 CLR 701, 709; *AMP Inc v Commissioner of Patents* (1974) 48 ALJR 278, 281. See also *Grove Hill Pty Ltd v Great Western Corp Pty Ltd* (2002) 55 IPR 257, [344].
904 *Welch Perrin & Co Pty Ltd v Worrel* (1961) 106 CLR 588, 612.
905 *Lockwood Security Products Pty Ltd v Doric Products Pty Ltd* (2004) 217 CLR 274, [10].

coincidence of language and mere assertion is insufficient disclosure on its own to satisfy the requirements for fair basis in s 40(3) of the *Patents Act 1990* (Cth). The inquiry is into what the body of the specification read as a whole discloses as the invention.[906]

The High Court in *Lockwood Security Products Pty Ltd v Doric Products Pty Ltd*[907] clarified that the consistory clause is to be considered, not in isolation, but with the rest of the specification. Hence, a claim that is based on the consistory clause will be fairly based only if the specification, when read as a whole, corresponds with that consistory clause, and therefore with the claim. The claim will not be fairly based if other parts of the specification show that the invention has a narrower scope than is asserted in the consistory clause.[908] In *Atlantis Corp Pty Ltd v Schindler*,[909] the specification when read as a whole described an invention that was limited to use as a sub-soil drainage system. The consistory clause and the claims had no such limitation as to use. Hence, the Full Federal Court held that the claims travelled beyond and were not fairly based on the matter described in the specification.[910]

10.13.12 Comparison with fair basis assessment: priority dates

The term 'fairly based' and its replacement 'supported by' serve two different functions in the *Patents Act 1990* (Cth). The first is to ensure that a claim is no wider than is warranted by the disclosure in the body of the specification.[911] The second is the priority function that was discussed in chapter 9. Despite these different functions, the courts have applied similar considerations in similar language to express the tests for fair basis in both contexts.[912] Nevertheless, prior to the *Raising the Bar* amendments, the application of the tests for the purposes of determining the relevant priority date for a claim cannot be completely analogous to the s 40(3) analysis.

First, the nature of the disclosures or descriptions is different. The s 40(3) requirement for 'internal' fair basis requires comparison between subject matter contained in the one complete specification. On the other hand, the priority date function or 'external' fair basis requires comparison between two documents that serve different purposes: a provisional and a complete specification. Before its amendment by the *Raising the Bar Act*, s 40(1) required that the provisional specification describe the invention, whereas s 40(2)(a) in its unamended form required that the complete specification describe the invention fully including the best method of its performance. Therefore, these provisions contemplated that the description in the provisional specification is less sophisticated. This description was not meant to be a

---

906 As to mere coincidence of language and fair basis see also: *Idenix Pharmaceuticals LLC v Gilead Sciences Pty Ltd* (2017) 134 IPR 1, [322]–[326].
907 (2004) 217 CLR 274.
908 Ibid [99]; *Atlantis Corp Pty Ltd v Schindler* (1997) 39 IPR 29; *Idenix Pharmaceuticals LLC v Gilead Sciences Pty Ltd* (2017) 134 IPR 1, [252].
909 (1997) 39 IPR 29.
910 Ibid 50 (Wilcox and Lindgren JJ).
911 *Patents Act 1990* (Cth) s 40(3); *CCOM Pty Ltd v Jiejing Pty Ltd* (1994) 51 FCR 260, 276.
912 *CCOM Pty Ltd v Jiejing Pty Ltd* (1994) 51 FCR 260, 280–1; *Rehm Pty Ltd v Websters Security Systems (International) Pty Ltd* (1988) 11 IPR 289, 304. See ch 9 at 9.11.4.

complete description: rather it is a fair disclosure of the invention, though it is recognised that this may be in a rough state.[913]

Second, subtle linguistic differences appeared in reference to the material with which a claim is to be compared. The internal fair basis comparison in s 40(3) was with reference to '*the matter described* in the application'.[914] In contrast, the external fair basis comparison in reg 3.12(1)(c) was with reference to 'matter *disclosed* in the specification'.[915] The addition of the definite article 'the' in s 40(3) and linguistic differences resulted in the Full Federal Court accepting greater flexibility in applying the test for external fair basis.[916]

These linguistic differences were removed by the *Raising the Bar* amendments to s 40(1) and (2)(a). Both the provisional and complete applications must 'disclose the invention in a manner which is clear enough and complete enough for the invention to be performed by a person skilled in the relevant art'.[917]

10.13.13 Claims must relate to one invention only: s 40(4)

The requirement that a complete specification must relate to one invention only is considered at examination.[918] It is not a ground of opposition, it cannot be the subject of re-examination and it is not available as a ground for revocation. Hence, if the fact that more than one invention is claimed in a specification is not detected at examination and prior to acceptance, it is possible that a patent may be granted where more than one invention is claimed.[919] The likely consequence is that there will be construction difficulties because it may not be possible to find one general principle that applies to all claims.[920]

---

[913] *Anaesthetic Supplies Pty Ltd v Rescare Ltd* (1994) 50 FCR 1, 20.
[914] Emphasis added.
[915] Emphasis added.
[916] *Multigate Medical Devices Pty Ltd v B Braun Melsungen AG* (2016) 117 IPR 1, [189]; *Coretell Pty Ltd v Australian Mud Company Pty Ltd* (2017) 250 FCR 155, [134].
[917] *Intellectual Property Laws Amendment (Raising the Bar) Act 2012* (Cth) sch 1 item 7. See above at 10.13.6.
[918] *Patents Act 1990* (Cth) s 45(1)(a).
[919] *Illinois Tool Works Inc v Autobars Co (Services) Ltd* [1972] FSR 67, 69.
[920] Ibid.

11

PATENTS FOR INVENTIONS: ALLOCATION OF RIGHTS AND OWNERSHIP, THE REGISTER AND DEALINGS

The principal theme that emerges in intellectual property regimes, with the exception of trade marks, is to vest ownership in the creator, but to vary this where creation is in the course of employment or pursuant to some other express contractual arrangement. The application process for obtaining the grant of a standard or innovation patent was described in chapter 9. In this chapter we discuss a variety of matters that relate to the entitlement to apply and be granted a patent, ownership and the allocation of rights, including the grant of interests in the Crown and compulsory licences, and the role of the Register.

11.1 Entitlement to grant

The *Patents Act 1990* (Cth) focuses on a person's entitlement to be granted the patent as distinct from the entitlement to apply for the grant of a patent. Any 'deception of the Crown as to entitlement to the invention or the identity of the true inventor destroys the foundation on which the patent is granted'.[1] A number of independent people or teams of people may be working on the same area of technology and arrive at the same invention. All may satisfy the technical requirements that qualify them as 'inventors' who would be entitled to a grant of patent under s 15. However, priority for grant of a patent is given to the first of the inventors to complete the work and file for protection.[2]

There is no strict requirement of entitlement to apply for the grant of a patent, as was the position under both the *Patents Act 1903* (Cth)[3] and the *Patents Act 1952* (Cth).[4] This contrasts with the position under the *Plant Breeder's Rights Act 1994* (Cth), for example, where the right to apply for plant breeder's rights is vested in the breeder as personal property.[5]

At present, a patent grant can be made only to an 'eligible person', that is a person within one of the following classes in s 15 of the *Patents Act 1990* who:

(a) is the inventor;
(b) would, on the grant of a patent for the invention, be entitled to have the patent assigned to that person;
(c) derives title to the invention from the inventor or the person mentioned in paragraph (b); or
(d) is the legal personal representative of [any of the above persons].

It is possible to have joint applications for a patent.[6] When there are joint inventors, a patent must be granted to all inventors or to persons claiming through them to avoid possible revocation on grounds of lack of entitlement.[7] Entitlement of more than one person to be granted a patent is assessed individually and not collectively, so that each joint applicant must individually satisfy the requirements in s 15(1). The reference to the 'patentee' in s 138(3)(a)

---

1 *JMVB Enterprises Pty Ltd v Camoflag Pty Ltd* (2005) 67 IPR 68, [129]; *Stack v Davies Shephard Pty Ltd* (2001) 108 FCR 422, 428–35.
2 *Patents Act 1990* (Cth) ss 3, 29, 43.
3 *Patents Act 1903* (Cth) s 32(3).
4 *Patents Act 1952* (Cth) s 34(1).
5 *Plant Breeder's Rights Act 1994* (Cth) s 25.
6 *Patents Act 1990* (Cth) s 31.
7 Ibid s 138(3)(a).

covers joint patentees. Hence, where a patent is granted to joint patentees, all must be entitled to the patent.[8]

The application for a standard patent will nominate the person to whom the patent is to be granted. Prior to the *Intellectual Property Laws Amendment (Raising the Bar) Act 2012* (Cth) taking effect in April 2013, the applicant had to explain the basis for this entitlement in a notice of entitlement that was filed before *acceptance* of the complete application.[9] This enabled applicants to 'defer exposing the basis of their entitlement to third parties' and could result in a delay in acceptance that 'may frustrate the legitimate concerns of third parties to resolve issues of ownership and unnecessarily increases the period of uncertainty for members of the public trying to determine the outcome of an application'.[10] A statement of entitlement is now incorporated in the approved form of the request for patent *examination*.[11] In the case of an innovation patent, the applicant makes an assertion as to entitlement to the invention in the patent request.

Disputes as to entitlement may arise before or after the grant of a patent. Prior to grant, it is possible to refer questions about entitlement to the Commissioner,[12] to oppose the grant of the patent on various grounds related to entitlement,[13] or to raise the issue of entitlement *following* an order made arising from court proceedings in relation to the patent.[14] Lack of entitlement to a patent is a ground for its revocation.[15] It is a matter for the party seeking revocation to establish lack of entitlement.[16] It is not sufficient to say that a patentee is entitled to the patent simply because they are identified as a nominated person in the patent request or because the grant has been made to that patentee.[17] Registration is not a source of entitlement; the *Patents Act 1990* (Cth) does not create a system of title by registration that is akin to a Torrens title system of registration of interests in real estate.[18]

Prior to the introduction of the *Intellectual Property Laws Amendment (Raising the Bar) Act 2012* (Cth), a grant to a person who is not an inventor or whose entitlement did not stem from an inventor would invalidate the patent, even if other joint patentees were properly entitled to the grant.[19] Invalidity arising from a grant to the wrong persons, due to a technical problem with establishing inventorship and ownership that was only discovered after grant, could not be corrected with a later assignment of the patent[20] or amendment to the patent or patent request to substitute the name of another person or persons as patentee.[21] The degree

---

8   *Patents Act 1990* (Cth) s 15; *University of British Columbia v Conor Medsystems Inc* (2006) 155 FCR 391.
9   *Patents Regulations 1991* (Cth) reg 3.1(2)(a) (end date 14 April 2013).
10 Explanatory Statement, Intellectual Property Legislation Amendment (Raising the Bar) Regulation 2013 (No 1) (Cth) sch 6 item 8.
11 *Patents Regulations 1991* (Cth) reg 3.15(2) (as part of the 'approved form').
12 *Patents Act 1990* (Cth) s 32 (joint applicants), s 36 (applicants and other interested parties).
13 Ibid ss 33, 59, 101M.
14 Ibid s 34.
15 Ibid s 138(3)(a).
16 *Sigma Pharmaceuticals (Australia) Pty Ltd v Wyeth* (2011) 119 IPR 194, [279].
17 *University of British Columbia v Conor Medsystems Inc* (2006) 155 FCR 391, [32]–[33] (Emmett J), [61]–[62] (Stone J).
18 Ibid [62] (Stone J).
19 *University of British Columbia v Conor Medsystems Inc* (2006) 155 FCR 391.
20 *Stack v Davies Shephard Pty Ltd* (2001) 108 FCR 422, [30]–[35].
21 *GS Technology Pty Ltd v Elster Metering Pty Ltd* (2008) 167 FCR 444, 460; *AstraZeneca AB v Apotex Pty Ltd* (2014) 226 FCR 324, [141], [179].

of complexity in the various statutory mechanisms that permit corrections to ownership and the resolution of ownership disputes prior to grant made it clear that statutory reform was necessary. A new s 22A that came into effect on 15 April 2013 specifies that a patent is not invalid and cannot be revoked merely because it was granted to the wrong person.[22] A new sub-s (4) was also added to s 138 to provide that a court must not order revocation of a patent on the ground of lack of entitlement unless it is satisfied that, in all the circumstances, it is just and equitable to do so.[23]

11.1.1 Criteria for inventorship

The term 'inventor' that appears in s 15(1)(a) is undefined in the 1990 legislation, but it is clear that it must be the actual or 'real inventor'[24] as distinct from a deemed inventor, such as one who imports an invention. It seems that the term 'inventor' relates to the invention so far as claimed.[25] Ultimately, while the broad principles are derived from decisions in the United States,[26] difficulties arise in their application, particularly when more than one person has worked with the invention and entitlement is contested.[27] The fact that it is contemplated that there will be further experiments for checking and testing, such as clinical trials, 'is not fatal to a conclusion that there is an existing invention'.[28]

Courts adopt a two-step process for determining the inventors that involves drawing a distinction between conception of the invention on the one hand and verification or reduction to practice on the other hand.[29] This latter term is understood to be in the nature of actions that themselves involve no contribution to the conception of the invention. However, in some cases, such as *Polwood Pty Ltd v Foxworth Pty Ltd*,[30] discussed below,[31] reduction of a concept to a working apparatus might be part of the overall invention. As inventorship is determined by an evaluation of who has made a material contribution to the *invention*,[32] the first step in identifying the inventors requires discerning the invention or concept of the invention that *underlies* the claims of the specification. This concept of the invention is not determined simply by reference to selected claims or individual integers in claims.[33] Second, each case will

---

[22] Explanatory Memorandum, Intellectual Property Laws Amendment (Raising the Bar) Bill 2011 (Cth) sch 6 item 31.
[23] See ch 12 at 12.13.2.
[24] *JMVB Enterprises Pty Ltd v Camoflag Pty Ltd* (2006) 154 FCR 348, [67]–[72].
[25] *Patents Act 1990* (Cth) ss 18, 33–35.
[26] *Burroughs Wellcome Co v Barr Laboratories Inc*, 40 F 3d 1223 (Fed Cir, 1994); *Apotex Inc v Wellcome Foundation Ltd* [2002] 4 SCR 153.
[27] Most entitlement disputes arise in actions brought under *Patents Act 1990* (Cth) s 32: see, for example, *Rozenblit v VR TEK Pty Ltd* (2013) 104 IPR 153; *Richwood Creek Pty Ltd v Williams* (2009) 82 IPR 385; *CSR Building Products Ltd v Abnoos* (2009) 81 IPR 641.
[28] *AstraZeneca AB v Apotex Pty Ltd* (2014) 226 FCR 324, [142]; *Wellcome Foundation Ltd v VR Laboratories (Australia) Pty Ltd* (1981) 148 CLR 262, 281; *Merck & Co Inc v Arrow Pharmaceuticals Ltd* (2006) 154 FCR 31, [104]–[108].
[29] *University of Western Australia v Gray* (2009) 179 FCR 346, [221], [237]; *Kafataris v Davis* (2016) 120 IPR 206, [62].
[30] (2008) 165 FCR 527, [33].
[31] At 11.1.1.2.
[32] See below at 11.1.1.1.
[33] *University of Western Australia v Gray* (2009) 179 FCR 346, [310]; *Polwood Pty Ltd v Foxworth Pty Ltd* (2008) 165 FCR 527, [60].

require detailed analysis of the *contributions of all relevant parties to that invention*.[34] This involves determining the contributions to the invention as described in the patent specification.[35] The investigation is assisted by reference to any formal research record book system, personal diaries and workbooks, notes and minutes of meetings as well as other evidence. A discussion of each feature follows.

11.1.1.1 The invention, conception of the invention or inventive concept

Section 40(4) of the *Patents Act 1990* (Cth) provides that a claim or claims must relate to one 'invention' only. In the context of entitlement and inventorship, the authorities refer variously to 'invention', 'inventive concept', 'conception of the invention' and 'concept of the invention'. The sense in which the term 'invention' is used in this subsection is likely to be equivalent to each of these terms and probably consistent with the meaning of 'invention' in the former s 40(2)(a), which the High Court held to be 'the embodiment which is described, and around which the claims are drawn'.[36] The following discussion assumes that the terms are interchangeable and are likely to have this meaning. Although a broad distinction applies between the conception of the invention on the one hand and mere verification or reduction to practice on the other, the point at which conception is complete will be fact-specific and often difficult to identify in contested cases. The Full Federal Court has made it clear that it cannot be said universally that 'an invention is complete only when one of ordinary skill in the art can perform it'.[37]

Some principles are, however, clear. First, the concept of the invention that underlies the claims is discerned from the whole patent specification, including but not limited to the claims.[38] The body of the specification describes the invention in this broad sense and should explain the inventive concepts involved. There is no claim-by-claim evaluation to identify who contributed which elements to each claim. Second, contribution to a claim without contributing to the conception of the invention itself, as discerned above, is not enough. Third, there may be more than one contributor to the invention (in which case there will be joint inventors) and more than one inventive contribution might be present in the invention that is described in the specification.[39]

11.1.1.2 The nature of the contribution

Various judicial questions attempt to explain the nature of the contribution that will justify a finding of inventorship, but it is clear that the putative inventor must have made a material contribution to the invention.[40] Does it have a 'material effect on the final concept of the

---

34 *University of Western Australia v Gray* (2009) 179 FCR 346, [247]–[248]; *Polwood Pty Ltd v Foxworth Pty Ltd* (2008) 165 FCR 527, [33].
35 *Polwood Pty Ltd v Foxworth Pty Ltd* (2008) 165 FCR 527, [35]; *University of Western Australia v Gray* (2009) 179 FCR 346, [247].
36 *Kimberly-Clark Australia Pty Ltd v Arico Trading International Pty Ltd* (2001) 207 CLR 1, [21]. The term 'invention' is used in a number of senses in the *Patents Act 1990* (Cth). For instance, in s 18 it means the invention as claimed in any claim.
37 *University of Western Australia v Gray* (2009) 179 FCR 346, [261].
38 Ibid [247]; *Polwood Pty Ltd v Foxworth Pty Ltd* (2008) 165 FCR 527, [60].
39 *Polwood Pty Ltd v Foxworth Pty Ltd* (2008) 165 FCR 527; *University of Western Australia v Gray (No 20)* (2008) 246 ALR 603, [1442].
40 *University of Western Australia v Gray* (2009) 179 FCR 346, [247]–[248].

invention'?[41] Would the final concept of the invention have come about without the involvement of that person?[42] Without their contribution, would the invention be 'less efficient, less simple, less economical, less something of benefit'?[43] When an invention is susceptible to a problem–solution analysis[44] it may be useful to ask who conceived the solution to a problem.[45] This approach was adopted in *Costa v GR & IE Daking Pty Ltd*,[46] where a Mr Geradis identified certain problems with the operation of a device used in the picking of vegetables and asked Mr Costa to build a machine that would solve the identified problems. The delegate of the Commissioner of Patents concluded that the invention only occurred because of the involvement of both parties. Gerardis identified the problem and 'had a general idea of what was required to solve the problem, [but] he did not necessarily know how to give effect to those ideas; the creation of the invention required the input of Costa'.[47] Costa would not have made the machine without being informed by Gerardis of base requirements for overcoming the identified problems with an existing machine. A finding of inventorship is inevitable if the contribution is inventive.[48] However, inventiveness of a contribution is not essential for the individual to be recognised as an inventor.[49] 'Rights in an invention are determined by objectively assessing contributions to the invention, rather than an assessment of the inventiveness of respective contributions.'[50]

In *Polwood Pty Ltd v Foxworth Pty Ltd*, the Full Federal Court found that a patent that claimed a method for production of potting mix using a 'steaming tube dual auger concept' and an apparatus for practising that method contained two interrelated but distinct aspects of the entire invention that were described in the specification. The court observed:

> There may be only one invention but it may be the subject of more than one inventive concept or inventive contribution. The invention may consist of a combination of elements. It may be that different persons contributed to that combination.[51]

In this case, Polwood devised the inventive concept underlying the method but Foxworth made an inventive contribution to the apparatus. There was no evidence that the concept devised by Polwood was sufficient in itself to encompass the apparatus that made it workable. Therefore, both Polwood and Foxworth were found to be joint inventors who were entitled equally to the patent, even though the contribution of Foxworth was far less in quantitative

---

41   *Polwood Pty Ltd v Foxworth Pty Ltd* (2008) 165 FCR 527, [52]; *Row Weeder Pty Ltd v Nielsen* (1997) 39 IPR 400, 403.
42   *JMVB Enterprises Pty Ltd v Camoflag Pty Ltd* (2005) 67 IPR 68, [132]; *Polwood Pty Ltd v Foxworth Pty Ltd* (2008) 165 FCR 527, [53]; *Harris v CSIRO* (1993) 26 IPR 469, 488; *Henrick v Granite Works Pty Ltd* (2008) 79 IPR 361, 368 [39].
43   *Harris v CSIRO* (1993) 26 IPR 469, 476, citing *Mueller Brass Co v Reading Industries Inc*, 352 F Supp 1357, 1372 (ED Pa, 1972).
44   This is not always the case: *Neobev Pty Ltd v Bacchus Distillery Pty Ltd (admin apptd) (No 3)* (2014) 104 IPR 249, [109]; *Aktiebolaget Hassle v Alphapharm Pty Ltd* (2002) 212 CLR 411; *Lockwood Security Products Pty Ltd v Doric Products Pty Ltd (No 2)* (2007) 235 CLR 173.
45   *Stack v Davies Shephard Pty Ltd* (2001) 108 FCR 422, [22].
46   (1994) 29 IPR 241, 246.
47   Ibid 246.
48   *Polwood Pty Ltd v Foxworth Pty Ltd* (2008) 165 FCR 527.
49   *Row Weeder Pty Ltd v Nielsen* (1997) 39 IPR 400, 406.
50   *JMVB Enterprises Pty Ltd v Camoflag Pty Ltd* (2005) 67 IPR 68, [132].
51   (2008) 165 FCR 527, [60].

terms than that of Polwood.[52] In cases such as this, neither party is entitled solely to a patent over the total invention unless there has been an assignment between them.[53] Each may be entitled to a patent over their own part (if it is otherwise patentable).[54]

Certain types of contribution do not amount to inventorship if the contribution was derived from the true inventor,[55] or is limited to:

- assistance in producing a workable embodiment of the invention but without providing an unexpected result or advantage;[56] or
- the suggestion of another example of the operation of the invention.[57]

Furthermore, a person is not an inventor if they merely follow another's instructions in performing experiments.[58]

11.1.1.3 Joint inventorship

It is clear from the above that an inventor does not have to conceive the entire concept of invention or even make an inventive contribution. What is required for joint inventorship is that each performs a step that materially contributes to the invention that emerges from all the steps taken together.[59] This assumes some form of cooperation among the parties. In fact, collaboration among the parties in developing the invention has been described as 'a relevant factor'[60] or a 'major consideration'.[61] When the invention arises from that collaborative effort 'it would ordinarily follow that the collaborators are joint inventors of the product of the collaboration'.[62] For instance, joint inventorship may arise when two people work together in circumstances where X follows Y's directions, but solves a problem not recognised by Y, or solves a recognised problem that Y could not solve, or produces an advantage or result not contemplated by Y.[63] The contribution of a co-inventor can occur at any stage in the development of the invention, as long as it materially contributed to the invention.[64] The roles of joint inventors are not necessarily equal and are qualitative rather than quantitative.[65] Subject to any agreement to the contrary, each is entitled to an equal undivided share in the patent.[66]

---

52 Ibid [33] (declaration as to identities of the eligible persons). See also *Neobev Pty Ltd v Bacchus Distillery Pty Ltd (admin apptd) (No 3)* (2014) 104 IPR 249, [108] for a useful summary of propositions formulated in *Polwood Pty Ltd v Foxworth Pty Ltd* (2008) 165 FCR 527.
53 *Stack v Davies Shephard Pty Ltd* (2001) 108 FCR 422, [21]; *JMVB Enterprises Pty Ltd v Camoflag Pty Ltd* (2005) 67 IPR 68, 94 [133].
54 *Stack v Davies Shephard Pty Ltd* (2001) 108 FCR 422, [14], [28]; *Polwood Pty Ltd v Foxworth Pty Ltd* (2008) 165 FCR 527.
55 *Polwood Pty Ltd v Foxworth Pty Ltd* (2008) 165 FCR 527, [52]; *Stack v Davies Shephard Pty Ltd* (2001) 108 FCR 422, [21].
56 *Henrick v Granite Works Pty Ltd* (2008) 79 IPR 361, 382 [112].
57 *Kafataris v Davis* (2016) 120 IPR 206, [75].
58 *Harris v CSIRO* (1993) 26 IPR 469, 476.
59 *McGill University v Bionomics Ltd* (2007) 72 IPR 149, [21], following *Primmcoy Pty Ltd v Teer* (2003) 60 IPR 164, [26] and *Monsanto Co v Kamp* (1967) 154 USPQ 259.
60 *Polwood Pty Ltd v Foxworth Pty Ltd* (2008) 165 FCR 527, [53].
61 *JMVB Enterprises Pty Ltd v Camoflag Pty Ltd* (2005) 67 IPR 68, [132].
62 *Polwood Pty Ltd v Foxworth Pty Ltd* (2008) 165 FCR 527, [34].
63 *Row Weeder Pty Ltd v Nielsen* (1997) 39 IPR 400, 406.
64 *McGill University v Bionomics Ltd* (2007) 72 IPR 149, 157.
65 *Polwood Pty Ltd v Foxworth Pty Ltd* (2008) 165 FCR 527, [33].
66 *Patents Act 1990* (Cth) s 16.

11.1.2 Entitled to have patent assigned to person: s 15(1)(b)

Section 15(1)(b) of the *Patents Act 1990* (Cth) applies to any enforceable assignment of the rights to the invention for which the patent is to be granted. The criteria in s 15(1)(b) encompass cases in which the applicant is not the person entitled to be granted the patent. The principal cases will be those of employment, where the applicant is the employee inventor who is under an express or implied obligation to assign present or future inventions to their employer. Those rights are determined by the express terms of any contract of employment and the common law and equitable principles that govern the employment relationship.[67] It may also apply to assignments of rights in patent applications, irrespective of whether the assignor was itself eligible for a grant of patent under s 15(1).[68]

The criteria in s 15(1)(b) will also cover those cases where an applicant has agreed in writing to assign the patent, or a part interest in the patent, when granted.[69] However, s 15 specifies that no formalities are necessary and an agreement could arise in writing or orally or be implied by the conduct of the parties.[70] An agreement could arise either before or after the application is filed by the assignor. This provision dispenses with the need for an actual assignment of rights in the application before grant.

11.1.3 Derives title to invention from inventor: s 15(1)(c)

This entitlement may arise where there is an express or implied agreement for the inventor to assign present or future inventions to another person. An assignment of rights in the invention will transfer title to the invention, with the result that the transferee becomes the eligible person under s 15(1)(c) to the exclusion of the inventor.[71] This assignment could arise before or after the invention is made, and either before[72] or after filing[73] an application for a patent.

Again, the most common circumstance will be that of employment, and will cover the case where the employer files the patent application for an employee invention or subsequently seeks amendment of the application. However, it is not restricted to employment relationships and can extend to any other circumstances where a person gains rights to the invention before grant.[74] A third party may acquire those rights either solely or together with the inventor

---

67 *Sterling Engineering Co Ltd v Patchett* [1955] AC 534, 543–4; *Richwood Creek Pty Ltd v Williams* (2010) 85 IPR 378, 380; *Spencer Industries Pty Ltd v Collins* (2003) 58 IPR 425; *Victoria University of Technology v Wilson* (2004) 60 IPR 392; *Kwan v Queensland Corrective Services Commission* (1994) 31 IPR 25.
68 *Foster's Australia Ltd v Cash's (Australia) Pty Ltd* (2013) 219 FCR 529, [99]–[100].
69 This was expressly provided in *Patents Act 1952* (Cth) s 64.
70 *University of British Columbia v Conor Medsystems Inc* (2006) 155 FCR 391, [37] (Emmett J); *Speedy Gantry Hire Pty Ltd v Preston Erection Pty Ltd* (1998) 40 IPR 543, 550; *Preston Erection Pty Ltd v Speedy Gantry Hire Pty Ltd* (1998) 43 IPR 74, 82 (*Patents Act 1952* (Cth) s 34(1)).
71 *Camilleri v Steel Foundations Ltd* (2003) AIPC 91-837, [37]; *Stack v Davies Shephard Pty Ltd* (2001) 108 FCR 422, [13]; *Sigma Pharmaceuticals (Australia) Pty Ltd v Wyeth* (2011) 119 IPR 194, [287].
72 *Speedy Gantry Hire Pty Ltd v Preston Erection Pty Ltd* (1998) 40 IPR 543, 548–9; *Preston Erection Pty Ltd v Speedy Gantry Hire Pty Ltd* (1998) 43 IPR 74, 81–2. As to an ineffective assignment, see *JMVB Enterprises Pty Ltd v Camoflag Pty Ltd* (2006) 154 FCR 348.
73 *Allaway v Lancome Investments Ltd* (2002) 58 IPR 346.
74 *Camilleri v Steel Foundations Ltd* (2003) AIPC 91-837 (implied assignment). This subsection is similar to s 34(1)(a) of the *Patents Act 1952* (Cth) (1960 addition primarily to cover employee inventions).

through voluntary assignment or devolution of law, through collaborative effort[75] where no formal agreement was negotiated for ownership of any resulting inventions,[76] or through purchase or other agreement. An example of an implied assignment is where an inventor of an existing invention incorporates a company to develop and exploit that invention and files the patent application in the name of the company.[77] Neither a joint patent request alone nor registration is a source of entitlement.[78] In contrast to the Torrens system of land registration that creates title by registration, the patent system relies on a prior entitlement for registration.[79]

As the subsection speaks of deriving title to the invention, it would apply in cases where the assignee is the applicant or becomes an applicant after opposition or other proceedings.[80] It will also apply in the case where the Commissioner directs a change in the patent application to include the name of a person claiming under an assignment or agreement.[81]

11.2 Ownership and co-ownership

Section 13(1) of the *Patents Act 1990* (Cth) gives the owner of the patent the exclusive right to exploit the invention and to authorise another person to do so. Section 13(2) provides that the exclusive rights are personal property and are capable of assignment and of devolution by law. These provisions comply with the obligations contained in art 28(2) of the *Agreement on Trade-Related Aspects of Intellectual Property*[82] (*TRIPS*), which requires member states to give patent owners the right to assign, or transfer by succession, the patent and to conclude licensing contracts.

11.2.1 The notion of co-ownership

Co-ownership can arise in a number of situations. It may arise when there are joint inventors who are entitled to own the intellectual property rights they create. For example, if two individual researchers each make a contribution to the inventive concept of a patentable invention, they will be co-owners of any patent that is granted upon their joint application. Co-ownership continues if each researcher assigns their respective rights to different third parties. In contrast, an assignment by both researchers to a common third party, such as a start-up company formed for the purpose of exploiting the patent, will result in sole ownership.

Co-ownership can also arise where X, the sole creator of a work or invention, deals with the invention in a way that splits ownership. For example, X may assign the rights to B and Z or

---

75   *Re Application by CSIRO and Gilbert* (1995) 31 IPR 67, 72–3.
76   *Row Weeder Pty Ltd v Nielsen* (1997) 39 IPR 400, 408; *Re Application by CSIRO and Gilbert* (1995) 31 IPR 67, 72.
77   *Preston Erection Pty Ltd v Speedy Gantry Hire Pty Ltd* (1998) 43 IPR 74; see also *Camilleri v Steel Foundations Ltd* (2003) AIPC 91-837.
78   *University of British Columbia v Conor Medsystems Inc* (2006) 155 FCR 391, [32] (Emmett J), [63] (Stone J).
79   Ibid [62] (Stone J).
80   *Patents Act 1990* (Cth) ss 59, 33. See also ss 34 and 35.
81   Ibid s 113.
82   *Marrakesh Agreement Establishing the World Trade Organization*, opened for signature 15 April 1994, 1867 UNTS 3 (entered into force 1 January 1995) annex 1C.

assign a portion of the rights to B only. In the first case, B and Z are now co-owners of the invention, whereas in the second example the co-owners are X and B.

11.2.2 Rights of co-owners

Where a patent is granted to two or more persons, they are each entitled to an equal undivided share in the patent, subject to any contrary agreement.[83] This means that they hold the patent as tenants in common in equal shares. Each is entitled to exploit the patent, by themselves or their agent,[84] for their own benefit and without the consent of the other co-owners.[85] This consent is required for the grant of a licence under the patent or to the assignment or mortgage of a share in the patent.[86] The general purpose of these provisions 'is to permit what might be called domestic enjoyment ... while not permitting large-scale commercial exploitation through the grant of licences'.[87] A third party will infringe the patent if they exercise any of the patentee's exclusive rights to exploit the invention without the authorisation of all co-owners.[88]

The *Patents Act 1990* (Cth) provides a degree of protection to purchasers (and those claiming through purchasers) from a co-owner of a patented product or a product of a patented process. The purchaser and those claiming through them can deal with the product as if it had been sold by all patentees.[89] The provisions of s 16 do not affect the rights and obligations of trustees and personal representatives or that arise out of either of those relationships.[90]

The consequence of these rules is that co-ownership of a patent is unlikely to suit inventors who have no ability to exploit the patent. Universities generally fall into this category, either because such activities are outside their powers or because they have inadequate skills and resources. Therefore, a university would be unwise to allow research to be conducted with a commercial entity that had the ability to exploit the invention itself without an express agreement to govern ownership and exploitation of any patentable inventions that result.[91]

11.2.3 Directions to co-owners

As co-owners of a patent have limited ability to exercise rights under the patent without the consent of the other co-owners, it is possible that all co-owners may fail to agree on how best to exploit or deal with the patent. The *Patents Act 1990* (Cth) provides a means for

---

83 *Patents Act 1990* (Cth) s 16(1)(a); *Young v Wilson* (1955) 72 RPC 351; *Polwood Pty Ltd v Foxworth Pty Ltd* (2008) 165 FCR 527, [66].
84 See *Henry Brothers (Magherafelt) Ltd v Ministry of Defence and Northern Ireland Office* [1999] RPC 442, 450.
85 *Patents Act 1990* (Cth) s 16(1)(b).
86 Ibid s 16(1)(c).
87 *Henry Brothers (Magherafelt) Ltd v Ministry of Defence and Northern Ireland Office* [1999] RPC 442, 449.
88 *Patents Act 1990* (Cth) s 13(1), sch 1 (definition of 'patentee'); *Acts Interpretation Act 1901* (Cth) s 23. On actions for infringement of patents, see *Patents Act 1990* (Cth) s 120.
89 *Patents Act 1990* (Cth) s 16(2).
90 *Patents Act 1990* (Cth) s 16(3).
91 See A. L. Monotti (with S. Ricketson), *Universities and Intellectual Property: Ownership and Exploitation* (New York: Oxford University Press, 2003) ch 5.

any co-owner to apply to the Commissioner for directions about dealing with the patent or an interest in it, the grant of licences under the patent and the exercise of a right under s 16 in relation to the patent.[92]

11.2.4 Grant of patent

A patent is granted to the nominated eligible person[93] and can be granted to two or more nominated persons jointly.[94] The grant to two or more persons jointly will result in co-ownership of a patent.[95] Where two co-inventors are each responsible for part of the invention, neither inventor is entitled to a patent over the entire invention[96] because they would then benefit from part of the invention that the other developed.

11.2.5 Proprietary rights in the patent

A patent gives the patentee exclusive rights that are personal property.[97] The rights are capable of assignment and devolution by law.[98] There is conflicting authority as to the status of a patent application. Section 15(1)(c) of the *Patents Act 1990* (Cth) clearly contemplates that the subject matter of the application is capable of assignment or other disposition to a party to whom a patent may be granted. One view is that an assignment of the rights in the application may amount to a present assignment of the future property in the granted patent when it comes into existence.[99] Such an agreement is specifically enforceable in equity. This is consistent with the view that regards the rights in the application as personal property on the basis that they amount to rights in future property.[100] It is also consistent with the observation of Yates J in *Sigma Pharmaceuticals (Australia) Pty Ltd v Wyeth* that the entitlement of an assignee who has since become registered owner of the patent 'derives from s 15(1)(c) of the Act, which, for its own purposes, treats an "invention" as a species of property'.[101] An invention is only information and the High Court has confirmed that there is no property in information per se.[102] Therefore, these authorities suggest that an invention becomes a species of property only because it is the subject of a patent application that, if successful, will result in the grant of personal property rights to exploit the invention. When the invention is divorced from the patent application it is merely information.

A number of sections in the *Patents Act 1990* (Cth) arguably provide further support for this suggestion that proprietary rights exist in the patent application or the invention that is the

---

92 *Patents Act 1990* (Cth) s 17.
93 Ibid s 61.
94 Ibid s 63.
95 Ibid s 16.
96 *Stack v Davies Shephard Pty Ltd* (2001) 108 FCR 422, [21]; *JMVB Enterprises Pty Ltd v Camoflag Pty Ltd* (2005) 67 IPR 68, [143]; *Polwood Pty Ltd v Foxworth Pty Ltd* (2008) 165 FCR 527, [36], [66].
97 *Patents Act 1990* (Cth) s 13.
98 Ibid s 13(2).
99 *Booth v Federal Commissioner of Taxation* (1987) 164 CLR 159, 165–6 (Mason CJ); *Norman v Federal Commissioner of Taxation* (1963) 109 CLR 9, 24–5 (Windeyer J).
100 *Hepples v Federal Commissioner of Taxation* (1990) 22 FCR 1, 24; *Camilleri v Steel Foundations Ltd* (2003) AIPC 91-837, [33].
101 (2011) 119 IPR 194, [287] ([126] Bennett and [133] Nicholas JJ concurring).
102 *Breen v Williams* (1996) 186 CLR 71.

subject of that application. First, the term of a granted patent commences from the date of the grant, which is the date of filing the complete specification.[103] Second, after grant of the patent, the patentee can start proceedings for infringement in respect of acts performed on and from the day on which the specification became open for inspection.[104] However, another explanation for these provisions is that the personal property rights arise on grant and are then backdated to have commenced on the date of the patent. No action can be taken for infringement that occurs while the application remains unpublished.

A contrasting approach denies that an application for a patent or the invention that is the subject of the application is a species of property.[105] As French J observed in *University of Western Australia v Gray (No 20)*:

> An application for a patent, whether made under the 1952 Act or the 1990 Act, is an application not a species of property right. Section 34(1)(fa) of the 1952 Act and s 15 of the 1990 Act both recognise that a right to take an assignment of a patent when granted may come into existence while an application is pending or before an application is made. Such a right may find its source in agreement or by operation of the general law. None of this confers on inventions or applications the character of property rights.[106]

11.3 Employee inventions

The *Patents Act 1990* (Cth) has no express provisions that deal with ownership of inventions created by employees in the course of their employment.[107] In the absence of an express agreement, the existence of an employer's rights is determined according to the general common law and the application of the equitable principles governing the employment relationship.[108] Australian legislation recognises the entitlement of an employer in s 15 as someone who is entitled to be assigned rights by the inventor on grant[109] or as a person who derives title to the invention from the inventor.[110] An employer may be able to claim entitlement to a grant of patent in place of the nominated person in any patent application.[111] It may also be able to request that an application proceed in its name when it would be entitled under an assignment or agreement or by operation of law to the patent when it is granted.[112]

Whether an invention made by an employee is the property of the employer will depend on many factors. These include:

---

103 *Patents Act 1990* (Cth) ss 61, 67.
104 Ibid s 57.
105 *University of British Columbia v Conor Medsystems Inc* (2006) 155 FCR 391, [39] (Emmett J), [101] (Bennett J).
106 (2008) 246 ALR 603, [1355].
107 *Patents Act 1990* (Cth) s 15. But note that *Patents Act 1977* (UK) ss 39–42 contain specific provisions that deal with inventions created by employees. For a general discussion of employee inventions in Australia, see Monotti, *Universities and Intellectual Property*, above n 91, [5.44]–[5.62].
108 See ch 8 at 8.6–8.7.
109 *Patents Act 1990* (Cth) s 15(1)(b).
110 Ibid s 15(1)(c).
111 Ibid s 36.
112 Ibid s 113.

- the nature of the invention;
- the duties that the employee is engaged to perform;
- the position that the employee occupies in the employer's operations; and
- the circumstances in which the invention is made.

In regard to the last point, relevant circumstances include whether it was made during the employer's time, whether there is a relationship of confidence, whether the invention will be useful to the employer's business, and whether the employee was responding to the employer's instructions in making a decision on the facts of the particular case at hand.[113]

It is important to note that the fact that the employee made the invention using the employer's materials and time does not necessarily lead to the conclusion that the employer should own the invention.[114]

11.3.1 Express provisions in the employment contract

In most cases the employment contract will contain an express term that governs ownership of employee inventions and entitlement will depend on the interpretation of that term. An express agreement may require the employee to assign to the employer all inventions that are made during employment.[115] Such a practice is considered to be 'wholly appropriate' in certain circumstances.[116] Indeed, if a company fails to insert any condition concerning the making of inventions in its employment contracts, courts are willing to imply a condition that is appropriate to safeguard the company's interests.[117]

The nature of the work done by the employee will suggest the type of clause that is appropriate. While an express or 'pre-assignment' clause is the most sensible approach to take when an employer expects its employees will invent, such clauses will attract the doctrine of restraint of trade and will be construed strictly against the employer.[118] The restrictions imposed must be reasonably necessary for the protection of the legitimate interests of the person imposing the restrictions and reasonable in reference to the interests of the public.[119]

---

[113] *Fine Industrial Commodities Ltd v Powling* (1954) 71 RPC 253, 257; *Worthington Pumping Engine Co v Moore* (1903) 20 RPC 41, 48–9; *Reiss Engineering Co Ltd v Harris* [1985] 14 IRLR 232; *Spencer Industries Pty Ltd v Collins* (2003) 58 IPR 425.

[114] *Mellor v William Beardmore & Co Ltd* (1927) 44 RPC 175, 191 (Lord Ormidale); *Kwan v Queensland Corrective Services Commission* (1994) 31 IPR 25, 33; *Re Charles Selz Ltd's Application* (1954) 71 RPC 158, 164; *Fine Industrial Commodities Ltd v Powling* (1954) 71 RPC 253, 257; *Greater Glasgow Health Board's Application* [1996] RPC 207; *Victoria University of Technology v Wilson* (2004) 60 IPR 392, [104].

[115] *Electrolux Ltd v Hudson* [1977] FSR 312.

[116] Ibid 321; *Leather Cloth Co v Lorsont* (1869) LR 9 Eq 345.

[117] *Electrolux Ltd v Hudson* [1977] FSR 312, 321–2.

[118] *Herbert Morris Ltd v Saxelby* [1916] 1 AC 688; *Triplex Safety Glass Co Ltd v Scorah* [1938] Ch 211. For the common law doctrine of restraint of trade, see *Thorsten Nordenfelt v Maxim Nordenfelt Guns & Ammunition Co* [1894] AC 535; *Amoco Australia Pty Ltd v Rocca Bros Motor Engineering Co Pty Ltd* (1973) 133 CLR 288; *Aerial Taxi Cabs Co-operative Society Ltd v Lee* (2000) 102 FCR 125; *Adamson v New South Wales Rugby League Ltd* (1991) 31 FCR 242; *Peters (WA) Ltd v Petersville Ltd* (2001) 205 CLR 126; *Australian Capital Territory v Munday* (2000) 99 FCR 72; J. D. Heydon, *The Restraint of Trade Doctrine* (3rd edn, Sydney: LexisNexis Butterworths, 2008).

[119] *Herbert Morris Ltd v Saxelby* [1916] 1 AC 688, 700 (Lord Atkinson); *Thorsten Nordenfelt v Maxim Nordenfelt Guns & Ammunition Co* [1894] AC 535; *Maggbury Pty Ltd v Hafele Australia Pty Ltd* (2001) 210 CLR 181.

They 'must afford adequate protection to the party in whose favour (the restraint) is imposed'.[120]

If the covenant fails to meet the test of reasonableness by being more than is adequate for the protection of the covenantee, it will not be enforced.[121] There is authority that restrictions will be enforceable where the employee accepts the restriction in return for an adequate level of remuneration during employment.[122] Adequacy of protection for the legitimate interests of the employer is measured at the time of entry into the restriction.[123]

11.3.2 Implied duty to assign inventions: the duty of good faith

There is necessarily to be implied into an employee's contract of service a term that the employee 'will serve his employer with good faith and fidelity'.[124] However, as Lord Greene MR stated in *Hivac Ltd v Park Royal Scientific Instruments Ltd*, 'the practical difficulty in any given case is to find exactly how far that rather vague duty of fidelity extends'.[125] This must be a 'question on the facts of each particular case'.[126] This duty requires the employee 'to carry out faithfully the work the employee is employed to do to the best of his ability'.[127] In general terms, a duty of good faith requires an employee to protect and promote the employer's interests and to refrain from acting contrary to its interests[128] or making a profit out of his or her trust or office.[129] This is reflected in the ability of an employer to restrain conduct undertaken with some deliberate and secret intention to do harm to the employer.[130] Even if an express covenant is declared unenforceable as an unreasonable restraint,[131] the employee remains bound by a duty of good faith to their employer.

---

120 *Herbert Morris Ltd v Saxelby* [1916] 1 AC 688, 707 (Lord Parker); *Tavener v Sheridan* [2000] FCA 219; *Petrofina (Great Britain) Ltd v Martin* [1966] Ch 146, 169; *Esso Petroleum Co Ltd v Harper's Garage (Stourport) Ltd* [1968] AC 269; *Quadramain Pty Ltd v Sevastapol Investments Pty Ltd* (1976) 133 CLR 390; C. Arup, 'What/whose knowledge? Restraints of trade and concepts of knowledge' (2012) 36 *Melbourne University Law Review* 369.
121 *Maggbury Pty Ltd v Hafele Australia Pty Ltd* (2001) 210 CLR 181 (confidential information). But see *Restraints of Trade Act 1976* (NSW).
122 See Heydon, *The Restraint of Trade Doctrine*, above n 118, 174–84.
123 *Lindner v Murdock's Garage* (1950) 83 CLR 628, 653 (Kitto J); *Amoco Australia Pty Ltd v Rocca Bros Motor Engineering Co Pty Ltd* (1973) 133 CLR 288, 318 (Gibbs J); *Bridge v Deacons* [1984] AC 705, 718. See Heydon, *The Restraint of Trade Doctrine*, above n 118, 94.
124 *Electrolux Ltd v Hudson* [1977] FSR 312, 326; *Wessex Dairies Ltd v Smith* [1935] 2 KB 80; *British Syphon Co Ltd v Homewood* [1956] 1 WLR 1190; *Hivac Ltd v Park Royal Scientific Instruments Ltd* [1946] Ch 169; *Robb v Green* [1895] 2 QB 315, 320 (A. L. Smith LJ); *Lancashire Fires Ltd v SA Lyons & Co Ltd* [1996] FSR 629, 648.
125 [1946] Ch 169, 174.
126 See also *French v Mason* [1999] FSR 597.
127 *Harris' Patent* [1985] RPC 19, 29; *Adamson v Kenworthy* (1932) 49 RPC 57.
128 *Hivac Ltd v Park Royal Scientific Instruments Ltd* [1946] Ch 169; *Independent Management Resources Pty Ltd v Brown* [1987] VR 605; *Robb v Green* [1895] 2 QB 315; *Wessex Dairies Ltd v Smith* [1935] 2 KB 80, 87.
129 *Keech v Sandford* (1726) Sel Cas Cha 61, 22 ER 629; *Keith Henry & Co Pty Ltd v Stuart Walker & Co Pty Ltd* (1958) 100 CLR 342, 350.
130 *Electrolux Ltd v Hudson* [1977] FSR 312, 328.
131 *Electrolux Ltd v Hudson* [1977] FSR 312; *Triplex Safety Glass Co Ltd v Scorah* [1938] Ch 211.

An important aspect of this duty is reflected in an implied term that the employer owns all inventions created in the performance of employment duties. The critical issue is to determine what the employee is paid to do.[132] Hence, it will apply only where the invention is made within the course and scope of the employee's work duties.[133] That implied term is invoked in the absence of an express term or where an express term is found to be invalid.[134] Hence, where a person is employed to solve a particular problem and creates an invention to achieve a solution, the employer will own that invention.[135] Similarly, this will occur where an employee is employed to make a technical design or proposal,[136] to make an improvement to the type of goods their employer manufactured[137] or to make or discover inventions.[138] In these circumstances, the invention flows directly from carrying out the duties that the employee is engaged to perform. However, while the general duty of good faith imposes an obligation to carry out faithfully the work they were employed to do to the best of their ability, it 'does not assist in the formulation of the actual duties which the employee is employed to do'.[139] These must be determined as a question of fact.[140] The employment duties can change over the course of employment and rights in any invention must be assessed with reference to the work performed at the relevant time. Therefore, although a person may not be employed to invent from the outset, it is open to an employer to change those duties by 'verbal instruction'.[141] The contractual validity of any directions to perform duties that involve a duty to invent will depend on whether the order was reasonable and lawful as being within the scope or course of employment.[142]

A duty to conduct research will not automatically vest ownership of an employee's inventions in the employer. It all depends on the nature of the research that the employee is retained to perform; this is taken from the nature of the employer's business and the nature of the research.[143]

A different position applies in the case of inventions created by academic employees of a university.[144] According to the Full Federal Court in *University of Western Australia v*

---

132 *Victoria University of Technology v Wilson* (2004) 60 IPR 392, [104].
133 See *University of Western Australia v Gray* (2009) 179 FCR 346, [148]–[173] (within context of a university); *Victoria University of Technology v Wilson* (2004) 60 IPR 392, 429; *Spencer Industries Pty Ltd v Collins* (2003) 58 IPR 425, 439; *MacKay v McKay* (2004) 63 IPR 441, 462; *Royal Children's Hospital v Alexander* [2011] APO 94.
134 *Sterling Engineering Co Ltd v Patchett* [1955] AC 534, 543–4.
135 *Adamson v Kenworthy* (1932) 49 RPC 57.
136 *British Reinforced Concrete Engineering Co v Lind* (1917) 34 RPC 101; *Barnet Instruments Ltd v Overton* (1949) 66 RPC 315; *Aneeta Window Systems (Vic) Pty Ltd v K Shugg Industries Pty Ltd* (1996) 34 IPR 95, 106.
137 *Sterling Engineering Co Ltd v Patchett* [1955] AC 534, 543–4.
138 *Triplex Safety Glass Co Ltd v Scorah* [1938] Ch 211.
139 *Harris' Patent* [1985] RPC 19, 29–30; *Adamson v Kenworthy* (1932) 49 RPC 57, 68.
140 See *Greater Glasgow Health Board's Application* [1996] RPC 207; *Vokes Ltd v Heather* (1945) 62 RPC 135, 136.
141 *Victoria University of Technology v Wilson* (2004) 60 IPR 392, 430.
142 M. Pittard, 'The innovative worker: Genius, accidental inventor or thief?' in M. Pittard, A. L. Monotti and J. Duns (eds), *Business Innovation and the Law: Perspectives from Intellectual Property, Labour, Competition and Corporate Law* (Cheltenham: Edward Elgar Publishing, 2013) ch 10.
143 *Re Charles Selz Ltd's Application* (1954) 71 RPC 158.
144 A. L. Monotti, 'Establishing clear rights in academic employee inventions in Australian universities: Lessons learnt from *University of Western Australia v Gray*' in M. Pittard, A. Monotti and

Gray,[145] academic employment is far removed from the types of employment relationships that gave rise to the common law implied term.[146] The distinctiveness of universities and academic employment within them was central to the court's decision to classify academic employment as a sub-class of employment contracts that do not attract the common law implication.[147] Hence, in the absence of an enforceable express term, an academic employee's duty to undertake unspecified research will not require them to assign to their employer any inventions that result from the performance of that research.

The policy and 'consequentialist considerations' that influenced this decision included:[148]

- An academic employee's general duty to carry out research does not necessarily incorporate a 'duty to invent'.
- Universities are created to serve public purposes and there was no evidence to suggest that commercial activities replace the traditional public function as an institution of higher education in favour of the pursuit of commercial purposes.
- The implication of an obligation of secrecy as of course would be an inevitable consequence of the implied term and would have 'quite significant collateral impact'[149] on the practices of academics. This was impossible to reconcile with the academic freedoms to publish (there were no constraints to keep anything secret) and to choose the subject and manner of research without being subject to the duty to invent and to collaborate with external organisations.
- The fact that it would be necessary to enter into collaborative arrangements with external organisations.

An additional factor may be the two-faceted character of the relationship where academics are both employees and members of the university. In the absence of an implied term in law, universities who require their academic employees to assign inventions must achieve this outcome with express contractual provisions that are both valid and enforceable. If an academic employee is bound to assign inventions that result from the performance of their research, there is some obiter to suggest that the nature of the research that an academic is engaged to perform will be judged according to the norm for their department; it is not informed by what happens in other parts of the university. Therefore, there is no duty to

---

J. Duns (eds), *Business Innovation and the Law* (Cheltenham: Edward Elgar Publishing, 2013) ch 5; A. L. Monotti, 'Is it time to codify principles for ownership of academic employee inventions? The disconnect between policy and the law' (2012) 38 *Monash University Law Review* 102; W. van Caenegem, '*VUT v Wilson, UWA v Gray* and university intellectual property policies' (2010) 21(3) *Australian Intellectual Property Journal* 148; C. Arup, 'Employee inventions: Labour law meets intellectual property' (2008) 21 *Australian Journal of Labour Law* 208; G. Moodie, '*Victoria University of Technology v Wilson & Ors*: The Supreme Court of Victoria tries some socio-legal analysis in reconceptualising the role of academics' (2004) 13 *Griffith Law Review* 225.

145 (2009) 179 FCR 346.
146 Ibid [173], [206].
147 Ibid [206]. See Monotti, *Universities and Intellectual Property*, above n 91.
148 *University of Western Australia v Gray* (2009) 179 FCR 346, [173]; *University of Western Australia v Gray (No 20)* (2008) 246 ALR 603, [1365]–[1366].
149 *University of Western Australia v Gray* (2009) 179 FCR 346, [190].

invent if the sort of research undertaken within the school in question is directed to the preparation and presentation of peer-reviewed learned papers.[150]

Once the employee is found to have breached the obligation of good faith and thereby become a trustee in relation to a secret discovery, 'he cannot avoid the obligations attached thereto, unless the beneficiaries release him either expressly or impliedly'.[151] Hence, an employee who leaves employment with a secret discovery holds this in trust for their employer, first as confidential information, and subsequently as the patented invention. It is only if the employer cannot protect the secret information under the doctrine of breach of confidence or under an enforceable express or implied covenant that the employee is free to use it.[152]

11.3.3 Fiduciary duties

It is necessary to distinguish between both the employee's contractual duty of good faith and the implied duty to assign inventions when they are created in pursuance of the employment duties (on the one hand) and such fiduciary duty (if any) as the employee may owe to an employer arising from the position occupied in the organisation.[153] Not all employees will owe fiduciary duties to their employers,[154] but where a duty exists it must accommodate itself to the terms of the contract of employment so that it is consistent with it and conforms to it. The fiduciary relationship cannot be superimposed on the contract so that it alters the operation that the contract was intended to have on its true construction.[155] Academic employees occupying senior and specific employment positions at the university have been found to owe such fiduciary duties to their university employer.[156] These fiduciary obligations to the university are similar to those of professional employees generally: a duty not to profit from their position at the expense of the employer, and a duty to avoid conflicts of interest and duty.[157] These duties require them to avoid work that could conflict with the interest of the employer.

In the course of its analysis of employee inventions, the Banks Committee in the United Kingdom made the following comments about the extent of this duty:

---

150   *Victoria University of Technology v Wilson* (2004) 60 IPR 392, 423.
151   *Triplex Safety Glass Co Ltd v Scorah* [1938] Ch 211, 218.
152   See ch 8 at 8.7.
153   *University of Nottingham v Fishel* [2000] ICR 1462, 1490 (Elias J); *Hospital Products Ltd v United States Surgical Corp* (1984) 156 CLR 41, 97 (Mason J); *Victoria University of Technology v Wilson* (2004) 60 IPR 392, 438; *Hivac Ltd v Park Royal Scientific Instruments Ltd* [1946] Ch 169; *Bayley & Associates Pty Ltd v DBR Australia Pty Ltd* [2013] FCA 1341, [238] (general manager). As to fiduciary relationships, see J. Glover, *Equity, Restitution and Fraud* (Sydney: LexisNexis Butterworths, 2004); P. Parkinson, 'Fiduciary obligations' in P. Parkinson (ed), *The Principles of Equity* (2nd edn, Sydney: Law Book Company, 2003) ch 10.
154   For example, *Woolworths Ltd v Olson* (2004) 184 FLR 121, [217]; *Aneeta Window Systems (Vic) Pty Ltd v K Shugg Industries Pty Ltd* (1996) 34 IPR 95, 106.
155   *Victoria University of Technology v Wilson* (2004) 60 IPR 392, 438; *Hospital Products Ltd v United States Surgical Corp* (1984) 156 CLR 41, 97 (Mason J); *University of Nottingham v Fishel* [2000] ICR 1462, 1491–2.
156   *Victoria University of Technology v Wilson* (2004) 60 IPR 392, 438.
157   *Chan v Zacharia* (1984) 154 CLR 178, 199.

It seems to be generally true to say that directors of companies and managers of businesses to whom no specific duties are allocated have a general duty to forward the interests of the company or business and will accordingly hold any inventions made during their employment (at least so far as they relate to the relevant business) in trust for the employer.[158]

To avoid a breach of duty and liability, a person occupying a fiduciary position who wishes to enter into a transaction that would otherwise amount to a breach of duty must make a full disclosure to the person to whom the duty is owed of all relevant facts known to the fiduciary, and that person must consent to the fiduciary's proposal.[159] In providing a remedy for a breach of fiduciary duty, it seems that the court would be prepared to recognise a constructive trust over the inventions up until innocent third-party interests became involved.[160]

Finally, where a term is implied to the effect that an employee holds an invention in trust for their employer, this obligation continues after employment.[161] Being confidential information until a patent application is made publicly available, this obligation is effectively another way of expressing an ex-employee's obligation to respect the confidentiality of their former employer's trade secrets.[162]

11.4 Crown use of patents for inventions
11.4.1 Introduction

The exclusive rights of a patentee to exploit the invention are circumscribed by a range of powers that the Crown reserves to itself under Chapter 17 of the *Patents Act 1990* (Cth).[163] The purpose of these provisions is to ensure that the Commonwealth and state governments have immediate access to inventions for the benefit of the services of the respective governments.[164] They provide the Crown with a statutory shield against a patent infringement action. Three principal obligations confine the legitimate scope of the Crown's retention of rights under

---

158 Board of Trade, *The British Patent System: Report of the Committee to Examine the Patent System and Patent Law* (Cmnd 4407, 1970) (Banks Committee) [443].
159 *Victoria University of Technology v Wilson* (2004) 60 IPR 392, 437; J. D. Heydon, M. D. Leeming and P. G. Turner, *Meagher, Gummow and Lehane's Equity: Doctrines and Remedies* (5th edn, Sydney: Butterworths, 2015).
160 *Victoria University of Technology v Wilson* (2004) 60 IPR 392.
161 *Triplex Safety Glass Co Ltd v Scorah* [1938] Ch 211.
162 See ch 8.
163 Intellectual Property Laws Amendment (Productivity Commission Response Part 2 and Other Measures) Bill 2019 (Cth) sch 2 increases the certainty and transparency of the operation of Chapter 17. The Bill was introduced into parliament in July 2019. The Senate, Economics Legislation Committee Report into the Bill recommended that the Bill be passed: see Senate, Economics Legislation Committee, Parliament of Australia, Intellectual Property Laws Amendment (Productivity Commission Response Part 2 and Other Measures) Bill 2019 (Report, September 2019). Its text was not available in time for detailed analysis to appear in this book, but occasional references appear in footnotes below. See generally Productivity Commission, *Compulsory Licensing of Patents* (Inquiry Report No 61, March 2013) ch 7; ACIP, *Review of Crown Use Provisions for Patents and Designs* (Final Report, November 2005). See also J. Nielsen, D. Nicol, J. Liddicoat and T. Whitton, 'Another missed opportunity to reform compulsory licensing and Crown use in Australia' (2014) 25 *Australian Intellectual Property Journal* 74.
164 *Stack v Brisbane City Council* (1995) 59 FCR 71, 84 (Cooper J). See also ACIP, *Review of Crown Use Provisions for Patents and Designs*, above n 163, [3.6.1].

Chapter 17. The first two are the international obligations in arts 30 and 31 of *TRIPS* and arts 17.9.7 and 17.9.3 of the *Australia–US Free Trade Agreement*[165] (*AUSFTA*). The third is that the Crown use provisions must be viewed in the context of the *Competition Principles Agreement*[166] between the Commonwealth and the states and territories.[167]

The powers that the Crown retains are to exploit patents without express authority of the patentee but subject to payment of agreed remuneration,[168] to compulsorily acquire patents,[169] and to acquire patents by way of assignment with or without valuable consideration.[170]

11.4.2 Exploitation of inventions by the Crown

There are extensive powers of the Commonwealth or a state to exploit the invention without permission at any time after a person applies for a patent for an invention. The exploitation will not infringe the rights in the application or the patent, provided that it is necessary for the proper provision of the services of the Commonwealth or the state within Australia.[171] Section 162 of the *Patents Act 1990* (Cth) recognises that both departments of government, and 'authorities' of the Commonwealth or states, perform and manage those services.[172]

There is no definition of 'authority of the Commonwealth' or 'authority of a State'. The Federal Court considered the meaning of 'authority of a State' in *Stack v Brisbane City Council*[173] in respect of the Brisbane City Council, a body corporate established under s 6 of the *City of Brisbane Act 1924* (Qld). The council has considerable autonomy and wide discretion in the exercise of its powers and functions within its territorial boundaries.[174] Cooper J concluded that there is no confinement of the phrase 'authority of a State' to the Crown or to those bodies that are so closely identified with the Crown to enjoy its immunity.[175] Rather, it has a wider scope. An authority will be 'an authority of a State' if its functions are

> 'impressed with the stamp of government' or if it has been given by the State the power to direct or control the affairs of others on behalf of the State. The role and involvement of the executive, through the Governor in Council or the appropriate Minister, is also a relevant factor.[176]

The primary focus is on government and the function of government. No one consideration is decisive, but a successful submission that an authority is not 'an authority of a State' requires a

---

165   Signed 18 May 2004, [2005] ATS 1 (entered into force 1 January 2005) (*AUSFTA*).
166   11 April 1995 (as amended to 13 April 2007) www.coag.gov.au.
167   See ACIP, *Review of Crown Use Provisions for Patents and Designs*, above n 163, [3.8].
168   *Patents Act 1990* (Cth) s 163. Intellectual Property Laws Amendment (Productivity Commission Response Part 2 and Other Measures) Bill 2019 (Cth) sch 2 item 7 repeals s 163 and introduces new ss 163 and 163A to implement additional requirements that must be satisfied before the relevant authority is exempt from infringement. See above n 163.
169   *Patents Act 1990* (Cth) s 171.
170   Ibid s 172.
171   Ibid s 163. This extends to exploitation for purposes outside Australia in the circumstances in s 168.
172   *General Steel Industries Inc v Commissioner for Railways (NSW)* (1964) 112 CLR 125, 133–4 (Barwick CJ); *Stack v Brisbane City Council* (1995) 59 FCR 71, 84.
173   (1995) 59 FCR 71, 84.
174   Ibid 83.
175   Ibid 77.
176   Ibid 78.

conclusion to be drawn from the legislation that the authority is not engaged in the work of government.[177] In the context of similar provisions in the *Patents Act 1952* (Cth), the High Court has found the Commissioner of Railways to be 'an authority of a State'.[178]

11.4.3 Scope of the exploitation right

The right for the Crown to exploit an invention includes the right to sell products that it makes in exercise of that right.[179] Purchasers of those products, and those claiming through them, can deal with the products as if the relevant authority is the patentee or nominated person.[180]

The exemption from infringement extends to exploitation of the invention by a person authorised in writing by the Commonwealth or a state.[181] Such authorisation can take place either before or after the act of exploitation and before or after the grant of patent.[182] Therefore, retrospective authorisation can immunise an otherwise infringing act. The nominated person or patentee may have already authorised a person to exploit the invention. If it so desires, the relevant authority can also authorise that person to exploit the invention under s 163 for its services. In this event, the terms of any licence agreement between the person and the patentee or nominated person do not bind the relevant authority, unless the Minister in the case of the Commonwealth, or the Attorney-General in the case of a state, approves those terms.[183]

11.4.4 'For the services of the Commonwealth or a State'

The exemption from infringement applies only where the exploitation is 'for the services of the Commonwealth or a State'. This includes a reference to the services of an authority of a state.[184]

The meaning of 'for the services of' was considered in *Stack v Brisbane City Council*.[185] A function of the Brisbane City Council is to supply reticulated water to the properties of its constituents. The council entered into a contract with a contractor for the supply of water meter assemblies that would be installed and connected to its pipes to measure the water supplied to those properties. The meters were to remain an asset of the council and were not to be resupplied to the respective landowners or used by them in any sense. George Stack claimed that the water meter assemblies incorporated a patented invention to which Stack was beneficially entitled and sought an injunction to restrain infringement. The council successfully relied

---

177   *Committee of Direction of Fruit Marketing v Australian Postal Commission* (1980) 144 CLR 577, 593–4 (Mason and Wilson JJ, Barwick CJ agreeing).
178   *General Steel Industries Inc v Commissioner for Railways (NSW)* (1964) 112 CLR 125, 132 (Barwick CJ). Intellectual Property Laws Amendment (Productivity Commission Response Part 2 and Other Measures) Bill 2019 (Cth) sch 2 item 6 repeals s 162 in consequence of item 25 which incorporates its terms into a new definition of 'relevant authority' in *Patents Act 1990* (Cth) sch 1. See above n 163.
179   *Patents Act 1990* (Cth) s 167(1).
180   Ibid s 167(2).
181   Ibid s 163(1).
182   Ibid s 163(2).
183   Ibid s 166.
184   *Stack v Brisbane City Council* (1995) 59 FCR 71, 84.
185   Ibid 84–5.

on Chapter 17 of the *Patents Act 1990* (Cth) as a defence to the infringement claim. Cooper J found that the use of the water meters as part of its supply of reticulated water was exploitation by the council as an authority of a state for the services of the council as such an authority.

The small number of cases in which this or a similar provision has been considered have all concerned the supply of an infringing item by a contractor for the direct use of an authority of the state or a government department.[186] It is not clear whether the purchase and resupply of an item by the state or department to a third party in competition with the patentee would be a use 'for the services of a State'.[187]

11.4.5 Obligations of the Crown

Although the relevant authority[188] can exploit the patent without prior notification to the patentee, it must inform the applicant and the nominated person (in the case of a patent application), or the patentee, of the exploitation as soon as practicable after its exploitation.[189] There is a continuing obligation to provide any information about the exploitation as is reasonably required. An exception to this obligation applies where it appears to the relevant authority that it would be contrary to the public interest to provide this information.

11.4.6 Procedures available to a patentee

If a patentee thinks that their invention has been exploited under s 163(1) of the *Patents Act 1990* (Cth), they can apply to a prescribed court for a declaration to that effect.[190] In the case of an innovation patent, no application is possible unless the patent has been certified.[191] The defendant relevant authority[192] can apply by way of counterclaim in the proceedings for revocation of the patent.[193]

11.4.7 Remuneration and terms for exploitation

There is a mechanism for determining the terms on which the relevant authority can exploit the invention without infringement. First, the parties can agree on terms or a method for determination of terms[194] before, during or after exploitation.[195] If they cannot reach agreement, then either party can apply to a prescribed court to determine the terms for exploitation and

---

186 *Pfizer Corp v Ministry of Health* [1965] AC 512; *General Steel Industries Inc v Commissioner for Railways (NSW)* (1964) 112 CLR 125.
187 *Pfizer Corp v Ministry of Health* [1965] AC 512; *Stack v Brisbane City Council* (1995) 59 FCR 71.
188 See *Patents Act 1990* (Cth) sch 1 (definition of 'relevant authority').
189 Ibid s 164.
190 Ibid s 169(1).
191 Ibid s 169(4).
192 Ibid s 169(2)(a).
193 Ibid s 169(2)(b), (3).
194 Ibid s 165(2). Intellectual Property Laws Amendment (Productivity Commission Response Part 2 and Other Measures) Bill 2019 (Cth) sch 2 item 11 repeals 165(2) and inserts a new s 165(2) to modify how remuneration is determined. See above n 163.
195 *Patents Act 1990* (Cth) s 165(3).

remuneration.[196] In fixing the terms, a court can take into account any compensation that a person interested in the invention or patent has received (directly or indirectly) for the invention from the relevant authority.[197]

11.4.8 Exploitation of invention to cease under court order

A nominated person or patentee can apply to a prescribed court for an order that exploitation cease.[198] The court may make an order subject to any conditions that it specifies, if it is satisfied that it is fair and reasonable to order that exploitation of the invention by the Crown is not, or is no longer, necessary for the proper provision of services of the Crown.[199] The court must ensure that the legitimate interests of the Crown are not adversely affected by the order.[200]

11.4.9 Supply of products by Commonwealth to foreign countries

The exemption from infringement in s 163 of the *Patents Act 1990* (Cth) applies to exploitation of an invention that is necessary for the proper provision of the services of the Commonwealth or a state within Australia.[201] This would include sales of products for use within Australia, but would not ordinarily extend protection to any export of products to another country. An exception applies where the Commonwealth has an agreement with a foreign country to supply it with products for its defence. In this case, the use of a product or process for the supply of that product is taken to be a use of the product or process for the services of the Commonwealth.[202] The Commonwealth or an authorised person can sell those products to the country under the agreement and can sell to any person any excess products that the country does not require.[203]

11.4.10 Acquisition of inventions or patents by the Commonwealth

The Governor-General may direct that a patent or an invention that is the subject of a patent application can be acquired by the Commonwealth.[204] All rights are transferred to and vested in the Commonwealth at the time the direction is given by force of s 171(2) of the *Patents Act 1990* (Cth).[205] Failing agreement as to the amount of compensation payable, either party can

---

196 Ibid ss 155(1), 165(2), sch 1.
197 Ibid s 165(4).
198 Ibid s 165A(1).
199 Ibid.
200 Ibid s 165A(2).
201 Ibid s 163(1), (3).
202 Ibid s 168(a).
203 Ibid s 168(b), (c).
204 Ibid s 171(1).
205 Ibid s 171(2); ss 173, 152 (notice); s 171(3)(b) (publication).

apply for court determination of the amount.[206] There are no recorded instances of the exercise of these powers of compulsory acquisition.[207] However, as the government can exercise rights in an invention without the need to acquire the patent, an acquisition may be necessary only where it seeks to exclude others from exploiting the invention.[208]

11.4.11 Assignments of inventions to the Commonwealth

An inventor, or an inventor's successor in title, may assign the invention and any patent granted, or to be granted, to the Commonwealth.[209] The assignment and all covenants and agreements are valid and effectual and can be enforced by proceedings in the name of the Minister even if no valuable consideration has been given for the assignment.[210]

11.4.12 Review of Crown use

The Crown use provisions have been invoked rarely in the past, and there is no evidence of Crown acquisition of patents. Nevertheless, the provisions were reviewed by the Australian Law Reform Commission in 2004 in its report *Genes and Ingenuity*,[211] by the Advisory Council on Intellectual Property (ACIP) in 2005,[212] and by the Productivity Commission in 2013 in the context of providing an alternative mechanism to compulsory licensing.[213] A focus of all reviews has been to clarify uncertainties in the existing provisions, the promotion of health care, and the need for increased transparency and accountability in the exercise of Crown use. The Productivity Commission report recommended changes in these areas that were implemented in sch 1 of the Intellectual Property Laws Amendment Bill 2013 (Cth). However, that schedule was removed from the Bill as it was eventually enacted in the form of the *Intellectual Property Laws Amendment Act 2015* (Cth). Following further consultation with stakeholders, amendments to the Crown use provisions appear in Intellectual Property Laws Amendment (Productivity Commission Response Part 2 and Other Measures) Bill 2019 (Cth) sch 2.[214]

11.5 Dealings with inventions
11.5.1 General principles

The path to commercial exploitation often involves dealings with patents and associated confidential information, know-how and data. A patent gives the patentee exclusive personal property rights in the invention that are capable of assignment and devolution by law.[215]

---

206 Ibid s 171(4).
207 Productivity Commission, *Compulsory Licensing of Patents*, above n 163, 164.
208 Ibid.
209 *Patents Act 1990* (Cth) s 172(1).
210 *Patents Act 1990* (Cth) s 172(2).
211 Australian Law Reform Commission, *Genes and Ingenuity: Gene Patenting and Human Health* (Report No 99, June 2004) ch 26.
212 ACIP, *Review of Crown Use Provisions for Patents and Designs*, above n 163. There was no government response on the grounds that no evidence of misuse of the provisions was available.
213 Productivity Commission, *Compulsory Licensing of Patents*, above n 163, ch 7.
214 The Bill was introduced into parliament in July 2019. See above n 163.
215 *Patents Act 1990* (Cth) s 13(2). See above at 11.2.5.

Section 13(1) of the *Patents Act 1990* (Cth) provides that the exclusive rights are to *exploit* the invention and to *authorise* another person to exploit the invention. The right to 'exploit' the patented invention is defined in the Dictionary to the Act to include a range of activities, such as to make, hire, sell, keep or import the invention, any one of which would amount to an exercise of the right to exploit. The owner of the patent can exploit the invention by exercising some or all of the exclusive rights themselves, by authorising another to do so, or by assigning ownership of the patent either in whole or in part. The patentee can deal with the patent as the absolute owner, subject only to any rights that appear in the Register as vested in another person.[216]

The usual way in which a person is authorised to exploit the patent is through contractual arrangements that involve the grant of a non-exclusive, sole or exclusive licence.[217] The possible scope of a licence corresponds with the range of actions that come within the exclusive rights of the patentee, the possibility for various fields of activity in which the rights are to be exercised, and the ability to fragment the patent area into segments. If the patentee imposes restrictions on subject matter other than the patented invention, this may have an adverse effect on competition. Chapter 14 of the *Patents Act 1990* (Cth) sets out conditions that will render a licence void. In addition, Part IV of the *Competition and Consumer Act 2010* (Cth) may also have an impact on certain agreements.[218] Until the repeal of s 51(3) of the *Competition and Consumer Act* in 2019,[219] conditional licensing or assignment of intellectual property benefited from an exemption from certain prohibitions in that Act.

If the licence so permits, a licensee may grant sub-licences that may be exclusive or non-exclusive in the limited field of the sub-licence.[220] A sub-licence cannot exceed the scope of the licence. Therefore, a licensee who is authorised to make products in Victoria cannot grant a sub-licence that authorises the sub-licensee to sell the products in Victoria.

It is rare for the licence to deal only with the subject matter of the patent. Normally the agreement would include provisions for transfer of know-how and the offer of technical assistance.[221]

11.5.2 Assignments

An assignment of a patent is a transfer of ownership. The patent can be assigned for a place in, or part of, the patent area. For example, it could be assigned in respect of Victoria. Also, a patentee may assign its rights in a patent by way of security for a loan. This may extend to

---

216 *Patents Act 1990* (Cth) s 189(1). See below at 11.8.
217 N. P. Stoianoff, F. Chilton and A. L. Monotti, *Commercialisation of Intellectual Property* (LexisNexis Butterworths, 2019).
218 *Australian Competition and Consumer Commission v Pfizer Australia Pty Ltd* (2018) 356 ALR 582.
219 Repealed by *Treasury Laws Amendment (2018 Measures No 5) Act 2019* (Cth) sch 4 item 1.
220 *Pacific Brands Sport & Leisure Pty Ltd v Underworks Pty Ltd* (2006) 149 FCR 395, 403 (context of an assignment of a sub-licence of a trade mark).
221 See generally Stoianoff, Chilton and Monotti, *Commercialisation of Intellectual Property*, above n 217, pt C ('Intellectual property licensing'); A. Stewart, P. Griffith, J. Bannister and A. Liberman, *Intellectual Property in Australia* (5th edn, Sydney: LexisNexis Butterworths, 2014) ch 22.

include any improvements to the patent that are made during the term of the loan.[222] To convey a legal interest in the patent, an assignment must be in writing and signed by or on behalf of the assignor and assignee.[223] However, the *Patents Act 1990* (Cth) does not prohibit the creation of equitable interests in patents.[224]

11.5.3 Exclusive licences

A licence may be non-exclusive, sole or exclusive. An exclusive licensee is defined in the *Patents Act 1990* (Cth) to mean

> a licensee under a licence agreement granted by the patentee and conferring on the licensee, or on the licensee and persons authorised by the licensee, the right to exploit the patented invention throughout the patent area to the exclusion of the patentee and all other persons.[225]

The correct classification of a licence as exclusive or otherwise is important for two reasons. First, it seems that an exclusive licence in a patent creates a proprietary interest in the patent.[226] This interest is created by the grant of the licence and not by registration.[227] In contrast, the rights under non-exclusive or sole licences are merely contractual.

Second, only the exclusive licensee has rights under s 120 of the *Patents Act 1990* (Cth), along with the patentee, to commence infringement proceedings against a third party[228] as well as rights to seek non-infringement declarations under Part 2 of Chapter 11 of the Act. However, the exclusive licensee who commences proceedings must join the patentee as a defendant unless joined as a plaintiff.[229] These rights cannot be exercised by the equitable owner of the patent.[230]

The High Court in *Re Imperial Chemical Industries Ltd; Ex parte British Nylon Spinners Ltd*[231] determined that only one exclusive licensee of a patent could be appointed under the *Patents Act 1952* (Cth). This was confirmed by the Full Federal Court in *Bristol-Myers Squibb Co v Apotex Pty Ltd (No 5)*.[232] Previously, there were conflicting authorities on whether this is also the position under the 1990 Act. At first instance in *Bristol-Myers*, Yates J disagreed with

---

222   *Buchanan v Alba Diagnostics Ltd* [2004] RPC 34. For the regulation of securities over intellectual property rights in general, see *Personal Property Securities Act 2009* (Cth); *Fermiscan Pty Ltd v James* [2009] NSWCA 355.
223   *Patents Act 1990* (Cth) s 14.
224   *Stack v Brisbane City Council (No 2)* (1996) 67 FCR 510, 513. See, for example, *Patents Act 1990* (Cth) ss 189(3), 196(1)(b)(ii).
225   *Patents Act 1990* (Cth) sch 1.
226   *Vitamins Australia Ltd v Beta-Carotene Industries Pty Ltd* (1987) 9 IPR 41, 48; *Eastland Technology Australia Ltd v Ritract Ltd* [2005] WASC 125, [18]; *Banks v Transport Regulation Board (Vic)* (1968) 119 CLR 222, 232 (proprietary nature of sole licences).
227   *Vitamins Australia Ltd v Beta-Carotene Industries Pty Ltd* (1987) 9 IPR 41, 48.
228   *Bristol-Myers Squibb Co v Apotex Pty Ltd (No 5)* (2013) 104 IPR 23, [424]–[440] (Yates J). See also *Pharmacia Italia SpA v Interpharma Pty Ltd* (2005) 67 IPR 397; *Orion Corp v Actavis Pty Ltd (No 3)* (2015) 116 IPR 102.
229   *Patents Act 1990* (Cth) s 120(2).
230   *Stack v Brisbane City Council (No 2)* (1996) 67 FCR 510, 513.
231   (1963) 109 CLR 336 (1952 Act); *Uprising Dragon Ltd v Benedict Trading & Shipping Pty Ltd* (1987) 16 FCR 93, 102 (1952 Act).
232   (2013) 104 IPR 23, [424]–[426].

the reasoning and conclusion of Holmes J in the Queensland Supreme Court in *Grant v Australian Temporary Fencing Pty Ltd*[233] that the definition of 'exclusive licensee' in the 1990 Act, when read in conjunction with the inclusive and distributive definition of 'exploit', is at least open to a construction that allows for a 'plurality of exclusive licences'.[234] Yates J concluded persuasively instead that s 13(1) recognises only two rights that are conferred by a patent: the right to exploit the invention and the right to authorise others to exploit the invention:

> The use of disjunctive language in the definition of 'exploit' to identify particular activities falling within the scope of the term does not create separate rights with respect to those activities. It merely recognises that the right to exploit covers a range of activities, any one of which, if undertaken, would amount to the exercise of the right to exploit.[235]

His Honour reasoned, therefore, that an exclusive licence can only arise when the patentee confers a single licence to exploit that precludes the patentee from exercising any rights, including the right to authorise others to exploit the invention.[236] A necessary consequence of this reasoning is that a licence that lists some but not all of the range of activities that comprise the right to exploit cannot confer an exclusive licence on the licensee.[237] The Full Federal Court accepted this reasoning in the appeal decision, stating: 'In our opinion, the definition of the word "exploit" describes the content of a right and is not intended to create separate rights in relation to each of the identified activities.'[238]

11.5.4 Non-exclusive and sole licences

A non-exclusive licence allows the patentee to continue to exploit the patent themself and to grant as many additional licences to exploit the invention over the same territory as the patentee deems appropriate. A non-exclusive licence may be a valuable tool for exploiting foundational patented research methods that the patentee seeks to disseminate as widely as possible among the research community. A sole licence is one where the patent owner shares the exclusive rights with the sole licensee. The patentee agrees not to grant another licence to anyone else. Neither a sole nor a non-exclusive licensee has rights to commence infringement proceedings against a third party.[239]

11.6 Compulsory licences
11.6.1 Application

The grant of monopoly rights offers the grantee the potential to use those rights in an abusive or anti-competitive manner that fails to meet the reasonable requirements of the public.

---

233 [2003] QSC 194.
234 *Bristol-Myers Squibb Co v Apotex Pty Ltd (No 5)* (2013) 104 IPR 23, [428]. See also *Pharmacia Italia SpA v Interpharma Pty Ltd* (2005) 67 IPR 397, [21].
235 *Bristol-Myers Squibb Co v Apotex Pty Ltd (No 5)* (2013) 104 IPR 23, [436], approved in *Blue Gentian LLC v Product Management Group Pty Ltd* (2014) 110 IPR 453, [235].
236 *Orion Corp v Actavis Pty Ltd (No 3)* (2015) 116 IPR 102 (interpretation of licence agreements).
237 Compare *Pharmacia Italia SpA v Interpharma Pty Ltd* (2005) 67 IPR 397, [21].
238 *Bristol-Myers Squibb Co v Apotex Pty Ltd (No 5)* (2015) 109 IPR 390, [105].
239 *Patents Act 1990* (Cth) s 120.

To provide some protection against abusive practices in exceptional cases, Chapter 12 of the *Patents Act 1990* (Cth) provides that any person can apply to the Federal Court for an order requiring the patentee to grant the applicant a licence to work the invention at any time after three years from the date of sealing of the patent.[240] In the case of an innovation patent, the patent must first be certified.[241] Few applications have been made for a compulsory licence and no application has been successful.[242] Although the costly and time-consuming process involved in obtaining a Federal Court order is identified as a factor for this rare use of the provisions, the Productivity Commission in its 2013 report *Compulsory Licensing of Patents* found no clear alternative that would maintain the quality of outcomes. Nevertheless, it concluded that a clear case exists to reform the criteria for a compulsory licence.[243] Schedule 4 of the Intellectual Property Laws Amendment (Productivity Commission Response Part 2 and Other Measures) Bill 2019 (Cth)[244] includes provisions to give effect to this recommendation.

11.6.1.1 Court is satisfied that certain conditions exist

In the event that an application is made, the court may make the order if it is satisfied either that there has been anti-competitive conduct[245] or that the following three conditions exist:

1. The applicant has tried for a reasonable period, but without success, to obtain an authorisation to work the invention on reasonable terms and conditions.[246]

2. The reasonable requirements of the public with respect to the patented invention have not been satisfied.[247]

3. The patentee has given no satisfactory reason for 'failing to exploit' the patent.[248]

'Failing to exploit' the patent does not refer to absolute failure to exploit, but failure to exploit the patent in a way that satisfies the reasonable requirements of the public. This is assessed at the time of the hearing.[249] A satisfactory reason might be that the applicant is not a person suitable to be a licensee, because maintenance of the reputation of the patented invention is a legitimate concern for the patentee and the court. Another may be that the delays resulted from designing a product that would suit the Australian market.[250]

---

240   Ibid s 133(1); *Patents Regulations 1991* (Cth) reg 12.1(1); *Amrad Operations Pty Ltd v Genelabs Technologies Inc* (1999) 45 IPR 447.
241   *Patents Act 1990* (Cth) s 133(1A).
242   Productivity Commission, *Compulsory Licensing of Patents*, above n 163, [6.1]; *Fastening Supplies Pty Ltd v Olin Mathieson Chemical Corp* (1969) 119 CLR 572; *Wissen Pty Ltd v Lown* (1987) 9 IPR 124; *Amrad Operations Pty Ltd v Genelabs Technologies Inc* (1999) 45 IPR 447.
243   Productivity Commission, *Compulsory Licensing of Patents*, above n 163, Terms of Reference.
244   The Bill was introduced into parliament in July 2019. See above n 163.
245   *Patents Act 1990* (Cth) s 133(2)(b) (contravention of *Competition and Consumer Act 2010* (Cth) pt IV or an application law, as defined in s 150A of that Act, in connection with the patent).
246   *Patents Act 1990* (Cth) s 133(2)(a)(i). See *Amrad Operations Pty Ltd v Genelabs Technologies Inc* (1999) 45 IPR 447 (a period of two years satisfied the reasonable period).
247   *Patents Act 1990* (Cth) s 133(2)(a)(ii). See *Wissen Pty Ltd v Lown* (1987) 9 IPR 124.
248   *Patents Act 1990* (Cth) s 133(2)(a)(iii) (the onus falls on the patentee). See *Amrad Operations Pty Ltd v Genelabs Technologies Inc* (1999) 45 IPR 447, 450; *Re Hatschek's Patents; Ex parte Zerenner* [1909] 2 Ch 68, 82.
249   *Fastening Supplies Pty Ltd v Olin Mathieson Chemical Corp* (1969) 119 CLR 572, 575–6.
250   Ibid 575.

Section 135 of the *Patents Act 1990* (Cth) sets out the circumstances in which the reasonable requirements of the public are not satisfied. They include:

- There is unfair prejudice to a trade or industry in Australia, or failure to reasonably meet the demand in Australia for the patented invention on reasonable terms.
- There is unfair prejudice to a trade or industry in Australia through the imposition of unfair conditions.
- The invention is not being worked on a commercial scale in Australia but is capable of being so worked.[251]

These provisions arguably operate as an incentive to a patentee to work the invention in ways that meet the reasonable requirements of the public.[252] Perhaps this has been effective, because no compulsory licences have been granted under the relevant patent legislation.[253] It is not in the patentee's interest to negotiate licences on unreasonable terms if the consequence could be an order from the court to grant a licence on terms imposed by the court.[254]

The Productivity Commission observed that the language in s 135 'conflates the reasonable requirements of the public with the interests of Australian industry' and is therefore 'inconsistent with promoting community-wide welfare'.[255] Its recommendation is to replace this 'reasonable requirements of the public' test with a new public interest test that would specify the conditions to be met.[256]

There are certain restrictions that operate on the terms of a compulsory licence. First, it is not possible to grant a compulsory exclusive licence.[257] Second, a compulsory licence can be assigned only in connection with an enterprise or goodwill in connection with which the licence is used.[258]

11.6.1.2 Court is satisfied that there is anti-competitive behaviour

The *Intellectual Property Laws Amendment Act 2006* (Cth) introduced a competition test which enables the court to also grant a remedy of a compulsory licence if the patentee is acting anti-competitively in contravention of Part IV of the *Competition and Consumer Act 2010* (Cth) or an application law as defined in s 150A of that Act.[259] The availability of this remedy under the *Patents Act 1990* (Cth) complements and is in addition to remedies that are available under the *Competition and Consumer Act 2010* (Cth).[260] This test implements the government response to recommendations of the Intellectual Property and Competition Review Committee that the existing tests should be retained and a competition test be added

---

251 *Patents Act 1990* (Cth) s 135(1), (2).
252 See Intellectual Property and Competition Review Committee, *Review of Intellectual Property Legislation under the Competition Principles Agreement* (Final Report, September 2000) 162.
253 Productivity Commission, *Compulsory Licensing of Patents*, above n 163, 3.
254 *Patents Act 1990* (Cth) s 133(3).
255 Productivity Commission, *Compulsory Licensing of Patents*, above n 163, finding 6.4.
256 Ibid rec 6.2. Intellectual Property Laws Amendment (Productivity Commission Response Part 2 and Other Measures) Bill 2019 (Cth) sch 4 would implement this recommendation. See above n 163.
257 *Patents Act 1990* (Cth) s 133(3)(a).
258 Ibid s 133(3)(b).
259 Ibid s 133(2)(b).
260 Further Explanatory Memorandum, Intellectual Property Laws Amendment Bill 2006 (Cth) sch 8 item 2. See *NT Power Generation Pty Ltd v Power and Water Authority* (2004) 219 CLR 90, 120–1.

as an additional ground on which a compulsory licence can be obtained. However, the Productivity Commission reached the opposite conclusion and recommended[261] the removal of s 133(2)(b) so that a compulsory licence based on restrictive trade practices would be available only under amendments to the *Competition and Consumer Act 2010* (Cth).[262]

11.6.2 Effect of compulsory licence on other patents

A patent grants the patentee the right to exclude others from exploiting the invention.[263] This is a negative right as opposed to a positive right to exploit the invention.[264] This concept is understood best in the context of an example. A patent for invention X may be granted because it satisfies all the grounds for validity in s 18 of the *Patents Act 1990* (Cth), but its exploitation will infringe a patent for invention Y unless patentee Y grants patentee X a licence. Patentee X has the right to exclude everyone else from performing invention X within the patent area. However, patentee Y enjoys similar rights in relation to invention X as its performance by an unlicensed third party also infringes invention Y. Consequently, the grant of a compulsory licence in respect of invention X has the potential to affect the rights of patentee Y.

The *Patents Act 1990* (Cth) deals with this possibility by requiring a court to make an order for a compulsory licence in respect of invention X only if it is satisfied that invention X involves an important technical advance of considerable economic significance on invention Y. If it is so satisfied, the order will require the grant of additional compulsory licences to allow invention X to be worked without infringement. The order will require the grant of a licence over invention X to the applicant. It will also require the grant of a licence over invention Y to the applicant insofar as it is necessary to work invention X. A further requirement for the order is that it must direct that the licence granted over invention Y may be assigned only if the applicant assigns the licence over invention X and only to the assignee of the licence over invention X.[265] If the patentee of invention Y so requires, the court must direct that they are granted a cross-licence on reasonable terms to work invention X.[266]

The current s 133(3B) does not restrict who can apply for a compulsory licence. Reform proposals limit the right to apply to the owner of invention X who is unable to work their invention without a licence from the owner of invention Y. This limitation is described as necessary to remove 'inequitable and illogical outcomes' that would arise when the applicant is a third party.[267]

---

261   Productivity Commission, *Compulsory Licensing of Patents*, above n 163, rec 6.1.
262   Intellectual Property Laws Amendment (Productivity Commission Response Part 2 and Other Measures) Bill 2019 (Cth) sch 4 item 6 does not implement the Productivity Commission recommendation but retains s 133(2)(b). See above n 163.
263   As to the practical limitations involved in compulsory licensing, see D. Nicol and J. Nielsen, 'The Australian medical biotechnology industry and access to intellectual property: Issues for patent law development' (2001) 23 *Sydney Law Review* 347, 372.
264   *Grain Pool of Western Australia v Commonwealth* (2000) 202 CLR 479, 513–14.
265   *Patents Act 1990* (Cth) s 133(3B)(c).
266   Ibid s 133(3B).
267   Explanatory Memorandum, Intellectual Property Laws Amendment (Productivity Commission Response Part 2 and Other Measures) Bill 2019 (Cth) 40. The Bill was introduced into parliament in July 2019. See above n 163.

11.6.3 Operation of the order

If a court makes an order in response to the application, it operates as if it were embodied in a deed granting a licence and executed by the patentee and all other relevant parties.[268] An order must not be made that is inconsistent with a treaty between the Commonwealth and a foreign country.[269]

11.6.4 Remuneration payable

In the event that a licence is granted to an applicant under a court order, the patentee is to be paid an amount of remuneration as is agreed between the patentee and the applicant. If there is no agreement, the patentee is to be paid an amount as is determined by the Federal Court to be just and reasonable having regard to the economic value of the licence.[270]

11.6.5 Revocation

It is possible for the patentee to revoke the compulsory licence without a court order if the patentee and the licensee are agreed. Alternatively, either party may apply to the Federal Court for revocation of the licence. The court may revoke the licence if it finds that the circumstances that justified the licence have ceased to exist and are unlikely to recur. In both situations, revocation is possible only if the legitimate interests of the licensee are not likely to be adversely affected by the revocation.[271]

The patentee and any person claiming an interest in the patent as exclusive licensee or otherwise can apply to the Federal Court for revocation of a patent, even though a compulsory licence is in existence. Such application can be made only after two years have expired from the date of the grant of the first compulsory licence in respect of a patent.[272]

11.6.6 Other circumstances for compulsory licence

A patent application may lapse or a patent may cease to apply in consequence of a failure to do one or more relevant acts within the prescribed time. If the reasons for this failure are beyond the control of the person concerned or are due to errors or omissions as set out in s 223 of the *Patents Act 1990* (Cth), the Commissioner must grant an extension of time upon application by the person concerned. This extension may be granted before or after the time has expired. Hence, it is possible for the lapsed patent application, and for a patent that has ceased, to be subsequently restored after an intervening period in which it would appear to a third party that no patent or application was in force. In these circumstances, a person who exploited or took

---

268   *Patents Act 1990* (Cth) s 133(4).
269   Ibid s 136.
270   Ibid s 133(5). Intellectual Property Laws Amendment (Productivity Commission Response Part 2 and Other Measures) Bill 2019 (Cth) sch 4 item 7 amends the standard to which the Federal Court must have regard: Explanatory Memorandum, Intellectual Property Laws Amendment (Productivity Commission Response Part 2 and Other Measures) Bill 2019 (Cth) 44–5 [236]–[241]. The Bill was introduced into parliament in July 2019. See above n 163.
271   *Patents Act 1990* (Cth) s 133(6).
272   Ibid s 134(1); *Patents Regulations 1991* (Cth) reg 12.2(1).

definite steps by way of contract or otherwise to exploit the invention because of the patentee's failure to do the relevant act within the time allowed can apply for a licence to exploit the invention by way of compensation and protection.[273] The cessation of the patent arising from the patentee's failure to do the relevant act as required must be linked with the applicant's reliance on this cessation for commencing steps to exploit the invention during this period. The section 'is not designed to protect a person who by happenstance takes steps to exploit a patent during a period in which it is ceased'.[274] This is an application as between the third party and the Commissioner, and the grant of a licence is accordingly between those parties. It is not between the patentee and the third party.[275] Hence, when the patent is restored, it is not necessarily a full restoration of rights. Rather it is a restoration of patent rights other than those rights accrued by third parties who have exploited the invention during its period of cessation, whether or not those rights are known to the patentee or Commissioner at the time of restoration.[276] The *Patents Act 1990* (Cth) also provides protection against infringement for an act that is committed in the intervening period between the lapse or cessation and its restoration.[277]

11.6.7 International requirements

Compulsory licensing is provided for in art 5A of the *Paris Convention for the Protection of Industrial Property*[278] and is further elaborated in art 31 of *TRIPS*. The latter provision is silent on the grounds on which a compulsory licence may be granted, but sets out the conditions that must be met for the grant of a licence without the authorisation of the right holder. The *Patents (World Trade Organization Amendments) Act 1994* (Cth), which became operational on 1 January 1995, amended the *Patents Act 1990* (Cth) to comply with this article.

Free trade agreements[279] vary in the extent to which they deal expressly with compulsory licensing. Article 17.9.7 of the *AUSFTA* (in force 1 January 2005) limits the circumstances in which a compulsory licence may be granted. These circumstances are:

- to remedy an anti-competitive practice;[280]
- cases of public non-commercial use, or of national emergency, or other circumstances of extreme urgency.[281]

---

273 *Patents Act 1990* (Cth) s 223(9); *Patents Regulations 1991* (Cth) reg 22.21.
274 *Law v Razer Industries Pty Ltd* (2010) 190 FCR 166, [27]; *Garden City Planters Pty Ltd v Vivre Veritas Pty Ltd* (2012) 99 IPR 403 (APO).
275 *HRC Project Design Pty Ltd v Orford Pty Ltd* (1997) 38 IPR 121 (licence terms).
276 Ibid 126; *Re Sanyo Electric Co Ltd and Commissioner of Patents* (1997) 36 IPR 470.
277 *Patents Act 1990* (Cth) s 223(10); *Patents Regulations 1991* (Cth) reg 22.11; *HRC Project Design Pty Ltd v Orford Pty Ltd* (1997) 38 IPR 121.
278 Opened for signature 14 July 1967, WIPO Lex No TRT/PARIS/001 (as amended 28 September 1979, entered into force 3 June 1984).
279 Australia's free trade agreements are listed on the website of the Department of Foreign Affairs and Trade, https://dfat.gov.au.
280 *AUSFTA* art 17.9.7(a).
281 Ibid art 17.9.7(b).

Chapter 12 of the *Patents Act 1990* (Cth) includes a provision that complies with the matter of anti-competitive conduct.[282] The circumstances in point (b) above are narrower than the circumstances set out in s 133 of the Act, in that they do not include any commercial use unless it is required by reason of a national emergency or other extreme urgency. This difference means that a narrower class of circumstances applies where one party has the protection of the *AUSFTA* because no order can be made under s 133 (or s 134) that is inconsistent with a treaty between the Commonwealth and a foreign country.

11.6.8 Patented pharmaceutical inventions

A 2001 World Trade Organization (WTO) ministerial, *Declaration on the TRIPS Agreement and Public Health*, recognised the 'gravity of the public health problems afflicting many developing and least-developed countries'.[283] The Declaration noted the difficulties for WTO members with insufficient or no manufacturing capacities in the pharmaceutical sector to make effective use of compulsory licensing under *TRIPS*, and instructed the Council for TRIPS to give effect to the terms of the Declaration. The General Council for TRIPS agreed in 2003 to an interim waiver to *TRIPS* to make it possible for those members to access pharmaceuticals made under compulsory licence in another country[284] and a permanent waiver was effected by the 2005 *TRIPS* Protocol. Australia formally accepted this amendment to *TRIPS* on 12 September 2007 and provisions implementing this commitment are contained in schs 1 and 2 of the *Intellectual Property Laws Amendment Act 2015* (Cth).

Schedule 1 of the *Intellectual Property Laws Amendment Act 2015* (Cth) implemented the interim waiver and *TRIPS* Protocol by introducing into Chapter 12 of the *Patents Act 1990* (Cth) 'amendments to enable countries to source generic versions of patented pharmaceuticals from Australia'[285] in accordance with its international obligations. The amendments in Part 3 of Chapter 12 give the Federal Court power to order the grant of a compulsory licence to an applicant to manufacture generic versions of a patented pharmaceutical invention to an eligible importing country.

11.7 Contracts
11.7.1 Void conditions

The patentee has the exclusive right to exploit the invention and to authorise another person to exploit the invention.[286] However, this exclusive right of exploitation is subject to some limited control in Chapter 14 of the *Patents Act 1990* (Cth) over the types of conditions that may be imposed in a contract relating to the sale or lease of, or licence to exploit, a patented

---

282   *Patents Act 1990* (Cth) s 133(2)(b).
283   WTO Doc MIN(01)/DEC/W/2 (14 November 2001).
284   *Implementation of Paragraph 6 of the Doha Declaration on the TRIPS Agreement and Public Health*, WTO Doc WT/L/540 (1 September 2003) (Decision of 30 August 2003) and WT/L/540/Corr.1.
285   Explanatory Memorandum, Intellectual Property Laws Amendment Bill 2014 (Cth) sch 1.
286   *Patents Act 1990* (Cth) s 13(1).

invention.[287] The word 'condition' refers to 'a term of a contract, whether it be a condition in the strict sense, a warranty or some other term'.[288]

There is no definition of a 'patented invention' but 'invention' is defined in the Act's Dictionary to mean 'any manner of new manufacture the subject of letters patent and grant of privilege within section 6 of the *Statute of Monopolies*, and includes an alleged invention'.[289] Hence, a patented invention would appear in this context to refer to an invention that is the subject of a granted patent.[290] In addition, a 'patented product' is defined to mean a product in respect of which a patent has been granted and is in force, and 'patented process' has a similar meaning.[291] Therefore, these provisions are concerned with contracts for sale or lease of, or a licence (referred to generically as 'licences') to exploit, a patented product or patented process. There is no precise definition of sale or lease, so these words would be given their usual meanings. This does not necessarily mean the strict legal definition and courts may look to the definition that parliament intended.[292] A licence means a licence to exploit, or to authorise the exploitation of, a patented invention.[293]

The restrictions on conditions that can be imposed are designed to prevent abuse of the monopoly by imposing restraints that go beyond the scope of the monopoly[294] and allow the patentee to 'obtain a collateral advantage'.[295] The purpose and effect of a similar provision in the *Patents and Designs Act 1907* (UK) was described by Lord Oaksey in *Tool Metal Manufacturing Co Ltd v Tungsten Electric Co Ltd* as being

> to prevent the licensor from limiting the right of the licensee to trade with others so as in effect to compel the licensee to trade with him.[296]

There are two types of prohibited condition in s 144 of the *Patents Act 1990* (Cth) that are necessarily void. The first type is the condition that restricts or prohibits the ability to use a third party's products or processes. The prohibition or restriction on 'use' does not extend to dealing in those products or processes.[297] An example of a void condition of this type is where X grants to Y a licence to use a patented process but prohibits Y from using a common chemical in that process that is supplied by Z. The second type is the condition that ties the right to exploit the patented invention to the purchase of other products from the licensor.[298] An example of such

---

[287] See C. Lawson, 'Tie-ins in the *Patents Act 1990* (Cth), s 144: Perhaps it's time to modernise?' (2010) 21 *Australian Intellectual Property Journal* 202.
[288] *Transfield Pty Ltd v Arlo International Ltd* (1980) 144 CLR 83, 100 (Mason J), citing *Thomas Hunter Ltd's Patent* [1965] RPC 416, 420.
[289] *Patents Act 1990* (Cth) sch 1 (definition of 'invention').
[290] Compare the meaning of this phrase in *Patents Act 1990* (Cth) s 145(1): *MPEG LA LLC v Regency Media Pty Ltd* (2014) 105 IPR 202, [28].
[291] *Patents Act 1990* (Cth) sch 1 (definitions of 'patented product' and 'patented process').
[292] In the context of plant breeder's patent rights, see *Sun World International Inc v Registrar, Plant Breeder's Rights* (1998) 87 FCR 405, 412.
[293] *Patents Act 1990* (Cth) sch 1 (definition of 'licence').
[294] *Tool Metal Manufacturing Co Ltd v Tungsten Electric Co Ltd* [1955] 1 WLR 761, 776 (Lord Oaksey).
[295] Ibid 770 (Viscount Simonds).
[296] Ibid 777.
[297] *Patents Act 1990* (Cth) s 144(1)(a); *Transfield Pty Ltd v Arlo International Ltd* (1980) 144 CLR 83, 92 (Stephen J), considering *Patents Act 1952* (Cth) s 112, the equivalent provision to s 144 of the 1990 Act.
[298] *Patents Act 1990* (Cth) s 144(1)(b).

a condition is where X grants Y a licence to use a patented process and requires Y to purchase from X a common unpatented chemical that is used in the process.

Either type of prohibited condition may take the form of an express or implied prohibition. An express positive obligation may carry with it an implied prohibition or restriction.[299] Hence, the licence of a patent to Y that includes a condition that Y purchase the common chemical from X impliedly prohibits Y obtaining those materials from Z, and vice versa.

In the case of an innovation patent, in addition to the preceding conditions, the imposition by Y of a condition is void if its effect is to prohibit X from applying for examination of the patent or to impose restrictions on the circumstances in which X may apply for examination.[300]

11.7.2 Conditions that are not void

Section 144(2) of the *Patents Act 1990* (Cth) provides that the imposition of an offending condition will not be void where X proves two facts:

- At the time of the contract, Y had the option of buying the product or obtaining a lease or licence on reasonable terms without the condition.
- The contract entitles Y to be relieved of the condition on the giving to X of three months' notice in writing and paying compensation.[301]

In addition, s 146 provides that the provisions in Chapter 12 do not affect certain conditions in contracts. First, the patentee is entitled to tie a person into the distribution of the patentee's goods to the exclusion of all others.[302] Second, Chapter 12 does not affect conditions in a contract for lease of or licence to exploit a patented product that reserves to the lessor or licensor the right to supply new parts of the patented product that are required to put or keep it in repair. For example, if X is the exclusive licensee to exploit an invention for a rubbish truck, a condition in the licence that requires X to purchase unpatented replacement parts for the truck will not be void under s 144(1)(b) if the supply is for the purposes of repair.

11.7.3 Defence to infringement proceedings

Any person who is sued for infringement of the patent can claim as a defence that the patented invention is, or was when the proceedings were started, the subject of a contract containing a provision inserted by the patentee that is void under s 144 of the *Patents Act 1990* (Cth). This condition does not have to be in a contract with the alleged infringer. All that is required is a contract in existence when the proceedings started that contains a void term inserted by the patentee.[303] The 'patentee' is defined as the person for the time being entered in the Register as the grantee or proprietor of a patent. Therefore, it is not a defence to establish the existence of a contract with a void condition that was inserted by an exclusive licensee of the patentee.

---

299   *Transfield Pty Ltd v Arlo International Ltd* (1980) 144 CLR 83, 93 (Stephen J).
300   *Patents Act 1990* (Cth) s 144(1A).
301   Ibid s 144(2).
302   Ibid s 146(a).
303   Ibid s 144(4).

It is not possible to remove the defence by removing the condition from the contract after proceedings have started. However, it is possible to remedy this defect prior to the commencement of proceedings. The patentee must offer the parties to that offending contract a new contract on the same terms but excluding the offending condition. Whether or not the parties to the contract accept the new contract, the existence of the offending contract no longer offers a person a defence to infringement.[304] The remedies that a patentee can seek for an infringement that occurs after the offer of the new contract are the usual remedies excluding damages or an account of profits for an infringement that was committed before the offer of a new contract.[305]

There is a provision that a person is not stopped from applying for or obtaining relief in any proceedings under the *Patents Act 1990* (Cth) just because they admit that the terms of sale were reasonable. Therefore, the reasonableness of the terms is not judged by the licensee's admission to this effect.[306]

11.7.4 Termination of contract after patent ceases to be in force

Section 145(1) of the *Patents Act 1990* (Cth) is aimed at anti-competitive conduct. It provides either party with the ability to terminate

> a contract relating to the lease of, or licence to exploit, *a patented invention* ... at any time after the patent, *or all the patents*, by which the invention was protected at the time the contract was made, have ceased to be in force.[307]

It applies despite anything to the contrary in the contract or in any other contract.[308] The object and purpose of this section has been said to be 'at least in part, ... to prevent the holder of a patent from taking potentially unfair advantage of the statutory monopoly conferred by a patent after it has expired'.[309] This would arise, for example, when the patentee required a licensee 'to bind himself, contractually, to pay royalties for a period longer than the life of the patent'.[310] However, the section is not designed to deny the contractual rights of the patent holder while a patent remains in force[311] and has the potential to be commercially unfair to both the patentee and the licensee in these circumstances. Courts need to exercise 'careful scrutiny' when one party seeks to invoke its provisions before all of the patents by which a patented invention is protected have expired.[312]

---

304   Ibid s 144(5).
305   Ibid s 144(5).
306   Ibid ss 144(3), 144(2)(a).
307   Emphasis added.
308   *Patents Act 1990* (Cth) s 145(2).
309   *MPEG LA LLC v Regency Media Pty Ltd* (2014) 105 IPR 202, [15], drawing an analogy with *Hansen v Magnavox Electronics Co Ltd* [1977] RPC 301, 308, 310 (a case in which foreign elements were not severable from the agreement).
310   *Hansen v Magnavox Electronics Co Ltd* [1977] RPC 301, 308 (Lord Denning MR), 310 (Ormrod J); *MPEG LA LLC v Regency Media Pty Ltd* (2014) 105 IPR 202, [17].
311   *MPEG LA LLC v Regency Media Pty Ltd* (2014) 105 IPR 202, [15].
312   Ibid [21].

The phrase 'patented invention' in s 145 is not defined. This is of no consequence if the contract relates to an invention that is protected by one Australian patent at the time the contract was made. It is clear that either party can terminate the contract on giving three months' notice in writing to the other party at any time after that patent has ceased to be in force.

However, the meaning of 'patented invention' in s 145 was shown to be of critical importance in a case[313] determining the lawful termination of a licence of multiple patent rights held in a patent pool and administered by a licensing administrator. A licensee is likely to enter into such an agreement as a matter of convenience for acquiring patent rights that are necessary for it to lawfully use an international standard in any product.[314] A patent pool licence avoids the need to negotiate separate licence agreements with the individual licensors of those patents. The case of *MPEG LA LLC v Regency Media Pty Ltd*[315] concerned the grant of a patent portfolio licence (PPL) to give Regency Media the rights necessary for compliance with the international standard relating to video data compression and data transport. The grant of rights covered three specified areas of technology: the MPEG-2 decoding products, the MPEG-2 encoding products, and the MPEG-2 packaged medium. Each specified area comprised a number of identified patents that were essential to the licensee's compliance with the relevant international standard and that had varying terms of duration. The agreement expressly provided that Regency Media could not terminate the agreement prior to December 2015. Some patents the subject of the PPL would necessarily have ceased to have effect prior to this date.

Regency Media terminated the entire agreement by letter in July 2012 before the expiry of all the Australian patents the subject of the agreement. When MPEG sought declaratory relief for unlawful termination of the PPL, Regency claimed its action was lawful within the terms of s 145. Although it was common ground that the agreement related to a 'patented invention', the parties disagreed on identifying the relevant 'patented invention' for the purposes of s 145.

Regency Media argued that the phrase 'patented invention' referred to a single patented invention: an 'invention' that is 'patented' upon grant. Thus, it contended, the agreement could be terminated when a single patent ceased to be in force despite the continuing existence of other patents the subject of the PPL.[316] MPEG disagreed and asserted that there were three 'patented inventions', namely, the three matters mentioned above: the MPEG-2 decoding products, the MPEG-2 encoding products, and the MPEG-2 packaged medium. If this were the position, s 145 could only be invoked when all the patents have expired.[317]

Although both approaches had merit, Flick J in the Federal Court preferred an interpretation that gave effect to the commercial agreement between the parties and did 'no disservice

---

313 *MPEG LA LLC v Regency Media Pty Ltd* (2014) 105 IPR 202.
314 The international standards developed by the International Organization for Standardization (ISO) are 'documents that provide requirements, specifications, guidelines or characteristics that can be used consistently to ensure that materials, products, processes and services are fit for their purpose': ISO, www.iso.org.
315 (2014) 105 IPR 202, [15].
316 Ibid [32].
317 Regency Media made no submission that the aggregation of individual patents to constitute each of these three matters (for example, the MPEG-2 decoding products) could not constitute a 'patented invention'.

to the object and purpose of s 145'. He rejected Regency Media's argument on the basis that the language of s 145 makes it clear that a patented invention can be protected by more than one patent in its reference to 'any time after the patent, *or all the patents*, by which the invention was protected at the time the contract was made, have *ceased* to be in force'.[318] He further rejected an argument that the phrase 'all of the patents' was referring to combination patents that include as part of the patented invention an integer or element that is itself patented. Instead, his Honour accepted the MPEG submission that each of the three identified matters constituted an 'invention' within its defined meaning – namely, the subject matter of the invention (manner of manufacture). The word 'patented' merely describes the 'invention' in that broad sense to which it refers. His Honour concluded that s 145 conferred no right of termination until all of the patents in respect of the 'patented inventions' identified in the PPL agreement have ceased to be in force.[319]

There was no discussion in *MPEG LA LLC v Regency Media Pty Ltd* of the application of s 145 to a contract that licenses technology protected by both Australian and overseas patents. It is possible that the definition of 'patent' in the Act's Dictionary – a standard patent or an innovation patent – may limit its application to Australian patents. If this is the case, it could permit termination of the entire licence after the last of the Australian patents ceases to be in effect, even if overseas patents remain in force. To avoid this outcome, agreements might be drafted to enable severance of the provisions that relate to Australian patents from the remainder of the agreement.[320]

11.8 The Register and official documents
11.8.1 Contents of the Register

The Australian Patent Office maintains a Register of Patents that contains separate parts for standard and innovation patents.[321] The Register may be kept wholly or partly by use of a computer. Particulars of standard and innovation patents in force, and other prescribed particulars, must be registered in the respective parts of the Register.[322] The Register must not contain notice of any trust relating to a patent or licence.[323] This does not prohibit the registration of a trustee, merely the notification of the trust, the status of the trustee or the details of the trust.[324] With the exception of 'security interests' over intellectual property, the Register establishes a means for establishing priority of interests in a patent. It also protects rights in a patent that are not proprietary because there is no requirement that the interest be proprietary for it to gain protection under this provision.[325] Security interests over intellectual

---

318　*MPEG LA LLC v Regency Media Pty Ltd* (2014) 105 IPR 202, [28], [39].
319　Ibid [6], [47].
320　For example, *Hansen v Magnavox Electronics Co Ltd* [1977] RPC 301, (Ormrod J, Lord Denning MR and Bridge LJ disagreeing).
321　*Patents Act 1990* (Cth) s 186.
322　Ibid s 187.
323　Ibid s 188; *Stack v Brisbane City Council (No 2)* (1996) 67 FCR 510, 513.
324　*Neobev Pty Ltd v Bacchus Distillery Pty Ltd (admin apptd) (No 3)* (2014) 104 IPR 249, [117].
325　*Patents Act 1990* (Cth) s 189(1).

property and their priority over other interests are determined according to the principles in the *Personal Property Securities Act 2009* (Cth) (*PPSA*) that came into effect on 30 January 2012. Even if a right that is a *PPSA* security interest is recorded on the Register, it has no effect on dealings with a patent over which the interest is secured.[326]

The prescribed particulars that require registration in the Register of Patents include:[327]

- an entitlement as mortgagee, licensee or otherwise to an interest in a patent;
- a transfer of an entitlement to a patent or licence, or to a share in a patent or licence;
- an extension of the term of a patent.

A person can file a copy of the document under which the interest is created but is not required to do so. If documents are filed, they must be available for inspection at the Patent Office.[328] The Register is a record of interests in a patent and does not create a system of title by registration as arises with interests in land registered under the Torrens title system. Registration per se is not the source of entitlement. Registration depends on entitlement as provided in s 15(1) of the *Patents Act 1990* (Cth) and is not the source of entitlement.[329] The interests themselves arise from the agreement between the parties.[330]

11.8.2 Inspection and access to the Register

The Register,[331] and all documents filed in connection with the registration of any of the above particulars,[332] must be available for inspection at the Patent Office by any person during the hours that it is open for business. In addition, the Commissioner may give any person information about a patent, an application for a patent that is open to public inspection, or any prescribed document or matter.[333]

11.8.3 False entries

There are criminal penalties for making or causing false entries to be made in the Register and for tendering in evidence a document that falsely purports to be a copy of or extract from an entry in the Register.[334] Persons who are aggrieved by omissions, errors and incorrect entries can apply to a prescribed court for rectification of the Register.[335]

---

326   Ibid s 189(2A).
327   *Patents Regulations 1991* (Cth) reg 19.1 contains the full list of prescribed particulars.
328   *Patents Act 1990* (Cth) s 193.
329   *University of British Columbia v Conor Medsystems Inc* (2006) 155 FCR 391, [62] (Stone J).
330   *Vitamins Australia Ltd v Beta-Carotene Industries Pty Ltd* (1987) 9 IPR 41, 53 (Kennedy J); *British Nylon Spinners Ltd v Imperial Chemical Industries Ltd* [1952] 2 All ER 780; *Clorox Australia Pty Ltd v International Consolidated Business Pty Ltd* (2005) 66 IPR 506, 509–10 [14] (exclusive licences).
331   *Patents Act 1990* (Cth) s 190.
332   Ibid s 193.
333   Ibid s 194.
334   Ibid s 191.
335   Ibid s 192.

11.8.4 Evidence

The Register is prima facie evidence of any particulars registered in it.[336] In the case of unregistered particulars, the general principle is that a document is not admissible in proceedings to prove title to a patent or to an interest in a patent.[337]

11.8.5 Power of patentee to deal with patent

The grant of a patent gives the patentee the exclusive rights to exploit the patent. Those rights are personal property and are capable of assignment and devolution by law.[338] It is the grant that is the source of the proprietary interest in the patent, rather than registration.[339] Registration only provides prima facie evidence of the particulars that are registered.[340] The Register does not affect the nature of the interest, only the extent to which it is enforceable against third parties.

The *PPSA*, which commenced on 30 January 2012,[341] established a single national law governing security interests in personal property and a single, searchable online register for personal property security. Amendments made to the *Patents Act 1990* (Cth) by the *Personal Property Securities (Consequential Amendment) Act 2009* (Cth) removed security interests recorded in the Register of Patents as well as unregistered security interests from the operation of Chapter 19. A 'security interest' is defined in s 12(1) of the *PPSA* to mean 'an interest in personal property provided for by a transaction that, in substance, secures payment or performance of an obligation'. The *PPSA* applies to all statutory intellectual property rights, including patents, and fundamentally changed the Australian law on personal property securities.[342] Significantly, a security interest does not include a licence.[343]

Section 189(1) of the *Patents Act 1990* (Cth) provides that the patentee can deal with interests in the patent as absolute owner, and give good discharges for any consideration for any dealing, subject only to the rights that appear from the Register to vest in another person. However, despite this subsection, s 189(2A)[344] provides that a recording in the Register of a *PPSA* security interest does not affect a dealing with the patent. Section 189(2) provides that a person who deals as a purchaser for value in good faith and without notice of any fraud on the part of the patentee takes subject only to those registered interests.[345] The consequences for

---

336 Ibid s 195. See also s 197.
337 Exceptions: ibid s 196(1)(a), (b)(i), (b)(ii).
338 Ibid ss 13, 61.
339 Ibid s 61(1).
340 Ibid s 195(1).
341 *Personal Property Securities (Migration Time and Registration Commencement Time) Determination* (Cth).
342 *Personal Property Securities Act 2009* (Cth) s 10. See R. Handler and M. Burrell, 'The *PPSA* and registered trade marks: When bureaucratic systems collide' (2011) 34(2) *University of New South Wales Law Journal* 600. See S. Pemberton and R. Chatwood, 'Using your IP to get finance? Implications of the *Personal Properties Securities Act 2009* for IP lawyers and their clients' (2010) 22 *Australian Intellectual Property Law Bulletin* 190; J. V. Swinson, 'Uncertainties and insecurities: Personal property security reform and its impact on intellectual property' (2006) 66 *Intellectual Property Forum* 12.
343 *Personal Property Securities Act 2009* (Cth) s 12(5).
344 Inserted by *Personal Property Securities (Consequential Amendment) Act 2009* (Cth) sch 2 item 9.
345 *Patents Act 1990* (Cth) s 189(2).

failure to register an interest therefore relate to priority of interests and enforceability of those interests against third parties. For example, if a patentee vested rights in a person who failed to register the details of those rights, and subsequently purports to transfer the patent without being subject to those rights, a purchaser in good faith for value without notice of any fraud on the part of the patentee will not be subject to those rights. Section 189(3) provides that equities in relation to a patent, with the exception of an equity that is a *PPSA* security interest, may be enforced against the patentee except to the prejudice of a purchaser in good faith for value.[346]

---

346   Ibid s 189(3), (4). See *Personal Property Securities Act 2009* (Cth) ch 2 pt 2.5 (taking personal property free of security interests), pt 2.6 (priority between security interests), ch 4 (enforcement of security interests).

12

PATENTS FOR INVENTIONS: EXPLOITATION, INFRINGEMENT AND REVOCATION

12.1 The role of the patent specification

A patent specification is a public instrument that contains the patentee's unilateral statement to the public of what are claimed as the essential features ('integers') of the invention.[1] The grant of the monopoly rights in a patent are balanced by the disclosure of the invention to the public.[2]

As a patent specification is directed to a person skilled in the art to which the specification relates, it can contain less detail than would be necessary if it were directed to a person not skilled in the relevant way. The patent specification itself is made up of several parts that have different functions.[3] The body, apart from the preamble, is there to instruct those skilled in the art concerned in the carrying out of the invention.[4] The claims identify the legal limits of the monopoly granted by the patent[5] and must define the invention in a way that is 'not reasonably capable of being misunderstood'.[6] Inadvertent or deliberate omissions from the claim have no protection.[7] In other words, what is not claimed is disclaimed.[8]

12.2 General principles for construction of patent specification

The patent specification is construed for a variety of purposes under the *Patents Act 1990* (Cth). Issues of validity under s 18 are determined with reference to the invention so far as claimed in any claim. Construction of the claim to identify its essential integers is critical to issues of novelty and inventive step. Construction of the whole specification is also necessary to determine the internal requirements of s 40 of the Act, such as sufficiency of description, and whether the claim is supported by matter disclosed in the specification.[9] Furthermore, it is always a question of whether the language of the claim covers the alleged infringement.[10]

---

1   For a discussion of the history of the patent specification, see D. J. Brennan, 'The evolution of English patent claims as property definers' [2005] 4 *Intellectual Property Quarterly* 361.
2   *Flexible Steel Lacing Co v Beltreco Ltd* (2000) 49 IPR 331, 347; *Rodi & Wienenberger AG v Henry Showell Ltd* [1969] RPC 367, 391–2 (Lord Upjohn).
3   *Kinabalu Investments Pty Ltd v Barron & Rawson Pty Ltd* [2008] FCAFC 178, [44].
4   *Decor Corp Pty Ltd v Dart Industries Inc* (1988) 13 IPR 385, 398 (Sheppard J).
5   *British United Shoe Machinery Co Ltd v A Fussell & Sons Ltd* (1908) 25 RPC 631, 650; *Walker v Alemite Corp* (1933) 49 CLR 643, 656–7.
6   *Flexible Steel Lacing Co v Beltreco Ltd* (2000) 49 IPR 331, 347, [72]; *Martin v Scribal Pty Ltd* (1954) 92 CLR 17, 59; *Welch Perrin & Co Pty Ltd v Worrel* (1961) 106 CLR 588, 610; *Populin v HB Nominees Pty Ltd* (1982) 41 ALR 471, 476; *Decor Corp Pty Ltd v Dart Industries Inc* (1988) 13 IPR 385, 400.
7   *Walker v Alemite Corp* (1933) 49 CLR 643, 656; *Flexible Steel Lacing Co v Beltreco Ltd* (2000) 49 IPR 331, 347; *Root Quality Pty Ltd v Root Control Technologies Pty Ltd* (2000) 49 IPR 225, 234; *Rodi & Wienenberger AG v Henry Showell Ltd* [1969] RPC 367, 380.
8   *Root Quality Pty Ltd v Root Control Technologies Pty Ltd* (2000) 49 IPR 225, 234; *Flexible Steel Lacing Co v Beltreco Ltd* (2000) 49 IPR 331, 347; *Walker v Alemite Corp* (1933) 49 CLR 643, 653; *Electric & Musical Industries Ltd v Lissen Ltd* [1938] 4 All ER 221, 224 (Lord Russell); *Populin v HB Nominees Pty Ltd* (1982) 41 ALR 471, 475.
9   The *Intellectual Property Laws Amendment (Raising the Bar) Act 2012* (Cth) introduced this concept in s 40(3) of the *Patents Act 1990* (Cth) by substituting the words 'supported by matter disclosed' for the words 'fairly based on the matter described' – the earlier concept of 'fair basis'.
10 *Sachtler GmbH & Co KG v RE Miller Pty Ltd* (2005) 65 IPR 605, citing *Improver Corp v Remington Consumer Products Ltd* [1990] FSR 181, 189–90; *PhotoCure ASA v Queen's University at Kingston* (2005) 64 IPR 314, 356.

Although it is stated that there are no special rules for the interpretation of patent specifications,[11] the reality is that courts have adapted the general principles for the interpretation of legal documents to take account of the special nature of the patent specification.[12] The body is there to instruct the skilled person in how to carry out the invention. Hence, the language used here is not so critical, provided it is understood by the skilled reader and does not mislead.[13] The claims that define the monopoly require careful scrutiny in the same way as documents that define legal rights are construed.[14] However, they exist within the larger document and must be read in that context.[15]

In *Decor Corp Pty Ltd v Dart Industries Inc*, Sheppard J distilled principles of construction from earlier authorities to provide a guide in 1988 for the construction of patent specifications.[16] Since then, later decisions have generally adopted these principles, either with or without adjustment or amplification according to the circumstances for decision.[17] The following represents a synthesis of the various rules that are uniformly regarded as well established:

1. A patent specification should be given a purposive, not a purely literal, construction.[18]
2. It is important to construe claims in a practical and commonsense manner.[19] Once the true meaning of the claim is arrived at by construing it within the context of the specification, it is not permissible to narrow or expand its scope 'by adding to those words glosses drawn from other parts of the specification',[20] unless they are expressly or by necessary implication picked up in the claim.[21] Integers cannot be added to a claim after reference to the context in which the claims appear.[22] A clear claim for one subject matter cannot be changed into a claim for a different subject matter.[23]

---

11 *Decor Corp Pty Ltd v Dart Industries Inc* (1988) 13 IPR 385, 391.
12 *H Lundbeck A/S v Alphapharm Pty Ltd* (2009) 177 FCR 151, 179 [118]–[120]; *PhotoCure ASA v Queen's University at Kingston* (2005) 64 IPR 314, 358.
13 *Decor Corp Pty Ltd v Dart Industries Inc* (1988) 13 IPR 385, 400.
14 Ibid.
15 *H Lundbeck A/S v Alphapharm Pty Ltd* (2009) 177 FCR 151, 179 [118]–[120]; *Kirin-Amgen Inc v Hoechst Marion Roussel Ltd* [2005] RPC 169.
16 (1988) 13 IPR 385, 400.
17 For some of the more recent distillations of the principles, see *ESCO Corp v Ronneby Road Pty Ltd* (2018) 131 IPR 1, [144]–[147]; *Sandvik Intellectual Property AB v Quarry Mining & Construction Equipment Pty Ltd* (2017) 126 IPR 427, [190]–[193]; *Product Management Group Pty Ltd v Blue Gentian LLC* (2015) 240 FCR 85, [34]–[41]; *Tramanco Pty Ltd v BPW Transpec Pty Ltd* (2014) 105 IPR 18, [174]–[175].
18 For example, *Novozymes A/S v Danisco A/S* (2013) 99 IPR 417, [13]; *Kirin-Amgen Inc v Hoechst Marion Roussel Ltd* [2005] RPC 169, [32]–[35]; *Decor Corp Pty Ltd v Dart Industries Inc* (1988) 13 IPR 385, 400.
19 *Tramanco Pty Ltd v BPW Transpec Pty Ltd* (2014) 105 IPR 18, [174]–[175] (Nicholas J); *Flexible Steel Lacing Co v Beltreco Ltd* (2000) 49 IPR 331.
20 *Kinabalu Investments Pty Ltd v Barron & Rawson Pty Ltd* [2008] FCAFC 178, [44]; *Fresenius Medical Care Australia Pty Ltd v Gambro Pty Ltd* (2005) 67 IPR 230, [44]; *Welch Perrin & Co Pty Ltd v Worrel* (1961) 106 CLR 588, 610; *Decor Corp Pty Ltd v Dart Industries Inc* (1988) 13 IPR 385, 391, 398; *Martin v Scribal Pty Ltd* (1954) 92 CLR 17, 97 (Taylor J).
21 *Martin v Scribal Pty Ltd* (1954) 92 CLR 17, 97 (Taylor J), affirmed (1956) 95 CLR 213; *Nesbit Evans Group Australia Pty Ltd v Impro Ltd* (1997) 39 IPR 56, 81.
22 *Fresenius Medical Care Australia Pty Ltd v Gambro Pty Ltd* (2005) 67 IPR 230, 236–7; *Minnesota Mining & Manufacturing Co v Beiersdorf (Australia) Ltd* (1980) 144 CLR 253; *Welch Perrin & Co Pty Ltd v Worrel* (1961) 106 CLR 588, 610.
23 *Electric & Musical Industries Ltd v Lissen Ltd* [1938] 4 All ER 221, 224–5; *Jupiters Ltd v Neurizon Pty Ltd* (2005) 65 IPR 86, [67].

The preferred embodiment cannot be used to introduce into definite words of a claim an additional definition or qualification of the invention.[24]

3. A construction according to which the invention will work is to be preferred to one according to which it may not do so.[25] Also, it is appropriate to construe the specification with an 'eye benevolent to the inventor',[26] while maintaining a construction that is reasonable and fair to both the patentee and the public.[27]

4. Purely verbal and grammatical questions are resolved according to ordinary principles of construction.[28] As a general rule, the terms of a specification should be accorded their ordinary English meaning.[29]

5. The proper construction of a specification is a matter of law.[30] As such, it is a matter for the court[31] and not for expert witnesses.[32]

6. The complete specification is not to be read in the abstract, but is to be construed in the light of the common general knowledge and the art before the priority date.[33] It is useful to recall here that the concept of common general knowledge is understood to include the information that the skilled person would retain in their mind,[34] as well as any information they know of and might refer to as a matter of course or habitually consult.[35]

7. The court is to place itself in the position of 'some person acquainted with the surrounding circumstances as to the state of [the] art and manufacture at the time'.[36] This hypothetical addressee of the patent specification is the non-inventive person skilled in the art or science to which the specification relates before the priority date.[37] Words are normally given the meaning that this skilled person would normally attach

---

24 *Erickson's Patent* (1923) 40 RPC 477, 491; *Rehm Pty Ltd v Websters Security Systems (International) Pty Ltd* (1988) 11 IPR 289, 298.
25 *Nesbit Evans Group Australia Pty Ltd v Impro Ltd* (1997) 39 IPR 56, 81; *Martin v Scribal Pty Ltd* (1954) 92 CLR 17, 97 (Taylor J); *Welch Perrin & Co Pty Ltd v Worrel* (1961) 106 CLR 588, 601–2 (Menzies J).
26 *Leonardis v Sartas No 1 Pty Ltd* (1996) 67 FCR 126, 149; *Martin v Scribal Pty Ltd* (1954) 92 CLR 17, 97 (Taylor J).
27 *Root Quality Pty Ltd v Root Control Technologies Pty Ltd* (2000) 49 IPR 225, 235–6.
28 *Flexible Steel Lacing Co v Beltreco Ltd* (2000) 49 IPR 331, 348; *Decor Corp Pty Ltd v Dart Industries Inc* (1988) 13 IPR 385, 400; *Welch Perrin & Co Pty Ltd v Worrel* (1961) 106 CLR 588, 610–11.
29 *Flexible Steel Lacing Co v Beltreco Ltd* (2000) 49 IPR 331, 350; *Electric & Musical Industries Ltd v Lissen Ltd* [1938] 4 All ER 221, 226; *Elconnex Pty Ltd v Gerard Industries Pty Ltd* (1991) 32 FCR 491, 512–13; *Minnesota Mining & Manufacturing Co v Beiersdorf (Australia) Ltd* (1980) 144 CLR 253, 279 (Aickin J).
30 *Decor Corp Pty Ltd v Dart Industries Inc* (1988) 13 IPR 385, 400; *Jupiters Ltd v Neurizon Pty Ltd* (2005) 65 IPR 86, [67].
31 *Minnesota Mining & Manufacturing Co v Beiersdorf (Australia) Ltd* (1980) 144 CLR 253, 270, 281 (Aickin J); *Jupiters Ltd v Neurizon Pty Ltd* (2005) 65 IPR 86, [67].
32 *Fei Yu (t/as Jewels 4 Pools) v Beadcrete Pty Ltd* (2014) 107 IPR 516, [31].
33 *Kimberly-Clark Australia Pty Ltd v Arico Trading International Pty Ltd* (2001) 207 CLR 1, [24].
34 *Minnesota Mining & Manufacturing Co v Beiersdorf (Australia) Ltd* (1980) 144 CLR 253, 292 (Aickin J).
35 *ICI Chemicals & Polymers Ltd v Lubrizol Corp Inc* (2000) 106 FCR 214, [57]; *ICI Chemicals & Polymers Ltd v Lubrizol Corp Inc* (1999) 45 IPR 577, 599–600; *Aktiebolaget Hassle v Alphapharm Pty Ltd* (2000) 51 IPR 375, 391; *PhotoCure ASA v Queen's University at Kingston* (2005) 64 IPR 314, 325. See ch 10 at 10.8.3.
36 *Kimberly-Clark Australia Pty Ltd v Arico Trading International Pty Ltd* (2001) 207 CLR 1, [24].
37 *Welch Perrin & Co Pty Ltd v Worrel* (1961) 106 CLR 588, 610; *Decor Corp Pty Ltd v Dart Industries Inc* (1988) 13 IPR 385, 397.

to them, having regard to the common general knowledge and to what is disclosed in the body of the specification.[38]

8. The construction of claims takes place in the context of the specification as a whole,[39] even if there is no apparent ambiguity in the claim.[40] The possibility that a word or phrase has more than one meaning, or is used in a technical or trade sense, may become evident only after reference to the specification as a whole. Hence, the body of the specification can be used to explain the background to the claims, to ascertain the meaning of technical terms,[41] to resolve ambiguities in the construction of the claims, and to explain, define or clarify obscure or doubtful language.[42] The rest of the specification can also help ascertain whether a word or expression requires clarification because the ordinary, or usual, meaning is not sufficiently precise.[43] The meaning of the words in the claims that are unclear may be defined or clarified by what is said in the body of the specification.[44]

9. In construing a claim, the court should disregard the infringing article.[45]

12.3 Claim construction
12.3.1 Introduction

As the function of the claims is to define the limits of the monopoly, 'the forbidden field must be found in the language of the claims, and not elsewhere'.[46] That forbidden field equates to the essential integers of the invention that are identified using a purposive approach to construction that is described below.[47] There is no infringement if an essential integer or

---

38 *Kimberly-Clark Australia Pty Ltd v Multigate Medical Products Pty Ltd* (2011) 92 IPR 21, [39]; *Jupiters Ltd v Neurizon Pty Ltd* (2005) 65 IPR 86, [67]; *Decor Corp Pty Ltd v Dart Industries Inc* (1988) 13 IPR 385, 391.
39 *Fresenius Medical Care Australia Pty Ltd v Gambro Pty Ltd* (2005) 67 IPR 230, [39]; *Decor Corp Pty Ltd v Dart Industries Inc* (1988) 13 IPR 385, 400; *Jupiters Ltd v Neurizon Pty Ltd* (2005) 65 IPR 86, [67].
40 *Flexible Steel Lacing Co v Beltreco Ltd* (2000) 49 IPR 331, 347–8; *Decor Corp Pty Ltd v Dart Industries Inc* (1988) 13 IPR 385, 410–11; *Clorox Australia Pty Ltd v International Consolidated Business Pty Ltd* (2006) 68 IPR 254, 260.
41 *Flexible Steel Lacing Co v Beltreco Ltd* (2000) 49 IPR 331, 347; *Martin v Scribal Pty Ltd* (1954) 92 CLR 17, 59.
42 *Fresenius Medical Care Australia Pty Ltd v Gambro Pty Ltd* (2005) 67 IPR 230, 236; *PhotoCure ASA v Queen's University at Kingston* (2005) 64 IPR 314, 358–9; *Interlego AG v Toltoys Pty Ltd* (1973) 130 CLR 461, 478–9; *Leonardis v Sartas No 1 Pty Ltd* (1996) 67 FCR 126, 148.
43 *Pharmacia Italia SPA v Mayne Pharma Pty Ltd* (2005) 66 IPR 84; *Minerals Separation North America Corp v Noranda Mines Ltd* (1952) 69 RPC 81, 96.
44 *Kimberly-Clark Australia Pty Ltd v Arico Trading International Pty Ltd* (2001) 207 CLR 1, [15]; *Welch Perrin & Co Pty Ltd v Worrel* (1961) 106 CLR 588, 610; *Interlego AG v Toltoys Pty Ltd* (1973) 130 CLR 461, 478.
45 *Bitech Engineering v Garth Living* (2010) 86 IPR 468, [26]; *GlaxoSmithKline Australia Pty Ltd v Reckitt Benckiser Healthcare (UK) Ltd* (2013) 305 ALR 363, 102, [60].
46 *Electric & Musical Industries Ltd v Lissen Ltd* [1938] 4 All ER 221, 224 (Lord Russell); *D'Arcy v Myriad Genetics Inc* (2015) 258 CLR 334, [14] (French CJ, Kiefel, Bell and Keane JJ).
47 *Catnic Components Ltd v Hill & Smith Ltd* [1982] RPC 183; *Kirin-Amgen Inc v Hoechst Marion Roussel Ltd* [2005] RPC 169.

feature is missing in an allegedly infringing article.[48] The fact that it is replaced with something of functional significance is irrelevant.[49] When the 'forbidden field' is taken in its entirety, it is of no consequence that an inessential integer is replaced with an equivalent.[50]

Some preliminary explanation of ways in which claims were formerly construed provides a context for why the purposive approach is now accepted as the preferred method. The early approach to construction of claims was one of literalism.[51] Technically, courts were required to construe the words of a claim in isolation and could refer to the body of the specification for clarification of the intended meaning only when a clear ambiguity in a word or phrase was present. However, sometimes ambiguity or lack of clarity in meaning only becomes evident when the words are construed within the context of the entire specification. A literal interpretation of the claim without its context could result in a narrow interpretation that would allow someone to remove their otherwise infringing product from the scope of the claim by making an 'immaterial variation'. For example, the literal meaning of the word 'vertical' when read in the claim in isolation could mean perpendicular. This would allow someone to design an immaterial variation that was a few degrees off the perpendicular in order to fall outside the scope of the claim. However, when the word 'vertical' is read in the context of a specification that is addressed to builders and engineers, it may be construed to include almost perpendicular and thus draw the immaterial variation within its scope as an infringing product.

Courts found ways of circumventing the type of colourable evasion that may result when claims are construed using a literal interpretation.[52] The United States developed a doctrine of equivalents. In the United Kingdom and Australia, courts abandoned literalism in favour of finding the 'pith and marrow' of a claim.[53]

12.3.2 'Pith and marrow'

The concept of 'pith and marrow' refers to the 'essence or substance'[54] of the invention and derives from a statement of James LJ in *Clark v Adie*.[55] However, the doctrine was always 'a bit vague' as to what this meant.[56] It was unclear initially whether the courts regarded it as a principle of construction that would assist in identifying the essential integers of the invention or whether it permitted an extension of protection outside the words of the claims by way of equivalence.[57] The United States doctrine of equivalents,[58] for example, does allow the patentee to extend protection outside the claims in this way.

---

48 *Populin v HB Nominees Pty Ltd* (1982) 41 ALR 471, 475.
49 *Fresenius Medical Care Australia Pty Ltd v Gambro Pty Ltd* (2005) 67 IPR 230, 245.
50 *Populin v HB Nominees Pty Ltd* (1982) 41 ALR 471, 475; *Sachtler GmbH & Co KG v RE Miller Pty Ltd* (2005) 65 IPR 605, 616.
51 *C Van der Lely NV v Bamfords Ltd* [1963] RPC 61.
52 Ibid 77 (Lord Reid).
53 *Kirin-Amgen Inc v Hoechst Marion Roussel Ltd* [2005] RPC 169, 188.
54 *Clark v Adie* (1875) 10 Ch App 667.
55 Ibid. See *Marconi v British Radio Telegraph & Telephone Co Ltd* (1911) 28 RPC 181, 217; *C Van Der Lely NV v Bamfords Ltd* [1963] RPC 61, 75, 78–80; *Radiation Ltd v Galliers & Klaerr Pty Ltd* (1938) 60 CLR 36, 52 (Dixon J); *Olin Corp v Super Cartridge Co Pty Ltd* (1977) 180 CLR 236, 246.
56 *Kirin-Amgen Inc v Hoechst Marion Roussel Ltd* [2005] RPC 169, 187.
57 Ibid.
58 *Graver Tank & Manufacturing Co Inc v Linde Air Products Co*, 339 US 605, 607 (Jackson J) (1950); *Royal Typewriter Co v Remington Rand Inc*, 168 F 2d 691, 692 (1948).

Irrespective of this historical uncertainty, there is no longer any sustainable concept of equivalence in Anglo-Australian law. According to Lord Hoffman in *Kirin-Amgen Inc v Hoechst Marion Roussel Ltd*, there is no wider concept of 'pith and marrow' that would allow a patent to extend to equivalents that go outside the scope of the claim.[59] This is also the position in Australia.[60] Moreover, to broaden the scope of the monopoly using any concept of equivalence is generally undesirable because the patentee may have chosen restrictive language and regarded it as essential for some reason that is not evident.[61]

'Pith and marrow' – a phrase that is rarely used – is now understood to equate with 'those novel features only that [the patentee] claims to be essential'[62] – namely, the essential integers of the claim. As Gibbs J stated in *Olin Corp v Super Cartridge Co Pty Ltd*,[63] the 'pith and marrow' is limited by the language of the claim.[64] Nevertheless, 'pith and marrow' is a device that allows the person construing a claim to reject an expressed feature in a claim as essential to the invention. In the United Kingdom, the default position is that everything in the language of the claim is regarded as essential.[65] This is also the favoured position in Australia.[66]

12.3.3 Purposive construction

As stated above,[67] it is generally accepted by Australian courts that a patent specification should be given a purposive, not a purely literal, construction. This principle of construction gives effect to what the skilled person would have understood the patentee to be claiming.[68] It is used both to identify the essential features of the invention and to construe their meaning in the context of the specification as a whole.[69] The purposive approach does not advocate the rejection of specific words that are chosen by the patentee in favour of some 'kind of divination which mysteriously penetrates beneath the language of the specification'.[70] Rather, it retains the significance of the language in the claims but rejects a literal interpretation that takes no account of the context. Importantly, it does not extend the patentee's monopoly to the 'ideas' disclosed in the specification.[71]

---

59 [2005] RPC 169, 187.
60 *Baygol Pty Ltd v Foamex Polystyrene Pty Ltd* (2005) 66 IPR 1.
61 Ibid 7; *Société Technique de Pulverisation Step v Emson Europe Ltd* [1993] RPC 513, 522.
62 *Catnic Components Ltd v Hill & Smith Ltd* [1982] RPC 183, 243 (Lord Diplock); *Fresenius Medical Care Australia Pty Ltd v Gambro Pty Ltd* (2005) 67 IPR 230, 245; *DSI Australia (Holdings) Pty Ltd v Garford Pty Ltd* (2013) 100 IPR 19, [126]–[132].
63 (1977) 180 CLR 236, 246.
64 See also *Rodi & Wienenberger AG v Henry Showell Ltd* [1969] RPC 367, 391–2 (Lord Upjohn); *Catnic Components Ltd v Hill & Smith Ltd* [1982] RPC 183; *Kirin-Amgen Inc v Hoechst Marion Roussel Ltd* [2005] RPC 169; *Baygol Pty Ltd v Foamex Polystyrene Pty Ltd* (2005) 66 IPR 1.
65 *Kirin-Amgen Inc v Hoechst Marion Roussel Ltd* [2005] RPC 169, 187.
66 *Fresenius Medical Care Australia Pty Ltd v Gambro Pty Ltd* (2005) 67 IPR 230; *Baygol Pty Ltd v Foamex Polystyrene Pty Ltd* (2005) 66 IPR 1, 14.
67 At 12.3.1 and 12.3.2.
68 *Kirin-Amgen Inc v Hoechst Marion Roussel Ltd* [2005] RPC 169, 187.
69 *Populin v HB Nominees Pty Ltd* (1982) 41 ALR 471, 476–7; *Rehm Pty Ltd v Websters Security Systems (International) Pty Ltd* (1988) 11 IPR 289, 301.
70 *Kirin-Amgen Inc v Hoechst Marion Roussel Ltd* [2005] RPC 169, 186.
71 *GlaxoSmithKline Australia Pty Ltd v Reckitt Benckiser Healthcare (UK) Ltd* (2013) 305 ALR 363, [60].

The House of Lords explained this approach in *Catnic Components Ltd v Hill & Smith Ltd* in the following way:

> The question in each case is: whether persons with a practical knowledge and experience of the kind of work in which the invention was intended to be used, would understand that strict compliance with a particular descriptive word or phrase appearing in a claim was intended by the patentee to be an essential requirement of the invention so that any variant would fall outside the monopoly claimed, even though it could have no material effect upon the way the invention worked.[72]

The context in which these statements were made was the interpretation of the phrase 'extending vertically' in a claim for a lintel used in the building and construction industries. It was clear that the phrase described an essential feature of the invention. The issue was whether the phrase as properly construed extended to a lintel that was slightly off the precisely vertical. This passage emphasises the role of the person skilled in the relevant art before the priority date in claim construction and rejects any role for 'the un-informed layperson or linguistically pedantic lawyer'.[73] However, this passage can also be used to explain why some judges in earlier decisions may not have accepted certain words in a claim as being essential to the invention. For example, the majority in *C Van der Lely NV v Bamfords Ltd*[74] regarded the requirement for dismounting 'foremost' rather than 'hindmost' wheels of a mechanical hay rake as an essential feature, whereas the dissenting judgment of Lord Reid saw the requirement for 'foremost' wheels to be dismounted as an inessential feature of the invention. Earlier jurisprudence would have explained the difference between the majority and Lord Reid in terms of 'literal' and 'pith and marrow' in the wider sense of equivalence. The House of Lords wiped away this apparent distinction by saying that the 'pith and marrow' of an invention equates to the essential features in a claim that are identified using a purposive construction of the words chosen by the patentee.

The general principles in *Catnic* were rephrased as a set of questions by Hoffman LJ in *Improver Corp v Remington Consumer Products Ltd*.[75] These questions, which came to be known as the *Improver* questions or the *Protocol*[76] questions, are as follows:

1. Does the variant have a material effect on the way the invention works? If yes, the variant is outside the claim. If no?

2. Would this (that is, the fact that the variant had no material effect) have been obvious at the date of publication of the patent to a reader skilled in the art? If no, the variant is outside the claim. If yes?

3. Would the reader skilled in the art nevertheless have understood from the language of the claim that the patentee intended that strict compliance with the primary meaning was an essential requirement of the invention? If yes, the variant is outside the claim.

---

72 [1982] RPC 183, 243 (Diplock LJ).
73 *Australian Mud Co Pty Ltd v Coretell Pty Ltd* (2010) 88 IPR 270, [26].
74 [1963] RPC 61.
75 [1990] FSR 181, 189.
76 From the *Protocol on the Interpretation of Article 69 EPC (European Patent Convention)*.

The types of cases where these guidelines might be useful are those that involve figures, measurements, angles and the like where some flexibility may be intended. This may arise when a maximum or minimum quantity is not precisely stated ('about') or where a term, such as 'extending vertically' is understood by the skilled reader to not require the precision of a right angle.[77] What is the standing of these rules in Australian jurisprudence? Some Australian courts have derived assistance from both *Catnic* and the *Improver* questions in deciding the ambit of the monopoly of a claim.[78] However, these 'rules' are no substitute for construction of the claim to ascertain the essential and inessential integers[79] and to interpret the language used. They can provide a guideline to the application of the purposive method of construction in individual difficult cases. Even in the United Kingdom, Lord Hoffmann cautioned in *Kirin-Amgen Inc v Hoechst Marion Roussel Ltd* that the *Protocol* questions are 'not a substitute for trying to understand what the person skilled in the art would have understood the patentee to mean by the language of the claim'.[80] The language chosen by the patentee is usually of critical importance to this question and the questions are asked only after the claim has been construed.[81]

It seems that a court may need to take the area of invention into account in its interpretation of claims. When the area is a particularly narrow one, and the inventive context is cramped, a narrow formulation is likely to be deliberate. Hence, it is not appropriate to take a claim carefully drawn to avoid invalidity and then permit a wider purposive construction of it for infringement purposes.[82] Sometimes, words are clear and unambiguous. For example, if the word 'concrete' is an essential element of the claimed invention, its interpretation cannot extend to mean plastic because 'concrete' in no sense can approximate to 'plastic'. The choice of this word shows a deliberate intention to leave materials such as plastic outside the claim.[83] On the other hand, words such as 'vertically', 'straight'[84] and 'solely' may mean different things in different contexts. They offer some scope for a purposive construction to provide a literal meaning or one that encompasses some sense of approximation[85] that is adequate to protect the patentee from others who make minimal changes to the patentee's invention.[86] The word

---

77 *Kirin-Amgen Inc v Hoechst Marion Roussel Ltd* [2005] RPC 169; *Austal Ships Pty Ltd v Stena Rederi AB* (2005) 66 IPR 420, 432, [71]–[72]; *Catnic Components Ltd v Hill & Smith Ltd* [1982] RPC 183; *Arrow Pharmaceuticals Ltd v Merck & Co Inc* (2004) 63 IPR 85, [116].
78 *Pharmacia Italia SPA v Mayne Pharma Pty Ltd* (2005) 66 IPR 84, 99; *Nesbit Evans Group Australia Pty Ltd v Impro Ltd* (1997) 39 IPR 56; *Root Quality Pty Ltd v Root Control Technologies Pty Ltd* (2000) 49 IPR 225; *PhotoCure ASA v Queen's University at Kingston* (2005) 64 IPR 314, 366–7; *Neurizon Pty Ltd v Jupiters Pty Ltd* (2004) 62 IPR 569, 600.
79 *Sachtler GmbH & Co KG v RE Miller Pty Ltd* (2005) 65 IPR 605, 619; *Clorox Australia Pty Ltd v International Consolidated Business Pty Ltd* (2006) 68 IPR 254, 263; *Baygol Pty Ltd v Foamex Polystyrene Pty Ltd* (2005) 66 IPR 1; *Breville Pty Ltd v Warehouse Group (Australia) Pty Ltd* (2005) 67 IPR 576, 584; *PhotoCure ASA v Queen's University at Kingston* (2005) 64 IPR 314, [206].
80 [2005] RPC 169, 194.
81 *Baygol Pty Ltd v Foamex Polystyrene Pty Ltd* (2005) 66 IPR 1.
82 *Jupiters Ltd v Neurizon Pty Ltd* (2005) 65 IPR 86, 100; *Grove Hill Pty Ltd v Great Western Corp Pty Ltd* (2002) 55 IPR 257, 334–5.
83 *Baygol Pty Ltd v Foamex Polystyrene Pty Ltd* (2005) 66 IPR 1, 5–7.
84 *Clorox Australia Pty Ltd v International Consolidated Business Pty Ltd* (2006) 68 IPR 254.
85 *Nesbit Evans Group Australia Pty Ltd v Impro Ltd* (1997) 39 IPR 56, 57–63 (Wilcox J).
86 *Catnic Components Ltd v Hill & Smith Ltd* [1982] RPC 183.

'solely' could mean 'completely solely' or 'effectively solely'.[87] The words 'water-tight manner' could mean 'absolutely' water-tight or 'effectively' water-tight.[88] The word 'flat' could include slightly concave.[89] A broader meaning of a word or phrase may be more likely where the court is satisfied that the other person has engaged in some degree of subterfuge.[90]

Patents might include what are commonly referred to as 'omnibus claims'. These typically define a monopoly by reference to examples or drawings in the specification that illustrate the invention.[91] The scope of omnibus claims is largely determined by the language of the claim, the context of the specification in which it appears, and the nature of the descriptions and drawings to which the claim refers.[92] However, defining inventions in this way has led to lack of clarity and scope of the monopoly claimed. The *Intellectual Property Laws Amendment (Raising the Bar) Act 2012* (Cth) (*Raising the Bar Act*) introduced s 40(3A) to require that claims must not rely on references to descriptions or drawings unless absolutely necessary to define the invention.

Another type of claim known as a 'Swiss-style claim' takes the following form: 'The use of compound X in the manufacture of a medicament for a specified (and new) therapeutic use.'[93] The Swiss developed this claim form for use in jurisdictions that require claims to be susceptible of industrial application but that exclude from patentability both a method of medical treatment of the human body and a new use for a known medicine. The Swiss-style claim avoids the exclusion of claiming a new use for an old medicine 'by characterising the manufacture of a pill for a new use as something that was "susceptible of industrial application".'[94] Such claims are 'seen as directed to the manufacture of a product and not to the use of the product for the newly identified purpose'.[95] In other words, in applying a purposive approach, a Swiss-style claim is not a claim to a pharmaceutical substance, but is a claim to a method or process.[96]

12.4 Exclusive rights of the patentee

12.4.1 Nature of exclusive rights

Under s 13(1) of the *Patents Act 1990* (Cth), the patentee has the exclusive rights, during the term of the patent, to exploit the invention and to authorise another person to exploit the

---

87   *Pharmacia Italia SPA v Mayne Pharma Pty Ltd* (2005) 66 IPR 84, 98.
88   *Elconnex Pty Ltd v Gerard Industries Pty Ltd* (1991) 32 FCR 491.
89   *Commonwealth Industrial Gases Ltd v MWA Holdings Pty Ltd* (1970) 180 CLR 160, 167.
90   Ibid; *Pharmacia Italia SPA v Mayne Pharma Pty Ltd* (2005) 66 IPR 84, 98.
91   *Britax Childcare Pty Ltd v Infa-Secure Pty Ltd (No 3)* [2012] FCA 1019, [23]; *GlaxoSmithKline Australia Pty Ltd v Reckitt Benckiser Healthcare (UK) Ltd* (2016) 120 IPR 406, [69]; *Raleigh Cycle Co Ltd v H Miller & Co Ltd* (1948) 65 RPC 141, 157.
92   *Britax Childcare Pty Ltd v Infa-Secure Pty Ltd (No 3)* [2012] FCA 1019, [24]; *Memcor Australia Pty Ltd v GE Betzdearborn Canada Co* (2009) 81 IPR 315, [22], citing *Lewis v Hall* (2005) 68 IPR 89, 93.
93   *Bristol-Myers Squibb Co v Baker Norton Pharmaceuticals Inc* [1999] RPC 253, [44]; *Actavis UK Ltd v Merck & Co Inc* [2009] 1 WLR 1186, [7]; *Apotex Pty Ltd v Sanofi-Aventis Australia Pty Ltd* (2013) 253 CLR 284, [248]; *Otsuka Pharmaceutical Co Ltd v Generic Health Pty Ltd (No 4)* (2015) 113 IPR 191, [101].
94   *Eli Lilly Canada Inc v Apotex Inc* (2008) 75 IPR 625, [20].
95   *Otsuka Pharmaceutical Co Ltd v Generic Health Pty Ltd* (2012) 291 ALR 763, [67].
96   *Commissioner of Patents v Abbvie Biotechnology Ltd* (2017) 253 FCR 436, [58]; *Otsuka Pharmaceutical Co Ltd v Generic Health Pty Ltd (No 4)* (2015) 113 IPR 191, [120].

invention within the patent area.[97] This is defined to mean Australia, the Australian continental shelf, the waters above the Australian continental shelf, and the airspace above Australia and the Australian continental shelf.[98] The exclusive rights are personal property and are capable of assignment and devolution by law.[99]

The dictionary in sch 1 of the 1990 Act provides that, unless the contrary intention appears, the word 'invention' means

> any manner of new manufacture the subject of letters patent and grant of privilege within section 6 of the *Statute of Monopolies*, and includes an alleged invention.

The word 'invention' is not used in a uniform way throughout the 1990 Act.[100] It is used in s 40 in the sense of 'the embodiment which is described and around which the claims are drawn'.[101] However, for the purposes of s 13(1) and the definition of 'exploit', as well as s 18,[102] the term must refer to the subject matter of a claim in the granted patent.[103]

The term 'exploit' in relation to an invention is defined in sch 1 of the *Patents Act 1990* (Cth) to include:

> (a) where the invention is a product – make, hire, sell or otherwise dispose of the product, offer[104] to make, sell, hire or otherwise dispose of it, use or import it, or keep it for the purpose of doing any of those things;
>
> (b) where the invention is a method or process – use the method or process or do any act mentioned in paragraph (a) in respect of a product resulting from such use.[105]

The exclusive rights can be exercised during the term of the patent. In the case of a standard patent, the term is twenty years from the date of the patent.[106] The term of an innovation patent is eight years from the date of the patent.[107] The date of the patent is the date of filing the complete specification unless determined otherwise under the regulations.[108] The only people who can exploit the invention are the patentee and those with the patentee's authorisation.[109]

12.4.2 Concept of an implied licence on sale

The purchaser of a patented article expects to have the control of it, but the patentee's exclusive rights could theoretically limit this control. Early English courts developed the

---

97	*Patents Act 1990* (Cth) s 13(3).
98	Ibid sch 1 (definition of 'patent area').
99	Ibid s 13(2).
100	*Kimberly-Clark Australia Pty Ltd v Arico Trading International Pty Ltd* (2001) 207 CLR 1, 13.
101	Ibid 14; *AMP Inc v Utilux Pty Ltd* (1971) 45 ALJR 123, 127.
102	*Kimberly-Clark Australia Pty Ltd v Arico Trading International Pty Ltd* (2001) 207 CLR 1, 13.
103	*Bristol-Myers Squibb Co v Apotex Pty Ltd (No 5)* (2013) 104 IPR 23, [434].
104	This term is given its ordinary meaning and is not confined to its contractual meaning: *Warner-Lambert Co LLC v Apotex Pty Ltd* (2017) 249 FCR 17, [15], [18]–[19].
105	*Patents Act 1990* (Cth) sch 1.
106	Ibid s 67. An extension of term is available for pharmaceutical substances: see ch 9 at 9.10.
107	Ibid s 68.
108	Ibid s 65; *Patents Regulations 1991* (Cth) reg 6.3.
109	*Patents Act 1990* (Cth) s 13(1).

concept of an implied licence granted by the patentee to explain why a purchaser should be able to deal with the tangible patented product in any way they please without infringement.[110] A patentee can exclude or modify the implied licence by express contrary agreement prior to sale, provided that the restrictions are brought to the notice of the purchaser at the time of purchase.[111] This requirement is not satisfied, for instance, when inbuilt technical limitations contained in a memory chip in a printer ink cartridge come to the notice of the purchaser after ownership is transferred.[112]

As to the scope of an implied licence on first sale, the Privy Council in *National Phonograph Co of Australia Ltd v Menck* presumed that 'the full right of ownership was meant to be vested in the purchaser'.[113] Members of the Full Federal Court in *Calidad Pty Ltd v Seiko Epson Corp* interpreted this expression as encompassing 'all the normal rights of an owner including the right to resell' or the 'right to use and the right to dispose of the patented article' and to import the patented article.[114] Any person who subsequently acquires products without actual knowledge of any conditions attached by the patentee at the time of the first sale is also entitled to assume a full licence in these terms.[115] However, the court confirmed that the scope of the implied licence does not extend to making a new embodiment of the claimed invention, either from scratch or by using parts of the purchased product.[116] Such actions would infringe the exclusive rights of the patentee, as would subsequent dealings with those modified products such as importation into Australia.[117]

12.4.3 No grant of positive rights

It is important to note that, despite its language, a patent grants no positive rights to the patentee. This was made clear by Lord Herschell LC in *Steers v Rogers*, where he stated:

> The truth is that letters patent do not give the patentee any right to use the invention – they do not confer upon him a right to manufacture according to his invention. That is a right which he would have equally effectually if there were no letters patent at all; only in that case all the world would equally have the right. What the letters patent confer is the right to exclude others from manufacturing in a particular way, and using a particular invention.[118]

---

110 *National Phonograph Co of Australia Ltd v Menck* (1911) 12 CLR 15; *Betts v Willmott* (1871) LR 6 Ch App 239, 245.
111 *National Phonograph Co of Australia Ltd v Menck* (1911) 12 CLR 15, 24; *Calidad Pty Ltd v Seiko Epson Corp* (2019) 142 IPR 381. See below at 12.5.1.
112 *Calidad Pty Ltd v Seiko Epson Corp* (2019) 142 IPR 381, [72] (Greenwood J), [91], [181] (Jagot J).
113 (1911) 12 CLR 15, 28.
114 (2019) 142 IPR 381, [82] (Greenwood J), [286] (Yates J). This judgment was not available in time for detailed analysis to appear in this book. Leave to appeal to the High Court was granted on 15 November 2019 (S239/2019).
115 *Calidad Pty Ltd v Seiko Epson Corp* (2019) 142 IPR 381, [42] (Greenwood J); *Austshade Pty Ltd v Boss Shade Pty Ltd* (2016) 118 IPR 93, [80]; *Roussel-Uclaf SA v Hockley International Ltd* [1996] RPC 441, 443.
116 *Calidad Pty Ltd v Seiko Epson Corp* (2019) 142 IPR 381, [164] (Jagot J).
117 Ibid. This aspect of the decision is noted briefly below at 12.5.4.
118 [1893] AC 232, 235.

The High Court confirmed in *Grain Pool of Western Australia v Commonwealth*[119] that our patent law is concerned with a monopoly identified in this way, and not with the conferral of 'positive authority'.

12.5 Direct infringement

Section 13(1) of the *Patents Act 1990* (Cth) and the definition of 'exploit' constitute a codification of the acts that were held to fall within the exclusive rights of the patentee under the *Patents Act 1952* (Cth).[120] The definition of 'exploit' removes some of the 'obscure language'[121] in which those rights were formulated – namely, 'exercise' and 'vend' – but retains the words 'make' and 'use'. These latter words carry the same meaning as given to them in the former legislation.[122] To avoid duplication, the meaning of the exclusive rights is discussed below in the context of infringement.

The *Patents Act 1990* (Cth) contains no express provision to define the acts that constitute an infringement of the patent.[123] Rather, infringement is implied when a person exercises any of the exclusive rights of the patentee without the patentee's authorisation. There is therefore a coincidence of language between that which defines the exclusive rights[124] on the one hand and that which defines infringing acts on the other. An inquiry into infringement therefore focuses on the language of the claims in the specification and whether the acts performed by the alleged infringer amount to an unauthorised exploitation of the invention as defined in a claim or claims of the complete specification.

There is a five-step process for determining infringement of a claim:

1. The patent specification is construed to determine the scope of the relevant claim or claims that define the 'invention' and the precise nature and extent of the rights claimed by the patentee.[125]

2. The product or process whose exploitation is alleged to infringe one or more of those claims is identified and compared to each claim independently to determine whether it contains all the essential integers of the relevant claim or claims. A person will infringe if he takes all essential integers of the claim.[126] There is no infringement if that product or process is missing one or more of those essential integers.[127]

---

119 (2000) 202 CLR 479, 513–14.
120 *Patents Act 1903* (Cth) s 62; *Patents Act 1952* (Cth) s 69.
121 Explanatory Memorandum, Patents Bill 1990 (Cth) cl 13 [23].
122 *Bedford Industries Rehabilitation Association Inc v Pinefair Pty Ltd* (1998) 40 IPR 438, 449, affirmed (1998) 87 FCR 458, 469 (Mansfield J).
123 Compare *Patents Act 1977* (UK) s 60(1) and 35 USC §271.
124 *Patents Act 1990* (Cth) s 13(1), sch 1 (definitions of 'exploit' and 'invention').
125 *Minnesota Mining & Manufacturing Co v Tyco Electronics Pty Ltd* (2001) 53 IPR 32, 57; *Lockwood Security Products Pty Ltd v Doric Products Pty Ltd (No 3)* (2005) 226 ALR 70, 80.
126 *Olin Corp v Super Cartridge Co Pty Ltd* (1977) 180 CLR 236, 246; *Seiko Epson Corp v Calidad Pty Ltd* (2017) 133 IPR 1, [170].
127 This exercise mirrors the novelty inquiry – the 'reverse infringement test'. See ch 10 at 10.6.8. It is not an infringement to substitute an equivalent for an essential integer: see, for example, *Coretell Pty Ltd v Australian Mud Company Pty Ltd* (2017) 250 FCR 155, [56]; *H Lundbeck A/S v Alphapharm Pty Ltd* (2009) 177 FCR 151, [93], [222].

3. For infringement, the actions that are performed in relation to that product or process must come within the meaning and scope of the exclusive rights of the patentee.
4. The actions must constitute an unauthorised exercise of those rights or amount to contributory infringement.
5. If the acts would otherwise infringe the patent, there may be a defence to infringement.

The first two steps involve construction of the claims, the principles for which were discussed above.[128] The remaining three steps are discussed next.

12.5.1 Exclusive right to make a patented product

To 'make' a patented product means to make something that has all the integers of the relevant claim in the specification.[129] Therefore, it is necessary to make the whole product, not its constituent parts. 'Making' is not complete 'until the final step is carried out which results in the complete infringing article'.[130] However, there is no need for the result to be produced in its ultimate commercial form.[131]

A patented product might be made as an integral step in the process of manufacture of a non-infringing product.[132] It seems it must play more than an 'unimportant or trifling part' in the manufacture.[133] However, it does not need to be something that is 'capable of immediate acceptance in the marketplace or of being turned to immediate commercial advantage'.[134] It is a question of fact whether there has been a relevant 'making' of the patented product in the process of manufacture of the ultimate non-infringing product.[135] For example, a majority of the Full Federal Court in *Pinefair Pty Ltd v Bedford Industries Rehabilitation Association Inc*[136] found that a patented garden-edging product was 'made' as an intermediate product in the process of manufacturing a non-infringing garden-edging product that consisted of split pine posts joined together with stapled plastic strips. The manufacturing process involved a continual mechanical process whereby the split pine posts passed along a conveyor belt as one continuous length of material. This passed through a variety of machines that performed functions of stapling and cutting, before emerging as the final non-infringing garden-edging product that was rolled and packaged into lengths for marketing. At one point in this continuous process, all the essential integers of the invention were present in a section of that continuous material that moved along the conveyor belt. The majority considered that an infringing product was 'made' even though the infringing section remained connected at both

---

128 At 12.3.
129 *Walker v Alemite Corp* (1933) 49 CLR 643, 650 (Rich J).
130 *Bedford Industries Rehabilitation Association Inc v Pinefair Pty Ltd* (1998) 40 IPR 438, 449, affirmed (1998) 87 FCR 458, 469 (Mansfield J).
131 *Pfizer Corp v Ministry of Health* [1965] AC 512, 571–3; *Pinefair Pty Ltd v Bedford Industries Rehabilitation Association Inc* (1998) 87 FCR 458, 469 (Mansfield J).
132 *Pinefair Pty Ltd v Bedford Industries Rehabilitation Association Inc* (1998) 87 FCR 458, 468.
133 Ibid; *Beecham Group Ltd v Bristol Laboratories Ltd (No 1)* [1978] RPC 153; *Saccharin Corp Ltd v Anglo-Continental Chemical Works Ltd* (1900) 17 RPC 307; *Dunlop Pneumatic Tyre Co Ltd v British & Colonial Motor Car Co* (1901) 18 RPC 313; *Pfizer Corp v Ministry of Health* [1965] AC 512.
134 *Pinefair Pty Ltd v Bedford Industries Rehabilitation Association Inc* (1998) 87 FCR 458, 463 (Foster J).
135 Ibid 466 (Mansfield J).
136 (1998) 87 FCR 458, 464–5 (Foster J), 469–71 (Mansfield J), 479 (Goldberg J dissenting).

ends to non-infringing material. A contrary view was taken on the facts by the dissenting judge, Goldberg J, who reasoned that the intermediary product must be a separate and freestanding product to be 'made'.

The exclusive right is to 'make' the invention. One way in which a person may infringe this right is to modify a purchased patented product in such a way as to reconstruct or remake it. The infringing nature of any modifications or alterations to the product is determined as a matter of fact and degree. Initially, the reasoning in United Kingdom decisions proceeded on the basis that the purchaser had an implied licence to repair the purchased products.[137] Resolution of an assertion of infringement focused generally on whether 'what has been done can fairly be termed a repair, having regard to the nature of the patented article'.[138] However, later decisions have rejected this concept of an implied licence to repair. Instead, they have focused on the language in the legislation itself – does the alleged infringer 'make' the article?

In the absence of Australian authority on this issue, two United Kingdom authorities provide useful comparative material for the purposes of analogy.[139] Both of the cases discussed below considered whether 'reconditioning' damaged patented products by replacing a worn or damaged part constitutes 'making' the patented product. The first decision, *United Wire Ltd v Screen Repair Services (Scotland) Ltd*,[140] concerned two patents for a screen that consisted of a metal frame to which two meshes of different sizes were secured so as to be at different tensions. The meshes were quickly torn whereas the frames had greater durability. The defendants reconditioned the screens by removing and replacing the meshes and stripping and recoating the wire frames. In construing the term 'make', the House of Lords rejected the former concept of an implied licence to repair as 'superfluous and possibly even confusing' on the basis that it has no relevance to an act that is outside the scope of the patentee's exclusive rights.[141] Lord Hoffman pointed out that the focus should be on whether the conduct amounts to making the product as claimed rather than whether it constitutes a repair to prolong the life of the article.[142] The conclusion on the facts of the case was:

> [The patented] product ceased to exist when the meshes were removed and the frame stripped down to the bare metal. What remained at that stage was merely an important component, a skeleton or chassis, from which a new screen could be made.[143]

The second case, the decision of the United Kingdom Supreme Court in *Schütz (UK) Ltd v Werit UK Ltd*,[144] provides guidance on specific considerations to take into account when determining the question. The patented product related to intermediate bulk containers that were of two-part construction: a metal cage on a pallet into which was fitted a plastic bottle for

---

137 *Solar Thomson Engineering Co Ltd v Barton* [1977] RPC 537.
138 Ibid 555 (Buckley LJ).
139 The authorities are discussed by Jagot and Yates JJ in *Calidad Pty Ltd v Seiko Epson Corp* (2019) 142 IPR 381, in the context of relevance to the scope of the implied licence on first sale and infringement through importation and sale of patented products that were modified and acquired overseas. The judgment was not available in time for analysis to appear in this book. Leave to appeal to the High Court was granted on 15 November 2019 (S239/2019). See below at 12.5.4.
140 [2000] 4 All ER 353.
141 Ibid 358.
142 Lord Bingham, ibid [56], adopted similar reasoning and all other Law Lords agreed.
143 *United Wire Ltd v Screen Repair Services (Scotland) Ltd* [2000] 4 All ER 353, [73].
144 [2013] UKSC 16.

storage and carriage of liquids. The cage had a longer life span than the bottles, so a reconditioning industry had developed to acquire discarded containers and refit either the bottles from the original manufacturer ('re-bottling') or the bottles from a different source ('cross-bottling'). Again, the issue was whether an infringement of the patent had occurred in the reconditioning process by making the patented product without authorisation.

Lord Neuberger PSC, with whom the other Lords and Lady agreed, confirmed that the correct approach requires the word 'makes' to be interpreted contextually (given the 'slippery nature of the meaning of the word') and with reference to a number of factors.[145] Relevant considerations were 'whether the bottle is such a *subsidiary part* of the patented article that its replacement, when required, does not involve making a new article',[146] and whether the worn-out part 'includes the inventive concept, or has a function that is closely connected with that concept'.[147] Although the bottle was large and was a necessary or integral part of the article, the combination of a number of factors led to the court concluding that its replacement did not amount to 'making' the patented article. These factors included that:

- its significantly lower life expectancy would raise an expectation for its replacement;
- it is a freestanding article that is physically easy to replace;
- it is relatively perishable; and
- it does not include any aspect of the inventive concept of the patent.[148]

The inventive concept related to the metal cage. Lord Neuberger distinguished the case before him from the facts in *United Wire*, identifying the exercise of the simple replacement of the bottle as being 'an exercise of a very different order' from the significant demolition and improvement work required in the reconditioning of the mesh screens the subject of *United Wire*.[149]

12.5.2 Exclusive right to use

Mere possession or mere purchase of an infringing product does not amount to infringement.[150] It is necessary to identify the additional ingredient that, combined with possession, makes up an infringement. As Lord Wilberforce commented in *Pfizer Corp v Ministry of Health*,[151] this is not easy to do from the reported cases. Prior to the *Patents Act 1990* (Cth), a variety of activities were identified in the context of infringement as within the broad concept of 'use'.[152] A number of these activities, such as importation and keeping products for a variety of purposes, are now separately itemised in the definition of 'exploit' in the *Patents Act 1990* (Cth),

---

145   Ibid [26]–[28].
146   Ibid [61] (emphasis added).
147   Ibid [67].
148   Ibid [78]. Note the comments of Burley J in *Seiko Epson Corp v Calidad Pty Ltd* (2017) 133 IPR 1, [175] as to the relevance of the inventive concept under Australian law in analysing modifications.
149   Ibid [71].
150   *British United Shoe Machinery Ltd v Simon Collier Ltd* [1910] 27 RPC 567, 572.
151   [1965] AC 512, 572.
152   The word 'use' also appears in *Patents Act 1990* (Cth) s 9 in the context of 'secret use': see ch 10. See also A. Monotti, 'To make an article for ultimate sale: The secret use provision in the *Patents Act 1990* (Cth)' [2005] 27 *European Intellectual Property Review* 446.

and will be discussed in that context. Although this separate itemisation could suggest that the word 'use' in the definition now only incorporates activities that are not expressly identified, this was denied by a majority of the Federal Court in *Azuko Pty Ltd v Old Digger Pty Ltd*.[153] In discussing the definition of 'exploit' in the Act's dictionary, Gyles J stated that '[i]t may be accepted that the various kinds of exploitation may overlap in different circumstances'.[154] As an example of the overlap, Gyles J stated that 'to sell goods might be seen as commercial use of the goods'.[155] The same reasoning could apply to other listed acts, such as to 'sell', 'hire', 'keep', 'dispose' or 'import'.[156] However, the majority expressly stated that the word 'use' does not overlap with the word 'make'. These are separate and distinct concepts.[157] In a strong dissenting judgment, Heerey J concluded to the contrary that to make an invention that is a product is also to use the invention.[158] Despite the expansive nature of the term 'use', some authority suggests that its meaning in the definition of exploit is qualified to apply to only 'commercial use'. In *Bedford Industries Rehabilitation Association Inc v Pinefair Pty Ltd*, von Doussa J applied the criterion for 'use' as 'taking commercial advantage of the invention to advance them into the market place'.[159] On appeal, Mansfield J agreed with his Honour's observations:

> From each of those judgments there emerges in my view an appropriate focus upon the market for the product the subject of the patent as the sole preserve of the respondent, so that manufacture and use of that product to the commercial advantage of the appellants would infringe the patent. It is apparent that the appellants were taking commercial advantage of the patent. They were doing so not in some peripheral or transitory way.[160]

The use of an invention 'as a transitory step in the production of an article which in its final form differs from the invention' falls within the scope of the concept of exploit, as long as it is not an unimportant or trifling part of the manufacture.[161]

12.5.3 Exclusive right to keep

Where the invention is a product, the definition of 'exploit' includes to keep it for the purpose of doing any of the other listed activities, such as making, sale, hire, importation or other form of disposal. This codifies the law that existed under the *Patents Act 1952* (Cth) as it applied to activities that involved keeping patented articles for some purpose. The following sets out the principles that will inform the interpretation of the word 'keep' in the context of keeping the article for the purpose of using it.

First, possession of articles by a trader or manufacturer for the purposes of a business is presumed to indicate that a user (and, therefore, possession of such articles) is prima facie

---

153 (2001) 52 IPR 75, 136.
154 Ibid.
155 Ibid.
156 Monotti, 'To make an article for ultimate sale', above n 152; *Monsanto Canada Inc v Schmeiser* [2004] 1 SCR 902.
157 *Azuko Pty Ltd v Old Digger Pty Ltd* (2001) 52 IPR 75, 136.
158 Ibid 113; Monotti, 'To make an article for ultimate sale', above n 152.
159 (1998) 40 IPR 438, 450.
160 *Pinefair Pty Ltd v Bedford Industries Rehabilitation Association Inc* (1998) 42 IPR 330, 341.
161 *Bedford Industries Rehabilitation Association Inc v Pinefair Pty Ltd* (1998) 40 IPR 438, 450–1.

infringement. This possession may be to hold the articles in stock for sale[162] or to make use of them as and when it would be beneficial to do so.[163] This presumption can be rebutted by the admitted fact of non-user.[164] There may be use of patented equipment through its possession, even though it has not been actually used. But this would require an intention to use it in the future, utility for the purposes of the business, and likelihood that it would be used.[165]

Second, there is a doctrine that an infringing use can occur when a patented article is kept as a 'standby'. An example might be possession of fire-extinguishing apparatus, the use being the actual provision of the means for extinguishment.[166] There is a distinction between use established through possession as a standby and possession in a way that could be viewed as a threat to infringe rather than infringement per se.[167] In this regard, it seems that the above example amounts to a use rather than an intention to infringe.[168]

Third, the courts have protected the rights of a mere carrier[169] and warehouseperson who does no more than store infringing goods for a consignor or consignee. Such actions do not amount to an infringing use.[170] Mere transport within the jurisdiction of a patented article from one place to another does not necessarily attract liability.[171] The additional ingredient necessary for 'use' of the patented product for the purposes of infringement is the derivation of some advantage arising from the merits in the patented article itself.[172] This would occur when the person transporting the articles is also carrying on a trade in those articles for profit.[173]

Another series of cases shows that the additional ingredient is satisfied when a patented article that is stored or transported is employed for the purpose for which it is designed. An example is the exhibition at a trade fair of cars fitted with tyres manufactured abroad in accordance with the patent specification for such tyres. Despite there being no intention to sell the car fitted with those patented tyres, the use was found to be infringing because the tyres were serving their intended purpose during the time they were exhibited.[174] Another example of this type of infringing use is the shipping of bottles of beer on which patented capsules were fitted to cover the corks and protect the beer. The bottles were shipped from Scotland to agents in England who then shipped them to other ports. Again, this use infringed the patent because the capsules were in 'active use for the very objects for which they were placed upon the bottles by the vendors'.[175]

---

162 *Pfizer Corp v Ministry of Health* [1965] AC 512, 573 (Lord Wilberforce).
163 *McDonald v Graham* [1994] RPC 407, 431; *Smith Kline French Laboratories Ltd v RD Harbottle (Mercantile) Ltd* [1980] RPC 363.
164 *British United Shoe Machinery Ltd v Simon Collier Ltd* [1910] 27 RPC 567, 572 (Lord Dunedin).
165 Ibid; *Pfizer Corp v Ministry of Health* [1965] AC 512, 556–7 (Lord Upjohn).
166 *British United Shoe Machinery Ltd v Simon Collier Ltd* [1910] 27 RPC 567, 572.
167 *Adair v Young* (1879) LR 12 Ch D 13, 19–20 (Brett LJ).
168 *Pfizer Corp v Ministry of Health* [1965] AC 512, 557 (Lord Upjohn).
169 *F Hoffmann-La Roche & Co AG v Harris Pharmaceuticals Ltd* [1977] FSR 200, 207; *Nobel's Explosives Co Ltd v Jones, Scott & Co* (1881) 17 Ch D 721.
170 *Smith Kline & French Laboratories Ltd v RD Harbottle (Mercantile) Ltd* [1980] RPC 363, 370.
171 *Pfizer Corp v Ministry of Health* [1965] 1 AC 512, 571 (Lord Wilberforce), 537 (Lord Reid), 548 (Lord Evershed), 550 (Lord Pearce).
172 *Badische Anilin & Soda Fabrik v Henry Johnson & Co* (1897) 14 RPC 919, 928.
173 *F Hoffmann-La Roche & Co AG v Harris Pharmaceuticals Ltd* [1977] FSR 200, 207; *Nobel's Explosives Co Ltd v Jones, Scott & Co* (1881) 17 Ch D 721, 741.
174 *Dunlop Pneumatic Tyre Co Ltd v British & Colonial Motor Car Co* (1901) 18 RPC 313, 315–16.
175 *Betts v Neilson* (1868) LR 3 Ch App 429, 439, affirmed (1871) LR 5 HL 1.

12.5.4 Exclusive right to import the invention

The *Patents Act 1952* (Cth) contained no express exclusive right to import the invention. However, the right was recognised by judicial interpretation of the exclusive right of the patentee to 'use' the invention in the phrase 'make, use, exercise and vend'. These earlier authorities provided that an unauthorised person who imports articles that embody the invention will use the invention and thereby infringe the patent.[176] The authorities prohibited unauthorised importation of the invention for purposes of sale or to hold in stock to be available against orders for the product, as well as for the purposes of export to another country.[177] This would include labelling and putting the imported product in packages ready for supply.[178] The conduct infringed the patent because it placed the importers in the position of traders of a patented article without the permission of the patentee. It gave them the opportunity to derive advantage that otherwise would have fallen to the patentee.

The right to import is now included within the definition of 'exploit' in sch 1 of the *Patents Act 1990* (Cth). If any rationale is necessary to justify its existence, it can be found in the absence of a requirement that an invention be actually worked in the jurisdiction. Where the invention is a product, the right is to import the product into Australia. A variety of circumstances exists in which unauthorised importation of articles that embody the invention may occur. There may be an attempt to import patented products that were purchased legitimately from someone other than the Australian patentee or with the patentee's authorisation. The manufacture of the articles in the country of export may infringe a local patent. The purchase may be on the express condition that the articles are not to be imported into Australia. The marketing of articles in the place of purchase may be without the express or implied permission of the local patentee. A third party who has no connection with the Australian patentee may have manufactured and sold the articles in a country in which no patent exists.[179]

Authorisation to import patented products that a patentee first sells overseas without restrictions on use is implied under the doctrine of an implied licence on sale.[180] However, a patentee may have the right to control or limit what may be done with those products when a person modifies the products prior to importation. In *Calidad Pty Ltd v Seiko Epson Corp*, the Full Federal Court determined the patentee's rights according to whether those modifications were within, or outside, the scope of the implied licence granted on sale.[181] That scope does not extend to making a new embodiment of the claimed invention, either from scratch or by using parts of the purchased product.[182]

Where the invention is a method or process, the patentee has the exclusive right to use the method or process to make a product in Australia, and among other things, to import

---

176   *Pfizer Corp v Ministry of Health* [1965] AC 512, 556 (Lord Upjohn); *British Motor Syndicate Ltd v Taylor & Son* [1901] 1 Ch 122, 133 (Vaughan Williams LJ).
177   *Pfizer Corp v Ministry of Health* [1965] AC 512, 573 (Lord Wilberforce).
178   Ibid.
179   Ibid; *Elmslie v Boursier* (1869–70) LR 9 Eq 217; *Von Heyden v Neustadt* (1880) 14 Ch D 230.
180   *National Phonograph Co of Australia Ltd v Menck* (1911) 12 CLR 15, 24; *Calidad Pty Ltd v Seiko Epson Corp* (2019) 142 IPR 381. See above at 12.4.2.
181   *Calidad Pty Ltd v Seiko Epson Corp* (2019) 142 IPR 381. The judgment was not available in time for detailed analysis of this issue to appear in this book. Leave to appeal to the High Court was granted on 15 November 2019 (S239/2019).
182   Ibid [164] (Jagot J).

into Australia products made anywhere using the method or process that is patented in Australia.[183] This provision codifies the common law, which construed the exclusive right to 'use' an invention as extending to the importation of a product where the use of the patented process is the last stage in the production of that product.[184] In *Saccharin Corp Ltd v Anglo-Continental Chemical Works Ltd*,[185] the defendant used a patented process outside England to produce toluene sulpho chloride. It then used this chemical in the production of saccharin that it imported into England. This use deprived the patentee of some of the profit and advantage of the invention and thus constituted infringement within the concept of the exclusive right to 'use' the invention. This common law prohibition requires the patented process to play more than 'an unimportant or trifling part in the manufacture abroad' of the imported product.[186] The definition of 'exploit' is sufficiently broad to also encompass the common law prohibition of importation of an article whose manufacture incorporated use of the patented process at any stage in its production. However, it has not been decided whether this common law doctrine is part of Australian patent law under the *Patents Act 1990* (Cth).[187]

The meaning of 'exploit' includes, where the invention is a product, 'to import it'. Although the definition is inclusive, Nicholas J has held that it would not extend the rights of the patentee to prohibit the importation of products that are made using the patented product abroad.[188]

12.5.5 Concept of parallel importation

The essence of parallel importation is the importation into Australia of patented products acquired lawfully overseas but without the express authorisation of the Australian patentee. This importation would be 'in parallel' with the authorised distribution channels. Whether parallel importation infringes the exclusive rights of the Australian patentee will depend on the actual or implied licences in the first sale and their effect in Australia. The common law provides that the unconditional sale of patented products by the patentee, or with their authorisation, exhausts the patentee's rights and gives the purchaser an implied licence to deal with the patented products in any way the purchaser pleases without infringement.[189] An implied licence of this kind is necessary to enable the purchaser to deal freely with the purchased goods in ways that would otherwise fall within the exclusive rights of the patentee. Although the exclusive rights of the patentee under the *Patents Act 1952* (Cth) to make, use, exercise and vend extended to importation, it was understood that the doctrine of implied

---

183   *Alphapharm Pty Ltd v H Lundbeck A/S* (2008) 76 IPR 618, [694]; *Otsuka Pharmaceutical Co Ltd v Generic Health Pty Ltd (No 4)* (2015) 113 IPR 191, [165]; *Warner-Lambert Co LLC v Apotex Pty Ltd (No 2)* (2018) 129 IPR 205, [167].
184   *Elmslie v Boursier* (1869–70) LR 9 Eq 217; *Wright v Hitchcock* (1870) LR 5 Exch 37; *Von Heyden v Neustadt* (1880) 14 Ch D 230; *Re Application of Eli Lilly & Co* [1982] 1 NSWLR 526, 533 (Wootten J).
185   (1900) 17 RPC 307, 319 (Buckley J).
186   *Wilderman v FW Berk & Co Ltd* [1925] Ch 116.
187   *Otsuka Pharmaceutical Co Ltd v Generic Health Pty Ltd (No 4)* (2015) 113 IPR 191, [178].
188   *Mylan Health Pty Ltd (formerly BGP Products Pty Ltd) v Sun Pharma ANZ Pty Ltd (formerly Ranbaxy Australia Pty Ltd)* (2019) 138 IPR 402, [315]–[318]. See also *Alphapharm Pty Ltd v H Lundbeck A/S* (2008) 76 IPR 618, [694]; *Beecham Group Ltd v Bristol Laboratories Ltd (No 1)* [1978] RPC 153; *Wilderman v FW Berk & Co Ltd* [1925] Ch 116.
189   *National Phonograph Co of Australia Ltd v Menck* (1911) 12 CLR 15, 24.

licences enabled a purchaser to freely import patented products that had been sold unconditionally overseas by the patentee or with their authorisation.[190]

It appears that the same position applies under the *Patents Act 1990* (Cth). An exclusive right of the patentee is to import the invention into Australia.[191] Section 13(1) of the *Patents Act 1990* (Cth) introduces the express right to authorise another person to exploit the invention. Authorisation may be express or implied. Express authorisation will be by way of an assignment of the patent or the grant of an exclusive or non-exclusive licence. Implied authorisation will arise from the circumstances that surround the manufacture and sale of products that embody the patented invention. There is nothing either in s 13(1) or in the definition of exploit that details the circumstances in which authorisation to import will be implied. However, the Explanatory Memorandum to the Patents Bill 1990 (Cth) made it clear that the right of a patentee to authorise exploitation was not intended 'to modify the operation of the law on infringement so far as it relates to subsequent dealings with a patented product after its first sale'. Clause 24 provided:

> [T]he question whether such a resale or importation constitutes an infringement in a particular case will continue to be determined as it is now, having regard to any actual or implied licences in the first sale and their effect in Australia, and to what is often known as the doctrine of 'exhaustion of rights' so far as it applies under Australian law.

To avoid infringement, an express or implied authorisation by the Australian patentee to import into Australia must be found in the terms of the first sale of the products that the person proposes to import. An unconditional sale made by the Australian patentee, or with their consent, is likely to amount to an implied authorisation by the Australian patentee to the importation of the products into Australia on the basis that the purchase carries an implied licence to use the products anywhere in the world.[192] It does not matter who sold the products to the importer, as long as the source was the patentee.

To avoid the imposition of this implied licence, a patentee can attach conditions to the sale of the goods prior to sale, and these will bind the purchaser when knowledge of those conditions is clearly brought home to the purchaser at the time of sale.[193] Hence, a person could impose a condition to prohibit importation of the legitimately acquired patented goods into Australia.[194]

12.5.6 Authorisation

It is an infringement not only to exploit the invention but also to authorise another person to exploit it. It is necessary to establish primary infringement to succeed with a claim of

---

[190] *Interstate Parcel Express Co Pty Ltd v Time-Life International (Nederlands) BV* (1977) 138 CLR 534, 540; *Betts v Willmott* (1871) LR 6 Ch App 239, 245; *United Wire Ltd v Screen Repair Services (Scotland) Ltd* [2000] 4 All ER 353, 357–8; T. A. Blanco White, *Patents for Inventions and the Protection of Industrial Designs* (4th edn, London: Stevens, 1974) [3.219], [10.104].

[191] *Patents Act 1990* (Cth) s 13(1) sch 1 (definition of 'exploit').

[192] *Betts v Willmott* (1871) LR 6 Ch App 239; *Société Anonyme des Manufactures de Glaces v Tilghman's Patent Sand Blast Co Ltd* [1884] LR 25 Ch D 1.

[193] Ibid.

[194] As to the effect of the modification of first-sold products prior to importation, see *Seiko Epson Corp v Calidad Pty Ltd* (2017) 133 IPR 1, discussed at 12.5.1 above.

authorisation of infringement.[195] However, an intention to infringe or knowledge that the conduct will infringe is not required.[196] The *Patents Act 1990* (Cth) defines 'exploit' in sch 1 but is silent as to the meaning of the separate and distinct concept of authorisation. A historic difference of judicial opinion as to the meaning of 'authorise' under patent law no longer exists. A narrow meaning of 'to give legal or formal warrant to (a person) to do; to empower, permit authoritatively'[197] has given way to the view that authorise has the meaning in copyright law that a person authorises an infringement if the person sanctions, approves or countenances the act of infringement.[198] This does not mean that authorisation under s 13(1) of the *Patents Act 1990* (Cth) has the same meaning as in s 101 of the *Copyright Act 1968* (Cth).[199] Yates J rejected an argument to this effect in *Bristol-Myers Squibb Co v Apotex Pty Ltd (No 5)*:

> I am unable to see the direct relevance of that provision to s 13(1) of the Act, which has no counterpart to s 101(1A) of the *Copyright Act*. Nevertheless, I will proceed on the basis that 'authorise' in s 13(1) was intended to have the judicially received meaning of that word in the context of the *Copyright Act* as at 1990.[200]

It is worth noting that the development of the copyright analogy took no account of the legislative origins of the *Patents Act 1990* (Cth) and in particular of its relationship with s 117, which provides specific circumstances in which a third-party supplier may become liable by way of contributory infringement.[201] The introduction of accessorial liability into s 13(1) through the express inclusion of authorisation as an exclusive right of the patentee is unexplained. In contrast, s 117 introduced contributory infringement following extensive review of the need for a patentee to enjoy a wider range of rights than are available under the common law joint tortfeasorship principles.[202] Although a potential risk exists of introducing unnecessary complexity into the law (as occurred in copyright law), this has not been realised to date. The factual circumstances in which courts have found authorisation of infringement also fall within either or both the protection offered by contributory infringement under s 117 and joint tortfeasorship at common law.[203]

Some examples of conduct that would amount to authorisation of infringement include:

- A person authorises the company of which they are a director to perform certain acts. Hence, for example, authorisation of infringement would apply to a director of a

---

195 *Apotex Pty Ltd v Les Laboratories Servier (No 2)* (2012) 293 ALR 272, [40].
196 *SNF (Australia) Pty Ltd v Ciba Specialty Chemicals Water Treatments Ltd* (2011) 92 IPR 46, [305]; *Inverness Medical Switzerland GmbH v MDS Diagnostics Pty Ltd* (2010) 85 IPR 525, [193]; *Streetworx Pty Ltd v Artcraft Urban Group Pty Ltd* (2014) 110 IPR 82, [394].
197 *Macquarie Dictionary* and *Shorter Oxford Dictionary* definitions, respectively, cited in *Bristol-Myers Squibb Co v FH Faulding & Co Ltd* (1998) 41 IPR 467, 488, discussed in *Caterpillar Inc v John Deere Ltd* (1999) 48 IPR 1, 11; *Advanced Building Systems Pty Ltd v Ramset Fasteners (Australia) Pty Ltd* (1995) AIPC 91-129, [39,200].
198 *University of New South Wales v Moorhouse* (1975) 133 CLR 1, 12, 20; *Multisteps Pty Ltd v Speciality Packaging Aust Pty Ltd* (2018) 132 IPR 399, [118]–[119].
199 *Bristol-Myers Squibb Co v FH Faulding & Co Ltd* (2000) 97 FCR 524, [97]; *Apotex Pty Ltd v Les Laboratories Servier (No 4)* (2010) 89 IPR 274, [14].
200 (2013) 104 IPR 23, [409].
201 The operation of s 117 is discussed below at 12.6.
202 See below at 12.6.
203 *Damorgold Pty Ltd v JAI Products Pty Ltd* (2014) 105 IPR 60; *Wake Forest University Health Sciences v Smith & Nephew Pty Ltd (No 2)* (2011) 92 IPR 496; *Inverness Medical Switzerland GmbH v MDS Diagnostics Pty Ltd* (2010) 85 IPR 525; *Caterpillar Inc v John Deere Ltd* (1999) 48 IPR 1.

corporation who 'expressly procures or directs the commission of a tort by a corporation'.[204] However, a director does not authorise infringement merely by their position,[205] participation in decision-making of the company, or meeting their expectations as a director.[206] In some cases, it may be necessary to consider whether the authorisation is by the director or by the company itself.[207]

- A parent company authorises its subsidiary to perform infringing acts.[208]
- A person manufactures and sells in kit form a product, to be assembled by the purchaser, that when assembled would infringe the patent.[209]
- There is conduct that satisfies either or both s 117 and the tort of joint tortfeasorship.[210]

Drawing on copyright authorities,[211] it seems that authorisation will not arise where there is:

- inactivity or failure to take steps to prevent infringement;[212]
- facilitation of infringing conduct or mere knowledge that infringing use is likely;[213]
- indifference to the occurrence of an infringing act (where there is no duty to intervene);[214] and
- no power to prevent the conduct.[215]

12.5.7 Liability as a joint tortfeasor through 'common design' or 'procurement'

Prior to the enactment of contributory infringement under s 117 of the *Patents Act 1990* (Cth), a person could facilitate infringement without penalty because such actions fell outside the scope of common law liability as a joint tortfeasor who acts in furtherance of a common design with the infringer[216] or 'procures' another to infringe.[217] The uncertain boundaries of

---

204   *King v Milpurrurru* (1996) 66 FCR 474, 486; *Kimberly-Clark Australia Pty Ltd v Arico Trading International Pty Ltd* (1998) 42 IPR 111, 129; *Walker v Alemite Corp* (1933) 49 CLR 643, 658 (Dixon J).
205   *Streetworx Pty Ltd v Artcraft Urban Group Pty Ltd* (2014) 110 IPR 82, [393].
206   *Blueport Nominees Pty Ltd v Sewerage Management Services Pty Ltd* (2015) 251 FCR 127, [123], [127].
207   *Root Quality Pty Ltd v Root Control Technologies Pty Ltd* (2000) 49 IPR 225, 262.
208   *Caterpillar Inc v John Deere Ltd* (1999) 48 IPR 1.
209   *Windsurfing International Inc v Petit* [1984] 2 NSWLR 196, 207.
210   For example, *Damorgold Pty Ltd v JAI Products Pty Ltd* (2014) 105 IPR 60 and the cases cited above at n 203.
211   *Apotex Pty Ltd v Les Laboratoires Servier (No 4)* (2010) 89 IPR 274, [31]–[32]; *Roadshow Films Pty Ltd v iiNet Ltd* (2011) 194 FCR 285, [24]–[34].
212   *Adelaide City Corporation v Australasian Performing Right Association Ltd* (1928) 40 CLR 481, 504.
213   *Australasian Performing Right Association Ltd v Metro on George Pty Ltd* (2004) 61 IPR 575, [18], citing *Australian Tape Manufacturers Association Ltd v Commonwealth* (1993) 176 CLR 480, 497–8.
214   *Adelaide City Corporation v Australasian Performing Right Association Ltd* (1928) 40 CLR 481, 497.
215   *Streetworx Pty Ltd v Artcraft Urban Group Pty Ltd* (2014) 110 IPR 82, [392].
216   *Morton-Norwich Products Inc v Intercen Ltd* [1978] RPC 501, 515–16; *Rotocrop International Ltd v Genbourne Ltd* [1982] FSR 241, 258–60; *Ryan v Lum* (1989) 16 NSWLR 518, 522; *BEST Australia Ltd v Aquagas Marketing Pty Ltd* (1988) 83 ALR 217, 220; *CBS Songs Ltd v Amstrad Consumer Electronics plc* [1988] AC 1013.
217   *Molnlycke AB v Procter & Gamble Ltd (No 4)* [1992] 1 WLR 1112, 1118–19; *Unilever plc v Gillette (UK) Ltd* [1989] RPC 583, 609–10; *Murex Diagnostics Australia Pty Ltd v Chiron Corp* (1995) 55 FCR 194, 206–9; *Caterpillar Inc v John Deere Ltd* (1999) 48 IPR 1, 9–10; *Rotocrop International Ltd v Genbourne Ltd*

tortious accessorial liability for infringement combined with its limitations were catalysts for enacting statutory liability for contributory infringement under s 117. Some brief outline of the common law doctrines that impose a high threshold for liability provides useful background to the discussion below of s 117.

Liability as a joint tortfeasor at common law requires personal direction of the acts that constitute infringement, so that the principal thereby makes 'himself a party to the act of infringement'.[218] The common design to infringe a patent may be between a supplier of goods and a consumer.[219] However, the more common scenario is that of the person who is found liable as a joint tortfeasor for acts committed by the company of which they are a director. The law is complex and unresolved.[220] Three principal tests for liability that are discussed in the cases are that the director:

- has directed or procured the infringing acts of the company;[221]
- 'was so personally involved in the commission of the unlawful act that it is just that he should be rendered liable';[222] or
- 'deliberately, wilfully or knowingly pursue[d] a course of conduct that was likely to constitute infringement or that reflected indifference to the risk of infringement'.[223]

One thing is clear: there is no necessary mental element for patent infringement, so a director does not have to know or have reason to know that the relevant acts constituted infringement of another party's patent.[224]

Liability at common law may arise also where the person induces, incites or procures another to infringe. This must go beyond mere facilitation of the doing of the act. The essence of the authorities is that there must be 'a procuring in the sense of persuading a party to commit the tort of infringing the patent'.[225] This may apply in some circumstances where a person

---

[1982] FSR 241, 259; *Ramset Fasteners (Australia) Pty Ltd v Advanced Building Systems Pty Ltd* (1999) 44 IPR 481, 497–8.

218   *Walker v Alemite Corp* (1933) 49 CLR 643, 658 (Dixon J); *Martin Engineering Co v Nicaro Holdings Pty Ltd* (1991) 20 IPR 241, 242; *CBS Songs Ltd v Amstrad Consumer Electronics plc* [1988] AC 1013, applied (1988) 11 IPR 1. See also A. L. Monotti, 'Liability for joint infringement of a method patent under Australian law' (2013) 35 *European Intellectual Property Review* 16; J. E. Liddicoat, 'Divided performance of patented methods in Australia: A call to codify procured infringement' (2018) 41(1) *University of New South Wales Law Journal* 252.

219   *Rotocrop International Ltd v Genbourne Ltd* [1982] FSR 241, 259–60; *Innes v Short & Beal* (1898) 15 RPC 449; *Damorgold Pty Ltd v JAI Products Pty Ltd* (2014) 105 IPR 60.

220   *Keller v LED Technologies Pty Ltd* (2010) 185 FCR 449; *Allen Manufacturing Co Pty Ltd v McCallum & Co Pty Ltd* (2001) 53 IPR 400. See also C. Wood, 'Liability of directors as joint tortfeasors in intellectual property matters' (2010) 21 *Australian Intellectual Property Journal* 164.

221   *Inverness Medical Switzerland GmbH v MDS Diagnostics Pty Ltd* (2010) 85 IPR 525; *Performing Right Society Ltd v Ciryl Theatrical Syndicate Ltd* [1924] 1 KB 1 (performing right society); *Microsoft Corp v Auschina Polaris Pty Ltd* (1996) 71 FCR 231, 246.

222   *Root Quality Pty Ltd v Root Control Technologies Pty Ltd* (2000) 49 IPR 225, [146] (Root Quality test).

223   *Mentmore Manufacturing Co Ltd v National Merchandising Manufacturing Co Inc* (1978) 89 DLR (3d) 195 (the Mentmore test).

224   *Allen Manufacturing Co Pty Ltd v McCallum & Co Pty Ltd* (2001) 53 IPR 400, [43]; *Inverness Medical Switzerland GmbH v MDS Diagnostics Pty Ltd* (2010) 85 IPR 525, [182].

225   *CCOM Pty Ltd v Jiejing Pty Ltd* (1993) 27 IPR 577, 626; *Dow Chemical AG v Spence Bryson & Co Ltd* [1982] FSR 397, 404; *Kalman v Packaging (UK) Ltd* [1982] FSR 406, 423–4.

supplies an unpatented product with instructions for use.[226] This might arise where there is no other use to which the components, or kit, as supplied, can be used or where the supplier provides comprehensive assembly instructions.[227] A remedy is available 'at least in circumstances where the whole of the relevant assembly is sold at the one time, albeit in parts'.[228] Hence, merely supplying materials with knowledge that the proposed use will infringe the patent does not amount to procurement.[229]

The provisions of the *Patents Act 1990* (Cth) have not excluded the possibility of liability as a joint tortfeasor or for procuring or inciting infringement.[230] However, it is likely that acts that satisfy these common law doctrines will come within the concept of authorisation in s 13(1) or s 117 that 'necessarily travels beyond the range of tortious accessory liability for infringement'[231] to encompass acts of contributory infringement.

12.6 Contributory infringement

12.6.1 Introduction

The doctrine of contributory infringement gives rights to the patentee to seek remedies from a person who does not infringe the patent directly, but who supplies another with the means to infringe the patent. The common cases in which a patentee may seek redress for contributory infringement of the patent include the supply of an unpatented component of a combination patent[232] and the supply of an unpatented product for use in a patented process.[233] In the latter case, the supplier will commonly attach instructions for performing the patented process.[234] Prior to the *Patents Act 1990* (Cth), the exclusive rights of the patentee did not extend to prevent such behaviour even though the 'infringer' sold materials for the purpose of infringing a patent and knew that the purchaser intended to use the product in a way that constitutes a

---

226 See *CCOM Pty Ltd v Jiejing Pty Ltd* (1993) 27 IPR 557, 627 (Cooper J) for a discussion of the relevant authorities; *Firth Industries Ltd v Polyglas Engineering Pty Ltd* (1975) 132 CLR 489, 497 (Stephen J); *Ryan v Lum* (1989) 16 NSWLR 518, 522; *Damorgold Pty Ltd v JAI Products Pty Ltd* (2014) 105 IPR 60. See below at 12.6 for a discussion of contributory infringement.
227 *Great Western Corp Pty Ltd v Grove Hill Pty Ltd* [2001] FCA 423, [30]; *Grove Hill Pty Ltd v Great Western Corp Pty Ltd* (2002) 55 IPR 257, [334]; *Windsurfing International Inc v Petit* [1984] 2 NSWLR 196; *Rotocrop International Ltd v Genbourne Ltd* [1982] FSR 241, 259–60; *Damorgold Pty Ltd v JAI Products Pty Ltd* (2014) 105 IPR 60.
228 *Grove Hill Pty Ltd v Great Western Corp Pty Ltd* (2002) 55 IPR 257, 341 (Gyles J).
229 *BEST Australia Ltd v Aquagas Marketing Pty Ltd* (1988) 83 ALR 217, 220; *Belegging-en-Exploitatiemaatschappij Lavender BV v Witten Industrial Diamonds Ltd* [1979] FSR 59, 65 (Buckley LJ).
230 *Bristol-Myers Squibb Co v FH Faulding & Co Ltd* (1998) 41 IPR 467, 489; *Bristol-Myers Squibb Co v FH Faulding & Co Ltd* (2000) 97 FCR 524, 559.
231 *Collins v Northern Territory* (2007) 161 FCR 549, [30] (French J).
232 For example, *Townsend v Haworth* (1875) 12 Ch D 831; (1879) 48 LJ Ch 770; *Dunlop Pneumatic Tyre Co Ltd v David Moseley & Sons Ltd* [1904] 1 Ch 612; *Walker v Alemite Corp* (1933) 49 CLR 643; *Windsurfing International Inc v Petit* [1984] 2 NSWLR 196.
233 For example, *Innes v Short & Beal* (1898) 15 RPC 449; *Firth Industries Ltd v Polyglas Engineering Pty Ltd* (1975) 132 CLR 489; *Rotocrop International Ltd v Genbourne Ltd* [1982] FSR 241; *BEST Australia Ltd v Aquagas Marketing Pty Ltd* (1988) 83 ALR 217.
234 For example, *Innes v Short & Beal* (1898) 15 RPC 449; *CCOM Pty Ltd v Jiejing Pty Ltd* (1993) 27 IPR 577; *Sartas No 1 Pty Ltd v Koukourou & Partners Pty Ltd* (1994) 30 IPR 479.

direct infringement of the patent.[235] The ability to sue third parties was limited to circumstances that fell within the concepts of 'procurement' and 'common design' that are discussed in the preceding section.

In its review of Australian patent law in 1984, the Industrial Property Advisory Committee recommended that

> in general the supply of goods whose only use would infringe a patent, or which are accompanied by a positive inducement for the ultimate consumer to perform actions which would innocently or knowingly infringe a patent, should itself be an infringement of the patent.[236]

The enactment of s 117 in the *Patents Act 1990* (Cth) introduced this concept of contributory infringement into Australian patent law to 'remove an area of uncertainty under Australian patent law and harmonise it with the laws of Australia's major trading partners'.[237] The section imposes liability on the supplier that would otherwise not exist without the need to prove an actual infringement by any person to whom the product is supplied in the circumstances of s 117. The section does not require that the product supplied is actually put to an infringing use. Completion of the act of supply constitutes infringement.[238] This is in contrast with liability as a joint tortfeasor or as a person who authorises infringement, which requires proof of direct infringement.[239] Section 117 makes no reference to the exclusive rights of the patentee. Rather, s 117(1) identifies the conduct and s 117(2) prescribes the conditions in which that conduct will infringe the patent.[240]

12.6.2 'Supply' of a 'product': s 117(1)

Section 117(1) of the *Patents Act 1990* (Cth) provides:

> If the use of a product by a person would infringe a patent, the supply of that product by one person to another is an infringement of the patent by the supplier unless the supplier is the patentee or licensee of the patent.

This language has been construed as imposing liability when '"the use of [the] product" by the person to whom it is supplied "would infringe [the] patent"'.[241] Infringement is determined as a factual matter with reference to the uses specified in s 117(2). This interpretation of s 117(1) only makes sense if the phrase 'use of a product by a person would infringe a patent' is

---

235 *Townsend v Haworth* (1875) 12 Ch D 831; (1879) 48 LJ Ch 770; *Dunlop Pneumatic Tyre Co Ltd v David Moseley & Sons Ltd* [1904] 1 Ch 612; *Walker v Alemite Corp* (1933) 49 CLR 643; A. Monotti, 'Contributory infringement of a process patent under the *Patents Act 1990*: Does it exist after *Rescare*?' (1995) 6 *Australian Intellectual Property Journal* 217.
236 Industrial Property Advisory Committee (IPAC), *Patents, Innovation and Competition in Australia* (Report, 1984) rec 33.
237 Explanatory Memorandum, Patents Bill 1990 (Cth) cl 117 [170]–[171].
238 *Collins v Northern Territory* (2007) 161 FCR 549, [61] (French J); *Generic Health Pty Ltd v Otsuka Pharmaceutical Co Ltd* (2013) 296 ALR 50, [104].
239 *Ramset Fasteners (Australia) Pty Ltd v Advanced Building Systems Pty Ltd* (1999) 44 IPR 481, 494–507.
240 *Northern Territory v Collins* (2008) 235 CLR 619, [21] (Gummow ACJ and Kirby J).
241 Ibid [21] (Gummow ACJ and Kirby J), [42] (Hayne J), [128] (Crennan J).

construed to refer to the person at the end of the supply chain.[242] For instance, it is understood that the supply of a generic drug will be to wholesalers or pharmacists through whose hands such products pass on their way to consumers.[243]

The word 'supply' is defined in sch 1 of the Act to include supply and offers to supply by way of sale, exchange, lease, hire or hire purchase. This definition is not exhaustive and 'in its ordinary meaning it encompasses any means by which something is passed from one person to another'.[244] A product may be supplied without payment and without any physical delivery of that product.[245] Its purpose 'is to define a field of liability for infringement' that extends beyond those who exploit the invention or are joint tortfeasors at common law.[246] An example of 'supply' within the meaning of s 117(1) is a licence that conferred on the licensee the right to enter land and sever standing timber and take that timber away.[247]

Early Federal Court authority including *Anaesthetic Supplies Pty Ltd v Rescare Ltd*[248] limited the meaning of 'product' in s 117(1) to a patented product or the product that resulted from the process patent. However, a majority of the Full Federal Court in *Bristol-Myers Squibb Co v FH Faulding & Co Ltd*[249] expressly rejected this limited meaning and construed a supplied product to be any product.[250] On the facts in *Bristol-Myers Squibb*, s 117(1) would cover the supply by Faulding of an unpatented drug, taxol, to doctors and hospitals together with a product information guide that recommended a method of administration that would (assuming validity) infringe two petty patents owned by Bristol-Myers Squibb. The court explained that to restrict the word 'product' to one that is itself patented or that resulted from the use of a patented process would not provide a remedy for this conduct and would leave s 117 'virtually, if not completely, otiose'.[251] There is no need for s 117 to provide the patentee with a remedy for this conduct because a person who supplies a patented product or a product that results from the use of a patented process directly infringes the patentee's exclusive right to exploit the invention.[252]

The High Court in *Northern Territory v Collins*[253] considered the meaning of s 117 in the context of an unusual set of circumstances. In this case, Vincent and Maryann Collins were the

---

242 This is the approach taken in the United Kingdom. See *KCI Licensing Inc v Smith & Nephew plc* [2010] EWCA Civ 1260, [53]; *Grimme Landmaschinenfabrik GmbH & Co KG v Scott* [2010] EWCA Civ 1110, [108].
243 *AstraZeneca AB v Apotex Pty Ltd* (2014) 226 FCR 324, [441].
244 *Northern Territory v Collins* (2008) 235 CLR 619, [134] (Crennan J).
245 *Collins v Northern Territory* (2007) 161 FCR 549, [71]–[72] (French J).
246 Ibid [71] (French J).
247 *Northern Territory v Collins* (2008) 235 CLR 619, [22] (Gummow ACJ and Kirby J), [55] (Hayne J), [137] (Crennan J).
248 (1994) 50 FCR 1, 24; *Sartas No 1 Pty Ltd v Koukourou & Partners Pty Ltd* (1994) 30 IPR 479, 495 (Gummow J); *Rescare Ltd v Anaesthetic Supplies Pty Ltd* (1992) 25 IPR 119, 154 (Gummow J); *Bristol-Myers Squibb Co v FH Faulding & Co Ltd* (1998) 41 IPR 467.
249 (2000) 97 FCR 524.
250 Ibid 555–60. This was the intention expressed in Explanatory Memorandum, Patents Bill 1990 (Cth) [170]–[171]. This interpretation was followed in *Leonardis v Theta Developments Pty Ltd* (2000) 78 SASR 376; *Prejay Holdings Ltd v Commissioner of Patents* [2002] FCA 881, [24]. See Monotti, 'Contributory infringement of a process patent under the *Patents Act 1990*', above n 235.
251 *Bristol-Myers Squibb Co v FH Faulding & Co Ltd* (2000) 97 FCR 524, 557.
252 Ibid; *Patents Act 1990* (Cth) s 13(1), sch 1 (definition of 'exploit').
253 (2008) 235 CLR 619.

registered proprietors of a patent for a method of producing essential oils from a species of cypress pine trees. They sued the Northern Territory for contributory infringement under s 117 in respect of the Territory's supply of timber from those trees to Australian Cypress Oil Co Pty Ltd (ACOC) whom the Collinses claimed had used the timber to extract the oils using their patented process. The alleged supply of the timber was said to arise from the grant of a licence by the Northern Territory to ACOC to enter a pine plantation and take the trees. ACOC was not a party to the action.

The Northern Territory framed a specific question for the court: 'is the supply of an input for a patented method or process (or resulting product) capable of attracting the operation of s 117(1) of the Act?'[254] No judge found it necessary to answer this question, but this does not mean they neglected the different question that arose in *Anaesthetic Supplies v Rescare* and *Bristol-Myers Squibb v Faulding*: 'what is the meaning of the word product in s 117(1) of the Act?'. Only Crennan J specifically addressed the differences in these earlier decisions on this issue, concluding that

> a consideration of the complete definition of 'exploit' in respect of a method or process indicates that there is no reason to deny the application of s 117 to a product (including, as here, an unpatented product) supplied by the supplier, preparatory to any carrying out of the patented method by a person to whom the product is supplied. The secondary materials referred to above show that the latter type of product was the main target of the legislation. The word 'product' in s 117 is not confined to a product resulting from the use of a patented method or process.[255]

Hayne J also concluded that the word 'product' in s 117(1) 'has its ordinary meaning and is not confined to a patented product or a product that is itself the result of applying a patented method or process'.[256] The remaining judges, Gummow ACJ and Kirby J in a joint judgment, and Heydon J, made no express comment on the meaning of 'product'. However, their willingness to apply s 117 to the supply of timber that is not produced by use of the patented method demonstrates implied acceptance that the word 'product' has its normal meaning.

More specifically, Gummow ACJ and Kirby J agreed with Hayne J and with his reasons for not attempting to answer the question framed by the Northern Territory. They did not disagree with his conclusion that the word 'product' has its ordinary meaning, and their observation that 'the fundamental duty of the court is to give meaning to the legislative command according to the terms in which it has been expressed' is consistent with giving a word like 'product' its ordinary meaning. Furthermore, their elaboration on his analysis and their willingness to evaluate whether the timber was a staple commercial product for the purposes of s 117(2)(b) presupposes that the conduct identified in s 117(1) is satisfied in the circumstances of the case. They expressly agreed with Hayne J that there 'was a "supply" of the timber within the meaning of s 117(1) of the Act'.[257] Although not stating the point expressly, the clear implication is that they accepted that the timber is a 'product' for the purposes of s 117(1). Heydon J agreed with Crennan J that the Northern Territory is protected by s 117(2)(b) and

---

254   Ibid [13].
255   Ibid [127].
256   Ibid [34].
257   Ibid [21]–[22].

with the reasons she gave for that conclusion.[258] While not directly agreeing with the above passage from her judgment, Heydon J suggested that s 117(2) (b) becomes relevant only when the conduct identified in s 117(1) is satisfied.

There has been no revival of the reasoning in *Anaesthetic Supplies* following *Northern Territory v Collins* and the question 'what is the meaning of the word product in s 117(1) of the Act?' no longer appears in later decisions that involve s 117 considerations.[259] When the infringement is alleged to arise from the supply of a generic pharmaceutical containing an active ingredient that has a variety of uses, Yates J decided that the 'product' for the purposes of s 117(1) is not the ingredient but the generic product whose only permitted use in Australia would not infringe the patented process.[260]

12.6.3 Infringing uses: s 117(2)

The use of a product by the person supplied with the product must be an infringing use, but only those infringing uses set out in s 117(2) will come within s 117 of the *Patents Act 1990* (Cth). These are the following:

(a) if the product is capable of only one reasonable use, having regard to its nature or design – that use; or
(b) if the product is not a staple commercial product – any use of the product, if the supplier had reason to believe that the person would put it to that use; or
(c) in any case – the use of the product in accordance with any instructions for the use of the product, or any inducement to use the product, given to the person by the supplier or contained in an advertisement published by or with the authority of the supplier.[261]

12.6.3.1 Section 117(2)(a)

Although the court refused a remedy under s 117 in *Anaesthetic Supplies Pty Ltd v Rescare Ltd*[262] due to the narrow interpretation of s 117(1), the facts of this case provide an example of circumstances in which a product is capable of only one reasonable use for the purposes of s 117(2)(a). The patent involved an invention for both an apparatus for administering continuous positive airways pressure via a face mask to treat obstructive sleep apnoea (product), and for the use of that apparatus in providing that treatment (process). As the face mask could have only one reasonable use – namely, the administration of continuous airways pressure – its unauthorised supply would amount to infringement of the process claims if the case were argued now. As the mask was itself the subject of the patent, its supply would also constitute a

---

258 Ibid [57].
259 *AstraZeneca AB v Apotex Pty Ltd* (2014) 226 FCR 324; *Generic Health Pty Ltd v Otsuka Pharmaceutical Co Ltd* (2013) 296 ALR 50; *Warner-Lambert Co LLC v Apotex Pty Ltd* (2014) 311 ALR 632; *Apotex Pty Ltd v Sanofi-Aventis Australia Pty Ltd* (2013) 253 CLR 284. See also *Fei Yu (t/as Jewels 4 Pools) v Beadcrete Pty Ltd* (2014) 107 IPR 516 (supply of glass beads for use as render on pools).
260 *Otsuka Pharmaceutical Co Ltd v Generic Health Pty Ltd (No 4)* (2015) 113 IPR 191, [188].
261 *Datadot Technology Ltd v Alpha Microtech Pty Ltd* (2003) 59 IPR 402, 406.
262 (1994) 50 FCR1.

direct infringement of the product claims. Infringement of the product claims does not require resort to s 117 when the patented product is supplied as a single assembled product.

12.6.3.2 Section 117(2)(b)

12.6.3.2.1 NOT A STAPLE COMMERCIAL PRODUCT

The requirement under s 117(2)(b) that the product is not a staple commercial product operates to limit liability for contributory infringement. The *Patents Act 1990* (Cth) contains no definition of 'staple commercial product'. The term would clearly cover common commercial raw material products, such as sugar, flour and salt. However, the concept is necessarily a question of fact[263] whose precise scope is likely to remain unclear. The following passage highlights why this might be the case:

> Too narrow an approach to the definition of product classes is likely to engender uncertainty in legitimate commercial markets about the scope of the patentee's protection. On the other hand too wide an approach could deprive the patentee of protection well within the language and policy of the statute. As with so many areas of legal taxonomy the boundaries to be drawn in product class definition will involve matters of evaluative judgment having regard to the legislative purpose.[264]

The statutory question is whether there is a 'staple commercial product'. The High Court provided some guidance as to the meaning of this phrase in *Northern Territory v Collins* in the reasoning that supported its decision that the timber supplied under licence by the Northern Territory to ACOC was a 'staple commercial product'. All members of the court adopted a liberal approach that is in line with that which applies in both the United Kingdom and the United States.[265] According to Crennan J, the phrase means 'a product supplied commercially for various uses'. She rejected any suggestion that the phrase mandated an inquiry as to whether there is 'an established wholesale or retail market'[266] or whether the product is 'generally available'.[267] Her conclusion that the timber was a staple commercial product arose from her broad classification of the timber as 'a naturally occurring raw material whether deliberately cultivated or not' being a species of timber that constituted 'a basic product commonly used for various purposes'. Apart from the licence agreement with ACOC, the timber was supplied 'on commercial terms to various licensees for a variety of non-infringing uses'.[268] While Hayne J agreed that there is no mandate to find the market, he doubted that a product could be a staple commercial product if there were not some market for its sale for various uses. His Honour observed that the phrase means 'an article of commerce

---

263 *AstraZeneca AB v Apotex Pty Ltd* (2014) 226 FCR 324, [430]. See, for example, *Theta Developments Pty Ltd v Leonardis* (2002) 59 IPR 368, 388 (a manufactured bottom cover spacer supplied for use in the construction industry is a staple commercial product).
264 *Collins v Northern Territory* (2007) 161 FCR 549, [70] (French J).
265 The term appears in s 60(3) of the *Patents Act 1977* (UK) but is also undefined. In 35 USC 271(c) a similar provision refers to 'and not a staple article or commodity of commerce'. See, for example, *Polysius Corp v Fuller Co*, 709 F Supp 560, 576 (ED Pa, 1989) (a non-staple article is 'one which was designed to carry out the patented process and has little or no utility outside of that process').
266 Compare *Collins v Northern Territory* (2007) 161 FCR 549, [156] (Branson and Sunberg JJ).
267 *Northern Territory v Collins* (2008) 235 CLR 619, [145] (Crennan J, Heydon J agreeing), [41] (Hayne J).
268 Ibid [141], [143]–[145] (Heydon J agreeing); *AstraZeneca AB v Apotex Pty Ltd* (2014) 226 FCR 324, [429].

that not only *can be used* in a variety of ways but also is *traded for use* in various ways'.[269] The judgment of Gummow ACJ and Kirby J appears to approve the observation of French J (as he then was) in the appealed decision of it being 'a product of the kind commonly available in trade or commerce and having more than one reasonable use'.[270]

The supply of generic versions of out-of-patent pharmaceutical compounds has triggered litigation in the area of contributory infringement under s 117 when the use of the generic product would infringe a patent claiming a new therapeutic use of the compound. Section 117(2)(a) cannot apply when there is more than one reasonable use of the compound. Section 117(2)(b) can apply only if the relevant pharmaceutical compound is classified as a staple commercial product.[271] Some further guidance in making this assessment appears in *AstraZeneca AB v Apotex Pty Ltd*.[272] An enlarged Full Federal Court rejected the argument that a compound known as rosuvastatin was a staple commercial product. The fact that a compound may be used for both infringing and non-infringing purposes is not conclusive: it is important to ask how widely the compound is used and for what range of purposes. In this case, the range of the possible uses was limited to prevention and treatment of cardiovascular disease and its associated risk factors. Despite evidence that rosuvastatin was prescribed for treatment of a number of other conditions, such as chronic renal disease and diabetes, such prescription would still be associated with treating or preventing cardiovascular disease in situations where the existence of these conditions imposed increased risk of it occurring.[273] The court was satisfied that rosuvastatin could not be 'characterised as either raw materials or basic products commonly used for a variety of purposes'.[274]

12.6.3.2.2 SUPPLIER HAD REASON TO BELIEVE THE PERSON WOULD PUT IT TO THAT USE

One difficulty facing patentees that s 117 was designed to ameliorate was the inability to identify consumers at the end of the supply chain who engage in an infringing use of products supplied to them by others.[275] Section 117 of the *Patents Act 1990* (Cth) does not require the patentee to identify any particular person or persons who the supplier has reason to believe will use the product in an infringing manner.[276] The determination of whether the supplier had reason to believe that some consumers[277] would engage in an infringing use of the product supplied is primarily a question of fact that requires proof on the balance of probabilities. This may be subjective (an actual belief) or objective (there are reasonable grounds to

---

269 Ibid [141] (emphasis in original).
270 *Collins v Northern Territory* (2007) 161 FCR 549, [70] (French J).
271 *AstraZeneca AB v Apotex Pty Ltd* (2014) 226 FCR 324, [431]; *Otsuka Pharmaceutical Co Ltd v Generic Health Pty Ltd* (2012) 291 ALR 763, [90]–[93] (prima facie case that Generic Health products are not staple commercial products). There is no suggestion that compounds supplied are a staple commercial product: *Warner-Lambert Co LLC v Apotex Pty Ltd* (2014) 311 ALR 632, [27]; *Generic Health Pty Ltd v Otsuka Pharmaceutical Co Ltd* (2013) 296 ALR 50, [2].
272 (2014) 226 FCR 324.
273 Ibid [431].
274 Ibid. See also *Otsuka Pharmaceutical Co Ltd v Generic Health Pty Ltd (No 4)* (2015) 113 IPR 191, [118]–[191].
275 IPAC, *Patents, Innovation and Competition in Australia*, above n 236, para 14.2.
276 *AstraZeneca AB v Apotex Pty Ltd* (2014) 226 FCR 324, [433].
277 Ibid [439].

believe).[278] Mere risk that this might occur is insufficient.[279] Bennett J observed in *Generic Health Pty Ltd v Otsuka Pharmaceutical Co Ltd*[280] that there must be a reasonable belief of a significant likelihood that infringing use *would* happen, and clearly the section would not apply where there is 'unlikely, freak or maverick use'. It is not sufficient that the supplier had reason to believe that a person *might* put the product to the infringing use.[281] Although instructions from the supplier at the time of supply as to an infringing use of the product make it easier to establish that there is a reason to believe that the person would put it to that use, this is not necessary for the purposes of s 117(2)(b). Such circumstances fall within s 117(2)(c).

Particular difficulties arise under s 117(2)(b) for a manufacturer or supplier of a generic version of an out-of-patent pharmaceutical compound when a method patent for a new therapeutic use for that compound remains in force. Even though the generic product is registered on the Australian Register of Therapeutic Goods for a specific non-infringing use, its supply or proposed supply can trigger an action for infringement under s 117(2)(b) when the product is not a 'staple commercial product' and when the supplier 'has reason to believe' that the person supplied would put it to an infringing use. In this type of case, the objective assessment under s 117(2)(b) must include reference to the specific registration of the product under the *Therapeutic Goods Act 1989* (Cth).[282] The Act provides that a product information form must accompany an application for registration.[283] This must include statements that indicate the treatments for which the drug is to be used.

The significance of the product information statement appears from the facts in *Apotex Pty Ltd v Sanofi-Aventis Australia Pty Ltd*.[284] A patent for the pharmaceutical compound leflunomide had expired but a current method patent covered its use in treating a skin condition known as psoriasis. Apotex applied successfully for registration of its generic leflunomide product known as Apo-Leflunomide in the Register for the treatment of rheumatoid arthritis and psoriatic arthritis. It stated in its approved product information document that the drug was indicated for the treatment of those two conditions but was 'not indicated for the treatment of psoriasis that is not associated with manifestations of arthritic disease'. Therefore, Apo-Leflunomide was not registered for use in treating psoriasis. In light of the express exclusionary statements in the approved product information, and in the absence of other evidence, the High Court determined as a question of fact that it could not be inferred that Apotex 'had reason to believe that the unpatented pharmaceutical substance, which it proposes to supply, would be used by recipients in accordance with the patented method'.[285]

These pharmaceutical cases expose a particular problem with the application of s 117(2)(b) where the product is supplied

---

278   *Generic Health Pty Ltd v Otsuka Pharmaceutical Co Ltd* (2013) 296 ALR 50, [34] (Emmett J), [103] (Bennett J), [135] (Greenwood J); *Collins v Northern Territory* (2007) 161 FCR 549, [66] (French J).
279   *AstraZeneca AB v Apotex Pty Ltd* (2014) 226 FCR 324, [432]–[433]; *Apotex Pty Ltd v AstraZeneca AB (No 4)* (2013) 100 IPR 285, [512].
280   (2013) 296 ALR 50.
281   Ibid [105]–[106].
282   *Apotex Pty Ltd v Sanofi-Aventis Australia Pty Ltd* (2013) 253 CLR 284, [296]–[298] (Crennan and Keifel JJ, Gageler J concurring).
283   *Therapeutic Goods Act 1989* (Cth) s 23(2)(ba).
284   (2013) 253 CLR 284.
285   Ibid [304]; *Generic Health Pty Ltd v Otsuka Pharmaceutical Co Ltd* (2013) 296 ALR 50, [105].

in large quantities for use by a large number of consumers where the first supplier in the relevant supply chain has reason to believe that some, but not all, of the consumers to whom the product might ultimately be supplied will put it to an infringing use.[286]

It seems that this problem can be resolved by courts using the flexibility that is inherent in designing the scope of injunctive relief. The Full Federal Court in *AstraZeneca AB v Apotex Pty Ltd* observed that if s 117(1) is engaged in such circumstances, then 'some consideration of proportionality as between the extent of the infringing use that is forecast and the scope of any injunctive relief is warranted'.[287] The court concluded:

> It seems to us that, all other things being equal, the more difficult it is for the patentee to establish that there is a likelihood of widespread infringing use, the more difficult it should be for the patentee to obtain injunctive relief in the broad terms restraining *any* supply of the relevant product.[288]

12.6.3.3 Section 117(2)(c)

Under s 117(2)(c) of the *Patents Act 1990* (Cth), the reference in s 117(1) to the use of a product by a person is a reference to the use of a product in accordance with any instructions for the use of the product given to the person by the supplier or contained in an advertisement published by or with the authority of the supplier. *Bristol-Myers Squibb Co v FH Faulding & Co Ltd*[289] provides an example of how s 117(2)(c)[290] may apply to contributory infringement of a process patent. Faulding sold and supplied the drug taxol to doctors and hospitals with product information that included directions for use in the treatment of patients suffering from cancer. The use of taxol by a medical practitioner in accordance with those instructions would infringe the patents. The Full Federal Court gave effect to that intention by making it clear that the 'product' referred to in s 117(1) can be any product that is supplied for an infringing use. The court decided on the facts that, assuming that the patent was valid, the supply of taxol in these circumstances constituted contributory infringement of the patent within s 117(2)(c).[291]

Hence, if the patent is for a product, both the product's use and its supply involve direct infringements. If the patent is for a process, the supply of a patented product for use in that process would again involve direct infringement of the product patent. Section 117 is not concerned with this direct infringement but with imposing liability on the supplier for providing the means to infringe the process patent. That means infringement may involve the supply

---

286 *AstraZeneca AB v Apotex Pty Ltd* (2014) 226 FCR 324, [443]. Compare *Mylan Health Pty Ltd (formerly BGP Products Pty Ltd) v Sun Pharma ANZ Pty Ltd (formerly Ranbaxy Australia Pty Ltd)* (2019) 138 IPR 402, [118].
287 *AstraZeneca AB v Apotex Pty Ltd* (2014) 226 FCR 324, [443].
288 Ibid [444].
289 (2000) 97 FCR 524.
290 *Datadot Technology Ltd v Alpha Microtech Pty Ltd* (2003) 59 IPR 402, 406 (innovation patent).
291 See also *Fei Yu v Beadcrete Pty Ltd* (2014) 107 IPR 516, [82]–[85]; *Product Management Group Pty Ltd v Blue Gentian LLC* (2015) 240 FCR 85, [128]–[133]. But in *Apotex Pty Ltd v Sanofi-Aventis Australia Pty Ltd* (2013) 253 CLR 284, [302]–[303], the High Court found no evidence of instructions that would engage s 117(2)(c).

of a patented product,[292] an unpatented product[293] or a product resulting from the use of patented process.[294] It is important not to confuse the issue of direct infringement with the operation of s 117.[295]

12.6.4 Infringement of a product patent by supply of component parts

Section 117(1) of the *Patents Act 1990* (Cth) refers to the 'use of a product' and supply of 'that product'. This raises the issue of the application of s 117 to a product patent. Clearly, the supply of a single or assembled product that infringes the claims in a patent is a direct infringement[296] but it also falls technically within the language of s 117.[297] At common law, a remedy is likely for the supply of a patented product as a kit of parts that the purchaser assembles in accordance with instructions.[298]

The supplier will escape liability at common law for supplying a part of a patented combination unless the supplier does this in furtherance of a common design with the consumer (joint tortfeasors) or as a secondary infringer who has aided, abetted, counselled or procured a purchaser to infringe the patent.[299]

There is little authority that considers the application of s 117 to the supply of a product that is used to infringe a product patent. In *Great Western Corp Pty Ltd v Grove Hill Pty Ltd*,[300] Kiefel J supported the application of s 117 to the supply of a component part of a patented product where all the necessary parts were provided. On appeal, Gyles J commented by way of obiter that he found it 'difficult to understand how [s 117] has anything to do with infringement of a product claim by commercial supply of an article'.[301]

Despite this expressed reservation, it is consistent with the rationales for the introduction of s 117 to apply its provisions to the supply of a component part of a patented product. A recent example where this arose concerned the application of s 117(2)(c) to a product claim for a structure having a reflective surface finish that comprised a 'plurality of glass beads and a cementious material providing the matrix for said glass beads'.[302] The respondent supplied only part of the claimed product – glass beads – with instructions to add the missing integer. The part is the 'product' for the purposes of s 117(1). A consumer who uses that part without authorisation to make the product would infringe the exclusive right of the patentee to make

---

292 *Anaesthetic Supplies Pty Ltd v Rescare Ltd* (1994) 50 FCR 1.
293 *Bristol-Myers Squibb Co v FH Faulding & Co Ltd* (2000) 97 FCR 524.
294 *Northern Territory v Collins* (2008) 235 CLR 619, [127] (Crennan J).
295 *Welcome Real-Time SA v Catuity Inc (No 2)* (2001) AIPC 91-736, [39,780]; *Prejay Holdings Ltd v Commissioner of Patents* [2002] FCA 881.
296 See above at 12.5.
297 Compare *Grove Hill Pty Ltd v Great Western Corp Pty Ltd* (2002) 55 IPR 257, [336] (Giles J).
298 *Windsurfing International Inc v Petit* [1984] 2 NSWLR 196; *Rotocrop International Ltd v Genbourne Ltd* [1982] FSR 241, 259–60; *Great Western Corp Pty Ltd v Grove Hill Pty Ltd* [2001] FCA 423, [30]; *Grove Hill Pty Ltd v Great Western Corp Pty Ltd* (2002) 55 IPR 257, 341.
299 See the discussion above at 12.5.7.
300 [2001] FCA 423.
301 *Grove Hill Pty Ltd v Great Western Corp Pty Ltd* (2002) 55 IPR 257, 341.
302 *Fei Yu v Beadcrete Pty Ltd* (2014) 107 IPR 516. See also *Blue Gentian LLC v Product Management Group Pty Ltd* (2014) 110 IPR 453, [208]–[210].

the product. Section 117 should apply if the infringing use satisfies one of the subparagraphs of s 117(2). It seems that supply of a component part that is capable of only being used to make the patented product will infringe, as will supply of a component part when the supplier has given the consumer instructions for use of the product, or any inducement to use the product in a way that infringes the patent, either directly or by means of published advertisement. Furthermore, if the component part is 'not a staple commercial product', its supply may also be an infringement if the supplier had reason to believe that the consumer would use it in an infringing way.

A further issue arises when a person supplies an entire product, such as a machine, which does not infringe a patent because it is missing an essential integer. However, a purchaser can readily remove or replace a part to make it fall within the claims of a patented product. This behaviour would amount to contributory infringement in the United Kingdom under s 60(2) of the *Patents Act 1977*.[303] It can be argued following the above reasoning that it may also amount to contributory infringement in Australia when the relevant use falls within one of the categories listed in s 117(2).

12.7 Misleading and deceptive conduct

Apart from infringement of the patent under the *Patents Act 1990* (Cth), a patentee may contravene s 18 of sch 2 of the *Competition and Consumer Act 2010* (Cth)[304] if it has engaged in conduct that was misleading or deceptive or likely to mislead or deceive. For example, a failure to warn customers that use of equipment in a particular way might constitute infringement of a patent may contravene s 18.[305]

12.8 Defences to infringement

Infringement requires that:

- the 'invention' falls within the scope of the claims of the patentee;
- the act falls within the scope of the patentee's exclusive rights;
- the act does not have the benefit of an express or implied exemption to infringement.[306]

Article 30 of the *Agreement on Trade-Related Aspects of Intellectual Property*[307] enables members to provide limited exceptions to the exclusive rights conferred by a patent provided that three conditions are met. The exceptions: (1) must not unreasonably conflict with a normal

---

303 *Grimme Landmaschinenfabrik GmbH & Co KG v Scott* [2010] EWCA Civ 1110; *KCI Licensing Inc v Smith & Nephew plc* [2010] EWCA Civ 1260.
304 Formerly *Trade Practices Act 1974* (Cth) s 52.
305 *Advanced Building Systems Pty Ltd v Ramset Fasteners (Australia) Pty Ltd* (1995) AIPC 91-129, [39,201].
306 Examples of some exemptions are found in *Patents Act 1990* (Cth) ss 118 (use in or on foreign vessels, aircraft or vehicles), 119 (prior use), 119B (regulatory approvals) and 119C (acts for experimental purposes).
307 *Marrakesh Agreement Establishing the World Trade Organization*, opened for signature 15 April 1994, 1867 UNTS 3 (entered into force 1 January 1995) annex 1C.

exploitation of the patent, (2) must not unreasonably prejudice the legitimate interests of the patent owner and (3) must take account of the legitimate interests of third parties.

The *Patents Act 1990* (Cth) provides express exceptions from infringement for prior use of an invention under s 119 and use in or on foreign vessels, aircraft or vehicles under s 118. Certain acts that are performed for the purposes of obtaining regulatory approval of pharmaceuticals are exempted from infringement by s 119A, which was introduced by the *Intellectual Property Laws Amendment Act 2006* (Cth).[308] Often referred to as 'springboarding of patents for pharmaceuticals', the amendments apply in relation to the exploitation, at or after the commencement of these provisions, of all patents in force after that time.[309]

12.8.1 Use in or on foreign vessels, aircraft or vehicles

The rights of the patentee are not infringed by using the patented invention on board a foreign vessel, in the body of the vessel, or in the machinery, tackle, apparatus and other accessories of the vessel, if that vessel comes only temporarily or accidentally into the patent area and the invention is used exclusively for the needs of the vessel.[310] A similar defence from infringement applies to use of an invention in the construction or working of a foreign aircraft or foreign land vehicle, or in the accessories of the aircraft or vehicle if the aircraft or foreign land vehicle comes only temporarily or accidentally into the patent area.[311]

These provisions are derived originally from art 5*ter* of the 1925 revision of the *Paris Convention for the Protection of Industrial Property (Paris Convention)*,[312] the purpose of which 'was to prevent national patents impinging upon foreign vessels coming into and out of territorial waters temporarily and also permanently if the cause was accidental'.[313] Although no Australian court has considered these provisions, 'temporarily' has been construed by the England and Wales Court of Appeal in the context of a similar provision in s 60(5)(d) of the *Patents Act 1977* (UK) to mean 'transient' or for a 'limited purpose'.[314] The court considered that the meaning of 'temporarily' had nothing to do with the frequency of visits so that the defence was available for use of the patented invention in a ferry that sailed regularly between Dublin in Ireland and Holyhead in Wales.[315]

12.8.2 Prior use of an invention: s 119

12.8.2.1 Overview

The patentee or a third party may use an invention before the priority date of the claim or claims. Subject to various exceptions that are available to the patentee,[316] use that makes the

---

308 *Intellectual Property Laws Amendment Act 2006* (Cth) sch 7.
309 Ibid sch 7 item 4.
310 *Patents Act 1990* (Cth) s 118(a).
311 Ibid s 118(b).
312 See *Stena Rederi AB v Irish Ferries Ltd* [2003] EWCA Civ 66, [16] for the legislative history.
313 Ibid [25].
314 Ibid [26].
315 Ibid [38].
316 *Patents Act 1990* (Cth) s 24; *Patents Regulations 1991* (Cth) regs 2.2, 2.2A–2.2D (regs 2.3 and 2.3 prior to 15 April 2013).

essential integers of the invention publicly available provides a ground for refusal to grant a patent, or in the case of a granted patent, a ground for its revocation.[317] There are different possible repercussions when the prior use is secret. The *Patents Act 1952* (Cth) provided that prior secret use, by either the patentee or a third party, was a ground for revocation of the patent.[318]

The *Patents Act 1990* (Cth) adopted a different policy approach and distinguished between prior secret use of the patentee and that of a third party. Prior secret use by or on behalf of the patentee is a ground for opposition and revocation of a patent.[319] On the other hand, prior secret use by a third party no longer provides grounds to revoke the patent. Instead, the *Patents Act 1990* introduced in s 119 the concept of a prior user right that may benefit third-party prior users.[320] The *Paris Convention* reserves to the domestic legislation of each contracting state the right to make provision for prior user rights.[321] A prior user right recognises some limitation on the patentee's rights as patentee. The nature of the right is independent of the patent and its existence stems only from a third party's use of the invention before the priority date of the claim or claims. The prior user right permits a would-be infringer who commenced an infringing activity before the priority date of a patent to continue to use the invention in specified ways without infringement. There are a number of justifications for granting a prior user right to a third party. First, the prior user will have expended its own capital in research and development on the invention without learning anything from the patentee.[322] The prior user right therefore prevents wasteful destruction of this existing investment. Second, the right protects the domestic manufacturing industry. It protects 'the person who has invested, put the product on the market, and provided good to the public by doing so'.[323] Third, a prior user right offers some measure of protection to the independent inventor while retaining the pre-eminent position of the patentee. Finally, the existence of prior user rights encourages the parties to negotiate mutually advantageous licensing agreements without the need to resort to litigation.

Schedule 6 of the *Intellectual Property Laws Amendment Act 2006* (Cth) repealed the former s 119 and substituted a new section that applies in relation to patents granted as a result of applications filed on or after commencement of the Schedule.[324] The former s 119 continues to apply to patents granted as a result of earlier applications. The principal differences are the following. Prior to its repeal, s 119 contained no geographical limitation, which suggested that acts anywhere in the world would trigger prior user rights. Also, the nature of the prior user right was much more limited than the current exemption that is described below. If a person

---

317 *Patents Act 1990* (Cth) ss 7(1), 18, 45(1)(b), 59(b), 138(3)(b), sch 1; *Nicaro Holdings Pty Ltd v Martin Engineering Co* (1990) 16 IPR 545.
318 *Patents Act 1952* (Cth) s 100(1)(l); S. Ricketson, *The Law of Intellectual Property* (Sydney: Law Book Company, 1984) 942–3.
319 *Patents Act 1990* (Cth) ss 9, 18(1)(d), 59, 138(3)(b).
320 For an analysis of prior user rights, see A. L. Monotti, 'Balancing the rights of the patentee and prior user of an invention: The Australian experience' [1997] 19 *European Intellectual Property Review* 351.
321 *Paris Convention* art 4(B).
322 See Franklin Pierce Law Centre, Fourth Biennial Patent System 'Prior User Rights' Panel discussion (1994) 34/DEA 117, 118–21 (Ms Strobel).
323 Ibid 414 (Mr Griswold).
324 *Intellectual Property Laws Amendment Act 2006* (Cth) sch 6 item 1 substituted the new s 119. Schedule 6 commenced on 28 September 2006.

gains the benefit of prior user rights under the former s 119, it by no means follows that they can act as though the patent did not exist.[325] The express reference in the former s 119 was to 'making a product or using a process'. This language may limit the rights of a prior secret user to these specific actions and thereby deny the third-party prior user the ability to continue other prior uses, such as sales or importation of the product or a product made using the process.[326] This narrow exemption is tantamount to extinguishing prior user rights in all but a small number of instances.

12.8.2.2 Current provision

The current s 119 provides a prior user right as an exemption from infringement where, immediately before the priority date of a claim, the person was exploiting[327] the product, method or process in the patent area or had taken definite steps (contractually or otherwise) to so exploit it. The person is not restricted to continuing to perform those acts that were performed before the priority date but can exploit the invention in any way without infringement.

It is likely that the judicial interpretation of similar provisions in the former s 119 continue to apply to the new section. Hence, if the claim relates to a product, it is not sufficient to have made part of the product alone to gain the benefit of this exemption.[328] Nor would it be sufficient to show that a person was still developing the product.[329] The concept of taking definite steps was illustrated by Heerey J in *Welcome Real-Time SA v Catuity Inc* with the following example:

> Assume a patented product consisting of components A, B and C. Immediately before the priority date an infringer: has drawings depicting the product; has actually made A; has on his premises the raw materials for component B; and has ordered the raw materials for component C. It can then be said that the infringer had taken definite steps to make that product. Conversely, it would not be sufficient that immediately before the priority date, the infringer has made A, has received the raw materials for B but is investigating whether C, D or E would be the preferable final component. And the infringer would be in no better position if, after the priority date, he in fact decided that C was preferable and then proceeded to manufacture a product consisting of A, B and C.[330]

The onus of establishing prior user rights is on the party claiming those rights.[331] The exemption from infringement does not apply if the person derived the invention from the patentee or the patentee's predecessor in title.[332] For example, a person has no exemption from infringement if information as to the subject matter of the invention was obtained from the patentee in the course of negotiations that subsequently break down. However, not all information that

---

325 *Welcome Real-Time SA v Catuity Inc* (2001) 113 FCR 110, 132.
326 Monotti, 'Balancing the rights of the patentee and prior user of an invention', above n 320.
327 This term is defined in a similar way as 'exploit' in *Patents Act 1990* (Cth) sch 1.
328 *CCOM Pty Ltd v Jiejing Pty Ltd* (1993) 27 IPR 577, 627 (Cooper J); *Welcome Real-Time SA v Catuity Inc* (2001) 113 FCR 110, 130.
329 *Welcome Real-Time SA v Catuity Inc* (2001) 113 FCR 110, 131.
330 Ibid 130.
331 Ibid.
332 *Patents Act 1990* (Cth) s 119(3).

derives from the patentee prevents the operation of the section. A person may be entitled to a prior user right when the information is made publicly available by or with the consent of the patentee in one of the prescribed circumstances mentioned in s 24(1)(a) of the *Patents Act 1990* (Cth). This may be, for example, when the person gains information about the invention by observing the patentee working it in public for the purposes of reasonable trial.[333]

Another instance where no exemption applies is if, before the relevant priority date of the claim, the person had stopped exploiting the product, method or process (except temporarily) in the patent area or had abandoned (except temporarily) the steps to exploit the product, method or process in the patent area.[334] Such an interlude may be necessary where, for example, a tested development in one aspect of a technology is put to one side, but not abandoned, while developments of other aspects are made and tested. It is not clear what is meant by 'temporarily' in this context. One interpretation is that the person must recommence the activity after a brief interlude. A broader interpretation would extend the concept to include an intention to recommence the activity. It would be a matter for the courts to determine on the facts of each case whether the requirements in s 119(2) are satisfied.[335] In contrast to the former s 119, the performance of the acts set out in s 119(1) before the priority date is now expressly limited to acts in the patent area.

There is judicial support for the proposition that s 119 'prescribes the protection to be afforded to a person who has previously used the process or product in question'.[336] It is clear that s 119 applies to prior secret activities.[337] However, the lack of any distinction between secret and public activities in the section raises the question whether the section also applies to prior public use that is sufficient to deprive an invention of novelty. The preferred position was expressed by Dowsett J in *Dyno Nobel Asia Pacific Ltd v Orica Australia Pty Ltd*:

> If such prior use were sufficient to deprive an invention of novelty, there would be little purpose in express protection of a person who has previously used it ... It is not presently necessary for me finally to determine this matter.[338]

In other words, the prior user would not be limited by the terms of s 119 and could seek revocation of the patent or counterclaim for revocation in the event that an infringement action is brought against them.[339] On this view, s 119 would only apply to specify the prior user rights that are available to the person who has used the invention in a way that does not deprive the invention of novelty.[340] The section gives prior user rights to the person who was making the product or using the product before the priority date but is silent as to whether those rights can be licensed or assigned. In the *Review of Intellectual Property Legislation under the*

---

333 *Patents Regulations 1991* (Cth) reg 2.2B (reg 2.2(d) prior to 15 April 2013).
334 *Patents Act 1990* (Cth) s 119(2). The form of s 119 prior to the *Intellectual Property Laws Amendment Act 2006* (Cth) included these concepts in s 119(4).
335 *Intellectual Property Laws Amendment Act 2006* (Cth) sch 6 item 1.
336 *Dyno Nobel Asia Pacific Ltd v Orica Australia Pty Ltd* (1999) 99 FCR 151, 214; *Welcome Real-Time SA v Catuity Inc* (2001) 113 FCR 110, 132.
337 Ibid; Monotti, 'Balancing the rights of the patentee and prior user of an invention', above n 320.
338 (1999) 99 FCR 151, 214.
339 This construction accords with the view of the European Communities in the World Trade Organization (WTO) Panel report *Canada – Patent Protection of Pharmaceutical Products: Complaint by the European Communities and Their Member States*, WTO Doc WT/DS114/R (17 March 2000) 54.
340 Compare *Welcome Real-Time SA v Catuity Inc* (2001) 113 FCR 110, 132.

Competition Principles Agreement, a majority of the Intellectual Property Competition and Review Committee considered that only the actual prior user should benefit from s 119 rights.[341] The government response concluded that assignees should have the benefit of rights, but not licensees. This is the effect of the 2006 amendment, which clarifies that a person may dispose of the whole of their entitlement under s 119(1) to another person.[342] The ability to grant licences is impliedly excluded. Furthermore, the defence under s 119 is limited to the infringer's own acts and does not cover the act of authorising another person to exploit the patent.[343]

12.8.3 Acts for obtaining regulatory approval of pharmaceuticals and non-pharmaceuticals

The subject matter of some patents requires regulatory approval prior to its exploitation. Consequently, there will be a delay in obtaining this approval before a competitor can enter the market unless the competitor can freely undertake regulatory studies on the invention prior to expiry of the patent term. The *Intellectual Property Laws Amendment Act 2006* (Cth) introduced in s 119A of the *Patents Act 1990* (Cth) an exemption from infringement for exploitation of a pharmaceutical patent solely for the purposes of obtaining the inclusion in the Australian Register of Therapeutic Goods of goods that are intended for therapeutic use and are not medical or therapeutic devices as defined in the *Therapeutic Goods Act 1989* (Cth).[344]

Regulatory approval is required for products other than pharmaceutical products, such as agricultural chemicals and certain medical devices. To recognise this anomaly, the *Raising the Bar Act* introduced an exemption from infringement in s 119B that applies to all technologies.[345]

12.8.4 Private acts

A patent grants no positive rights or positive authority to the patentee.[346] Hence, it is a mistake to analyse the rights of the patentee to exclude others as if they are absolute. However, the *Patents Act 1990* (Cth) contains no express limitation on the scope of the rights that the patentee can exercise. Therefore, if there is to be any limitation on the scope of the rights or any exemption from infringement for this type of activity, it must be found in the common law. The monopoly power with respect to inventions was granted originally as an exception to enhance trade and commerce and to overcome common law restraints. Therefore, it is more

---

341   Intellectual Property Competition and Review Committee (IPCRC), *Review of Intellectual Property Legislation under the Competition Principles Agreement* (Final Report, September 2000).
342   *Patents Act 1990* (Cth) s 119(4).
343   *Vehicle Monitoring Systems Pty Ltd v SARB Management Group Pty Ltd (No 2)* (2013) 101 IPR 496, [103].
344   *Therapeutic Goods Act 1989* (Cth) s 119A came into operation on 25 October 2006; *Alphapharm Pty Ltd v H Lundbeck A/S* (2008) 76 IPR 618, [643], [647].
345   *Intellectual Property Laws Amendment (Raising the Bar) Act 2012* (Cth) sch 2 item 1. The new section applies in relation to acts done on or after the commencement of sch 2 (15 April 2012) in relation to patents granted before, on or after that commencement.
346   *Grain Pool of Western Australia v Commonwealth* (2000) 202 CLR 479, 513–14; *National Phonograph Co of Australia Ltd v Menck* (1911) 12 CLR 15, 22; *Steers v Rogers* [1893] AC 232, 235 (Lord Herschell LC).

likely that the rights of exclusion for the patentee are limited to acts that would be 'acts injurious to the patentee'.[347] This is likely to be injurious in some broad commercial sense, such as when the activities interfere with the patentee's entitlement in trade and commerce[348] to 'enjoy the whole profit and advantage from time to time accruing by reason of the said invention'.[349]

If the common law has defined the exclusive rights of the patentee with reference in some way to the commercial purpose for which the act is performed, it is at least arguable that the performance of acts for private or non-commercial purposes would be outside the scope of the patentee's rights. Such a 'use' would not amount to 'taking advantage of the invention to advance [the user] in the marketplace'[350] and would not be acts injurious to the patentee. Hence, it is arguable that it would be outside the scope of the patentee's exclusive rights to license an invention for such use. By analogy, limitations on the exclusive rights of a patentee for non-commercial uses were thought to exist under the *Patents Act 1949* (UK), the legislation on which the *Patents Act 1952* (Cth) was modelled.[351] The *Patents Act 1977* (UK) now includes an express exemption from infringement for acts that 'are done privately and for purposes which are not commercial'.

12.8.5 Experimental and research use

Apart from acts that are performed for purely private and personal purposes, some limited acts that are performed for experimental and research purposes may also be outside the scope of the patentee's exclusive rights.[352] The difficulty is to identify the scope of such limitations. Prior to the enactment of the *Patents Act 1977* (UK), United Kingdom commentators generally assumed that certain experimentation on an invention might not infringe a patent, based on the obiter dicta of Jessel MR in *Frearson v Loe*, which is as follows:

> [N]o doubt if a man makes things merely by way of *bona fide* experiment, and not with the intention of selling and making use of the thing so made for the purpose of which a patent has been granted, but with the view of improving upon the invention the subject of the patent, or with the view of seeing whether an improvement can be made or not, that is not an invasion of the exclusive rights granted by the patent.[353]

---

347 *Minter v Williams* (1835) 4 AD & E 250, 256; 31 ER 781, 783. It is also implicit in IPCRC, *Review of Intellectual Property Legislation under the Competition Principles Agreement*, above n 341, 25.
348 *Grant v Commissioner of Patents* (2005) 67 IPR 1; *Attorney-General (Cth) v Adelaide Steamship Co Ltd* [1913] AC 781, 793.
349 These words appear in former United Kingdom patent grants and appeared originally in s 6 of the *Statute of Monopolies*.
350 *Bedford Industries Rehabilitation Association Inc v Pinefair Pty Ltd* (1998) 40 IPR 438, 450 (von Doussa J), quoted and affirmed (1998) 87 FCR 458, 469 (Mansfield J); *Monsanto Co v Stauffer Chemical Co (NZ) Ltd* [1984] FSR 559, 566 (Eichelbaum J) ('is one of advantage in a commercial sense'); *Smith Kline & French Laboratories Ltd v Attorney-General (NZ)* (1991) 22 IPR 143, 145 (Cooke P), 146 (Hardie Boys J); *Pfizer Corp v Ministry of Health* [1965] AC 512, 569 (Lord Wilberforce).
351 Blanco White, *Patents for Inventions*, above n 190, [3.204] n 65; Ricketson, *The Law of Intellectual Property*, above n 318, 985.
352 A. Monotti, 'Limitations on the scope of a patentee's exclusive rights in the context of third party experimental uses' (2006) 29 *University of New South Wales Law Journal* 63; A. Monotti, 'The Australian experimental use exemption: A current overview' (2009) 12 *Journal of World Intellectual Property* 422.
353 (1878) 9 Ch D 48, 66–7.

A variety of later decisions that refer to this exemption are consistent with the view that patents may not grant exclusive rights over all uses of the invention. Although no case provides any exemption from infringement on its own facts, each provides some insight into the limitations that apply to the exercise of the patentee's exclusive rights from the inherent nature of a patent. Some of these limitations are the following:

- the performance of acts without a view to profit, but with the view of improving on the invention the subject of the patent, or with the view of seeing whether an improvement can be made or not;[354]
- an experiment for the purpose of ascertaining the proportions or properties of the invention;[355] and
- experiments for testing an invention and inspecting the nature of the products it produces with no intention to sell the machine or the products.[356]

There is some suggestion that an educational use of an invention will infringe. However, the authority that is cited for this view does not extend to this extreme and should be treated with caution. In *United Telephone Co v Sharples*,[357] Kay J commented by way of obiter that the use of an invention for instruction of young persons who are admitted into the business to learn the business would be an infringing use. The posited uses were 'to let them use, to let them experiment with, to let them, if they please, pull in pieces'.[358] However, the facts of the case involved a business in which the defendant was using a cheaper infringing product to instruct pupils in the business. This saved the expense of using the patented telephone for the same purpose. It was the purchase of the infringing telephone that was in issue, not the use to which it was put. Although the defendant raised this instructional use within the business as a defence to infringement, Kay J did not believe that the defendants used it in this way. Therefore, any obiter as to instructional use was inevitably coloured by the particular circumstances of the case. The defendants had purchased infringing products for whatever purpose they proposed within their business. They deprived the patentee of the purchase price of the patented telephone.

The position may be different if the instruction is in an educational institution and does not involve the purchase of an infringing product for this purpose. For example, the demonstration to undergraduate students of how a patented process works involves no derivation of commercial advantage or profit and should not be a use that the patentee can restrain.

The changes made under the *Patents Act 1990* (Cth) to the definition of the exclusive rights of the patentee were made with the intention of simplifying the language used. There was no intention to restrict those rights in any way, or to remove any limitations that the previous law recognised either as binding precedent or by way of policy.[359] Hence, it is arguable that the exclusive rights to exploit are limited in the ways set out above. Although the scope of the

---

354   *Frearson v Loe* (1878) 9 Ch D 48; *Proctor v Bayley & Son* (1888) 6 RPC 106, 109.
355   *Muntz v Foster* (1844) 2 WPC 93.
356   *Molins & Molins Machine Co Ltd v Industrial Machine Co Ltd* (1936) 54 RPC 94, 108; *F Hoffmann-La Roche & Co AG v Harris Pharmaceuticals Ltd* [1977] FSR 200, 202–3.
357   (1885) 2 RPC 12.
358   Ibid 15.
359   Explanatory Memorandum, Patents Bill 1990 (Cth) cl 13 [25].

rights will remain the subject of debate,[360] there is some degree of consensus among the Australian Law Reform Commission and the Advisory Council on Intellectual Property that some exemption from infringement may exist.[361] In light of uncertainty about the extent to which patent rights impinge on freedom to do research, and the adverse effect that this uncertainty may have on innovation and dissemination of technical knowledge, both bodies recommended amendment of the *Patents Act 1990* (Cth) to include an express exemption that does not affect the continuation of any existing common law exemption.[362] The *Raising the Bar Act* introduced an express exemption in s 119C. The Explanatory Memorandum accompanying the Bill makes it clear that s 119C aims to enhance certainty for the research community. It also makes clear that '[t]he amendments explicitly preserve any implicit experimental use defence that may be found by a court. The addition of an explicit exemption is not intended to detract in any way from any existing protection that researchers may enjoy'.[363]

Section 119C(1) came into operation on 15 April 2012[364] and provides that 'a person may, without infringing a patent, do an act that would infringe the patent apart from this subsection, if the act is done for experimental purposes relating to the subject matter of the invention'. Hence, it is necessary to draw on the exemption only when the act would otherwise infringe an exclusive right of the patentee. According to the Explanatory Memorandum:

> It is intended that 'experimental' be given its ordinary English meaning. The exemption should apply to tests, trials and procedures that a researcher or follow-on innovator undertakes as part of discovering new information or testing a principle or supposition.[365]

To enhance certainty, s 119C(2) provides that experimental purposes relating to the subject matter of the invention include, but are not limited to:

- determining the properties of the invention;
- determining the scope of a claim relating to the invention;
- improving or modifying the invention;
- determining the validity of the patent or of a claim relating to the invention; and
- determining whether the patent for the invention would be, or has been, infringed by the doing of an act.

---

360   Australian Law Reform Commission (ALRC), *Gene Patenting and Human Health* (Issues Paper No 27, July 2003); Advisory Council on Intellectual Property (ACIP), *Patents and Experimental Use* (Options Paper, February 2004); ACIP, *Patents and Experimental Use* (Final Report, 2005). See also New Zealand Ministry of Economic Development, *An Experimental Use Exception for the Patents Act: Analysis of Submissions* (June 2006).
361   ALRC, *Genes and Ingenuity: Gene Patenting and Human Health* (Report No 99, June 2004) [13.78]; ACIP, *Patents and Experimental Use* (Final Report, October 2005) [8.3].
362   See Monotti, 'Limitations on the scope', above n 352.
363   Explanatory Memorandum, Intellectual Property Laws Amendment (Raising the Bar) Bill 2011 (Cth) sch 2 item 1.
364   *Intellectual Property Laws Amendment (Raising the Bar) Act 2012* (Cth) sch 2 pt 2. This section applies to acts done on or after 15 April 2012 in relation to patents granted before, on or after that commencement.
365   Explanatory Memorandum, Intellectual Property Laws Amendment (Raising the Bar) Bill 2011 (Cth) sch 2 item 1.

Arguably these activities should be outside the exclusive rights of the patentee in any event and freely available to all, so their express mention must carry no implied expansion of the current scope of the patentee's rights. Furthermore, it is clear from the Explanatory Memorandum that these exemptions are 'not intended to detract in any way from any existing protection that researchers may enjoy'.[366]

The range of exempted acts does not extend to any research use of inventions (which was the type of use that provoked the various inquiries into experimental use) and in particular would not extend to use of inventions as research tools. As the Explanatory Memorandum noted:

> Research tools are often used exclusively or primarily in research. If the experimental use exemption were to apply to such tools it would substantially diminish the economic incentive to develop better research tools.[367]

The Explanatory Memorandum clarifies a number of other issues regarding the intended scope of the new provision, including the following:

- Activities need not be undertaken solely for experimental purposes. Where research is undertaken for mixed purposes, the exemption should apply where the predominant purpose is 'gaining new knowledge or testing a principle or supposition about the invention'. An example is an activity directed to improving a patented invention, even though the person had in mind commercialising the improvement in future.
- The exemption is not intended to apply where the purpose is predominantly commercial, such as 'making and using the invention to test the likely commercial demand for a product'.
- The exemption is intended to cover circumstances where 'experiments inherently include the subject matter of a patent, perhaps as part of a larger or more complex experiment, but the researcher is unaware of the existence of the patent'.

12.9 Infringement proceedings

Although the exclusive rights commence on the date of the patent, it is only unauthorised acts done by third parties after the application for a standard patent has become open for public inspection that can be the subject of infringement proceedings.[368] No infringement proceedings in respect of an act can be commenced until the patent is granted on the application.[369] In the case of an innovation patent, no proceedings can be commenced until the patent is certified.[370]

The patentee or an exclusive licensee can commence infringement proceedings in a prescribed court or in another court having jurisdiction to hear and determine the matter.[371]

---

366 Ibid.
367 Ibid.
368 *Patents Act 1990* (Cth) ss 55, 57, 120.
369 Ibid s 57(3).
370 Ibid ss 120(1A), 101E.
371 Ibid s 120(1). See below at 17.9.

If the exclusive licensee institutes proceedings, the patentee must be joined as a defendant unless joined as a plaintiff. The patentee pays no costs if they are joined as a defendant unless they enter an appearance and take part in the proceedings.[372] Proceedings must be commenced within three years of the day on which the relevant patent is granted or within six years from the day on which the infringing act is done, whichever ends later.[373] A defendant to an infringement action can apply by way of counterclaim in the proceedings for revocation of the patent.[374] Special provisions apply to the burden of proof when the infringement action initiated by the patentee or exclusive licensee relates to a patented process for obtaining a product. A defendant who claims to have used a non-infringing process bears the burden of proving this if the court is satisfied of two things: first, that it is very likely that the defendant used the patented process; and, second, that the patentee or exclusive licensee has been unable through the use of reasonable steps to find out the process used.[375] The court is to take into account the defendant's legitimate interests in having business and manufacturing secrets protected in deciding how the defendant is to provide this evidence.[376]

12.10 Relief for infringement

Relief for infringement includes an injunction[377] and damages or an account of profits at the option of the plaintiff.[378] If there is more than one plaintiff, each must make the same election.[379] A court may also award additional damages in patent infringement actions after having regard to matters that include the flagrancy of the infringement and the need to deter similar infringements of patents.[380]

In order to prevent damage to the plaintiff's intellectual property interests, it may be necessary to obtain an interlocutory injunction preventing the defendant's conduct until the full trial of the matter.[381] The date from which a person is entitled to relief from infringement of a standard patent is the date of the patent.[382] In the case of an innovation patent, relief is entitled from the date of the grant of patent in suit.[383] Hence, a person cannot infringe an innovation in respect of acts performed prior to grant. There is also provision for the court to make orders for inspection of anything in or on any premises, on the application of either

---

372 Ibid s 120(2), (3).
373 Ibid s 120(4).
374 Ibid s 121.
375 Ibid s 121A.
376 Ibid s 121A(3).
377 As to availability of a springboard injunction in patent cases, see *Streetworx Pty Ltd v Artcraft Urban Group Pty Ltd* (2015) 110 IPR 544.
378 *Patents Act 1990* (Cth) s 122(1). As to the methodological approach to quantification of damages, see *Generic Health Pty Ltd v Bayer Pharma AG* (2018) 137 IPR 1.
379 *Spring Form Inc v Toy Brokers Ltd* [2002] FSR 17.
380 *Patents Act 1990* (Cth) s 122(1A), introduced by *Intellectual Property Laws Amendment Act 2006* (Cth).
381 *Federal Court of Australia Act 1976* (Cth) s 23; *Samsung Electronics Co Ltd v Apple Inc* (2011) 286 ALR 257 (an appeal from an interlocutory decision). See ch 17 at 17.2.3 for general principles. See also C. Lawson, 'The interlocutory injunction dilemma in patent infringement and invalidity disputes' (2010) 21 *Australian Intellectual Property Journal* 73.
382 *Patents Act 1990* (Cth) s 57; *Coretell Pty Ltd v Australian Mud Co Pty Ltd* (2017) 250 FCR 155, [58].
383 *Coretell Pty Ltd v Australian Mud Co Pty Ltd* (2017) 250 FCR 155, [68], [97], [104], rejecting the construction in *Britax Childcare Pty Ltd v Infa-Secure Pty Ltd (No 3)* [2012] FCA 1019.

party.[384] The court may refuse to award damages or make an order for account of profits if the defendant satisfies the court that, at the date of the infringement, they were not aware and had no reason to believe that a patent for the invention existed.[385] However, the defendant is presumed to be aware of the existence of the patent if patented products, marked so as to indicate that they are patented in Australia, were sold or used in the patent area to a substantial extent before the date for the infringement.[386] The court's power to grant relief by way of injunction is unaffected by the defendant establishing that infringement was innocent.[387]

12.11 Non-infringement declarations

The effect of obtaining a non-infringement declaration is that liability is limited in the event that the doing of an act is found to infringe the claim.[388] It can therefore assist people who are unable to get clear legal advice, or an assurance from a patentee, that their activities would not infringe a patent. The *Raising the Bar Act* introduced a number of changes to ss 125–7 to remedy difficulties arising from the statutory provisions in force before 15 April 2013.[389]

In relation to an application for non-infringement declarations, the applicant must join the patentee as a respondent.[390] Furthermore, the application can be made despite an assertion by the patentee that the doing of the act would infringe the claim.[391] No declaration will be made unless the applicant:

- has sought in writing, but failed to obtain, a written admission from the patentee that the doing of the act has not infringed or would not infringe the patent;
- has provided the patentee with full written particulars of the act done or proposed to be done; and
- has undertaken to pay a reasonable sum for the patentee's expenses in obtaining advice.[392]

12.12 Unjustified threats of infringement proceedings

A person who is threatened by anyone with infringement or similar proceedings by means of circulars, advertisements or otherwise can apply to a court having jurisdiction for:

---

384 *Patents Act 1990* (Cth) s 122(2).
385 Ibid s 123(1); *Coretell Pty Ltd v Australian Mud Company Pty Ltd* (2017) 250 FCR 155, [105]–[107] (innovation patent). As to exercise of the discretion, see *H Lundbeck A/S v Sandoz Pty Ltd* (2018) 137 IPR 408, [343]–[348].
386 *Patents Act 1990* (Cth) s 123(2).
387 Ibid s 123(3). See J. E. Liddicoat, 'Re-evaluating innocent infringement in Australia: Patent numbers and virtual marking' (2014) 25 *Australian Intellectual Property Journal* 18.
388 *Patents Act 1990* (Cth) s 127.
389 *Occupational & Medical Innovations Ltd v Retractable Technologies Inc* (2008) 77 IPR 570, [5]. See the discussion in M. Davison, A. Monotti and L. Wiseman, *Australian Intellectual Property Law* (3rd edn, Melbourne: Cambridge University Press, 2016) [15.11].
390 *Patents Act 1990* (Cth) s 125(3).
391 *Patents Act 1990* (Cth) ss 125(2), 55.
392 *Patents Act 1990* (Cth) s 126(1)(a), (b).

- a declaration that the threats are unjustifiable;
- an injunction to discontinue the threats; and
- recovery of any damages sustained as a result of the threats.

The person making the threats need not be interested in or entitled to the patent or a patent application. It is not a threat to make a mere notification of the existence of a patent or application for a patent, although to do so coupled with a statement that 'our clients are prepared to protect their interests with the utmost vigour' has been held to be a threat.[393] A notification that 'further action will be taken by ... against other infringers if necessary' has been regarded as no more than a 'general warning'.[394] In the case of threats made in respect of standard patents or an application for a standard patent, the person who makes the threat bears the burden of satisfying the court that there is no unjustified threat. They may do so, for example, by showing that the acts in question infringed or would infringe a claim that the applicant has not shown to be invalid.[395] When no infringement arises, the threats will be unjustifiable.[396] A similar provision applies in relation to threats made in respect of a certified innovation patent.[397] Certain threats that are made in relation to an innovation patent application or an innovation patent are always unjustifiable. These are threats made by a person whose innovation patent application has not been determined, or a person who has an uncertified innovation patent.[398] A court has discretion to award declaratory and injunctive relief pursuant to s 128 of the *Patents Act 1990* (Cth)[399] and to award additional damages under s 128(1A) after having regard to matters that include the flagrancy of the infringement and the need to deter similar infringements of patents.[400]

The respondent to an action for unjustified threats can counterclaim for relief for infringement of the patent to which the threats relate.[401] The applicant can apply in the same proceedings for revocation of the patent.[402] In the case of an innovation patent, it must first be certified. No legal practitioner or patent attorney can be liable for unjustified threats in respect of an act done in their professional capacity on behalf of a client but the client cannot avoid liability by arguing that their lawyer made the threat, not them.[403]

---

393   Patents Act 1990 (Cth) s 131. See *Rosedale Associated Manufacturers Ltd v Airfix Products Ltd* [1956] RPC 360. See also *Lido Manufacturing Co Pty Ltd v Meyers & Leslie Pty Ltd* [1964] 5 FLR 443; *U & I Global Trading (Australia) Pty Ltd v Tasman-Warajay Pty Ltd* (1995) 60 FCR 26, 32.
394   *Damorgold Pty Ltd v Blindware* (2017) 130 IPR 1, [406].
395   Patents Act 1990 (Cth) ss 129, 59.
396   *Uniline Australia Ltd v S Briggs Pty Ltd* (2009) 81 IPR 42, [116], [119].
397   Patents Act 1990 (Cth) s 129A(3); *SNF (Australia) Pty Ltd v Ciba Specialty Chemicals Water Treatments Ltd* (2011) 92 IPR 46, [329].
398   Patents Act 1990 (Cth) s 129A(1).
399   *Occupational & Medical Innovations Ltd v Retractable Technologies Inc* (2007) 73 IPR 312, 325; *BLH Engineering & Construction Pty Ltd v Pro 3 Products Pty Ltd* (2015) 114 IPR 105.
400   Patents Act 1990 (Cth) s 128(1) was introduced by *Intellectual Property Laws Amendment (Productivity Commission Response Part 1 and Other Measures) Act 2018* (Cth) sch 2 pt 8 item 200 (commenced 24 February 2019).
401   Patents Act 1990 (Cth) s 130(1).
402   Ibid s 130(2).
403   Ibid s 132; *HVE Electric Ltd v Cufflin Holdings Ltd* [1964] RPC 149, 158; *Wanem Pty Ltd v Tekiela* (1990) 19 IPR 435, 444.

12.13 Revocation of patents

12.13.1 Statutory provisions

The Minister and any other person may apply to a prescribed court for revocation of the patent on a number of other grounds that are set out in s 138(3) of the *Patents Act 1990* (Cth). In the case of an innovation patent, no application is possible unless the patent had been certified.[404] Revocation involves annulment of patent rights where it is found that the rights should not have been granted.[405]

Section 138(3) provides for the court in its discretion to revoke the patent either wholly or so far as it relates to a claim on one or more of the following grounds:[406]

- that the patentee is not entitled to the patent;[407]
- that the invention is not a patentable invention;[408]
- that the patent was obtained by fraud, false suggestion or misrepresentation;[409]
- that an amendment of the patent request or complete specification was made or obtained by fraud, false suggestion or misrepresentation;[410]
- that the specification does not comply with s 40(2) or (3).[411]

The ground in s 138(3)(b) that the invention is not a patentable invention will be established if the invention does not satisfy the requirements in s 18 or 18(1A). Those requirements are discussed in chapter 10. The requirements of s 40(2) and (3) are also discussed in that chapter. The remaining grounds – namely, lack of entitlement and the effect of fraud, false suggestion and misrepresentation – are discussed below.[412] A defendant to an infringement action can apply by way of counterclaim in the proceedings for revocation of the patent.[413]

A brief mention of a range of other grounds on which a patent can be revoked is appropriate in this overview of the statutory provisions. In the case of a patent of addition, the revocation of the patent for the main invention usually results in the patent of addition becoming an independent patent for the unexpired part of the term of the patent for the main invention.[414] In addition, a patent can be revoked after grant of a compulsory licence[415] and after the Commissioner has accepted a patentee's offer to surrender a patent.[416]

---

404 *Patents Act 1990* (Cth) s 138(1A).
405 *Stack v Brisbane City Council* (1999) 47 IPR 525, [50].
406 Until the repeal of s 138(3)(c) by the *US Free Trade Agreement Implementation Act 2004* (Cth) sch 8 item 5, revocation was possible where a condition in a granted patent was unfulfilled or subsequently breached.
407 *Patents Act 1990* (Cth) s 138(3)(a).
408 Ibid s 138(3)(b).
409 Ibid s 138(3)(d).
410 Ibid s 138(3)(e).
411 Ibid s 138(3)(f).
412 At 12.13.2 and 12.13.3.
413 *Patents Act 1990* (Cth) s 121. As to infringement proceedings, see above at 12.9.
414 *Patents Act 1990* (Cth) s 85.
415 Ibid s 134. See ch 11.
416 Ibid s 137.

12.13.2 Lack of entitlement

Section 138(3)(a) of the *Patents Act 1990* (Cth) provides that a ground of revocation is that the patentee is not entitled to the patent at the time of its grant, regardless of any later assignment of rights.[417] The respondent bears the onus of establishing the ground of lack of entitlement.[418]

This ground of revocation reflects the common law principle that deception of the Crown as to entitlement to the invention or the identity of the true inventor destroys the foundation on which the patent is granted.[419] Entitlement stems from the inventor.[420] Hence, this inquiry is the same as that which is followed to determine ownership and involves objective assessment of the identity of the inventor[421] and of whether the entitlement of the inventor or inventors has been assigned or transmitted to another party.[422] When the original grantee remains the registered patentee at the time of the proceedings, their entitlement will be determined according to their eligibility under s 15 of the Act. If the registered patentee is different from the original grantee at the time of the proceedings, entitlement still remains to be determined with reference to the eligibility of the original grantee under s 15.[423] It is not sufficient to say that a patentee is entitled to the patent simply because they are identified as a nominated person in the patent request or because the grant has been made to that patentee.[424] Registration is not a source of entitlement; the *Patents Act 1990* (Cth) does not create a system of title by registration that is akin to a Torrens title system of registration of interests in real estate.[425]

Patent ownership issues can be complicated. Honest mistakes in identifying those who are entitled to be granted the patent have resulted in revocation of patents when the mistakes were not detected until after the grant of the patent to the wrong party. Even when errors were detected prior to grant, the mechanisms for correcting and resolving the issues were unnecessarily complex. These harsh consequences arising from the operation of s 138(3)(a) were alleviated by the *Raising the Bar* reforms. A new s 22A specifies that a patent is not invalid merely because the patent is granted to the wrong person.[426] At the same time, a new sub-s (4) was added to s 138 to provide that a court must not revoke a patent for incorrect entitlement unless it is satisfied that, in all the circumstances, it is just and equitable to do so. Section 138(4) applies in relation to applications for revocation orders made on or after 15 April 2013, whether the patent was granted before, on or after that day.[427] The intention of both amendments is 'to provide that the default remedy for a defect in entitlement is not revocation of the

---

[417] *University of British Columbia v Conor Medsystems Inc* (2006) 155 FCR 391; *Stack v Davies Shephard Pty Ltd* (2001) 108 FCR 422, [34]; *AstraZeneca AB v Apotex Pty Ltd* (2014) 226 FCR 324, [158].
[418] *Ryan v Lum* (1989) 16 NSWLR 518, 523; *George C Warner Laboratories Pty Ltd v Chemspray Pty Ltd* (1967) 41 ALJR 75; *JMVB Enterprises Pty Ltd v Camoflag Pty Ltd* (2005) 67 IPR 68, [128].
[419] *Stack v Davies Shephard Pty Ltd* (2001) 108 FCR 422, 428–33.
[420] *Patents Act 1990* (Cth) s 15(1). See ch 11.
[421] See ch 11 at 11.1.1 (criteria for inventorship).
[422] *Patents Act 1990* (Cth) s 15(1)(b)–(d). See ch 11 at 11.1.2 and 11.1.3.
[423] *Stack v Brisbane City Council* (1999) 47 IPR 525, [51].
[424] *University of British Columbia v Conor Medsystems Inc* (2006) 155 FCR 391, [32]–[33] (Emmett J), [61]–[62] (Stone J).
[425] Ibid [62] (Stone J).
[426] Inserted by *Intellectual Property Laws Amendment (Raising the Bar) Act 2012* (Cth) sch 6 item 31.
[427] The relevant time is when revocation orders are actually applied for in court and not when an application for such orders is filed in the Registry: *AstraZeneca AB v Apotex Pty Ltd* (2014) 226 FCR 324, [183]–[184].

patent'.[428] Nevertheless, notwithstanding the enactment of s 22A, revocation proceedings that include the basis of lack of entitlement require a court to consider s 138(3)(a) and to decide whether it is just and equitable to revoke the patent.[429]

The reference to the 'patentee' in s 138(3)(a) covers joint patentees. Hence, where a patent is granted to joint patentees, all must be entitled to the patent.[430] The ground for revocation is made out if one of several patentees is not entitled because a grant can be made only to the inventor or a person who claims under the inventor. It is not necessary for all joint patentees to lack entitlement for this ground to succeed.[431] The time at which entitlement is assessed for the purposes of a revocation order is not clear. There is authority that suggests it is the time of the grant in cases where the original grantee remains the registered patentee at the time of the proceedings.[432]

12.13.3 Fraud and false suggestion or misrepresentation

The public must be fairly given possession of the invention.[433] Hence, a ground for revocation under s 138(3)(d) of the *Patents Act 1990* (Cth) is that the patent was obtained by fraud, false suggestion or misrepresentation.[434] A further ground in s 138(3)(e) is that an amendment of the patent request or the complete specification was made or obtained by fraud, false suggestion or misrepresentation. A deliberate intent to deceive is not a necessary ingredient of the provisions.[435] These grounds are based on equitable notions of good faith, fairness, conscionable conduct and honesty.[436] Neither of the two grounds outlined above is considered at examination; nor is either available for pre-grant opposition. The respondent bears the onus of establishing the ground.[437] 'Fraud' has its common law meaning. It would include conduct that is engaged in so as to induce a state of mind in the Commissioner as to a matter concerning the patent, or the application for the patent, that the patentee either knows is untrue or is recklessly indifferent as to its truth or falsity. The conduct can include omissions.[438] The words 'false

---

428   Explanatory Memorandum, Intellectual Property Laws Amendment (Raising the Bar) Bill 2011 (Cth) sch 6 item 75.
429   *AstraZeneca AB v Apotex Pty Ltd* (2014) 226 FCR 324, [179]–[191] (concerning an appeal from an application for revocation order that was determined prior to 15 April 2013 when s 138(4) had not yet come into force).
430   *Patents Act 1990* (Cth) s 15; *Stack v Davies Shephard Pty Ltd* (2001) 108 FCR 422, [21]; *Stack v Brisbane City Council* (1999) 47 IPR 525, [51].
431   *Conor Medsystems Inc v University of British Columbia (No 2)* (2006) 68 IPR 217, [19]; *JMVB Enterprises Pty Ltd v Camoflag Pty Ltd* (2005) 67 IPR 68, [133].
432   *Conor Medsystems Inc v University of British Columbia (No 2)* (2006) 68 IPR 217, [19]; *Stack v Brisbane City Council* (1999) 47 IPR 525, 536 (Cooper J, by implication).
433   *Adhesives Pty Ltd v Aktieselskabet Dansk Gaerings-Industri* (1935) 55 CLR 523, 546 (Evatt J); *Nesbit Evans Group Australia Pty Ltd v Impro Ltd* (1997) 39 IPR 56, 99.
434   *Prestige Group (Australia) Pty Ltd v Dart Industries Inc* (1990) 26 FCR 197 (for the history of the expression 'false suggestion or representation'); *Apotex Pty Ltd v Les Laboratories Servier* [2013] FCA 1426, [201].
435   *Prestige Group (Australia) Pty Ltd v Dart Industries Inc* (1990) 26 FCR 197; *Pfizer Overseas Pharmaceuticals v Eli Lilly & Co* (2005) 68 IPR 1, [394].
436   As to false suggestion and representation, see *Prestige Group (Australia) Pty Ltd v Dart Industries Inc* (1990) 26 FCR 197, 198.
437   *Ryan v Lum* (1989) 16 NSWLR 518, 520; *George C Warner Laboratories Pty Ltd v Chemspray Pty Ltd* (1967) 41 ALJR 75; *Speedy Gantry Hire Pty Ltd v Preston Erection Pty Ltd* (1998) 40 IPR 543, 549.
438   *Apotex Pty Ltd v Les Laboratories Servier* [2013] FCA 1426, [191].

suggestion' are akin to equitable fraud.[439] That is, it must be 'a misrepresentation so material that it can be said that the Crown has been deceived'.[440] While some causal nexus (connection) is required between the challenged conduct and the patent grant, there is no requirement to establish that, in its absence, the patent would not have been granted.[441] The word 'misrepresentation' has been construed to 'bear its natural and ordinary meaning, of an objectively incorrect statement, unqualified by the word "false"'.[442]

There is a certain degree of overlap between obtaining a patent by fraud, false suggestion or misrepresentation and other separately defined grounds of revocation, such as absence of entitlement,[443] lack of patentability through inutility and noncompliance with s 40 of the Act. For example, an incorrect statement to the Commissioner as to the identity of the inventor in a patent application that is later granted will make the patent susceptible to revocation on the ground of false suggestion or misrepresentation.[444] In circumstances where it is proved that the inventor knew of the anticipation by a third party, it could be found that the patentee's suggestion that they were the true inventor may amount to a false suggestion.[445] In addition, a false statement as to the results that can be obtained may expose the patent to revocation on grounds of both lack of utility and obtaining the patent by false suggestion. The presence of sub-s (3)(d) and (e) in s 138 nevertheless demonstrates the intention that it has some independent role that should be allowed to develop without judicial circumscription.[446]

For the fraud, false suggestion or misrepresentation to invalidate, it must have materially contributed to the Commissioner's decision to grant the patent, or have been a material, inducing factor which led to the grant,[447] even if other factors were also influential,[448] so that it can be said that the Crown was deceived.[449] Merely showing that a statement is false will not of itself be 'sufficient reason to draw an inference that the suggestion or representation

---

439   *Prestige Group (Australia) Pty Ltd v Dart Industries Inc* (1990) 26 FCR 197, 201 (Lockhart J), citing *Morgan v Seaward* (1837) 2 M & W 544, 561; 150 ER 874, 880–1; *Kromschroder AG's Patent* [1960] RPC 75, 83–4; *Re Parry-Husband's Application* [1965] RPC 382, 386.
440   *Re Alsop's Patent* (1907) 24 RPC 733, 753; *JMVB Enterprises Pty Ltd v Camoflag Pty Ltd* (2005) 67 IPR 68, [135].
441   *Prestige Group (Australia) Pty Ltd v Dart Industries Inc* (1990) 26 FCR 197, 201 (Lockhart J), 218 (Gummow J); *Ranbaxy Australia Pty Ltd v Warner-Lambert Co LLC* (2008) 77 IPR 449, [82].
442   *Apotex Pty Ltd v Les Laboratories Servier* [2013] FCA 1426, [192].
443   *Conor Medsystems Inc v University of British Columbia (No 2)* (2006) 68 IPR 217, 223; *JMVB Enterprises Pty Ltd v Camoflag Pty Ltd* (2005) 67 IPR 68, 97.
444   *JMVB Enterprises Pty Ltd v Camoflag Pty Ltd* (2005) 67 IPR 68, [136]; *Atlantis Corp Pty Ltd v Schindler* (1997) 39 IPR 29, 54; *Martin v Scribal Pty Ltd* (1954) 92 CLR 17, 67–9, 93; *R v Commissioner of Patents; Ex parte Martin* (1953) 89 CLR 381, 398–9 (Williams ACJ).
445   *Jupiters Ltd v Neurizon Pty Ltd* (2005) 65 IPR 86, [135].
446   Ibid 199 (Lockhart J), 218 (Gummow J), referring to s 100(1) of the 1952 Act.
447   *Ranbaxy Australia Pty Ltd v Warner-Lambert Co LLC* (2008) 77 IPR 449, [82]; *Albany Molecular Research Inc v Alphapharm Pty Ltd* (2011) 90 IPR 457; *Apotex Pty Ltd v Les Laboratories Servier* [2013] FCA 1426, [201].
448   *Pfizer Overseas Pharmaceuticals v Eli Lilly & Co* (2005) 68 IPR 1, [394]; *Prestige Group (Australia) Pty Ltd v Dart Industries Inc* (1990) 26 FCR 197, 201 (Lockhart J), 218 (Gummow J); *Ranbaxy Australia Pty Ltd v Warner-Lambert Co LLC* (2008) 77 IPR 449, [82].
449   *Re Alsop's Patent* (1907) 24 RPC 733, 753; *Prestige Group (Australia) Pty Ltd v Dart Industries Inc* (1990) 26 FCR 197, 200 (Lockhart J); *JMVB Enterprises Pty Ltd v Camoflag Pty Ltd* (2005) 67 IPR 68, [135]; *Valensi v British Radio Corp Ltd (No 1)* [1972] FSR 273, 311.

contributed to the decision to grant the patent'.[450] It may be a relevant factor that the Commissioner chooses not to give evidence, but this is not decisive.[451] In some situations, the contribution to the decision to grant a patent might be inferred if this was objectively a likely outcome and the patent was in fact granted.[452]

Generally, representations may be made in the patent specification or during the patent application process.[453] Representations made in the specification may be as to the results that the invention can achieve. There is a distinction between false promises of results that will also amount to a lack of utility and correct representations of the results accompanied by false statements of the purposes for which the results can be used.[454] In the latter case, provided that there are purposes for which the results are useful,[455] the promise will only invalidate the patent if it amounts to a material false suggestion or representation on which the patent was obtained. A false representation as to the meaning of a technical term in the specification may also be a false suggestion or representation.[456] Representations made during the patent application process might arise in correspondence with the Commissioner of Patents in response to examiners' reports,[457] and in an appeal brief filed in connection with a basic application.[458] Examples where no misrepresentation was found include an applicant's bona fide but incorrect submission to the Patent Office as to the proper construction or effect of a piece of prior art,[459] and a misrepresentation by an applicant that it was the assignee of the inventor who was entitled on other grounds to make the application.[460]

A 'mere puff' or expression of an 'over-sanguine and erroneous view of its character' will not invalidate the patent.[461] Neither will a false representation in a specification that the skilled person would understand to reflect the position held by the inventors only (there being no suggestion that the statement was false to the knowledge of the inventors), as opposed to an objective statement. For example, a statement that a step was impossible or that a course of

---

450 *Ranbaxy Australia Pty Ltd v Warner-Lambert Co LLC* (2008) 77 IPR 449, [137]; *Sigma Pharmaceuticals (Australia) Pty Ltd v Wyeth* (2011) 119 IPR 194, [114]; *Apotex Pty Ltd v Warner-Lambert Co LLC (No 2)* (2016) 122 IPR 17, [156].

451 *ICI Chemicals & Polymers Ltd v Lubrizol Corp Inc* (2000) 106 FCR 214, [89]–[97]; *WM Wrigley Jr Co v Cadbury Schweppes Pty Ltd* (2005) 66 IPR 298, [123]–[130]; *Ranbaxy Australia Pty Ltd v Warner-Lambert Co LLC* (2008) 77 IPR 449, [83]; *Sigma Pharmaceuticals (Australia) Pty Ltd v Wyeth* (2011) 119 IPR 194, [114].

452 *Synthetic Turf Development Pty Ltd v Sports Technology International Pty Ltd* [2004] FCA 1179, [2]; *WM Wrigley Jr Co v Cadbury Schweppes Pty Ltd* (2005) 66 IPR 298, [123]–[130]; *Albany Molecular Research Inc v Alphapharm Pty Ltd* (2011) 90 IPR 457, [213]; *Morellini v Mizzi Family Holdings Pty Ltd* (2016) 116 IPR 411, [107]–[108].

453 *Prestige Group (Australia) Pty Ltd v Dart Industries Inc* (1990) 26 FCR 197, 201 (Lockhart J).

454 Ibid 200.

455 *Re Alsop's Patent* (1907) 24 RPC 733, 753.

456 *Prestige Group (Australia) Pty Ltd v Dart Industries Inc* (1990) 26 FCR 197; *ICI Chemicals & Polymers Ltd v Lubrizol Corp Inc* (2000) 106 FCR 214.

457 *Prestige Group (Australia) Pty Ltd v Dart Industries Inc* (1990) 26 FCR 197; *ICI Chemicals & Polymers Ltd v Lubrizol Corp Inc* (2000) 106 FCR 214; *Ranbaxy Australia Pty Ltd v Warner-Lambert Co LLC* (2008) 77 IPR 449; *Albany Molecular Research Inc v Alphapharm Pty Ltd* (2011) 90 IPR 457, [213].

458 *Prestige Group (Australia) Pty Ltd v Dart Industries Inc* (1990) 26 FCR 197, 218 (Gummow J).

459 Ibid.

460 *Speedy Gantry Hire Pty Ltd v Preston Erection Pty Ltd* (1998) 40 IPR 543, 544; *R v Commissioner of Patents; Ex parte Martin* (1953) 89 CLR 381.

461 Blanco White, *Patents for Inventions and the Protection of Industrial Designs*, above n 190, [4.405].

inquiry was fruitless does not amount to a false suggestion merely because it can be later shown to be possible or fruitful.[462] A representation that was material to abandoned claims need not and should not result in revocation of the remaining claims, even if it did materially induce the grant.[463]

12.13.4 Litigation: parties to proceedings

In proceedings for revocation of patents (and compulsory licences), the patentee and the exclusive licensee are parties to the proceedings. Section 139(1) also provides that any person claiming an interest in the patent as 'exclusive licensee *or otherwise*' is a party to the proceedings.[464] This phrase encompasses not only an exclusive licensee but also

> a person who claims an interest in the exclusive right to do the things referred to in the definition of 'exploit' in respect of the product in question in the patent area, not being the patentee (who is mentioned expressly) and not being necessarily an exclusive licensee.[465]

---

462   *Sigma Pharmaceuticals (Australia) Pty Ltd v Wyeth* (2011) 119 IPR 194, [113].
463   *ICI Chemicals & Polymers Ltd v Lubrizol Corp Inc* (2000) 106 FCR 214, 245.
464   Emphasis added.
465   *Emory University v Biochem Pharma Inc* (1998) 86 FCR 1.

13

PLANT BREEDER'S RIGHTS

13.1 Introduction

Most modern laws that protect new plant varieties derive from the 1961 *International Convention for the Protection of New Varieties of Plants* (*UPOV*), which was subsequently revised in 1972, 1978 and 1991.[1] The *UPOV* Conventions provide a system that enables breeders to recoup some of the associated costs of bringing a plant into cultivation through the grant of exclusive rights in the reproductive and propagating material of a new plant variety.[2] By way of balance, others can use protected varieties for further breeding of new varieties.[3] This regime provides additional benefits for contracting states: the ability to control the reproduction and maintenance of their own plant varieties[4] as well as the improvement of access to new varieties from other countries. Following an extensive debate,[5] Australia adopted the minimum standards in *UPOV 1978* and enacted them in the form of the *Plant Variety Rights Act 1987* (Cth). Some years later, Australia adopted[6] and implemented the provisions of the 1991 revision of the Convention (*UPOV 1991*) in the *Plant Breeder's Rights Act 1994* (Cth) (*PBRA*).[7] The *Intellectual Property Laws Amendment (Productivity Commission Response Part 1 and Other Measures) Act 2018* (Cth) made both substantive and procedural amendments to the *PBRA*, all of which are in effect at the date of publication. The principal substantive reforms relate to essentially derived varieties, unjustified threats of infringement, and discretion to award additional damages. The text below presents the law following these amendments. IP Australia is responsible for the administration of the *PBRA*.[8]

This chapter provides an overview of the nature of plant breeder's rights, including some brief discussion of the technical background. It explains some fundamental concepts and outlines the procedures for obtaining the grant of a plant breeder's right.

13.2 Plant breeding: technical background

Plants are classified in hierarchical levels using Latin terminology, with the species forming the basis of the classification. The main levels are termed, in Latin, *divisio, classis, ordo, familia,*

---

1. Opened for signature 2 December 1961 (as revised 1972, 1978 and 1991). See Anon, 'The 1961 Act' (1962) 1 *Industrial Property* 5–14; N. Byrne, 'Plant breeder's rights' in J. Lahore, J. Garnsey and A. Dufty, *Patents Trade Marks and Related Rights* (Sydney: LexisNexis Butterworths, 2001) [29,010]–[29,020].
2. G. Tritton, *Intellectual Property in Europe* (London: Sweet & Maxwell, 2002) ch 6.
3. Expert Panel on Breeding, *Clarification of Plant Breeding Issues under the Plant Breeder's Rights Act 1994* (December 2002) http://www.anbg.gov.au.
4. Tritton, *Intellectual Property in Europe*, above n 2, ch 6.
5. Senate Standing Committee on National Resources, *Plant Variety Rights* (Parliamentary Paper No 63, May 1984); A. Lazenby, *Australia's Plant Breeding Needs* (Report to the Minister for Primary Industry, 1986).
6. See Senate Standing Committee on Rural and Regional Affairs, *Report on the Consideration of a Bill Referred to the Committee: Plant Breeder's Rights Bill 1994* (1994) app 3, attachment 1; N. Byrne, *Legal Protection of Plants in Australia under Patent and Plant Variety Rights Legislation* (Australian Patent Office, 1990).
7. Constitutional validity was upheld in *Grain Pool of Western Australia v Commonwealth* (2000) 202 CLR 479.
8. The earlier position appears in M. Davison, A. Monotti and L. Wiseman, *Australian Intellectual Property Law* (3rd edn, Melbourne: Cambridge University Press, 2016).

genus, species. Examples of the common names for species include roses, apples, wheat and potatoes. A species may have many different varieties. Plant breeder's rights (PBR) exist in 'propagating material' of a particular plant variety, being material that can produce another plant with the same essential characteristics, such as the shape and colour of a seed, flower, leaf or fruit.[9] Propagating material includes seeds, bulbs, tubers, spores and seedlings, as well as cuttings and cell lines.

The meaning of 'plant' extends beyond its natural meaning of broad types of botanical specimen to include all fungi and algae, but expressly excludes bacteria, bacteroids,[10] mycoplasmas,[11] viruses,[12] viroids[13] and bacteriophages.[14] The term 'plant variety'[15] concerns the detailed characteristics of a specifically defined group of plants of the lowest known rank within a species. It includes a 'hybrid', which is a combination of two or more genotypes[16] of the same or different groups or taxa,[17] but excludes a combination comprising a scion[18] grafted on to a root stock. For example, crossing two varieties of pure-breeding carrot would produce hybrid progeny that would contain the genetic material that was present in both parents.[19] Hence, the progeny of a hybrid are no longer pure-breeding but will have a variety of traits that reflect their genetic makeup. The term 'plant variety' also includes a plant grouping despite the fact that the genome of the plants in that plant grouping has been altered by the introduction of genetic material that is not from plants.[20] A plant variety is defined by the expression of the characteristics resulting from the genotype of each individual within that plant grouping. It is distinguished from any other plant grouping by the expression of at least one of those characteristics and can be considered as a functional unit because of its suitability for being propagated unchanged.

'Propagation' is defined to mean 'the growth, culture or multiplication of that organism or component, whether by sexual or asexual means'.[21] 'Sexual propagation' means the exchange of genetic material between parents to produce a new generation. The most common form of sexual propagation is with seeds. Asexual propagation involves vegetative propagation using such techniques as cuttings, layering, division, grafting, budding and tissue culture.

9	*Plant Breeder's Rights Act 1994* (Cth) s 3(1) (definition of 'propagating material').
10	Any of various structurally modified bacteria, such as those occurring on the root nodules of leguminous plants.
11	Genus of small bacteria that lack cell walls.
12	Any of various simple sub-microscopic parasites of plants, animals and bacteria that often cause disease. Unable to replicate without a host cell, viruses are typically not considered living organisms.
13	Smallest known infectious pathogens.
14	A virus capable of infecting and lysing bacterial cells. Also called 'phage'.
15	*Plant Breeder's Rights Act 1994* (Cth) s 3(1) (definition of 'plant variety'). See also International Union for the Protection of New Varieties of Plants (UPOV), *Explanatory Notes on the Definition of Variety under the 1991 Act of the UPOV Convention* (UPOV/EXN/VAR1, 2010).
16	The genetic makeup of an organism or a group of organisms.
17	In biology, the term 'taxa' is used to denote groups or ranks in the classification of organisms – for example, classes, orders, families, genera or species.
18	A detached shoot or twig containing buds from a woody plant, used in grafting.
19	Mendel's law.
20	*Plant Breeder's Rights Act 1994* (Cth) s 6.
21	Ibid s 3(1) (definition of 'propagation').

13.3 Subject matter of PBR

There is no protection under the *PBRA* for breeding the variety.[22] Instead, the *PBRA* provides certain exclusive rights – PBR – in relation to propagating material of a protected plant variety.[23] In certain circumstances, the PBR extends beyond propagating material to varieties that are essentially derived from the protected variety,[24] certain derived plant varieties,[25] harvested material,[26] and products obtained from harvested material.[27] The nature of each form of protection and the circumstances in which it applies are discussed below in the context of the nature of PBR.

13.4 Registrability and grant of PBR

Regardless of how the plant variety originates, it must satisfy the specified criteria in s 43 of the *PBRA*. To be registrable, a plant variety must have a breeder; be distinctive, uniform and stable (DUS criteria); and not have been exploited by or with the permission of the breeder, or if so, only recently.[28] It must also be given a name.[29] Before granting PBR, the Registrar of Plant Breeder's Rights must also be satisfied of other matters listed in s 44, including the entitlement of the applicant to make the application. These criteria are discussed in the following sections. In the interests of harmonisation, the Council of the International Union for the Protection of New Varieties of Plants (UPOV) provides guiding principles for members of the union to apply in examination of DUS criteria.[30]

13.4.1 The variety has a breeder

The objective of plant breeding or plant improvement is to produce new, distinct, uniform and stable genetic structures. To be a breeder, the person must have bred the variety.[31] This person could be, for example, a gardener, horticulturist, farmer or scientist. The normal meaning of 'breeding' encompasses the wide range of methodologies that breeders use, such as cross-fertilisation of closely or distantly related species, progressive plant selection and genetic engineering.[32] It also extends to new methodologies that continue to evolve.[33] Proof of breeding relates to comparisons with the source population or parents. However, it does not

---

22   *Grain Pool of Western Australia v Commonwealth* (2000) 202 CLR 479, 510.
23   *Plant Breeder's Rights Act 1994* (Cth) s 11.
24   Ibid ss 12, 40, 41. See below at 13.7.2.
25   Ibid s 13. See below at 13.7.3.
26   Ibid s 14. See below at 13.7.4.
27   Ibid s 15. See below at 13.7.5.
28   Ibid s 43.
29   Ibid s 27.
30   UPOV, *General Introduction to the Examination of Distinctness, Uniformity and Stability and the Development of Harmonized Descriptions of New Varieties of Plants* (TG/1/3, April 2002).
31   *Plant Breeder's Rights Act 1994* (Cth) s 3(1). The *Plant Variety Rights Act 1987* (Cth) contained no definition of breeding; instead, 'originator' was the term used.
32   UPOV, *The Notion of Breeder and Common Knowledge in the Plant Variety Protection System Based upon the UPOV Convention* (Position Paper CAJ/44/2, August 2002) 2, 3.
33   Expert Panel, *Clarification of Plant Breeding Issues*, above n 3, 9.

include the simple multiplication and testing of an existing variety in a different environment, as this material will not be distinct from the existing known variety.[34] Nor does it extend to a mere discovery.

The *PBRA* contains no definition of 'bred' but defines 'breeding' in s 5 to include 'a reference to the discovery of the plant together with its use in selective propagation so as to enable the development of the new plant variety'.[35] This concept of 'breeding' is one that has created uncertainties within the plant breeding community. In 2002, an Expert Panel on Breeding addressed many of these uncertainties in its report *Clarification of Plant Breeding Issues under the Plant Breeder's Rights Act 1994*.

13.4.1.1 Meaning of 'discovery'

The Expert Panel concluded, following advice of the Australian Government Solicitor, that 'discovery' in s 5 means merely the act of 'finding a physical specimen of plant which was previously unknown to the general public'.[36] The advice worked through various questions that related to the meaning of discovery in s 5 of the *PBRA* and drew the following conclusions:

1. 'Discovering' a plant means finding a physical specimen of a plant rather than identifying its particular characteristics.[37]
2. More than one person can 'discover' a plant as long as it has not become common knowledge.[38]
3. A person does not 'discover' a plant if someone else provided them with particulars of its existence, a cutting or something similar.[39]
4. Where the plant is found is irrelevant to the question of whether it is 'discovered'. Ownership of the physical specimen is different from ownership of the intellectual property rights in the plant variety.[40]
5. Discovery of the plant variety is an independent inquiry from that of the DUS criteria.[41] DUS criteria relate to the plant variety, whereas discovery relates to the plant.
6. Discovery of a plant in the wild can constitute a 'discovery'.[42]

The Panel concurred with this advice. In addition, it considered that, in the absence of information to the contrary, the 'discoverer' is the first to file for PBR protection.[43]

13.4.1.2 Meaning of selective propagation

The Expert Panel considered that 'selective propagation' has its normal biological meaning, which requires a clear difference in at least one characteristic between the plant variety and its

---

34 UPOV, *The Notion of Breeder and Common Knowledge*, above n 32, [9].
35 *Plant Breeder's Rights Act 1994* (Cth) s 5(1).
36 Expert Panel, *Clarification of Plant Breeding Issues*, above n 3, app 1 [13].
37 Ibid [24].
38 Ibid [18].
39 Ibid [20].
40 Ibid [28].
41 Ibid [34].
42 Ibid [35].
43 Expert Panel, *Clarification of Plant Breeding Issues*, above n 3, 7.

parents or source population.[44] In the context of its discovery in the wild, it is only established where the new variety is different from the immediate breeding population from which the 'discovered plant' originated. For example, the new variety may have green and gold variegated leaves whereas the source population has green leaves. A person is not entitled to protection of the discovered variety that is propagated unchanged.[45]

13.4.2 The variety is distinct

A plant variety is distinct if it is clearly distinguishable from any other variety whose existence is a matter of common knowledge at the time of filing the application.[46] The ways in which the variety is shown to be distinct can include such things as growth habit, height, shape of leaves and flowers, colour and size of seeds, leaves and stamens, and time of flowering or harvest.

13.4.2.1 Common knowledge

There is no exhaustive definition of common knowledge in the *PBRA*. Section 43 provides that a variety will be treated as one of common knowledge if an application for PBR in that variety has been lodged in a contracting party and the application is proceeding, or has led, to the grant of PBR.[47]

UPOV guidelines identify further specific aspects that would establish the variety as one of common knowledge, namely:

- Propagating or harvested material has been commercialised.
- A detailed description has been published.
- Living plant material exists in a publicly accessible plant collection.[48]

Comparison is not limited to varieties that satisfy the conditions in s 43(1) for a grant of PBR. Rather, the *PBRA* permits a direct comparison with all varieties of common knowledge as long as they meet the criteria set out in the definition of 'plant variety' in s 3(1). Although accessing some of this type of material may be problematic, a grant can be revoked when new information comes to light that establishes the prior existence of a plant variety of common knowledge that is indistinguishable from the registered variety. Delegate Hulse applied the UPOV guidelines in *Majestic Selections Pty Ltd v Bushland Flora*[49] to conclude that a pre-existing *Lomandra* plant variety was one of common knowledge due to prior sales of plants within that variety. This new information provided grounds for revocation[50] of a registered *Lomandra* variety, 'Lime Tuff', on the basis that the latter was not shown to be distinct within the meaning of s 43(2).[51]

---

44 Ibid.
45 UPOV, *Explanatory Notes on the Definition of Breeder under the 1991 Act of the UPOV Convention* (UPOV/EXN/BRD/1, 2013) [9].
46 *Plant Breeder's Rights Act 1994* (Cth) s 43(2). See s 30(2), which does not limit comparisons to varieties of common knowledge for the purposes of acceptance of an application.
47 Ibid s 43(8), (9).
48 UPOV, *General Introduction to the Examination of Distinctness, Uniformity and Stability*, above n 30, [5.2.2].
49 [2016] APBRO 1.
50 *Plant Breeder's Rights Act 1994* (Cth) s 50(1).
51 *Majestic Selections Pty Ltd v Bushland Flora* [2016] APBRO 1.

13.4.3 The variety is uniform

Uniformity is tested across plants in one generation of the variety. A plant variety is uniform if, subject to the variation that may be expected from the particular features of its propagation, it is uniform in its relevant characteristics on propagation.[52] Some low degree of variation is permitted to maintain genetic diversity that would be reduced if absolute uniformity is required. Uniformity is established through test growing.[53] If the test growing shows lack of uniformity, it will be necessary to repeat the testing in relation to the next generation. The numbers of generations of breeding that may be necessary to produce uniformity will depend on the type of breeding method. For example, cloned material will produce uniformity in the first generation. On the other hand, breeding that uses methods of cross-pollination may require a second generation to prove uniformity.

13.4.4 The variety is stable

Stability is tested across plants in one generation of the variety. As with uniformity, stability is established through test growing.[54] A plant variety is stable if its relevant characteristics remain unchanged after repeated propagation.[55] Lack of uniformity will necessarily mean that the repeat generation will not be stable.

13.4.5 The variety has not been exploited or has only recently been exploited

A plant variety is registrable if the variety has not been exploited or has been only recently exploited in Australia or in the territory of another contracting party by the breeder or with their authorisation.[56] This is regarded as the 'novelty' requirement for PBR. However, unlike the concept of novelty in patent law,[57] the *PBRA* equivalent requires exploitation of propagating material as distinct from public exposure. The variety is taken not to have been exploited if no plant material of the variety has been sold to another person by, or with the consent of, the breeder prior to the filing date of the application.[58] Therefore, growth of plants alone would not constitute exploitation of the variety. 'Plant material' in relation to a plant variety is defined in s 43(10) of the *PBRA* to mean propagating material, harvested material and products obtained from harvested material.[59]

The plant variety is taken to have been only recently exploited if there were no authorised sales in Australia more than one year before the date of lodging the application for PBR. If X and Y independently breed the same variety and X has sold the variety in Australia for more than twelve months before Y's priority date without Y's consent, that will not affect Y's novelty.

---

52 *Plant Breeder's Rights Act 1994* (Cth) s 43(3).
53 Ibid ss 34(1), 37, 38, 41 (essential derivation for PBR-protected varieties), s 41E (essential derivation for non-PBR-protected second varieties).
54 Ibid s 34(4)(b).
55 Ibid s 43(4).
56 Ibid s 43(6).
57 See ch 10 at 10.6.
58 *Plant Breeder's Rights Act 1994* (Cth) s 43(5).
59 Ibid s 43(10) defines 'variety' as having the same meaning as it has in *UPOV 1991*.

In the case of sales outside Australia, the period is more than six years (trees or vines) or more than four years (any other case) before the priority date.[60] This operates effectively as a 'grace period' within which the breeder can make the plant variety publicly available by way of sale anywhere in the world without losing the ability to gain PBR protection. The breeder may sell plant material before lodging a PBR application to test market the variety. While this may be a useful tactic to explore whether registration is sensible, it risks another breeder gaining priority with an earlier application.

The definition of 'sell' includes letting on hire and exchanging by way of barter.[61] The Full Federal Court considered the meaning of 'sale' under s 14 of the *Plant Variety Rights Act 1987* (Cth) in *Sun World International Inc v Registrar, Plant Breeder's Rights*.[62] The relevant transactions involved the sale of Sugraone grapevines for vineyard development, such sales being subject to a variety of restrictions on the use to which the grower could put the plant or reproductive material. The court held that 'sell' and 'sale' are not confined to an unconditional transfer of the absolute property in the plant or propagating material for consideration limited to money.[63] It reasoned that the legislative definition of 'sell' showed a parliamentary intention to interpret 'sell' in a very wide sense that would include sales where the price may be low or nominal, where the sale was part of a larger transaction and where restrictive covenants are imposed. This reasoning is equally applicable to the *PBRA* in view of the identical definition of 'sell' in both Acts. Hence, 'sale' extends to transactions that have wider commercial purposes than simply the unconditional disposition of the plant material for money. It may be that some consideration in money may be required, but it is enough for it to be 'low or nominal'.[64] It is immaterial that the exchange occurs privately, to the public, to wholesalers, in small numbers or below market value.

Amendments to s 43 of the *PBRA* in 2002 introduced a number of specific instances of sales that do not amount to an exploitation of the plant variety. The principal purpose of these was to ensure that the widespread practice of testing varieties in farmers' paddocks before lodging an application for PBR would not destroy the registrability of the plant variety being tested.[65] The following are instances of non-exploitation:

- The sale is by the breeder to another person in circumstances where the sale is a part of, or related to, another transaction under which the right of the breeder to make application for PBR in that plant variety is sold to that other person.[66] For example, X sells his vineyard with its vines, which include the new variety for which an application is pending or to be made.
- The sale is for the sole purpose of multiplying plant material of that variety on behalf of the breeder and the agreement for the sale provides that immediately after the plant material is multiplied, property in the new plant material vests in the breeder.[67]

---

60   *Plant Breeder's Rights Act 1994* (Cth) s 43(6).
61   Ibid s 3(1).
62   (1998) 87 FCR 405.
63   Ibid 412–13.
64   Ibid 413.
65   Explanatory Memorandum, Plant Breeder's Rights Amendment Bill 2002 (Cth).
66   *Plant Breeder's Rights Act 1994* (Cth) s 43(7).
67   Ibid s 43(7A).

- The sale is part of an agreement under which the person agrees to use plant material for the sole purpose of evaluating the variety in one or more of field tests, laboratory trials, small-scale processing trials and tests or trials prescribed for the purposes of s 43(7B).[68]
- The sale only involves plant material that is a by-product or surplus product of any trials and is sold without identification of the plant variety of the plant material and for the sole purpose of final consumption.[69]

13.4.6 Time at which the variety must meet the DUS criteria

A breeder of a 'plant variety' may make an application for the grant of PBR in the variety.[70] The definition of 'plant variety' alone does not confirm that the requirements for the variety to be distinct, uniform and stable must be present at the time of application. It is necessary to refer to other sections of the *PBRA* to ascertain this.

Section 26(2)(e) of the Act provides that the application must include, among other things, a brief description of a plant of the variety, which usually includes a photograph, that is sufficient to establish a prima facie case that the variety is distinct from other varieties of common knowledge.[71] Hence it seems that the plant variety must be distinct at the time of lodging the application. The application makes no reference to the requirements for qualities of uniformity and stability. A test growing of the variety is required to establish those particulars, details of which must be lodged with the Registrar not later than twelve months after acceptance of the application.[72] Hence, if the test growing establishes that this variety is distinct, uniform and stable, it will have possessed these characteristics at the time the application was lodged. Although there is no express requirement that the plant variety possess these characteristics at the time of the application, it will not be registered unless the test growing establishes each characteristic.[73] Therefore, for all practical purposes, the plant variety must be distinct, uniform and stable at the time the application is lodged.

13.5 PBR applications

The process for obtaining a grant of PBR involves an application that is subjected to a formalities check prior to acceptance, followed by a substantive examination, the right for objections and grant. The process is relatively cheap and easy to secure in comparison with applications made under the patent system.[74] The applicant may withdraw an application at any time.[75]

---

68 Ibid s 43(7B).
69 Ibid s 43(7C).
70 Ibid s 24(1).
71 Ibid s 26(2)(e).
72 Ibid s 34(6).
73 Ibid s 43.
74 Ibid pt 3.
75 Ibid s 33(1).

13.5.1 Right to apply for PBR

It is the breeder, or their successor in title, who has the right to apply for PBR in a plant variety.[76] This right is personal property and is capable of assignment and of transmission by will or by operation of law.[77] Any of these events may occur either before making the application[78] or after its acceptance and before concluding examination.[79] The successor in title is a person to whom the right of the breeder to make application for PBR in that variety has been assigned, or transmitted by will or by operation of law.[80] An assignment of a right to apply for PBR must be in writing signed by or on behalf of the assignor.[81] The grant of PBR is open to any breeder[82] throughout the world in respect of any new variety irrespective of where it was bred.[83]

There may be more than one person who breeds the same new plant variety, either jointly or independently of others.[84] In this case, the *PBRA* recognises each as a breeder.[85] In the case of independent breeders, each has the right to apply for PBR, but the first to file the application has priority over the others for consideration of their application.[86] Although the other breeders may still file separate applications or retain their right to do so, the grant of PBR in that variety to another breeder results in a cessation of those rights.[87] Hence, the right to apply for PBR is a proprietary interest that may blossom into the separate proprietary interest in the form of PBR. On the other hand, it may cease upon the grant of PBR to another.

In the case of two or more persons breeding a plant jointly, a PBR application must be by all breeders jointly or by one or more breeders jointly with the consent in writing of the other breeders.[88] If PBR is granted to persons who make a joint application, the PBR is granted to them jointly.[89] There are no defined criteria for being joint breeders. It is likely to require some form of collaboration as is evident from s 5(2) of the *PBRA*, which provides that both the person who discovers a plant and another person who uses it in selective propagation so as to enable the development of the new plant variety are joint breeders of the new variety.

Employers' rights in their employees' work are protected. If a person breeds the variety as an employee, it is the employer who is defined as the 'breeder' and as the person entitled to make application for and to be granted PBR.[90] However, it is not just employers who are granted this vicarious status of 'breeder' – any body (whether corporate or unincorporated)

---

76 Ibid s 24(1).
77 Ibid s 25(1).
78 Ibid s 25(1).
79 Ibid s 31(1).
80 Ibid s 3(1).
81 Ibid s 25(2).
82 Exceptions: ibid s 60(1).
83 Ibid s 24(2).
84 Ibid ss 3, 5(2), 24(3), (4).
85 Ibid s 3(1).
86 Ibid s 28(3).
87 Ibid s 48.
88 Ibid s 24(3), (4).
89 Ibid ss 44(11), 45(1) Note. *Intellectual Property Laws Amendment (Productivity Commission Response Part 1 and Other Measures) Act 2018* (Cth) sch 2 pt 9 item 212.
90 *Plant Breeder's Rights Act 1994* (Cth) s 3.

may be granted this status and associated benefits when one or more of its members breeds the variety in the course of performing duties as a member.[91]

An odd distinction arises between individual breeders and joint breeders. If an individual breeder breeds the variety in the course of performing duties *or functions* as a member or employee of a body, the body of which that person is a member or employee is the breeder. However, it seems that the employer or other body is the breeder only where two people jointly breed the variety in the course of performing duties as a member or employee of that body. There is no reference to 'in the course of performing ... functions'.[92] This seems to be an oversight rather than a deliberate distinction.

13.5.2 Form of application for PBR

The written application must contain certain particulars, including a brief description of the variety, its name and the name of the person (qualified person) who can verify the particulars in the application and supervise any test growing of the plant variety to establish that it is distinct, uniform and stable.[93] As mentioned above, the brief description of the variety must be sufficient to establish a prima facie case that the variety is distinct from other varieties of common knowledge.[94] This is the standard for registrability set out in s 43 of the *PBRA*. An applicant provides a more detailed description after the application is accepted and when the test growing trial is complete.[95]

The name of the variety in the application must comply with certain requirements.[96] It must be a word or words (invented or not) with or without letters or figures.[97] It must not be likely to deceive or cause confusion; must not be contrary to law, scandalous or prohibited by regulations; or must not be a trade mark, registered or sought, in respect of live plants, plant cells and plant tissues.[98] Among the other requirements in s 27 of the *PBRA* is that the name must comply with the International Code of Botanical Nomenclature and subsidiary codes.[99] If a PBR has been granted already in another contracting party, the Australian application must use the name under which the PBR was first granted.[100] If that name is noncompliant with Australian requirements, a compliant synonym must be included in the application.[101]

13.5.3 Priority dates

Generally, the date on which a person lodges an application for PBR is its priority date.[102] However, the person might be entitled to an earlier priority date where the application arises from an earlier foreign application.[103]

---

91 Ibid s 3(1).
92 Ibid.
93 Ibid ss 26, 34(4).
94 Ibid s 26(2)(e).
95 Ibid s 34.
96 Ibid s 27(1).
97 Ibid s 27(4).
98 Ibid s 27(5).
99 Ibid s 27(6); *International Code of Nomenclature for Cultivated Plants 1995*.
100 *Plant Breeder's Rights Act 1994* (Cth) s 27(2)(a).
101 Ibid s 27(2)(b), (3).
102 Ibid s 28(1).
103 Ibid s 29.

13.5.4 Acceptance and rejection

The Registrar must accept the application if satisfied that it complies with s 26 requirements, that no earlier application exists, and that a prima facie case exists 'for treating the plant variety as distinct from other varieties.'[104] The Registrar must reject the application if not satisfied of these matters.[105] As noted above,[106] the application requires a brief description of a plant of the variety that is sufficient to establish a prima facie case that the variety is distinct from other varieties *of common knowledge*. In contrast, acceptance of the application requires a prima facie case for treating the plant variety as distinct from *other varieties* (without restriction to those of common knowledge).[107]

13.5.5 Variation of the application after acceptance

In addition to allowing variation of an application to reflect the assignment or transmission of the right to apply,[108] there is a general provision that allows an applicant, after acceptance and before conclusion of the examination, to request that the Registrar vary the application. The Registrar does not have to accede to the request.[109]

13.5.6 Application after acceptance: substantive examination and test growing requirements

Following acceptance, the applicant must provide a detailed description of the plant variety that contains particulars of:

- the characteristics that distinguish the variety from other plant varieties the existence of which is a matter of common knowledge; and
- any test growing that has been carried out.

A test growing of the plant variety is carried out and supervised by the approved qualified person nominated in the application to establish that the variety is distinct, uniform and stable.[110]

After a PBR examiner has provided independent verification of the trial, the results are verified by the qualified person as part of the detailed description or specification of the variety that is provided to the Registrar.[111] The results of the test growing are published in the *Plant Varieties Journal* insofar as they demonstrate the characteristics of the variety, but evidence of uniformity and stability is not published.

---

104   Ibid s 30(2).
105   Ibid s 30(3), (4), (5).
106   At 13.5.2.
107   *Plant Breeder's Rights Act 1994* (Cth) s 30(2).
108   Ibid s 31(1).
109   Ibid ss 31(5), (6), 32.
110   Ibid ss 26(2)(i), 34(4), 37, 38. Test growing may also be required when a grantee of PBR applies for a declaration that another variety is essentially derived from the initial variety: at ss 41, 41E.
111   Ibid s 34(1), (6).

13.5.7 Objections

A person may make a written objection to an accepted application if they consider that their commercial interests would be affected by the grant of that PBR to the applicant.[112] This invitation to the public to comment on accepted applications is a critical part of protecting the public interest against invalid registrations.

13.5.8 Access to the application and any objection

An application for PBR in a plant variety and any objection lodged in respect of that application (including that detailed description) is open for inspection.[113] This includes access to any detailed description of the plant variety given in support of the application. However, there is limited access[114] to the information referred to in s 26(2)(ga) of the *PBRA* – that is, the names of the parent varieties used in the breeding program, including the names by which each is known or sold in Australia, and particulars of any PBR granted in respect of each parent.

13.5.9 Status of accepted applications

The rights of the applicant commence from the day the application is accepted but no action or proceeding can be taken for an infringement of those rights unless and until PBR is finally granted to the person under s 44 of the *PBRA*.[115]

13.5.10 Deposit of propagating material

Prior to grant, the applicant must deposit propagating material of the plant variety for storage in an approved plant genetic resource centre.[116] The quantity must be sufficient to enable survival of that variety.[117] The *PBRA* empowers the person in charge of a genetic resource centre to maintain the viability of propagating material stored at that centre.[118] The intention of the *PBRA* is that the delivery of the material for storage to another site that is not owned by the applicant does not pass property in the material to the owner of the site.[119] In many cases, the material will be stored at the applicant's nursery or premises, in which case their ownership of that material is clear. The Registrar can use the stored material for the purposes of the *PBRA*, including the purposes of s 19 – namely, for ensuring reasonable public access to a plant variety.[120]

In addition to genetic resource centres, the *PBRA* provides for storage of plant specimens in specified herbariums.[121] Storage of plant specimens in a herbarium is mandatory in the case of

---

112   Ibid s 35.
113   Ibid s 36.
114   Ibid s 36(3).
115   Ibid s 39.
116   Ibid ss 3(1), 44(1)(b)(vii).
117   Ibid s 44(7).
118   Ibid s 70(2).
119   Ibid s 44(8).
120   Ibid s 44(9).
121   Ibid ss 3(1), 71.

a plant variety that is a species indigenous to Australia.[122] However, the Registrar may also require the supply of a satisfactory specimen plant of any other variety to the herbarium.[123]

13.6 Grant of PBR

13.6.1 Requirements

The Registrar must grant PBR to the applicant if the application meets all the requirements of s 44(1)(b) of the *PBRA*, namely:

> (i) there is such a variety [the subject of the application]; and
> (ii) the variety is a registrable plant variety within the meaning of section 43; and
> (iii) the applicant is entitled to make the application; and
> (iv) the grant of that right is not prohibited by this Act; and
> (v) that right has not been granted to another person; and
> (vi) the name of the variety complies with section 27; and
> (vii) propagating material of that variety has been deposited for storage, at the expense of the applicant, in a genetic resource centre approved by the Registrar; and
> (viii) if the Registrar so requires, a satisfactory specimen plant of the variety has been supplied to the herbarium;[124] and
> (ix) all fees payable under this Act in respect of the application, examination and grant have been paid ...

No grant or refusal to grant PBR in a plant variety is possible until at least six months after the detailed description of the variety is published.[125] Hence, PBR arise from registration. The proprietary right that exists prior to registration is merely a right to apply for PBR.[126] If the PBR is granted to persons who make a joint application for the right, the right is to be granted to those persons jointly.[127]

The *PBRA* contains a procedure whereby the Minister may impose conditions on a proposed or existing grant of PBR.[128]

13.6.2 Entry of details in the Register

The Registrar must enter certain details of PBR in the Register of Plant Varieties,[129] including conditions imposed by the Minister on PBR under s 49 of the *PBRA*.

---

122 Ibid s 44(2).
123 Ibid s 44(1)(b)(viii).
124 Ibid ss 3, 71.
125 Ibid s 44(4), (5).
126 See above at 13.5.1.
127 *Plant Breeder's Rights Act 1994* (Cth) s 44(11).
128 Ibid s 49.
129 Ibid s 46.

13.6.3 Effect of grant of PBR

The PBR system operates as a first-to-file system, so that the first application to be filed for a particular plant variety has precedence over any later application. Upon the grant of PBR, any other person who was entitled to apply for the right in the same variety loses that entitlement and can claim no interest in the right.[130] If that person had already made an application, they cease to be entitled to have their application considered and can claim no interest in the right that is granted.[131] Hence, the proprietary interest in the nature of the right to apply for PBR ceases upon the grant of PBR in that variety to another. However, the person who loses rights in a plant variety in these circumstances may still challenge the validity of the grant if grounds are available.[132] If appropriate, that person can also seek a declaration that the plant variety in which PBR is granted is essentially derived from another plant variety in which the person holds PBR.[133]

13.6.4 Term of protection

Registration provides a term of monopoly protection in Australia for a fixed period that commences on the day that the grant of PBR is made.[134] The term is twenty-five years for trees and vines, and twenty years for any other plant varieties.[135]

Where a PBR in an initial variety extends to cover another plant variety that is declared to be an essentially derived variety of the initial variety,[136] the PBR in the initial variety extends to the derived variety from the day on which the declaration is made until the day on which the PBR in the initial variety ends.[137]

Where the PBR in an initial variety extends to cover any dependent varieties, the term of protection for the dependent plant variety commences on the date of the grant of PBR in the initial variety, or the day on which the dependent variety comes into existence, whichever is later. The term ends at the time that the PBR in the initial variety ceases.[138]

13.7 Rights in PBR
13.7.1 General nature of PBR in propagating material

The grant of the breeder's rights provides the breeder with exclusive proprietary rights in the reproductive and propagating material of that new plant variety, not in any new processes for its production. Patents provide the relevant intellectual property regime to protect new processes. In general, the grantee of PBR can do or license another person to do any of the

---

130   Ibid s 48(1)(a).
131   Ibid s 48(1)(b).
132   Ibid s 48(2).
133   Ibid ss 48(2)(c), 40.
134   Ibid s 22(1).
135   Ibid s 22(2).
136   Ibid ss 12, 40, 41, 41A–41F. See below at 13.7.2.
137   Ibid ss 12, 22(5).
138   Ibid s 22(4).

following acts in relation to propagating material of the variety. Under s 11, the grantee has the exclusive right to:

(a) produce or reproduce the material;
(b) condition the material for the purpose of propagation;[139]
(c) offer the material for sale;
(d) sell the material;
(e) import the material;
(f) export the material;
(g) stock the material for [any of the above purposes].

By analogy with similar provisions in the *Patents Act 1990* (Cth), mere possession of propagating material would not be an exclusive right of the grantee. The exclusive right to condition the material can be for the purpose of preparing the material for propagation or sale.[140] The exclusive right to sell has been interpreted broadly, and is not limited to unconditional transfers of the propagating material solely in return for money consideration.[141] Although expressed in terms of exclusive rights to do certain acts, the *PBRA* does not confer on the grantee the right to perform these acts – they could do them anyway – but without a grant for PBR this ability would not be exclusive.[142] A grant of PBR confers the right to exclude others from performing these acts and to require licences from those persons that the breeder allows to exploit the variety commercially. Therefore, it is possible for a grantee of PBR to have these rights restricted by the application of other legislation. For example, there may be legislation that prohibits the use of that variety in food, or the growing of that variety because it is a genetically modified organism or a noxious weed.

The rights extend to essentially derived varieties, certain derived varieties, harvested material and products obtained from harvested material.[143] The practical effect of extending rights to essentially derived and certain derived varieties is to give the grantee of PBR the power to prevent the owners of those varieties from exploiting them in Australia without a licence. It does not give the grantee of PBR exclusive rights to exploit those varieties themselves.[144]

13.7.2 Extension beyond propagating material: essentially derived varieties

Generally, acts done in relation to a protected plant variety for the purpose of breeding other plant varieties do not infringe PBR.[145] However, there is an exception where the new variety is

---

139 For example, the seed may need to be cleaned or coated with a range of fungicides or germinated prior to planting, as is the case with rice.
140 *Cultivaust Pty Ltd v Grain Pool Pty Ltd* (2005) 147 FCR 265, 267. See *Plant Breeder's Rights Act 1994* (Cth) s 3(1) (definition of 'conditioning').
141 *Plant Breeder's Rights Act 1994* (Cth) s 3(1) (definition of 'sell'); *Sun World International Inc v Registrar, Plant Breeder's Rights* (1998) 87 FCR 405. See above at 13.4.5.
142 *Grain Pool of Western Australia v Commonwealth* (2000) 202 CLR 479, 513–14.
143 *Plant Breeder's Rights Act 1994* (Cth) ss 12–15.
144 *Grain Pool of Western Australia v Commonwealth* (2000) 202 CLR 479.
145 *Plant Breeder's Rights Act 1994* (Cth) s 16.

declared to be an essentially derived variety (EDV) of a registered variety. By way of explanation, an EDV may arise in the following way. Person Y may use a protected variety of tomato (Tomato X) to create a new variety of tomato (Tomato Y). The grantee of PBR in Tomato X (Person X), or the exclusive licensee of the grantee, can apply to the Registrar for a declaration that Tomato Y is essentially derived from Tomato X in certain circumstances and if certain characteristics are present in Tomato Y.[146] Tomato Y is taken to be essentially derived from Tomato X if it:

- is predominantly derived from Tomato X;
- retains the essential characteristics that result from the genotype or combination of genotypes of Tomato X; and
- does not exhibit any important (as distinct from cosmetic) features that differentiate it from Tomato X.[147]

In other words, Tomato Y is effectively a copy of Tomato X.[148] What effect does a declaration of Tomato Y as an EDV of Tomato X have on Persons X and Y? The exclusive rights of the grantee of PBR in a variety, although cast in positive terms, are rights to exclude others from the performance of the acts listed in s 11 of the *PBRA*.[149] Assuming that Tomato Y is a PBR-protected variety, even though technically each breeder can perform the acts listed in s 11, that performance could be restrained by the other breeder. As Tomato Y is effectively a copy of Tomato X, Person X can continue to exploit their PBR in Tomato X and can prevent Person Y exploiting PBR in Tomato Y.[150] Person Y can exploit Tomato Y commercially only under licence from Person X. Similarly, Person X is not authorised to exploit Tomato Y; Person X can merely restrain others, including Person Y, from doing so. Both Persons X and Y can exclude third parties from the unauthorised performance of any of the acts in s 11 in relation to Tomato Y.

An application for EDV under s 40 of the *PBRA* was restrained originally by two criteria:

- Only the grantee of PBR in the initial variety could apply to the Registrar for an EDV.
- The second variety had to be either registered or the subject of registration (PBR-protected varieties).

Various reviews[151] identified a gap in this protection: a person could avoid an EDV declaration by not filing a PBR application for their own plant variety. The reviewers recommended extending the scope of EDV declarations to varieties that are not the subject of a PBR application or grant (non-PBR-protected second varieties). The *Intellectual Property Laws Amendment (Productivity Commission Response Part 1 and Other Measures) Act 2018* (Cth) implemented this recommendation to close the gap and essentially to protect the breeder

---

146   Ibid s 12.
147   Ibid s 4.
148   For a discussion of essentially derived varieties in Australia, see Expert Panel, *Clarification of Plant Breeding Issues*, above n 3, 19–24.
149   *Grain Pool of Western Australia v Commonwealth* (2000) 202 CLR 479.
150   Expert Panel, *Clarification of Plant Breeding Issues*, above n 3, 21.
151   Productivity Commission, *Intellectual Property Arrangements* (Inquiry Report No 78, September 2016) 423; Advisory Council on Intellectual Property, *Review of Enforcement of Plant Breeder's Rights* (Final Report, January 2010) 9; Expert Panel, *Clarification of Plant Breeding Issues*, above n 3, 23.

against such 'copycat' breeding.[152] The Act also extended to an 'eligible person' – defined as the grantee of PBR in a variety, or an exclusive licensee of such a grantee – the right to make an application for an EDV declaration under s 40 (PBR-protected varieties) or s 41A (non-PBR-protected second varieties) of the *PBRA*.[153] This extension is consequential upon amendments that allow exclusive licensees to take infringement actions under s 54.[154]

Hence, a declaration that a second variety is essentially derived from the initial variety is available in both PBR-protected varieties and non-PBR-protected second varieties.[155] It is worth noting that the Registrar must convert a s 41A application to a s 40 application if a PBR application is made for the second variety before a declaration is decided.[156]

Both s 40 and s 41A applications are subject to two qualifications. First, the initial variety must not itself have been declared to be essentially derived from another PBR-protected variety.[157] Second, an application for an EDV declaration in relation to the second variety does not prevent another eligible person from also applying for an EDV declaration in that second variety.[158]

13.7.3 Extension beyond propagating material: certain dependent plant varieties

Rights of the grantee of PBR in an initial variety also extend to what are called 'dependent varieties'. There are two classes of plant varieties that meet this definition. The first is any other plant variety that is not clearly distinguishable from the initial variety but is clearly distinguishable from any plant variety that was common knowledge at the time of grant of PBR in the initial variety.[159] Therefore, it must be the same or similar to the initial variety but different from any other commonly known plants. The second is any other plant variety whose reproduction requires the repeated use of the initial variety or a dependent variety.[160] The variety to which PBR extends may exist at the time PBR is granted or may come into existence at a later date.[161] The *PBRA* provides no formal procedure for declaring any varieties as dependent plant varieties.

Therefore, unless the dependent variety is protected with a patent, the grantee of PBR in the initial variety can exercise the rights in s 11 and can exclude all others, including the breeder of that dependent variety or the variety that requires its repeated use, from exercising those rights without authorisation.

152　*Intellectual Property Laws Amendment (Productivity Commission Response Part 1 and Other Measures) Act 2018* (Cth) sch 1 pt 2 (commenced 24 February 2019).
153　See below at 13.10.2 on licences.
154　See below at 13.14.1 on actions for infringement.
155　*Plant Breeder's Rights Act 1994* (Cth) ss 40, 41 (PBR-protected), ss 41A–41F (non-PBR-protected second varieties).
156　Ibid s 41G.
157　Ibid ss 40(2), (6), 41A(2).
158　Ibid ss 40(1C), 41A(8).
159　Ibid s 13(a).
160　Ibid s 13(b).
161　Ibid s 13.

13.7.4 Extension beyond propagating material: harvested material

Under s 14(1) of the *PBRA*, the PBR of the grantee extends to harvested material if three prerequisites are established:

(a) propagating material of a plant variety covered by PBR is produced or reproduced without the authorisation of the grantee; and
(b) the grantee does not have a reasonable opportunity to exercise the grantee's right in relation to the propagating material; and
(c) material is harvested from the propagating material.

The effect of s 14(1) is that s 11 operates in relation to that harvested material as if it were propagating material. Therefore, the grantee's rights under s 11 may extend beyond propagating material (seed) to harvested non-propagating material (pumpkin). As the Full Federal Court noted in *Cultivaust Pty Ltd v Grain Pool Pty Ltd*,[162] these sections make sense in a context where the harvested material would not otherwise be propagating material. However, some propagating material, such as grains, produce a harvest that is itself propagating material. Although it may have other uses, such as for animal feed or human consumption, the harvested grains are within the definition of 'propagating material' in s 3(1) of the Act. Section 14 applies also to this harvested material that is itself propagating material.[163]

Section 14 operates in the following way. First, propagating material is produced or reproduced without authorisation of the grantee of PBR. For example, X might save seed from a previous crop of pumpkins without the authorisation of the grantee from whom the seed was purchased. Even if the seed is saved pursuant to the exemption in s 17 of the *PBRA* (farmers' rights), its use to grow pumpkins for commercial purposes or to give a bag of seed to a neighbour, for example, is not authorised by the grantee for the purposes of s 14(1).

The second prerequisite is that the grantee does not have a reasonable opportunity to exercise the grantee's right in relation to that unauthorised pumpkin seed.[164] This will occur, for instance, if X has already grown the second crop of pumpkins before the grantee becomes aware of the unauthorised production of the seed. Third, material is harvested from the crop grown using that unauthorised seed. This could be pumpkins or further seed. If all prerequisites are satisfied and no other exemption from infringement applies (such as where the acts are performed for private and non-commercial purposes),[165] the grantee can exercise the rights set out in s 11 in relation to the pumpkins themselves, even though they may not be within the meaning of propagating material. Section 14(1) deems the harvested material (pumpkins or seed) to be propagating material for the purposes of s 11. The grantee can also exercise rights set out in s 11 in relation to any further seed that is harvested, either because s 14(1) deems it as

---

162 (2005) 147 FCR 265.
163 *Cultivaust Pty Ltd v Grain Pool Pty Ltd* (2004) 62 IPR 11, affirmed (2005) 147 FCR 265, 268. See also Explanatory Memorandum, Plant Breeder's Rights Bill 1994 (Cth) cl 25.
164 Plant Breeder's Rights Act 1994 (Cth) s 14(1)(b). The meaning of 'reasonable opportunity' was discussed in *Cultivaust Pty Ltd v Grain Pool Pty Ltd* (2005) 147 FCR 265, 267, 277. See also UPOV, *Explanatory Notes on Acts in Respect of Harvested Material under the 1991 Act of the UPOV Convention* (UPOV/EXN/HRV/1, 2013) [12], [13].
165 Plant Breeder's Rights Act 1994 (Cth) s 16.

propagating material or because it is propagating material within the definition of that phrase and no other section qualifies the operation of the grantee's rights.[166] The advances in breeding have the effect that there is limited harvested material that would be outside the meaning of 'propagating material' in s 3. Hence, s 14(1) may have limited application if the grantee can rely directly on s 11 to exercise those rights.

13.7.5 Extension beyond propagating material: products obtained from harvested material

Section 15 of the *PBRA* operates to extend rights of the breeder one further step down the production chain to products – such as pumpkin soup – that are made using the pumpkins that are harvested from the crop grown using that unauthorised seed. Hence, s 15 enables the grantee to exercise the rights set out in s 11 in relation to the soup, even though it is not propagating material. However, the extension of rights applies only where the same three prerequisites required in s 14(1) are established,[167] with the additional prerequisite that the grantee does not have, in the circumstances set out in s 14, a reasonable opportunity of exercising the grantee's rights in the harvested material before the products are made.

13.7.6 Concept of exhaustion of rights

The *PBRA* sets the limit at which PBR are in effect exhausted. Section 23 relates to the disposition and use of a first-generation crop from propagating material that was lawfully acquired.[168] It deals with the sale of seed and what can be done with the harvest from that crop. Its operation would be subject to any express or implied conditions in the agreement that governed the sale. As a general proposition, a PBR does not extend to any act referred to in s 11 in relation to propagating material of the variety, or of any essentially derived or dependent variety, that takes place after that propagating material has been sold by the grantee or with the grantee's consent. Therefore, a sale of carrot seeds partially exhausts the PBR in those carrot seeds. The purchaser can plant them, and harvest and sell the carrots. In the case of a crop such as barley where the seed is the same as the harvest, the sale of the seed will, by implication, authorise the sale of the barley for non-reproductive purposes.[169]

However, there is not a complete exhaustion of rights after such sales. PBR continue to apply in two circumstances. The first concerns any act in relation to the propagating material that involves further production or reproduction of the propagating material.[170] Growing the purchased carrot seed, and allowing the carrot crop to go to seed for the purpose of harvesting and selling seed, would be excluded from this exemption in s 23. The same is true where the purchaser grows the barley and sells the harvest for further propagation. To avoid infringement, it would be necessary for the sale to include a licence from the grantee to perform these

---

166   Ibid ss 16, 17, 18, 19, 23.
167   See above at 13.7.4.
168   The Full Federal Court expressed no view on the specific operation of s 23(1) in *Cultivaust Pty Ltd v Grain Pool Pty Ltd* (2005) 147 FCR 265, 268.
169   *Cultivaust Pty Ltd v Grain Pool Pty Ltd* (2004) 62 IPR 11, 48, 50.
170   Plant Breeder's Rights Act 1994 (Cth) s 23(4); *Cultivaust Pty Ltd v Grain Pool Pty Ltd* (2004) 62 IPR 11, 53.

acts. An exemption is provided to a person engaged in farming activities, who is permitted by s 17(1) to save a sufficient amount of that seed and condition it for use for their own propagation purposes to produce second and subsequent harvests. In addition, any person, including a farmer, is entitled under s 16 to perform certain acts for private, experimental or breeding purposes without those acts constituting an infringement of PBR.

The second circumstance in which PBR continue to apply is the unauthorised export of the purchased propagating material for a purpose other than final consumption to a country that does not provide PBR in relation to that variety.

Section 23 does not deal with the sale of second and subsequent generation crops, assuming they are grown from farm-saved seed from lawfully acquired propagating material. The seed used for the second-generation crop is not 'sold by the grantee'. According to Mansfield J in *Cultivaust*,[171] this section complements the extension in ss 14 and 15. Hence, s 23 would not exclude from the operation of s 11 all subsequent generations of crops from seed originally purchased from the grantee of PBR.[172] The Full Federal Court considered that Mansfield J had dealt with s 23 in a way that 'appears unexceptionable'.[173] However, it expressed no view on the section's specific operation in the scheme of the *PBRA*.

13.8 Limitations on PBR

The exclusive rights of the breeder set out in s 11 of the *PBRA* as applicable to propagating material of a variety are extended by ss 12–15 to essentially derived varieties, dependent varieties, harvested material and products made using harvested material. These rights are subject to the limitations in ss 16–18.

13.8.1 Private, experimental or breeding purposes

It is compulsory under art 15(1) of *UPOV 1991* to exempt certain acts from infringement. These are contained in s 16 of the *PBRA*, and fall into three categories:

- acts done privately and for non-commercial purposes;
- acts done for experimental purposes;
- acts done for the purpose of breeding other plant varieties.

It is important to note that s 16 is concerned with acts that would otherwise be infringing acts. It qualifies the operation of the breeder's exclusive rights that are set out in ss 11–15 of the *PBRA* and the acts require no authorisation of the breeder.

Neither *UPOV 1991* nor the *PBRA* contains definitions of 'privately and for non-commercial purposes' or 'experimental purposes'. However, UPOV Explanatory Notes assist with understanding the scope of the exception for 'acts done privately and for non-commercial purposes'. The exception requires those acts to be of both a private and a non-commercial nature. Hence, saving seed on a farmer's own holding might be a private act but if it is saved for commercial

---

171 *Cultivaust Pty Ltd v Grain Pool Pty Ltd* (2004) 62 IPR 11.
172 Ibid 53–4.
173 *Cultivaust Pty Ltd v Grain Pool Pty Ltd* (2005) 147 FCR 265, 277.

purposes it would be outside the exception. Examples of acts that may fall within the exception include an amateur gardener propagating a variety for the use only of their family or a farmer propagating a food crop for consumption only by their family and dependents living on the farm.[174]

It seems that the phrase 'experimental purposes' encompasses something other than or in addition to acts done for the purpose of breeding other varieties, as there is the separate category for that class of acts. It is likely that the word 'experimental' would be given its usual meaning, so that it would include such things as trials and investigations. It is likely that experiments that have a commercial objective are also within this exemption, as there is otherwise nothing to differentiate its scope from the category of use for private and non-commercial purposes.[175]

Generally, it is not an infringement of PBR to use the variety for further breeding.[176] The *PBRA* contains two exceptions to this proposition. One is where that protected variety is used repeatedly in commercial production as would occur in the case of a parent of a hybrid variety.[177] The other is where the new variety that is bred is declared to be an essentially derived variety.[178]

13.8.2 Farmer's rights

Article 15(2) of *UPOV 1991* gives members the right to provide an optional exception within reasonable limits and subject to the safeguarding of the legitimate interests of the breeder to

> restrict the breeder's right in relation to any variety in order to permit farmers to use for propagating purposes, on their own holdings, the product of the harvest which they have obtained by planting, on their own holdings, the protected variety, or a variety covered by Article 14(5)(a)(i) or (ii).

This exemption, which is usually referred to as a farmer's exemption to save seed or other propagating material, is additional to the exempted acts set out in art 15(1) of *UPOV 1991*. Its focus is small, subsistence farmers, and not commercial growers.

The traditional practice of farmers before the advent of breeder's rights was to collect seeds from a past crop and condition and sow the saved seed to produce future crops. A farmer may therefore need only purchase seed once. Arguably, there is something inherently unfair if a farmer can buy seeds for one crop but thereafter provide no further recompense to the breeder. On the other hand, complete freedom to save and deal with saved seed or other propagating material has an inhibiting effect on investment in breeding certain types of plant varieties.

The central issue for policymakers in designing protection for breeders was to determine the extent to which this practice should occur in respect of PBR-protected varieties. Breeders have a few options available to protect their investment. They can charge a premium for the

---

174   UPOV, *Explanatory Notes on Exceptions to the Breeder's Right Under the 1991 Act of the UPOV Convention* (UPOV/EXN/EXC/1, 2009) [5]–[7].
175   Byrne, 'Plant breeder's rights', above n 1, [29,090].
176   UPOV, *Explanatory Notes on Exceptions to the Breeder's Right*, above n 174, [9]–[11].
177   *Plant Breeder's Rights Act 1994* (Cth) s 13.
178   Ibid s 12.

first sale of seed to recoup profit for the breeding endeavour, but risk lower sales if the seed is too expensive. Alternatively, they can abstain from breeding varieties that are at risk and focus on breeding hybrid varieties that have 'an inherent biological solution to the problem'.[179] Farmers who want to retain the past freedoms and reduce the costs of crop production could purchase non-protected seed, but will then be excluded from accessing new and improved varieties.

UPOV 1991 gives member states two options for dealing with this issue. One option favours breeders and limits exemptions from infringement to those listed in art 15(1) of the convention.[180] It is an infringement of PBR to save seed of the protected variety for any other purposes without authorisation. The other option is to provide farmers with a limited right to save seed and other propagating material but not at the expense of the legitimate interests of the breeder.

The *PBRA* takes the latter approach. Section 17 provides farmers with the capacity to use seed that they have generated for planting and use on their own holdings without infringement. It does not provide for what the farmer may do with propagating material that is generated from farm-saved seed beyond its further use as farm-saved seed.[181] This is the province of ss 11, 14 and 15, as qualified by the exemptions in ss 16 and 18. The combination of the farm-saved seed exemption in s 17 and the rights in ss 11, 14 and 15 enables the growers to share the risks with the breeder. A moderate charge is made for the seed and subsequent profitability for both farmers and breeders is dependent on the quality of the seed. If the seed produces poor crops, both end-point royalties and profits will be low. The converse is also true: excellent crops will provide benefits for both growers and breeders. Breeders are able to learn the outcomes of their variety and use this knowledge in further plant breeding endeavours. These rights are more easily established through contract, and end-point royalties are commonly used in the industry.

Sub-paragraphs (a)–(c) of s 17(1) set out the conditions for the operation of the exemption and the material that is going to be the subject of the exemption, while sub-paras (d) and (e) specify the extent of the exemption. There are three aspects of sub-para (a). First, the exemption applies only to a person who is engaged in farming activities. Hence, it has no application to research scientists in a university, for example, unless they are involved in farming activities. Second, that person legitimately obtains propagating material either by purchase or by previous operation of s 17. Section 17 would not apply to a voluntary release of seed to farmers for the purpose of trialling and testing. Nor would it apply to a farmer who obtains a bag of seeds over the fence from their neighbour. Third, that material must be acquired for use in farming activities. It would have no application to seed purchased for the private vegetable garden on the farm. Section 16(a) provides exemptions for saving and propagating seed in those circumstances. A farmer who buys seed for use in their farming activities will satisfy s 17(1)(a).

Sub-para (c) of s 17(1) specifies that it is the propagating material that the farmer harvests from the crop grown with legitimately acquired seed that is the subject of sub-paras (d) and (e). These latter provisions specify the acts that would otherwise infringe the breeder's rights that the farmer may perform without constituting an infringement. These allow the farmer to

---

179 Byrne, 'Plant breeder's rights', above n 1, [27,127], [29,090].
180 See above at 13.8.1.
181 *Cultivaust Pty Ltd v Grain Pool Pty Ltd* (2004) 62 IPR 11, 49.

condition so much of the material as is required for the farmer's use for reproductive purposes or the reproduction of that further material. Therefore, the exemption enables farmers to keep back seed indefinitely from previous crops and plant it on their own land. The exemption from infringement is limited to the use of seed for their own reproductive purposes – to grow the crop on their own land – and to retain sufficient further seed for future reproductive purposes. Section 17 does not indicate what the grower can do with propagating material generated from farm-saved seed beyond its further use as farm-saved seed. It does not permit the farmer to offer any harvested propagating material from those legitimately grown crops for sale, or to sell it or perform any of the other acts listed in s 11. Furthermore, s 17 does not say what a farmer can do with any non-propagating material that is harvested or with products made from that harvested material. To discern this, reference is necessary to ss 14 and 15, which are discussed above.[182]

13.8.3 Breeder's rights in harvested material and products from crops grown with farm-saved seed

Section 14(1) of the *PBRA* applies only to a crop that is grown from propagating material that is produced or reproduced without authorisation. Hence, it does not apply to purchased propagating material that is used for the purposes authorised expressly or impliedly by the terms of sale. The unconditional sale of seed carries with it an implied authorisation to sow the seed, grow and harvest the crop, and use the harvest.

In the absence of any limitation on the scope of s 14(1), all material harvested from crops grown with farm-saved seed would be subject to its provisions. Section 14(2) limits the operation of s 14(1) by reference to s 17(1) of the Act and directs that the part of the harvest that is retained as farm-saved seed is not subject to its provisions.[183] If the conditions in s 14(1) are satisfied, the PBR in propagating material extends to all the second and subsequent generations of the crop that are produced except for that portion that is saved under s 17.[184] Section 14(1) is available to deal with all harvested material, irrespective of whether it is propagating material or non-propagating material. However, where the harvested material is also propagating material, breeders can rely on s 11 to exercise PBR, without the need to resort to s 14(1). Section 15 is then available if products are made from that harvested material before the grantee can exercise their rights in relation to that harvested material. If the harvested material is itself propagating material (such as wheat), and is made into products (such as flour and bread) before the grantee can exercise rights in relation to that material, it is necessary for the grantee to rely on s 14 to deem the harvested material as propagating material before s 15 can apply to the products.

13.8.4 Other restrictions on rights

Section 18 of the *PBRA* provides a form of compulsory licence for a person who is authorised by or under a Commonwealth, state or territory law to do an act referred to in s 11. To gain this

---

182 At 13.7.4 and 13.7.5, respectively.
183 *Cultivaust Pty Ltd v Grain Pool Pty Ltd* (2005) 147 FCR 265, 268.
184 *Cultivaust Pty Ltd v Grain Pool Pty Ltd* (2004) 62 IPR 11, 49.

exemption from infringement, it is necessary for the person, before doing the act, either to pay equitable remuneration to the grantee of PBR in the plant variety or an exclusive licensee of the grantee, or to make arrangements for such payment. To avoid infringement, the person must reach an agreement with the grantee of PBR or an exclusive licensee of the grantee as to the amount to be paid, or have the amount determined by the court, before the act is performed. This exemption from infringement in no way limits the rights that farmers have under s 17.[185]

If a person performs an act in relation to protected propagating material and pays or makes arrangements for payment of equitable remuneration as required by s 18, the exclusive rights of the grantee of the PBR, or an exclusive licensee of the grantee, are partially extinguished in the same way as if there had been a sale of the propagating material.[186]

13.8.5 Reasonable public access

The grantee must take all reasonable steps to ensure that there will be reasonable public access to the propagating material of the protected variety.[187] This obligation is satisfied if propagating material of reasonable quality is available to the public at reasonable prices, or as gifts to the public, in sufficient quantities to meet demand.[188]

The *PBRA* provides a form of compulsory licensing in s 19 to ensure that the public has reasonable access to the plant variety. It cannot be activated during the period of two years after the grant of PBR in a plant variety.[189] Furthermore, it does not apply in relation to a plant variety that the Registrar certifies, in writing, at the time of the grant of PBR, to have no direct use as a consumer product.[190] In the circumstances provided in s 19, the Registrar may license a person to sell propagating material of plants of that variety, or to produce propagating material of plants of that variety for sale during such period as considered appropriate and on such terms and conditions (including the provision of reasonable remuneration to the grantee) as the Registrar considers would be granted by the grantee in the normal course of business.[191]

13.9 Ownership and co-ownership

A PBR in a plant variety is granted to the applicant. This will be the breeder who made the application or the person to whom the breeder's right to make application for PBR in that variety has been assigned, or transmitted by will or by operation of law.[192] In the event that an application for PBR is made jointly,[193] the PBR is granted to those persons jointly.[194] Hence they hold the interest as joint tenants rather than as tenants in common in equal shares. In

---

185 *Plant Breeder's Rights Act 1994* (Cth) s 18(2).
186 Ibid s 23(3).
187 Ibid s 19(1).
188 Ibid s 19(2).
189 Ibid s 19(4).
190 Ibid ss 19(11), 77.
191 Ibid s 19(3).
192 See above at 13.5.1.
193 Ibid s 24(3).
194 Ibid s 44(11).

consequence, the interest of a joint tenant in PBR would pass to the surviving joint tenant on death.

A PBR is personal property and, subject to any conditions imposed under s 49, is capable of assignment, or of transmission by will or by operation of law.[195] Where a PBR is granted to the breeders jointly pursuant to a joint application,[196] it appears that neither breeder can exercise the exclusive rights for his or her own commercial purposes without the other's authorisation.[197]

13.10 Exploiting PBR: licensing and other forms

13.10.1 Assignment of PBR

An assignment of PBR (otherwise than because of the order of a court) does not have effect unless it is in writing signed by, or on behalf of, the assignor and assignee.[198] If a PBR in a particular plant variety is granted to a person, X, and another person, Y, was entitled, at law or in equity, to an assignment of the right to make an application for the PBR, then Y is entitled to an assignment of the PBR.[199] A possible scenario where this might arise is where the grant of PBR is to an employee who bred the variety in the course of performing duties of employment. In the absence of an agreement with the employer to the contrary, the employer is entitled to an assignment of PBR.[200]

13.10.2 Licences

A grantee of PBR may give another person an exclusive or non-exclusive licence in that right. An exclusive licensee is defined to mean

> a licensee under a licence granted by the grantee that confers on the licensee, or on the licensee and persons authorised by the licensee, PBR in the plant variety to the exclusion of the grantee and all other persons.[201]

Any such licence binds every successor in title to the interest of that grantee to the same extent as it was binding on the grantee.[202] There is no requirement to enter particulars of licences in the Register of Plant Varieties. As it is only the grantee or an exclusive licensee of the grantee of PBR who has the right to exclude others from the activities listed in s 11, and to take infringement proceedings,[203] a non-exclusive licensee has no power in this regard unless appropriate rights are included in the licence agreement.

---

195 Ibid s 20(1).
196 Ibid s 45(2).
197 Ibid s 53.
198 Ibid s 20(2).
199 Ibid s 48(3).
200 Ibid s 3(1) (definition of 'breeder').
201 Ibid s 3(1).
202 Ibid s 20(3).
203 Ibid s 54(1).

The grantee of PBR is entitled to sell seed subject to a licence that grants rights to produce or reproduce that seed for commercial purposes. The licence can also include the imposition of a production levy on the first and subsequent generations of crops. Hence, the grantee could sell barley to purchaser X on condition that X pays an agreed amount per tonne of barley that is harvested from the initial crop and from all subsequent crops that are grown using farm-saved seed.[204] There has been no judicial determination as to whether the licence can also impose as a term of sale that the grower must not retain any of the harvested crop for further use as propagating material. Such a term would be inconsistent with the express right in s 17 of the *PBRA*.[205]

13.11 Revocation of PBR

The Registrar must revoke PBR when the conditions set out in s 50(1) are present. The Registrar may act on their own initiative or upon receipt of a written application. Such application may be made by a person whose interests are affected by the grant of PBR in a plant variety, or by the making of a declaration that a plant variety is an essentially derived variety.[206] There are two grounds that mandate revocation by the Registrar. The first is that the Registrar becomes satisfied that facts existed that would have resulted in the refusal to grant the right or make the declaration if the Registrar had known of those facts at that time.[207] The second ground is the non-payment of fees.[208] The Registrar also has discretion to revoke PBR in a variety on a number of grounds.[209] Any decision to revoke or refuse to revoke PBR or a declaration as to an essentially derived variety is reviewable by the Administrative Affairs Tribunal under s 77.[210]

A defendant to an infringement action can counterclaim for revocation of PBR on two grounds. The first is that the variety was not a new plant variety.[211] This is not an express ground for revocation under s 50(1). The second is similar to that provided in s 50(1) – namely, that facts exist that would have resulted in the refusal of the grant of that right if they had been known to the Registrar before the grant of the right.[212] It is not clear what the first ground adds to the second, if anything. If the facts demonstrate that the variety was not new, then this information would have resulted in a refusal to grant PBR.

13.12 Surrender of PBR

Surrender of PBR may occur voluntarily by written notice to the Registrar[213] or in consequence of failure to pay the prescribed annual fee for renewal.[214]

---

204   *Cultivaust Pty Ltd v Grain Pool Pty Ltd* (2004) 62 IPR 11, 42.
205   Ibid.
206   *Plant Breeder's Rights Act 1994* (Cth) s 50(8).
207   Ibid s 50(1)(a). See *Majestic Selections Pty Ltd v Bushland Flora* [2016] APBRO 1 (Delegate N Hulse).
208   *Plant Breeder's Rights Act 1994* (Cth) s 50(1)(b).
209   Ibid s 50(2).
210   Ibid s 50(10).
211   Ibid s 54A(1)(a).
212   Ibid s 54A(1)(b).
213   Ibid s 52.
214   Ibid s 51(2).

13.13 Infringement of rights

13.13.1 What amounts to infringement?

A person infringes the exclusive rights of the grantee[215] of PBR in a plant variety if they:

- do any act in s 11 of the *PBRA* in respect of the variety or of a dependent variety without, or not in accordance with, the grantee's authorisation;[216]
- claim the right to do any act in s 11 in respect of the variety or of a dependent variety without, or not in accordance with, the grantee's authorisation;[217]
- use a name of the variety that is entered in the Register in relation to any other plant variety of the same plant class or a plant of any other variety of the same plant class.[218]

If the evidence falls short of establishing the use of the name, it may be possible to make out a case of contravention of misleading and deceptive conduct under s 18 of sch 2 of the *Competition and Consumer Act 2010* (Cth).[219]

In the case where an essentially derived variety is a PBR-protected variety, the person requires the authorisation of both the grantee of the initial variety (from which the essentially derived variety is derived) and the grantee of the essentially derived variety, to avoid infringement of PBR in that variety.[220]

13.13.2 Exemptions from infringement

The *PBRA* contains a number of exemptions from infringement, discussed above in the context of limitations on the breeder's rights.[221] These exempt:

- acts that are done privately and for non-commercial purposes, for experimental purposes or for the purposes of breeding other varieties;[222]
- farmers' rights to save, condition and use propagating material for their own purposes;[223]
- performance of acts with legislative authority upon payment of equitable remuneration to the grantee;[224]
- licensing of PBR by the Registrar in circumstances where the grantee has taken all reasonable steps to ensure reasonable public access to the plant variety;[225] and
- acts that take place after propagating material has been sold by the grantee or with the grantee's consent or licensed under s 18.[226]

---

215 This term includes a person who has, by assignment or transmission, become the holder of that right (ibid s 53(3)) and an exclusive licensee (ibid s 53(4)).
216 *Plant Breeder's Rights Act 1994* (Cth) s 53(1)(a).
217 Ibid s 53(1)(b).
218 Ibid ss 53(1)(c), 53(1A).
219 *Buchanan Turf Supplies Pty Ltd v Premier Turf Supplies Pty Ltd* [2003] FCA 230. *Competition and Consumer Act 2010* (Cth) sch 2 s 18 was formerly *Trade Practices Act 1974* (Cth) s 52.
220 *Plant Breeder's Rights Act 1994* (Cth) s 53(2).
221 At 13.8.
222 *Plant Breeder's Rights Act 1994* (Cth) s 16.
223 Ibid s 17.
224 Ibid s 18.
225 Ibid s 19.
226 Ibid s 23.

13.13.3 Prior user rights

It is possible for two breeders, X and Y, to have bred the same plant variety independently of each other, but only one grant is possible in relation to that variety.[227] If X is first to file the application, the prior existence of Y's variety may prevent registration by X if it is a variety of common knowledge. As discussed above,[228] specific aspects that would establish Y's variety as one of common knowledge include commercialisation of propagating or harvested material. Hence, any prior sales by Y of plants within her variety will render that variety one of common knowledge and thus render X's variety not distinct.[229]

Assuming that X is successful in the application, Y's variety will be regarded as a dependent variety over which the PBR to X extends under s 13. If Y wants to exploit the variety commercially, it is necessary for Y to obtain a licence from X.

13.14 Enforcement of rights
13.14.1 Actions for infringement

Only the grantee or an exclusive licensee of the grantee of PBR in a plant variety can begin an action for infringement of PBR in the Federal Court or the Federal Circuit Court.[230] If an exclusive licensee brings the action, he must make the grantee a defendant to the action unless the grantee is joined as a plaintiff.[231] Provisional protection for the variety arises when the application for PBR is accepted.[232] While no proceedings can be commenced for infringement until the grant of the PBR,[233] a grantee may have a right of action in respect of an act that was committed at any time from the acceptance of the PBR application.[234]

The infringement of PBR in a variety under s 53 may be the subject of criminal prosecution under s 74(1), even if an infringement action has been brought against the person under s 54.

A defendant in an infringement action can counterclaim for revocation on the grounds that the variety was not a new plant variety or on the grounds of the existence of facts that would have resulted in a refusal of the grant of PBR had the Registrar had prior knowledge of them.[235]

13.14.2 Non-infringement declarations

The Federal Court or Federal Circuit Court may make a declaration as to non-infringement in proceedings issued by a person who wants to perform an act described in s 11 of the *PBRA* in relation to propagating material of a protected plant variety.[236] A person can apply for such a

---

227 Ibid s 45(1).
228 At 13.4.2.1.
229 *Majestic Selections Pty Ltd v Bushland Flora* [2016] APBRO 1 (Delegate N Hulse).
230 *Plant Breeder's Rights Act 1994* (Cth) s 54(1).
231 Ibid ss 54(2), (3).
232 Ibid s 39(1).
233 Ibid s 39(6).
234 Ibid s 39(1), (6).
235 Ibid s 54A.
236 Ibid s 55(1).

declaration whether or not there has been an assertion of infringement of that right and must join the grantee as a respondent in those proceedings.[237] No declaration can be made unless the person has been unsuccessful in obtaining an admission of non-infringement from the grantee.[238] The proceedings must not consider the validity of a grant of PBR in a plant variety.[239] Furthermore, the making of, or refusal to make, a declaration has no implications as to validity or otherwise of the grant of PBR.[240]

13.14.3 Unjustified threats of infringement proceedings

The *Intellectual Property Laws Amendment (Productivity Commission Response Part 1 and Other Measures) Act 2018* (Cth) introduced s 57A into the *PBRA* to give to a person threatened with infringement proceedings the right to apply to the Federal Court or the Federal Circuit Court for:

- a declaration that the threats are unjustified;[241]
- an injunction; and
- recovery of any damages sustained as a result of the threats.[242]

Each court has discretion to award additional damages for flagrantly unjustified threats.[243] No relief is to be granted where the acts complained of would infringe the PBR in the variety.[244] The respondent in s 57A proceedings for unjustified threats can counterclaim for relief for infringement of PBR in the variety.[245] A legal practitioner who acts professionally on behalf of a client is not liable to s 57A proceedings.[246]

13.14.4 Jurisdiction

The Federal Court and the Federal Circuit Court have jurisdiction with respect to matters in which infringement actions may be brought under the *PBRA*.[247] The Administrative Appeals Tribunal has the power to review decisions by the Minister under s 49(2) (imposition of conditions on PBR), and various other decisions of the Registrar made under the *PBRA*.[248]

---

237 Ibid ss 55(2), (7). The reference to 'grantee' in s 55 includes an exclusive licensee of the grantee: at s 55(8).
238 Ibid ss 55(3).
239 Ibid s 55(5).
240 Ibid s 55(6).
241 Mere notification of the existence of PBR is not a threat of proceedings: Ibid s 57D.
242 *Intellectual Property Laws Amendment (Productivity Commission Response Part 1 and Other Measures) Act 2018* (Cth) sch 2 pt 8 item 202. The application of s 57A is limited to threats made on or after the commencement of sch 3 pt 8 (24 February 2019): at sch 2 pt 8 item 209(4) (commenced 24 February 2019).
243 *Plant Breeder's Rights Act 1994* (Cth) s 57A(2). See below at 13.16.
244 Ibid s 57B.
245 Ibid s 57C.
246 Ibid s 57E.
247 Ibid s 56(1), (2) (Federal Court), s 56A(1), (2) (Federal Circuit Court).
248 Ibid s 77.

13.14.5 Offences and conduct by directors, servants and agents

The *PBRA* provides for criminal sanctions with respect to infringement offences[249] and certain false statements and false representations.[250] The fact that an action for infringement is brought under s 54 does not prevent a prosecution under s 74 for the same infringing conduct. Section 75 provides for false statements in documents given to the Registrar and for false representations to another person that the representor is the grantee of PBR, or as to the scope of protection for a plant variety, or that PBR has been granted. There are also provisions that deal with the conduct of directors, servants and agents in proceedings for an offence under s 74 or s 75.[251]

13.15 The Register

The Registrar of Plant Breeder's Rights[252] must keep a Register of Plant Varieties[253] available for inspection at any reasonable time.[254] The PBR database is on the IP Australia website. The following must be entered in the Register:

- particulars of the grant of PBR and of derived variety and essentially derived variety declarations;[255]
- particulars of revocation of PBR in accordance with s 50 of the *PBRA*;[256]
- an order of a court given under s 54A(2) revoking PBR;[257]
- surrender of PBR pursuant to non-payment of fees;[258] and
- details of an assignment or transmission of rights.[259]

The Registrar has powers introduced in s 62A to rectify the Register, on application by any person or otherwise, when the Registrar is satisfied of any of the circumstances set out in s 62A.[260]

13.16 Remedies

The relief that the Federal Court or Federal Circuit Court may award to the grantee or the exclusive licensee of the grantee of PBR in an action or proceeding for infringement includes

---

249 Ibid s 74.
250 Ibid s 75.
251 Ibid s 76.
252 Ibid s 58.
253 Ibid s 61.
254 Ibid s 62.
255 Ibid s 46.
256 Ibid s 51(1)(a).
257 Ibid s 51(1)(b).
258 Ibid s 51(3). Section 52 does not require a voluntary surrender to be entered on the Register.
259 Ibid s 21.
260 Ibid 62A applies to all grants of PBR and entries in the Register irrespective of when grants or entries were made: *Intellectual Property Laws Amendment (Productivity Commission Response Part 1 and Other Measures) Act 2018* (Cth) sch 2 pt 9 item 217 (commenced 24 February 2019).

an injunction and, at the option of the plaintiff, either damages or an account of profits.[261] Amendments under the *Intellectual Property Laws Amendment (Productivity Commission Response Part 1 and Other Measures) Act 2018* (Cth) give each court discretion, having regard to a range of criteria, to award additional damages for an infringement of PBR. The criteria include flagrancy, the need for a deterrent effect, the conduct of the infringer and the benefits accrued from their conduct. Additional damages can be awarded only in relation to conduct engaged in, on or after the commencement of the amendments.[262]

In the case of an innocent infringement, the court may refuse to award damages or to make an order for an account of profits.[263] Innocent infringement will occur where the person satisfies the court that they were not aware of, and had no reasonable grounds for suspecting the existence of PBR at the time of the infringement. However, the person is taken to be so aware if propagating material of plants of the plant variety, labelled so as to indicate that PBR is held in the variety in Australia, has been sold to a substantial extent before the date of the infringement.[264] The unqualified reference to sales in s 57(2) is not limited to Australia; the material could have been sold anywhere in the world. Inadequate labelling can therefore reduce the effectiveness of future and existing rights. IP Australia provides industry guidelines for labelling and requires that only recommended versions of the logo and standardised wording are used.

13.17 Relationships between PBR and other intellectual property regimes

Article 27(3)(b) of the *Agreement on Trade-Related Aspects of Intellectual Property*[265] (*TRIPS*) provides that members have an obligation to protect plant varieties either by patents or under an effective sui generis system or by any combination thereof. *UPOV* is a sui generis system for plant variety protection and many member states, including Australia, model their statutory plant variety protection schemes on this convention. Although *TRIPS* provides its members with the option of choosing either patent protection or plant varieties protection, many states including Australia provide both forms of protection for plants.

13.17.1 PBR and patents

The *PBRA* and the patent system are not mutually exclusive but use different criteria for access to their protection. Patents protect inventions that are new and not obvious. They provide an incentive and reward for invention. They generally protect processes or components of a variety, such as gene sequences. In contrast, the PBR system is available to protect propagating material

---

261 *Plant Breeder's Rights Act 1994* (Cth) s 56(3).
262 *Intellectual Property Laws Amendment (Productivity Commission Response Part 1 and Other Measures) Act 2018* (Cth) sch 2 pt 11 items 221–3 inserting s 56(3A) (Federal Court) and s 56A(3A) (Federal Circuit Court) (commenced 24 February 2019).
263 *Plant Breeder's Rights Act 1994* (Cth) s 57(1).
264 Ibid s 57(2).
265 *Marrakesh Agreement Establishing the World Trade Organization*, opened for signature 15 April 1994, 1867 UNTS 3 (entered into force 1 January 1995) annex 1C (*Agreement on Trade-Related Aspects of Intellectual Property*).

of the plant variety. It protects varieties that have been made publicly available (as long as they are not common knowledge) and is not designed to protect non-obvious results. The right protects the time expended in the development of the plant variety, not in its invention.

There is a potential conflict between these two regimes that results from the fundamental requirement under the *PBRA* for a protected variety to be made available without restriction for further breeding. In contrast, the *Patents Act 1990* (Cth) provides limited exemptions from infringement of a patent under s 119C when the acts are done for experimental purposes relating to the subject matter of the invention.[266] Prior to the introduction of s 119C, concern was expressed that the insertion of a patented gene into a plant variety that is then registered may activate restrictions on the accessibility of the plant for further breeding purposes and thereby undermine the *PBRA*.[267] The extent to which this remains a risk will depend upon the acts performed and the scope of exemptions under s 119C. The various exemptions that are contained in the *PBRA*, such as exemption for farm-saved seed and exemption for private and non-commercial purposes, have no express counterparts in the *Patents Act 1990*.

13.17.2 PBR and trade marks

The name that is given to a plant variety is a generic name to describe the variety and as such must be able to be used freely by the public. In contrast to a trade mark, the plant variety name has no purpose to distinguish the trade origin of the plant variety. The requirement for freedom of use of the name means that the name of a plant variety must not be or include a trade mark that is registered or whose registration is being sought under the *PBRA* in respect of live plants, plant cells and plant tissues.[268] However, a grantee of PBR can use a trade mark in conjunction with a plant variety name provided that each has equal prominence with the other.[269]

13.18 Other international conventions

Other international conventions or treaties deal with plant genetic resources in ways that create linkages and conflicts with the PBR system. These include the *Convention on Biological Diversity*[270] and the *International Treaty on Plant Genetic Resources for Food and Agriculture 2001*.[271]

---

266 *Patents Act 1990* (Cth) s 119C; Advisory Council on Intellectual Property, *Patents and Experimental Use* (Final Report, October 2005); Australian Law Reform Commission, *Genes and Ingenuity: Gene Patenting and Human Health* (Report No 99, June 2004) ch 13. See ch 12 at 12.8.5.
267 C. Lawson, 'Patents and plant breeder's rights over plant genetic resources for food and agriculture' (2004) 32 *Federal Law Review* 107; M. Rimmer, 'Franklin Barley: Patent law and plant breeder's rights' (2003) 10 *Murdoch University Electronic Journal of Law* 1.
268 *Plant Breeder's Rights Act 1994* (Cth) s 27(5)(e).
269 See IP Australia, 'Plant breeder's rights FAQs: Variety Names' www.ipaustralia.gov.au.
270 Opened for signature 5 June 1992, 1760 UNTS 79 (entered into force 29 December 1993). The convention was adopted by the Intergovernmental Negotiating Committee for a Convention on Biological Diversity, during its Fifth Session (Nairobi 11–22 May 1992). Signed by Australia on 5 June 1992; ratified 18 June 1992.
271 Opened for signature 3 November 2001, 2400 UNTS 303 (entered into force 29 June 2004). The Food and Agriculture Organization of the United Nations (FAO) Conference, at its Thirty-First Session (November 2001), through Resolution 3/2001, approved the treaty. Australia signed the treaty on 10 June 2002.

PART IV

TRADE MARKS

14

PASSING OFF

14.1 History of passing off

A typical passing off situation is one in which the defendant represents that its product originates from or is in some way associated with the plaintiff or the plaintiff's business when that is not the case.[1] It may do this by adopting some business indicia of the plaintiff, such as an identical or similar business name or sign associated with the plaintiff's product; but, as we will see, there are many different scenarios that fit that general description of passing off and the tort has also developed well beyond that basic proposition. We will also see that the understanding of the tort is complicated by its historical evolution. Its complicated history relates to the fact that the tort was recognised by both common law courts and courts of equity but they exhibited considerable differences in both their approach to the theoretical underpinnings of the tort and their approach to remedies for passing off. These historical differences continue to inform and complicate the development and application of the tort. An understanding of that history is essential to understanding the present-day formulation of passing off. It is also essential to understanding the various functions of registered trade marks, a statutory system of intellectual property that evolved from the tort of passing off.

14.1.1 Common law and passing off

Common law courts perceived passing off as a form of fraud and placed greater emphasis on the 'fraud' aspect of passing off. They were therefore concerned with representations by traders that deceived consumers about the trade origin of goods. However, unlike the tort of fraud, it was not the recipient of the fraudulent misrepresentation, the consumer, who brought the action. Instead, it was the injured trader who brought the passing off action because the trader was injured when consumers were deceived into believing that the goods being sold originated from the trader, when in fact they did not. This common law tort became far more powerful when the requirement of intention to deceive, a necessary element of the tort of fraud, was dropped well over a century ago and the nature of the misrepresentations recognised as founding the action expanded dramatically during the twentieth century.

14.1.2 Equity and passing off

Courts of equity were more concerned with the property aspect of passing off. Consequently, they focused on the property interest of a trader who was injured as a result of the defendant's conduct. The property interest in question is today recognised as the business reputation of the plaintiff. This emphasis of equity on the property interest of the plaintiff had considerable implications for the tort as well. First, it meant that courts of equity were not concerned about the element of intention that dominated the tort of fraud and therefore early common law approaches to passing off. Second, the emphasis on the property interest of the plaintiff has probably led to an inclination on the part of courts to more readily find the misrepresentation

---

1   See *Stone & Wood Group Pty Ltd v Intellectual Property Development Corp Pty Ltd* [2018] FCAFC 29, [7]–[9] for the distinction between a representation that the goods are the goods of another party and a representation that the goods have some relevant association or connection with the goods of another party.

that is still a necessary part of the tort. By being easily convinced that a misrepresentation has occurred, courts then quickly move to protect the plaintiff's reputation. Indeed, some commentators have suggested that passing off has metamorphosed into a tort of unfair competition that prevents misappropriation of another's business reputation, even in the absence of a misrepresentation. Some comments by English and Australian judges have strengthened this suggestion.[2] While this is not yet the case in Australia,[3] the courts have certainly widened their view of what may constitute the necessary misrepresentation and appear to be quite quick to find a misrepresentation by the defendant, especially in character merchandising cases. The property-based emphasis on passing off was the precursor of the registered trade mark system in which a registered owner may acquire property rights in a trade mark. However, it needs to be remembered that in that system the property is in the trade mark itself whereas, with passing off, the relevant property is the plaintiff's business reputation, which may be indicated by a trade mark but is separate from it.

Common law and equity also took different approaches to remedies. While the common law dropped the requirement of intention for a successful passing off action, case law to this day suggests that damages for passing off will not be awarded unless intention is proved. Often that will be overcome by advising the defendant that they are engaging in passing off, at which point any subsequent passing off may be regarded as intentional. Equity, with its emphasis on the protection of property interests, made its remedies of injunctions and accounting of profits available regardless of proof of any intentional misconduct on the part of the defendant.

14.2 Elements of passing off

A comprehensive definition of passing off is probably impossible due to the way in which it has developed and expanded with generations of common law decisions. As Gummow J has stated, 'the law of passing off contains sufficient nooks and crannies to make it difficult to formulate any satisfactory definition in short form'.[4] Nevertheless, various formulations are commonly referred to, including the five-part test adopted in the *Pub Squash* decision[5] from *Erven Warnink BV v J Townend & Sons (Hull) Ltd*:

> (1) a misrepresentation (2) made by a trader in the course of trade (3) to prospective customers of his or ultimate consumers of his goods or services supplied by him (4) which is calculated to injure the business or goodwill of another trader (in the sense that this is a reasonably foreseeable consequence) and (5) which causes actual damage to a business or goodwill of the trader by whom the action is brought or (in a quia timet action) will probably do so.[6]

---

2 *Bollinger v Costa Brava Wine Co Ltd* [1960] Ch 262; *Hogan v Koala Dundee Pty Ltd* (1988) 20 FCR 314 (Pincus J); A. Kamperman Sanders, *Unfair Competition Law: The Protection of Intellectual and Industrial Creativity* (New York: Oxford University Press, 1997).
3 *Moorgate Tobacco Co Ltd v Philip Morris Ltd (No 2)* (1984) 156 CLR 414.
4 *ConAgra Inc v McCain Foods (Australia) Pty Ltd* (1992) 33 FCR 302, 357.
5 *Cadbury Schweppes Pty Ltd v Pub Squash Co Ltd* [1980] 2 NSWLR 851.
6 *Erven Warnink BV v J Townend & Sons (Hull) Ltd (Advocaat* case) [1979] AC 731, 742.

These five criteria can be and often are whittled down to three basic elements of passing off:

- a business reputation or goodwill of the plaintiff;
- a misrepresentation by the defendant; and
- damage or the possibility of damage to the plaintiff's reputation or goodwill as a consequence of the misrepresentation.[7]

However, it must be quickly added that while all these elements must be present for a successful passing off action, not all situations involving these elements constitute passing off. Consequently, these shorthand lists of criteria of passing off are only a guide as to whether a passing off action is available.[8] One important aspect of the requirements is that the misrepresentation will take advantage of the plaintiff's goodwill by, for example, inaccurately suggesting some association between the defendant and the plaintiff or between one of them and the product of the other. For example, in character merchandising cases, the alleged misrepresentation is usually that the defendant's conduct has somehow suggested that the celebrity plaintiff has endorsed or otherwise associated themselves with the defendant or the defendant's product. In contrast, a misleading statement by a defendant that the plaintiff's products are unreliable in some way would not constitute passing off, although it may constitute some other cause of action, such as injurious falsehood, or contravene a statutory provision, such as s 18 of sch 2 of the *Competition and Consumer Act 2010* (Cth).[9] With those aspects of the definition of passing off in mind, we can move to a more detailed consideration of the individual elements of the tort and thereby explain in context the difficulties with the definition that are more abstractly referred to above.

14.3 The reputation of the plaintiff

As indicated above, the courts of equity in particular emphasised the property protection aspects of passing off. For some time, there was considerable controversy as to where the property right subsisted. It was initially thought that property resided in the actual sign or business indicium used by the plaintiff in the course of its business. Hence, it was suggested that if the plaintiff sold Spalding footballs, the property lay in the word 'Spalding'. It was not until the decision in *AG Spalding & Brothers v AW Gamage Ltd*[10] in the early twentieth century that a definitive judicial statement was made that defined the property right in question.

In that case, the House of Lords held that the relevant property right was not in the name 'Spalding' itself but in the business goodwill associated with the name that had been acquired by the use of it in a business context over many years. There are a number of implications of such an approach. One implication is that while there is usually some indicia of the plaintiff's reputation, such as a trade name or trade mark, the focus of this element of the action will be on the plaintiff proving the extent of its reputation. The indicium will simply be a sign indicating that reputation to consumers and the means by which consumers are advised that

---

7   *Reckitt & Colman Products Ltd v Borden Inc* [1990] 1 All ER 873, 890; *ConAgra Inc v McCain Foods (Australia) Pty Ltd* (1992) 33 FCR 302, 357–8 (Gummow J).
8   *Erven Warnink BV v J Townend & Sons (Hull) Ltd* (*Advocaat* case) [1979] AC 731, 742.
9   Formerly *Trade Practices Act 1974* (Cth) s 52.
10   (1915) 32 RPC 273.

the product in question originates in some way from the plaintiff. Consequently, in order to prove its reputation, the plaintiff will have to adduce evidence of issues such as:

- the time it has been in the market;
- the nature and amount of promotion it has undertaken – for example, the nature and extent of advertising in and through various media such as radio, television, newspaper and trade exhibitions;
- details of its sales network, including the number of outlets and/or distributors;
- the geographical extent of its business;
- the volume of its sales in both numbers and dollar value;
- use of a relevant domain name for a website and details of the extent of the usage of the website by potential customers;
- any other evidence of its reputation with its customers or in the wider community. This evidence may include survey evidence undertaken as part of the business or specifically for the purpose of litigation.[11]

The above factors need to be considered in the context of the relevant reputation. For example, the reputation may be that of a celebrity and evidence of that reputation would include details of the nature and extent of the celebrity's public exposure via mass media, social media or other means. Television ratings surveys may be of relevance in this context.[12]

A further implication of the emphasis on the plaintiff's reputation is that passing off can be used to protect a reputation associated with almost any indicium of a business and it therefore casts its net beyond trade names and even the now widely defined trade marks to include such things as a business' get-up and market image. Hence, the design and shape of products might be protected as may the colour scheme of franchised restaurants if they are associated in the minds of consumers with one particular trader.[13] More abstract indicia of a business' reputation may also be the subject of protection. A possible advantage of this is that protection will be conferred on indicia that are not capable of registration as trade marks. For example, in the *Pub Squash* case,[14] the plaintiff claimed its lemon-flavoured soft drink was exclusively associated through its extensive radio and television advertising with a romantic ideal of country pubs. The plaintiff therefore objected to the defendant entering the lemon-flavoured soft drink market with 'Pub Squash', which was also marketed in a can with a representation of the swinging doors of some old hotels.[15]

---

11 M. Sylvester and C. Sgourakis, 'Survey evidence: Improving probative value in IP and trade practices cases' (2005) 18(1) *Australian Intellectual Property Law Bulletin* 1. See *Cadbury Schweppes Pty Ltd v Darrell Lea Chocolate Shops Pty Ltd (No 4)* (2006) 229 ALR 136. See also Federal Court of Australia, *Survey Evidence Practice Note*, 25 October 2016, on the use of survey evidence. See also V. Huang, K. Weatherall and E. Webster, 'The use of survey evidence in Australian trade mark and passing off cases' in A. T. Kenyon, N. Wee Loon and M. Richardson (eds), *The Law of Reputation and Brands in the Asia Pacific* (Cambridge University Press, 2012) 181, 197, reviewing hundreds of cases and finding that submission of survey evidence has 'limited impact on the results in these cases'.
12 See, for example, *Amalgamated Television Services Pty Ltd v Clissold* (2000) 52 IPR 207.
13 See, for example, *Canadian Shredded Wheat Co Ltd v Kellogg Co of Canada Ltd* [1938] 1 All ER 618; *Kellogg Co v National Biscuit Co*, 305 US 111 (1938); and *Jerry's Famous Deli Inc v Papanicolaou*, 383 F 3d 998 (9th Cir, 2004).
14 *Cadbury Schweppes Pty Ltd v Pub Squash Co Pty Ltd* [1980] 2 NSWLR 851.
15 For further discussion see below at 14.3.7.

Of course, in each case, the plaintiff will have to demonstrate that it has a business reputation associated exclusively with the indicium in question as it is this reputation that is the basis of the action. In the *Pub Squash* case, the plaintiff failed because it was unable to prove that its product had yet become exclusively associated in the minds of consumers with the general idea of country pubs and their ambience.[16]

These issues are discussed in more detail in the sections below dealing with different types of reputations.

14.3.1 Location of reputation

One issue that has frequently arisen is whether it is sufficient for a business to have a reputation in the jurisdiction where it claims passing off has occurred or whether it must demonstrate that it has actually traded there and consequently has goodwill there. Goodwill has various definitions but is usually referred to as 'the attractive force that brings in custom'.[17] Hence, the critical distinction between reputation and goodwill is that the former simply requires the trader's business to be known in the jurisdiction while the latter requires the business to be operating in the jurisdiction and presently supplying its goods or services to people in the jurisdiction. The issue is increasingly relevant in a globalised trading environment where global communications via the internet and other formats, such as international magazines and cable television, have increasingly led to the establishment of reputations without corresponding goodwill. For example, both Whirlpool and Calvin Klein have brought litigation in India against the users of their well-known trade marks. Their litigation was complicated by the fact that neither company had actually traded in India at the time of the alleged infringing action. Despite this, not surprisingly, the trade marks were well known among Indian consumers as a consequence of the global marketing campaigns by both plaintiffs.[18] The Indian courts decided that the reputation of those multinational corporations in India was sufficient to found a successful passing off action. In contrast, a Jamaican court found in favour of a local Jamaican restaurant named McDonald's that was established before the McDonald's chain of restaurants was established there but after the chain's reputation was established in Jamaica.[19]

Originally, English and Australian case law required the plaintiff to demonstrate that it actually traded in the relevant jurisdiction and English case law appears to still take that position.[20] However, the distinction led to increasingly difficult decisions about what constitutes trading in the jurisdiction. For example, in the *Sheraton* case,[21] the plaintiff was successful

---

16 United States decisions include *The Coca-Cola Co v Gemini Rising Inc*, 346 F Supp 1183 (ED NY, 1972); *Dallas Cowboys Cheerleaders Inc v Pussycat Cinema Ltd*, 604 F 2d 200 (2nd Cir, 1979); *Clairol Inc v Boston Discount Center of Berkley Inc*, 608 F 2d 1114 (6th Cir, 1979); *Rex Wayne Bell v Starbucks US Brands Corp*, 389 F Supp 2d 766 (SD Tex, 2005); *Motor Improvements Inc v AC Spark Plug Co*, 80 F 2d 385 (6th Cir, Mich, 1935); and *K Taylor Distilling Co v Food Center of St Louis Inc*, 31 F Supp 460 (ED Mo, 1940).
17 Lord Macnaghten in *Inland Revenue Commissioners v Muller & Co's Margarine Ltd* [1901] AC 217.
18 *Whirlpool Trade Mark* [1997] FSR 905 (India); *Calvin Klein Inc v International Apparel Syndicate* [1995] FSR 515.
19 *McDonald's Corp v McDonald's Corp Ltd* [1997] FSR 200.
20 *Jian Tools for Sales Inc v Roderick Manhattan Group Ltd* [1995] FSR 924; *Hotel Cipriani Srl v Cipriani (Grosvenor Street) Ltd* [2010] EWCA Civ 110.
21 *Sheraton Corp of America v Sheraton Motels* [1964] RPC 202.

on the basis that people in England were able to book a room in an American Sheraton hotel from England and therefore trading occurred in England. More tenuously, in the *Crazy Horse Saloon* case,[22] the plaintiff was successful in opposing the establishment of a London nightclub called the Crazy Horse Saloon on the basis of the reputation it had for its Paris nightclub of the same name. The justification for the decision seemed to be that Londoners were likely to actually cross the channel to visit the Parisian nightclub and therefore it had goodwill in London. The most curious of these decisions was probably the *Budweiser* case,[23] which involved a conflict between a Czech Budweiser beer and the American Budweiser beer. The evidence demonstrated that the American beer had a reputation in England and that considerable amounts of the American beer were bought and consumed on what appeared to be English soil. However, because the sale and consumption actually occurred on American military bases, the consumer market for the beer was restricted to those who frequented those establishments and the court declined to prevent the sale of the Czech beer in England. The difficulty with these decisions was that it made little sense to protect business goodwill where trading in the jurisdiction had been minimal although the plaintiff's reputation in the jurisdiction led to consumers being misled, while refusing relief where the plaintiff had not yet begun trading but its reputation in the jurisdiction was such that consumers were still misled.

In Australia, case law equivocated on the issue for many years. An early High Court decision found in favour of General Motors when the defendant adopted that name in the full knowledge that General Motors was about to enter the Australian car market although it had not yet done so at the time of the defendant's actions. The court placed considerable emphasis on the fact that the defendant knew of General Motors' intention to enter the Australian market and had intentionally traded off that fact.[24] The issues also arose in the context of businesses that developed a goodwill in one or more states but an enterprising defendant adopted their name or business indicia in another state where they had not yet started business. For example, in the *Budget Rent A Car* case,[25] the plaintiff had a thriving business in most Australian states but the defendant commenced its Budget rental business in the Northern Territory before the plaintiff started its operations there. The plaintiff was successful on the grounds that it had commenced business activities in the Northern Territory before the defendant began to use the name Budget Rent A Car; moreover, a considerable number of its prospective customers in Darwin were people who had travelled there from other parts of Australia where its business was well established. Consequently, the respondent had a reputation in the Northern Territory under the names Budget Rent A Car and Budget Rent A Car System, which it was entitled to protect.

In *Fletcher Challenge Ltd v Fletcher Challenge Pty Ltd*,[26] Powell J in the New South Wales Supreme Court on an interlocutory application adopted the view that 'the relevant question is "does the plaintiff have the necessary reputation?" rather than "does the plaintiff itself carry on business here?"'.[27] On the other hand, the Full Federal Court in the *Taco Bell* decision[28] came

---

22   *Alain Bernadin & Cie v Pavilion Properties Ltd* [1967] RPC 581.
23   *Anheuser-Busch Inc v Budejovicky Budvar* (1984) 4 IPR 260.
24   *Turner v General Motors (Australia) Pty Ltd* (1929) 42 CLR 352.
25   *BM Auto Sales Pty Ltd v Budget Rent A Car System Pty Ltd* (1976) 12 ALR 363.
26   [1981] 1 NSWLR 196.
27   Ibid 205.
28   *Taco Co (Australia) Inc v Taco Bell Pty Ltd* (1982) 42 ALR 177.

down on the side of the need for goodwill in the jurisdiction when a local Bondi restaurant used the same name for its Mexican food restaurant as that used in the United States by a large chain of Mexican restaurants. In that case, though, there was no evidence of intention to mislead consumers. The combined effect of these cases seemed to be that intent to deceive would be sufficient in the absence of goodwill provided the plaintiff had a reputation, while the existence of goodwill would be sufficient to overcome a lack of intention to mislead. Again, the cases display the dichotomous historical roots of passing off.

Definitive authority on the point came in the Full Federal Court decision of *ConAgra Inc v McCain Foods (Australia) Pty Ltd*.[29] In that case, ConAgra, an American corporation that had not commenced to trade in Australia, objected to the use of the term 'Healthy Choice' to describe frozen dinners produced by the defendant in Australia. The plaintiff's Healthy Choice meals were well known in America. The court unanimously held that the plaintiff did not have to prove that it traded in Australia in order for it to succeed in a passing off provided its reputation in Australia was sufficient to prove that use of 'Healthy Choice' by the defendant would mislead consumers. As a matter of evidence, the court held that the plaintiff's reputation in Australia was insufficient to justify a passing off action but the general point that reputation in Australia is sufficient was clearly acknowledged.

The strong obiter view expressed in the *ConAgra* decision was confirmed by the Full Federal Court in *Knott Investments v Winnebago Industries Inc*.[30] The American manufacturer of Winnebago motor homes had not traded in Australia but it had a reputation in the relevant market in Australia. It was successful in its action.

14.3.2 Ownership of reputation

Determining the actual owner of the relevant reputation may also be an issue in some situations. For example, if a famous actor plays a particular film character, who has the right to prevent passing off involving the wrongful association of that character by the defendant with its product? Is it the actor who 'is' that character or the producers of the film? The issue arose in the *Alvin Purple* case[31] and in the *Crocodile Dundee* case.[32] The issue is usually resolved in advance by contractual arrangement between the parties but difficulties may arise if this is not done and the issue will come down to a question of fact as to who 'owns' the reputation in question.

14.3.3 Joint ownership of reputation

One of the extensions of the passing off action has been in the area of joint ownership of the necessary business reputation. Hence, a reputation may be jointly 'owned' by a number of traders. A clear example of this is the *Spanish Champagne* case.[33] As the name suggests, the case involved the objection of a champagne maker to the use of the term 'Spanish Champagne' for sparkling wine made in Spain. The plaintiff's claim was that the term 'Champagne' could

---

29 (1992) 33 FCR 302.
30 (2013) 211 FCR 449.
31 *Hexagon Pty Ltd v Australian Broadcasting Commission* (1975) 7 ALR 233.
32 *Pacific Dunlop Ltd v Hogan* (1989) 23 FCR 553.
33 *Bollinger v Costa Brava Wine Co Ltd* [1960] Ch 262.

only apply to sparkling wine made in the Champagne district of France. Danckwerts J accepted this proposition and that the defendant's use of the term 'Spanish Champagne' was misleading[34] but there was an issue as to whether the plaintiff had the necessary reputation to found the action. The complication here was that it was not the only maker of champagne. Danckwerts J held that the reputation associated with the term 'Champagne' was shared by all of the champagne makers of the relevant French winemaking region.[35] Consequently, any or all of them could bring an action against any person who used the term in a misleading manner.

A similar case was the *Advocaat* case,[36] which was referred to above[37] in the context of the definition of passing off. The difference was that the reputation in question was not based on the shared geographical origin of the product in question but on other qualities commonly associated with the product. In that case, the defendant made an alcoholic drink that it called 'advocaat'. Its drink was made with eggs and wine whereas 'real' advocaat was and still is traditionally made with eggs and brandy, a fortified wine that is more expensive to make due to the extra distilling process and also due to higher government taxes often imposed on strong liquor. One of the makers of traditional advocaat objected to the defendant's use of the term 'advocaat'. The House of Lords accepted the proposition that advocaat is made with brandy, not wine, and the defendant was precluded from calling its product advocaat. Again, the court held that the reputation was shared by all makers of advocaat and that any or all could bring an action to prevent misuse of the term.

The matter can become contentious when there is disagreement as to what are the relevant qualities of the product indicated by the word in question. For example, there is some disagreement about whether Prosecco is the name of a grape variety or the name of a wine from a particular area in Italy.[38]

14.3.4 Dual ownership: honest concurrent user and use of own name

A situation different from where a group of traders share the reputation associated with a particular product's qualities and its name is where two traders have independently used the same or a very similar trade name or indicium of their respective reputations. These situations differ from the *Spanish Champagne* and *Advocaat* decisions in that the reputations are quite distinct and separate although they may have arisen from a common origin. A number of cases have endorsed the possibility of honest concurrent use, including some decisions from the nineteenth century where separate traders acquired the reputation associated with a particular trade name, often by inheritance. They then proceeded to trade under that same name and, in doing so, obviously acquired their own individual reputations associated with the name.[39]

---

34 See below at 14.4.2 for a discussion as to why the term 'Spanish Champagne' was misleading.
35 A similar conclusion was reached in relation to the term 'sherry' in *Vine Products Ltd v McKenzie & Co Ltd (No 3)* [1969] RPC 1, although the plaintiff in that case was ultimately unsuccessful due to the very lengthy delay in seeking injunctive relief.
36 *Erven Warnink BV v J Townend & Sons (Hull) Ltd* [1979] AC 731.
37 At 14.2.
38 M. Davison, C. Henckels and P. Emerton, '*In vino veritas*: The dubious legality of the EU's claims to exclusive use of the term "Prosecco"' (2019) 29(3) *Australian Intellectual Property Journal* 110.
39 *Dent v Turpin* (1861) 2J & H 139, 70 ER 1003; *Southorn v Reynolds* (1865) 12 LT 75.

Later decisions have endorsed the idea that honest concurrent use may lead to the plaintiff failing to obtain a remedy and the concept is certainly relevant in the arena of registered trade marks.[40] The exact basis of it as a defence to passing off is uncertain. In some cases, the issue has rested on acquiescence by the plaintiff to the defendant's conduct[41] while in others it has been justified on the basis that the existence of two reputations associated with similar indicia is not sufficiently misleading to justify either party being denied the exploitation of their reputation.[42] While that approach has been criticised,[43] the tort's concern with both misleading behaviour and the property of traders in their reputation may well justify the conclusion that in the case of honest concurrent user, the tort has simply not been made out and that consumers are both aware of and accept the possibility that two traders may have legitimate interests. In this regard, passing off may differ from s 18 of sch 2 of the *Competition and Consumer Act 2010* (Cth)[44] which is clearly focused on misleading conduct, and honest concurrent use is not a defence to a contravention of the standard previously laid down by s 52 of the *Trade Practices Act 1974* (Cth).[45] However, even in those cases, there is a discernible tendency for judges to find that the defendant's conduct is confusing but not misleading, or to attribute any deception of consumers to their own assumptions about entitlements to the use of the indicium in question rather than the defendant's conduct.[46]

Similar cases in relation to a business name suggest that a person is entitled to carry on a business under their own name where they are doing so honestly although they are not entitled to use the name as a trade mark. For example, in *Parker-Knoll Ltd v Knoll International Ltd*,[47] the House of Lords took such an approach in the face of strong dissent from Lord Denning who supported a more general defence of the use of one's own name provided it was done honestly by, for example, avoiding contractions that resulted in greater similarities with the plaintiff.

The uncertainty surrounding issues such as these is an ongoing reflection of the difficulties that the courts experience in balancing the concerns of passing off with the two principles of prevention of misleading consumers and protecting the reputations of traders. In most situations, the two principles work effectively in tandem. In these instances, there is an inevitable clash between them, and the courts must balance one against the other. Not surprisingly, in the course of doing so, some confusion and differences in approach emerge from the judgments as to the basis for achieving that balance. Hence, some resolve the issue by determining that the likelihood of deception is insufficient to justify a remedy[48] while others more openly support a clear defence for those with legitimately acquired reputations, even when deception arises.

---

40 See, for example, *GE Trade Mark* [1973] RPC 297 (Lord Diplock); *Ausdoc Office Pty Ltd v Complete Office Supplies Pty Ltd* (1996) 136 ALR 659, 664.
41 *Dominion Rent A Car Ltd v Budget Rent A Car Systems (1970) Ltd* [1987] 2 NZLR 395.
42 *Habib Bank Ltd v Habib Bank AG Zurich* [1982] 99 RPC 1, 24.
43 See, for example, M. Davison and I. Horak, *Shanahan's Australian Law of Trade Marks and Passing Off* (5th edn, Sydney: Thomson Reuters, 2012) 701.
44 Formerly *Trade Practices Act 1974* (Cth) s 52.
45 *Peter Isaacson Publications v Nationwide News Pty Ltd* (1984) 6 FCR 289.
46 *McWilliam's Wines Pty Ltd v LS Booth Wine Transport* (1992) 25 NSWLR 723.
47 [1962] RPC 265.
48 See, for example, *EV Hawtin Ltd v John F Hawtin & Co Ltd* [1960] RPC 95.

Of course, these cases are also complicated by their individual facts and circumstances such that consideration needs to be given to various other issues, such as whether the defendant has acted in some way that lessens its entitlement to protection of its reputation. Examples of this may include deliberately altering its name or adopting a contraction that results in greater deception.[49]

14.3.5 Reputation in descriptive words and insignia: secondary meanings

Many and probably the majority of the indicia used by plaintiffs to develop the reputation of their products are inherently distinctive in the sense that they do not in any way describe the products or are not related to the shape or function of those products. In those circumstances, it is relatively easy for the plaintiff to associate its products exclusively with those inherently distinctive indicia and thereby develop the necessary reputation.

On the other hand, the indicia in question may, at least at the time of their initial use, be descriptive in nature or a functional aspect of the shape of the plaintiff's goods. These indicia may develop a secondary meaning to consumers so that the indicia may either indicate the plaintiff's products or operate in their normal, descriptive sense. The context of the use will determine whether the original, primary meaning of the indicia is at work or whether it is this secondary meaning that is in operation.

The potential breadth of passing off is partly revealed by cases that demonstrate the means by which a descriptive term may come to be associated exclusively with the plaintiff, effectively preventing competitors from using the term. One of the oldest and clearest examples of this is the decision in *Reddaway v Banham*.[50] The plaintiff made and sold belting for machinery that it called 'Camel Hair Belting'. Not surprisingly, the belting was made of camel hair. For many years, it was the only supplier of such belting and the only company to use the term.

The defendant started to compete with the plaintiff and also called its belting made of camel hair 'Camel Hair Belting'. The House of Lords held that the plaintiff had established a reputation associated with the term such that buyers of that product associated the term exclusively with the plaintiff. Consequently, use of the term by the defendant suggested that its product was associated with or originated from the plaintiff and was unlawful.

On the other hand, the plaintiff must demonstrate that its use of the descriptive term has been so extensive, pervasive and exclusive that consumers associate the term with the plaintiff and no other trader. This is no easy task and the plaintiff has failed in cases such as *McCain International Ltd v Country Fair Foods Ltd*,[51] where the plaintiff objected to the defendant's use of the term 'oven chips', which the plaintiff had originally coined and used. The extent and nature of its use had not been sufficient to associate the largely descriptive term exclusively with it. In part, this was due to the plaintiff's use of its name and trade mark, McCain's, in conjunction with the term, thus emphasising the descriptive nature of the expression.

---

[49] For example, *Parker-Knoll Ltd v Knoll International* [1962] RPC 265; *Hotel Cipriani Srl v Cipriani (Grosvenor Street) Ltd* [2010] EWCA Civ 110.
[50] [1896] AC 199.
[51] [1981] RPC 69.

The defendant also differentiated its product by using its trade mark in conjunction with 'oven chips'.

Potato chips and the description of the method of cooking them have also been the subject of litigation in two Australian decisions[52] with varying outcomes. The plaintiff in both cases had a significant reputation as a consequence of it being the first in Australia to sell kettle chips that were cooked in a particular manner that imparted a particular flavour. Competitors soon adopted the method of cooking that was clearly within their rights but the dispute arose as to the manner in which they labelled their kettle chips. In the case where the plaintiff was successful,[53] the defendant's use of 'Kettle Chips' was conspicuous in part because of the extent to which its packaging minimised its own trade mark, Smith's, a well-known trade mark in respect of potato chips that was usually displayed far more prominently. The net effect was that it was found to be using 'Kettle Chips' as an indication of the business origin of the chips and therefore its use was deceptively suggesting that the chips originated from the plaintiff. In contrast, in the other case,[54] the defendant used its indicator of origin 'Thins', which was also well known, in a prominent manner so as to indicate the origin of the chips and the term 'kettle cooked' was only being used to indicate the method of cooking. Similarly, in *Pacific Publications Pty Ltd v IPC Media Pty Ltd*,[55] the plaintiff failed to demonstrate that its magazine was exclusively associated with the words in the title 'Home Beautiful' to justify preventing the defendant from using the title '25 Beautiful Homes'. It was able to satisfy the court that the defendant should be restrained from using that title in conjunction with instructions to newsagents to place the two magazines together and from using a substantial number of the plaintiff's photographs in its magazine.[56]

On the other hand, the matter can become complicated when one party is effectively the first to create the term describing the product. The issue arose in *Stone & Wood Group Pty Ltd v Intellectual Property Development Corp Pty Ltd*[57] where the plaintiff was the first or at least one of the first beer brewers to develop a style of beer called 'Pacific Ale'. As the expression was held to be a description of a type of beer, albeit one that evoked calmness and a relaxed beach lifestyle, the plaintiff was unsuccessful in preventing use of the term by another brewer.

14.3.6 Reputation in packaging and appearance

As already indicated, passing off has broadened to include protection of reputation associated with many different forms of indicia. The section above considered the possibility that normally descriptive words could be indicators of that reputation. In addition to or instead of words, the packaging and appearance of a product can also indicate the reputation of the supplier of the goods. A famous example of this is the uniquely shaped Coca-Cola bottle, which is recognisable throughout most of the world. As with words, the more inherently distinctive the packaging or appearance is, the quicker it may become associated exclusively

---

52 *Pepsico Australia Pty Ltd v Kettle Chip Co Pty Ltd* (1996) 135 ALR 192; *Apand Pty Ltd v Kettle Chip Co Pty Ltd* (1994) 52 FCR 474.
53 *Apand Pty Ltd v Kettle Chip Co Pty Ltd* (1994) 52 FCR 474.
54 *Pepsico Australia Pty Ltd v Kettle Chip Co Pty Ltd* (1996) 135 ALR 192.
55 (2003) 57 IPR 28.
56 See also *European Ltd v Economist Newspaper Ltd* [1996] FSR 431, affirmed [1998] FSR 283.
57 [2018] FCAFC 29.

with the reputation of one trader. However, extensive use is still required before this will occur and it is not in itself sufficient that the shape is unique or quite unusual. This is because while the initial use of such shapes is likely to attract consumer attention, it does not necessarily do so on the basis that the shape indicates the trade origin of the product but that the product has a shape that attracts interest.[58]

In *The Coca-Cola Co v PepsiCo Inc (No 2)*,[59] Coca-Cola alleged that a Pepsi cola bottle indicated an association between Pepsi's business and Coca-Cola's business for various reasons, including the similarity of Pepsi's bottle to the Coke bottle. The action was unsuccessful because the reputation of Coca-Cola's bottle was in respect of the combination of all of the features of its bottle rather than just the outline or silhouette of its bottle. Consequently, differences between the two bottles, such as a wave pattern in the middle of the Pepsi bottle, sufficiently differentiated the two bottles to refute passing off in respect of those consumers who made purchasing decisions by reference to bottle shape alone. In addition, other consumers differentiated the two products by reference to considerations other than the bottle shapes, such as the well-known word brands of both products.

As seen above, descriptive words can become the relevant indicator of reputation and the position is the same with 'descriptive' or functional packaging and appearance. In *William Edge & Sons Ltd v William Niccolls & Sons Ltd*,[60] the plaintiff successfully objected to the defendant placing its 'washing blue' at the end of a stick that was used to dunk the blue into laundry. It did so because it had been the sole supplier of washing blue in that way for a number of years and those who did the laundry at that time, often poorly paid and uneducated washerwomen, identified the plaintiff's product purely by reference to its shape and the stick used. Consequently, the defendant's use of its name on very similar packaging did not have the desired effect of differentiating its product from that of the plaintiff in the eyes of its users.

A later and more controversial example of this is the House of Lords decision in *Reckitt & Colman Products Ltd v Borden Inc*.[61] In that case, the plaintiff objected to the defendant packaging its lemon juice in a yellow, lemon-shaped container. The action was successful despite the 'descriptive' nature of such packaging because the plaintiff had been the sole retailer of yellow, lemon-shaped lemon juice containers for a number of years.[62] While the Law Lords regretted the result due to its anti-competitive implications, they considered that the facts before them left them no choice but to find for the plaintiff.

In both cases, the critical point was that consumers had come to exclusively identify the packaging in question with the plaintiff's product as a consequence of extended exclusive use. In the latter case, the exclusivity of use was achieved in part by the plaintiff routinely threatening legal action against any company adopting similar packaging; and the longer the

---

58   M. Davison, 'Shape trade marks: The role and relevance of functionality and aesthetics in determining their registrability' (2004) 15 *Australian Intellectual Property Journal* 106; *Wal-Mart Stores Inc v Samara Brothers Inc* (2000) 529 US 205.
59   (2014) 109 IPR 429.
60   [1911] AC 693.
61   [1990] 1 All ER 873.
62   See *Cadbury Schweppes Pty Ltd v Darrell Lea Chocolate Shops Pty Ltd (No 4)* (2006) 229 ALR 136 (where the Federal Court found against Cadbury, which claimed that the colour purple was identified solely with its chocolate packaging).

threats resulted in potential competitors avoiding such use, the firmer was the plaintiff's position until, when ultimately challenged in court, it became unassailable.

On the other hand, as seen with the *Pepsico*[63] case concerning kettle-cooked chips discussed above,[64] the defendant's prominent use of its own well-known indicator of reputation might negative a finding of passing off. In *Koninklijke Philips Electronics NV v Remington Products Australia*,[65] Philips objected to Remington selling electric triple-headed rotary shavers. Philips had done so exclusively for many years until Remington began to do so and Philips claimed that consumers identified triple-headed rotary shavers exclusively with it. Philips sued for trade mark infringement and on the basis of passing off. Both at first instance and on appeal, the Federal Court concluded that Remington's prominent use of its well-known trade mark rebutted any suggestion that the similar shape of its razors suggested an association with Philips. In addition, the functional nature of the shape diminished Philips' case as the shape was partly used to achieve the required function of shaving effectively and partly used to indicate the reputation of the maker. Consumer awareness of the functionality of the shape would result in them at least considering the possibility that another maker had simply entered the market for providing razors of that shape.

14.3.7 Reputation of marketing image

It is possible for a plaintiff to prove that it has a reputation associated with a particular marketing image. These cases represent some of the more difficult passing off cases as there is considerable difficulty in determining the point at which a general marketing image should be considered to be associated exclusively with the plaintiff. A famous case considering this issue is the *Pub Squash* decision.[66] The plaintiff released its Solo lemon squash onto the market with an intensive advertising campaign identifying its drink with the ambience of country hotels. Its advertisements contained statements, read out in a slow, Australian accent, such as 'Just like the lemon squash that pubs used to make'. When Pub Squash, a rival lemon squash, was released with a similar marketing theme, the plaintiff objected on the grounds that doing so deceived consumers. Ultimately, the plaintiff was unsuccessful because no individual company had an exclusive right to the use of such general images. However, such a finding must be restricted to the particular facts of the case as, presumably, the issue was one of fact, not law, as to whether Solo was associated exclusively in the eyes of the public with the particular image. Just as with descriptive terms, repeated and exclusive use of a general image may result in it acquiring a secondary meaning related to the plaintiff's products.

14.3.8 Reputation in personality

In recent times, a common use of passing off has been to prevent unpaid exploitation of an actual or fictitious public personality. Associating products with particular celebrities has become prevalent in the marketing industry and the courts have for some time recognised

---

63   *Pepsico Australia Pty Ltd v Kettle Chip Co Pty Ltd* (1996) 135 ALR 192.
64   At 14.3.5.
65   (2000) 100 FCR 90.
66   *Cadbury Schweppes Pty Ltd v Pub Squash Co Ltd* [1980] 2 NSWLR 851.

that such celebrities have valuable business reputations. Australian case law has protected those reputations via passing off for several decades and the 'character merchandising cases' as they have become known are a well-established part of passing off jurisprudence.

One of the earliest examples of character merchandising in Australia was *Henderson v Radio Corp Pty Ltd*[67] where a professional dancing couple objected to the use of a photograph containing their images on the cover of a record of dance music. In more recent times, Olympic athletes such as Gary Honey and Kieren Perkins, and television personalities (for example, Sue Smith) have objected to the use of their image on posters, publications and advertisements, and popular music artists have objected to the sale of unauthorised T-shirts bearing their names.[68]

The 'character' in character merchandising can and often does go beyond the real-life person in question to include the character portrayed in films or television. Examples of this include litigation involving Paul Hogan and his film character Crocodile Dundee from the film series of the same name. In one of those cases, the objection was to a television advertisement in which the male character was dressed like, spoke like and acted like Crocodile Dundee. However, few if any viewers believed the person in question was Paul Hogan himself and so the real objection was to the use of the Crocodile Dundee character. Of course, that in turn leads to a question of who 'owns' the character or in the context of passing off who possesses the reputation indicated by the character. For example, in earlier litigation relating to a movie and television series character, 'Alvin Purple', a question arose as to whether the actor who played the part of Alvin Purple had a right to object to another person playing that part.[69] This issue is discussed above[70] in relation to ownership of reputation. The character in question may also be an animated or puppet character, such as the puppets from the children's program *Sesame Street*.[71]

Protection may even extend beyond celebrities and the characters that they portray to the fictional items used by fictional characters. In the *Duff Beer* case,[72] the defendant was restrained from selling the beer drunk by Homer Simpson on cartoon show *The Simpsons*.

14.3.9 Abandonment of reputation

Once established, it is possible for a reputation to be lost in various ways. Businesses decline or cease trading for various reasons and there is then an issue about the point at which they no longer have a reputation that founds a passing off action. The decision in *Ad Lib Club Ltd v Granville*[73] probably represents the height of the courts' willingness to protect a dwindling reputation. In that case, the owners of the defunct Ad Lib nightclub were able to argue that its reputation remained five years after it had been closed down due to noncompliance with local

---

67 (1960) 60 SR (NSW) 576.
68 *Honey v Australian Airlines Ltd* (*Gary Honey* case) (1990) 18 IPR 185; *10th Cantanae Pty Ltd v Shoshana Pty Ltd* (*Sue Smith* case) (1987) 79 ALR 299; *Talmex Pty Ltd v Telstra Corp Ltd* [1997] 2 Qd R 444; *MK Hutchence v South Sea Bubble Co Pty Ltd* (1986) 64 ALR 330.
69 *Hexagon Pty Ltd v Australian Broadcasting Commission* (1975) 7 ALR 233.
70 At 14.3.2.
71 *Children's Television Workshop Inc v Woolworths Ltd* (1981) 1 NSWLR 273.
72 *Twentieth Century Fox Film Corp v South Australian Brewing Co Ltd* (1996) 66 FCR 451.
73 [1972] RPC 673.

council town planning requirements. They claimed that they had not reopened due to a lack of suitable premises that would overcome the council's objections. While the decision may be questionable on the basis that either the former owners were not serious about obtaining new premises or such premises did not exist, the general proposition that a residual reputation will be protected has been accepted in numerous other cases.[74]

An Australian example of the principle is found in the Full Federal Court decision in *Mark Foys Pty Ltd v TVSN (Pacific) Ltd*.[75] Mark Foys was a well-known Sydney department store that had closed down. The plaintiff acquired the rights to the business store but had not yet commenced trading under that name. It successfully objected to the registration and use of the domain name 'markfoys.com' and the use of images of the old Mark Foys' business on the defendant's website.

14.4 The misrepresentation

With some idea of the necessary reputation to found a passing off action and the possible indicia of this reputation, we can now turn our attention to the nature and types of misrepresentation concerning this reputation that attract the attention of passing off. One of the undefined and more difficult issues is identifying the test for a misrepresentation in this context.

14.4.1 Misrepresentation, confusion and deception

The courts regularly use different terms, such as misrepresentation, deception and confusion, interchangeably when speaking about passing off. Unfortunately, there appears to be little consistency in the use of the different terms and so it is important to appreciate the different ways in which the terms are used. One possible meaning of 'confusion' is deception and thus the two terms are interchangeable. However, a distinction is usually drawn between 'confusion' and 'deception' on the basis that 'confusion' leads to consumers having cause to wonder whether the two products that they are considering are related in some way whereas 'deception' requires them to draw the wrongful conclusion that the two products are in fact associated in some way. When it comes to misrepresentation and deception, one commonly drawn distinction is that the former does not necessarily involve any intent on the part of the representor whereas deception may require intent to mislead. Again, the terms are often used interchangeably and deception does not necessarily denote an intention to mislead.

In the context of passing off, deception, in the sense that it denotes an intention to mislead, is relevant because it still seems to be the case that an intention to deceive is a prerequisite for obtaining damages for passing off. This situation is a lingering consequence of the common law emphasis on fraud referred to at the beginning of this chapter. Equity's emphasis on

---

74 See, for example, *Ramsay v Nicol* [1939] VLR 330; *Bayer Pharma Pty Ltd v Henry York & Co Pty Ltd* [1964] FSR 143 (SC NSW); *Ad Lib Club Ltd v Granville* [1972] RPC 673 (Ch D); *Berkeley Hotel Co Ltd v Berkeley International (Mayfair) Ltd* [1972] RPC 237 (Ch D); *AA Levey v Henderson-Kenton (Holdings) Ltd* [1974] RPC 617 (Ch D); *Star Industrial Co Ltd v Yap Kwee Kor* [1976] FSR 256, 270 (PC from Singapore); *Thermawear Ltd v Vedonis Ltd* [1982] RPC 44 (Ch D); *Heller Financial Services Ltd v Brice* (1987) 9 IPR 469 (SC Qld); *ACI Australia Ltd v Glamour Glaze Pty Ltd* (1988) 11 IPR 269 (FC); *WMC Ltd v Westgold Resources NL* (1997) 39 IPR 319.
75 (2000) 104 FCR 61.

property interests means that the equitable remedies of permanent and quia timet injunctions are obtainable in the absence of intention to mislead.

From an evidentiary perspective, intention to mislead is also highly relevant simply because if the defendant intended to mislead consumers it is but one further short step to concluding that the defendant was successful in its intention. Documentation obtained during discovery processes may constitute the 'smoking gun' that demonstrates an intention to mislead. For example, in the *Duff Beer* case,[76] marketing documentation prepared for the defendant demonstrated its clear intention to trade off the reputation of *The Simpsons* and was unsurprisingly referred to by the trial judge. On the other hand, while intention to mislead is relevant it does not inevitably lead to the conclusion that misleading conduct has in fact taken place. In the *Pub Squash* case,[77] the court found an intention to mislead but also found that the intention had not been successfully implemented and reaffirmed the point that while it is a short step from intending to mislead to actually misleading, it is a step that must have actually been taken. It should also be borne in mind that when a competitor has captured a market share in some way, other firms will be looking to recapture part of that market and will intend to sail as close to the wind as they can legally without deceiving consumers. It then becomes a question as to whether they have achieved that objective or crossed the line.[78]

The difficulty with terminology is further complicated by consideration of the processes by which consumers make their decisions. For example, deception may occur initially, especially with small, cheap items or in other circumstances, such as undertaking an internet search that reveals multiple websites in response to a particular search. This initial deception may be relatively quickly remedied before a purchase is completed or an internet shopper spends any significant time at a particular website. The question then arises as to the degree to which courts will tolerate this initial deception. There is also an issue about the extent to which the courts will require consumers to take some steps to protect themselves from being deceived, summed up somewhat insensitively by the statement that the courts do not assist 'a moron in a hurry'. Hence, while the expression of the relevant legal tests of deception and confusion are relatively straightforward, the actual application of those tests in any given factual situation may be quite difficult. In addition, it seems the case that policy considerations influence judges' decisions about whether to make a finding of deception or 'mere confusion', particularly in cases where the business indicium in question has a primary descriptive meaning and the question is whether it has acquired a secondary, distinctive meaning associated exclusively with the plaintiff. The concern with preventing monopolisation of descriptive words and packaging appears to result in more decisions where the finding is one of 'mere confusion' or that consumers are responsible for their own deception by not taking sufficient care or making assumptions about the legal entitlements to use of particular terms.[79]

---

76 *Twentieth Century Fox Film Corp v South Australian Brewing Co Ltd* (1996) 66 FCR 451. See also *Clipsal Australia Pty Ltd v Clipso Electrical Pty Ltd (No 3)* [2017] FCA 60.
77 *Cadbury Schweppes Pty Ltd v Pub Squash Co Pty Ltd* [1980] 2 NSWLR 851.
78 See, for example, 'Hill of Grace' and 'Hill of Gold' in *CA Henschke & Co v Rosemount Estates Pty Ltd* (2000) 52 IPR 42.
79 *McWilliam's Wines Pty Ltd v McDonald's System of Australia Pty Ltd* (1980) 33 ALR 394; *Lego System A/S v Lego M Lemelstrich Ltd* [1983] FSR 155.

14.4.2 The target of the representation

A critical issue in determining whether the defendant's conduct is misleading will be determining the target audience of the representation. Most representations will be to the public at large and so the test will be whether a substantial number of members of the public would be misled by the defendant's conduct.[80] This necessarily includes those with imperfect knowledge of the type of goods being sold. For example, in the *Spanish Champagne* case,[81] it was argued that consumers could not be misled by the description of the defendant's sparkling wine as 'Spanish Champagne' because, by definition, real champagne comes from the district of that name in France. Therefore, well-informed consumers of sparkling wine would not have been misled by the label.

However, many consumers with some interest in sparkling wine would have been aware that champagne was a description of a type of sparkling wine with renowned qualities but they would not necessarily have been aware that the term had a specific geographic connotation. Consequently, they would have believed that Spanish champagne was 'real' champagne.

On the other hand, the representation may be directed at a very discrete section of the public and that section may have specific knowledge that will eliminate any possibility of deception. While most products are available to the public at large, some are bought almost exclusively on the recommendation of professionals who are far more likely to be aware of subtle differences between competing products. For example, in *Hodgkinson & Corby Ltd v Wards Mobility Services Ltd*,[82] the plaintiff objected to the fact that the defendant sold cushions with a very similar design to that of the plaintiff. Both cushions were designed for use in wheelchairs but wheelchair users made their purchasing decisions almost exclusively on the recommendation of occupational therapists who were very familiar with both products. Their advanced knowledge of the two products precluded the possibility of deception. In addition, many similarities in design were the necessary result of the identical function performed by both cushions and the plaintiff's shape was as much an indicator of the function it performed as it was of the plaintiff's reputation.

Evidence as to what is the actual market and who makes up that market could be important. In *Clipsal Australia Pty Ltd v Clipso Electrical Pty Ltd (No 3)*,[83] the defendant claimed that the relevant market consisted entirely of electricians and wholesalers, not end consumers. Consequently, the prospects of deception were eliminated. The difficulty with the argument was that a relevant part of the market was end consumers and some of these consumers insisted on certain branded parts being used by their electrical contractors.

14.4.3 Misrepresentations of the trade origin of goods

The 'standard' misrepresentation in passing off is one that adopts the plaintiff's indicia of its reputation, such as a trade mark, trade name or get-up. The most obvious example of this type of misrepresentation is the production of counterfeit products bearing the plaintiff's trade mark

---

80 *Reckitt & Colman Products Ltd v Borden Inc* [1990] 1 All ER 873, 881.
81 *Bollinger v Costa Brava Wine Co Ltd* [1960] Ch 262.
82 [1995] FSR 169.
83 [2017] FCA 60.

and in those cases there is really no significant issue as to whether passing off has occurred as well as infringement of the plaintiff's registered trade mark.

More difficult circumstances arise where the indicium in question is descriptive in some way and there the issue becomes whether the defendant has used it in such a way as to indicate the trade origin of its product or simply to describe its product. The decisions concerning kettle-cooked chips discussed above[84] exemplify the potential difficulty. It is impossible to emphasise too much that the individual circumstances of both the plaintiff's and the defendant's use must be carefully considered to determine whether misleading conduct has occurred.

Alternatively, the defendant will either adopt very similar indicia or somehow associate its indicia with that of the plaintiff. An example of the latter situation is the decision in *Wingate Marketing v Levi Strauss & Co*.[85] In that case, the defendant suggested that its product had the same trade origin as that of the plaintiff by selling second-hand Levi jeans and pronouncing its trade mark for them ('Revise') as 'Ree-vise' to rhyme with 'Levi's'.

14.4.4 Different quality of goods

One variation of the 'standard' form of passing off is where the defendant correctly states that the goods in question are associated with the plaintiff but incorrectly states the nature of that association. In *AG Spalding & Brothers v AW Gamage Ltd*,[86] the defendant represented that it was selling the top of the range Spalding soccer ball when it was in fact selling Spalding's cheaper soccer ball. Spalding successfully argued passing off because the defendant's misrepresentation deceptively traded off its goodwill in respect of its more expensive soccer balls.

14.4.5 Character merchandising

The character merchandising cases are interesting examples of the creativity of the common law in adapting and expanding the tort of passing off to accommodate and protect new marketing practices. They also involve consideration of some of the most difficult conceptual issues, particularly in relation to whether consumers are misled by the defendant's actions.

Early English decisions were opposed to character merchandising cases on several grounds. Up to that time, passing off actions had involved direct competitors. Consequently, it was easier to identify the relevant misrepresentation, whereas with character merchandising the general complaint is that the defendant has misrepresented the plaintiff's endorsement of the defendant's product. This aspect of passing off was temporarily ensconced in an irrebuttable proposition that the plaintiff and defendant had to be in a common field of activity. In *McCulloch v Lewis A May (Produce Distributors) Ltd*,[87] a well-known children's radio identity, Uncle Mac, was unsuccessful when he objected to a breakfast cereal producer using radio advertisements with a sound-alike voiceover that suggested the plaintiff had read the advertisement. The court stated:

---

84   At 14.3.5.
85   (1994) 49 FCR 89.
86   (1915) 32 RPC 273.
87   [1947] 2 All ER 845.

> I am satisfied that there is discoverable in all of those [cases] in which the court has intervened this factor, namely, that there was a common field of activity in which, however remotely, both the plaintiff and the defendant were engaged and that it was the presence of this factor that accounted for the jurisdiction of this court.[88]

Like many judicial statements, this was elevated almost to the status of legislative edict, when the better approach would have been to simply acknowledge that the extent to which the plaintiff and defendant occupied a common field of activity is relevant to whether consumers would be deceived but is not determinative of the issue. Certainly, in today's economy, celebrities endorse all sorts of products about which they know little or nothing, yet consumers either rely on those endorsements or at least pay some attention to them. Hence, a misleading representation that a celebrity endorses a product would, in fact, deceive consumers. This reality has led to the abandonment of a strict requirement of a common field of activity although it is still relevant to asking the question whether consumers are deceived by the defendant's conduct.[89]

In Australia, the first character merchandising case was *Henderson v Radio Corp Pty Ltd*.[90] Radio Corporation sold a record of ballroom dancing music and on the cover it placed a photograph of the Hendersons. Unknown to Radio Corporation, the Hendersons were a reasonably successful ballroom dancing team and teachers of ballroom dancing. They objected to the use of their photograph on the cover of the record without permission and were successful. Evatt CJ and Myers J explained:

> [The appellant] claims that a court of equity has no power to restrain the appellant from falsely representing that the respondents can prove that their professional reputation has thereby been injured or that in some other way their capacity to earn money by the practice of their profession has thereby been impaired. We do not think this is the law.
>
> It is true that the coercive power of the court cannot be invoked without proof of damage, but the wrongful appropriation of another's professional or business reputation is an injury in itself, no less, in our opinion, than the appropriation of their goods or money. The professional recommendation of the respondents was and still is theirs, to withhold or bestow at will, but the appellant has wrongfully deprived them of the right to do so and of the payment of reward on which, if they had been minded to give their approval to the appellant's record, they could have insisted.[91]

The decision was somewhat controversial for several reasons. One was that the Hendersons could only be recognised from a certain angle and their presence in the photograph was by no means highly prominent. Nevertheless, the court found that the Hendersons had been deprived of the opportunity to charge for the use of their reputation in the ballroom dancing industry.

The difficulty with the decision and some later character merchandising cases is proving that consumers would be misled into thinking that the celebrities in question would have been paid for their involvement in the promotion of the defendant's products and that they actively

---

88　Ibid 851 (per Wynn-Parry J).
89　*Lego System A/S v Lego M Lemelstrich Ltd* [1983] FSR 155.
90　(1960) 60 SR (NSW) 576.
91　Ibid 595.

endorse the product. In fact, the reality is that many consumers do not turn their mind to the issue. Nor do they care whether payment has been made if the product in question bears the logo or image that they are seeking. For example, in one case the band INXS successfully objected to the sale of unauthorised INXS T-shirts that bore their name, but it must be questionable whether consumers really cared whether they were authorised or not.[92]

Nevertheless, the courts have demonstrated a willingness to find a misrepresentation of this sort with minimal evidence although they still hold to the requirement of some form of misrepresentation. In *Pacific Dunlop v Hogan*,[93] Paul Hogan sued in respect of a television advertisement for Grosby shoes. The advertisement consisted of a variation of the famous knife scene from the movie *Crocodile Dundee*. A character, dressed as Crocodile Dundee, was accosted by a thief who demanded his wallet. When urged by his companion to look at the thief's shoes, the Crocodile Dundee character said 'Those aren't shoes, these are shoes' and then proceeded to kick the thief. The advertisement ended by identifying the brand of the shoes. At first instance and on appeal, three of the four Federal Court judges accepted that Pacific Dunlop had misled television viewers by implying that Hogan, as the 'true' Crocodile Dundee, endorsed the shoes and had been paid to do so. These findings were made despite the fact that the majority of witnesses acknowledged that they did not believe that the Crocodile Dundee character in the advertisement looked anything like Paul Hogan and there was no clear view expressed by them that they thought Hogan had been paid for the use of the Dundee look-alike.

In the Full Court, Burchett J observed that the real deception lay not so much in any implication of Hogan's endorsement of the product but in a less direct but nevertheless effective means of associating Hogan with it:

> Character merchandising through television advertisements should not be seen as setting off a logical train of thought in the minds of television viewers ... An association of some desirable character with the product proceeds more subtly to foster favourable inclination towards it, a good feeling about it, an emotional attachment to it. No logic tells the consumer that boots are better because Crocodile Dundee wears them ... The whole importance of character merchandising is the creation of an association of the product with the character, not the making of precise representations.[94]

Such an approach goes close to adopting unfair competition principles that prevent the appropriation of a celebrity's reputation without payment, even in the absence of any deception in the way the celebrity's image is used. Indeed, in other litigation involving Hogan, Pincus J noted that the real problem with the defendant's action was that it involved 'wrongful appropriation of a reputation or, more widely, wrongful association of goods with an image properly belonging to the [plaintiff]'.[95] While this emphasis on the unfair competition aspects of the case has been explicitly rejected, one is left with the reality that proving a misrepresentation

---

[92] *MK Hutchence v South Sea Bubble Co Pty Ltd* (1986) 64 ALR 330. But see also *Arsenal Football Club plc v Reed (No 2)* [2003] All ER (D) 289 (May).
[93] *Pacific Dunlop Ltd v Hogan (Crocodile Dundee* case) (1989) 23 FCR 553.
[94] Ibid 583.
[95] *Hogan v Koala Dundee Pty Ltd* (1988) 20 FCR 314, 325.

is not particularly difficult due to the courts leaning towards protecting the reputation of celebrities.[96]

Other character merchandising cases really come quite close to requiring payment for the non-misleading use of celebrity reputation. In particular, cases objecting to the sale of merchandise bearing the names or photographs of celebrities are successful on the grounds that the merchandise is not endorsed or approved by those celebrities. Yet these decisions are questionable as consumers may be interested in getting the picture or the name on a T-shirt or other merchandise without necessarily being concerned about whether it is authorised merchandise. A case from the United Kingdom primarily concerned with registered trade marks illustrates the point. In that case, the defendant sold football merchandise bearing the trade marks of the Arsenal football club. His defence to the trade mark infringement action was that the use of the name Arsenal on the merchandise did not suggest that the football club had sanctioned the application of the brand or that the merchandise was official Arsenal merchandise. Instead, consumers were simply after scarves and other merchandise bearing the name and Arsenal colours without necessarily caring if they were official. This argument was accepted by the trial judge, Laddie J, although there were other issues related to the infringement of the registered trade mark that are not relevant in the context of passing off and the first-instance decision was ultimately reversed.[97]

On the other hand, the adherence to the requirement of misrepresentation is demonstrated by cases such as those involving Gary Honey[98] and Sue Smith.[99] Gary Honey was an Olympic silver medallist. Without his permission, an airline company used a photograph of him in competition on posters that it distributed to travel agents and schools. The airline's name was clearly printed at the foot of each poster. In addition, a religious organisation used the photograph on the cover of one of its religious publications. Actions against both organisations were unsuccessful on the grounds that there was insufficient evidence that people would assume that Honey had approved of the use of his photo or had otherwise endorsed the products or the organisations. In light of decisions involving Olympic athletes,[100] Honey may consider himself unlucky as his case may have been clouded by the unusual 'amateur' status of Olympic athletes at the time, which may have affected a court's preparedness to believe others would consider him to have been paid for endorsement. It is also the case that, partly as a consequence of decisions such as those in the *Hogan* cases, the practice of paying celebrities has, in fact, become commonplace in recent years, thus ensuring that the public now assumes payment has been provided when a celebrity's image is used. Arguably, the law created the belief that is now the basis of the misrepresentation in such cases.

14.5 Passing off and the internet

In recent years, one of the most common forms of passing off has been via various uses of the internet. In particular, defendants have used identical or misleadingly similar domain names to

---

96   M. Davison and M. Kennedy, 'Proof of deception and character merchandising cases' (1990) 16 *Monash University Law Review* 111.
97   *Arsenal Football Club plc v Reed (No 2)* [2003] 3 All ER 865.
98   *Honey v Australian Airlines Ltd* (*Gary Honey* case) (1990) 18 IPR 185.
99   *10th Cantanae Pty Ltd v Shoshana Pty Ltd* (*Sue Smith* case) (1987) 79 ALR 299.
100 *Talmex Pty Ltd v Telstra Corp Ltd* (*Kieren Perkins* case) [1997] 2 Qd R 444.

direct internet traffic to their websites. An understanding of these issues first requires a brief explanation of the domain name system.

The internet is a network of computers that permit the distribution of information from any computer to any of the other computers in the network. In order to ensure that information reaches its correct destination or that a computer user can reach a particular site on the internet, each computer needs its own unique computer-readable address, which is initially in the form of a series of numbers. However, like many telephone numbers, these numbers can also be 'translated' into a name called a domain name or uniform resource locator (URL), such as 'www.nike.com'. Obviously, these names are far easier to remember than the actual underlying numerical sequences.

14.5.1 Domain names

A domain name or URL is assigned by various domain name registrars that are appointed by the Internet Corporation for Assigned Names and Numbers (ICANN). The domain names are divided into various parts or levels. The first level is the internet protocol, such as 'www', standing for world wide web. The second level is the secondary top-level domain (sTLD), which is the critical identifier of the domain name and the part that is the subject of the dispute. The third level is the generic top-level domain (gTLD), such as '.com' or '.net'. There may also be an individual country code top-level domain (ccTLD), such as '.au'. The general rule for allocating domain names is 'First come, first served', although some country code domain names, such as the '.au' domain names, impose some other prerequisites that require the applicant for registration to demonstrate its connection with both Australia and the particular generic top-level domain. For example, an applicant seeking a '.com.au' has to prove it is an Australian commercial entity by producing evidence, such as proof of registration of an Australian business name or an Australian company name.

The consequence of these unique internet addresses is that they work both as a means of ensuring the physical functioning of the internet and as a means of easily identifying a particular site and attracting internet users to that site. It is this latter function that attracts the attention of passing off and trade mark considerations, especially given the necessary uniqueness of every domain name and the communication power of the internet.

The use and abuse of domain name registration may take one or more of several forms. One previously common practice was to register one or more domain names consisting of well-known registered trade marks or the names of well-known celebrities. These domain names were then 'warehoused' by the registrant in the hope that the trade mark owners or celebrities would pay to acquire the domain names in question.

Passing off cases have responded to such behaviour by providing plaintiffs with the means to obtain injunctive relief very quickly. A seminal case on the point is the decision in *British Telecommunications v One-in-a-Million*.[101] The defendant in that case had registered and warehoused a number of well-known domain names, such as 'www.marksandspencer.com'. The plaintiffs contended that the mere act of registration of the domain names by the defendant constituted passing off and sought an injunction requiring them to transfer registration of the

---

101 [1998] NLJR 1179.

relevant domain names to the plaintiffs. The Court of Appeal (England and Wales) agreed with the plaintiffs for two reasons. First, the registers of domain names are publicly available. Any member of the public seeking the identity of the registrant of a domain name such as www.marksandspencer.com would be able to discover that it was registered in the name of the defendant. Consequently, the defendant had already engaged in deceptive conduct as the register then wrongly represented an association between the defendant and Marks & Spencer. Second, the act of registration was considered to constitute the 'creation of an instrument of deception' by the defendant. Consequently, the defendant was preparing to engage in fraudulent conduct. In such circumstances, equity has long recognised the right to a quia timet injunction, an injunction to prevent impending damage before it actually occurs. Consequently, the court was prepared to grant relief immediately to prevent such a situation arising. This aspect of the decision was based on the 'creation of an instrument of deception' by the defendant.

In addition to warehousing, a domain name might be used to attract internet users to a website in various ways. For example, internet search engines will identify the website when internet users search for the relevant term, such as 'Nike'. Many users, looking for information about Nike products, may even type 'www.nike.com' directly into the internet address box of the relevant browser. The effect will be that they will be directed to a website that has nothing to do with Nike Inc. The passing off implications of such a situation are obvious. In addition, attempts are often made to use misleadingly similar domain names, such as 'www.niki.com', again in the hope of attracting internet users who mistype an address or in the hope that similar names will be picked up by internet search engines.

One potential domain name scenario involves more innocent activity. It is entirely possible that two different legal entities would have separate but equally valid reasons for registering exactly the same domain name. In such circumstances, the first to acquire registration will be entitled to retain it, despite the objections of the second.[102] For example, in *Prince plc v Prince Sports Group Inc*,[103] an American sports goods company with a strong reputation for its trade mark 'Prince' objected to the registration and use of 'www.prince.com' by a United Kingdom company that sold computer products. While the American company had a bigger reputation for Prince than the United Kingdom company, each was entitled to use the term in respect of their very different products and the United Kingdom company was entitled to continue to use the domain name that it had registered first.

14.5.2 Australian passing off cases and the internet

Several Australian cases have dealt with domain name disputes. In *Architects (Australia) Pty Ltd v Witty Consultants Pty Ltd*,[104] Architects Australia objected to the domain name www.architectsaustralia.com.au, which was used by the defendant to provide a web-based directory of Australian architects. The plaintiff had provided an architecture service in southeast Queensland for some twenty years prior to the defendant's registration of the domain name. Chesterman J in the Queensland Supreme Court found that the term 'Architects

---

102 *Pitman Training Ltd v Nominet UK* (1997) 38 IPR 341.
103 [1998] FSR 21.
104 [2002] QSC 139.

Australia' was distinctive of the plaintiff's business, even though its goodwill and reputation were geographically restricted while the defendant's website would obviously be available on a worldwide basis. A disclaimer on the website was also considered to be ineffective. The decision is somewhat surprising as it seems to downplay the reality that more than one entity may have a legitimate interest in the one domain name and that internet users are aware of that possibility. On the other hand, the judgment did place some emphasis on the finding that 'Architects Australia' was not purely descriptive.

A later case that more specifically addressed the nature of the internet was the decision in *Sydney Markets Ltd v Sydney Flower Market Pty Ltd*.[105] Both the plaintiff and the defendant had registered domain names containing the words 'Sydney flower market' and both used that descriptive term in their trading. The court declined to find for either the plaintiff or the defendant in its cross-claim but was prepared to require both parties to place disclaimers on their websites, and said: 'Whilst disclaimers ... are often regarded as insufficient to avoid the public being misled, the same considerations are not applicable in the case of a web site.'[106] The decision reflects a preparedness of courts to acknowledge the nature of the internet, the potentially inherently confusing aspects of its operation and the understanding of the internet's users of those confusing aspects.

In other cases, it has been abundantly obvious that the registrant of the relevant domain name has no interest in the domain name other than the opportunity it provides to seek to extract a transfer fee from a company with a legitimate interest in the name. In those circumstances, the registration of the domain name is likely to constitute either passing off or a breach of s 18 of sch 2 of the *Competition and Consumer Act 2010* (Cth), the former s 52 of the *Trade Practices Act 1974* (Cth). The decision in *CSR Ltd v Resource Capital Australia Pty Ltd*[107] is an example where the registrant registered names such as csrsugar.com and csrsugar.com.au despite having no interest in conducting business in the sugar industry. The Federal Court ordered the relevant domain names to be transferred to CSR on the basis that the registration of the domain names by the registrant breached s 52 of the *Trade Practices Act* as it then was.[108] An even more obvious case of misleading conduct was *Australian Competition and Consumer Commission v Chen*[109] in which the defendant registered Sydneyopera.org and proceeded to sell tickets to events at the Sydney Opera House by representing that the website was the official website of the Sydney Opera Trust.

There has also been an important passing off case involving use of the internet other than misleading use of domain names. In *Ward Group Pty Ltd v Brodie & Stone plc*,[110] the plaintiff objected to the sale of a product called Restoria via English websites. The plaintiff had a reputation for Restoria in Australia. It was concerned that it was possible for Australian consumers to buy the English version of Restoria, which was produced by an English company unrelated to the plaintiff via the website, and that they might do so believing that they were acquiring it from the Australian company. While the court accepted that a 'trap order' by the

---

105 (2002) ATPR (Digest) 46-216.
106 Ibid [152].
107 (2003) 128 FCR 408.
108 See also *Macquarie Bank Ltd v Seagle* (2005) 146 FCR 400.
109 (2003) 132 FCR 309.
110 (2005) 143 FCR 479.

plaintiff demonstrated the capacity of consumers to buy the product via the internet, it formed the conclusion that no damage would be done to the plaintiff's reputation by the defendant's activities because there was no evidence that Australian consumers had or would be likely to obtain the product via the websites. The price of the product in England was considerably greater than the price charged by the plaintiff in Australia and the website offered many products for sale of which Restoria was but one. Those findings of fact may not be replicated in similar cases and later courts may be more inclined to accept the likelihood of damage to the plaintiff's reputation.

14.5.3 Uniform dispute resolution policy

Despite the ability of passing off cases to adapt to domain name disputes, the extent to which domain names were abused led to the development of administrative procedures to deal with 'abusive registration'. The objective of these procedures is to deal with the most obvious cases of inappropriate registration of domain names quickly and cheaply. To that end, ICANN established a *Uniform Domain Name Dispute Resolution Policy*[111] (*UDRP*) and an associated dispute resolution process that came into effect in 2000.

The *UDRP* works via a contract signed by every domain name registrant, which requires registrants to submit to the *UDRP* and its associated processes. The complaint is made to one of the dispute resolution service providers approved by ICANN, which in turn assigns the matter to one of its many accredited panellists who have expertise in trade mark and passing off issues. (The most popular of these dispute resolution service providers is the World Intellectual Property Organization, or WIPO.)[112]

The dispute is resolved 'on the papers' via the written submissions of the parties. A complainant under the *UDRP* has to satisfy a three-part test:

- The domain name in question is identical, or confusingly similar, to a trade mark or service mark in which the complainant has rights.
- The domain name registrant has no rights or legitimate interests in respect of the domain name.
- The domain name has been registered and is being used in bad faith.

A very considerable jurisprudence has arisen through the written decisions of panellists and many have constituted precedents that have been relied on by other panellists, despite the fact that this is obviously not a common law court system and decisions are not binding on later panellists. Nevertheless, a number of issues relating to interpretation of the *UDRP* seem to have been settled via this process of relying on prior decisions. In addition, WIPO has conducted three overviews of all of the decisions made by panellists and prepared overview reports that distil the essence of decisions on important matters that have been in contention from time to time. The consequence is that the panellists and all parties to such disputes have a wealth of prior decisions at their disposal as well as clear summaries of the overall trends in decisions to draw on.[113]

---

111   Opened for signature on 26 August 1999 (entered into force on 24 October 1999).
112   See, for example, A. Roy, 'Internet domain name dispute resolution in Australia' (2014) 36 *European Intellectual Property Review* 492.
113   See WIPO, 'WIPO Overview of WIPO Panel Views on Selected *UDRP* Questions, Third Edition ("WIPO Jurisprudential Overview 3.0")' www.wipo.int.

For example, the expression 'a trade mark or service mark in which the complainant has rights' has been interpreted to include unregistered trade marks that have acquired goodwill or a reputation through use. Consequently, a number of well-known celebrities have been able to successfully argue that they have grounds to bring a complaint. The actress Julia Roberts was one of the first celebrities to win such a case[114] in the face of some controversy about whether the *UDRP* should have been applied to such situations. In any event, the effect of such decisions is to apply the *UDRP* to many passing off situations.

The second element of a complaint – namely, proving that the registrant has no rights or legitimate interest in a domain name – can be difficult because of the problems associated with proving a negative. The panel decisions have tended to place the onus on a registrant to demonstrate they have such a right or interest once the complainant asserts the lack of such an interest.[115] The *UDRP* provides a non-exhaustive list of particular examples of rights or legitimate interests, such as the bona fide offering of goods or services or that the registrant is commonly known by the domain name.[116]

The third element of the complaint – namely, that the domain name has been registered and is being used in bad faith – has also generated some controversy surrounding its interpretation. The main difficulty with the wording of this requirement is that it is conjunctive and so the complainant needs to demonstrate both bad faith registration and bad faith use. The latter requirement immediately generates some potential difficulties where domain names are 'warehoused' but not used. One of the earliest decisions dealt with the issue by providing that the act of registration and passive holding may meet the bad faith element if other factors are present.[117] For example, the complainant had a very strong reputation while the registrant had given no evidence of any good faith use or intended good faith use and had actively concealed and falsified its contact details. The total effect of these circumstances was that it was impossible to envisage any use that would be in good faith.

If a complainant is successful, a panellist may order either the deregistration of the domain name or the transfer of the domain name to the complainant. The relevant domain name registrar is then bound by that decision. There is no appeal process under the *UDRP*. However, any party may bring court proceedings either during or after the process and the result of such proceedings would 'trump' any decision pursuant to the *UDRP* processes. As the *UDRP* is only aimed at clear cases of abusive registration, such proceedings would be necessary if, for example, the registrant was able to demonstrate some interest in the domain name but, on balance, its continued use would deceive consumers by suggesting an association with the complainant. The court decision in *Architects (Australia) Pty Ltd v Witty Consultants Pty Ltd*,[118] discussed above,[119] is an example of such a situation where the dispute resolution policy would probably not have resulted in a change of ownership of the domain name but the court was prepared to find for the plaintiff.

---

114   *Julia Fiona Roberts v Russell Boyd* D2000-0210 (WIPO, 29 May 2000).
115   Ibid 648.
116   Ibid 649–50.
117   *Telstra Corp Ltd v Nuclear Marshmallows* D2000-0003 (WIPO, 18 February 2000).
118   [2002] QSC 139.
119   At 14.5.2.

14.5.4 Australian uniform dispute resolution policy

Australia has its own dispute resolution policy (*auDRP*) in relation to '.au' domain names administered by the .au Domain Administration Ltd (auDA).[120] There are far fewer disputes concerning '.au' domain names for several reasons. First, the demand for '.au' domain names is considerably less than it is for open domains such as '.com' domain names. Second, auDA imposes requirements on potential registrants that limit the potential for future disputes. Those seeking a '.com.au' domain name have to demonstrate that they are a commercial entity with some connection with Australia by providing proof of such connection, such as the ownership of an Australian trade mark or registration of a business or company.[121]

The *auDRP* is similar to the *UDRP* but, having been formulated after it, has avoided some of the difficulties associated with the *UDRP*'s interpretation. For example, it does not require both bad faith registration and bad faith use of a domain name. Either will be sufficient. Recently, an overview of *auDRP* decisions was published that is similar in nature to the two WIPO overviews of *UDRP* decisions.[122]

14.5.5 Meta-tags

Meta-tags are hidden computer code placed in the computer software code of websites. The meta-tags may contain keywords, such as trade marks, that indicate the nature of the content of the website. On occasion, these meta-tags have included trade marks that either have nothing to do with the content of the website or are the trade marks of competitors of the website owners. While internet users do not see the meta-tags, it was common practice for internet search engines to rely on the meta-tags for the purposes of identifying a website as one that met the search criteria of users. The internet search results would then include the website with the relevant meta-tags and internet users could be deceived, at least initially, by the suggestion that the website met their search criteria.

Several American decisions relating to the use of meta-tags have had different outcomes, which indicates some of the difficulties that courts have in dealing with the new commercial environment created by the internet. For example, in *Brookfield Communications Inc v West Coast Entertainment Corp*,[123] the plaintiff objected to the use of the meta-tag 'MovieBuff' in the defendant's website coding. The court found for the plaintiff on the grounds of 'initial interest confusion'. While consumers would not have been ultimately misled and would not have purchased the defendant's product believing that it was the plaintiff's product, they would have been initially directed to the defendant's website. Consequently, the defendant deceptively interested the consumers in its product. The decision has been criticised for failing to recognise the reality of internet searching, which invariably throws up false leads, and the capacity of internet users to adapt to that difficulty and quickly sift through a list of websites to determine the ones that suit their needs.[124]

---

120   See auDA's website www.auda.org.au for details of the organisation.
121   See auDA's website www.auda.org.au for details of the requirements for registration within the different second-level domains for '.au' domain names.
122   See auDA, '*auDRP* overview', www.auda.org.au/policies/audrp/audrp-overview.
123   174 F 3d 1036 (9th Cir, 1999).
124   J. A. Rajzer, 'Misunderstanding the internet: How courts are overprotecting trademarks used in meta tags' (2001) *Michigan State University Law Review* 427.

Other decisions have been less critical of the use of meta-tags and less open to the application of the 'initial interest' test.[125] For example, in *Playboy Enterprises v Welles*,[126] a former *Playboy* centrefold was permitted to use the meta-tag 'Playboy' in her website because her website quite legitimately referred to her involvement with *Playboy* magazine.

At least one Australian Federal Court decision has granted an injunction preventing a defendant from using another's trade mark as a meta-tag embedded within its website.[127] The use was part of a range of uses of the trade mark that contributed to a finding of misleading or deceptive conduct by the defendant.

In any event, the extent of the abuse of meta-tags has been so great that internet search engine operators have changed their searching practices to place far less reliance on meta-tags in determining the identity of websites that meet a user's search request.[128]

14.5.6 Keyword advertising

Another, and possibly the most contentious, issue is the use of keyword advertising to generate advertising results that may be misleading or deceptive. This practice involves the use of an internet search engine that arranges its computer indexing in such a way that if internet searchers type in particular keywords, which may include a particular trade mark with a significant reputation, the search engine may display the advertisements for related or competing products. Alternatively, the search engine may display the websites of competing products as well as or instead of the website of the trader that may be researched by the internet user.

The results of the search are usually displayed as 'organic' results or 'sponsored' results with weblinks to various websites. The former are results created without the intervention of an advertiser paying for its advertisement to be displayed in response to searches made by reference to particular keywords. The latter are results that are the consequence of payment by an advertiser to ensure that its advertisement comes up in response to a search involving the relevant keywords.

Separate issues may arise relating to the liability of the advertiser on the one hand and the search engine operator on the other hand. In the former situation, there is no doubt that the advertiser controls the advertisement that is revealed as a consequence of the keyword search. Consequently, if the resulting advertisement is found to constitute passing off or misleading or deceptive conduct, the advertiser will clearly be liable. For example, one decision involved the purchase of the keywords 'harvey world travel'.[129] When a consumer searched for those words, a sponsored link was shown with the heading 'Harvey Travel' followed by a brief statement about flights, hotels and packages together with a web link to statravel.com.au, the website of a rival to Harvey World Travel. It was agreed that such conduct was misleading and deceptive conduct by STA Travel. A different result may have been arrived at if the sponsored advertisement clearly indicated that the link was not to Harvey World Travel but a different

---

125 *Bihari v Gross*, 119 F Supp 2d 309 (SD NY, 2000).
126 279 F 3d 796 (9th Cir, 2002).
127 *Mantra Group Pty Ltd v Tailly Pty Ltd (No 2)* (2010) 183 FCR 450.
128 See, for example, V. Huang, 'Liability for 'invisible' use of trade marks on the internet' (2018) 28 *Australian Intellectual Property Journal* 51, 54.
129 *Google Inc v Australian Competition and Consumer Commission* (2013) 249 CLR 435.

travel agency altogether. Internet users are accustomed to differentiating between organic and sponsored search results. In doing so, they would be aware of the very real possibility that sponsored links shown in response to their searching would not necessarily link to the particular company that they may have been researching. On the other hand, if, as was the situation in that case, the sponsored link suggests that it does link to the company being researched when it does not, a finding of misleading or deceptive conduct would not be difficult to establish.

An example of the former is the decision in *Lift Shop Pty Ltd v Easy Living Home Elevators Pty Ltd*.[130] In that case, the plaintiff owned and had a reputation for the name 'Liftshop' in respect to home elevators. It objected to sponsored links by a rival that read as below:

> **Easy Living Lifts | Home Elevators | ←Lift Shop – Lift Shop→**
> www.easy-living.com.au
> At Easy Living home elevators website you will find details on all of our lifts and home elevators here, which will help you achieve the easy living you deserve.

The Federal Court found that the use of the term 'Lift Shop' as two separate words in the context of the sponsored links that clearly referred to Easy Living did not amount to passing off or misleading or deceptive conduct.

In *Google Inc v Australian Competition and Consumer Commission*[131] the High Court addressed the more complex question of whether Google was responsible for deceptive advertising in circumstances where it accepted the advertisement 'placed' by STA Travel. The High Court took the view that Google was not relevantly different from owners of other advertising media forms, such as newspapers or broadcasts, that publish or broadcast the advertisements of customers.[132] No reasonable search engine user would have concluded that the sponsored links generated by a search for 'harvey world travel' were endorsed or adopted by Google.

14.6 Effect of disclaimers

As seen in cases such as the *Sydney Flower Market* case[133] discussed above[134] and *Wells Fargo v WhenU.com*,[135] disclaimers may be particularly effective in the internet environment where internet users are used to the 'vagaries' of the internet. In theory, a disclaimer might dispel any misleading aspect of a defendant's conduct in almost any circumstances. In practice, the courts have tended to be cautious about accepting the efficacy of disclaimers because, as was said in the *Stone Ales* case: 'Thirsty folk want beer, not explanations.'[136]

---

130   [2013] FCA 900.
131   (2013) 249 CLR 435.
132   Ibid [69].
133   *Sydney Markets Ltd v Sydney Flower Market Pty Ltd* (2002) ATPR (Digest) 46-216.
134   At 14.5.2.
135   293 F Supp 2d 734 (ED Mich, 2003).
136   *Montgomery v Thompson* [1891] AC 217.

Some of the difficulties with disclaimers include the following:

- A potential purchaser's focus is on the product being considered for purchase rather than the disclaimer. How carefully a consumer will examine a product and take notice of disclaimers will depend on a number of issues, such as the price of the product and the likelihood that consumers will have the time or inclination to notice a disclaimer. For example, in *Abundant Earth Pty Ltd v R & C Products Pty Ltd*,[137] a disclaimer was ineffective primarily because the product in question, mustard, was a relatively inexpensive item and consumers would not notice it in their brief consideration before taking it from the supermarket shelf.
- A disclaimer, especially in relation to services, may not be passed on from one customer to another but the misrepresentation might be. For example, in *Bridge Stockbrokers Ltd v Bridges*,[138] a disclaimer would be ineffective because similarly named stockbrokers would be spoken about by name by customers but they would not repeat any disclaimer.
- A disclaimer may imply that there is something wrong or unethical about the services of the other trader. Again, in *Bridge Stockbrokers*,[139] a disclaimer to the effect that a stockbroker was in no way associated with another named stockbroker may have suggested some impropriety on the part of that stockbroker rather than dispelling any deception arising from their similar names.
- Depending on the product, a disclaimer may be misinterpreted, thus failing to negative the misleading nature of the defendant's conduct and the suggestion of an association with the plaintiff. In the *Duff Beer* case,[140] the defendant offered to provide a disclaimer on the cans of 'Duff' beer that it sold. Duff beer is the fictitious beer drunk by Homer Simpson on the cartoon show *The Simpsons*. One problem with the proposed disclaimer was that those familiar with the quirky humour of the show may have thought that the disclaimer was a joke and actually affirmed the connection with *The Simpsons*.

Nevertheless, there are instances where a disclaimer or appropriate label has been considered sufficiently effective to rebut any alleged misrepresentation. One of the most widely cited decisions in this respect is *Parkdale Custom Built Furniture Pty Ltd v Puxu Pty Ltd*.[141] In that case, a majority of the High Court held that similarities in the shape of furniture and the potential for deception flowing from those similarities were overcome by the defendant's label, which was located at the bottom of cushions in chairs and sofas. These unassuming disclaimers, which were no more than the defendant's own label with its own name, were deemed effective because the cost of the furniture in question was such that consumers could be expected to inspect the furniture carefully before making purchasing decisions. Again, policy decisions are implicit within the decision as it required a decision about the standard of care required of consumers, a decision about the point at which any deception might be dispelled and whether that point was too far into the purchasing process. It was probably influenced by a desire not to provide a monopoly right over particular shapes.

---

137   (1985) 7 FCR 233.
138   (1984) 4 FCR 460.
139   Ibid.
140   *Twentieth Century Fox Film Corp v South Australian Brewing Co Ltd* (1996) 66 FCR 451.
141   (1982) 149 CLR 191.

In other cases, sufficiently explicit disclaimers have been effective, as in *Sony Music Australia Ltd v Tansing*[142] where unauthorised sound recordings of musical performances were made and then sold with very large, unambiguous warnings that the recordings were not authorised by the performers. At the time, Australia did not recognise performers' rights and the plaintiff's only cause of action in passing off was negatived by the disclaimer.

A more recent example of a disclaimer being accepted by the Federal Court as part of the terms of an injunction against conduct regarded as misleading or deceptive is the disclaimer in *Knott Investments v Winnebago Industries Inc*.[143] Knott Investments sold motor homes under the Winnebago trade mark in Australia for many years while the Winnebago trade mark was well known as the trade mark of an American company that first made Winnebago motor homes. In a passing off action, the Full Federal Court decided to permit the Australian company to continue to use the Winnebago trade mark, provided that all vehicles carried this notice: 'This vehicle was not manufactured by, or by anyone having any association with, Winnebago of the United States.' The Australian company was also required to obtain a written acknowledgment from its customers that its products were not associated with the American company. In deciding on an injunction that included the use of the disclaimers in question, the court noted: 'The relief should be such that the Court is satisfied it will prevent deception.'[144] Consequently, the issue is not so much whether a disclaimer should be required but what impact a disclaimer would have in the context of all the circumstances under which the sale of products would occur.

14.7 A holistic perspective

The culmination of these points is that the existence or otherwise of passing off depends on an examination of all aspects of the plaintiff's reputation and the defendant's conduct. This confirms the point made above that what is protected is the plaintiff's reputation rather than any particular commercial indicia associated with the reputation. So the mere use of that or similar indicia by the defendant in a commercial context will not necessarily constitute passing off. The real question will be whether, in all the circumstances of the case, the defendant has made some misrepresentation that would suggest an association between itself and the plaintiff that might damage the plaintiff's interests. In the same way that the use of commercial indicia does not of itself constitute passing off, the use of a disclaimer cannot of itself prevent a finding of passing off without looking at the entire situation in context. Hence, not only are disclaimers relevant but a number of other issues, such as the location and extent of the plaintiff's reputation, whether the business indicium in question is descriptive in nature, the intention of the defendant and the entirety of its conduct, will be examined.

For example, in *The Coca-Cola Co v PepsiCo Inc (No 2)*[145] the Federal Court was at pains to identify the precise details of the source or sources of the plaintiff's reputation in circumstances in which it complained about the production by PepsiCo of a similarly shaped bottle. Consequently, the court was careful to note the extent to which consumers relied on indicia such as

---

142   (1993) 27 IPR 649.
143   (2013) 211 FCR 449.
144   Ibid [22].
145   (2014) 109 IPR 429.

word trade marks rather than bottle shape to distinguish products. In addition, it noted the extent to which the plaintiff relied on the precise combination of features in its bottle and contrasted them with all of the features of PepsiCo's bottle. Finally, the court pointed out the similarities of the contexts in which the two soft drinks were sold or likely to be sold, including the similarity of colour of the contents of the bottle and the quick decision-making process of consumers in relation to relatively small priced items.

14.8 Damage

The final element of passing off is the requirement of either damage or a likelihood of damage. The sufficiency of a likelihood of damage is, again, an indication of equity's influence on passing off with its willingness to issue quia timet injunctions where no damage has yet occurred but the defendant's actions or proposed actions suggest that it will. The reality is that once a reputation is proved and the court accepts the existence of some misrepresentation, damage or a likelihood of it is an almost inevitable consequence. Hence, a misrepresentation that goods originate from the plaintiff when they do not has the obvious implication that the plaintiff will lose the business of those who were seeking its goods.

In addition, if the quality of the defendant's products is less than that of the plaintiff's or even just different, then the plaintiff's reputation will inevitably suffer. Examples of this situation include the *Advocaat*[146] and *Spanish Champagne*[147] cases where the defendant's product was clearly different from the plaintiff's and probably inferior in quality. Similarly, in *AG Spalding & Brothers v AW Gamage Ltd*,[148] the misrepresentation was that the soccer balls sold by the defendant were Spalding's high-quality balls when, in fact, they were not. Again, the impact on the plaintiff's reputation is clear and obvious.

Other types of damage might flow from the diversion of custom through 'initial deception'. This type of damage often occurs in relation to domain names where customers discover reasonably quickly that they are not at the website that they are seeking, but by that time their attention has been diverted to the defendant's website and its products.

In relation to character merchandising, the damage to the plaintiff is either the loss of licence fees[149] or damage to the celebrity's reputation from association with a product that it does not wish to be associated with. For example, in the *Duff Beer* case,[150] Twentieth Century Fox's main objection to the sale of Duff beer was not any loss of potential licence fees but concern that *The Simpsons* would be perceived as sponsoring alcohol and that it might be encouraging young viewers to drink alcohol. This objection was based on both the commercial considerations that *The Simpsons* is a family show and the loss of parental support would be damaging, and the deontological perspective that those associated with the show did not in fact want to be promoting such products, regardless of the potential licence fees and commercial advantages that might flow from doing so. As indicated in the discussion above concerning

---

146   *Erven Warnink BV v J Townend & Sons (Hull) Ltd* [1979] AC 731.
147   *Bollinger v Costa Brava Wine Co Ltd* [1960] Ch 262.
148   (1915) 32 RPC 273.
149   See also *Winnebago Industries Inc v Knott Investments Pty Ltd (No 4)* [2015] FCA 1327 for a discussion of a licence fee in assessing damages
150   *Twentieth Century Fox Film Corp v South Australian Brewing Co Ltd* (1996) 66 FCR 451.

the nature of the relevant misrepresentation, the possibility of such damage seems to fuel the likelihood of the court finding a misrepresentation.

One case where the plaintiff failed because the court was not satisfied of damage or the likelihood of it was the decision in *Ward Group Pty Ltd v Brodie & Stone plc*.[151] The facts of that case are provided above.[152] The court concluded that, as the plaintiff was the only person to have ordered the relevant product from an overseas website, it had not been damaged. Further, it found that as the product was readily available in Australia from the plaintiff and it was considerably cheaper if obtained from the plaintiff rather than the overseas website in question, the likelihood of Australian consumers buying it through the website was remote. Consequently, the likelihood of damage was so small that an injunction was not justified. This aspect of the decision may be questionable. Products sold over the internet are often more expensive than products sold in a physical store. Yet internet users are willing to pay the higher price in return for convenience and privacy.

14.9 Statutory causes of action

There are numerous statutory standards of conduct[153] imposed on traders that approximate the standard of conduct required by passing off. The most widely known and used of these provisions is s 18 of sch 2 of the *Competition and Consumer Act 2010* (Cth), which was commonly known as s 52(1) of the *Trade Practices Act 1974* (Cth) until a change of name and rearrangement of section numbers took place on 1 January 2011. It provides that 'a person must not, in trade or commerce, engage in conduct that is misleading or deceptive or is likely to mislead or deceive'. While s 18 of sch 2 affects much conduct that is not passing off, there would be few instances of passing off that would not contravene the section. A general analysis of the wording of the section and other provisions is necessary to understand both its breadth and some of its limitations before undertaking a more detailed analysis of its application to passing off situations.

14.9.1 Application of the legislation

Due to the limits on the constitutional powers of the Commonwealth, the application of the former *Trade Practices Act* was limited. The application of the former s 52 was limited to conduct by corporations and other conduct by individuals that could be brought within other constitutional powers of the Commonwealth. For example, interstate trade can be regulated by the Commonwealth and was caught by s 52. In time, the individual states passed legislation that largely mirrored the Commonwealth legislation and applied to the conduct of individuals operating within a state.

---

151 (2005) 143 FCR 479. See also *Lifeplan Australia Friendly Society Ltd v Woff* [2016] FCA 248, [411]–[412], for another example where damages were not found.
152 At 14.5.2.
153 The provisions imposing the standard of conduct and other provisions providing for liability for failing to comply with it are usually separate. For example, the enforcement provisions that are applicable to a breach of *Competition and Consumer Act 2010* (Cth) sch 2 s 18 and specify the possible remedies for the breach are contained in other provisions of sch 2 of that legislation.

As at the beginning of 2011, the Australian Consumer Law regime came into effect such that the one set of consumer laws applies throughout Australia. The details of the regime and the interrelationship between Commonwealth and state legislation are not the subject of this book. However, for our purposes, it is sufficient to note that any conduct by any person in trade or commerce that is misleading or deceptive or likely to mislead or deceive will be caught by some legislative provision.

14.9.2 'In trade or commerce'

While conduct may be in the course of trade or commerce, not all of such conduct is necessarily 'in trade or commerce'. The leading case on the interpretation of this phrase is *Concrete Constructions (NSW) Pty Ltd v Nelson*.[154] In that case, a foreman advised an employee that a grill separating him from a lift shaft was firmly attached. The employee leaned on it, it gave way and he fell. The High Court held that the conduct in question was not 'in trade or commerce' as opposed to being conduct in the course of trade or commerce and that the employee could therefore not rely on s 52 as a basis for recovering damages for his injuries. The limitation is unlikely to affect many, if any, passing off situations although there has been one passing off case involving a dispute between two churches with the same name about which was the 'true' church. The use of the church name may not have been regarded as being in trade or commerce.[155]

14.9.3 'Engage in conduct'

This broad phrase catches almost all conduct. It certainly does not require any express oral or written representation and the entire conduct will be taken into account. Silence may also constitute conduct for these purposes as s 2(2)(a) and (b) of sch 2 expressly states that a reference to engaging in conduct shall be read as a reference to doing or refusing to do any act. Section 2(2)(c) of sch 2 further clarifies that a reference to refusing to do an act includes a reference to refraining (otherwise than inadvertently) from doing that act.

14.9.4 'Misleading or deceptive'

This expression raises again some of the issues about terminology used in the passing off decisions. A few points can be made with clarity about this expression. First, the courts have made it clear that conduct that is confusing does not breach s 18 of sch 2 of the *Competition and Consumer Act 2010* (Cth). Hence, if a defendant's conduct causes a person to wonder about the correct state of affairs rather than to be actually misled as to that state of affairs, they will not be in breach of the section and the courts have regularly made this point.[156] Again, as pointed out earlier in the chapter when discussing this terminology, while the distinction is relatively easy to make in theory, in practice, it is quite difficult to apply. The manner in which

---

154 (1990) 169 CLR 594.
155 *Attorney-General (NSW) ex rel Elisha v Holy Apostolic and Catholic Church of the East (Assyrian) Australia New South Wales Parish Association* (1989) 14 IPR 609.
156 *Parkdale Custom Built Furniture Pty Ltd v Puxu Pty Ltd* (1982) 149 CLR 191; *Campomar SL v Nike International Ltd* (2000) 202 CLR 45.

the distinction is applied suggests that policy considerations are either directly or indirectly taken into account, and hence a finding of 'confusion' rather than being misled often occurs in cases relating to descriptive terms (for example, 'Office Cleaning Business'), where there is an understandable reluctance to confer exclusive rights to the use of the term. In addition, such decisions also require a policy decision about the particular point in trade at which the confusing or misleading conduct or is to be evaluated. Consequently, one is often left with the impression that a finding of 'confusing' conduct rather than 'misleading or deceptive conduct' is a justification for a policy-based outcome rather than the explanation of what actually occurred.

Second, intention is not relevant to a finding of a breach of the section.[157] Conduct will be misleading even if it was not intended to be misleading. This leaves open the question of the distinction between 'misleading' and 'deceptive' conduct. Basic statutory interpretation principles would suggest that the two terms must have different meanings for to state otherwise would leave one of the terms otiose. No authoritative satisfactory distinction between the terms has been made apart from one suggestion put forward by French J in *Bridge Stockbrokers Ltd v Bridges*.[158] In that case, he suggested that deceptive conduct would include conduct that was deliberately confusing. In other words, if a defendant intentionally generated confusion, then its conduct would be deceptive but not misleading. Similarly, misleading conduct would involve more than confusion but need not involve any intent to mislead on the part of the defendant. The suggestion has not yet been unequivocally adopted by other judges.

The actual determination of whether conduct is misleading or deceptive is the subject of a four-step approach referred to by the Full Federal Court in the *Taco Bell* case.[159] The test is frequently quoted and it is summarised below with some added points derived from later cases.

1. It is possible to identify the relevant section of the public (which may be the public at large) that is or was the target of the defendant's conduct.

2. The matter is considered by reference to all who come within that section of the public. Consequently, if the conduct was aimed at a particularly knowledgeable section of the public, it would be less likely to mislead. An example might be specialist medical equipment that looks similar to other such equipment but which is purchased only by or on the recommendation of medical professionals with a keen understanding of the differences between the products.[160]

3. Evidence that some of the people have been misled or deceived will be relevant but not determinative of the issue as the test is objective and even if people have been deceived this may be because they may be regarded as unusually gullible or because they had made certain false assumptions for which the defendant should not be held responsible.[161]

---

157   *Hornsby Building Information Centre Pty Ltd v Sydney Building Information Centre Ltd* (1978) 140 CLR 216.
158   (1984) 4 FCR 460.
159   *Taco Co (Australia) Inc v Taco Bell Pty Ltd* (1982) 42 ALR 177, 202–3.
160   *Hodgkinson & Corby Ltd v Wards Mobility Services Ltd* [1995] FSR 169.
161   *McWilliam's Wines Pty Ltd v McDonald's System of Australia Pty Ltd* (1980) 33 ALR 394.

4. The reason for any deception must be determined and it must be attributable to the defendant's conduct rather than some other cause, such as some assumption that the plaintiff is the only person with the legal right to use certain words or indicia.[162]

14.10 Comparison with passing off

The courts have constantly pointed out that the former equivalent of s 18 of sch 2 of the *Competition and Consumer Act 2010* (Cth) was to be applied on its own terms and that its interpretation was not to be controlled by passing off principles.[163] Section 18 of sch 2 is concerned exclusively with the prevention of misleading conduct whereas passing off also has a concern with the plaintiff's reputation and, in some circumstances (for example, honest concurrent use), the defendant's reputation. While as a matter of law the differences between the two are clear, as a matter of practice, the overlap between the section and passing off is very considerable and it will be a rare case where passing off exists but no breach of the section has occurred. Not surprisingly, the application of the section in circumstances that are similar to passing off has resulted in at least reference to if not reliance on passing off principles in many instances. Nevertheless, a number of distinctions can be quickly made between them:

- Any person may bring an action pursuant to s 18 of sch 2; they do not need to prove that they own any reputation or goodwill. This may be of assistance where there is any doubt as to who is the proper owner of the reputation, such as where the reputation relates to a famous screen character identified with a particular actor but the production company may also claim or be alleged to be the owner in question.
- Intention is clearly not necessary to obtain damages for a breach of the section pursuant to s 236 of sch 2 of the *Competition and Consumer Act 2010*. It probably is for damages for passing off.
- There are other significant differences in the remedies available for the two different actions. The potential remedies for a breach are quite broad in nature but do not include either an account of profit or punitive damages.
- In theory, various 'defences' recognised by passing off cases, such as the use of one's own name or honest concurrent use, are not available as it has a blanket prohibition against misleading and deceptive conduct. In practice, such defences may well manifest themselves less specifically in decisions that find that the defendant's conduct is confusing rather than misleading and a similar effect may be achieved.
- There may be a breach without necessarily a passing off action. For example, if two similar businesses adopted the same indicia recently and virtually simultaneously, neither may have the necessary reputation to sustain an action in passing off but both may be engaging in misleading conduct.[164]

---

162   Ibid; *Lego Australia Pty Ltd v Paul's (Merchants) Pty Ltd* (1982) 42 ALR 344.
163   *Parkdale Custom Built Furniture Pty Ltd v Puxu Pty Ltd* [1982] HCA 44.
164   *Peter Isaacson Publications v Nationwide News Pty Ltd* (1984) 6 FCR 289.

- If there are discretionary reasons for declining an application for an injunction against passing off, these are less likely to be relevant when considering an injunction to prevent further breaches of s 18 of sch 2. For example, a plaintiff's delay in protecting its own interests in preventing passing off may result in an unsuccessful application. In contrast, the section lays down a statutory standard of conduct of corporations and there is a public interest in preventing contraventions of that standard. Consequently, such breaches are more likely to be the subject of an injunction, regardless of the plaintiff's conduct.

14.10.1 Sections 29, 33 and 34 of sch 2

In addition to the general provision in s 18 of sch 2, other provisions of sch 2 of the *Competition and Consumer Act 2010* (Cth) also have an effect that is similar to the tort of passing off. The conduct proscribed by these provisions constitutes more specific examples of misleading and deceptive conduct and as such is a subset of s 18 of sch 2. The major difference between these provisions and s 18 of sch 2 is that a breach of the standard of conduct laid out in s 18 attracts only civil liability whereas a breach of the other provisions also attracts criminal liability.

In particular, s 29(c) and (d) prevents a corporation from representing that either it or its goods or services have any sponsorship, approval or affiliation that it or they do not have. Section 30(c) and (d) imposes similar prohibitions in respect of the sale or grant of interests in land. In addition, s 34 prevents a corporation from engaging in conduct that is liable to mislead the public as to the characteristics of its services.

14.10.2 Comparison with trade mark infringement

There are numerous critical distinctions between misleading or deceptive conduct and passing off on the one hand and trade mark infringement on the other hand. In particular, while the fact that a party may be exercising its freedom to use its registered trade mark will excuse it from infringing some other trade mark, it will not exempt the party from liability for passing off or engaging in misleading or deceptive conduct. The High Court decision in *Campomar v Nike*[165] made that clear. The defendant in that case had acquired registration of 'Nike' for deodorants many years before the Nike sports company acquired both registration of and a reputation associated with the word Nike in respect of sports clothing and equipment. After the sports company acquired its reputation, the defendant sold the product 'Nike Sports Deodorant'. As the defendant held a valid trade mark registration for Nike for deodorant, it was immune from any action for trade mark infringement. However, its conduct was found to be misleading or deceptive by the High Court, and the fact that it was using its trade mark in respect of goods for which that trade mark was registered did not make the defendant immune from such a finding.

14.11 Remedies

Pre-trial remedies, such as Anton Piller orders and interlocutory injunctions, are discussed in chapter 17. Pecuniary remedies for passing off include damages or an account of profits.

---

165 *Campomar SL v Nike International Ltd* (2000) 202 CLR 45.

As passing off is a tort, the generally applicable principle is to calculate damages by reference to the position that the plaintiff would have been in if the tort had not been committed.[166] In the context of passing off, the plaintiff will have suffered lost sales if it is in direct competition with the defendant. The plaintiff may also suffer a loss of reputation if the defendant's products are inferior and, even if they are not inferior, some diminution of the value of the plaintiff's reputation will ensue.

If the plaintiff and the defendant are not in direct competition, the diminution of reputation may still apply. In addition, the plaintiff may have lost the opportunity to or been inhibited from expanding into the area of commerce in which the defendant operates. Alternatively, the plaintiff may have lost the opportunity to be paid a licence fee for the use of its goodwill.[167]

In the case of character merchandising, the loss of a licence fee that would otherwise be payable will be relevant.[168] Again, in these instances, there may also be a loss of reputation if the plaintiff is associated with a product that may harm its general image. For example, in the *Duff Beer* case, the plaintiff creators of *The Simpsons* were keen to ensure that their cartoon show was not associated with the promotion of alcohol consumption because of a potential audience backlash.[169]

The balance of authority holds that damages, or at least substantial damages, will not be paid for passing off unless the defendant's conduct was either fraudulent or, at the least, it had notice of the plaintiff's interests and persisted in its passing off after receipt of that notice. This requirement is, in part, a remnant of the common law approach to passing off that is based on fraud. In addition, it has the effect of conferring some protection on the multitude of parties that may be unwittingly guilty of passing off. In particular, in theory, every retailer of goods that are passed off as being those of the plaintiff is liable for passing off. A similar requirement of knowledge is applicable in claims for an account of the profits obtained from passing off.[170] On the other hand, as with most torts, exemplary damages are available where there has been a deliberate and blatant disregard for the plaintiff's rights.[171]

The principle that damages are not payable for passing off in the absence of fraud is reflected in s 230(2) of the *Trade Marks Act 1995* (Cth). It deals with the situation where the defendant is a party to a passing off action arising out of the use by the defendant of a registered trade mark in its capacity as owner or authorised user of that trade mark. In such circumstances, damages may not be awarded against the defendant if the defendant was unaware and had no reasonable means of finding out that the trade mark of the plaintiff was in use and that when the defendant became aware of the existence and nature of the plaintiff's

---

166 For a detailed discussion of English cases on damages for passing off and registered trade marks, see *Kerly's Law of Trade Marks and Trade Names* (13th edn, London: Sweet and Maxwell, 2001) [18-139]–[18-158].
167 *Lego System A/S v Lego M Lemelstrich Ltd* [1983] FSR 155.
168 *Henderson v Radio Corp Pty Ltd* (1960) 60 SR (NSW) 576; *Hogan v Pacific Dunlop Ltd* (1988) 83 ALR 403. See also *Winnebago Industries Inc v Knott Investments Pty Ltd (No 4)* [2015] FCA 1327.
169 *Twentieth Century Fox Film Corp v South Australian Brewing Co Ltd* (1996) 66 FCR 451. It appears that the policy of not being associated with alcohol has since been reversed as licences have been given by Fox for Duff beer.
170 *Apand Pty Ltd v Kettle Chip Co Pty Ltd* (1994) 52 FCR 474.
171 *Flamingo Park Pty Ltd v Dolly Dolly Creations Pty Ltd* (1986) 6 IPR 431, 456–7; *GM Holden Ltd v Paine* (2011) 281 ALR 406, [94]–[98].

trade mark, he or she immediately ceased to use the trade mark in relation to the goods or services in relation to which it was used by the plaintiff.

In contrast to damages for passing off, damages for a breach of provisions such as s 18 of sch 2 of the *Competition and Consumer Act 2010* (Cth) are recoverable in the absence of fraud or notice. The standards of conduct laid down by statute do not require any form of mens rea on the part of the defendant. In addition, s 236 of sch 2 (damages) and pt 5-2 of sch 2 generally, which state the available remedies for a breach, impose no requirement of fraud or knowledge before the remedies can be given.

The usual test for damages for a breach of s 18 of sch 2 is the same tortious standard that applies to passing off – namely, what position would the plaintiff have been in but for the misleading or deceptive conduct?[172] General damages can be given for loss of business profits without evidence of particular losses from particular transactions.[173] In addition, general damages can be given for loss of reputation under s 236 of sch 2.[174]

However, as the relevant legislative provisions circumscribe the available remedies, plaintiffs must find justification in those sections for any remedy that they seek. Section 236 of sch 2, the primary section dealing with damages, provides for the recovery of loss or damage. As exemplary damages are punitive in nature rather than compensatory, they are not available under that section.[175] Similarly, pt 5-2 of sch 2 generally relates to orders designed to compensate for loss or damage and so exemplary damages are not available under those provisions either.

---

[172] *Gates v City Life Mutual Assurance Society Ltd* (1986) 160 CLR 1; *Yorke v Ross Lucas Pty Ltd* (1982) 45 ALR 299.
[173] *Prince Manufacturing Inc v ABAC Corp Australia Pty Ltd* (1984) 4 FCR 288.
[174] *Flamingo Park Pty Ltd v Dolly Dolly Creation Pty Ltd* (1986) 6 IPR 431; *Brabazon v Western Mail Ltd* (1985) 58 ALR 712.
[175] *Musca v Astle Corp Pty Ltd* (1988) 80 ALR 251; *Mayne Nickless Ltd v Multigroup Distribution Services Pty Ltd* (2001) 114 FCR 108.

15

REGISTERED TRADE MARKS

15.1 History of registered trade marks

The registration of trade marks was a reasonably natural development beyond the law of passing off. While passing off or its statutory equivalents have and still have numerous advantages, they are inadequate in some respects as a means of facilitating the exploitation of signs used to indicate the origin of goods or services or as a means of defining and regulating property rights.

The first United Kingdom trade mark legislation was passed in 1875,[1] and the Australian colonies followed the legislative lead of the United Kingdom in due course. All of the Australian colonies had their own trade marks legislation at the time of Federation and the first federal trade marks legislation was the *Trade Marks Act 1905* (Cth), which largely mirrored then United Kingdom legislation. The next Australian legislation was the *Trade Marks Act 1955* (Cth), which also largely mirrored the United Kingdom legislation of 1938, although some key differences were emerging at that time.[2]

Since then, Australia has enacted two more trade marks Acts although only one of them ever came into effect. The *Trade Marks Act 1994* (Cth) was intended to come into effect on 1 January 1996 but it contained a number of flaws and it was deemed more appropriate to simply repeal it before it came into operation. It was replaced by the present legislation, the *Trade Marks Act 1995* (Cth), which did come into effect on 1 January 1996. The new legislation and the 1994 legislation were a response to a number of issues, including some requirements under the *Agreement on Trade-Related Aspects of Intellectual Property*[3] (*TRIPS*) that were not met by the 1955 legislation and a government report on trade mark law to the Minister for Science and Technology, usually referred to as the Working Party Report, which made a number of recommendations concerning Australian trade mark legislation.[4] In addition, by this time, United Kingdom legislation had gone its own way in response to the requirement to comply with European Union standards and Directives.

The net result is that the current legislation is significantly different from the 1955 legislation and quite different from current United Kingdom legislation. However, the new legislation has been described as an evolution rather than a revolution, at least in relation to the nature of a trade mark. The move away from reliance on the lead of the United Kingdom has meant that the current legislation and the case law interpreting it have drawn on an eclectic group of factors. These include long-held principles of trade marks established under the legislation of 1905 and 1955 that have been retained, albeit modified in some respects; developments in marketing practice that were reflected in the Working Party Report; *TRIPS* requirements, including the requirement to provide greater protection for geographical indications and well-known trade marks that are registered; and case law from both Europe and the United States. To a limited extent, the interpretation of the legislation is also affected by the wording of

---

1 *Trade Marks Registration Act 1875* (UK).
2 M. Davison and I. Horak, *Shanahan's Australian Law of Trade Marks and Passing Off* (56th edn, Sydney: Thomson Reuters, 2016) 9 ff.
3 *Marrakesh Agreement Establishing the World Trade Organization*, opened for signature 15 April 1994, 1867 UNTS 3 (entered into force 1 January 1995) annex 1C.
4 Working Party to Review the Trade Marks Legislation, *Recommended Changes to the Australian Trade Marks Legislation* (Department of Science and Technology, 1992).

its immediate predecessor, the *Trade Marks Act 1994* (Cth).[5] The references to legislation in the remainder of this chapter will be to the 1995 Act unless otherwise stated.

15.2 Drawbacks of passing off

The registration of trade marks overcomes a number of the drawbacks of passing off actions in protecting the position of traders. These drawbacks include:

- The plaintiff needs to prove its reputation on every occasion. The costs of doing so will be considerable as it requires proof of matters such as geographical distribution, promotion costs, time in the market, volume of sales, the degree of customer recognition of one's trade mark, the views of those in the industry and myriad other issues.
- Passing off does not protect investment in preparing to establish a reputation, such as devising a marketing strategy and preparing advertising, as opposed to the reputation that results when those strategies are actually put in place. This leaves the possibility of another person 'gazumping' a trader by actually adopting the same or a similar sign to indicate its products after a trader has invested in the preparation of advertising and other marketing strategies but before that trader has actually implemented those strategies and established a reputation associated with that sign.
- The plaintiff must prove a misrepresentation by the defendant. While the case law has taken an expansive view of what constitutes a misrepresentation, the issue is ultimately one for assessment by the presiding judge in the context of the impact of the totality of the defendant's conduct on consumers. The rights granted to owners of registered trade marks are less dependent on the particular circumstances in which the defendant uses its allegedly infringing sign. Consequently, proving infringement of registered trade marks is often easier than proving passing off.
- In contrast to registered trade marks, property exists in the reputation associated with a sign rather than the sign itself. It is therefore difficult to license others to use the sign and probably impossible to sell rights to use the sign without selling the goodwill of the business.
- There is no public register of which signs can be used by whom. This generates difficulties for parties who wish to avoid unintentionally infringing upon the rights of others.

Various features of the registered trade mark system overcome these difficulties by doing away with the requirement for an existing reputation, at least with inherently distinctive trade marks, and treating registered trade marks as property in their own right.[6] The exclusive rights conferred on trade mark owners then enable the owners to expend time and money on preparing promotion campaigns with the intention to acquire a reputation associated with

---

5   *Koninklijke Philips Electronics NV v Remington Products Australia Pty Ltd* (2000) 100 FCR 90.
6   See *Trade Marks Act 1995* (Cth) s 21, which states that a trade mark is personal property; and s 41(3), which refers to a trade mark's inherent distinctiveness as a decisive factor in whether or not a trade mark is capable of distinguishing the designated goods or services from the goods or services of other persons.

the trade marks without fear of being 'gazumped'. They also make it easy for owners to license and sell the trade marks, without the need to transfer the goodwill of their business.[7]

15.3 Functions of trade marks

There are several functions of trade marks that influence the law relating to them.[8] The most traditional explanation of trade marks is that they act as an indicator of the origin of the goods or services in relation to which they are used. This view permeates Australian trade mark law and was expressly acknowledged in the definition of a trade mark in s 6 of the 1955 legislation, which provided that a trade mark was

> [a] mark used or proposed to be used in relation to goods or services for the purpose of indicating ... a connexion in the course of trade between the goods or services and a person who has the right, either as proprietor or as registered user, to use the mark ...

In the current legislation, that role of trade marks is expressed slightly differently as 'a sign used or intended to be used, to distinguish goods or services dealt with or provided in the course of trade by a person from goods or services so dealt with or provided by any other person'. Judicial comment to date suggests that the different definition in the new legislation has not made any fundamental change in the nature of a trade mark.[9]

15.3.1 Reducing search costs

In any event, a related function of a registered trade mark is the function of indicating in shorthand form the quality of a product to consumers. In this way, the trade mark reduces what economists refer to as the search costs of consumers. This means that instead of having to consider each product anew when they are buying, they need only refer to their knowledge of the product provided through the trade mark. Hence, the trade mark Coca-Cola indicates a black, cola-flavoured, caffeine-infused soft drink with a distinctive taste. Consumers searching for those particular characteristics need only search for the Coca-Cola trade mark.

These functions of registered trade marks are functions that are consistent with consumer protection objectives. They aid consumers by reducing their search costs and reduce the possibility of confusion and deception by making it easier for traders to distinguish their products from the products of other traders.

---

7   *Trade Marks Act 1995* (Cth) s 106(3).
8   F. I. Schechter, 'The rational basis of trade mark protection' (1927) 40 *Harvard Law Review* 813; M. Gabay, 'The role of trademarks in consumer protection and development in developing countries' [1987] *Industrial Property* 102; S. Carter, 'The trouble with trademark' (1990) 99 *Yale Law Journal* 759; W. Landes and R. Posner, 'The economics of trademark law' (1988) 78 *The Trademark Reporter* 267; T. Stevens, 'ACIP review of trade mark enforcement' (2004) 7 *Australian Intellectual Property Law Journal* 50.
9   See, for example, *E & J Gallo Winery v Lion Nathan Australia Pty Ltd* (2010) 241 CLR 144, [41]–[43].

15.3.2 Managing property interests

On the other hand, trade marks are a form of property in their own right[10] and provisions such as those relating to assignment and licensing indicate the extent to which they are treated as tradable commodities. The manner in which restrictions on assignment and licensing have been loosened with each new piece of trade mark legislation confirms this treatment of trade marks as property.[11] It is this property aspect of trade marks that has become increasingly important as trade marks such as the Coca-Cola trade mark and many other famous trade marks may have a life force of their own that is independent of the products with which they are associated. The image associated with such trade marks is such that they will and can sell almost any product. So, the importance and value of the trade mark exceeds its capacity to distinguish one product from another and it becomes a tradable commodity in its own right. This function of trade marks is one reason for demands for extra protection for famous or well-known trade marks and s 120(3), one of the infringement provisions in the Act, accommodates these demands to some extent. Owners of well-known trade marks may seek protection for their property that extends beyond protection from the use of similar or identical trade marks in circumstances where consumers are likely to be deceived or confused. They may want protection that will prevent any tarnishment or blurring of their trade mark, even in the absence of any possibility of deception or confusion of consumers; such protection is provided in the United States and the European Union via the anti-dilution provisions of the *Lanham (Trademark) Act*[12] and the *Trade Marks Directive*.[13] Whether such protection is conferred by s 120(3) of the current Australian legislation is still open to interpretation.

The end result is that the trade mark legislation is a mix of provisions relating to pro-consumer objectives and the regulation of the ownership and exploitation of property rights in trade marks. The pro-consumer objectives are designed to limit confusion or deception and to facilitate the provision of information to consumers. Examples of these objectives are the provisions requiring trade marks to be distinctive[14] and the prevention of registration of trade marks with connotations that may be likely to deceive or cause confusion.[15] The provisions relating to the ownership and exploitation of property are often consistent with but sometimes in conflict with the pro-consumer provisions. For example, the legislation tolerates the existence of some confusion in the prior continuous user and honest concurrent user provisions.[16]

15.3.3 Promoting the product

A further function of the trade mark is to act as a means of promoting the product in relation to which it is used. The promotional function has two aspects to it. One aspect is to increase demand for the particular brand of the product in question. The other aspect is to increase

---

10	*Trade Marks Act 1995* (Cth) s 21(1).
11	Davison and Horak, *Shanahan's Australian Law of Trade Marks and Passing Off*, above n 2, 589 ff.
12	15 USC § 1125 (1946).
13	*Directive (EU) 2015/2436 of the European Parliament and of the Council of 16 December 2015 to Approximate the Laws of the Member States Relating to Trade Marks* [2015] OL J 336/1, art 10(2)(c).
14	*Trade Marks Act 1995* (Cth) s 41.
15	Ibid s 43.
16	Ibid s 44(3)–(4).

demand for the underlying product in question with a corresponding benefit for all owners of trade marks relating to that product. It is this latter aspect that is the target of the Australian tobacco plain packaging legislation, which has an objective of reducing the appeal of tobacco products and thus decreasing demand.[17]

15.4 Overview of the registration process

In order to obtain registration, the relevant application has to be submitted to the Registrar of Trade Marks. The trade mark is identified clearly in the application as are the goods and/or services in respect of which registration is sought. Registration is granted for specific trade marks in respect of specified goods and/or services. For the purposes of maintaining the Register of Trade Marks and facilitating the searching of the Register, goods and services are categorised within particular classes although the application itself needs to be more specific than simply identifying the class within which registration is being sought. It must identify with precision those particular goods or services that will be used in conjunction with the trade mark.

The application will also have a priority date that is relevant for the purposes of its eligibility for registration in the event of a conflict with another trade mark application. For example, if applications for similar trade marks for similar goods were lodged at about the same time, the trade mark with the earlier priority date would most likely receive registration.[18] As a general rule, the date of lodgement of the application will be the priority date but there are some important exceptions to that general rule. For example, if an earlier application for registration of the same trade mark has been made in any one of a large number of countries within six months of the Australian application, the priority date of the Australian application will be the day of the original application in that other country.[19] Other circumstances that may affect the priority date of an application could be an application under the *Madrid Protocol*[20] lodged prior to a separate Australian application by another party[21] and what is called a divisional application.[22]

The trade mark application is then examined to see if it meets the requirements for registration. This process often involves correspondence between the examiner and the applicant, with clarification of the application and the provision of any necessary evidence from the applicant. If accepted, the fact of acceptance is published and a period of time is then available for opposition to the registration on any or all of the grounds specified in the legislation. If there is no successful opposition to the accepted trade mark, it will be registered. Registration is initially for ten years and is renewable for further periods of ten years upon payment of the necessary fees. Once registered, there are also various grounds on which a trade mark may be removed from the Register or the Register may be rectified. In particular, a

---

17 *Tobacco Plain Packaging Act 2011* (Cth) s 3(2)(a).
18 *Trade Marks Act 1995* (Cth) s 44.
19 *Trade Marks Act 1995* (Cth) s 72.
20 *Protocol Relating to the Madrid Agreement Concerning the International Registration of Marks*, opened for signature 12 November 2007, WIPO Lex No TRT/MADRIDP-GP/001 (as amended 12 November 2007, entered into force 1 September 2008).
21 See *Trade Marks Regulations 1995* (Cth) pt 17A.
22 See *Trade Marks Act 1995* (Cth) pt 4 div 3.

trade mark is liable for removal for non-use or the Register may be rectified if the trade mark should never have been registered and has not subsequently become eligible for registration.

Each of the acceptance and opposition stages is subject to appeals to the Federal Court and possibly the High Court.[23] Consequently, some of the important litigation in the area is between the Registrar and an applicant whose application has been denied or between an opponent and the Registrar when an opposition has been unsuccessful before the Registrar.

From a practical point of view, applicants and opponents need to be very aware of the legislative time frames for the submission of documentation – these govern, for example, the supply of additional information and the process for filing an opposition. In addition, trade mark owners need to maintain a watching brief on trade marks that have been accepted by the Registrar in case it is necessary to lodge an opposition to a competitor's trade mark. Obviously, it is also important to ensure that trade mark registrations are renewed when required. Hence, even after registration of a trade mark, considerable ongoing 'maintenance' needs to occur in order to ensure the trade mark retains its value to its owner.

15.5 Definition of a trade mark

Obviously, in order for an application to be successful, it must relate to a trade mark. Section 17 defines a trade mark as 'a sign used, or intended to be used, to distinguish goods or services dealt with or provided in the course of trade by a person from goods or services so dealt with or provided by any other person'. This definition of a trade mark is critical to an understanding of not just what may be registered as a trade mark but also other trade mark issues, such as what conduct constitutes an infringement of a trade mark. Consequently, a detailed examination and dissection of the definition of a trade mark is necessary.

15.6 Definition of a sign

A sign is inclusively defined in s 6 as including 'the following or any combination of the following, namely, any letter, word, name, signature, numeral, device, brand, heading, label, ticket, aspect of packaging, shape, colour, sound or scent'.[24] The inclusive wording of the definition and case law on the point suggests that almost anything capable of being perceived by any one or more of a human being's senses is a sign. Anything that could be seen, heard, smelled, felt or even tasted is a sign. For example, the feel or texture of goods may be registrable even though 'texture' is not specifically listed in the definition.

The terms 'letter, word, name, signature, numeral' are self-explanatory and the term 'device' refers to any form of artistic representation, such as logos, drawings, pictures or even diagrams. The terms 'brand, heading, label and ticket' are not so much references to types of signs but more the means by which a sign (such as a word, numeral or device) might be physically associated with goods. 'Brands' are burnt into goods such as cigar boxes, 'headings'

---

23   See *Woolworths Ltd v BP plc (No 2)* (2006) 154 FCR 97 for a discussion of the appeal process concerning opposition.
24   For further reference, see P. Loughlan, 'The concept of "sign" in Australian trade mark law' (2005) 16 *Australian Intellectual Property Law Journal* 95.

are the trade marks of textiles woven into the top or bottom of the material, 'labels' are usually affixed to goods in such a way as to be permanently affixed whereas 'tickets' are loosely attached by, say, string and intended to be removed, usually after purchase.[25]

15.6.1 Aspect of packaging, shape

It has always been the case that a particular aspect of packaging or even some part of the product itself may constitute a trade mark. For example, in *Re Application by Hamish Robertson & Co Ltd*,[26] a crest on a seal on the neck of a bottle of alcohol was found to be a 'very unusual and quite distinctive' trade mark.[27]

The case law took a different view of the situation where the sign in question was the entirety of the packaging or the product. It required the trade mark to be 'something capable of being described and depicted apart from the goods' for which it was a trade mark.[28]

While this principle is relatively easily stated, its application in some circumstances was a more complex matter. For example, in the High Court decision of *Smith Kline & French Laboratories (Australia) Ltd v Registrar of Trade Marks*,[29] registration was sought for the colour scheme of a pharmaceutical capsule in which half of the capsule was coloured and the other half was transparent so as to reveal the multicoloured pellets of medicine contained inside the capsule. Kitto J refused registration on the basis that the trade mark could not be described and depicted apart from the capsule itself. When the very same facts came before the House of Lords, the House of Lords held that in the particular case, the colour scheme was separate from the goods in respect of which it was to be used.

While the application of the principle is difficult in some circumstances, both Australian and English law agreed that a consequence of this principle was that a trade mark could not have consisted of the entirety of the shape of the product in relation to which it was used. Pursuant to this principle, the shape of the well-known Lifesaver confectionery was denied registration in Australia,[30] and in the United Kingdom the House of Lords unequivocally refused protection for the shape of the Coca-Cola bottle on the grounds that the bottle simply was not a trade mark.[31]

Under the new legislation, a sign may include 'shape' and therefore may include the entire shape of either goods or the packaging in which they come. The relationship between this new addition to the definition of a sign ('mark' under the old legislation) and the requirement that a

---

25   S. Ricketson, *Intellectual Property: Cases, Materials and Commentary* (3rd edn, Sydney: LexisNexis Butterworths, 2005) 937.
26   (1998) 13 IPR 69.
27   Ibid 73.
28   *The Coca-Cola Co v All-Fect Distributors Ltd* (1999) 96 FCR 107, 116; *Smith Kline & French Laboratories (Australia) Ltd v Registrar of Trade Marks* (1967) 116 CLR 628, 640. But see also the United Kingdom decision in *Smith Kline v Registrar of Trade Marks* [1976] RPC 511 where the same facts resulted in the opposite decision. See also M. Davison, 'Shape trade marks: The role and relevance of functionality and aesthetics in determining their registrability' (2004) 15 *Australian Intellectual Property Journal* 231; J. Baird, '"This mark is so attractive – it should be free for all to use!" An Australian perspective on functional shape marks' (2003) 52 *Intellectual Property Forum* 26.
29   *Smith Kline & French Laboratories (Australia) Ltd v Registrar of Trade Marks* (1967) 116 CLR 628.
30   *Life Savers (Australasia) Ltd's Application* (1952) 22 AOJP 3106.
31   *Coca-Cola Trade Marks* [1986] FSR 472.

trade mark be something separate from the goods themselves has been the subject of comment by the Full Federal Court on two occasions. While the distinction between a trade mark and the product to which it is applied remains in theory, it seems to have been reformulated. The reformulation appears to take the view that the trade mark will be separate from the goods if the shape is not essential to and is separate from the function of the goods. If the trade mark owner can demonstrate that the shape in question is different from the product itself in the sense that the function of the product does not determine the shape, registration is available.

In a trade mark case between Remington and Philips, the Full Federal Court considered the infringement of a trade mark consisting of a two-dimensional representation of Philips' three-headed rotary shaver. In doing so, it commented on the registrability of the actual shape itself although that issue was not directly before the court.[32] The court appeared to express the view that the shape itself would not be registrable because of its importance to the function of the shaver. Burchett J stated:

> But that is not to say that the 1995 Act has invalidated what Windeyer J said in *Smith Kline*. The special cases where a shape of the goods may be a mark are cases falling within, not without, the principle he expounded. For they are cases where the shape that is a mark is 'extra', added to the inherent form of the particular goods as something distinct which can denote origin. The goods can still be seen as having, in Windeyer J's words, 'an existence independently of the mark' which is imposed upon them.[33]

In the *Kenman Kandy* case[34] the Full Court considered the registration of the shape of a lolly as a trade mark for that lolly. Stone J adopted the above statement from the *Philips* decision and explained:

> The concerns expressed in both *Philips v Remington* [Full Federal Court] and *Philips v Remington* [High Court (England and Wales)] about the prospect of trade marks creating monopolies related only to the registration of trade marks that would restrict access to functional features or innovations, and for this reason were well founded. It is this concern that finds expression in the requirement that a trade mark be something added to the inherent form of goods. The 'inherent form' of goods, in my view, can only refer to those aspects of form that have functional significance.[35]

Consequently, the entire shape of goods will be a sign and considered separate from the goods provided that the shape is not functional. The proviso that a functional shape cannot be a trade mark is questionable in light of the role of s 41(3) (formerly s 41(6)) and this issue is discussed below at 15.7.4. However, what is clear is that the 'sign' in question and the shape of the goods in relation to which it is used may be one and the same. The decision in *Kenman Kandy* is itself quite specific authority for that proposition, as in that case the Full Federal Court held that the entire shape of the bug-shaped lolly was registrable as a trade mark.

---

32   *Koninklijke Philips Electronics NV v Remington Products Australia Pty Ltd* (2000) 100 FCR 90.
33   Ibid 104.
34   *Kenman Kandy Australia Pty Ltd v Registrar of Trade Marks* (2002) 122 FCR 494.
35   Ibid [137]. See also *Global Brand Marketing Inc v YD Pty Ltd* (2008) 76 IPR 161, [61].

In addition, a search of the Register will show the registration of trade marks, such as:

- the Rubik's Cube (reg no 707482);
- the semi-spherical shape of a Kettle barbeque (reg no 7036222);
- the shape of the pens and pencils in a pen and pencil shape (reg no 719912);
- the shape of a bottle for perfume (reg no 627798); and
- the triangular box shape of Toblerone chocolate (reg no 706797).

15.6.2 Colour

Several hundred colours or combinations of colours are presently registered, such as:

- orange for personal communication technology (reg no 820452);
- orange for sparkling wine (reg no 704779);
- sky blue for electrical tools (reg no 585856);
- purple for block and boxed chocolate (reg no 1120614); and
- green and yellow applied as the predominant colours to fasciae of buildings, petrol pumps and signage boards for service station services (reg no 728555).

Unlike the situation with shapes, the colour of the goods and the goods themselves are usually quite distinct although the peculiar facts in the *Smith Kline* decisions[36] demonstrate that this may not always be the case.[37]

15.6.3 Sounds

Numerous sounds have been registered although often in combination with words. Hence, McCain Foods Pty Ltd has registered the high-pitched ping of a microwave when used to intersperse the words 'Ah McCain, ('Ping') You've Done It Again'. Music that has been registered or in respect of which applications for registration have been made includes:

- the sound of 'Greensleeves' for Mr Whippy ice cream (reg no 876931);
- the traditional musical start to Twentieth Century Fox movies (reg no 891830);
- a wolf whistle followed by the sound of an exploding bottle for alcoholic beverages (reg no 924027);
- the 'Happy Little Vegemites' tune by Kraft (reg no 941362); and
- 'Sproing' for floor coverings (reg no 738848).

---

36 Cited above at n 28.
37 L. Eade, 'Looking at smells and sounds: Graphical representation of new trade marks' (2003) 16 *Australian Intellectual Property Journal* 33; J. McCutcheon, 'How many colours in the rainbow? The registration of colour per se under Australian trade mark law' (2004) 26 *European Intellectual Property Review* 27; L. Eade, 'Puce as a trade mark: Acquired distinctiveness of colour trade marks' (2004) 16 *Australian Intellectual Property Law Bulletin* 121.

15.6.4 Scents

The scent of *Eucalyptus radiata* has been registered for golf tees (reg no 1241420). Various other applicants have been unsuccessful for various reasons. These include:

- the scent of musk for perfume: rejected (reg no 727820);
- a eucalyptus scent for laundry detergent: rejected (reg no 7622286); and
- the scent of coffee for suntan lotion: rejected (reg no 821444).

As with colours, the scent of the product and the product itself are usually clearly distinguishable although an interesting question is whether the scent of a perfume could be a sign in relation to that perfume.

The end result of the new definition and the reinterpretation of the principle in the *Smith Kline* decision[38] in light of the new definition of a sign is that it is very easy to demonstrate that something is a 'sign' and other aspects of the definition will be more important to determining registrability.

15.7 'Used or intended to be used'

In order to be a trade mark, the owner must use a sign or intend to use it *as a trade mark*: that is, in order to distinguish its products from other products.[39] There are a number of aspects of intent that need to be borne in mind.

15.7.1 Unconditional intention

The intent need not involve a plan to use the trade mark within a specific time frame provided there is an unconditional intention to use the trade mark at some point in the future.[40] A conditional intention to use the trade mark if favourable market conditions arise is not sufficient. For example, in the *Rawhide* case,[41] the applicant for registration sought to register 'Rawhide' for various goods in the hope that the American television series of that name would be shown in the United Kingdom, thus giving the trade mark some quick publicity without the need for any investment from the trade mark owner. As use of the trade mark was conditional on the show coming to the United Kingdom, the applicant did not have the required intention.

The intention must be a bona fide intention and 'sham' use simply to acquire rights in relation to the trade mark will not constitute either use or intention to use for the purposes of the definition. Hence, when a cigarette company used the trade mark 'Nerit' for several thousand cigarettes but then discontinued their manufacture in accordance with a

---

38   *Smith Kline & French Laboratories (Australia) Ltd v Registrar of Trade Marks* (1967) 116 CLR 628.
39   For further reference, see L. Bently and R. Burrell, 'The requirement of trade mark use' (2002) 13 *Australian Intellectual Property Journal* 181; R. Burrell, 'The requirement of trade mark use: Recent developments in Australia' (2005) 16 *Australian Intellectual Property Journal* 231; T. Stevens, 'Trade marks ownership and sharp business' (2004) *Australian Intellectual Property Law Bulletin* 4.
40   *Re Ducker's Trade Mark* (1928) 45 RPC 397, 402; *Food Channel Network Pty Ltd v Television Food Network GP* (2010) 185 FCR 9.
41   *Rawhide Trade Mark* [1962] RPC 133.

predetermined plan to do so, its registration of 'Nerit' was revoked for lack of the necessary intention to seriously market those cigarettes.[42]

15.7.2 Objective test of intention

The intended use must be use that is objectively regarded as use as a trade mark. As we will see later, not every use of a trade mark is use *as* a trade mark and the issue of what constitutes such use arises again and again in trade mark law. In this context, it is not sufficient for the trade mark owner to put the trade mark on its goods. It must actually do so in a way that differentiates its products from other products. For example, in *Johnson & Johnson v Unilever Australia Ltd*,[43] the plaintiff used the trade mark 'caplets' in relation to its paracetamol medication, which consisted of a tablet in the shape of a capsule. As 'caplets' was at least partly descriptive in nature, it was argued that the plaintiff's use did not distinguish its goods from other goods but simply described the nature of the products being sold. The plaintiff argued that it was sufficient that it subjectively intended to use the trade mark as a trade mark even though it may not have used it in that manner. The Federal Court rejected this argument and held that the relevant 'intent to use' required an intention to use the trade mark in a manner that would be objectively considered to be use as a trade mark.

In reality, the requirement of intention to use is difficult to disprove in the absence of a 'smoking gun' confession or some other clear evidence. It is usually proved by an actual lack of use that will eventually be grounds for removal in its own right after the relevant statutory period of time.[44]

15.7.3 Use by others

Section 27(1)(b)(ii) and (iii) sets out some limited circumstances in which the applicant need not intend to use the trade mark themselves provided other requirements are met. It is sufficient to meet the requirement of intention if the applicant has authorised or intends to authorise another person to use the trade mark or intends to assign the trade mark to a body corporate that is about to be constituted with a view to the use by that body corporate.[45] The former situation arises where an owner intends to license one or more people to produce and market the product in question and the owner only intends to exercise some form of control over the use of the trade mark applied to the product.[46] Unlike the situation under the previous legislation, it appears that it is not necessary for the applicant to have identified the particular person who will be licensed to use the trade mark.[47] The latter situation permits a promoter of a company about to be formed to acquire assets such as a trade mark and then transfer it to the company after it is established.

---

42   *Imperial Group Ltd v Philip Morris & Co Ltd* [1982] FSR 72.
43   [1994] AIPC 91-038.
44   For further reference, see T. Stevens, 'The use of multiple trade marks' (2005) 18 *Australian Intellectual Property Law Bulletin* 22.
45   *Trade Marks Act 1995* (Cth) s 27(1).
46   See ch 16 at 16.18 for discussion of licensing.
47   *Pussy Galore Trade Mark* [1967] RPC 265.

15.8 Distinguishing goods or services

The phrase 'to distinguish goods or services dealt with or provided in the course of trade by a person from goods or services so dealt with or provided by any other person' goes to the essence of what it means to use a sign as a trade mark and has already been addressed in the previous section in the discussion of intention. As seen above, almost anything is a sign. The key issue will be whether it is being used or is intended to be used in such a way as to distinguish the goods or services of the person using the trade mark from other goods and services. Thus, the capacity of a trade mark to achieve this task of distinguishing goods or services from other goods or services is a critical requirement to its initial registration and its continued registration. As we will see later, if it loses that capacity after registration, it may be removed from the Register.

The capacity of a trade mark to distinguish one product from another product must be an immediate capacity in the sense that the trade mark must have the distinguishing effect immediately upon use, not some time after it has been used repeatedly and acquired distinctiveness at some indeterminate time in the future.[48]

To put it in colloquial terms, the trade mark must say to a consumer: 'When you see this trade mark, you are seeing a sign of the goods or services of a particular person. You may not know the identity of that particular person but you will know that it is a particular person who has a specific and unique relationship to those goods and services.'

Consequently, the relevant sign must be used in such a way as to indicate a trade connection between the person using the trade mark and the goods or services in relation to which it is used. In this way, trade marks retain their traditional function of indicating the origin of goods or services and a trade mark continues to be what it was originally intended to be, namely, 'a badge of origin'. This point was made by the Full Court in *The Coca-Cola Co v All-Fect Distributors Ltd* when it stated:

> Use 'as a trade mark' is use of the mark as a 'badge of origin', in the sense that it indicates a connection in the course of trade between goods and the person who applies the mark to the goods ... That is the concept embodied in the definition of 'trade mark' in s 17.[49]

As demonstrated by this statement, to date the courts' consideration of the phrase has been restricted to interpreting it by reference to the traditional concept of a trade mark and stating that it has the same meaning and effect, at least in the context of use by the trade mark owner, as the old definition under the 1955 legislation. Consequently, the new definition of a trade mark continues to adopt the traditional view of a trade mark as a sign that indicates the trade origin of the goods or services in relation to which it is used.

15.8.1 'Dealt with or provided'

While this phrase has not yet been directly examined by courts, it is reasonably certain that it will be interpreted widely. If a trade mark is to distinguish goods and services by indicating a

---

48 *Cantarella Brothers Pty Ltd v Modena Trading Pty Ltd* (2014) 315 ALR 4, [85] (Gageler J); *Thomson v B Seppelt & Sons Ltd* (1925) 37 CLR 305. See also *Bayer Pharma Pty Ltd v Farbenfabriken Bayer AG* (1965) 120 CLR 285, 332–3.
49 (1999) 96 FCR 10, [19].

connection or association between it and its user, then the nature of that connection or association – the dealing with or provision in the course of trade – may be any one or more of a broad range of connections. Section 3 of the *Trade Marks Act 1905* (Cth) specified the various forms of connection between goods or services and the user of the trade mark as 'manufacturing, selection, certification, dealing with or offering for sale'. This expression was broadened to the general concept of 'indicating a connection' in the 1955 Act and then that expression was replaced by the present expression of 'dealt with or provided'. While there is a return to the term 'dealing with', the tenor of the legislation suggests that it is in fact as least as broad as 'indicating a connection' in the 1955 Act.

The case law under previous legislation provides a long list of 'connections' that are likely to be sufficient to qualify as relevant dealings for the purposes of the Act and these cases demonstrate that almost any dealing with goods or services prior to them reaching the consumer will suffice. This approach is consistent with the function of trade marks to indicate the trade origin of the product in question but recognises that the relevant trade origin may be any one of a number of different forms of connection with the end product. For example, in *Major Brothers v Franklin & Son*,[50] a market salesman had a trade mark that he applied to baskets containing the fruit he sold for selected growers. The act of selecting the growers for whom he sold was a sufficient connection between him and the goods he sold to justify his ownership of the trade mark. Other dealings indicated by the trade mark may include the manufacturing of the goods, their retailing, the selection of the goods to be sold or the control over the use of the trade mark exercised by a trade mark owner who has licensed the use of the trade mark.[51]

15.8.2 'In the course of trade'

The course of trade is a very broad expression and refers to almost any form of commercial dealing in goods or services prior to 'consumption'.[52] Hence it will include offering or advertising for sale, leasing or offering for lease and even preparing goods for export without any intention that they be displayed or made available in Australia. For example, in *James Minifie & Co v Edwin Davey & Sons*,[53] the plaintiff's trade mark was placed on bags of flour without its permission. The bags were transported to the docks under cover for export but the High Court still found that this constituted use of the trade mark in the course of trade.

The primary activity that would not be 'in the course of trade' might be importation for personal use or consumption. For example in *Oakley Inc v Franchise China Pty Ltd*,[54] the defendant imported sunglasses with the plaintiff's trade mark. It claimed that its intention was solely to give them to its employees as gifts. The Federal Court stated that if that was the case, the importation would not be use in the course of trade although it did not accept the

---

50   (1908) 25 RPC 406.
51   See *Estex Clothing Manufacturers Pty Ltd v Ellis & Goldstein Ltd* (1967) 116 CLR 254. See also *Settef SpA v Riv-Oland Marble Co (Vic) Pty Ltd* (1987) 10 IPR 402 (SC Vic); *Transport Tyre Sales Pty Ltd v Montana Tyres Rims & Tubes Pty Ltd* (1999) 93 FCR 421; *Asia Television Ltd v Yau's Entertainment Pty Ltd* (2000) 49 IPR 264 (overturned on appeal but not on this point).
52   *Oakley Inc v Franchise China Pty Ltd* (2003) 58 IPR 452.
53   (1933) 49 CLR 349.
54   (2003) 58 IPR 452.

defendant's claim that was the situation. Similarly in *WD & HO Wills (Australia) Ltd v Rothmans Ltd*,[55] an order placed overseas for cigarettes for consumption rather than resale in Australia did not constitute dealing with them in the course of trade. However, even situations such as those would have to be examined individually to ascertain whether the vendor was actively dealing with Australian consumers and therefore the vendor was using the trade mark in Australia, even though its business operations were outside Australia.

One area of uncertainty in this regard is the situation where the defendant is, for example, selling over the internet with an intention to deal all over the world. Australian decisions have held that in such circumstances there is no use in Australia unless and until the vendor accepts an online offer from Australia to purchase the goods in question or the vendor uses its website to specifically target Australian consumers.[56]

15.8.3 'By a person'

It is clear that while the person who deals with the goods or provides them in the course of trade must be a particular person, consumers need not know the identity of that person. In fact, more often than not, consumers will not know the name of the owner of a trade mark.

In the context of the current definition, the person using the sign as a trade mark is not necessarily the owner of the trade mark. For example, an authorised user (licensee) is also using the trade mark when they produce, distribute or otherwise deal with the trade marked goods in a manner contemplated by the licence agreement.

The person in question may even be an infringer who uses a registered trade mark on counterfeit goods. Such a person is also using the trade mark as they are using the sign or signs in question to distinguish their counterfeit goods from other goods. Of course, that particular use is an infringing use pursuant to s 120. However, the point to note here is that reference needs to be made back to the definition of a trade mark in numerous, quite different circumstances for various purposes.

15.9 Ownership

The legislation clearly contemplates that someone may own a trade mark even before an application for registration is lodged and certainly before registration occurs. For example, s 27(1) states, in part, that 'a person may apply for the registration of a trade mark ... if the person claims to be the owner of the trade mark'. The obvious implication of this is that ownership of a trade mark or at least ownership of the right to seek registration of it may be acquired prior to or at the time of applying for registration. An examination of the case law confirms the point and there are several ways in which the case law has recognised ownership of a trade mark for which registration is being sought.

---

55 (1956) 94 CLR 182.
56 *Ward Group Pty Ltd v Brodie & Stone plc* (2005) 143 FCR 479; *International Hair Cosmetics Group Pty Ltd v International Hair Cosmetics Ltd* [2011] FCA 339.

15.9.1 First use in Australia

In particular, it is clear that first use of the trade mark in Australia almost invariably leads to the user being the person with the right to obtain registration. Use in this context need only be minimal use as a trade mark and it is certainly not necessary that it be sufficient to create a reputation.[57] For example, in *Thunderbird* the sale of one boat with the relevant trade mark was sufficient.[58] Similarly, the distribution of advertising brochures or even the use of the trade mark on a price list will suffice,[59] as well as dispatching trade marked goods to Australia in response to an order by a potential distributor;[60] although dispatching goods to an Australian consumer for consumption has been held not to constitute such use.[61] This latter situation needs to be considered in the context of a pre-internet world where the consumer initiated the sale, the overseas manufacturer was not attempting to inject its product into the Australian market and would not have sent any of its product there but for the fact that the Australian consumer sought it out. A more recent decision concerning sales over the internet found that trade mark use occurred at the point at which the overseas website operator accepted an offer from an Australian consumer made via the relevant website.[62]

The High Court decision in *Gallo v Lion Nathan*[63] may also complicate the issue of first use of a trade mark in Australia. The case did not deal with ownership directly. Instead, the key issue was whether a registered trade mark owner had used its trade mark in Australia even though it had no knowledge that its trade marked goods had been sold here. The owner marked and sold its wine overseas. Some of that wine had then been bought by another party that imported the wine into Australia and sold it here. The defendant in that case claimed that these sales in Australia did not constitute use in Australia and the trade mark should be removed from the Register due to non-use by its owner. The High Court held that use occurs even without a trade mark owner intentionally injecting the goods into the Australian market or even being aware that sales of its marked goods had occurred.[64] The clear implication is that whenever an importer sells marked goods in Australia, the owner of that trade mark will be using it in Australia, even without their knowledge. The further implication is that this use would justify a claim of ownership of the trade mark on the basis of first use and, in such circumstances, the overseas owner is also the owner in Australia.

While a minimal amount of actual use will suffice to substantiate ownership, use preparatory to trading in Australia will not suffice. Hence, in *Moorgate Tobacco v Philip Morris*,[65] the High Court found that providing samples of cigarettes that the plaintiff proposed to sell in Australia and correspondence referring to the proposed trade mark did not constitute use in Australia.

---

57 *Moorgate Tobacco Co Ltd v Philip Morris Ltd (No 2)* (1984) 156 CLR 414.
58 *Thunderbird Products Corp v Thunderbird Marine Products Pty Ltd* (1974) 131 CLR 592.
59 *Alexander v Tait-Jamison* (1993) 28 IPR 103.
60 *Re Yanx Registered Trade Mark; Ex parte Amalgamated Tobacco Corp Ltd* (1951) 82 CLR 199.
61 *Rothmans Ltd v WD & HO Wills (Australia) Ltd* (1955) 92 CLR 131; *WD & HO Wills (Australia) Ltd v Rothmans Ltd* (1956) 94 CLR 182.
62 *Ward Group Pty Ltd v Brodie & Stone plc* (2005) 143 FCR 479. See also *International Hair Cosmetics Group Pty Ltd v International Hair Cosmetics Ltd* [2011] FCA 339.
63 *E & J Gallo Winery v Lion Nathan Australia Pty Ltd* (2010) 241 CLR 144.
64 Ibid., [51].
65 *Moorgate Tobacco Co Ltd v Philip Morris Ltd (No 2)* (1984) 156 CLR 414.

In order for a dispute concerning ownership on the basis of first use in Australia to be an issue, the two trade marks in question must be identical or, at the very least, substantially identical. If not, the issue for registration is not one of ownership.[66] In addition, the use of the identical or substantially identical trade marks must be in respect of the same goods or services or goods and services of the same kind. As noted in the overview of the registration process, registration is granted in respect of specified goods and services and there is no necessary objection to the same or a very similar trade mark being used in respect of different goods or services by different owners. While such circumstances may raise other objections to registration that are considered later, ownership is not one of them.

The need for ownership to be based on first use of either an identical trade mark or a substantially identical one in respect of the same goods or services or goods or services of the same kind is exemplified by the Full Federal Court decision in *Colorado Group Ltd v Strandbags Group Pty Ltd*.[67] In relation to the issue of identity of the trade marks, the Full Federal Court held that the word Colorado, by itself, was not sufficiently identical to the word Colorado used in conjunction with a simple mountain motif that was akin to a triangle.[68]

In relation to the issue of goods of the same kind, the court held that this was a far narrower concept than goods of the same description. Essentially, the goods must be of the same nature but they may be smaller or bigger. For example, a hatchet is of the same kind as an axe.

> That backpacks are a type or style of bag does not answer the question as to whether they should be viewed as essentially the same goods as any bag or receptacle. The backpack is a bag with straps to be worn on the back. It is not essentially the same or the same kind of thing as other bags, handbags, purses or wallets. The task is not to identify the genus into which the goods upon which the mark was used fall, but to identify the goods.[69]
>
> ...
>
> I cannot agree that handbags are the same kind of thing as wallets and purses. All three items are receptacles, but wallets and purses tend to be the same object (generally for men and women respectively) used for the same purpose – to carry money, cards (mainly credit cards), receipts and the like. Handbags often fulfil a wider purpose. I accept that wallets and purses are the same kind of thing and, indeed, both sides approached the appeal on this basis.[70]

The limitation of ownership to either the identical trade mark or a substantially identical trade mark means that careful consideration might have to be given to the issue of substantial identity as opposed to deceptive similarity, a different and broader concept that is relevant in various contexts such as infringement and the application of s 44.

15.9.2 Distributorship arrangements

A common scenario is where an overseas manufacturer arranges for distribution of its trade marked goods into Australia and, at some later stage, the distributor seeks registration of the

---

66 *Mirage Studios v Thompson* (1994) 28 IPR 517.
67 (2007) 164 FCR 506.
68 Ibid [110].
69 Ibid [90].
70 Ibid [94].

trade mark in Australia. In such circumstances, the overseas manufacturer will be considered the true owner of the trade mark and it will retain the right to seek registration unless and until others can demonstrate that it has lost that right. For example, in the *Riv-Oland* case,[71] an Italian marble manufacturer arranged for its marble to be exported to Australia and distributed through an Australian company. The distributorship arrangement dissolved relatively quickly and no marble was imported into Australia for some years. The Australian distributor then manufactured its own Australian marble, used the 'Riv-Oland' trade mark and subsequently sought to register that trade mark. The Italian manufacturer and exporter successfully objected to the registration on the grounds that its first use entitled it to registration. The rights flowing from that first use would only be lost if the distributor could demonstrate that they had been lost by sale, gift, abandonment or possibly as the result of estoppel if the distributor had acted to its detriment in reliance on some implied representation that it was permitted to use the trade mark. In the circumstances, the court was not satisfied that any of these grounds had been established.

There are a number of other cases in which overseas manufacturers have prevailed in a battle for ownership with Australian distributors. The High Court decision in *Gallo v Lion Nathan*, discussed above,[72] would appear to further strengthen the position of the overseas maker of the goods who applies its trade mark to the goods.

However, the Australian distributor may be successful if it can demonstrate that it was the real user of the trade mark in Australia and the overseas manufacturer was simply that, a manufacturer who provided the goods in question as directed by the distributor. For example, in *James North Australia Pty Ltd v Blundstone Pty Ltd*,[73] the Australian applicant for registration had selected the goods (shoes) for sale in Australia and requested the application of the trade mark to the goods by the manufacturer. The Australian company was the owner of the trade mark as a consequence of its selection of the shoes for sale in Australia and its direction as to the trade mark to be applied to them. In *Challenge Engineering Ltd v Fitzroy Milk Tanks Pty Ltd*,[74] an Australian company imported some milking machinery from New Zealand and subsequently sought registration of the trade mark under which the machinery was sold. In the absence of evidence that the New Zealand manufacturer intended to export its machinery to Australia and trade in Australia, the Australian importer was successful. The outcome in similar cases may be altered by the High Court decision in *Gallo v Lion Nathan*. If use can occur without intention to use in Australia, it is likely that the starting point would be that the overseas manufacturer would be held to have used the trade mark in Australia unless the circumstances of the importation were akin to those in the *James North* case where the trade mark was chosen by the distributor and applied at its direction.

15.9.3 Creation or adoption of an overseas trade mark

In the absence of prior use of the trade mark in Australia, the very act of seeking registration is itself some evidence of ownership. In these circumstances, the applicant will be the author of

---

71   *Riv-Oland Marble Co (Vic) Pty Ltd v Settef SpA* (1988) 19 FCR 569.
72   At 15.9.1.
73   (1978) 18 IPR 596.
74   (1997) 40 IPR 647.

the trade mark. One form of authorship is to create or devise the trade mark. This may be done by inventing a new word, logo or other sign. An example is Exxon, which is an invented word. Alternatively, the applicant may adopt an existing word, logo or sign from another area of social discourse. Actual use of the sign as a trade mark in Australia is not necessary before seeking registration.

Another possibility is adopting a trade mark in use overseas. Adopting trade marks from overseas may be a legitimate means of acquiring ownership of a trade mark in Australia. For example, in *Aston v Harlee Manufacturing Co*,[75] the Australian applicant adopted the trade mark of soft ice cream that he had found in America. Prior to doing so, he corresponded with the American company with the intention of becoming its licensee but attempts at negotiating such a licence came to nothing. As the trade mark had not been used in Australia by the American company, he was free to use it in Australia. The reverse situation occurred in the United States when a company registered 'Ugg boots' in the United States despite the significant use of that term in Australia.[76]

Australian courts have openly acknowledged the possibility of adopting overseas trade marks, even where doing so involved sharp practice. In *Moorgate Tobacco v Philip Morris Ltd (No 2)*,[77] the plaintiff and the defendant had lengthy negotiations with a view to the defendant acting as the plaintiff's distributor. When negotiations started to break down, the defendant sought registration of the trade mark that it knew the plaintiff was proposing to use. As there had been no use of the trade mark in Australia and there were no other legal grounds on which the plaintiff could object to the defendant's actions, such as breach of confidential information, fraud or breach of any fiduciary relationship, the plaintiff was unable to prevent the registration by the defendant.[78]

15.9.4 Persons who can own a trade mark

An owner must be a person having legal personality unless the application is for a collective trade mark.[79] For example, an unincorporated association could not apply for a standard trade mark.

15.10 Certification trade marks

There are three types of trade marks other than the standard trade mark that may be registered: certification, collective and defensive trade marks. Certification trade marks are defined in s 169 as:

---

75 (1960) 103 CLR 391.
76 See S. Joseph, 'When an ugg boot is no longer an ugg boot' [2004] *Art and Law* 7; and L. Eade, 'Uggly side of trade marks' (2004) 17 *Australian Intellectual Property Law Bulletin* 12. For further discussion on protection of well-known trade marks in Australia, see K. Maharaj, 'Well known trade marks in Australia and other jurisdictions' (2005) 17 *Australian Intellectual Property Law Bulletin* 147; and W. Burnett, 'Protecting well known trade marks in Australia and other jurisdictions' (2005) 17 *Australian Intellectual Property Law Bulletin* 155.
77 (1984) 156 CLR 414.
78 The result in *Moorgate Tobacco Co Ltd v Philip Morris Ltd (No 2)* may have been different under the current legislation, which affords a ground of opposition on the basis that the application was made in bad faith. However, the general proposition remains true: adopting an overseas trade mark that has not yet been used in Australia and does not have a reputation in Australia is frequently permissible.
79 *Trade Marks Act 1995* (Cth) s 27(2)(c), (2A).

A sign used, or intended to be used, to distinguish goods or services:

(a) dealt with or provided in the course of trade; and
(b) certified by a person [the owner], or by another person approved by that person, in relation to quality, accuracy or some other characteristic, including (in the case of goods) origin, material or mode of manufacture;

from other goods or services dealt with or provided in the course of trade but not so certified.

The objective of a certified trade mark is to certify the characteristics or standards of the products in relation to which the trade mark is used. The trade origins of the goods may be and often are quite diverse but each of the different goods will have the relevant characteristic and the trade mark will certify that to be the case. For example, the National Heart Foundation has registered a certification trade mark consisting of a white 'tick' inside a red circle and the words 'National Heart Foundation Approved'[80] for numerous different foodstuffs. The food items in question are produced and distributed by many different producers with both their standard trade marks and the National Heart Foundation's certification trade mark. The certification trade mark indicates that the food in question meets clearly defined, objective criteria, such as the percentage of fat and/or sugar in the product in question. Other certification trade marks may certify the geographical origin of the goods.

Another feature of certification trade marks is that the rules for obtaining the right to use the certification trade mark must make it possible for any trader that complies with the rules to obtain the right. Consequently, any trader that sells produce that meets the National Heart Foundation's health standards may use the certification trade mark upon payment of the relevant licensing fee and compliance with the relevant rules.

These aspects of certification trade marks are confirmed by ss 171 and 172. Section 171 confers on the owner of a certification trade mark the exclusive rights to use and to allow another person to use the certification trade mark but only in accordance with the rules governing the use of the certification trade mark. Section 172 gives an approved user the right to use the certification trade mark in accordance with the rules.

15.10.1 Requirements for registration

The different nature of certification trade marks means that the requirements for their registration are different from standard trade marks. For example, the nature of the necessary distinctiveness is not that prescribed in s 41 for standard trade marks but that stated in s 177 – namely, that the trade mark must be capable of distinguishing goods or services certified by the applicant or an approved certifier from goods or services not so certified.[81]

In addition, the application must include the rules for use of the trade mark in its application[82] and they must provide for various matters, including:

---

80   See, for example, trade mark reg no 498180.
81   *Trade Marks Act 1995* (Cth) ss 170, 177(1).
82   Ibid s 173.

- the cases in which goods or services are to be certified and the conditions under which approved users are to be allowed to use the certification trade mark; and
- settlement of any dispute arising from a refusal to certify goods or services or to allow the use of the certification trade mark.

Once examined by the Registrar, the application and the rules for use of the certification trade mark are considered by the Australian Competition and Consumer Commission (ACCC) to determine whether the applicant or its approved certifiers is or are competent to certify the goods or services in question, whether the rules would not be to the detriment of the public and whether they are satisfactory having regard to the principles of what were formerly Parts IV, IVA and V of the *Trade Practices Act 1974* (Cth) and what are now Part IV, sch 2 pt 2-2 and sch 2 pt 3-1 of the *Competition and Consumer Act 2010* (Cth).[83] These parts relate to the restrictive trade practices, unconscionable conduct and consumer protection provisions of that legislation. The ACCC will require documentation[84] that demonstrates that the proposed certification is consistent with consumer protection principles, such as evidence of the form and extent of testing of the product or service and procedures for ongoing quality control. It will also require information concerning any potential anti-competitive aspects of the application. One of the concerns will be that the certification trade mark would not be used to exclude or discriminate against some potential authorised users. For example, the ACCC would not permit rules that do not guarantee that any person complying with the relevant rules would be given approved user status. This would include ensuring that effective and impartial dispute resolution procedures are in place. In addition, the ACCC would ensure that none of the rules infringed Part IV provisions by, for example, setting prices or requiring approved users to obtain their supplies from a prescribed source or sources.

There is limited case law relating to certification trade marks and much of it has been overtaken by the more complex and specific provisions of the new legislation, which gives the ACCC a large role in approving certification trade marks. For example, two British cases presented conflicting views as to whether the owner of a certification trade mark had to engage in ongoing supervision of approved users or whether it was sufficient for them to simply ensure at the outset of approved use that the approved users met the necessary requirements.[85] The nature of the rules required by the express provisions of s 173 and the ACCC's requirements now make it clear that the obligation of the owner is an ongoing one to ensure that either it or its certified approvers continue to monitor the proper use of the trade mark. In addition, s 88(2)(c) provides for rectification of the Register on the grounds that 'because of circumstances applying at the time when the application for rectification is filed, the use of the trade mark is likely to deceive or cause confusion'. If the required monitoring did not take place, the unmonitored use of the trade mark by multiple parties would result in the trade mark failing to meaningfully certify the same characteristics and, therefore, its use would be likely to deceive or cause confusion.

---

83   Ibid s 175; *Trade Marks Regulations 1995* (Cth) reg 16.6.
84   Details of the role and requirements of the Australian Competition and Consumer Commission (ACCC) can be found at www.accc.gov.au.
85   *Union Nationale Inter-Syndicate des Marques Collectives Application* (1922) 39 RPC 346; *'Sea Island Cotton' Certification Trade Marks* [1989] RPC 87.

15.10.2 Certification by other means

The relatively complex nature of the process for registration of certification trade marks and the extent of scrutiny undertaken by the ACCC are such that some owners may bypass the process by relying on extensive use of their certification trade mark and passing off principles. For example, the National Heart Foundation certification trade mark had a significant reputation prior to registration and therefore could have been protected by passing off. It could also have been protected by copyright on the basis that the logo was an original artistic work.

15.11 Collective trade marks

Collective trade marks were introduced into Australian trade mark law as a consequence of Australia being a signatory to *TRIPS*. Collective trade marks are the trade marks used or intended to be used by members of an association to distinguish their goods or services from goods or services dealt with or provided by persons who are not members of the association.[86] Originally, collective trade marks could only be registered by unincorporated associations but that position has now been altered so that both unincorporated associations and legal persons constituting associations can apply for registration.[87]

Due to the legislative history that required applicants to be unincorporated associations, many collective trade marks are owned by such associations. Examples include an association of industry superannuation funds that has registered 'Industry Super Funds: Your Fund Your Future' (reg no 679462) and an association of agricultural producers that has registered 'Montasio' for cheese from the Montasio region in Italy (reg no 681415).

15.12 Defensive trade marks

A trade mark that is already registered as a standard trade mark may also be registered as a defensive trade mark.[88] Defensive trade marks differ from standard trade marks in a number of respects:

- Defensive trade marks are usually registered in respect of goods or services for which the trade mark is *not* presently registered.
- There is no requirement to either use or intend to use the defensive trade mark in respect of those goods or services for which the defensive registration is applied.[89]
- Registration as a defensive trade mark is not subject to removal for non-use.[90]

The purpose of the defensive registration is to prevent another party from using a well-known trade mark for goods or services in respect of which the trade mark is not registered. For example, famous trade marks such as 'Coke' and 'Levi's'[91] are registered as defensive trade

---

[86] *Trade Marks Act 1995* (Cth) s 162.
[87] Ibid ss 6, 27(2A).
[88] Ibid s 185(1).
[89] Ibid s 186.
[90] Ibid ss 185(2), 186.
[91] See, for example, trade mark reg no 337300; trade mark reg no 279015.

marks in respect of goods for which their owners do not intend to use those goods and therefore do not wish to obtain standard trade mark registration. Failure to obtain defensive registration may not be a large problem for an owner because the use by others of those trade marks in respect of those goods or services could be prevented via passing off or the infringement provisions in s 120(3) and their registration could probably be prevented by reliance on s 60. Nevertheless, defensive registration constitutes a form of 'forward defence'. Once the defensive registration is in place, the owner can be confident that applications for the trade mark or substantially identical or deceptively similar trade marks will be rejected by the Registrar. In addition, any actual use by a third party of such trade mark in respect of goods or services for which defensive registration has been obtained would constitute an infringement of s 120(1), a far easier form of infringement to prove than infringement under s 120(3). The owner of the defensive registration would also have the benefit of s 120(2), which is also an easier form of infringement to prove.

In order to obtain defensive registration, the applicant needs to meet the following requirements:

- The trade mark must already be registered as a standard trade mark.
- It must have been used in relation to all or any of the goods or services in respect of which it is registered as a standard trade mark.
- The extent of its use is such that its use in relation to other goods or services would indicate a connection between those other goods or services and the registered owner.[92]

The third of these requirements is the most difficult for an applicant to meet. It is not sufficient simply to demonstrate that it has a reputation in respect of the goods or services for which the trade mark is registered and used. The applicant needs to go further and demonstrate that the reputation has 'spilled over' to such an extent that if another person used it on the other goods or services for which defensive registration is sought, consumers would be likely to conclude that the applicant had expanded its business and use of its trade mark to those other goods or services. If the reputation of the trade mark is quite specifically associated with particular goods or services, defensive registration maybe denied. For example, in *Ferodo Ltd's Application*,[93] Evershed J rejected defensive registration for 'Ferodo' in respect of pharmaceuticals and tobacco despite the fact that it had a considerable reputation in respect of brake and clutch linings.

> [G]enerally speaking the more special in character those goods are and the more limited their market, the less likely will be the inference required ... to be drawn in relation to goods of a very different kind.[94]

Similarly, in *Re Vono's Application*,[95] the British Registry refused defensive registration for toilet preparation, cosmetic preparations and essential oils and soaps, despite its reputation in respect of items such as furniture and bedding. The application was further compromised by the opponent's registration of 'Vono' for medicinal powders, ointments and pills, which were

---

92   *Trade Marks Act 1995* (Cth) s 185(1).
93   [1945] Ch 334.
94   Ibid 338.
95   (1949) 66 RPC 305 (UK Reg).

probably more analogous to the categories of defensive registration than the applicant's registration for its standard trade mark.

Conversely, if the standard trade mark has been used both extensively and across a wide category of goods (or a category of goods with a wide impact beyond the immediate commercial field), prospects of defensive registration increase. For example, in *AT&T Corp's Application*,[96] AT&T's registration and extensive use of its trade mark for telecommunications goods and services was the basis for successful defensive registration for a very wide variety of goods and services, such as electronic education and entertainment services, insurance and financial services and surgical, medical, dental and veterinary instruments. Similarly, 'Viagra' has received defensive registration for an extremely large range of goods.[97]

The latter two decisions are also indicative of a more liberal approach to defensive registration that flows in part from the presumption in favour of applications and a change of wording in the new legislation that only requires that the use of the trade mark by another suggests a 'likelihood of connection' rather than 'a likelihood of connection in the course of trade'. The connection in question may flow from the possibility that the use is a licensed use, the owner might be sponsoring or endorsing the goods or services or might have entered into a joint venture with another company.[98]

Other factors that may favour an applicant include situations where the trade mark is inherently distinctive and there is no reason why any other trader would wish to use that trade mark in relation to any goods or services. 'Viagra' is an example of such a trade mark.[99]

While defensive registration has not been common to date, the more liberal approach to it is likely to lead to an increased reliance on it. In addition, the wording of the provisions in relation to defensive registration is similar to s 120(3), the infringement provision relating to well-known trade marks. It is likely that the interpretation of the defensive registration provisions will affect the interpretation of s 120(3) and vice versa.

15.13 Overview of requirements at examination of standard trade mark applications

A trade mark application is first examined by the Registrar. If the requirements at the examination stage are met, the trade mark is accepted by the Registrar but there is then an opportunity for any person to oppose the registration of the trade mark. The grounds for opposition include most of the requirements that are to be met at the examination stage and other, specified grounds of opposition.

At the examination stage, the Registrar must accept the application unless satisfied that one or more grounds for rejection exist or the application has not been made in accordance with

---

96   [2001] ATMO 96.
97   *Re Pfizer Products Inc* (2004) 61 IPR 165.
98   *AT&T Corp's Application* [2001] ATMO 96.
99   *Re Pfizer Products Inc* (2004) 61 IPR 165.

the legislation.[100] While the onus is on the Registrar to be satisfied of grounds for rejection, rather than on the applicant to demonstrate grounds for acceptance, the wording of the legislation makes it clear that if the Registrar is so satisfied, the Registrar must reject the application if the ground of rejection is established. The only exception to this is s 39(2) where the Registrar has some discretion. The grounds for rejecting an application at the examination stage are set out in div 2 of Part 4:

- The trade mark contains or consists of a sign that regulations made pursuant to s 18 decree must not be used as a trade mark (s 39(1)).
- The application *may* be rejected if it contains or consists of a sign prescribed for the purposes of s 39(2) or a sign so nearly resembling such a sign or a sign referred to in s 39(1) as to be likely to be taken for it (s 39(2)).
- The trade mark cannot be represented graphically (s 40).
- The trade mark is not capable of distinguishing the applicant's goods or services from the goods or services of other persons (s 41).
- The trade mark contains or consists of scandalous matter or its use would be contrary to law (s 42).
- Because of some connotation that the trade mark or a sign contained in the trade mark has, the use of the trade mark would be likely to deceive or cause confusion (s 43).
- The trade mark must not be substantially identical with or deceptively similar to an existing registered trade mark that is registered in respect of similar goods or closely related services (s 44). If the trade mark does not meet this requirement, it may still be eligible for registration under the honest concurrent user or prior user provisions in s 44(3) and (4).

15.14 National signs not to be used as trade marks

Schedule 2 of the *Trade Marks Regulations 1995* (Cth) specifies the signs that may not be registered as trade marks. It includes signs such as 'Austrade', 'Olympic Champion' and 'Returned Soldier'. The use of these signs as or in a trade mark is completely prohibited. The protection of various national icons has also been the subject of much debate and a report by the Advisory Council on Intellectual Property.[101]

15.15 Signs prescribed under s 39(2)

Regulation 4.15 of the *Trade Marks Regulations 1995* (Cth) prescribes the relevant signs. They include words such as 'Patent', 'Copyright' and 'Plant Breeder's Rights', representations of the coats of arms, flags or seals of Australian governments, and emblems of Australian cities, towns and public authorities. As this ground for rejection is discretionary, it is conceivable that a trade

---

100 *Trade Marks Act 1995* (Cth) s 33. See the discussion of s 41 concerning the onus of proof of distinctiveness of a trade mark below at 15.17.

101 See Advisory Council on Intellectual Property, *The Protection of National Icons* (Final Report, December 2002).

mark may be accepted if one of the prescribed signs is part of the trade mark but if the trade mark consists entirely of the prescribed sign it is highly unlikely that it will be accepted.[102]

15.16 Trade mark cannot be represented graphically: s 40

This requirement of s 40 really relates to technical issues concerning the maintenance of the Register and facilitating the searching of the Register.[103] Searching of the Register is done by computer, so the relevant search results must obviously be in digital form. As a matter of practice, every sign can be represented graphically in some way or another. Hence, sounds are described in words via the use of onomatopoeia although recordings of the sounds can also be obtained from the Register. Scents are also described in words as are colours. The effect of this requirement is essentially to ensure that the Registrar has the power to require representation of unusual signs in ways that are consistent with the Registrar's obligation to maintain an easily accessible and searchable register. The obligation to graphically represent a trade mark is one matter that is entirely within the Registrar's discretion. Unlike the other grounds for examination, it is not a ground of opposition that the trade mark cannot be represented graphically.[104]

15.17 Trade mark not distinguishing goods or services: s 41

This requirement of s 41 goes to the essence of a trade mark and is intimately bound up with the definition of a trade mark in s 17 in that a sign cannot 'distinguish goods or services dealt with or provided in the course of trade by a person from goods or services so dealt with or provided by any other person' unless it is distinctive. Section 41 is worded such that a trade mark is considered to be distinctive unless it fails to meet all of three separate tests of distinctiveness, although the actual wording of s 41(2) provides that a trade mark is to be considered distinctive unless either s 41(3) or s 41(4) applies to the trade mark. The previous wording of s 41 and the wording of s 33, which presumes registrability of a trade mark unless a ground for refusing registration is made out,[105] created some uncertainty as to whether the applicant must prove distinctiveness.[106]

It is clear now that the trade mark will be considered distinctive unless the Registrar is satisfied that it does not meet any of the three standards or tests for distinctiveness. Those three standards are discussed below.

---

102 O. Morgan, 'National icons and the *Trade Marks Act 1995*' (2004) 15 *Australian Intellectual Property Journal* 94.
103 See IP Australia, 'Australian Trade Mark Search' https://search.ipaustralia.gov.au/trademarks/search/quick.
104 *Trade Marks Act 1995* (Cth) s 40.
105 R. Burrell and M. Handler, 'Rethinking the presumption of registrability in trade mark law' (2012) 38 *Monash University Law Review* 148.
106 *Chocolaterie Guylian NV v Registrar of Trade Marks* (2009) 180 FCR 60; *Sports Warehouse Inc v Fry Consulting Pty Ltd* (2010) 186 FCR 519.

15.17.1 Inherent distinctiveness

First, the trade mark may be sufficiently inherently adapted to distinguish the goods or services to justify registration without any further inquiry or examination.[107] Finn J in *Austereo Pty Ltd v DMG Radio (Australia) Pty Ltd*[108] summarised principles concerning inherent adaptability to distinguish by referring to and quoting from four cases on the issue. The principles are set out below.

> Inherent adaptability is something which depends on the nature of the trade mark itself ... and is therefore not something that can be acquired; the inherent nature of the trade mark itself cannot be changed by use or otherwise.[109]

While this focus on the trade mark itself is necessary, it also needs to be borne in mind that the distinctiveness of any particular sign will depend on the goods or services in relation to which it is to be used. For example, the crocodile symbol may be inherently distinctive for Lacoste shirts but less distinctive, if at all, for shoes and handbags made of crocodile skin.

> While inherent adaptation to distinguish requires attention to be focused on the mark itself, and is intended to stand in sharp contrast to a mark's capacity to distinguish arising from use, the notion of 'the mark itself' does not exclude from consideration the nature of the range of goods within the class or classes in respect of which registration is sought, or the various ways in which the mark might, within the terms of the registration, be used in relation to those goods. Indeed, those matters must be taken into account.[110]

The test has also been cast in negative terms in cases decided under both the 1955 legislation and the current provisions:

> The ultimate question in applying [the test] is whether the mark, considered apart from the effects of registration, is such that by its use the applicant is likely to attain its object of thereby distinguishing its goods from the goods of others.[111]
>
> ...
>
> [T]he question whether a mark is adapted to distinguish [is to] be tested by reference to the likelihood that other persons, trading in goods of the relevant kind and being actuated only by proper motives – in the exercise, that is to say, of the common right of the public to make honest use of words forming part of the common heritage, for the sake of the signification which they ordinarily possess – will think of the word and want to use it in connexion with similar goods *in any manner which would infringe a registered trade mark granted in respect of it*.[112]

Some further explanation of that test is required. It is not sufficient to just show that another trader, properly motivated, may wish to use the sign in question for it to be denied registration on the basis of lack of distinctiveness. The starting point is to determine the original

---

107 *Trade Marks Act 1995* (Cth) s 41(3).
108 (2004) 209 ALR 93.
109 *Burger King Corp v Registrar of Trade Marks* (1973) 128 CLR 417, 424 (Gibbs CJ).
110 *Kenman Kandy Australia Pty Ltd v Registrar of Trade Marks* (2002) 122 FCR 494, [84] (Lindgren J).
111 Ibid [47].
112 Ibid [85] (emphasis in original). Lindgren J was citing the comments of Kitto J in *Clark Equipment Co v Registrar of Trade Marks* (1964) 111 CLR 511, 514.

signification or meaning of the sign to consumers. Once that is determined, consideration is given to whether another trader may legitimately wish to use it to distinguish their goods. The point was explained by a majority of the High Court in *Cantarella Brothers Pty Ltd v Modena Trading Pty Ltd* as follows:

> As shown by the authorities in this Court, the consideration of the 'ordinary signification' of any word or words (English or foreign) which constitute a trade mark is crucial, whether (as here) a trade mark consisting of such a word or words is alleged not to be registrable because it is not an invented word and it has 'direct' reference to the character and quality of goods, or because it is a laudatory epithet or a geographical name, or because it is a surname, or because it has lost its distinctiveness, or because it never had the requisite distinctiveness to start with. Once the 'ordinary signification' of a word, English or foreign, is established an enquiry can then be made into whether other traders might legitimately need to use the word in respect of their goods. If a foreign word contains an allusive reference to the relevant goods it is prima facie qualified for the grant of a monopoly. However, if the foreign word is understood by the target audience as having a directly descriptive meaning in relation to the relevant goods, then prima facie the proprietor is not entitled to a monopoly of it. Speaking generally, words which are prima facie entitled to a monopoly secured by registration are inherently adapted to distinguish.[113]

The case involved trade marks 'oro' and 'cinque stelle' for coffee. Those Italian words mean 'gold' and 'five stars' when translated to English. The majority of the High Court was unconvinced that the Italian words would convey those meanings to the average Australian consumer and so they were found to be inherently distinctive although the English words 'gold' and 'five stars' would not be inherently distinctive.

The test requires some 'fleshing out', which is provided to some extent by the comments in *Ocean Spray Cranberries Inc v Registrar of Trade Marks*, referred to by Finn J in the *Austereo* case:[114]

> Trade marks that are not inherently adapted to distinguish goods or services are mostly trade marks that consist wholly of a sign that is ordinarily used to indicate:
>
> (a) the kind, quality, quantity, intended purpose, value, geographical origin, or some other characteristic, of goods or services.[115]

This quote from the *Ocean Spray* case gives some context to the reference to the 'common heritage' in the *Kenman Kandy* decision but debate still remains as to what should be regarded as part of the commons available to all to use to describe their products. In *Kenman Kandy*,[116] the members of the Full Court disagreed on whether the shape of the applicant's 'bug' should be considered part of a commons available to all to use, with the majority siding with the view that the commons was not unduly degraded by permitting registration in that case.

---

113 *Cantarella Bros Pty Ltd v Modena Trading Pty Ltd* (2014) 315 ALR 4, [71].
114 *Austereo Pty Ltd v DMG Radio (Australia) Pty Ltd* (2004) 209 ALR 93.
115 *Ocean Spray Cranberries Inc v Registrar of Trade Marks* (2000) 47 IPR 579, [29]–[30].
116 *Kenman Kandy Australia Pty Ltd v Registrar of Trade Marks* (2002) 122 FCR 494.

In any event, the legislation leaves the interpretation of the concept of inherent adaptability to distinguish to the courts and so the principles cited above are critical to an understanding of it. However, the understanding of those principles is best achieved by referring to individual cases or generally accepted categories of inherently distinctive trade marks. Under the 1955 Act, inherent adaptability to distinguish was the only basis for proving the necessary distinctiveness, at least for trade marks registered under Part A of the old Register[117] and the 1955 Act provided a list of the types of signs (called 'marks' under that legislation)[118] that would be regarded as inherently distinctive. Those same signs would also be inherently distinctive under the 1995 Act and are therefore worthy of discussion here. They included the following.

(1) The name of a person represented in a special or particular manner and the signature of the applicant or some predecessor in business

For example, in *Standard Cameras Ltd's Application*,[119] the trade mark for a camera store consisted of the name 'Robin Hood' represented so that the R depicted an archer holding a bow in the shooting position and the D was a target with an arrow stuck in it. However, in *Fanfold Ltd's Application*,[120] registration of the name Fanfold 'in ordinary block type in the form of a slight arch and having a faint scroll underneath' was rejected as it was not considered to be a special or particular manner.

(2) Invented words

A genuinely invented word will be inherently distinctive. For example, 'Exxon' is an invented word not known to any language and is clearly inherently distinctive. However, inventiveness does not automatically flow from the fact that the word is not in the dictionary. For example, 'Rohoe' for a rotary hoe was rejected by the High Court because farmers would readily identify it as referring to the goods in question.[121]

(3) Words not having direct reference to the characteristics or qualities of the goods or services in question

A word or words need not be invented to be distinctive. For example, 'Nike', the name of the Greek goddess of victory, is inherently distinctive for sportswear, primarily because it does not describe the goods in question. Case law indicates that the words may make some covert and skilful allusion to or be suggestive of the characteristics or qualities of the goods or services without being considered to be a direct reference to those characteristics or qualities. For example, the High Court accepted 'Tub Happy' for clothes capable of being washed in a washing machine.[122] Similarly, a majority of the High Court accepted 'oro' and

---

117 Part A trade marks had greater protection than Part B trade marks, which had a lesser degree of inherent distinctiveness. There is no equivalent of Parts A and B in the present Register. It is not divided into parts, although it can be searched for standard, certification, collective and defensive trade marks.
118 *Trade Marks Act 1955* (Cth) s 6(1).
119 (1952) 69 RPC 125.
120 (1928) 45 RPC 325.
121 *Howard Auto-Cultivators Ltd v Webb Industries Pty Ltd* (1946) 72 CLR 175.
122 *Mark Foy's Ltd v Davies Co-op & Co Ltd* (1956) 95 CLR 190.

'cinque stelle' for coffee as being inherently distinctive trade marks, although they mean 'gold' and 'five star' in Italian, on the basis that the ordinary signification of those words from the perspective of Australian consumers was not a direct reference to the characteristics of coffee.[123] On the other hand, the High Court previously rejected 'Whopper' for hamburgers.[124]

(4) Words that are not, according to their ordinary meanings, geographical names or surnames

Many words may be used as names or refer to some geographical location but the issue is whether they are regarded as such according to their ordinary meaning. For example, 'Free' for cigarettes was rejected by the Registrar on the grounds that a substantial number of people had the family name 'Free'. On appeal, the Federal Court held that the word was not normally regarded as a name and registration was allowed.[125] The court also held that the Registrar's practice of determining whether a trade mark was a name according to its ordinary meaning by counting the prevalence of the name on the electoral roll was an inappropriate means of determining the issue. Similarly, many words may be geographical terms but not according to their ordinary meaning. For example, 'Farah' for shirts was accepted because few consumers would be aware that there is a river of the same name in Afghanistan.[126] Even if they were aware of this fact, it is unlikely that they would have associated the geographical place with the goods or services in question. The stereotypical example of this is 'North Pole' for bananas but actual cases include the acceptance of 'Bali' for bras because the Indonesian island of Bali is not associated with bras (although the trade mark was rejected for other reasons).[127] On the other hand, registrations of Bohemia and Bohemia Crystal for crystal glassware were revoked as Bohemia is a place in the Czech Republic and known for crystal.[128] Similarly, Moroccanoil for hair and skin care products was considered by the Full Court to be completely lacking in any inherent distinctiveness,[129] as too was Primary Health Care for operating health services.[130]

(5) Any other distinctive mark

With the extended definition of a sign in s 6 and the relaxation of the need for physical separation between a trade mark and the goods in relation to which it is used, many more signs, such as shapes, may now be considered to be inherently distinctive. For example, in *Kenman Kandy* the Full Court held that the shape of a lolly could be and was inherently distinctive as a trade mark for the lolly itself.[131]

---

123 *Cantarella Brothers Pty Ltd v Modena Trading Pty Ltd* (2014) 315 ALR 4.
124 *Burger King Corp v Registrar of Trade Marks* (1973) 128 CLR 417.
125 *Companhia Souza Cruz Industria & Comercio v Rothmans of Pall Mall (Australia) Ltd* (1998) 41 IPR 497.
126 *'Farah' Trade Mark* [1978] FSR 234.
127 *Berlei Hestia Industries v Bali Co Inc* (1973) 129 CLR 353.
128 *Bohemia Crystal Pty Ltd v Host Corp Pty Ltd* [2018] FCA 235.
129 *Aldi Foods Pty Ltd v Moroccanoil Israel Ltd* [2018] FCAFC 93.
130 *Primary Health Care Ltd v Commonwealth* [2017] FCAFC 174.
131 *Kenman Kandy Australia Pty Ltd v Registrar of Trade Marks* (2002) 122 FCR 494.

15.17.2 Partial inherent distinctiveness: use and intended use

Section 41(4) refers to a situation where, when the trade mark is not sufficiently inherently distinctive to justify registration on that ground alone, the Registrar may take the view that a combination of some inherent adaptability to distinguish and actual or intended use by the applicant will result in the trade mark being sufficiently adapted to distinguish. The trade mark must have some inherent distinctiveness but need not have much. For example, 'fine form' for lingerie was accepted pursuant to this test.[132] It should be noted that while some use will almost certainly be required for s 41(4), the applicant may rely on evidence of its intention to use the trade mark in question. Consequently, evidence of marketing plans and advertising campaigns may assist to get an application over the line.

15.17.3 Distinctiveness through use

Finally, if a trade mark has no inherent distinctiveness whatsoever the Registrar may take the view that even though the trade mark is not inherently adapted to distinguish at all, its actual use by the applicant may have been so extensive that it does in fact distinguish the applicant's goods or services from other goods or services.[133] Signs such as words that may initially be purely descriptive or single colours that have no innate distinctiveness may become registered after sufficient use. For example, 'Beautiful' for perfume was accepted in *Re Estee Lauder Cosmetics Ltd*[134] on the basis of its extensive use. Similarly, 'Oregon' for power tools has been accepted despite it obviously being a geographical name.[135] The colour 'orange' has been accepted for sparkling wines on the basis of the extensive use of a plain orange label[136] and substantial advertising, as was the colour 'terracotta' for hose fittings. In this latter example, the colour was held not to be inherently adapted to distinguish under s 41(3); however, Mansfield J did find on evidence that it was factually distinctive.[137]

The proof of use must be quite extensive. 'Sakata' for rice biscuits was initially refused on the basis that 'Sakata' is a city in Japan and rice biscuits are likely to be associated with a Japanese city.[138] Similarly, in *Ocean Spray Cranberries Inc v Registrar of Trade Marks*,[139] 'classic' when used in the context of Ocean Spray Classic Cranberry Juice was not considered to have acquired a secondary meaning, mainly because the extensive use of 'classic' was not use as a trade mark. Hence, it is not sufficient just to prove that the sign has been used

---

132   *Gazal Apparel Pty Ltd v Fine Lines Extraordinary Apparel Pty Ltd* (2000) AIPC 91-543 (prior to amendment of s 41; the relevant test was then set out in s 41(5)). See also *Master Plumbers & Mechanical Services Association (Australia) v Master Plumbers & Mechanical Contractors Association (NSW)* (2003) 60 IPR 156; *Monaco v TGSG Group Pty Ltd* (2001) 51 IPR 191; *Re Application by SPHC(IP) Pty Ltd* (2001) 49 IPR 655.
133   More precisely, bearing in mind the onus of proof, s 41(3) of the *Trade Marks Act 1995* (Cth) now provides that a trade mark will be considered not to be distinctive under s 41(3) if it has no inherent distinctiveness and it has not been used to such an extent as to make it distinctive.
134   (2000) 50 IPR 131.
135   *Blount Inc v Registrar of Trade Marks* (1998) 83 FCR 50.
136   *Re Application by Veuve Clicquot Ponsardin, Maison Fondee En 1772* (1999) 45 IPR 525.
137   *Philmac Pty Ltd v Registrar of Trade Marks* (2002) 126 FCR 525.
138   *Re Sakata Rice Snacks (Australia) Pty Ltd* (1998) 43 IPR 378.
139   (2000) 47 IPR 579.

extensively. It must have been used in such a way that consumers would recognise the use as indicating the origin of the goods or services in question, that is, as a trade mark.[140] For example, a particular colour may be used extensively on packaging but the reason for that use and the perception of that use by consumers must be considered. In *Re Application by Notetry Ltd*,[141] the colours yellow and silver were used on vacuum cleaners but such colours are commonly used on vacuum cleaners. In addition, the manufacturer's word trade mark 'Dyson' was prominently displayed on the goods and the Registrar rejected the proposition that consumers associated the colours with the applicant's vacuum cleaners and no others. Consumers identified the applicant's goods by reference to the name 'Dyson' and the colours were more decorative than indicative of the origin of the goods.

Similarly, in *Re Multix Pty Ltd*,[142] the colour red was rejected as a trade mark for aluminium foil because, again, the applicant's word trade mark had been displayed prominently and it was this trade mark that consumers associated with the applicant's aluminium foil. Such trade marks are often euphemistically referred to as 'limping' trade marks because they limp behind the dominant trade mark. However, the term has not been officially adopted and each case needs to be examined on its merits as there is no reason why consumers would not associate a particular product with two different signs, especially if one is a word sign and the other a colour or shape.

15.17.4 Functional shapes

One of the contentious areas of registration is the registration of the shape of products as a trade mark. It is contentious because if an applicant acquires trade mark registration for a functional shape, its competitors may well be disadvantaged by being unable to use that shape for their products. The end result may be a diminution in competition as owners use their registration more for the purpose of acquiring a monopoly over functional shapes than for the intended legislative purpose of indicating the origin of their goods. The opportunity to obtain what is, in effect, perpetual protection via trade mark registration makes the registration of functional shapes as trade marks a far more attractive proposition than acquiring limited protection for ten years under designs legislation.

The legislation makes no express reference to the registration of functional shapes. In Australia, some attempt was previously made to deal with the issue. Section 39 of the 1994 Act provided a separate ground of refusal of registration of a shape 'if the trade mark consists wholly or principally of the shape, or some other characteristic, possessed, because of their nature, by the goods, or a shape, or some other characteristic, that the goods must have if a particular technical result is to be obtained'.

No equivalent of s 39 appears in the current legislation and so the issue is left to case law. The issue has been discussed in detail by the Full Federal Court in two decisions.[143] In both

---

140 For example, *Apple Inc v Registrar of Trade Marks* [2014] FCA 1304, where 'app store' was found not to be distinctive despite considerable use by Apple Inc.
141 (1999) 45 IPR 547.
142 (1999) 47 IPR 153.
143 *Koninklijke Philips Electronics NV v Remington Products Australia Pty Ltd* (2000) 100 FCR 90; *Kenman Kandy Australia Pty Ltd v Registrar of Trade Marks* (2002) 122 FCR 494. See also Davison, 'Shape trade marks', above n 28, 231; J. Luck, 'The registrability of shapes of goods as trade marks: A commentary on

cases, the court took the view that the question of functionality is mediated via the issue of distinctiveness and the definition of a trade mark in s 17. For example, Burchett J in *Philips v Remington* considered that the deletion of s 39 from the repealed legislation of 1994 was not important. This was because

> [n]o change being contemplated to the nature of trade mark use, it followed that neither 'a shape possessed because of their nature, by the goods nor a shape that the goods must have if a particular technical result is to be obtained' (the categories of shape identified in s 39) could distinguish the goods of one trade source from the similar goods of another; and therefore such a shape could not function as a trade mark. Indeed, it is hard to imagine how such a shape of the goods themselves could be used, or be intended to be used, for the purpose set out in s 17 – its use would inevitably be nothing other than part of the use of the commodity itself. Section 39 was omitted from the *Trade Marks Act 1995* because it was unnecessary.[144]

Stone J reiterated the point in *Kenman Kandy*, when stating that '[a] shape dictated by the nature of or function of the goods would not be capable of distinguishing between one trader and another in those goods'.[145]

While the simple proposition that either functional shapes are not trade marks or they can never be distinctive seems simple enough, the actual application of that principle is more difficult. Does it mean that shapes with any degree of functionality are disqualified from registration or only those where the shape in question is the only shape capable of performing the function in question? For example, the Philips triangulated, triple-headed rotary shaver could be made so that the rotary razors are in a direct line rather than a triangle shape and such a razor could perform the same shaving function although possibly not as well or easily. Similarly, there are many different types of bottle shapes that may achieve the same function of holding and facilitating the pouring of liquids. Presumably, not all bottle shapes are to be excluded from registration even though every bottle is functional. The Coca-Cola bottle is an obvious example of a shape that is both functional and aesthetically pleasing. In short, the issue will usually be what is the degree of functionality of a shape rather than whether it is functional at all.

A further difficulty is that it is not clear from the judgments in those two cases why distinctiveness or a trade mark 'function' of distinguishing the goods of the user from other goods cannot be acquired by extensive use in the absence of any inherent distinctiveness and therefore registration may occur via s 41(3).[146] Some passing off cases demonstrate the point

---

this part of the Full Federal Court's judgment in *Philips v Remington*' (2001) 12 *Australian Intellectual Property Journal* 12. For further reference, see M. Richardson, 'Shape trade marks in Australian courts' (2001) 12 *Australian Intellectual Property Journal* 5; R. Burrell and H. B. Smith, 'Shaving the *Trade Marks Directive* down to size' (2000) 63 *Modern Law Review* 570.

144 *Koninklijke Philips Electronics NV v Remington Products Australia Pty Ltd* (2000) 100 FCR 90, 103.
145 *Kenman Kandy Australia Pty Ltd v Registrar of Trade Marks* (2002) 122 FCR 494, [43] (French J). See also *Sebel Furniture Ltd v Acoustic & Felts Pty Ltd* (2009) 80 IPR 244.
146 Davison, 'Shape trade marks', above n 28, 231; J. Baird, 'The registrability of functional shape marks' (2002) 13 *Australian Intellectual Property Journal* 218. See also Baird, 'This mark is so attractive', above n 28, 26; J. McCutcheon, 'Monopolised product shapes and factual distinctiveness under s 41(6) of the *Trade Marks Act 1995* (Cth)' (2004) 15 *Australian Intellectual Property Journal* 18.

that functional shapes can acquire a secondary, distinctive meaning via extensive use[147] and there is no obvious reason why this can never be done for registration purposes in the light of the extended definition of a sign, the adoption of use criteria for determining distinctiveness in s 41(3) and the absence of any express prohibition on the registration of functional shapes.

In any event, it is clear that non-functional shapes can be registered on the basis of either their inherent distinctiveness or their use. In *Kenman Kandy*, registration was sought for a bug-eyed, insect-like shape of confectionery although the shape was not that of any particular insect and had been 'invented'. The Registrar rejected the application on the grounds that it was not inherently distinctive and, as the shape had not been used, registration on other bases was impossible.

However, in the eventual appeal to the Full Federal Court, the majority rejected this argument, holding that there was no basis in the legislation for the view that the shape of goods could not be inherently distinctive. It rejected the proposition that the number of potential shapes of an item is so limited that any trader actuated by honest motives may be inclined to adopt the shape in question. Whether the particular shape in *Kenman Kandy* was in fact inherently distinctive is a matter for debate and the first-instance decision in this case held that the shape, while not that of any particular insect, was not inherently distinctive. Since it had six legs and the large, neotenous eyes that so often attract children, it may be questionable whether it really was an invented shape in the same way that 'Rohoe' was not an invented word.

In dissent, Lindgren J suggested that the shape of confectionery could not be inherently distinctive as consumers, particularly children, would not recognise the shape as indicating the origin of the goods in question but simply regard it as an interesting and possibly attractive shape that would invite their attention.[148] Drawing on United States Supreme Court authority, Lindgren J stated:

> Although it is unnecessary to do so for the purpose of deciding the present case, I make the following further observations. In *Wal-Mart Stores Inc v Samara Bros Inc* (2000) 529 US 205, Justice Scalia, delivering the opinion of the United States Supreme Court, stated (at 213):
>
>> In the case of product design, as in the case of color, we think consumer predisposition to equate the feature with the source does not exist. Consumers are aware of the reality that, almost invariably, even the most unusual of product designs – such as a cocktail shaker shaped like a penguin – is intended not to identify the source, but to render the product itself more useful or more appealing.[149]

In any event, the final legal position is that the shape of a product may be registered on the basis of inherent distinctiveness. However, if the shape is functional, it seems that it may not be registered although the definition of 'functional' in this context remains to be determined. In addition, it is not clear why distinctiveness of functional shapes cannot be acquired through use and s 41(3).[150]

---

147 *William Edge & Sons Ltd v William Niccolls & Sons Ltd* [1911] AC 693.
148 *Kenman Kandy Australia Pty Ltd v Registrar of Trade Marks* (2002) 122 FCR 494.
149 Ibid 524.
150 Note, for example, the registration for the shape of a kettle-shaped barbecue grill, which was accepted pursuant to the previous s 41(6), the equivalent of s 41(3) under the current legislation: reg no 703633.

The Australian situation contrasts sharply with the position in the European Union and the United States. Both those jurisdictions have express prohibitions on the registration of certain shape trade marks. These express prohibitions have been introduced because the difficulties with registration of functional shapes probably cannot be overcome via the use of standard trade mark criteria. The problems relate to competition issues outside the usual trade mark law paradigm and so restrictions on registration of such trade marks need to go beyond the usual criteria for registration.[151] For example, art 4(1)(e) of the European Union's *Trade Marks Directive* states:

> (1) The following shall not be registered, or if registered, shall be liable to be declared invalid:
>
> ...
>
> (e) signs which consist exclusively of:
>   (i) the shape, or another characteristic, which results from the nature of the goods themselves, or
>   (ii) the shape, or another characteristic, of goods which is necessary to obtain a technical result, or
>   (iii) the shape, or another characteristic, which gives substantial value to the goods; ...[152]

The United States also has specific legislation on the topic as s 2(e)(5) of the *Lanham (Trademark) Act*[153] which provides that a trade mark will not be registered if 'it consists of a mark which ... comprises any matter that, as a whole, is functional'.

In both these pieces of legislation, the emphasis is not on the issue of distinctiveness of the trade marks but on the function that the shape may play, and the intention of the prohibitions is to prevent the monopolisation of functional shapes via trade mark registration.

15.17.5 Colour trade marks

As discussed earlier,[154] a colour or combination of colours is a sign. It will be difficult, if not impossible, to establish that a single colour is inherently distinctive and the applicant will have to rely on s 41(6) to demonstrate distinctiveness.

Even then, the applicant faces considerable difficulties. It must demonstrate the following: 'the use of the colour in the manner described in the application has ... constituted use of the colour as a trade mark. The second issue is whether the trade mark applied for does in fact distinguish the applicant's products, having regard to evidence concerning the actual use of the colour as a trade mark.'[155]

---

151 M. Davison, 'Shape trade marks: Problems and solutions' (2004) 15 *Australian Intellectual Property Journal* 106.
152 *Directive (EU) 2015/2436 of the European Parliament and of the Council of 16 December 2015 to Approximate the Laws of the Member States Relating to Trade Marks* [2015] OL J 336/1.
153 15 USC § 1125 (1946).
154 At 15.6.2.
155 *Woolworths Ltd v BP plc (No 2)* (2006) 154 FCR 97, [81], citing with approval *Philmac Pty Ltd v Registrar of Trade Marks* (2002) 126 FCR 525, [548].

Hence, in the *Multix* trade mark application,[156] the Registrar declined registration on the grounds that although the colour red had been extensively used in the applicant's packaging, it had not been used as a trade mark and there was insufficient evidence that consumers associated the colour with the applicant's product. A factor in that decision was the applicant's use of its various word trade marks to identify the product to consumers.

In addition, in *Woolworths Ltd v BP (No 2)*, the Full Federal Court denied registration of

> the colour green as shown in the representation on the application applied as the predominant colour to the fascias of buildings, petrol pumps, signage boards – including poster boards, pole signs and price boards – and spreaders, all used in service station complexes for sale of the goods and supply of the services covered by the registration.[157]

In reaching its decision, the Full Court noted that while the applicant had used the colour green extensively as its predominant colour, it had done so in combination with the colour yellow. The court held: 'Green, alone, was not used as a trade mark in the parts of the service stations referred to in the endorsements.'[158]

On the other hand, in decisions such as *Philmac Pty Ltd v Registrar of Trade Marks*,[159] the Federal Court was convinced that the applicants' use of a terracotta colour for polypipe fittings justified registration pursuant to the then s 41(6) (now s 41(3)). In addition, the Registrar has permitted registration of a single colour in a number of circumstances.[160]

15.18 Scandalous trade marks: s 42

Few trade marks are rejected on the grounds that they contain or consist of scandalous matter. Hence, trade marks that may be sexually offensive, such as 'Good girls do swallow' and 'FCUK', have gained registration despite their capacity to offend.[161] Offending or shocking matter is regarded as something different from scandalous matter. The requirement is most likely to operate in the area of religious or racial matters. Hence, 'Jesus' and 'Mecca' have been rejected for some goods. Similarly, racially scandalous trade marks like 'black boy' for shoe polish are certain to be rejected. The goods or services in respect of which registration is sought may also be relevant. For example, 'Porn Star' for children's clothing would be clearly inappropriate.[162]

---

156   *Re Application by Multix Pty Ltd* (2004) 64 IPR 128.
157   (2006) 154 FCR 97, [7].
158   Ibid [81], citing with approval *Philmac Pty Ltd v Registrar of Trade Marks* (2002) 126 FCR 525, [105].
159   (2002) 126 FCR 525.
160   For example, *Veuve Clicquot Ponsardin, Maison Fondee en 1772* [1999] ATMO 29 (when 'orange' was registered for sparkling wine).
161   See also *Cosmetic, Toiletry and Fragrance Association Foundation v Fanni Barns Pty Ltd* (2003) 57 IPR 594, where 'Look Good + Feel Good = Root Good' was considered offensive but not scandalous.
162   For further reference, see P. Loughlan, 'Oh yuck! The registration of scandalous trade marks' (2005) 61 *Intellectual Property Forum* 38; S. Givoni, 'Pushing the boundaries: Scandalous trade marks' (2004) 17 *Australian Intellectual Property Law Bulletin* 21.

15.19 Use contrary to law: s 42

The use of some trade marks would be contrary to law and if an opponent can prove that to be so, registration will be denied. The key word here is 'would', not 'could' or 'might'. The use of the trade mark must necessarily contravene some law in order for this provision to apply; hence it would not be sufficient to show that use of the trade mark may involve misleading or deceptive conduct as that would depend on the particular circumstances of its use.[163]

The Registrar is not restricted to considering trade mark law in this context and must consider any laws that would be contravened by the use of the trade mark. In *Advantage-Rent-A-Car v Advantage Car Rental Pty Ltd*,[164] the plaintiff claimed that the trade mark in question contained an artistic work and that it owned the copyright in the artistic work. Consequently, use of the trade mark by the defendant would have required reproduction of the artistic work and a breach of copyright law. The Federal Court held that the Registrar was required to consider all laws, including copyright, not just trade mark laws or passing off considerations.[165]

There are numerous federal and state laws that place prohibitions on the use of particular signs for various reasons and this legislation may also come into play when considering the application of s 42. Much of this legislation relates to major sporting events and the protection of indicia relating to those events. Details of these types of legislative controls on business indicia are discussed below.

15.20 Deceptive or confusing trade marks: s 43

Section 43 states that an application may be refused 'if, because of some connotation that the trade mark or a sign contained in the trade mark has, the use of trade mark would be likely to deceive or cause confusion'. The word 'connotation' is defined in the *Shorter Oxford Dictionary* as 'something implied as a condition or accompaniment or an association or idea suggested by a word in addition to its primary meaning'. The purpose of s 43 is to permit the Registrar to reject the application if there is any aspect of it which necessarily suggests the likelihood of deception or confusion.

As a general rule, the application will, on its face, reveal the potential confusion or deception and thus bear the relevant connotation. For example, while a trade mark might be distinctive, it might also suggest that the goods in relation to which it is used have qualities that they do not in fact possess. The equivalent provision in the 1955 legislation was used to reject 'Orlwoola' for goods that were not made of wool,[166] 'Vitamin' for soap that contained no vitamins[167] and 'Bubble-up' for beverages that were non-aerated.[168] A recent application for

---

163   *Primary Health Care Ltd v Commonwealth* [2017] FCAFC 174, [411]
164   (2001) 52 IPR 24.
165   Ibid 30. See also *Neumann v Sons of the Desert SL* [2008] FCA 1183, [31].
166   *Re Trade Mark 'Orlwoola'* (1909) 26 RPC 850.
167   *Kitchen & Sons Pty Ltd v Inman* (1939) AOJP 1383.
168   *Seven-Up Co v Bubble Up Co Inc* (1987) 9 IPR 259.

'Himalayan Spring Water – Bottled in the Sacred Himalayas of Nepal to the vibrational chanting of Tibetan Monks' was only accepted on the condition that the bottling in fact took place in that location while a recording of the chanting occurred.[169] One can also readily imagine trade marks that would be dangerously deceptive, such as 'Scrumptious' for toilet cleaner or even attractive scents that might encourage a young child to consume the product. On the other hand, the alleged connotation was not established in *Carlton United Breweries v Royal Crown Co Inc*,[170] where Carlton unsuccessfully argued that 'draft' necessarily referred to beer on tap. The Hearing Officer did not agree and found that use of the word 'draft' for bottled soft drink did not constitute a deceptive or confusing connotation.

In *Primary Health Care Ltd v Commonwealth*,[171] two judges of the Full Federal Court noted that the primary meaning of a trade mark is its connection between the goods or services in question and the trade mark owner.[172] As such, it must be distinctive within the meaning of s 41. The question for s 43 purposes is whether it has a secondary meaning or connotation and, if so, whether that connotation is likely to deceive or cause confusion. In that case, 'Primary Health Care' was considered to have such a connotation as it suggested or implied that the service would be the provision of health care to individuals when, in fact, the service was that of operating medical centres within which doctors and other medical practitioners operated. The latter were providing the primary health care, not the trade mark owner.

In addition to these situations where the trade mark suggests a quality that is in fact absent, the trade mark may also suggest other associations that it does not in fact have. Consequently, in *Clissold v Amalgamated Television Services Pty Ltd*,[173] the trade mark 'Home and Away' was rejected for soap as *Home and Away* is a well-known television soap opera. Similarly, in *Durkan v Twentieth Century Fox Film Corp*,[174] 'Braveheart' for a musical was rejected because of the connotation that it might be associated with the movie of the same name. On the other hand, in *RS Components Ltd v Holophane Corp*,[175] the court did not consider that RSL for electrical components would have the connotation of an association with the Returned Services League.

The cases referred to in the previous paragraph often involve attempts to rely on the provision when there is a conflict between two trade marks. The Full Federal Court has indicated that in those circumstances the better approach is to resolve such conflicts by reference to s 44 or s 60 in opposition proceedings.[176] Nevertheless, it appears that the Registrar has continued to refer to s 43 in such circumstances in cases where the connotation arises from a particular reputation that has resulted in a term such as 'Braveheart' entering into

---

169   Trade mark reg no 1261293.
170   (2001) 53 IPR 599.
171   [2017] FCAFC 174
172   See the judgments of Greenwood J and Kratzmann J.
173   (2000) 52 IPR 207.
174   (2000) 47 IPR 651.
175   (1999) 46 IPR 451.
176   See *Woolworths Ltd v Registrar of Trade Marks* (1998) 45 IPR 445, affirmed (1999) 45 IPR 411. See also J. Luck, 'Distinctiveness, deceptive and confusing marks under the *Trade Marks Act 1955*' (1996) 7 *Australian Intellectual Property Journal* 97; *Trade Marks Office Manual of Practice and Procedure* [29.1]–[29.2].

the general language.[177] Consequently, it is likely that s 43 will continue to be referred to by both the Registrar and opponents in such circumstances.

The term 'likely' is used in this and other provisions such as s 60. In these contexts, it means a 'real possibility' as opposed to a remote possibility or the civil standard of proof of 'more likely than not'.[178]

15.21 Trade marks identical or similar to existing trade marks: s 44

This provision, which specifies that 'the trade mark must not be substantially identical with or deceptively similar to an existing registered trade mark', requires the Registrar to compare the proposed trade mark with existing registered trade marks and trade mark applications that have an earlier priority date. Each aspect of the provision, particularly the requirements of 'substantially identical with or deceptively similar to' on the one hand and 'similar goods or closely related services' on the other hand needs to be considered separately. However, a global assessment of the two aspects of the provision also needs to be undertaken as both aspects often involve questions of degree rather than 'yes/no' propositions.[179] For example, two trade marks may be a little bit deceptively similar and the goods in relation to which they are to be used may be a little bit similar. A global assessment would suggest that the applicant's trade mark be registered in such circumstances whereas if the two trade marks were quite deceptively similar and to be used in respect of very similar or identical goods, registration would be denied.

The legal terms used in this section appear in other parts of the 1995 Act, such as s 120 on infringement. Consequently, an understanding of the terms is critical both for the purposes of determining registration and for other purposes such as determining infringement. Some of the cases referred to below were decided in the context of infringement rather than registration.

15.21.1 Substantially identical with

Determining whether trade marks are substantially identical involves a side-by-side comparison of them:

> In considering whether marks are substantially identical they should, I think, be compared side by side, their similarities and differences noted and the importance of these assessed

---

177 *Durkan v Twentieth Century Fox Film Corp* (2000) 47 IPR 651.
178 See, for example, the comments of French J in *Registrar of Trade Marks v Woolworths Ltd* (1999) 45 IPR 411, 426. In considering the phrase 'likely to deceive or cause confusion', his Honour observed: 'The use of the word "likely" in this context does not import a requirement that it be more probable than not that the mark has that effect. The probability of deception or confusion must be finite and non-trivial. There must be a "real tangible danger of it occurring".' See also *Southcorp Wines Pty Ltd v Coy* [2001] AIPC 91-715; *Leroy SA v Regal Grange Pty Ltd* (2001) 51 IPR 199; *Spiral Foods Ltd v Valio Ltd* (2000) 50 IPR 473.
179 *Woolworths Ltd v Registrar of Trade Marks* (1998) 45 IPR 445, affirmed (1999) 45 IPR 411.

having regard to the essential features of the registered mark and the total impression of resemblance or dissimilarity that emerges from the comparison.[180]

This comparison therefore takes account of any visual similarities but it also takes account of other similarities, such as the way in which the two trade marks are pronounced.

In undertaking the comparison, emphasis would also be placed on the distinctive aspects of the signs in question. For example, many word trade marks may contain prefixes or suffixes that are common to the particular goods or services in question and therefore they would be largely discounted. Similarly, the emphasis in pronunciation of English words tends to be on the first syllable and so greater emphasis would be placed on identity or near identity of those syllables.

Substantial identity cannot be proven simply by demonstrating that one trade mark is contained within another trade mark. It is necessary to compare the entirety of the two trade marks. For example, in *Angoves Pty Ltd v Johnson*,[181] 'St Agnes Liquor Store' was not considered substantially identical to 'St Agnes'. Similarly, in *SAP (Australia) Pty Ltd v Sapient Australia Pty Ltd*,[182] 'Sapient College' was held not to be substantially identical to 'Sapient'.

On the other hand, more recent decisions of the Full Federal Court have created some controversy by referring to the 'dominant cognitive cues' within the respective trade marks. For example, 'Harbour Lights' has been held to be substantially identical to another sign consisting of those words together with a semi-circle of golden stars above them with stars of different sizes and the words 'a new star shines' underneath 'Harbour Lights'.[183] The Full Court held that the dominant cognitive cue was in the words 'Harbour Lights' and the other signs were not sufficient to demonstrate a lack of substantial identity. While the two trade marks were almost certainly also deceptively similar, the issue of substantial identity might have considerable relevance in the context of a dispute about ownership and first use.

15.21.2 Or deceptively similar to

Deceptive similarity is a broader test than that for substantial identity and there is a far higher likelihood of a finding of deceptive similarity than of substantial identity. Indeed, it is difficult to think of an example where two trade marks would be substantially identical but not deceptively similar. In contrast, there are many examples where courts have found trade marks to be deceptively similar but not substantially identical.

Section 10 provides that 'a trade mark is taken to be "deceptively similar" to another trade mark if it so nearly resembles that other trade mark that it is likely to deceive or cause confusion'. The case law relating to the term makes it clear that the test is not a side-by-side test but one of calculating the residual impression that the trade marks would leave on consumers. One needs to consider the potential effect of the two trade marks on consumers

---

180   *Shell Co of Australia Ltd v Esso Standard Oil (Australia) Ltd* (1963) 109 CLR 409, 414–15.
181   (1982) 66 FLR 216, 230.
182   (1999) 48 IPR 593.
183   *Accor Australia & New Zealand Hospitality Pty Ltd v Liv Pty Ltd* [2017] FCAFC 56. See also *Pham Global Pty Ltd v Insight Clinical Imaging Pty Ltd* [2017] FCAFC 83.

if they saw the two trade marks at different times. *Jafferjee v Scarlett*[184] provides a good example of the point. In that case, the plaintiff had already registered a trade mark for flour consisting of an athlete breasting the finishing tape in a foot race. The defendant's trade mark for flour consisted of a picture of an athlete throwing a javelin. A side-by-side comparison of the two trade marks quickly revealed their differences and negatived a finding of substantial identity. However, the general impression left by the two trade marks flowing from their very similar theme would be and was found to be deceptively similar. Consumers who saw the first trade mark one week and then saw the other trade mark the next week would be caused to wonder whether the two products were the same or at least likely to come from the same source.[185] The meaning of 'likely' is 'a real, tangible danger' rather than a mere possibility or a requirement of 'more likely than not'.[186]

When considering the net impression of the two trade marks, the courts have referred to various tests although it is important to regard them as assisting in determining the issue of deceptive similarity rather than being strict legal doctrines to be applied. Hence, when speaking of the net impression of two competing trade marks, courts bear in mind the imperfect recollection of consumers and take into account not just the visual and aural similarities between the two trade marks but also the ideas evoked by the two trade marks. *Jafferjee v Scarlett*[187] is a classic example of the evocation of similar ideas leading to a finding of deceptive similarity.

On the other hand, some ideas are common to the goods or services in respect of which the trade marks are used or simply common to trade description in general. If the two trade marks in *Jafferjee v Scarlet*[188] had involved devices such as a picture or drawing of a field of wheat or sheaves of wheat, the similarities would not have led consumers to wonder whether the two products came from the same origin. The connection of wheat with flour would be obvious and consumers would regard it as entirely possible that there would be two trade marks with similar concepts.

Similarly, the use of words of a general laudatory nature in the competing trade marks is unlikely to generate difficulties. For example, in *Cooper Engineering Co Pty Ltd v Sigmund Pumps Ltd*,[189] the High Court permitted both Rain King and Rainmaster for water sprinklers. The use of words such as 'King' and 'master' both implied superiority but that general concept is and should be open to all trade mark owners.

When comparing the two trade marks, account needs to be taken of not only visual similarities and the effect of the ideas evoked by the two trade marks but also any aural similarities. For example, in *Wingate Marketing Pty Ltd v Levi Strauss & Co*,[190] the defendant's trade mark of 'Revise' was considered deceptively similar to 'Levi's' because it pronounced its trade mark 'Ree-vise' in order to rhyme with 'Levi's'.

---

184 (1937) 57 CLR 115.
185 *Woolworths Ltd v Registrar of Trade Marks* (1998) 45 IPR 445, affirmed (1999) 45 IPR 411.
186 Ibid.
187 (1937) 57 CLR 115.
188 Ibid.
189 (1952) 86 CLR 536.
190 (1994) 49 FCR 89.

Consequently, the determination of deceptive similarity depends on an analysis of the visual and aural aspects of the two trade marks and the idea or impression given to a consumer. Either of these factors may lead to a finding of deceptive similarity or a combination of the two may lead to that conclusion.

15.21.3 The context of the comparison

Some care needs to be taken in considering the particular circumstances in which the comparison is being made. The test of deceptive similarity is a separate one from that of enquiring whether the applicant's use would constitute passing off. In a passing off context, consideration is given to the entirety of the defendant's conduct in the light of the plaintiff's actual reputation. In contrast, the test of deceptive similarity focuses on a comparison of the two trade marks and their potential use within the scope of their registration if both were registered.

This approach, in turn, eliminates from consideration a number of factors. For example, the applicant for registration cannot rely on the fact that it intends to target a different market sector from that targeted by the owner of the other trade mark. In *Berlei v Bali*,[191] the applicant for registration of Bali-bra argued that its trade mark would not be deceptively similar to the existing trade mark of Berlei for bras because its bras were expensive and Berlei bras were much cheaper. This argument, while relevant to a passing off claim, was not relevant to deceptive similarity because registration entitled Berlei to seek out the top end of the market and Bali-bra's registration would not be limited to expensive bras. Similarly, the use of a disclaimer while relevant to passing off would be irrelevant to the question as to whether two trade marks are deceptively similar.[192]

The existing reputation of either trade mark owner should be irrelevant to the issue.[193] Two cases appear to contradict that proposition but they, in turn, have also been questioned by case authority. In *Woolworths Ltd v Registrar of Trade Marks*,[194] the Full Federal Court had to consider whether the words 'Woolworths Metro' accompanied by a device of blue wavy lines was deceptively similar to an existing registration for 'Metro'. The Registrar argued that s 44 operated at the examination stage and did not involve evidence of the reputation of the trade marks. Consequently, the Registrar submitted that the reputation of Woolworths was irrelevant to the inquiry. However, the majority of the Full Court held that the considerable national notoriety of 'Woolworths' was highly relevant in comparing the two trade marks. A similar view was expressed by the Full Court in *The Coca-Cola Co v All-Fect Distributors Ltd*.[195] In that case, Coca-Cola sued for infringement of its trade mark of the two-dimensional representation of its well-known bottle when All-Fect sold a cola-flavoured confectionery with an arguably deceptively similar shape. In the course of identifying a number of factors relating to the issue of

---

191   *Berlei Hestia Industries v Bali Co Inc* (1973) 129 CLR 353.
192   See *Knott Investments Pty Ltd v Winnebago Industries Inc* (2013) 211 FCR 449 for an example where a disclaimer was accepted as avoiding misleading or deceptive conduct but trade mark infringement was not in question at the time of the decision.
193   M. Davison, 'Reputation in trade mark infringement: Why some courts think it matters and why it should not' (2010) 38 *Federal Law Review* 231.
194   (1998) 45 IPR 445, affirmed (1999) 45 IPR 411.
195   (1999) 96 FCR 107.

whether the two trade marks were deceptively similar, the Full Court added that the reputation of the Coca-Cola trade mark was a factor in deciding that the two were deceptively similar.

This aspect of both these decisions is questionable, at least to some degree. In the *Henschke* case,[196] which was decided after the *Woolworths* decision, the Full Court indicated that *Woolworths* was limited to its particular facts and that the principle espoused there would only be operative where the reputation was of such a nature and extent that judicial notice could be taken of the reputation. Even this acceptance of the relevance of the reputation of the trade mark may be going too far. Similarly, the reliance of the Full Court on the reputation of the Coca-Cola trade mark is highly questionable although there were clearly other aspects of the two trade marks that justified a finding of deceptive similarity in that case.

The issue has been addressed more recently by the Full Court in *Australian Meat Group Pty Ltd v JBS Australia Pty Ltd*,[197] albeit in the context of infringement proceedings, with the Full Court endorsing the decision in *Henchke*.

A more widely accepted point arising from the *Woolworths* decision is that the comparison must be between the two actual trade marks and not some abbreviation or diminutive of them. Consequently, the comparison was to be between the entire trade mark of Woolworths Metro with the device of wavy lines and Metro rather than just the words 'Woolworths Metro' and 'Metro'. A similar point was made in *SAP Australia Pty Ltd v Sapient Australia Pty Ltd*.[198]

15.21.4 Similar goods

If the two trade marks are substantially identical or deceptively similar, a further consideration is whether the goods of the two parties are similar, or if one party provides services and the other goods, the goods and services are closely related. Goods are similar if they are the same or they are of the same description as the other goods.[199]

As a general rule, there will be no difficulty in determining whether the goods in question are the same although the courts have tended to take a relatively narrow approach to this issue.[200] Consequently, they have not regarded rum to be the same product as a rum cocktail.[201]

The expression 'of the same description' is not defined in the legislation and resort must be had to case law on the topic. The basic test is whether purchasers would regard the goods as having the same trade origin if they were sold under the same or deceptively similar trade marks. While the class in which the goods are registered is relevant, it is quite possible for goods to be of the same description but not registered in the same class and also possible that they be registered in the same class but not be goods of the same description.

The case law has identified a number of criteria to refer to in determining the issue. The three most basic and most often cited criteria are those cited by Romer J in *Jelinnek's Application*,[202] namely:

---

196   *CA Henschke & Co v Rosemount Estates Pty Ltd* (2000) 52 IPR 42.
197   [2018] FCAFC 207.
198   (1999) 48 IPR 593.
199   *Trade Marks Act 1995* (Cth) s 14(1).
200   *Colorado Group Ltd v Strandbags Group Pty Ltd* (2007) 164 FCR 506.
201   *Daiquiri Rum Trade Mark* [1969] RPC 600.
202   (1946) 63 RPC 59.

- the nature of the goods;
- their uses; and
- the trade channels through which they are bought and sold.

These criteria were adopted by the High Court in *Southern Cross Refrigerating Co v Toowoomba Foundry Pty Ltd*,[203] although the court also pointed out that not all three criteria need to be present.[204] In that case, the High Court held that dairy farming milk refrigeration equipment and farm windmills were not goods of the same description even though they were sold through the same channels to the same customers.

In order to apply those three criteria, one can physically compare the goods and their physical characteristics. The case law suggests that the physical similarities need to be capable of being reasonably narrowly drawn. For example, just because two products are both edible is not in itself sufficient. Hence, edible oils and fats and margarine on the one hand have been held not to be of the same description as bread, yeast and bakery products.[205] On the other hand, soya bean–based extracts and beverages have been treated as being of the same description as processed vegetables.[206] Coffee, tea and cocoa within Class 30 have been treated as being of the same description as other similar beverages adapted for health promotion within Class 5, such as green tea, and beer and wine have been held to be goods of the same description.[207] Similarly, when considering the purpose or uses of the goods, it is not sufficient if the two goods are used in association with each other. For example, in the *Jelinnek* case itself, shoes and shoe polish were not considered to be goods of the same description.

When considering the trade channels through which they are bought and sold, several issues may be considered, including the following:

- whether the goods are likely to be made by the same manufacturer;
- whether they are likely to be distributed by the same wholesale houses;
- whether they are likely to be sold in the same shops, during the same seasons and to the same customers; and
- whether those in the trade regard the goods as being of the same description.

15.21.5 Similar services

There has been little judicial consideration of the term 'similar services'. As with goods, similar services are services that are the same or are of the same description.[208] *MID Sydney Pty Ltd v Australian Tourism Co Ltd*[209] makes it clear that the principles applied in relation to

---

203   (1954) 91 CLR 592.
204   Ibid 606.
205   *George Weston Foods Ltd v Peerless Holding Pty Ltd* (1999) 48 IPR 145.
206   *Sunrider Corp v Vitasoy International Holdings Ltd* [2009] ATMO 42.
207   *General Nutrition Investment Co v Little Vienna Pty Ltd* [2009] ATMO 44; *E & J Gallo Winery v Lion Nathan Australia Pty Ltd* (2009) 175 FCR 386.
208   *Trade Marks Act 1995* (Cth) s 14(2).
209   (1998) 90 FCR 236.

determining whether goods are of the same description should be adapted to the inquiry in relation to whether services are of the same description.

The decision adds the point that when comparing services, one should focus primarily on a comparison of the totality of the two services rather than the individual aspects of those services. In that case the relevant comparison was between the services of hotel management and management of office space. A number of aspects of the relevant services are identical. For example, both require the provision and maintenance of building infrastructure and services. On the other hand, one service focuses on the accommodation needs of short-term guests while the other focuses on the long-term needs of office tenants. Consequently, the Federal Court was of the view that the overriding differences between the two services meant that they were not of the same description. In addition, the court noted that the people who provided the two services were not from the same industry, thus reinforcing the court's conclusion.

Perhaps in contrast, there are decisions of the Registrar that have held that alcoholic beverage bar services and a discotheque are services of the same description[210] as are the reselling of computer hardware and computer software and systems services.[211] In both cases, the relevant consumers of the services would be the same and likely to seek them simultaneously. For example, a night out on the town may well involve a visit to a bar and a night club while someone in the market for a computer system would require both a supplier of hardware and a supplier of software and systems services.

15.21.6 Closely related goods and services

The concept of closely related goods and services acknowledges the relevance of the relationship between goods and services in consumers' consideration of whether particular goods and services may come from the same source. Usually, the service will involve some sort of interaction with the relevant goods, such as 'the installation, operation, maintenance or repair of' the allegedly closely related goods. Hence, coffins and funeral services are closely related as are the rental and maintenance of tractors.[212]

15.21.7 A global assessment

The final decision will depend on a combination of the two basic issues of similarity of the two trade marks and the nature of the goods or services in respect of which they are to be used. In *Woolworths Ltd v Registrar of Trade Marks*,[213] the two trade marks were considered somewhat deceptively similar for reasons already explained but the extent of that deception was not considered great. In addition, while the goods of Metro were considered closely related to the retailing services of Woolworths Metro's stores, again the degree of relation was not particularly close. Consequently, the combined deceptive similarity and closeness of relationship between the relevant goods and services was considered so low as to justify registration.

---

210   *Weller Hotels & Taverns Pty Ltd v TGI Friday's Inc* (1994) 30 IPR 631; *SPL Worldgroup (Australia) Pty Ltd v Shimmersea (Australia) Pty Ltd* (1998) 43 IPR 641.
211   *SPL Worldgroup (Australia) Pty Ltd v Shimmersea (Australia) Pty Ltd* (1998) 43 IPR 641.
212   *Caterpillar Inc v Amco (Vic) Pty Ltd* (2000) 49 IPR 407.
213   (1998) 45 IPR 445, affirmed (1999) 45 IPR 411.

French J expressed the issue this way when he said:

> In the end there is one practical judgment to be made. Whether any resemblance between different trade marks for goods and services renders them deceptively similar will depend upon the nature and degree of that resemblance and the closeness of the relationship between the services and the goods in question. It will not always be necessary to dissect that judgment into discrete and independent conclusions about the resemblance of marks and the relationship of goods and services.[214]

15.22 Honest concurrent user

Even if the trade mark offends s 44(1) or s 44(2), registration may still be permitted under either s 44(3) or s 44(4). Section 44(3) confers a discretion on the Registrar to accept the application of an honest concurrent user of a substantially identical or deceptively similar trade mark.[215] This provision is an example of the willingness of the registered trade mark system to tolerate some actual or potential confusion or deception in order to accommodate the property interests of trade mark owners.

'Honesty' in this context means that the applicant is not seeking to trade off the reputation or goodwill of the existing registered person.[216] The applicant may know of the registered trade mark and its use by the registered owner but that will not in itself dispel a finding of honesty. If it did, one letter to the applicant would deprive it of the necessary honesty.

Honesty is necessary but not sufficient to justify registration.[217] Once the Registrar is satisfied that there has been honest concurrent use of the two trade marks, regard will be had to a number of factors, such as:

- the extent of use by both parties;
- the degree of likelihood of confusion;
- the balance of convenience; and
- other special circumstances, including the effect of any conditions or limitations that the Registrar might impose on the applicant's registration.

For example, in *Alexander Pirie & Sons Ltd's Application*,[218] the court took account of the fact that the applicant had developed its business quite substantially while the existing registrant's business had not grown for some time. This disparity in the extent of the use by the two parties outweighed other considerations, such as the degree of likelihood of confusion. Hence, the court was prepared to accept the registration of both 'Abbermill' and 'Hammermill' for stationery as the balance of convenience favoured the applicant. On the other hand, the actual

---

214 *Registrar of Trade Marks v Woolworths Ltd* (1999) 45 IPR 411.
215 If the trade marks are identical and the application is in respect of the same goods or services, the issue then becomes one of ownership, and registration pursuant to *Trade Marks Act 1995* (Cth) s 44(3) would be impossible.
216 *Tivo Inc v Vivo International Corp Pty Ltd* [2012] FCA 252 and on appeal in *Vivo International Corp Pty Ltd v Tivo Inc* [2012] FCAFC 159.
217 *PB Foods Ltd v Malanda Dairy Foods Ltd* (1999) 47 IPR 47.
218 [1933] All ER 956.

use need not be great although it will be compared to the use of the first registered trade mark. In *PB Foods Ltd v Malanda Dairy Foods Ltd*,[219] the registrant had only used its trade mark concurrently for five weeks but the first registered trade mark had only been used for ten, thus negating the argument that the extent of the applicant's use did not justify registration.

In *Brook v Canon Kabushiki Kaisha*,[220] the Registrar was prepared to tolerate a quite considerable degree of likelihood of confusion when accepting 'Cannon' despite the pre-existing registration for 'Canon' and rejecting the argument that potential purchasers would easily differentiate between the two because one was the name of a piece of artillery while the other was the name of a Church law.[221] Again, other factors weighed the balance of convenience in the applicant's favour. In particular, while the existing 'Canon' was widely used in relation to cameras and other products, it had not been widely used in relation to goods of the same description as those in respect of which application was sought. Consequently, the applicant's greater use of its trade mark in respect of those goods weighed in its favour.

On the other hand, some market circumstances might suggest that while the two trade marks may appear to be deceptively similar, the particular purchasers of the products in question may not necessarily be deceived. In *Totally and Permanently Disabled Soldiers' Association v Australian Federation of Totally and Permanently Incapacitated Ex-Service Men & Women Ltd*,[222] the Registrar permitted the honest concurrent registration application by the Australian TPI Federation of a trade mark that included the words 'TPI' and 'Totally and Permanently Disabled Soldiers' Association'. This was done in the face of an existing trade mark with the same letters and words that had been registered by the TPD Association because there was a long history of acrimony between the two separate associations that both represented permanently and disabled soldiers. As those likely to rely on the trade marks would be well aware of the two separate organisations, the likelihood of actual confusion would be relatively small and it would also be inappropriate to favour one organisation over the other given their history. In *Western Australia's Application*,[223] consideration was given to the fact that registration was being sought for a Black Swan device and the Black Swan is an emblem of Western Australia.

As s 44(3) permits the Registrar to impose conditions and limitations on the honest concurrent use, this will also be relevant in determining whether to exercise the discretion to register the trade mark. For example, in *PB Foods Ltd v Malanda Dairy Foods Ltd*,[224] the applicant had used 'Choc Chill' for flavoured milk in Western Australia from April 1992 but the opponent had used 'Chill' for the same product in Queensland from late February 1992. The Registrar imposed a condition that the registration of 'Choc Chill' be restricted to Western Australia.

---

219   (1999) 47 IPR 47.
220   (1994) 30 IPR 525.
221   This decision was later altered in *Canon Kabushiki Kaisha v Brook* (1996) 69 FCR 401 on the grounds that the goods in question were not goods of the same description. Hence s 44 did not apply and the initial decision to permit registration was therefore affirmed.
222   (2001) 52 IPR 626.
223   (1934) AOJP 557.
224   (1999) 47 IPR 47.

The discretion might also be exercised by limiting the description of goods for which honest concurrent registration is permitted. An example of that occurring was *Caesarstone Ltd v Ceramiche Caesar SpA (No 2)*.[225]

While the Registrar has a discretion to register pursuant to s 44(3), the discretion only gives the Registrar the capacity to override objections to registration on the basis of either s 44(1) or s 44(2). There may still be objections to registration on the basis of other sections, such as s 60 or s 58. For example, it is not clear how two different parties could both be treated as the owners of exactly the same registered trade mark for exactly the same goods or services. On the other hand, s 58A only operates to oppose a registration based on s 44(4) which is discussed in the next section. The fact that an opponent might have first used a deceptively similar or substantially identical trade mark will not prevent the operation of s 44(3).[226]

15.23 Prior continuous user

Section 44(4) applies if the Registrar is satisfied that the applicant or its predecessor in title has continuously used their trade mark on similar goods or closely related services since before the priority date for the registration of the other trade mark. If the Registrar is so satisfied, the registration cannot be rejected because of the mere existence of the other trade mark although there may still be difficulties flowing from other sections, such as s 60. In order to be successful, the applicant must demonstrate that its use has been continuous and that continuous use has been in relation to the goods or services for which it is seeking registration.

What constitutes continuous use will depend on the nature of the goods or services offered and standard market conditions but the user has to do more than show they have not abandoned their trade mark.[227] For example, in infringement proceedings in *Hy-Line Chicks Pty Ltd v Swifte*,[228] the defendant relied on the equivalent defence of prior continuous user because it had sold eggs and dressed poultry under its trade mark of 'Hi-Line' for several years prior to the priority date of registration of the plaintiff's 'Hy-Line'. However, its sales of live poultry only commenced after the plaintiff's priority date and so the defence was only applicable in respect of eggs and dressed poultry.

While s 44(4) does not expressly confer a discretion on the Registrar to impose conditions or limitations, case law under previous legislation suggests that the Registrar is free to exercise the general powers to do so pursuant to s 33 or s 55.[229] Consequently, the registration could be restricted to the particular geographical area where the prior continuous user has operated. This approach is probably justified on the basis that s 44(4) restricts the Registrar to not relying on the existence of the existing trade mark as a ground for rejecting the application of the prior continuous user. Therefore, it does not address any issues associated with the reputation of that other trade mark or issues such as the extent of its use. These issues, which are external to the operation of s 44(4), may justify the imposition of conditions or limitations.

---

225 [2018] FCA 1096.
226 *Caesarstone Ltd v Ceramiche Caesar SpA (No 2)* [2018] FCA 1096.
227 *Smith Bartlet & Co v British Pure Oil Grease & Carbide Co Ltd* (1934) 51 RPC 157.
228 (1966) 115 CLR 159.
229 *John Fitton & Co Ltd's Application* (1949) 66 RPC 110; *Hy-Line Chicks Pty Ltd v Swifte* (1966) 115 CLR 159.

15.24 Other legislation

There are a number of other pieces of legislation that relate to the registration and/or use of business indicia. Each piece of legislation needs to be carefully considered to identify the rights conferred by the legislation and the relationship of those rights to the trade mark legislation.

15.24.1 Protection of sporting events

Much of the relevant legislation is specifically enacted to provide protection for indicia associated with major sporting events. For example, specific legislation was enacted for the purposes of the Sydney Olympics and the Melbourne Commonwealth Games.[230] The legislation identifies particular indicia associated with the particular event. It then imposes certain restrictions on the use of those indicia, such as any use that would suggest that the user is sponsoring the event in question.

Similarly, the *Australian Grand Prix Act 1994* (Vic) protects Grand Prix indicia, including the expressions 'Grand Prix', 'Formula One', 'What a Great Place for the Race' and 'What a Great Place for the Great Race'. Only the Grand Prix Corporation may supply or authorise for supply goods marked with Grand Prix insignia or use Grand Prix insignia for the purpose of promoting the supply of goods or services or assume a name or description that includes Grand Prix insignia. Similar legislation existed in Queensland in respect of the Indy Race that was run on the Gold Coast for some years. That legislation even went so far as to confer property rights to the relevant organising body over illegal merchandise by giving the body the right to sue for conversion.

15.24.2 Business names

One of the related forms of legislation that creates the greatest confusion is business name legislation.[231] The greatest error made in relation to the registration of a business name is the assumption that such registration confers rights on the registrant. It does not.[232] It merely provides immunity from prosecution for failing to register a business name.[233] Prior to the passing of Commonwealth legislation on the issue, each state and territory had its own legislation[234] that required business operators to register their business name if they intended to use a business name other than their own.

---

230 *Sydney 2000 Games (Indicia and Images) Protection Act 1996* (Cth); *Commonwealth Games Arrangements Act 2001* (Vic); and more generally *Olympic Insignia Protection Act 1987* (Cth) and amending legislation of 1994. For further reference, see T. Altobelli, 'Learning the lessons of history: Disputes and the Olympic Games' (1999) 22 *University of New South Wales Law Journal* 843; J. Sebel and D. Gyngell, 'Protecting Olympic gold: Ambush marketing and other threats to Olympic symbols and indicia' (1999) 22 *University of New South Wales Law Journal* 691.
231 Business names are governed by federal law, in the form of the *Business Names Registration Act 2011* (Cth).
232 *Business Names Registration Act 2011* (Cth) s 17.
233 Ibid s 18.
234 *Business Names Act 1963* (ACT); *Business Names Act 2002* (NSW); *Business Names Act 1963* (NT); *Business Names Act 1962* (Qld); *Business Names Act 1996* (SA); *Business Names Act 1962* (Tas); *Business Names Act 1962* (Vic); *Business Names Act 1962* (WA).

The Commonwealth legislation mirrors the intent of the previous state and territory legislation but does away with the inconvenience of having to register a business name in multiple jurisdictions. The basic objective behind business names legislation is to ensure that parties dealing with an entity that uses a business name know or can easily ascertain the identity of the legal entity or entities behind the business name. For example, if one is dealing with XYZ Plumbing, that name does not reveal whether one is dealing with a sole trader, a partnership or a company and, if so, the identity of that sole trader, partnership or company. Searchable business name registration provides that information to the public.

Letters of demand to other traders that assert any positive right flowing from business name registration are based on a fundamental error. Several cases have involved injunctions preventing registrants from continuing to trade under the relevant name and requiring them to relinquish their business name registration when the continued use of that business name would involve deception.[235]

There are two indirect benefits from registration of a business name that may assist a registrant. One is the impact that registration has on the right to obtain registration of a '.com .au' domain name. Under the rules relating to entitlement to such domain names, the registration of a business name is one basis on which an applicant can claim a particular '.com.au' domain name.[236] The other potential benefit is that registration may be of some small, limited evidentiary value in demonstrating that a business has been operating for a particular period of time and that, in turn, may be relevant in passing off proceedings or to provide minimal assistance to support a claim of first use of a trade mark.

15.24.3 Wine Australia Act 2013

In 1993, Australia introduced legislation relating to European Union and Australian geographical indications for wine. The legislation lists a large number of European and Australian geographical indications for wines and either prohibits their use on wine that does not originate from the relevant region or sets out a time frame for phasing out their use. For example, geographical indications such as 'Burgundy' may no longer be used on Australian wines. In 2010, further amendments to sch 1 of the *Australian Wine and Brandy Corporation Regulations 2010* (Cth) (as it then was) were made relating to other geographical indications, including 'champagne', 'port' and 'sherry'.

The rights conferred on these geographical indications for wine are over and above the rights conferred on all geographical indications by the *Trade Marks Act 1995* (Cth). For example, the Act preserves the position of traders who have continuously used a geographical indication since before the introduction of the Act.[237] No such concession was made to wine growers under the *Australian Wine and Brandy Corporation Amendment Act 1993* (Cth) (as

---

235   *Lone Star Steakhouse & Saloon Inc v Zurcas* (2000) 48 IPR 325; *Caterpillar Loader Hire (Holdings) Pty Ltd v Caterpillar Tractor Co* (1983) 77 FLR 139; *Franconi Holdings Ltd v Gunning* (1982) 1 SR (WA) 341; *Australian Marketing Development Pty Ltd v Australian Interstate Marketing Pty Ltd* [1972] VR 219; *JH Coles Pty Ltd v Need* (1933) 49 CLR 499 .
236   See .au Domain Administration, *Domain Name Eligibility and Allocation Policy Rules for the Open 2LDs* (Policy No 2005-01, 2005) www.auda.org.au. For further reference, see A. Grant, 'Cybersquatting: The case of famous marks' (2001) 14 *Australian Intellectual Property Law Bulletin* 92.
237   *Trade Marks Act 1995* (Cth) s 61(2)(c).

it then was). In *Comite Interprofessionnel des Vins des Cotes de Provence v Bryce*,[238] a Tasmanian wine grower was required to cease his use of the term 'Provence' in respect of his Tasmanian wines despite having used the term for many years. The relevant legislation is now titled the *Wine Australia Act 2013* (Cth).

15.24.4 Protection for particular industries

Some particular industries also have specific legislation protecting their indicia. For example, s 66 of the *Banking Act 1959* (Cth) prohibits the use of terms such as 'bank', 'banker' and 'banking' by anyone running a financial business unless they have the approval of the Australian Prudential Regulation Authority to do so. More recently, the Victorian government conferred exclusive rights over the word 'casino' when it enacted the *Gaming Machine Control (Amendment) Act 1993* (Vic). This legislation prevents the use of the word 'casino' by any business involved in gaming, such as the provision of poker machines, except for Crown Casino, which paid a substantial licence fee for its right to establish a casino in Victoria.

15.25 Overview of grounds of opposition

If an application is accepted after examination by the Registrar, any person has the opportunity of opposing the registration of the trade mark. The grounds of opposition to registration are identified in div 2 of Part 5 of the Act. The rationale for some grounds being grounds of opposition but not grounds for rejection by the Registrar at the examination stage is relatively straightforward. The nature of the inquiries made by the Registrar at the time of examination is primarily restricted to matters that can be resolved by reference to the application itself, the Register and matters of general knowledge. For example, distinctiveness can be assessed by reference to the application and supporting evidence from the applicant of use or intended use.

Opposition proceedings often involve issues such as the opponent providing evidence of the actual reputation of its trade mark, which is relevant to provisions such as s 60. However, opponents are also able to challenge the Registrar's view that a trade mark application should be accepted and all bar one of the grounds for the Registrar rejecting an application may also be grounds for opposition.

The grounds of opposition are as follows:

- The ground is any of the grounds on which the Registrar may reject an application, except the requirement that the trade mark be capable of being graphically represented, which is exclusively within the remit of the Registrar (s 57). These grounds have been discussed above in relation to the requirements for registration.[239]
- The applicant is not the owner of the trade mark (s 58) or, if the applicant relied on s 44(4) (prior continuous user), the opponent establishes that the applicant was not a prior

---

238 (1996) 69 FCR 450.
239 At 15.14 to 15.21.

continuous user within the meaning of s 44(4) (s 58A). The issue of ownership was addressed above.[240]
- The applicant is not intending to use the trade mark (s 59). This issue was discussed above[241] in relation to the definition of a trade mark.
- The trade mark is substantially identical with or deceptively similar to another trade mark that has acquired a reputation in Australia and because of that reputation, the use of the applicant's trade mark would be likely to deceive or cause confusion (s 60).
- The trade mark contains or consists of a sign that is a geographical indication for goods and none of the exceptions in s 61 are applicable (s 61).
- The application or supporting documentation was amended contrary to the Act and the Registrar accepted the application for registration on the basis of evidence or representations that were false in material particulars (s 62).
- The application was made in bad faith (s 62A).

15.26   Another trade mark's prior reputation: s 60

Section 60 prevents registration because 'another trade mark had before the priority date ... acquired a reputation in Australia and because of [that] reputation ... the use of the applicant's trade mark would be likely to deceive or cause confusion'. The section overlaps s 44 but it contains some key differences that can be quickly identified. These overlaps and differences mean that some applications for registration will be caught by both provisions while others may be caught by one but not by the other.

The first key difference between s 44 and s 60 is that the opponent's trade mark need not be registered in Australia or indeed anywhere in the world although it may be registered. The only requirement is that the trade mark has a reputation in Australia. It may even be possible that the trade mark has not been used in Australia but has a 'slop over' reputation. In *Radio Corp Pty Ltd v Disney*,[242] the applicant was denied registration of 'Mickey Mouse' and 'Minnie Mouse' for radio sets and kits although Walt Disney had not himself used the trade marks in Australia.

A second key point is that likelihood of deception or confusion must flow from the actual reputation of the opponent's trade mark when compared with the potential use within the scope of the registration that is being sought. This differs from s 44, which is more focused on the potential uses of the two trade marks within the scope of the registration. Section 60 is focused on what the opponent has in fact done with their trade mark to date and the reputation flowing from that use. A weak reputation will not be sufficient to establish a likelihood of deception or confusion.[243]

---

240   At 15.9.
241   At 15.7.
242   (1937) 57 CLR 448.
243   *Anchorage Capital Partners Pty Ltd v ACPA Pty Ltd* [2018] FCAFC 6.

A related point is that the use of the opponent's trade mark and its consequent reputation need not relate to goods or services that are similar to or closely related to the goods or services for which registration is being sought by the applicant. While s 60 is therefore broader than s 44 in this respect, it still remains the case that the goods or services for which the reputation exists will be relevant to the question of whether the applicant's use of its trade mark would be likely to deceive or cause confusion. For example, the opponent's reputation may be strong and there may be wide consumer awareness of it but the reputation may be restricted to a relatively small range of goods or services. Of course, some trade marks may be sufficiently well known, even in respect of only one product, that their reputation may lead to the conclusion that almost any use of the trade mark would be likely to deceive or cause confusion. The extensive defensive registrations conferred on 'Viagra'[244] indicate such a possibility. So too does the decision in *Twentieth Century Fox Film Corp v Die Hard*[245] in which 'Die Hard' was rejected for optical goods, surfboards and skateboards, items well removed from the setting of the *Die Hard* movie.

On the other hand, if the reputation is both strong and broad in the sense that it relates to a range of goods, consumers may more quickly be caused to wonder whether there is a relationship of some kind between the users of the two trade marks in question. The *Toowoomba Foundry*[246] case exemplifies the point. In that case, the opponent had an established reputation for 'Southern Cross' in respect of a variety of goods, such as milking machinery and well-drilling equipment. While the applicant's goods, refrigeration equipment, were not considered to be goods of the same description and therefore the statutory equivalent of s 44 under previous legislation was not applicable, the opponent's reputation in respect of a wide variety of goods was sufficient to deny registration.

The decision also demonstrates that even where goods are not of the same description, there will be an issue as to the degree to which they are unrelated. In that case, while the High Court ultimately decided that the goods in question were not of the same description there was a detailed analysis of the issue, and the degree of difference between the goods, while sufficient to conclude that they were not of the same description, was not particularly great. For example, both sets of products were sold via the same trade channels to the same customers. This degree of similarity, while not sufficient to bring the previous equivalent of s 44 into play, did influence the application of the then equivalent of s 60.

In contrast, in *Notaras v Barcelona Pty Ltd*,[247] the use of 'Atomic' for coffee machines did not present a problem for use of Atomic for coffee beans and other related coffee items as the goods were considered significantly different. Coffee machines are relatively expensive items and specialist in nature as opposed to consumable items such as coffee beans.

The definition of 'likely' in this context means 'a real, tangible possibility'[248] and not the civil standard of proof of 'more likely than not'. The reference to 'confusion' means that it will

---

244   See above at 15.12.
245   (2001) 52 IPR 455.
246   *Southern Cross Refrigerating Co v Toowoomba Foundry Pty Ltd* (1954) 91 CLR 592.
247   [2019] FCA 4
248   *Registrar of Trade Marks v Woolworths Ltd* (1999) 45 IPR 411, 426 (French J).

be sufficient if consumers, having regard to the actual reputation of the opponent and the potential use of the trade mark by the applicant, might be caused to wonder if the products of two traders are associated.[249]

Further, the trade mark for which registration is being sought may already have a reputation in Australia at the time of the application for registration. This will not necessarily mean that the application will escape s 60. It is possible that the opponent and the applicant both have a reputation in Australia. The opponent's reputation need not be an exclusive reputation in order for confusion to be likely to arise if the applicant uses its trade mark.[250] Finally, due to amendments introduced by the *Trade Marks Amendment Act 2006* (Cth), the two trade marks in question need not be substantially identical or deceptively similar. Obviously, the degree of similarity between the trade marks will be relevant to whether the applicant's use would be likely to deceive or cause confusion but the degree of similarity will be but one issue in determining the ultimate question. It is possible, for example, that a pre-existing well-known trade mark may have such a reputation that the use of a later trade mark that is not substantially identical or deceptively similar may still be likely to deceive or cause confusion.

15.26.1 Relationship with honest concurrent user and prior continuous user provisions

Neither s 60 nor s 44(3) or (4) makes any direct reference to the relationship between s 60 and the honest concurrent user and prior continuous user provisions. While the issue was never fully resolved under the previous legislation, the balance of authority[251] and the common law history of the defence of honest concurrent use suggested that the provision under the previous legislation was subject to the honest concurrent use provisions. The position under the Act is different. Kenny J in *McCormick & Co Inc v McCormick*[252] held that the provisions in s 44 could not be used to overcome an opposition to registration based on s 60.[253] In particular, Kenny J noted that the two provisions are in quite different parts of the Act. Section 44 relates primarily to the examination stage and the similarity between two trade marks to be used in respect of similar goods, while s 60 relates to the opposition stage and a comparison of the opponent's reputation with the applicant's trade mark application.

The Trade Marks Legislation Review recommended an amendment to s 60 to allow honest concurrent and/or prior use as a basis for permitting registration in the face of s 60, but that has not been implemented to date.[254]

---

249 *Southern Cross Refrigerating Co v Toowoomba Foundry Pty Ltd* (1954) 91 CLR 592, 608.
250 *Optical 88 Ltd v Optical 88 Pty Ltd (No 2)* (2010) 275 ALR 526.
251 See *McCormick & Co Inc v McCormick* (1998) 42 IPR 515 for a discussion of previous case law on the point.
252 (2001) 51 IPR 102.
253 See *Optical 88 Ltd v Optical 88 Pty Ltd (No 2)* (2010) 275 ALR 526, [187], which followed the decision in *McCormick & Co Inc v McCormick* (1998) 42 IPR 515.
254 IP Australia, *Trade Marks Legislation Review* (Paper 3, September 2004) 12.

15.27 Geographical indications: s 61

This provision was introduced as a requirement of *TRIPS* to provide specific protection for geographical indications. In addition, there is other legislation relating to the protection of geographical indications for Australian and European geographical indications for wine.[255]

15.27.1 Definition of a geographical indication

Section 6 defines a geographical indication 'in relation to goods originating in a particular country or in a region or locality of that country' as meaning

> a sign recognised in that country as a sign indicating that the goods:
>
> (a) originated in that country, region or locality; and
> (b) have a quality, reputation or other characteristic attributable to their geographical origin.

A few points can be made about the definition. First, the definition refers to 'signs' not just words. Consequently, while most geographical indications are words, any sign could act as a geographical indication. Second, the definition relates only to goods, not services. Third, the geographical indication need only be recognised in the country from which the goods in relation to which it is used originate. It need not be recognised in Australia as a geographical indication here. So the possibility arises that a trade mark may be opposed on the basis that it contains or consists of a geographical indication from overseas even if it is not known at all in Australia. However, the 'recognition' in question must be some formal recognition by the legal system of that country. It is not sufficient that the term is regarded by consumers or the relevant industry as a geographical indication. Consequently, there either needs to be some form of registration as a geographical indication or case law that recognises the geographical indication.[256]

Finally, there are some difficult aspects of the definition of geographical indication that need to be kept in mind. It is necessary, but not sufficient, that the sign indicate the geographical origin of the goods. It must also indicate that the goods have some 'quality, reputation or other characteristic attributable to their geographical origin'. The goods must be known for that quality, reputation or characteristic and the sign in question must indicate it. For example, 'Burgundy' indicates a wine from the Burgundy region of France and 'Edam' may indicate a type of cheese from Edam in the Netherlands but 'French' for wine and 'Dutch' for cheese are not likely to be geographical indications because there is no specific quality, reputation or other characteristic attributable to their geographical origin. The point is further exemplified by

---

255 *Wine Australia Act 2013* (Cth). For further reference, see M. Davison, C. Henckels and P. Emerton. '*In vino veritas*: The dubious legality of the EU's claims to the exclusive use of the term "Prosecco"' (2019) 29(3) *Australian Intellectual Property Journal* 110; S. Stern, 'The conflict between geographical indications and trade marks: Australia once again heads down the garden path' (2005) 61 *Intellectual Property Forum* 28; M. Handler, 'The EU's geographical indications agenda and its potential impact on Australia' (2004) 15 *Australian Intellectual Property Journal* 173.

256 *Bavaria NV v Bayerischer Brauerbund eV* (2009) 177 FCR 300.

the decision in *Esteban Zone Industrielle v Digital Crown Holdings*,[257] in which the Registrar rejected the argument that Paris was a geographical indication for perfume. It therefore becomes critical to the existence and recognition of the geographical indication that the users of it be able to provide evidence of the specific characteristics of their product attributable to the relevant geographical area. For this reason, the vast majority of geographical indications relate to food or wine where the argument can be and is made that the food or wine has unique characteristics because of the climate, soil or combination of both in the relevant geographical area.

On the other hand, the reference to 'reputation' in the definition means that human factors can be the necessary characteristic if the reputation in question is one based on human activity in such a way that the reputation is associated with a particular region. Examples might be 'Swiss' for watches or 'Sheffield' for cutlery.

15.27.2 Interpretation

In addition to the difficulties with the definition of a geographical indication, there are potential problems with the wording of s 61. Section 61(1) provides that opposition may be based on the ground that the trade mark contains or consists of a sign that is a geographical indication for goods originating in an area other than the area from which the trade mark applicant's goods originate. Two main points need to be made. First, s 61(1) only refers to a trade mark that contains or consists of a sign that is a geographical indication, not to a sign that may also be substantially identical with or deceptively similar to that geographical indication. In *Bavaria NV v Bayerischer Bauerbund eV*,[258] the applicant wished to register the words 'Bavaria Holland' together with a device mark for beer and the opponent had rights in Germany in relation to the term 'Bayerisches Bier', registered in the European Union as a geographical indication for beer. Bayerisches Bier means Bavarian beer in English but the lack of identity between the applicant's trade mark and the opponent's geographical indication was held to be fateful to opposition under s 61. Second, if the goods of the trade mark applicant do actually originate from the same geographical area as the goods associated with the geographical indication, the wording of s 61(1) suggests that it would not be grounds for opposing registration. Hence, Edam for cheese that is actually from Edam could not be successfully opposed on the basis of s 61. This suggestion is confirmed by s 61(2), which provides that the opposition fails if the application establishes that the relevant goods originated in the place identified by the geographical indication. Of course, other provisions, particularly s 41 and its requirement for distinctiveness, may still operate to prevent the registration of the trade mark.

A strict reading of the original s 61(1) would have meant that an opposition could have been maintained even if the trade mark was being sought for goods other than those for which the geographical indication is known. The *Trade Marks Amendment Act 2006* (Cth) changed that situation such that the opposition could only be successful if the geographical indication in question is used for goods that are similar to the goods in respect of which registration is sought. In addition, the legislation amended the meaning of 'originate' in the context of wine or

---

257   (2004) 64 IPR 122.
258   (2009) 177 FCR 300.

spirits to bring the definition into line with the definition in the *Australian Grape and Wine Authority Act 2013 (Cth)* (now the *Wine Australia Act 2013* (Cth)).

15.27.3 Exceptions

There are a number of exceptions to s 61(1) contained in sub-ss (2) and (3). Section 61(2)(b) and (c) provides that the opposition will fail if the sign has ceased to be used as a geographical indication in the country from where goods indicated by the geographical indication originated. Section 61(2)(c) constitutes a 'grandfathering' provision that preserves the rights of users of the sign in good faith prior to 1 January 1996 (the date of implementation of *TRIPS* requirements in Australia) or prior to the day the sign was recognised as a geographical indication in its country of origin, whichever is the later.

Some of the points made above can be demonstrated by reference to the facts in a decision under the previous legislation. In *Cantarella Brothers Pty Ltd v Kona Coffee Roastery & Equipment Supplies Pty Ltd*,[259] an existing registrant for 'Vittoria' for coffee objected to the use of 'Kona Coffee Vitoria Blend' for coffee. An infringement action was brought under the previous legislation, which contained no reference to geographical indications. The defendant, perhaps curiously, conceded that it was using 'Vitoria' as a trade mark but claimed that it had a defence on the grounds that it was using the term to describe the character or quality of its goods. In particular, it argued that as its coffee came from the Brazilian region near the port of Vitoria, the word was descriptive of the character of its coffee. Einfeld J rejected the argument because 'Vitoria' had no descriptive significance in Australia as few, if any, Australians were familiar with the term as describing a type of Brazilian coffee.

Under the current Act, the arguments may have been different. 'Vitoria' would be arguably a geographical indication for coffee in Brazil although it would have to be formally recognised as such in Brazil by the Brazilian legal system. However, its lack of recognition in Australia would be irrelevant to its capacity to prevent registration of 'Vitoria' for coffee in respect of coffee not from that region. On the other hand, a literal reading of s 61 would lead to the conclusion that it could not prevent the registration of 'Vitoria' for coffee because the two words are not the same although they are substantially identical. In addition, the prior use of 'Vitoria' would save its registration under the grandfathering provisions of s 61.

15.28 Application made in bad faith

Section 62A makes it possible to oppose an application made in bad faith. The precise scope of this ground of opposition is not entirely clear, either in Australia or in the European Community,[260] and it may overlap with other grounds of opposition, such as a lack of intention to use the trade mark.[261] Examples of bad faith applications given in the Explanatory Memorandum to

---

259 (1993) 28 IPR 176.
260 For example, *Gromax Plasticulture Ltd v Don & Low Nonwovens Ltd* [1999] RPC 367, where Lindsay J declined to define the concept but did say at 379 that it 'includes dishonesty and also dealings that fall short of the standards of acceptable commercial behaviour'. In *Demon Ale Trade Mark* [2000] RPC 345, Hobbs QC said that it can involve behaviour that 'otherwise involves no breach of any duty, obligation, prohibition or requirement that is legally binding'.
261 *Home Box Office Inc v Florenca* (2010) 90 IPR 164.

the amending legislation are where the applicant identifies an overseas trade mark, registers it and then immediately seeks to sell it to the overseas owner. Alternatively, they monitor new business activities and register trade marks identical with or similar to the names used for those activities with the intention of threatening the business operation with trade mark infringement.[262]

There have been a number of Trade Mark Office decisions relating to the provision. In *Hard Coffee Pty Ltd v Hard Coffee Main Beach Pty Ltd*,[263] the Hearing Officer found that the s 62A ground had been made out where an applicant sought registration of trade marks that were deceptively similar to business names of the vendor of a business the applicant had purchased. The contract of sale expressly reserved for the vendor intellectual property rights in the relevant business names:

> For an assessment of 'bad faith' as it applies to such a situation it would appear that there would need to be an element of intentional dishonesty or a deliberate attempt to mislead the Registrar in some way in the claim made by means of the application.[264]

However, while actual dishonesty will be sufficient for a finding of bad faith, it does not appear to be a necessary condition. It seems that the test is a combination of objective and subjective factors.[265] It would be sufficient if a reasonable person in the position of the applicant would be aware that they should not apply for the trade mark. For example, in *Bombala Council v Peter Wilkshire*,[266] the applicant applied to register trade marks despite the fact that he had agreed in settlement terms relating to Federal Court litigation not to interfere with the opponent's rights to the trade marks in question.

This proposition seems to have been confirmed by the Federal Court in *Fry Consulting Pty Ltd v Sports Warehouse Inc (No 2)*:

> The words 'bad faith' suggest a mental state. Clearly when considering the question of whether an application to register is made in bad faith all the circumstances will be relevant. However the court must decide whether the knowledge of the applicant was such that his decision to apply for registration would be regarded as in bad faith by persons adopting proper standards.[267]

In that case, aspects of the applicant's conduct were considered to be consistent with bad faith, including the adoption of a trade mark that was knowingly very similar to the opponent's trade mark. However, a written offer to cease use if the opponent provided evidence of its exclusive entitlement to use of its trade mark was not responded to in any meaningful time and the applicant also made some slight alterations to its trade mark by adding a logo device and the word 'Australia'. On balance, the finding was that the opponent had therefore not met its onus

---

262 Explanatory Memorandum, Trade Marks Amendment Bill 2006 (Cth) cl 4.12.
263 [2009] ATMO 26.
264 Ibid [11].
265 *Fry Consulting Pty Ltd v Sports Warehouse Inc (No 2)* (2012) 201 FCR 565, [147] ff.
266 [2009] ATMO 33.
267 (2012) 201 FCR 565, [26].

of demonstrating bad faith. Similarly, in *Dunlop Aircraft Tyres Ltd v The Goodyear Tire & Rubber Co*, the fact that the applicant had requested a licence of the relevant trade marks was not in itself evidence of bad faith given that the applicant also sought the removal of the existing registration of the trade marks for non-use.[268]

On the other hand, in *Clipsal Australia Pty Ltd v Clipso Electrical Pty Ltd (No 3)*,[269] the applicant sought to register Clipso in a market where Clipsal was a well-known trade mark. The applicant was held to be acting dishonestly, thus meeting and exceeding the element of subjectivity required. In addition, the conduct met the objective requirement of being something falling short of acceptable commercial behaviour.[270]

15.29 Overview of rectification of the Register

Once registered, a trade mark entry on the Register may be amended or cancelled in circumstances prescribed in Part 8 of the Act. Some of the circumstances are such that the Registrar may make the relevant decision to amend or cancel whereas other circumstances are exclusively within the consideration of the courts.

15.30 Amendment or cancellation by the Registrar

Division 1 of Part 8 permits the Registrar to make the following amendments or cancellations:

- The Registrar may correct any errors or omissions made in entering any particular in the Register (s 81).
- The Registrar may amend the Register as required as a consequence of any change in the classification of goods or services for the purposes of the Act (s 82).
- The Registrar may agree to amend the representation of the trade mark if it does not substantially affect the identity of the originally registered trade mark (s 83(1)(a)).
- At the written request of a registered owner, the Registrar may agree to various types of small amendments to particulars concerning any goods or services in respect of which the trade mark is registered (s 83(1)(b)) and other particulars relating to the trade mark (s 83(1)(c)) provided they do not have the effect of extending the rights of the registered owner apart from those amendments.
- The Registrar may make amendments required in order for use of the trade mark to be consistent with any Australian obligation under an international agreement when that obligation did not exist at the time of registration (s 83A).

---

268   [2018] FCA 1014.
269   [2017] FCA 60.
270   Ibid [97].

- The Registrar must cancel the registration of a trade mark if the registered owner requests it (s 84).
- As a consequence of the *Intellectual Property Laws Amendment Act 2006* (Cth), the Registrar has a broad power to cancel any registration within twelve months of that registration (s 84A).

The circumstances in which the Registrar alters the Register are relatively rare. Most of the case law surrounding decisions by the Registrar relates to applications for amendment of the representation of the trade mark. As a general rule, these applications under the present and previous legislation have been declined as the Registrar takes a strict approach to whether alterations to the representation affect the identity of the originally registered trade mark. The concern here is that any change may lead to conflict with other trade marks. In addition, the alteration may inappropriately bypass the examination process and indirectly confer an extended priority date. In *Lawson's Application*,[271] a request to alter the propeller device within a trade mark was rejected because the new representation would not be easily recognised as a propeller device, 'but something that eludes a precise description ... It follows, of course, that the altered mark could be in conflict with other marks on the Register or those awaiting registration'.[272] Decisions under previous legislation took a similar approach.

Amendments of particulars relating to any goods or services are usually undertaken when the owner wishes to limit its existing registration. For example, a registration for desks, tables and chairs might be restricted to business desks and business chairs but could not be extended to 'furniture'.

As the trade mark is the exclusive property of the owner, the owner is entitled to abandon that property by requiring the Registrar to remove the trade mark from the Register. An owner may wish to deregister a trade mark as part of a settlement of actual or pending litigation, such as an application for removal for non-use or rectification. Alternatively, it may simply wish to stop using the trade mark.

As a consequence of the *Intellectual Property Laws Amendment Act 2006* (Cth), the Registrar now has the power to reverse a decision to register a trade mark at any time within twelve months after registration. A new s 84A was added to the Act under which the Registrar may revoke the registration if the Registrar is satisfied that the trade mark should not have been registered and it is reasonable to do so. The circumstances to be taken into account in determining this are set out in s 84A and include errors or omissions that led directly or indirectly to the registration and any relevant obligations of Australia under an international agreement. One circumstance in which the power may be exercised is where a trade mark is registered but a *Madrid Protocol* application is then received that has an earlier priority date. In addition, s 84B, which was introduced in the 2006 legislation, requires revocation of the trade mark in certain circumstances where the Registrar has failed to take account of a notice of opposition.

---

[271] *Re Lawson* [2001] AIPC 91-693.
[272] Ibid 39,361.

15.31 Overview of rectification by the court

While the Registrar may amend the Register in the limited circumstances described above[273] and the exercise of that power is subject to appeal to the Federal Court,[274] there are some instances in which only the Federal Court may order the amendment or rectification of the Register. These circumstances are described in div 2 of Part 8 of the Act. The applicant in each case must be 'an aggrieved person'.

- An applicant may apply for the entry of particulars that are wrongly omitted or correcting any error in an entry in the Register (s 85).
- Cancellation or removal of amendment of any entry may be made on the ground that a condition or limitation entered in the Register has been contravened (s 86).
- An entry may be amended or cancelled as a consequence of a trade mark becoming 'generic'. Sections 24 and 25 provide details of the circumstances in which a registered owner may lose their exclusive rights as a consequence of the 'genericisation' of his or her trade mark (s 87).[275]
- An application for cancellation, removal or amendment of an entry wrongly made or remaining or the entering of any condition or limitation can be made on the various grounds set out in s 88(2).[276]

15.31.1 Aggrieved person

In a number of instances, the applicant has no standing unless it is an aggrieved person. There is no simple or exhaustive definition of 'an aggrieved person'.[277] The requirement is designed to prevent common informers or strangers proceeding wantonly but it is to be interpreted liberally.[278] In *Health World Ltd v Shin-Sun Australia Pty Ltd*,[279] the majority of the High Court held that it is sufficient that the two parties are in the same trade in that they trade in the class of goods in respect of which the challenged mark is registered.[280] In that case, the registered owner of 'Inner Health Plus' sold probiotic powder and the registered owner of 'Health Plus' sold natural health supplements derived from squalene and shark cartilage and from beeswax.

Yet even the requirement to be in the same trade is not absolutely essential. For example, in *Campomar SL v Nike International Ltd*,[281] the owner of the well-known Nike trade mark for sporting shoes and goods objected to a long-standing registration of Nike for deodorant. It was

---

273 At 15.30.
274 *Trade Marks Act 1995* (Cth) s 83(2).
275 For further reference, see J. Nurton, 'How to avoid genericization' (2002) 123 *Managing Intellectual Property* 14.
276 For further reference, see J. McCutcheon, 'Rectification of the Trade Marks Register on grounds existing at the time of application to rectify: An analysis of sections 88(2)(a) and (c) and 89 of the *Trade Marks Act 1995* (Cth)' (2002) 13 *Australian Intellectual Property Journal* 199.
277 *Trade Marks Act 1995* (Cth) ss 85, 86, 87, 88. Section 181 is the equivalent of s 88 in relation to certification trade marks. The requirement of being aggrieved used to apply in non-use proceedings.
278 *Health World Ltd v Shin-Sun Australia Pty Ltd* (2010) 240 CLR 590, [27].
279 (2010) 240 CLR 590.
280 Ibid [45].
281 (2000) 202 CLR 45.

held to be an aggrieved person because of the potential impact on its broad reputation in spite of the fact that the applicant did not sell or wish to sell Nike deodorant. The extension of infringement under s 120(2) and (3), the more liberal view of defensive registration and the relaxation of licensing arrangements mean that it is even more likely that situations such as in the *Nike* case will lead to traders being aggrieved or more easily demonstrating that they are aggrieved.

With these general principles in mind, some examples of 'being aggrieved' then include the following:

- The parties are in the same trade and they each trade in the class of goods in respect of which the challenged mark is registered.
- A party may have a desire to use the trade mark itself or a substantially identical or deceptively similar one in relation to similar goods or services. For this reason, a person may be aggrieved only in relation to particular goods or services rather than all goods or services for which registration exists.[282]
- There is actual use of the trade mark itself or a substantially identical or deceptively similar one in relation to dissimilar goods or services where the applicant has established a broad reputation for its trade mark even though it may not wish to trade in the goods or services in respect of which rectification is sought.
- The aggrieved person has been the subject of threats of proceedings for trade mark infringement, passing off or a breach of s 18 of sch 2 of the *Competition and Consumer Act 2010* (Cth).[283]

15.32 Errors and omissions: s 85

This ground for amendment relates primarily to relatively minor amendments. There was case authority under previous legislation to suggest that it could extend to substituting the true owner of the trade mark for that of a wrongfully registered claimant,[284] such as where the wrong company in a corporate group has been named as the applicant and the applicant is, in effect, the trustee of the real owner. However, case law under the current legislation suggests that if the wrong person makes the original application, it should be abandoned and a new application started afresh.[285]

15.33 Contravention of conditions or limits: s 86

This ground is self-explanatory. Examples of such conditions or limitations may include geographical limitations imposed at the time of registration on the basis of honest concurrent

---

282 *Ritz Hotel Ltd v Charles of the Ritz Ltd* (1988) 15 NSWLR 158.
283 *New South Wales Dairy Corporation v Murray Goulburn Co-operative Co Ltd* (1989) 14 IPR 75.
284 *Figgins Holdings Pty Ltd v Registrar of Trade Marks* (1995) 59 FCR 147; *Aquaculture Corp v New Zealand Green Mussel Co Ltd (No 2)* (1986) 10 IPR 319, 344 (HC NZ); *Lincoln Industries Ltd v Wham-O Manufacturing Co* (1984) 3 IPR 115, 155–6 (CA NZ), where substitution was refused as the Registrar was not before the court.
285 *SPI Spirits (Cyprus) Ltd v Diageo Australia Ltd (No 6)* (2008) 77 IPR 62.

use. As with all grounds, there is a general discretion not to remove the trade mark from the Register, and if the relevant breach is cured this would be relevant to the exercise of the discretion.

15.34 Effect of ss 24 and 25 on s 87

The effect of s 87 can only be appreciated by acquiring an understanding of the operation of ss 24 and 25. Those two provisions describe particular circumstances in which a registered owner may lose their exclusive rights in respect of their registered trade mark as a consequence of their trade mark effectively becoming generic. Close attention is needed to the wording of the provisions as they do not actually use the term 'generic'. In particular, the relevant test is not so much whether consumers regard the trade mark as generic but whether 'the trade mark consists of, or contains, a sign that, after the date of registration of the trademark, becomes generally accepted within the relevant trade as the sign that describes or is the name of an article, substance or service'.[286]

The emphasis is on the use within the relevant trade rather than the use by consumers. So evidence of how retailers, wholesalers, manufacturers and advertisers use the sign will be the key issue. Of course, the use by consumers will still be relevant as their use will influence and be the precursor of a change in the use of the sign in the relevant trade. Partly for this reason, trade mark owners often vociferously object to dictionary entries in new editions that refer to registered trade marks as the general word for an article. For example, the word 'esky' is clearly identified in dictionaries such as the *Macquarie* and *Shorter Oxford* as a trade mark although the latter describes it as 'proprietary in Australia', implying that it may be generic elsewhere. The common references to an 'esky' rather than an esky cooler certainly suggest that the term is considered by many consumers as the word for the article in question rather than a word for a particular brand of that article. In contrast, according to the *Shorter Oxford* 'ugg boots' is a generic term in Australia although it is the subject of trade mark registration in the United States.

In order for s 24(1) to be operative, the sign in question must describe or be the name of the relevant article, substance or service. Case law under the previous legislation held that an equivalent provision was not applicable if the word in question was only part of the description in question. For example, in *FH Faulding & Co Ltd v Imperial Chemical Industries of Australia & New Zealand Ltd*,[287] the trade mark 'Barrier' for skin protective creams did not fall foul of s 56 of the 1955 Act because the relevant term used in the industry was 'Barrier Cream'. The dissenting judge in that case considered that the use of the word 'Barrier' as an adjective was enough to invoke the section.

The wording of s 24(1) is slightly different. It refers to the sign describing the article, not to the sign being 'the description'. As adjectives describe but are not necessarily themselves 'the description' of an article, the minority view in the *Faulding* case may well be applicable under the new provision. In any event, one clear difference between s 24(1) and the previous

---

286 *Trade Marks Act 1995* (Cth) s 24(1).
287 (1964) 112 CLR 537.

provision is that s 24(1) refers to a 'sign' not just a word. So it is quite possible for any sort of sign, such as a shape trade mark, to be generic.[288] Section 24(2) and (3) sets out the consequences if a sign does meet the test laid down in s 24(1). If the trade mark consists of the sign, the registered owner does not have any exclusive rights to use the trade mark.[289] If the trade mark contains the sign, the owner has no exclusive rights to use that sign. The court may determine the day on which the sign meets the test in s 24(1) and the trade mark owner therefore loses exclusive rights in relation to it from that day.[290]

Section 25 deals with a specific type of genericism. It deals with the situation where a trade mark consists of or contains a sign that describes or is the name of an article or substance that was formerly exploited under a patent or a service formerly provided as a patented process. If the sign is the only commonly known way to describe or identify the article, substance or service two years or more after the patent has expired, then the trade mark owner loses its exclusive rights to use the sign. This provision exists because during the term of a patent, the patent owner is unlikely to be subject to s 24. The nature of the patent monopoly is such that by definition no other person can make or sell the patented product and so the patent owner's trade mark will almost necessarily be distinctive and not generic during the patent period. Once the patent expires, other traders become free to make and sell the product but not to use the patent owner's trade mark, which may have become the name of the product as well. The provision encourages patent owners to develop a sign trade mark that is separate from the shape or name of their product during both the patent period and after it because failure do so may lead to the application of s 25. For example, in *Mayne Industries Pty Ltd v Advanced Engineering Group Pty Ltd*,[291] the trade mark in question consisted of the shape of a 'fence dropper', designed to be inserted into a fence so as to engage the horizontal wires of the fence and ensure that each horizontal wire is kept at the same distance apart. The fence dropper itself had been the subject of an Australian patent. The trade mark for the patented product (that is, the shape of the product) was held to describe the patented product within the meaning of s 25 and Greenwood J held that the trade mark was not entitled to further protection because of s 25.

In addition to the loss of exclusive rights to use the sign pursuant to s 24 or s 25, s 87 provides the court with a power to amend or cancel the registration of the trade mark if either s 24 or s 25 applies. If the trade mark contains or consists of the relevant generic sign, s 87(1) empowers the court to cancel the registration or remove or amend any entry relating to the trade mark. If the trade mark does not consist of the sign but only contains it, the court may allow the trade mark to remain on the Register subject to any condition or limitation that the court may impose. This ground for rectification, which is in itself discretionary,[292] is also subject to the fault provision in s 89 discussed below.[293]

---

288   *Mayne Industries Pty Ltd v Advanced Engineering Group Pty Ltd* (2008) 166 FCR 312.
289   *Trade Marks Act 1995* (Cth) s 24(2).
290   Ibid s 24(4).
291   (2008) 166 FCR 312.
292   See the discussion below at 15.37 on the general discretion not to rectify.
293   At 15.41. See Nurton, 'How to avoid genericization', above n 275, 14.

15.35 Cancellation, removal or amendment: s 88(2)

There is some overlap in the wording of this provision as the cancellation of a trade mark also involves the removal of an entry. Of course, an 'entry' may entail other matters, such as assignments or claims to interests in and rights in trade marks.

The reference to entries wrongly made obviously refers to the initial addition of the entry to the Register and therefore relates to objections to the initial entry. For example, if one of the grounds of opposition could have been made out at the time of registration but the relevant process was not undertaken, the registration of the trade mark was wrongly made. The reference to entries wrongly remaining on the Register relates to events since the entry was made. For example, it is possible that the use of a trade mark may become likely to deceive or cause confusion because of events since registration.

15.36 Transitional provisions and presumptive validity

Under the previous legislation, trade marks registered in Part A of the old Register received presumptive validity once they had been registered for seven years or more.[294] This meant that the original registration could not be challenged unless one of three specific grounds was first made out. The current legislation provides that this protection from an attack on the original registration remains for those trade marks registered in Part A of the old register pursuant to the previous legislation.[295] As many trade marks fall into this category, it was considered necessary to 'grandfather' this protection in the current legislation.

Consequently, s 234(2) provides that the original registration of such trade marks cannot be challenged after seven years unless it is shown that:

- the original registration was obtained by fraud;
- the registration of the trade mark would be contrary to s 28 of the *Trade Marks Act 1955* (Cth); or
- the trade mark did not, at the commencement of the proceedings, distinguish the goods or services of the registered owner in relation to which the trade mark is used from the goods or services of other persons.

It is important to note that while the applicant for rectification must prove that one or more of these three requirements is met, the meeting of that requirement is not in itself sufficient to justify rectification. The applicant must first meet one of the three requirements to overcome presumptive validity and then meet one of the grounds for rectification.

---

[294] *Trade Marks Act 1955* (Cth) s 61(1).
[295] *Trade Marks Act 1995* (Cth) s 234.

15.36.1 Fraud

Fraud involves some form of active deception of either the Registrar or a third party, such as a person who would have opposed the registration but for the fraud. For example, the owner may have fraudulently informed another person that they were not going to proceed with an application for registration.

15.36.2 Contrary to s 28 of the repealed legislation

Section 28 of the previous legislation was the subject of many tortured attempts at interpretation because of its ambiguous wording.[296] The most important paragraph of s 28 was s 28(a), which provided that registration should be denied 'if the use of the trade mark would be likely to deceive or cause confusion'. There were two controversial aspects of the paragraph. One was whether the provision had both immediate and prospective effect such that the test could be applied both at the time of application for registration and after registration for rectification purposes. For example, a trade mark may not be likely to deceive or cause confusion at the time of registration but post-registration circumstances may lead to such a situation. The other issue was whether, if paragraph (a) had prospective effect for rectification purposes, paragraph (a) was qualified by some requirement of blameworthy conduct on the part of the registered owner that was responsible for the trade mark becoming likely to deceive or cause confusion. This second issue is addressed in s 89 of the current legislation.

The first issue concerning s 28(a), whether it had prospective effect, was not finally resolved until after it was repealed in the High Court decision of *Campomar SL v Nike International Ltd*.[297] In that case, the High Court held that s 28(a) only applied to the initial registration of a trade mark and had no prospective operation. For the purposes of s 234 of the current legislation, this means that in order to overcome presumptive validity, an applicant for rectification must demonstrate that, at the time of the application for registration, the trade mark was likely to deceive or cause confusion.[298] This test is largely a conflation of the existing tests in ss 43 and 60.

15.36.3 Not distinctive when proceedings commence

The third ground on which presumptive validity may be overcome is that at the time of the application for rectification, the trade mark does not actually distinguish the goods or services of the owner. Trade marks registered under Part A of the old Register needed to be inherently distinctive and thus, if the current legislation had applied to their original registration, they would have been registered pursuant to s 41(3). In order for this ground for overcoming presumptive validity to apply, the trade mark either must have never been inherently distinctive and has not since gained distinctiveness through use or has lost its inherent distinctiveness. The latter would be difficult to establish. It is also worth noting that while presumptive validity may be overcome on this ground, loss of distinctiveness is not itself a ground for rectification

---

296   *Campomar SL v Nike International Ltd* (2000) 202 CLR 45; *New South Wales Dairy Corporation v Murray Goulburn Co-operative Co Ltd* (1990) 171 CLR 363.
297   (2000) 202 CLR 45.
298   *Toddler Kindy Gymbaroo Pty Ltd v Gymboree Pty Ltd* (2000) 100 FCR 166, 192.

and the applicant will also need to demonstrate that some particular ground in s 88(2) has been made out. There may be some overlaps between the grounds in s 88(2) and the grounds for overcoming presumptive validity, but not necessarily.

15.37 General discretion not to rectify

In any event, whether the trade mark has the protection of presumptive validity or not, the wording of the relevant rectification sections, which state that the court 'may' order rectification, appears to confer a discretion on the court not to order rectification even if the relevant ground is found to be established. In overturning some authority to the contrary such as that of Branson J in *Eos (Australia) Pty Ltd v Expo Tomei Pty Ltd*,[299] the Full Federal Court has held that there is a general discretion not to cancel registration even if one or more of the grounds for doing so have been found.[300] The general discretion exists in addition to a very specific discretion created by s 89.

15.38 Grounds for opposition

If any presumptive validity can be overcome or the trade mark in question does not qualify for presumptive validity, s 88(2)(a) permits rectification on any of the grounds on which the registration of the trade mark could have been opposed under div 2 of Part 5. Consequently, a trade mark is, in a sense, liable to de facto opposition proceedings at any time after its registration. Issues such as ownership and distinctiveness can be revisited at any time as can conflicts with other trade marks pursuant to ss 44 and 60. For example, in *Yarra Valley Dairy Pty Ltd v Lemnos Foods Pty Ltd*,[301] the trade mark 'Persian Fetta' was removed on the basis that those words had never had the necessary distinctiveness within the meaning of s 41. In *Toddler Kindy Gymbaroo Pty Ltd v Gymboree Pty Ltd*[302] rectification was ordered because at the time of the application for registration, use of the trade mark would have been likely to deceive or cause confusion because of the reputation of a prior trade mark and registration should have been denied due to s 60. A similar finding was made in *Tivo Inc v Vivo International Corp Pty Ltd*[303] and on appeal in that case.[304]

A more recent example of rectification on this basis was the decision in *Knott Investments Pty Ltd v Winnebago Industries Inc*.[305] An American company first used the trade mark 'Winnebago' in the United States and acquired a worldwide reputation for the trade mark, including a reputation for it in Australia despite not using it in Australia. An Australian company used the trade mark for some years and acquired registration of it before the American company finally launched litigation. At first instance, the trade mark registration of the Australian company was cancelled on the grounds that use of it would be contrary to law within the

---

299   (1998) 42 IPR 277.
300   *Anchorage Capital Partners Pty Ltd v ACPA Pty Ltd* [2018] FCAFC 6, [149]
301   (2010) 191 FCR 297.
302   (2000) 100 FCR 166.
303   [2012] FCA 252.
304   *Vivo International Corp Pty Ltd v Tivo Inc* [2012] FCAFC 159.
305   (2013) 211 FCR 449.

meaning of s 42. It may be that any alternative argument based on s 60 may also have been effective. In any event, the registration was cancelled because a ground of opposition existed at the time of registration, even though registration took place many years prior to the application for rectification. The American company has now obtained registration of 'Winnebago'.[306]

However, even if the original registration should not have taken place and rectification is granted on that basis, the cancellation of the trade mark does not operate retrospectively. Any infringement of the trade mark prior to cancellation is still actionable.[307]

15.39 Fraud, false suggestion or misrepresentation

Section 88(2)(c) and (e) provides for rectification where an amendment to an application for registration was obtained or an entry in the Register was made as a result of fraud, false suggestion or misrepresentation. Previous legislation referred only to 'fraud', not false suggestion or misrepresentation. However, the expression has been used in patent legislation and it obviously goes beyond deliberate deceit as is the case with fraud.[308] In relation to the use of the term in patent legislation, Lockhart J stated:

> The words 'false suggestion or representation' are of wide import. The statutory ground ... is based on equitable notions of good faith, fairness, conscionable conduct and honesty.[309]

The only case where the expression has been considered in relation to the current legislation is the *Montana* case.[310] That case was one involving an application for rectification on the basis that an assignee had obtained registration via an assignment without revealing to the Registrar a collateral agreement between the assignee and the assignor. Under the collateral agreement, the assignor of the trade mark retained very considerable control over the trade mark pursuant to which the assignor could demand the re-assignment of the trade mark. At first instance, Wilcox J held that if the Registrar had been aware of the control retained by the assignor, the Registrar would probably not have registered the assignment. Consequently, withholding the details of the agreement, while submitting a standard assignment, constituted the necessary false suggestion or misrepresentation. On appeal, this decision was reversed because the agreement related to control over, not title to, the trade mark and the Registrar would have registered the assignment even if made aware of the collateral arrangement. Nevertheless, the general principles espoused at first instance concerning the nature of false suggestion and misrepresentation are useful to the interpretation of these provisions.

---

306   Trade mark reg no 1349326.
307   *Deckers Outdoor Corp v Farley (No 2)* (2009) 176 FCR 33.
308   *Prestige Group (Australia) Pty Ltd v Dart Industries Inc* (1990) 26 FCR 197.
309   Ibid 198.
310   *Transport Tyre Sales Pty Ltd v Montana Tyres Rims & Tubes Pty Ltd* (1999) 93 FCR 421 (discussed in the context of parallel importing in ch 16 at 16.7).

15.40 Use likely to deceive or cause confusion

Section 88(2)(c) permits rectification where, due to circumstances arising since the registration of the trade mark, the use of the trade mark is likely to deceive or cause confusion. This ground is or at least was intended[311] to be the equivalent of the prospective operation claimed for s 28(a) of the previous legislation even though s 28(a) itself was ultimately held not to have such prospective operation.[312]

The circumstances in which s 88(2)(c) may arise are where the use of the trade mark or a substantially identical or deceptively similar one by another or other traders has led to a situation where the use of the registered trade mark is now likely to deceive or cause confusion. Often, the conduct by those other traders that has resulted in that situation arising was infringing conduct. The question then is whether the registered owner should lose its registration as a result of the infringing conduct of another person. This issue is addressed in s 89, discussed below. However, another possibility is that the registered owner has consented to another using its trade mark but has failed to supervise or control the use by that other person. The result is that the use of the trade mark now indicates that the relevant goods or services may come from more than one source. This in turn generates the necessary likelihood of deceit or confusion that justifies rectification.

In *Health World Ltd v Shin-Sun Australia Pty Ltd*[313] the trade mark in question was owned by Shin-Sun Australia Pty Ltd. It allowed Nature's Hive Pty Ltd to use its trade mark but did not control or supervise that use in any way. The shareholders of Shin-Sun were the parents of the majority shareholder, their daughter, in Nature's Hive. The daughter was the general manager of both companies but the differences in shareholdings meant that the two companies were quite distinct and the uncontrolled use of the trade mark by Nature's Hive meant that further use of the trade mark was likely to deceive or confuse.

15.41 Rectification not granted if registered owner not at fault

Section 89 confers a specific discretion on the court not to order rectification pursuant to ss 87, 88(2)(a) and 88(2)(c) 'if the registered owner satisfies the court that the ground relied on by the applicant has not arisen through any act or fault of the registered owner'. The provision is designed to protect an owner from rectification proceedings where the grounds for rectification have arisen through the unlawful conduct of infringers of the trade mark.[314]

The case law dealing with the previous legislation imported into its interpretation a concept of blameworthy conduct in the context of rectification. The judicial consideration of the concept has a lengthy and complex history. Regrettably, a detailed analysis of that history

---

311 Working Party to Review the Trade Mark Legislation, *Recommended Changes*, above n 3, 94–5.
312 *Campomar SL v Nike International Ltd* (2000) 202 CLR 45.
313 (2008) 75 IPR 478.
314 For further reference, see McCutcheon, 'Rectification of the Trade Marks Register', above n 276.

often leads to greater confusion than clarification of the issue. The pinnacle of that confusion was scaled in a High Court decision where multiple and conflicting opinions were expressed about the nature of blameworthy conduct in the context of s 28(a) of the previous legislation.[315]

Section 89 was a response to this confusion but in reality it is more a codification of that confusion than anything else. The main difficulty with the section is that it provides no definition of 'act or fault' of the registered owner. In addition, the wording of the phrase itself introduces difficulties. 'Act' suggests positive action rather than failure to act. In turn, this suggests that 'fault' involves omission but there are other possible interpretations. The word 'fault' may stand in contradistinction to 'act', thus suggesting that the act need not involve any fault, despite the heading to the section. The section also refers to 'act or fault' of the registered owner, rather than any 'act or fault' of a predecessor, so there is an issue as to whether the conduct of a predecessor in title is relevant.

Eventually, regard will have to be had to the various judicial references to 'blameworthy conduct' in cases dealing with s 28 of the previous legislation even though that term is not adopted in the Act. Here again, there is confusion. The main Australian decision relating to the issue is *New South Wales Dairy Corporation v Murray Goulburn Co-operative Co Ltd*.[316] The case involved a dispute concerning the word trade marks 'Moo' and 'Moove' for flavoured milk. Moo was registered in 1966 and assigned in 1987 to Murray Goulburn Co-operative, which then started to use Moo for the first time in relation to flavoured milk. Moove was registered well after Moo but use of it for flavoured milk commenced in 1979. Moove should probably never have been registered because of the existence of Moo on the Register. However, because it was registered and used, the New South Wales Dairy Corporation sought to have Moo removed from the Register on the basis that its continued use would be likely to deceive or cause confusion – that is, that the situation had changed since registration as a consequence of the use of Moove.

Two different concepts of 'blameworthy conduct' emerged from the High Court decision. Mason CJ and Brennan J adopted a general view of blameworthy conduct as any conduct

> (whether by act or omission) on the part of a registered proprietor or his predecessor in title which he knew or ought to have known would result in the likelihood that the use of the mark would deceive or cause confusion and which has in fact caused or contributed to that result.[317]

For those two judges, blameworthy conduct was constituted by:

- extensive use of Moo after extensive use of Moove;
- failure to object to the use of Moove; and
- the lengthy period of non-use.

Dawson and Toohey JJ took a different view of blameworthy conduct. They believed that the legislative basis for the requirement flowed from s 28(d) of the previous legislation, which read

---

315 *New South Wales Dairy Corporation v Murray Goulburn Co-operative Co Ltd* (1990) 171 CLR 363.
316 Ibid.
317 Ibid 391 (Brennan J).

that '[a] mark which would otherwise be not entitled to protection in a court of justice shall not be registered as a trade mark'. Both judges read s 28(a) and (d) conjunctively and interpreted s 28(d) as referring to general equitable principles. Consequently, for them the test of blameworthy conduct was whether the owner's conduct was such that a court of equity would deny injunctive relief against infringement of the trade mark. Such a test is not easily met and not surprisingly they did not consider that the owner of Moo had engaged in blameworthy conduct. In particular, they emphasised the fact that the owners of Moo did not believe that there was any problem with the use of both Moo and Moove, which raises an issue as to whether 'fault' in s 89 involves an objective or subjective test of fault. Their Honours also considered that as non-use was addressed comprehensively in other provisions of the legislation, it was not relevant in the context of s 28. A similar argument could apply in relation to the present s 89.

The wording of the present s 89 would seem to adopt the approach of Mason CJ and Brennan J, at least in relation to the issue of the impact of equitable principles, as none of the wording of s 28(d) has been adopted. On the other hand, several ambiguities remain, including:

- the extent to which non-use might be relevant given what appears to be a code in relation to non-use;
- the meaning of 'act', in contradistinction to 'fault'; and
- whether and to what extent the conduct of a predecessor in title is relevant. It may be that the question is to what extent an assignee is expected to inquire into the past conduct of the assignor. Omission to make inquiries about use or steps to stamp out infringing conduct by the predecessor in title may be relevant to the issue of 'fault' on the part of the registered owner.

A decision of the Full Federal Court casts some light on the interpretation of s 89. In *Knott Investments Pty Ltd v Winnebago Industries Inc*[318] the registered owner attempted to resist an application for cancellation of its registration pursuant to s 88(2)(a). The specific ground of opposition relied on was that the use of the trade mark was contrary to law because another company had a reputation associated with the trade mark, which inevitably led to its use constituting misleading or deceptive conduct. The trade mark owner claimed that its registration was not due to any act or omission on its part as the other company had failed to assert its rights in relation to the trade mark.

The Full Court rejected this argument on several bases. One basis was that an agreement between the two parties included an undertaking not to seek registration of the trade mark. In addition, the Full Court noted that s 60 specifically envisaged the situation where an owner of the same or a similar trade mark has a reputation at the time of the application for registration. To deny rectification on the grounds that this ground had not been exercised would leave little room for the operation of s 88(2)(a), which specifically envisages that opposition proceedings were not initiated at the time of registration.

It should also be noted that unlike s 28 of the previous legislation, s 89 applies to rectification pursuant to genericism and all of the grounds for rectification that are set out in

---

[318] (2013) 211 FCR 449.

s 88. This complicates the issue even more. For example, the genericisation process necessarily involves infringement of the trade mark and a failure by the registered owner to prevent infringement is a primary reason for the trade mark becoming generic. The difficulty a court then faces is that the very basis for rectification of the Register necessarily involves a failure on the part of the registered owner to take sufficient action against infringement, yet the court has still to consider the discretion under s 89 if it is to have any meaning with respect to all of the grounds for rectification set out in s 88.

In any event, s 89(2) goes on to provide that in making a decision under subs (1), the court must also take into account any matter that is prescribed and any other matter that the court considers relevant. The prescribed matters are set out in reg 8.2 as:

(a) the extent to which the public interest will be affected if registration is not cancelled;
(b) whether any circumstances that gave rise to the application have ceased to exist;
(c) the extent to which the trade mark distinguished the relevant goods and/or services before the circumstances giving rise to the application arose;
(d) whether there is any order or other remedy, other than an order for rectification, that would be adequate in the circumstances.[319]

15.42 Removal for non-use

A basic proposition of trade mark law is that if you don't use it, you lose it.[320] Part 9 of the Act provides that a registered trade mark will be liable for removal if it is not used for the relevant periods prescribed in the legislation. Authorised use by a licensee is deemed to be used by the owner pursuant to s 8 but the corollary of that is if the licensee's use is not authorised use, the owner cannot rely on that use to resist an application for removal.[321] An applicant has five years from the date of registration to use the trade mark in Australia, and after that initial five-year period has expired any three-year period of non-use in Australia renders the trade mark liable for removal. Non-use of the trade mark includes not using it in good faith in Australia.[322] Consequently, sham use intended to merely forestall an application for removal for non-use will be ineffective.[323]

The relevant three-year period of non-use is for a three-year period ending one month prior to the filing of the application for non-removal. This delay is intended to provide an opportunity for an applicant to demand that the registered owner agree either to the removal of its trade mark from the Register or to the assignment of the trade mark. If neither occurs, the application can still be made within one month and use after the receipt of the demand will not assist the owner.

Applications for removal may be made by any person although until 2006, the applicant had to be aggrieved.[324]

---

319   *Trade Marks Regulations 1995* (Cth) reg 8.2.
320   For further reference, see Bently and Burrell, 'The requirement of trade mark use', above n 39, 181; Burrell, 'The requirement of trade mark use: Recent developments in Australia', above n 39, 231.
321   *Lodestar Anstalt v Campari America LLC* [2016] FCAFC 92.
322   *Trade Marks Act 1995* (Cth) s 92(4)(a).
323   *Imperial Group Ltd v Philip Morris & Co Ltd* [1982] FSR 72.
324   See the discussion of an aggrieved person above at 15.31.1.

Once the application is made, the matter is dealt with by the Registrar although the Registrar has the power to refer the matter to a prescribed court.[325] If the application is unopposed, the Registrar must remove the trade mark from the Register.[326]

As proving a negative, namely non-use, is difficult, if not impossible, the onus lies on the opponent to prove use of the trade mark. The relevant use must have been in relation to the goods or services in respect of which the trade mark is registered. Consequently, the trade mark may be removed in respect of some goods or services but not others.

Section 100(2) and (3) identifies some circumstances in which the allegation of non-use is rebutted. For example, it is sufficient if the opponent uses the trade mark or the trade mark with additions or alterations that do not substantially affect its identity. Recent decisions that take a slightly broader view of what constitutes substantial identity might be relevant in this context.[327] However, in *Dunlop Aircraft Tyres Ltd v The Goodyear Tire & Rubber Co*,[328] the use of a composite trade mark that included the relevant registered trade mark was not sufficient to avoid removal for non-use.[329] Alternatively, if the trade mark has been assigned during the relevant period but the assignment has not been recorded on the Register, the Registrar or the court may form the view that use by the assignee should be treated as use by the trade mark owner. Case law on the point identifies several principles to be considered by courts in determining whether it would be reasonable to regard the assignee's use as that of the registered owner. The first of these principles is the public interest in preventing deception of the public but this public interest may itself be counterbalanced by the public interest in the preservation of an established mark.[330] In addition, the assignee's title to the trade mark and its use in good faith may well overcome the importance of enforcing technical defects in that title, particularly if the only consequence would be that the assignee would simply restart the registration process with a very strong prospect of obtaining registration.[331]

Section 100(3)(c) also provides a specific exemption from removal for non-use if the owner establishes that it did not use the trade mark during the period because of 'circumstances (whether affecting traders generally or only the registered owner of the trade mark) that were an obstacle to the use of the trade mark during that period'. Under the previous legislation, the relevant circumstances had to affect all traders in the particular trade, not just an individual trader. Examples of such circumstances included delays in obtaining health department approval for products[332] and post-war restrictions on imports.[333]

The Act has a more lenient approach with its reference to circumstances that may affect only the registered owner. However, the circumstances must be circumstances of a trading nature and they must arise externally to the registered owner. For example, it appears that the trader could not rely on financial difficulties or illness.[334]

---

325   *Trade Marks Act 1995* (Cth) s 94.
326   Ibid s 97.
327   See ch 16 at 16.1.4.
328   [2018] FCA 1014.
329   Ibid [122]–[144].
330   *Paragon Shoes Pty Ltd v Paragini Distributors (NSW) Pty Ltd* (1988) 13 IPR 323, 346.
331   Ibid.
332   *Pierre Fabre SA v Marion Laboratories Inc* (1986) 7 IPR 387 (Reg).
333   *Aktiebolaget Manus v RJ Fullwood & Bland Ltd* (1949) 66 RPC 71 (CA).
334   *Woolly Bull Enterprises Pty Ltd v Reynolds* (2001) 107 FCR 166, 180.

15.42.1 General discretion

In addition to the specific circumstances set out in s 100, a general discretion resides with the Registrar and the court under s 101 not to remove the trade mark from the Register even if the relevant period of non-use is made out. An example under the Act of the exercise of that discretion is the decision in *CA Henschke & Co v Rosemount Estates Pty Ltd*.[335] The relevant trade mark for wine had been used by a partnership of which the registered owner was a member. After the death of the registered owner, the partnership continued to use the trade mark but the trade mark was not transferred to the beneficiaries of the estate for a number of years. Consequently, the trade mark was not used by the registered owner who was deceased or his executors but by the remaining members of the partnership.

At first instance and on appeal, the Federal Court found that the relevant use had been authorised by the executors and therefore constituted use for the purposes of the Act.[336] However, as this finding was contentious, both the first instance judge and the Full Court went on to find that even if the use had not been authorised, the general discretion not to remove the trade mark for non-use would be exercised. The decision to that effect was based on several principles that were similar to, if not the same as, those referred to above in relation to the use by an unregistered assignee. In particular, no significant deception had occurred as a consequence of the partners, rather than the executors, using the trade mark and little would have been achieved by removal of the trade mark as the executors could simply have reapplied for registration and they had an unimpeachable title to it.

15.42.2 Changes to non-use under the *Trade Marks Amendment Act 2006*

The *Trade Marks Amendment Act 2006* (Cth) altered the pre-existing provisions in some respects. First, it clarified the pre-existing provisions by providing that if use has occurred in only a restricted area (and therefore not occurred outside that area), future use may be restricted to that area.[337] Trade marks for restaurants are an example of such a situation. The legislation also clarified the fact that use of the trade mark on goods of the same description or closely related services would be relevant to the exercise of the Registrar's discretion whether to remove the trade mark from the Register.[338]

---

335   (2000) 52 IPR 42.
336   Ibid.
337   *Trade Marks Act 1995* (Cth) s 102.
338   Ibid s 101(4).

16
EXPLOITATION OF REGISTERED TRADE MARKS

16.1 Overview of infringement of trade marks

The rights of an owner of a registered trade mark are stated in s 20(1)[1] to be the exclusive right to use the trade mark and to authorise other persons to use the trade mark in relation to goods and/or services in respect of which the trade mark is registered. This general commercial freedom of the owner to use a trade mark is subject to government restrictions on that use.[2] In addition, s 20(2) provides that the registered owner has the right to obtain relief under the Act if the trade mark has been infringed.

The manner in which the exclusivity of use of a trade mark is conferred on a trade mark owner is established by the infringement provisions, which confer a right to prevent others from using the trade mark or a similar trade mark in particular circumstances. Section 120(1)–(3) provides three different circumstances in which a registered owner may sue for infringement. However, before turning to the individual aspects of each subsection, a number of general features of the three different forms of infringement can be identified and examined.

16.1.1 Use as a trade mark

Each of the forms of infringement requires that the defendant uses, as a trade mark, a sign that is substantially identical with or deceptively similar to the plaintiff's registered trade mark. As with so many aspects of the legislation, use as a trade mark is a critical issue and it needs to be considered here in the context of infringement.

The 1955 Act[3] did not expressly require the defendant to use the trade mark as a trade mark in order to constitute infringement but the case law on the topic made it abundantly clear that such a requirement was implied in the legislation. The leading High Court decision on the point was *Shell Co of Australia Ltd v Esso Standard Oil (Australia) Ltd*.[4] In that case, Esso objected to a television advertisement of Shell. Esso had registered as a trade mark a device being a cartoon-like person in the shape of an oil drop. Facial features, such as eyes, had been placed in the top part of the oil drop to give it the appearance of an oil man. Shell's advertisement consisted of an oil drop that constantly changed shape throughout the advertisement while a voice-over promoted various aspects of Shell. For very brief periods during the advertisement, the oil drop assumed a shape that was very similar to Esso's oil drop man.

The High Court held that despite the similarity between the two oil drops, Shell's brief portrayal of its oil drop man was not use as a trade mark. In other words, when seeing that oil drop man for the very brief period during the television advertisement, consumers would not perceive that Shell was using it to indicate a connection between it and the petrol being advertised. Instead, the oil drop man was being used only to tell the story of Shell's petrol, rather than as a sign that, when seen, indicated Shell's petrol and nobody else's.

---

1   In this chapter, all references to legislative provisions are references to the *Trade Marks Act 1995* (Cth), unless otherwise indicated.
2   *JT International SA v Commonwealth* (2012) 250 CLR 1.
3   *Trade Marks Act 1955* (Cth).
4   (1963) 109 CLR 409.

The issue may be contrasted with the European Union law in relation to trade mark infringement as demonstrated in the English decision of *Arsenal Football Club plc v Reed*.[5] In that case, Reed was sued for infringement of the Arsenal Football Club's trade marks when he sold unauthorised items, such as Arsenal shirts and scarves. He argued that his use of 'Arsenal' was not one that indicated the trade origin of the products in question and as such he was not using the trade mark as a trade mark. While the court agreed with his contention, it held that the English law on the topic, as amended pursuant to the relevant European Union Directive, no longer required use of the trade mark as a trade mark. In the circumstances of that particular case, it was sufficient that he was using the Arsenal trade mark in the course of trade and that his actions would affect the role of the trade mark as operating as a guarantee of origin.[6]

16.1.2 Use as descriptive term rather than as trade mark

Another example under the 1955 legislation is the decision in *Johnson & Johnson (Australia) Pty Ltd v Sterling Pharmaceuticals Pty Ltd*.[7] In that case, the Federal Court found that 'Caplets' for paracetamol had been used by the defendant to simply describe the shape of its product (a tablet in the shape of a capsule) rather than to indicate its connection with the product. Consequently, the use was not use as a trade mark. Curiously, this finding was made at the same time as a finding that the defendant had not established the defence in s 64 of the 1955 legislation, which permitted the 'use in good faith by a person of a description of the character or quality of his goods or services'. The defence failed because the defendant was not using 'Caplets' in good faith, which seems to be inconsistent with a finding that it was not using the term as a trade mark. The decision seems explicable only on the basis that there was an intention to trade off the plaintiff's reputation, thus negativing good faith, but the defendant had not in fact actually achieved its intention because its use was not actually as a trade mark.

At the same time, the plaintiff avoided an action for removal for non-use on the basis that its use of 'Caplets' was use as a trade mark because it had placed the symbol ® next to the word, thus demonstrating to consumers that the word indicated a connection between the plaintiff and the goods in question.

The need to demonstrate that the use in question is use as a trade mark becomes even more relevant in the context of the expansion of the categories of signs accepted for registration and the expansion of the test of distinctiveness to include distinctiveness acquired through use. For example, where the alleged infringement involves the use of the shape of a product, the defendant may well argue that it is using the shape in a functional manner rather than as a trade mark.

The decision in *Philips v Remington*[8] is an example of this situation. In that case, Philips alleged that Remington's sale of triple-headed rotary shavers infringed its two-dimensional

---

5   [2003] RPC 9.
6   *Arsenal Football Club plc v Reed* [2003] RPC 9. Article 5(1) of the *First Council Directive 89/104/EEC of 21 December 1988 to Approximate the Laws of the Member States Relating to Trademarks* [1989] OJ L 40/1, as it then was, provided that the trademark owner had the right to 'prevent all third parties not having his consent from using in the course of trade; any sign which is identical with the trade mark in relation to goods or services which are identical with those for which the trade mark is registered'.
7   (1991) 30 FCR 326.
8   *Koninklijke Philips Electronics NV v Remington Products Australia Pty Ltd* (2000) 100 FCR 90.

device trade mark, which depicted a triple-headed rotary shaver. Remington successfully argued at first instance and on appeal that its use of the shape in question was not use as a trade mark.

The registration of descriptive words on the basis of their acquisition of secondary meaning also 'invites' defendants to argue that they are using such trade marks with their descriptive meaning rather than their secondary, acquired meaning. Two cases involving the Kettle Chip Company demonstrate the issue.[9] Kettle owned the trade mark 'Kettle' for its chips, which were hand-cooked chips cooked slowly in large kettles. Two of its competitors adopted the same manner of cooking but they also adopted the word 'Kettle' in their packaging. For example, Apand described its chips as Smith's Country Kettle chips although it is important to note that the previously prominent trade mark 'Smith's' was represented in smaller type than usual and smaller than the words 'Country Kettle'. Kettle successfully brought an action for passing off and a breach of s 52 of the *Trade Practices Act* (Cth) as it then was on the basis that the arguably descriptive word 'Kettle' had acquired a secondary meaning. The action was successful as the Full Federal Court was satisfied that the defendant had deceptively represented to consumers an association between its chips and the plaintiff by its use of the word 'Kettle'.

In contrast, when the plaintiff later brought trade mark infringement proceedings against Pepsico Australia for its description of its chips as 'Thins Double Crunch Kettle Cooked Chips', the action was unsuccessful. The trade mark 'Thins' had been used by the defendant for some time and the Full Court accepted that its use of Kettle was a descriptive use of the manner of cooking the chips, not as a sign distinguishing the defendant's chips from any other chips.

The matter may be further complicated by the possibility that the defendant is using the sign in question as both a trade mark and a decorative element for its products. The two uses are not mutually exclusive, and in *Adidas AG v Pacific Brands Footwear Pty Ltd (No 3)*[10] the court held that the defendant's stripes on the side of its sports shoes were being used both to distinguish its sports shoes from others and as a decorative element for those shoes.

16.1.3 Sign used to distinguish goods and services from others

The requirement of use of a trade mark as a trade mark also means that the relevant question is whether the defendant has used the substantially identical or deceptively similar sign to distinguish its goods from other goods. The question is not whether it has used the sign to distinguish the goods by suggesting they are the goods of the trade mark owner. The point is illustrated by the decision of the Full Federal Court in *The Coca-Cola Co v All-Fect Distributors Ltd*[11] (the *Coca-Cola* case). In that case, the defendant produced and distributed a cola-flavoured lolly. When unwrapped and rolled out, the lolly allegedly looked like the shape of

---

9   *Apand Pty Ltd v Kettle Chip Co Pty Ltd* (1994) 52 FCR 474; *Pepsico Australia Pty Ltd v Kettle Chip Co Pty Ltd* (1996) 135 ALR 192. The first of these decisions was based on passing off and breach of s 52 of the *Trade Practices Act 1974* (Cth) as it then was but the result would have been similar if the action had been based on trade mark infringement.
10 (2013) 308 ALR 74, [61].
11 (1999) 96 FCR 107.

the well-known Coca-Cola bottle. Coca-Cola sued for infringement of the two-dimensional shape of its bottle. At first instance, Merkel J held that the defendant had not used the lolly shape as a trade mark. The basis of that argument was that consumers would not look at the shape in question and then think that it indicated the product of Coca-Cola, the owner of the registered owner.

On appeal, the Full Court rejected that reasoning and said that the real issue in determining 'use as a trade mark' was whether the sign in question indicated a connection between the defendant and the goods in relation to which the sign was used and not whether it indicated a connection between the defendant and the registered trade mark owner:

> The question at this stage is not whether the respondent has used a sign so as to indicate a connection between it and the appellant. It is whether the use indicates a connection between the confectionery and the respondent. So it does not assist the respondent to demonstrate by reference to the packaging that the suggested connection is with Efruti rather than Coca-Cola.[12]

The point made by the Full Court is in keeping with the definition of a trade mark, which refers to 'a person' using a sign to distinguish their goods from other goods. The person[13] in question may be the infringer and it is not necessary for consumers to believe that it is the actual owner or someone with a right to use the trade mark, such as a licensee who is using the trade mark to distinguish the goods or services from other goods or services. This proposition is also justified by the fact that infringement of a registered trade mark is possible even before it is used or acquires any reputation. If the approach adopted in the first instance decision in the Coca-Cola case was adhered to, the registered owner would rarely be in any better position than if it relied on passing off.

Another case involving the same trade mark involved litigation between Coca-Cola and PepsiCo Inc about the shape of a bottle used by Pepsi to sell its cola.[14] At first instance, Besanko J found that Pepsi was using its particular bottle shape as a trade mark but, importantly, that the use included use of all of its bottle's features, including a wave-like ribbing in the middle of the bottle. In contrast, the outline or silhouette of the Pepsi bottle was found not to be used as a trade mark. The issue of trade mark use was critical in its own right and for the purpose of defining with some precision exactly what sign or combination of signs was substantially identical with or deceptively similar to the registered trade mark. It is only that particular sign or combination of signs that could infringe the registered trade mark because only it was being used as a trade mark.

16.1.4 Substantially identical with or deceptively similar to

A further requirement common to the three forms of infringement is that the sign used as a trade mark by the defendant must be substantially identical with or deceptively similar to the plaintiff's trade mark.

---

12   Ibid 119.
13   'Person' includes a body of persons, whether incorporated or not: *Trade Marks Act 1995* (Cth) s 6.
14   *The Coca-Cola Co v PepsiCo Inc (No 2)* (2014) 109 IPR 429.

The definitions and applications of these terms have already been addressed in some detail in chapter 15 in the context of registrability.[15] The same principles apply in the context of infringement.[16]

In relation to 'substantially identical' and 'deceptively similar', the Full Court in the *Coca-Cola* case stated:

> In order to determine whether marks are substantially identical they should be compared side by side, their similarities and differences noted and the importance of these similarities and differences assessed having regard to the essential features of the registered mark and the total impression of resemblance or dissimilarity that emerges from the comparison ...[17]

Whether one device mark 'resembles' another involves an assessment of the visual impression made by the two marks when compared.

In contrast, the likelihood of deception or confusion in the context of deceptive similarity involves an assessment of what would be the probable visual impression on customers or potential customers that would be produced as a result of the 'notional normal and fair use' of the marks.[18]

The meaning of 'substantial identity' has been considered in two other Full Federal Court decisions in recent years which have generated some controversy on the topic and suggested a possible widening of its scope. Both decisions refer to the 'dominant cognitive cues' in the two trade marks being compared. One resulted in a view that the words 'Harbour Lights' were the dominant cognitive cues in the two trade marks although the second trade mark also contained five gold stars of different sizes arranged in a semi-circle above those words together with the words 'A New Star Shines' below them.[19] In the second case, both trade marks for optometry services had the word 'insight' and devices that suggested eyes in the context of optometry services.[20] Again, the Full Court referred to dominant cognitive cues. Arguably, the decisions focused too greatly on the word signs rather than the totality of the two trade marks when considering substantial identity. On the other hand, the finding in *Anchorage Capital*[21] that Anchorage Capital and Anchorage Capital Partners were substantially identical seems unexceptional.

Deceptive similarity was considered in some detail in the *Coca-Cola* case.[22] After deciding that the two signs were not substantially identical because 'a total impression of similarity does not emerge from a comparison of the two marks, and accordingly the shape of the confectionery is not substantially identical with the contour bottle mark',[23] the Full Court went on to assess the issue of deceptive similarity in the context of the particular circumstances:

---

15   See ch 15 at 15.21.
16   *The Coca-Cola Co v All-Fect Distributors Ltd* (1999) 96 FCR 107.
17   Ibid 121.
18   Ibid 122.
19   *Accor Australia & New Zealand Hospitality Pty Ltd v Liv Pty Ltd* [2017] FCAFC 56.
20   *Pham Global Pty Ltd v Insight Clinical Imaging Pty Ltd* [2017] FCAFC 83.
21   *Anchorage Capital Partners Pty Ltd v ACPA Pty Ltd* [2018] FCAFC 6.
22   *The Coca-Cola Co v All-Fect Distributors Ltd* (1999) 96 FCR 107.
23   Ibid 121.

Whether a mark is deceptively similar to another depends on a combination of visual impression and judicial estimation of the effect likely to be produced in the course of the ordinary conduct of affairs ... Taking into account the 'imperfect recollection' that customers may have of the contour bottle mark, and the fact that the 'idea' suggested by the mark is more likely to be recalled than its precise details, the factors that have led us to conclude that the features of the confectionery are likely to cause confusion in consumers, that is to say, cause them to wonder whether it might be the case that the confectionery comes from the same source as Coca-Cola are these:

- The contour bottle is extremely well known;[24]
- There are similarities between the features of the confectionery and the contour bottle mark ... [the court then described those similarities in detail];
- To a greater or lesser degree depending on the feature, the respondent has taken all significant features of the contour bottle mark;
- The word COLA on the confectionery, though not itself a mark, reinforces the link between the confectionery and Coca-Cola that is conveyed by the shape of the confectionery;
- When fresh, the lower half of the confectionery is the same colour as Coca-Cola, again reinforcing the link referred to.[25]

The key features of the Coca-Cola bottle shape (apart from the fact that the bottle is well known) were referred to in a later decision involving Coca-Cola and PepsiCo but then compared with the Pepsi bottle ('the Carolina bottle'), which was found to have the following features:

(1) the Carolina Bottle has a gently curving waist at a higher point than that in the mark and does not have an abrupt pinch near the base;
(2) the Carolina Bottle has a cylindrical shoulder, not a curved shoulder;
(3) the Carolina Bottle has a frustoconical neck, not a curved neck;
(4) the Carolina Bottle has a twist top enclosure, not a cap lid seal; and
(5) the Carolina Bottle has a distinctive horizontal embossed wave pattern across the bottom half of the bottle.[26]

Consequently, while the Pepsi bottle had been used as a trade mark, it was found not to be deceptively similar to the Coca-Cola trade mark because of the different and distinctive features of the Pepsi bottle.

16.1.5 Relevance of the defendant's conduct

Some aspects of the context in which the defendant uses its sign will be relevant to the question of infringement and those aspects may increase or decrease the prospects of a finding of infringement. On the other hand, as the relevant inquiry is not the same as passing off, there are various aspects of the defendant's conduct that will not be relevant. For example, in

---

24 See below at 16.1.6 concerning this aspect of the judgment.
25 Ibid 123.
26 *The Coca-Cola Co v PepsiCo Inc (No 2)* (2014) 109 IPR 429, [247].

Wingate Marketing Pty Ltd v Levi Strauss & Co,[27] the defendant used the sign 'Revise' to indicate its connection with second-hand Levi jeans. On its face, Revise was very different from Levi's. The situation changed when the defendant started to pronounce Revise as 'Ree-vise' so as to rhyme with 'Levi's'. Hence, its sign was transformed by the defendant's own conduct into a deceptively similar trade mark.

On the other hand, the presence of other signs or the actual manner in which the defendant uses its sign may determine whether the use is use as a trade mark. For example, in *Philips v Remington*,[28] Remington's prominent use of its own trade mark 'Remington' was relevant to determining the question whether its triple-headed rotary shaver was being used as a trade mark. In contrast, in *FH Faulding & Co Ltd v Imperial Chemical Industries of Australia & New Zealand Ltd*,[29] the defendant's use of the word 'Barrier' to describe its own cream infringed 'Barrier Cream' because its packaging emphasised the word in larger print than surrounding words, thus leading to a finding of use as a trade mark as the emphasis on 'Barrier' was designed to ensure that it was the sign by reference to which consumers distinguished the defendant's goods from other goods.

The defendant's conduct described above focuses on the particular use by the defendant of the relevant sign in question. Another example of a relevant context in which the defendant uses its sign is the decision in *Adidas AG v Pacific Brands Footwear Pty Ltd (No 3)*,[30] where the defendant placed stripes on the side of its sports shoe facing away from the other shoe. The evidence that this position was the common position for placing signs used as trade marks, such as the Nike swoosh trade mark, was relevant to a finding that the defendant was using its stripes as a trade mark.

Other extrinsic issues relating to the context of the use by the defendant are far less likely to impact on the question of infringement, even though they would be relevant in a passing off context. For example, if the defendant's advertising is aimed at a different market demographic or at developing a different image, these factors would not affect the question of infringement, at least in the context of s 120(1).[31] Similarly, it is extremely difficult to envisage how the use of a disclaimer by an alleged infringer under s 120(1) would defeat an infringement action, whereas it may be sufficient to stave off a finding of passing off.[32]

16.1.6 Relevance of the plaintiff's trade mark's reputation

Given the nature of the infringement provisions and the scheme of the legislation, it would seem that the reputation or lack of reputation of the plaintiff's trade mark would be irrelevant to the question of substantial identity or deceptive similarity. The legislation confers property rights on a registered owner in respect of the sign that is registered as a trade mark and does not require use before registration. Infringement is not dependent on the reputation of the

---

27 (1994) 49 FCR 89.
28 *Koninklijke Philips Electronics NV v Remington Products Australia Pty Ltd* (2000) 100 FCR 90.
29 (1964) 112 CLR 537.
30 (2013) 308 ALR 74.
31 M. Davison, 'Reputation in trade mark infringement: Why some courts think it matters and why it should not' (2010) 38 *Federal Law Review* 231.
32 See *Knott Investments Pty Ltd v Winnebago Industries Inc* (2013) 211 FCR 449 for such a disclaimer.

registered trade mark (at least in relation to s 120(1) and probably (2) as well),[33] as the issue is one of comparison of the two trade marks in an objective sense or a likelihood of deception or confusion, given the similarities of the two trade marks.

However, several decisions of the Full Federal Court have indicated that the reputation of the plaintiff's trade mark may be relevant to a finding of deceptive similarity, both in the context of infringement proceedings and pursuant to s 44(1) and (2) for registration purposes. The relevance of the reputation of the trade mark for s 44 purposes was discussed in chapter 15,[34] particularly in the discussion of *Registrar of Trade Marks v Woolworths Ltd*.[35] In relation to infringement, in the *Coca-Cola* case the Full Court listed a number of factors that led to its finding of deceptive similarity. Most of these factors related to the physical similarities between the trade mark and the defendant's sign.[36] Yet the first factor named by the court was that Coca-Cola's bottle shape is extremely well known. This suggests that the possibility of deceptive similarity is increased if the plaintiff's trade mark is well known. However, that possibility is complicated by later cases that suggest the exact opposite. They suggest that if the plaintiff's trade mark is very well known, this decreases the likelihood of deceptive similarity because consumers who know the plaintiff's trade mark well will easily perceive differences between it and the defendant's allegedly infringing sign.[37]

The Full Court retreated to some extent from the position seemingly adopted in the *Coca-Cola* case in *CA Henschke & Co v Rosemount Estates Pty Ltd*,[38] but the fame of the trade mark may still be relevant if it can be proven to be very famous as opposed to just famous. It seems the fame must be so great that consumers generally must be taken to be familiar with it. The *Henschke* case involved an infringement action involving the plaintiff's trade mark for wine, 'Hill of Grace', and the defendant's trade mark for its wine, 'Hill of Gold'. The first instance judge refused to take into account any evidence of the very considerable reputation of 'Hill of Grace' among keen wine drinkers. On appeal, the Full Court stated:

> [W]e do not think that their Honours, by that brief reference [the reference in the *Coca-Cola* case to the reputation of Coca-Cola's well-known trade mark] are to be taken to have decided that reputation evidence, of the kind which is undoubtedly relevant in a passing off action, is generally relevant to a question of deceptive similarity.[39]
>
> ... [I]n assessing the nature of a consumer's imperfect recollection of a mark, the fact that the mark, or perhaps an important element of it, is notoriously so ubiquitous and of such long standing that consumers generally must be taken to be familiar with it and with its use in relation to particular goods or services is a relevant consideration. It is unnecessary to consider whether the cases are authority for precisely that proposition. All that is necessary for present purposes is to hold, as we would, that they are authority for no wider proposition in relation to the relevance, on a question of deceptive similarity in

---

33   The reputation of the plaintiff's trade mark would obviously be relevant to the *Trade Marks Act 1995* (Cth): s 120(3). See *Lone Star Steakhouse & Saloon Inc v Zurcas* (2000) 48 IPR 325; *The Coca-Cola Co v All-Fect Distributors Ltd* (1999) 96 FCR 107.
34   See ch 15 at 15.21.3.
35   (1999) 45 IPR 411.
36   *The Coca-Cola Co v All-Fect Distributors Ltd* (1999) 96 FCR 107.
37   *Mars Australia Pty Ltd v Sweet Rewards Pty Ltd* (2009) 81 IPR 354.
38   (2000) 52 IPR 42.
39   Ibid 63.

proceedings where it is alleged under s 120(1) that a registered mark has been infringed, of evidence as to the reputation attaching to the mark. A wider proposition would not, in our view, be consistent with the earlier, and binding authority to which we have referred.[40]

The above quotes suggest that the Full Court's position is now that evidence of the trade mark's reputation, at most, will be relevant only if the evidence demonstrates that the trade mark is notoriously ubiquitous, and the Full Court found that 'Hill of Grace' was not so notorious or ubiquitous.

The matter is further complicated by the fact that in the *Woolworths* case, the ubiquity of the trade mark was considered to be a factor in finding a lack of deceptive similarity[41] but in the *Coca-Cola* case, it added to a finding of deceptive similarity. Since those two cases, later, seemingly contradictory, decisions on the legal position were given at first instance.[42] The position taken in the *Henschke* case and the apparent retreat from the decision in the *Coca-Cola* case was affirmed by the Full Court in *Australian Meat Group Pty Ltd v JBS Australia Pty Ltd*:

> Consistently with the nature of the test of deceptive similarity and the authorities to which we have referred, it is not easy to see what relevance the reputation an applicant may have in a particular mark ... has in an action for infringement brought in reliance on s 120(1) ...[43]

16.2   Section 120(1)

Section 120(1) applies when the defendant uses as a trade mark a sign that is substantially identical with or deceptively similar to the plaintiff's trade mark in relation to goods or services for which the plaintiff's trade mark is registered. The concepts of 'use as a trade mark' and 'substantially identical and deceptively similar' have already been discussed.[44] There may be an issue of fact as to whether the defendant's goods or services are the same as those in respect of which the plaintiff has registered its trade mark. The courts have tended to take a narrow approach to this issue in the past and are unlikely to change that approach, given the new, expanded forms of infringement in s 120(2) and (3).

---

40   Ibid 64.
41   *Woolworths Ltd v Registrar of Trade Marks* (1998) 45 IPR 445, affirmed (1999) 45 IPR 411. The dissenting judge in that case considered that, if relevant at all, the reputation of Woolworths increased the prospect of a finding of deceptive similarity between Woolworths Metro and Metro.
42   *Adidas AG v Pacific Brands Footwear Pty Ltd (No 3)* (2013) 308 ALR 74, [86], where Robertson J stated that 'the strength or the "fame" of a trade mark must be taken into account in assessing the imperfect recollection of the relevant trade mark which was relevant in the deceptive similarity test' and *Louis Vuitton Malletier v Sonya Valentine Pty Ltd* (2013) 106 IPR 203, [34], where Jessup J found that the plaintiff's trade mark did not reach the high bar required by the Full Court in *Henschke*.
43   [2018] FCAFC 207, [45].
44   At 16.1.1 and 16.1.4 above, respectively.

16.2.1 The goods or services for which the trade mark is registered

For example, in the *Daiquiri Rum Trade Mark* case,[45] the House of Lords decided that a registration for rum did not include rum cocktails; and the British Registrar decided that wire-reinforced plastic tubing were not the same goods as flexible tubing made wholly or principally of metal.[46] On the other hand, stationery has been held to include metal staples.[47] Some insight into this issue may come from the Full Federal Court decision in *Colorado Group Ltd v Strandbags Group Pty Ltd*,[48] which, in the context of ownership, referred to the need for goods to be of the same kind, as opposed to goods of the same description, and that, for example, a hatchet would be the same kind of good as an axe.[49] If the goods or services are found not to be the same as those for which registration has occurred, there is a strong likelihood that s 120(2) will apply.

16.3 Section 120(2)

Section 120(2) applies when the infringing conduct relates to use of a substantially identical or deceptively similar sign in relation to goods of the same description or closely related services. Alternatively, the defendant might use its infringing sign in relation to services of the same description or closely related goods, depending on whether the plaintiff's trade mark is registered for goods or services.

Unlike s 120(1), s 120(2) provides that a person is not taken to have infringed the trade mark if 'the person establishes that using the sign as the person did is not likely to deceive or cause confusion'. At first sight, this provision suggests that s 120(2) is little more than a codification of a particular form of passing off or a specific type of contravention of s 18 of sch 2 of the *Competition and Consumer Act 2010* (Cth). This impression is incorrect and there are several important differences between this form of infringement and passing off. First, the onus of proof is on the defendant as it is the defendant who must establish the lack of a likelihood of deception or confusion. Second, a likelihood of confusion must be negatived. While the passing off case law is itself confusing about the relevant standard (confusion or deception), the higher standard required of defendants is clearly contemplated here in that they must negative both confusion and deception. Similarly, the provision differs from s 18 of sch 2 of the *Competition and Consumer Act 2010* (Cth) by its express reference to confusion whereas s 18 of sch 2 requires deception or misleading conduct to occur and numerous cases have stated that confusion is insufficient.

Finally, and probably most importantly, the particular examination is an examination of the defendant's conduct in the light of the potential as well as the actual use by the plaintiff of its trade mark. In a passing off situation, it is only the plaintiff's actual reputation at the time of the alleged passing off that is relevant to determining whether deception has occurred. The

---

45 [1969] RPC 600.
46 *Vac-U-Flex Trade Mark* [1965] FSR 176.
47 *Ofrex Ltd v Rapesco Ltd* [1963] RPC 169.
48 (2007) 164 FCR 506.
49 See ch 15 at 15.9.1.

provision focuses on the future as well as the past by expressly referring to whether the use *is* likely to deceive or cause confusion. Hence, while the defendant is free to refer to any aspect of the circumstances surrounding its use of the sign, it cannot rely on the particular use by the trade mark owner to date. For example, the trade mark owner may not have used the trade mark at all at the time of the alleged infringement or it may have an established reputation for selling its goods at bargain prices. In such circumstances, the defendant cannot rely on factors such as the plaintiff's lack of reputation or an argument that, unlike the plaintiff, its products are targeted at the expensive end of the market. Instead, it has to demonstrate that its actual conduct would not be likely to confuse or deceive in the future, even in the context of the full scope of the potential use by the plaintiff of its trade mark.

The defence was discussed at first instance and on appeal to the Full Federal Court in *Gallo v Lion Nathan*.[50] Lion Nathan sold beer with a sign used as a trade mark that was deceptively similar to Gallo's trade mark for wine. At first instance, the defence in s 120(2) was held to apply because the shapes of the bottles were different, the emphasis in Lion Nathan's marketing was on the 'refreshing' qualities of its beer, and the products were sold in quite separate parts of liquor stores, with beer being sold primarily from the cold room. The difficulty with such an approach was that Gallo could, in the future, market its wine as refreshing, alter the shape of its bottle and ensure that it was sold from cold rooms. On appeal, the Full Court held that that these factors did not offset the likelihood of deception or confusion arising from Lion Nathan selling beer called Barefoot Radler while Gallo sold wine called Barefoot. The Full Court also noted that neither party suggested that the way in which Gallo had actually used its trade mark was relevant to the defence.

16.4   Section 120(3)

Section 120(3) provides additional protection for registered, well-known trade marks over and above that given in s 120(1) and (2) for all trade marks. Its precise meaning is unclear. One view is that it is little more than a particular form of passing off or a breach of s 18 of sch 2 of the *Competition and Consumer Act 2010* (Cth).[51] Another view is that it is a form of anti-dilution provision designed to provide protection to well-known trade marks as property in their own right and regardless of any possibility of confusion or deception of consumers.[52] The subsection itself is based on the wording of art 16(2) and (3) of the *Agreement on Trade-Related Aspects of Intellectual Property*[53] (*TRIPS*) and broadly reflects the wording of that article although that provides little assistance in its interpretation either. Below is a brief description of anti-dilution in other jurisdictions. Thereafter appears an analysis of the sub-paragraphs and key terms in s 120(3) together with a discussion of the different possible interpretations of it.

---

50   *E & J Gallo Winery v Lion Nathan Australia Pty Ltd* (2008) 77 IPR 69 and *E & J Gallo Winery v Lion Nathan Australia Pty Ltd* (2009) 175 FCR 386.
51   M. Handler, 'Trade mark dilution in Australia?' [2007] *European Intellectual Property Review* 307–18, republished in (2007) 70 *Intellectual Property Forum* 36–49.
52   M. Gonsalves and P. Flynn, 'Dilution down under: The protection of well-known trade marks in Australia' [2006] *European Intellectual Property Review* 174.
53   *Marrakesh Agreement Establishing the World Trade Organization*, opened for signature 15 April 1994, 1867 UNTS 3 (entered into force 1 January 1995) annex 1C.

16.4.1 Anti-dilution

The United States and the European Union have specific legislative provisions known as anti-dilution provisions. The basic premise of anti-dilution provisions is that infringement of a well-known trade mark may occur in the absence of any deception or confusion of consumers. For example, art 10(2)(c) of the *European Trade Marks Directive*[54] prevents a person from using any sign 'where use of that sign without due cause takes unfair advantage of, or is detrimental to, the distinctive character or the repute of the trade mark'. In addition, the amendments to the *Lanham (Trademark) Act*[55] via the United States *Federal Trademark Dilution Act of 1995* and subsequent amendments in 2006 protect famous trade marks by prohibiting 'the lessening of the capacity of a famous mark to identify and distinguish goods or services'. The rationale for anti-dilution provisions is firmly grounded in a property-based approach to trade marks, which perceives well-known trade marks as valuable commodities in their own right having a very considerable 'pulling power' regardless of the goods or services with which they are associated.[56] It is this capacity to attract attention, rather than the capacity of the trade mark to indicate origin, characteristics or quality of a product that is protected by anti-dilution laws.

The actual interpretation and application of anti-dilution provisions has been the cause of considerable confusion, with it often being regarded as 'merely a different and more subtle kind of likelihood of confusion'[57] and many cases from the United States are not clear as to the nature of anti-dilution. Part of the difficulty flows from the fact that the one act by the defendant may simultaneously constitute dilution of the property right of the trade mark and traditional infringement by constituting conduct that may deceive or confuse consumers. Separating the dilution from the 'standard' infringement may be difficult. Further difficulty in interpreting the American decisions flows from the fact that the test for standard infringement under American trade mark law is based on a finding of confusion or deception that is akin to passing off.

There are two commonly acknowledged forms of dilution: blurring and tarnishment. Blurring occurs where consumers identify the famous trade mark and the defendant's sign with two different sources or origins of two different goods. As they are aware that the origins are different origins, there is no confusion involved but a dilution of the value of the famous trade mark as an exclusive identifier of its goods.

The thesis is that if those who are aware of the accused use identify the mark with products sold both under the famous mark and by the accused user, then that indicates a duality of sources identified by the famous mark – evidence of blurring.[58]

---

[54] Directive (EU) 2015/2436 of the European Parliament and of the Council of 16 December 2015 to Approximate the Laws of the Member States Relating to Trade Marks [2015] OL J 336/1.
[55] 15 USC § 1125 (1946).
[56] F. Schechter, 'The rational basis of trademark protection' (1927) *Harvard Law Review* 813.
[57] J. McCarthy, 'The American experience with trademark anti-dilution law' (2004) 15 *Australian Intellectual Property Journal* 70, 73. For Australian and New Zealand perspectives, see T. Stevens, 'Dilution in Australia: Waiting in the wings' (2004) 16 *Australian Intellectual Property Law Bulletin* 129; A. Sims, 'Dilution in New Zealand: The effects of the tarnishment limb of dilution on free speech' (2001) 32 *Victoria University of Wellington Law Review* 103.
[58] McCarthy, 'The American experience with trademark anti-dilution law', above n 57, 79–80.

An example of such blurring might be branding spring water as Champagne spring water or candy as Rolex candies. In both cases, there may also be traditional infringement in that there is the likelihood of deception or confusion due to the use of deceptively similar trade marks and the pre-existing reputation of the well-known trade mark but even in the absence of that there is dilution of the distinctive characteristics of the well-known trade mark.

Tarnishment is where a defendant tarnishes the positive associations with a famous trade mark. For example, the domain name of the website adultsrus.com, which sold adult sexual products, was held to tarnish the famous trade mark Toys 'R' Us.[59] As with blurring, consumers would not consider the adultsrus products to come from or be associated with Toys 'R' Us. Nevertheless, the use of 'adultsrus' would have a negative impact on the famous trade mark.

It has been suggested that s 120(3) may be interpreted as an anti-dilution provision and the High Court has indicated that some aspects of the previous legislation were intended to confer some anti-dilution protection on trade marks, although such comments were not made in the context of infringement proceedings but rectification proceedings pursuant to s 28 of the 1955 legislation.[60] On the other hand, there are good reasons to believe the provision is not an anti-dilution provision; these are discussed below.

16.4.2 Well known

The plaintiff's first requirement under s 120(3) is to prove that its trade mark is well known in Australia. A well-known trade mark is not defined in the legislation although some minimal assistance is provided by s 120(4), which prescribes that one 'must take account of the extent to which the trade mark is known within the relevant sector of the public, whether as a result of the promotion of the trade mark or for any other reason'. Consequently, a trade mark may be well known even if it is only known within 'the relevant sector'. The World Intellectual Property Organization (WIPO) has developed some criteria for determining the 'relevant sector', including:

(i) actual or potential consumers of the type of goods or services in relation to which the trade mark is used;
(ii) persons involved in channels of distribution of the type of goods or services; and
(iii) business circles dealing with the type of goods and/or services.[61]

WIPO has also stated that the trade mark need not be well known by the public at large in order to be a well-known trade mark.[62] However, it should be noted that being well known is but one element of s 120(3) and a trade mark that is well known only in the relevant sector will have far greater difficulty satisfying the other requirements of s 120(3) than one that is generally well known by the public at large.

---

59 *Toys 'R' Us Inc v Akkaoui*, 40 USPQ 2d 1836 (ND Cal, 1996).
60 *Campomar SL v Nike International Ltd* (2000) 202 CLR 45.
61 *Joint Recommendation Concerning Provisions on the Protection of Well-Known Marks* art 2(2), adopted by the Assembly of the Paris Union for the Protection of Industrial Property and the General Assembly of WIPO at the Thirty-Fourth Series of Meetings of the Assemblies of the Member States of WIPO, 20–29 September 1999. Available at WIPO, 'Joint Recommendation Concerning Provisions on the Protection of Well-Known Marks' (1999) www.wipo.int.
62 Ibid art 2(3).

WIPO has also developed other relevant criteria for identifying well-known trade marks. In addition to the criterion already stated in s 120(4), they are:

1. the duration, extent and geographical area of any use of the mark;
2. the duration, extent and geographical area of any promotion of the mark, including advertising or publicity and the presentation, at fairs or exhibitions, of the goods and/or services to which the mark applies;
3. the duration and geographical area of any registrations, and/or any applications for registration, of the mark, to the extent that they reflect use or recognition of the mark;
4. the record of successful enforcement of rights in the mark, in particular, the extent to which the mark was recognized as well known by competent authorities;
5. the value associated with the mark.[63]

Other factors may include attempts to register the trade mark as a domain name by other than the registered owner of the trade mark.

Cases concerning s 120(3) have identified a number of well-known trade marks, including:

- the famous Coca-Cola bottle shape;[64]
- 'Nintendo', the trade mark for computer games;[65]
- 'Virgin';[66]
- 'San Remo';[67] and
- 'Google'.[68]

Some guidance may also be gained from the treatment of applications for registration of defensive trade marks as it is highly unlikely that a trade mark could gain defensive registration unless it is well known. However, the reverse may not be the case as just because it is well known does not mean that it will gain defensive registration.[69]

16.4.3 Used in relation to unrelated goods or services

If the trade mark is found to be well known, the next requirement is that the defendant must have used a sign that is substantially identical with or deceptively similar to the plaintiff's trade mark as a trade mark in relation to unrelated goods or services. Unrelated goods and services are ones that are not of the same description or closely related to the goods or services for which the well-known trade mark is registered. In other words, neither s 120(1) nor s 120(2) applies to the situation in question.

---

63   Ibid art 2(1)(b).
64   *The Coca-Cola Co v All-Fect Distributors Ltd* (1998) 43 IPR 47; *The Coca-Cola Co v All-Fect Distributors Ltd* (1999) 96 FCR 107.
65   *Nintendo Co Ltd v CARE* (2000) 52 IPR 34.
66   *Virgin Enterprises Ltd v Klapsas* (2002) AIPC 91-670.
67   *San Remo Macaroni Co Pty Ltd v San Remo Gourmet Coffee Pty Ltd* (2000) 50 IPR 321.
68   *Google LLC v Weeks* [2018] FCCA 3150.
69   See *Trade Marks Act 1995* (Cth) ss 33 and 185 regarding defensive trade marks, and the comments in *Re Pfizer Products Inc* (2004) 61 IPR 165.

However, as with concepts such as 'goods of the same description' or 'closely related services', the concept of 'unrelated goods or services' is one of degree.[70] In other words, goods may be totally unrelated, largely unrelated or insufficiently related to be considered goods of the same description. Arguably, while the goods or services in question must be unrelated for s 120(3) to apply, the less 'unrelated' they are, the more likely it is that other elements of s 120(3) will be satisfied.

16.4.4 Indicating a connection with the owner

The third requirement is that 'because the trade mark is well known, the sign would be likely to be taken as indicating a connection between the unrelated goods or services and the registered owner of the trade mark'. This requirement is different from and additional to the requirement that the defendant use the trade mark as a trade mark. In the *Coca-Cola* case,[71] the Full Court found that using the trade mark as a trade mark involves the defendant using the trade mark to indicate that it has a connection with the goods or services in question. It also stated that this is a separate proposition from using the trade mark to indicate a connection between the plaintiff and the goods or services in question. Consequently, in that case, decided pursuant to s 120(2), the plaintiff did not have to demonstrate that the defendant's use of its sign indicated a connection between the goods and Coca-Cola. If the matter had been determined under s 120(3), the plaintiff would have had to demonstrate that was the case.

The interpretation of these words in s 120(3) will turn very much on the meaning of the word 'connection'. There are at least two possible meanings. One is consistent with and tied into an interpretation of s 120(3), which identifies the subsection as the equivalent of passing off. The other is consistent with s 120(3) being an anti-dilution provision.

The interpretation consistent with a passing off type of provision is as follows. The question is whether consumers would look at the sign in question and think 'that sign indicates to me that these goods (or services) are connected with whoever owns that well-known mark with which I am so familiar'. In addition, the sign would indicate that it is distinguishing the goods of whoever is using the goods (the defendant) from other goods and is therefore being used as a trade mark. This situation will be most likely to arise in circumstances where the sign being used is identical or nearly identical to the owner's trade mark. By using a very similar sign, consumers would be likely to make the necessary connection between the sign, the goods for which it is used and the owner. Consumers who are aware of the well-known trade mark would then assume some connection between the owner and the goods in question such as one of the following:

- The owner has itself expanded its branding to new products.
- The owner has entered into an authorised use arrangement.
- The owner has entered into a strategic alliance with another company, body or entity in order to produce the goods in question.[72]

---

70 *Registrar of Trade Marks v Woolworths Ltd* (1999) 45 IPR 411.
71 *The Coca-Cola Co v All-Fect Distributors Ltd* (1999) 96 FCR 107.
72 These forms of connection are also relevant to applications for defensive registration. See *AT&T Corp's Application* [2001] ATMO 96.

The application of this particular interpretation can be considered in the context of the facts of the *Coca-Cola* case. If the goods in question in the case had been unrelated to aerated beverages, s 120(3) infringement would arguably *not* have occurred. The primary reason for such an outcome would have been that the defendant's sign, while being deceptively similar to the shape trade mark of the Coca-Cola bottle design, was not identical or even substantially identical.[73] The differences between the two were so great that consumers would probably not have believed that Coca-Cola had entered the confectionery market, either by itself or via some arrangement with another company. At most, consumers would think that the user of the sign was trying to trade off the well-known trade mark by attracting people's attention.

On the other hand, if the sign used by the defendant had been the same or very similar to the Coca-Cola trade mark, consumers would have easily drawn the necessary conclusions for s 120(3) to apply. The first would be the one in fact drawn by the Full Court – namely, that whoever had used the sign was saying to consumers, 'When you see this sign, you are seeing my goods and not the goods of anyone else'. This would constitute the use of the sign as a trade mark sufficient for the purposes of s 120(1) or s 120(2). In addition, the use of the sign would send another message to consumers: 'These goods are provided, endorsed, licensed by or have some other connection with the company that owns the well-known trade mark of the shape of a Coca-Cola bottle.'

The second interpretation of s 120(3), based on an anti-dilution approach, would suggest that the necessary connection is simply that the sign used by the defendant brings the plaintiff's well-known trade mark to mind and therefore reminds the consumer of the plaintiff's trade mark. Consequently, there is a connection between the unrelated goods or services and the registered owner even though no consumer would think that the defendant's goods are endorsed, supplied or associated in a business sense with the defendant's product. Again this interpretation could be applied to the facts of the *Coca-Cola* case. Upon seeing the defendant's sign, a hypothetical consumer would be reminded of Coca-Cola. The consumer may not think that the sign indicates that the goods are those of Coca-Cola and, indeed, may be quite sure that they are not because of the dissimilarities; but the similarities are sufficient for the creation of a sufficient connection to bring the owner of the Coca-Cola trade mark to mind. This hypothetical consumer then believes that two similar signs are used in two different products, thus blurring or diluting the value of the registered trade mark as envisaged in anti-dilution situations.

Whichever interpretation of connection is taken, some assistance in determining the necessary connection for these purposes may also come from the provisions dealing with defensive registration. Section 185(1) requires an applicant for defensive registration to demonstrate that the use of the applicant's trade mark would be likely to be taken to indicate that there is a connection between those goods or services for which defensive registration is sought and the applicant. Consequently, it is a reasonable assumption that the 'connection' required for the purposes of s 185 is the same 'connection' required for s 120(3). The close relationship between the defensive registration provisions and s 120(3) was argued strongly by

---

73 *The Coca-Cola Co v All-Fect Distributors Ltd* (1998) 43 IPR 47, 57; *The Coca-Cola Co v All-Fect Distributors Ltd* (1999) 96 FCR 107, 122.

the applicant before the Registrar in *Re Pfizer Products Inc*,[74] and while not yet accepted by any court, the argument has considerable merit.

In addition, regardless of whichever interpretation of 'connection' is adopted, while this element of s 120(3) requires that the sign would be likely to be taken as indicating a connection between the goods and the owner 'because the trade mark is well known', other factors would almost certainly be taken into account. In particular, as already explained, the likelihood of the necessary connection being made increases as the similarity between the defendant's sign and the owner's trade mark increases. So too does that likelihood increase if the goods and services in question are not too 'unrelated'.

16.4.5 Owner's interests adversely affected

Finally, the registered owner must demonstrate that because the sign would be likely to be taken as indicating a connection between the unrelated goods or services and the registered owner, the interests of the registered owner are likely to be adversely affected.

If, in fact, all the previous elements of s 120(3) are proven, it is hard to imagine circumstances in which the interests of the registered owner would not be likely to be adversely affected in some way. This again suggests that the meaning of 'adversely affected' depends on whether the provision is an equivalent of passing off or an anti-dilution provision.

If the provision is a passing off provision, the affected interests may include one or more of the following:

- loss of the opportunity to penetrate or greater difficulty in penetrating the market for the goods or services being supplied by the defendant;
- loss of licensing fees that could have been demanded from the defendant in return for use of the deceptively similar sign; and
- loss of custom generally if the defendant's product is perceived as being of inferior quality and customers then have less regard for goods or services bearing the plaintiff's trade mark.

It is important to note that it is sufficient for the owner to demonstrate a likelihood that its interests would be adversely affected. As the defendant will have an incentive to make a short-term gain by cutting corners on costs and quality and trading off the wrongful connection with the trade mark owner, the likelihood of an adverse effect on the owner will almost always be significant.

If the provision is an anti-dilution provision, an adverse effect is inevitable. In addition to the adverse effects mentioned in the previous paragraph, there is the general dilution of the value of the plaintiff's trade mark. The constant use of a similar trade mark by others, even if done in a non-confusing or non-deceptive way, dilutes the image conveyed or hoped to be conveyed by the trade mark owner.

16.4.6 Anti-dilution or passing off?

While the actual purpose of s 120(3) is not clear, on balance it is probably not an anti-dilution provision. First, the requirement of a connection between the defendant's goods or services

---

74 (2004) 61 IPR 165.

and the owner suggests the need for some actual deceit or confusion of consumers although a wide reading of the term may include some form of non-deceptive but powerful psychological association between the goods and the well-known trade mark.[75]

Second, while the *Coca-Cola* decision was based on s 120(2) not s 120(3), an important comment from the Full Court on the relationship between the two subsections clearly indicates that s 120(3) is not an anti-dilution provision:

> [S]ub-sections (2) and (3) are mutually exclusive – the former dealing with 'goods of the same description ...' and the latter with 'goods ... that are not of the same description ...'[76]

Subsection (2) is clearly not an anti-dilution provision. This fact is demonstrated by the defence contained in it that the defendant will not have infringed 'if the person establishes that using the sign as the person did is not likely to deceive or cause confusion'. It is highly unlikely that parliament intended to confer antidilution protection when the defendant uses its deceptively similar or substantially identical sign on unrelated goods but declined to confer such protection when the defendant uses its sign in relation to goods of the same description. There would be no good reason for such an approach.

Third, an anti-dilution provision could have been achieved more easily by simply omitting the requirement of 'a connection' and adopting wording similar to either the American or European Union provisions. The lack of a clear indication from the legislature suggests that it would be inappropriate for a court to take such a broad approach to the rights of trade mark owners, which goes beyond anything previously considered at common law. The clear rejection of a tort of unfair competition in Australian case law suggests that a legislative decision to overturn that view would have been signalled far more clearly.

Fourth, there is no ground of opposition to registration on the basis that an opponent's trade mark would be diluted by the use of the trade mark for which registration is sought. Section 60 is based on a finding of likelihood of deception or confusion. Both the United States and the European Community prevent registration on the basis that a trade mark might dilute a well-known trade mark. It would be curious if Australian law permitted the registration of a trade mark that may dilute a well-known trade mark but then had an anti-dilution infringement provision. Section 120(1)(e) provides a defence to infringement if a person uses a right to use a trade mark given to a person under the present legislation. Consequently, a diluting sign may be registered because there is no express ground on which to oppose its registration and, once registered, the owner would be entitled to use that trade mark in a manner that dilutes the mark because such use would be neither an infringement of the well-known trade mark nor passing off.

16.4.7 Comparison with passing off

If s 120(3) is not an anti-dilution provision, it is not easy to identify any circumstances in which infringement based on s 120(3) would not also constitute passing off or a breach of s 18 of

---

75 B. Fitzgerald and E. Sheehan, 'Trademark dilution and the commodification of information: Understanding the cultural command' (1999) 3 *Macquarie Law Review* 61.
76 *The Coca-Cola Co v All-Fect Distributors Ltd* (1999) 96 FCR 107, [44].

sch 2 of the *Competition and Consumer Act 2010* (Cth). In this context, both require an actual reputation in Australia and an unauthorised association or connection with the plaintiff.

16.5 Oral use of a trade mark

With the above principles in mind, we can turn to consideration of some specific examples of trade mark use that may constitute trade mark infringement and that raise their own specific legal issues. Under the 1955 Act, infringing use of a trade mark had to be in some tangible form and hence oral infringement was not possible. Section 7(2) overcomes this by providing that 'if a trade mark consists of the following, or any combination of the following, namely, any letter, word, name or numeral, any aural representation of the trade mark is, for the purposes of this Act, a use of the trade mark'. Hence, radio advertisements, spruiking on the footpath and wrongful use of the trade mark when taking orders over the telephone may constitute infringement.

16.6 Two-dimensional device infringed by three-dimensional shape

As two-dimensional device signs are obviously registrable, one issue that may arise is whether a three-dimensional reproduction of that two-dimensional device may constitute an infringing sign. A similar issue may arise in copyright in determining whether a three-dimensional item infringes the copyright in a two-dimensional artistic work. The decision in *Philips v Remington*[77] clearly demonstrates that infringement may occur in such circumstances. At first instance and on appeal, the Federal Court accepted that Philip's two-dimensional representation of its triple-headed rotary razor may have been infringed by Remington's actual, three-dimensional triple-headed rotary razor although the actual use by Remington of its razor was not considered to be use 'as a trade mark' and therefore not an infringing use.

16.7 Parallel importing

Parallel importation involves several steps. First, goods are produced overseas and a trade mark is applied to them there with the consent of the owner of that trade mark, which is registered in the relevant overseas country. Second, those goods are put on the market overseas. Third, the goods are bought by an Australian importer who then imports the goods into Australia for resale without the consent of the owner of the Australian trade mark. These imported goods then compete with the goods placed on the market in Australia by or with the consent of the owner of the Australian trade mark.

The current position is controlled by s 122A which only came into effect in late 2018. Prior to then, the position was controlled by s 123 of the Act, as it then was. Section 122A is a lengthy and complex provision. Its primary objective is to ensure the legality of parallel importing but,

---

[77] *Koninklijke Philips Electronics NV v Remington Products Australia Pty Ltd* (2000) 100 FCR 90.

as with any legislative provision, it must be applied by reference to the particular facts being considered in any infringement action.

In order to understand how s 122A is likely to operate, it is important to have an understanding of the previous history of parallel importing and the difficulties that arose from previous case law, as it is those difficulties that the provision is intended to address.

All but two cases decided under the 1955 legislation permitted parallel importing on the basis that parallel importing did not involve use of the trade mark as a trade mark by the importer. Consequently, the trade mark owner failed to establish infringement. These decisions were, in turn, influenced by an underlying theory that trade mark rights are exhausted once trade marked products are initially sold on the open market. The opposing theory is that of territoriality, which treats the rights of trade mark owners as being restricted to the particular territory or jurisdiction for which they have acquired registration. While these theories are relevant to the policy debate about the appropriateness or otherwise of parallel importing, the legality or otherwise of the practice must be determined by reference to the current legislative provisions.[78]

The case law position changed with the introduction of the 1995 Act. Section 123 of the 1955 legislation provided, in part:

> In spite of section 120, a person who uses a registered trade mark in relation to goods that are similar to goods in respect of which the trade mark is registered does not infringe the trade mark if the trade mark has been applied to, or in relation to, the goods by, or with the consent of, the registered owner of the trade mark.

The first parallel importing case decided under the 1995 Act was *Transport Tyre Sales Pty Ltd v Montana Tyres Rims & Tubes Pty Ltd*.[79] In that case, the plaintiff (Montana Tyres) objected to the parallel importation of car tyres that were branded with the trade mark 'Ohtsu' and other trade marks. Ohtsu tyres were made in Japan by the company of the same name and Montana had an exclusive Australian distributorship arrangement with Ohtsu. At the time that Transport Tyres commenced to parallel import Ohtsu tyres that it obtained in Singapore, Ohtsu was the registered owner in Australia of the trade mark 'Ohtsu'. Soon after Transport Tyres commenced importing Ohtsu tyres, Ohtsu assigned the trade mark to Montana. Montana then instituted proceedings against Transport, alleging that the importation and sale of Ohtsu tyres by Transport both prior to and after the assignment of the trade mark to Montana constituted infringement.

The assignment of the trade mark was subject to a contractual requirement that Montana reassign the trade mark to Ohtsu as soon as the distributorship arrangement between it and Ohtsu came to an end.

The Full Federal Court held that the importer was using the trade mark as a trade mark. While the majority of cases under the previous legislation had held otherwise, those cases were questionable. However, while finding that the importer was using the trade mark as a trade mark, it did not actually explain why it was now making such a finding in the face of the previous cases, especially given that the concept of use as a trade mark is the same under the

---

78 *Paul's Retail Pty Ltd v Lonsdale Australia Ltd* (2012) 294 ALR 72.
79 (1999) 93 FCR 421.

current legislation as under the previous legislation. Nevertheless, this case and subsequent cases have held that a parallel importer is using the trade mark as a trade mark and is, therefore, prima facie infringing the trade mark.[80]

The Full Court then went on to decide that the importation prior to the assignment did not constitute infringement because of the effect of s 123(1).

As Ohtsu had applied the trade mark to those tyres and it was the trade mark owner in Australia at that time, s 123(1) applied to prevent a finding of infringement. The Full Court rejected an argument by Montana that while the sign applied to all the tyres in Japan was identical, it should regard the same sign as constituting a different trade mark, depending on the intended destination of any particular tyre. Montana claimed that if a tyre marked 'Ohtsu' was intended for the Singapore market, then that 'Ohtsu' sign was the Singaporean trade mark 'Ohtsu', not the Australian trade mark 'Ohtsu'.[81] Consequently, the trade mark owner had not applied 'the' trade mark to the tyres imported by Transport Tyres as 'the' trade mark it was using was the Australian trade mark, not the Singaporean trade mark. This argument was supported by the reference to the application of 'the trade mark' rather than the sign or signs constituting the trade mark. This suggests that the provision may be referring to something with a legal rather than a physical identity.

Nevertheless, the Full Court rejected the argument and pointed out that a trade mark is also a physical manifestation:

> A physical manifestation, or sign, may be registered. When the Act speaks of a 'trade mark' it is concerned only with something which is capable of being a sign, albeit a sign which is used or intended to be used to distinguish goods or services from other goods or services in the course of trade.[82]

Consequently, the importation of tyres prior to the assignment to Transport Tyres was lawful.

The importation of tyres after the assignment was never considered by the Full Court because Montana provided Transport Tyres with an undertaking to cease further exports and so the matter was resolved out of court. If it had not been resolved, the question[83] would have been whether Montana could have argued that the trade mark had been applied to the tyres with Transport Tyres' consent. Such consent could either be express or implied and, as a general rule, there will be no express consent, especially in circumstances such as where the intention of a conditional assignment is to actually prevent parallel importing.

So the consent needed to be inferred from the conduct of the owner of the Australian trade mark. A critical point here is that the relevant consent would be to the application in Japan by Ohtsu of the 'Ohtsu' trade mark, not whether Transport Tyres consented to the use of its trade mark by importation into Australia or any other dealing with the tyres once branded.

After the *Montana* decision, the issue was not whether the importer was using the trade mark as a trade mark but whether the defendant could prove that the registered owner of the

---

80   For example, *Paul's Retail Pty Ltd v Lonsdale Australia Ltd* (2012) 294 ALR 72.
81   A similar argument was successful in the United Kingdom in *Colgate Palmolive v Markwell Finance Ltd* [1989] RPC 497.
82   *Transport Tyres Sales Pty Ltd v Montana Tyres Rims & Tubes Pty Ltd* (1999) 93 FCR 421, 436.
83   M. Davison, 'Parallel importing of trade marked goods: An answer to the unasked question' (1999) *Australian Intellectual Property Journal* 146.

trade mark had either applied the trade mark to the goods or consented to the application of the trade mark to the goods. Various strategies were adopted by registered owners to ensure that they did not apply the trade mark to the goods and to negative any suggestion of an implied consent to the application of the trade mark. One such strategy was that of assigning the trade mark to the local Australian distributor with the consequence that the assignor was the party applying the trade mark, not the new registered owner. The onus then fell on the defendant to prove consent to the application of the trade mark.

In the context of the *Montana* decision, the implication of such consent could have flowed from various factors:[84]

- Transport Tyres was relying on the global reputation of Ohtsu to sell the tyres.
- The continued sale of the Ohtsu tyres throughout the world by Ohtsu was therefore to Transport Tyres' advantage, thus leading to an implication that it was consenting to that continuing.
- The assignment agreement required Transport Tyres to do nothing that might damage the international reputation of Ohtsu tyres and provided for termination of the distributorship agreement if that condition was breached.
- Transport Tyres effectively remained under the control of the Japanese company via the assignment agreement although its relationship was contractual rather than corporate. It is inconceivable that it would have or could have directed Ohtsu to stop applying the 'Ohtsu' trade marks to tyres. If it had, the distributorship arrangement would have been terminated and the trade mark reassigned to Ohtsu.

Later cases made the position difficult for parallel importers. For example, in *Brother Industries Ltd v Dynamic Supplies Pty Ltd*,[85] Tamberlin J stated in obiter that production and marking of goods by another company in the same corporate group would not, of itself, constitute consent to the application of the trade mark. Alternatively, the Australian registered owner may argue that an overseas licensee had produced more items than that permitted under its licence. Consequently, the owner did not consent to the application of the trade mark to those items produced over and above the number in the licence agreement.

From a practical point of view, an importer inspecting the goods in question was unable to differentiate between goods produced and marked by a licensee in accordance with its contractual restrictions and such goods produced outside those restrictions. Since the onus was on the importer to prove the relevant consent of the trade mark owner, it was not in a position to know the legality of its actions until it actually imported them and the matter was litigated. By then, of course, it was too late for the importer to avoid being successfully sued for infringement.

One further response of trade mark owners to the potential use of s 123 was to attempt to exclude the possibility of a claim that they had consented to the application of the trade mark to certain products by a licensee who had been given limited authority to place the trade mark on some goods but not others. Typically, the licence agreement would provide that the licensee only had authority to mark goods produced by it or under its supervision that had

---

84   Ibid 152.
85   (2007) 163 FCR 530.

been produced solely for the purpose of sale in the territory defined by the licence agreement. Consequently, if the overseas licensee then made and marked goods intended for a territory other than the territory defined by the licence agreement, the trade mark owner could not be considered to have consented to the application of the trade mark to those goods.

One case that exemplified this situation was *Paul's Retail Pty Ltd v Lonsdale Australia Ltd*.[86] In that case, a licensee of the owner of the Australian trade mark had a licence to arrange for the production and marking of goods to be sold within defined territory in Europe. In fact, it arranged for the production and marking of the relevant goods in China and for transfer of property in those goods to another party in China, rather than the territory designated in the licence agreement. Consequently, the application of the trade mark by the licensee had been done outside the conditions of its licence and the Australian trade mark owner could not be said to have consented to the application of the trade mark to those goods.

On the other hand, if the goods were produced in accordance with the licence conditions and those goods subsequently make their way onto the Australian market, s 123 did apply. The relevant issue was the consent at the time of the application of the trade mark, not the trade mark owner's objection to importation after application, with consent, had occurred.[87]

In addition, the wording of s 123, as it then was, permitted the repackaging of some goods in some circumstances if the relevant trade mark was originally placed on the goods by or with the consent of the registered owner. In *Scandinavian Tobacco Group Eersel BV v Trojan Trading Co Pty Ltd*,[88] the defendant obtained some cigars in their original packaging. The trade marks had been applied to the packaging. In order to comply with Australia's laws on packaging of tobacco products, the cigars were removed from their packaging and placed in new packaging produced by the defendant that complied with the Australian packaging laws. The Full Court held that this conduct was lawful under s 123.

16.7.1 Parallel importing and exclusive licensees

It seems to make no difference to the legality of parallel importing that the Australian distributor was an exclusive licensee of the trade mark owner. However, in such circumstances, if the trade mark owner sold its goods to the importer with the knowledge that they would be imported into Australia, the licensee could sue the owner for breach of contract. It could also sue the purchaser for inducing breach of contract if the purchaser knew of the licensing arrangement.[89]

16.7.2 Section 122A

Section 122A is intended to address the types of problem associated with the onus of proof on defendants, limited licences restricting the place of sale of goods, conditional assignments, different members of the same corporate group using a trade mark, and other problems that

---

86 (2012) 294 ALR 72. See also *Sporte Leisure Pty Ltd v Paul's International Pty Ltd (No 3)* (2010) 275 ALR 258.
87 *Facton Ltd v Toast Sales Group Pty Ltd* (2012) 205 FCR 378.
88 [2016] FCAFC 91.
89 *Delphic Wholesalers v Elco Food Co* (1987) 8 IPR 545.

create legal obstacles to parallel importing. For example, the issue of onus of proof is addressed by introducing a test of a reasonable person who made reasonable inquiries in relation to a trade mark prior to using it.[90] The inquiries relate to whether a relevant person applied or consented to the application of the trade mark to the goods.

In addition, the category of 'a relevant person' is massively expanded when compared to the old s 123 which only referred to the registered owner. Relevant people now include the registered owner, an authorised user, a person permitted to use the trade mark by the registered owner, a person with significant influence over the use of the trade mark by the registered owner, or an associated entity – within the meaning of the *Corporations Act 2001* (Cth) – of another relevant person.[91] A person with significant influence over the use of the trade mark would probably include a previous assignor of the trade mark who retains a contractual right to its reassignment in certain circumstances.

Further, the concept of consent has been broadly defined in s 122A(2). For example, consent subject to a condition that the goods are to be sold only in a foreign country or consent that can be reasonably inferred from the conduct of a relevant person comes within the meaning of consent for these purposes.

The net result is that the onus of proof is met by making reasonable inquiries as to whether there was consent to the application of the trade mark to the goods. The consent could be given by any one of a wide range of people, including licensees, members of the same corporate group as the trade mark owner, and those with significant influence over the trade mark owner such as assignors with a contractual right to reassignment.

It is also important to note that s 122A does not only apply in circumstances where there is importation of goods into Australia. It refers to any goods to which the trade mark has been applied by or with the consent of the relevant person and the reasonable inquiries of any person in relation to the trade marks.

16.7.3 Parallel importing and passing off

While parallel importing may not infringe a registered trade mark, it may still constitute passing off or a breach of s 18 of sch 2 of the *Competition and Consumer Act 2010* (Cth) if there is a material difference between the characteristics or qualities of the two trade marked products – that is, those intended for overseas use or consumption and those intended for Australian use or consumption. For example, in *Colgate Palmolive v Markwell Finance Ltd*,[92] objections to parallel importing were founded on the fact that Colgate toothpaste from Brazil was made with chalk as an abrasive whereas the English Colgate toothpaste contained a more expensive and superior abrasive. Consumers, accustomed to the English Colgate, may have been deceived into believing that the two products were of equal quality. Similarly, in *Star Micronics Pty Ltd v Five Star Computers Pty Ltd*[93] the importation of computer printers was prevented on the grounds that the imported printers operated on different electrical voltages and were therefore of little use in Australia.

---

90   *Trade Marks Act 1995* (Cth) s 122A(1)(b), (c).
91   Ibid s 122A(c).
92   [1989] RPC 497.
93   (1991) 22 IPR 473.

16.8 Second-hand goods

As a general rule, once trade marked goods have been sold to a consumer, the trade mark on them is no longer being used as a trade mark. In addition, s 122A would now apply to second-hand goods so as to make resale possible without infringement occurring.

In very rare circumstances, this situation may change if the goods are resold as second-hand goods with the trade mark still in place. In those circumstances, it is possible, but unlikely, that the very nature of the goods may have been altered to such an extent that they can no longer be regarded as originating from the trade mark owner. In that event, the retention of the trade mark on the goods while displaying them for sale would result in the seller of the second-hand goods using the trade mark to distinguish its goods from other goods. Such a use would be an infringing use. To take an extreme hypothetical example, if a defendant took pairs of Levi jeans that were washed, torn, embroidered, altered and then sewn together in order to make curtains and the Levi badge was retained on those curtains, it would be arguable that what is being sold is the defendant's curtains and that the retention of the Levi badges may constitute an infringing use of the Levi trade mark under s 120(3).

Section 134(2) of the *Trade Marks Act 1994* (Cth) provided that the sale of second-hand goods would not constitute infringement of a registered trade mark originally applied to them if:

(a) the person clearly indicates that the goods are second-hand; or
(b) the changes, alterations or repairs ... are not so extensive or fundamental that the goods can no longer reasonably be regarded as possessing the main characteristics, qualities, or attributes inherent to the goods when they were new.

No equivalent of s 134(2) of the 1994 Act appears in the current legislation although s 134(2) was probably an attempt to codify the first instance decision in *Wingate Marketing Pty Ltd v Levi Strauss & Co*.[94] In that case, the defendant sold second-hand Levi jeans that had been stonewashed, torn, embroidered and in some cases cut off to make shorts. One of several claims by Levi was that the sale of the second-hand goods constituted an infringement of the Levi trade mark. At first instance, it was held that jeans that had been worn or damaged, or worn or damaged and repaired, were not fundamentally changed and, therefore, no infringement had taken place. On the other hand, stonewashed, patched, cut-off, dyed and painted jeans had been fundamentally changed so as to be a different product and therefore the retention of the Levi trade mark constituted an infringing use when reselling those jeans. The position would be somewhat akin to creating a new product and then placing the Levi trade mark on it.

On appeal, the Full Federal Court held that the sale of the second-hand jeans did not constitute use of the trade mark as a trade mark. The Levi trade mark indicated the trade origin of the jeans. The fact that they had been substantially altered did not alter the reality of that origin and hence the trade mark was not being used, by the defendant, as a trade mark. The judges did acknowledge the possibility that, depending on the circumstances of sale, consumers may have been misled and that Levi Strauss may have had an action for passing off or a

---

94   (1994) 49 FCR 89.

breach of s 52 of the *Trade Practices Act 1974* (Cth) as it then was. The omission of s 134 of the 1994 Act from the current legislation therefore suggests that the view of the Full Court that the sale of second-hand goods does not constitute infringement of a trade mark is probably the relevant law in Australia today. Yet the matter is further complicated by an obscure reference to second-hand goods in s 7(4), which states that 'use of a trade mark in relation to goods means use of the trade mark upon, or in physical or other relation to, the goods (including second-hand goods)'. The provision provides no further elucidation and it does not state that this use is use 'as a trade mark' as opposed to merely use of a trade mark. Consequently, its effect on the legality of selling second-hand goods is not clear.

In any event, the combined effect of the case law and s 122A is that the sale of second-hand goods will very rarely constitute infringement. Perhaps the only circumstances where infringement will occur is where the goods have been so dramatically altered that they are in a sense 'new' goods and the plaintiff's trade mark has been left on the new goods.

16.9 Trade mark infringement and the internet

The passing off implications of various uses of the internet are considered in some detail in chapter 14. In the context of infringement of registered trade marks, the primary issue to address would be whether the particular internet use of the plaintiff's trade mark is use 'as a trade mark'. For example, does the registration of a well-known trade mark as a domain name constitute use of that trade mark as a trade mark?

The need to demonstrate for the purposes of infringement that the trade mark has been used for goods and services so as to distinguish those goods and services from other goods and services suggests that mere registration of a domain name, by itself, would not constitute use of a trade mark as a trade mark. The domain name would have to be used on a website that deals with or provides goods or services in the course of trade before a conclusion could be reached that the domain name is being used as a trade mark.[95] Even then, there would need to be evidence associating the domain name to the goods or services sold or advertised via the website. For example, in *CSR Ltd v Resource Capital Australia Pty Ltd*,[96] the defendant had registered a domain name with the trade mark 'CSR' in it but had not used the domain name to sell any products, let alone sugar products for which CSR is widely known. Consequently, while a finding of passing off was made, there was no finding of trade mark infringement because there had been no use as a trade mark of 'CSR' in relation to any goods or services, let alone those for which CSR was registered.

In contrast, in *Mantra Group Pty Ltd v Tailly Pty Ltd (No 2)*,[97] the defendant was found to have used domain names containing the relevant registered trade mark or substantially identical trade marks in combination with website content that used the relevant trade marks as trade marks. Consequently, infringement was found to have occurred.

---

95   See the comments in *CSR Ltd v Resource Capital Australia Pty Ltd* (2003) 128 FCR 408.
96   (2003) 128 FCR 408.
97   (2010) 183 FLR 450.

The use of trade marks as meta-tags, primarily for the purpose of attracting the attention of internet search engines, is unlikely to constitute use as a trade mark because the meta-tag would not, by itself, be use of the trade mark to distinguish the goods or services advertised or sold at that website from other goods or services. In *Mantra Group* the defendant's extensive use of meta-tags consisting of the plaintiff's trade marks was not considered to constitute trade mark use but it was relevant to whether other uses of the plaintiff's trade marks were in good faith for the purposes of describing its services.

In keeping with the views expressed in the *CSR* and the *Mantra Group* decisions, in relation to the use of domain names and meta-tags, the use of keyword advertising is also unlikely, by itself, to constitute infringing trade mark use. As with those decisions, the trade mark owner would need to point to some content within the resulting keyword advertisement that, in combination with the trade mark used within the keywords, constitutes use as a trade mark.

A more recent case dealing with use of a trade mark in the context of websites is *Lift Shop Pty Ltd v Easy Living Home Elevators Pty Ltd*.[98] The plaintiff owned the trade mark, which consisted of one word, 'Liftshop', presented in a slightly fancy form. The defendant recrafted its website with the intention of optimising its recognition by internet search engines in response to various types of searches by consumers. In doing so, it added the words 'Lift Shop' to the title of its website and used those words in the keywords to describe itself and its website so that those keywords appeared above its website in response to various searches. The Full Federal Court found that while the sign 'Lift Shop' was deceptively similar to the registered trade mark 'Liftshop' in stylised form, the defendant had not used 'Lift Shop' as a trade mark but as a means of describing the goods and services that it offered.

One important issue that can arise as a consequence of advertising and sale via the internet is whether a foreign website is using a trade mark in Australia, which is a necessary condition for any infringement action. For example, an Australian company may have legitimately adopted a foreign trade mark for its product and then both it and the overseas owner of the trade mark establish websites that advertise the same product with the same trade mark or even facilitate sale of it via the website. Some case law suggests that overseas sales to Australian consumers with no intention that they be resold in Australia does not constitute use in Australia but the situation may be different where an overseas seller is actively seeking out Australian consumers. It is possible that trade mark owners may need to restrict the sales of their products to jurisdictions in which they have registration of the trade mark.[99]

The first Australian case to date relating to the issue is the decision in *Ward Group Pty Ltd v Brodie & Stone plc*,[100] although the particular facts of the case affect its precedential value to some extent. The Ward Group owned the trade mark 'Restoria' for a hair restoration product in Australia. Brodie & Stone plc owned the same trade mark for the same product in the United Kingdom. Some of Brodie & Stone's customers in the United Kingdom sold Restoria via their websites. The relevant action for trade mark infringement was brought against Brodie & Stone but in order to have any prospect of success, the Ward Group needed to prove that the website operators were using the trade mark in Australia.

---

98 (2014) 311 ALR 207.
99 *Ward Group Pty Ltd v Brodie & Stone plc* (2005) 143 FCR 479.
100 Ibid.

Merkel J held that the website operators were using the trade mark in Australia at the point at which they accepted orders from Australian consumers but not prior to that point in time. The operators offered a number of goods through their websites and the websites clearly envisaged sales to Australians as payment methods included paying in Australian dollars. Merkel J's view was that as they offered numerous products via their websites, they were not specifically offering Restoria to Australians unless and until an order for it was made and they accepted the order. He then concluded that as the relevant orders that constituted the alleged infringement had been initiated by the Australian trade mark owner, the use in question was permitted as a consequence of s 123 of the Act.[101]

The case therefore stands for the proposition that offering a trade marked product via an overseas website may not of itself constitute use of that trade mark in Australia, especially if the product is but one of several products on offer. However, use of the trade mark in Australia will occur at the point at which the website operator accepts an order from an Australian consumer.

In contrast, a New Zealand decision of *DB Breweries v Domain Name Co Ltd*[102] suggests that merely holding a domain name for the purpose of resale may constitute grounds for a mandatory injunction requiring the registrant of the domain name to transfer it to the trade mark owner, at least on an interlocutory basis. In that case, the defendant registered db.nz.com while the plaintiff was the owner of the trade mark 'db', a well-known New Zealand beer. The court ordered the transfer of the domain name to the plaintiff on the basis that attempts to sell the domain name may have been the precursor to it being used to trade goods or services on the relevant website. The interlocutory nature of the decision may suggest that it would have limited application in Australia.

16.10   Breach of certain restrictions: s 121

Section 121 permits a registered owner to place restrictions on altering, removing or obliterating its trade mark or applying another trade mark in certain prescribed situations. In order to take advantage of this power, the registered owner or an authorised user must display on the goods or on their packaging a notice prohibiting the relevant act. For example, the notice may prohibit a person from altering, or partially removing or obliterating, any representation of the trade mark applied to the goods or used in physical relation to them.[103]

However, the scope of s 121 is quite limited. The relevant notice only affects a person if they own the goods in question, undertake the prohibited act in the course of trade, and actually knew of the notice before they acquired the goods.[104] In addition, if the owner became the owner of the goods through a person who acquired them without being aware of the notice, the notice is not binding on them even if they knew of the notice at the time of acquiring the goods.[105]

---

101   See the discussion of s 123 below at 16.13.
102   (2001) 52 IPR 280.
103   *Trade Marks Act 1995* (Cth) s 121(2).
104   Ibid s 121(3), (4).
105   Ibid s 121(4)(b).

As it is difficult to prove that the owner of the goods had actual knowledge of the notice and the notice will take up valuable advertising and get-up space, it is not surprising that very few such notices are placed on goods.[106]

16.11 Groundless threats of legal proceedings

Section 129 confers a right of action on a person who is accused of infringing a registered trade mark. In those circumstances, the plaintiff (the threatened person) may obtain a declaration that the defendant has no grounds for the threat and/or an injunction restraining the person from continuing to make the threat, and they may also recover damages as a consequence of the threat. For example, the threatened person may desist from making and distributing its goods in response to the threat or its distributors may have declined to continue distributing the goods as a consequence of the threat. In those circumstances, the potential damage to the threatened person is significant.

The courts have been quick to find a threat to bring an infringement action. For example, in *Prince plc v Prince Sports Group Inc*,[107] an English court found an American company had made groundless threats of trade mark infringement. The United States company wrote to an English company complaining about its use of the domain name 'www.Prince.com'. The American company had an established reputation in both the United States and the United Kingdom for its sporting goods. However, the English company had a registration for 'Prince' for computer products. The letters were perceived as constituting a groundless threat to bring infringement proceedings in the United Kingdom even though the American company claimed that its letters related to use of the domain name in the United States.

Similar provisions relating to groundless threats appear in almost all Australian intellectual property legislation[108] and so the case law relating to those provisions may also be drawn upon. For example, in *U & I Global Trading (Australia) Pty Ltd v Tasman-Warajay Pty Ltd*, a case involving groundless threats of patent infringement proceedings, Cooper J laid down the general test of a threat as

> whether the language would convey to any reasonable person that the author of the letter in the present case intended to bring proceedings for infringement against the person said to be threatened. It is not necessary that there be direct words that action would be taken.[109]

In that case, the defendant's statement that 'upon the registration of the patent, we reserve our right to sue for any past infringements of the patent' was held to be an unjustified threat even though the defendant may have obtained the right to sue at some future time.

---

106 See *County Laboratories Ltd v J Mindel Ltd* [1957] 1 Ch 295.
107 [1998] FSR 21.
108 For example, *Copyright Act 1968* (Cth) s 202; *Circuit Layouts Act 1989* (Cth) s 46; *Patents Act 1990* (Cth) ss 128–32.
109 (1995) 60 FCR 26, 31.

However, there are some important differences between the groundless threat provisions relating to trade marks and other groundless threat provisions.[110] In particular, s 129(5) provides:

> An action may not be brought, or (if brought) may not proceed, under this section if the registered owner of the trade mark, or an authorised user of the trade mark having power to bring an action for infringement of the trade mark, with due diligence, brings and pursues an action against the threatened person for infringement of the trade mark.

The institution of proceedings by the trade mark owner may therefore avoid some consequences of an action brought pursuant to s 129(1). The critical issue is whether the trade mark infringement action is brought with due diligence. There is no clearly identifiable point in time at which the owner will be held to have failed to have acted with due diligence. In *Transport Tyres Pty Ltd v Montana Tyres Rims & Tubes Pty Ltd*,[111] the Full Court held that it was sufficient for the owner to seek to file its claim within two months of the first directions hearing in relation to the alleged infringer's claim under s 129. In that case, the threatened party started proceedings two days after receiving the threat and the owner decided that it did not need to take its own action until after the first return date of the s 129 proceedings. The Full Court agreed and decided that for the purposes of that case, the time for determining 'due diligence' ran from the first return date of the s 129 action, although previous authority suggests that time runs from the making of the threat.[112]

In some contrast, the plaintiff in *Stone & Wood Group Pty Ltd v Intellectual Property Development Corp Pty Ltd*[113] did not commence infringement proceedings at the same time as it commenced passing off proceedings. It then delayed pleading infringement until the claim for groundless threats was made. The Full Court refused leave to appeal from a finding of groundless threats.

The effect of s 129 is therefore twofold. Trade mark owners need to be very careful about sending letters of demand that allege infringement and should not do so unless they are willing and able to institute proceedings immediately. If an action for groundless threats is brought, they need to be able to respond by bringing their own proceedings relatively quickly and, even then, the situation might be complicated if an obvious opportunity to initiate proceedings such as an action based on a passing off claim existed prior to the groundless threat proceedings. In order to prevent an order for damages pursuant to s 129, it may even be necessary to institute proceedings.

16.12 Acts not constituting infringement

Section 122 lists a number of types of conduct that are deemed not to constitute infringement. Interestingly, these provisions are not described as defences to infringement. The reason for this is that the conduct in question probably would not constitute use of a trade mark as a trade

---

110 N. Weston and M. Davison, 'Groundless threats of trade mark infringement: How to avoid getting court' (2000) *Australian Intellectual Property Journal* 151–61.
111 (1999) 93 FCR 421.
112 *Challender v Royle* (1887) 36 Ch D 425.
113 [2018] FCAFC 29.

mark and therefore would not be infringing conduct, even in the absence of these provisions. Consequently, many, if not all, of these provisions should be regarded as simply clarifying the types of conduct that are not infringing conduct.

16.12.1 In good faith

A number of the provisions refer to the use of a name, place of business or sign in good faith. 'In good faith' in this context is probably similar to the meaning of 'honest' in the honest concurrent user provisions in s 44(3). Hence, good faith will not exist where the respondent is engaging in sharp conduct with an eye to wrongly divert business.[114] On the other hand, use may still be in good faith if the defendant knows about the plaintiff's trade mark, provided that the defendant is not attempting to trade off the reputation associated with the plaintiff's trade mark and is not being wilfully blind to the possibility of confusion.[115] In *Baume & Co Ltd v AH Moore Ltd*, the United Kingdom Court of Appeal described the concept of good faith ('bona fide' being the actual term in question) in relation to the use by a trader of their own name as follows:

> The mere fact in itself that a trader is using his own name which too closely resembles a registered trade name of which he is aware does not prevent the user from being 'bona fide', provided that the trader honestly thought that no confusion would arise and if he had no intention of wrongfully diverting business to himself by using the name. The truth is that a man is either honest or dishonest in his motives, there is no such thing, so far as we are aware, as constructive dishonesty.[116]

Consequently, simply informing the defendant of the owner's registration will not necessarily deprive the defendant's actions of their 'good faith' character.[117]

Despite this authority, some Federal Court decisions have suggested the good faith defences in s 122 are intended to deal with situations where a trader chances to use 'a word or words which trespass upon another's trade mark of the existence of which the trader was unaware'.[118] In any event, repeated use of the plaintiff's trade mark, such as multiple uses within meta-tags for a website or within the content of a website in a context where the use is not a descriptive use, may well negative good faith.[119]

In *Pham Global Pty Ltd v Insight Clinical Imaging Pty Ltd*,[120] the defendant changed its name to one similar to the plaintiff's and the Full Court rejected the proposition that this change was done in good faith.

---

[114] *Australian Postal Corporation v Digital Post Australia* (2013) 308 ALR 1, [74].
[115] Ibid [94].
[116] [1958] Ch 907, 921.
[117] *Parker-Knoll Ltd v Knoll International Britain (Furniture & Textiles) Ltd* [1961] RPC 346, 363; *Optical 88 Ltd v Optical 88 Pty Ltd (No 2)* (2010) 275 ALR 526, [163]. But see the comments in *Anheuser-Busch Inc v Budejovicky Budvar* (2002) 56 IPR 182, [216]–[218], where there was wilful blindness to the possibility of confusion.
[118] *Kettle Chip Co Pty Ltd v Pepsico Australia Pty Ltd* (1995) 132 ALR 286, 304; *Mantra Group Pty Ltd v Tailly Pty Ltd (No 2)* (2010) 183 FCR 450, [94].
[119] *Mantra Group Pty Ltd v Tailly Pty Ltd (No 2)* (2010) 183 FCR 450.
[120] [2017] FCAFC 83.

16.12.2 Good faith use of a name: s 122(1)(a)

The provisions of s 122(1)(a) or their predecessors have been interpreted reasonably generously from a defendant's perspective. For example, in *Hy-Line Chicks Pty Ltd v Swifte*,[121] the defendant was entitled to call its premises the 'Hi-Line Poultry Farm and Hatchery' in the face of the plaintiff's registration of Hy-Line. In addition, the name of the business may include the geographical location of the business. Consequently, in *Angoves Pty Ltd v Johnson*,[122] the defendant was permitted to call its store the St Agnes Liquor Store because it was located in the St Agnes shopping centre in the suburb of St Agnes. The provision is also one of the few that actually constitutes a genuine defence as, without the defence, the defendant's actions would almost certainly constitute infringement. In *Optical 88 Ltd v Optical 88 Pty Ltd (No 2)*,[123] the defendant adopted the name 'Optical 88' for its business and was permitted to continue to do so, in spite of very similar registered trade marks being held by the plaintiff. Similarly, in *Australian Postal Corporation v Digital Post Australia*,[124] Digital Post Australia was found to be using its name in good faith, although Digital Post Australia was also found not to be deceptively similar to Australia Post. In contrast, in *Pham Global Pty Ltd v Insight Clinical Imaging Pty Ltd*,[125] the name adopted appeared to be adopted in bad faith and the provision was inapplicable for that reason.

16.12.3 Good faith use of a sign: s 122(1)(b)

Use in good faith to indicate '(i) the kind, quality, quantity, intended purpose, value, geographical origin, or some other characteristic, of goods or services' does not constitute infringement. The circumstances in which this provision would be applicable are quite limited. It imposes a good faith requirement, whereas the same conduct contemplated by the provision, in the absence of good faith, would not constitute use 'as a trade mark'. For example, in *Johnson & Johnson (Australia) Pty Ltd v Sterling Pharmaceuticals Pty Ltd*,[126] the defendant used the plaintiff's trade mark 'Caplets' and successfully defended infringement proceedings on the basis that its use of the word was descriptive of its product, capsule-shaped tablets, and therefore not use as a trade mark. This decision was in spite of the finding that the defendant had actually intended to trade off the plaintiff's reputation and that the equivalent of this provision under the 1955 legislation was consequently not applicable due to a lack of good faith.

In addition, 'good faith' in this context does not mean that it is sufficient for the defendant to show that it believed it was entitled to use the words in question. As with use of a name, there must be an intention not to confuse or to trade off the reputation of the plaintiff. An intention to do this coupled with a belief that it has been done without infringing the trade mark is not 'good faith'.[127]

---

[121] (1966) 115 CLR 159.
[122] (1982) 66 FLR 216.
[123] (2010) 275 ALR 526.
[124] (2013) 308 ALR 1.
[125] [2017] FCAFC 83.
[126] (1991) 30 FCR 326.
[127] *Kettle Chip Co Pty Ltd v Pepsico Australia Pty Ltd* (1995) 132 ALR 286.

The new approach to distinctiveness in s 41(5) and (6), which allows registration of descriptive signs that acquire a secondary significance, means that this provision may well be used successfully more often than it was under previous legislation. A defendant will presumably argue that they used a descriptive term in its primary descriptive sense rather than in its secondary trade mark sense. Of course, that argument will be tied closely to the more general argument that no use as a trade mark has occurred at all.

For example, in *Accor Australia & New Zealand Hospitality Pty Ltd v Liv Pty Ltd* the Full Federal Court rejected the application of s 122(1)(b) by finding:

> The marks used by the respondents were not used 'to indicate' the 'geographical origin' of 'the services'. The marks were used to identify *a connection*, in the course of trade, between the operator of the business providing the services and the services.[128]

Similarly, in *Samuel Smith & Son Pty Ltd v Pernod Ricard Winemakers Pty Ltd* Charlesworth J stated 'Pernod Ricard intended to use the sign BAROSSA SIGNATURE *both* to indicate the relevant characteristic *and* to distinguish its goods from those of other traders' in rejecting the application of the provision.[129]

The words 'geographical origin' have been held to refer to relatively broad localities such as suburbs, town or districts. They do not extend to refer to the name of a particular building. For example, in *Mantra Group Pty Ltd v Tailly Pty Ltd (No 2)*,[130] the defendant referred to 'Circle on Cavill', the name of the twin towers at the Gold Coast containing some apartments for which it acted as the letting agent. Reeves J held that the name of an apartment building is not the 'geographical' origin of the services. The defendant was unable to rely on the defence relating to name of business because it actually conducted its business at a place distant from the building in question.

16.12.4 Good faith used to indicate purpose: s 122(1)(c)

This provision would apply in circumstances where a trader is attempting to indicate that its product can be used in conjunction with another trader's trade marked goods. For example, it is acceptable to describe one's product as 'compatible with' a particular trade marked product as was the case in *Gillette Co v Pharma-Goods Australia Pty Ltd*.[131] Again, one needs to consider the actual use in question, so an undue emphasis on the word 'Gillette' by bigger or bolder print and more subdued printing of 'compatible with' may have led to a contrary result. Use in such a way would both negative a finding of 'good faith' and negative an argument that the defendant was not using the trade mark as a trade mark.

16.12.5 Use of trade mark for comparative advertising: s 122(1)(d)

Comparative advertising is a clear example of a situation that does not constitute use of a trade mark as a trade mark under the Australian legislation. Perhaps for this reason, there is no

---

128 [2017] FCAFC 56, [353] (emphasis in original).
129 [2016] FCA 1515, [119] (emphasis in original).
130 (2010) 183 FCR 450, [83]–[88].
131 (1997) 38 IPR 509.

requirement that the defendant demonstrate good faith. It involves advertising in which a trader compares its product with that of another trader and emphasises the advantages of its product over those of another trader's product. For example, if Pepsi advertises that it is cheaper than Coca-Cola, it is not using Coca-Cola to distinguish its goods from any other goods. It is simply referring to the price of Coca-Cola and using Pepsi as its trade mark. Under previous United Kingdom legislation, comparative advertising did constitute infringement of a trade mark,[132] although no such finding was ever made under any Australian legislation and this provision emphasises that comparative advertising is not an infringement of a registered trade mark. Of course, if done deceptively by making a false or misleading comparison, comparative advertising may contravene s 18 of sch 2 of the *Competition and Consumer Act 2010* (Cth).[133]

16.12.6 Exercising right to use trade mark: s 122(1)(e)

Once registered, a person has the rights of a registered owner, which include the right to use the trade mark for the goods or services for which it is registered.[134] The legislation obviously contemplates the registration of trade marks that may be substantially identical with or deceptively similar to other trade marks in some circumstances. The honest concurrent user and prior continuous user provisions are examples but it is also possible that a deceptively similar trade mark may be registered by error. In those circumstances, the plaintiff would have to first undertake rectification proceedings and then institute infringement proceedings for any use by the defendant after the defendant's trade mark has been taken off the Register. An example of such a situation was *Clipsal Australia Pty Ltd v Clipso Electrical Pty Ltd (No 3)*[135] where the defendant's trade mark was removed from the Register but conduct prior to removal could not constitute infringement.

16.12.7 Defendant may obtain registration of similar trade mark: s 122(1)(f)

This provision permits a court to decline a finding of infringement in circumstances such as those where the defendant may have grounds for rectification of the Register and obtaining registration of the trade mark in its own right. For example, if the defendant is the true owner of the trade mark and the plaintiff has wrongly obtained registration, this provision could be applied.[136] It also applies where the trade mark used by the defendant is sufficiently different from the trade mark that the defendant's trade mark may also be registered, but that is unlikely to be necessary as in such circumstances the defendant will not have used a substantially identical or deceptively similar trade mark.[137]

---

132 *Trade Marks Act 1938* (UK) s 4(1)(b). See *Bismag v Amblins* [1940] Ch 667; *Montana Wines Ltd v Villa Maria Wines Ltd* [1985] FSR 400.
133 *Gillette Australia Pty Ltd v Energizer Australia Pty Ltd* (2002) 193 ALR 629.
134 *Trade Marks Act 1995* (Cth) s 20.
135 [2017] FCA 60.
136 *Trade Marks Act 1995* (Cth) s 122(1)(f).
137 *Aldi Stores Ltd Partnership v Frito-Lay Trading Co GmbH* (2001) 54 IPR 344.

Section 122(1)(f) may have originally been intended to also apply in circumstances where the defendant was using a substantially identical or deceptively similar trade mark and its use constituted honest concurrent use that would entitle it to registration on that basis under s 44(3). However, the actual wording of the provision refers to 'the trade mark' – namely, the trade mark registered in the name of the plaintiff. Comments were made by Moore J in *Unilever Australia Ltd v PB Foods Ltd*[138] to the effect that s 122(1)(f) may not cover situations such as honest concurrent use. In response, s 122(1)(fa) was introduced. It refers to the situation where the court is of the opinion that the defendant would obtain registration of its substantially identical or deceptively similar trade mark.

Since the defendant must convince the court that it would obtain registration, it would need to demonstrate that all the requirements for registration would be met. Hence, in *Aldi Stores Ltd Partnership v Frito-Lay Trading Co GmbH*,[139] the defendant could not rely on this defence to justify its use of 'Cheezy Twists' because that trade mark was purely descriptive and there had been insufficient use to justify registration on the basis of s 41(6).[140] Similarly, in *Optical 88 Ltd v Optical 88 Pty Ltd (No 2)*,[141] while the defendant was able to establish honest concurrent use, the plaintiff's reputation for its trade marks in Australia meant that registration would be denied by s 60. Consequently, while the defendant's ongoing use was permitted pursuant to the defence in s 122(1)(a), the defence under this provision was not available to it.

16.12.8 Non-infringement due to condition or limitation: s 122(1)(g)

As the plaintiff's original registration may be restricted by the imposition of some condition or limitation, the plaintiff's exclusive rights of use are similarly restricted and it would need to demonstrate that it is those rights that have been infringed by the defendant. For example, if registration were limited to Western Australia, the plaintiff would have to demonstrate that the alleged infringement occurred there as the exclusive right of use granted by registration would be limited to that region.

16.12.9 Disclaimers: s 122(1)(h)

Section 122(2) provides:

> If a disclaimer has been registered in respect of a part of a registered trade mark, a person does not infringe the trade mark by using that part of the trade mark.

Disclaimers are voluntary but, if actually made, the owner has no exclusive rights in relation to the part disclaimed.

---

138   (1999) 47 IPR 358.
139   (2001) 54 IPR 344.
140   A similar problem arose for the defendant in *Electrolux Ltd v Electrix Ltd (No 2)* (1954) 71 RPC 23. On appeal in *Frito-Lay Trading Co GmbH v Aldi Stores Ltd Partnership* (2001) 52 IPR 410, the defendant succeeded on the basis that the two trade marks were not deceptively similar.
141   (2010) 275 ALR 526.

16.13 Trade mark applied by or with consent of registered owner

The operation of s 123 may have an impact on both parallel importing and the sale of second-hand goods. These issues have been discussed above.[142] As s 123 only applies when the trade mark is applied to similar goods and services, it does not apply if the trade mark owner applies its trade mark to goods or services that are dissimilar to those for which it has registration. However, even in those circumstances, it will still be difficult for the trade mark owner to demonstrate that the defendant has used the trade mark as its trade mark if the goods or services did in fact originate with the owner via application of the trade mark or consent to the application of the trade mark. As already pointed out in the section on parallel importing, the 'trade mark' in the context of s 123 is the physical sign rather than the legal entity manifested by the sign.[143]

Section 123 is different from an issue of consent to use of the trade mark as it is obviously possible to consent to the original application of the trade mark but to refuse consent to the later use of the trade mark. However, in *Ward Group v Brodie & Stone plc*,[144] Merkel J seemed to suggest that the section also encompasses consent to the use of the trade mark. The facts of the case are discussed above[145] in relation to infringement over the internet but, briefly, the only sales into Australia via overseas websites were trap orders made by the plaintiff. Merkel J noted:

> [A] quite different situation would arise when goods bearing the mark are being offered for sale by an overseas vendor to the world at large and a trap purchase is made by a purchaser in Australia, who not only procures the sale and delivery of the goods in Australia but also procures the sole use of the infringing mark by the overseas vendor in Australia. In that situation, but for the trap purchase, no use of the mark in Australia would have occurred. In those circumstances it would be difficult for the trap purchaser, whose conduct was the sole cause of the use of the infringing mark in Australia, to contend that it has not consented to that use.
>
> ... It follows that I am satisfied ... that, as that conduct has been consented to by the Ward Group, that use was not an infringing use under s 120(1) by reasons of s 123(1) of the *TMA*.[146]

16.14 Prior continuous use defence: s 124

Under s 44(4), an applicant may acquire registration on the basis that they are a prior continuous user of a substantially identical or deceptively similar trade mark. This section provides a defence to an unregistered prior continuous user on similar grounds to those on which registration may be granted.[147]

---

142 At 16.7 and 16.8, respectively.
143 *Transport Tyre Sales Pty Ltd v Montana Tyres Rims & Tubes Pty Ltd* (1999) 93 FCR 421.
144 (2005) 143 FCR 479.
145 At 16.9.
146 (2005) 143 FCR 479, 492–3.
147 *Optical 88 Ltd v Optical 88 Pty Ltd (No 2)* (2010) 275 ALR 526.

16.15 No damages for infringement during non-use period: s 127

If the defendant has applied for the removal of the plaintiff's trade mark for non-use, no damages for infringement will be granted for any infringement occurring during the critical period – that is, the period of non-use on which the removal application is based.

16.16 Remedies

Chapter 17 discusses various remedies, such as injunctions and account of profits. The plaintiff has the option of seeking damages or an account of profits for infringement.[148] One exception to this proposition is that if the defendant has sought the trade mark's removal for non-use, the court may not award damages or an account of profits for infringement during the period of non-use by the plaintiff. The principles for awarding damages for infringement of a registered trade mark are similar to those that apply in respect of passing off,[149] except that a defendant should be aware of the existence of a registered trade mark. Consequently, a defendant would be unable to argue lack of knowledge of the plaintiff's rights. In any event, the case law indicates that damages may be awarded even for what is claimed to be innocent infringement.[150]

The basic proposition is that damages for infringement are designed to put the plaintiff in the position they would have been in if the infringement had not occurred. The main principle is therefore what damage has been done to the value of the defendant's trade mark, but a starting point will be the licence fee that the owner would have required from a defendant.[151] But other factors may well be taken into account. For example, the sale of inferior goods by the defendant will damage the plaintiff's goodwill[152] and the plaintiff may be forced to 'incur expenditure on advertising to counteract the effect of the defendant's conduct' or 'putting on notice foreign manufacturers of infringing materials'.[153]

The *Intellectual Property Laws Amendment (Raising the Bar) Act 2012* (Cth) introduced additional damages into s 126(2) of the *Trade Marks Act 1995* (Cth). Such damages are designed to deter infringers and to punish them for flagrant infringement rather than to compensate the trade mark owner for its losses.[154] Relevant factors listed in s 126(2) are:

---

148   *Trade Marks Act 1995* (Cth) s 126.
149   See *Kerly's Law of Trade Marks and Trade Names* (13th edn, London: Sweet & Maxwell, 2001) [18-139]–[18-158] for a detailed discussion of case law concerning such damages.
150   *Colbeam Palmer Ltd v Stock Affiliates Pty Ltd* (1968) 122 CLR 25, 35–6.
151   J. Phillips, *Trade Mark Law: A Practical Anatomy* (Oxford: Oxford University Press, 2003) [14.84], citing *Reed Executive plc v Reed Business Information Ltd* [2003] Info TLR 660 (unreported) (HC). See also *Stoke-on-Trent City Council v W & J Wass Ltd* [1988] 1 WLR 1406; *Meters Ltd v Metropolitan Gas Meters Ltd* (1911) 29 RPC 157.
152   *Alexander v Henry* (1895) 12 RPC 360.
153   *Kerly's Law of Trade Marks and Trade Names*, above n 149, [18-148]. See also *AG Spalding & Brothers v AW Gamage Ltd* (1915) 32 RPC 273; *Dormeuil Freres SA v Feraglow* [1990] RPC 449.
154   See *Hugo Boss Trade Mark Management GmbH & Co Kg v Sasalili Oxford Fia* (2014) 110 IPR 74, where the defendant demonstrated indifference to letters of demand and did not alter its conduct, despite being advised in writing that it was infringing the registered trade mark.

(a) the flagrancy of the infringement; and
(b) the need to deter similar infringements of registered trade marks; and
(c) the conduct of the party that infringed the registered trade mark that occurred:
  (i) after the act constituting the infringement; or
  (ii) after that party was informed that it had allegedly infringed the registered trade mark; and
(d) any benefit shown to have accrued to that party because of the infringement; and
(e) all other relevant matters.

16.17 Assignment of trade marks

Originally, common law or unregistered trade marks could not be assigned unless the goodwill associated with the business giving rise to their reputation was also transferred at the same time. This position was a logical consequence of the fact that, at common law, a trader has property in the goodwill associated with a trade mark but no property in the trade mark itself.

This approach to the assignment of trade marks was followed in the early trade mark legislation but successive trade mark legislation has progressively reduced the restrictions on the assignment of trade marks.[155] Prior to the 1955 Act, assignments were only valid if assigned together with the goodwill of the business with which the trade mark was associated.

Under s 82(1) of the 1955 Act, assignment without goodwill was made possible for the first time. Section 82(2) of that legislation placed some limitations on such assignments, in particular if the assignor continued to use a substantially identical or deceptively similar trade mark on goods or services of the same description or 'of such a description that the public is likely to be deceived by the use of the trade mark by the assignor and assignee upon their respective goods or services'.

Section 106(3) of the current legislation permits the assignment of trade marks without the associated goodwill and there are no provisions such as s 82(2) of the 1955 legislation. In addition, assignments may be partial in that they may apply to only some of the goods and/or services for which the trade mark is registered.[156] However, if the assignor continues to use identical or similar trade marks in respect of similar or closely related goods or services, it and its assignee run the risk that their trade marks will be subject to rectification proceedings pursuant to s 82(2)(b), which permits rectification of the Register if 'because of circumstances applying at the time an application for rectification is filed, use of the relevant trade mark is likely to deceive or cause confusion'.

16.17.1 Process of assignment

Section 106(1) permits the assignment or transmission[157] of a registered trade mark or 'a trade mark whose registration is being sought'. Assignments will often be made pursuant to a

---

155   M. Davison and I. Horak, *Shanahan's Australian Law of Trade Marks and Passing Off* (Thomson Reuters, 6th edn, 2016) 589 ff.
156   *Trade Marks Act 1995* (Cth) s 106(2).
157   Ibid s 6 defines transmission as: '(a) transmission by operation of law; or (b) devolution on the personal representative of a deceased person; or (c) any other kind of transfer except assignment.'

contract but need not be for consideration. In order to be registered, assignments and transmissions need to be in the prescribed form and supported by documents evidencing the assignment or transmission, such as a deed of assignment or a will indicating who is to receive the testator's trade mark. The transmission of trade marks may occur via the legal effect of wills, mergers of business or the sale of assets in the administration of bankruptcy. The Registrar has to be satisfied that the relevant documentation constitutes an assignment or evidence of transmission.[158] The matter could become complicated in circumstances such as where the person seeking to become the registered owner claims that the trade mark was held on trust for another entity and the assignment in question is from the trustee in bankruptcy of that entity.[159]

It is unlikely that an oral assignment will be effective in either law or equity because property legislation in all states provides that even the disposition of equitable interests must be in writing and signed by the assignor.[160]

> The reference in s 106(1) to an assignment of a 'trade mark whose registration is being sought' simply means that the assignee adopts the rights of the assignor in respect of the trade mark for which registration is being sought. If the original applicant, the assignor, was not entitled to registration, the assignee will not be in any better position. For example, if the wrong person originally filed the application because they were not the true owner, the flaw in the application is not remedied by any assignment pursuant to s 106. The application must be made afresh.[161]

Section 107 requires the assignor or the assignee to register an assignment although the consequences of failing to do so are not spelled out and no time limit is imposed for doing so. Failure to register the assignment may have serious consequences because presumably the still-registered owner would not be using the trade mark any longer and the trade mark would eventually be liable for removal for non-use. Difficulties may also arise as a consequence of the assignor giving a new assignment or there being an appearance of transmission of the still-registered trade mark from the registered owner to any other entity.[162]

Once an assignment is submitted for registration, the Registrar must notify any person who has claimed an interest in or right in respect of the trade mark pursuant to Part 11 of the 1995 Act. Unless those people consent to the assignment or a court orders otherwise, the assignment will not be registered for two months.[163] While the registration of the assignment can be delayed for two months, it is unlikely that licensees could prevent the assignment, even if their claim to an interest has been recorded pursuant to Part 11, unless they are in a direct contractual relationship with the assignee.

---

158 See, for example, *Mediaquest Communications LLC v Registrar of Trade Marks* (2012) 205 FCR 205.
159 Ibid.
160 But see *Acorn Computer Ltd v MCS Microcomputer Systems Pty Ltd* (1984) 6 FCR 277, where an oral agreement for consideration for the assignment of copyright was considered effective to confer an equitable interest on the payee.
161 *SPI Spirits (Cyprus) Ltd v Diageo Australia Ltd (No 6)* (2008) 77 IPR 62.
162 Ibid 394–5. See *Re Applications of Tashounidis* (1995) 35 IPR 305. The effect of that decision has probably been altered as a consequence of the amendment to s 22 of the Act pursuant to the *Trade Marks Amendment Act 2006* (Cth). Section 22 now provides that the registered owner may deal with the trade mark subject only to any rights appearing in the Register to be vested in another person.
163 *Trade Marks Regulations 1995* (Cth) reg 10.4.

On the other hand, the assignee may well take the trade mark subject to the licence as s 22 provides that while the registered owner may deal with the trade mark as its absolute owner, it may only do so subject to any rights appearing in the Register to be vested in another person.

16.17.2 Assignment of certification trade marks

Certification trade marks can only be assigned with the permission of the Australian Competition and Consumer Commission (ACCC).[164] In such circumstances, the ACCC will have to be satisfied of the same matters relating to the assignee as it was in relation to the assignor's original registration.[165]

16.17.3 Assignment of collective trade marks

Collective trade marks may not be assigned or transmitted[166] because, by definition, they are unique to and solely identifiable with the particular unincorporated organisation that sought and obtained their original registration.

16.17.4 Assignment of defensive trade marks

Defensive trade marks may be assigned but only with the standard trade mark in question, as the Registrar may cancel the defensive registration if the trade mark is not otherwise registered in the name of the registered owner of the defensive trade mark.[167]

16.18 Licensing of trade marks

The common law originally had an antagonistic attitude towards the licensing of trade marks and the view was held that any licensing arrangements would invalidate a trade mark as the licensing would result in deception or confusion of the public.[168] However, the complex nature of modern commerce has led to a greater acceptance of licensing arrangements[169] and it is now appreciated and understood that more than one person may have a connection with a trade mark.[170] The 1955 legislation introduced registered user provisions that permitted registration of licensees provided the Registrar was satisfied that the use by the proposed user would not be contrary to the public interest.[171] In effect, this meant that the Registrar had to be

---

164   *Trade Marks Act 1995* (Cth) s 180. Section 180A deals with the assignment of an unregistered certification trade mark.
165   Ibid s 180(3).
166   Ibid s 166.
167   Ibid s 189.
168   See *Bowden Wire Ltd v Bowden Brake Co Ltd* (1914) 31 RPC 385.
169   For further reference, see M. Yastreboff, 'Managing the transfer of "house" brands: Licensing and trade mark splitting' (2002) 13 *Australian Intellectual Property Journal* 87. The author argues that a combination of licensing and assignment provides a more effective outcome for corporate entities that own well-known house brands and are looking to restructure, sell or relocate assets within the group. See also T. Gyopar, 'Trade mark licence or franchise agreement: How much control is too much control?' (2004) 17 *Australian Intellectual Property Law Bulletin* 98.
170   *Pioneer Electronic Corp v Registrar of Trade Marks* (1977) 137 CLR 670.
171   *Trade Marks Act 1955* (Cth) s 74(3).

convinced of the ongoing connection of the owner with the trade mark and the licence agreement had to be lodged with the Registrar.[172] This statutory acceptance of licensing in certain situations was taken further by case law. A number of cases held that the registration of licensing arrangements was not compulsory.[173] These cases held that the critical issue was not whether the licensed use was registered or not via the registered user provisions, but whether the registered owner ensured that the licensee's use did not deceive the public.

The current legislative provisions concerning the licensing of registered trade marks and the associated case law are very accommodating to licensing arrangements although some conditions still do apply to it. As a consequence of the previous case law recognising even unregistered licences, the registered user provisions of the previous legislation have been abolished and the recording of licensing arrangements is now purely voluntary. The critical consideration in determining the effect of licensing arrangements on the validity of a trade mark is whether the registered owner has exercised control over the licensee. Such licensees are referred to as authorised users.

Section 8(1) provides:

> A person is an authorised user of a trade mark if the person uses the trade mark in relation to goods or services under the control of the owner of the trade mark.

The purpose of the control requirement was explained by Graham J in the *General Electric* case:

> The really important point is that the public should recognize that the symbol or word in question is being used as a trade mark by someone who is responsible for the product being what it is and having the quality which it in fact has ... This is why it is important that proprietors of trade marks should retain adequate control over the quality of their product and should by careful advertising and use of their marks ensure that the public do not attribute to marks meanings which may lead to confusion.[174]

16.18.1 Quality control

The critical issue then becomes what are the forms of control that will avoid the confusion that Graham J spoke of. Section 8(3)–(5) provides non-exhaustive definitions of 'control'. Subsection (3) provides:

> If the owner of a trade mark exercises quality control over goods or services:
>
> (a) dealt with or provided in the course of trade by another person; and
> (b) in relation to which the trade mark is used;
>
> the other person is taken ... to use the trade mark ... under the control of the owner.

The quality control in question may involve issues such as auditing the licensee's production processes. Alternatively, the registered owner may produce the products itself and license the

---

172   Ibid s 74(2).
173   For example, *Pioneer Electronic Corp v Registrar of Trade Marks* (1977) 137 CLR 670 (in Australia); *Bostitch Trade Mark* [1963] RPC 183 (in England).
174   *General Electric Co v General Electric Co Ltd* [1969] RPC 418, 448 (Ch D).

distribution process, as was the case in *Pioneer Electronic Corp v Registrar of Trade Marks*.[175] Obviously, the licensing agreement should state and reflect the respective roles of the licensor and licensee and provide the licensor with the necessary power to exercise control by, for example, granting access to the licensee's premises and inspection of the goods that it is selling. It is also necessary that the licensor actually exercise the power of control as it is the actual act of control, rather than the contractual power to exercise it, which is necessary.

This proposition was affirmed by a Full Court sitting with five justices in *Lodestar Anstalt v Campari America LLC*.[176] The licence for the relevant trade mark for wine was a perpetual, exclusive licence subject to the licensee's obligation to ensure that the wine was 'of a quality at least sufficient to obtain a continuing approval of the wine for export by the Australian Wine and Brandy Corporation (AWBC)'. The licence gave the licensor power to request samples of the wine every year and to submit the wine to the AWBC for the purpose of determining if the wine met that standard. The evidence was that the AWBC very rarely found a wine did not meet the required standard for export.

The difficulty for Campari, the assignee of the licensor, was that neither it nor its predecessor in title ever took any step to ascertain whether the licensee's wine met the relevant standard adopted in the licence agreement. Consequently, there was no control of the use of the trade mark and, therefore, the trade mark was liable to removal for non-use. The fact that the standard was a low standard was not a problem; as stated by Greenwood J, 'What matters is whether a quality benchmark was selected as an expression of the necessary control and the parties truly acted upon it'.[177]

Another example of a failure to exercise such control is provided by the decision in *Health World Ltd v Shin-Sun Australia Pty Ltd*,[178] previously discussed in chapter 15.[179] In that case, the registered owner permitted another company to use its trade mark but exercised no control over that use. Consequently, the trade mark was vulnerable to cancellation pursuant to s 88(2)(c) on the basis that the use of the trade mark was now likely to deceive or cause confusion.

16.18.2   Financial control

Section 8(4) provides that financial control over a licensee will constitute the necessary control. Often this involves the use of the trade mark by one member of a corporate group of companies. Some authority suggests that in such circumstances the registered owner need be either the company through which the group of companies is managed and controlled or the company that actually uses the trade mark.[180] However, other authority suggests that it is sufficient if there are close links between the companies in question and the trade mark is being used as a 'house mark' on behalf of the whole group.[181] For example in *Polo Textile*

---

175   (1977) 137 CLR 670.
176   [2016] FCAFC 92.
177   Ibid [13].
178   (2008) 75 IPR 478.
179   At 15.40.
180   *Ritz Hotel Ltd v Charles of the Ritz Ltd* (1988) 15 NSWLR 158, 199–201.
181   *Revlon Inc v Cripps & Lee Ltd* [1980] FSR 85; *Polo Textile Industries v Domestic Textile Corp Pty Ltd* (1993) 42 FCR 227.

Industries v Domestic Textile Corp Pty Ltd,[182] Polo Textile Industries was the registered owner of the trade mark. The shares in it were acquired by Gamble Holdings Pty Ltd but the trade mark was actually used under an informal, implied licensing arrangement by Keith Gamble Pty Ltd, a company owned by Gamble Holdings. Burchett J found that the close relationship between the three companies was such that the use of the trade mark by Keith Gamble Pty Ltd did not result in any deception.[183]

16.18.3 Other forms of control

The somewhat liberal view of 'control' in that decision, which was based on the 1955 legislation, is also reflected to some extent in s 8(5), which further opens up the concept of control by stating that sub-ss (3) and (4) do not limit the concept of control. An example of such other forms of control comes from the decision in *CA Henschke & Co v Rosemount Estates Pty Ltd*.[184] The case involved an unusual set of circumstances. Cyril Henschke was the registered owner of the relevant trade mark for wine. Prior to his death, he and his partners used the trade mark but his surviving partners continued to use the trade mark after his death even though ownership of the trade mark was not transferred to the executors for over ten years. The Full Federal Court was sceptical of the proposition that the executors were actually exercising quality control over the use of the trade mark. Yet, the Full Court was prepared to accept that in the peculiar business and personal circumstances of the family-run business they were exercising sufficient control to meet the requirements of the legislation although the exact nature of that control was not spelled out by either the executors or the court itself.

Consequently, the main forms of control are quality control over the goods and services dealt with by the licensee and financial control over the licensee itself but other forms of control may be acceptable as the real issue is whether the use of the trade mark by the licensee deceives consumers. Such use will be deceptive if the registered owner fails to maintain its connection with the trade mark but it seems that connection need only be slight in order to meet the control requirement and avoid invalidation of the trade mark.[185] As noted in the discussion of the *Lodestar* decision above,[186] while that connection might be slight, it must nevertheless exist and be demonstrated to have been maintained by the licensor.

16.18.4 Franchising

In addition to the Act's provisions concerning licensing, there are now provisions of the *Competition and Consumer Act 2010* (Cth) that regulate franchising, a form of business activity that almost invariably includes the licensing of one or more trade marks.

---

182   (1993) 42 FCR 227.
183   Ibid 239. See also *TGI Friday's Minnesota Inc v TGI Friday's Australia Pty Ltd* (1999) 48 IPR 65.
184   (2000) 52 IPR 42.
185   *CA Henschke & Co v Rosemount Estates Pty Ltd* (2000) 52 IPR 42, 72–3.
186   At 16.18.1.

16.18.5 Assignment of licences

Difficulties may arise where either the licensor or the licensee wishes to assign its licence interest. One Full Federal Court decision determined that it is possible for a trade mark licence to be assigned by either the licensor or the licensee but there are potential difficulties with doing so that need to be considered.[187] In particular, while assignment is possible in theory, the trade mark licence in question and the relationship between the parties may be such that the assignment is invalid.

In *Pacific Brands Sport & Leisure Pty Ltd v Underworks Pty Ltd*,[188] Underworks objected to a purported termination of a trade mark licence by Pacific Brands. The original licence agreement had been between Underworks, as licensee, and Sara Lee Apparel Pty Ltd but Sara Lee had assigned the licence to Pacific Brands.

The majority held that the licence agreement did not explicitly authorise assignment of the licence interest. In addition, some of the provisions of the licence[189] and the context in which it was executed led to the conclusion that the licensor/licensee relationship was of such a personal nature that it could not be assigned. In particular, the new licensor, Pacific Brands, was a competitor of Underworks, which necessarily generated tension in relation to a range of contractual matters, such as agreeing on new products and the provision of sensitive business information.[190]

The key lesson to be learned from the decision is the importance of dealing with the issue at the time of preparing and executing the relevant licence. An explicit understanding about the basis on which assignment can take place may be critical to the validity of any assignment.

16.19 Voluntary recording of interests and claims

Part 11 of the Act permits parties that claim they have an interest in or right in respect of a trade mark to record the particular of that claim in the Register. This step can only be taken with the consent of the registered owner as s 113(1) requires the application for the recording of the particulars to be made by the person and the registered owner together.

Two particular rights or interests that are likely to be recorded are those of licensees and of lenders who have taken some form of security over the trade mark in question. While the trade marks legislation is relevant, the position in relation to security taken over trade marks is now very much affected by the *Personal Property Securities Act 2009* (Cth) (see further below).

The actual effect of recording interests or rights is not entirely clear. Section 116 provides that the fact that a record has been made is 'not proof or evidence that the person has that right or interest' so, unlike the Torrens system of land title, the fact of registration does not itself prove or constitute ownership of the right or interest. However, the presence of the entry would constitute notice to third parties of the interest or right being claimed and this may be

---

187   *Pacific Brands Sport & Leisure Pty Ltd v Underworks Pty Ltd* (2006) 149 FCR 395.
188   Ibid.
189   See ibid [65], in particular.
190   See ibid [58].

relevant in circumstances where, for example, there are competing claims to the trade mark. The precise relevance of the notice would depend on issues such as the legal status of the right or interest being claimed. If the right is merely a contractual right but not a legal or equitable proprietary right, the provision of the notice may be of little effect.

The other effect of the recording is that the Registrar is required to notify the person in question of various dealings with the trade mark.[191] In particular, they must be notified of any assignment of the trade mark and, unless the person with the claimed interest consents, the assignment cannot be registered for two months.[192] The two-month period would provide an opportunity to bring court proceedings in respect of any dispute between the assignee and anyone with the claimed interest or right.

Changes to s 22 of the 1995 Act in 2006 have significantly increased the importance of and need for recording some interests on the Register. Section 22 previously provided that a registered owner of a trade mark 'may, subject only to any rights vested in another person, deal with the trade mark as its absolute owner and give in good faith discharges for any consideration for that dealing'. The amended section now provides that the registered trade mark owner is able to deal with the trade mark subject only to any rights 'appearing in the Register to be' vested in another person. Consequently, failure to be noted on the Register may result in the registered owner dealing with bona fide third parties to the detriment of any person who has not noted their interests on the Register.[193]

However, the situation in respect of security interests over registered trade marks is, in some ways, more simple and, in others, more complex. In order for a security interest over a trade mark to have priority over competing interests, the security interest needs to be registered pursuant to the *Personal Property Securities Act 2009* (Cth). Recording such an interest under the *Trade Marks Act 1995* (Cth) is now of little assistance unless that registration has also occurred, although the requirement for the Registrar to notify a person who has recorded an interest is of some ongoing value.[194]

16.20 International treaty obligations

There are a number of international treaties that have an impact on Australian trade mark law. Some affect the substantive law while others deal with procedural and administrative matters relating to the registration process and the maintenance of the Register.

The main treaty affecting substantive matters is *TRIPS*, which requires members to implement various provisions of the *Paris Convention for the Protection of Industrial Property*.[195] *TRIPS* also imposes some additional requirements. For example, the protection provided for

---

191 *Trade Marks Act 1995* (Cth) s 111.
192 *Trade Marks Regulations 1995* (Cth) reg 10.4.
193 *Trade Marks Act 1995* (Cth) s 22(2A) provides that registering a personal security interest on the Register of Trade Marks does not affect dealings with that trade mark. Registration of a personal security interest needs to be done through the personal security legislation discussed herein.
194 R. Burrell and M. Handler, 'The PPSA and registered trade marks: When bureaucratic systems collide' (2011) 34 *University of New South Wales Law Journal* 600. Note that s 22 has been amended since the article was published.
195 Opened for signature 14 July 1967, WIPO Lex No TRT/PARIS/001 (as amended 28 September 1979, entered into force 3 June 1984).

well-known trade marks in s 120(3) goes beyond the provisions of the *Paris Convention* and the provisions in *TRIPS* concerning geographical indications do not appear in the *Paris Convention*. At the time of writing, an appeal is in progress relating to a major World Trade Organization (WTO) dispute between Australia and two appellant nations over Australia's plain packaging legislation for tobacco products. The dispute has already resulted in a detailed decision of the WTO Panel on ten grounds of complaint pursuant to *TRIPS* and as eight of those grounds have not been appealed, it constitutes a detailed and authoritative examination of at least those eight grounds.[196]

There are three main international agreements that affect procedural matters. The *Nice Agreement Concerning the International Classification of Goods and Services for the Purposes of the Registration of Marks*[197] is, as its lengthy title suggests, an agreement designed to standardise the classification of goods and services for the purposes of organising registers in different countries so that the relevant classes in the different countries will be the same. The *Trademark Law Treaty*[198] also relates to some procedural issues concerning registration of trade marks. Finally, the *Protocol Relating to the Madrid Agreement Concerning the International Registration of Marks*[199] allows applicants to lodge the one application for registration of a trade mark in a multitude of jurisdictions. The application is lodged with WIPO in Geneva and then forwarded to individual national offices for examination. The application is then assessed by each individual national office in accordance with its own laws but, once accepted, various matters such as changes in the owner's details can be addressed in all jurisdictions via the one document.

---

196 Panel Report, *Australia – Certain Measures Concerning Trademarks, Geographical Indications and Other Plain Packaging Requirements Applicable to Tobacco Products and Packaging*, WTO Docs WT/DS435, WT/DS441/R, WT/DS458/R, WT/DS467/R (28 June 2018).
197 Opened for signature 28 September 1979, WIPO Lex No TRT/NICE/001 (as amended 28 September 1979, entered into force 6 September 1982).
198 Opened for signature 27 October 1994, WIPO Lex No TRT/TLT/001 (entered into force 1 August 1996).
199 Opened for signature 12 November 2007, WIPO Lex No TRT/MADRIDP-GP/001 (as amended 12 November 2007, entered into force 1 September 2008).

PART V

ENFORCEMENT OF RIGHTS

17

REMEDIES AND MISCELLANEOUS ISSUES

17.1 Introduction

There are some aspects of the intellectual property regimes that are common to all the regimes. Some of the remedies available for alleged breaches of intellectual property rights fall into this category. In addition, there are some other laws that affect the intellectual property laws in a relatively uniform manner. For example, the restrictive trade practices provisions of Part IV of the *Competition and Consumer Act 2010* (Cth) apply equally to all owners of intellectual property, subject to one or two variations.

The purpose of this chapter is to deal with most of those aspects. The chapter commences with a discussion of available remedies for infringement. After dealing with remedies, the chapter deals with a number of other miscellaneous issues, such as the relationship between intellectual property and restrictive trade practices.

17.2 Pre-trial remedies

The nature of the various forms of intellectual property is such that it is relatively easy and inexpensive to engage in infringing behaviour that can have devastating effects on the value of the intellectual property in question. Consequently, it is important to have an understanding of the types of action that can be taken to protect intellectual property and, in particular, action that can be taken before trial to preserve the intellectual property owner's position.

17.2.1 Anton Piller orders

One order specifically created to deal with the conduct of unscrupulous intellectual property infringers is the Anton Piller order, named after the first case to grant such an order.[1] The objective of an Anton Piller order is to secure evidence of infringement that would otherwise probably be destroyed by the defendant prior to trial. Such orders are given in ex parte proceedings (without the other party being present or even aware of the proceedings). In the *Anton Piller* case itself, Lord Denning stated that such an order can be made

> but it should only be made where it is essential that the plaintiff should have inspection so that justice can be done between the parties: and when, if the defendant were forewarned, there is a grave danger that vital evidence will be destroyed, that papers will be burnt or lost or hidden, or taken beyond the jurisdiction, and so the ends of justice be defeated; and when the inspection would do no real harm to the defendant or his case.[2]

An Anton Piller order authorises the plaintiff to take various steps such as:

- entering the defendant's premises to seize allegedly infringing material and machinery used to produce infringing material;
- seizing evidence of infringement and its effects such as lists of distributors, bank accounts and other financial documents demonstrating the nature and extent of the defendant's activities; and
- requiring the defendant to respond to various questions relating to its activities.

---

1   *Anton Piller KG v Manufacturing Processes Ltd* (1976) Ch 55.
2   Ibid 61.

The order is often made in respect of suspected fly-by-night operators such as those who sell pirate CDs or fake trade-marked products. As the precise identification of such operators is difficult, it is possible to obtain orders by reference to a general description of the people in question such as 'the woman with dark hair staffing the third stall from the right when facing north'.

Despite the initial insistence by the courts that Anton Piller orders only be granted in extreme cases, courts have been willing to assume that documents or articles will be destroyed if the defendant's conduct is 'of clandestine or criminal dealings'.[3] Some orders relating to breaches of confidentiality obligations have been made where there was a prima facie case of a breach and relative ease in destroying evidence such as emails containing the relevant documentation.[4]

One case has gone even further. In *Universal Music Australia Pty Ltd v Sharman License Holdings Ltd*,[5] an order was granted and a subsequent application for its discharge denied even though the court accepted that there was no evidence of a deliberate intention to destroy evidence. The case related to the operation of a peer-to-peer file sharing system. The plaintiff sought an Anton Piller order to record transitory computer information that would be overwritten or lost by the ordinary operation of computer systems. Wilcox J stated:

> [W]here the case sought to be made by a party depends upon demonstrating the operation of a dynamic scheme, it is difficult to see any alternative to the taking of 'snapshots' of the scheme in operation, thereby preserving evidence of what the dynamic system was doing at the moment of inspection . . . [M]aterial may be lost without destructive intent. If that is so, it is not to the point that the respondents . . . have not deliberately destroyed documents containing static data . . .[6]

While the circumstances in which an order will be made therefore appear to have been expanded, the draconian nature of such orders still requires a number of safeguards so as to prevent them becoming, in effect, private search warrants. In particular, safeguards are built into the procedure by which such orders are granted and the obligations placed on the plaintiff's legal representatives and provisions in the orders relating to the manner in which the order is to be executed. When bringing an application, solicitors have an obligation of full disclosure to the court of any matters that may affect the court's decision.[7]

The provisions of the order will be also quite specific as to the process by which it must be executed. In particular, it will specify the hours at which the order may be executed, thus preventing 'knocks on the door at dawn', and in the Federal Court there is a requirement that

---

3   S. D. Simpson, D. L. Bailey and E. K. Evans, *Discovery and Interrogatories* (2nd edn, Sydney: Butterworths, 1990) 279. See *Star Micronics Pty Ltd v General Synthetics Pty Ltd* (Unreported, No V G390 of 1991 Fed No 868) and *Microsoft Corp v Goodview Electronics Pty Ltd* (1999) FCA 754 for examples of the refusal of an application for an Anton Piller order.
4   *Liberty Financial Pty Ltd v Scott* [2002] FCA 345.
5   (2005) 222 FCR 465.
6   Ibid [77].
7   *Universal Music Australia Pty Ltd v Sharman License Holdings Ltd* (2005) 222 FCR 465; *Liberty Financial Pty Ltd v Scott* [2002] FCA 345.

an independent solicitor be in attendance to advise the defendant about the nature of the order and generally to supervise the execution of the order.[8]

In addition, solicitors are required to make a detailed inventory of anything that is seized and to ensure that nothing is seized that is not encompassed within the order. Items wrongly seized should be returned if subsequent inspection of them demonstrates that they were wrongly seized and solicitors should inspect the documents quickly to ascertain whether they have been correctly seized.[9] They will be personally liable for any failure in this regard. Some solicitors who have failed to meet their strict obligations under Anton Piller orders have faced considerable fines.

In the event of the defendant refusing to comply with an order, the plaintiff is not permitted to obtain entry by force. The plaintiff's recourse in such circumstances is to bring an action against the defendant for contempt of court.

One of the potential difficulties with Anton Piller orders is that the plaintiff's civil action and the evidence obtained via an Anton Piller order may affect possible criminal proceedings. This in turn has led to claims that a defendant is entitled to resist Anton Piller orders on the grounds that to do otherwise would involve self-incrimination and the defendant is entitled to claim privilege in such circumstances. The Practice Note issued by the Federal Court in relation to Anton Piller orders contains a standard form of order with clauses that permit a party to object to the unconditional disclosure of such evidence.[10] The defendant is required to prepare an affidavit referring to the information required to be disclosed to which objection is taken. The affidavit must then be delivered to the court in a sealed envelope. A separate affidavit must be served on the plaintiff setting out the basis of the objection.

The case law provides that the defendant can refuse discovery and to answer any interrogatories on the basis of common law privilege against self-incrimination.[11] However, the privilege does not extend to a right to refuse entry or the inspection and seizure of material. In addition, the position becomes complicated if the order is directed against a corporation. In such circumstances, the corporation cannot rely on privilege to refuse discovery or production of documents, either for itself or on the grounds that compliance with the order will incriminate its director.[12] From a practical perspective, objections are addressed via the process relating to the filing of the sealed envelope referred to above.

17.2.2 Representative orders

A development of Anton Piller orders involves orders against as yet unidentified individuals who are likely to be engaging in infringing conduct in a public place. A representative order differs from an Anton Piller order in that it does not involve entry into private property and the identity of the defendant is not known in any way. The most common situation is where there is a legitimate concern that illegal merchandise will be sold outside concert venues. In *Tony*

---

8   Federal Court of Australia, *Search Orders Practice Note*, 26 October 2016.
9   *Flocast Australia Pty Ltd v Purcell (No 3)* (2000) 52 IPR 147.
10 Federal Court of Australia, *Search Orders Practice Note*, above n 8.
11 *Rank Film Distributors Ltd v Video Information Centre* [1982] AC 380; *Howard v Reid* (1993) 31 NSWLR 298; *Spedley Securities Ltd (in liq) v Bond Brewing Investment Pty Ltd* (1991) 9 ACLC 522.
12 *Microsoft Corp v CX Computer Pty Ltd* (2002) AIPC 91-780.

Blain Pty Ltd v Jamieson[13] an order was made in respect of any such activity in the vicinity of concerts by the band Metallica. A representative order was made preventing the sale of illegal merchandise and authorising the seizure of such merchandise from any person engaged in that activity within a defined radius of the concerts.

17.2.3 Interlocutory injunctions

In order to prevent damage to the plaintiff's intellectual property interests, it may be necessary to obtain an interlocutory injunction preventing the defendant's conduct until the full trial of the matter. The decision on such an application may also have the effect of resolving the matter completely. There may be minimal commercial point in taking the matter to a full trial if, for example, the defendant effectively has to close down its business as a consequence of the injunction and the view is expressed at the interlocutory level that the plaintiff appears to have a strong case.

There has been considerable judicial and extra-judicial debate as to the relevant criteria to be applied in Australia, with apparently conflicting authorities referring to the need for the plaintiff to demonstrate a prima facie case[14] while others referred to the need to only demonstrate a serious issue for trial.[15] The High Court addressed these two conflicting tests in *Australian Broadcasting Corporation v O'Neill*.[16] Gummow and Hayne JJ stated:

> By using the phrase 'prima facie case', their Honours [in *Beecham Group Ltd v Bristol Laboratories Pty Ltd*] did not mean that the plaintiff must show that it is more probable than not that at trial the plaintiff will succeed; it is sufficient that the plaintiff show a sufficient likelihood of success to justify in the circumstances the preservation of the status quo pending the trial ... With reference to the first inquiry, the Court [in *Beecham*] continued, in a statement of central importance for this appeal:
>
>> How strong the probability needs to be depends, no doubt, upon the nature of the rights [the plaintiff] asserts and the practical consequences likely to flow from the order he seeks.[17]

Gummow and Hayne JJ went on to say:

> When *Beecham* and *American Cyanamid* [*Co v Ethicon*] are read with an understanding of the issues for determination and an appreciation of the similarity in outcome, much of the assumed disparity in principle between them loses its force ... However, a difference between this Court in *Beecham* and the House of Lords in *American Cyanamid* lies in the apparent statement by Lord Diplock that, provided the court is satisfied that the plaintiff's claim is not frivolous or vexatious, then there will be a serious question to be tried and this will be sufficient. The critical statement by his Lordship is '[t]he court no doubt must be satisfied that the claim is not frivolous or vexatious; in other words, that there is a serious

---

13   (1993) AIPC 90-990.
14   *Beecham Group Ltd v Bristol Laboratories Pty Ltd* (1968) 118 CLR 618, 662.
15   *American Cynamid Co v Ethicon Ltd* [1975] AC 396.
16   (2006) 227 CLR 57.
17   Ibid 65 (citations omitted).

question to be tried' ... Those statements do not accord with the doctrine in this Court as established by *Beecham* and should not be followed.[18]

The two criteria of a prima facie case and the balance of convenience are interrelated. The balance of convenience is tipped in the plaintiff's favour to some degree by it providing an undertaking to pay the damages incurred by the defendant as a consequence of the injunction if the plaintiff is ultimately unsuccessful at trial.[19]

On the other hand, the defendant may be able to argue that the payment of damages by it would be sufficient to overcome the injury to the plaintiff's interests flowing from the alleged infringement. This is unlikely to be the case in trade mark or passing off issues where the risk of permanent damage to the plaintiff's reputation is considerable. But in, for example, copyright cases where the real issue is a failure to pay licence fees, the courts may be less willing to provide injunctive relief on the grounds that damages would be adequate to meet the plaintiff's requirements. Even here the issue may be clouded if there is evidence of the defendant's inability to pay or the rearrangement of its affairs to avoid payment.[20]

Other factors that the courts take into account in determining the balance of convenience include:

- the impact of an injunction (or lack thereof) on the businesses of the plaintiff and the defendant. In that regard, the tendency is to protect the existing, established business rather than new businesses;
- the probable time between the interlocutory application and final trial of the matter; and
- the conduct of the parties.

As with all applications for injunctions, the court has a discretion and the plaintiff's delay or other conduct contributing to a lack of 'clean hands' may be relevant to the exercise of that discretion. However, this does not mean that the plaintiff must necessarily be quick to launch proceedings. It is entitled to observe the defendant's activities, gather evidence, obtain legal advice and engage in negotiations before starting litigation. Injunctions have rarely been denied in passing off actions due to delay. They have been denied more often in patent infringement cases. The real issue is not so much the delay itself but whether the delay makes it unjust to now grant the injunction.

17.3 Permanent injunctions

One of the most sought-after final remedies is a permanent injunction as the plaintiff will seek to enforce its exclusive rights in relation to the intellectual property. Each piece of intellectual

---

18   Ibid 71 (citations omitted).
19   See Federal Court of Australia, *Usual Undertaking as to Damages Practice Note*, 15 October 2016 for an example of such an undertaking.
20   *Paramount Design v Awaba Group* (2003) AIPC 91-331. See also *Johnson v Mortgage Processing Centre* [2003] FMCA 483; *MG Distribution Pty Ltd v Luthra* [2004] FMCA 1027.

property legislation specifically provides for an injunction, as does the *Competition and Consumer Act 2010* (Cth) in respect of misleading and deceptive conduct.[21]

Once the infringement is established, the grant of an injunction is very likely although it remains discretionary and it may be declined in some circumstances[22] – for example, if the defendant has clearly now refrained from the infringing conduct[23] or damages are adequate to meet the plaintiff's needs.

In addition, a court may decline to grant an injunction against an overseas defendant if there is no clear means of enforcing the injunction. For example, in *Australian Competition and Consumer Commission v Chen*,[24] the Federal Court was initially disinclined to grant an injunction against an American citizen in respect of his misleading or deceptive conduct due to the lack of any procedure for registering and enforcing such an injunction via American courts. However, the injunction was granted on the basis that the existence of such an order was likely to influence the relevant American consumer protection authorities to take action against the defendant if the misleading conduct persisted.

Various orders may be made in support of an injunction to deprive the defendant of the means by which it has and may in the future infringe the plaintiff's intellectual property rights. Consequently, orders may be made for the delivery up or destruction of infringing items or the obliteration of offending material such as trade marks. The *Copyright Act 1968* (Cth) has specific provisions enabling such an order on the basis that, in certain circumstances, the copyright owner is to be treated as the owner of infringing items and entitled to remedies by way of the tort of conversion.[25]

Other specific injunctive relief that might be obtained includes a requirement that a defendant cancel or change a company name registration and remove an advertisement from the Yellow Pages.[26]

17.4 Groundless threats

Each piece of intellectual property legislation has provisions that provide for certain consequences if groundless threats are made to bring litigation in respect of alleged infringement of intellectual property rights.[27] The targets of such threats may initiate their own action and seek declarations and damages flowing from the threats. For example, a trader may cease trading as a consequence of a claim that they are infringing intellectual property rights and suffer considerable damage as a consequence of that cessation. In such circumstances, the maker of the threat may be liable for damages if the threats are unfounded.

21	For example, *Copyright Act 1968* (Cth) s 115(2); *Circuit Layouts Act 1989* (Cth) s 27(2); *Designs Act 2003* (Cth) s 77; *Patents Act 1990* (Cth) s 122(1); *Trade Marks Act 1995* (Cth) s 126; *Plant Breeder's Rights Act 1994* (Cth) s 56(3).
22	See *eBay v MercExchange*, 126 S Ct 1837 (2006). See also G. Wilkinson, 'Stop! In the name of equity' (2006) 19 *Australian Intellectual Property Law Bulletin* 37.
23	*Australian Competition and Consumer Commission v Chen* (2003) 132 FCR 309.
24	Ibid.
25	*Copyright Act 1968* (Cth) s 116.
26	*Buildcorp Contracting NSW Pty Ltd v Build Corp Construction Pty Ltd* [2019] FCA 90
27	See, for example, *Trade Marks Act 1995* (Cth) s 129. See also N. Weston and M. Davison, 'Groundless threats of trade mark infringement proceedings: How to avoid getting court' (2000) *Australian Intellectual Property Journal* 151–61.

17.5 Damages

The calculation of damages in intellectual property cases is difficult and the courts have reflected this difficulty by retaining some flexibility in their assessment.[28] By and large, the issue for the court is the diminution in the value of the owner's property as a consequence of the infringement. In the context of copyright and patents, this will often take the form of lost earnings resulting from either a loss of business that the plaintiff would otherwise have had by selling directly to the defendant's customers or a loss of licence fees that it would have extracted from the defendant for use of its intellectual property. The position is different with trade marks and passing off as the defendant's conduct not only deprives the owner of the trade mark or the relevant reputation of those earnings but may also damage the owner's reputation and therefore the capacity of that reputation to produce future earnings.

In some circumstances, the defendant's intention will be relevant to the question of damages. For example, damages are not awarded in passing off unless the defendant was aware of the plaintiff's rights. The various legislative schemes have different approaches to the question of innocence. The copyright and circuit layouts legislation do not permit damages where the defendant was not aware, and had no reasonable grounds for suspecting, that they were engaging in infringing conduct. These provisions probably relate to the fact that copyright and circuit layouts are not registered and so the possibility of innocent infringement is greater than in other regimes. In addition, the copyright, trade mark, patent, designs and circuit layouts legislation takes into account the nature of the defendant's conduct in deciding whether to award exemplary damages under the relevant provisions.[29]

The patent, designs and plant breeder's rights statutes grant a discretion to a court to refuse damages where the defendant did not know and could not reasonably have known of the existence of the plaintiff's right. This onus on the defendant may be difficult to meet given that ownership of all three of the types of intellectual property in question can be relatively easily verified via searches of the relevant registers.

Details of the various approaches to calculation of damages for breaches of the different intellectual property rights are discussed in the respective chapters.

17.6 Account of profits

A successful plaintiff may seek either damages or an account of profits[30] although the latter is an equitable remedy and the court has discretion to refuse to award an account of profits.[31] For

---

28 See, for example, *Interfirm Comparison (Australia) Pty Ltd v Law Society of New South Wales* [1975] 2 NSWLR 104. Compare *Seager v Copydex Ltd (No 2)* [1969] 2 All ER 718.
29 *Copyright Act 1968* (Cth) s 115; *Circuit Layouts Act 1989* (Cth) s 27; *Designs Act 2003* (Cth) s 75(3); *Patents Act 1990* (Cth) s 122(1A); *Trade Marks Act 1995* (Cth) s 126(2); *Plant Breeder's Rights Act 1994* (Cth) s 56(3).
30 For example, *Copyright Act 1968* (Cth) s 115(2).
31 *Colbeam Palmer Ltd v Stock Affiliates Pty Ltd* (1968) 122 CLR 25, 34–5 (Windeyer J).

example, if the dispute relates to confidential information that could have been obtained from a consultant, the damages would be the relevant fee and an account may be denied.[32] They are mutually exclusive remedies:[33]

> The distinction between an account of profits and damages is that by the former the infringer is required to give up his ill-gotten gains to the party whose rights he has infringed: by the latter he is required to compensate the party wronged for the loss he has suffered. The two computations can obviously yield different results, for a plaintiff's loss is not to be measured by the defendant's gain, nor a defendant's gain by the plaintiff's loss. Either may be greater, or less, than the other.[34]

The calculation of the defendant's profit as a consequence of its infringing conduct may be fraught with difficulties. Only the profit attributable to the infringement is recoverable and it needs to be separate from non-infringing activity undertaken or non-infringing parts of the product supplied by the defendant. For example, in *Colbeam Palmer Ltd v Stock Affiliates Pty Ltd*,[35] the defendant sold goods with the plaintiff's trade marks. The value of the goods themselves had to be deducted from the proceeds of sale of the wrongly trade-marked goods. Similarly, in *Dart Industries Inc v Décor Corp Pty Ltd*,[36] the defendant was only liable in respect of the value of the press button seals on its plastic kitchen canisters. The seals infringed the plaintiff's patent but the body of the canisters did not infringe and their value was not taken into account in determining the profit attributable to infringement. In addition, allowance needs to be made 'for the defendant's skill, exertions and acumen'.[37]

The defendant's overheads associated with the sale of the infringing material and infringing activity also need to be taken into account, and both overheads specifically attributable to the activity and the defendant's general business overheads need to be considered.[38] Consequently, while the defendant cannot claim opportunity costs, profits forgone as a consequence of engaging in the infringing activity rather than some other business activity, it can still claim the 'cost of the overheads which sustained the capacity that would have been utilized by an alternative product and that was in fact utilized by the infringing product'.[39] The position may be different if the plaintiff could demonstrate that the infringing production had occurred using excess manufacturing capacity and that general overheads would have been incurred even if the infringing activity had not been engaged in.

A case where the defendant used excess capacity to produce infringing material was *Apand Pty Ltd v Kettle Chip Co Pty Ltd*.[40] In that case the defendant had engaged in passing off by selling 'Country Kettle' chips when the plaintiff had a considerable reputation for Kettle chips. At trial, Burchett J only allowed a small percentage of the defendant's general overheads

---

32   B. Kercher and M. Noone, *Remedies* (2nd edn, Sydney: LBC Information Service, 1990) 275; *Seager v Copydex Ltd* [1967] 2 All ER 415.
33   *Colbeam Palmer Ltd v Stock Affiliates Pty Ltd* (1968) 122 CLR 25, 32 (Windeyer J).
34   Ibid.
35   Ibid.
36   [1994] FSR 567.
37   Kercher and Noone, *Remedies*, above n 32, 276; *Hoechst Celanese International Corp v BP Chemicals Ltd* [1999] RPC 203.
38   *Dart Industries Inc v Décor Corp Pty Ltd* [1994] FSR 567.
39   Ibid.
40   (1999) 88 FCR 568.

or indirect costs on the grounds that those expenses would have been incurred in any event on producing an alternative, non-infringing product but that a less successful non-infringing product would not have recovered the same percentage of expenses. Consequently, it was that latter and lower percentage of expenses that was permitted on the grounds that the defendant was really utilising surplus capacity to produce the infringing product.

A further and unusual aspect of the *Kettle Chip* decision was the fact that the defendant sold part of its business, including goodwill, prior to the passing off action. Consequently, the sale price included a capital sum in respect of the goodwill of the unregistered trade mark 'Country Kettle'. As the use of that mark constituted the passing off in question, the defendant made a capital gain from its illegal activities. A proportion of the sale price of the business attributable to the illegally obtained goodwill was included in the account of profits.

The defendant bears the onus of proving any costs that it claims should be deducted from the revenue gained as a result of the infringement.[41] In addition, the defendant cannot claim any wages or director's fees by way of remuneration for engaging in the infringing activities. Hence, in *Liquideng Farm Supplies Pty Ltd v Liquid Engineering 2003 Pty Ltd*,[42] the defendant was denied his claim of $1000 per week by way of wages for his work associated with selling the infringing items.

These aspects of an application for an account of profits generate some uncertainty and disputes about the accounting methods to be employed and the precise figures to be derived from such methods. The case law acknowledges that mathematical exactitude is not necessary and, in the end, a reasonable approximation will be made.[43] On the other hand, the degree of complexity in assessing an account will be a relevant factor for the court in exercising its discretion to order an account of profit.[44]

17.7 Criminal liability

The statutory regimes for intellectual property have provision for criminal offences for some types of infringement. As the criminal charges relate to blatant and, usually, commercial infringements of intellectual property rights, they are not the subject of detailed discussion in this book. In the case of trade marks, for example, it is arguable that some of the criminal provisions generate a civil right on the grounds that there is a statutory duty owed to a trade mark owner not to engage in the criminal conduct in question but that issue has not been resolved as yet.[45]

17.8 Customs seizure

Some of the intellectual property legislation also has provisions for the seizure of infringing material by Australian Customs.[46] Again, those provisions are not dealt with in detail in this book.

---

41   *Liquideng Farm Supplies Pty Ltd v Liquid Engineering 2003 Pty Ltd* (2009) 175 FCR 26.
42   Ibid.
43   *My Kinda Town Ltd v Soll* [1982] FSR 147, 159.
44   *Docker v Somes* (1834) 39 ER 1095.
45   *British American Tobacco Exports v Trojan Trading Co Pty Ltd* (2010) 90 IPR 392.
46   *Trade Marks Act 1995* (Cth) pt 13; *Copyright Act 1968* (Cth) pt V div 7.

17.9 Jurisdiction

Due to the constitutional structure of Australia and the difficulties associated with the federal system, the rules concerning jurisdiction in relation to intellectual property matters are complex. However, as a matter of practice, the vast majority of intellectual property matters are dealt with, at first instance, by either the Federal Circuit Court (formerly the Federal Magistrates Court) or the Federal Court. The relevant Commonwealth intellectual property statutes confer jurisdiction on the Federal Court in relation to the regimes created by those statutes.

Hence, the Federal Court has jurisdiction in relation to copyright, trade marks, designs, circuit layouts, patents, plant breeder's rights and matters under the *Competition and Consumer Act 2010* (Cth). Part of this jurisdiction is conferred on the Federal Circuit Court, which has jurisdiction in relation to copyright, trade marks, plant breeder's right and matters under the *Competition and Consumer Act 2010*. It is possible to transfer matters to and from the Federal Court and the Federal Circuit Court.

A difficulty might arise with intellectual property matters that are not based on Commonwealth statutes but on common law or equity. These matters include passing off and actions in respect of confidential information. The Federal Court and Federal Circuit Court will not have jurisdiction in relation to actions for breach of confidential information or passing off unless they can rely on the concept of accrued jurisdiction. Under this concept, each court may deal with an action that is associated with another cause of action over which it does have express jurisdiction. For example, the same facts may give rise to an action for both a breach of s 18 of sch 2 of the *Competition and Consumer Act 2010* (Cth) and passing off. In such circumstances, the courts, exercising their jurisdiction in relation to the consumer law action, could also hear the associated claim relating to passing off. Acquiring jurisdiction over a matter based on claims to confidential information may be more difficult for the Federal Court.

The state and territory Supreme Courts have jurisdiction over common law matters such as passing off and actions in respect of confidential information. They also have jurisdiction over most of the other areas of intellectual property although, in practice, most claims are made in the Federal Court or the Federal Circuit Court. The territory Supreme Courts have some limits placed on their jurisdiction. For example, in patent matters, the territory courts can only deal with revocation of a patent owned by a resident of the territory or a company with its principal place of business there.[47] Similar restrictions are imposed in respect of designs[48] and trade marks.[49] In addition, the Federal Court and Federal Circuit Courts have between them exclusive jurisdiction in relation to plant breeder's rights.[50]

---

47   *Patents Act 1990* (Cth) s 155.
48   *Designs Act 2003* (Cth) s 84.
49   *Trade Marks Act 1995* (Cth) s 195.
50   *Plant Breeder's Rights Act 1994* (Cth) s 54.

17.10 Intellectual property and freedom of competition

The nature of intellectual property is that it tends towards some form of restriction of competition although one of the justifications for it is that the provision of some limited exclusive rights ultimately promotes a competitive economy. Inevitably, there are therefore some tensions between intellectual property laws and freedom of competition. The intellectual property laws themselves are designed to provide a balance between the need for protection of exclusive rights of owners and the preservation of competition. The lengthy debates concerning the appropriateness of parallel importing are but one example of this tension.[51] In addition to the tensions contained within the intellectual property rules themselves, Part IV of the *Competition and Consumer Act 2010* (Cth) has provisions that prohibit certain restrictive trade practices, as well as a provision in s 51(3) that provides some specific exemptions for certain contractual arrangements relating to intellectual property

A detailed analysis of the provisions in Part IV is beyond the scope of this book but a brief overview of those provisions and their potential impact on intellectual property can be provided. Part IV has some provisions that prohibit certain types of conduct without any inquiry into the purpose or effects of the conduct or into the position in the market of the parties engaging in it. These prohibitions, which focus exclusively on the conduct of the defendant, are known as *per se* prohibitions and cover activities such as price fixing[52] and resale price maintenance.[53]

Other prohibitions in Part IV require a consideration of a number of different factors. As with *per se* prohibitions, the conduct of the defendant is relevant but other factors include the degree of market power that the defendant has, the purpose of its conduct and/or the effect of the conduct on competition. For example, s 46 prohibits use of substantial market power for the purpose, effect or likely effect of substantially lessening competition. These prohibitions are referred to as rule of reason prohibitions.

17.10.1 *Per se* prohibitions

The most commonly considered *per se* prohibitions in the *Competition and Consumer Act 2010* (Cth) are those against cartel conduct such as price fixing and the separate prohibition in s 48 against resale price maintenance. Price fixing occurs where competitors agree on the price at which they will sell their respective products. Other cartel provisions relate to matters such as provisions in contracts, arrangements or understandings for the restriction of production or supply of goods or services or the allocation of customers or suppliers or exclusive geographical areas between competitors. The cartel provisions are aimed at horizontal arrangements in which at least two of the parties are or, but for the provisions, would be competitors.

---

51 Prices Surveillance Authority (PSA), *Book Prices* (Report Nos 24 and 25, 1989); PSA, *The Prices of Sound Recordings* (Report No 35, 1990); PSA, *Prices of Computer Software* (Report Nos 44 and 46, 1992); Intellectual Property and Competition Review Committee, *Review of Intellectual Property Legislation under the Competition Principles Agreement* (Final Report, September 2000) (*Ergas Committee Report*).
52 *Competition and Consumer Act 2010* (Cth) ss 45AD
53 Ibid s 48.

Intellectual property owners are therefore unlikely to be caught by these provisions unless they are entering into arrangements with competitors.

In the context of the exercise of intellectual property rights in a manner that might contravene Part IV of the Act, provisions relating to how vertical arrangements operate might have particular relevance. Intellectual property owners might have to take particular care when formulating licence agreements or having discussions surrounding conduct by their licensees. For example, resale price maintenance occurs where a supplier dictates or attempts to dictate to its customers the price at which they may resell the products in question.

A particular concern for owners of trade marks is that they might be liable for resale price maintenance if they refuse to supply their goods to certain retailers, especially discount retailers. Care needs to be taken to ensure that the refusal to supply is not the result of attempts to dictate the resale price by retailers.

17.10.2 Rule of reason prohibitions

Most of the rule of reason prohibitions only apply if the defendant has a substantial degree of power in a market. As a general rule, the ownership of one piece of intellectual property will not of itself give the owner a substantial degree of market power.[54] Even the ownership of a number of items of intellectual property may not result in the acquisition of substantial market power. For example, in *Universal Music Australia Pty Ltd v Australian Competition and Consumer Commission*,[55] the Full Federal Court found that neither of two music companies, Universal Music and Warner Brothers, had a substantial degree of market power as a consequence of their copyright entitlements in respect of popular music. Although each had exclusive rights to many popular sound recordings, the transitory nature of that popularity meant that according to the court they did not possess a substantial degree of market power as consumers could quickly and easily choose to acquire other music. A similar view would probably be taken that ownership of any one trade mark does not confer substantial market power on the owners as there are substitute products that consumers may choose if their preferred option becomes too expensive. For example, if Nike shoes are excessively priced, other brands such as Adidas, Asics and Brooks would become more popular.

There is the possibility that a single patent may confer a significant degree of market power if it is extremely inventive and of great commercial value and it is not possible to easily patent around it. However, such patents are rare.[56]

A lack of substantial market power may not prevent a contravention of some of the rule of reason prohibitions. Despite the findings of a lack of substantial market power in the *Universal Music* case mentioned above, both defendants were found guilty of exclusive dealing by threatening to refuse to supply retailers with their sound records with the purpose of substantially lessening competition. After parallel importing of sound recordings was legalised under copyright legislation, the two companies attempted to coerce music retailers into obtaining their sound recordings exclusively from them. They threatened not to supply those retailers if they acquired any of their stock from overseas through parallel importing. The Full Federal

---

54   *Broderbund Software Inc v Computermate Products (Australia) Pty Ltd* (1991) 22 IPR 215.
55   (2003) 131 FCR 529.
56   *Murex Diagnostics Australia Pty Ltd v Chiron Corp* (1995) 55 FCR 194, 196.

Court found that this conduct did not have the effect of substantially lessening competition because the defendants did not have a substantial degree of market power. However, it did find that their intention was to substantially lessen competition and this purpose was sufficient to contravene the exclusive dealing provisions.

On the other hand, in some circumstances the ownership or control of a considerable number of patents or copyrights by one competitor may confer a substantial degree of market power. Alternatively, by acting in collaboration with other owners, they may jointly have a substantial degree of market power. An example of the former is copyright collecting societies. For example, APRA AMCOS has an effective monopoly in respect of the public performance of sound recordings as, without a licence from APRA, it is virtually impossible to conduct a business, such as a nightclub, that requires or involves playing music in public. One case was brought against APRA under s 46 by a nightclub operator that claimed APRA's refusal to provide it with a licence constituted a misuse of its market power with the purpose of preventing the nightclub operator from competing in the nightclub market.[57] While the action was unsuccessful as APRA's refusal stemmed quite rightly from the plaintiff's failure to pay licence fees rather than any anti-competitive purpose, the case still demonstrates the potential anti-competitive effects of collective control of intellectual property.

17.10.3 Abolition of exemptions under s 51(3)

At the time of writing, specific exemptions from the operation of some sections in Part IV of the *Competition and Consumer Act 2010* (Cth) were given to conditions of licences of various forms of intellectual property under s 51(3) but those exemptions were abolished in September 2019.[58] Activities such as patent cross-licensing with problematic conditions might be affected by the repeal.[59] In particular, the repeal might have ramifications for existing arrangements that were in place prior to the repeal because the provisions in Part IV prevent not only entering into prohibited arrangements but also giving effect to such provisions. Consequently, arrangements that were originally not prohibited might now be caught if they continue to be implemented.[60]

---

57   *Australasian Performing Right Association Ltd v Ceridale Pty Ltd* (1990) 19 IPR 1.
58   *Treasury Laws Amendment (2018 Measures No 5) Act 2019*(Cth). The only reported case considering the exemption is *Transfield Pty Ltd v Arlo International Ltd* (1980) 144 CLR 83.
59   M. Diffey, J. Oliver and K. Diwell, 'End of an era: Repeal of s 51(3) of the *CCA* and implications for your IP' (Minter Ellison, 6 November 2018) www.minterellison.com.
60   R. De Boos, 'Proposed removal of intellectual property safe harbour a potential nightmare' (Davies Collison Cave, 14 January 2019) https://dcc.com.

INDEX

acts not constituting infringement of trade mark, 673
  disclaimers, 678
  exercising right to use trade mark, 677
  good faith use of a name, 675
  good faith use of a sign, 675–6
  good faith use to indicate purpose, 676
  in good faith, 674–5
  non-infringement due to condition or limitation, 678
  registration of similar trade mark by defendant, 677–8
  use of trade mark for comparative advertising, 676–7
Advisory Council on Intellectual Property (ACIP)
  review of Crown use of patents and designs, 422
  review of designs system, 198–200, 216
  review of innovation patent system, 293–4, 355
  review of patentable subject matter, 308, 320, 322, 381
Anti-Counterfeiting Trade Agreement (ACTA), 45–6
anti-dilution of trade marks, 654–5
  blurring, 655–6
  in Europe and USA, 655–6
  passing off and, 660–2
  tarnishment, 656
Anton Piller orders, 694–6
application for patent, procedure for
  acceptance and publication, 276–7
  application, 274–5
  examination, 275–6
  grant of patent, 278
  innovation patents, 278–9
  opposition, 277–8
  pre-examination, 275
  re-examination, 278
application for patent, types of
  Convention applications, 271–2, 283
  divisional applications, 273
  patents of addition, 273
  PCT applications, 272–3, 283
application for plant breeder's rights, 501
  acceptance, 504
  access to application and objections, 505
  deposit of propagating material, 505–6
  form of application, 502–3
  objections, 505
  priority dates, 503
  rejection, 504
  right to apply, 502–3

  status of accepted applications, 505
  substantive examination and test growing requirements after acceptance, 504–5
  variation of application after acceptance, 504
APRA AMCOS, 111, 706
artistic works
  artistic craftsmanship, 60–2
  authorship, 77
  buildings, 59
  copyright, 57–62
  defence to infringement of copyright, 160–1
  derogatory treatment, 173
  drawings, 58
  duration of copyright protection, 101–2
  engravings, 59
  first ownership rights, 86
  industrial application of corresponding designs, 217–18
  originality, 67–74
  paintings, 57
  photographs, 59
  registration of corresponding designs, 216–17
  sculptures, 58
artist's resale rights, 185–8
assessment of inventive step, patents, 356
  commercial success, 363
  common general knowledge, 358–60
  expectation of success, 363–5
  expert evidence tainted by hindsight, 361
  information skilled person could ascertain, understand and regard as relevant, 360–1
  long-felt want and its successful solution, 362–3
  objection to reliance on hindsight, 366
  obviousness, 356
  person skilled in relevant art, 356–8
  problem and solution, 365–6
  secondary factors in obviousness assessment, 361–6
  standard required, 361
assignment of trade marks, 681
  certification trade marks, 683
  collective trade marks, 683
  defensive trade marks, 683
  process, 681–3
.au Domain Administration Ltd, 556
Audio-Visual Copyright Society, 111
AUSFTA, 43
Australasian Mechanical Copyright Owners' Society (AMCOS), 111
Australasian Performing Right Association (APRA), 111

Australia–United States Free Trade Agreement (AUSFTA), 9, 19, 35, 169, 181–3, 372, 381, 418, 430
Australian Communications and Media Authority (ACMA), 39
Australian Competition and Consumer Commission (ACCC), 112, 135, 589, 683
Australian Law Reform Commission (ALRC)
  on design law, 197
  review of copyright and digital economy, 38, 93, 109, 143, 166
  review of designs system, 197, 206
  review of gene patenting, 167, 308, 317, 322, 422
Australian Official Journal of Designs, 202, 339
Australian Official Journal of Patents (*Official Journal*), 275, 277, 279
Australian Register of Therapeutic Goods, 281–2, 471, 479
Australian Society of Authors (ASA), 133
Australian uniform dispute resolution policy, 556
authorship
  commissioned works, 83–4
  Crown copyright, 84–5
  duration of copyright protection, 101–2
  exceptions to first ownership, 80–5
  first ownership rights, 76–80
  joint authorship, 78–9
  journalists, 82–3
  literary, dramatic, muscial and artistic works, 77
  nature of rights, 85–92
  orphan works, 80
  right of commercial rental, 92
  right of reproduction, 86–8
  right to communicate work to public, 89–91
  right to make adaptation of work, 91–2
  right to perform work in public, 88–9
  right to publish work, 88
  technological protection measures, 92–101
  works created by employees, 81–2

Beijing Treaty, 44–5
Berne Convention, 15–16, 33, 41–3, 65, 134, 136–7, 159, 169, 186
bilateral agreements, 17–18
breach of confidence, 222–3
  after employment, 249–54
  damages, 260–1
  defences, 254–8
  duration of obligation, 244–6
  during employment, 248–9
  elements. *See* elements of breach of confidence
  entitlement, 246–8
  equitable obligations, 244
  express contractual obligations, 244
  international dimensions, 262–3
  origins of equitable doctrine, 224–6
  public interest in disclosure, 254–8
  relationship to copyright, 262
  relationship to patents, 261–2
  remedies, 258–61
  subsistence of obligations alongside comparable contractual obligations, 223–4
  See also confidential information
broadcast copyright, 63–4
  originality, 74
  reform, 46
broadcasts
  initial owners of copyright, 78
  statutory licences, 107
  unauthorised access to encoded broadcasts, 100–1
Budapest Treaty, 288–9, 300, 386

certification trade marks, 587–8
  assignment, 683
  certification by other means, 590
  requirements for registration, 588–90
character merchandising, 547–50
cinematograph films. *See* films
circuit layouts, 188–9
  duration, 191
  exceptions and defences, 192–3
  exclusive rights, 190
  exploitation, 191
  infringement, 191
  innocent commercial exploitation, 192–3
  overlap with copyright and design protection, 194
  ownership, 191
  remedies, 193
  subsistence, 190
claim construction, patents, 444–5
  pith and marrow, 445–6
  purposive construction, 446–9
competition and intellectual property law, 704
  abolition of exemptions, 706
  per se prohibitions, 704–5
  rule of reason prohibitions, 705–6
compilations
  copyright, 52
compulsory licences, patents
  application, 425–8
  court satisfied conditions exist, 426–7
  court satisfied of anti-competitive behaviour, 427–8
  effect on other patents, 428–9
  international requirements, 430–1
  operation of court order, 429
  other circumstances for, 429–30

    patented pharmaceutical inventions, 431
    remuneration payable, 429
    revocation, 429
computer programs
    copyright, 52–5
    defences to infringement of copyright, 161–2
    validity of patents, 302–3
confidential information, 10–11
    business or trade secrets, 234
    circumstances that import an obligation of confidence, 235–6
    disclosure by the confidant, 245
    disclosure by the confider, 244
    disclosure by third party after confidence is imposed, 245
    encrypted information, 236–7
    entitlement to confidence, 246–8
    ideas, 230–1
    illegal eavesdropping, 237
    inadvertent acquisition of written confidences, 238–9
    inadvertent eavesdropping, 237
    information based on public knowledge and ideas, 234
    necessary quality of confidence, 229–35
    relative secrecy and public domain, 231–4
    springboard principle, 259–60
    surreptitious acquisition through theft or use of telephoto lens, 239
    telephone tapping, 237
    verbal confidences, 237–8
confidentiality. *See* breach of confidence
contracts, patents
    conditions that are not void, 433
    defence to infringement proceedings, 433–4
    termination after patent ceases to be in force, 434–6
    void conditions, 431–3
contributory infringement of patents, 464–5
    infringing uses, 468–73
    not a staple commercial product, 469–70
    product has only one reasonable use, 468–9
    supplier believes person would put product to infringing use, 470–2
    supply of a product, 465–8
    supply of component parts, 473–4
    use of product in accordance with instructions for use, 472–3
copyright, 9–10
    natural rights arguments for, 29–30
    utilitarian arguments for, 28–9
Copyright Agency, 107–11, 163, 187
copyright collecting societies, 110–11
copyright law
    administration of copyright licences, 41

    authorship. *See* authorship
    British legacy, 31–2
    criteria for protection of creations. *See* subsistence, copyright
    digital economy and online piracy, 38–9
    disability access, 40
    exploitation of copyright work. *See* exploitation of copyright
    fair dealing. *See* fair dealing, copyright
    film directors' rights, 36
    first ownership of copyright. *See* first ownership, copyright
    history in Australia, 30–41
    infringement. *See* infringement of copyright
    introduction to, 26–7
    justifications for, 27–30
    overlap with circuit layouts protection, 194
    overlap with design law, 216–18
    relationship to breach of confidence, 262
    reprographic reproduction, 33–4
    resale royalty rights, 37–8
    technological protection measures. *See* technological protection measures, copyright
copyright law reform, 32–41
    AUSFTA commitments, 35
    CLRC reviews, 34
    digital agenda reforms, 34–5, 92
    Franki Committee, 33–4
    future reforms, 46–7, 167
    modernisation, 40–1
    Productivity Commission review, 39–40
    reports since 2000, 34
    Spicer Committee, 33
    WIPO commitments, 35
Copyright Law Review Committee (CLRC), 34, 53, 84, 111, 166
Copyright Tribunal of Australia, 111–12
Crown copyright, 84–5, 102
    statutory licences, 107
Crown use of patents, 417–18
    acquisition of inventions or patents, 421–2
    assignment of inventions to Commonwealth, 422
    exploitation of inventions, 418–19
    exploitation to cease under court order, 421
    for services of Commonwealth or a State, 419–20
    obligations of Crown, 420
    procedures available to patentees, 420
    remuneration and terms for exploitation, 420
    review of, 422

Crown use of patents (cont.)
  scope of exploitation right, 419
  supply of products to foreign countries, 421

damages, 700
  breach of confidence, 260–1
  copyright infringement, 138
  trade mark infringement, 680–1
database protection, 7, 14, 43
defences to infringement of copyright, 143
  artistic works, 160–1
  commercial research, 167
  computer programs, 161–2
  contracting out of copyright defences, 165–7
  educational uses, 159–60
  exceptions for archives, libraries and key cultural institutions, 157–9
  films, 164
  format shifting, 155–7
  future reforms, 167
  government uses, 163
  legal materials, 163
  organisations assisting persons with a disability, 160
  public interest, 165
  reading or recitation in public, 163
  sound recordings, 164
  temporary and incidental reproductions, 162–3
  time shifting, 154–5
defences to infringement of design law
  consent and parallel importation, 214
  Crown use and supply, 214
  overall appearance of a product, 213–14
  'repair' defence, 213
  right of repair for spare parts defence, 211–14
defences to infringement of patents, 474–5
  acts for obtaining regulatory approval of pharmaceuticals and non-pharmaceuticals, 479
  contracts, 433–4
  experimental and research use, 480–3
  prior use of an invention, 475–9
  private acts, 479–80
  use in or on foreign vessels, aircraft or vehicles, 475
design law, 10
  criteria for protection, 203–9
  definition of design, 203–6
  history, 197–9
  new and distinctive designs, 206–9
  overlap with circuit layouts protection, 194
  overlap with copyright, 216–18
  ownership of designs, 200, 209
  product aspect of designs, 205–6
  registration. *See* design registration
  rights of design owners, 209
  spare parts, 206
  visual features of design, 204–5
design registration, 199–200
  certification, 202
  duration of protection, 203
  post-registration examination, 203
  priority date, 202
  publication of application, 202
  request for registration or publication, 201
  requirements of application, 201
  who can apply, 200
digital agenda reforms, 34–5, 92
direct infringement of copyright, 113
  act done on whole or part of copyright work, 116–20
  activities within owner's control, 113
  alleged infringing work derived from copyright work, 114–16
  authorisation, 120–31
  liability of internet service providers, 123–31
direct infringement of patents, 452–3
  authorisation, 460–2
  exclusive right to import invention, 458–9
  exclusive right to keep, 456–8
  exclusive right to make patented product, 453–5
  exclusive right to use, 455–6
  liability as joint tortfeasor through common design or procurement, 462–4
  parallel importation, 459–60
disability access, 40
disclosure without consent, patents, 338–9
  general grace period, 343–4
  publication before learned society, 340–1
  showing, use and publication at recognised exhibition, 339–40
  working invention in public for purposes of reasonable trial, 341–3
domain names, 19, 550, 553–6, 561, 618
dramatic works
  authorship, 77
  copyright, 55–7
  derogatory treatment, 172
  duration of copyright protection, 101–2
  first ownership rights, 85
  originality, 67–74

educational lending rights, 194
elements of breach of confidence, 226–8
  identification of information with specificity, 228–9
  information given or received to import an obligation of confidence, 235–9
  information with necessary quality of confidence, 229–35

need to show detriment, 242–3
reasonableness of obtaining remedy, 243
scope of obligation, 241–2
unauthorised use of disclosure of information, 239–41
See also confidential information
elements of passing off
damage or likelihood of damage, 561–2
definition of passing off, 531–2
employee inventions, 411–12
duty of good faith, 413–16
express provisions in employment contract, 412–13
fiduciary duties, 416–17
employees
breach of confidence during employment, 248–9
breach of confidence when employment ends, 249–54
copyright over works created by, 81–2
equitable principles of confidence, 252–4
express terms to control disclosure of information, 250–1
implied duty of good faith, 251–2
enforcement of plant breeder's rights
actions for infringement, 521
jurisdiction, 522
non-infringement declarations, 521–2
offences and conduct by directors, servants and agents, 523
remedies, 523–4
unjustified threats of infringement proceedings, 522
entitlement to be granted a patent, 401–3
criteria for inventorship. *See* inventorship criteria for patents
derives title to invention from inventor, 407–8
patent assigned to a person, 407
European Patent Convention, 289–90
exceptions to first ownership, 80
commissioned works, 83
Crown copyright, 84–5
works created by employees, 81–2
works created by journalists, 82–3
exceptions to infringement of copyright
archives, libraries and key cultural institutions, 157–9
artistic works, 160–1
computer programs, 161–2
educational uses, 159–60
films, 164
government uses, 163
legal materials, 163
public interest, 165
reading or recitation in public, 163

sound recordings, 164
exceptions to infringement of design law
consent and parallel importation, 214
Crown use and supply, 214
overall appearance of a product, 213–14
'repair' defence, 213
exploitation of copyright
assignment, 104–5
collective administration, 110–12
compulsory or statutory licences, 106–10
educational statutory licences, 107–10
express licences, 105
implied licences, 106
licences, 105–10
exploitation of patents without infringement
exploitation to cease under court order, 421
remuneration and terms for exploitation, 420
supply of products to foreign countries, 421
exploitation of trade marks
anti-dilution provisions. *See* anti-dilution of trade marks
indicating connection with owner, 658–60
owner's interests adversely affected, 660
unrelated goods and services, 657–8
use as a trade mark, 644–5
use as descriptive term not trade mark, 645–6
well-known trade marks, 656–7
express exclusions from patentability
contrary to law, 381–2
international obligations, 382–3
mere mixtures, 382
plants and animals, 380–1

fair dealing, copyright, 143–4
access by persons with a disability, 151
criticism or review, 146–8
dealing must be 'fair', 151–4
parody or satire, 149–51
permitted purposes, 144
professional advice and legal proceedings, 149
reporting news, 148–9
research or study, 144–6
film directors' rights, 36
films
copyright, 62
defences to infringement of copyright, 164
derogatory treatment, 172
duration of copyright protection, 102
first ownership rights, 86
initial owners of copyright, 77
originality, 74
first ownership, copyright
authorship and, 76–80
exceptions to. *See* exceptions to first ownership
Franki Committee, 33–4, 121, 144, 152–3

functions of trade marks, 572
  managing property interests, 573
  promotion of product, 573–4
  reducing search costs, 572–3

genes and biological materials, patents, 307–13
geographical origins of goods or services, 618–19, 623–5
goods and services, distinguishing by trade marks, 581
  by a person, 583
  dealt with or provided, 581–2
  in the course of trade, 582–3
grant of plant breeder's rights
  effect of, 507
  entry of details in Register, 506
  requirements, 506

harmonisation of intellectual property procedures, 18

Indigenous communal moral rights, 38, 180
indirect infringement of copyright, 131
  books, 132–3
  electronic publications and computer programs, 135–6
  non-infringing accessories to the article, 136–7
  parallel importation, 131
  sound recordings, 133–5
Industrial Property Advisory Committee (IPAC), 300, 465
infringement of copyright, 112–13
  additional damages, 138
  conversion or detention, 139
  criminal offences, 141–2
  damages, 138
  defences. *See* defences to infringement of copyright
  direct. *See* direct infringement of copyright
  exceptions to. *See* execeptions to infringement of copyright
  groundless threats to sue, 140–1
  indirect. *See* indirect infringement of copyright
  injunctions, 137–8
  innocent infringement, 139
  relief for, 137–42
infringement of design law, 209
  defences. *See* defences to infringement of design law
  exceptions. *See* exceptions to infringement of design law
  primary infringement, 209–11
  remedies, 215–16
  secondary infringement, 211
  unjustified threats, 215–16

infringement of patents
  contributory infringement. *See* contributory infringement of patents
  defences. *See* defences to infringement of patents
  direct infringement. *See* direct infringement of patents
  disclosure without consent. *See* disclosure without consent, patents
  misleading and deceptive conduct, 474
  proceedings. *See* infringement of patents, proceedings for
infringement of patents, proceedings for, 483–4
  non-infringement declarations, 485
  relief for infringement, 484–5
  unjustified threats of, 485–7
infringement of plant breeder's rights
  exemptions from, 520–1
  prior use rights, 521
  what amounts to infringement, 520
infringement of trade marks
  acts not constituting. *See* acts not constituting infringement of trade mark
  breach of certain restrictions, 671–2
  damages, 680–1
  groundless threats of legal proceedings, 674–5
  internet and, 669–71
  no damages for infringement during non-use period, 680
  oral use of trade mark, 662
  overview, 644
  passing off and, 566
  prior continuous use defence, 679
  remedies, 680–1
  second-hand goods, 668–9
  two-dimensional device infringed by three-dimensional shape, 662
innovative step, patents, 347–8
  differences to inventive step, 355–6
  level of advance and assessment, 354–5
  prior art base and information for comparative purposes, 353–4
  relationship with novelty, 346–7
  statutory requirements, 348–50
  time at which innovative step raised, 348
intellectual property
  freedom of competition and. *See* competition and intellectual property law
  nature of, 4
  regimes, 11–12
  theories of, 4–8
Intellectual Property Competition and Review Committee, 189, 479
intellectual property law
  constitutional issues in Australia, 20–1

criminal liability and, 702
customs seizure and, 702
diversity and complexity, 8
history in Australia, 19–20
incentive to create or dissemination, 6
internationalisation, 15–19
jurisdiction, 703
natural or personality rights, 5
property aspect, 5
protection for investment, 7
remedies. *See* remedies
rent seeking, 7
technological change and, 13–14
internal requirements for patent specifications
   application to end with claims defining invention, 394
   best method, 391–3
   claims supported by matter disclosed in specification, 395–7
   claims to relate to one invention only, 399
   clarity and succinctness, 394–5
   comparison with fair basis assessment, 398–9
   consistory clause and fair basing, 397–8
   construction of specification, 386–7
   evolution of specification and function of claims, 383–4
   priority date, 398–9
   provisional specifications, 387–8
   relations to other grounds of invalidity, 387
   requirement to fully describe invention, 388–91
   stages for consideration, 387
   statutory provisions for, 384–6
   time for meeting requirement to fully describe invention, 393–4
International Code of Botanical Nomenclature, 503
international influences on copyright law
   ACTA, 45–6
   AUSFTA, 9, 35, 43
   Beijing Treaty, 44–5
   Berne Convention, 15, 33, 41–3
   harmonisation of procedures, 18
   investor–state dispute settlement, 18
   Marrakesh Treaty, 44
   Paris Convention, 15
   plurilatural and bilateral agreements, 17–18
   Rome Convention, 42–3
   TRIPS Agreement, 42
   Universal Copyright Convention, 42
   WIPO internet treaties, 43
   World Intellectual Property Organization (WIPO), 35
International Patent Cooperation Union, 272
Internet Corporation for Assigned Names and Numbers (ICANN)
   uniform dispute resolution policy, 554–6

inventive step, patents, 347–8
   differences to innovative step, 355–6
   elements of assessment. *See* assessment of inventive step, patents
   prior art base and information for comparitive purposes, 350–3
   relationship with novelty, 346–7
   statutory requirements, 348–50
   time at which inventive step raised, 348
inventorship criteria for patents, 403–4
   invention, conception of the invention or inventive concept, 404
   joint inventorship, 406–7
   nature of contribution, 404–6
investor–state dispute settlement, 18
IP Australia, 199, 268–9, 272, 278, 309, 322, 353, 494, 524
   Designs Office, 199
   on Hague Agreement, 199

jurisdiction
   intellectual property regimes, 703–4
   plant breeder's rights, 522

keyword advertising, 557–8

licences, patents, 422–3
   compulsory licences. *See* compulsory licences, patents
   exclusive licences, 424–5
   non-exclusive licences, 425
   sole licences, 425
licensing of trade marks, 683–4
   assignment of licences, 687
   financial control, 685–6
   franchising, 686
   other forms of control, 686
   quality control, 684–5
limitations on plant breeder's rights, 513
   farmer's rights, 514–16
   harvested material and products from crops grown with farm-saved seed, 516
   other restrictions, 516–17
   private, experimental or breeding purposes, 513–14
   reasonable public access, 517
literary works, 50–5
   authorship, 77
   copyright, 50–5
   derogatory treatment, 172
   duration of copyright protection, 101–2
   first ownership rights, 85
   originality, 67–74

Madrid Protocol, 689
manner of manufacture, patents
   application of *NRDC* principles, 300–2
   background to meaning of, 295–7
   computer-implemented methods, 303–7
   computer programs, 302–3
   discoveries, ideas, intellectual information and other unpatentable subject matter, 318–20
   genes and biological materials, 307–13
   methods of medical treatment for humans, 313–18
   NRDC case, 297–300
   reform proposals, 320
   time at which manner of manufacture raised, 295
Marrakesh Treaty, 44
meta-tags, 556–7
misleading and deceptive conduct
   Competition and Consumer Act 2010 and, 474
   passing off and, 565–6
   patent infringement and, 474
misrepresentation, passing off, 544
   character merchandising, 547–50
   confusion and deception and, 544–6
   quality of goods, 547
   target of representation, 546
   trade origin of goods and, 546–7
moral rights, 169–71
   basis of, 6
   consent, 178–9
   Indigenous communal moral rights, 38, 180
   limits on, 176–9
   performers' rights, 183–5
   remedies, 179–80
   right of attribution, 171–2
   right of integrity, 172–5
   right to object to false attribution, 175–6
   treatment 'reasonable in all the circumstances', 176–8
musical works
   authorship, 77
   copyright, 57
   derogatory treatment, 172
   duration of copyright protection, 101–2
   first ownership rights, 85
   originality, 67–74
   statutory licences, 107

names, 51–2
natural rights
   as argument for copyright, 29–30
   intellectual property law and, 5
Nice Agreeement, 689
novelty, patents, 323
   by way of selection, 345–6
   innovative step, relationship with. *See* innovative step, patents
   inventive step, relationship with. *See* inventive step, patents
   non-consensual disclosure, 344–5
   prior art base, 327–8
   prior information made publicly available, 329–30
   prohibition on mosaics, 337–8
   relationship with secret use, 373–4
   skilled addressee, 328
   statutory requirements, 324–6
   test for anticipation. *See* test for anticipation, patents
   time at which novelty is raised, 323–4
   time at which to construe and read documentary disclosures, 326–7

ownership of patents, 408
   assignment, 423–4
   directions to co-owners, 409
   grant of patent, 410
   notion of co-ownership, 408–9
   proprietary rights in the patent, 410–11
   rights of co-owners, 409
ownership of trade marks, 583–4
   creation or adoption of overseas trade marks, 586–7
   distributorship arrangements, 585–6
   first use in Australia, 584–5
   persons who can own, 587

parallel importation, 40
   passing off and, 667–8
parallel importation, copyright
   books, 132–3
   infringement of copyright, 133–5
   non-infringing accessories to the article, 136–7
   sound recordings, 133–5
parallel importation, designs
   consent and, 214
parallel importation, patents
   patented products, 459–60
parallel importation, trade marks, 662–6
   licences and, 666–7
Paris Convention, 15, 262, 271, 287, 339, 430, 475–6, 688
passing off, 12
   anti-dilution of trade marks and, 660–2
   common law and, 530–1
   comparison with misleading or deceptive conduct, 565–6
   comparison with trade mark infringement, 566
   effect of disclaimers, 558–60

elements of. *See* elements of passing off
equity and, 530–1
history of, 530–1
holistic perspective, 560–1
internet and. *See* passing off and the internet
misrepresentation. *See* misrepresentation, passing off
parallel importation and, 667–8
remedies, 566–8
statutory causes of action. *See* statutory causes of action, passing off
trade marks and, 571–2
passing off and the internet, 550–1
   Australian cases, 552–4
   Australian uniform dispute resolution policy, 556
   domain names, 551–2
   keyword advertising, 557–8
   meta-tags, 556–7
   uniform dispute resolution policy, 554–6
Patent Law Treaty, 290
patent specification
   general principles for construction of, 441–4
   internal requirements for. *See* internal requirements for patent specifications
   role, 441
patentees, exclusive rights
   implied licence on sale, 450–1
   nature of exclusive rights, 449–50
   no grant of positive rights, 451–2
patents for invention, 11, 265–6
   application procedure. *See* application for patent, procedure for
   application types. *See* application for patent, types of
   assignments, 423–4
   breach of confidence and, 261–2
   ceasing of, 286
   claim construction. *See* claim construction, patents
   combination patents, 271
   complete applications, 283
   contracts. *See* contracts, patents
   co-ownership. *See* ownership of patents
   Crown use of. *See* Crown use of patents
   dealings with inventions, general principles, 422–3
   development of patent law in Australia, 268–9
   employee inventions. *See* employee inventions
   entitlement to be granted. *See* entitlement to be granted a patent
   exclusive rights of patentees. *See* patentees, exclusive rights
   exploitation without infringement. *See* exploitation of patents without infringement
   express exclusions from patentability. *See* express exclusions from patentability
   grant of, 278, 410
   infringement of. *See* infringement of patents
   innovation patents, 270, 278–9, 370
   international treaties and conventions, 286–90
   inventorship criteria. *See* inventorship criteria for patents
   lapsing of, 286
   licences for. *See* licences, patents
   origins of protection, 266–8
   ownership. *See* ownership of patents
   patent specifications. *See* patent specification
   pharmaceutical substances, term extension, 280–2
   plant breeder's rights and, 524–5
   power of patentees, 438–9
   priority dates, requirements, 282–4
   priority dates, role, 285–6
   priority documents, 283–5
   rationales for protection, 269–70
   Register. *See* Register of Patents
   revocation. *See* revocation of patents
   selection patents, 271
   specification. *See* patent specification
   standard patents, 270
   term of, 279
   types of patents, 270–1
   validity. *See* validity, patents
   withdrawal of, 286
performers' rights, 181–3
   moral rights, 183–5
plant breeder's rights, 11–12, 494
   applications. *See* application for plant breeder's rights
   assignment, 518
   certain dependent plant varieties, 510–11
   essentially derived varieties, 508–10
   exhaustion of rights, 512–13
   exploitation of, 518–19
   general nature in propogating material, 507–8
   grant of. *See* grant of plant breeder's rights
   harvested material, 511–12
   infringement. *See* infringement of plant breeder's rights
   international conventions or treaties, 525
   licences, 518–19
   limitations on. *See* limitations on plant breeder's rights
   ownership and coownership, 517–18
   products obtained from harvested materials, 512
   Register of Plant Varieties, 523
   registrability of plant varieties. *See* registrability of plant varieties

plant breeder's rights (cont.)
  relationship to patents,
    524–5
  relationship to trade marks, 525
  relationship with other intellectual property
    regimes, 524–5
  revocation, 519
  rights in, 507–13
  subject matter, 496
  surrender of, 519
  technical background of plant breeding, 494–6
  term of protection, 507
Plant Varieties Journal, 504
plurilateral and bilateral agreements, 17–18
presumptive validity, trade marks, 633–4
  contrary to *Trade Marks Act 1955* s 28, 634
  fraud, 634
  not distinctive when proceedings commence,
    634–5
Productivity Commission
  on compulsory licensing of patents, 422, 427–8
  on Hague Agreement, 199
  review of intellectual property arrangements,
    39–41, 80, 133, 143, 166, 294, 355
  review of parallel importation provisions, 132–3
public interest defences
  breach of confidence, 254–8
  infringement of copyright, 165
public lending rights, 194
published editions
  copyright, 64, 74
  first ownership rights, 86
  original owners of copyright, 78

rectification of trade marks Register, 627
  aggrieved person, 629–30
  amendment or cancellation by Registrar, 627–9
  cancellation, removal or amendment, 633
  contravention of conditions or limits, 630
  court order, 629–30
  errors and omissions, 630
  fraud, false suggestion or misrepresentation,
    636–7
  general discretion not to rectify, 635
  grounds for opposition, 635–6
  presumptive validity. *See* presumptive validity,
    trade marks
  registered owner at fault, 637–40
  trade mark becoming generic, 631–2
  use likely to deceive or cause
    misrepresentation, 637
Register of Patents
  contents, 436–7
  evidence, 438
  false entries, 437
  inspection and access to, 437
  power of patentee to deal with patent, 438–9
Register of Plant Varieties, 506, 518, 523
registered trade marks. *See* trade marks, registered
registrability of plant varieties, 496
  distinctiveness of variety, 498
  meaning of discovery, 497
  meaning of selective propagation, 497
  stability of variety, 499
  time at which the variety must meet the DUS
    criteria, 501
  uniformity of variety, 499
  variety has a breeder, 496–7
  variety not exploited or only recently exploited,
    499–501
remedies, 694
  account of profits, 700–2
  Anton Piller orders, 694–6
  breach of confidence, 260–1
  damages, 700
  enforcement of plant breeder's rights,
    523–4
  enforcement of trade mark infringement
    remedies, 680–1
  groundless threats of legal proceedings,
    699–700
  interlocutory injunctions, 697–8
  passing off, 566–8
  permanent injunctions, 698–9
  pre-trial remedies, 694–8
  representative orders, 696–7
removal of trade mark for non-use, 640–2
  general discretion not to remove, 642
  under *Trade Marks Amendment Act 2006*,
    642
reputation of plaintiff
  abandonment of reputation, 543–4
  dual ownership, 537–9
  elements of passing off, 532–4
  joint ownership of reputation, 536–7
  location of reputation, 534–6
  ownership of reputation, 536
  reputation in descriptive words and insignia,
    539–40
  reputation in packaging and appearance,
    540–2
  reputation in personality, 542–3
  reputation of marketing image, 542
revocation of patents
  fraud and false suggestion or misrepresentation,
    489–92
  lack of entitlement, 488–9
  parties to litigation proceedings, 492
  statutory provisions, 487–8
Rome Convention, 42–3

Screenrights, 111
secret use, patents, 372–3
　grace period, 379
　meaning of secret, 374
　meaning of use, 374–6
　onus of proof, 378
　rationale, 373
　relationship with novelty, 373–4
　use for purpose other than trade or commerce, 378
　use for reasonable trial or experiment, 376–7
　use occurring in confidential disclosure, 377–8
　use on behalf of government, 378
signs and exploitation of trade marks
　goods or services for which trade mark registered, 652–3
　likelihood of deception or confusion, 653–4
　relevance of defendant's conduct, 649–50
　relevance of plaintiff's trade mark's reputation, 650–2
　substantially identical or deceptively similar to, 647–9
　use to distinguish goods and services, 646–7
signs as trade marks
　colour, 578
　definition, 575–6
　intent to use, 579–81
　objective test of intention, 580
　packaging and shape, 576–8
　scents, 579
　sounds, 578–9
　unconditional intention to use, 579–80
　use by others, 580–1
sound recordings
　copyright, 62
　defences to infringement of copyright, 164
　duration of copyright protection, 102
　first ownership rights, 86
　infringement of copyright, 133–5
　initial owners of copyright, 77
　originality, 74
　statutory licences, 107
Spicer Committee, 33
statutory causes of action, passing off, 562
　application of legislation, 562–3
　engage in conduct, 563
　in trade or commerce, 563
　misleading or deceptive conduct, 563–5
subsistence, copyright, 49
　artistic works, 57–62
　Australian connection, 65–7
　compilations, 52
　computer programs, 52–5
　dramatic works, 55–7
　literary works, 50–5
　musical works, 57

names, 51–2
originality, 67–74
recorded in material form, 64
subject matter, 49–50
subject matter other than works, 62–4, 74
tables, 52
titles, 51–2
works, 50–62
Substantive Patent Law Treaty, 290

tables
　copyright, 52
technological change
　intellectual property law and, 13–15
technological protection measures, copyright, 36–7, 92–4
　aiding and abetting in circumvention, 96–7
　anti-circumvention, 94–9
　circumventing an access control TPM, 94–6
　criminal actions, 98
　defences to liability for criminal actions, 99
　providing a circumvention service, 97–8
　rights management information, 99–100
　unauthorised access to encoded broadcasts, 100–1
test for anticipation, patents
　anticipation through prior use, 334–5
　general principles, 330–4
　implict disclosure and inevitable outcome, 335–7
titles, 51–2
trade mark applications, grounds of opposition to registration, 619–20
　application made in bad faith, 625–7
　geographical indications, 623–5
　prior reputation of another trade mark, 620–2
　relationship with honest concurrent and prior continuous user, 622
trade mark applications, identical or similar to existing trade marks, 607
　closely related goods and services, 613
　context of comparison, 610–11
　deceptive similarity, 608–10
　global assessment, 613–14
　honest concurrent user, 614–16
　prior continuous user, 616–17
　similar goods, 611–12
　similar services, 612–13
　substantially identical with, 607–8
trade mark applications, requirements at examination of, 592–3
　applications identical or similar to existing trade marks. See trade mark applications, identical or similar to existing trade marks
　business names, 617–18
　colour trade marks, 603–4

Index　717

trade mark applications, requirements at examination of (cont.)
    deceptive or confusing trade marks, 605–7
    distinctiveness through use, 599–600
    functional shapes, 600–3
    geographical indications for wine, 618–19
    graphical representation, 594
    inherent distinctiveness, 595–9
    national signs prohibition, 593
    partial inherent distinctiveness, 599
    prescribed signs, 593–4
    protection for particular industries, 619
    protection of sporting events, 617
    scandalous matter, 604–5
    use contrary to law, 605
trade marks, registered, 12–13
    acts not constituting infringement. *See* acts not constituting infringement of trade mark
    assignment. *See* assignment of trade marks
    certification trade marks. *See* certification trade marks
    collective trade marks, 590, 683
    defensive trade marks, 590–2, 683
    definition, 575
    distinguishing goods and services. *See* goods and services, distinguishing by trade marks
    exploitation of. *See* exploitation of trade marks
    functions of. *See* functions of trade marks
    grounds of opposition to registration. *See* trade mark applications, grounds of opposition to registration
    history, 570–1
    infringement. *See* infringement of trade marks
    international treaty obligations, 688–9
    licensing of. *See* licensing of trade marks
    ownership of. *See* ownership of trade marks
    passing off and, 571–2
    rectification of Register. *See* rectification of trade marks Register
    registration process, 574–5
    relationship to plant breeder's rights, 525
    removal for non-use. *See* removal of trade mark for non-use
    requirements at examination of application. *See* trade mark applications, requirements at examination of
    signs as. *See* signs as trade marks
    types, 587

voluntary recording of interests and claims, 687–8
traditional knowledge
    intellectual property aspects, 46
TRIPS Agreement, 42, 287–8, 570, 590 688
    anti-dilution of trade marks, 654
    circuit layout protection, 189
    enforcement of intellectual property agreements, 16–17
    express exclusions from patentability, 382–3
    on compulsory licensing of patents, 430–1
    protection of confidential information, 262–3

uniform dispute resolution policy
    Australian, 556
    ICANN, 554–6
Universal Copyright Convention (UCC), 42

validity, patents
    concept of invention, 294–5
    contrary to law or generally inconvenient, 320–3
    internal requirements for patent specifications. *See* internal requirements for patent specifications
    manner of manufacture. *See* manner of manufacture, patents
    novelty. *See* novelty, patents
    statutory requirements, 292
    threshold quality of inventiveness, 366–70
    two-tier system, 292–4
    utility, 370–2
Viscopy, 111

World Intellectual Property Organization (WIPO), 16, 35, 689
    broadcast copyright, 46
    intellectual property aspects of traditional knowledge, 46
    internet treaties, 43
    moral rights protection for audiovisual performers, 183
    proposed Substantive Patent Law Treaty, 290
    Washington Treaty, 189
World Trade Organization (WTO), 689